LEARNSMART ADVANTAGE WORKS

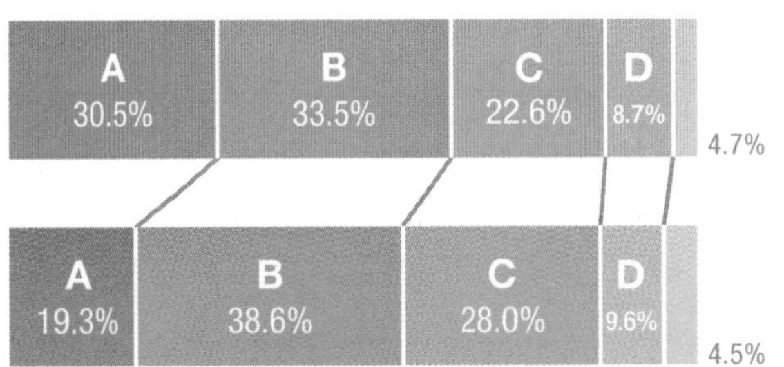

Without LearnSmart

More C students earn B's

*Study: 690 students / 6 institutions

Over 20% more students pass the class with LearnSmart

*A&P Research Study

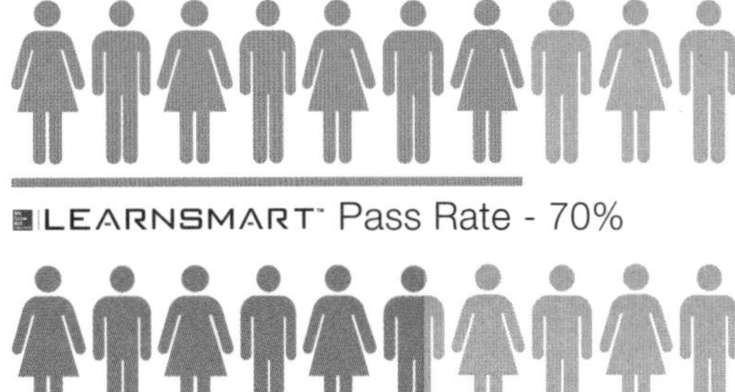

LEARNSMART Pass Rate - 70%

Without LearnSmart Pass Rate - 57%

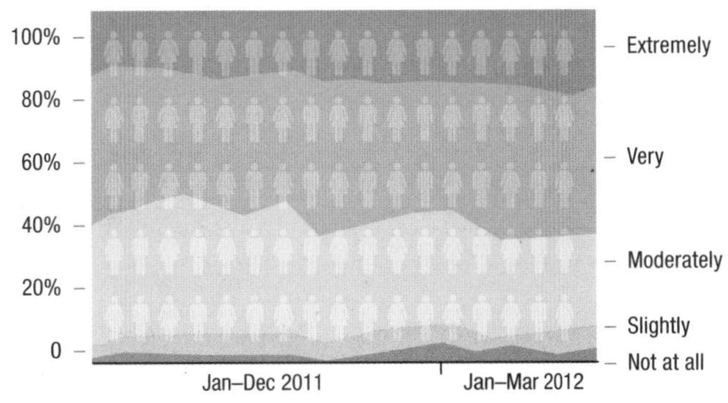

More than 60% of all students agreed LearnSmart was a very or extremely helpful learning tool

*Based on 750,000 student survey responses

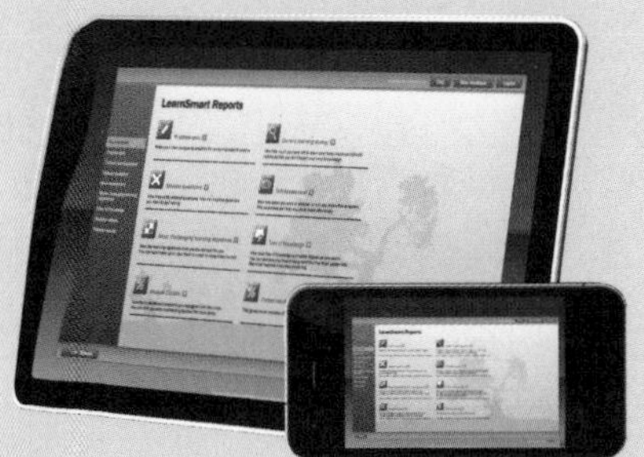

> AVAILABLE ON-THE-GO

http://bit.ly/LS4Apple

http://bit.ly/LS4Droid

How do you rank against your peers?

What you know (green) and what you still need to review (yellow), based on your answers.

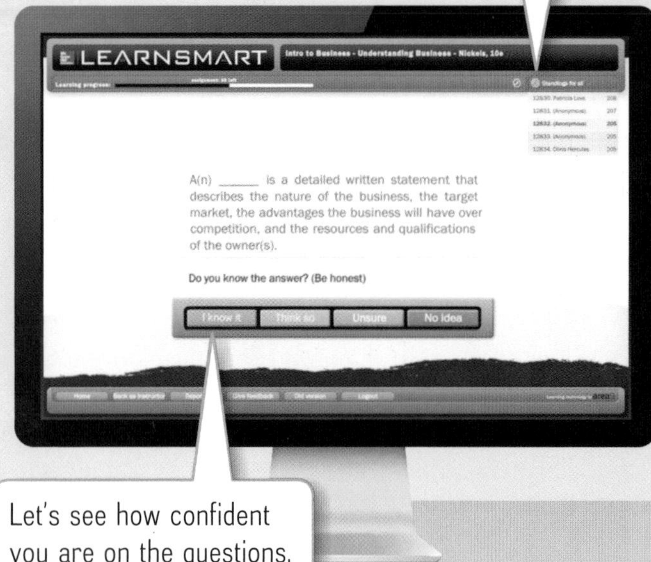

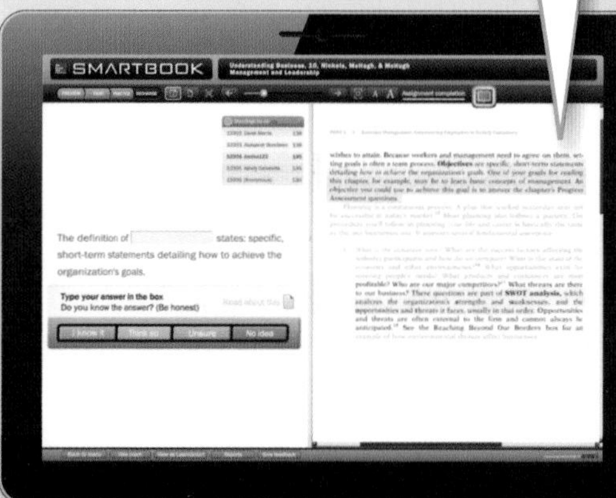

Let's see how confident you are on the questions.

COMPARE AND CHOOSE WHAT'S RIGHT FOR YOU

	BOOK	LEARNSMART	ASSIGNMENTS	
connect plus+	✓	✓	✓	LearnSmart, assignments, and SmartBook—all in one digital product for maximum savings!
connect plus+ Looseleaf	✓	✓	✓	Pop the pages into your own binder or carry just the pages you need.
connect plus+ Bound Book	✓	✓	✓	The #1 Student Choice!
SMARTBOOK™ Access Code	✓	✓		The first and only book that adapts to you!
LEARNSMART™ ADVANTAGE Access Code		✓		The smartest way to get from a B to an A.
CourseSmart eBook	✓			Save some green and some trees!
create™	✓	✓	✓	Check with your instructor about a custom option for your course.

> Buy directly from the source at www.ShopMcGraw-Hill.com.

PERSONAL FINANCE

ELEVENTH EDITION

The McGraw-Hill/Irwin Series in Finance, Insurance, and Real Estate

Stephen A. Ross
Franco Modigliani Professor of Finance and Economics
Sloan School of Management
Massachusetts Institute of Technology
Consulting Editor

FINANCIAL MANAGEMENT

Block, Hirt, and Danielsen
Foundations of Financial Management
Fifteenth Edition

Brealey, Myers, and Allen
Principles of Corporate Finance
Eleventh Edition

Brealey, Myers, and Allen
Principles of Corporate Finance, Concise
Second Edition

Brealey, Myers, and Marcus
Fundamentals of Corporate Finance
Seventh Edition

Brooks
FinGame Online 5.0

Bruner
Case Studies in Finance: Managing for Corporate Value Creation
Seventh Edition

Cornett, Adair, and Nofsinger
Finance: Applications and Theory
Third Edition

Cornett, Adair, and Nofsinger
M: Finance
Second Edition

DeMello
Cases in Finance
Second Edition

Grinblatt (editor)
Stephen A. Ross, Mentor: Influence through Generations

Grinblatt and Titman
Financial Markets and Corporate Strategy
Second Edition

Higgins
Analysis for Financial Management
Tenth Edition

Kellison
Theory of Interest
Third Edition

Ross, Westerfield, and Jaffe
Corporate Finance
Tenth Edition

Ross, Westerfield, Jaffe, and Jordan
Corporate Finance: Core Principles and Applications
Fourth Edition

Ross, Westerfield, and Jordan
Essentials of Corporate Finance
Eighth Edition

Ross, Westerfield, and Jordan
Fundamentals of Corporate Finance
Tenth Edition

Shefrin
Behavioral Corporate Finance: Decisions that Create Value
First Edition

White
Financial Analysis with an Electronic Calculator
Sixth Edition

INVESTMENTS

Bodie, Kane, and Marcus
Essentials of Investments
Ninth Edition

Bodie, Kane, and Marcus
Investments
Tenth Edition

Hirt and Block
Fundamentals of Investment Management
Tenth Edition

Jordan and Miller
Fundamentals of Investments: Valuation and Management
Seventh Edition

Stewart, Piros, and Heisler
Running Money: Professional Portfolio Management
First Edition

Sundaram and Das
Derivatives: Principles and Practice
First Edition

FINANCIAL INSTITUTIONS AND MARKETS

Rose and Hudgins
Bank Management and Financial Services
Ninth Edition

Rose and Marquis
Financial Institutions and Markets
Eleventh Edition

Saunders and Cornett
Financial Institutions Management: A Risk Management Approach
Eighth Edition

Saunders and Cornett
Financial Markets and Institutions
Fifth Edition

INTERNATIONAL FINANCE

Eun and Resnick
International Financial Management
Seventh Edition

REAL ESTATE

Brueggeman and Fisher
Real Estate Finance and Investments
Fourteenth Edition

Ling and Archer
Real Estate Principles: A Value Approach
Fourth Edition

FINANCIAL PLANNING AND INSURANCE

Allen, Melone, Rosenbloom, and Mahoney
Retirement Plans: 401(k)s, IRAs, and Other Deferred Compensation Approaches
Eleventh Edition

Altfest
Personal Financial Planning
First Edition

Harrington and Niehaus
Risk Management and Insurance
Second Edition

Kapoor, Dlabay, and Hughes
Focus on Personal Finance: An active approach to help you develop successful financial skills
Fourth Edition

Kapoor, Dlabay, and Hughes
Personal Finance
Eleventh Edition

Walker and Walker
Personal Finance: Building Your Future
First Edition

PERSONAL FINANCE

ELEVENTH EDITION

JACK R. KAPOOR

College of DuPage

LES R. DLABAY

Lake Forest College

ROBERT J. HUGHES

Dallas County Community Colleges

MELISSA M. HART

Contributing Author, North Carolina State University

PERSONAL FINANCE, ELEVENTH EDITION

Some ancillaries, including electronic and print components, may not be available to customers outside the United States.

This book is printed on acid-free paper.

1 2 3 4 5 6 7 8 9 0 DOW/DOW 1 0 9 8 7 6 5 4

ISBN 978-0-07-786164-3
MHID 0-07-786164-7

Senior Vice President, Products & Markets: *Kurt L. Strand*
Vice President, Content Production & Technology Services: *Kimberly Meriwether David*
Managing Director: *Douglas Reiner*
Executive Brand Manager: *Chuck Synovec*
Executive Director of Development: *Ann Torbert*
Development Editor II : *Jennifer Lohn Upton*
Director of Digital Content: *Doug Ruby*
Digital Development Editor: *Meg B. Maloney*
Executive Marketing Manager: *Melissa S. Caughlin*
Director, Content Production: *Terri Schiesl*
Content Project Manager: *Daryl Horrocks*
Buyer II: *Debra R. Sylvester*
Design: *Matthew Baldwin*
Cover Image: ©*KidStock/Getty Images and Rudi Sebastian/Getty Images*
Senior Content Licensing Specialist: *Jeremy Cheshareck*
Typeface: *10/12 Times Roman*
Compositor: *Laserwords Private Limited*
Printer: *R. R. Donnelley*

Library of Congress Cataloging-in-Publication Data

Kapoor, Jack R., 1937-
Personal finance/Jack R. Kapoor, College of DuPage, Les R. Dlabay, Lake Forest College, Robert J. Hughes, Dallas County Community Colleges, Melissa M. Hart, contributing author, North Carolina State University.—Eleventh edition.
pages cm.—(The McGraw-Hill/Irwin series in finance, insurance, and real estate)
Includes index.
ISBN 978-0-07-786164-3 (alk. paper)—ISBN 0-07-786164-7 (alk. paper)
1. Finance, Personal. I. Title.
HG179.K37 2015
332.024—dc23

2013044253

www.mhhe.com

To the memory of my parents, Ram and Susheela Kapoor; and to my wife, Theresa; and my children, Karen, Kathryn, and Dave

To the memory of my parents, Mary and Les Dlabay; and to my wife, Linda; and my children, Carissa and Kyle

To my mother, Barbara Y. Hughes; and my wife, Peggy

To my husband, David Hart; and my children, Alex and Madelyn

About the Authors

Jack R. Kapoor, EdD

College of DuPage

Jack Kapoor is a professor of business and economics in the Business and Technology Division of the College of DuPage, Glen Ellyn, Illinois, where he has taught business and economics since 1969. He received his BA and MS from San Francisco State College and his EdD from Northern Illinois University. He previously taught at Illinois Institute of Technology's Stuart School of Management, San Francisco State University's School of World Business, and other colleges. Professor Kapoor was awarded the Business and Technology Division's Outstanding Professor Award for 1999–2000. He served as an assistant national bank examiner for the U.S. Treasury Department and has been an international trade consultant to Bolting Manufacturing Co., Ltd., Mumbai, India.

Dr. Kapoor is known internationally as a coauthor of several textbooks, including *Business:* A *Practical Approach* (Rand McNally), *Business* (Houghton Mifflin), *Business and Personal Finance* (Glencoe), and *Focus on Personal Finance* (McGraw-Hill). He served as a content consultant for the popular national television series *The Business File: An Introduction to Business* and developed two full-length audio courses in business and personal finance. He has been quoted in many national newspapers and magazines, including *USA Today, U.S. News & World Report,* the *Chicago Sun-Times, Crain's Small Business,* the *Chicago Tribune,* and other publications.

Dr. Kapoor has traveled around the world and has studied business practices in capitalist, socialist, and communist countries.

Les R. Dlabay, EdD

Lake Forest College

Teaching about the "Forgotten Majority" (the more than 3 billion people living on $2 or less a day) is a priority of Les Dlabay, professor of business at Lake Forest College, Lake Forest, Illinois. He believes our society can improve global business development through volunteer time, knowledge sharing, and financial donations. In addition to writing several textbooks, Dr. Dlabay teaches accounting and various international business courses. His hobbies include a collection of cereal packages from over 100 countries and paper currency from 200 countries, which are used to teach about economic, cultural, and political aspects of international business environments.

His research involves informal and alternative financial services, microfinance, and value chain facilitation in base-of-the-pyramid (BoP) market settings. Dlabay has presented more than 300 workshops and seminars for teachers and community organizations. He serves on the boards of Bright Hope International (www.brighthope.org), which emphasizes microenterprise development through microfinance programs, and Andean Aid (www.andeanaid.org), which provides tutoring assistance to school-age children in Colombia and Venezuela. Professor Dlabay has a BS (Accounting) from the University of Illinois, Chicago; an MBA from DePaul University; and an EdD in Business and Economic Education from Northern Illinois University. He has twice received the Great Teacher award at Lake Forest College.

Robert J. Hughes, EdD

Dallas County Community Colleges

Financial literacy! Only two words, but Bob Hughes, professor of business at Dallas County Community Colleges, believes that these two words can literally change people's lives. Whether you want to be rich or just manage the money you have, the ability to analyze financial decisions and gather financial information are skills that can always be improved. In addition to writing several textbooks, Dr. Hughes has taught personal finance, introduction to business, business math, small business management, small business finance, and accounting since 1972. He also served as a content consultant for two popular national television series, *It's Strictly Business* and *Dollars & Sense: Personal Finance for the 21st Century,* and is the lead author for a business math project utilizing computer-assisted instruction funded by the ALEKS Corporation. He received his BBA from Southern Nazarene University and his MBA and EdD from the University of North Texas. His hobbies include writing, investing, collecting French antiques, art, and travel.

Melissa M. Hart, CPA

North Carolina State University

Melissa Hart is a permanent lecturer in the Poole College of Management at North Carolina State University. She was inducted into the Academy of Outstanding Teachers in 2012. She teaches courses in personal finance and corporate finance and has developed multiple ways to use technology to introduce real-life situations into the classroom and the distance education environment. Spreading the word about financial literacy has always been a passion of hers. It doesn't stop at the classroom. Each year she shares her common sense approach of "No plan is a plan" with various student groups, clubs, high schools, and outside organizations. She is a member of the North Carolina Association of Certified Public Accountants (NCACPA) where she serves on the Accounting Education Committee. She received her BBA from the University of Maryland and an MBA from North Carolina State University. Prior to obtaining an MBA, she worked eight years in public accounting in auditing, tax compliance, and consulting. Her hobbies include keeping up with her family's many extracurricular activities as well as working on various crafts. She travels extensively with her family to enjoy the many cultures and beauty of the state, the country, and the world.

Preface

KAPOOR
DLABAY
HUGHES
HART

11th Edition

Dear Personal Finance Professors and Personal Finance Students,

Just for a moment consider how the following questions affect you and your students.

Which direction is our economy headed?
Will the housing market regain its strength?
What type of investments should you choose for a long-term investment program?
How do you manage your money during an economic crisis or an economic recovery?

For most people, the answers to the above questions affect not only their financial security, but also their quality of life. In fact, for many individuals the financial crisis of 2007–2009 was a wake-up call that forced them to examine how they managed their personal finances. Until recently, for example, Americans had both the highest rate of homeownership and the highest concentration of wealth in housing ever recorded. And yet, easy access to credit and rapidly rising home values forced our personal savings rate to plunge to the lowest level since the 1930s. To make matters worse, many Americans lost their jobs and were forced to use their savings to pay everyday expenses. As the economy has begun to improve, many people now must rebuild their financial security.

As authors and teachers, we believe it is important to help people develop a plan to achieve financial security. While the 11th edition of *Personal Finance* does not guarantee that each student will be able to get the ideal job or become a millionaire, it does provide the information needed to take advantage of opportunities and to help manage personal finances. As in previous editions, we address the changing financial needs and challenges that students face on a daily basis. The 11th edition of *Personal Finance* provides a wealth of information about career planning; money management; taxes; consumer credit, including college loans; housing; legal protection; insurance; investments; retirement planning; and estate planning. By teaching students how to make informed choices, we believe you can encourage them to build a foundation of financial security.

For 11 editions, we have been keenly aware that our customers are students and professors. With each revision, we have asked professors for suggestions that will help them teach better and help students learn more efficiently. And with each edition, we have incorporated these suggestions and ideas to create what has become a best-selling personal finance textbook. We are also proud to say that we have included extensive student feedback in our text and instructional package. We do sincerely **thank you** for your suggestions, ideas, and support.

A text and instructional package should always be evaluated by the people who use it. We encourage you to e-mail us if you have comments, suggestions, or would like more information about the new edition. Finally, we invite you to examine the visual guide that follows to see how the new edition of *Personal Finance* and instructional package can help your students obtain financial security and success.

Welcome to the new 11th edition of *Personal Finance.*

Sincerely,

Jack Kapoor
kapoorj@cod.edu

Les Dlabay
dlabay@lakeforest.edu

Bob Hughes
bhughes@dcccd.edu

Melissa Hart
mmhart@ncsu.edu

Acknowledgments

The extensive feedback and thoughtful comments provided by the following instructors greatly contributed to the quality of the 11th edition of *Personal Finance.*

David A. Dumpe, *Kent State University*
Caroline Fulmer, *University of Alabama*
Paul Gregg, *University of Central Florida*
Monte Hill, *Northern Virginia Community College*
Jim Livingston, *Weber State University*
KT Magnusson, *Salt Lake Community College*
Robert B. McCalla, *University of Wisconsin – Madison*
Tammi Metz, *Mississippi State University*
Noel Morris, *University of Arkansas*
Jeff C. Parsons, *California State University – Fullerton*
Mehmet Sencicek, *Albertus Magnus College*
Harold Williamson, *University of South Alabama*
Helen Davis, *Jefferson Community College*
Jeffrey Schultz, *Christian Brothers University*
Joan Ryan, *Clackamas Community College*
Joe Howell, *Salt Lake Community College*
Kerri McMillan, *Clemson University*
Laura Perault, *Southeastern Louisiana University*
Laurie Hensley, *Cornell University*
Mark Clark, *Collin College*
Martin Welc, *Saddleback College*
Melissa Rueterbusch, *Mott Community College*
Paul Gregg, *University of Central Florida*
Ronald VanWey, *Tarrant County College District*
Sally Proffitt, *Tarrant County College Northeast*
Sharon Parker, *Clackamas Community College*
Ted Ondracek, *Coastline Community College*
Terri Conzales-Kreisman, *Delgado Community College*
Yuhong Fan, *Weber State University*
Diane Andrews-Hagan, *Ohio Business College*
Jeff Guernsey, *Cedarville University*
Ken Mergl, *Arapahoe Community College*
Rod Thirion, *Pikes Peak Community College*
Ron Christner, *Loyola University, New Orleans*
Sharon Meyer, *Pikes Peak Community College*
Thomas Severance, *Mira Costa College*

Many talented professionals at McGraw-Hill Higher Education have contributed to the development of *Personal Finance,* 11th Edition. We are especially grateful to Michele Janicek, Chuck Synovec, Jennifer Upton, Melissa Caughlin, Daryl Horrocks, Debra Sylvester, Matt Baldwin, Cara Hawthorne, Jeremy Cheshareck, Joyce Chappetto, and Ira Roberts.

In addition, Jack Kapoor expresses special appreciation to Theresa and Dave Kapoor, Kathryn Thumme, and Karen and Joshua Tucker for their typing, proofreading, and research assistance. Les Dlabay would also like to thank Jason Ross, Gene Monterastelli, Bryna Mollinger, and Kevin Smith for their help reviewing the manuscript. Finally, we thank our wives and families for their patience, understanding, encouragement, and love throughout the years.

PERSONAL FINANCE OFFERS YOU EVERYTHING YOU HAVE ALWAYS EXPECTED . . . AND MORE!

The primary purpose of this book is to help you apply the personal finance practices you learn from the book and from your instructor to your own life. The following *new* features of the tenth edition expand on this principle. You can use them to assess your current personal financial literacy, identify your personal finance goals, and develop and apply a personal finance strategy to help you achieve those goals. (*For a complete list of all of the features in* Personal Finance, *11th ed., refer to the Guided Tour on pages xxi–xxvi.)*

NEW EDUCATION FINANCING APPENDIX

One of the biggest financial decisions that you will make in your life is whether or not to go to college, and how to finance that expense if you do choose to go. The new Appendix A covers applying for student loans and scholarships, key terms and forms, and the different types of financial aid available. Key resource websites are also highlighted.

NEW DASHBOARD FEATURE

Are you on track to meet your financial goals? It can be tough to tell sometimes. The new Finance Dashboard feature is designed to help students recognize where they're at on the continuum of financial health and to help students that aren't up to speed understand where to start and what they need to do to get to a stable and prosperous future.

Chapter	*Selected Topics*	Benefits for the Teaching–Learning Environment
Chapter 1	*New visual:* The financial system	Provides students with an overview of the financial intermediaries and markets that facilitate personal financial decisions.
	Revised visual: Financial goals and activities for various life situations	Provides expanded and reorganized coverage of foundation and life situation specific financial goals and activities.
	New feature: How to . . . Select a path to financial security	Contrasts easy and appropriate financial actions to guide students to long-term financial security and reduce emotional stress.
	Revised content: Time value of money	Explains future value and present value calculations using several methods: formula, time value of money tables, financial calculator, and spreadsheet software.
	New Dashboard feature	Provides an overview of emergency savings funds.
	New case: You Be the Financial Planner	Allows students an opportunity to assess various financial situations and recommend courses of action.
Chapter 2	*New content:* The "skills gap"	Informs students of the difference between skills needed by employers and the skills possessed by applicants.
	Updated content: Career trends	Provides an update on the careers expected to have the most demand in the future.
	Revised content: Entrepreneurial career options	Encourages students to become small business owners such as *social entrepreneurs* to mix traditional business practices with innovation to address concerns such as hunger, disease, poverty, and education.
	New feature: How to . . . Update Your Career Activities	Emphasizes both the career planning actions from the past that are still valid along with other actions to compete in a changing employment market.
	New content: Business cards in an age of social media	Offers insights about the importance of business cards in an age of various online networking tools.
	New content: Connecting experience and organizational needs	Assists students in better communicating their background in relation to the job description in their cover letter, résumé, or interview.
	Revised content: Developing a résumé	Provides enhanced and reorganized coverage of résumé content, types, preparation, and submission.
	New visual: Résumé makeover	Communicates actions that may be taken to update and restructure a résumé.
	New content: Your career brand	Provides suggestions for creating and communicating a professional image.
	Revised visual: Cover letter	Includes a bulleted link to highlight and communicate key experiences and competencies.
	New content: Preparing for a Skype interview	Suggests actions to take when preparing for and participating in an online interview.
	New content: How to . . . prepare for a case interview	Offers an overview of actions to take when required to use your analytical and decision-making abilities in a job interview.
	New Dashboard feature	Provides a template for developing career contacts.

Chapter	*Selected Topics*	Benefits for the Teaching–Learning Environment
Chapter 3	*New content:* Storing financial documents "in the cloud"	Provides guidelines for electronically storing and maintaining a system for personal financial documents.
	Revised visual: Where to keep your financial records	Suggests a format for a computerized system for personal financial documents.
	New feature: How to . . . Conduct a Money Management SWOT Analysis	Allows students to identify and assess their money management strengths, weaknesses, opportunities, and threats.
	New examples: Calculating net work and a budget variance	Presents specific numeric examples for determining net worth and a budget variance.
	New Dashboard feature	Outlines how to keep a basic cash budget.
	New case: "Adjusting the Budget"	Provides students an opportunity to make recommendations to revise a household budget.
Chapter 4	*Updated content:* Recent tax law changes	Updates students on the key changes for planning a tax strategy and for filing their income tax return.
	Expanded content: Tax rates	Demonstrates how to calculate total tax due using a tax bracket schedule.
	Expanded content: Alternative minimum tax (AMT)	Updates students on key changes for AMT exemption limits.
	Expanded content: Filing status considerations	Describes a situation where a *marriage penalty or bonus* could occur and how this amount would be calculated.
	Revised feature: Filing taxes online	Updates students on the most recent methods to file their taxes online.
	Revised feature: Tax scams	Provides a listing of the most recent tax scams.
	Revised box feature: Financial Planning Calculations	Provides revised calculations for short-term and long-term capital gains example.
	New content: 529 education savings plans	Describes how a 529 education savings plan can offer significant tax savings.
	New Dashboard feature	Provides a graphic of how proper tax planning and organization can ensure that you pay your "fair share."
	Revised Financial Planning Case	Includes revised numbers for calculating the Financial Planning case.
Chapter 5	*New visual:* Financial institutions and banking services	Presents an overview of deposit financial institutions, nondeposit institutions, nonbank financial service providers, and high-cost financial service providers.
	New visual: Mobile banking	Details the payment, transfer, deposit, and other services available through mobile banking.
	New visual: Expanding prepaid debit card services	Provides an overview of prepaid debit card "loading" methods, uses, and fees.
	Expanded content: The "Unbanked" and High-Cost Financial Services	Updates coverage of pawnshops, check-cashing outlets, payday loans, rent-to-own centers, and car title loans.
	Updated content: Types of CDs	Offers revised coverage of various types of certificates of deposit.
	Updated content: FDIC insurance	Presents updated information on recent changes for federal deposit insurance.
	New content: Failing to reconcile your bank account	Warns of potential dangers as a result of not preparing a bank reconciliation.
	New Dashboard feature	Provides an overview of healthy saving.
	New case: Evaluating Banking Services	Allows students to assess alternative financial services for use in various situations.

Chapter	Selected Topics	Benefits for the Teaching–Learning Environment
Chapter 6	*New Content:* Changes in perception about credit.	Provides information why many people use credit to live beyond their means, and why past generations used it sparingly.
	New content: Advantages of credit	Describes how most major cards provide benefits, such as accidental death insurance, collision damage waiver, roadside services, gift cards, etc., at no extra cost.
	New content: Advantages of credit	Includes information that some credit cards extend the manufacturer's warranty by up to one year when their credit card is used.
	New content: Disadvantage of credit	Points out that if you choose to make a minimum payment, it may take decades to pay off the credit card balance and hefty interest.
	Updated Exhibit 6-2: Volume of Consumer Credit	Shows that the volume of consumer credit has reached new highs in 2012.
	Updated Exhibit 6-3 Credit card holders and credit cards held	Provides updated statistics about credit card holders and credit cards held in 2012.
	Updated Did You Know feature	Provides updated statistics about 191 million debit card holders and how they use their cards.
	New coverage: Use of smart phones	Describe how some phones are now equipped to make purchases. Retailers such as Starbucks have apps that are scannable bar codes to quickly pay using a mobile phone.
	Revised content: What's "phishing"?	Includes expanded information on "phishing" in the Financial Planning for Life's Situations box.
	Updated Exhibit 6-4: Calculating debt-payments-to-income ratio	Gives updated information on how to calculate debt payments-to-income ratio with new figures.
	New content: VantageScore 3.0	Provides information on new VantageScore 3.0. Introduced in 2013, it features a score range of 300–850 and does not count debt collection accounts that have been paid off.
	New Did You Know feature	Informs how to obtain free credit report updates from Credit Sesame and free daily monitoring of Trans Union report from Credit Karma.
	Updated Did You Know feature	Points out Consumer Sentinel Network identity theft complaints by victims' age in 2012.
	Updated Exhibit 6-12: Consumer credit laws	Provides updated information about federal government agencies that enforce consumer credit laws.
	New Dashboard feature	Explains the importance of debt payments-to-income ratio in determining creditworthiness.
Chapter 7	*New Content:* Predatory lending	Defines predatory lending and how these lenders exploit lower-income and minority borrowers.
	Revised content: Expensive loans	Provides revised and updated examples.
	Updated Did You Know feature	Gives updated information for using a credit card in a foreign country.
	Revised content: Cost of credit and expected inflation	Provides updated information about cost of credit and expected inflation.
	Updated Exhibit 7-6 Bankruptcy filings	Includes new statistics for U.S. consumer bankruptcy filings for 2010–2012.

Chapter	*Selected Topics*	Benefits for the Teaching–Learning Environment
Chapter 7 (Cont.)	*Revised content:* Chapter 7 bankruptcy	Provides revised Chapter 7 bankruptcy filing court fees.
	New Dashboard feature	Explains the importance of paying bills in a timely manner.
Chapter 8	*New visual:* Buying influences and wise spending strategies.	Presents an overview of factors that influence buying and actions that may be taken for wise shopping decisions.
	New feature: Net present value of buying a hybrid car	Provides a framework to assess various consumer purchases in terms of the time value of money.
	New example: Upside down	Presents a numeric examples for a situation in which the balance of an auto loan exceeds the value of the vehicle.
	New visual: Resolving consumer complaints	Offers detailed actions for obtaining assistance when facing a consumer problem situation.
	New Dashboard feature	Lays out a plan to minimize unplanned spending.
Chapter 9	*Expanded content:* Leases	Offers suggestions for negotiating the terms of a lease that may be considered unacceptable.
	Expanded content: Mortgage payment calculation	Presents a numeric example for determining a mortgage payment along with contrasting calculation methods using a formula, financial calculator, and spreadsheet software.
	Expanded content: Interest-only mortgages	Offers an overview and warning regarding interest-only mortgages.
	Updated content: Closing costs	Suggests revised amounts that might be encountered for home purchase settlement costs.
	Updated coverage: Short sales	Provides an overview of factors to consider when making a decision about being involved in a short sale.
	New Dashboard feature	Provides a plan to build mortgage equity.
Chapter 10	*New content:* "Disaster Blaster"	Describes the simulator created by the Institute for Business and Home Safety to test the wind-resistance of structural modifications for homes.
	Updated exhibit: Automobile insurance minimum limits	Lists the minimum limits by state for bodily injury and property damage liability coverages.
	New example: Deductible	Presents a specific numeric example for determining the amount paid for a claim for comprehensive and collision insurance.
	New content: Crash damage	Provides a comparison of the safety and damage caused by larger and smaller vehicles in a crash.
	New Dashboard feature	Outlines how to secure adequate personal property insurance coverage.
Chapter 11	*Revised Content:* Health care debate	Cautions that even though the U.S. Supreme Court upheld the Affordable Care Act in 2012, the debate still continues.
	Revised coverage: High medical costs	Provides revised and updated information on runaway health care costs.
	Updated Exhibit 11-1: National health expenditures	Highlights the U.S. national health expenditures from 1960 to 2018.
	Updated coverage: Health insurance and financial planning	Explains that although we spent over $3.1 trillion on health care in 2013, the number of Americans without basic health insurance has been growing.
	New boxed feature: Financial Planning for Life's Situations	Describes the important provisions of COBRA's continuation coverage.
	Updated coverage: Types of health insurance coverage	Explains that a good health insurance plan should pay at least 80 percent for out-of-pocket expenses after a yearly deductible of $1,000 per person or $2,000 per family.

Chapter	*Selected Topics*	Benefits for the Teaching–Learning Environment
Chapter 11 (Cont.)	*Updated coverage:* Long term care insurance	Provides new statistics about the cost of long term care insurance.
	Updated Did You Know feature	Shows the 2012 average costs of Long-term care in nursing homes and other such facilities.
	New coverage: Private insurance companies	Describes that as of September 23, 2012, all health insurance companies and group health plans are required to provide a summary of health plan's benefits and coverage.
	New Exhibit 11-4: Summary of Benefits and Coverage	Provides a Uniform Summary of Benefits and Coverage under the new Affordable Healthcare Act.
	New coverage: PPOs	Explains that starting in 2014, a new type of non-profit, consumer-run health insurers will offer health insurance.
	New coverage: The Health Insurance Marketplaces	Describes that starting in 2014, the Health Insurance Marketplaces will make buying healthcare coverage easier and more affordable.
	New Financial Planning for Life's Situation boxed feature	Provides a checklist of seven steps that you can take to get ready now for the Health Insurance Marketplaces.
	New content: Medicare	Describes that according to the CMS, since 2010 Medicare Advantage premiums have decreased by 10 percent and enrollment has increased by 28 percent.
	Expanded content: Medicare	Explains that while Medicare enjoys broad support among seniors and the general public, it faces a number of policy challenges including its affordability.
	New Did You Know feature	Describes that Medicare enrollment has increased from 19 million in 1966 to over 50 million in 2013.
	New Did You Know feature	Provides information about downloading a computer file of your claims data and add your personal health information to share with your health care providers and family.
	New content: Medigap	Provides sources on how to get more information about Medigap policies.
	New coverage: Health insurance and the Patient Protection and Affordable Care Act (ACA)	Describes the major provisions of the ACA that take effect by January 2014. Is a government-run health care system that provides universal health care to all the most ethical?
	New coverage: Pros and cons of the ACA	Explains the pros and cons of the Affordable Care Act.
	New content: The Food and Drug Administration	Provides information about the new websites maintained by the FDA and Medicare.
	New Dashboard feature	Explains the importance of disability insurance in your financial plan.
Chapter 12	*Updated content:* Life insurance	Provides updated information on life insurance policies and their face value as of 2012.
	Revised Exhibit 12-1	Illustrates expectations of life and expected deaths based on sex and age in 2010.
	New Exhibit 12-2: Life expectancy and education	Presents a new graphic that compares life expectancy with education level attained.
	New Did You Know?	Provides information on the amount of hours and equivalent wage of a stay-at-home mom.

Chapter	*Selected Topics*	Benefits for the Teaching–Learning Environment
Chapter 12 (Cont.)	*Expanded content:* Online calculators and apps to calculate life insurance	Provides additional methods to calculate insurance needs using updated online calculators and apps.
	Revised coverage: Decreasing term insurance	Describes the use of decreasing term insurance as well as some common alternatives.
	Revised Did You Know?	Updates the average face amount of individual life insurance policies purchased.
	Revised Exhibit 12-7	Provides updated information for individual, group, and credit life insurance.
	New Did You Know?	Provides information about the most common insurance rider: waiver of premium.
	New Financial Planning Calculation feature:	Describes the effect of inflation on a life insurance policy using time value of money calculations.
	New information: Underwriting	Includes new information about the use of underwriting.
	Revised Financial Planning Calculation feature:	Updated calculations for determining the cost of insurance.
	New content: Payout options	Includes coverage of payout options for life insurance.
	New Dashboard feature	Provides a graphic of how much insurance is needed based upon various life stages.
Chapter 13	*New content:* Why you should pay your bills on time	Provides information about why an individual should pay recurring bills on time and what happens if bills aren't paid.
	Updated coverage: The need to manage credit card debt	Includes revised statistics about how many Americans use credit cards and how much they owe.
	New content: Basic information on economics	Defines economics and the business cycle and how the economy can affect an individual's personal finances and investment activities.
	New Did You Know	Points out trends for American consumer debt.
	New content: Priority of investment goals	Describes how many employers have eliminated or reduced their matching provisions in 401(k) or 403(b) retirement plans during the recent economic crisis.
	Revised content: The time value of money	Includes more streamlined coverage of how to calculate the time value of money.
	New examples: Real-world examples	Uses real-world companies including Apple, J.M. Smuckers, Borders Books, Shutterfly, and Biogen Idec to illustrate key topics in the chapter.
	Updated statistics: Value of long-term investments	Provides updated statistics about the performance of stocks and bonds for the period 1926 to 2013.
	Updated Did You Know	Gives updated information for different income levels for people in the United States.
	New Dashboard feature	Explains the importance of developing measurable investment goals and performing a financial checkup.
Chapter 14	*New content:* Why people invest in stocks	Explains the psychological reasons why people choose stocks for a long-term investment program.
	New content: How to make a decision to buy or sell stocks	Provides some specific steps to help individuals make a decision to buy or sell a stock.
	Updated information: Income from dividends	Explains the importance of the record date for a quarterly dividend distribution for Chevron.

Chapter	*Selected Topics*	Benefits for the Teaching–Learning Environment
	Updated Exhibit 14-2 Sample stock transaction	Illustrates how investors can make money with a stock investment in The Walt Disney Corporation.
	New Exhibit 14-5: Stock information from the Internet	Describes the type of information provided by the Yahoo! Finance website for the Gap Corporation.
	Updated Did You Know	Provides new information about historical values for the Dow Jones Industrial Average for the period December 2007 through December 2012.
	New Exhibit 14-7: Value Line research information	Illustrates the type of detailed research information for Dollar Tree, Inc. available from the Value Line professional advisory service
	New coverage: Stock market bubbles	Defines a stock market bubble and describes how it can affect the value of an investment.
	Updated coverage: Numerical measures	Provides updated examples for all examples in the section Numerical Measures that Influence Investment Decisions.
	New box feature: Financial Planning Calculations	Illustrates how the time value of money can affect the value of a stock investment.
	Updated boxed feature: Financial Planning Calculations	Includes current statistics for the Boeing Company that are used to illustrate the price/earnings to growth (PEG) ratio calculation.
	Updated Exhibit 14-8: Typical commission charges	Shows current commission charges for some popular online brokerage firms.
	New information: Limit orders	Illustrates how a limit order can be used to specify a price to buy or sell stock in Macy's.
	New Did You Know	Gives an explanation of how Wall Street got its name.
	Revised Exhibit 14-9: Dollar-cost averaging	Includes seven years of investments instead of four years for the dollar-cost averaging example.
	New example: Margin transactions	Provides an example of how investors can increase their profits by using margin.
	New material: Selling short	Provides new material and an example on the selling short process that investors can use to increase profits.
	New Dashboard feature	Points out why investors need to save money before they begin investing.
	New time value of money problems	Adds new problems that illustrate how the time value of money can affect investment returns and cumulative dividend amounts.
	New Financial Planning Case	Allows students a chance to increase their ability to research a stock investment in Dollar Tree, Inc. and is based on the Value Line research information contained in Exhibit 14-7.
Chapter 15	*New Example:* Convertible bonds	Includes information about Ford Motor Company's convertible bond issue.
	Updated Did You Know	Provides updated information for the yields on high-quality corporate bonds.
	New material: The psychology of investing in bonds	Adds a new section on the psychology of investing in bonds and specific reasons why investors choose bonds.
	Revised Example: Interest calculation	Shows students how to calculate the interest for a $1,000 AT&T bond that pays 5.50 percent annual interest.

Chapter	*Selected Topics*	Benefits for the Teaching–Learning Environment
Chapter 15 (Cont.)	*New boxed feature:* Financial Planning Calculations	Illustrates how reinvesting annual interest amounts can make a difference because of the time value of money.
	Updated Example: Dollar appreciation for a bond	Shows how a bond's value can change because of changes in overall interest rates in the economy.
	Updated Exhibit 15-2: Sample Corporate Bond Transaction	Describes how bond investors can make money with an investment in a DuPont bond.
	Revised Content: Government securities	Addresses the quality of securities issued by the U.S. government.
	Updated Did You Know	Provides information about yields for 10-year treasury notes from 1990 to February 2013.
	Revised Exhibit 15-4: Tax-exempt yields	Includes equivalent yields for all tax brackets including the recently added 39.6 percent bracket.
	Revised Exhibit 15-5: Bond information	Gives information from the Yahoo! Finance website about an American Express bond.
	Revised Exhibit 15-6: Bond Ratings	Provides revised information about the bond ratings provided by Moody's and Standard and Poor's.
	Revised Examples: Yields	Includes current dollar values for all the examples in the section Bond-Yield Calculations.
	Revised box feature: Financial Planning Calculations	Gives current financial information for AT&T that can be used to calculate the times interest earned ratio.
	New Dashboard feature	Explains the reasons why people—even young investors—choose bonds for their investment program.
	Revised Financial Planning Case	Includes current prices for the possible investments provided in the case.
Chapter 16	*New Example:* Janus Enterprise fund	Illustrates how one person made money by investing in the Janus Enterprise fund.
	Updated Content: Fund statistics	Provides new statistics about the people who invest in mutual funds.
	Expanded Coverage: Fund history	Adds new material about the history of mutual fund investing
	Updated Did You Know	Includes current information about the age of investors who own mutual funds.
	New Exhibit 16-1: Fund diversification	Shows the type of stocks and securities included in the Invesco Growth and Income fund.
	New information: Number of funds	Provides current numbers for exchange-traded, closed-end, and open-end funds.
	Updated Exhibit 16-2: Fund fee table	Illustrates the fee table for the Davis New York Venture fund.
	New Example: A fund objective	Provides the fund objective for the Vanguard Growth Equity fund.
	New box feature: Time value of money	Ties the time value of money to fund investing.
	New Did You Know	Illustrates the reasons why people invest in funds.
	Expanded coverage: Fund managers	Adds material about the role of a fund manager during both good and bad economic times.
	New Did You Know	Provides information about the Morningstar "Star" ratings system.

Chapter	*Selected Topics*	Benefits for the Teaching–Learning Environment
Chapter 16 (Cont.)	*Updated Exhibit 16-4:* Large funds	Updates information about three large funds: The Vanguard Group, Fidelity Investments, and American Funds.
	Expanded coverage: Professional advisory services	Provides more information and an example of the type of research information about funds that is available on the Morningstar website.
	New Exhibit 16-6: Information from Money Magazine	Shows a portion of the "Money 70 Best Mutual Funds and ETFs" article from *Money* Magazine.
	Updated Example: Fidelity Stock Selector fund	Provides current price information used to illustrate a capital gains distribution for the Fidelity Stock Selector fund.
	New Example: Withdrawals	Adds an example of a withdrawal when an investor receives a portion of asset growth during an investment period.
	New Dashboard feature	Points out that even with the professional management and diversification that funds offer, investors must still evaluate fund investments.
	New Financial Planning Case	Asks students to conduct research about a fund and then decide if they would invest money in the fund they chose.
Chapter 17	*Updated Did You Know feature*	Shows that home ownership in the United States soared to a historic high of 69.1 percent in 2005, but it dropped to 65.4 percent in 2012.
	Updated Did You Know feature	Illustrates that home ownership is very low for people under 35, but it rises sharply as people enter their mid-30s.
	Revised, updated content: Home as an investment	Explains that about $7 trillion in household wealth was lost as average house prices decreased by nearly 33 percent from their peak in 2007.
	New Exhibit 17-2: U.S. home sales	Shows that recent economic indicators suggest that the worse of the housing crisis is over.
	New Exhibit 17-3A: House price declines	Displays the peak-to-trough home price declines for each state during the housing bust.
	New Exhibit 17-3B: Increases in house prices	Displays the increase in house prices since prices bottomed out in each state through June 2012.
	Revised, updated content: Vacation home	Provides updated information about the characteristics of vacation home investors.
	New Financial Planning for Life's Situations boxed feature	Cautions that investing in a foreclosure may be profitable, but make sure to protect your own property from being foreclosed.
	New content: REITs	Explains that REITs invest in apartment buildings, hospital, hotels, industrial facilities, nursing homes, and other properties.
	Updated Did You Know feature	Illustrates how REITs invest in all types of properties (in 2012).
	Revised and updated Financial Planning for Life's Situations feature	Provides new information about Uncle Sam and His Family (the government securities).
	New coverage: Disadvantages of real estate investments	Points out that beginning in 2013, a new 3.8 percent tax on some investment income is imposed to fund the Affordable Care Act.

Chapter	*Selected Topics*	Benefits for the Teaching–Learning Environment
Chapter 17 (Cont.)	*Revised and updated coverage:* Precious metals	Provides the latest information on the recent rise and fall in the prices of gold, silver, platinum, palladium, and rhodium.
	Updated Exhibit 17-4: Gold prices	Illustrates how the price of gold has fluctuated from 1976 to 2012.
	Revised and updated Did You Know feature	Shows the biggest producers of gold in the world (2011).
	New Financial Planning for Life's Situations boxed feature	Questions if gold is a solid investment, and if so, what are several ways to invest in it.
	New Dashboard feature	Explains the importance of investment diversification by including a variety of assets in your portfolio.
Chapter 18	*New content:* Why retirement planning?	Explains that as baby boomers near and enter their retirement years, they will encounter a unique set of challenges unlike those any previous generation has faced.
	Revised content: Starting early	Provides most current information about the importance of starting early.
	New content: The power of compounding	Shows the power of compounding at different annual rates of return over different time periods.
	Revised content: Financial Planning for Life's Situations feature	Defines a qualified domestic relations order (QDRO) and cautions that there is no single "best" way to divide retirement benefits in a QDRO.
	Updated Exhibit 18-4: Older household expenditures	Illustrates how an "average" older household spends its money (2011).
	Revised Did You Know feature	Illustrates who receives Social Security benefits (2012).
	Revised Did You Know feature	Provides updated information on monthly Social Security benefits in 2013.
	Revised content: The future of Social Security	Cautions that according to the 2012 Trustees Report, Social Security is not sustainable over the long term at current benefit and tax rates.
	Updated Exhibit 18-8: The future of Social Security	Shows that the number of workers per beneficiary has plummeted since 1945.
	Updated coverage: Defined-contribution plan	Describes new contribution limits for 2013.
	Updated coverage: Regular and Roth IRAs	Provides new contribution limits for regular and Roth IRAs for 2013.
	New content: Keogh plans	Provides an expanded discussion of Keogh plans and SEP-IRAs.
	New content: Financial Planning for Life's Situation boxed feature	Adds a timeline for retirement in the retirement checklist.
	New Dashboard feature	Explains the importance of exploring your options in retirement savings opportunities now that traditional pensions and other employer-funded investment plans have become increasingly rare.

Chapter	*Selected Topics*	Benefits for the Teaching–Learning Environment
Chapter 19	*Revised content:* New lifestyles	Provides the latest available information about gift and estate tax exemptions.
	New content: Social media will	Explains the importance of preparing a social media will, if social media is part of your daily life.
	New content: Credit-shelter trust	Points out that a married couple will not pay any estate tax if their estate is less than $10.5 million in 2013.
	Revised content: Federal and State Estate Taxes	Provides the latest available information about gift taxes (2013).
	New content: Estate Taxes	Points out that under the American Taxpayer Relief Act of 2012 (ATRA), the surviving spouse's estate in excess of $10.5 million (in 2013) faces estate tax of 40 percent.
	Updated Exhibit 19-6: Estate tax law changes	Shows the highest tax rates, gift exemption, and GST tax exemption amounts from 2001 to 2013.
	New Dashboard feature	Explains the importance of estate planning to ensure that you have a secure future for yourself and your loved ones.

ASSURANCE OF LEARNING

Many educational institutions today are focused on the notion of assurance of learning, an important element of some accreditation standards. *Personal Finance, 11th ed.,* is designed specifically to support your assurance of learning initiatives with a simple, yet powerful, solution.

Each test bank question for *Personal Finance, 11th ed.,* maps to a specific chapter learning outcome/objective listed in the text. You can use the test bank software to easily query for learning outcomes/objectives that directly relate to the learning objectives for your course. You can then use the reporting features of the software to aggregate student results in similar fashion, making the collection and presentation of assurance of learning data simple and easy.

GUIDED TOUR

Chapter Opener: The chapter opener contains new features that serve as the chapter road map at a glance!

What Will This Mean for Me?

A short summary of why this chapter is important. Also, what students can expect to learn from it and apply to their own personal financial plan.

Learning Objectives	What will this mean for me?
LO1-1 Analyze the process for making personal financial decisions. **LO1-2** Assess personal and economic factors that influence personal financial planning. **LO1-3** Develop personal financial goals. **LO1-4** Calculate time value of money situations associated with personal financial decisions. **LO1-5** Identify strategies for achieving personal financial goals for different life situations.	Every person has some money. However, the amounts and individual needs and choices are diverse. You now have the opportunity to learn about varied financial paths for avoiding common money mistakes. Your knowledge and actions will move you toward financial security. Despite economic uncertainty, you will be able to use wise financial strategies in every stage of your life to achieve your personal goals.

Learning Objectives

A summary of learning objectives is presented at the start of each chapter. These objectives are highlighted at the start of each major section in the chapter and appear again in the end-of-chapter summary. The learning objectives are also used to organize the end-of-chapter problems and activities, as well as materials in the *Instructor's Manual* and *Test Bank*. Problems in CONNECT can also be organized using the objectives.

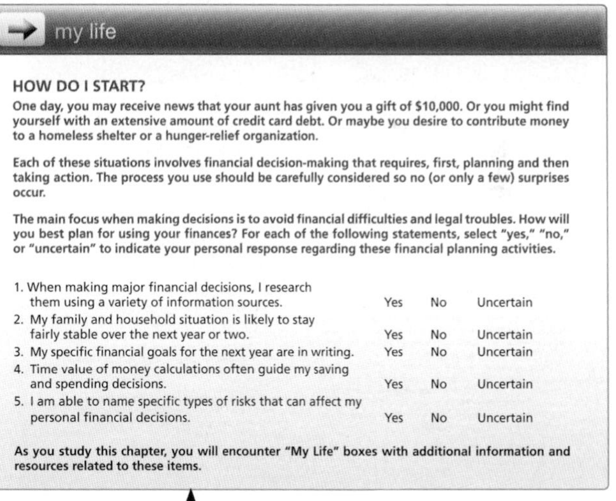

my life

HOW DO I START?

One day, you may receive news that your aunt has given you a gift of $10,000. Or you might find yourself with an extensive amount of credit card debt. Or maybe you desire to contribute money to a homeless shelter or a hunger-relief organization.

Each of these situations involves financial decision-making that requires, first, planning and then taking action. The process you use should be carefully considered so no (or only a few) surprises occur.

The main focus when making decisions is to avoid financial difficulties and legal troubles. How will you best plan for using your finances? For each of the following statements, select "yes," "no," or "uncertain" to indicate your personal response regarding these financial planning activities.

1. When making major financial decisions, I research them using a variety of information sources.	Yes	No	Uncertain
2. My family and household situation is likely to stay fairly stable over the next year or two.	Yes	No	Uncertain
3. My specific financial goals for the next year are in writing.	Yes	No	Uncertain
4. Time value of money calculations often guide my saving and spending decisions.	Yes	No	Uncertain
5. I am able to name specific types of risks that can affect my personal financial decisions.	Yes	No	Uncertain

As you study this chapter, you will encounter "My Life" boxes with additional information and resources related to these items.

My Life

The My Life concept begins with the chapter opener. It presents students with an engaging scenario that relates what they're about to learn to their own lives. The follow-up questions are designed to get students thinking about how involved they currently are in their personal finances and to motivate them to try new beneficial practices in their own personal finance life. The My Life Boxes throughout the chapters and the Learning Objectives in the chapter summary expand on this concept.

Boxed features are used in each chapter to build student interest and highlight important topics. Three different types of boxed features are used.

How To . . .

The How To . . . boxes fit in with the application-driven themes of *Personal Finance*. Each box highlights a personal finance issue and walks students through how to navigate the situation.

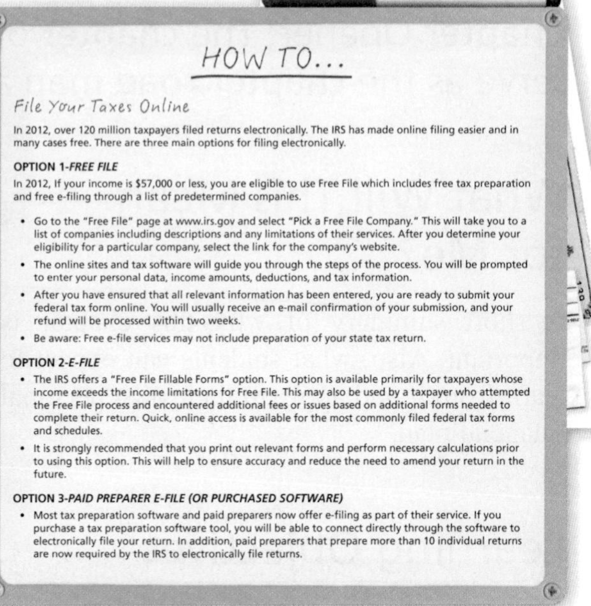

HOW TO...

File Your Taxes Online

In 2012, over 120 million taxpayers filed returns electronically. The IRS has made online filing easier and in many cases free. There are three main options for filing electronically.

OPTION 1-*FREE FILE*

In 2012, if your income is $57,000 or less, you are eligible to use Free File which includes free tax preparation and free e-filing through a list of predetermined companies.

- Go to the "Free File" page at www.irs.gov and select "Pick a Free File Company." This will take you to a list of companies including descriptions and any limitations of their services. After you determine your eligibility for a particular company, select the link for the company's website.
- The online sites and tax software will guide you through the steps of the process. You will be prompted to enter your personal data, income amounts, deductions, and tax information.
- After you have ensured that all relevant information has been entered, you are ready to submit your federal tax form online. You will usually receive an e-mail confirmation of your submission, and your refund will be processed within two weeks.
- Be aware: Free e-file services may not include preparation of your state tax return.

OPTION 2-*E-FILE*

- The IRS offers a "Free File Fillable Forms" option. This option is available primarily for taxpayers whose income exceeds the income limitations for Free File. This may also be used by a taxpayer who attempted the Free File process and encountered additional fees or issues based on additional forms needed to complete their return. Quick, online access is available for the most commonly filed federal tax forms and schedules.
- It is strongly recommended that you print out relevant forms and perform necessary calculations prior to using this option. This will help to ensure accuracy and reduce the need to amend your return in the future.

OPTION 3-*PAID PREPARER E-FILE (OR PURCHASED SOFTWARE)*

- Most tax preparation software and paid preparers now offer e-filing as part of their service. If you purchase a tax preparation software tool, you will be able to connect directly through the software to electronically file your return. In addition, paid preparers that prepare more than 10 individual returns are now required by the IRS to electronically file returns.

Financial Planning for Life's Situations

This box offers information that can assist students when faced with special situations and unique financial planning decisions. Many emphasize the use of Internet sources.

Financial Planning for Life's Situations

WHAT'S "PHISHING"?

You open an e-mail and see messages like these: "We suspect an unauthorized transaction on your account. To ensure that your account is not compromised, please click the link below and confirm your identity." "During our regular verification of accounts, we could not verify your information. Please click here to update and verify your information." "Our records indicate that your account was overcharged. You must call us within 7 days to receive your refund." These senders are "phishing" for your information to commit fraud.

Regulatory agencies have published a brochure, *Internet Pirates Are Trying to Steal Your Information*, to assist you in identifying and preventing a new type of Internet fraud known as "phishing." With this type of scam, you receive fraudulent e-mail messages that appear to be from your financial institution. The messages often appear authentic and may include the institution's logo and marketing slogans.

These messages usually describe a situation that requires immediate attention and state that your accounts will be terminated unless you verify your personal information by clicking on a provided Web link. The Web link then takes you to a screen that asks for confidential information, including:

- Account numbers.
- Social Security numbers.
- Passwords.
- Place of birth.
- Other information used to identify you.

Those perpetrating the fraud then use this information to access your accounts or assume your identity.

The brochure advises consumers:

- If you're not sure the e-mail is legitimate, go to the company's site by typing in a Web address that you know is authentic.
- If you think the e-mail message might be fraudulent, *do not* click on any embedded link within the e-mail. The link may contain a virus.
- Do not be intimidated by e-mails that warn of dire consequences for not following the sender's instructions.
- If you do you fall victim to a phishing scam, act immediately to protect yourself by alerting your financial institution, placing fraud alerts on your credit files, and monitoring your account statements closely.
- Report suspicious e-mails or calls from third parties to the Federal Trade Commission, either through the Internet at www.consumer.gov/idtheft or by calling 1-877-IDTHEFT.

The brochure is on the Office of the Comptroller of the Currency's website, www.occ.gov/consumer/phishing.htm.

Source: Federal Trade Commission, www.consumer.ftc.gov/articles/0003-phishing, March 6, 2013.

Financial Planning Calculations

This feature presents more than 90 mathematical applications relevant to personal financial situations.

Financial Planning Calculations

ANNUAL PERCENTAGE YIELD

The Truth in Savings law requires that financial institutions report in advertisements, if a rate is quoted, and to savings plan customers the annual percentage yield (APY). The formula for APY is

$$\text{APY} = 100\left[(1 + \text{Interest/Principal})^{365/\text{days in term}} - 1\right]$$

The *principal* is the amount of funds on deposit. *Interest* is the total dollar amount earned during the term on the principal. *Days in term* is the actual number of days over which interest is earned.

When the number of days in the term is 365 (that is, where the stated maturity is 365 days) or where the account does not have a stated maturity, the APY formula is simply

$$\text{APY} = 100\,(\text{Interest/Principal})$$

APY provides a consistent comparison for savings plans with different interest rates, different compounding frequencies, and different time periods. APY may be easily viewed in terms of a $100 deposit for a 365-day year. For example, an APY of 6.5 percent would mean $6.50 interest for a year.

Margin notes provide connections to supplementary information. While the Did You Know? feature provides interesting statistics and tips in personal financial planning. The Practice Quiz feature provides an ongoing assessment tool.

Key Terms

Key terms appear in bold type and in the margin definition boxes. The terms and their page references are also listed at the end of each chapter.

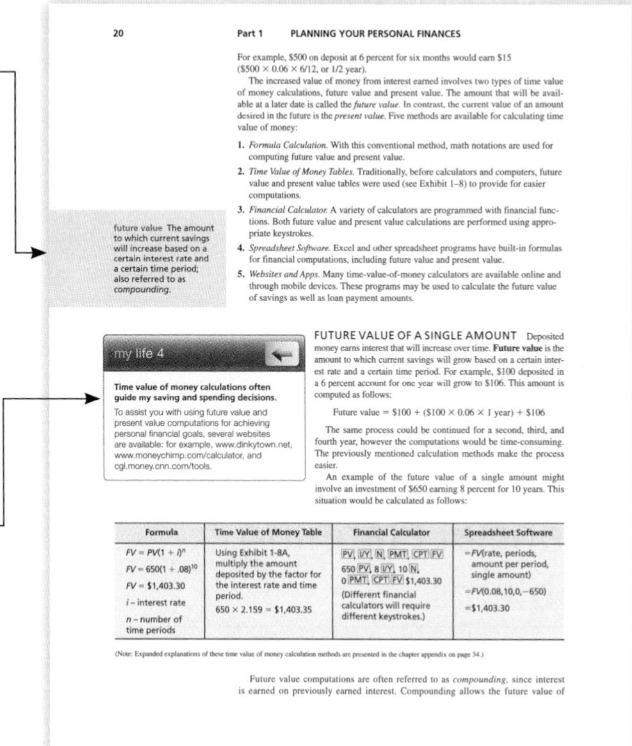

20 Part 1 PLANNING YOUR PERSONAL FINANCES

For example, \$500 on deposit at 6 percent for six months would earn \$15 (\$500 × 0.06 × 6/12, or 1/2 year).

The increased value of money from interest earned involves two types of time value of money calculations, future value and present value. The amount that will be available at a later date is called the *future value*. In contrast, the current value of an amount desired in the future is the *present value*. Five methods are available for calculating time value of money:

1. *Formula Calculation.* With this conventional method, math notations are used for computing future value and present value.
2. *Time Value of Money Tables.* Traditionally, before calculators and computers, future value and present value tables were used (see Exhibit 1–8) to provide for easier computations.
3. *Financial Calculator.* A variety of calculators are programmed with financial functions. Both future value and present value calculations are performed using appropriate keystrokes.
4. *Spreadsheet Software.* Excel and other spreadsheet programs have built-in formulas for financial computations, including future value and present value.
5. *Websites and Apps.* Many time-value-of-money calculators are available online and through mobile devices. These programs may be used to calculate the future value of savings as well as loan payment amounts.

future value The amount to which current savings will increase based on a certain interest rate and a certain time period; also referred to as *compounding*.

my life 4

Time value of money calculations often guide my saving and spending decisions.

To assist you with using future value and present value computations for achieving personal financial goals, several websites are available: for example, www.dinkytown.net, www.moneychimp.com/calculator, and cgi.money.cnn.com/tools.

FUTURE VALUE OF A SINGLE AMOUNT Deposited money earns interest that will increase over time. **Future value** is the amount to which current savings will grow based on a certain interest rate and a certain time period. For example, \$100 deposited in a 6 percent account for one year will grow to \$106. This amount is computed as follows:

Future value = \$100 + (\$100 × 0.06 × 1 year) + \$106

The same process could be continued for a second, third, and fourth year, however the computations would be time-consuming. The previously mentioned calculation methods make the process easier.

An example of the future value of a single amount might involve an investment of \$650 earning 8 percent for 10 years. This situation would be calculated as follows:

Formula	Time Value of Money Table	Financial Calculator	Spreadsheet Software
$FV = PV(1 + i)^n$ $FV = 650(1 + .08)^{10}$ $FV = \$1,403.30$ i – interest rate n – number of time periods	Using Exhibit 1-8A, multiply the amount deposited by the factor for the interest rate and time period. 650 × 2.159 = \$1,403.35	PV, I/Y, N, PMT, CPT FV 650 PV, 8 I/Y, 10 N, 0 PMT, CPT FV \$1,403.30 (Different financial calculators will require different keystrokes.)	=FV(rate, periods, amount per period, single amount) =FV(0.08,10,0,−650) =\$1,403.30

(Note: Expanded explanations of these time value of money calculation methods are presented in the chapter appendix on page 34.)

Future value computations are often referred to as *compounding*, since interest is earned on previously earned interest. Compounding allows the future value of

My Life Boxes

My Life boxes appear next to material that relates back to the opening My Life scenario and the Learning Objectives. These boxes offer useful tips and possible solutions to help students better manage their finances.

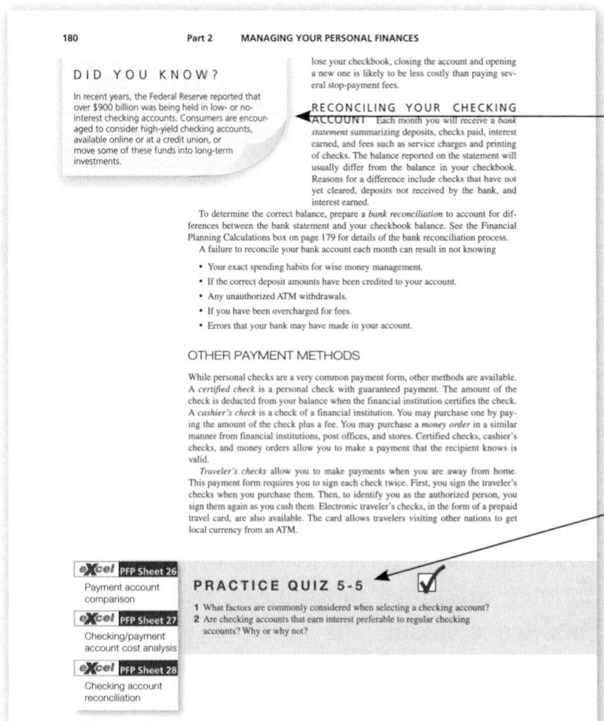

180 Part 2 MANAGING YOUR PERSONAL FINANCES

DID YOU KNOW?

In recent years, the Federal Reserve reported that over \$900 billion was being held in low- or no-interest checking accounts. Consumers are encouraged to consider high-yield checking accounts, available online or at a credit union, or move some of these funds into long-term investments.

lose your checkbook, closing the account and opening a new one is likely to be less costly than paying several stop-payment fees.

RECONCILING YOUR CHECKING ACCOUNT Each month you will receive a *bank statement* summarizing deposits, checks paid, interest earned, and fees such as service charges and printing of checks. The balance reported on the statement will usually differ from the balance in your checkbook. Reasons for a difference include checks that have not yet cleared, deposits not received by the bank, and interest earned.

To determine the correct balance, prepare a *bank reconciliation* to account for differences between the bank statement and your checkbook balance. See the Financial Planning Calculations box on page 179 for details of the bank reconciliation process.

A failure to reconcile your bank account each month can result in not knowing

- Your exact spending habits for wise money management.
- If the correct deposit amounts have been credited to your account.
- Any unauthorized ATM withdrawals.
- If you have been overcharged for fees.
- Errors that your bank may have made in your account.

OTHER PAYMENT METHODS

While personal checks are a very common payment form, other methods are available. A *certified check* is a personal check with guaranteed payment. The amount of the check is deducted from your balance when the financial institution certifies the check. A *cashier's check* is a check of a financial institution. You may purchase one by paying the amount of the check plus a fee. You may purchase a *money order* in a similar manner from financial institutions, post offices, and stores. Certified checks, cashier's checks, and money orders allow you to make a payment that the recipient knows is valid.

Traveler's checks allow you to make payments when you are away from home. This payment form requires you to sign each check twice. First, you sign the traveler's checks when you purchase them. Then, to identify you as the authorized person, you sign them again as you cash them. Electronic traveler's checks, in the form of a prepaid travel card, are also available. The card allows travelers visiting other nations to get local currency from an ATM.

eXcel PFP Sheet 26 Payment account comparison

eXcel PFP Sheet 27 Checking/payment account cost analysis

eXcel PFP Sheet 28 Checking account reconciliation

PRACTICE QUIZ 5-5

1 What factors are commonly considered when selecting a checking account?
2 Are checking accounts that earn interest preferable to regular checking accounts? Why or why not?

Did You Know?

Each chapter contains several *Did You Know?* features with fun facts, information, and financial planning assistance.

Practice Quiz

The *Practice Quiz* at the end of each major section provides questions to help students assess their knowledge of the main ideas covered in that section. As shown here, many of these quizzes include references to related Personal Financial Planning sheets, offered both in Excel and in hard copy at the back of the book.

A variety of end-of-chapter features are offered to support the concepts presented throughout each chapter.

Finance Dashboard and My Life Stages

There are increasing numbers of nontraditional students taking personal finance. The **new** Dashboard feature provides students of all ages with a high-level snapshot outlining how to evaluate progress in achieving mastery of the chapter concepts in real life. The My Life Stages box at the end of each chapter provides personal finance action items for students of all ages.

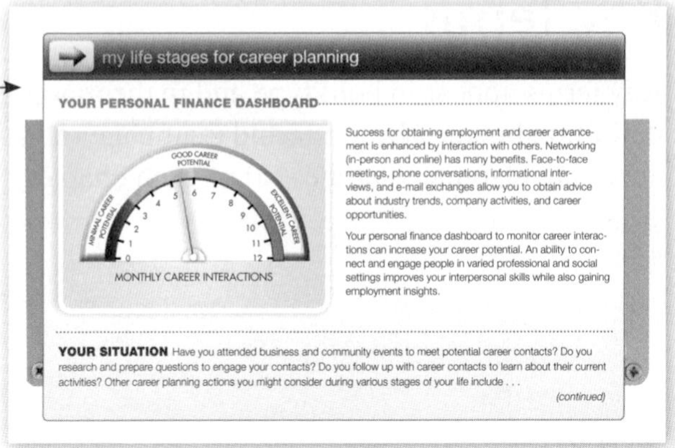

my life stages for career planning

YOUR PERSONAL FINANCE DASHBOARD

Success for obtaining employment and career advancement is enhanced by interaction with others. Networking (in-person and online) has many benefits. Face-to-face meetings, phone conversations, informational interviews, and e-mail exchanges allow you to obtain advice about industry trends, company activities, and career opportunities.

Your personal finance dashboard to monitor career interactions can increase your career potential. An ability to connect and engage people in varied professional and social settings improves your interpersonal skills while also gaining employment insights.

YOUR SITUATION Have you attended business and community events to meet potential career contacts? Do you research and prepare questions to engage your contacts? Do you follow up with career contacts to learn about their current activities? Other career planning actions you might consider during various stages of your life include . . .

(continued)

Financial Planning Problems

With more added to this edition, these problems allow students to apply their quantitative analysis of personal financial decisions.

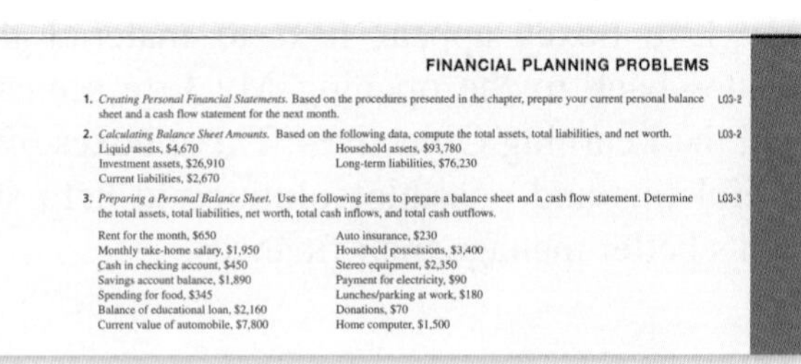

FINANCIAL PLANNING PROBLEMS

1. *Creating Personal Financial Statements.* Based on the procedures presented in the chapter, prepare your current personal balance sheet and a cash flow statement for the next month. LO3-2
2. *Calculating Balance Sheet Amounts.* Based on the following data, compute the total assets, total liabilities, and net worth. LO3-2
   Liquid assets, $4,670 — Household assets, $93,780
   Investment assets, $26,910 — Long-term liabilities, $76,230
   Current liabilities, $2,670
3. *Preparing a Personal Balance Sheet.* Use the following items to prepare a balance sheet and a cash flow statement. Determine the total assets, total liabilities, net worth, total cash inflows, and total cash outflows. LO3-3

Rent for the month, $650	Auto insurance, $230
Monthly take-home salary, $1,950	Household possessions, $3,400
Cash in checking account, $450	Stereo equipment, $2,350
Savings account balance, $1,890	Payment for electricity, $90
Spending for food, $345	Lunches/parking at work, $180
Balance of educational loan, $2,160	Donations, $70
Current value of automobile, $7,800	Home computer, $1,500

Financial Planning Activities

The *Financial Planning Activities* provide methods of researching and applying financial planning topics.

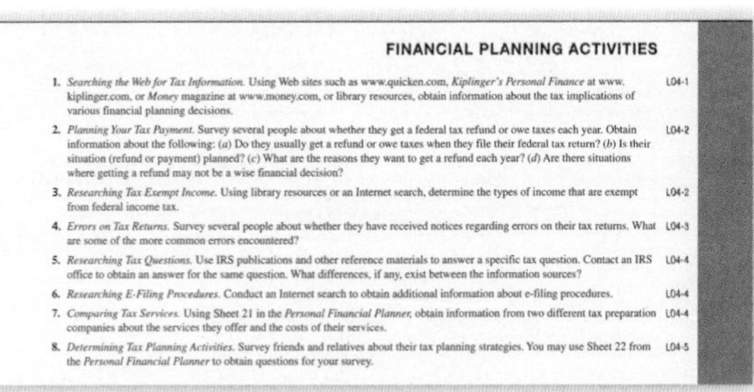

FINANCIAL PLANNING ACTIVITIES

1. *Searching the Web for Tax Information.* Using Web sites such as www.quicken.com, *Kiplinger's Personal Finance* at www.kiplinger.com, or *Money* magazine at www.money.com, or library resources, obtain information about the tax implications of various financial planning decisions. LO4-1
2. *Planning Your Tax Payment.* Survey several people about whether they get a federal tax refund or owe taxes each year. Obtain information about the following: (*a*) Do they usually get a refund or owe taxes when they file their federal tax return? (*b*) Is their situation (refund or payment) planned? (*c*) What are the reasons they want to get a refund each year? (*d*) Are there situations where getting a refund may not be a wise financial decision? LO4-2
3. *Researching Tax Exempt Income.* Using library resources or an Internet search, determine the types of income that are exempt from federal income tax. LO4-2
4. *Errors on Tax Returns.* Survey several people about whether they have received notices regarding errors on their tax returns. What are some of the more common errors encountered? LO4-3
5. *Researching Tax Questions.* Use IRS publications and other reference materials to answer a specific tax question. Contact an IRS office to obtain an answer for the same question. What differences, if any, exist between the information sources? LO4-4
6. *Researching E-Filing Procedures.* Conduct an Internet search to obtain additional information about e-filing procedures. LO4-4
7. *Comparing Tax Services.* Using Sheet 21 in the *Personal Financial Planner,* obtain information from two different tax preparation companies about the services they offer and the costs of their services. LO4-4
8. *Determining Tax Planning Activities.* Survey friends and relatives about their tax planning strategies. You may use Sheet 22 from the *Personal Financial Planner* to obtain questions for your survey. LO4-5

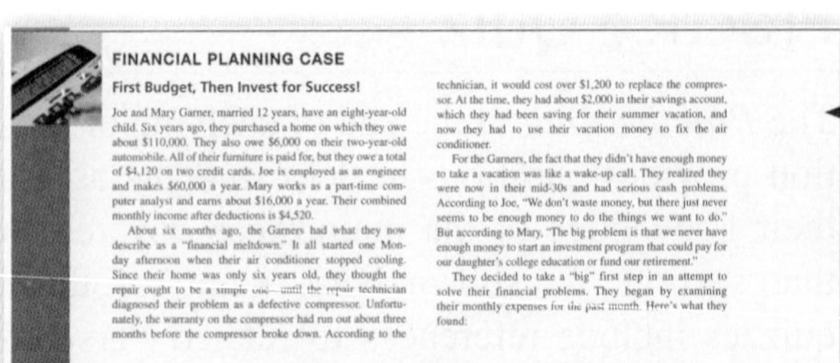

FINANCIAL PLANNING CASE

First Budget, Then Invest for Success!

Joe and Mary Garner, married 12 years, have an eight-year-old child. Six years ago, they purchased a home on which they owe about $110,000. They also owe $6,000 on their two-year-old automobile. All of their furniture is paid for, but they owe a total of $4,120 on two credit cards. Joe is employed as an engineer and makes $60,000 a year. Mary works as a part-time computer analyst and earns about $16,000 a year. Their combined monthly income after deductions is $4,520.

About six months ago, the Garners had what they now describe as a "financial meltdown." It all started one Monday afternoon when their air conditioner stopped cooling. Since their home was only six years old, they thought the repair ought to be a simple one—until the repair technician diagnosed their problem as a defective compressor. Unfortunately, the warranty on the compressor had run out about three months before the compressor broke down. According to the technician, it would cost over $1,200 to replace the compressor. At the time, they had about $2,000 in their savings account, which they had been saving for their summer vacation, and now they had to use their vacation money to fix the air conditioner.

For the Garners, the fact that they didn't have enough money to take a vacation was like a wake-up call. They realized they were now in their mid-30s and had serious cash problems. According to Joe, "We don't waste money, but there just never seems to be enough money to do the things we want to do." But according to Mary, "The big problem is that we never have enough money to start an investment program that could pay for our daughter's college education or fund our retirement."

They decided to take a "big" first step in an attempt to solve their financial problems. They began by examining their monthly expenses for the past month. Here's what they found:

Financial Planning Case

Students are given a hypothetical personal finance dilemma and data to work through to practice concepts they have learned from the chapter. A series of questions helps students to use analytic and critical thinking skills while reinforcing chapter topics.

Personal Financial Planner in Action

This feature provides long- and short-term financial planning activities per the concepts learned within the chapter, and links each to relevant Personal Financial Planner sheets (located at the end of the book) and websites for further personal financial planning.

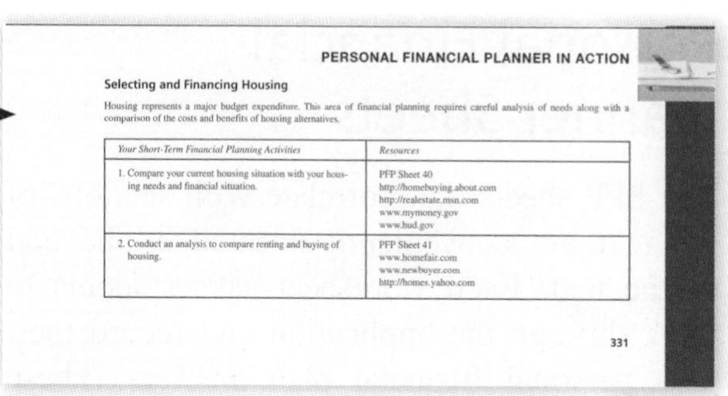

PERSONAL FINANCIAL PLANNER IN ACTION

Selecting and Financing Housing

Housing represents a major budget expenditure. This area of financial planning requires careful analysis of needs along with a comparison of the costs and benefits of housing alternatives.

Your Short-Term Financial Planning Activities	*Resources*
1. Compare your current housing situation with your housing needs and financial situation.	PFP Sheet 40 http://homebuying.about.com http://realestate.msn.com www.mymoney.gov www.hud.gov
2. Conduct an analysis to compare renting and buying of housing.	PFP Sheet 41 www.homefair.com www.newbuyer.com http://homes.yahoo.com

331

Continuing Case

The continuing case gives students the opportunity to apply course concepts in a life situation. This feature encourages students to evaluate the changes that affect a family and then respond to the resulting shift in needs, resources, and priorities through the questions at the end of each case.

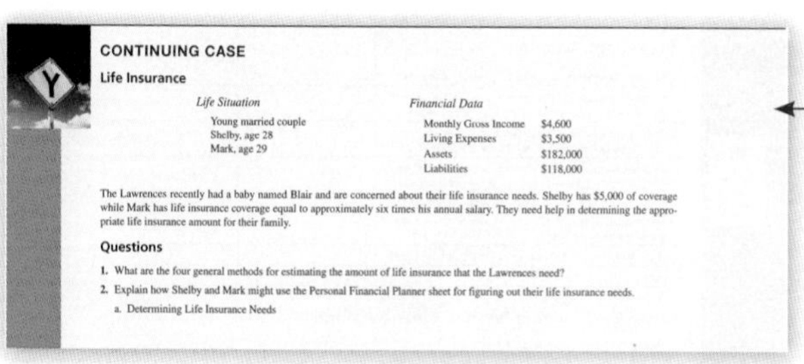

CONTINUING CASE

Life Insurance

Life Situation	*Financial Data*	
Young married couple	Monthly Gross Income	$4,600
Shelby, age 28	Living Expenses	$3,500
Mark, age 29	Assets	$182,000
	Liabilities	$118,000

The Lawrences recently had a baby named Blair and are concerned about their life insurance needs. Shelby has $5,000 of coverage while Mark has life insurance coverage equal to approximately six times his annual salary. They need help in determining the appropriate life insurance amount for their family.

Questions

1. What are the four general methods for estimating the amount of life insurance that the Lawrences need?
2. Explain how Shelby and Mark might use the Personal Financial Planner sheet for figuring out their life insurance needs.
   a. Determining Life Insurance Needs

Daily Spending Diary

Do you buy a latte or a soda every day before class? Do you and your friends meet for a movie once a week? How much do you spend on gas for your car each month? Do you try to donate to your favorite local charity every year?

These everyday spending activities might go largely unnoticed, yet they have a significant effect on the overall health of an individual's finances. The Daily Spending Diary sheets (in Appendix D and online) and end-of-chapter activities offer students a place to keep track of *every cent they spend* in any category. Careful monitoring and assessing of these daily spending habits can lead to better control and understanding of students' personal finances.

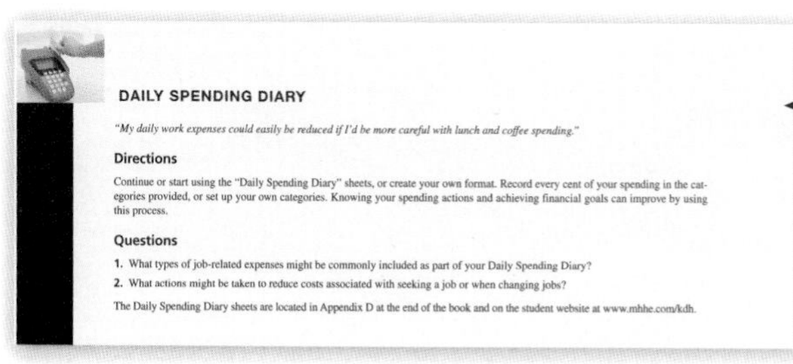

DAILY SPENDING DIARY

"My daily work expenses could easily be reduced if I'd be more careful with lunch and coffee spending."

Directions

Continue or start using the "Daily Spending Diary" sheets, or create your own format. Record every cent of your spending in the categories provided, or set up your own categories. Knowing your spending actions and achieving financial goals can improve by using this process.

Questions

1. What types of job-related expenses might be commonly included as part of your Daily Spending Diary?
2. What actions might be taken to reduce costs associated with seeking a job or when changing jobs?

The Daily Spending Diary sheets are located in Appendix D at the end of the book and on the student website at www.mhhe.com/kdh.

Persona
feature
adapte

Personal Financial Planner Sheets

The PFP sheets that correlate with sections of the text are conveniently located at the end of the text. Each worksheet asks students to work through the application and record their own personal financial plan answers. These sheets apply concepts learned to students' personal situation and serve as a road map to their personal financial future. Students can fill them out, submit them for homework, and keep them filed in a safe spot for future reference!

Key websites are provided to help students research and devise their personal financial plan, and the "What's Next for Your Personal Financial Plan?" section at the end of each sheet challenges students to use their responses to plan the next level, as well as foreshadow upcoming concepts. NEW to this edition, the authors recommend favorite apps to help students master the relevant contents.

Look for one or more PFP icons next to many Practice Quizzes. The icons direct students to the Personal Financial Planner sheet that corresponds with the preceding section.

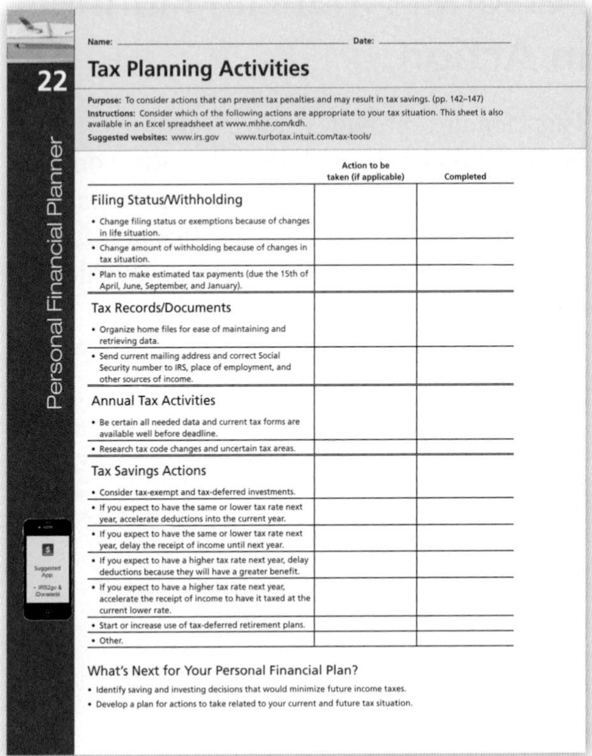

22 Personal Financial Planner

Name: ____________ Date: ____________

Tax Planning Activities

Purpose: To consider actions that can prevent tax penalties and may result in tax savings. (pp. 142–147)

Instructions: Consider which of the following actions are appropriate to your tax situation. This sheet is also available in an Excel spreadsheet at www.mhhe.com/kdh.

Suggested websites: www.irs.gov www.turbotax.intuit.com/tax-tools/

	Action to be taken (if applicable)	Completed
Filing Status/Withholding		
• Change filing status or exemptions because of changes in life situation.		
• Change amount of withholding because of changes in tax situation.		
• Plan to make estimated tax payments (due the 15th of April, June, September, and January).		
Tax Records/Documents		
• Organize home files for ease of maintaining and retrieving data.		
• Send current mailing address and correct Social Security number to IRS, place of employment, and other sources of income.		
Annual Tax Activities		
• Be certain all needed data and current tax forms are available well before deadline.		
• Research tax code changes and uncertain tax areas.		
Tax Savings Actions		
• Consider tax-exempt and tax-deferred investments.		
• If you expect to have the same or lower tax rate next year, accelerate deductions into the current year.		
• If you expect to have the same or lower tax rate next year, delay the receipt of income until next year.		
• If you expect to have a higher tax rate next year, delay deductions because they will have a greater benefit.		
• If you expect to have a higher tax rate next year, accelerate the receipt of income to have it taxed at the current lower rate.		
• Start or increase use of tax-deferred retirement plans.		
• Other.		

Suggested App:
• IRS2go &
iDonatedit

What's Next for Your Personal Financial Plan?

- Identify saving and investing decisions that would minimize future income taxes.
- Develop a plan for actions to take related to your current and future tax situation.

SUPPLEMENTS

Few textbooks provide such innovative and practical instructional resources for both students and teachers. The comprehensive teaching–learning package for *Personal Finance* includes the extensive tools housed on the book's website.

Online Learning Center (OLC): www.mhhe.com/kdh

The Online Learning Center (OLC) contains access to Web-based study tools and instructor resources created for this text. OLCs can be delivered in multiple ways—through the textbook website (www.mhhe.com/kdh), through PageOut (see below), or within a course management system like Blackboard, WebCT, TopClass, and eCollege. They can also be easily accessed through McGraw-Hill's CONNECT. Ask your campus representative for more details.

For Instructors

The ***Instructor Edition*** of the OLC holds all supplementary material, including the Instructor's Manual, Test Bank, computerized testing software, PowerPoint, and related Web links:

- The *Instructor's Manual* includes a "Course Planning Guide" with instructional strategies, course projects, and supplementary resource lists. The "Chapter Teaching Materials" section of the *Instructor's Manual* provides a chapter overview, the chapter objectives with summaries, introductory activities, and detailed lecture outlines with teaching suggestions. This section also includes concluding activities, ready-to-duplicate quizzes, supplementary lecture materials and activities, and answers to concept checks, end-of-chapter problems, and cases.
- The *Test Bank,* revised by Montgomery Hill, *Northern Virginia Community College,* consists of almost 2,000 true–false, multiple-choice, and essay questions. Each test item is tagged with a corresponding learning objective, topic, level of difficulty, page number, and Blooms category. Use these tags to easily and effectively customize your test bank.
- *Computerized Testing Software*—McGraw-Hill's EZ Test is a flexible and easy-to-use electronic testing program. The program allows instructors to create tests from book-specific items. It accommodates a wide range of question types, and instructors may add their own questions. Multiple versions of the test can be created, and any test can be exported for use with course management systems such as WebCT, BlackBoard, or PageOut. EZ Test Online gives you a place to easily administer your EZ Test–created exams and quizzes online. The program is available for Windows and Macintosh environments.
- Chapter *PowerPoint Presentations* revised by Michelle Grant, *Bossier Parish Community College,* offers more than 300 visual presentations that may be edited and manipulated to fit a particular course format.

ONLINE SUPPORT FOR STUDENTS AND INSTRUCTORS

The student edition of the OLC contains many helpful study tools.

For Students

Self-Study Quizzes
Quizzes consist of 10–15 self-grading multiple choice questions on important chapter topics. They reveal a score instantly as well as hints to help students solve questions they answered incorrectly. Each chapter contains a chapter quiz as well as pre- and posttest quizzes so that students can thoroughly gauge their understanding of the material.

Narrated Student PowerPoint, Revised by Michelle Grant, *Bossier Parish Community College*
Every student learns differently and the *Narrated PowerPoint* was created with that in mind! The interactive chapter presentations are part of the online premium content package and can be purchased. They guide students through understanding key topics and principles by presenting real-life examples based on chapter content.

And More!

Personal Finance Telecourse

If you teach personal finance as a telecourse, this text is a perfect fit! A telecourse program is available from Coastline Community College titled *Dollars $ & Sense: Personal Finance for the 21st Century* that is based on the Kapoor, Dlabay, and Hughes text. The program includes 26 thirty-minute videotapes, which you purchase directly from Coast by contacting Lynn Dahnke, Marketing Director, Coast Learning Systems, 11460 Warner Ave., Fountain Valley, CA 92708, (800) 547-4748 or www.CoastLearning.org. The course also has a *Telecourse Study Guide* available that connects the videos to the text.

PACKAGE OPTIONS

You may also package your text with a variety of other learning tools that are available for your students:

MCGRAW-HILL *CONNECT™ FINANCE*

Less Managing. More Teaching. Greater Learning. McGraw-Hill *Connect™ Finance* is an online assignment and assessment solution that connects students with the tools and resources they'll need to achieve success. *Connect™* helps prepare students for their future by enabling faster learning, more efficient studying, and higher retention of knowledge.

McGraw-Hill *Connect™ Finance* Features *Connect™ Finance* offers a number of powerful tools and features to make managing assignments easier, so faculty can spend more time teaching. With *Connect™ Finance,* students can engage with their coursework anytime and anywhere, making the learning process more accessible and efficient. *Connect™ Finance* offers you the features described below.

Simple assignment management With *Connect™ Finance,* creating assignments is easier than ever, so you can spend more time teaching and less time managing. The assignment management function enables you to

- Create and deliver assignments easily with selectable end-of-chapter problems and test bank items.
- Streamline lesson planning, student progress reporting, and assignment grading to make classroom management more efficient than ever.
- Go paperless with the eBook and online submission and grading of student assignments.

Smart grading When it comes to studying, time is precious. *Connect™ Finance* helps students learn more efficiently by providing feedback and practice material when they need it, where they need it. When it comes to teaching, your time is also precious. The grading function enables you to

- Have assignments scored automatically, giving students immediate feedback on their work and side-by-side comparisons with correct answers.
- Access and review each response; manually change grades or leave comments for students to review.
- Reinforce classroom concepts with practice tests and instant quizzes.

Instructor library The *Connect™ Finance* Instructor Library is your repository for additional resources to improve student engagement in and out of class. You can select and use any asset that enhances your lecture.

Student study center The *Connect™ Finance* Student Study Center is the place for students to access additional resources. The Student Study Center

- Offers students quick access to lectures, practice materials, eBooks, and more.
- Provides instant practice material and study questions, easily accessible on the go.

Student progress tracking *Connect™ Finance* keeps instructors informed about how each student, section, and class is performing, allowing for more productive use of lecture and office hours. The progress-tracking function enables you to

- View scored work immediately and track individual or group performance with assignment and grade reports.
- Access an instant view of student or class performance relative to learning objectives.

Lecture capture through Tegrity Campus For an additional charge Lecture Capture offers new ways for students to focus on the in-class discussion, knowing they can revisit important topics later. This can be delivered through Connect or separately. See below for more details.

McGraw-Hill *Connect™ Plus Finance* McGraw-Hill reinvents the textbook learning experience for the modern student with *Connect™ Plus Finance.* A seamless integration of an eBook and *Connect™ Finance, Connect™ Plus Finance* provides all of the *Connect™ Finance* features plus the following:

- An integrated eBook, allowing for anytime, anywhere access to the textbook.
- Dynamic links between the problems or questions you assign to your students and the location in the eBook where that problem or question is covered.
- A powerful search function to pinpoint and connect key concepts in a snap.

In short, *Connect™ Finance* offers you and your students powerful tools and features that optimize your time and energies, enabling you to focus on course content, teaching, and student learning. *Connect™ Finance* also offers a wealth of content resources for both instructors and students. This state-of-the-art, thoroughly tested system supports you in preparing students for the world that awaits.

For more information about Connect™, go to www.mcgrawhillconnect.com, or contact your local McGraw-Hill sales representative.

Diagnostic and adaptive learning of concepts: LearnSmart Students want to make the best use of their study time. The LearnSmart adaptive self-study technology within *Connect Finance* provides students with a seamless combination of practice, assessment, and remediation for every concept in the textbook. LearnSmart's intelligent software adapts to every student response and automatically delivers concepts that advance the student's understanding while reducing time devoted to the concepts already mastered. The result for every student is the fastest path to mastery of the chapter concepts. LearnSmart

- Applies an intelligent concept engine to identify the relationships between concepts and to serve new concepts to each student only when he or she is ready.
- Adapts automatically to each student, so students spend less time on the topics they understand and more time on those they have yet to master.
- Provides continual reinforcement and remediation but gives only as much guidance as students need.
- Integrates diagnostics as part of the learning experience.
- Enables you to assess which concepts students have efficiently learned on their own, thus freeing class time for more applications and discussion.

Mc Graw Hill Education | SMARTBOOK™

SmartBook™ uses McGraw-Hill Education's market-leading adaptive technology to provide an ultra-efficient reading and learning experience for students. Students have access to a "smart" eBook, customized to highlight the most important concepts in the chapter and those that the individual student is yet to master. As the student reads, the reading material constantly adapts to ensure the student is focused on the content he or she needs most to close knowledge gaps.

Broken into separate modules that have students read, practice the material they just learned, and review material they have covered previously to improve knowledge retention, SmartBook is a next-generation study tool that is proven to improve student learning outcomes and understanding of the material.

Tegrity Campus: Lectures 24/7

Tegrity Campus is a service that makes class time available 24/7 by automatically capturing every lecture in a searchable format for students to review when they study and complete assignments. With a simple one-click start-and-stop process, you capture all computer screens and corresponding audio. Students can replay any part of any class with easy-to-use browser-based viewing on a PC or Mac.

Educators know that the more students can see, hear, and experience class resources, the better they learn. In fact, studies prove it. With Tegrity Campus, students quickly recall key moments by using Tegrity Campus's unique search feature. This search helps students efficiently find what they need, when they need it, across an entire semester of class recordings. Help turn all your students' study time into learning moments immediately supported by your lecture.

To learn more about Tegrity watch a two-minute flash demo at **http://tegritycampus.mhhe.com**.

McGraw-Hill Customer Care Contact Information

At McGraw-Hill, we understand that getting the most from new technology can be challenging. That's why our services don't stop after you purchase our products. You can e-mail our product specialists 24 hours a day to get product-training online. Or you can search our knowledge bank of Frequently Asked Questions on our support website. For customer support, call **800-331-5094,** or visit **www.mhhe.com/support**. One of our technical support analysts will be able to assist you in a timely fashion.

Brief Contents

Contents

1

Planning Your Personal Finances

2 Managing Your Personal Finances

5

Investing Your Financial Resources

chapter 1

Personal Finance Basics and the Time Value of Money

Learning Objectives

LO1-1 Analyze the process for making personal financial decisions.

LO1-2 Assess personal and economic factors that influence personal financial planning.

LO1-3 Develop personal financial goals.

LO1-4 Calculate time value of money situations associated with personal financial decisions.

LO1-5 Identify strategies for achieving personal financial goals for different life situations.

What will this mean for me?

Every person has some money. However, the amounts and individual needs and choices are diverse. You now have the opportunity to learn about varied financial paths for avoiding common money mistakes. Your knowledge and actions will move you toward financial security. Despite economic uncertainty, you will be able to use wise financial strategies in every stage of your life to achieve your personal goals.

my life

HOW DO I START?

One day, you may receive news that your aunt has given you a gift of $10,000. Or you might find yourself with an extensive amount of credit card debt. Or maybe you desire to contribute money to a homeless shelter or a hunger-relief organization.

Each of these situations involves financial decision-making that requires, first, planning and then taking action. The process you use should be carefully considered so no (or only a few) surprises occur.

The main focus when making decisions is to avoid financial difficulties and legal troubles. How will you best plan for using your finances? For each of the following statements, select "yes," "no," or "uncertain" to indicate your personal response regarding these financial planning activities.

1. When making major financial decisions, I research them using a variety of information sources.	Yes	No	Uncertain
2. My family and household situation is likely to stay fairly stable over the next year or two.	Yes	No	Uncertain
3. My specific financial goals for the next year are in writing.	Yes	No	Uncertain
4. Time value of money calculations often guide my saving and spending decisions.	Yes	No	Uncertain
5. I am able to name specific types of risks that can affect my personal financial decisions.	Yes	No	Uncertain

As you study this chapter, you will encounter "My Life" boxes with additional information and resources related to these items.

The Financial Planning Process

LO1-1

Analyze the process for making personal financial decisions.

Being "rich" means different things to different people. Some define wealth as owning many expensive possessions and having a high income. People may associate being rich with not having to worry about finances or being able to pay bills. For others, being rich means they are able to donate to organizations that matter to them.

How people get rich also varies. Starting a successful business or pursuing a high-paying career are common paths to wealth. However, frugal living and wise investing can also result in long-term financial security. In recent years, many have discovered that the quality of their lives should be measured in terms of something other than money and material items. A renewed emphasis on family, friends, and serving others has surfaced.

Most people want to handle their finances so that they get full satisfaction from each available dollar. To achieve this and other financial goals, people first need to identify and set priorities. Both financial and personal satisfaction are the result of an organized process that is commonly referred to as *personal money management* or *personal financial planning.*

personal financial planning The process of managing your money to achieve personal economic satisfaction.

Personal financial planning is the process of managing your money to achieve personal economic satisfaction. This planning process allows you to control your financial situation. Every person, family, or household has a unique financial position, and any financial activity therefore must also be carefully planned to meet specific needs and goals.

A comprehensive financial plan can enhance the quality of your life and increase your satisfaction by reducing uncertainty about your future needs and resources. The specific advantages of personal financial planning include

- Increased effectiveness in obtaining, using, and protecting your financial resources throughout your life.
- Increased control of your financial affairs by avoiding excessive debt, bankruptcy, and dependence on others for economic security.
- Improved personal relationships resulting from well-planned and effectively communicated financial decisions.
- A sense of freedom from financial worries obtained by looking to the future, anticipating expenses, and achieving your personal economic goals.

We all make hundreds of decisions each day. Most of these decisions are quite simple and have few consequences. Some are complex and have long-term effects on our personal and financial situations. Personal financial activities involve three main decision areas:

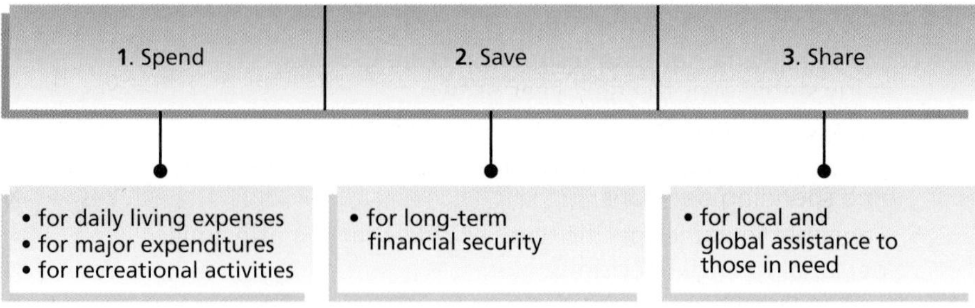

While everyone makes decisions, few people consider how to make better decisions. As Exhibit 1-1 shows, the financial planning process is a logical, six-step procedure that can be adapted to any life situation.

Exhibit 1-1

The financial planning process

STEP 1: DETERMINE YOUR CURRENT FINANCIAL SITUATION

First, determine your current financial situation regarding income, savings, living expenses, and debts. Preparing a list of current asset and debt balances and amounts spent for various items gives you a foundation for financial planning activities. The personal financial statements discussed in Chapter 3 will provide the information needed to match your goals with your current income and potential earning power.

EXAMPLE: Step 1

Within the next two months, Kent Mullins will complete his undergraduate studies with a major in global business development. He has worked part-time in various sales jobs. He has a small savings fund ($1,700) and over $8,500 in student loans. What additional information should Kent have available when planning his personal finances?

How about you? Depending on your current (or future) life situation, what actions might you take to determine your current financial situation?

STEP 2: DEVELOP YOUR FINANCIAL GOALS

Several times a year, you should analyze your financial values and goals. This activity involves identifying how you feel about money and why you feel that way. Are your feelings about money based on factual knowledge or on the influence of others?

Are your financial priorities based on social pressures, household needs, or desires for luxury items? How will economic conditions affect your goals and priorities? The purpose of this analysis is to differentiate your needs from your wants.

Specific financial goals are vital to financial planning. Others can suggest financial goals for you; however, *you* must decide which goals to pursue. Your financial goals can range from spending all of your current income to developing an extensive savings and investment program for your future financial security.

EXAMPLE: Step 2

Kent Mullins has several goals, including paying off his student loans, obtaining an advanced degree in global business management, and working in Latin America for a multinational company. What other goals might be appropriate for Kent?

How about you? Depending on your current (or future) life situation, describe some short-term or long-term goals that might be appropriate for you.

STEP 3: IDENTIFY ALTERNATIVE COURSES OF ACTION

Financial choices require periodic evaluation.

Developing alternatives is crucial when making decisions. Although many factors will influence the available alternatives, possible courses of action usually fall into these categories:

- *Continue the same course of action.* For example, you may determine that the amount you have saved each month is still appropriate.
- *Expand the current situation.* You may choose to save a larger amount each month.
- *Change the current situation.* You may decide to use a money market account instead of a regular savings account.
- *Take a new course of action.* You may decide to use your monthly savings budget to pay off credit card debts.

Not all of these categories will apply to every decision; however, they do represent possible courses of action. For example, if you want to stop working full time to go to school, you must generate several alternatives under the category "Take a new course of action."

Creativity in decision making is vital for effective choices. Consideration of many alternatives will help you make more effective and satisfying decisions. For instance, most people believe they must own a car to get to work or school. However, they should consider other alternatives such as public transportation, carpooling, renting a car, shared ownership of a car, or a company car.

Remember, when you decide not to take action, you elect to "do nothing," which can be a dangerous alternative.

DID YOU KNOW?

According to the National Endowment for Financial Education, 70 percent of major lottery winners end up with financial difficulties. These winners often squander the funds awarded them, while others overspend. Many end up declaring bankruptcy. Having more money does not mean you will make better financial choices.

EXAMPLE: Step 3

Kent Mullins has several options available for the near future. He could work full time and save for graduate school; he could go to graduate school full time by taking out an additional loan; or he could go to school part time and work part time. What additional alternatives might he consider?

How about you? Depending on your current (or future) life situation, list various alternatives for achieving the financial goals you identified in the previous step.

STEP 4: EVALUATE YOUR ALTERNATIVES

Next, you need to evaluate possible courses of action, taking into consideration your life situation, personal values, and current economic conditions. How will the ages of dependents affect your saving goals? How do you like to spend leisure time? How will changes in interest rates affect your financial situation?

CONSEQUENCES OF CHOICES Every decision closes off alternatives. For example, a decision to invest in stock may mean you cannot take a vacation. A decision to go to school full time may mean you cannot work full time. **Opportunity cost** is what you give up by making a choice. This cost, commonly referred to as the trade-off of a decision, cannot always be measured in dollars. It may refer to the money you forgo by attending school rather than working, but it may also refer to the time you spend shopping around to compare brands for a major purchase. In either case, the resources you give up (money or time) have a value that is lost.

opportunity cost What a person gives up by making a choice.

Decision making will be an ongoing part of your personal and financial situation. Thus, you will need to consider the lost opportunities that will result from your decisions. Since decisions vary based on each person's situation and values, opportunity costs will differ for each person.

EVALUATING RISK Uncertainty is a part of every decision. Selecting a college major and choosing a career field involve risk. What if you don't like working in this field or cannot obtain employment in it? Other decisions involve a very low degree of risk, such as putting money in an insured savings account or purchasing items that cost only a few dollars. Your chances of losing something of great value are low in these situations.

In many financial decisions, identifying and evaluating risk are difficult (see Exhibit 1-2). The best way to consider risk is to gather information based on your experience and the experiences of others, and to use financial planning information sources.

FINANCIAL PLANNING INFORMATION SOURCES When you travel, you might use a GPS or a map. Traveling the path of financial planning requires a different kind of map. Relevant information is required at each stage of the decision-making process. This book provides the foundation you need to make appropriate personal financial planning decisions. Changing personal, social, and economic conditions will require that you continually supplement and update your knowledge. Exhibit 1-3 offers an overview of the informational resources available when making personal financial decisions.

When making major financial decisions, I research them using a variety of information sources.

Always consider information from several sources when making financial decisions. In addition to various websites, see Appendix B for other financial planning resources.

Exhibit 1-2

Types of risk

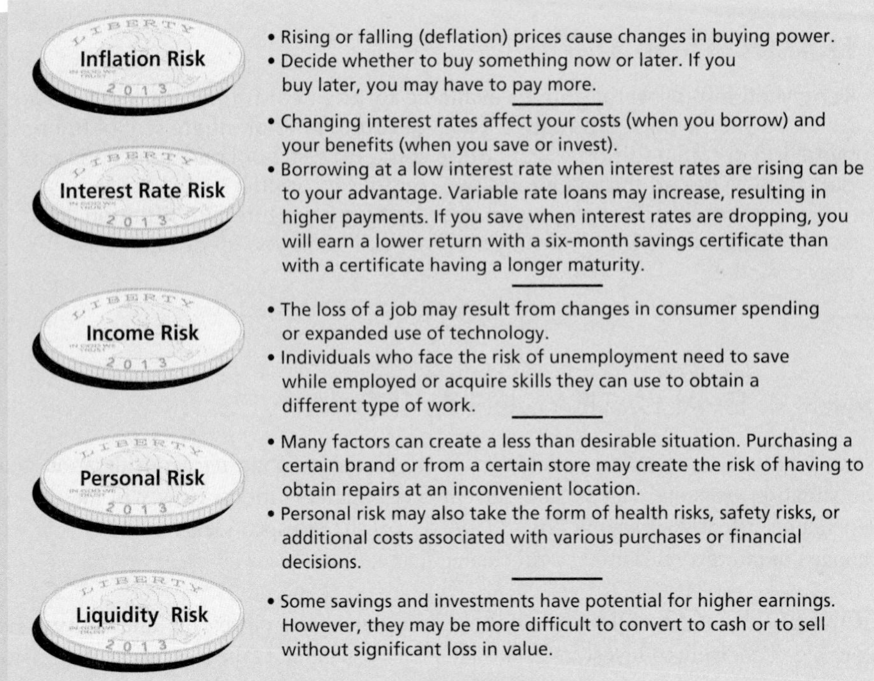

Exhibit 1-3

Financial planning information sources

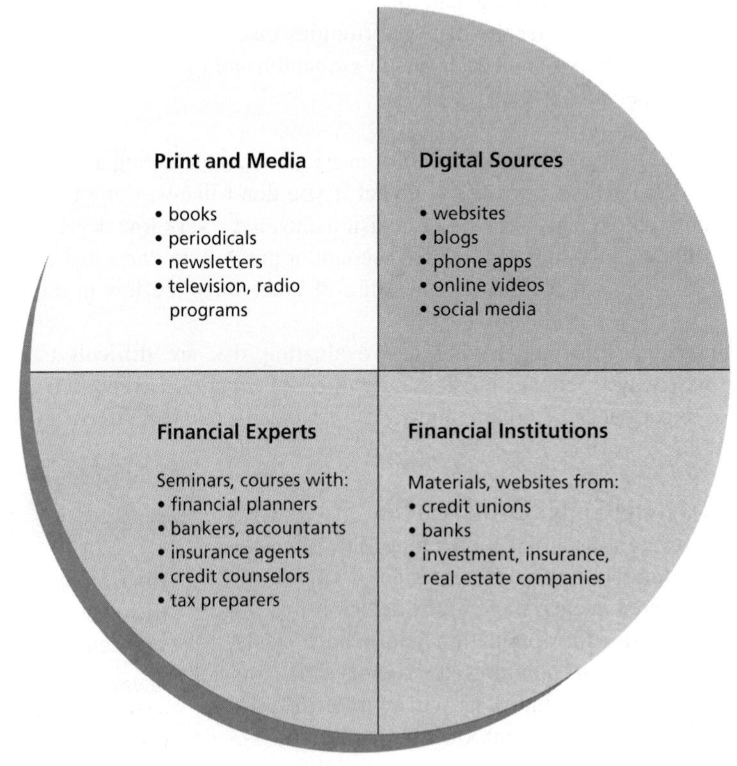

EXAMPLE: Step 4

As Kent Mullins evaluates his alternative courses of action, he must consider his income needs for both the short term and the long term. He should also assess career opportunities with his current skills and his potential with advanced training. What risks and trade-offs should Kent consider?

How about you? Depending on your current (or future) life situation, what types of risks might you encounter in your various personal financial activities?

STEP 5: CREATE AND IMPLEMENT YOUR FINANCIAL ACTION PLAN

This step of the financial planning process involves developing an action plan that identifies ways to achieve your goals. For example, you can increase your savings by reducing your spending or by increasing your income through extra time on the job. If you are concerned about year-end tax payments, you may increase the amount withheld from each paycheck, file quarterly tax payments, shelter current income in a tax-deferred retirement program, or buy municipal securities. As you achieve your short-term or immediate goals, the goals next in priority will come into focus.

To implement your financial action plan, you may need assistance from others. For example, you may use the services of an insurance agent to purchase property insurance or the services of an investment broker to purchase stocks, bonds, or mutual funds.

EXAMPLE: Step 5

Kent Mullins has decided to work full time for a few years while he (1) pays off his student loans, (2) saves money for graduate school, and (3) takes a couple of courses in the evenings and on weekends. What are the benefits and drawbacks of this choice?

How about you? Depending on your current (or future) life situation, describe the benefits and drawbacks of a financial situation you have encountered during the past year.

STEP 6: REVIEW AND REVISE YOUR PLAN

Financial planning is a dynamic process that does not end when you take a particular action. You need to regularly assess your financial decisions. You should do a complete review of your finances at least once a year. Changing personal, social, and economic factors may require more frequent assessments.

When life events affect your financial needs, this financial planning process will provide a vehicle for adapting to those changes. Regularly reviewing this decision-making process will help you make priority adjustments that will bring your financial goals and activities in line with your current life situation.

DID YOU KNOW?

Most financial planning professionals have a code of ethics, but not all abide by these principles. To avoid financial difficulties and potential fraud, make sure your financial planner strictly applies industry policies regarding confidentiality, integrity, objectivity to prevent a conflict of interest, and a commitment to continuing education.

EXAMPLE: Step 6

Over the next 6 to 12 months, Kent Mullins should reassess his financial, career, and personal situations. What employment opportunities or family circumstances might affect his need or desire to take a different course of action?

How about you? Depending on your current (or future) life situation, what factors in your life might affect your personal financial situation and decisions in the future?

PFP Sheet 1
Personal data

eXcel PFP Sheet 2
Financial institutions and advisers

PRACTICE QUIZ 1-1

1 What are the main elements of every decision we make?
2 What are some risks associated with financial decisions?
3 What are some common sources of financial planning information?
4 Why should you reevaluate your actions after making a personal financial decision?

Influences on Personal Financial Planning

LO1-2

Assess personal and economic factors that influence personal financial planning.

Many factors influence daily financial decisions, ranging from age and household size to interest rates and inflation. Three main elements affect financial planning activities: life situation, personal values, and economic factors.

LIFE SITUATION AND PERSONAL VALUES

my life 2

My family and household situation is likely to stay fairly stable over the next year or two.

Many personal, social, and economic factors can affect your life situation. Refer to Exhibit 1-6 (p. 17) for further information on financial goals and personal finance activities for various life situations.

People in their 20s spend money differently than those in their 50s. Personal factors such as age, income, household size, and personal beliefs influence spending and saving patterns. Life situation or lifestyle is created by a combination of factors.

As our society changes, different types of financial needs evolve. Today people tend to get married at a later age, and more households have two incomes. Many households are headed by single parents. More than 2 million women provide care for both dependent children and parents. We are also living longer; over 80 percent of all Americans now living are expected to live past age 65.

The **adult life cycle**—the stages in the family and financial needs of an adult—is an important influence on your financial activities and decisions. Your life situation is also affected by marital status, household size, and employment, as well as events such as

adult life cycle The stages in the family situation and financial needs of an adult.

- Graduation (at various levels of education).
- Engagement and marriage.
- The birth or adoption of a child.
- A career change or a move to a new area.
- Dependent children leaving home.
- Changes in health.
- Divorce.
- Retirement.
- The death of a spouse, family member, or other dependent.

In addition to being defined by your family situation, you are defined by your **values**—the ideas and principles that you consider correct, desirable, and important. Values have a direct influence on such decisions as spending now versus saving for the future or continuing school versus getting a job.

values Ideas and principles that a person considers correct, desirable, and important.

economics The study of how wealth is created and distributed.

THE FINANCIAL SYSTEM AND ECONOMIC FACTORS

The financial system and daily economic activities influence personal financial decisions. As shown in Exhibit 1-4, money in an economy flows from providers of funds to users of funds through intermediaries and financial markets. The buying and selling of investments occur in these financial settings.

While some investments are physical items (houses, land, gold, rare coins), others represent borrowing or ownership. A *security* is a financial instrument that represents debt or equity. *Debt securities,* such as bonds, represent money borrowed by companies or governments. These debt securities are often bought as an investment. In contrast, *equity securities* (stock) represent ownership in a corporation. Shares of stock are also bought by investors. In addition to stocks and bonds, other examples of securities include mutual funds, certificates of deposit (CDs), and commodity futures.

In most societies, the forces of supply and demand set prices for securities, goods, and services. **Economics** is the study of how wealth is created and distributed. The economic environment includes various institutions, including business, labor, and government, that work together to satisfy needs and wants.

Various government agencies regulate financial activities (see Exhibit 1-4). The Federal Reserve System, the central bank of the United States, has significant economic responsibility. *The Fed,* as it is often called, maintains an adequate money supply. This is achieved by influencing borrowing, interest rates, and the buying or selling of government securities. The Fed attempts to make adequate funds available for consumer spending and business expansion while keeping interest rates and consumer prices at an appropriate level.

Exhibit 1-4 The Financial System

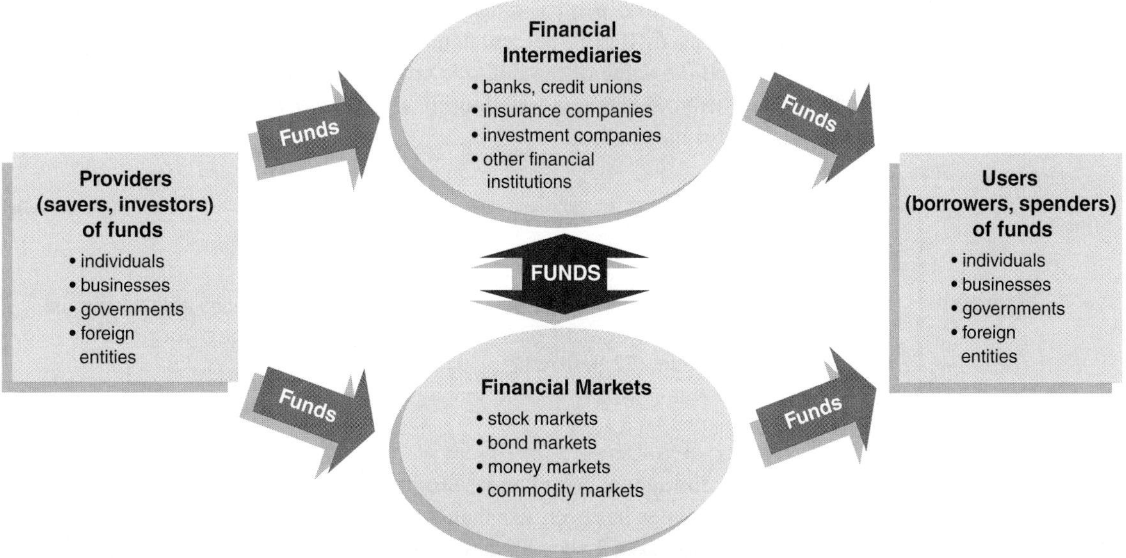

Financial Regulators: Federal Reserve System, Federal Deposit Insurance Corporation, National Credit Union Administration, Office of the Comptroller of the Currency, Consumer Financial Protection Bureau, Securities and Exchange Commission, state banking agencies, state insurance agencies.

GLOBAL INFLUENCES The global economy also influences personal finance. An economy is affected by both the financial activities of foreign investors and competition from foreign companies. American businesses compete against foreign companies for the spending dollars of American consumers.

When the value of exports of U.S.-made goods is lower than the value of imported goods, more U.S. dollars leave the country than the dollar value of foreign currency coming into the United States. This reduces the funds available for domestic spending and investment. Also, if foreign companies decide not to invest their dollars in the United States, the domestic money supply is reduced. This reduced money supply can result in higher interest rates. A *trade deficit* also affects the value of a nation's money and the cost of items being purchased by consumers.

ECONOMIC CONDITIONS Various economic conditions (see Exhibit 1-5) influence financial decisions. Personal financial decisions are most closely influenced by consumer prices, consumer spending, and interest rates.

inflation A rise in the general level of prices.

1. Consumer Prices **Inflation** is a rise in the general level of prices. In times of inflation, the buying power of the dollar decreases. For example, if prices increased 5 percent during the last year, items that cost $100 one year ago would now cost $105. This means it now takes more money to buy the same amount of goods and services.

The main cause of inflation is an increase in demand without a comparable increase in supply. For example, if people have more money to spend because of pay increases or borrowing but the same amounts of goods and services are available, the increased demand can bid up prices for those goods and services.

Inflation is most harmful to people living on fixed incomes. Due to inflation, retired people and others whose incomes do not change are able to afford fewer goods and services.

Inflation can also adversely affect lenders of money. Unless an adequate interest rate is charged, amounts repaid by borrowers in times of inflation have less buying power than the money they borrowed. If you pay 4 percent interest on a loan and the inflation rate is 6 percent, the dollars you pay the lender have lost buying power. For this reason, interest rates rise in periods of high inflation.

The rate of inflation varies. During the late 1950s and early 1960s, the annual inflation rate was in the 1 to 3 percent range. During the late 1970s and early 1980s, the cost of living increased 10 to 12 percent annually. At a 12 percent annual inflation rate, prices double (and the value of the dollar is cut in half) in about six years. To find out how fast prices (or your savings) will double, use the *rule of 72:* Just divide 72 by the annual inflation (or interest) rate.

EXAMPLE: Rule of 72

An annual inflation rate of 4 percent, for example, means prices will double in 18 years (72 ÷ 4 = 18). Regarding savings, if you earn 6 percent, your money will double in 12 years (72 ÷ 6 = 12).

More recently, the annual price increase for most goods and services as measured by the consumer price index has been less than 2 percent. The *consumer price index (CPI),* published by the Bureau of Labor Statistics, is a measure of the average change in the prices urban consumers pay for a fixed "basket" of goods and services. For current CPI information, go to www.bls.gov.

Inflation rates can be deceptive. Most people face *hidden* inflation since the cost of necessities (food, gas, health care), on which they spend most of their money, may rise

Exhibit 1-5 Changing economic conditions and financial decisions

Economic Factor	What It Measures	How It Influences Financial Planning
Consumer prices	The buying power of a dollar; changes in inflation.	If consumer prices increase faster than your income, you are unable to purchase the same amount of goods and services; higher consumer prices also cause higher interest rates.
Consumer spending	The demand for goods and services by individuals and households.	Increased consumer spending is likely to create more jobs and higher wages; high levels of consumer spending and borrowing may push up consumer prices and interest rates.
Interest rates	The cost of money; the cost of credit when you borrow; the return on your money when you save or invest.	Higher interest rates make buying on credit more expensive; higher interest rates make saving and investing more attractive and discourage borrowing.
Money supply	The dollars available for spending in our economy.	Interest rates tend to decline as more people save and invest; but higher saving (and lower spending) may also reduce job opportunities.
Unemployment	The number of people without employment who are willing and able to work.	People who are unemployed should reduce their debt level and have an emergency savings fund for living costs while out of work; high unemployment reduces consumer spending and job opportunities.
Housing starts	The number of new homes being built.	Increased home building results in more job opportunities, higher wages, more consumer spending, and overall economic expansion.
Gross domestic product (GDP)	The total value of goods and services produced within a country's borders, including items produced with foreign resources.	The GDP provides an indication of a nation's economic viability, resulting in employment and opportunities for increased personal wealth.
Trade balance	The difference between a country's exports and its imports.	If a country exports more than it imports, the balance of payments deficit can result in price changes for foreign goods.
Dow Jones Average, S&P 500, other stock market indexes	The relative value of stocks represented by the index.	These indexes provide an indication of the general movement of stock prices.

at a higher rate than the cost of nonessential items. This results in a *personal* inflation rate that is higher than the government's CPI.

Deflation, a decline in prices, can also have damaging economic effects. As prices drop, consumers expect they will go even lower. As a result, they cut their spending, which causes damaging economic conditions. While widespread deflation is unlikely, certain items may be affected, and their prices will drop.

2. Consumer Spending Total demand for goods and services in the economy influences employment opportunities and the potential for income. As consumer purchasing increases, the financial resources of current and prospective employees expand. This situation improves the financial condition of many households.

HOW TO...

Select a Path to Financial Security

Do you feel stress when you think about money? Are your financial decisions influenced by emotions rather than valid information? Do you often have disagreements about money?

To address these and other financial concerns, two paths exist for your daily money decisions.

The *easy* path involves little thinking, no planning, and minimal effort, usually resulting in wasted money and financial difficulties. In contrast, the *appropriate* path takes some time and effort, but results in lower stress and personal financial security.

It is EASY to...		*...but APPROPRIATE to...*
...spend without planning.	⇨	...save for emergencies and the future.
...overuse credit cards.	⇨	...maintain a low level of debt.
...avoid insurance coverage.	⇨	...have a risk management plan.
...select investments carelessly.	⇨	...research to avoid investment scams.
...make decisions on your own.	⇨	...communicate with others.

You can easily start to move yourself from *easy mistakes* to *appropriate actions* with these steps:

1. *Do something.* Start small, such as saving a small amount each month. Or decide to reduce your credit card use.
2. *Avoid excuses.* Do not tell yourself that "I don't have time" or "It's what everyone else is doing."
3. *Rate your current situation.* Indicate on this scale where you are currently in relation to the two available paths:

   Spender — Saver

   Financial difficulties — Financial security

4. *Set your mission.* Create a *personal finance mission statement* to communicate your personal values, financial goals, and future vision. This paragraph (or list or drawing or other format) will remind you and family members of your desired path for financial security. The wording describes where you want to be, and how you will get there. Develop your financial mission statement by talking with those who can help guide your actions. Your personal finance mission statement may include phrases such as "My financial mission is to change my spending habits for . . . ," ". . . to better understand my insurance needs . . . ," or "to donate (or volunteer) to local community service organizations."

Choosing to take the appropriate actions can result in reduced emotional stress, improved personal relationships, and increased financial security.

In contrast, reduced spending causes unemployment, since staff reduction commonly results from a company's reduced financial resources. The financial hardships of unemployment are a major concern of business, labor, and government. Retraining programs, income assistance, and job services can help people adjust.

3. Interest Rates In simple terms, interest rates represent the cost of money. Like everything else, money has a price. The forces of supply and demand influence interest rates. When consumer saving and investing increase the supply of money, interest rates tend to decrease. However, as consumer, business, government, and foreign borrowing increase the demand for money, interest rates tend to rise.

Interest rates affect your financial planning. The earnings you receive as a saver or an investor reflect current interest rates as well as a *risk premium* based on such factors as the length of time your funds will be used by others, expected inflation, and the extent of uncertainty about getting your money back. Risk is also a factor in the interest rate you pay as a borrower. People with poor credit ratings pay a higher interest rate than people with good credit ratings. Interest rates influence many financial decisions. Current interest rate data may be obtained at www.federalreserve.gov.

1 How do age, marital status, household size, employment situation, and other personal factors affect financial planning?
2 How might the uncertainty of inflation make personal financial planning difficult?
3 What factors influence the level of interest rates?

Monitoring current economic conditions

Developing Personal Financial Goals

LO1-3

Develop personal financial goals.

Since the United States is one of the richest countries in the world, it is difficult to understand why so many Americans have money problems. The answer seems to be the result of two main factors. The first is poor planning and weak money management habits in areas such as spending and the use of credit. The other factor is extensive advertising, selling efforts, and product availability. Achieving personal financial satisfaction starts with clear financial goals.

TYPES OF FINANCIAL GOALS

Two factors commonly influence your financial aspirations for the future. The first is the time frame in which you would like to achieve your goals. The second is the type of financial need that drives your goals.

TIMING OF GOALS What would you like to do tomorrow? Believe it or not, that question involves goal setting, which may be viewed in three time frames.

1. *short-term goals,* such as saving for a vacation or paying off small debts, will be achieved within the next year.
2. *intermediate goals* have a time frame from one to five years.
3. *long-term goals* involve financial plans that are more than five years off, such as retirement, money for children's college education, or the purchase of a vacation home.

A variety of personal and financial goals will motivate your actions.

Long-term goals should be planned in coordination with short-term and intermediate ones. Setting and achieving short-term goals is the basis for achieving long-term goals. For example, saving for a down payment to buy a house is an intermediate goal that can be a foundation for a long-term goal: owning your own home.

Goal frequency is another ingredient in the financial planning process. Some goals, such as vacations or money for gifts, may be set annually. Other goals, such as a college education, a car, or a house, occur less frequently.

GOALS FOR DIFFERENT FINANCIAL NEEDS A goal of obtaining increased career training is different from a goal of saving money to pay a semi-annual auto insurance premium. *Consumable-product goals* usually occur on a periodic basis and involve items that are used up relatively quickly, such as food, clothing, and entertainment. Such purchases, if made unwisely, can have a negative effect on your financial situation.

Durable-product goals usually involve infrequently purchased, expensive items such as appliances, cars, and sporting equipment; these consist of tangible items. In contrast, many people overlook *intangible-purchase goals.* These goals may relate to personal relationships, health, education, and leisure. Goal setting for these life circumstances is also necessary for your overall well-being.

DID YOU KNOW?

A survey conducted by the Consumer Federation of America (CFA) estimates that more than 60 million American households will probably fail to realize one or more of their major life goals largely due to a lack of a comprehensive financial plan. In households with annual incomes of less than $100,000, savers who say they have financial plans report about twice as much savings and investments as savers without plans.

GOAL-SETTING GUIDELINES

An old saying goes, "If you don't know where you're going, you might end up somewhere else and not even know it." Goal setting is central to financial decision making. Your financial goals are the basis for planning, implementing, and measuring the progress of your spending, saving, and investing activities. Exhibit 1-6 on page 17 offers typical goals and financial activities for various life situations.

Your financial goals should take a S-M-A-R-T approach, in that they are:

S—*specific,* so you know exactly what your goals are so you can create a plan designed to achieve those objectives.

M—*measurable* with a specific amount. For example, "Accumulate $5,000 in an investment fund within three years" is more measurable than "Put money into an investment fund."

A—*action-oriented,* providing the basis for the personal financial activities you will undertake. For example, "Reduce credit card debt" will usually mean actions to pay off amounts owed.

R—*realistic,* involving goals based on your income and life situation. For example, it is probably not realistic to expect to buy a new car each year if you are a full-time student.

T—*time-based,* indicating a time frame for achieving the goal, such as three years. This allows you to measure your progress toward your financial goals.

my life 3

My specific financial goals for the next year are written down.

Having specific financial goals in writing that you review on a regular basis is the foundation of successful personal financial planning. To start (or continue) creating and achieving your financial goals, use "Financial Planning for Life's Situations: Developing Financial Goals" on page 18.

Exhibit 1-6 Financial goals and activities for various life situations

Foundation Financial Goals and Activities		
• Obtain appropriate career training. • Create an effective financial recordkeeping system. • Develop a regular savings and investment program.	• Accumulate an appropriate emergency fund. • Purchase appropriate types and amounts of insurance coverage. • Create and implement a flexible budget.	• Evaluate and select appropriate investments. • Establish and implement a plan for retirement goals. • Make a will and develop an estate plan.

Specialized Financial Goals and Activities for Various Life Situations			
Young, Single (18–35)	**Young Couple with Children under 18**	**Single Parent with Children under 18**	**Young Dual-Income Couple, No Children**
• Establish financial independence. • Obtain disability insurance to replace income during prolonged illness. • Consider home purchase for tax benefit.	• Carefully manage increased need for the use of credit. • Obtain an appropriate amount of life insurance for the care of dependents. • Use a will to name guardian for children.	• Obtain appropriate health, life, and disability insurance. • Contribute to savings and investment fund for college. • Name a guardian for children and make other estate plans.	• Coordinate insurance coverage and other benefits. • Develop investment program for changes in life situation (larger house, children). • Consider tax-deferred contributions to retirement fund.
Unmarried Couple, No Children	**Older Couple (50+), No Dependent Children**	**Mixed-Generation Elderly Individuals and Children under 18**	**Older (50+), Single Person, No Dependent Children**
• Plan joint and individual band and credit accounts. • Communicate budgeting attitude differences. • Discuss and share joint and individual financial goals. • Consider a home purchase with a property agreement.	• Review financial assets and estate plans. • Consider household budget changes several years prior to retirement. • Plan retirement housing, living expenses, recreational activities, and part-time work.	• Obtain long-term care, life, disability insurance coverage. • Use dependent care service. • Provide for handling finances of elderly if they become ill. • Consider splitting investment cost—elderly get income while alive, principal to survivors.	• Make arrangement for long-term health care coverage. • Review will and estate plan. • Plan retirement living facilities, living expenses, and activities. • Monitor investments to consider current financial needs and market conditions.

1 What are examples of long-term goals?
2 What are the five main characteristics of useful financial goals?

PFP Sheet 4
Setting personal financial goals

DEVELOPING FINANCIAL GOALS

Based on your current situation or expectations for the future, create one or more financial goals based on this process:

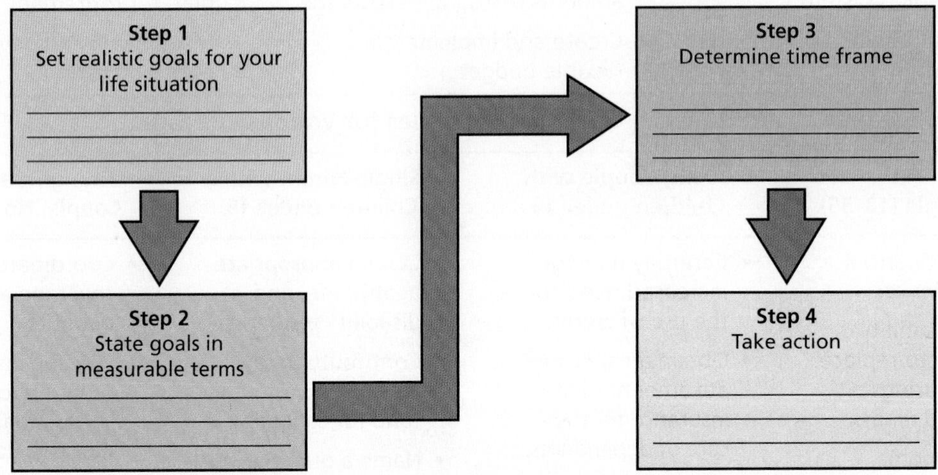

See Personal Financial Planner Sheet 4 to plan and implement your financial goals.

Opportunity Costs and the Time Value of Money

LO1-4

Calculate time value of money situations associated with personal financial decisions.

Have you noticed that you must give up something when you make choices? In every financial decision, you sacrifice something to obtain something else that you consider more desirable. For example, you might forgo current buying to invest funds for future purchases or long-term financial security. Or you might gain the use of an expensive item now by making credit payments from future earnings. These *opportunity costs* may be viewed in terms of both personal and financial resources (see Exhibit 1-7).

PERSONAL OPPORTUNITY COSTS

An important personal opportunity cost involves time that, when used for one activity, cannot be used for other activities. Time used for studying, working, or shopping will not be available for other uses. The allocation of time should be viewed like any decision: select your use of time to meet your needs, achieve your goals, and satisfy personal values.

Other personal opportunity costs relate to health. Poor eating habits, lack of sleep, or avoiding exercise can result in illness, time away from school or work, increased health care costs, and reduced financial security. Like financial resources, your personal resources (time, energy, health, abilities, knowledge) require careful management.

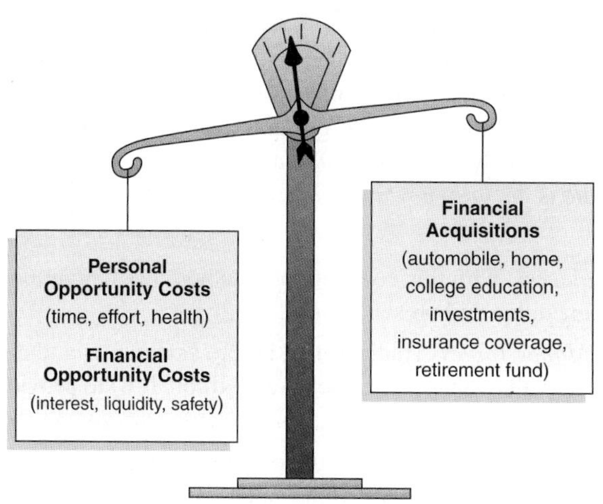

Exhibit 1-7

Opportunity costs and financial results should be assessed when making financial decisions

FINANCIAL OPPORTUNITY COSTS

Would you rather have $100 today or $105 a year from now? How about $120 a year from now instead of $100 today? Your choice among these alternatives will depend on several factors, including current needs, future uncertainty, and current interest rates. If you wait to receive your money in the future, you want to be rewarded for the risk. The **time value of money** calculates increases in an amount of money as a result of interest earned. Saving or investing a dollar instead of spending it today results in a future amount greater than a dollar. Every time you spend, save, invest, or borrow money, you should consider the time value of that money as an opportunity cost. Spending money from your savings account means lost interest earnings; however, what you buy with that money may have a higher priority than those earnings. Borrowing to make a purchase involves the opportunity cost of paying interest on the loan, but your current needs may make this trade-off worthwhile.

time value of money Increases in an amount of money as a result of interest earned.

The opportunity cost of the time value of money is also present in these financial decisions:

- Setting aside funds in a savings plan with little or no risk has the opportunity cost of potentially higher returns from an investment with greater risk.
- Having extra money withheld from your paycheck in order to receive a tax refund has the opportunity cost of the lost interest the money could earn in a savings account.
- Making annual deposits in a retirement account can help you avoid the opportunity cost of having inadequate funds later in life.
- Purchasing a new automobile or home appliance has the potential benefit of saving you money on future maintenance and energy costs.

INTEREST CALCULATIONS Three amounts are required to calculate the time value of money for savings in the form of interest earned:

1. The amount of the savings (commonly called the *principal*).
2. The annual interest rate.
3. The length of time the money is on deposit.

These three items are multiplied to obtain the amount of interest. Simple interest is calculated as follows:

Amount in savings	×	Annual interest rate	×	Time period	=	Interest

For example, \$500 on deposit at 6 percent for six months would earn \$15 (\$500 × 0.06 × 6/12, or 1/2 year).

The increased value of money from interest earned involves two types of time value of money calculations, future value and present value. The amount that will be available at a later date is called the *future value.* In contrast, the current value of an amount desired in the future is the *present value.* Five methods are available for calculating time value of money:

1. *Formula Calculation.* With this conventional method, math notations are used for computing future value and present value.
2. *Time Value of Money Tables.* Traditionally, before calculators and computers, future value and present value tables were used (see Exhibit 1–8) to provide for easier computations.
3. *Financial Calculator.* A variety of calculators are programmed with financial functions. Both future value and present value calculations are performed using appropriate keystrokes.
4. *Spreadsheet Software.* Excel and other spreadsheet programs have built-in formulas for financial computations, including future value and present value.
5. *Websites and Apps.* Many time-value-of-money calculators are available online and through mobile devices. These programs may be used to calculate the future value of savings as well as loan payment amounts.

future value The amount to which current savings will increase based on a certain interest rate and a certain time period; also referred to as *compounding.*

my life 4

Time value of money calculations often guide my saving and spending decisions.

To assist you with using future value and present value computations for achieving personal financial goals, several websites are available: for example, www.dinkytown.net, www.moneychimp.com/calculator, and cgi.money.cnn.com/tools.

FUTURE VALUE OF A SINGLE AMOUNT Deposited money earns interest that will increase over time. **Future value** is the amount to which current savings will grow based on a certain interest rate and a certain time period. For example, \$100 deposited in a 6 percent account for one year will grow to \$106. This amount is computed as follows:

Future value = \$100 + (\$100 × 0.06 × 1 year) + \$106

The same process could be continued for a second, third, and fourth year, however the computations would be time-consuming. The previously mentioned calculation methods make the process easier.

An example of the future value of a single amount might involve an investment of \$650 earning 8 percent for 10 years. This situation would be calculated as follows:

Formula	Time Value of Money Table	Financial Calculator	Spreadsheet Software
$FV = PV(1 + i)^n$ $FV = 650(1 + .08)^{10}$ $FV = \$1,403.30$ i – interest rate n – number of time periods	Using Exhibit 1-8A, multiply the amount deposited by the factor for the interest rate and time period. 650 × 2.159 = \$1,403.35	PV, I/Y, N, PMT, CPT FV 650 PV, 8 I/Y, 10 N, 0 PMT, CPT FV \$1,403.30 (Different financial calculators will require different keystrokes.)	=*FV*(rate, periods, amount per period, single amount) =*FV*(0.08,10,0,−650) =\$1,403.30

(Note: Expanded explanations of these time value of money calculation methods are presented in the chapter appendix on page 34.)

Future value computations are often referred to as *compounding,* since interest is earned on previously earned interest. Compounding allows the future value of

Exhibit 1-8

Time value of money tables (condensed)

A. Future Value of $1 (single amount)

Year	Percent 5%	6%	7%	8%	9%
5	1.276	1.338	1.403	1.469	1.539
6	1.340	1.419	1.501	1.587	1.677
7	1.407	1.504	1.606	1.714	1.828
8	1.477	1.594	1.718	1.851	1.993
9	1.551	1.689	1.838	1.999	2.172
10	1.629	1.791	1.967	2.159	2.367

B. Future Value of a Series of Annual Deposits (annuity)

Year	Percent 5%	6%	7%	8%	9%
5	5.526	5.637	5.751	5.867	5.985
6	6.802	6.975	7.153	7.336	7.523
7	8.142	8.394	8.654	8.923	9.200
8	9.549	9.897	10.260	10.637	11.028
9	11.027	11.491	11.978	12.488	13.021
10	12.578	13.181	13.816	14.487	15.193

C. Present Value of $1 (single amount)

Year	Percent 5%	6%	7%	8%	9%
5	0.784	0.747	0.713	0.681	0.650
6	0.746	0.705	0.666	0.630	0.596
7	0.711	0.665	0.623	0.583	0.547
8	0.677	0.627	0.582	0.540	0.502
9	0.645	0.592	0.544	0.500	0.460
10	0.614	0.558	0.508	0.463	0.422

D. Present Value of a Series of Annual Deposits (annuity)

Year	Percent 5%	6%	7%	8%	9%
5	4.329	4.212	4.100	3.993	3.890
6	5.076	4.917	4.767	4.623	4.486
7	5.786	5.582	5.389	5.206	5.033
8	6.463	6.210	5.971	5.747	5.535
9	7.108	6.802	6.515	6.247	5.995
10	7.722	7.360	7.024	6.710	6.418

Note: See the appendix at the end of this chapter for more complete future value and present value tables.

a deposit to grow faster than it would if interest were paid only on the original deposit. The sooner you make deposits, the greater the future value will be. Depositing $1,000 in a 5 percent account at age 40 will give you $3,387 at age 65. However, making the $1,000 deposit at age 25 would result in an account balance of $7,040 at age 65.

FUTURE VALUE OF A SERIES OF DEPOSITS Many savers and investors make regular deposits. An *annuity* is a series of equal deposits or payments. To determine the future value of equal yearly savings deposits time value of money tables can be used (see Exhibit 1-B). For this table to be used, and for an annuity to exist, the deposits must earn a constant interest rate. For example, if you deposit $50 a year at 7 percent for six years, starting at the end of the first year, you will have $357.65 at the end of that time ($50 × 7.153). The Financial Planning Calculations box on page 23 presents examples of using future value to achieve financial goals.

PRESENT VALUE OF A SINGLE AMOUNT Another aspect of the time value of money involves determining the current value of an amount desired in the future. **Present value** is the current value for a future amount based on a particular interest rate for a certain period of time. Present value computations, also called *discounting,* allow you to determine how much to deposit now to obtain a desired total in the future. For example, using the present value table (Exhibit 1-C), if you want $1,000 five years from now and you earn 5 percent on your savings, you need to deposit $784 ($1,000 × 0.784).

present value The current value for a future amount based on a certain interest rate and a certain time period; also referred to as *discounting.*

DID YOU KNOW?

If you invest $2,000 a year (at 9 percent) from ages 31 to 65, these funds will grow to $470,249 by age 65. However, if you save $2,000 a year (at 9 percent) for only 9 years from ages 22 to 30, at age 65 this fund will be worth $579,471! Most important: Start investing something now!

PRESENT VALUE OF A SERIES OF DEPOSITS You may also use present value computations to determine how much you need to deposit now so that you can take a certain amount out of the account for a desired number of years. For example, if you want to take $400 out of an investment account each year for nine years and your money is earning an annual rate of 8 percent, you can see from Exhibit 1-D that you would need to make a current deposit of $2,498.80 ($400 × 6.247).

Additional details for the formulas, tables, and other methods for calculating time value of money are presented in the chapter appendix on page 34.

Time value of money calculations

PRACTICE QUIZ 1-4

1 How can you use future value and present value computations to measure the opportunity cost of a financial decision?
2 Use the time value of money tables in Exhibit 1-8 to calculate the following:
   a. The future value of $100 at 7 percent in 10 years.
   b. The future value of $100 a year for six years earning 6 percent.
   c. The present value of $500 received in eight years with an interest rate of 8 percent.

TIME VALUE OF MONEY CALCULATIONS FOR ACHIEVING FINANCIAL GOALS

Achieving specific financial goals may require making regular savings deposits or determining an amount to be invested. By using time value of money calculations, you can compute the amount needed to achieve a financial goal.

Situation 1. Jonie Emerson has two children who will start college in 10 years. She plans to set aside $1,500 a year for her children's college education during that period and estimates she will earn an annual interest rate of 5 percent on her savings. What amount can Jonie expect to have available for her children's college education when they start college?

Formula	Time Value of Money Table	Financial Calculator	Spreadsheet Software
$FV = \text{Annuity}\ \frac{(1+i)^n - 1}{i}$ $FV = \frac{1{,}500(1+.05)^{10} - 1}{.05}$ FV = $18,866.85	Using Exhibit 1-B, multiply the amount deposited by the factor for the interest rate and time period. 1,500 × 12.578 = $18,867	PV, I/Y, N, PMT, CPT FV 0 PV, 5 I/Y, 10 N, 1,500 PMT, CPT FV $18,866.84 (Different financial calculators will require different keystrokes.)	= FV(rate, periods, amount per period, amount) = FV(0.05,10,−1,500) = $18,866.84

Conclusion. Based these calculations, if Jonie deposits $1,500 a year at an annual interest rate of 5 percent, she would have $18,867 available for her children's college education.

Situation 2. Don Calder wants to have $50,000 available in 10 years as a reserve fund for his parents' retirement living expenses and health care. If he earns an average of 8 percent on his investments, what amount must he invest today to achieve this goal?

Formula	Time Value of Money Table	Financial Calculator	Spreadsheet Software
$PV = \frac{FV}{(1+i)^n}$ $PV = \frac{50{,}000}{(1+.08)^{10}}$ FV = $23,159.94	Using Exhibit 1-C, multiply the amount desired by the factor for the interest rate and time period. 50,000 × 0.463 = $23,150	FV, N, I/Y, PMT, CPT PV 50,000 FV, 10 N, 8 I/Y, 0 PMT, CPT PV $23,159.67 (Different financial calculators will require different keystrokes.)	= PV(rate, periods, payment, future value amount, type) = PV(0.08,10,0,−50,000) = $23,159.67

Conclusion. Don needs to invest approximately $23,160 today for 10 years at 8 percent to achieve the desired financial goal.

(Note: Expanded explanations of these time value of money calculation methods are presented in the chapter appendix on page 34.)

Achieving Financial Goals

LO1-5

Identify strategies for achieving personal financial goals for different life situations.

Throughout life, our needs usually can be satisfied with the intelligent use of financial resources. Financial planning involves deciding how to obtain, protect, and use those resources. By using the eight major areas of personal financial planning to organize your financial activities, you can avoid many common money mistakes.

COMPONENTS OF PERSONAL FINANCIAL PLANNING

This book is designed to provide a framework for the study and planning of personal financial decisions. Exhibit 1-9 presents an overview of the eight major personal financial planning areas. To achieve a successful financial situation, you must coordinate these components through an organized plan and wise decision making.

OBTAINING (CHAPTER 2) You obtain financial resources from employment, investments, or ownership of a business. Obtaining financial resources is the foundation of financial planning, since these resources are used for all financial activities.

EXAMPLE: Online Sources for Obtaining

Many guidelines for effective career planning and professional development may be obtained at www.rileyguide.com and www.monster.com.

PLANNING (CHAPTERS 3, 4) Planned spending through budgeting is the key to achieving goals and future financial security. Efforts to anticipate expenses and financial decisions can also help reduce taxes. The ability to pay your fair share of taxes—no more, no less—is vital to increasing your financial resources.

EXAMPLE: Online Sources for Planning

Budgeting is an ongoing activity, and tax planning should not occur only around April 15. For assistance, go to www.money.com, www.20somethingfinance.com, and www.irs.gov.

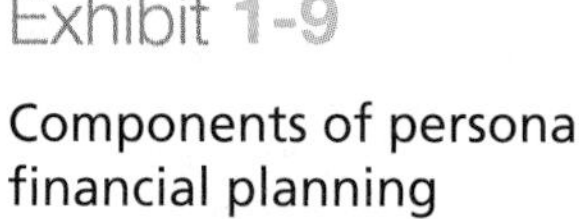

Exhibit 1-9

Components of personal financial planning

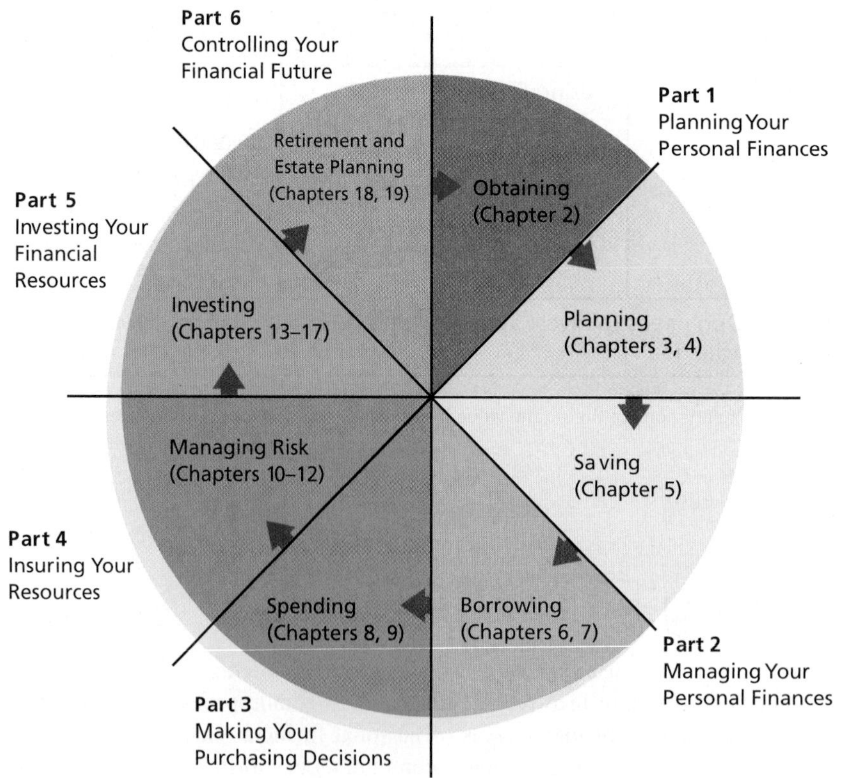

SAVING (CHAPTER 5) Long-term financial security starts with a regular savings plan for emergencies, unexpected bills, replacement of major items, and the purchase of special goods and services, such as a college education, a boat, or a vacation home. Once you have established a basic savings plan, you may use additional money for investments that offer greater financial growth.

An amount of savings must be available to meet current household needs. **Liquidity** refers to the ability to readily convert financial resources into cash without a loss in value. The need for liquidity will vary based on a person's age, health, and family situation. Savings plans such as interest-earning checking accounts, money market accounts, and money market funds earn money on your savings while providing liquidity.

liquidity The ability to readily convert financial resources into cash without a loss in value.

bankruptcy The legal status of a person who is not able pay debts owed.

EXAMPLE: Online Sources for Saving

Fast updates on savings rates and other banking services are available at www.bankrate.com and www.banx.com.

BORROWING (CHAPTERS 6, 7) Maintaining control over your credit-buying habits will contribute to your financial goals. The overuse and misuse of credit may cause a situation in which a person's debts far exceed the resources available to pay those debts. **Bankruptcy** is the legal status of a person who is not able pay debts owed. Federal laws exist that allow you to either restructure your debts or remove certain debts. However, the people who declare bankruptcy each year may have avoided this trauma with wise spending and borrowing decisions. Chapter 7 discusses bankruptcy in detail.

EXAMPLE: Online Sources for Borrowing

Current rates for credit cards, personal loans, and other types of credit are available at www.bankmonitornotes.com, www.consumercredit.com and www.bankrate.com.

SPENDING (CHAPTERS 8, 9) Financial planning is designed not to prevent your enjoyment of life but to help you obtain the things you want. Too often, however, people make purchases without considering the financial consequences. Some people shop compulsively, creating financial difficulties. You should detail your living expenses and your other financial obligations in a spending plan. Spending less than you earn is the only way to achieve long-term financial security.

EXAMPLE: Online Sources for Spending

Consumer buying information is available at www.consumerworld.org and www.consumer.gov. Over 70 percent of car buyers research purchases online at websites such as www.autoweb.com and autos.msn.com. Prospective home buyers can obtain financing online at www.hsh.com and www.eloan.com.

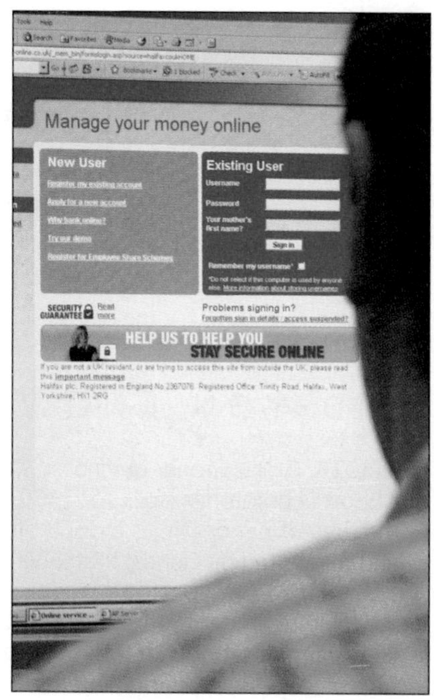

The planning component of personal finance provides a foundation for other activities.

MANAGING RISK (CHAPTERS 10–12) Adequate insurance coverage is another component of personal financial planning. Certain types of insurance are commonly overlooked in financial plans. For example, the number of people who suffer disabling injuries or diseases at age 50 is greater than the number who die at that age, so people may need disability insurance more than they need life insurance. Yet surveys reveal that most people have adequate life insurance but few have disability insurance. The insurance industry is more aggressive in selling life insurance than in selling disability insurance, thus putting the burden of obtaining adequate disability insurance on you.

Many households have excessive or overlapping insurance coverage. Insuring property for more than it is worth may be a waste of money, as may both a husband and a wife having similar health insurance coverage.

EXAMPLE: Online Sources for Managing Risk

Insurance planning assistance and rate quotes may be obtained at personalinsure .about.com and www.carinsurance.com.

INVESTING (CHAPTERS 13–17) While many types of investment vehicles are available, people invest for two primary reasons. Those interested in *current income* select investments that pay regular dividends or interest. In contrast, investors who desire *long-term growth* choose stocks, mutual funds, real estate, and other investments with potential for increased value in the future.

You can achieve investment diversification by including a variety of assets in your *portfolio*—for example, stocks, bond mutual funds, real estate, and collectibles such as rare coins. Obtaining general investment advice is easy; however, it is more difficult to obtain specific investment advice to meet your individual needs and goals.

EXAMPLE: Online Sources for Investing

"Information is power"—this is especially true when investing. You can obtain company information and investment assistance at finance.yahoo.com, www.fool.com, and www.marketwatch.com.

DID YOU KNOW?

In 1935, Grace Groner purchased three shares of Abbott Laboratories stock for $180. In 2010, at the time of her death, as a result of stock splits and reinvested dividends, that initial investment was worth $7 million. These funds are now available to students at Lake Forest College, which Groner attended, to provide grants for service learning during internships and foreign study programs.

RETIREMENT AND ESTATE PLANNING (CHAPTERS 18, 19) Most people desire financial security upon completion of full-time employment. But retirement planning also involves thinking about your housing situation, your recreational activities, and possible part-time or volunteer work.

Transfers of money or property to others should be timed, if possible, to minimize the tax burden and maximize the benefits for those receiving the financial resources. A knowledge of property transfer methods can help you select the best course of action for funding current and future living costs, educational expenses, and retirement needs of dependents.

EXAMPLE: Online Sources for Retirement and Estate Planning

Whether you are 40 years or 40 minutes away from retiring, you can obtain assistance at retireplan.about.com, www.aarp.org, and www.estateplanning-links.com.

DEVELOPING A FLEXIBLE FINANCIAL PLAN

A **financial plan** is a formalized report that summarizes your current financial situation, analyzes your financial needs, and recommends future financial activities. You can create this document on your own, seek assistance from a financial planner, or use a money management software package. Exhibit 1-10 offers a framework for developing and implementing a financial plan, along with examples for several life situations.

financial plan A formalized report that summarizes your current financial situation, analyzes your financial needs, and recommends future financial activities.

Exhibit 1-10 Financial planning in action for different life situations

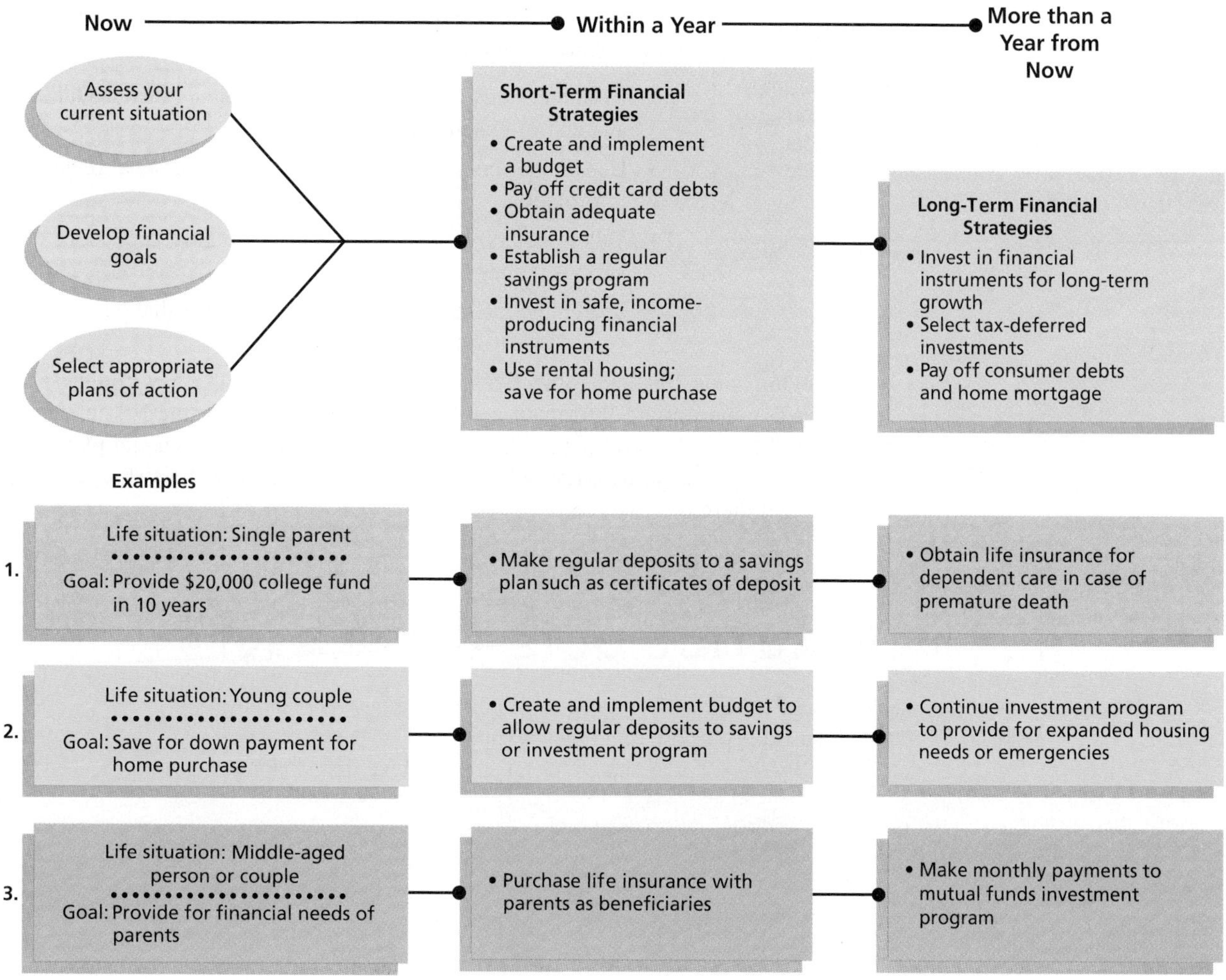

IMPLEMENTING YOUR FINANCIAL PLAN

You must have a plan before you can implement it. However, once you have clearly assessed your current situation and identified your financial goals, what do you do next?

The most important strategy for success is to develop financial habits that contribute to both short-term satisfaction and long-term financial security, including the following:

1. Using a well-conceived spending plan will help you stay within your income while you save and invest for the future. The main source of financial difficulties is overspending.
2. Having appropriate insurance protection will help you prevent financial disasters.
3. Becoming informed about tax and investment alternatives will help you expand your financial resources.

my life 5

I am able to name specific types of risks that can affect my personal financial decisions.

All decisions involve risk. Some risks are minor with limited consequences. Others can have long-term effects. Inflation and interest rates will influence your financial decisions. Information on changing economic conditions is available at www.bls.gov, www.federalreserve.gov, and www.bloomberg.com.

STUDYING PERSONAL FINANCE

Within each chapter of this book are various learning devices to help you build knowledge. The *Personal Financial Planner* sheets provide a framework for creating and implementing your financial activities. The website (www.mhhe.com/kdh) connects you to additional resources and activities. As you move into the following chapters, we recommend that you:

- Read and study the book carefully. Use the Practice Quizzes and end-of-chapter activities.
- Use online sources and apps for the latest personal finance information.
- Talk to others, experts and friends, who have knowledge of various money topics.
- Search the Internet for answers to questions that result from your desire to know more.

Achieving your financial objectives requires two things: (1) a willingness to learn and (2) appropriate information sources. *You* must provide the first element; the material that follows will provide the second. For successful financial planning, know where you are now, know where you want to be, and be persistent in your efforts to get there.

PRACTICE QUIZ 1-5

1 What are the main components of personal financial planning?
2 What is the purpose of a financial plan?
3 Identify some common actions taken to achieve financial goals.

my life stages for financial planning

YOUR PERSONAL FINANCE DASHBOARD

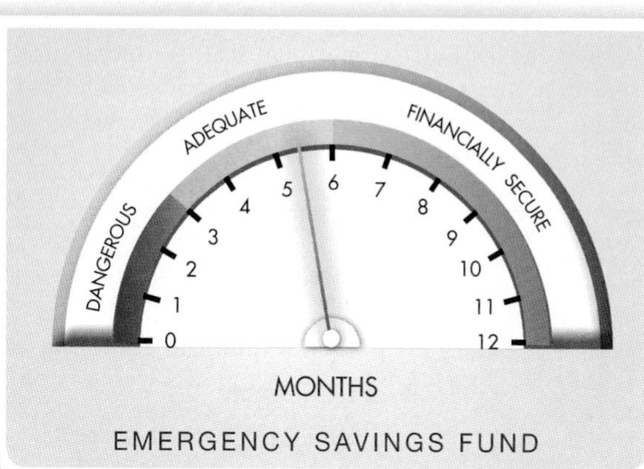

The creation of an emergency fund is often overlooked. Financial advisers suggest saving three to six months of living expenses for unexpected situations. A larger amount may be needed if you are self-employed or a full-time student.

Your emergency fund can be measured with a *dashboard, a* tool used by organizations to monitor *key performance indicators* such as delivery time, product defects, or customer complaints. As an individual, you can use a *personal finance dashboard* to assess your financial situation. As with driving, a personal finance dashboard allows you to keep track of your progress to a destination.

YOUR SITUATION Have you started your emergency fund? Do you make progress each month? Where is the needle on your Personal Finance Dashboard for an emergency fund? Other personal financial planning actions you might consider during various stages of your life include . . .

. . . in college

- Develop wise budgeting habits
- Create a regular savings program
- Establish a plan for wise use of banking services and credit

. . . in my 20s

- Pay off any college loans
- Increase amounts saved and invested
- Continue proper spending and credit habits

. . . in my 30s and 40s

- Assess progress toward long-term financial goals
- Evaluate needed insurance as a result of changes in household or financial situation

. . . in my 50s and beyond

- Assess need for long-term health care coverage
- Review will and estate plan
- Consider various activities, locations for retirement

SUMMARY OF LEARNING OBJECTIVES

LO1-1

Analyze the process for making personal financial decisions.
When making major financial decisions, use a variety of information sources to implement the personal financial planning process: (1) determine your current financial situation, (2) develop financial goals, (3) identify alternative courses of action, (4) evaluate alternatives, (5) create and implement a financial action plan, and (6) review and revise the financial plan.

LO1-2

Assess personal and economic factors that influence personal financial planning.
Financial goals and financial planning decisions are affected by a person's life situation (income, age, household size, health) and personal values, and by economic factors (prices, interest rates, and employment opportunities).

LO1-3

Develop personal financial goals.

The financial goals you develop should take a S-M-A-R-T approach with goals that are: Specific, Measurable, Action-oriented, Realistic, and Time-based.

LO1-4

Calculate time value of money situations associated with personal financial decisions.

Every decision involves a trade-off with things given up. Personal opportunity costs include time, effort, and health. Financial opportunity costs are based on time value of money calculations. Future value and present value calculations enable you to measure the increased value (or lost interest) that results from a saving, investing, borrowing, or purchasing decision.

LO1-5

Identify strategies for achieving personal financial goals for different life situations.

Successful financial planning requires specific goals combined with spending, saving, investing, and borrowing strategies based on your personal situation and various social and economic factors, especially inflation and interest rates.

KEY TERMS

adult life cycle 10
bankruptcy 25
economics 11
financial plan 27
future value 20
inflation 12
liquidity 25
opportunity cost 7
personal financial planning 4
present value 22
time value of money 19
values 11

SELF-TEST PROBLEMS

1. The Rule of 72 provides a guideline for determining how long it takes your money to double. This rule can also be used to determine your earning rate. If your money is expected to double in 12 years, what is your rate of return?
2. If you desire to have $10,000 in savings eight years from now, what amount would you need to deposit in an account that earns 5 percent?

Self-Test Solutions

1. Using the Rule of 72, if your money is expected to double in 12 years, you are earning approximately 6 percent (72 ÷ 12 years = 6 percent).
2. To calculate the present value of $10,000 for eight years at 5 percent, use Exhibit 1-8C, p. 21 (or Exhibit 1-C, p. 44): $10,000 × 0.677 = $6,770.

FINANCIAL PLANNING PROBLEMS

(Note: Some of these problems require the use of the time value of money tables in the chapter appendix.)

L01-2 1. *Calculating the Future Value of Property.* Ben Collins plans to buy a house for $220,000. If that real estate is expected to increase in value by 3 percent each year, what will its approximate value be seven years from now?

L01-2 2. *Using the Rule of 72.* Using the rule of 72, approximate the following amounts.

a. If the value of land in an area is increasing 6 percent a year, how long will it take for property values to double?

b. If you earn 10 percent on your investments, how long will it take for your money to double?

c. At an annual interest rate of 5 percent, how long will it take for your savings to double?

L01-2 3. *Determining the Inflation Rate.* In 2006, selected automobiles had an average cost of $16,000. The average cost of those same automobiles is now $28,000. What was the rate of increase for these automobiles between the two time periods?

4. *Computing Future Living Expenses.* A family spends 48,000 a year for living expenses. If prices increase by 2 percent a year for the next three years, what amount will the family need for their living expenses after three years? L01-2

5. *Calculating Earnings on Savings.* What would be the yearly earnings for a person with $8,000 in savings at an annual interest rate of 2.5 percent? $$$(LO1.4) L01-4

6. *Computing the Time Value of Money.* Using time value of money tables, calculate the following. L01-4

   a. The future value of $450 six years from now at 7 percent.

   b. The future value of $900 saved each year for 10 years at 8 percent.

   c. The amount a person would have to deposit today (present value) at a 6 percent interest rate to have $1,000 five years from now.

   d. The amount a person would have to deposit today to be able to take out $600 a year for 10 years from an account earning 8 percent.

7. *Calculating the Future Value of a Series of Amounts.* Elaine Romberg prepares her own income tax return each year. A tax preparer would charge her $80 for this service. Over a period of 10 years, how much does Elaine gain from preparing her own tax return? Assume she can earn 3 percent on her savings. L01-4

8. *Calculating the Time Value of Money for Savings Goals.* If you desire to have $20,000 for a down payment for a house in five years, what amount would you need to deposit today? Assume that your money will earn 5 percent. L01-4

9. *Calculating the Present Value of a Series.* Pete Morton is planning to go to graduate school in a program of study that will take three years. Pete wants to have $15,000 available each year for various school and living expenses. If he earns 4 percent on his money, how much must be deposited at the start of his studies to be able to withdraw $15,000 a year for three years? L01-4

10. *Using the Time Value of Money for Retirement Planning.* Carla Lopez deposits $3,200 a year into her retirement account. If these funds have an average earning of 9 percent over the 40 years until her retirement, what will be the value of her retirement account? L01-4

11. *Calculating the Value of Reduced Spending.* If a person spends $15 a week on coffee (assume $750 a year), what would be the future value of that amount over 10 years if the funds were deposited in an account earning 3 percent? L01-4

12. *Calculating the Present Value of Future Cash Flows.* A financial company advertises on television that they will pay you $60,000 now in exchange for annual payments of $10,000 that you are expected to receive for a legal settlement over the next 10 years. If you estimate the time value of money at 10 percent, would you accept this offer? L01-4

13. *Calculating the Potential Future Value of Savings.* Tran Lee plans to set aside $2,400 a year for the next six years, earning 4 percent. What would be the future value of this savings amount? L01-4

14. *Determining a Loan Payment Amount.* If you borrow $8,000 with a 5 percent interest rate, to be repaid in five equal yearly payments, what would be the amount of each payment? (*Note:* Use the present value of an annuity table in the chapter appendix.) L01-4

FINANCIAL PLANNING ACTIVITIES

1. *Determining Personal Risks.* Talk to friends, relatives, and others about their personal financial activities. Ask about potential risks involved with making financial decisions. What actions might be taken to investigate and reduce these risks? L01-1

2. *Using Financial Planning Experts.* Prepare a list of financial planning specialists (investment advisers, credit counselors, insurance agents, real estate brokers, tax preparers) in your community who can assist people with personal financial planning. L01-1, 1-2

3. *Analyzing Changing Life Situations.* Ask friends, relatives, and others how their spending, saving, and borrowing activities changed when they decided to continue their education, change careers, or have children. L01-2

4. *Researching Economic Conditions.* Use library resources, such as *The Wall Street Journal,* www.businessweek.com, or other websites to determine recent trends in interest rates, inflation, and other economic indicators. Information about the consumer price index (measuring changes in the cost of living) may be obtained at www.bls.gov. Report how this economic information might affect your financial planning decisions. L01-2

5. *Setting Financial Goals.* Ask friends, relatives, and others about their short-term and long-term financial goals. What are some of the common goals for various personal situations? Using Sheet 3 in the *Personal Financial Planner,* create one short-term and one long-term goal for people in these life situations: *(a)* a young single person, *(b)* a single parent with a child age 8, *(c)* a married person with no children, and *(d)* a retired person. L01-3

6. *Comparing Alternative Financial Actions.* What actions would be necessary to compare a financial planner who advertises "One Low Fee Is Charged to Develop Your Personal Financial Plan" and one that advertises "You Are Not Charged a Fee, My Services Are Covered by the Investment Company for Which I Work"? L01-4, 1-5

FINANCIAL PLANNING CASE

You Be the Financial Planner

At some point in your life you may use the services of a financial planner. However, your personal knowledge should be the foundation for most financial decisions. For each of these situations, determine actions you might recommend:

Situation 1: Fran and Ed Blake, ages 43 and 47, have a daughter who is completing her first year of college and a son three years younger. Currently they have $42,000 in savings and investment funds set aside for their children's education. With increasing education costs, they are concerned whether this amount is adequate. In recent months, Fran's mother has required extensive medical attention and personal care assistance. Unable to live alone, she is now a resident of a long-term care facility. The cost of this service is $4,750 a month, with annual increases of about 5 percent. While a major portion of the cost is covered by Social Security and her pension, Fran's mother is unable to cover the entire cost. In addition, Fran and Ed are concerned about saving for their own retirement. While they have consistently made annual deposits to a retirement fund, current financial demands may force them to access some of that money.

Situation 2: "While I knew it might happen someday, I didn't expect it right now." This was the reaction of Patrick Hamilton when his company merged with another organization and moved its offices to another state, resulting in him losing his job. Patrick does have some flexibility in his short-term finances since he has three months of living expenses in a saving account. However, "three months can go by very quickly," as Patrick noted.

Situation 3: Nina Resendiz, age 23, recently received a $12,000 gift from her aunt. Nina is considering various uses for these unexpected funds including paying off credit card bills from her last vacation or setting aside money for a down payment on a house. Or she might invest the money in a tax-deferred retirement account. Another possibility is using the money for technology certification courses to enhance her earning power. Nina also wants to contribute some of the funds to a homeless shelter and a world hunger organization. She is overwhelmed by the choices and comments to herself, "I want to avoid the temptation of wasting the money on impulse items. I want to make sure I use the money on things with lasting value."

Questions

1. For each situation, identify the main financial planning issues that need to be addressed.
2. What additional information would you like to have before recommending actions in each situation?
3. Based on the information provided and your assessment of the situation, what actions would you recommend for the Blakes, Patrick, and Nina?

PERSONAL FINANCIAL PLANNER IN ACTION

Starting Your Financial Plan

Planning is the foundation for success in every aspect of life. Assessing your current financial situation, along with setting goals is the key to successful financial planning.

Your Short-Term Financial Planning Activities	*Resources*
1. Prepare a list of personal and financial information for yourself and family members. Also create a list of financial service organizations that you use.	PFP Sheets 1, 2 www.money.com www.kiplinger.com
2. Set financial goals related to various current and future needs.	PFP Sheet 4 http://financialplan.about.com
3. Monitor current economic conditions (inflation, interest rates) to determine possible actions to take related to your personal finances.	PFP Sheet 3 www.federalreserve.gov www.bls.gov
Your Long-Term Financial Planning Activities	*Resources*
1. Based on various financial goals, calculate the savings deposits necessary to achieve those goals.	PFP Sheet 5 www.dinkytown.net
2. Identify various financial planning actions for you and other household members for the next two to five years.	Exhibit 1-6, p. 17; text pages 23–28 www.moneycentral.msn.com

CONTINUING CASE

Getting Started

Life Situation	*Financial Data*
Single	Monthly Income $1,750
Age 21	Living Expenses $1,210
No dependents	Personal property $7,300
College student	Savings $2,000
	Student loan $3,000
	Credit card debt $2,400

Shelby Johnson has a flair for grooming dogs and cats. She hopes to open her own pet salon when she graduates from college. She is currently completing her sophomore year in business while working at a local pet store. Shelby has been living with a roommate (Melinda) in an apartment near her work in order to reduce her living expenses. However, she continually uses her credit card to make ends meet.

Her personal property consists of a 2005 car ($5,550) that gets great gas mileage, a television set with a DVD player ($400), a digital camera ($50), a laptop computer ($400), clothing ($300), and some furnishings valued at $600 (bed, dresser, lamp, clock, couch) with a total value of $7,300.

Questions

1. Given her current situation, list various personal financial decisions that Shelby may be considering at this point in her life.
2. Describe what short-term, intermediate and long-term goals Shelby should develop using "Setting Personal Financial Goals" (Sheet 3) located at the back of this book.
3. What types of time value of money calculations would be helpful for Shelby?

DAILY SPENDING DIARY

"I first thought this process would be a waste of time, but the information has helped me become much more careful of how I spend my money."

Directions

Nearly everyone who has taken the effort to keeping a Daily Spending Diary has found it beneficial. While at first the process may seem tedious, after awhile, recording this information becomes easier and faster.

Using the "Daily Spending Diary" sheets, record every cent of your spending each day in the categories provided. Or you may create your own format to monitor your spending. You can indicate the use of a credit card with (CR). This experience will help you better understand your spending patterns and identify desired changes you might want to make in your spending habits.

Analysis Questions

1. What did your Daily Spending Diary reveal about your spending habits? What areas of spending might you consider changing?
2. How might your Daily Spending Diary assist you when identifying and achieving financial goals?

The Daily Spending Diary sheets are located in Appendix D at the end of the book and on the student website at www.mhhe.com/kdh.

chapter 1 appendix
Time Value of Money

- "If I deposit $10,000 today, how much will I have for a down payment on a house in five years?"
- "Will $2,000 saved each year give me enough money when I retire?"
- "How much must I save today to have enough for my children's college education?"

The *time value of money,* more commonly referred to as *interest,* is the cost of money that is borrowed or lent. Interest can be compared to rent, the cost of using an apartment or other item. The time value of money is based on the fact that a dollar received today is worth more than a dollar that will be received one year from today, because the dollar received today can be saved or invested and will be worth more than a dollar a year from today. Similarly, a dollar that will be received one year from today is currently worth less than a dollar today.

The time value of money has two major components: future value and present value. *Future value* computations, which are also referred to as *compounding,* yield the amount to which a current sum will increase based on a certain interest rate and period of time. *Present value,* which is calculated through a process called *discounting,* is the current value of a future sum based on a certain interest rate and period of time.

In future value problems, you are given an amount to save or invest and you calculate the amount that will be available at some future date. With present value problems, you are given the amount that will be available at some future date and you calculate the current value of that amount. Both future value and present value computations are based on basic interest rate calculations.

Interest Rate Basics

Simple interest is the dollar cost of borrowing or earnings from lending money. The interest is based on three elements:

- The dollar amount, called the *principal.*
- The *rate of interest.*
- The amount of *time.*

The formula and financial calculator computations are as follows:

Interest Rate Basics	
Formula	**Financial Calculator***
Interest = Principal × Rate of interest (annual) × Time (years)	Interest = Amount × Rate × Number of (or portion of) years
The interest rate is stated as a percentage for a year. For example, you must convert 12 percent to either 0.12 or 12/100 before doing your calculations. The time element must also be converted to a decimal or fraction. For example, three months would be shown as 0.25, or 1/4 of a year. Interest for 2½ years would involve a time period of 2.5.	

Formula	Financial Calculator*
Example A: Suppose you borrow $1,000 at 5 percent and will repay it in one payment at the end of one year. Using the simple interest calculation, the interest is $50, computed as follows:	
$50 = $1,000 × 0.05 × 1 (year)	$50 = 1000 × .05 × 1
Example B: If you deposited $750 in a savings account paying 8 percent, how much interest would you earn in nine months? You would compute this amount as follows:	
Interest = $750 × 0.08 × 3/4 (or 0.75 of a year) = $45	−750 [PV], 8 [I/Y], 9/12 = .75 [N], 0 [PMT], [CPT] [FV] 795. 795 − 750 = 45

*NOTE: These financial calculator notations may require slightly different keystrokes when using various brands and models.

SAMPLE PROBLEM 1

How much interest would you earn if you deposited $300 at 6 percent for 27 months?

(Answers to sample problems are on page 39.)

SAMPLE PROBLEM 2

How much interest would you pay to borrow $670 for eight months at 12 percent?

Future Value of a Single Amount

The future value of an amount consists of the original amount plus compound interest. This calculation involves the following elements:

FV = Future value

PV = Present value

i = Interest rate

n = Number of time periods

The formula and financial calculator computations are as follows:

Future Value of a Single Amount		
Formula	**Table**	**Financial Calculator**
$FV = PV(1 + i)^n$	FV = PV (Table factor)	[PV], [I/Y], [N], [PMT], [CPT] [FV]
Example C: The future value of $1 at 10 percent after three years is $1.33. This amount is calculated as follows:		
$1.33 = $(1.001 + 0.10)³	Using Exhibit 1-A: $1.33 = $1.00(1.33)	1 [PV], 10 [I/Y], 3 [N], 0 [PMT], [CPT] [FV] 1.33

Future value tables are available to help you determine compounded interest amounts (see Exhibit 1-A on page 42). Looking at Exhibit 1-A for 10 percent and three years, you can see that $1 would be worth $1.33 at that time. For other amounts, multiply the table factor by the original amount. This process may be viewed as follows:

Future value (rounded)	$1		$1.10		$1.21		FV = $1.33
		Interest $0.10		Interest $0.11		Interest $0.12	
After year	0		1		2		3

Future Value of a Single Amount		
Formula	**Table**	**Financial Calculator**
Example D: If your savings of \$400 earns 12 percent, compounded *monthly*, over a year and a half, use the table factor for 1 percent for 18 time periods; the future value would be:		
$\$478.46 = \$400(1 + 0.01)^{18}$	$\$478.40 = \$400(1.196)$	400 [PV], 12/12 = 1 [I/Y], 1.5 × 12 = 18 [N], 0 [PMT], [CPT] [FV] 478.46
Excel formula notation for future value of a single amount	= FV(rate, nper, pmt, pv, type)	
	Example D solution =FV(0.01,18,0, −400) = 478.46	

SAMPLE PROBLEM 3

What is the future value of \$800 at 8 percent after six years?

SAMPLE PROBLEM 4

How much would you have in savings if you kept \$200 on deposit for eight years at 8 percent, compounded *semiannually?*

Future Value of a Series of Equal Amounts (an Annuity)

Future value may also be calculated for a situation in which regular additions are made to savings. The formula and financial calculator computations are as follows:

Future Value of a Series of Payments		
Formula	**Table**	**Financial Calculator**
$FV = \text{Annuity}\,\frac{(1+i)^n - 1}{i}$	Using Exhibit 1-B: Annuity × Table factor	[PMT], [N], [I/Y], [PV], [CPT] [FV]
This calculation assumes that (1) each deposit is for the same amount, (2) the interest rate is the same for each time period, and (3) the deposits are made at the end of each time period.		
Example E: The future value of three \$1 deposits made at the end of the next three years, earning 10 percent interest, is \$3.31. This is calculated as follows:		
$\$3.31 = \$1\,\frac{(1+0.10)^3 - 1}{0.10}$	Using Exhibit 1-B: \$3.31 = \$1 × 3.31	−1 [PMT], 3 [N], 10 [I/Y], 0 [PV], [CPT] [FV] 3.31
This may be viewed as follows:		

Future value (rounded)		\$1	\$2.10	*FV* = \$3.31
	Deposit \$1 Interest 0	Deposit \$1 Interest \$0.10	Deposit \$1 Interest \$0.21	
After year	0	1	2	3

Future Value of a Series of Payments		
Formula	**Table**	**Financial Calculator**
Example F: If you plan to deposit $40 a year for 10 years, earning 8 percent compounded annually, the future value of this amount is:		
$\$579.46 = \frac{\$40(1+0.08)^{10}-1}{0.08}$	Using Exhibit 1-B $579.48 = $40(14.487)	−40 [PMT], 10 [N], 10 [I/Y], 0 [PV], [CPT] [FV] 579.46
Excel formula notation for future value of a series	=FV(rate, nper, pmt)	
	Example F solution =FV(0.08,10,−40) = 579.46	

SAMPLE PROBLEM 5

What is the future value of an annual deposit of $230 earning 6 percent for 15 years?

SAMPLE PROBLEM 6

What amount would you have in a retirement account if you made annual deposits of $375 for 25 years earning 12 percent, compounded annually?

Present Value of a Single Amount

If you want to know how much you need to deposit now to receive a certain amount in the future, the formula and financial calculator computations are as follows:

Present Value of a Single Amount		
Formula	**Table**	**Financial Calculator**
$PV = \frac{FV}{(1+i)^n}$	Using Exhibit 1-C: PV = FV(Table Factor)	[FV], [N], [I/Y], [PMT], [CPT] [PV]
Example G: The present value of $1 to be received three years from now based on a 10 percent interest rate is calculated as follows:		
$\$0.75 = \frac{\$1}{(1+0.10)^3}$	Using Exhibit 1-C: $0.75 = $1(0.751)	1 [FV], 3 [N], 10 [I/Y], 0 [PMT], [CPT] [PV] .75131

This may be viewed as follows:

Future value (rounded)	$0.75	$0.83	$0.91	$1
	Discount (interest) $0.075 →	Discount (interest) $0.0825 →	Discount (interest) $0.0905 →	
After year	0	1	2	3

Present value tables are available to assist you in this process (see Exhibit 1-C on page 44). Notice that $1 at 10 percent for three years has a present value of $0.75. For amounts other than $1, multiply the table factor by the amount involved.

Example H: If you want to have $300 seven years from now and your savings earn 10 percent, compounded *semiannually* (which would be 5 percent for 14 time periods), finding how much you would have to deposit today is calculated as follows:		
$\$151.52 = \frac{\$300}{(1+0.05)^{14}}$	Using Exhibit 1-C: $151.50 = $300(0.505)	300 [FV], 7 × 2 = 14 [N], 10/2 = 5 [I/Y], 0 [PMT], [CPT] [PV] 151.52
Excel formula notation for present value of a single amount	=PV(rate, nper, pmt, fv, type)	
	Example H solution: =PV(0.05,14, 0,−300) = 151.52	

SAMPLE PROBLEM 7

What is the present value of $2,200 earning 15 percent for eight years?

SAMPLE PROBLEM 8

To have $6,000 for a child's education in 10 years, what amount should a parent deposit in a savings account that earns 12 percent, compounded *quarterly?*

Present Value of a Series of Equal Amounts (an Annuity)

The final time value of money situation allows you to receive an amount at the end of each time period for a certain number of periods. The formula and financial calculator computations are as follows:

Present Value of a Series of Payments		
Formula	**Table**	**Financial Calculator**
$PV = \text{Annuity} \times \dfrac{1 - \dfrac{1}{(1+i)^n}}{i}$	Using Exhibit 1-D: PV = Annuity(Table factor)	[PMT], [N], [I/Y], [FV], [CPT] [PV]
Example I: The present value of a $1 withdrawal at the end of the next three years would be $2.49, for money earning 10 percent. This would be calculated as follows:		
$\$2.49 = \$1 \left[\dfrac{1 - \dfrac{1}{(1+0.10)^3}}{0.10} \right]$	Using Exhibit 1-D: $2.49 = $1(2.487)	1 [PMT], 3 [N], 10 [I/Y], 0 [FV], [CPT] [PV] 2.48685
This may be viewed as follows: 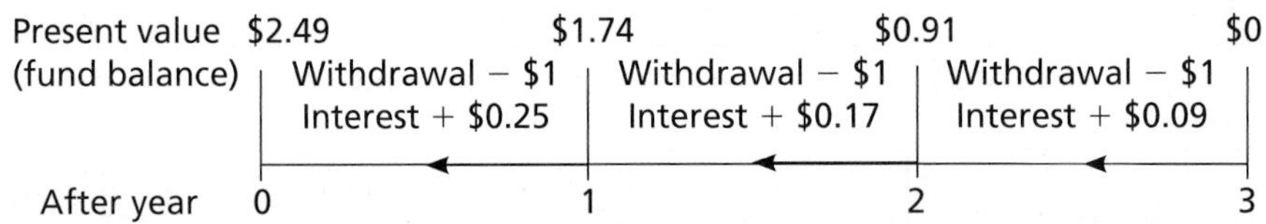 This same amount appears in Exhibit 1-D on page 45 for 10 percent and three time periods. To use the table for other situations, multiply the table factor by the amount to be withdrawn each year.		
Example J: If you wish to withdraw $100 at the end of each year for 10 years from an account that earns 14 percent, compounded annually, what amount must you deposit now?		
$\$521.61 = \$100 \left(\dfrac{1 - \dfrac{1}{(1+0.14)^{10}}}{0.14} \right)$	Using Exhibit 1-D: $521.60 = $100(5.216)	100 [PMT], 10 [N], 14 [I/Y], 0 [FV], [CPT] [PV] 521.61
Excel formula notation for present value of a series	=PV(rate, nper, pmt)	
	Example J solution =PV(0.14,10,−100) = 521.61	

SAMPLE PROBLEM 9

What is the present value of a withdrawal of $200 at the end of each year for 14 years with an interest rate of 7 percent?

SAMPLE PROBLEM 10

How much would you have to deposit now to be able to withdraw $650 at the end of each year for 20 years from an account that earns 11 percent?

Using Present Value to Determine Loan Payments

Present value tables (Exhibit 1–D) can also be used to determine installment payments for a loan as follows:

Present Value to Determine Loan Payments	
Table	**Financial Calculator**
$\frac{\text{Amount borrowed}}{\text{Present value of a series table factor (Exhibit 1-D)}}$ = Loan payment	[PV], [I/Y], [N], [FV], [CPT] [PMT]
Example K: If you borrow $1,000 with a 6 percent interest rate to be repaid in three equal payments at the end of the next three years, the payments will be $374.11. This is calculated as follows:	
$\frac{\$1,000}{2.673} = \$374.11$	1000 [PV], 6 [I/Y], 3 [N], 0 [FV], [CPT] [PMT] 374.10981
Excel formula notation for determining loan payment amount	=PMT(rate, nper, pv)
	Example K solution =PMT(.06,3,1000) = $374.11

SAMPLE PROBLEM 11

What would be the annual payment amount for a $20,000, 10-year loan at 7 percent?

Answers to Sample Problems (based on TVM tables)

1. $300 × 0.06 × 2.25 years (27 months) = $40.50.
2. $670 × 0.12 × 2/3 (of a year) = $53.60.
3. $800(1.587) = $1,269.60. (Use Exhibit 1-A, 8%, 6 periods.)
4. $200(1.873) = $374.60. (Use Exhibit 1-A, 4%, 16 periods.)
5. $230(23.276) = $5,353.48. (Use Exhibit 1-B, 6%, 15 periods.)
6. $375(133.33) = $49,998.75. (Use Exhibit 1-B, 12%, 25 periods.)
7. $2,200(0.327) = $719.40. (Use Exhibit 1-C, 15%, 8 periods.)
8. $6,000(0.307) = $1,842. (Use Exhibit 1-C, 3%, 40 periods.)
9. $200(8.745) = $1,749. (Use Exhibit 1-D, 7%, 14 periods.)
10. $650(7.963) = $5,175.95. (Use Exhibit 1-D, 11%, 20 periods.)
11. $20,000/7.024 = $2,847.38. (Use Exhibit 1-D, 7%, 10 periods.)

Time Value of Money Application Exercises

1. **(Present value of an annuity)** You wish to borrow $18,000 to buy a new automobile. The rate is 8.6% over four years with monthly payments. Find the monthly payment. (Answer: $444.52)
2. **(Present value of an annuity)** How much money must your rich uncle give you now to finance four years of college, assuming an annual cost of $48,000 and an interest rate of 6% (applied to the principal until disbursed)? (Answer: $166,325.07)
3. **(Present value of a single amount)** How much money must you set aside at age 20 to accumulate retirement funds of $100,000 at age 65, assuming a rate of interest of 7%? (Answer: $4,761.35)
4. **(Future value of a single amount)** If you deposit $2,000 in a 5-year certificate of deposit at 5.2%, how much will it be worth in five years? (Answer: $2,576.97)
5. **(Future value of a single amount)** If you deposit $2,000 in a 5-year certificate of deposit at 5.2% with quarterly compounding, how much will it be worth in five years? (Answer: $2,589.52)
6. **(Future value of an annuity)** You choose to invest $50/month in a 401(k) that invests in an international stock mutual fund. Assuming an annual rate of return of 9%, how much will this fund be worth if you are retiring in 40 years? (Answer: $234,066.01)
7. **(Future value of an annuity)** If, Instead, you invest $600/year in a 401(k) that invests in an international stock mutual fund. Assuming an annual rate of return of 9%, how much will this fund be worth if you are retiring in 40 years? (Answer: $202,729.47)

Time Value of Money Calculation Methods: A Summary

The time value of money may be calculated using a variety of techniques. When achieving specific financial goals requires regular deposits to a savings or investment account, the computation may occur in one of several ways. For example, Bonnie Keller plans to deposit $10,000 in an account for the next 10 years. She estimates these funds will earn an annual rate of 5 percent. What amount can Bonnie expect to have available after 10 years?

Method	Process, Results
Formula Calculation The most basic method of calculating the time value of money involves using a formula.	For this situation, the formula would be: $PV(1 + i)^n = FV$ The result should be $10,000 (1 + 0.05)^{10} = $16,288.95
Time Value of Money Tables Instead of calculating with a formula, time value of money tables are available. The numeric factors presented ease the computational process.	Using the table in Exhibit 1-A: $10,000 Future value of $1, 5%, 10 years $10,000 × 1.629 = $16,290
Financial Calculator A variety of financial calculators are programmed with various financial functions. Both future value and present value calculations may be performed using the appropriate keystrokes.	Using a financial calculator, the keystrokes would be: Amount −10,000 [PV] Time periods 10 [N] Interest rate 5 [I] Result [FV] $16,288.94
Spreadsheet Software Excel and other software programs have built-in formulas for various financial computations, including time value of money.	When using a spreadsheet program, this type of calculation would require this format: = FV(rate, periods, amount per period, single amount) The results of this example would be: = FV(0.05, 10, 0, −10,000) = $16,288.95
Time Value of Money Websites and Apps Many time-value-of-money calculators are also available online and for smartphones. These web-based programs perform calculations for the future and present value of savings as well as determining loan payment amounts.	Some easy-to-use calculators for computing the time value of money and other financial computations are located at • www.kiplinger.com/tools • www.dinkytown.net • http://tcalc.timevalue.com/ • cgi.money.cnn.com/tools

NOTE: The slight differences in answers are the result of rounding.

Exhibit 1-A Future value (compounded sum) of $1 after a given number of time periods

Period	1%	2%	3%	4%	5%	6%	7%	8%	9%	10%	11%
1	1.010	1.020	1.030	1.040	1.050	1.060	1.070	1.080	1.090	1.100	1.110
2	1.020	1.040	1.061	1.082	1.103	1.124	1.145	1.166	1.188	1.210	1.232
3	1.030	1.061	1.093	1.125	1.158	1.191	1.225	1.260	1.295	1.331	1.368
4	1.041	1.082	1.126	1.170	1.216	1.262	1.311	1.360	1.412	1.464	1.518
5	1.051	1.104	1.159	1.217	1.276	1.338	1.403	1.469	1.539	1.611	1.685
6	1.062	1.126	1.194	1.265	1.340	1.419	1.501	1.587	1.677	1.772	1.870
7	1.072	1.149	1.230	1.316	1.407	1.504	1.606	1.714	1.828	1.949	2.076
8	1.083	1.172	1.267	1.369	1.477	1.594	1.718	1.851	1.993	2.144	2.305
9	1.094	1.195	1.305	1.423	1.551	1.689	1.838	1.999	2.172	2.358	2.558
10	1.105	1.219	1.344	1.480	1.629	1.791	1.967	2.159	2.367	2.594	2.839
11	1.116	1.243	1.384	1.539	1.710	1.898	2.105	2.332	2.580	2.853	3.152
12	1.127	1.268	1.426	1.601	1.796	2.012	2.252	2.518	2.813	3.138	3.498
13	1.138	1.294	1.469	1.665	1.886	2.133	2.410	2.720	3.066	3.452	3.883
14	1.149	1.319	1.513	1.732	1.980	2.261	2.579	2.937	3.342	3.797	4.310
15	1.161	1.346	1.558	1.801	2.079	2.397	2.759	3.172	3.642	4.177	4.785
16	1.173	1.373	1.605	1.873	2.183	2.540	2.952	3.426	3.970	4.595	5.311
17	1.184	1.400	1.653	1.948	2.292	2.693	3.159	3.700	4.328	5.054	5.895
18	1.196	1.428	1.702	2.026	2.407	2.854	3.380	3.996	4.717	5.560	6.544
19	1.208	1.457	1.754	2.107	2.527	3.026	3.617	4.316	5.142	6.116	7.263
20	1.220	1.486	1.806	2.191	2.653	3.207	3.870	4.661	5.604	6.727	8.062
25	1.282	1.641	2.094	2.666	3.386	4.292	5.427	6.848	8.623	10.835	13.585
30	1.348	1.811	2.427	3.243	4.322	5.743	7.612	10.063	13.268	17.449	22.892
40	1.489	2.208	3.262	4.801	7.040	10.286	14.974	21.725	31.409	45.259	65.001
50	1.645	2.692	4.384	7.107	11.467	18.420	29.457	46.902	74.358	117.390	184.570

Period	12%	13%	14%	15%	16%	17%	18%	19%	20%	25%	30%
1	1.120	1.130	1.140	1.150	1.160	1.170	1.180	1.190	1.200	1.250	1.300
2	1.254	1.277	1.300	1.323	1.346	1.369	1.392	1.416	1.440	1.563	1.690
3	1.405	1.443	1.482	1.521	1.561	1.602	1.643	1.685	1.728	1.953	2.197
4	1.574	1.630	1.689	1.749	1.811	1.874	1.939	2.005	2.074	2.441	2.856
5	1.762	1.842	1.925	2.011	2.100	2.192	2.288	2.386	2.488	3.052	3.713
6	1.974	2.082	2.195	2.313	2.436	2.565	2.700	2.840	2.986	3.815	4.827
7	2.211	2.353	2.502	2.660	2.826	3.001	3.185	3.379	3.583	4.768	6.276
8	2.476	2.658	2.853	3.059	3.278	3.511	3.759	4.021	4.300	5.960	8.157
9	2.773	3.004	3.252	3.518	3.803	4.108	4.435	4.785	5.160	7.451	10.604
10	3.106	3.395	3.707	4.046	4.411	4.807	5.234	5.696	6.192	9.313	13.786
11	3.479	3.836	4.226	4.652	5.117	5.624	6.176	6.777	7.430	11.642	17.922
12	3.896	4.335	4.818	5.350	5.936	6.580	7.288	8.064	8.916	14.552	23.298
13	4.363	4.898	5.492	6.153	6.886	7.699	8.599	9.596	10.699	18.190	30.288
14	4.887	5.535	6.261	7.076	7.988	9.007	10.147	11.420	12.839	22.737	39.374
15	5.474	6.254	7.138	8.137	9.266	10.539	11.974	13.590	15.407	28.422	51.186
16	6.130	7.067	8.137	9.358	10.748	12.330	14.129	16.172	18.488	35.527	66.542
17	6.866	7.986	9.276	10.761	12.468	14.426	16.672	19.244	22.186	44.409	86.504
18	7.690	9.024	10.575	12.375	14.463	16.879	19.673	22.091	26.623	55.511	112.460
19	8.613	10.197	12.056	14.232	16.777	19.748	23.214	27.252	31.948	69.389	146.190
20	9.646	11.523	13.743	16.367	19.461	23.106	27.393	32.429	38.338	86.736	190.050
25	17.000	21.231	26.462	32.919	40.874	50.658	62.669	77.388	95.396	264.700	705.640
30	29.960	39.116	50.950	66.212	85.850	111.070	143.370	184.680	237.380	807.790	2,620.000
40	93.051	132.780	188.880	267.860	378.720	533.870	750.380	1,051.700	1,469.800	7,523.200	36,119.000
50	289.000	450.740	700.230	1,083.700	1,670.700	2,566.200	3,927.400	5,998.900	9,100.400	70,065.000	497,929.000

Exhibit 1-B Future value (compounded sum) of $1 paid in at the end of each period for a given number of time periods (an annuity)

Period	1%	2%	3%	4%	5%	6%	7%	8%	9%	10%	11%
1	1.000	1.000	1.000	1.000	1.000	1.000	1.000	1.000	1.000	1.000	1.000
2	2.010	2.020	2.030	2.040	2.050	2.060	2.070	2.080	2.090	2.100	2.110
3	3.030	3.060	3.091	3.122	3.153	3.184	3.215	3.246	3.278	3.310	3.342
4	4.060	4.122	4.184	4.246	4.310	4.375	4.440	4.506	4.573	4.641	4.710
5	5.101	5.204	5.309	5.416	5.526	5.637	5.751	5.867	5.985	6.105	6.228
6	6.152	6.308	6.468	6.633	6.802	6.975	7.153	7.336	7.523	7.716	7.913
7	7.214	7.434	7.662	7.898	8.142	8.394	8.654	8.923	9.200	9.487	9.783
8	8.286	8.583	8.892	9.214	9.549	9.897	10.260	10.637	11.028	11.436	11.859
9	9.369	9.755	10.159	10.583	11.027	11.491	11.978	12.488	13.021	13.579	14.164
10	10.462	10.950	11.464	12.006	12.578	13.181	13.816	14.487	15.193	15.937	16.722
11	11.567	12.169	12.808	13.486	14.207	14.972	15.784	16.645	17.560	18.531	19.561
12	12.683	13.412	14.192	15.026	15.917	16.870	17.888	18.977	20.141	21.384	22.713
13	13.809	14.680	15.618	16.627	17.713	18.882	20.141	21.495	22.953	24.523	26.212
14	14.947	15.974	17.086	18.292	19.599	21.015	22.550	24.215	26.019	27.975	30.095
15	16.097	17.293	18.599	20.024	21.579	23.276	25.129	27.152	29.361	31.772	34.405
16	17.258	18.639	20.157	21.825	23.657	25.673	27.888	30.324	33.003	35.950	39.190
17	18.430	20.012	21.762	23.698	25.840	28.213	30.840	33.750	36.974	40.545	44.501
18	19.615	21.412	23.414	25.645	28.132	30.906	33.999	37.450	41.301	45.599	50.396
19	20.811	22.841	25.117	27.671	30.539	33.760	37.379	41.446	46.018	51.159	56.939
20	22.019	24.297	26.870	29.778	33.066	36.786	40.995	45.762	51.160	57.275	64.203
25	28.243	32.030	36.459	41.646	47.727	54.865	63.249	73.106	84.701	98.347	114.410
30	34.785	40.588	47.575	56.085	66.439	79.058	94.461	113.280	136.310	164.490	199.020
40	48.886	60.402	75.401	95.026	120.800	154.760	199.640	259.060	337.890	442.590	581.830
50	64.463	84.579	112.800	152.670	209.350	290.340	406.530	573.770	815.080	1,163.900	1,668.800

Period	12%	13%	14%	15%	16%	17%	18%	19%	20%	25%	30%
1	1.000	1.000	1.000	1.000	1.000	1.000	1.000	1.000	1.000	1.000	1.000
2	2.120	2.130	2.140	2.150	2.160	2.170	2.180	2.190	2.200	2.250	2.300
3	3.374	3.407	3.440	3.473	3.506	3.539	3.572	3.606	3.640	3.813	3.990
4	4.779	4.850	4.921	4.993	5.066	5.141	5.215	5.291	5.368	5.766	6.187
5	6.353	6.480	6.610	6.742	6.877	7.014	7.154	7.297	7.442	8.207	9.043
6	8.115	8.323	8.536	8.754	8.977	9.207	9.442	9.683	9.930	11.259	12.756
7	10.089	10.405	10.730	11.067	11.414	11.772	12.142	12.523	12.916	15.073	17.583
8	12.300	12.757	13.233	13.727	14.240	14.773	15.327	15.902	16.499	19.842	23.858
9	14.776	15.416	16.085	16.786	17.519	18.285	19.086	19.923	20.799	25.802	32.015
10	17.549	18.420	19.337	20.304	21.321	22.393	23.521	24.701	25.959	33.253	42.619
11	20.655	21.814	23.045	24.349	25.733	27.200	28.755	30.404	32.150	42.566	56.405
12	24.133	25.650	27.271	29.002	30.850	32.824	34.931	37.180	39.581	54.208	74.327
13	28.029	29.985	32.089	34.352	36.786	39.404	42.219	45.244	48.497	68.760	97.625
14	32.393	34.883	37.581	40.505	43.672	47.103	50.818	54.841	59.196	86.949	127.910
15	37.280	40.417	43.842	47.580	51.660	56.110	60.965	66.261	72.035	109.690	167.290
16	42.753	46.672	50.980	55.717	60.925	66.649	72.939	79.850	87.442	138.110	218.470
17	48.884	53.739	59.118	65.075	71.673	78.979	87.068	96.022	105.930	173.640	285.010
18	55.750	61.725	68.394	75.836	84.141	93.406	103.740	115.270	128.120	218.050	371.520
19	63.440	70.749	78.969	88.212	98.603	110.290	123.410	138.170	154.740	273.560	483.970
20	72.052	80.947	91.025	102.440	115.380	130.030	146.630	165.420	186.690	342.950	630.170
25	133.330	155.620	181.870	212.790	249.210	292.110	342.600	402.040	471.980	1,054.800	2,348.800
30	241.330	293.200	356.790	434.750	530.310	647.440	790.950	966.700	1,181.900	3,227.200	8,730.000
40	767.090	1,013.700	1,342.000	1,779.100	2,360.800	3,134.500	4,163.210	5,529.800	7,343.900	30,089.000	120,393.000
50	2,400.000	3,459.500	4,994.500	7,217.700	10,436.000	15,090.000	21,813.000	31,515.000	45,497.000	80,256.000	165,976.000

Exhibit 1-C Present value of $1 to be received at the end of a given number of time periods

Period	1%	2%	3%	4%	5%	6%	7%	8%	9%	10%	11%	12%
1	0.990	0.980	0.971	0.962	0.952	0.943	0.935	0.926	0.917	0.909	0.901	0.893
2	0.980	0.961	0.943	0.925	0.907	0.890	0.873	0.857	0.842	0.826	0.812	0.797
3	0.971	0.942	0.915	0.889	0.864	0.840	0.816	0.794	0.772	0.751	0.731	0.712
4	0.961	0.924	0.885	0.855	0.823	0.792	0.763	0.735	0.708	0.683	0.659	0.636
5	0.951	0.906	0.863	0.822	0.784	0.747	0.713	0.681	0.650	0.621	0.593	0.567
6	0.942	0.888	0.837	0.790	0.746	0.705	0.666	0.630	0.596	0.564	0.535	0.507
7	0.933	0.871	0.813	0.760	0.711	0.665	0.623	0.583	0.547	0.513	0.482	0.452
8	0.923	0.853	0.789	0.731	0.677	0.627	0.582	0.540	0.502	0.467	0.434	0.404
9	0.914	0.837	0.766	0.703	0.645	0.592	0.544	0.500	0.460	0.424	0.391	0.361
10	0.905	0.820	0.744	0.676	0.614	0.558	0.508	0.463	0.422	0.386	0.352	0.322
11	0.896	0.804	0.722	0.650	0.585	0.527	0.475	0.429	0.388	0.350	0.317	0.287
12	0.887	0.788	0.701	0.625	0.557	0.497	0.444	0.397	0.356	0.319	0.286	0.257
13	0.879	0.773	0.681	0.601	0.530	0.469	0.415	0.368	0.326	0.290	0.258	0.229
14	0.870	0.758	0.661	0.577	0.505	0.442	0.388	0.340	0.299	0.263	0.232	0.205
15	0.861	0.743	0.642	0.555	0.481	0.417	0.362	0.315	0.275	0.239	0.209	0.183
16	0.853	0.728	0.623	0.534	0.458	0.394	0.339	0.292	0.252	0.218	0.188	0.163
17	0.844	0.714	0.605	0.513	0.436	0.371	0.317	0.270	0.231	0.198	0.170	0.146
18	0.836	0.700	0.587	0.494	0.416	0.350	0.296	0.250	0.212	0.180	0.153	0.130
19	0.828	0.686	0.570	0.475	0.396	0.331	0.277	0.232	0.194	0.164	0.138	0.116
20	0.820	0.673	0.554	0.456	0.377	0.312	0.258	0.215	0.178	0.149	0.124	0.104
25	0.780	0.610	0.478	0.375	0.295	0.233	0.184	0.146	0.116	0.092	0.074	0.059
30	0.742	0.552	0.412	0.308	0.231	0.174	0.131	0.099	0.075	0.057	0.044	0.033
40	0.672	0.453	0.307	0.208	0.142	0.097	0.067	0.046	0.032	0.022	0.015	0.011
50	0.608	0.372	0.228	0.141	0.087	0.054	0.034	0.021	0.013	0.009	0.005	0.003

Period	13%	14%	15%	16%	17%	18%	19%	20%	25%	30%	35%	40%	50%
1	0.885	0.877	0.870	0.862	0.855	0.847	0.840	0.833	0.800	0.769	0.741	0.714	0.667
2	0.783	0.769	0.756	0.743	0.731	0.718	0.706	0.694	0.640	0.592	0.549	0.510	0.444
3	0.693	0.675	0.658	0.641	0.624	0.609	0.593	0.579	0.512	0.455	0.406	0.364	0.296
4	0.613	0.592	0.572	0.552	0.534	0.515	0.499	0.482	0.410	0.350	0.301	0.260	0.198
5	0.543	0.519	0.497	0.476	0.456	0.437	0.419	0.402	0.320	0.269	0.223	0.186	0.132
6	0.480	0.456	0.432	0.410	0.390	0.370	0.352	0.335	0.262	0.207	0.165	0.133	0.088
7	0.425	0.400	0.376	0.354	0.333	0.314	0.296	0.279	0.210	0.159	0.122	0.095	0.059
8	0.376	0.351	0.327	0.305	0.285	0.266	0.249	0.233	0.168	0.123	0.091	0.068	0.039
9	0.333	0.300	0.284	0.263	0.243	0.225	0.209	0.194	0.134	0.094	0.067	0.048	0.026
10	0.295	0.270	0.247	0.227	0.208	0.191	0.176	0.162	0.107	0.073	0.050	0.035	0.017
11	0.261	0.237	0.215	0.195	0.178	0.162	0.148	0.135	0.086	0.056	0.037	0.025	0.012
12	0.231	0.208	0.187	0.168	0.152	0.137	0.124	0.112	0.069	0.043	0.027	0.018	0.008
13	0.204	0.182	0.163	0.145	0.130	0.116	0.104	0.093	0.055	0.033	0.020	0.013	0.005
14	0.181	0.160	0.141	0.125	0.111	0.099	0.088	0.078	0.044	0.025	0.015	0.009	0.003
15	0.160	0.140	0.123	0.108	0.095	0.084	0.074	0.065	0.035	0.020	0.011	0.006	0.002
16	0.141	0.123	0.107	0.093	0.081	0.071	0.062	0.054	0.028	0.015	0.008	0.005	0.002
17	0.125	0.108	0.093	0.080	0.069	0.060	0.052	0.045	0.023	0.012	0.006	0.003	0.001
18	0.111	0.095	0.081	0.069	0.059	0.051	0.044	0.038	0.018	0.009	0.005	0.002	0.001
19	0.098	0.083	0.070	0.060	0.051	0.043	0.037	0.031	0.014	0.007	0.003	0.002	0
20	0.087	0.073	0.061	0.051	0.043	0.037	0.031	0.026	0.012	0.005	0.002	0.001	0
25	0.047	0.038	0.030	0.024	0.020	0.016	0.013	0.010	0.004	0.001	0.001	0	0
30	0.026	0.020	0.015	0.012	0.009	0.007	0.005	0.004	0.001	0	0	0	0
40	0.008	0.005	0.004	0.003	0.002	0.001	0.001	0.001	0	0	0	0	0
50	0.002	0.001	0.001	0.001	0	0	0	0	0	0	0	0	0

Exhibit 1-D Present value of $1 received at the end of each period for a given number of time periods (an annuity)

Period	1%	2%	3%	4%	5%	6%	7%	8%	9%	10%	11%	12%
1	0.990	0.980	0.971	0.962	0.952	0.943	0.935	0.926	0.917	0.909	0.901	0.893
2	1.970	1.942	1.913	1.886	1.859	1.833	1.808	1.783	1.759	1.736	1.713	1.690
3	2.941	2.884	2.829	2.775	2.723	2.673	2.624	2.577	2.531	2.487	2.444	2.402
4	3.902	3.808	3.717	3.630	3.546	3.465	3.387	3.312	3.240	3.170	3.102	3.037
5	4.853	4.713	4.580	4.452	4.329	4.212	4.100	3.993	3.890	3.791	3.696	3.605
6	5.795	5.601	5.417	5.242	5.076	4.917	4.767	4.623	4.486	4.355	4.231	4.111
7	6.728	6.472	6.230	6.002	5.786	5.582	5.389	5.206	5.033	4.868	4.712	4.564
8	7.652	7.325	7.020	6.733	6.463	6.210	5.971	5.747	5.535	5.335	5.146	4.968
9	8.566	8.162	7.786	7.435	7.108	6.802	6.515	6.247	5.995	5.759	5.537	5.328
10	9.471	8.983	8.530	8.111	7.722	7.360	7.024	6.710	6.418	6.145	5.889	5.650
11	10.368	9.787	9.253	8.760	8.306	7.887	7.499	7.139	6.805	6.495	6.207	5.938
12	11.255	10.575	9.954	9.385	8.863	8.384	7.943	7.536	7.161	6.814	6.492	6.194
13	12.134	11.348	10.635	9.986	9.394	8.853	8.358	7.904	7.487	7.103	6.750	6.424
14	13.004	12.106	11.296	10.563	9.899	9.295	8.745	8.244	7.786	7.367	6.982	6.628
15	13.865	12.849	11.939	11.118	10.380	9.712	9.108	8.559	8.061	7.606	7.191	6.811
16	14.718	13.578	12.561	11.652	10.838	10.106	9.447	8.851	8.313	7.824	7.379	6.974
17	15.562	14.292	13.166	12.166	11.274	10.477	9.763	9.122	8.544	8.022	7.549	7.102
18	16.398	14.992	13.754	12.659	11.690	10.828	10.059	9.372	8.756	8.201	7.702	7.250
19	17.226	15.678	14.324	13.134	12.085	11.158	10.336	9.604	8.950	8.365	7.839	7.366
20	18.046	16.351	14.877	13.590	12.462	11.470	10.594	9.818	9.129	8.514	7.963	7.469
25	22.023	19.523	17.413	15.622	14.094	12.783	11.654	10.675	9.823	9.077	8.422	7.843
30	25.808	22.396	19.600	17.292	15.372	13.765	12.409	11.258	10.274	9.427	8.694	8.055
40	32.835	27.355	23.115	19.793	17.159	15.046	13.332	11.925	10.757	9.779	8.951	8.244
50	39.196	31.424	25.730	21.482	18.256	15.762	13.801	12.233	10.962	9.915	9.042	8.304

Period	13%	14%	15%	16%	17%	18%	19%	20%	25%	30%	35%	40%	50%
1	0.885	0.877	0.870	0.862	0.855	0.847	0.840	0.833	0.800	0.769	0.741	0.714	0.667
2	1.668	1.647	1.626	1.605	1.585	1.566	1.547	1.528	1.440	1.361	1.289	1.224	1.111
3	2.361	2.322	2.283	2.246	2.210	2.174	2.140	2.106	1.952	1.816	1.696	1.589	1.407
4	2.974	2.914	2.855	2.798	2.743	2.690	2.639	2.589	2.362	2.166	1.997	1.849	1.605
5	3.517	3.433	3.352	3.274	3.199	3.127	3.058	2.991	2.689	2.436	2.220	2.035	1.737
6	3.998	3.889	3.784	3.685	3.589	3.498	3.410	3.326	2.951	2.643	2.385	2.168	1.824
7	4.423	4.288	4.160	4.039	3.922	3.812	3.706	3.605	3.161	2.802	2.508	2.263	1.883
8	4.799	4.639	4.487	4.344	4.207	4.078	3.954	3.837	3.329	2.925	2.598	2.331	1.922
9	5.132	4.946	4.772	4.607	4.451	4.303	4.163	4.031	3.463	3.019	2.665	2.379	1.948
10	5.426	5.216	5.019	4.833	4.659	4.494	4.339	4.192	3.571	3.092	2.715	2.414	1.965
11	5.687	5.453	5.234	5.029	4.836	4.656	4.486	4.327	3.656	3.147	2.752	2.438	1.977
12	5.918	5.660	5.421	5.197	4.988	4.793	4.611	4.439	3.725	3.190	2.779	2.456	1.985
13	6.122	5.842	5.583	5.342	5.118	4.910	4.715	4.533	3.780	3.223	2.799	2.469	1.990
14	6.302	6.002	5.724	5.468	5.229	5.008	4.802	4.611	3.824	3.249	2.814	2.478	1.993
15	6.462	6.142	5.847	5.575	5.324	5.092	4.876	4.675	3.859	3.268	2.825	2.484	1.995
16	6.604	6.265	5.954	5.668	5.405	5.162	4.938	4.730	3.887	3.283	2.834	2.489	1.997
17	6.729	6.373	6.047	5.749	5.475	5.222	4.988	4.775	3.910	3.295	2.840	2.492	1.998
18	6.840	6.467	6.128	5.818	5.534	5.273	5.033	4.812	3.928	3.304	2.844	2.494	1.999
19	6.938	6.550	6.198	5.877	5.584	5.316	5.070	4.843	3.942	3.311	2.848	2.496	1.999
20	7.025	6.623	6.259	5.929	5.628	5.353	5.101	4.870	3.954	3.316	2.850	2.497	1.999
25	7.330	6.873	6.464	6.097	5.766	5.467	5.195	4.948	3.985	3.329	2.856	2.499	2.000
30	7.496	7.003	6.566	6.177	5.829	5.517	5.235	4.979	3.995	3.332	2.857	2.500	2.000
40	7.634	7.105	6.642	6.233	5.871	5.548	5.258	4.997	3.999	3.333	2.857	2.500	2.000
50	7.675	7.133	6.661	6.246	5.880	5.554	5.262	4.999	4.000	3.333	2.857	2.500	2.000

chapter 2

Financial Aspects of Career Planning

Learning Objectives

LO2-1 Describe activities associated with career planning and advancement.

LO2-2 Evaluate factors that influence employment opportunities.

LO2-3 Implement employment search strategies.

LO2-4 Assess financial and legal concerns related to obtaining employment.

LO2-5 Analyze techniques available for career growth and advancement.

What will this mean for me?

Financial planning involves spending, saving, and sharing your economic resources. Your ability to obtain these funds will depend on your career planning activities. Preparing for and obtaining work has become an ongoing need as a changing job market creates new opportunities and challenges. Development of a portfolio of career skills and technical competencies will help ensure continuing employment success.

my life

WORK TO LIVE, OR LIVE TO WORK?

Few decisions in life will affect you to a greater extent than your choice of employment. Your income, amount of leisure time, travel opportunities, and the people with whom you associate will be greatly influenced by your work situation.

As you start (or expand) your career planning activities, consider the following statements. For each, indicate if you "agree," are "neutral," or "disagree" related to your current situation regarding career planning activities.

1. I understand my personal interests and abilities that could create a satisfying work life.	Agree	Neutral	Disagree
2. My actions keep me informed of various factors that influence employment opportunities in our society.	Agree	Neutral	Disagree
3. I have the ability to ask other people questions that provide me with information about career planning activities and employment opportunities.	Agree	Neutral	Disagree
4. Salary would be the important factor for me when accepting an employment position.	Agree	Neutral	Disagree
5. I sometimes think about what type of employment situation I would like to have three or five years from now.	Agree	Neutral	Disagree

As you study this chapter, you will encounter "My Life" boxes with additional information and resources related to these items.

Career Choice Factors

LO2-1

Describe activities associated with career planning and advancement.

"Only two days until the weekend." "Just ten more minutes of sleep!" "Oh no!" "Excellent!" These are some common responses to "It's time to get up for work."

Have you ever wondered why some people find great satisfaction in their work while others only put in their time? As with other personal financial decisions, career selection and professional growth require planning. The average person changes jobs, or even careers, five or more times during a lifetime. Most likely, therefore, you will reevaluate your choice of a job on a regular basis.

The lifework you select is a key to your financial well-being and personal satisfaction. You may select a **job,** an employment position obtained mainly to earn money. Many people work in one or more jobs during their lives without considering their interests or opportunities for advancement. Or you may select a **career,** a commitment to a profession that requires continued training and offers a clear path for occupational growth.

job An employment position obtained mainly to earn money, without regard for interests or opportunities for advancement.

career A commitment to a profession that requires continued training and offers a clear path for occupational growth.

TRADE-OFFS OF CAREER DECISIONS

While many factors affect living habits and financial choices, your employment probably affects daily decisions the most. Your income, business associates, and leisure time are a direct result of the work you do.

Like other decisions, career choice and professional development alternatives have risks and opportunity costs. In recent years, many people have placed family and personal fulfillment above monetary reward and professional recognition. Career choices require periodic evaluation of trade-offs related to personal, social, and economic factors. For example:

- Some people select employment that is challenging and offers strong personal satisfaction rather than employment in which they can make the most money.
- Some people refuse a transfer or a promotion that would require moving their families to a new area or reducing leisure time.
- Many parents opt for part-time employment or flexible hours to allow more time with children.
- Many people give up secure job situations because they prefer to operate their own businesses.

Time with family members may be an important influence on career decisions.

CAREER TRAINING AND SKILL DEVELOPMENT

Your level of formal training affects financial success. Exhibit 2-1 shows the influence of education on lifetime earnings. The statistics in this exhibit do not mean you will automatically earn a certain amount because you have a college degree. More education increases your *potential* earning power and reduces your chances of being unemployed. Other factors, such as field of study, experiences, and the job market, also influence future income.

The skills gap—the difference between skills needed by employers and the skills possessed by applicants—is an ongoing concern. Also missing in many job hunters are *employability skills,* which refer to the basic capabilities necessary for obtaining, maintaining, and advancing in a work situation. The training you obtain may be viewed in two main categories:

1. **Technical skills.** Specialized career training refers to technical skills for a specific profession. This training includes competencies in fields such as information technology, accounting, law, engineering, health care, education, real estate, insurance, and law enforcement.

Exhibit 2-1

Education and income

Earning a professional or doctorate degree could be worth over $3.6 million in income over 40 years:

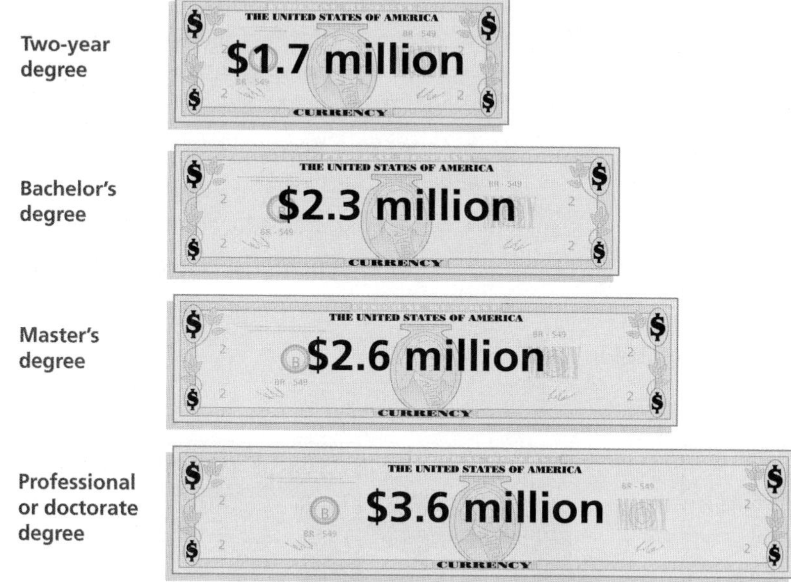

Source: Georgetown University, Center on Education and the Workforce

2. **General skills.** In addition to technical training, managers, employers, and career counselors stress the importance of traits adaptable to most work situations, sometimes called *social intelligence.* While some of these abilities can be acquired in school, others require experience in work or organizational settings. The general competencies that successful people commonly possess include:
   - An ability to work well with others in a variety of settings.
   - Taking initiative to overcome obstacles and meet challenges.
   - An interest in reading and continuing learning.
   - A willingness to cope with conflict and adapt to change.
   - An awareness of accounting, finance, and marketing fundamentals.
   - A knowledge of technology and computer software.
   - An ability to solve problems creatively in team settings.
   - A knowledge of research techniques and resource materials.
   - Effective written and oral communication skills.
   - An understanding of both personal motivations and the motivations of others.

These competencies give people flexibility, making it easier to move from one organization to another and to successfully change career fields. How are you working to develop these traits?

PERSONAL FACTORS

You may identify a satisfying career using guidance tests that measure abilities, interests, and personal qualities. Aptitude tests, interest inventories, and other types of career assessment tests are available at school career counseling offices and online.

DID YOU KNOW?

Prospective workers who are most successful possess technical skills (such as computer use and financial analysis), have the ability to communicate effectively, and work well in team settings.

DEVELOPING A CAREER ACTION PLAN

Your career plan might start with a personal S-W-O-T analysis, in which you identify your:

Strengths, which are the skills and experiences that set you apart from others.

Weaknesses involve personal areas in need of improvement.

Opportunities are social, economic, technological, global, and organizational trends for employment.

Threats are factors that limit employment opportunities, such as changing technology and global competition.

Next, for one of the following career development activities, describe your plans and actions using the steps below.

- Assess your personal and career interests.
- Identify and expand career skills.
- Obtain required education and career training.
- Apply for a potential employment position.

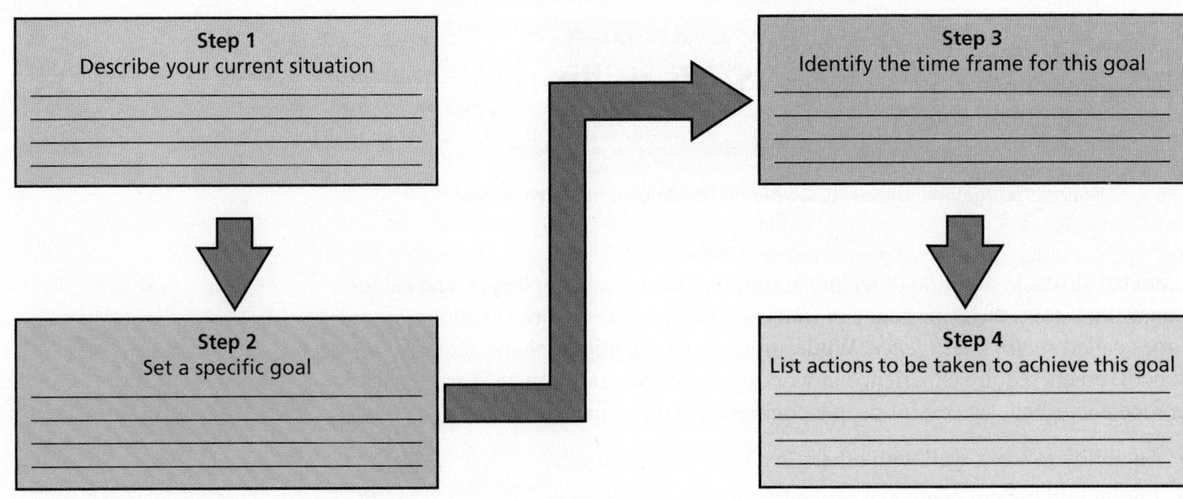

Aptitudes are natural abilities that people possess. The ability to work well with numbers, problem-solving skills, and physical dexterity are examples of aptitudes.

Interest inventories determine the activities that give you satisfaction. These instruments measure qualities related to various types of work. People with strong social tendencies may be best suited for careers that involve dealing with people, while people with investigative interests may be best suited for careers in research areas.

Test results will not tell you which career to pursue. However, these assessments will indicate your aptitudes and interests. Another important dimension of career selection is your personality. Do you perform best in structured or high-pressure situations, or do you prefer unstructured or creative work environments? Sample career assessments may be located through an online search for "career interest inventory" and "career interest survey."

my life 1

I understand my personal interests and abilities that could create a satisfying work life.

You might ask people who know you well to point out some of your interests and abilities. This information may be used to start your career planning activities using the "Financial Planning for Life's Situations: Developing a Career Action Plan" feature.

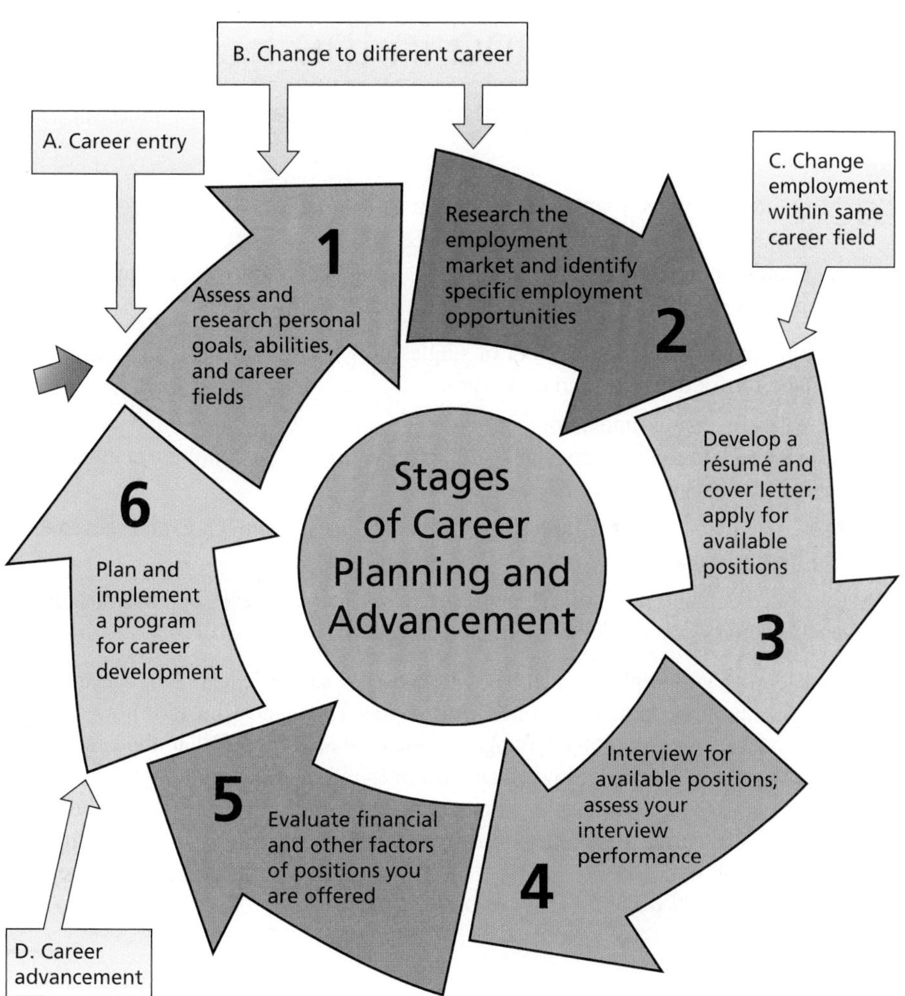

Exhibit 2-2

Stages of career planning and advancement

CAREER DECISION MAKING

Changing personal and social factors will require you to continually assess your work situation. Exhibit 2-2 provides an approach to career planning, advancement, and career change. As you can see, the different entry points depend on your personal situation. For example, people established in a certain career field may start at point C (Change employment within same career field) or D (Career advancement).

Your career goals will also affect how you use this process. If you desire more responsibility on the job, for example, you may obtain advanced training or change career fields. This process is a suggested framework for planning, changing, or advancing in a career.

PRACTICE QUIZ 2-1

1 How does a job differ from a career?
2 What opportunity costs are associated with career decisions?
3 What skills would be of value in most employment situations?

Career Opportunities: Now and in the Future

LO2-2

Evaluate factors that influence employment opportunities.

Your job search should start with an assessment of the career choice factors shown in Exhibit 2-3.

SOCIAL INFLUENCES

Various demographic and geographic trends influence employment opportunities. Demographic trends affecting the job market include the following:

- Continuing growth in the number of single and working parents expands the demand for food service and child care.
- Increases in leisure time among various segments of the population, resulting in an increased interest in personal health, physical fitness, technology, and recreational products and services.
- As people live longer, the demand for travel services, health care, and retirement facilities increases.
- Expanded demand for employment training services increases opportunities for teachers, corporate trainers, and related careers.

In considering geographic areas, be sure to assess salary levels. Average incomes are high in such metropolitan areas as Boston, New York, and Chicago; however, the prices of food, housing, and other living expenses are also high. What appears to be a big salary may actually mean a lower standard of living than in a geographic area with lower salaries and lower living costs. For example, in recent years, the cost of living for a single employee earning $30,000 annually was 60 percent higher in the District of Columbia than the national city average. In contrast, the cost of living in Fayetteville, Arkansas, was only 90 percent of the national city average.

EXAMPLE: Geographic Cost of Living Differences

To compare living costs and salaries in different cities, you may use the following "Geographic Buying Power" formula:

$$\begin{matrix}\text{City 1} \\ \text{City 2}\end{matrix} \quad \frac{\text{Index number} \times \text{Salary}}{\text{Index number}} = \text{\$ buying power}$$

For example,

$$\begin{matrix}\text{Chicago} \\ \text{Omaha}\end{matrix} \quad \frac{123 \times \$30{,}000}{93.3} = \$39{,}550$$

A person earning $30,000 in Omaha, Nebraska, would need to earn $39,550 in Chicago to have comparable buying power. Information to compare geographic cost-of-living differences is available at www.bls.gov and www.erieri.com.

ECONOMIC CONDITIONS

High interest rates, price increases, or decreased global demand for goods and services can affect career opportunities. While you cannot eliminate the effects of economic factors on employment trends, these factors affect some businesses more than others. For example, high interest rates reduce employment in housing-related industries, since people are less likely to buy homes when interest rates are high.

DID YOU KNOW?

In recent years, nearly 80 percent of new jobs in the U.S. economy occurred in companies with fewer than 100 employees.

Exhibit 2-3

Factors influencing your career opportunities

INDUSTRY TRENDS

While career opportunities have dwindled in some sectors of our economy, opportunities in other sectors have grown. Service industries that are expected to continue to have the greatest employment potential include

Technology influences career opportunities and required employment skills.

- *Information technology*—systems analysts, database administrators, web and software developers, network operations managers, and repair personnel and service technicians.
- *Health care*—medical assistants, physical therapists, home health workers, biotech analysts, laboratory technicians, registered nurses, dental hygienists, and health care administrators.
- *Medical technology*—microbiologists, food and drug inspectors, pharmaceutical salespersons, public health specialists, medical laboratory managers, clinical pathologists, and toxicologists.
- *Environmental services*—environmental auditors, environmental consultants, water quality analysts, sustainability analysts, energy analysts, and urban planners.
- *Business services*—social media consultants, foreign language translators, employee benefit managers, operations consultants, and research data analysts.
- *Social services*—child care workers, elder care coordinators, family counselors, and social service agency administrators.
- *Sales and retailing*—social media promotion developers, marketing representatives, and sales managers with technical knowledge in the areas of electronics, medical products, and financial services.
- *Hospitality and food services*—resort and hotel administrators, food service managers, online customer service representatives, and meeting planners.

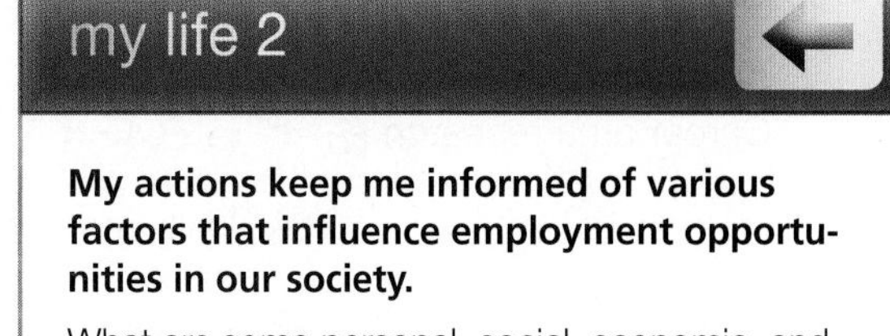

My actions keep me informed of various factors that influence employment opportunities in our society.

What are some personal, social, economic, and technological factors you might consider when planning the direction for your career?

Financial Planning for Life's Situations

ENTREPRENEURIAL CAREER OPTIONS

People start their own businesses for two main reasons: (1) reduced career opportunities in their field and (2) a desire for greater control of their work environment. Over 20 million people in the United States operate their own businesses. These range from home-based sales and consulting services to small manufacturing enterprises and technology support. In recent years, a strong interest in *social entrepreneurship* has surfaced. Social entrepreneurs mix traditional business practices with innovation to address social concerns such as hunger, disease, poverty, and education.

GETTING STARTED

If you are planning to start a business, consider three main issues. First, become knowledgeable about your product or service. Next, identify potential customers, select an appropriate location, and study competitors. Finally, consider your financial resources. Most entrepreneurs use a combination of personal funds and loans.

QUALITIES OF SUCCESSFUL ENTREPRENEURS

Would running your own business be an appropriate career for you? That depends on your personality and abilities. Are you a highly motivated, confident individual? Do you have the ability to manage different phases of a business? Are you someone who enjoys challenges and is willing to take risks?

In addition, skills commonly viewed as vital for entrepreneurial success include: sales and marketing knowledge; effective written and oral communication ability; an understanding of accounting and financial management of cash flows; an ability to motivate and coordinate the work of others; effective and efficient management of your time; and a creative vision for success.

BUSINESS PLAN ELEMENTS

The foundation for success is a business plan, which is used to communicate the vision and purpose of an enterprise. This document, containing detailed financial projections, product information, and a marketing plan, is a vital tool for business planning and operations. Websites with information on business plans include www.bplans.com, www.businessplans.org, and entrepreneurs.about.com.

To obtain assistance about starting a business, contact a lawyer, local banker, accountant, or insurance agent. Additional information about running your own business may be obtained from the Small Business Administration (www.sba.gov), the Association for the Self-Employed (www.nase.org), Startup Journal (www.startupjournal.com), and SCORE (www.score.org).

- *Management and human resources*—clerical supervisors, recruiters, interviewers, employee benefit administrators, and employment service workers.
- *Education*—corporate trainers, special education teachers, adult education instructors, educational administrators, and teachers for elementary, secondary, and postsecondary schools.
- *Financial services*—risk assessment managers, actuaries, accountants, investment brokers, and others with a knowledge of accounting, finance, economics, and taxes.

Future business demands will include expanded reading and communication skills. More and more employees are being required to read scientific and technical journals and financial reports and to write speeches and journal articles. Your career success is likely to depend on communication skills, computer skills, and the ability to communicate in more than one language.

Career area research sheet

PRACTICE QUIZ 2-2

1 What are some demographic and economic factors that affect career opportunities?
2 How does technology affect available employment positions?

Employment Search Strategies

LO2-3

Implement employment search strategies.

Most people have heard about job applicants who sent hundreds of résumés with very little success, while others get several offers. What are the differences between these two groups? The answer usually involves an ability to expand one's experiences and use job search techniques effectively.

OBTAINING EMPLOYMENT EXPERIENCE

A common concern among people seeking employment is a lack of work experience. Many opportunities are available to obtain work-related training.

PART-TIME EMPLOYMENT Summer and part-time work can provide experience along with the chance to see if you enjoy a particular career field. The increased use of temporary employees has opened up opportunities to obtain experience in different career areas. More and more workers are taking advantage of temporary job assignments as a channel to a full-time position. Working as a "temp" can give you valuable experience as well as contacts in various employment fields.

VOLUNTEER WORK Involvement in community organizations can provide excellent opportunities to acquire skills, establish good work habits, and make contacts. Volunteering to work at the gift shop of a museum, for example, gives you experience in retailing. You may participate in a recycling project, assist at a senior center, or help supervise youth activities at a park district. These activities will help you obtain organizational skills.

INTERNSHIPS In very competitive fields, an internship can give you needed experience. During an internship, you can make contacts about available jobs. Applying for an internship is similar to applying for a job. Most colleges and universities offer internships as part of their academic programs.

CAMPUS PROJECTS Class assignments and campus activities are frequently overlooked as work-related experience. You can obtain valuable career skills on campus from experience in

- Managing, organizing, and coordinating people and activities as an officer or a committee chairperson of a campus organization.
- Public speaking in class, campus, and community presentations.
- Goal setting, planning, supervising, and delegating responsibility in community service and class team projects.
- Financial planning and budgeting gained from organizing fund-raising projects, managing personal finances, and handling funds for campus organizations.
- Conducting research for class projects, community organizations, and campus activities.

USING CAREER INFORMATION SOURCES

Career planning, like other financial decisions, is enhanced by relevant information. Exhibit 2-4 provides an overview of the main career information sources.

Most libraries offer many career information sources. The *Occupational Outlook Handbook* covers all aspects of career planning and provides detailed information on

Exhibit 2-4

Career information sources

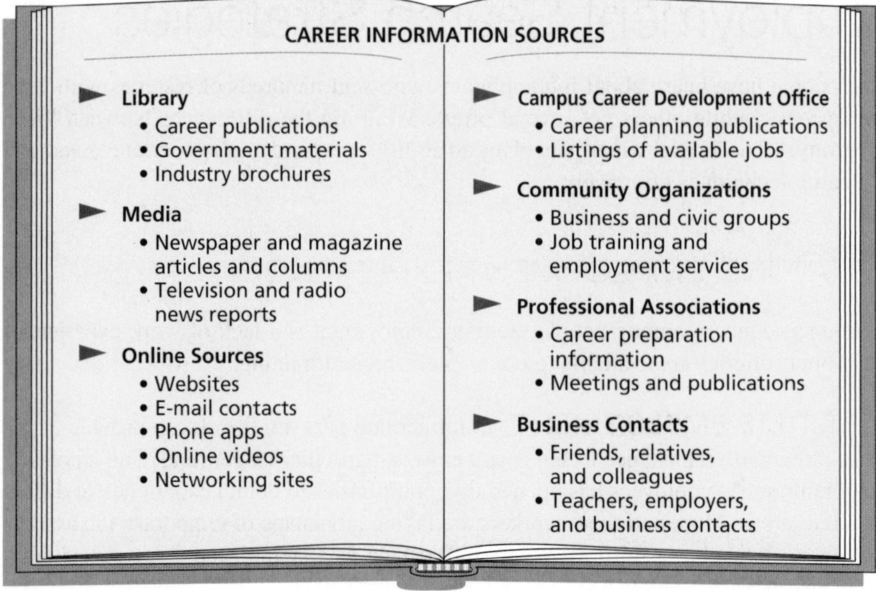

various career clusters. This and other government publications are available online. Most newspapers offer articles and columns about job searches and career trends. News sources also report on economic and social influences on careers. Extensive information related to job opportunities, preparing a résumé, interviewing, and other career planning topics may be found online. Your school probably has a career development office with resources and services on career planning topics, creating a résumé, and preparing for an interview.

CAREER DEVELOPMENT OFFICE This office will have services for career planning and can assist you in creating a résumé and preparing for an interview.

networking The process of making and using contacts for obtaining and updating career information.

NETWORKING **Networking** is the process of making and using contacts to obtain and update career information. Every person you talk to is a potential contact who may provide career assistance. These activities can be especially valuable, because about 70 percent of professionals find positions through personal contacts and networking, while responding to job ads accounts for only about 15 percent of jobs. The main sources of networking include:

1. **Community organizations.** Every community has business and civic groups you can use in your career search. Public meetings featuring industry leaders and business owners provide opportunities to become acquainted with local businesspeople.
2. **Professional associations.** All professions have organizations to promote their career areas. These organizations include the American Marketing Association, the Council of Supply Chain Management Professionals, the Association of Women in International Trade, and the National Restaurant Association. The *Encyclopedia of Associations,* as well as an online search, can help you identify organizations related to careers in which you are interested. Many of these organizations have a reduced membership fee for students.
3. **Business contacts.** Professional contacts can advise you about career preparation and job opportunities. Friends, relatives, people you meet through community and professional organizations, and people you meet through school, work, religious services, or other activities are all potential business contacts.

HOW TO...

Update Your Career Activities

While many career planning actions from the past are still valid, you should consider others to compete in a changing employment market.

When you want to...	Previously, people would...	Today, you can also...
Obtain career planning assistance.	Talk with others in career fields in which you are interested.	Acquire guidance from online contacts, videos, and webinars.
Develop potential career contacts.	Go to professional meetings, seminars, and community events.	Use social media, such as LinkedIn, to connect with professional contacts.
Follow up with networking contacts	Talk by phone or send an e-mail.	Stay in contact on LinkedIn and through other social media networks.
Gain entry-level career experience.	Part-time employment, volunteer work, and community service activities.	Participate in virtual volunteering, online communities, and online tutorials.
Identify employment opportunities.	Obtain leads from contacts, media, and positions in your current organization.	Connect through your online network to enhance other sources of employment.
Create a cover letter.	Highlight experiences related to the specific job or organizational needs.	Create a Q letter with bulleted items to communicate your specific experiences for a position.
Communicate your key skills on a résumé.	Include a career objective on their résumé.	Use a career profile or summary of skills and abilities.
Submit a résumé.	Mail or drop off at a company's office to make a personal contact.	Send by e-mail or posting on a website.
Prepare for an interview.	Talk to others for interview tips; participate in mock interviews.	Create a video to have others critique your poise and professionalism.
Conduct company research.	Talk to people who have worked at the organization or who have done business with them.	Use LinkedIn, Twitter, Facebook, blogs to study the company and people who will interview you.
Participate in an interview.	Meet face to face.	Take part in a Skype interview or a video conference.

(continued)

HOW TO... Continued

When you want to...	Previously, people would...	Today, you can also...
Follow up after an interview.	Send a handwritten note or e-mail to express appreciation and to reinforce your interest in the available position.	Send a work sample, evidence of your experience, such as a news article or report, or link to your e-portfolio.
Achieve career advancement training.	Participate in on-the-job training, professional seminars, graduate study.	Participate in webinars and online courses.
Develop and promote a personal brand.	Use business cards to communicate your organization and title.	Develop an online presence with a summary of unique experiences and competencies; use a personal website to convey your potential work contribution.

Your online presence can be a valuable asset for your career planning activities. Be sure to avoid actions that might present you in less than a professional manner. To communicate an appropriate online image, consider these actions:

- DO get connected to various LinkedIn.com and other professional networking sites.
- DON'T put items online that create an inappropriate image; search your name to assess online presence.
- DO use keywords for capabilities and experiences expected in the industry in which you work.
- DON'T post your résumé online arbitrarily; select websites appropriate for your specific job search.
- DO regular follow-ups with online contacts; share current news and ideas on industry trends.
- DON'T join online groups in which you will not be an active participant.
- DO create a blog to enhance your online image and to communicate areas of expertise.

Additional career planning information is available at: www.jobhuntersbible.com www.rileyguide.com jobsearch.about.com college.monster.com www.careerbuilder.com www.careerpath.com www.monster.com www.find-your-dream-career.com www.career-success-for-newbies.com "Smart Career Planning" and "Career Planning Forum" on LinkedIn.com

(*Note:* about.me allows you to connect a personal website, blog, and social media sites in one location.)

For effective networking: (1) prepare and practice a 30-second summary of your abilities and experience; (2) volunteer for committees and events of professional organizations; and (3) ask questions to get others to talk about themselves and their experiences.

Although contacts may not be able to hire you, if jobs are available they might refer you to the right person. They can also help you get an **informational interview,** a meeting at which you gather information about a career or an organization. When planning and using informational interviews, consider the following:

informational interview A company visit or meeting at which one gathers information about a career or an organization.

- Prepare a list of industries and organizations for which you would like to work. Talk to family, friends, co-workers, and others for names of people you might contact.
- Prepare a list of open-ended questions that will help you obtain information about current trends in the industry and potential employment opportunities.
- Make an appointment for a 20-minute meeting; emphasize to the person that the meeting is for information only.
- Try to interact with the person at his or her place of work to gain better awareness of the work environment.
- Follow up with a thank-you note and, if possible, send some information (such as an article) that might be of interest to your contact.

An e-mail informational "interview" may be used in some settings. Be sure your questions are open-ended and focused on various career and industry topics. Send your e-mail request to a specific person. As a follow-up to the e-mail response, you may also want to meet in person or talk by telephone.

my life 3

I have the ability to ask other people questions that provide me with information about career planning activities and employment opportunities.

Develop some questions that you might ask in an informational interview. These questions should reflect your current knowledge of a career field and should lead the person you interview to provide additional information. The best questions usually start with "How," "What," "Why," "Describe," or "Explain."

EXAMPLE: Business Cards in an Age of Social Media

While several apps are available as an alternative to business cards, these networking tools are still expected in many settings. Some things to remember:

- Keep the format simple with necessary contact information.
- Create a brief, yet descriptive, tagline to communicate your unique skills.
- Use the back of your card to list competencies and accomplishments, or to have a translation of your card for international business activities.
- Several apps are available to scan and store business cards.

IDENTIFYING JOB OPPORTUNITIES

Before you apply for employment, you need to identify job openings that match your interests and abilities.

JOB ADVERTISEMENTS Advertisements for employment opportunities were previously found in newspapers and other print media. While some still exist, nearly all job listings are now online. In addition to newspaper websites, also check for available positions offered through professional organizations, trade associations, and other online sources. For opportunities in a specific career field, refer to the website of specialized publications such as *Advertising Age, Marketing*

DID YOU KNOW?

An *elevator speech,* also called an *elevator pitch,* is a short, persuasive, focused summary of your unique experiences and skills used when networking. This talk should be conversational (not forced), memorable, and sincere. The use of an engaging idea or question can help keep the conversation going.

DID YOU KNOW?

When encountering unemployment and other difficult career situations, take these actions: (1) acknowledge stress, anxiety, frustration, and fear; (2) eat properly and exercise; (3) determine sources of emergency funds; cut unnecessary spending; (4) maintain a positive outlook to communicate confidence; (5) connect with others in professional and social settings; (6) consider part-time work, consulting, and volunteering to expand your contacts and career potential.

News, the *Journal of Accountancy*, and *American Banker*. Since a large portion of available jobs may not be advertised to the general public, other job search techniques are critical.

CAREER FAIRS Career fairs, commonly held on campuses and at convention centers, offer an opportunity to contact several firms in a short time span. Be prepared to quickly communicate your potential contributions to an organization. By making yourself memorable to the recruiter, you are likely to be called for a follow-up interview. Be ready to ask specific questions about the organizations in which you are interested. Additional information on career fairs may be obtained at www.nationalcareerfairs.com.

EMPLOYMENT AGENCIES Another possible source of job leads is employment agencies. These for-profit organizations match job hunters with prospective employers. Often the hiring company pays the fee charged by the employment agency; however, be careful when you are asked to pay a fee and have no guarantee of a job. Be sure you understand any contracts before signing them.

Government-supported employment services are also available. Contact your state employment service or your state department of labor for further information.

job creation The development of an employment position that matches your skills with the needs of an organization.

JOB CREATION After researching a particular organization or industry, present how your abilities would contribute to that organization. **Job creation** involves developing an employment position that matches your skills with the needs of an organization.

As you develop skills in areas you enjoy, you may be able to create a demand for your services. For example, a person who enjoyed researching business and economic trends was hired by a major corporation to make presentations for its managers at various company offices. Or people with an ability to design promotions and advertising might be hired by a nonprofit organization that needs to enhance its public visibility.

A career fair provides an opportunity to contact many prospective employers.

OTHER JOB SEARCH METHODS Your ability to locate existing and potential employment positions is limited only by your imagination and initiative. Commonly overlooked sources of jobs include the following:

- Visit organizations where you would like to work, and make face-to-face contacts. Create an impression that you are someone who can contribute. Calling or visiting before 8 a.m. or after 4 p.m. increases your chance of talking to someone who is not busy.
- Successful organizations continually look for quality employees. An online search can provide names of organizations that employ people with your qualifications.
- Be in contact with alumni who work in your field. Graduates who are familiar with your school and major can help you focus your career search.

To improve your job search efforts, work as many hours a week *getting* a job as you expect to work each week *on* the job. Maintaining an ongoing relationship with contacts can be a valuable source of information about future career opportunities.

APPLYING FOR EMPLOYMENT

Many qualified people never get the job they deserve without a presentation of skills and experiences. This process usually involves three main elements.

1. The **résumé,** a summary of education, training, experience, and qualifications, provides prospective employers with an overview of your potential contributions to an organization.
2. A **cover letter** is the correspondence you send with a résumé to communicate your interest in a job and to obtain an interview.
3. The *interview* is the formal meeting used to discuss your qualifications in detail.

résumé A summary of a person's education, training, experience, and other job qualifications.

cover letter A letter that accompanies a résumé and is designed to express interest in a job and obtain an interview.

When connecting your background and potential contributions to the needs of an organization in a résumé, cover letter, or interview, consider how these examples achieve that purpose:

A prospective employer requires that you have:	Experiences, competencies, you have:	A connection you might make on a résumé or in an interview:
• Research experience	• Class research project for case study in Eastern Europe.	• Researched potential markets in Eastern Europe for company expansion.
• Leadership skills	• Summer camp coordinator for youth sports.	• Coordinated camp volunteers for youth sports program.
• Marketing background	• Prepared marketing proposal during internship.	• Developed marketing proposal for community service organization.

Most important is to communicate how your experiences will contribute to the future needs and success of the organization.

For expanded coverage of résumés, cover letters, and interview strategies, see the appendix at the end of this chapter.

Making career contacts

PRACTICE QUIZ 2-3

1 How can a person obtain employment-related experiences without working in a job situation?
2 What types of career information sources can be helpful in identifying job opportunities?
3 How does the information in a cover letter differ from the information in a résumé?

Financial and Legal Aspects of Employment

LO2-4

Assess financial and legal concerns related to obtaining employment.

"We would like you to work for us." When offered an employment position, you should examine a range of factors. Carefully assess the organization, the specific job, and the salary and other benefits.

ACCEPTING AN EMPLOYMENT POSITION

Before accepting a position, do additional research about the job and the company. Request information about your specific duties and job expectations. If someone currently has a similar position, ask to talk to that person. If you are replacing a person who is no longer with the company, obtain information about the circumstances of that person's departure.

THE WORK ENVIRONMENT Investigate the work environment. The term *corporate culture* refers to management styles, work intensity, dress codes, and social interactions within an organization. For example, some companies have rigid lines of communication, while others have an open-door atmosphere. Are the values, goals, and lifestyles of current employees similar to yours? If not, you may find yourself in an uncomfortable situation.

Consider company policies and procedures for salary increases, evaluations of employees, and promotions. Talking with current workers can help you obtain this information.

FACTORS AFFECTING SALARY Your initial salary will be influenced by your education and training, company size, and salaries for comparable positions. To ensure a fair starting salary, talk to people in similar positions and research salary levels.

To improve your value on the job and to enhance your salary potential:

- Ask your supervisor for professional development suggestions.
- Obtain additional training; request additional duties.
- Take initiative to exceed performance expectations.
- Talk with co-workers to obtain ideas for contributing to team and organizational success.

DID YOU KNOW?

The main factors college graduates consider when choosing an employer are: enjoyment of the work, integrity of the organization, potential for advancement, benefits, and job location.

EVALUATING EMPLOYEE BENEFITS

Escalating health care costs, changing family situations, and concerns about retirement have increased the attention given to supplementary compensation benefits.

MEETING EMPLOYEE NEEDS In recent years, nonsalary employee benefits have expanded to meet the needs of different life situations. The increasing number of two-income and single-parent households has resulted in a greater need for child care benefits and leaves of absence. The need for elder care benefits for employees with dependent parents or grandparents has also increased. Other common employee benefits designed to meet varied life situation needs include:

- Flexible work schedules.
- Work-at-home arrangements (telecommuting).
- Legal assistance.
- Counseling for health, emotional, and financial needs.
- Exercise and fitness programs.

SELECTING EMPLOYEE BENEFITS

Commonly recommended employee benefits for various life situations are shown here:

Single, No Children	Young Family	Single Parent	Married, No Children	Mixed-Generation Household
• Disability income insurance • Health insurance • Retirement program • Educational assistance, such as tuition reimbursement	• Comprehensive health insurance • Life insurance • Child care services	• Health insurance • Life insurance • Disability income insurance • Dependent care benefits	• Health insurance • Retirement program • Maternity coverage and parental leave (young couple) • Long-term health care (older couple)	• Health and disability insurance • Child care services • Elder care benefits

Based on your current life situation or expectations for the future, list the employee benefits that would be most important to you.

Life Situation	Desired Employee Benefits

Such benefits not only enhance the quality of an employee's life but are also profitable for organizations because happier, healthier workers have fewer absences and a higher level of productivity.

Cafeteria-style employee benefits are programs that allow workers to base their job benefits on a credit system and personal needs. Flexible selection of employee benefits has become common. A married employee with children may opt for increased life and health insurance, while a single parent may use benefit credits for child care services. The Financial Planning for Life's Situations box on this page can help you plan benefits. As with any financial decision, employee benefits involve a trade-off, or opportunity cost.

cafeteria-style employee benefits Programs that allow workers to base their job benefits on a credit system and personal needs.

Many organizations offer *flexible spending plans,* also called *expense reimbursement accounts.* This arrangement allows you to set aside part of your salary for paying medical or dependent care expenses. These funds are not subject to income or Social Security taxes. However, money not used for the specified purpose is forfeited. Therefore, you must carefully plan the amount to be designated for a flexible spending plan.

Similarly, a *medical-spending account (Archer MSA)* or a *health savings account (HSA)* allows paying health care costs with pretax dollars. These have two components: (1) health insurance coverage with a high deductible, and (2) a tax-deferred

Salary would be the important factor for me when accepting an employment position.

While salary is important, research findings consistently rate several other factors higher for a person deciding to accept a position. Talk to people in various stages of their careers to obtain information about factors they have considered when selecting an employment position.

savings account for medical expenses. Money in this account may be used for other purposes; however, the amount is taxed, along with a tax penalty based on age and health condition. While MSAs and HSAs have tax-saving implications, the high deductible may not be affordable for many households.

When matching dependent health care needs and medical insurance plans, consider the following:

- Types of services available and location of health care providers.
- Direct costs (insurance premiums) to you.
- Anticipated out-of-pocket costs (deductibles and coinsurance amounts).

As people live longer, various retirement programs are increasing in importance. In addition to Social Security benefits, some employers contribute to a pension plan. *Vesting* is the point at which retirement payments made by the organization on your behalf belong to you even if you no longer work for the organization. Vesting schedules vary, but all qualified plans (those for which an employer may deduct contributions to the plan for tax purposes) must (1) be 100 percent vested on completion of five years of service or (2) have 20 percent vesting after three years and full vesting, in stages, after seven years. Vesting refers only to the employer's pension contributions; employee contributions belong to the employees regardless of the length of their service with the organization.

Workers are commonly allowed to make personal contributions to company-sponsored retirement programs. These plans usually involve a variety of investments, making it easy for employees to create a diversified portfolio for their retirement funds.

COMPARING BENEFITS Two methods used to assess the monetary value of employee benefits are market value calculations and future value calculations.

Market value calculations determine the specific monetary value of employee benefits—the cost of the benefits if you had to pay for them. For example, you may view the value of one week's vacation as 1/52 of your annual salary, or you may view the value of a life insurance benefit as what it would cost you to obtain the same coverage. You can use this method to determine the difference between two job offers with different salaries and employee benefits.

Future value calculations, as discussed in Chapter 1, enable you to assess the long-term worth of employee benefits such as pension programs and retirement plans. For example, you can compare the future value of payments contributed to a company retirement fund to that of other saving and investment options.

You should also take tax considerations into account when you assess employment benefits. A *tax-exempt* benefit is one on which you won't have to pay income tax, but a *tax-deferred* benefit requires the payment of income tax at some future time, such as at retirement. When assessing employment compensation and benefits, consider their taxability, since an untaxed benefit of lower value may be worth more than a benefit of higher value that is subject to taxation (see the Financial Planning Calculations box).

DID YOU KNOW?

Many employers use credit reports as hiring tools. Federal law requires that job applicants be told if credit histories are being used in the hiring process. You can check your credit report at www.annualcreditreport.com.

YOUR EMPLOYMENT RIGHTS

Employees have legal rights both during the hiring process and on the job. For example, an employer cannot refuse to hire a woman or terminate her employment because of pregnancy, nor can it force her to go on leave at an arbitrary point during her pregnancy. In addition, a woman who stops working due to pregnancy must get full credit

Financial Planning Calculations

TAX-EQUIVALENT EMPLOYEE BENEFITS

Employee benefits that are nontaxable have a higher financial value than you may realize. A $100 employee benefit on which you are taxed is not worth as much as a nontaxable $100 benefit. This formula is used to calculate the *tax-equivalent value* of a nontaxable benefit:

$$\frac{\text{Value of the benefit}}{(1 - \text{Tax rate})}$$

For example, receiving a life insurance policy with a nontaxable annual premium of $350 is comparable to receiving a taxable employee benefit worth $486 if you are in the 28 percent tax bracket. This tax-equivalent amount is calculated as follows:

$$\frac{\$350}{1 - 0.28} = \frac{\$350}{0.72} = \$486$$

A variation of this formula, which would give the *after-tax value* of an employee benefit, is

$$\text{Taxable value of the benefit } (1 - \text{Tax rate})$$

For the above example, the calculation would be

$$\$486\ (1 - 0.28) = \$486(0.72) = \$350$$

In other words, a taxable benefit with a value of $486 would have an after-tax value of $350 since you would have to pay $136 ($486 × 0.28) in tax on the benefit.

These calculations can help you assess and compare different employee benefits within a company or in considering different jobs. Remember to also consider the value of employee benefits in terms of your personal and family needs and goals.

for previous service, accrued retirement benefits, and accumulated seniority. Other employment rights include the following:

- A person may not be discriminated against in the employment selection process on the basis of age, race, color, religion, sex, marital status, national origin, mental or physical disabilities, or sexual orientation.
- Minimum-wage and overtime pay legislation apply to individuals in certain work settings.
- Worker's compensation (for work-related injury or illness), Social Security, and unemployment insurance are required benefits.

1 How does a person's life situation determine the importance of certain employee benefits?
2 What methods can be used to measure the monetary value of employee benefits?

Employee benefits comparison

Long-Term Career Development

LO2-5

Analyze techniques available for career growth and advancement.

A job is for today, but a career can be for a lifetime. Will you always enjoy the work you do today? Will you be successful in the career you select? These questions cannot be answered right away; however, certain skills and attitudes can lead to a fulfilling work life.

Every day you can perform duties that contribute to your career success. Communicating and working well with others will enhance your chances for financial advancement and promotion. Flexibility and openness to new ideas will expand your abilities, knowledge, and career potential.

Develop efficient work habits. Use lists, goal setting, and time management techniques. Combine increased productivity with quality. All of your work activities should reflect your best performance. This extra effort will be recognized and rewarded.

Finally, learn to anticipate problems and areas for action. Creativity and a willingness to assist others can help the entire organization and contribute to your work enjoyment and career growth.

TRAINING OPPORTUNITIES

Many technology-work situations did not exist a few years ago. Many of the job skills you will need in the future have yet to be created. Your desire for increased education is a primary determinant of your career success and financial advancement. Continue to learn about new technology, diverse cultures, and the global economy.

Various methods for updating and expanding your knowledge are available. Formal methods may include company programs, seminars and webinars offered by professional organizations, and graduate and advanced college courses. Some companies encourage and pay for continuing education.

Informal methods for updating and expanding your knowledge include reading and discussion with colleagues. Online sources offer a wealth of information on business, economic, and social trends. Informal meetings with co-workers and associates from other companies can also be a valuable source of career information.

CAREER PATHS AND ADVANCEMENT

As with other financial decisions, career choices must be reviewed in light of changing values, goals, economic conditions, and social trends. As Exhibit 2-5 on page 67 shows, you will move through a series of career stages, each with specific tasks and challenges. A successful technique for coping with the anxieties associated with career development is to gain the support of an established person in your field. A **mentor** is an experienced employee who serves as a teacher and counselor for a less experienced person in a career field. A relationship with a mentor can provide such benefits as personalized training, access to influential people, and emotional support during difficult times.

mentor An experienced employee who serves as a teacher and counselor for a less experienced person in a career field.

Your efforts to attract a mentor start with excellent performance. Show initiative, be creative, and be alert to meeting the needs of others. Maintain visibility and display a desire to learn and grow by asking questions and volunteering for new assignments.

A prospective mentor should be receptive to assisting others and to helping them grow in both the technical and social areas of a career. Many organizations have formal mentor programs with an experienced employee assigned to oversee the career development of a newer employee. Some mentor relationships involve retired individuals who desire to share their knowledge and experience.

CHANGING CAREERS

At some time in their lives, most workers change jobs. Millions of career moves occur each year. People change jobs to obtain a better or different position within the same career field or to move into a new career field. Changing jobs may be more difficult than selecting the first job. Unless their present situation is causing mental stress or physical illness, most people are unwilling to exchange the security of an existing position for the uncertainty of an unfamiliar one.

The following may be indications that it is time to move on:

- Low motivation toward your current work.
- Physical or emotional distress caused by your job.

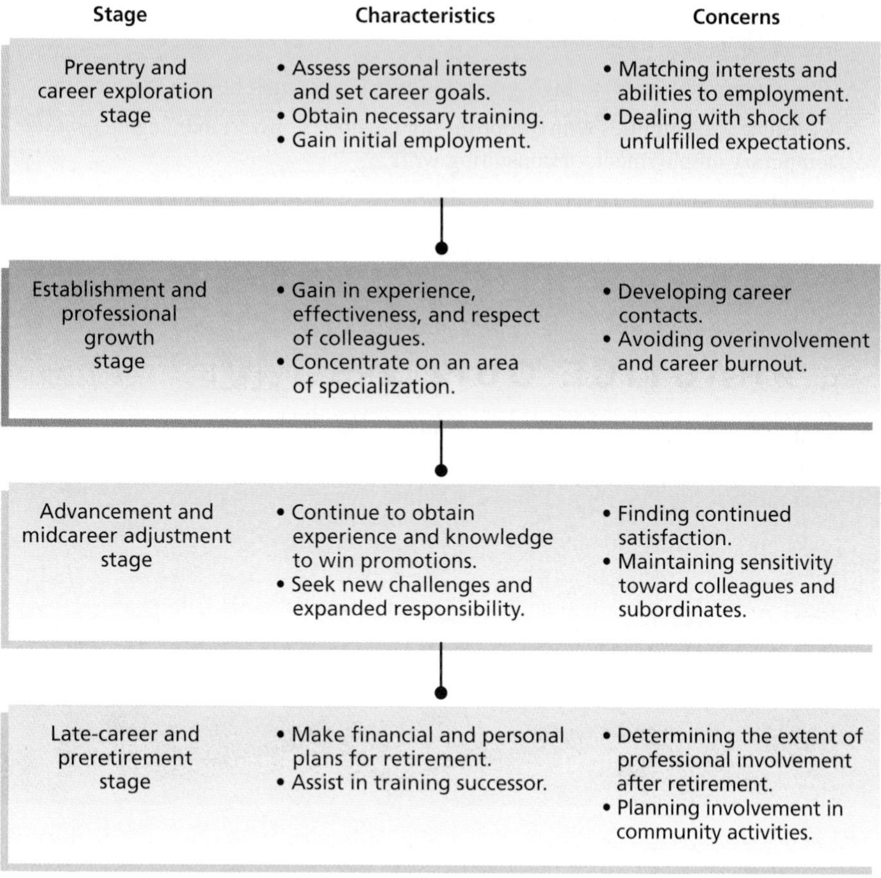

Stage	Characteristics	Concerns
Preentry and career exploration stage	• Assess personal interests and set career goals. • Obtain necessary training. • Gain initial employment.	• Matching interests and abilities to employment. • Dealing with shock of unfulfilled expectations.
Establishment and professional growth stage	• Gain in experience, effectiveness, and respect of colleagues. • Concentrate on an area of specialization.	• Developing career contacts. • Avoiding overinvolvement and career burnout.
Advancement and midcareer adjustment stage	• Continue to obtain experience and knowledge to win promotions. • Seek new challenges and expanded responsibility.	• Finding continued satisfaction. • Maintaining sensitivity toward colleagues and subordinates.
Late-career and preretirement stage	• Make financial and personal plans for retirement. • Assist in training successor.	• Determining the extent of professional involvement after retirement. • Planning involvement in community activities.

Exhibit 2-5

Stages of career development: characteristics and concerns

- Consistently poor performance evaluations.
- A lack of social interactions with co-workers.
- Limited opportunity for salary or position advancement.
- A poor relationship with your superior.

A decision to change careers may require minor alterations in your life (such as going from retail sales to industrial sales), or it may mean extensive retraining and starting at an entry level in a new field. As with every other financial decision, no exact formula exists for deciding whether you should make a career change. However, follow these guidelines. First, carefully assess the financial and personal costs and benefits of changing careers in relation to your needs and goals and those of your household. Giving up benefits such as health insurance may be costly to a family, but the expanded career opportunities in a new field may be worth the trade-off. Then determine whether a career change will serve your needs and goals and those of other household members.

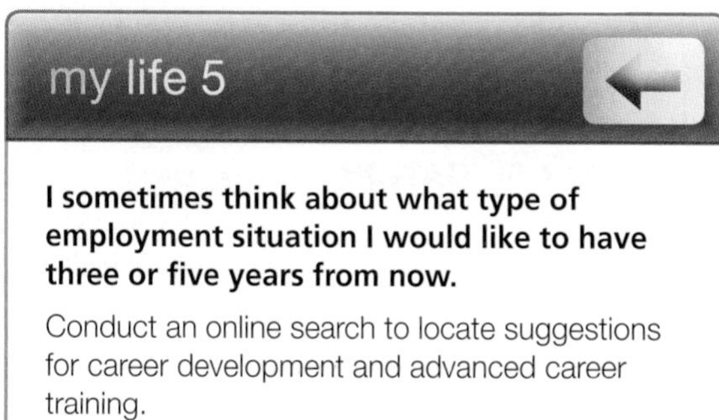

my life 5

I sometimes think about what type of employment situation I would like to have three or five years from now.

Conduct an online search to locate suggestions for career development and advanced career training.

In most industries, long-term job security is a thing of the past. Company mergers, downsizing, technology, and economic conditions may result in forced career changes. Layoffs cause emotional and financial stress for individuals and families. To cope with job termination while seeking new employment, counselors recommend that you

- Maintain appropriate eating, sleep, and exercise habits.
- Get involved in family and community activities; new career contacts are possible anywhere.

- Improve your career skills through personal study, online classes, or volunteer work.
- Target your job search to high-growth industries or small businesses.
- Consider opportunities with nonprofit organizations, government agencies, temporary employment, or consulting work.
- Target your skills and experience to the needs of an organization.

Career development and advancement

PRACTICE QUIZ 2-5

1 What types of activities would you recommend for people who desire career advancement and professional growth?
2 What factors should a person consider before changing jobs or career fields?

my life stages for career planning

YOUR PERSONAL FINANCE DASHBOARD

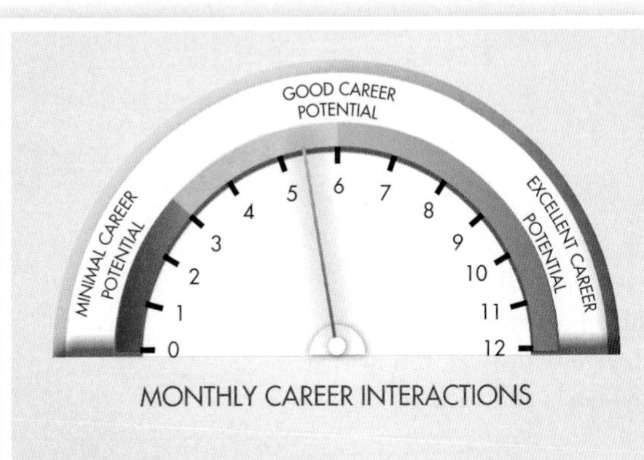

Success for obtaining employment and career advancement is enhanced by interaction with others. Networking (in-person and online) has many benefits. Face-to-face meetings, phone conversations, informational interviews, and e-mail exchanges allow you to obtain advice about industry trends, company activities, and career opportunities.

Your personal finance dashboard to monitor career interactions can increase your career potential. An ability to connect and engage people in varied professional and social settings improves your interpersonal skills while also gaining employment insights.

YOUR SITUATION Have you attended business and community events to meet potential career contacts? Do you research and prepare questions to engage your contacts? Do you follow up with career contacts to learn about their current activities? Other career planning actions you might consider during various stages of your life include . . .

(continued)

my life stages for career planning *(concluded)*

...in college

- Obtain career competencies in class, work, and volunteer situations
- Explore various career fields
- Make contacts with people in various career fields
- Create résumé and career portfolio

...in my 20s

- Revise résumé and career portfolio
- Apply for employment positions
- Expand and update career network contacts
- Consider advanced degree study programs

...in my 30s and 40s

- Reassess career situation and employee benefits based on life situation
- Obtain additional training and career advancement skills
- Update résumé

...in my 50s and beyond

- Serve as a mentor for younger workers
- Evaluate needed changes in employee benefits
- Increase contributions to retirement plans, as appropriate

SUMMARY OF LEARNING OBJECTIVES

LO2-1

Describe activities associated with career planning and advancement.

An understanding of your personal interests and abilities is the basis of a satisfying work life. Career planning and advancement involve the following stages and activities: (1) assess and research personal goals, abilities, and career fields; (2) evaluate the employment market and identify specific employment opportunities; (3) develop a résumé and cover letter for use in applying for available positions; (4) interview for available positions; (5) evaluate financial and other elements of the positions you are offered; and (6) plan and implement a program for career development.

LO2-2

Evaluate factors that influence employment opportunities.

Take actions to keep informed of various factors that influence employment opportunities in our society. Consider the selection of a career in relation to personal abilities, interests, experience, training, and goals; social influences affecting employment, such as demographic trends; changing economic conditions; and industrial and technological trends.

LO2-3

Implement employment search strategies.

Your ability to ask questions of others that provide information about career planning activities and employment opportunities is the basis of successful career planning and development. Also consider the following: Obtain employment or related experiences by working part-time or by participating in campus and community activities. Use career information sources to learn about employment fields and identify job opportunities. Prepare a résumé and cover letter that effectively present your qualifications for a specific employment position. Practice interview skills that project enthusiasm and competence.

LO2-4

Assess financial and legal concerns related to obtaining employment.

While salary may be viewed by some as the important factor when accepting an employment position, also evaluate the work environment and compensation package. Assess employee benefits on the basis of their market value, future value, and taxability and your personal needs and goals. Prospective and current employees have legal rights with regard to fair hiring practices and equal opportunity on the job.

LO2-5

Analyze techniques available for career growth and advancement.

When considering your employment situation three to five years from now, identify informal and formal education and training opportunities that are available to further your professional development and facilitate career changes.

KEY TERMS

KEY FORMULAS

Page	Topic	Formula
52	Geographic buying power	Geographic buying $= \frac{\text{City 1}}{\text{City 2}} \quad \frac{\text{Index number} \times \text{Salary}}{\text{Index number}}$
		Example:
		$= \frac{123 \times 50{,}000}{98.8}$
		$= \$62{,}247$
65	Tax-equivalent employee benefits	Tax-equivalent of a nontaxable $= \frac{\text{Value of the benefit}}{(1 - \text{Tax rate})}$
		Example:
		$= \frac{\$1{,}250}{(1 - 0.28)}$
		$= \$1{,}736$

SELF-TEST PROBLEMS

1. Time value of money calculations are used to determine the value of potential retirement benefits. If a person deposits $1,800 a year in a retirement account earning 6 percent for 20 years, what would be the future value of that account?
2. A non-taxable employee benefit has a greater value than the stated amount. What would be the tax equivalent value of a non-taxable employee benefit of $392? Assume a 30 percent tax rate.

Self-Test Solutions

1. Using the future value of a series (annuity) table on page 35, the result would be $66,214.80 ($1,800 × 36.786).
2. To determine the tax equivalent value, divide the amount by one minus the tax rate. In this situation, $392 would be divided by 0.70 (1 − 0.3), resulting in $560.

FINANCIAL PLANNING PROBLEMS

1. *Determining the Future Value of Education.* Jenny Franklin estimates that as a result of completing her master's degree, she will earn $7,000 a year more for the next 40 years. LO2-1

   a. What would be the total amount of these additional earnings?

   b. What would be the *future value* of these additional earnings based on an annual interest rate of 6 percent? (Use Table 1–B in the Chapter 1 Appendix.)

2. *Comparing Living Costs.* Brad Edwards is earning $45,000 a year in a city located in the Midwest. He is interviewing for a position in a city with a cost of living 12 percent higher than where he currently lives. What is the minimum salary Brad would need at his new job to maintain the same standard of living? LO2-2

3. *Calculating Future Value of Salary.* During a job interview, Pam Thompson is offered a salary of $28,000. The company gives annual raises of 4 percent. What would be Pam's salary during her fifth year on the job? LO2-3

4. *Computing Future Value.* Calculate the future value of a retirement account in which you deposit $2,000 a year for 30 years with an annual interest rate of 6 percent. (Use the tables in the Chapter 1 appendix.) LO2-4

5. *Comparing Taxes for Employee Benefits.* Which of the following employee benefits has the greater value? Use the formula given in the Financial Planning Calculations box on page 65 to compare these benefits. (Assume a 28 percent tax rate.) LO2-4

   a. A nontaxable pension contribution of $4,300 or the use of a company car with a taxable value of $6,325.

   b. A life insurance policy with a taxable value of $450 or a nontaxable increase in health insurance coverage valued at $340.

6. *Comparing Employment Offers.* Bill Mason is considering two job offers. Job 1 pays a salary of $36,500 with $4,500 of nontaxable employee benefits. Job 2 pays a salary of $34,700 and $6,120 of nontaxable benefits. Which position would have the higher monetary value? Use a 28 percent tax rate. LO2-4

7. *Calculating the After-Tax Value of Employee Benefits.* Helen Meyer receives a travel allowance of $180 each week from her company for time away from home. If this allowance is taxable and she has a 30 percent income tax rate, what amount will she have to pay in taxes for this employee benefit? LO2-4

8. *Future Value of Advanced Training.* Ken Braden estimates that taking some classes would result in earning $3,500 more a year for the next 30 years. Based on an annual interest rate of 4 percent, calculate the future value of these classes. LO2-5

9. *Comparing the Value of a Career Change.* Marla Opper currently earns $50,000 a year and is offered a job in another city for $56,000. The city she would move to has 8 percent higher living expenses than her current city. What quantitative analysis should Marla consider before taking the new position? LO2-5

FINANCIAL PLANNING ACTIVITIES

1. *Researching Career Planning Activities.* Talk to several people about influences on their current employment situation. How did various personal, economic, and social factors affect their career choices and professional development? LO2-1

2. *Conducting an Informational Interview.* Arrange an informational interview at a local company or with a business contact you have made. Prepare questions related to needed skills in this employment field, current trends for the industry, and future prospects for this career area. LO2-2

3. *Searching the Web for Benefit Information.* Using a Web search or the library, obtain information about various employee benefits such as health insurance, retirement plans, child care, life insurance, and tuition reimbursement. LO2-3

4. *Analyzing Employee Benefits.* Talk with people employed in various types of organizations. Prepare a list of the most common types of employee benefits received by workers. Using Sheet 12 in the *Personal Financial Planner,* obtain information about various employee benefits from current or prospective employers. LO2-4

5. *Obtaining Career Advancement Information.* Talk with people employed in various types of careers (large company, international business, individual entrepreneur, nonprofit, government) about the training and professional development activities they have found most valuable. Create a list of competencies, skills, and technical abilities that you would like to develop over the next few years. What actions will you take to obtain those proficiencies? LO2-5

6. *Preparing for an Interview.* Based on library and Internet research and experiences of others, obtain information about effective interviewing techniques. Prepare a video that presents appropriate and inappropriate actions one might take when preparing for and participating in an interview. (Chapter 2 appendix.)

FINANCIAL PLANNING CASE

Which Job? Are You Sure?

"Wow, you mean you have three job offers? How did that happen?"

"I'm not quite sure, Joan," responded Alexia. "I guess I just carefully prepared for my job search."

"Ahhh . . . could you be a bit more specific for those of us who have no job offers?" asked Joan.

"After researching various organizations, I tried to match my abilities and experiences to their needs," Alexia continued. "Then, in addition to my résumé, I sent a portfolio with samples of my research work and creative projects."

"OK, Alex, which of the three jobs are you going to take?" asked Joan.

"Again, I'm not quite sure. I've created a comparison of the three to help me decide," Alexia replied.

"Let me see that!" exclaimed Joan. "Wow, you take this career search stuff seriously!"

Job Offer Comparison	Position A	Position B	Position C
Position description, organization	Advertising account assistant for international promotions with global company with offices in 17 countries.	Marketing assistant for a medium-sized equipment company; sales offices in eight southeastern states.	Public relations director in local office of national nonprofit organization assisting low-income families with food and housing.
Salary situation	$46,000; performance reviews and salary increases every six months for first two years, then annually.	$43,500; annual bonus based on percentage of company sales increase.	$38,500, with annual salary increases of 3 to 5 percent.
Vacation time (paid)/year	Two weeks (first year); additional two days for each year of service.	One week after six months on the job; two additional days for each six months of service.	Two weeks (paid); additional unpaid leave time up to four weeks a year.
Health insurance coverage	Employer pays 80 percent of health premiums for doctors on list of insurance company.	Employer pays for HMO coverage with some flexibility of doctors.	Employer pays 60 percent of health premiums; employee selects own doctor.
Retirement fund	Employer contributes 5 percent of salary; additional contributions allowed.	Employer matches employee contributions (up to 10 percent).	Employer pays 2 percent of salary; employee may make tax-deferred contributions.
Educational opportunities	On-site training seminars to update employees on global cultures and advertising trends.	Tuition reimbursement (up to $6,000 a year) for graduate courses.	Two trips a year to seminars on topics related to nonprofit organizations.

Questions

1. What steps might Alexia take when deciding which position to accept?
2. What additional factors would you consider when selecting an employment position?
3. Which employment position would you recommend for her? Why?

PERSONAL FINANCIAL PLANNER IN ACTION

Planning Your Career

Your selection of a career and professional development activities will influence many aspects of your life, including financial resource availability, leisure time, living location, and acquaintances.

Your Short-Term Financial Planning Activities	*Resources*
1. Explore various career areas in relation to your interests, abilities, and goals.	PFP Sheets 6, 7 www.mappingyourfuture.org www.jobbankinfo.org www.hotjobs.yahoo.com
2. Develop a résumé and sample cover letter for use in a job search.	PFP Sheets 8, 9 www.job-hunt.org www.rileyguide.com www.careerjournal.com
3. Research prospective employers and develop a strategy for effective interviewing.	PFP Sheets 10, 11 www.jobhuntersbible.com www.careerbuilder.com www.businessweek.com/careers/index.htm
Your Long-Term Financial Planning Activities	*Resources*
1. Analyze employee benefits based on your current and possible future financial needs.	PFP Sheet 12 www.benefitnews.com www.dol.gov/ebsa
2. Develop a plan of action for professional development. Consider starting your own business.	PFP Sheet 13 www.sba.gov www.inc.com www.startupjournal.com

CONTINUING CASE

Career Decision

Life Situation	*Financial Data*
Single	Monthly Income $1,750
Age 21	Living Expenses $1,210
No dependents	Personal property $7,300
College student	Savings $2,000
	Student loan $3,000
	Credit card debt $2,400

Shelby Johnson's current employment position, a grooming specialist for a local pet store, provides her with a lot interesting activities each day. While she is not part of management, she does have the opportunity to use various communication skills, record business transactions, and use current technology tools. Shelby especially enjoys working with the pets and their owners to achieve a pleasing experience.

Her income is based on an hourly wage which can result in financial stress during times of inflation. She has previously used her credit cards to help make ends meet each month. However, the experience she is gaining will be especially valuable when she opens her own pet salon in the future.

Questions

1. Given her current situation, identify some positive and negative aspects of her current career.
2. What suggestions do you think Shelby should consider related to her current and future career activities.
3. Describe how Shelby might use the following Personal Financial Planner sheets for career planning: Résumé Worksheet and Preparing for an Interview.

DAILY SPENDING DIARY

"My daily work expenses could easily be reduced if I'd be more careful with lunch and coffee spending."

Directions

Continue or start using the "Daily Spending Diary" sheets, or create your own format. Record every cent of your spending in the categories provided, or set up your own categories. Knowing your spending actions and achieving financial goals can improve by using this process.

Questions

1. What types of job-related expenses might be commonly included as part of your Daily Spending Diary?
2. What actions might be taken to reduce costs associated with seeking a job or when changing jobs?

The Daily Spending Diary sheets are located in Appendix D at the end of the book and on the student website at www.mhhe.com/kdh.

chapter 2 appendix

Résumés, Cover Letters, and Interviews

Developing a Résumé

Every business must present its product or service to potential customers in an effective manner. In the same way, you must market yourself to prospective employers by developing a résumé, creating a letter to obtain an interview, and interviewing for available positions.

RÉSUMÉ ELEMENTS

A résumé is a summary of your education, training, experience, and other work qualifications. This personal information sheet is usually an essential component in your employment search. The main elements are typically as follows:

1. THE PERSONAL DATA SECTION

Prepare a heading with your name, address, telephone number, and e-mail address. Both school and home addresses and telephone numbers may be appropriate. Do not include your birth date, sex, height, weight, or photograph in a résumé unless they apply to specific job qualifications.

2. THE CAREER OBJECTIVE SECTION

Be sure to clearly focus your objective to each specific employment situation. A vague career objective will be meaningless to a prospective employer, and one that is too specific might prevent you from being considered for another position within the organization. Your career objective may be omitted from the résumé and best communicated in your cover letter. As an alternative, consider a "Career Profile" or a "Career Summary" section with a synopsis of your distinctive skills and experiences.

> **DID YOU KNOW?**
>
> Résumés often include vague words such as *competent, creative, flexible, motivated,* or *team player.* Instead, give specific examples of your experiences and achievements to better communicate these capabilities.

3. THE EDUCATION SECTION

This section should include dates, schools attended, fields of study, and degrees earned. Courses directly related to your career field may be highlighted with information about research activities, team projects, and presentation experiences. If your grade point average is exceptionally high, include it to demonstrate your ability to excel.

4. THE EXPERIENCE SECTION

In this section, list organizations, dates of service, and responsibilities for all previous employment, work-related school activities, and community service. Highlight computer skills, technical abilities, and other specific competencies that are in demand by organizations. Use action verbs to communicate how your experience and talents will benefit the organization (see Exhibit 2-A). Focus this information on results and

Exhibit 2-A

Action verbs to effectively communicate career-related experiences

accomplishments, not characteristics. Consider using the S-T-A-R format to communicate your experiences and achievements:

S	Situation, or the setting	Fund-raising coordinator for campus organization
T	Task, your duties	Prepared a plan to raise funds for social service agency.
A	Actions you took	Administered a team that solicited donations on campus.
R	Result, the outcome	Donations of over $2,000 to a homeless shelter.

On your résumé, this experience might be presented as follows:

- Coordinated fund-raising campaign to raise funds for social service agency, resulting in over $2,000 in donations to a homeless shelter.

The S-T-A-R format may also be used when communicating your experiences during an interview.

5. THE RELATED INFORMATION SECTION

List honors or awards to communicate your ability to produce quality work. List interests and activities that relate to your career. Information on hobbies and other interests, can communicate a well-rounded individual.

REFERENCES

At this time, you should also prepare a list of *references,* people who can verify your skills and competencies. These individuals may include teachers, previous employers, supervisors, or business colleagues. Be sure to obtain permission from the people you plan to use as references. While references are usually not included on a résumé, have this information available when a prospective employer requests it. Your reference list should the person's name, title, organization, and contact information (address, phone, e-mail).

When selecting references, choose people who will give a balanced view of your strengths and areas that need improvement. Be sure your references offer a consistent story that confirms your version of your work history. Finally, your references should be people with credibility and integrity.

TYPES OF RÉSUMÉS

Three main types of résumés are commonly used:

1. The *chronological résumé* presents your education, work experience, and other information in a reverse time sequence (the most recent item first). Many people find it to be the best vehicle for presenting their career qualifications. Exhibit 2-B provides an example of a chronological résumé along with suggestions on how to create a more effective presentation.

DID YOU KNOW?

To more effectively communicate qualifications, job candidates are supplementing their résumés with *infographics*. This visual representation of information and data can highlight skills and experiences. Infographics may especially be appropriate when applying for visual or creative positions, or when you want to quickly convey extensive information. Remember this device does not replace a traditional résumé. However, this visual can possibly put you ahead of other applicants in the initial screening process.

Exhibit 2-B Résumé makeover

CHAD BOSTWICK
bostwc@unsoark.edu
Phone: (407) 555-1239

SCHOOL ADDRESS
234B Weber Drive (Apt. 6)
Jasper, MO 54321

HOME ADDRESS
765 Cannon Lane
Benton, KS 67783

CAREER SUMMARY

Customer service specialist in health care industry. Effective training, technology capabilities. Qualified in team building and innovation development. Planned and implemented strategies to increase customer satisfaction by over 20 percent.

BEFORE: CAREER OBJECTIVE
An entry-level position in medical or health care administration.

EDUCATION

Bachelor of Science in Business Administration and Health Care Marketing, University of South Arkansas, June 2015.
Associate of Arts, Medical Technician Assistant, Arrow Valley Community College, Arlington, Kansas, June 2013.

...also consider including relevant class experiences, such as:
- coordinated team research project to identify health care opportunities in Asian markets.

ORGANIZATIONAL EXPERIENCE

Patient account clerk, University Hospital, Jasper,Missouri, November 2014 – present
- Researched accounts to reduce uncollectible amounts by 12 percent
- Created collection method to improve accounts receivable turnover
- Trained newly hired billing clerks in database applications

BEFORE:
Researched overdue accounts, created collection method for faster accounts receivable turnover, assisted in training billing clerks.

Sales data clerk, Jones Medical Supply Company, Benton, Kansas, January–August 2013
- Maintained inventory records, processed customer records
- Supervised quality control of entry-level data clerks

CAMPUS ACTIVITIES

Newsletter editor, University of South Arkansas chapter of Financial Management Association, January–June 2015
- Managed editorial staff to research, design, and publish online newsletter
- Researched and prepared news stories on financial industry trends

BEFORE:
Newsletter editor, University of South Arkansas chapter of Financial Management Association, January–June 2015.

Tutor for business statistics and computer lab, 2013–2015
- Coordinated review sessions for exams and homework assignments
- Developed problems and case studies to supplement course materials

HONORS

College of Business Community Service Award, University of South Arkansas, June 2015
Arrow Valley Health Care Society Scholarship, June 2013

2. The *functional résumé* is suggested for people with diverse skills and time gaps in their experience. This format emphasizes abilities and skills in categories such as communication, supervision, project planning, human relations, and research. Each section provides information about experiences and qualifications. This type of résumé is appropriate when changing careers or if your recent experiences are not directly related to the position for which you are applying.
3. A *combination résumé* brings together the chronological and functional types. With this blended format, you first highlight skills and experience relevant to the position. This is followed by your employment history section, which reports specific experiences that match the requirements for the job.

Thousands of résumés are submitted each day. To stand out, applicants have tried various creative approaches. Employers report receiving résumés in the form of comic strips, "wanted" posters, advertisements, and menus, and résumés attached to balloons, pizzas, and plants. Some of these were effective; however, most employers view them as frivolous. A creative approach may be appropriate for jobs in advertising, journalism, photography, and public relations.

In recent years, additional types of résumés, and alternatives to résumés, have surfaced; these include:

- A *targeted résumé* is designed for a specific job and highlights the capabilities and experiences most appropriate to the available position. The format is usually similar to the chronological or functional along with a very specific career objective.
- A *targeted application letter,* describing specific experiences and accomplishments, can be used in some situations. After researching a position and the organization, communicate how your specific skills will benefit the organization. Within your letter (or e-mail), present a bulleted list with short descriptions of your specific experiences that relate to the available position.
- A *career portfolio* can provide tangible evidence of your experience and competencies. Using a print or digital format, you might include a résumé, cover letter, answers to sample interview questions, and letters of recommendation. In addition, research reports, presentations, creative works, and published articles for class projects or campus activities can effectively communicate your abilities.
- A video résumé should be prepared in an expert manner. Be sure to dress professionally. Don't read; talk as if you were in an in-person interview setting. Be concise, make eye contact, and show enthusiasm.

Some career planning experts suggest that résumés are becoming online "living entities." Your *social résumé* will involve the use of LinkedIn, Twitter, and other social media networks to communicate your career competencies. Expect to interact with hiring managers through social networks before applying for a position using one or more of these strategies:

- A LinkedIn profile highlights career achievements and competencies. Your ability to provide a vibrant profile will enhance your employment potential.
- Twitter creates an opportunity to communicate your unique skills and personal brand while linking prospective employers to your website or other professional networking sites.
- QR (quick response) codes may be appropriate in some settings, especially a technology-related position. Be sure to also include your website.
- Pinterest allows online posting of your résumé, photos, videos, and other visuals to communicate career competencies, expertise, and achievements.
- Consider showing what others have to say about you. Your recommendations on LinkedIn can provide a foundation for further discussion in the application process.

RÉSUMÉ PREPARATION

No exact formula exists; however, a résumé must be presented in a professional manner. The use of bulleted items, bold type, and short sentences improves readability. Be sure to read your résumé on a phone or tablet since many hiring managers review *résumés* on a mobile device.

Limit your résumé to one page. Send a two-page résumé only if you have enough material to fill three pages; then use the most relevant information to prepare an impressive two-page presentation.

Use a format that highlights how your background will contribute to an organization's needs. Remember, résumés are usually scanned for key words related to education and technical expertise. The words and phrases used should be based the job description and industry. Some commonly used words to impress a prospective employer include "foreign language skills," "software certification," "research experience," "problem-solving," "leadership," "team projects," and "overseas experience." Avoid overused and vague words such as "team player," "energetic," "results focused," "confident," "creative," and "professional." Also, instead of just listing your ability to use various software packages (such as Excel or PowerPoint), describe how these tools were used to research information or to present findings for a specific project.

Résumé worksheet

When preparing an online résumé, consider the following:

- Keep the format simple; avoid bold type, underlines, italics, and tabs. If you do use various formatting styles, save your résumé as a PDF.
- Avoid attached files that may be difficult to open.
- Use keywords (especially nouns) for the specific employment position and industry.
- When filling out fields for name, address, phone number, e-mail, and other information, paste only plain text to avoid formatting problems.

Résumés posted online may be viewed by your current employer, whom you may not want to know about your job search. Also, some suggest putting a date on your résumé so your current boss will not think your résumé from two years ago is for a current job search.

For an improved résumé, seek guidance in preparing and evaluating your résumé. Counselors, the campus career services office, and friends may find errors and suggest improvements.

RÉSUMÉ SUBMISSION

Traditionally, résumés have been mailed or hand delivered. When presenting a résumé in person, you have an opportunity to observe the organizational environment and make a positive impression about your career potential. Today, however, most résumés are submitted online.

Most résumé posting sites are free. Never pay a large fee; scam artists have set up phony websites with an online payment system to defraud people. Be cautious of sites not based in the country in which you desire to work. Only post to sites with jobs in the geographic region of interest to you, and for which you qualify.

Résumés sent by e-mail should be addressed to a specific person with a subject line referencing the specific job. Your e-mail should include a cover letter to introduce yourself and to encourage the recipient to read your résumé. Properly format your résumé and include it in the body of the e-mail.

DID YOU KNOW?

Identity theft can occur using an online résumé. Do not put your Social Security number on your résumé. Thieves will often contact you and pretend to be a prospective employer in an effort to obtain other personal information.

Follow up with a call or e-mail to reinforce your qualifications and interest. Ask about how and when to follow up on your status in the job search process.

EXAMPLE: Your Career Brand

Your professional image, or "brand," should:

- Communicate unique skills, experiences, and competencies.
- Provide a vision of your potential contribution to an employer.
- Have a consistent message online, in print, and elsewhere.
- Involve ongoing actions that communicate your image, such as "collaborator" or "international expert."

Creating a Cover Letter

Your résumé must be targeted to a specific organization and job. A *cover letter* is designed to express your interest in a job and help you obtain an interview. This letter accompanies your résumé and usually consists of an introductory paragraph, one or two development paragraphs, and a concluding paragraph.

INTRODUCTION

The introductory paragraph should get the reader's attention. Indicate your reason for writing by referring to the job or type of employment in which you are interested. Communicate what you have to offer the organization based on your experience and qualifications. If applicable, mention the name of the person who referred you to this organization.

DID YOU KNOW?

The *Q letter* (*Q* for qualifications) provides a side-by-side comparison of your experiences and abilities with the job requirements. The two coordinated lists allow you to be quickly rated as a viable candidate for the position.

DEVELOPMENT

The development section should highlight the aspects of your background that specifically qualify you for the job. Refer the employer to your résumé for more details. At this point, elaborate on experiences and training. Connect your skills and background to specific organizational needs.

CONCLUSION

Planning a cover letter

The concluding paragraph should request action from the employer. Ask for the opportunity to discuss your qualifications and potential with the employer in more detail; in other words, get an interview! Include information to make contacting you convenient, such as telephone numbers, e-mail address, and the times when you are available. Close your letter by summarizing how you can benefit the organization.

Prepare a personalized cover letter (see Exhibit 2-C) for each position. Be sure to address (or e-mail) the letter to the appropriate person in the organization. In the subject line of an e-mail, state the job title for which you are applying.

A résumé and cover letter are your ticket to the interview. You may possess outstanding qualifications and career potential, but you need an interview to communicate this information. The time, effort, and care you take to present yourself will help you achieve your career goal.

Exhibit 2-C

Sample Cover Letter

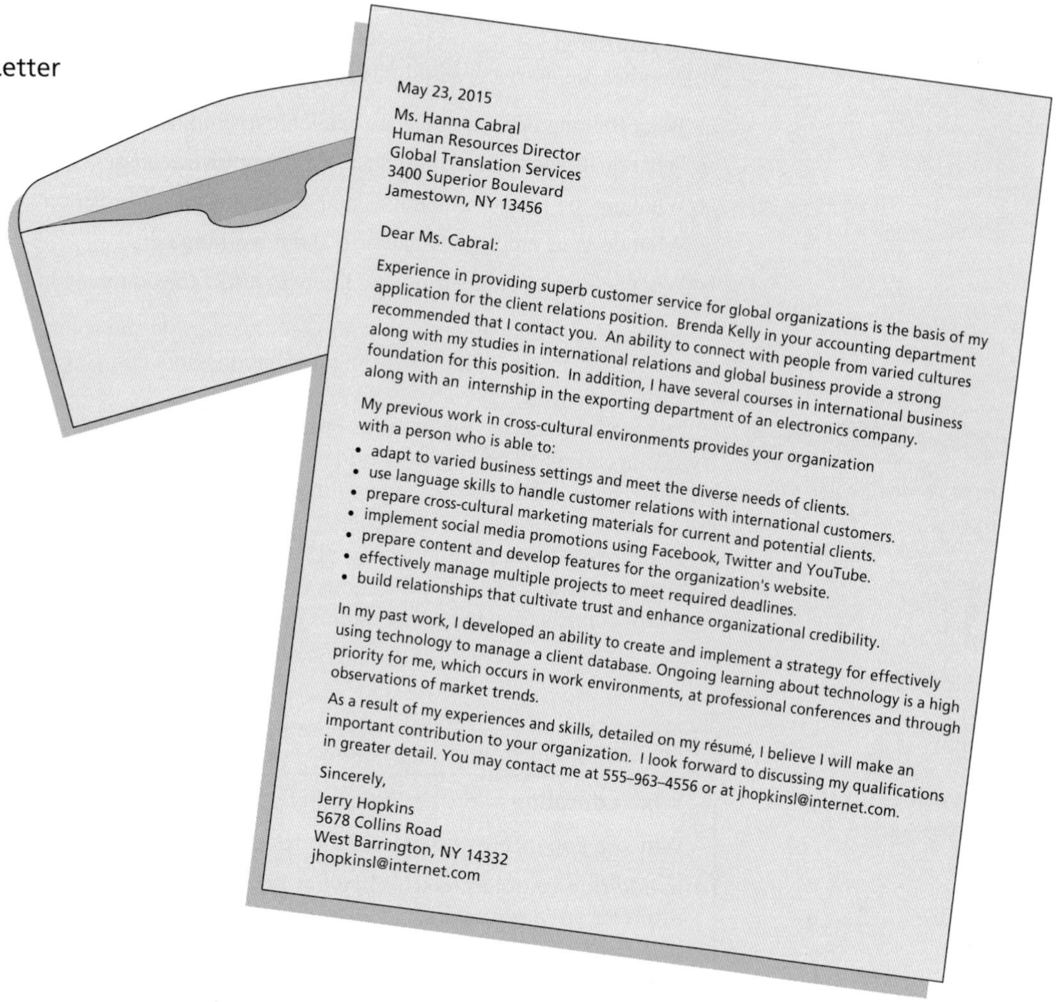

May 23, 2015

Ms. Hanna Cabral
Human Resources Director
Global Translation Services
3400 Superior Boulevard
Jamestown, NY 13456

Dear Ms. Cabral:

Experience in providing superb customer service for global organizations is the basis of my application for the client relations position. Brenda Kelly in your accounting department recommended that I contact you. An ability to connect with people from varied cultures along with my studies in international relations and global business provide a strong foundation for this position. In addition, I have several courses in international business along with an internship in the exporting department of an electronics company.

My previous work in cross-cultural environments provides your organization with a person who is able to:

- adapt to varied business settings and meet the diverse needs of clients.
- use language skills to handle customer relations with international customers.
- prepare cross-cultural marketing materials for current and potential clients.
- implement social media promotions using Facebook, Twitter and YouTube.
- prepare content and develop features for the organization's website.
- effectively manage multiple projects to meet required deadlines.
- build relationships that cultivate trust and enhance organizational credibility.

In my past work, I developed an ability to create and implement a strategy for effectively using technology to manage a client database. Ongoing learning about technology is a high priority for me, which occurs in work environments, at professional conferences and through observations of market trends.

As a result of my experiences and skills, detailed on my résumé, I believe I will make an important contribution to your organization. I look forward to discussing my qualifications in greater detail. You may contact me at 555-963-4556 or at jhopkinsl@internet.com.

Sincerely,

Jerry Hopkins
5678 Collins Road
West Barrington, NY 14332
jhopkinsl@internet.com

The Job Interview

"Why should we hire you?" This may be an unexpected question; however, you may need to answer it. The interview phase of job hunting is limited to candidates who possess the specific qualifications the employer wants. Being invited for an interview puts you closer to receiving a job offer.

PREPARING FOR THE INTERVIEW

Prepare for your interview by obtaining additional information about your prospective employer. The best sources of company information include

- Library resources such as annual reports or recent articles.
- Online searches of company and industry information.
- Observations during company visits.
- Observations of company products in stores or other places.
- Informal interviews with current and past employees.
- Conversations with people knowledgeable about the company or industry.

Researching a prospective employer

During your research, try to obtain information about the organization's past and current activities. Facts about its operations, competitors, recent successes, planned expansion, and personnel policies will be helpful when you discuss your potential contributions to the organization.

Another preinterview activity is preparing questions you might ask, such as

- What training opportunities are available to employees who desire advancement?
- What qualities do your most successful employees possess?
- What are the main expectations and challenges of this position?
- What do your employees like best about working here?
- What actions of competitors are likely to affect the company in the near future?

Also, prepare questions about your specific interests and about the organization with which you are interviewing. Request information about company policies and employee benefits.

Preparing for an interview

Successful interviewing requires practice. By using a video camera or working with friends, you can develop the confidence needed for effective interviewing. Work to organize ideas, speak clearly and calmly, and communicate enthusiasm. Prepare specific answers regarding your strengths. Many campus organizations and career placement offices offer opportunities for practice by conducting mock interviews. Prepare concise answers for specific questions (see Exhibit 2-D) explaining how your experience will contribute to the future of the company. Also, practice stories that demonstrate

Exhibit 2-D

Interview questions you should expect

Education and Training Questions
What education and training qualify you for this job?
Why are you interested in working for this organization?
In addition to going to school, what activities have helped you expand your interests and knowledge?
Behaviorial, Competency-Based Questions
In what types of situations have you done your best work?
Describe the supervisors who motivated you most.
Which of your past accomplishments are you most proud of?
Have you ever had to coordinate the activities of several people?
Describe some people whom you have found difficult to work with.
Describe a situation in which your determination helped you achieve a specific goal.
Describe situations in which you demonstrated creativity.
Personal Qualities Questions
What are your major strengths?
What are your major weaknesses? What have you done to overcome your weaknesses?
What do you plan to be doing 3 or 5 years from now?
Which individuals have had the greatest influence on you?
What traits make a person successful?
How well do you communicate your ideas orally and in writing?
How would your teachers and your past employers describe you?

your skills in various settings. If appropriate, plan to bring photos or other evidence of your past efforts.

Career counselors suggest having a "theme" for interview responses to focus on your key qualifications. Throughout the interview, come back to the central idea that communicates your potential contributions to the organization.

As you get ready for the interview, keep in mind that proper dress and grooming are important. Current employees are the best source of information about how to dress. In general, dress more conservatively than employees do. A business suit is usually appropriate for both men and women. Avoid trendy and casual styles, and don't wear too much jewelry. Confirm the time and location of the interview. Be sure you have correct directions to the interview location.

Take copies of your résumé, your reference list, work samples, and paper for taking notes during the interview. Plan to arrive about 10 minutes earlier than your appointed time.

EXAMPLE: Preparing for a Skype Interview

1. Prepare as you would for any other interview.
2. Test your computer connection in advance; avoid WiFi use.
3. Eliminate visual distractions that might be seen by the interviewer.
4. Locate the webcam at eye level to avoid distorted face angles.
5. Go online early to communicate punctuality and readiness.
6. Maintain eye contact with the webcam to project confidence and professionalism.
7. Tape notes and questions on a wall behind the camera to avoid looking down.

THE INTERVIEW PROCESS

A *screening interview* is an initial, usually brief, meeting with applicants that reduces the pool of job candidates. In the screening interview, interviewees are processed on the basis of overall impression and a few general questions. Screening interviews may be conducted on college campuses by corporate recruiters or by telephone. A screening interview by phone will require stronger verbal communication since there is no eye contact or body language. Success qualifies you for additional consideration by the employer.

Organizations are expanding the use of online screening interviews in which applicants provide basic personal and background information. In addition, these "e-interviews" may ask you to respond to questions such as "Would you rather have structure or flexibility in your work?" and "What approach do you use to solve difficult problems?" Computerized interviewing may also be used to test an applicant's ability in job-related situations such as those that a bank teller or retail clerk might encounter.

Once you are judged to be a strong candidate for a job, your next interview can last from one hour to several days. The *selection interview,* which is reserved for the finalists in the job search, may involve a series of activities, including responses to questions, meetings with several people on the staff, and a seminar presentation.

DID YOU KNOW?

In situational interviewing, candidates for a sales position may be asked to interact with a potential customer. Prospective employees for Southwest Airlines participate in a "job audition." This starts the moment they apply, with extensive notes from the initial phone call. During the flight to the interview, gate agents, flight attendants, and other company employees are instructed to pay special attention to the candidate's behaviors. Thus, the candidate is being observed constantly, similar to their job setting. The process also includes giving a talk to a large group. Bored or distracted audience members are disqualified. This selection process has been shown to reduce employee turnover and increase customer satisfaction.

The first part of the selection interview usually occurs in an informal setting. This arrangement is designed to help you relax and to establish rapport. Next, a brief discussion of the available position may take place. The main part of the interview involves questions to assess your abilities, potential, and personality. Interviews may include situations or questions to determine how you react under pressure. Remain calm. Answer clearly in a controlled manner. In the last portion of the interview, you are usually given an opportunity to ask questions.

An interviewer *cannot* ask:

- Where you were born.
- Your age.
- If you have any disabilities.
- About marital status, religion, or responsibility for children, or other personal information protected by law.

However, an interviewer *can* ask:

- If you have the legal right to work in the United States indefinitely.
- You to prove you are over 18, if there is a minimum age requirement for the job.
- If you have the physical ability to perform the job for which you have applied.
- If there are any days or times when you can't work.

Behavioral interviewing is used to better evaluate an applicant's on-the-job potential. In these situations, prospective employees are asked how they might handle various work situations. Behavioral interview questions typically begin with "describe" or "tell me about . . ." to encourage interviewees to better explain their work style.

Most interviewers conclude the selection interview by telling you when you can expect to hear from them. While waiting, consider doing two things. First, send a follow-up letter or e-mail within a day or two expressing your appreciation for the opportunity to interview. If you don't get the job, this thank-you letter can make a positive impression that improves your chances for future consideration. Second, do a self-evaluation of your interview performance. Write down the areas that you could improve. Try to remember the questions you were asked that were different from what you expected.

Finally, the more interviews you have, the better you will present yourself. And the more interviews you have, the better the chance of being offered a job.

EXAMPLE: Asking for the Job

Near the conclusion of an interview, show your enthusiasm and desire for the position by asking for the job:

- "I believe my experiences would contribute to the continued success of your organization. Is there any additional information you need from me?"
- "Based on my abilities in the area of _____, am I the appropriate fit for this position?"
- "This job is of great interest to me. What additional information would convince you that I'm the right person?"
- "Since my background and skills seem very appropriate for the position, what additional steps will be involved in the selection process?"

HOW TO...

Prepare for a Case Interview

"The client believes that declining profits are the result of new competitors. How might the company determine if this is the actual cause?" This question reflects what you might encounter in a *case interview,* which is commonly used by consulting firms and other organizations as part of the interview process and may involve this sequence:

A screening interview designed to determine your overall qualifications for the available position. → *A behavioral interview* allows you to explain how your training, experiences, and achievements prepare you for the position. → *A case interview* assesses problem-solving and analytical abilities for providing conclusion and recommunications.

A case interview gives a prospective employee an opportunity to demonstrate a capacity to think in a structured, creative manner when presented with a real-world problem. These case situations may address topics such as competition, joint ventures, raising capital, and supply chain management or present a candidate with an open-ended question. When involved in a case interview, consider these actions:

1. Listen and read carefully to understand the background and the main problem of the situation.
2. Develop a framework to organize your analysis and to show the relationship among key issues.
3. Consider alternative courses of action to show varied approaches and versatility in thinking.
4. Use quantitative and qualitative evidence to support your analysis and suggested actions.
5. Clearly communicate your analysis process, conclusions, and recommendations.

Take these actions for improved success in a case interview:

- Prepare by using practice cases online and researching the organization's culture.
- Talk with people who have experienced the case interview process.
- Ask questions of the interviewer to clarify key points.
- Stay focused on the key question for the situation and main issues.
- Avoid stock answers; popular frameworks and buzzwords may not be appropriate.
- Emphasize the process, analysis, and actions rather than finding the "right" answer.
- Prepare by researching current business events and organizational trends.
- Practice the process with others who are willing to help.

Extensive resources on case interviews are available at www.caseinterview.com or search online for "preparing for case interviews."

chapter 3

Money Management Strategy: Financial Statements and Budgeting

Learning Objectives

LO3-1 Recognize relationships among financial documents and money management activities.

LO3-2 Develop a personal balance sheet and cash flow statement.

LO3-3 Create and implement a budget.

LO3-4 Relate money management and savings activities to achieve financial goals.

What will this mean for me?

When difficult economic conditions occur, people will often need to draw upon past savings. The average person in the United States saves less than four cents of every dollar earned. This lack of saving results in not having adequate funds for financial emergencies and long-term financial security. Effectively planning your spending and saving decisions provides a foundation for wise money management today and financial prosperity in the future.

my life

SAVING IS THE ONLY PATH FOR FINANCIAL SUCCESS

"Money not going out is like money coming in!" Reducing your spending will result in lower credit card debt, more money for emergencies, and funds for long-term investing.

From a budgeting perspective, "if you only spend money on things you *really need,* you always have money for things you really want." Very often in our society, people use the word *need* when they really mean *want.* As a result, overspending, increased debt, and lower saving and investing occur.

What are your money management habits? You can now start to assess your money management knowledge and skills. For each of the following statements, circle the choice that best describes your current situation.

1. My money management activities are most valuable to help me
   a. avoid credit problems.
   b. achieve financial goals.
   c. enjoy spending for daily needs.
2. My system for organizing personal financial records could be described as
   a. nonexistent . . . I have documents that are missing in action!
   b. basic . . . I can find most stuff when I need to!
   c. very efficient . . . better than the Library of Congress!
3. The details of my cash flow statement are
   a. simple . . . "money coming in" and "money going out."
   b. appropriate for my needs . . . enough information for me.
   c. very informative . . . I know where my money goes.

(continued)

4. My budgeting activities could be described as
   a. "I don't have enough money to worry about where it goes."
   b. "I keep track of my spending on my smartphone."
   c. "I have a written plan for spending and paying my bills on time."
5. The status of my savings goals could be described as
   a. "Good progress is being made."
   b. "If I save $100 more, I'll have $100!"
   c. "What is a savings goal?"

As you study this chapter, you will encounter "My Life" boxes with additional information and resources related to these items.

Successful Money Management

LO3-1

Recognize relationships among financial documents and money management activities.

"Each month, I have too many days and not enough money. If the month were only 20 days long, budgeting would be easy." Most of us have heard a comment like this when it comes to budgeting and money management.

Your daily spending and saving decisions are at the center of financial planning. You must coordinate these decisions with your needs, goals, and personal situation. When people watch a baseball or football game, they usually know the score. In financial planning, knowing the score is also important.

Maintaining financial records and planning your spending are essential to successful personal financial management. The time and effort you devote to these recordkeeping activities will yield benefits. **Money management** refers to the day-to-day financial activities necessary to manage current personal economic resources while working toward long-term financial security.

money management
Day-to-day financial activities necessary to manage current personal economic resources while working toward long-term financial security.

OPPORTUNITY COST AND MONEY MANAGEMENT

Daily decision making is a fact of life, and trade-offs are associated with each choice made. Selecting an alternative means you give up something else. In terms of money management decisions, examples of trade-off situations, or *opportunity costs,* include the following:

- Spending money on current living expenses reduces the amount you can use for saving and investing for long-term financial security.
- Saving and investing for the future reduce the amount you can spend now.
- Buying on credit results in payments later and reduces the amount of future income available for spending.
- Using savings for purchases results in lost interest earnings and an inability to use savings for other purposes.
- Comparison shopping can save you money and improve the quality of your purchases but uses up something of value you cannot replace: your time.

As you plan and implement various money management activities, you need to assess financial and personal costs and benefits associated with financial decisions.

my life 1

I understand the value of money management activities.

Many online sources are available to provide money management information. Locate a blog that you consider reliable for obtaining money management guidance.

Exhibit 3-1 Money management activities

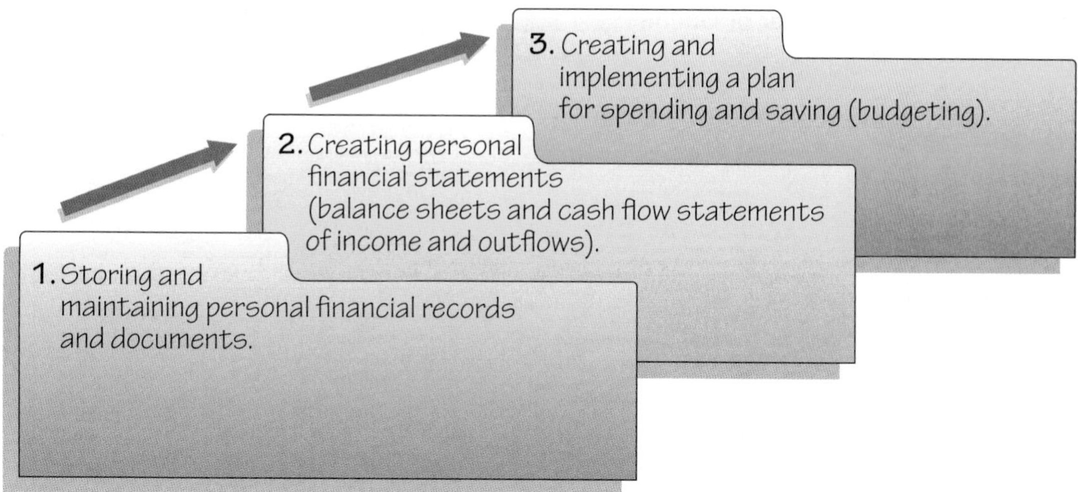

COMPONENTS OF MONEY MANAGEMENT

As Exhibit 3-1 shows, three major money management activities are interrelated. First, personal financial records and documents are the foundation of systematic resource use. These provide written evidence of business transactions, ownership of property, and legal matters. Next, personal financial statements enable you to measure and assess your financial position and progress. Finally, your spending plan, or *budget,* is the basis for effective money management.

A Personal Financial Records System

Invoices, credit card statements, insurance policies, and tax forms are used to document various personal financial activities. An organized system of financial records provides a basis for (1) handling daily business activities, such as bill paying; (2) planning and measuring financial progress; (3) completing required tax reports; (4) making effective investment decisions; and (5) determining available resources for current and future spending.

Most financial records are kept in one of three places: a home file, a safe deposit box, or a computer. A home file should be used to keep records for current needs and documents with limited value. Your home file may be a series of folders, a file cabinet, or even a box. Whatever method you use, your home file should be organized to allow quick access to needed documents and information, which can easily be organized into 10 categories (see Exhibit 3-2). These groups correspond to the major topics covered in this book. You may not need to use all of these records and documents at present. As your financial situation changes, you will add others.

DID YOU KNOW?

In the United States, people keep various documents and valuables in 30 million safe deposit boxes in banks and other financial institutions. While these boxes are usually very safe, each year a few people lose the contents of their safe deposit boxes through theft, fire, or natural disasters. Such losses are usually, but not always, covered by the financial institution's insurance.

Exhibit 3-2 Where to keep your financial records

Home Files, Home Computer or Online

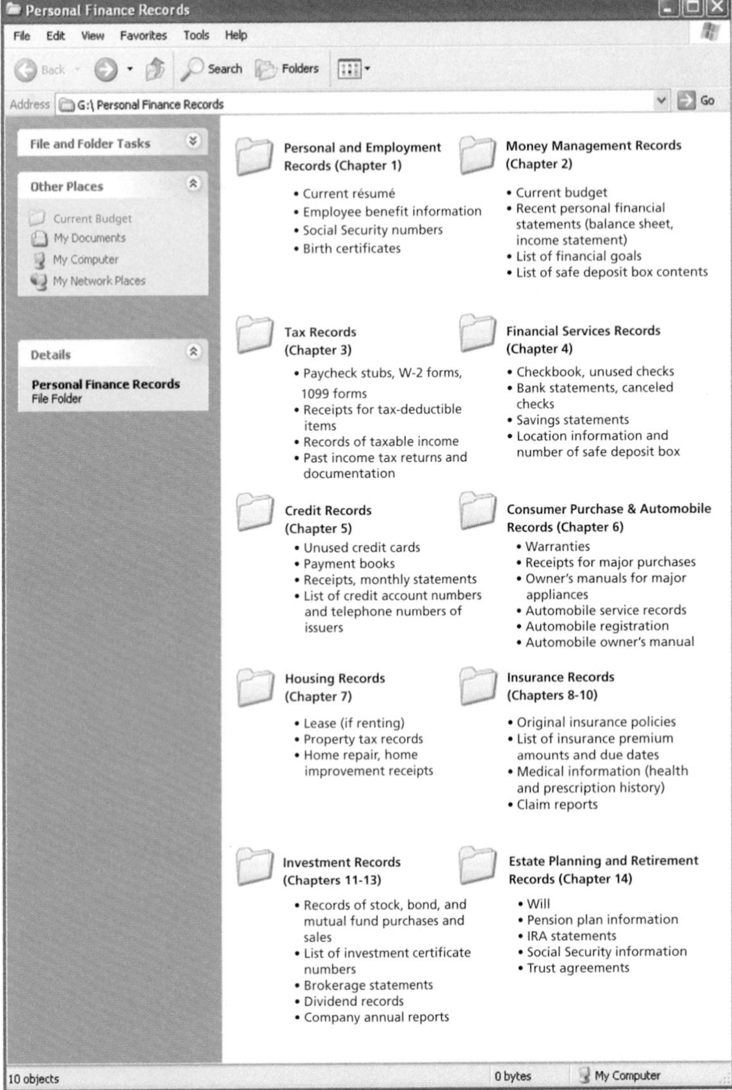

Source: © Microsoft 2013. Screen capture reprinted with permission.

Safe Deposit Box or Fireproof Home Safe

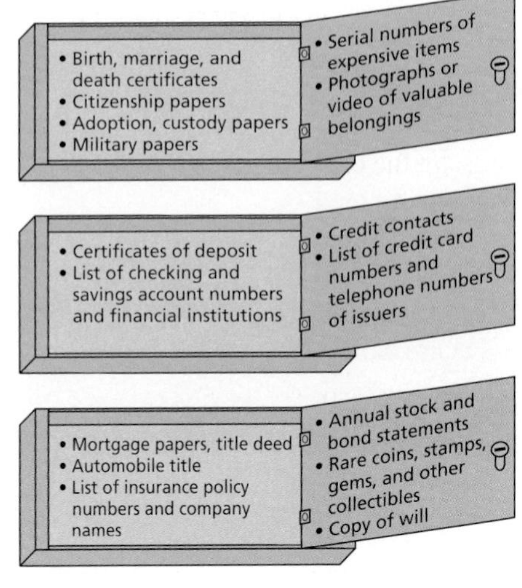

Computer, Tablet, Phone

What Not to Keep . . .

Wastebasket

Shredder

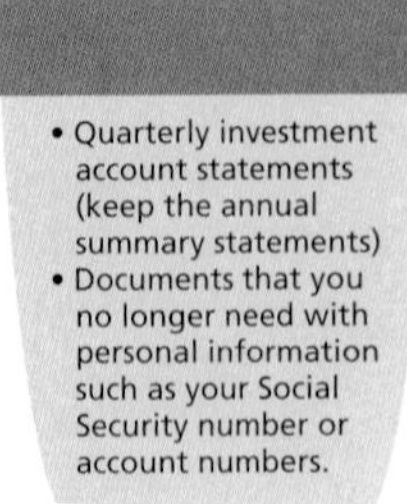

Computer recycle bin

Empty recycle bin on regular basis. Make sure personal data files are completely erased.

Important financial records and valuable articles should be kept in a location that provides better security than a home file. A **safe deposit box** is a private storage area at a financial institution with maximum security for valuables and difficult-to-replace documents. Access to the contents of a safe deposit box requires two keys. One key is issued to you; the other is kept by the financial institution where the safe deposit box is located. Items commonly kept in a safe deposit box include an annual stock investment statement, contracts, a list of insurance policies, and valuables such as rare coins and stamps. These documents may also be kept in a fireproof home safe.

safe deposit box A private storage area at a financial institution with maximum security for valuables.

As more documents are provided electronically, and people are storing financial records "in the cloud," consider the following actions:

- Download copies of all statements and forms to your local storage area using a logical system of files and folders.
- Back up files on external media or use an online backup service.
- Secure data with complex passwords and encryption.
- Scan copies of documents so you no longer need to keep paper versions
- Take appropriate action to completely erase files when discarding items no longer needed.

Hard copies may still be required, such as car titles, birth certificates, property deeds, and life-insurance policies. Original receipts may be needed for returns or warranty service.

How long should you keep personal finance records? Records such as birth certificates, wills, and Social Security data should be kept permanently. Records of property and investments should be kept as long as you own these items. Federal tax laws dictate the length of time you should keep tax-related information. Copies of tax returns and supporting data should be saved for seven years. Normally, an audit will go back only three years; however, under certain circumstances, the Internal Revenue Service may request information from further back. Financial experts recommend keeping documents related to the purchase and sale of real estate indefinitely.

PRACTICE QUIZ 3-1

1 What opportunity costs are associated with money management activities?
2 What are the three major money management activities?
3 What are the benefits of an organized system of financial records and documents?
4 What suggestions would you give for creating a system for organizing and storing financial records and documents?

Financial documents and records

Personal Financial Statements

LO3-2

Develop a personal balance sheet and cash flow statement.

Every journey starts somewhere. You need to know where you are before you can go somewhere else. Personal financial statements tell you the starting point of your financial journey.

Most of the financial documents we have discussed come from financial institutions, business organizations, or the government. Two documents that you create yourself, the personal balance sheet and the cash flow statement, are called *personal financial statements.* These reports provide information about your current financial position and present a summary of your income and spending. The main purposes of personal financial statements are to

- Report your current financial position in relation to the value of the items you own and the amounts you owe.
- Measure your progress toward your financial goals.
- Maintain information about your financial activities.
- Provide data you can use when preparing tax forms or applying for credit.

THE PERSONAL BALANCE SHEET: WHERE ARE YOU NOW?

balance sheet A financial statement that reports what an individual or a family owns and owes; also called a *net worth statement.*

assets Cash and other property with a monetary value.

liquid assets Cash and items of value that can easily be converted to cash.

The current financial position of an individual or a family is a common starting point for financial planning. A **balance sheet**, also called a *net worth statement* or *statement of financial position,* reports what you own and what you owe. You prepare a personal balance sheet to determine your current financial position using the following process:

Items of value (what you own)	−	Amounts owed (what you owe)	=	Net worth (your wealth)

For example, if your possessions are worth $4,500 and you owe $800 to others, your net worth is $3,700.

STEP 1: LIST ITEMS OF VALUE Available cash and money in bank accounts combined with other items of value are the foundation of your current financial position. **Assets** are cash and other tangible property with a monetary value. The balance sheet for Rose and Edgar Gomez (Exhibit 3-3) lists their assets under four categories:

1. **Liquid assets** are cash and items of value that can easily be converted to cash. Money in checking and savings accounts is liquid and is available to the Gomez family for current spending. The cash value of their life insurance may be borrowed if needed. While assets other than liquid assets can also be converted into cash, the process is not quite as easy.
2. *Real estate* includes a home, a condominium, vacation property, or other land that a person or family owns.
3. *Personal possessions* are a major portion of assets for most people. Included in this category are automobiles and other personal belongings. While these items have value, they may be difficult to convert to cash. You may decide to list your possessions on the balance sheet at their original cost. However, these values probably need to be revised over time, since a three-year-old television set, for example, is worth less now than when it was new. Thus, you may wish to list your possessions at their current value (also referred to as *market value*). This method takes into account the fact that such things as a home or rare jewelry may increase in value over time. You can estimate current value by looking at ads for the selling price of comparable automobiles, homes, or other possessions. Or you may use the services of an appraiser.
4. *Investment assets* are funds set aside for long-term financial needs. The Gomez family will use their investments for such things as financing their

DID YOU KNOW?

Poorly organized financial records can result in *hidden* assets such as U.S. savings bonds, old life insurance policies with a cash value, dormant savings accounts, old investments, and unused gift cards.

Exhibit 3-3 Creating a personal balance sheet

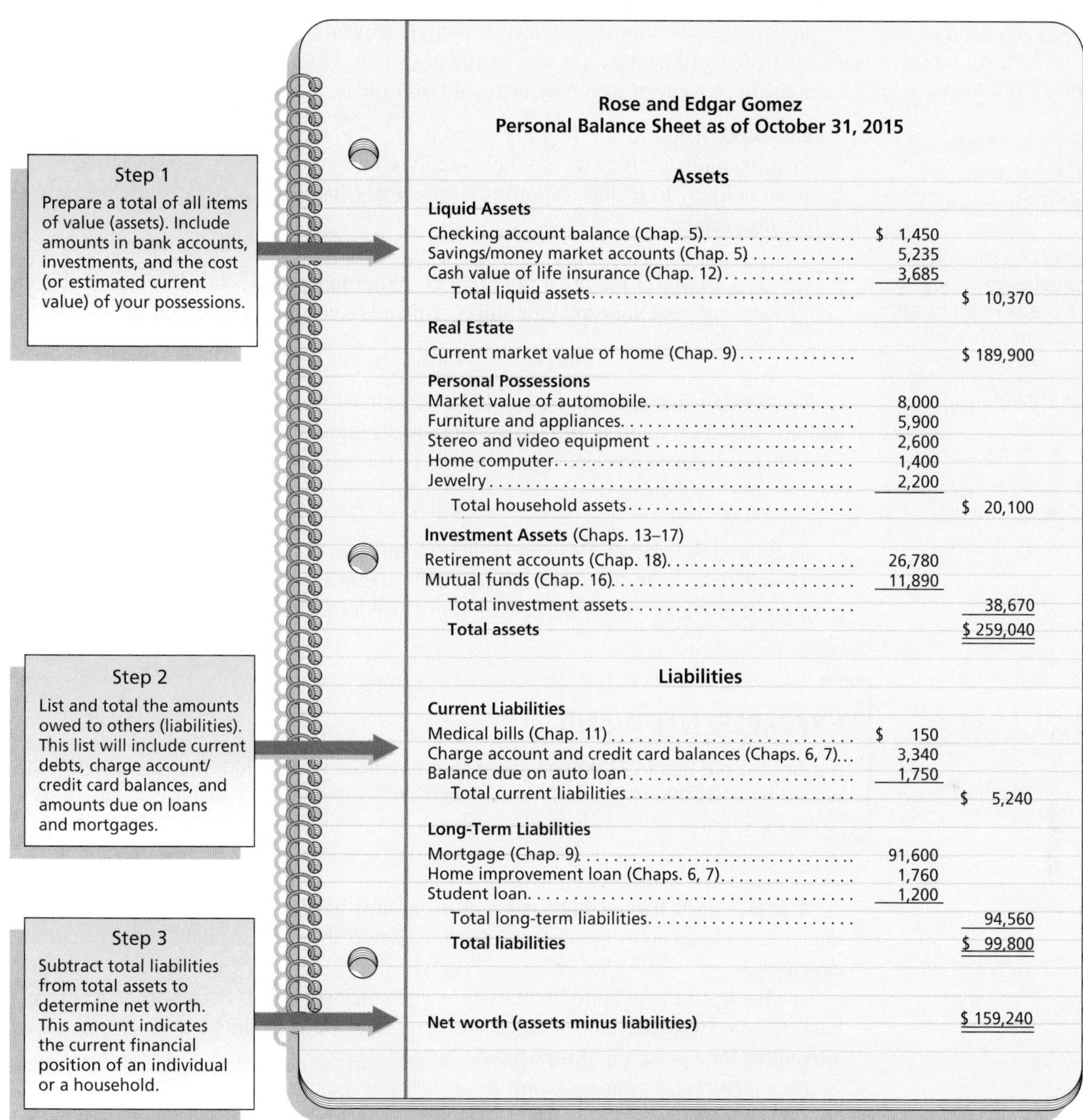

Rose and Edgar Gomez
Personal Balance Sheet as of October 31, 2015

Assets		
Liquid Assets		
Checking account balance (Chap. 5)	$ 1,450	
Savings/money market accounts (Chap. 5)	5,235	
Cash value of life insurance (Chap. 12)	3,685	
Total liquid assets		$ 10,370
Real Estate		
Current market value of home (Chap. 9)		$ 189,900
Personal Possessions		
Market value of automobile	8,000	
Furniture and appliances	5,900	
Stereo and video equipment	2,600	
Home computer	1,400	
Jewelry	2,200	
Total household assets		$ 20,100
Investment Assets (Chaps. 13–17)		
Retirement accounts (Chap. 18)	26,780	
Mutual funds (Chap. 16)	11,890	
Total investment assets		38,670
Total assets		$ 259,040
Liabilities		
Current Liabilities		
Medical bills (Chap. 11)	$ 150	
Charge account and credit card balances (Chaps. 6, 7)	3,340	
Balance due on auto loan	1,750	
Total current liabilities		$ 5,240
Long-Term Liabilities		
Mortgage (Chap. 9)	91,600	
Home improvement loan (Chaps. 6, 7)	1,760	
Student loan	1,200	
Total long-term liabilities		94,560
Total liabilities		$ 99,800
Net worth (assets minus liabilities)		$ 159,240

Note: Various asset and liability items are discussed in the chapters listed next to them.

children's education, purchasing a vacation home, and planning for retirement. Since investment assets usually fluctuate in value, the amounts listed should reflect their value at the time the balance sheet is prepared.

STEP 2: DETERMINE AMOUNTS OWED Looking at the total assets of the Gomez family, you might conclude that they have a strong financial position. However, their debts must also be considered. **Liabilities** are amounts owed to others but do not include items not yet due, such as next month's rent. A liability is a debt you owe now, not something you may owe in the future. Liabilities fall into two categories:

liabilities Amounts owed to others.

current liabilities Debts that must be paid within a short time, usually less than a year.

1. **Current liabilities** are debts you must pay within a short time, usually less than a year. These liabilities include such things as medical bills, tax payments, insurance premiums, cash loans, and charge accounts.

long-term liabilities Debts that are not required to be paid in full until more than a year from now.

net worth The difference between total assets and total liabilities.

insolvency The inability to pay debts when they are due because liabilities far exceed the value of assets.

2. **Long-term liabilities** are debts you do not have to pay in full until more than a year from now. Common long-term liabilities include auto loans, educational loans, and mortgages. A *mortgage* is an amount borrowed to buy a house or other real estate that will be repaid over a period of usually 15 years or more. Similarly, a home improvement loan may be repaid over the next 5 to 10 years.

The debts listed in the liability section of a balance sheet represent the amount owed at the moment; they do not include future interest payments. However, each debt payment is likely to include a portion of interest. Chapters 6 and 7 discuss the cost of borrowing further.

STEP 3: COMPUTE NET WORTH Your **net worth** is the difference between your total assets and your total liabilities. This relationship can be stated as

Assets − Liabilities = Net worth

Net worth is the amount you would have if all assets were sold for the listed values and all debts were paid in full. Also, total assets equal total liabilities plus net worth. The balance sheet of a business is commonly expressed as

Assets = Liabilities + Net worth

As Exhibit 3-3 shows, Rose and Edgar Gomez have a net worth of $159,240. Since very few people, if any, liquidate all assets, the amount of net worth has a more practical purpose: It provides a measurement of your current financial position.

EXAMPLE: Net Worth

If a household has $193,000 of assets and liabilities of $88,000, the net worth would be $105,000 ($193,000 minus $88,000).

A person may have a high net worth but still have financial difficulties. Having many assets with low liquidity means not having the cash available to pay current expenses.

Insolvency is the inability to pay debts when they are due; it occurs when a person's liabilities far exceed available assets. Bankruptcy, discussed in Chapter 7, may be an alternative for a person in this position.

You can increase your net worth in various ways, including

- Increasing your savings.
- Reducing spending.
- Increasing the value of investments and other possessions.
- Reducing the amounts you owe.

Remember, your net worth is *not* money available for use but an indication of your financial position on a given date.

EVALUATING YOUR FINANCIAL POSITION

A personal balance sheet helps you measure progress toward financial goals. Your financial situation improves if your net worth increases each time you prepare a balance sheet. It will improve more rapidly if you are able to set aside money each month for savings and investments. As with net worth, the relationship among various balance sheet items can give an indication of your financial position.

THE CASH FLOW STATEMENT: WHERE DID YOUR MONEY GO?

Each day, financial events can affect your net worth. When you receive a paycheck or pay living expenses, your total assets and liabilities change. **Cash flow** is the actual inflow and outflow of cash during a given time period. Income from employment will probably represent your most important *cash inflow;* however, other income, such as interest earned on a savings account, should also be considered. In contrast, payments for items such as rent, food, and loans are *cash outflows.*

A **cash flow statement**, also called a *personal income and expenditure statement* (Exhibit 3-4 on page 96), is a summary of cash receipts and payments for a given period, such as a month or a year. This report provides data on your income and spending patterns, which will be helpful when preparing a budget. A checking account can provide information for your cash flow statement. Deposits to the account are your *inflows;* checks written, online payments, and debit card purchases are your *outflows.* Of course, in using this system, when you make cash payments or purchases, you must also note these amounts for your cash flow statement.

The process for preparing a cash flow statement is

Total cash received during the time period	−	Cash outflows during the time period	=	Cash surplus or deficit

cash flow The actual inflow and outflow of cash during a given time period.

cash flow statement A financial statement that summarizes cash receipts and payments for a given period.

income Inflows of cash to an individual or a household.

take-home pay Earnings after deductions for taxes and other items; also called *disposable income.*

discretionary income Money left over after paying for housing, food, and other necessities.

STEP 1: RECORD INCOME Creating a cash flow statement starts with identifying the cash received during the time period involved. **Income** is the inflows of cash for an individual or a household. For most people, the main source of income is money received from a job. Other common income sources include

- Wages, salaries, and commissions.
- Self-employment business income.
- Savings and investment income (interest, dividends, rent).
- Gifts, grants, and scholarships.
- Government payments, such as Social Security, public assistance, and unemployment benefits.
- Amounts received from pension and retirement programs.
- Alimony and child support payments.

In Exhibit 3-4, notice that Lin Ye's monthly salary (or *gross income*) of $4,350 is her main source of income. However, she does not have use of the entire amount. **Take-home pay**, also called *net pay,* is a person's earnings after deductions for taxes and other items. Lin's deductions for federal, state, and Social Security taxes are $1,250. Her take-home pay is $3,196. This amount, plus earnings from savings and investments, is the income she has available for use during the current month.

Take-home pay is also called *disposable income,* the amount a person or household has available to spend. **Discretionary income** is money left over after paying for housing, food, and other necessities. Studies report that discretionary income ranges from less than 5 percent for people under age 25 to more than 40 percent for older people.

Daily purchasing decisions influence cash outflows and long-term financial goals.

STEP 2: RECORD CASH OUTFLOWS Cash payments for living expenses and other items make up the second component of a cash flow statement. Lin Ye divides

Exhibit 3-4 Creating a cash flow statement of income and outflows

Step 1
For a set time period (such as a month), record your income from various sources, such as wages, salary, interest, or payments from the government.

Step 2
Develop categories and record cash payments for the time period covered by the cash flow statement.

Step 3
Subtract the total outflows from the total inflows. A positive number (surplus) represents the amount available for saving and investing. A negative number (deficit) represents the amount that must be taken out of savings or borrowed.

Lin Ye
Cash Flow Statement for the Month Ended September 30, 2015

Income (cash inflows)				
Salary (gross income)		$4,350		
Less deductions				
Federal income tax	$810			
State income tax	108			
Social Security	332			
Total deductions		$1,250		$3,100
Interest earned on savings				34
Earnings from investments				62
Total income				$3,196
Cash Outflows				
Fixed Expenses				
Rent		$1,150		
Loan payment		216		
Cable television		52		
Monthly train ticket		196		
Life insurance		32		
Apartment insurance		23		
Total fixed outflows			$1,669	
Variable Expenses				
Food at home		260		
Food away from home		168		
Clothing		150		
Telephone		52		
Electricity		48		
Personal care (dry cleaning, laundry, cosmetics)		66		
Medical expenses		85		
Recreation/entertainment		100		
Gifts		70		
Donations		80		
Total variable outflows			1,079	
Total outflows				$2,748
Cash surplus + (or deficit −)				+$448
Allocation of Surplus				
Emergency fund savings				168
Savings for short-term/intermediate financial goals				80
Savings/investing for long-term financial security				200
Total surplus				$448

her cash outflows into two major categories: fixed expenses and variable expenses. While every individual and household has different cash outflows, these main categories, along with the subgroupings Lin uses, can be adapted to most situations.

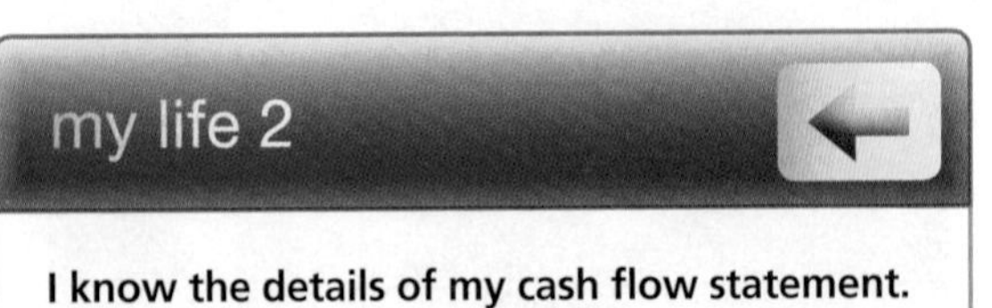

I know the details of my cash flow statement.

In what ways might the "Daily Spending Diary" (at the end of each chapter) be of value when preparing a personal cash flow statement?

1. *Fixed expenses* are payments that do not vary from month to month. Rent or mortgage payments, installment loan payments, cable television service fees, and a monthly train ticket for commuting to work are examples of constant or fixed cash outflows.

For Lin, another type of fixed expense is the amount she sets aside each month for payments due once or twice a year. For example, Lin pays $384 every March for life insurance. Each month, she records a fixed outflow of $32 for deposit in a special savings account so that the money will be available when her insurance payment is due.

Financial Planning Calculations

RATIOS FOR EVALUATING FINANCIAL PROGRESS

Financial ratios provide guidelines for measuring the changes in your financial situation. These relationships can indicate progress toward an improved financial position.

Ratio	Calculation	Example	Interpretation
Debt ratio	Liabilities divided by net worth	\$25,000/\$50,000 = 0.5	Shows relationship between debt and net worth; a low debt ratio is best.
Current ratio	Liquid assets divided by current liabilities	\$4,000/\$2,000 = 2	Indicates \$2 in liquid assets for every \$1 of current liabilities; a high current ratio is desirable to have cash available to pay bills.
Liquidity ratio	Liquid assets divided by monthly expenses	\$10,000/\$4,000 = 2.5	Indicates the number of months in which living expenses can be paid if an emergency arises; a high liquidity ratio is desirable.
Debt-payments ratio	Monthly credit payments divided by take-home pay	\$540/\$3,600 = 0.15	Indicates how much of a person's earnings goes for debt payments (excluding a home mortgage); most financial advisers recommend a debt/payments ratio of less than 20 percent.
Savings ratio	Amount saved each month divided by gross income	\$648/\$5,400 = 0.12	Financial experts recommend monthly savings of 5–10 percent.

Based on the following information, calculate the ratios requested:

Liabilities \$12,000

Liquid assets \$2,200

Monthly credit payments \$150

Monthly savings \$130

Net worth \$36,000

Current liabilities \$550

Take-home pay \$900

Gross income \$1,500

1. Debt ratio ______________________
2. Current ratio ______________________
3. Debt-payments ratio ______________________
4. Savings ratio ______________________

Analysis: How do these ratios compare with the guidelines mentioned in the "Interpretation" column above?

Answers: (1) \$12,000/\$36,000 = 0.33; (2) \$150/\$900 = 0.166; (3) \$2,200/\$550 = 4.0; (4) \$130/\$1,500 = 0.086, 8.66 percent

2. *Variable expenses* are flexible payments that change from month to month. Common examples of variable cash outflows are food, clothing, utilities (such as electricity, telephone, cable, and Internet), recreation, medical expenses, gifts, and donations. The use of a checkbook or some other recordkeeping system is necessary for an accurate total of cash outflows.

DID YOU KNOW?

About one-fourth of Americans have no emergency fund, while about 40 percent have less than three months expenses saved. Only about 25 percent of people have six months or more in their fund.

STEP 3: DETERMINE NET CASH FLOW

The difference between income and outflows can be either a positive (*surplus*) or a negative (*deficit*) cash flow. A deficit exists if more cash goes out than comes in during a given month. This amount must be made up by withdrawals from savings or by borrowing.

When you have a cash surplus, as Lin did (Exhibit 3-4), this amount is available for saving, investing, or paying off debts. Each month, Lin sets aside money for her *emergency fund* in a savings account that she would use for unexpected expenses or to pay living costs if she did not receive her salary. She deposits the rest of the surplus in savings and investment plans that have two purposes. The first is the achievement of short-term and intermediate financial goals, such as a new car, a vacation, or reenrollment in school; the second is long-term financial security—her retirement.

A cash flow statement provides the foundation for preparing and implementing a spending, saving, and investment plan. The cash flow statement reports the *actual* spending of a household. In contrast, a budget, which has a similar format, considers both *projected* income and spending.

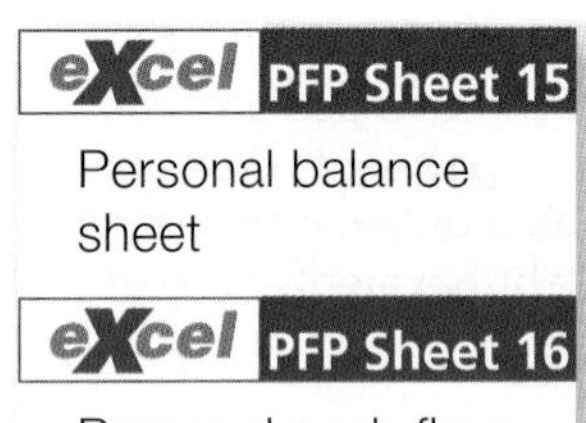

Personal balance sheet

eXcel PFP Sheet 16

Personal cash flow statement

PRACTICE QUIZ 3-2

1 What are the main purposes of personal financial statements?
2 What does a personal balance sheet tell about your financial situation?
3 How can you use a balance sheet for personal financial planning?
4 What information does a cash flow statement present?

Budgeting for Skilled Money Management

LO3-3

Create and implement a budget.

budget A specific plan for spending income.

A **budget**, or *spending plan,* is necessary for successful financial planning. The common financial problems of overusing credit, lacking a regular savings program, and failing to ensure future financial security can be minimized through budgeting. The main purposes of a budget are to help you:

- Live within your income.
- Spend your money wisely.
- Reach your financial goals.
- Prepare for financial emergencies.
- Develop wise financial management habits.

With a budget, you will be in control of your life. Without a budget, others will be in control, such as those to whom you owe money. Use a budget to tell your money where to go, rather than having overspending and debt control your life. Budgeting may be viewed in four major phases, as shown in Exhibit 3-5.

THE BUDGETING PROCESS

The financial statements and documents discussed earlier in this chapter are the starting point for money management activities. A personal balance sheet is an effective scorecard for measuring financial progress. An improved net worth as a result of increased

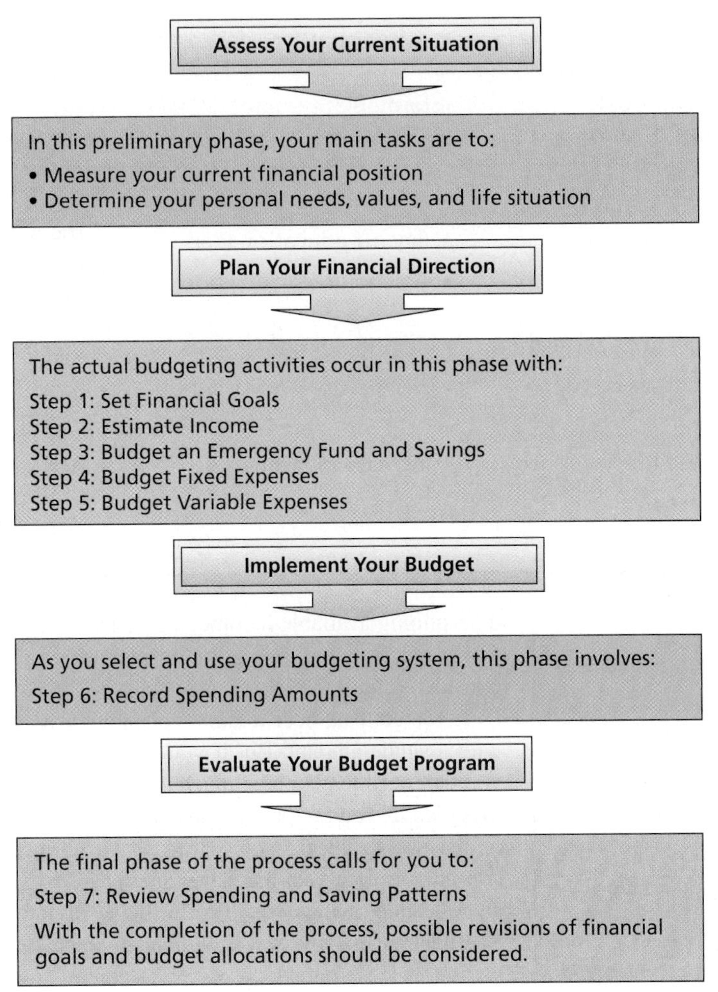
Assess Your Current Situation

In this preliminary phase, your main tasks are to:
• Measure your current financial position
• Determine your personal needs, values, and life situation

Plan Your Financial Direction

The actual budgeting activities occur in this phase with:
Step 1: Set Financial Goals
Step 2: Estimate Income
Step 3: Budget an Emergency Fund and Savings
Step 4: Budget Fixed Expenses
Step 5: Budget Variable Expenses

Implement Your Budget

As you select and use your budgeting system, this phase involves:
Step 6: Record Spending Amounts

Evaluate Your Budget Program

The final phase of the process calls for you to:
Step 7: Review Spending and Saving Patterns
With the completion of the process, possible revisions of financial goals and budget allocations should be considered.

Exhibit 3-5

Creating and implementing a budget

assets or decreased debt are evidence of a better financial position. A regular assessment of your financial standing is one of the foundation elements of budgeting activities, which involves these steps:

STEP 1: SET FINANCIAL GOALS Future plans are an important dimension of your financial direction. Financial goals are plans for future activities that require you to plan your spending, saving, and investing. Exhibit 3-6 gives examples of common financial goals based on life situation and time.

As discussed in Chapter 1, financial goals should take a S-M-A-R-T approach with goals that are: **S**pecific, **M**easurable, **A**ction-oriented, **R**ealistic, and **T**ime-based. Your personal financial statements and budgeting allow you to achieve your financial goals with

1. Your balance sheet: reporting your current financial position—where you are now.
2. Your cash flow statement: telling you what you received and spent over the past month.
3. Your budget: planning spending and saving to achieve financial goals.

STEP 2: ESTIMATE INCOME As Exhibit 3-7 shows, you should next estimate available money for a given time period. A common budgeting period is a month, since many payments, such as rent or mortgage, utilities, and credit cards, are due each month. In

DID YOU KNOW?

The main budgeting mistakes people make are failing to save, never creating a budget, underestimating expenses, and not planning for large costs (vacations, auto repairs).

Exhibit 3-6 Common financial goals

Personal Situation	Short-Term Goals (less than 1 year)	Intermediate Goals (1–5 years)	Long-Term Goals (over 5 years)
Single person	• Complete college • Pay off auto loan	• Take a vacation to Europe • Pay off education loan • Attend graduate school	• Buy a vacation home in the mountains • Provide for retirement income
Married couple (no children)	• Take an annual vacation • Buy a new car	• Remodel home • Build a stock portfolio	• Buy a retirement home • Provide for retirement income
Single parent (young children)	• Increase life insurance • Increase savings	• Increase investments • Buy a new car	• Accumulate a college fund for children • Move to a larger home

Maintaining income and expense records makes the budgeting process easier.

determining available income, include only money that you are sure you'll receive. Bonuses, gifts, or unexpected income should not be considered until the money is actually received.

If you get paid once a month, planning is easy since you will work with a single amount. But if you get paid weekly or twice a month, you will need to plan how much of each paycheck will go for various expenses. If you get paid every two weeks, plan your spending based on the two paychecks you will receive each month. Then, during the two months each year that have three paydays, you can put additional amounts into savings, pay off some debts, or make a special purchase.

Budgeting income may be difficult if your earnings vary by season or your income is irregular, as with sales commissions. In these situations, attempt to estimate your income based on the past year and on your expectations for the current year. Estimating your income on the low side will help you avoid overspending and other financial difficulties.

STEP 3: BUDGET AN EMERGENCY FUND AND SAVINGS To set aside money for unexpected expenses as well as future financial security, the Fraziers (see Exhibit 3-7) have budgeted several amounts for savings and investments. Financial advisers suggest that an *emergency fund* representing three to six months of living expenses be established for use in periods of unexpected financial difficulty. This amount will vary based on a person's life situation and employment stability. A three-month emergency fund is probably adequate for a person with a stable income or secure employment, while a person with erratic or seasonal income may need to set aside an emergency fund sufficient for six months or more of living expenses.

The Fraziers also set aside an amount each month for their automobile insurance payment, which is due every six months. Both this amount and the emergency fund are put into a savings account. The *time value of money,* discussed in Chapter 1, refers to increases in an amount of money as a result of interest earned. Savings methods for achieving financial goals are discussed later in this chapter.

DID YOU KNOW?

According to Lynnette Khalfani (www.themoneycoach.net), LIFE is the major budget buster:

- L is "Listed" expenses (housing, utilities, food, clothing) that are underestimated.
- I involves "Impulse buying," whether in stores or online.
- F are "Forgotten" bills, such as annual insurance payments.
- E are "Emergencies," such as unexpected auto or home repairs.

Exhibit 3-7 The Fraziers develop and implement a monthly budget

Step 1 Set financial goals.

Step 2 Estimate expected income from all sources; this amount is to be allocated among various outflow categories.

Step 3 Budget amount for an emergency fund, periodic expenses, and financial goals.

Step 4 Budget set amounts that you are obligated to pay.

Step 5 Budget estimated amounts to be spent for various household and living expenses.

Step 6 Record actual amounts for inflows and outflows. Compare actual amounts with budgeted amounts to determine variances.

Step 7 Evaluate whether revisions are needed in your spending and savings plan.

Monthly Budget

Financial goals: increase emergency fund; avoid credit card debt.

	Budgeted Amounts (dollars)	Budgeted Amounts (percent)	Actual Amounts	Variance
Projected Inflows (income)				
Salary	2874	100	2874	—
Projected Outflows (disbursements)				
Emergency Fund and Savings:				
Emergency fund savings	115	4	115	—
Savings for auto insurance	29	1	29	—
Savings for vacation	57	2	57	—
Savings for investments	57	2	57	—
Total savings	258	9	258	—
Fixed Expenses				
Mortgage payment	518	18	518	—
Property taxes	115	4	115	—
Auto loan payment	144	5	144	—
Life insurance	29	1	29	—
Total fixed expenses	806	28	806	—
Variable expenses				
Food	402	14	417	-15
Utilities (telephone, heat, electric, water)	172	6	164	+8
Clothing	116	4	93	+23
Transportation (automobile operation, repairs, public transportation)	460	16	471	-11
Personal and health care	172	6	163	+9
Entertainment	172	6	201	-29
Reading, education	86	3	78	+8
Gifts, donations	144	5	150	-6
Personal allowances, miscellaneous expenses	86	3	90	-4
Total variable expenses	1810	63	1827	-17
Total outflow	2874	100	2891	-17

A very common budgeting mistake is to save only the amount left at the end of the month. When you do that, you often have *nothing* left for savings. Since savings are vital to long-term financial security, advisers suggest that an amount be budgeted as a fixed expense.

STEP 4: BUDGET FIXED EXPENSES Definite obligations make up this portion of a budget. As Exhibit 3-7 shows, the Fraziers have fixed expenses for housing, taxes, and loan payments. They make a monthly payment of $29 for life insurance. The budgeted total for the Fraziers' fixed expenses is $806, or 28 percent of estimated available income.

You will notice that a budget has a similar format to the previously discussed cash flow statement. A budget, however, involves *projected* or planned income and expenses. The cash flow statement reports the *actual* income and expenses.

Assigning amounts to spending categories requires careful consideration. The amount you budget for various items will depend on your current needs and plans for the future. The following sources can help you plan your spending:

- Your cash flow statement.
- Consumer expenditure data from the Bureau of Labor Statistics.

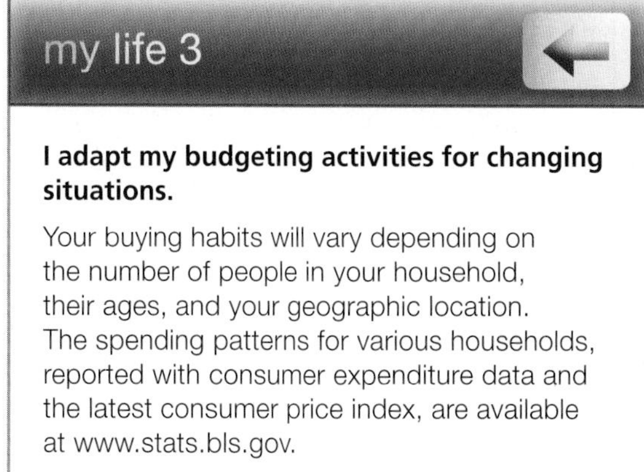
my life 3

I adapt my budgeting activities for changing situations.

Your buying habits will vary depending on the number of people in your household, their ages, and your geographic location. The spending patterns for various households, reported with consumer expenditure data and the latest consumer price index, are available at www.stats.bls.gov.

- Articles in magazines such as *Kiplinger's Personal Finance Magazine* and *Money.*
- Estimates of future income and expenses and anticipated changes in inflation rates.

Exhibit 3-8 provides suggested budget allocations for different life situations. Although this information can be of value when creating budget categories, maintaining a detailed record of your spending for several months is a better source for your personal situation. However, don't become discouraged. Use a simple system, such as a notebook or your checkbook. This "spending diary" will help you know where your money is going. Remember, a budget is an *estimate* for spending and saving intended to help you make better use of your money, not to reduce your enjoyment of life.

STEP 5: BUDGET VARIABLE EXPENSES Planning for variable expenses is not as easy as budgeting for savings or fixed expenses. Variable expenses will fluctuate by household situation, time of year, health, economic conditions, and a variety of other factors. A major portion of the Fraziers' planned spending—over 60 percent of their budgeted income—is for variable living costs.

The Fraziers base their estimates on their needs and desires for the items listed and on expected changes in the cost of living. The *consumer price index (CPI)* is a measure of the general price level of consumer goods and services in the United States. This government

DID YOU KNOW?

For ideas to cut your spending, go to www.clarkhoward.com, http://money.msn.com/saving-money-tips, www.debtproofliving.com, and www.thefrugalshopper.com.

Exhibit 3-8 Typical after-tax budget allocations for different life situations

Budget Category	Student	Working Single (no dependents)	Couple (children under 18)	Single Parent (young children)	Parents (children over 18 in college)	Couple (over 55, no dependent children)
Housing (rent or mortgage payment; utilities; furnishings and appliances)	0–25%	30–35%	25–35%	20–30%	25–30%	25–35%
Transportation	5–10	15–20	15–20	10–18	12–18	10–18
Food (at home and away from home)	15–20	15–25	15–25	13–20	15–20	18–25
Clothing	5–12	5–15	5–10	5–10	4–8	4–8
Personal and health care (including child care)	3–5	3–5	4–10	8–12	4–6	6–12
Entertainment and recreation	5–10	5–10	4–8	4–8	6–10	5–8
Reading and education	10–30	2–4	3–5	3–5	6–12	2–4
Personal insurance and pension payments	0–5	4–8	5–9	5–9	4–7	6–8
Gifts, donations, and contributions	4–6	5–8	3–5	3–5	4–8	3–5
Savings	0–10	4–15	5–10	5–8	2–4	3–5

Sources: Bureau of Labor Statistics (stats.bls.gov); *American Demographics; Money; The Wall Street Journal.*

statistic indicates changes in the buying power of a dollar. As consumer prices increase due to inflation, people must spend more to buy the same amount. Changes in the cost of living will vary depending on where you live and what you buy.

As mentioned in Chapter 1, the *rule of 72* can help you budget for price rises. At a 2 percent inflation rate, prices will double in 36 years (72/2). However, at a 6 percent inflation rate, prices will double in 12 years (72/6).

budget variance The difference between the amount budgeted and the actual amount received or spent.

deficit The amount by which actual spending exceeds planned spending.

surplus The amount by which actual spending is less than planned spending.

STEP 6: RECORD SPENDING AMOUNTS After you have established your spending plan, you will need to keep records of your actual income and expenses similar to those you keep in preparing an income statement. In Exhibit 3-7, notice that the Fraziers estimated specific amounts for income and expenses. These are presented under "Budgeted Amounts."

The family's actual spending was not always the same as planned. A **budget variance** is the difference between the amount budgeted and the actual amount received or spent. The total variance for the Fraziers was a $17 **deficit**, since their actual spending exceeded their planned spending by this amount. The Fraziers would have had a **surplus** if their actual spending had been less than they had planned.

EXAMPLE: Budget Variance

If a family budgets $380 a month for food and spends $363, this would result in a $17 budget *surplus*. However, if the family spent $406 on food during the month, a $26 budget *deficit* would exist.

Variances for income should be viewed as the opposite of variances for expenses. Less income than expected would be a deficit, while more income than expected would be a surplus.

Spending more than planned for an item may be justified by reducing spending for another item or putting less into savings. However, it may be necessary to revise your budget and financial goals.

STEP 7: REVIEW SPENDING AND SAVING PATTERNS Like most decision-making activities, budgeting is a circular, ongoing process. You will need to review and perhaps revise your spending plan on a regular basis.

Review Your Financial Progress The results of your budget may be obvious: having extra cash in checking, falling behind in your bill payments, and so on. However, such obvious results may not always be present. Occasionally, you will have to evaluate (with other household members, if appropriate) and review areas where spending has been more or less than expected.

As Exhibit 3-9 shows, you can prepare an annual summary to compare actual spending with budgeted amounts. This type of summary may also be prepared every three or six months. A spreadsheet computer program can be useful for this purpose. The summary will help you see areas where changes in your budget may be necessary. This review process is vital to both successful short-term money management and long-term financial security.

DID YOU KNOW?

Households can save money each month by cutting insurance costs, adopting wise grocery shopping habits, using less energy, switching to a less expensive cable or phone plan, and avoiding the fees and high payments that come with debt. They can also choose not to receive a tax refund at the end of the year, and instead have less taxes withheld every month. These actions may end up saving households an additional $500 a month or more!

Exhibit 3-9 An annual budget summary

Microsoft Excel

File Edit View Insert Format Tools Data Window Help Acrobat

O1 = Annual Totals

	A	B	C	D	E	F	G	H	I	J	K	L	M	N	O	P
1			Actual Spending (cash outflows)												Annual Totals	
2	**Item**	**Monthly Budget**	**Jan.**	**Feb.**	**Mar**	**Apr**	**May**	**June**	**July**	**Aug.**	**Sept.**	**Oct**	**Nov.**	**Dec.**	**Actual**	**Budgeted***
3	Income	2,730	2,730	2,730	2,730	2,940	2,730	2,730	2,730	2,730	2,850	2,850	2,850	2,850	33,450	32,760
4	Savings	150	150	150	200	150	90	50	30	100	250	250	150	40	1,610	1,800
5	Mortgage/Rent	826	826	826	826	826	826	826	826	826	826	826	826	826	9,912	9,912
6	Housing Costs (insurance, utilities)	190	214	238	187	176	185	'88	146	178	198	177	201	195	2,283	2,280
7	Telephone	50	43	45	67	56	54	52	65	45	43	52	49	47	618	600
8	Food (at home)	280	287	277	245	234	278	267	298	320	301	298	278	324	3,407	3,360
9	Food (away from home)	80	67	78	84	87	123	'09	89	83	67	76	83	143	1,089	960
10	Clothing	100	98	78	123	156	86	76	111	124	87	95	123	111	1,268	1,200
11	Transportation (auto operation, public transportation)	340	302	312	333	345	297	287	390	373	299	301	267	301	3,807	4,080
12	Credit payments	249	249	249	249	249	249	249	249	249	249	249	249	249	2,988	2,988
13	Insurance (life, health, other)	45	___	___	135	___	___	'35	___	___	135	___	___	135	540	540
14	Health care	140	176	145	187	122	111	'56	186	166	134	189	193	147	1,912	1,680
15	Recreation	80	67	98	123	98	67	45	87	98	65	87	87	111	1,033	960
16	Reading, education	40	32	54	44	34	39	54	12	38	54	34	76	45	516	480
17	Gifts, donations	100	102	110	94	87	123	89	95	94	113	87	99	134	1,227	1,200
18	Personal miscellaneous expense	60	89	45	67	54	98	59	54	49	71	65	90	56	797	720
19	**Total**	2,730	2,702	2,705	2,964	2,674	2,626	2,642	2,638	2,743	2,892	2,786	2,771	2,864	33,007	32,760
20	**Surplus (deficit)**		28	25	(234)	266	104	88	92	(13)	(42)	64	79	(14)	443	------

Sheet1 Sheet2 Sheet3

Ready NUM

Source: © Microsoft 2013. Screen capture reprinted with permission.

Revise Your Goals and Budget Allocations What should you cut first when a budget shortage occurs? This question doesn't have easy answers, and the answers will vary for different household situations. The most common overspending areas are entertainment and food, especially away-from-home meals. Purchasing less expensive brand items, buying quality used products, avoiding credit card purchases, and renting rather than buying are common budget adjustment techniques. When having to cut household budgets, reduced spending most often occurs for vacations, dining out, cleaning and lawn services, cable/Internet service, and charitable donations.

At this point in the budgeting process, you may also revise your financial goals. Are you making progress toward achieving your objectives? Have changes in personal or economic conditions affected the desirability of certain goals? Have new goals surfaced that should be given a higher priority than those that have been your major concern? Addressing these issues while creating an effective saving method will help ensure accomplishment of your financial goals.

CHARACTERISTICS OF SUCCESSFUL BUDGETING

Having a spending plan will not eliminate financial worries. A budget will work only if you follow it. Changes in income, expenses, and goals will require changes in your spending plan. Money management experts advise that a successful budget should be

- *Well planned.* A good budget takes time and effort to prepare. Planning a budget should involve everyone affected by it. Children can learn important money management lessons by helping to develop and use the family budget.

- *Realistic.* If you have a moderate income, don't immediately expect to save enough money for an expensive car or a lavish vacation. A budget is designed not to prevent you from enjoying life but to help you achieve what you want most.
- *Flexible.* Unexpected expenses and changes in your cost of living will require a budget that you can easily revise. Also, special situations, such as two-income families or the arrival of a baby, may require an increase in certain types of expenses.
- *Clearly communicated.* Unless you and others involved are aware of the spending plan, it will not work. The budget should be written and available to all household members.

TYPES OF BUDGETING SYSTEMS

Although your checkbook and online payments summary may give you a fairly complete picture of your expenses, these records do not serve the purpose of planning for spending. A *budget* requires that you outline how you will spend available income. The following are commonly used budgeting systems:

1. A *mental budget* exists only in a person's mind. This simple system may be appropriate if you have limited resources and minimal financial responsibilities. An "in your head" budget can be dangerous when you forget the amounts you plan to spend on various items.
2. A *physical budget* involves envelopes, folders, or containers to hold money or slips of paper representing amounts allocated for spending categories. This system allows you to actually see where your money goes. Envelopes would contain the amount of cash or a note listing the amount to be used for food, rent, clothing, auto payment, entertainment, and other expenses.
3. A *written budget* allows you provide a detailed plan for spending. This type of budget can be in a notebook or on accounting paper or a budget record book available in office supply stores. A common written budget format is a spreadsheet that has several monthly columns for comparing budgeted and actual amounts for various expense items.
4. A *computerized budgeting system* may be developed using spreadsheet software. Excel budget templates may be located online. Or, you may use money management software such as *Quicken* (www.quicken.com). In addition to creating a budget, these programs are capable of doing other financial planning tasks.
5. An *online budget* may be used through a website such as mint.com. In addition, banks, credit unions, brokerage firms, and other financial institutions have various budgeting and personal financial management tools on their websites.
6. A *budgeting app* on your cell phone or tablet has various money management features. Costs range from free downloads to a few dollars.

Your decision for a budgeting system will depend on your personal situation and your preference for maintaining information. The most important consideration when choosing a system is to find one that provides accurate and timely information for helping you achieve your financial goals.

1 What are the main purposes of a budget?
2 How does a person's life situation affect goal setting and amounts allocated for various budget categories?
3 What are the main steps in creating a budget?
4 What are commonly recommended qualities of a successful budget?
5 What actions might you take when evaluating your budgeting program?

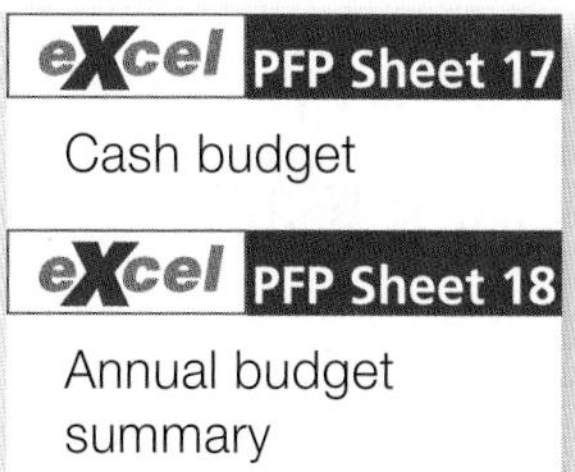

HOW TO...

Conduct a Money Management SWOT Analysis

SWOT (**s**trengths, **w**eaknesses, **o**pportunities, **t**hreats) is a planning tool used by companies and other organizations. This technique can also be used for your money management and budgeting activities. Listed below are examples of possible items for each SWOT category. Now, in the area provided, determine your strengths, weaknesses, opportunities, and threats related to budgeting and money management. Do online research and talk with others to get ideas for your personal SWOT items.

Internal (Personal) Factors	External (Economic, Social) Influences
Strengths	**Opportunities**
• Saving 5–10 percent of income • Informed on personal finance topics • No credit card debt • Flexible job skills *Your strengths:* ____________ ____________	• Phone apps for monitoring finances • Part-time work to supplement income • Availability of no-fee bank account • Low-interest-rate education loan *Potential opportunities:* ____________ ____________
Weaknesses	**Threats**
• High level of credit card debt • No emergency fund • Automobile in need of repairs • Low current cash inflow *Your weaknesses:* ____________ ____________	• Lower market value of retirement fund • Possible reduced hours at part-time job • Reduced home market value • Increased living costs (inflation) *Potential threats:* ____________ ____________

Creating a money management SWOT analysis is only a start. Next you need to select actions to build on your strengths, minimize your weaknesses, take advantage of opportunities, and avoid being a victim of threats. Through research and innovation, weaknesses and threats can become strengths and opportunities.

Money Management and Achieving Financial Goals

LO3-4

Relate money management and savings activities to achieving financial goals.

Your personal financial statements and budget allow you to achieve your financial goals with

1. Your balance sheet: reporting your current financial position—where you are now.
2. Your cash flow statement: telling you what you received and spent over the past month.
3. Your budget: planning spending and saving to achieve financial goals.

People commonly prepare a balance sheet on a periodic basis, such as every three or six months. Between those points in time, your budget and cash flow statement help you plan and measure spending and saving activities. For example, you might prepare a balance sheet on January 1 and July 1. Your budget would serve to plan your spending and saving between these points in time, and your cash flow statement of income and outflows would document your actual spending and saving. This relationship may be illustrated in this way:

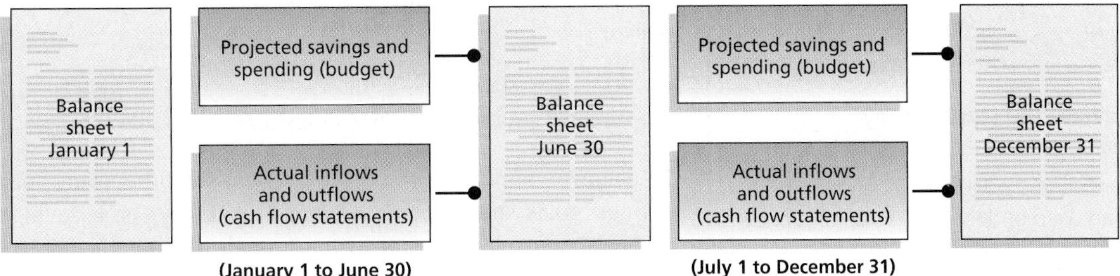

Changes in your net worth result from cash inflows and outflows. In periods when your outflows exceed your inflows, you must draw on savings or borrow (buy on credit). When this happens, lower assets (savings) or higher liabilities (due to the use of credit) result in a lower net worth. When inflows exceed outflows, putting money into savings or paying off debts will result in a higher net worth.

IDENTIFYING SAVING GOALS

Saving current income (as well as investing, which is discussed in Chapters 13–17) is the basis for an improved financial position and long-term financial security. Common reasons for saving include:

- To create an emergency fund for irregular and unexpected expenses.
- To pay for the replacement of expensive items, such as appliances or an automobile, or to have money for a down payment on a house.
- To buy expensive items such as electronics or sports equipment or to pay for a vacation.
- To provide for long-term expenses such as the education of children or retirement.
- To earn income from the interest on savings for use in paying living expenses.

Specific savings activities contribute to achieving long-term financial goals.

SELECTING A SAVING TECHNIQUE

For many years, the United States has ranked lowest among industrial nations in savings rate. Low savings affect personal financial situations. Studies reveal that the majority of Americans do not have an adequate amount set aside for emergencies.

Since most people find saving difficult, financial advisers suggest these methods to make it easier:

1. Write a check each payday to deposit in a separate savings account. Or use an automatic payment or a smartphone app to electronically transfer an amount to savings. This deposit can be a percentage of income, such as 5 or 10 percent, or a specific dollar amount.
2. *Payroll deduction* is available through most places of employment. With this system, an amount is deducted from your salary and deposited in savings.

DID YOU KNOW?

For years, co-workers were amused by a woman who carried a brown bag lunch to her job each day. That woman later retired in financial comfort and lived her later years in beachfront property. A daily coffee and muffin can add up to over $1,300 a year.

3. Saving coins or spending less on certain items can help you save. Each day, put your change in a container. You can also increase your savings by taking a sandwich to work instead of buying lunch or refraining from buying snacks or magazines.

How you save is far less important than making regular periodic savings deposits that will help you achieve financial goals. Small amounts of savings can grow faster than most people realize.

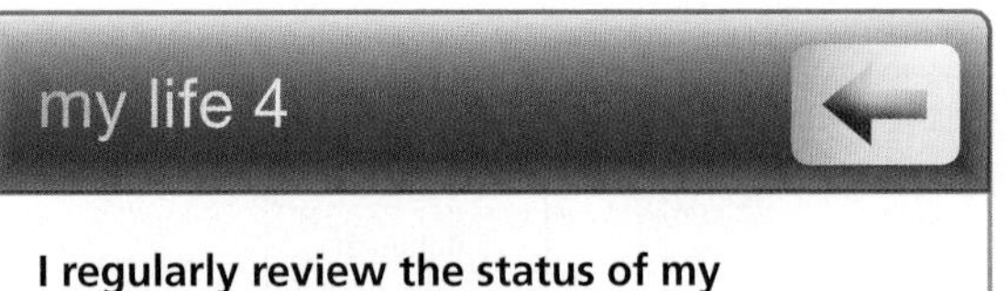

I regularly review the status of my saving goals.

Reaching your financial goals will depend on the savings method used and the time value of money. How do the examples shown in Exhibit 3-10, Using Savings to Achieve Financial Goals, relate to your current or future life situation?

CALCULATING SAVINGS AMOUNTS

To achieve your financial objectives, you should convert your savings goals into specific amounts. Your use of a savings or investment plan is vital to the growth of your money. As Exhibit 3-10 shows, using the time value of money calculations, introduced in Chapter 1, can help you calculate progress toward achieving your financial goals.

PFP Sheet 19

College education cost analysis, savings plan

PRACTICE QUIZ 3-4

1 What are some suggested methods to make saving easy?
2 What methods are available to calculate amounts needed to reach savings goals?

Exhibit 3-10

Using savings to achieve financial goals

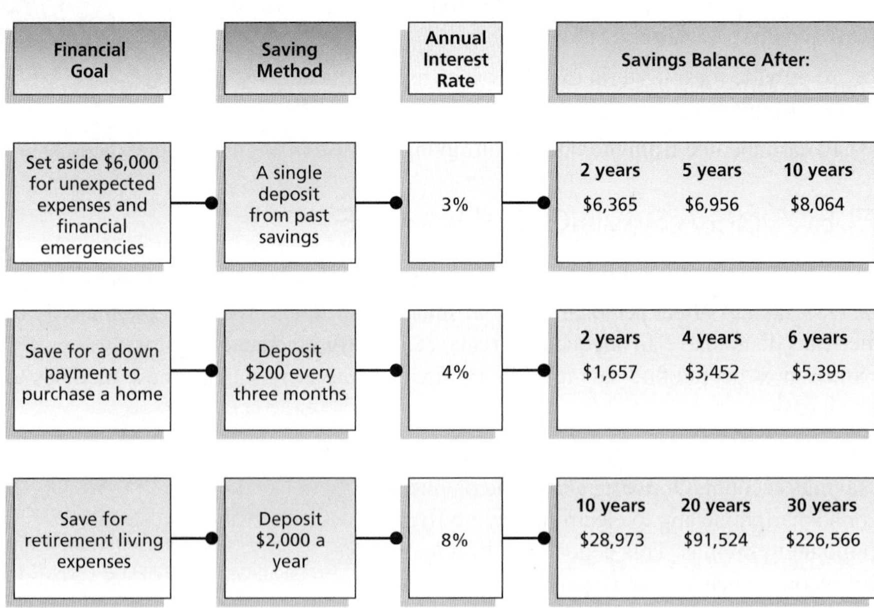

Financial Goal	Saving Method	Annual Interest Rate	Savings Balance After:		
Set aside $6,000 for unexpected expenses and financial emergencies	A single deposit from past savings	3%	2 years $6,365	5 years $6,956	10 years $8,064
Save for a down payment to purchase a home	Deposit $200 every three months	4%	2 years $1,657	4 years $3,452	6 years $5,395
Save for retirement living expenses	Deposit $2,000 a year	8%	10 years $28,973	20 years $91,524	30 years $226,566

my life stages for money management

YOUR PERSONAL FINANCE DASHBOARD

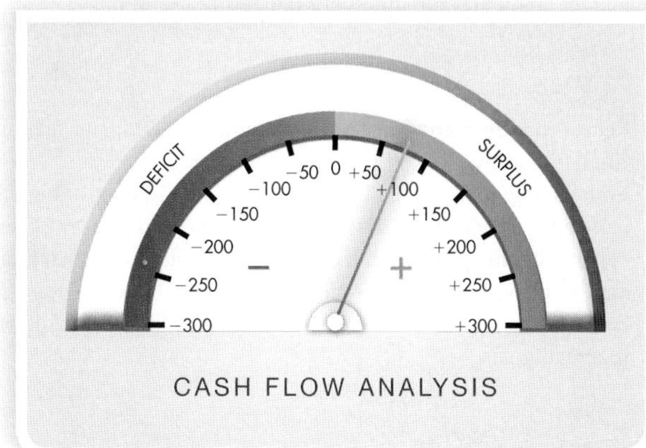

A personal finance dashboard with key performance indicators can help you monitor your financial situation and guide you toward financial independence. A monthly cash flow analysis will help you achieve various financial goals.

By comparing your cash inflows (income) and cash outflows (spending), you will determine if you have a *surplus* or *deficit.* A surplus allows you to save more or pay off debts. A deficit reduces your savings or increases the amount you owe.

YOUR SITUATION Do you maintain a record of cash inflows and outflows? Does your cash flow situation reflect a deficit with unnecessary spending? How can you reduce spending to improve your cash flow situation? Other money management actions you might consider during various stages of your life include. . .

. . . in college

- Maintain spending diary to monitor daily finances
- Create a system for financial records and documents
- Use a budget that includes savings

. . . in my 20s

- Create a personal balance sheet and income statement on an annual basis
- Accumulate an appropriate emergency fund
- Revise budget

. . . in my 30s and 40s

- Update personal financial statements
- Begin investment program for funding children's education
- Adapt budget to changing household needs

. . . in my 50s and beyond

- Determine potential changes in daily spending needs during retirement
- Consider increased savings and contributions to retirement plans

SUMMARY OF LEARNING OBJECTIVES

LO3-1

Recognize relationships among financial documents and money management activities.

Successful money management requires effective coordination of personal financial records, personal financial statements, and budgeting activities. Your system for organizing personal financial records and documents is the foundation of effective money management. This structure should provide ease of access as well as security for financial documents that may be impossible to replace.

LO3-2

Develop a personal balance sheet and cash flow statement.

A personal balance sheet, also known as a *net worth statement,* is prepared by listing all items of value (assets) and all amounts owed to others (liabilities). The difference between your total assets and your total liabilities is your net worth. A cash flow statement, also called a *personal income and expenditure statement,* is a summary of cash receipts and payments for a given period, such as a month or a year. This report provides data on your income and spending patterns.

LO3-3

Create and implement a budget.

Your budgeting activities should involve a process with four phases: (1) assessing your current personal and financial situation, (2) planning your financial direction by setting financial goals and creating budget allowances, (3) implementing your budget, and (4) evaluating your budgeting program.

LO3-4

Relate money management and savings activities to achieve financial goals.

Your saving goals should be based on the relationship among the personal balance sheet, cash flow statement, and budget. Saving current income provides the basis for achieving long-term financial security. Future value and present value calculations may be used to compute the increased value of savings for achieving financial goals.

KEY TERMS

assets 92
balance sheet 92
budget 98
budget variance 103
cash flow 95
cash flow statement 95
current liabilities 93
deficit 103
discretionary income 95
income 95
insolvency 94
liabilities 93
liquid assets 92
long-term liabilities 94
money management 88
net worth 94
safe deposit box 91
surplus 103
take-home pay 95

KEY FORMULAS

Page	Topic	Formula
92	Net worth	Net worth = Total assets − Total liabilities *Example:* = \$125,000 − \$53,000 = \$72,000
95	Cash surplus (or deficit)	Cash surplus (or deficit) = Total inflows − Total outflows *Example:* = \$5,600 − \$4,970 = \$630 (surplus)
97	Debt ratio	Debt ratio = Liabilities/Net worth *Example:* = \$7,000/\$21,000 = 0.33

Page	Topic	Formula
97	Current ratio	Current ratio = Liquid assets/Current liabilities *Example:* = \$8,500/\$4,500 = 1.88
97	Liquidity ratio	Liquidity ratio = Liquid assets/Monthly expenses *Example:* = \$8,500/\$3,500 = 2.4
97	Debt-payments ratio	Debt-payments ratio = Monthly credit payments/Take-home pay *Example:* = \$760/\$3,800 = 0.20
97	Savings ratio	Savings ratio = Amount saved per month/Gross monthly income *Example:* = \$460/\$3,800 = 0.12

SELF-TEST PROBLEMS

1. The Hamilton household has \$145,000 in assets and \$63,000 in liabilities. What is the family's net worth?
2. Harold Daley budgeted \$210 for food for the month of July. He spent \$227 on food during July. Does he have a budget surplus or deficit, and what amount?

Self-Test Solutions

1. Net worth is determined by assets (\$145,000) minus liabilities (\$63,000) resulting in \$82,000.
2. The budget *deficit* of \$17 is calculated by subtracting the actual spending (\$227) from the budgeted amount (\$210).

FINANCIAL PLANNING PROBLEMS

1. *Creating Personal Financial Statements.* Based on the procedures presented in the chapter, prepare your current personal balance sheet and a cash flow statement for the next month. L03-2
2. *Calculating Balance Sheet Amounts.* Based on the following data, compute the total assets, total liabilities, and net worth. L03-2

   Liquid assets, \$4,670
   Investment assets, \$26,910
   Current liabilities, \$2,670
   Household assets, \$93,780
   Long-term liabilities, \$76,230

3. *Preparing a Personal Balance Sheet.* Use the following items to prepare a balance sheet and a cash flow statement. Determine the total assets, total liabilities, net worth, total cash inflows, and total cash outflows. L03-3

   Rent for the month, \$650
   Monthly take-home salary, \$1,950
   Cash in checking account, \$450
   Savings account balance, \$1,890
   Spending for food, \$345
   Balance of educational loan, \$2,160
   Current value of automobile, \$7,800
   Auto insurance, \$230
   Household possessions, \$3,400
   Stereo equipment, \$2,350
   Payment for electricity, \$90
   Lunches/parking at work, \$180
   Donations, \$70
   Home computer, \$1,500

Telephone bill paid for month, $65	Value of stock investment, $860
Credit card balance, $235	Clothing purchase, $110
Loan payment, $80	Restaurant spending, $130

LO3-2 **4.** *Computing Balance Sheet Amounts.* For each of the following situations, compute the missing amount.

a. Assets $45,000; liabilities $12,600; net worth $_____.

b. Assets $78,980; liabilities $_____; net worth $13,700.

c. Assets $44,280; liabilities $12,965; net worth $_____.

d. Assets $_____; liabilities $38,345; net worth $53,795.

LO3-2 **5.** *Calculating Financial Ratios.* The Fram family has liabilities of $128,000 and a net worth of $340,000. What is their debt ratio? How would you assess this?

LO3-2 **6.** *Determining Financial Progress.* Carl Lester has liquid assets of $2,680 and current liabilities of $2,436. What is his current ratio? What comments do you have about this financial position?

LO3-3 **7.** *Determining Budget Variances.* Fran Bowen created the following budget:

Food, $350	Clothing, $100
Transportation, $320	Personal expenses and recreation, $275
Housing, $950	

She actually spent $298 for food, $337 for transportation, $982 for housing, $134 for clothing, and $231 for personal expenses and recreation. Calculate the variance for each of these categories, and indicate whether it was a *deficit* or a *surplus.*

LO3-3 **8.** *Calculating the Effect of Inflation.* Bill and Sally Kaplan have an annual spending plan that amounts to $36,000. If inflation is 3 percent a year for the next three years, what amount will the Kaplans need for their living expenses three years from now?

LO3-4 **9.** *Computing the Time Value of Money for Savings.* Use future value and present value calculations (see Chapter 1 appendix) to determine the following.

a. The future value of a $400 savings deposit after eight years at an annual interest rate of 3 percent.

b. The future value of saving $11,800 a year for five years at an annual interest rate of 4 percent.

c. The present value of a $6,000 savings account that will earn 3 percent interest for four years.

LO3-4 **10.** *Calculating Present Value of a Savings Fund.* Hal Thomas wants to establish a savings fund from which a community organization could draw $800 a year for 20 years. If the account earns 3 percent, what amount would he have to deposit now to achieve this goal?

LO3-4 **11.** *Future Value of Reduced Spending.* Brenda plans to reduce her spending by $80 a month. Calculate the future value of this increase in saving over the next 10 years. (Assume an annual deposit to her savings account, and an annual interest rate of 5 percent.)

LO3-4 **12.** *Future Value of Savings.* Kara George received a $4,000 gift for graduation from her uncle. If she deposits the entire amount in an account paying 3 percent, what will be the value of this gift in 15 years?

FINANCIAL PLANNING ACTIVITIES

LO3-1 **1.** *Researching Money Management Information.* Talk to two or three people regarding wise and poor money management actions they have taken in their lives, and about the system they use to keep track of various financial documents and records. Based on this information, what actions might you take now or in the future?

LO3-2 **2.** *Creating Personal Financial Statements.* Using Sheets 15 and 16 in the *Personal Financial Planner,* or some other format you find online, prepare a personal balance sheet and cash flow statement.

LO3-1, 3-3 **3.** *Researching Money Management Apps.* Conduct research to identify various budgeting and money management apps. Determine the features, ease of operation, and information provided by these apps. Which app would you consider using for your budgeting and money management activities?

LO3-3 **4.** *Analyzing Budgeting Situations.* Discuss with several people how the budget in Exhibit 3-7 might be changed based on various budget variances. If the household faced a decline in income, what spending areas might be reduced first?

LO3-4 **5.** *Analyzing Saving Habits.* Talk to a young single person, a young couple, and a middle-aged person about their financial goals and saving habits. What actions do they take to determine and achieve various financial goals?

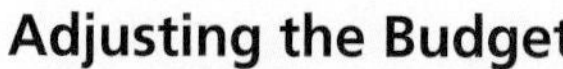

Adjusting the Budget

In a recent month, the Constantine family had a budget deficit, which is something they want to avoid so they do not have future financial difficulties. Jason and Karen Constantine, and their children (ages 10 and 12), plan to discuss the situation after dinner this evening.

While at work, Jason was talking with his friend Ken Lopez. Ken had been a regular saver since he was very young, starting with a small savings account. Those funds were then invested in various stocks and mutual funds. While in college, Ken was able to pay for his education while continuing to save between $50 and $100 a month. He closely monitored his spending. Ken realized that the few dollars here and there for snacks and other minor purchases quickly add up.

Today, Ken works as a customer service manager for the online division of a retailing company. He lives with his wife and their two young children. The family's spending plan allows for all their needs and also includes regularly saving and investing for the children's education and for retirement.

Jason asked Ken, "How come you never seem to have financial stress in your household?"

Ken replied, "Do you know where your money is going each month?"

"Not really," was Jason's response.

"You'd be surprised by how much is spent on little things you might do without," Ken responded.

"I guess so. I just don't want to have to go around with a notebook writing down every amount I spend," Jason said in a troubled voice.

"Well, you have to take some action if you want your financial situation to change," Ken countered.

That evening, the Constantine family met to discuss their budget situation:

Current Spending		Suggested Budget	
Rent	$950	Rent	$ ____
Electricity, water	120	Electricity, water	____
Telephone	55	Telephone	____
Cable, Internet	125	Cable, Internet	____
Food (at home)	385	Food (at home)	____
Food (away)	230	Food (away)	____
Auto payment	410	Auto payment	____
Gas, oil changes	140	Gas, oil changes	____
Insurance	125	Insurance	____
Clothing	200	Clothing	____
Personal, gifts	185	Personal, gifts	____
Donations	50	Donations	____
Savings	35	Savings	____
Total spending	$3,010	Total budgeted	$ ____
Total monthly amount available	$2,800	Total monthly amount available	$2,800
Surplus (deficit)	($210)	Surplus (deficit)	$ ____

Questions

1. What situations might have created the budget deficit for the Constantine family?
2. What amounts would you suggest for the various categories for the family budget?
3. Describe additional actions for the Constantine family related to their budget or other money management activities.

PERSONAL FINANCIAL PLANNER IN ACTION

Personal Financial Statements and a Spending Plan

Money management activities are the basis for most financial planning activities. Creation of a financial document filing system, a personal balance sheet, a cash flow statement, and a budget provide you with tools for setting, implementing, and achieving financial goals.

Your Short-Term Financial Planning Activities	*Resources*
1. Develop a filing system to organize your financial records and documents.	PFP Sheet 14 www.quicken.com www.kiplinger.com
2. Create a personal balance sheet and a personal cash flow statement.	PFP Sheets 15, 16 www.money.com www.lifeadvice.com
3. Based on your current financial situation, set short-term financial goals and develop a budget. Monitor your spending for various categories.	PFP Sheets 17, 18 www.betterbudgeting.com www.mymoney.gov www.mint.com
4. Accumulate an appropriate amount for an emergency fund.	www.clevelandsaves.org www.choosetosave.org
Your Long-Term Financial Planning Activities	*Resources*
1. Set long-term financial goals related to education, housing, or retirement.	PFP Sheet 19 www.statefarm.com/lifevents/lifevents.htm www.dinkytown.net
2. Develop a savings plan, such as automatic withdrawals, to achieve long-term financial goals.	Text pages 107–108 www.asec.org

CONTINUING CASE

Money Management Activities

Life Situation	*Financial Data*
Single Age 21 No dependents College student	Monthly Income (after taxes) $1,450 Personal property $7,300 Savings $2,000 Student loan $3,000 Credit card debt $2,400 Rent $400 Utilities $75 Car insurance $100 Cell phone $50 Credit card payment $40 Gas/Car maintenance $100 Cable/Internet $45 Groceries $300 Clothing $50 Gifts & donations $50

Since Shelby has a fixed income each month, she has been using her credit card to make ends meet. Although she pays the minimum required by the credit card company each month, her credit card debt is rising at an alarming rate. She knows that she is not clear on where all of her money is going but she is glad to be able to share expenses with her roommate, Melinda. She does have a small amount of savings, but she is not sure it is enough if an emergency were to occur.

Questions

1. Since a budget is made up of fixed expenses and variable expenses, identify which of Shelby's expenses fall into each category. Then total each category and compare it to her monthly income to determine if she has a surplus or deficit.
2. Based on the information above, how much should Shelby have in an emergency fund? What steps should she take to reach this amount?
3. Describe how Shelby might use the following Personal Financial Planner sheets for assessing her financial condition (Creating a Personal Balance Sheet, Creating a Personal Cash Flow Statement, and Developing a Personal Budget).

DAILY SPENDING DIARY

"I am amazed how little things can add up. However, since I started keeping track of all my spending, I realized that I need to cut down on some items so I can put some money away into savings."

Directions

Continue or start using the "Daily Spending Diary" sheets, or create your own format, to record *every cent* of your spending in the categories provided. This experience will help you better understand your spending patterns and help you plan for achieving financial goals.

Analysis Questions

1. What information from your Daily Spending Diary might encourage you to reconsider various money management actions?
2. How can your Daily Spending Diary assist you when planning and implementing a budget?

The Daily Spending Diary sheets are located in Appendix D at the end of the book and on the student website at www.mhhe.com/kdh.

chapter 4

Planning Your Tax Strategy

Learning Objectives

LO4-1 Describe the importance of taxes for personal financial planning.

LO4-2 Calculate taxable income and the amount owed for federal income tax.

LO4-3 Prepare a federal income tax return.

LO4-4 Identify tax assistance sources.

LO4-5 Select appropriate tax strategies for various financial and personal situations.

What will this mean for me?

Changing economic and political environments often result in new tax regulations, some of which may be favorable for you while others are not. An important element of tax planning is your refund. Each year, more than 90 million American households receive an average tax refund of over $2,700 for a total of over $230 billion. Invested at 5 percent for a year, these refunds represent over $11.5 billion in lost earnings. By having less withheld and obtaining a smaller refund, you can save and invest these funds for your benefit during the year.

my life

PAY ONLY YOUR FAIR SHARE

Taxes are often viewed as a confusing aspect of personal financial planning. However, with a little effort, the basic elements of taxes can be understood.

THE MAIN FOCUS

The main focus when planning and paying your taxes is to pay your fair share based on current tax laws. What action do you commonly take regarding taxes? For each of the following statements, select "agree" or "disagree" to indicate your personal response regarding these tax-planning activities:

1. I have a good knowledge of the various taxes paid in our society.	Agree	Disagree
2. My tax records are organized to allow me to easily find needed information.	Agree	Disagree
3. I am able to file my taxes on time each year.	Agree	Disagree
4. My tax returns have never been questioned by the Internal Revenue Service.	Agree	Disagree
5. I stay informed on proposed tax changes being considered for my current tax filing status.	Agree	Disagree

As you study this chapter, you will encounter "My Life" boxes with additional information and resources related to these items.

Taxes and Financial Planning

LO4-1

Describe the importance of taxes for personal financial planning.

Taxes are an everyday financial fact of life. You pay some taxes every time you get a paycheck or make a purchase. However, most people concern themselves with taxes only in April. With about one-third of each dollar you earn going to taxes, an effective tax strategy is vital for successful financial planning. Understanding tax rules and regulations can help you reduce your tax liability.

The U.S. Bureau of the Census reports that about two out of three American households have no money left after paying for taxes and normal living expenses. For most of us, taxes are a significant factor in financial planning. Each year, the Tax Foundation determines how long the average person works to pay taxes. In recent years, "Tax Freedom Day" came in Mid-April. This means that the time people worked from January 1 until Mid-April represents the portion of the year worked to pay their taxes.

This financial obligation includes the many types of taxes discussed later in this section. To help you cope with these taxes, common goals related to tax planning include

- Knowing the current tax laws and regulations that affect you.
- Maintaining complete and appropriate tax records.
- Making purchase and investment decisions that can reduce your tax liability.

Target your tax planning efforts toward paying your fair share of taxes while taking advantage of tax benefits appropriate to your personal and financial situation.

The principal purpose of taxes is to finance government activities. As citizens, we expect government to provide services such as police and fire protection, schools, road maintenance, parks and libraries, and safety inspection of food, drugs, and other products. Most people pay taxes in four major categories: taxes on purchases, taxes on property, taxes on wealth, and taxes on earnings.

TAXES ON PURCHASES

excise tax A tax imposed on specific goods and services, such as gasoline, cigarettes, alcoholic beverages, tires, and air travel.

You probably pay *sales tax* on many of your purchases. This state and local tax is added to the purchase price of products. Many states exempt food and drugs from sales tax to reduce the economic burden of this tax on the poor. In recent years, all but five states (Alaska, Delaware, Montana, New Hampshire, and Oregon) have had a general sales tax. An **excise tax** is imposed by the federal and state governments on specific goods and services, such as gasoline, cigarettes, alcoholic beverages, tires, air travel, and telephone service.

DID YOU KNOW?

According to the Tax Foundation (www.taxfoundation.org), Alaska, New Hampshire, Delaware, Tennessee, and Alabama were the most "tax-friendly" states. In contrast, Vermont, Maine, New York, Rhode Island, and Ohio had the highest taxes as a percentage of income.

TAXES ON PROPERTY

Real estate property tax is a major source of revenue for local governments. This tax is based on the value of land and buildings. The increasing amount of real estate property taxes is a major concern of homeowners. Retired people with limited pension incomes may encounter financial difficulties if local property taxes increase rapidly.

Some areas also impose *personal property taxes.* State and local governments may assess taxes on the value of automobiles, boats, furniture, and farm equipment.

TAXES ON WEALTH

An **estate tax** is imposed on the value of a person's property at the time of his or her death. This federal tax is based on the fair market value of the deceased individual's investments, property, and bank accounts less allowable deductions and other taxes. Estate taxes are discussed in greater detail in Chapter 19.

Money and property passed on to heirs may also be subject to a state tax. An **inheritance tax** is levied on the value of property bequeathed by a deceased person. This tax is paid for the right to acquire the inherited property.

estate tax A tax imposed on the value of a person's property at the time of his or her death.

inheritance tax A tax levied on the value of property bequeathed by a deceased person.

For 2013, individuals are allowed to give money or items valued at $14,000 or less in a year to a person without being subject to taxes. Gift amounts greater than $14,000 are subject to federal tax. Amounts given for the payment of tuition or medical expenses are not subject to federal gift taxes. Some states impose a gift tax on amounts that a person, before his or her death, transfers to another person, because the action may have been intended to avoid estate and inheritance taxes.

Real estate property taxes are the major revenue source for local government.

TAXES ON EARNINGS

The two main taxes on wages and salaries are Social Security and income taxes. The Federal Insurance Contributions Act (FICA) created the Social Security tax to fund the old-age, survivors, and disability insurance portion of the Social Security system and the hospital insurance portion (Medicare). Chapters 11 and 18 discuss various aspects of Social Security.

Income tax is a major financial planning factor for most people. Some workers are subject to federal, state, and local income taxes. Currently, only seven states do not have a state income tax.

Throughout the year, your employer will withhold income tax payments from your paycheck, or you may be required to make estimated tax payments if you own your own business. Both types of payments are only estimates of your income taxes. You may need to pay an additional amount, or you may get a tax refund. The following sections will assist you in preparing your federal income tax return and planning your future tax strategies.

I have a good knowledge of the various taxes paid in our society.

Prepare a list of the various taxes you pay in our society. This list might include fees and charges associated with various licenses and government services.

1 How should you consider taxes in your financial planning?
2 What types of taxes do people frequently overlook when making financial decisions?

Income Tax Fundamentals

LO4-2

Calculate taxable income and the amount owed for federal income tax.

The starting point for preparing your taxes is proper documentation. You are required to keep records to document tax deductions. Maintaining an organized system that allows you to quickly access this documentation is essential. Later, we will discuss how long you should keep these documents and will recommend ways to create an organized system.

Each year, millions of Americans are required to pay their share of income taxes to the federal government. The process involves computing taxable income, determining the amount of income tax owed, and comparing this amount with the income tax payments withheld or made during the year.

taxable income The net amount of income, after allowable deductions, on which income tax is computed.

earned income Money received for personal effort, such as wages, salary, commission, fees, tips, or bonuses.

investment income Money received in the form of dividends, interest, or rent from investments. Also called *portfolio income.*

passive income Income resulting from business activities in which you do not actively participate.

exclusion An amount not included in gross income.

tax-exempt income Income that is not subject to tax.

tax-deferred income Income that will be taxed at a later date.

adjusted gross income (AGI) Gross income reduced by certain adjustments, such as contributions to an individual retirement account (IRA) and alimony payments.

tax shelter An investment that provides immediate tax benefits and a reasonable expectation of a future financial return.

STEP 1: DETERMINING ADJUSTED GROSS INCOME

Taxable income is the net amount of income, after allowable deductions, on which income tax is computed. Exhibit 4-1 presents the components of taxable income and the process used to compute it.

TYPES OF INCOME Most, but not all, income is subject to taxation. Your gross, or total, income can consist of three main components:

1. **Earned income** is money received for personal effort. Earned income is usually in the form of wages, salary, commission, fees, tips, or bonuses.
2. **Investment income** (sometimes referred to as *portfolio income*) is money received in the form of dividends, interest, or rent from investments.
3. **Passive income** results from business activities in which you do not actively participate, such as a limited partnership.

Other types of income subject to federal income tax include alimony, awards, lottery winnings, and prizes. Cameron Clark once won $30,533 in prizes on the television game show *Wheel of Fortune.* In addition to paying California sales tax of $1,154, Cameron had to sell the car stereo, ping-pong table, camping gear, water ski equipment, bass guitar, and art drawing table and chair he won to pay the federal income tax. He did get to keep the Toyota, Honda scooter, Gucci watches, and Australian vacation.

Total income is also affected by exclusions. An **exclusion** is an amount not included in gross income. For example, the foreign earned income exclusion allows U.S. citizens working and living in another country to exclude a certain portion ($97,600, as of 2013) of their incomes from federal income taxes.

Exclusions are also referred to as **tax-exempt income,** or income that is not subject to tax. For example, interest earned on most state and city bonds is exempt from federal income tax. **Tax-deferred income** is income that will be taxed at a later date. The earnings on an individual retirement account (IRA) are an example of tax-deferred income. While these earnings are credited to the account now, you do not pay taxes on them until you withdraw them from the account.

ADJUSTMENTS TO INCOME **Adjusted gross income (AGI)** is gross income after certain reductions have been made. These reductions, called *adjustments to income,* include contributions to an IRA or a Keogh retirement plan, penalties for early withdrawal of savings, and alimony payments. Adjusted gross income is used as the basis for computing various income tax deductions, such as medical expenses.

Certain adjustments to income, such as tax-deferred retirement plans, are a type of tax shelter. **Tax shelters** are investments that provide immediate tax benefits and a reasonable expectation of a future financial return. In recent years, tax court rulings and

Exhibit 4-1 Computing taxable income and your tax liability

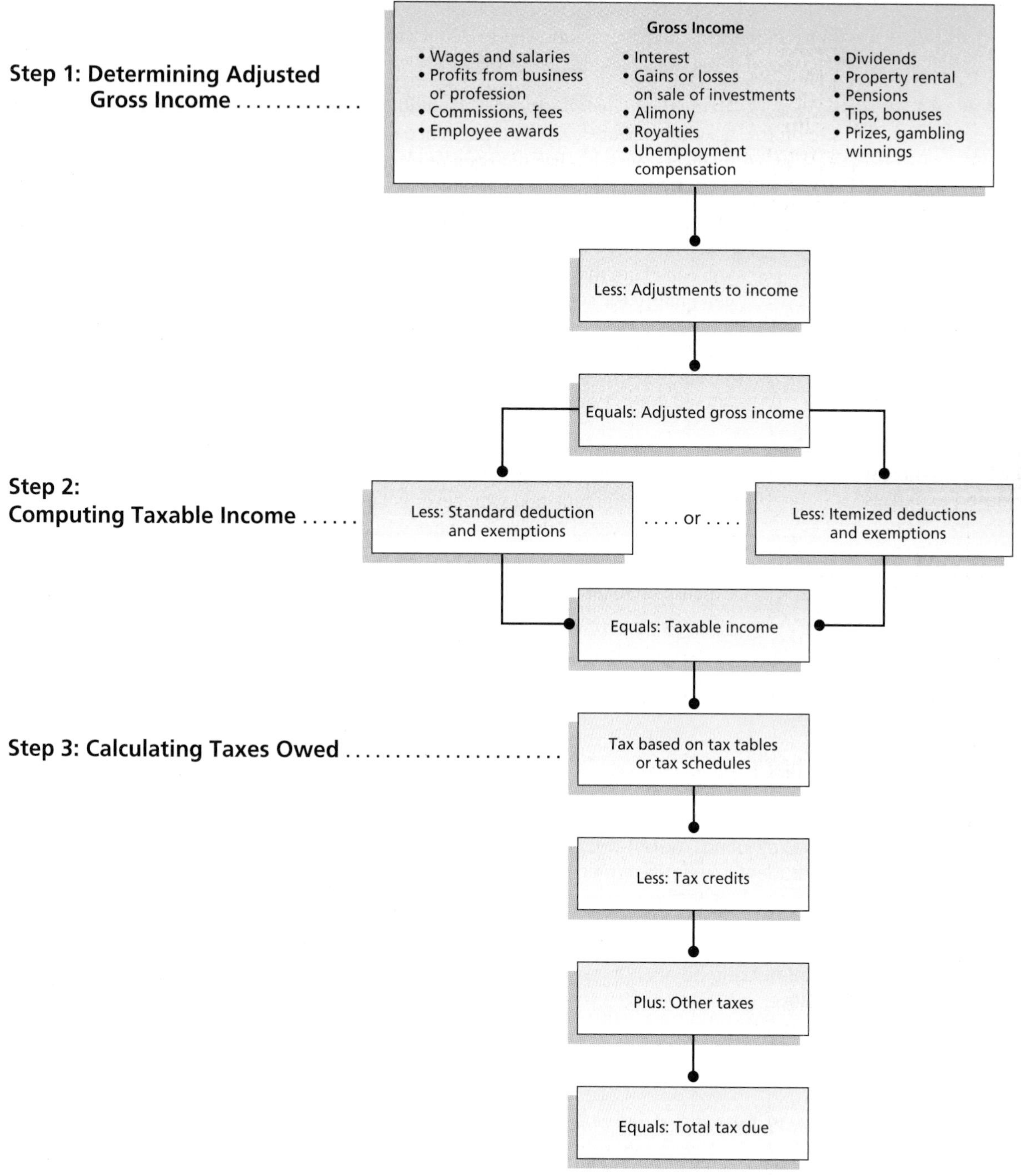

changes in the tax code have disallowed various types of tax shelters that were considered excessive.

STEP 2: COMPUTING TAXABLE INCOME

tax deduction An amount subtracted from adjusted gross income to arrive at taxable income.

DEDUCTIONS A **tax deduction** is an amount subtracted from adjusted gross income to arrive at taxable income. Every taxpayer receives at least the **standard deduction,** a set amount on which no taxes are paid. As of 2013, single people receive a standard deduction of $6,100 (married couples filing jointly receive $12,200). Blind people and individuals 65 and older receive higher standard deductions.

Many people qualify for more than the standard deduction. **Itemized deductions** are expenses a taxpayer is allowed to deduct from adjusted gross income. Common itemized deductions include the following:

- *Medical and dental expenses,* including doctors' fees, prescription medications, hospital expenses, medical insurance premiums, hearing aids, eyeglasses, and medical travel that has not been reimbursed or paid by others. This deduction is equal to the amount by which the medical and dental expenses exceed 10 percent (as of 2013) of adjusted gross income. If your AGI is $20,000, for example, you must have more than $2,000 in unreimbursed medical and dental expenses before you can claim this deduction. If your medical and dental bills amount to $2,600, you qualify for a $600 deduction.

standard deduction A set amount on which no taxes are paid.

itemized deductions Expenses that can be deducted from adjusted gross income, such as medical expenses, real estate property taxes, home mortgage interest, charitable contributions, casualty losses, and certain work-related expenses.

Note: The 10 percent threshold is an increase in 2013 from the long-standing 7.5 percent threshold. The 10 percent threshold will only apply to persons under 65 years old until 2017.

- *Taxes*—state and local income tax, real estate property tax, and state or local personal property tax. You may also deduct an amount for state sales tax instead of your state income tax, whichever is larger—but not both. This deduction will benefit taxpayers in the seven states without a state income tax.
- *Interest*—mortgage interest, home equity loan interest, and investment interest expense up to an amount equal to investment income.
- *Contributions* of cash or property to qualified charitable organizations. Contribution totals greater than 20 percent of adjusted gross income are subject to limitations.
- *Casualty and theft losses*—financial losses resulting from natural disasters, accidents, or unlawful acts. Deductions are for the amount exceeding 10 percent of AGI, less $100, for losses *not* reimbursed by an insurance company or other source. (California residents commonly report casualty losses due to earthquake damage.)
- *Moving expenses* when a change in residence is associated with a new job that is at least 50 miles farther from your former home than your old main job location. Deductible moving expenses include only the cost of transporting the taxpayer and household members and the cost of moving household goods and personal property.

DID YOU KNOW?

The most frequently overlooked tax deductions are state sales taxes, reinvested dividends, out-of-pocket charitable contributions, student loan interest paid by parents, moving expense to take first job, military reservists' travel expenses, child care credit, estate tax on income in respect of a decedent, state tax you paid last spring, refinancing points, and jury pay paid to employer.

- *Job-related and other miscellaneous expenses* such as unreimbursed job travel, union dues, required continuing education, work clothes or uniforms, investment expenses, tax preparation fees, and safe deposit box rental (for storing investment documents). The total of these expenses must exceed 2 percent of adjusted gross income to qualify as a deduction. Such miscellaneous expenses as gambling losses to the extent of gambling winnings and physical or mental disability expenses that limit employability are not subject to the 2 percent limit.

The standard deduction *or* total itemized deductions, along with the value of your exemptions (see the next section), is subtracted from adjusted gross income to obtain

IS IT TAXABLE INCOME? IS IT DEDUCTIBLE?

Certain financial benefits individuals receive are not subject to federal income tax. Indicate whether each of the following items would or would not be included in taxable income when you compute your federal income tax.

Is it taxable income?	Yes	No
1. Lottery winnings	____	____
2. Child support received	____	____
3. Worker's compensation benefits	____	____
4. Life insurance death benefits	____	____
5. Municipal bond interest earnings	____	____
6. Bartering income	____	____

Indicate whether each of the following items would or would not be deductible when you compute your federal income tax.

Is it deductible?	Yes	No
7. Life insurance premiums	____	____
8. Gym membership	____	____
9. Fees for traffic violations	____	____
10. Mileage for driving to volunteer work	____	____
11. An attorney's fee for preparing a will	____	____
12. Income tax preparation fee	____	____

Note: These taxable income items and deductions are based on the 2013 tax year and may change due to changes in the tax code.

Answers: 1, 6, 10, 12—yes; 2, 3, 4, 5, 7, 8, 9, 11—no.

your taxable income. In past years, pre-2006, there was a limitation on itemized deductions for high-income taxpayers. Starting in 2013, some of the limitation rules have been reinstated. The new rules state that taxpayers must reduce their total itemized deductions by 3 percent of the excess of their adjusted gross income over specified thresholds. The thresholds are as follows: $300,000 if married filing jointly, $250,000 for a single taxpayer, and $150,000 for married filing separately. (*Note:* There are some exceptions for medical expenses, investment interest, casualty and theft losses, and gambling losses.)

Financial advisers recommend a filing system (see Exhibit 4-2) for organizing receipts and other tax documents. Canceled checks (or electronic copies of checks) can serve as proof of payment for such deductions as charitable contributions, medical expenses, and business-related expenses. Travel expenses can be documented in a daily log with records of mileage, tolls, parking fees, food and lodging costs.

Generally, you should keep tax records for three years from the date you file your return. However, you may be held responsible for providing back documentation up to six years. This means keep documentation from tax year 2013, that is filed in 2014, until 2020. Records such as copies of past tax returns and home ownership documents should be kept indefinitely.

My tax records are organized to allow me to easily find needed information.

To assist you in organizing your tax records, you need to be aware of what is taxable income and what is deductible. See the Financial Planning for Life's Situations above.

Exhibit 4-2 A tax recordkeeping system

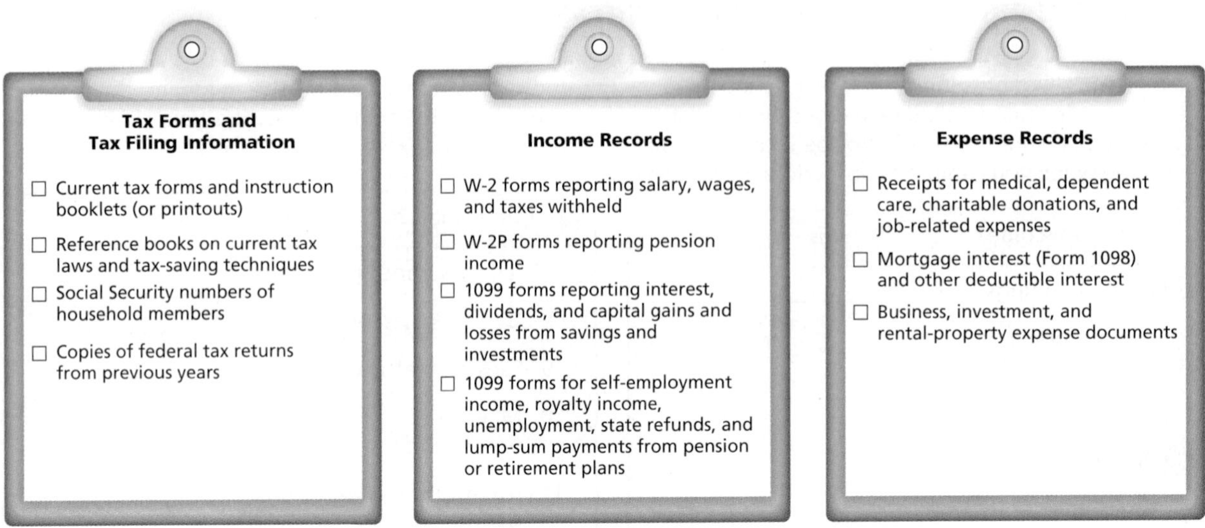

exemption A deduction from adjusted gross income for yourself, your spouse, and qualified dependents.

EXEMPTIONS An **exemption** is a deduction from adjusted gross income for yourself, your spouse, and qualified dependents. A dependent must not earn more than a set amount unless he or she is under age 19 or is a full-time student under age 24; you must provide more than half of the dependent's support; and the dependent must reside in your home or be a specified relative and must meet certain citizenship requirements. The Social Security number of each dependent must be reported on the tax return, regardless of age.

For 2013, taxable income was reduced by $3,900 for each exemption claimed. This amount is revised annually based on inflation. Increased exemptions and standard deductions eliminate or reduce the taxes many low-income Americans pay. For 2013, a family of four did not have to pay federal income tax on the first $27,800 of gross income ($12,200 for the standard deduction and $15,600 for four exemptions). After deducting the amounts for exemptions, you obtain your taxable income, which is the amount used to determine taxes owed.

EXAMPLE: Taxable Income

Calculating taxable income involves the following steps:

1 Gross income (wages, profits, dividends, interest, other income)	$ 78,210
2 Less: Adjustments to income (retirement plan contributions)	– $ 4,500
3 Equals: Adjusted gross income	= $ 73,710
4 Less: Itemized deductions (or standard deduction) and exemptions	– $ 16,410 – $ 15,600
5 Equals: Taxable income	= $ 41,700

STEP 3: CALCULATING TAXES OWED

Your taxable income is the basis for computing the amount of your income tax. The use of tax rates and the benefits of tax credits are the final phase of the tax computation process.

TAX RATES Use your taxable income in conjunction with the appropriate tax table or tax schedule. For several years previous to 1987, there were 14 tax rates, ranging from 11 to 50 percent. For 2013, the seven-rate system for federal income tax was as follows:

Rate on Taxable Income	Single Taxpayers	Married Taxpayers Filing Jointly	Head of Households
10%	Up to $8,925	Up to $17,850	Up to $12,750
15	$8,925–$36,250	$17,850–$72,500	$12,750–$48,600
25	$36,250–$87,850	$72,500–$146,400	$48,600–$125,450
28	$87,850–$183,250	$146,400–$223,050	$125,450–$203,150
33	$183,250–$398,350	$223,050–$398,350	$203,150–$398,350
35	$398,350–$400,000	$398,350–$450,000	$398,350–$425,000
39.6	$400,000 +	$450,000 +	$425,000+

A separate tax rate schedule exists for married persons who file separate income tax returns.

The 10, 15, 25, 28, 33, 35 and 39.6 percent rates are referred to as **marginal tax rates.** These rates are used to calculate tax on the last (and next) dollar of taxable income. After deductions and exemptions, a person in the 28 percent tax bracket pays 28 cents in taxes for every dollar of taxable income in that bracket.

marginal tax rate The rate used to calculate tax on the last (and next) dollar of taxable income.

CALCULATING YOUR TAX Each of the tax rates represents a range of income levels. These are often referred to as *brackets.* To calculate the tax on a specific amount of income, you must calculate the tax from each of the brackets as you progress up to your taxable income. (*Note:* This is the tax calculated prior to additional credits or other taxes, such as self-employment tax.)

The diagram below illustrates the calculation of the income tax due if your filing status is *Married Filing Jointly* and you have a taxable income of $125,000. You and your spouse are in the 25 percent tax bracket. Although most computer programs will automatically calculate the tax owed, it is helpful to understand the process to calculate the tax due. (*Note:* For this assumption, we will assume that there is no other income at different rates, such as capital gains.)

Tax calculated from each tax bracket (10%, 15% & 25%) are added to equal the total tax due

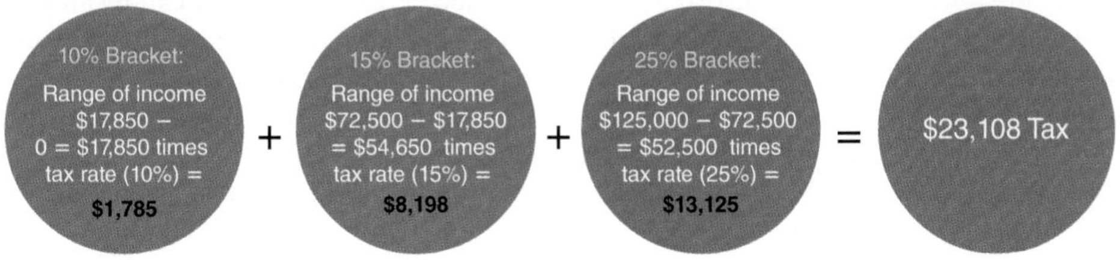

Financial Planning Calculations

TAX CREDITS VERSUS TAX DEDUCTIONS

Many people confuse *tax credits* with *tax deductions.* Is one better than the other? A tax *credit,* such as eligible child care or dependent care expenses, results in a dollar-for-dollar reduction in the amount of taxes owed. A *tax deduction,* such as an itemized deduction in the form of medical expenses, mortgage interest, or charitable contributions, reduces the taxable income on which your taxes are based.

Here is how a $100 tax credit compares with a $100 tax deduction:

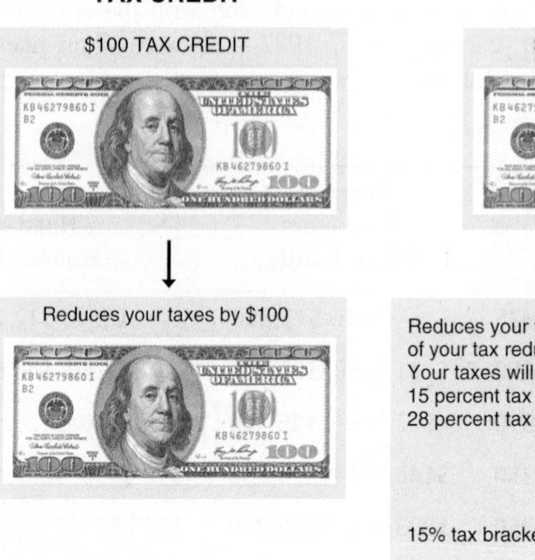

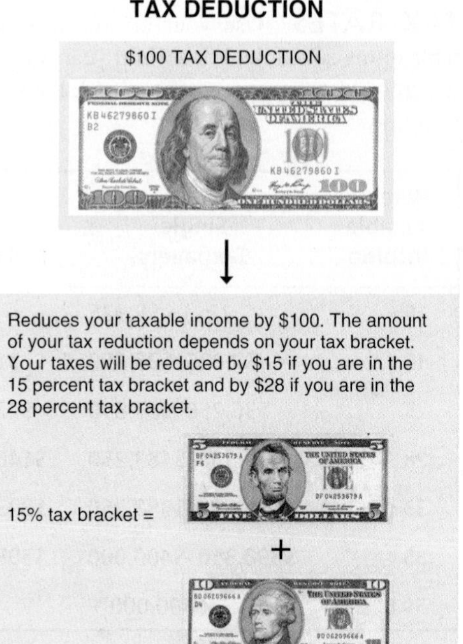

As you might expect, tax credits are less readily available than tax deductions. To qualify for a $100 child care tax credit, you may have to spend $500 in child care expenses. In some situations, spending on deductible items may be more beneficial than qualifying for a tax credit. A knowledge of tax law and careful financial planning will help you use both tax credits and tax deductions to maximum advantage.

average tax rate Total tax due divided by taxable income.

In contrast, the **average tax rate** is based on the total tax due divided by taxable income. Except for taxpayers in the 10 percent bracket, this rate is less than a person's marginal tax rate. For example, a person with taxable income of $40,000 and a total tax bill of $4,200 would have an *average tax rate* of 10.5 percent ($4,200 ÷ $40,000). Self-employed people are likely to have a higher average tax rate due to self-employment taxes, which include payments toward future Social Security benefits.

Taxpayers with high amounts of certain deductions and various types of income may be subject to an additional tax. The *alternative minimum tax (AMT)* is designed to ensure that those who receive tax breaks also pay their fair share of taxes. The AMT was originally designed to prevent those with high incomes from using special tax breaks to pay little in taxes. Some of these special tax breaks that can result in a person paying the AMT include high levels of deductions for state and local taxes, interest on second mortgages, medical expenses, and other deductions. Other items that can trigger the AMT are incentive stock options, long-term capital gains, and tax-exempt interest. AMT rules state that the taxpayer starts with gross income but excludes many of the tax breaks, which makes the taxable income much higher.

There are a few caveats to the AMT, an exemption is allowed for a certain portion of income. This exemption in previous years was not inflation adjusted. As income levels rose, more people were exposed to the AMT tax. The American Taxpayer Relief Act of 2012 now provides for annually adjusting the exemption due to inflation. For tax year 2013, the exemptions are $80,800 for married couples filing jointly, $51,900 for single and head of household filers, and $40,400 for married people filing separately. Additional information about the AMT may be obtained at www.irs.gov.

TAX CREDITS The tax owed may be reduced by a **tax credit,** an amount subtracted directly from the amount of taxes owed. One example of a tax credit is the credit given for child care and dependent care expenses. This amount lowers the tax owed by an individual or a couple. A tax credit differs from a deduction in that a *tax credit* has a full dollar effect in lowering taxes, whereas a *deduction* reduces the taxable income on which the tax liability is computed. (See the Financial Planning Calculations box, on the previous page.)

tax credit An amount subtracted directly from the amount of taxes owed.

Low-income workers can benefit from the *earned-income credit (EIC).* This federal tax regulation, for working parents with taxable income under a certain amount ($51,567 in 2013 for three or more children), can result in a tax credit of up to $6,044. Families that do not earn enough to owe federal income taxes are also eligible for the EIC. When these families file a tax return and attach Schedule EIC, they receive a check from the IRS for the amount of their credit.

Other recent tax credits have included:

- Foreign tax credit to avoid double taxation on income taxes paid to another country.
- Child and dependent care expense credit to cover qualifying expenses to pay for someone else to care for your child under age 13 or dependent (e.g., disabled older child, spouse, or parent) who could not care for themselves.
- Retirement savings tax credit to encourage investment contributions to individual and employer-sponsored retirement plans by low- and middle-income taxpayers.
- Adoption tax credit to cover qualifying expenses when adopting a child.
- American Opportunity and Lifetime Learning tax credits to help offset college education expenses.
- Mortgage interest tax credit for low-income, first-time home buyers.
- Energy-savings tax credit when purchasing various energy-efficient products or renewable home energy systems.
- Elderly and disabled tax credit assists low-income people age 65 or older, and those under age 65 retired with a permanent disability and taxable disability income.

During recent economic difficulties, other tax credits were used to stimulate business activity, some of which may be extended in the future. Tax preparation software will guide you in identifying current tax credits for which you may qualify.

MAKING TAX PAYMENTS

You will make your payment of income taxes to the federal government in one of two ways: through payroll withholding or through estimated tax payments.

WITHHOLDING The pay-as-you-go system requires an employer to deduct federal income tax from your pay and send it to the government. The withheld amount is based on the number of exemptions and the expected deductions claimed on the W-4 form. For example, a married person with children would have less withheld than a single person with the same salary, since the married person will owe less tax at year-end.

After the end of the year, you will receive a W-2 form (see Exhibit 4-3), which reports your annual earnings and the amounts that have been deducted for federal income tax, Social Security, and, if applicable, state income tax. A copy of the W-2 form is filed with your tax return to document your earnings and the amount you have paid in taxes. The difference between the amount withheld and the tax owed is either the additional amount you must pay or the refund you will receive.

Regarding wise financial decisions for your tax refund:

DID YOU KNOW?

An estimated 15 million people are self-employed, an equivalent of 1 in 9 workers. These self-employed people file Schedule C requiring payment for Social Security and Medicare taxes. However, they will also be eligible for various business deductions against their income.

DON'T		DO
DON'T have excessive withholding that results in a large refund.	→	DO have an amount from each paycheck deposited in a savings or investment account.
DON'T use your refund for impulse purchases.	→	DO use the funds to reduce high-interest credit card debt.
DON'T leave the amount of the refund in your checking account.	→	DO make contributions to retirement and college-savings plans.

Exhibit 4-3 W-2 form

a Employee's social security number | OMB No. 1545-0008 | Safe, accurate, FAST! Use IRS e-file | Visit the IRS website at www.irs.gov/efile

b Employer identification number (EIN)	1 Wages, tips, other compensation	2 Federal income tax withheld
37 - 19876541	23,972.09	2,678.93
c Employer's name, address, and ZIP code	3 Social security wages 23,972.09	4 Social security tax withheld $1,486.27
Information Data, Inc. 9834 Collins Blvd. Benton, NJ 08734	5 Medicare wages and tips $23,972.09	6 Medicare tax withheld $347.60
	7 Social security tips	8 Allocated tips
d Control number 123-45-6789	9	10 Dependent care benefits
e Employee's first name and initial Last name Suff.	11 Nonqualified plans	12a See instructions for box 12
Barbara Victor 124 Harper Lane Parmont, NJ 07819	13 Statutory employee ☐ Retirement plan ☐ Third-party sick pay ☐	12b
	14 Other	12c
f Employee's address and ZIP code		12d

15 State	Employer's state ID number	16 State wages, tips, etc.	17 State income tax	18 Local wages, tips, etc.	19 Local income tax	20 Locality name
	37 - 19876541	$23,972.09	$599.30			

Form **W-2** Wage and Tax Statement

Department of the Treasury—Internal Revenue Service

Copy B—To Be Filed With Employee's FEDERAL Tax Return.
This information is being furnished to the Internal Revenue Service.

Students and low-income individuals may file for exemption from withholding if they paid no federal income tax last year and do not expect to pay any in the current year. Dependents may not be exempt from withholding if they have $300 or more of unearned income (ex: interest) and if the earned income (ex: wages) will be more than $850. Being exempt from withholding results in not having to file for a refund and allows you to make more use of your money during the year. However, even if federal income tax is not withheld, Social Security taxes will still be deducted.

ESTIMATED PAYMENTS People with income from savings, investments, independent contracting, royalties, and lump-sum payments from pensions or retirement plans have their earnings reported on Form 1099. People in these situations and others who do not have taxes withheld may be required to make tax payments during the year (April 15, June 15, September 15, and January 15 as the last payment for the previous tax year). These payments are based on the person's estimate of taxes due at year-end. Underpayment or failure to make these estimated payments can result in penalties and interest charges. These penalties are usually avoided if withholding and estimated payments total more than your tax liability for the previous year or at least 90 percent of the current year's tax.

EXAMPLE: Refund or Amount Owed?

Taxes owed or a refund?

(1) Compare withholding amount and payments made during the year with	$2,225
(2) taxes due as calculated on your 1040 form, which	$1,926
(3) would result in a REFUND of	$ 299

However when withholding and payments are less than the amount of taxes due. An additional amount must be paid by April 15.

DEADLINES AND PENALTIES

Most people are required to file their federal income tax return each April 15. If you are not able to file on time, you can use Form 4868 to obtain an automatic six-month extension. This extension is for the 1040 form and other documents, but it does not delay your payment liability. You must submit the estimated amount owed along with Form 4868 by April 15. Failure to file on time can result in a penalty of 5 percent for just one day.

People who make quarterly deposits for estimated taxes must submit their payments by April 15, June 15, and September 15 of the current tax year, with the final payment due by January 15 of the following year.

The IRS can impose penalties and interest for violations of the tax code. Failure to file a tax return can result in a 25 percent penalty in addition to the taxes owed.

Underpayment of quarterly estimated taxes requires paying interest on the amount you should have paid. Underpayment due to negligence or fraud can result in penalties of 50 to 75 percent. The good news is that if you claim a refund several months or years late, the IRS will pay you interest. Refunds must be claimed within three years of filing the return or within two years of paying the tax.

Current income tax estimate

PRACTICE QUIZ 4-2

1 How does tax-exempt income differ from tax-deferred income?
2 What information is needed to compute taxable income?
3 When would you use the standard deduction instead of itemized deductions?
4 What is the difference between your marginal tax rate and your average tax rate?
5 How does a tax credit affect the amount owed for federal income tax?

Filing Your Federal Income Tax Return

LO4-3

Prepare a federal income tax return.

As you stare at those piles of papers, you know it's time to do your taxes! Submitting your federal income tax return requires several decisions and activities. First, you must determine whether you are required to file a return. Next, you need to decide which basic form best serves your needs and whether you are required to submit additional schedules or supplementary forms. Finally, you must prepare your return.

WHO MUST FILE?

Every citizen or resident of the United States and every U.S. citizen who is a resident of Puerto Rico is required to file a federal income tax return if his or her income is above a certain amount. The amount is based on the person's *filing status* and other factors such as age. For example, single persons under 65 had to file a return on April 15, 2013 (for tax year 2012), if their gross income exceeded $9,750, single persons over 65 had to file if their gross income exceeded $11,200. The amount at which you are required to file will change each year based on changes in the standard deduction and in the allowed personal exemptions. If your gross income is less than this amount but taxes were withheld from your earnings, you will need to file a return to obtain a refund.

Your filing status is affected by such factors as marital status and dependents. The five filing status categories are as follows:

- *Single*—never-married, divorced, or legally separated individuals with no dependents.
- *Married, filing joint return*—combines the income of a husband and a wife.
- *Married, filing separate returns*—each spouse is responsible for his or her own tax. Under certain conditions, a married couple can benefit from this filing status.
- *Head of household*—an unmarried individual or a surviving spouse who maintains a household (paying for more than half of the costs) for a child or a dependent relative.
- *Qualifying widow or widower*—an individual whose spouse died within the past two years and who has a dependent; this status is limited to two years after the death of the spouse.

In some situations, you may have a choice of filing status. In such cases, compute your taxes under the available alternatives to determine the most advantageous filing status.

The *marriage penalty* often occurs for couples that have similar income levels. The *penalty* is the amount of additional tax that a couple will pay using a *married, filing joint* status versus a *single* filing status. It is important to note that couples who are married on the last day of the year are considered married for the entire year. A *marriage bonus* can also occur if the income levels of each person are vastly different as well. Want to calculate the amount of the penalty or bonus? The Tax Policy Center has an online calculator that you can access at http://taxpolicycenter.org/taxfacts/marriagepenaltycalculator.cfm.

WHICH TAX FORM SHOULD YOU USE?

Although about 800 federal tax forms and schedules exist, you have a choice of three basic forms when filing your income tax (see Exhibit 4-4). Recently about 20 percent of taxpayers used Form 1040EZ or Form 1040A; about 60 percent used the regular Form 1040. Your decision in this matter will depend on your type of income, the amount of your income, the number of your deductions, and the complexity of your tax situation. Most tax preparation software programs will guide you in selecting the appropriate 1040 form.

DID YOU KNOW?

The Internal Revenue Service oversees more than 17,000 pages of laws and regulations with about 500 different tax forms.

COMPLETING THE FEDERAL INCOME TAX RETURN

The major sections of Form 1040 (see Exhibit 4-5 on page 133) correspond to tax topics discussed in the previous sections of this chapter:

1. *Filing status and exemptions.* Your tax rate is determined by your filing status and allowances for yourself, your spouse, and each person you claim as a dependent.
2. *Income.* Earnings from your employment (as reported by your W-2 form) and other income, such as savings and investment income, are reported in this section of Form 1040.
3. *Adjustments to income.* As discussed later in the chapter, if you qualify, you may deduct contributions (up to a certain amount) to an individual retirement account (IRA) or other qualified retirement program.
4. *Tax computation.* In this section, your adjusted gross income is reduced by your itemized deductions (see Exhibit 4-6) or by the standard deduction for your tax situation. In addition, an amount is deducted for each exemption to arrive at your taxable income. That income is the basis for determining the amount of your tax (see Exhibit 4-7 on page 136).
5. *Tax credits.* Any tax credits for which you qualify are subtracted at this point.
6. *Other taxes.* Any special taxes, such as self-employment tax, are included at this point.
7. *Payments.* Your total withholding and other payments are indicated in this section.
8. *Refund or amount you owe.* If your payments exceed the amount of income tax you owe, you are entitled to a refund. If the opposite is true, you must make an additional payment. Taxpayers who want their refunds sent directly to a bank record the necessary account information directly on Form 1040, 1040A, or 1040EZ.
9. *Your signature.* Forgetting to sign a tax return is one of the most common filing errors.

I am able to file my taxes on time each year.

The latest federal income tax forms and instructions are available at www.irs.org. Information about state income taxes may be obtained at www.taxadmin.org.

Exhibit 4-4 Selecting a 1040 form

FORM 1040EZ

You may use Form 1040EZ if:

- You are single or married filing a joint return, under age 65, and claim no dependents.
- Your income consisted only of wages, salaries, and tips and not more than $1,500 of taxable interest.
- Your taxable income is less than $100,000.
- You do not itemize deductions or claim any adjustments to income or any tax credits.

Form 1040EZ — Department of the Treasury—Internal Revenue Service — Income Tax Return for Single and Joint Filers With No Dependents (99) — OMB No. 1545-0074

FORM 1040A

This form would be used by people who have less than $100,000 in taxable income from wages, salaries, tips, unemployment compensation, interest, or dividends and use the standard deduction. With Form 1040A, you can also take deductions for individual retirement account (IRA) contributions and a tax credit for child care and dependent care expenses. If you qualify for either Form 1040EZ or Form 1040A, you may wish to use one of them to simplify filing your tax return. You may not want to use either the Form 1040EZ or Form 1040A if Form 1040 allows you to pay less tax.

Form 1040A — Department of the Treasury—Internal Revenue Service — U.S. Individual Income Tax Return (99) — OMB No. 1545-0074

FORM 1040

Form 1040 is an expanded version of Form 1040A that includes sections for all types of income. You are required to use this form if your income is over $100,000 or if you can be claimed as a dependent on your parents' return *and* you had interest or dividends over a set limit.

Form 1040 allows you to itemize your deductions. You can list various allowable expenses (medical costs, home mortgage interest, real estate property taxes) that will reduce taxable income and the amount you owe the government. Consider all the possible adjustments to income, deductions, and tax credits for which you may qualify.

Form 1040 — Department of the Treasury—Internal Revenue Service (99) — U.S. Individual Income Tax Return — OMB No. 1545-0074

FORM 1040X

This form is used to amend a previously filed tax return. If you discover income that was not reported, or if you find additional deductions, you should file Form 1040X to pay the additional tax or obtain a refund.

FORM 1040NR and FORM 1040NR-EZ

These forms are designed for nonresident aliens living in the United States; resident aliens file Form 1040, 1040A, or 1040EZ. The status of a taxpayer may be determined using the 1040NR instructions. Most international students and others not claiming any dependents, and income under $100,000 can use Form 1040NR-EZ. Additional information about these forms is available at www.irs.gov.

FILING STATE INCOME TAX RETURNS

All but seven states (Alaska, Florida, Nevada, South Dakota, Texas, Washington, and Wyoming) have a state income tax. In most states, the tax rate ranges from 1 to 10 percent and is based on some aspect of your federal income tax return, such as adjusted gross income or taxable income. For further information about the income tax in your state, contact the state department of revenue. States usually require income tax returns to be filed when the federal income tax return is due. For help in planning your tax activities, see Exhibit 4-8 on page 137.

Exhibit 4-5 Federal income tax return—Form 1040

1. Your marriage and household situation will affect your taxable income and tax rate.

2. Your earnings and other sources of income will be reported in this section.

3. Adjusted gross income results from certain deductions and will be used as a basis for computing other deductions.

Form **1040** Department of the Treasury—Internal Revenue Service (99)
U.S. Individual Income Tax Return
OMB No. 1545-0074 IRS Use Only—Do not write or staple in this space.
See separate instructions.

Your first name and initial	Last name	Your social security number
Howard M.	Kemp	567 89 1234
If a joint return, spouse's first name and initial	Last name	Spouse's social security number
Julia A.	Kemp	345 67 8912

Home address (number and street). If you have a P.O. box, see instructions. 8901 Arbor Ridge Court — Apt. no.

▲ Make sure the SSN(s) above and on line 6c are correct.

City, town or post office, state, and ZIP code. If you have a foreign address, also complete spaces below (see instructions). Firestone, CO 80520

Foreign country name | Foreign province/state/county | Foreign postal code

Presidential Election Campaign Check here if you, or your spouse if filing jointly, want $3 to go to this fund. Checking a box below will not change your tax or refund. ☐ You ☐ Spouse

Filing Status

Check only one box.

1 ☑ Single
2 ☐ Married filing jointly (even if only one had income)
3 ☐ Married filing separately. Enter spouse's SSN above and full name here. ▶
4 ☐ Head of household (with qualifying person). (See instructions.) If the qualifying person is a child but not your dependent, enter this child's name here. ▶
5 ☐ Qualifying widow(er) with dependent child

Exemptions

6a ☑ **Yourself.** If someone can claim you as a dependent, **do not** check box 6a — Boxes checked on 6a and 6b: 2
b ☑ **Spouse**
c **Dependents:**

(1) First name Last name	(2) Dependent's social security number	(3) Dependent's relationship to you	(4) ✓ if child under age 17 qualifying for child tax credit (see instructions)
Cameron Kemp	123 45 6789	Son	☐
Lewis Kemp	891 23 4567	Son	☐
Ariana Kemp	678 91 2345	Daughter	☐
			☐

No. of children on 6c who: • lived with you: 3 • did not live with you due to divorce or separation (see instructions)
Dependents on 6c not entered above
If more than four dependents, see instructions and check here ▶ ☐
d Total number of exemptions claimed — Add numbers on lines above ▶ 5

Income

Attach Form(s) W-2 here. Also attach Forms W-2G and 1099-R if tax was withheld.

If you did not get a W-2, see instructions.

Enclose, but do not attach, any payment. Also, please use **Form 1040-V.**

Line	Description	Line	Amount
7	Wages, salaries, tips, etc. Attach Form(s) W-2	7	126,205 —
8a	**Taxable** interest. Attach Schedule B if required	8a	315 —
b	**Tax-exempt** interest. **Do not** include on line 8a — 8b		
9a	Ordinary dividends. Attach Schedule B if required	9a	415
b	Qualified dividends — 9b		
10	Taxable refunds, credits, or offsets of state and local income taxes	10	
11	Alimony received	11	
12	Business income or (loss). Attach Schedule C or C-EZ	12	
13	Capital gain or (loss). Attach Schedule D if required. If not required, check here ▶ ☐	13	
14	Other gains or (losses). Attach Form 4797	14	
15a	IRA distributions 15a — b Taxable amount	15b	
16a	Pensions and annuities 16a — b Taxable amount	16b	
17	Rental real estate, royalties, partnerships, S corporations, trusts, etc. Attach Schedule E	17	
18	Farm income or (loss). Attach Schedule F	18	
19	Unemployment compensation	19	
20a	Social security benefits 20a — b Taxable amount	20b	
21	Other income. List type and amount	21	
22	Combine the amounts in the far right column for lines 7 through 21. This is your **total income** ▶	22	126,935 —

Adjusted Gross Income

Line	Description	Line	Amount	Line	Amount
23	Educator expenses	23			
24	Certain business expenses of reservists, performing artists, and fee-basis government officials. Attach Form 2106 or 2106-EZ	24			
25	Health savings account deduction. Attach Form 8889	25			
26	Moving expenses. Attach Form 3903	26			
27	Deductible part of self-employment tax. Attach Schedule SE	27			
28	Self-employed SEP, SIMPLE, and qualified plans	28			
29	Self-employed health insurance deduction	29			
30	Penalty on early withdrawal of savings	30			
31a	Alimony paid b Recipient's SSN ▶	31a			
32	IRA deduction	32	5,000 —		
33	Student loan interest deduction	33			
34	Tuition and fees. Attach Form 8917	34			
35	Domestic production activities deduction. Attach Form 8903	35			
36	Add lines 23 through 35			36	5,000 —
37	Subtract line 36 from line 22. This is your **adjusted gross income** ▶			37	121,935 —

For Disclosure, Privacy Act, and Paperwork Reduction Act Notice, see separate instructions. Cat. No. 11320B Form **1040**

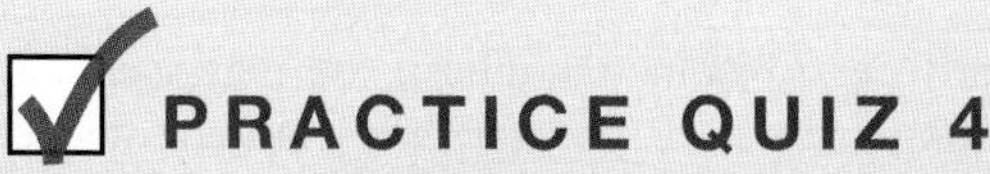

PRACTICE QUIZ 4-3

1. In what ways does your filing status affect preparation of your federal income tax return?
2. What factors affect your choice of a 1040 form?

Exhibit 4-5 continued

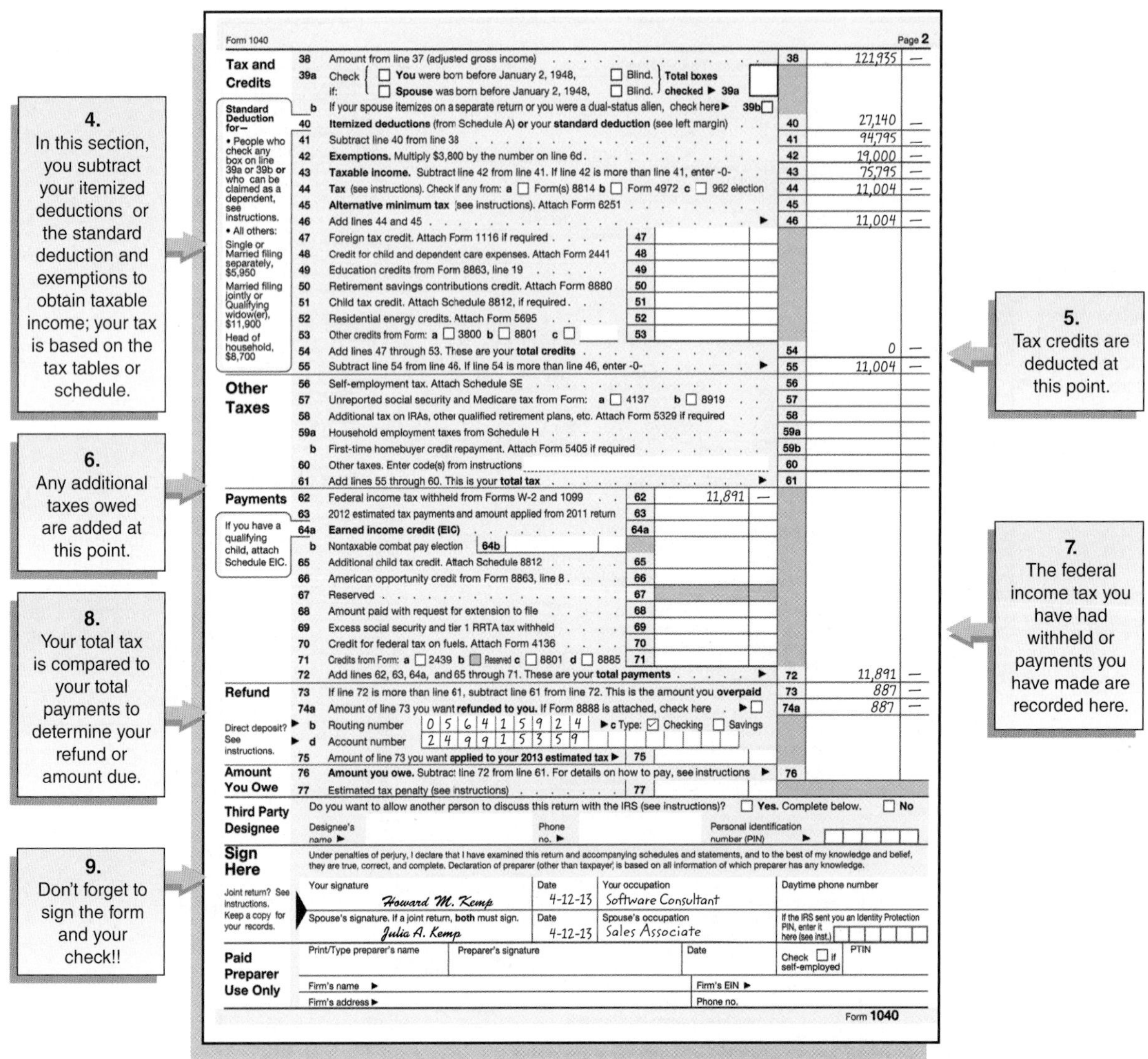

Form 1040 Page **2**

Tax and Credits

Standard Deduction for— • People who check any box on line 39a or 39b **or** who can be claimed as a dependent, see instructions. • All others: Single or Married filing separately, $5,950 Married filing jointly or Qualifying widow(er), $11,900 Head of household, $8,700

Line	Description	Box	Amount	Line	Amount
38	Amount from line 37 (adjusted gross income)			38	121,935 —
39a	Check if: ☐ **You** were born before January 2, 1948, ☐ Blind. ☐ **Spouse** was born before January 2, 1948, ☐ Blind. **Total boxes checked** ▶ 39a ☐				
b	If your spouse itemizes on a separate return or you were a dual-status alien, check here ▶ 39b ☐				
40	**Itemized deductions** (from Schedule A) **or** your **standard deduction** (see left margin)			40	27,140 —
41	Subtract line 40 from line 38			41	94,795 —
42	**Exemptions.** Multiply $3,800 by the number on line 6d			42	19,000 —
43	**Taxable income.** Subtract line 42 from line 41. If line 42 is more than line 41, enter -0-			43	75,795 —
44	**Tax** (see instructions). Check if any from: **a** ☐ Form(s) 8814 **b** ☐ Form 4972 **c** ☐ 962 election			44	11,004 —
45	**Alternative minimum tax** (see instructions). Attach Form 6251			45	
46	Add lines 44 and 45 ▶			46	11,004 —
47	Foreign tax credit. Attach Form 1116 if required	47			
48	Credit for child and dependent care expenses. Attach Form 2441	48			
49	Education credits from Form 8863, line 19	49			
50	Retirement savings contributions credit. Attach Form 8880	50			
51	Child tax credit. Attach Schedule 8812, if required	51			
52	Residential energy credits. Attach Form 5695	52			
53	Other credits from Form: **a** ☐ 3800 **b** ☐ 8801 **c** ☐	53			
54	Add lines 47 through 53. These are your **total credits**			54	0 —
55	Subtract line 54 from line 46. If line 54 is more than line 46, enter -0- ▶			55	11,004 —

Other Taxes

Line	Description	Box	Amount	Line	Amount
56	Self-employment tax. Attach Schedule SE			56	
57	Unreported social security and Medicare tax from Form: **a** ☐ 4137 **b** ☐ 8919			57	
58	Additional tax on IRAs, other qualified retirement plans, etc. Attach Form 5329 if required			58	
59a	Household employment taxes from Schedule H			59a	
b	First-time homebuyer credit repayment. Attach Form 5405 if required			59b	
60	Other taxes. Enter code(s) from instructions			60	
61	Add lines 55 through 60. This is your **total tax** ▶			61	

Payments

If you have a qualifying child, attach Schedule EIC.

Line	Description	Box	Amount	Line	Amount
62	Federal income tax withheld from Forms W-2 and 1099	62	11,891 —		
63	2012 estimated tax payments and amount applied from 2011 return	63			
64a	**Earned income credit (EIC)**	64a			
b	Nontaxable combat pay election 64b				
65	Additional child tax credit. Attach Schedule 8812	65			
66	American opportunity credit from Form 8863, line 8	66			
67	Reserved	67			
68	Amount paid with request for extension to file	68			
69	Excess social security and tier 1 RRTA tax withheld	69			
70	Credit for federal tax on fuels. Attach Form 4136	70			
71	Credits from Form: **a** ☐ 2439 **b** ☐ Reserved **c** ☐ 8801 **d** ☐ 8885	71			
72	Add lines 62, 63, 64a, and 65 through 71. These are your **total payments** ▶			72	11,891 —

Refund

Line	Description	Box	Amount	Line	Amount
73	If line 72 is more than line 61, subtract line 61 from line 72. This is the amount you **overpaid**			73	887 —
74a	Amount of line 73 you want **refunded to you.** If Form 8888 is attached, check here ▶ ☐			74a	887 —
▶ b	Routing number 0 5 6 4 1 5 9 2 4 ▶ **c** Type: ☑ Checking ☐ Savings				
▶ d	Account number 2 4 9 9 1 5 3 5 9				
75	Amount of line 73 you want **applied to your 2013 estimated tax** ▶	75			

Direct deposit? See instructions.

Amount You Owe

Line	Description	Box	Amount	Line	Amount
76	**Amount you owe.** Subtract line 72 from line 61. For details on how to pay, see instructions ▶			76	
77	Estimated tax penalty (see instructions)	77			

Third Party Designee Do you want to allow another person to discuss this return with the IRS (see instructions)? ☐ **Yes.** Complete below. ☐ **No**

Designee's name ▶ Phone no. ▶ Personal identification number (PIN) ▶

Sign Here Under penalties of perjury, I declare that I have examined this return and accompanying schedules and statements, and to the best of my knowledge and belief, they are true, correct, and complete. Declaration of preparer (other than taxpayer) is based on all information of which preparer has any knowledge.

Joint return? See instructions. Keep a copy for your records.

Your signature	Date	Your occupation	Daytime phone number
Howard M. Kemp	4-12-13	Software Consultant	
Spouse's signature. If a joint return, both must sign.	**Date**	**Spouse's occupation**	**If the IRS sent you an Identity Protection PIN, enter it here (see inst.)**
Julia A. Kemp	4-12-13	Sales Associate	

Paid Preparer Use Only

Print/Type preparer's name	Preparer's signature	Date	Check ☐ if self-employed	PTIN
Firm's name ▶		Firm's EIN ▶		
Firm's address ▶		Phone no.		

Form **1040**

Note: These forms were used in a recent year; the current forms may not be exactly the same. Obtain current income tax forms and current tax information from your local IRS office, post office, public library, or at www.irs.gov.

LO4-4

Identify tax assistance sources.

Tax Assistance and the Audit Process

In the process of completing your federal income tax return, you may seek additional information or assistance. After filing your return, you may be identified for a tax audit. If this happens, several policies and procedures protect your rights.

TAX INFORMATION SOURCES

As with other aspects of personal financial planning, many resources are available to assist you with your taxes. The IRS offers a wide variety of services to taxpayers. Libraries and bookstores offer books and other publications that are updated annually.

IRS SERVICES If you wish to do your own tax return or just to expand your knowledge of tax regulations, the IRS has several methods of assistance:

Exhibit 4-6 Schedule A for itemized deductions—Form 1040

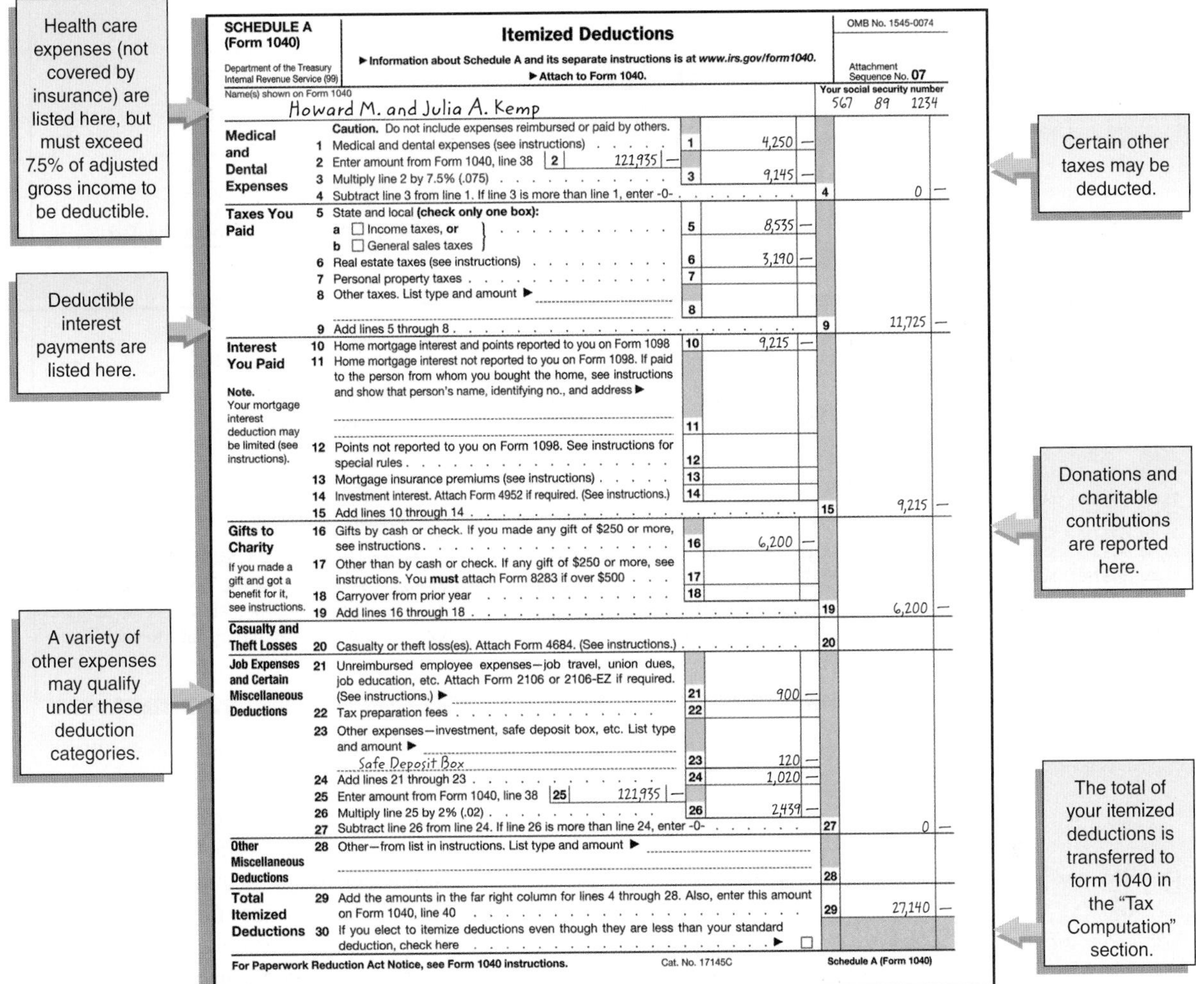

SCHEDULE A (Form 1040) — **Itemized Deductions** — OMB No. 1545-0074

Department of the Treasury, Internal Revenue Service (99) ▶ Information about Schedule A and its separate instructions is at www.irs.gov/form1040. ▶ Attach to Form 1040. Attachment Sequence No. 07

Name(s) shown on Form 1040: Howard M. and Julia A. Kemp — Your social security number: 567 89 1234

Medical and Dental Expenses		Caution. Do not include expenses reimbursed or paid by others.				
	1	Medical and dental expenses (see instructions)	1	4,250 —		
	2	Enter amount from Form 1040, line 38 [2] 121,935 —				
	3	Multiply line 2 by 7.5% (.075)	3	9,145 —		
	4	Subtract line 3 from line 1. If line 3 is more than line 1, enter -0-			4	0 —
Taxes You Paid	5	State and local (check only one box): a ☐ Income taxes, or b ☐ General sales taxes	5	8,535 —		
	6	Real estate taxes (see instructions)	6	3,190 —		
	7	Personal property taxes	7			
	8	Other taxes. List type and amount ▶	8			
	9	Add lines 5 through 8			9	11,725 —
Interest You Paid	10	Home mortgage interest and points reported to you on Form 1098	10	9,215 —		
Note. Your mortgage interest deduction may be limited (see instructions).	11	Home mortgage interest not reported to you on Form 1098. If paid to the person from whom you bought the home, see instructions and show that person's name, identifying no., and address ▶	11			
	12	Points not reported to you on Form 1098. See instructions for special rules	12			
	13	Mortgage insurance premiums (see instructions)	13			
	14	Investment interest. Attach Form 4952 if required. (See instructions.)	14			
	15	Add lines 10 through 14			15	9,215 —
Gifts to Charity	16	Gifts by cash or check. If you made any gift of $250 or more, see instructions	16	6,200 —		
If you made a gift and got a benefit for it, see instructions.	17	Other than by cash or check. If any gift of $250 or more, see instructions. You **must** attach Form 8283 if over $500	17			
	18	Carryover from prior year	18			
	19	Add lines 16 through 18			19	6,200 —
Casualty and Theft Losses	20	Casualty or theft loss(es). Attach Form 4684. (See instructions.)			20	
Job Expenses and Certain Miscellaneous Deductions	21	Unreimbursed employee expenses—job travel, union dues, job education, etc. Attach Form 2106 or 2106-EZ if required. (See instructions.) ▶	21	900 —		
	22	Tax preparation fees	22			
	23	Other expenses—investment, safe deposit box, etc. List type and amount ▶ Safe Deposit Box	23	120 —		
	24	Add lines 21 through 23	24	1,020 —		
	25	Enter amount from Form 1040, line 38 [25] 121,935 —				
	26	Multiply line 25 by 2% (.02)	26	2,439 —		
	27	Subtract line 26 from line 24. If line 26 is more than line 24, enter -0-			27	0 —
Other Miscellaneous Deductions	28	Other—from list in instructions. List type and amount ▶			28	
Total Itemized Deductions	29	Add the amounts in the far right column for lines 4 through 28. Also, enter this amount on Form 1040, line 40			29	27,140 —
	30	If you elect to itemize deductions even though they are less than your standard deduction, check here ▶ ☐				

For Paperwork Reduction Act Notice, see Form 1040 instructions. Cat. No. 17145C Schedule A (Form 1040)

1. *Publications.* The IRS offers hundreds of free booklets and pamphlets. You can obtain these publications at a local IRS office, by mail request, or by a telephone call to the office listed in your tax packet or your local telephone directory. Especially helpful is *Your Federal Income Tax* (IRS Publication 17). You may obtain IRS publications and tax forms by calling 1-800-TAX-FORM, online at www.irs.gov, or by fax at 703-368-9694.
2. *Recorded messages.* The IRS Tele-Tax system allows you access to about 150 telephone tax tips covering everything from filing requirements to reporting gambling income. Your push-button phone gives you 24-hour-a-day access to this recorded information. Telephone numbers can be found in your tax packet or your telephone directory, or call 1-800-829-4477.
3. *Phone hot line.* You can obtain information about specific problems through an IRS-staffed phone line. The appropriate telephone number is listed in your local telephone directory, or call 1-800-829-1040. You are not asked to give your name when you use this service, so your questions are anonymous.
4. *Walk-in service.* You can visit your local or district IRS office to obtain assistance with your taxes. More than 400 of these facilities are available to taxpayers. Be aware, however, that information IRS employees provide is not always reliable. Various studies in recent years have reported incorrect answers over 30 percent of the time. You are still liable for taxes owed even if you based your calculations on information provided by IRS employees.

Exhibit 4-7 Tax tables and tax rate schedules

Tax Table

If line 43 (taxable income) is—		And you are—			
At least	But less than	Single	Married filing jointly *	Married filing separately	Head of a household
		Your tax is—			
75,000					
75,000	**75,050**	14,786	10,816	14,897	13,401
75,050	**75,100**	14,799	10,829	14,911	13,414
75,100	**75,150**	14,811	10,841	14,925	13,426
75,150	**75,200**	14,824	10,854	14,939	13,439
75,200	**75,250**	14,836	10,866	14,953	13,451
75,250	**75,300**	14,849	10,879	14,967	13,464
75,300	**75,350**	14,861	10,891	14,981	13,476
75,350	**75,400**	14,874	10,904	14,995	13,489
75,400	**75,450**	14,886	10,916	15,009	13,501
75,450	**75,500**	14,899	10,929	15,023	13,514
75,500	**75,550**	14,911	10,941	15,037	13,526
75,550	**75,600**	14,924	10,954	15,051	13,539
75,600	**75,650**	14,936	10,966	15,065	13,551
75,650	**75,700**	14,949	10,979	15,079	13,564
75,700	**75,750**	14,961	10,991	15,093	13,576
75,750	**75,800**	14,974	11,004	15,107	13,589
75,800	**75,850**	14,986	11,016	15,121	13,601
75,850	**75,900**	14,999	11,029	15,135	13,614
75,900	**75,950**	15,011	11,041	15,149	13,626
75,950	**76,000**	15,024	11,054	15,163	13,639

* This column must also be used by a qualifying widow(er).

Tax Rate Schedules

Schedule Y-1—If your filing status is **Married filing jointly** or **Qualifying widow(er)**

If your taxable income is: Over—	But not over—	The tax is:	of the amount over—
$0	$17,400	.... 10%	**$0**
17,400	70,700	**$1,740.00 + 15%**	**17,400**
70,700	142,700	**9,735.00 + 25%**	**70,700**
142,700	217,450	**27,735.00 + 28%**	**142,700**
217,450	388,350	**48,665.00 + 33%**	**217,450**
388,350	....	**105,062.00 + 35%**	**388,350**

Use **only** if your taxable income (Form 1040, line 43) is $100,000 or more. If less, use the **Tax Table.** Even though you cannot use the Tax Rate Schedules below if your taxable income is less than $100,000, all levels of taxable income are shown so taxpayers can see the tax rate that applies to each level.

Note: These were the federal income tax rates for a recent year. Current rates may vary due to changes in the tax code and adjustments for inflation. Obtain current income tax booklets from your local IRS office, post office, bank, public library, or at www.irs.gov.

5. *Interactive tax assistant.* The IRS has developed an interactive tool that allows taxpayers to get answers to a number of common as well as challenging questions. The system is designed to ask probing questions based upon a variety of tax laws. This can be a very detailed query that may generate additional questions for the taxpayer to ensure that they are receiving correct information based on their specific question.
6. DVD. The Internal Revenue Service also sells a DVD with over 2,000 tax forms, publications, and frequently asked questions.

In addition, the IRS has videos, free speakers for community groups, and teaching materials for schools to assist taxpayers.

DID YOU KNOW?

Volunteer Income Tax Assistance (VITA) offers free tax help to low- and moderate-income taxpayers who cannot prepare their own tax returns. Certified volunteers provide this service at community centers, libraries, schools, shopping malls, and other locations. Most locations also offer free electronic filing. To locate the nearest VITA site call 1-800-829-1040.

TAX PUBLICATIONS Each year, several tax guides are published and offered for sale. These publications include *J. K. Lasser's Your Income Tax, The Ernst & Young Tax Guide,* and the *U.S. Master Tax Guide.* You can purchase them online or at local stores.

THE INTERNET As with other personal finance topics, extensive information may be found on the Internet. The Internal Revenue Service (www.irs.gov) is a good starting point. Personal finance magazines, such as *Kiplinger's Personal Finance* and *Money,* as well as other financial planning information services, offer a variety of tax information. In addition, the websites of companies that sell tax software and tax-related organizations can be useful.

Exhibit 4-8 Tax-planner calendar

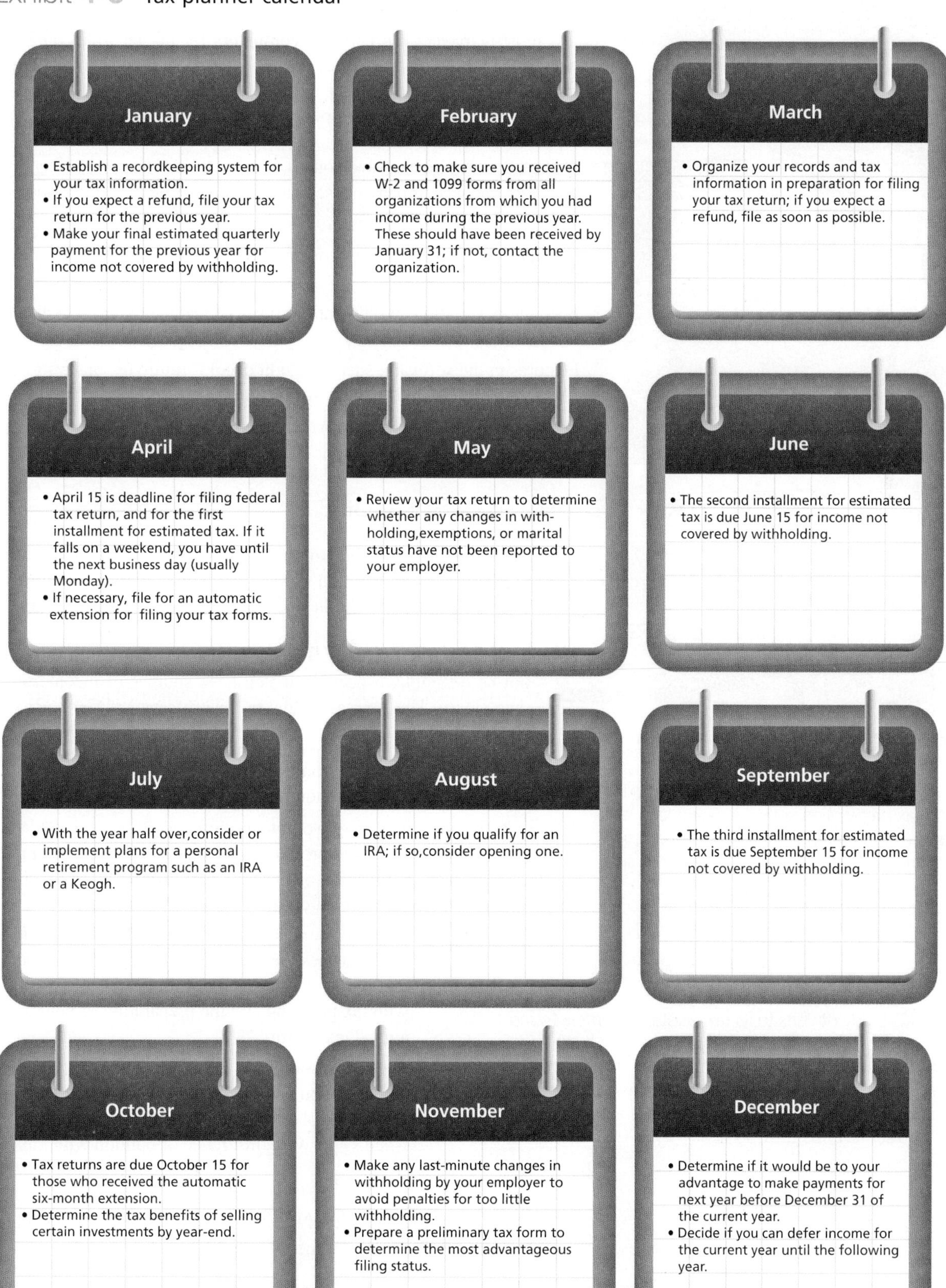

Note: Children born before the end of the year give you a full year exemption, so plan accordingly!

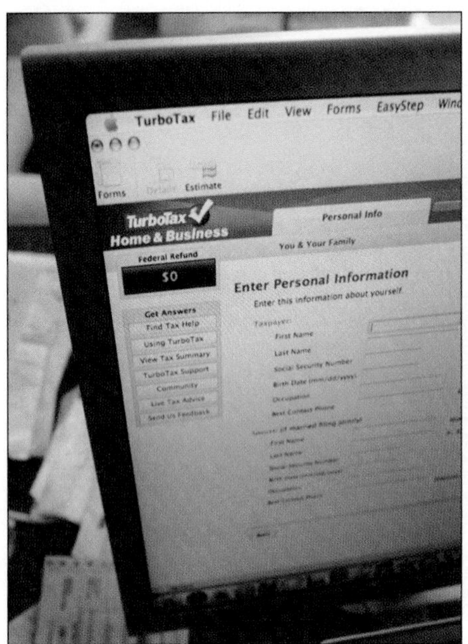

Software can reduce tax return preparation time and effort.

TAX PREPARATION SOFTWARE

Today, most taxpayers use personal computers for tax recordkeeping and tax form preparation. A spreadsheet program can be helpful in maintaining and updating income and expense data. Software packages such as *TaxCut* and *TurboTax* allow you to complete needed tax forms and schedules to either print for mailing or file online.

Using tax software can save you 10 or more hours when preparing your Form 1040 and accompanying schedules. When selecting tax software, consider the following factors:

1. Your personal situation—are you employed or do you operate your own business?
2. Special tax situations with regard to types of income, unusual deductions, and various tax credits.
3. Features in the software, such as "audit check," future tax planning, and filing your federal and state tax forms online.
4. Technical aspects, such as the hardware and operating system requirements, and online support that is provided.

TAX PREPARATION SERVICES

Over 40 million U.S. taxpayers pay someone to do their income taxes. The fee for this service can range from $40 at a tax preparation service for a simple return to more than $2,000 to a certified public accountant for a complicated return.

my life 4

My tax returns have never been questioned by the Internal Revenue Service.

You reduce your chance of a tax audit when using tax preparation software. Conduct a Web search to obtain information about various tax software as well as the cost of these programs.

TYPES OF TAX SERVICES Doing your own taxes may not be desirable, especially if you have sources of income other than salary. The sources available for professional tax assistance include the following:

- Tax services range from local, one-person operations to national firms with thousands of offices, such as H&R Block.
- Enrolled agents—government-approved tax experts—prepare returns and provide tax advice. You may contact the National Association of Enrolled Agents at 1-800-424-4339 for information about enrolled agents in your area.
- Many accountants offer tax assistance along with other business services. A certified public accountant (CPA) with special training in taxes can help with tax planning and the preparation of your annual tax return.
- Attorneys usually do not complete tax returns; however, you can use an attorney's services when you are involved in a tax-related transaction or when you have a difference of opinion with the IRS.

DID YOU KNOW?

An IRS study of visits to its tax assistance centers found that 19 of 26 tax returns (83 percent) had been incorrectly prepared by IRS employees. The agency reported that 17 of the 19 inaccurately prepared fictitious returns would have resulted in incorrect refunds totaling nearly $32,000.

EVALUATING TAX SERVICES When planning to use a tax preparation service, consider these factors:

- What training and experience does the tax professional possess?
- How will the fee be determined? (Avoid preparers who earn a percentage of your refund.)
- Does the preparer suggest you report various deductions that might be questioned?

HOW TO...

File Your Taxes Online

In 2012, over 120 million taxpayers filed returns electronically. The IRS has made online filing easier and in many cases free. There are three main options for filing electronically.

OPTION 1-*FREE FILE*

In 2012, If your income is $57,000 or less, you are eligible to use Free File which includes free tax preparation and free e-filing through a list of predetermined companies.

- Go to the "Free File" page at www.irs.gov and select "Pick a Free File Company." This will take you to a list of companies including descriptions and any limitations of their services. After you determine your eligibility for a particular company, select the link for the company's website.
- The online sites and tax software will guide you through the steps of the process. You will be prompted to enter your personal data, income amounts, deductions, and tax information.
- After you have ensured that all relevant information has been entered, you are ready to submit your federal tax form online. You will usually receive an e-mail confirmation of your submission, and your refund will be processed within two weeks.
- Be aware: Free e-file services may not include preparation of your state tax return.

OPTION 2-*E-FILE*

- The IRS offers a "Free File Fillable Forms" option. This option is available primarily for taxpayers whose income exceeds the income limitations for Free File. This may also be used by a taxpayer who attempted the Free File process and encountered additional fees or issues based on additional forms needed to complete their return. Quick, online access is available for the most commonly filed federal tax forms and schedules.
- It is strongly recommended that you print out relevant forms and perform necessary calculations prior to using this option. This will help to ensure accuracy and reduce the need to amend your return in the future.

OPTION 3-*PAID PREPARER E-FILE (OR PURCHASED SOFTWARE)*

- Most tax preparation software and paid preparers now offer e-filing as part of their service. If you purchase a tax preparation software tool, you will be able to connect directly through the software to electronically file your return. In addition, paid preparers that prepare more than 10 individual returns are now required by the IRS to electronically file returns.

- Will the preparer represent you if your return is audited?
- Is tax preparation the main business activity, or does it serve as a front for selling other financial products and services?

Additional information about tax preparers may be obtained at the websites for the National Association of Enrolled Agents (www.naea.org) and the National Association of Tax Professionals (www.natptax.com).

TAX SERVICE WARNINGS Even if you hire a professional tax preparer, you are responsible for supplying accurate and complete information. Hiring a tax preparer will not guarantee that you pay the *correct* amount. A study conducted by *Money* magazine of 41 tax preparers reported fees ranging from $375 to $3,600, with taxes due ranging from $31,846 to $74,450 for the same fictional family. If you owe more tax because

TAX SCAM WARNINGS FROM THE IRS

Alan Newell was attracted to the idea of reducing his taxes by running a business out of his home. However, the bogus home-based business promoted in an online advertisement did not qualify for a "home office" deduction.

Vanessa Elliott liked the idea of increasing the refund she would receive from her federal income tax return. For a fee, she would be informed of additional tax deductions to lower her taxable income. Vanessa avoided the offer since the refund was promised without any knowledge of her tax situation.

Ken Turner was informed that he had won a prize that required payment of the income tax on the item before it would be shipped to him. While taxes are usually due on large prizes, the amount would not be paid until later.

Fortunately, Alan, Vanessa, and Ken did not fall for these deceptive offers. These three situations are some of the many common tax scams that cost consumers billions of dollars each year. The Internal Revenue Service warns taxpayers to never give out personal and financial information without proper identification by the IRS employee.

Each year, the IRS releases its annual list of the "Dirty Dozen Tax Scams." This is a listing of the most prevalent tax scams that have occurred in the past year. For 2013, a portion of the listing includes:

IDENTITY OR FINANCIAL THEFT

- An official-looking, but phony, letter or e-mail is sent in an attempt to trick a taxpayer into disclosing personal information and bank account numbers. This is also referred to as *phishing*. The most common tactic is informing a person that they are entitled to a tax refund from the IRS. This usually requires that the recipient reveal personal information to claim the money. During 2012, the IRS prevented the issuance of $20 billion of fraudulent refunds, including those related to identity theft.

RETURN PREPARER FRAUD

- Due to complex tax laws, nearly 60 percent of taxpayers hire someone to prepare their tax returns. Incidence of refund fraud and identity theft due to unscrupulous preparers is on the rise. One important reminder is that preparers should always sign the tax returns and enter their IRS Preparer Tax Identification Numbers (PTINs).

SOCIAL SECURITY OR TAX RETURN "FREE MONEY"

- An offer to obtain a refund of the Social Security taxes paid during a person's lifetime. The taxpayer is asked to pay a "paperwork" fee of $100. The law does not allow such a refund. Schemes that promise large refunds or "free money" to people with little or no income and those that would normally not have a filing requirement have also been on the rise.

CHARITABLE ORGANIZATIONS FRAUD

- Due to the prevalence of natural disasters over the past years, scam artists have spent a lot of effort impersonating charities to get money as well as private information. This may include phone calls or e-mail solicitations. The IRS recommends donating to recognized charities. Also, don't give or send cash.

As with any fraud, consumers should be cautious. The opportunity to make fast money can end up being very expensive. Information about misuse of IRS insignia, seals, and symbols as well as to identify theft related to taxes may be obtained at www.ustreas.gov/tigta. Suspected tax fraud can be reported using IRS Form 3949-A, which is available at IRS.gov, or by calling 1-800-829-3676.

Source: "Dirty Dozen Tax Scams," www.irs.gov

your return contains errors or you have made entries that are not allowed, it is your responsibility to pay that additional tax, plus any interest and penalties.

Beware of tax preparers and other businesses that offer your refund in advance. These "refund anticipation loans" frequently charge very high interest rates for this type of consumer credit. Studies reveal interest rates sometimes exceeding 300 percent (on an annualized basis).

WHAT IF YOUR RETURN IS AUDITED?

The Internal Revenue Service reviews all returns for completeness and accuracy. If you make an error, your tax is automatically refigured and you receive either a bill or a refund. If you make an entry that is not allowed, you will be notified by mail.

Exhibit 4-9 How to avoid common filing errors

- Organize all tax-related information for easy access.
- Follow instructions carefully. Many people deduct total medical and dental expenses rather than the amount of these expenses that exceeds 7.5 percent of adjusted gross income. (10 percent starting in 2013)
- Use the proper tax rate schedule or tax table column.
- Be sure to claim the correct number of exemptions and the correct amounts of standard deductions.
- Consider the alternative minimum tax that may apply to your situation. Be sure to pay self-employment tax and tax on early IRA withdrawals.
- Check your math and accuracy of software data entries several times.
- Sign your return (both spouses must sign a joint return), or the IRS won't process it.
- Be sure to include the correct Social Security number(s) and to record amounts on the correct lines.
- Attach necessary documentation, such as your W-2 forms and required supporting schedules.
- Make the check payable to "United States Treasury."
- Put your Social Security number, the tax year, and a daytime telephone number on your check—and be sure to sign the check!
- Keep a copy of your return.
- Put the proper postage on your mailing envelope.
- Finally, check everything again—and file on time! Care taken when you file your income tax can result in "many happy returns."

A **tax audit** is a detailed examination of your tax return by the IRS. In most audits, the IRS requests more information to support the entries on your tax return. Be sure to keep accurate records to support your return. Keep receipts, canceled checks, and other evidence to prove amounts that you claim. Avoiding common filing mistakes (see Exhibit 4-9) helps to minimize your chances of an audit.

tax audit A detailed examination of your tax return by the Internal Revenue Service.

WHO GETS AUDITED? About 1 percent of all tax filers—1.4 million people—are audited each year. While the IRS does not reveal its basis for auditing returns, several indicators are evident. People who claim large or unusual deductions increase their chances of an audit.

Tax advisers suggest including a brief explanation or a copy of receipts for deductions that may be questioned. Individuals with high incomes who report large losses due to tax shelters or partnerships, or who have had their tax returns questioned in the past, may also be targeted for an audit.

TYPES OF AUDITS The simplest and most common type of audit is the *correspondence audit.* This mail inquiry requires you to clarify or document minor questions about your tax return. You usually have 30 days to provide the requested information.

The *office audit* requires you to visit an IRS office to clarify some aspect of your tax return. This type of audit usually takes an hour or two.

The *field audit* is more complex. An IRS agent visits you at your home, your business, or the office of your accountant to have access to your records. A field audit may be done to verify whether an individual has an office in the home as claimed.

The IRS also conducts more detailed audits for about 50,000 taxpayers. These range from random requests to document various tax return items to line-by-line reviews by IRS employees.

DID YOU KNOW?

The *Sacramento Bee* reported that Aaron Zeff, of Sacramento, California, was visited by IRS agents to collect delinquent taxes amounting to . . . 4 cents! While he sent in checks to cover $202.31 in interest and penalties, the late payment wiped out all but 4 cents of the tax obligation. Zeff did not understand why he was never informed of the late payment due before he was visited by the agents.

YOUR AUDIT RIGHTS When you receive an audit notice, you have the right to request time to prepare. Also, you can ask the IRS for clarification of items being questioned. When you are audited, use the following suggestions:

- Decide whether you will bring your tax preparer, accountant, or lawyer.
- Be on time for your appointment; bring only relevant documents.
- Present tax records and receipts in a logical, calm, and confident manner; maintain a positive attitude.
- Make sure the information you present is consistent with the tax law.
- Keep your answers aimed at the auditor's questions. Answer questions clearly and completely. Be as brief as possible; you can never tell an auditor too little.

People under stress tend to talk too much. IRS auditors are trained to create silence and listen in case the taxpayer blurts out damaging information. The five best responses to questions during an audit are "Yes," "No," "I don't recall," "I'll have to check on that," and "What specific items do you want to see?"

If you disagree with the results of an audit, you may request a conference at the Regional Appeals Office. Although most differences of opinion are settled at this stage, some taxpayers take their cases further. A person may go to the U.S. tax court, the U.S. claims court, or the U.S. district court. Some tax disputes have gone to the U.S. Supreme Court.

Income tax preparer comparison

PRACTICE QUIZ 4-4

1 What are the main sources available to help people prepare their taxes?
2 What actions can reduce the chances of an IRS audit?
3 What appeal process do taxpayers have if they disagree with an audit decision of the IRS?

Tax Planning Strategies

LO4-5

Select appropriate tax strategies for various financial and personal situations.

Most people want to pay their fair share of taxes—no more, no less. They do this by practicing **tax avoidance,** the use of legitimate methods to reduce one's taxes. In contrast, **tax evasion** is the use of illegal actions to reduce one's taxes. To minimize taxes owed, follow these guidelines:

- If you expect to have the *same* or a *lower* tax rate next year, *accelerate deductions* into the current year. Pay real estate property taxes or make your January mortgage payment in December. Make charitable donations by December 31.

Exhibit 4-10 Special tax situations

Business in your home	• You may deduct any ordinary and necessary expenses related to starting and maintaining your business, including a portion of your rent or mortgage if that portion of your home is used exclusively for business. • It must be your principal place of business. (Individuals who are employed elsewhere and claim an office at home are likely to be challenged by the IRS on this deduction.)
Divorced persons	• Child support payments have no tax consequences. They are neither deductible by the payer nor included in the recipient's income. • Alimony is tax deductible by the payer and must be included as income by the recipient. • Exemptions for children are generally claimed by the parent who has custody for a longer period during the tax year.
Single parents	• A single parent may claim "head of household" filing status, which has greater advantages than "single" status. • Working parents may qualify for a child care tax credit. • Low-income families may qualify for the earned-income credit (EIC).
Retired persons	• Individuals over age 59½ may withdraw tax-deferred funds from a retirement plan without penalty. Of course, these funds must be reported as ordinary income. • As of 2012, retirees with total incomes, including Social Security, exceeding \$44,000 (couples) and \$34,000 (singles) pay income tax on up to 85 percent of their Social Security benefits. Those with incomes between \$25,000 and \$34,000 (singles) or \$32,000 and \$44,000 (couples) continue to be taxed on up to 50 percent of their benefits.

Note: Individual circumstances and changes in the tax laws can affect these examples.

- If you expect to have a *lower* or the *same* tax rate next year, *delay the receipt of income* until next year. This means income will be taxed at a lower rate or at a later date.
- If you expect to have a *higher* tax rate next year, consider *delaying deductions,* since they will have a greater benefit. A \$1,000 deduction at 28 percent lowers your taxes \$280; at 33 percent, your taxes are lowered \$330.
- If you expect to have a *higher* tax rate next year, *accelerate the receipt of income* to have it taxed at the current lower rate.

tax avoidance The use of legitimate methods to reduce one's taxes.

tax evasion The use of illegal actions to reduce one's taxes.

As Exhibit 4-10 shows, people in different life situations can take advantage of various tax rules. When considering financial decisions in relation to your taxes, remember that purchasing, investing, and retirement planning are the areas most heavily affected by tax laws.

CONSUMER PURCHASING

The buying decisions most directly affected by taxes are the purchase of a residence, the use of credit, and job-related expenses.

PLACE OF RESIDENCE Owning a home is one of the best tax shelters. Both real estate property taxes and interest on the mortgage are deductible (as itemized deductions) and thus reduce your taxable income. While renting may seem less expensive than owning, the after-tax cost of owning a home often makes owning financially advantageous. Chapter 9 presents specific calculations for comparing renting and buying.

CONSUMER DEBT Current tax laws allow homeowners to borrow for consumer purchases. You can deduct interest on loans (of up to $100,000) secured by your primary or secondary home up to the actual dollar amount you have invested in it—the difference between the market value of the home and the amount you owe on it. These *home equity loans,* which are *second mortgages,* are discussed in greater detail in Chapters 6 and 9. Current tax laws allow you to use that line of credit to buy a car, consolidate credit card or other debts, or finance other personal expenses. Some states place restrictions on home equity loans. A person may also claim a deduction for interest expense on qualified education loans.

JOB-RELATED EXPENSES As previously mentioned, certain work expenses, such as union dues, some travel and education costs, and business tools, may be included as itemized deductions. Job search expenses are also deductible if you incur them when seeking employment in your current occupational category. Such expenses may include transportation to interviews, résumé preparation and duplication, and employment agency or career counseling fees. Remember, only the portion of these expenses that exceeds 2 percent of adjusted gross income is deductible. Expenses related to finding your first job or obtaining work in a different field are not deductible.

HEALTH CARE EXPENSES *Flexible spending accounts (FSA),* a type of health savings account, allow you to reduce your taxable income when paying for medical expenses or child care costs. Workers are allowed to put pretax dollars into these employer-sponsored programs. These "deposits" result in a lower taxable income. Then, the funds in the FSA may be used to pay for various medical expenses and dependent care costs. A drawback of the FSA is that any account funds must be used to pay for expenses incurred before year's end or the money is lost.

DID YOU KNOW?

Each year, over 90,000 taxpayers do not receive their refunds. The undeliverable checks total over $60 million, an average of more than $600 per check. These refund checks were returned by the post office because it was unable to deliver them. Taxpayers due a refund may contact the IRS at 1-800-829-1040.

INVESTMENT DECISIONS

A major area of tax planning involves the wide variety of decisions related to investing.

TAX-EXEMPT INVESTMENTS Interest income from municipal bonds, which are issued by state and local governments, and other tax-exempt investments is not subject to federal income taxes. While municipal bonds have lower interest rates than other investments, the *after-tax* income may be higher. For example, if you are in the 28 percent tax bracket, earning $100 of tax-exempt income would be worth more to you than earning $125 in taxable investment income. The $125 would have an after-tax value of $90: $125 less $35 (28 percent of $125) for taxes. Interest on EE savings bonds is exempt from federal income tax if it is used to pay tuition at a college, university, or qualified technical school. Chapter 5 gives further details.

TAX-DEFERRED INVESTMENTS Although, from a tax standpoint, tax-deferred investments, whose income will be taxed at a later date, are less beneficial than tax-exempt investments, they also have financial advantages. According to basic opportunity cost, paying a dollar in the future instead of today gives you the opportunity to invest (or spend) it now. Examples of tax-deferred investments include

- *Tax-deferred annuities,* usually issued by insurance companies. These investments are discussed in Chapter 19.
- *Section 529 savings plans* are state-run, tax-deferred plans to set aside money for a child's education. The 529 is like a prepaid tuition plan in which you invest to cover future education costs. The 529 plans differ from state to state.
- *Retirement plans* such as IRA, Keogh, or 401(k) plans. The next section discusses the tax implications of these plans.

Capital gains, profits from the sale of a capital asset such as stocks, bonds, or real estate, are also tax deferred; you do not have to pay the tax on these profits until the asset is sold. *Long-term* capital gains (on investments held more than a year) will be taxed at a rate that is lower than ordinary income. For 2013, the rates are as follows:

capital gains Profits from the sale of a capital asset such as stocks, bonds, or real estate

Current Tax Bracket	Capital Gain Tax Rate
10% & 15%	0%
25%, 28%, 33%, 35%	15%
39.6%	20%

Certain assets, however, such as art, antiques, stamps, and other collectibles, are taxed at 28 percent.

Short-term capital gains (on investments held for less than a year) are taxed as ordinary income (see the Financial Planning Calculations box on page 146).

The sale of an investment for less than its purchase price is, of course, a *capital loss.* Capital losses can be used to offset capital gains and up to $3,000 of ordinary income. Unused capital losses may be carried forward into future years to offset capital gains or ordinary income up to $3,000 per year.

Capital gains of $500,000 on the sale of a home may be excluded by a couple filing a joint return ($250,000 for singles). This exclusion is allowed each time a taxpayer sells or exchanges a principal residence—however, only once every two years.

SELF-EMPLOYMENT Owning your own business has certain tax advantages. Self-employed persons may deduct expenses such as health and life insurance as business costs. However, business owners have to pay self-employment tax (Social Security) in addition to the regular tax rate.

CHILDREN'S INVESTMENTS In past years, parents made investments on their children's behalf and listed the children as owners. This process, known as *income shifting,* attempted to reduce the taxable income of parents by shifting the ownership of investments to children in lower tax brackets. A child under 18 with investment income of more than $1,900 (as of 2013) is taxed at the parent's top rate. For investment income under $1,900, the child receives a deduction of $950 and the next $950 is taxed at his or her own rate, which is probably lower than the parent's rate. This income-shifting restriction does not apply to those 19 and older, so it is not possible to take advantage of income shifting with them.

RETIREMENT AND EDUCATION PLANS

A major tax strategy is the use of tax-deferred retirement and education plans such as individual retirement arrangements (IRAs), Keogh plans, 401(k) plans, and education savings accounts.

SHORT-TERM AND LONG-TERM CAPITAL GAINS

You will pay a lower tax rate on the profits from stocks and other investments if you hold the asset for more than 12 months. As of 2013, a taxpayer in the 28 percent tax bracket would pay $420 in taxes on a $1,500 short-term capital gain (assets held for less than a year). However, that same taxpayer would pay only $225 on the $1,500 (a 15 percent capital gains tax) if the investment were held for more than a year.

	Short-Term Capital Gain (assets held less than a year)	Long-Term Capital Gain (assets held a year or more)
Capital gain	$1,500	$1,500
Capital gains tax rate	28%	15%
Capital gains tax	$420	$225
Tax savings		$195

my life 5

I stay informed on proposed tax changes being considered for my current tax filing status.

Your attempts to continually update your knowledge of income taxes will help you make better informed financial decisions. Ask several people about the actions they take to stay informed and to reduce the amount paid in taxes.

TRADITIONAL IRA When IRAs were first established, every working person was allowed to deduct up to $2,000 per year for IRA contributions. The contributions to and earnings from these accounts are not taxed until they are withdrawn. Today the regular IRA deduction is available only to people who do not participate in employer-sponsored retirement plans or who have an adjusted gross income under a certain amount. As of 2013, the IRA contribution limit was $5,500. Older workers, age 50 and over, are allowed to contribute up to $6,500 as a "catch up" to make up for lost time saving for retirement.

In general, amounts withdrawn from deductible IRAs are included in gross income. An additional 10 percent penalty is usually imposed on withdrawals made before age 59½ unless the withdrawn funds are on account of death or disability, for medical expenses, or for qualified higher education expenses.

Variations of the IRA include the Simplified Employee Pension (SEP) Plan and the Savings Incentive Match Plans for Employees (SIMPLE Plans). These plans are designed for people who are self-employed and small business owners.

ROTH IRA The Roth IRA also allows a $5,500 (as of 2013) annual contribution, which is not tax deductible; however, the earnings on the account are tax free after five years. The funds from the Roth IRA may be withdrawn before age 59½ if the account owner is disabled, or for the purchase of a first home ($10,000 maximum).

Deductible IRAs provide tax relief up front as contributions reduce current taxes. However, taxes must be paid when the withdrawals are made from the deductible IRA. In contrast, the Roth IRA does not have immediate benefits, but the investment grows in value on a tax-free basis. Withdrawals from the Roth IRA are exempt from federal and state taxes.

COVERDELL EDUCATION SAVINGS ACCOUNT The Education Savings Account is designed to assist parents in saving for the education of their children. Once again, the annual contribution (limited to $2,000) is not tax deductible and is limited to taxpayers with an adjusted gross income under a certain amount. However, as with the Roth IRA, the earnings accumulate tax free.

529 PLAN The 529 plan is another type of education savings plan that helps parents save for the college education of their children. Almost every state has a 529 plan available. There is no federal tax deduction, but the earnings grow tax free and there are no taxes when the money is taken out of the account for qualified educational expenses. In addition, you do not have to invest in the plan for your home state, but there may be tax advantages in doing so. Many states allow their residents to deduct contributions to their state plans up to a specified maximum. Make sure to check out the investment choices and performance before investing.

KEOGH PLAN If you are self-employed and own your own business, you can establish a Keogh plan. This retirement plan, also called an HR10 plan, may combine a profit-sharing plan and a pension plan of other investments purchased by the employee. In general, with a Keogh, people may contribute 25 percent of their annual income, up to a maximum of $51,000 (as of 2013), to this tax-deferred retirement plan.

401(K) PLAN The part of the tax code called 401(k) authorizes a tax-deferred retirement plan sponsored by an employer. This plan allows you to contribute a greater tax-deferred amount ($17,500 in 2013) than you can contribute to an IRA. Older workers, age 50 and over, are allowed to contribute up to $23,000. However, most companies set a limit on your contribution, such as 15 percent of your salary. Many employers provide a matching contribution in their 401(k) plans. For example, a company may contribute 50 cents for each $1 contributed by an employee up to a certain percentage of income. This results in an immediate 50 percent return on your investment.

Tax planners advise people to contribute as much as possible to a Keogh or 401(k) plan since (1) the increased value of the investment accumulates on a tax-free basis until the funds are withdrawn and (2) contributions reduce your adjusted gross income for computing your current tax liability. Chapter 18 discusses retirement plans in greater detail.

TAX-SAVINGS STRATEGIES: A SUMMARY

Someone once said that "death and taxes are the only certainties of life." Changing tax laws seem to be another certainty. Each year, the IRS modifies the tax form and filing procedures. In addition, Congress often passes legislation that changes the tax code. These changes require that you regularly determine how to take best advantage of the tax laws for personal financial planning. Some guidelines to consider when selecting effective personal tax strategies include the following:

- Time the receipt of income and payment of taxable expenses in relation to your current and future tax rate.
- Take advantage of tax credits for which you qualify.
- Maximize contributions to tax-deferred retirement programs.
- Consider tax-exempt investments, such as municipal bonds.
- Defer capital gains and accelerate capital losses.
- Take advantage of the tax benefits of owning your own business.
- Plan purchases, such as a house or health care, with tax implications in mind.
- Search out all possible itemized deductions.

Carefully monitor your personal tax strategies to best serve both your daily living needs and your long-term financial goals.

Tax planning activities

PRACTICE QUIZ 4-5

1 How does tax avoidance differ from tax evasion?

2 What common tax-saving methods are available to most individuals and households?

my life stages for tax planning

YOUR PERSONAL FINANCE DASHBOARD

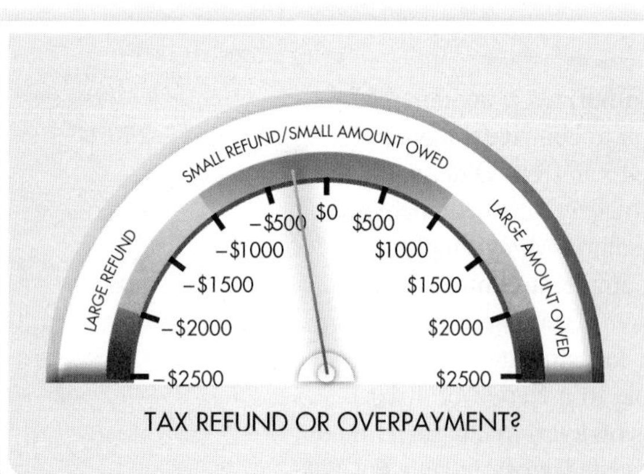

Another indicator of your financial health is your ability to organize and prepare key documents to maximize your tax situation. Whether you prepare your tax return or take it to someone to prepare, you need to have all of the key documents to pay your "fair share." You also need to monitor your tax situation throughout the year. This means understanding your tax situation and being aware of any changes.

YOUR SITUATION Do you owe taxes each year? Do you receive an excessive tax refund? Other personal financial planning actions you might consider during various stages of your life include:

... in college

- Maintain a system for tax documents
- Estimate a suitable withholding amount to avoid a large refund or large amount owed
- Develop an understanding for preparing your own tax return

... in my 20s

- Sign up for your employer's tax-deferred retirement plan
- Consider buying a home or other actions for possible tax savings
- Revise withholding amounts based on family changes

... in my 30s and 40s

- Consider increased contributions to tax-deferred retirement plans
- Investigate various tax-exempt investments
- Research tax credits for which you may qualify

... in my 50s and beyond

- Contribute larger "catch up" amounts to retirement plan
- Assess financial and tax implications of withdrawals from tax-deferred retirement plans
- Determine age at which Social Security benefits will start

SUMMARY OF LEARNING OBJECTIVES

LO4-1

Describe the importance of taxes for personal financial planning.

Your knowledge of the varied taxes paid in our society will provide an understanding of your tax planning, which can influence spending, saving, borrowing, and investing decisions. Knowing tax laws and maintaining accurate tax records allows you to take advantage of appropriate tax benefits. An awareness of income taxes, sales taxes, excise taxes, property taxes, estate taxes, inheritance taxes, gift taxes, and Social Security taxes is vital for successful financial planning.

LO4-2

Calculate taxable income and the amount owed for federal income tax.

Organized tax records allow you to easily find needed information when calculating taxable income, which is determined by subtracting adjustments to income, deductions, and allowances for exemptions from gross income. Your total tax liability is based on the published tax tables or tax schedules, less any tax credits.

LO4-3

Prepare a federal income tax return.

To file your taxes on time each year requires that you understand the major sections of Form 1040, which are (1) your filing status, (2) exemptions, (3) income from all sources, (4) adjustments to your income, (5) standard deduction or itemized deductions, (6) tax credits for which you qualify, (7) other taxes you owe, (8) amounts you have withheld or paid in advance, and (9) your refund or the additional amount you owe.

LO4-4

Identify tax assistance sources.

You reduce questions by the Internal Revenue Service about your tax return by using the main sources of tax assistance: IRS services and publications, other tax publications, the Internet, computer software, and professional tax preparers such as commercial tax services, enrolled agents, accountants, and attorneys.

LO4-5

Select appropriate tax strategies for different financial and personal situations.

Learning new tax information may reduce your tax burden when you carefully plan financial decisions related to consumer purchasing, debt, investments, and retirement planning.

KEY TERMS

adjusted gross income (AGI) 122
average tax rate 126
capital gains 145
earned income 120
estate tax 119
excise tax 118
exclusion 120
exemption 124
inheritance tax 119
investment income 120
itemized deductions 122
marginal tax rate 125
passive income 120
standard deduction 122
taxable income 120
tax audit 141
tax avoidance 142
tax credit 127
tax deduction 122
tax-deferred income 120
tax evasion 142
tax-exempt income 120
tax shelter 121

SELF-TEST PROBLEMS

1. A person had $3,245 withheld for federal income taxes, and had a tax liability of $3,400. Would this be a refund or an additional amount due for what amount?
2. Based on the following information, what is the amount of taxable income?

Gross salary	$62,155	Interest earnings	$200
Dividend income	$145	One personal exemption	$3,900
Itemized deductions	$10,200		

Answers to Self-Test Problems

1. To determine the amount of refund or additional tax due, compare the amount of tax liability with the amount withheld. The $3,400 tax liability minus the $3,245 would result in an additional tax due of $155.
2. Taxable income is calculated by adding salary, income, and dividends, and then subtracting itemized deductions and exemptions. $62,155 + $200 + $145 − $3,900 − $10,200 = $48,400

FINANCIAL PLANNING PROBLEMS

LO4-2 1. *Computing Taxable Income.* Ross Martin arrived at the following tax information:

Gross salary, $52,145

Interest earnings, $205

Dividend income, $65

One personal exemption, $3,900

Itemized deductions, $9,250

Adjustments to income, $1,200

What amount would Ross report as taxable income?

LO4-2 2. *Determining Tax Deductions.* If Lola Harper had the following itemized deductions, should she use Schedule A or the standard deduction? The standard deduction for her tax situation is $6,100.

Donations to church and other charities, $2,050

Medical and dental expenses exceeding 10 percent of adjusted gross income, $330

State income tax, $690

Job-related expenses exceeding 2 percent of adjusted gross income, $1,610

LO4-2 3. *Calculating Tax Deductions.* Kaye Blanchard is 72 years old. She has $30,000 of adjusted gross income and $8,000 of qualified medical expenses. She will be itemizing her tax deductions this year. How much of a tax deduction will Kaye be able to deduct?

LO4-2 4. *Comparing Tax Deductions and Credits.* Imari Brown is attending community college. She has $1,000 of education expenses. She claims herself on her tax return. She is trying to decide between the tuition and fees deduction or an education credit. If Imari is in the 15% tax bracket, which should she choose?

LO4-2 5. *Calculating Average Tax Rate.* What would be the average tax rate for a person who paid taxes of $4,864.14 on a taxable income of $39,870?

LO4-2 6. *Determining a Refund or Taxes Owed.* Based on the following data, would Ann and Carl Wilton receive a refund or owe additional taxes?

Adjusted gross income: $46,686

Itemized deductions: $11,420

Child care tax credit: $80

Federal income tax withheld: $4,784

Amount for personal exemptions: $7,300

Tax rate on taxable income: 15 percent

LO4-2 7. *Indexing Exemptions for Inflation.* Each year, the Internal Revenue Service adjusts the value of an exemption based on inflation (and rounds to the nearest $50). In a recent year, if the exemption was worth $3,800 and inflation was 2.7 percent, what would be the amount of the exemption for the upcoming tax year?

LO4-2 8. *Determining a Tax Refund.* If $4,026 was withheld during the year and taxes owed were $4,050, would the person owe an additional amount or receive a refund? What is the amount?

LO4-2 9. *Opportunity Cost of Tax Refunds.* If 400,000 people each receive an average refund of $2,400, based on an interest rate of 4 percent, what would be the lost annual income from savings on those refunds?

10. *Selecting Federal Tax Forms.* Which 1040 form should each of the following individuals use? L04-3

a. A high school student with an after-school job and interest earnings of $480 from savings accounts.

b. A college student who, due to ownership of property, is able to itemize deductions rather than take the standard deduction.

c. A young, entry-level worker with no dependents and income only from salary.

11. *Using Federal Tax Tables.* Using the tax table in Exhibit 4-7, determine the amount of taxes for the following situations: L04-3

a. A head of household with taxable income of $75,750.

b. A single person with taxable income of $75,052.

c. A married person filing a separate return with taxable income of $75,926.

12. *Comparing Taxes on Investments.* Would you prefer a fully taxable investment earning 8.1 percent or a tax-exempt investment earning 6.1 percent? (Assume a 28 percent tax rate) Why? L04-5

13. *Capital Gains.* Samuel Jenkins made two investments, the first was 13 months ago and the second was two months ago. He just sold both investments and has capital gain of $2,000 on each. If Samuel is in the 28 percent tax bracket, what will be the amount of capital gains tax on each investment? L04-5

14. *Future Value of a Tax Savings.* On December 30, you decide to make a $1,500 charitable donation. If you are in the 28 percent tax bracket, how much will you save in taxes for the current year? If you deposit that tax savings in a savings account for the next five years at 4 percent, what will be the future value of that account? L04-5

15. *Tax Deferred Retirement Benefits.* If a person with a 28 percent tax bracket makes a deposit of $5,000 to a tax deferred retirement account, what amount would be saved on current taxes? L04-5

FINANCIAL PLANNING ACTIVITIES

1. *Searching the Web for Tax Information.* Using websites such as www.quicken.com, *Kiplinger's Personal Finance* at www.kiplinger.com, or *Money* magazine at www.money.com, or library resources, obtain information about the tax implications of various financial planning decisions. L04-1

2. *Planning Your Tax Payment.* Survey several people about whether they get a federal tax refund or owe taxes each year. Obtain information about the following: (*a*) Do they usually get a refund or owe taxes when they file their federal tax return? (*b*) Is their situation (refund or payment) planned? (*c*) What are the reasons they want to get a refund each year? (*d*) Are there situations where getting a refund may not be a wise financial decision? L04-2

3. *Researching Tax Exempt Income.* Using library resources or an Internet search, determine the types of income that are exempt from federal income tax. L04-2

4. *Errors on Tax Returns.* Survey several people about whether they have received notices regarding errors on their tax returns. What are some of the more common errors encountered? L04-3

5. *Researching Tax Questions.* Use IRS publications and other reference materials to answer a specific tax question. Contact an IRS office to obtain an answer for the same question. What differences, if any, exist between the information sources? L04-4

6. *Researching E-Filing Procedures.* Conduct an Internet search to obtain additional information about e-filing procedures. L04-4

7. *Comparing Tax Services.* Using Sheet 21 in the Personal Financial Planner, obtain information from two different tax preparation companies about the services they offer and the costs of their services. L04-4

8. *Determining Tax Planning Activities.* Survey friends and relatives about their tax planning strategies. You may use Sheet 22 from the Personal Financial Planner to obtain questions for your survey. L04-5

FINANCIAL PLANNING CASE

A Single Father's Tax Situation

Ever since his wife's death, Eric Stanford has faced difficult personal and financial circumstances. His job provides him with a good income but keeps him away from his daughters, ages 8 and 10, nearly 20 days a month. This requires him to use in-home child care services that consume a large portion of his income. Since the Stanfords live in a small apartment, this arrangement has been very inconvenient.

Due to the costs of caring for his children, Eric has only a minimal amount withheld from his salary for federal income taxes. This makes more money available during the year, but for the last few years he has had to make large payments in April—another financial burden.

Although Eric has created an investment fund for his daughters' college education and for his retirement, he has not sought to select investments that offer tax benefits. Overall, he needs to look at several aspects of his tax planning activities to find strategies that will best serve his current and future financial needs.

Eric has assembled the following information for the current tax year:

Earnings from wages	$99,520
Interest earned on savings	$150
IRA deduction	$4,000
Checking account interest	$80
Three exemptions	$3,900 each
Current standard deduction for filing status	$8,950
Amount withheld for federal income tax	$10,178
Tax credit for child care	$600
Filing status	Head of household

Questions

1. What are Eric's major financial concerns in his current situation?
2. In what ways might Eric improve his tax planning efforts?
3. Is Eric typical of many people in our society with regard to tax planning? Why or why not?
4. What additional actions might Eric investigate with regard to taxes and personal financial planning?
5. Calculate the following

   a. What is Eric's taxable income? (Refer to Exhibit 4-1, page 121.)

   b. What is his total tax liability? (Use Exhibit 4-7, page 136.) What is his average tax rate?

   c. Based on his withholding, will Eric receive a refund or owe additional tax? What is the amount?

PERSONAL FINANCIAL PLANNER IN ACTION

Tax Planning Activities

Taxes are an important factor of financial planning. Various actions can be taken to reduce the time and money that go toward taxes.

Your Short Term Financial Planning Activities	*Resources*
1. Develop a system for filing and storing various tax records related to income, deductible expenses, and current tax forms.	See Exhibit 4-2 (p. 124) www.turbotax.com www.taxsoft.com
2. Using the IRS and other websites, identify recent changes in tax laws that may affect your financial planning decisions.	www.irs.gov www.1040.com

3. Using current IRS tax forms and tax tables, estimate your tax liability for the current year.	PFP Sheet 20 www.irs.gov www.taxadmin.org
4. Compare the cost of tax preparation services.	PFP Sheet 21 www.ey.com/us/tax www.hrblock.com
Your Long-Term Financial Planning Activities	*Resources*
1. Identify saving and investing decisions that would minimize future income taxes.	PFP Sheet 22 www.ustaxcourt.gov
2. Develop a plan for actions to take related to your current and future tax situation.	Text pages www.taxlogic.com

CONTINUING CASE

Taxes

Life Situation

Single
Age 21
No dependents
College student

Financial Data

Monthly Income $1,750
Living Expenses $1,210
Personal property $7,300
Savings $2,000
Student loan $3,000
Credit card debt $2,400

Shelby Johnson has been working at a local pet store in the grooming department. She has just received her W-2 statement from her employer so that she can prepare her taxes. Her tax withheld from her paycheck is normally greater than the tax owed as calculated on her tax return. In the past, she has used her tax refund to build up her wardrobe with a shopping spree. However, as she gets closer to graduating she is reconsidering this behavior and needs help deciding on a better alternative.

Questions

1. Given her current situation, list some suggestions on what Shelby should do with a tax refund of $800.
2. Based on her current and future life situation, what tax planning strategies should she consider?
3. Describe how Shelby might use the Personal Financial Planner sheet entitled "Tax Planning Activities" to help her tax situation.

DAILY SPENDING DIARY

"Sales tax on various purchases can really increase the amount of my total spending."

Directions

Continue your "Daily Spending Diary" to record and monitor your spending in various categories. Your comments should reflect what you have learned about your spending patterns and help you consider possible changes you might want to make in your spending habits.

Questions

1. What taxes do you commonly pay that are reflected (directly or indirectly) in your Daily Spending Diary?
2. How might you revise your spending habits to better control or reduce the amount you pay in taxes?

The Daily Spending Diary sheets are located in Appendix D at the end of the book and on the student website at www.mhhe.com/kdh.

chapter 5

Financial Services: Savings Plans and Payment Accounts

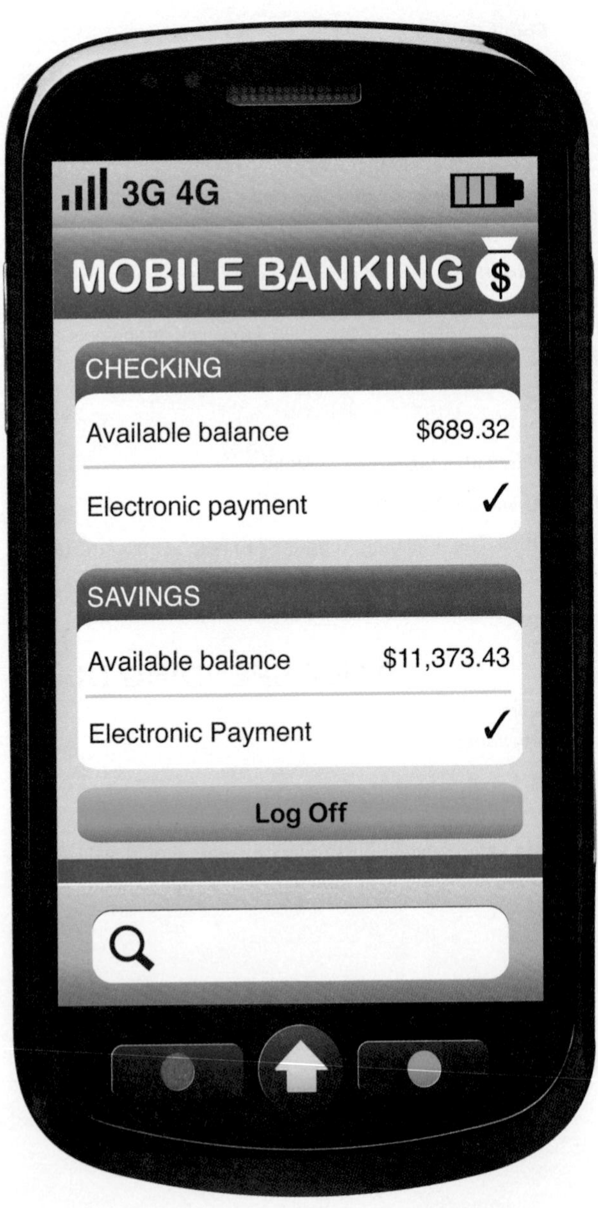

Learning Objectives

LO5-1 Analyze factors that affect the selection and use of financial services.

LO5-2 Compare the types of financial institutions.

LO5-3 Compare the costs and benefits of various savings plans.

LO5-4 Identify the factors used to evaluate different savings plans.

LO5-5 Compare the costs and benefits of different types of payment accounts.

What will this mean for me?

As many financial institutions face economic difficulties, some banking costs for consumers remain high. ATM fees can range from nothing to as high as $4 per cash withdrawal. If you are charged two $1 transaction fees a week and could invest your money at 5 percent, this convenience will cost you more than $570 over a five-year period. Your knowledge of financial service costs can save you thousands of dollars over a lifetime.

my life

BANKING BASICS

The variety and sources of financial services can be overwhelming. Extensive numbers of savings, checking, and credit plans are offered from local banks and online financial institutions. Your efforts to understand the costs associated with various banking services can result in large savings and improved personal financial planning.

What are your attitudes toward financial services? For each of the following statements, indicate the choice that best describes your current situation.

1. The financial service about which I'm least informed is
   a. online banking services.
   b. certificates of deposit and other savings plans.
   c. checking accounts and other payment methods.
2. My primary financial service activity involves the use of
   a. a bank or credit union.
   b. mobile banking and ATMs.
   c. a check-cashing outlet.
3. The most appropriate savings plan for my current situation is a
   a. regular savings account.
   b. money market account.
   c. certificate of deposit.

(continued)

4. When selecting a savings plan, my main concern is
   a. bank location and availability of cash machines.
   b. federal deposit insurance coverage.
   c. rate of return.
5. My checking account balance is
   a. updated in my records after every check written and deposit made.
   b. based on a rough estimate in my checkbook.
   c. only known by my financial institution.

As you study this chapter, you will encounter "My Life" boxes with additional information and resources related to these items.

Financial Services for Financial Planning

LO5-1

Analyze factors that affect the selection and use of financial services.

More than 20,000 banks, savings and loan associations, credit unions, and other financial institutions provide payment, savings, and credit services. Today, *banking* may mean a credit union, an ATM, or a phone app to transfer funds. While some financial decisions relate directly to goals, your daily activities require other financial services. Exhibit 5-1 is an overview of the varied financial services and institutions available for managing cash flows and achieving financial goals.

Lending practices, foreclosures, higher fees, and tougher account requirements have created a different environment for financial services. You will find more emphasis on consolidation of accounts and mobile banking while you encounter lower savings rates and higher loan and credit card rates.

MANAGING DAILY MONEY NEEDS

Buying groceries, paying the rent, and completing other routine spending activities require a cash management plan. Cash, check, credit card, debit card, and online/mobile transfer are the common payment choices. Mistakes made frequently when managing current cash needs include (1) overspending as a result of impulse buying and using credit; (2) having insufficient liquid assets to pay current bills; (3) using savings or borrowing to pay for current expenses; (4) failing to put unneeded funds in an interest-earning savings account or investment program.

Information on various financial services is available from many sources.

No matter how carefully you manage your money, at some time you will need more cash than you have available. To cope in that situation, you have two basic choices: liquidate savings or borrow. A savings account, certificate of deposit, mutual fund, or other investment may be accessed when you need funds. Or a credit card cash advance or a personal loan may be appropriate. Remember, however, that both using savings and increasing borrowing reduce your net worth and your potential to achieve long-term financial security.

TYPES OF FINANCIAL SERVICES

Banks and other financial institutions offer services to meet a variety of needs. These services fall into four main categories.

Exhibit 5-1 Financial institutions and banking services

DEPOSIT FINANCIAL INSTITUTIONS
- Commercial bank
- Credit union
- Savings and loan association
- Mutual savings bank

NON-DEPOSIT INSTITUTIONS
- Life insurance company
- Investment company
- Brokerage firm
- Credit card company
- Finance company
- Mortgage company

TYPES OF FINANCIAL SERVICES	
Cash Availability • Check cashing • ATM/debit cards • Traveler's checks • Foreign currency exchange	**Payment Services** • Checking account • Online payments • Cashier's checks • Money orders
Savings Services • Regular savings account • Money market account • Certificates of deposit • U.S. savings bonds	**Credit Services** • Credit cards, cash advances • Auto loans, education loans • Mortgages • Home equity loans
Investment Services • Individual retirement accounts (IRAs) • Brokerage service • Investment advice • Mutual funds	**Other Services** • Insurance; trust service • Tax preparation • Safe deposit boxes • Budget counseling • Estate planning

HIGH-COST FINANCIAL SERVICE PROVIDERS
- Pawnshop
- Check-cashing outlet
- Payday loan company
- Rent-to-own center
- Car title loan company

NON-BANK FINANCIAL SERVICE PROVIDERS
- Retailer stores (prepaid debit cards, other services)
- Online banking service provider (E*Trade Bank)
- Online payment services (PayPal)
- P2P (peer-to-peer) lending intermediaries

1. SAVINGS Safe storage of funds for future use is a basic need for everyone. These services, commonly referred to as *time deposits,* include money in savings accounts and certificates of deposit. Selection of a savings plan is commonly based on the interest rate earned, liquidity, safety, and convenience, which are discussed later in the chapter.

2. CASH AVAILABILITY AND PAYMENT SERVICES The ability to transfer money to other parties is a necessary part of daily business activities. Checking accounts and other payment methods, commonly called *demand deposits,* are also covered later in the chapter.

3. BORROWING Most people use credit at some time during their lives. Credit alternatives range from short-term accounts, such as credit cards and cash loans, to long-term borrowing, such as a home mortgage. Chapters 6 and 7 discuss the types and costs of credit.

4. INVESTMENTS AND OTHER FINANCIAL SERVICES Insurance protection, investing for the future, real estate purchases, tax assistance, and financial planning are additional services you may need for successful financial management. With some financial plans, someone else manages your funds. A **trust** is a legal

trust A legal agreement that provides for the management and control of assets by one party for the benefit of another.

agreement that provides for the management and control of assets by one party for the benefit of another. This type of arrangement is most commonly created through a commercial bank or a lawyer. Parents who want to set aside certain funds for their children's education may use a trust. The investments and money in the trust are managed by a bank, and the necessary amounts go to the children for their educational expenses. Trusts are covered in more detail in Chapter 19.

asset management account An all-in-one account that includes savings, checking, borrowing, investing, and other financial services for a single fee; also called a *cash management account.*

To simplify the array of financial services and to attract customers, many financial institutions offer all-in-one accounts. An **asset management account,** also called a *cash management account* or a *wealth management account* provides a complete financial services program for a single fee. Investment brokers and other financial institutions offer this all-purpose account, which usually includes a checking account, a debit-credit card, online banking, mobile apps, as well as a line of credit for obtaining quick cash loans. These accounts also provide access to stocks, bonds, mutual funds, and other types of investments.

A consolidated financial services account has the potential benefits of:

- Keeping track of your money in a single location.
- Fewer monthly and quarterly statements.
- Lower fees for maintaining a large balance with one financial institution.
- Simplified tax reporting with all dividends and interest on one 1099 form.
- Ease of communicating your financial situation to family members.

ONLINE AND MOBILE BANKING

Banking online and through wireless mobile systems continues to expand (see Exhibit 5-2). While most traditional financial institutions offer online banking services, web-only banks have also become strong competitors. For example, E*Trade Bank operates online while also providing customers with access to ATMs. These "e-banks" and "e-branches" provide nearly every needed financial service.

Financial service activities through your smartphone or tablet has three access methods: (1) text banking, providing account information and conducting transactions

Exhibit 5-2 Mobile banking services

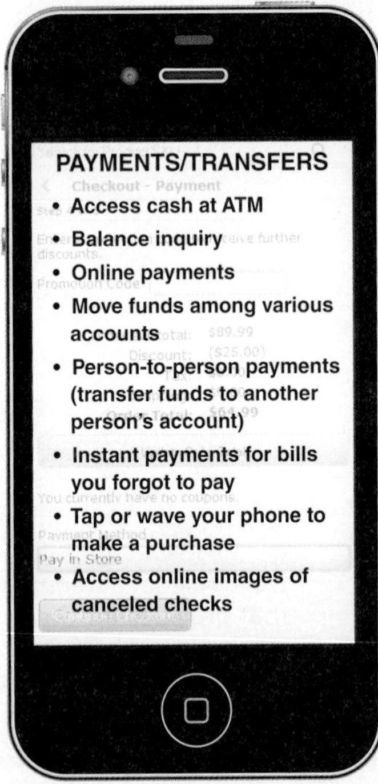

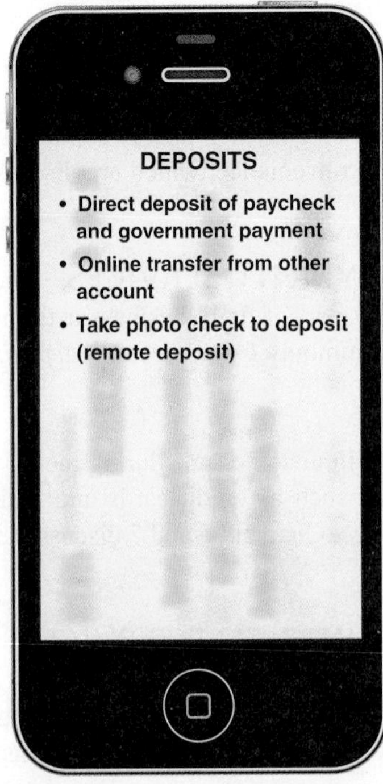

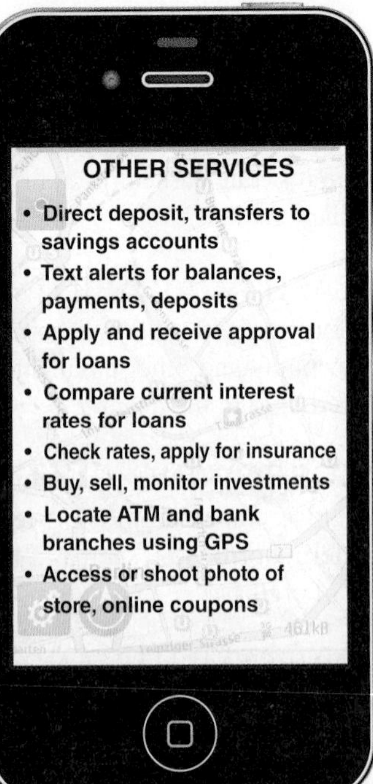

through text messages; (2) mobile web banking with Internet access of the financial institution's website; and (3) banking apps for performing various types of transactions.

Mobile and online banking provide the benefits of convenience and saving time along with instant information access. However, concerns of privacy, security of data, ease of overspending, costly fees, and online scams must also be considered.

More traditional electronic banking can occur through an **automatic teller machine (ATM),** also called a *cash machine,* which can facilitate various types of transactions. To minimize ATM fees, compare several financial institutions. Use your own bank's ATM to avoid surcharges and withdraw larger amounts to avoid fees on several small transactions.

automatic teller machine (ATM) A computer terminal used to conduct banking transactions; also called a *cash machine.*

The **debit card,** or *cash card,* that activates ATM transactions may also be used to make purchases. A debit card is in contrast to a *credit card,* since you are spending your own funds rather than borrowing additional money. A lost or stolen debit card can be expensive. If you notify the financial institution within two days of the lost card, your liability for unauthorized use is $50. However, you can be liable for up to $500 of unauthorized use if you wait up to 60 days to notify your bank. After 60 days, your liability can be the total amount in your account, and even more if your card is linked to other bank accounts.

debit card A plastic access card used in computerized banking transactions; also called a *cash card.*

However, some card issuers use the same rules for lost or stolen debit cards as for credit cards: a $50 maximum. Of course, you are not liable for unauthorized use, such as a con artist using your account number to make a purchase. Remember to report the fraud within 60 days of receiving your statement to protect your right not to be charged for the transaction.

PREPAID DEBIT CARDS

Prepaid debit cards have become the fastest growing payment method. For many consumers, these cards (see Exhibit 5-3) are being used instead of traditional banking services. Prepaid debit cards are issued by many financial service providers including traditional financial institutions, retailers (such as Walmart), and non-bank companies specifically created to provide this financial service.

A major concern with prepaid debit cards can be the extensive fees that a user encounters due to few current regulations for these financial products. Beware of fees that may include an activation fee, a monthly fee, a transaction fee, a cash withdrawal (ATM) fee, a balance-inquiry fee, a fee to add funds, a dormancy fee, and others.

However, the expanded use of prepaid cards has resulted in lower consumer debt since the debit card can help control spending and buying on credit. With credit cards you "pay later," with debit cards you "pay now," and with prepaid cards you "pay before."

Exhibit 5-3 Expanding prepaid debit card services

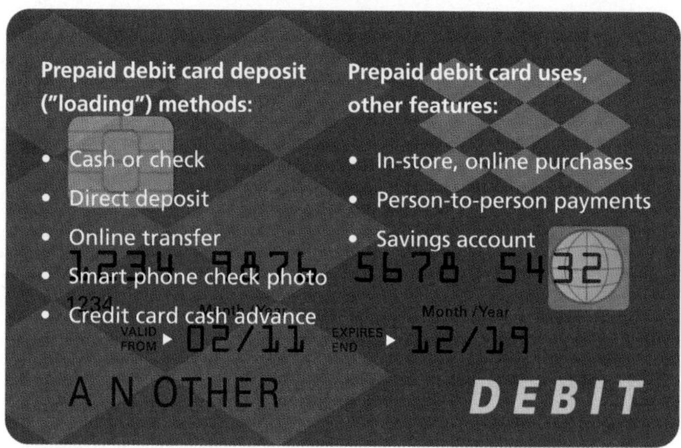

Some prepaid cards have celebrity endorsements, such as Suze Orman, Magic Johnson, and Justin Bieber, which does not mean a better deal for consumers. Comparisons of features and fees for prepaid debit cards are available at www.nerdwallet.com.

DID YOU KNOW?

Personalized ATM visits are becoming more common with primary transaction options based on your last two or three visits. The screen may also display a "Happy Birthday" message on your special day. However, don't expect the bank's CEO to be singing you birthday wishes.

OPPORTUNITY COSTS OF FINANCIAL SERVICES

When making decisions about spending and saving, consider the trade-off between current satisfaction and long-term financial security. Consider the opportunity cost—what you give up—when you evaluate, select, and use financial services. Common trade-offs related to financial services include the following:

- Higher returns for long-term savings will usually be achieved at the cost of *low liquidity,* the inability to obtain your money quickly.
- The convenience of a 24-hour automatic teller machine or a bank branch office near your home or place of work should be considered against service fees.
- The "no-fee" checking account that requires a non-interest-bearing $500 minimum balance means lost interest of nearly $400 at 6 percent compounded over 10 years.

You should evaluate costs and benefits in both monetary and personal terms to choose the financial services that best serve your needs.

my life 1

I am well informed about various financial services.

To be better informed on current financial services, conduct an Internet search of various online banks. Obtain information on various services that might be of value to you now or in the future. How could changing interest rates affect your decision to use various types of financial services?

FINANCIAL SERVICES AND ECONOMIC CONDITIONS

Changing interest rates, rising consumer prices, and other economic factors also influence financial services. For successful financial planning, be aware of the current trends and future prospects for interest rates (see Exhibit 5-4). You can learn about these trends and prospects by reading *The Wall Street Journal* (www.wsj.com), business periodicals such as *Businessweek* (www.businessweek.com), *Forbes* (www.forbes.com), *Fortune* (www.fortune.com), and other online finance sources.

Exhibit 5-4

Changing interest rates and decisions related to financial services

When interest rates are rising...

- Use long-term loans to take advantage of current low rates.
- Select short-term savings instruments to take advantage of higher rates when they mature.

When interest rates are falling...

- Use short-term loans to take advantage of lower rates when you refinance the loans.
- Select long-term savings instruments to "lock in" earnings at current high rates.

1 What is the relationship between financial services and overall financial planning?
2 What are the major categories of financial services?
3 Why shouldn't you select financial services only on the basis of monetary factors?
4 How do changing economic conditions affect the use of financial services?

Planning the use of financial services

Financial Institutions

LO5-2

Compare the types of financial institutions.

Many businesses, such as insurance companies, investment brokers, and credit card companies, have become involved in financial services previously limited to banks. Banks have also expanded their competitive efforts by opening offices that specialize in financial services such as investments, insurance, or real estate.

Despite changes in the banking environment, many familiar financial institutions still serve your needs. Most of these institutions have expanded their services. As previously shown in Exhibit 5-1 (on page 157), financial institutions may be viewed in the categories of deposit institutions, non-deposit institutions, non-bank financial service providers, and high-cost financial service providers.

DEPOSIT INSTITUTIONS

The financial institutions that most people use serve as intermediaries between suppliers (savers) and users (borrowers) of funds. These deposit-type institutions include commercial banks, savings and loan associations, mutual savings banks, and credit unions.

COMMERCIAL BANKS A **commercial bank** offers a full range of financial services, including checking, savings, and lending, along with many other services. Commercial banks are organized as corporations, with investors (stockholders) providing the needed capital for the bank to operate. National banks are chartered by the federal government and state banks by state governments. State-chartered banks are usually subject to fewer regulations than federally-chartered banks.

commercial bank A financial institution that offers a full range of financial services to individuals, businesses, and government agencies.

SAVINGS AND LOAN ASSOCIATIONS While the commercial bank traditionally served businesses and individuals with large amounts of money, the **savings and loan association (S&L)** specialized in savings accounts and loans for mortgages. Today, savings and loan associations also offer checking accounts, expanded savings plans, loans to businesses, and other investment and financial planning services.

savings and loan association (S&L) A financial institution that traditionally specialized in savings accounts and mortgage loans.

MUTUAL SAVINGS BANKS A **mutual savings bank** is owned by depositors and, like the traditional savings and loan association, specializes in savings accounts and mortgage loans. Mutual savings banks are located mainly in the northeastern United States. Unlike the profits of other types of financial institutions, the profits of a mutual savings bank go to the depositors, usually paying higher rates on savings.

mutual savings bank A financial institution that is owned by depositors and specializes in savings accounts and mortgage loans.

UNDERSTANDING INTEREST RATES

When people discuss higher or lower interest rates, they could be talking about one of many types. Some interest rates refer to the cost of borrowing by a business; others refer to the cost of buying a home. Your awareness of various types of interest rates can help you plan your spending, saving, borrowing, and investing. The accompanying table describes some commonly reported interest rates and gives their *annual average* for selected years.

Using the business section of a newspaper, *The Wall Street Journal,* the website of the Federal Reserve System (www.federalreserve.gov), or other business information sources, obtain current numbers for some or all of these interest rates. How might the current trend in interest rates affect your financial decisions?

	1985	1990	1995	2000	2005	2009	2012	Current
Prime rate—an indication of the rate banks charge large corporations	9.93%	10.01%	8.83%	9.23%	6.19%	3.25%	3.25%	_____%
Discount rate—the rate financial institutions are charged to borrow funds from Federal Reserve banks	7.69	6.98	5.21	5.73	4.19	0.50	0.75	_____
T-bill rate—the yield on short-term (13-week) U.S. government debt obligations	7.48	7.51	5.51	5.66	3.15	0.15	0.09	_____
Treasury bond rate—the yield on long-term (20-year) U.S. government debt obligations	10.97	8.55	6.96	6.23	4.64	4.11	2.54	_____
Mortgage rate—the amount individuals are paying to borrow for the purchase of a new home	11.55	10.13	7.95	8.06	5.86	5.04	3.66	_____
Corporate bond rate—the cost of borrowing for large U.S. corporations	11.37	9.32	7.59	7.62	5.23	5.31	3.67	_____
Certificate of deposit rate—the rate for six-month time deposits at savings institutions	8.25	8.17	5.93	6.59	3.73	0.87	0.44	_____

Source: Federal Reserve Statistical Release: *Selected Interest Rates* (H-15), www.federalreserve.gov.

credit union A user-owned, nonprofit, cooperative financial institution that is organized for the benefit of its members.

CREDIT UNIONS A **credit union** is a user-owned, nonprofit, cooperative financial institution. Traditionally, credit union members had to have a common bond such as work, church, or community affiliation. As the common bond restriction was loosened, the membership of credit unions increased. Today more than 80 million people belong to over 9,000 credit unions in the United States.

THE "UNBANKED" AND HIGH-COST "SHADOW" FINANCIAL SERVICES

Would you pay $8 to cash a $100 check? Or pay $20 to borrow $100 for two weeks? Many people who do not have bank accounts (especially low-income consumers) make use of financial service companies that charge very high fees and excessive interest rates. An estimated 17 million people in the United States are "unbanked," using a variety of alternative services rather than having a bank account. Another 20 percent of the population are "underbanked" and make use of many of these services in addition to having a bank account.

PAWNSHOPS

Loans through a pawnshop are based on the value of tangible possessions such as jewelry or other valuable items. Many low- and moderate-income families use these organizations to obtain cash loans quickly. Pawnshops charge higher fees than other financial institutions. Thousands of consumers are increasingly in need of small loans—usually $50 to $75, to be repaid in 30 to 45 days. Pawnshops have become the "neighborhood bankers" and the "local shopping malls," since they provide both lending and retail shopping services, selling items that owners do not redeem. While states regulate pawnshops, the interest rates charged can range from 3 percent a month to over 100 percent for a year.

CHECK-CASHING OUTLETS

Most banks will not cash a check unless you have an account. The more than 6,000 check-cashing outlets (CCOs) charge anywhere from 1 to 20 percent of the face value of a check; the average cost is 2 to 3 percent. However, for a low-income family, that can be a significant portion of the total household budget. CCOs, sometimes called *currency exchanges,* offer other services, including electronic tax filing, money orders, private postal boxes, utility bill payment, and the sale of transit tokens. These services are usually less costly at other types of financial service providers.

PAYDAY LOANS

Many consumer organizations caution against using payday loans, also referred to as *cash advances, check advance loans, postdated check loans,* and *delayed deposit loans.* Desperate borrowers pay annual interest rates of as much as 780 percent and more to obtain needed cash from payday loan companies. The most frequent users of payday loans are workers who have become trapped by debts or poor financial decisions.

In a typical payday loan, a consumer writes a personal check for $115 to borrow $100 for 14 days. The payday lender agrees to hold the check until the next payday. This $15 finance charge for the 14 days translates into an annual percentage rate of 391 percent. Some consumers "roll over" their loans, paying another $15 for the $100 loan for the next 14 days. After a few rollovers, the finance charge can exceed the amount borrowed. To prevent this exploitation, some employers are offering to pay advances through payroll provider services. The loans have rates in the 9 to 18 percent range.

RENT-TO-OWN CENTERS

Rental businesses offer big-screen televisions, seven-piece bedroom sets, kitchen appliances, and computers. The rent-to-own (RTO) industry is defined as stores that lease products to consumers who can own the item if they complete a certain number of monthly or weekly payments. A $600 computer can result in $1,900 of payments. RTO purchases can result in annual interest rates of over 300 percent.

CAR TITLE LOANS

When in need of money, people with poor credit ratings might obtain a cash advance using their automobile title as security for a high-interest loan. These loans, usually due in 30 days, typically have a cost similar to payday loans, often exceeding 200 percent. While the process is simple, the consequences can be devastating with the repossession of your car.

All of these expensive financial service providers should be avoided. Instead, make an effort to properly manage your money and use the services of a reputable financial institution, such as a credit union.

Each year, surveys conducted by consumer organizations and others report lower fees for checking accounts, lower loan rates, and higher levels of user satisfaction for credit unions compared to other financial institutions. Most credit unions offer credit cards, mortgages, home equity loans, direct deposit, cash machines, safe deposit boxes, and investment services.

my life 2 

My primary financial service activities are clearly identified

Comparing financial situations requires time to identify various services and costs based on your life situation. Credit unions consistently offer a low-cost alternative for financial services. For additional information about credit unions, go to www.cuna.org.

OTHER FINANCIAL INSTITUTIONS

Financial services are also available from institutions such as life insurance companies, investment companies, brokerage firms, finance companies, credit card companies, and mortgage companies.

LIFE INSURANCE COMPANIES While the main purpose of life insurance is to provide financial security for dependents, many life insurance policies contain savings and investment features. Chapter 12 discusses these policies. In recent years, life insurance companies have expanded their financial services to include investment and retirement planning.

money market fund A savings–investment plan offered by investment companies, with earnings based on investments in various short-term financial instruments.

INVESTMENT COMPANIES Investment companies, also referred to as *mutual funds,* offer banking-type services. A common service of these organizations is the **money market fund,** a combination savings–investment plan in which the investment company uses your money to purchase a variety of short-term financial instruments. Unlike accounts at most banks, savings and loan associations, and credit unions, investment company accounts are not covered by federal deposit insurance. Investors in money market funds are usually allowed to write a limited number of checks, providing the convenience of liquidity.

BROKERAGE FIRMS These organizations employ investment advisers and financial planners, and serve as agents between the buyer and seller for stocks, bonds, and other investment securities. Their earnings come from commissions and fees. Expanded financial services are available from brokerage firms, including checking accounts and online banking.

FINANCE COMPANIES Making loans to consumers and small businesses is the main function of finance companies. These loans have short and intermediate terms with higher rates than most other lenders charge. Some finance companies have expanded their activities to offer other financial planning services.

CREDIT CARD COMPANIES Specializing in funding short-term retail lending is the focus of credit card companies. These networks, including VISA, MasterCard, and Discover, have also expanded into other banking and investing services.

MORTGAGE COMPANIES Mortgage companies are organized primarily to provide loans to purchase homes. Chapter 9 discusses the activities of mortgage companies.

DID YOU KNOW?

Bankrate.com suggests these actions to minimize fees: (1) avoid overdraft charges of nearly $30 each by linking your checking account to savings; (2) use ATMs that are in your bank's system; (3) search for true "free" checking accounts with a low minimum balance requirement; and (4) consider doing your banking at a credit union, where lower fees, lower borrowing rates, and higher rates for savings are usually offered.

COMPARING FINANCIAL INSTITUTIONS

As you use financial services, decide what you want from the organization that will serve your needs. With the financial marketplace constantly changing, you must assess the various services and other factors before selecting an organization. Exhibit 5-5 provides guidelines for selecting a financial institution.

Exhibit 5-5

Choosing a financial institution

STEP 1. List your most important features for a financial institution, related to:
- ***Services:*** checking, savings accounts; deposit insurance; loans; investments; mobile app
- ***Costs, fees, earnings:*** checking minimum balance, ATM fees; credit rates; savings rates
- ***Convenience:*** branch locations, hours; ATM locations; customer service; rewards program
- ***Online, mobile banking:*** ease of operation; services; privacy, security; other fees

STEP 2. Rank the top three or four specific features based on their importance to you.

STEP 3. Prepare a list of local, national, and online financial institutions (include the address, phone, and website).

STEP 4. Conduct three types of research: (1) talk with people who have used various financial institutions; (2) conduct online research on the services, policies, and fees; and (3) visit, as appropriate, the financial institution to observe the environment and to talk with staff members.

Additional research actions may include:
- Determining the minimum balance to avoid monthly service charges.
- Obtaining a fee disclosure statement, savings rate sheet, and sample loan application.
- Assessing whether the deposit insurance and online banking services meet your needs.

STEP 5. Balance your needs with the information collected, and decide where you will do business. You may use more than one financial institution to take advantage of the best services offered by each. This action gives you flexibility to move your money if the fees at one place increase. Talk with a manager if you believe a fee was charged unfairly; the bank may reverse the charge to keep you as a customer. "Switch kits" are available to make changing banks easier. These forms and authorization letters facilitate a smooth transition of direct deposits and automatic payments from one financial institution to another.

Note: Personal Financial Planner sheets 23, 25, 26, and 27, at the end of the book, can be used for this process. Also, a fee disclosure form is available at www.pewtrusts.org/safechecking.

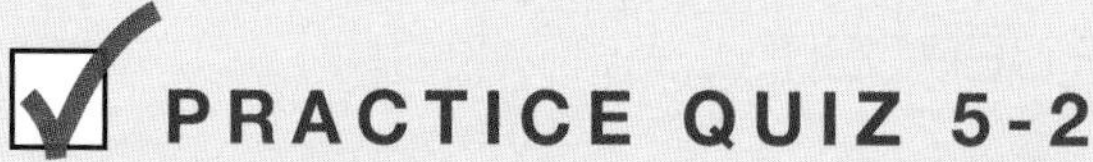

1 What are examples of deposit financial institutions?
2 What factors do consumers usually consider when selecting a financial institution?

Savings Plans

LO5-3

Compare the costs and benefits of various savings plans.

As Chapter 3 emphasized, a savings program is needed to achieve financial goals. Evaluating various savings plans is the starting point of this process. An overview of savings alternatives is presented in Exhibit 5-6.

REGULAR SAVINGS ACCOUNTS

Regular savings accounts usually involve a low or no minimum balance. Savers receive a monthly or quarterly statement with a summary of transactions. A regular savings account usually allows you to withdraw money as needed. Banks, savings and loan

Exhibit 5-6 Savings alternatives

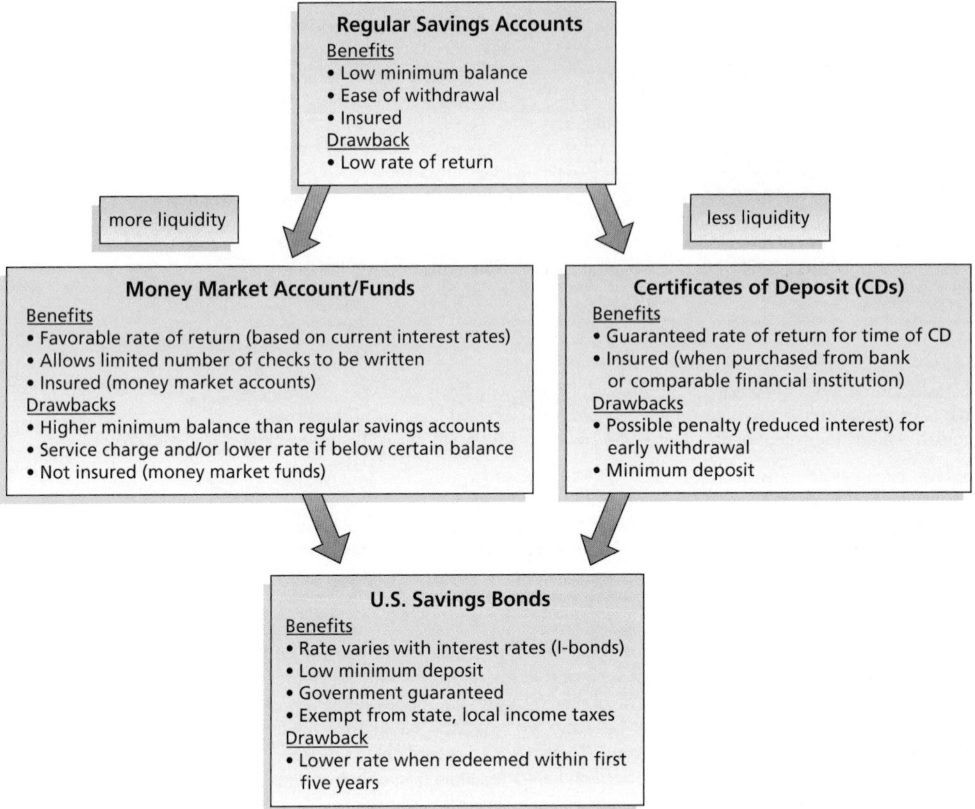

associations, and other financial institutions offer regular savings accounts. At a credit union, these savings plans are called **share accounts.**

share account A regular savings account at a credit union.

certificate of deposit (CD) A savings plan requiring that a certain amount be left on deposit for a stated time period to earn a specified interest rate.

CERTIFICATES OF DEPOSIT

Higher earnings are commonly available to savers when they leave money on deposit for a set time period. A **certificate of deposit (CD)** is a savings plan requiring that a certain amount be left on deposit for a stated time period (ranging from 30 days to five or more years) to earn a specific rate of return. These time deposits can be an attractive and a safe savings alternative. However, most financial institutions impose a penalty for early withdrawal of CD funds. For CDs of one year or less, the penalty is usually three months of interest. CDs of more than a year will likely have a fine of six-months' interest, while a five-year CD can result in a penalty as high as 20 to 25 percent of the total interest to maturity on the account.

TYPES OF CDs While traditional certificates of deposit continue to be the most popular, financial institutions offer other types of CDs:

1. *Rising-rate* or *bump-up CDs* may have higher rates at various intervals, such as every six months. However, beware of ads that highlight a higher rate in the future. This rate may be in effect only for the last few months of an 18- or 24-month CD.
2. *Liquid CDs* offer an opportunity to withdraw money without a penalty. However, you will likely be required to maintain a minimum balance in the account. This type

of CD may have other restrictions such as a waiting period before any funds can be withdrawn or a limit on the number of withdrawals allowed.

3. *A zero-coupon CD* is purchased at a deep discount (a small portion of the face value) with no interest payments. Your initial small deposit ($5,000, for example) grows to the maturity value of the CD ($10,000) in 10 years, which is approximately a 6 percent annual return.
4. *Indexed CDs* have earnings based on the stock market. In times of strong stock performance, your earnings can be higher than those on other CDs. At other times, however, you may earn no interest and may even lose part of your savings. A CD based on the consumer price index can result in higher returns as inflation increases.
5. *Callable CDs* start with higher rates and usually have long maturities, as high as 10 to 15 years. With this savings option, if interest rates drop, the bank may "call" (close) the account after a set period, such as one or two years. When the call option is exercised, the saver receives the original deposit amount and any interest that has been earned.

Beware of *promotional CDs,* which attempt to attract savers with gifts or special rates. Be sure to balance the value of the item against the lost interest.

MANAGING CDs When saving with a CD or *rolling over* a CD (buying a new one at maturity), carefully assess all earnings and costs. Do not allow your financial institution to automatically roll over your money into another CD for the same term. If interest rates have dropped, you might consider a shorter maturity. Or if you believe rates are at a peak and you won't need the money for some time, obtain a CD with a longer term.

Consider creating a CD *portfolio* with CDs maturing at different times, for example, $2,000 in a three-month CD, $2,000 in a six-month CD, $2,000 in a one-year CD, and $2,000 in a two-year CD. This will give you some degree of liquidity and flexibility when you reinvest your funds.

Don't hesitate to buy CDs online from a financial institution in another state. You might earn as much as a full percentage point higher than with your local bank. Also, when interest rates stay low, consider other savings alternatives such as savings bonds, mutual funds, and government securities. Current information about CD rates at various financial institutions may be obtained at www.bankrate.com.

MONEY MARKET ACCOUNTS AND FUNDS

With increased demand for higher savings rates, financial institutions created a savings plan with a floating interest rate. A **money market account** is a savings account that requires a minimum balance and has earnings based on market interest rates. Money market accounts may allow you to write a limited number of checks to make large payments or to transfer money to other accounts. Money market accounts may impose a fee when you go below the required minimum balance.

Both money market accounts and money market funds offer earnings based on current interest rates, and both have minimum-balance restrictions and allow check writing. The major difference is in safety. Money market *accounts* at banks and credit unions are covered by federal deposit insurance. This is not true of money market *funds,* which are a product of investment companies. Since money market funds invest mainly in short-term (less than a year) government and corporate securities, however, they are usually quite safe.

money market account A savings account offered by banks, savings and loan associations, and credit unions that requires a minimum balance and has earnings based on market interest rates.

my life 3

I am aware of the most appropriate savings plan for my current situation.

An extensive number of savings alternatives are available for various financial goals and life situations. You can obtain current rates for CDs and other savings plans at www.bankrate.com. For the latest rates and information on U.S. savings bonds, go to www.savingsbonds.gov.

SAVINGS BONDS

U.S. savings bonds are a low-risk savings program guaranteed by the federal government that have been used to achieve various financial goals. The Treasury Department offers various programs for buying savings bonds.

EE BONDS Series EE bonds may be purchased for any amount greater than $25, Electronic EE bonds are purchased online at face value; for example, you pay $50 for a $50 bond. These bonds may be purchased for any amount you desire, such as $143.58, giving savers more flexibility.

Paper savings bonds, while no longer issued at financial institutions, are still available through payroll savings plans or by using part or all of your federal tax refund. Paper EE bonds are sold at half the face value, and may be purchased for set values ranging from $25 to $5,000, with maturity values of $50 to $10,000. Paper savings bonds continue to be redeemed at financial institutions. If a savings bond has been lost or stolen, it can be reissued in either a paper or electronic format. To locate savings bonds issued since 1974, go to www.treasuryhunt.gov.

DID YOU KNOW?

To earn more interest on your savings: (1) compare local and online banks and credit unions; (2) combine several savings accounts to create a larger amount that might qualify for a higher rate; (3) search for special rates on checking accounts or specialty CDs. Helpful websites include bankrate.com, depositaccounts.com, and checkingfinder.com.

EE bonds increase in value as interest accrues monthly and compounds semiannually. If you redeem the bonds before five years, you forfeit the latest three months of interest; after five years, you are not penalized. A bond must be held for one year before it can be cashed. Series EE bonds continue to earn interest for 30 years. The main tax advantages of series EE bonds are: the interest earned is exempt from state and local taxes, and federal income tax on earnings is not due until the bonds are redeemed.

Redeemed series EE bonds may be exempt from federal income tax if the funds are used to pay tuition and fees at a college, university, or qualified technical school for yourself or a dependent. The bonds must be purchased by an individual who is at least 24 years old, and they must be issued in the names of one or both parents. This provision is designed to assist low- and middle-income households; people whose incomes exceed a certain amount do not qualify for this tax exemption.

HH BONDS Series HH bonds, which are no longer sold, were *current-income* bonds with interest deposited electronically to your bank account every six months. This interest was taxed as current income on a person's federal tax return, but exempt from state and local taxes.

I BONDS The I bond has an interest rate based on two components: (1) a fixed rate for the life of the bond, and (2) an inflation rate that changes twice a year. Every six months a new, fixed base rate is set for new bonds. The additional interest payment is recalculated twice a year, based on the current annual inflation rate. I bonds are sold in any amount over $25, and are purchased at face value. As with EE bonds, the minimum holding period is one year. Interest earned on I bonds is added to the value of the bond and received when you redeem your bond. I bonds have the same tax and education benefits as EE bonds.

A person may purchase up to $10,000 worth of electronic savings bonds of each series (EE and I bonds) a year. for a total of $20,000. This amount applies to any person,

FINANCIAL SERVICES IN OTHER CULTURES

Recent arrivals from other countries may be familiar with financial services that would seem unusual to most people in our society. Many of these banking activities resulted from a lack of access to formal financial institutions.

Rotating savings and credit associations (RoSCAs) exist in over 70 countries in settings where people cannot obtain loans. These community-based groups allow people otherwise unable to save or obtain credit to pay for household expenses or business costs. These informal lending groups involve members pooling their funds with each member taking a turn to use the funds. At the RoSCA meetings, usually held weekly or monthly, group members make their payments. The full amount collected at each meeting goes to one person. Then, at the next meeting, another person obtains the funds, until each person has a turn. RoSCAs have various names. In Cameroon and other French-speaking countries, they are *tontines.* In India, they are *chit funds, tandas* in Mexico, and *osusu* in Nigeria.

The transfer of funds to family members in other countries may occur through informal networks called a *hawala.* Often used by migrant workers from the Middle East, Africa, and Asia to send remittances home, the *hawala* involves a network of brokers in cities around the world. Transactions take place on an honor basis with the broker earning a fee.

In India, the postal service has been the main provider of banking and other financial services since 1854. Using the brand name "India Post," this government-operated enterprise offers savings accounts, money transfers, money orders, life insurance, and mutual funds through more than 150,000 offices. More recently, India Post allows customers to electronically transfer funds to pay bills at any postal service office.

so parents may buy an additional $25,000 in each child's name. Savings bonds are commonly registered with one of three ways: (1) single owner, (2) two owners, either as co-owners or with one as primary owner, or (3) with a beneficiary, who takes ownership of the bond when the original owner dies.

A TreasuryDirect account at www.treasurydirect.gov provides the benefits of

- 24-hour access to buy, manage, and redeem series EE and I electronic savings bonds.
- Converting series EE and I paper savings bonds to electronic through the SmartExchange feature.
- Purchasing electronic savings bonds as a gift.
- Enrolling in a payroll savings plan for purchasing electronic bonds.
- Investing in other Treasury securities such as bills, notes, bonds, and TIPS (Treasury Inflation-Protected Securities).
- Eliminating the risk that your savings bonds will be lost, stolen, or damaged.

Additional information and current value calculations may be obtained at www.savingsbonds.gov.

1 What are the main types of savings plans offered by financial institutions?
2 How does a money market *account* differ from a money market *fund?*
3 What are the benefits of U.S. savings bonds?

Using savings to achieve financial goals

Evaluating Savings Plans

LO5-4

Identify the factors used to evaluate different savings plans.

Your selection of a savings plan will be influenced by various factors, as shown in Exhibit 5-7.

RATE OF RETURN

Earnings on savings can be measured by the **rate of return,** or *yield,* the percentage of increase in the value of your savings from earned interest. For example, a $100 savings account that earned $3 after a year would have a rate of return, or yield, of 3 percent. This rate of return was determined by dividing the interest earned ($3) by the amount in the savings account ($100).

rate of return The percentage of increase in the value of savings as a result of interest earned; also called *yield.*

compounding A process that calculates interest based on previously earned interest.

annual percentage yield (APY) The percentage rate expressing the total amount of interest that would be received on a $100 deposit based on the annual rate and frequency of compounding for a 365-day period.

COMPOUNDING The yield on your savings usually will be greater than the stated interest rate. **Compounding** refers to interest that is earned on previously earned interest. Each time interest is added to your savings, the next interest amount is computed on the new balance in the account. Future value and present value calculations, introduced in Chapter 1, take compounding into account.

The more frequent the compounding, the higher your rate of return will be. For example, $100 in a savings account that earns 6 percent compounded annually will increase $6 after a year. But the same $100 in a 6 percent account compounded daily will earn $6.19 for the year. Although this difference may seem slight, large amounts held in savings for long periods of time will result in far higher differences (see Exhibit 5-8).

TRUTH IN SAVINGS The *Truth in Savings* law (Federal Reserve Regulation DD) requires financial institutions to disclose the following information on savings account plans:

- Fees on deposit accounts.
- The interest rate.
- The annual percentage yield (APY).
- Other terms and conditions of the savings plan.

Truth in Savings (TIS) defines **annual percentage yield (APY)** as the percentage rate expressing the total amount of interest that would be received on a $100 deposit

Exhibit 5-7

Selecting a savings plan

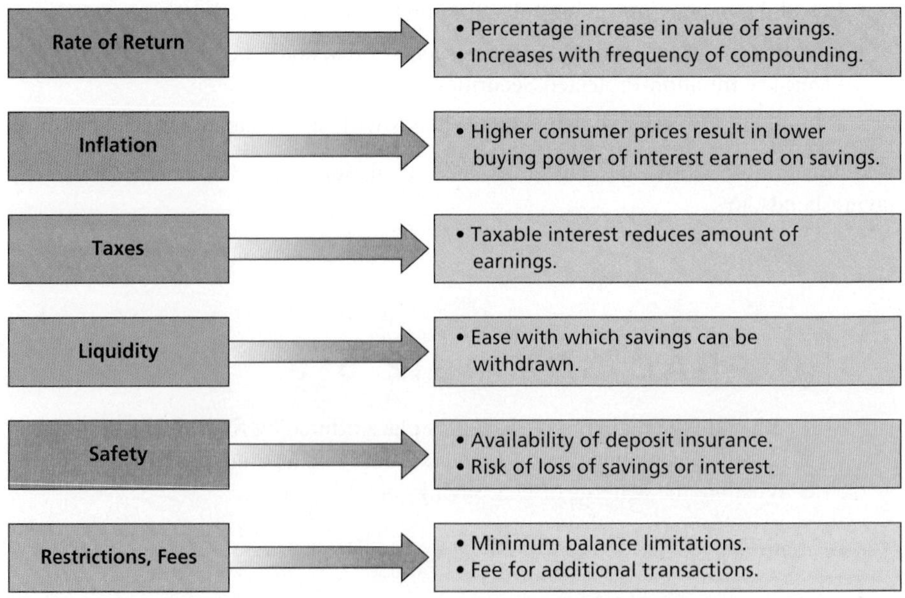

Financial Planning Calculations

ANNUAL PERCENTAGE YIELD

The Truth in Savings law requires that financial institutions report in advertisements, if a rate is quoted, and to savings plan customers the annual percentage yield (APY). The formula for APY is

$$\text{APY} = 100\left[(1 + \text{Interest/Principal})^{365/\text{days in term}} - 1\right]$$

The *principal* is the amount of funds on deposit. *Interest* is the total dollar amount earned during the term on the principal. *Days in term* is the actual number of days over which interest is earned.

When the number of days in the term is 365 (that is, where the stated maturity is 365 days) or where the account does not have a stated maturity, the APY formula is simply

$$\text{APY} = 100\ (\text{Interest/Principal})$$

APY provides a consistent comparison for savings plans with different interest rates, different compounding frequencies, and different time periods. APY may be easily viewed in terms of a \$100 deposit for a 365-day year. For example, an APY of 6.5 percent would mean \$6.50 interest for a year.

based on the annual rate and frequency of compounding for a 365-day period. This law defines a year as 365 days rather than 360, 366, or some other number. TIS eliminates the confusion caused by the more than 8 million variations of interest calculation methods previously used by financial institutions. APY reflects the amount of interest a saver should expect to earn. (See the Financial Planning Calculations box above for additional information on APY.)

EXAMPLE: Annual Percentage Yield

When the number of days in the term is 365 (that is, where the stated maturity is 365 days) or where the account does not have a stated maturity, the APY formula is simply

$$\begin{aligned}\text{APY} &= 100\left(\frac{\text{Interest}}{\text{Principal}}\right)\\ &= 100\left(\frac{66}{1{,}200}\right)\\ &= 100\ (0.055) = 5.5\%\end{aligned}$$

	Compounding Method			
End of Year	Daily	Monthly	Quarterly	Annually
1	\$10,832.78	\$10,830.00	\$10,824.32	\$10,800.00
2	11,743.91	11,728.88	11,716.59	11,664.00
3	12,712.17	12,702.37	12,682.41	12,597.12
4	13,770.82	13,756.66	13,727.85	13,604.89
5	14,917.62	14,898.46	14,859.46	14,693.28
Annual yield	8.33%	8.30%	8.24%	8.00%

Exhibit 5-8

Compounding frequency affects the savings yield

Shorter compounding periods result in higher yields. This chart shows the growth of \$10,000, five-year CDs paying the same rate of 8 percent, but with different compounding methods.

In addition to setting the formula for computing the annual percentage yield, Truth in Savings (1) requires disclosure of fees and APY earned on any statements provided to customers, (2) establishes rules for advertising deposit accounts, and (3) restricts the method of calculating the balance on which interest is paid. Financial institutions are also required to calculate interest on the full principal balance in the account each day.

INFLATION

The rate of return you earn on your savings should be compared with the inflation rate. When the inflation rate was over 10 percent, people with money in savings accounts earning 5 or 6 percent were experiencing a loss in the buying power of that money. In general, as the inflation rate increases, the interest rates offered to savers also increase. This gives you an opportunity to select a savings option that will minimize the loss in value of your dollars on deposit.

TAX CONSIDERATIONS

Like inflation, taxes reduce interest earned on savings. For example, a 10 percent return for a saver in a 28 percent tax bracket means a real return of 7.2 percent (the Financial Planning Calculations feature on page 173 shows how to compute the after-tax savings rate of return). As discussed in Chapter 4 and discussed further in Chapter 18, several tax-exempt and tax-deferred savings plans and investments can increase your real rate of return.

Also, remember that taxes usually are not withheld from taxable savings and investment income. Consequently, you may owe additional taxes at year-end as a result of earnings on savings.

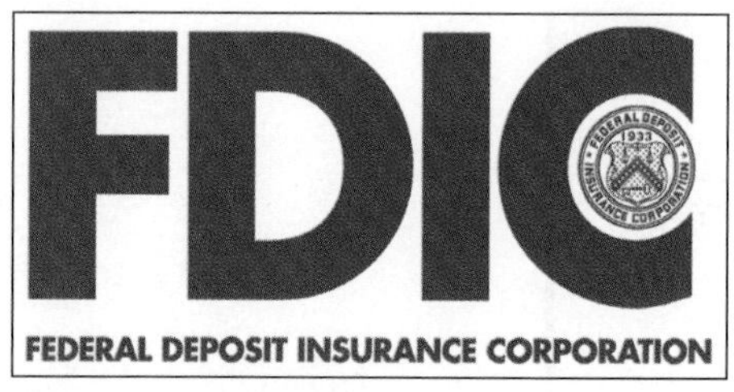

Federal deposit insurance reduces the risk of saving for consumers.

LIQUIDITY

Liquidity allows you to withdraw your money on short notice without a loss of principal or fees. Some savings plans impose penalties for early withdrawal or have other restrictions. With certain types of savings certificates and accounts, early withdrawal may be penalized by a loss of interest or a lower earnings rate.

You should consider the degree of liquidity you desire in relation to your savings goals. To achieve long-term financial goals, many people trade off liquidity for a higher return.

> **my life 4**
>
> **I understand the major factors to consider when selecting a savings plan.**
>
> While several factors should be considered when selecting a savings plan, safety is often a major one. Beware that some "shadow" banking services (money-market funds, reloadable prepaid cards) are not covered by federal deposit insurance; additional information is available at www.fdic.gov.

SAFETY

Most savings plans at banks, savings and loan associations, and credit unions are insured by agencies affiliated with the federal government. The Federal Deposit Insurance Corporation (FDIC) coverage prevents a loss of money due to the failure of the insured institution. Credit unions may obtain deposit insurance through the National Credit Union Association (NCUA). Some state-chartered credit unions have opted for a private insurance program. While some financial institutions have failed in recent years, savers with deposits covered by federal insurance have not lost any money. Depositors have either been paid, or have had the accounts taken over by a financially stable institution.

Financial Planning Calculations

AFTER-TAX SAVINGS RATE OF RETURN

The taxability of interest on your savings reduces your real rate of return. In other words, you lose some portion of your interest to taxes. This calculation consists of the following steps:

1. Determine your top tax bracket for federal income taxes.
2. Subtract this rate, expressed as a decimal, from 1.0.
3. Multiply the result by the yield on your savings account.
4. This number, expressed as a percentage, is your after-tax rate of return.

For example,

1. You are in the 28 percent tax bracket.
2. $1.0 - 0.28 = 0.72$.
3. If the yield on your savings account is 6.25 percent, $0.0625 \times 0.72 = 0.045$.
4. Your after-tax rate of return is 4.5 percent.

You may use the same procedure to determine the *real rate of return* on your savings based on inflation. For example, if you are earning 6 percent on savings and inflation is 5 percent, your real rate of return (after inflation) is 5.7 percent: $0.06 \times (1 - 0.05) = 0.057$.

The FDIC insures amounts of up to $250,000 per depositor per insured financial institution. Coverage amounts that exceed the limit are possible by using different ownership categories, such as individual, joint, and trust ownership accounts. For example, a joint account, held by two people, would be covered up to $500,000, with each account owner having $250,000 of coverage. Remember, however, that different branch offices count as the same institution, and mergers in the financial service industry may bring accounts from different banks together.

The FDIC and NCUA also provide deposit insurance for certain retirement accounts, up to $250,000, including traditional IRAs, Roth IRAs, Simplified Employee Pension (SEP) IRAs, and Savings Incentive Match Plans for Employees (SIMPLE) IRAs as well as self-directed Keogh accounts and various plans for state government employees. Of course, this coverage applies only to retirement accounts in financial institutions insured by the FDIC and NCUA.

To determine if all of your deposits are insured, use the Electronic Deposit Insurance Estimator (EDIE) at www.fdic.gov/edie/index.html. This feature includes a step-by-step tutorial with depositor situations for different types of accounts and different ownership. Information about credit union deposit coverage is available at www.ncua.gov. Since not all financial institutions have federal deposit insurance, investigate this matter when you are selecting a savings plan. Additional information on the regulation and consumer protection aspects of financial institutions is included in Appendix C.

EXAMPLE: Deposit Insurance

If you have a $562,000 joint account with a relative in an FDIC insured financial institution, $31,000 of your savings will not be covered by federal deposit insurance.

One-half of the $562,000 exceeds the $250,000 limit by $31,000.

Savings plan comparison

PRACTICE QUIZ 5-4

1 When would you prefer a savings plan with high liquidity over one with a high rate of return?
2 What is the relationship between compounding and the future value of an amount?
3 How do inflation and taxes affect earnings on savings?

Payment Methods

LO5-5

Compare the costs and benefits of different types of payment accounts.

While check writing still accounts for many consumer transactions, various electronic payment methods are now commonly used (Exhibit 5-9).

ELECTRONIC PAYMENTS

Transactions not involving cash, checks, or credit cards have expanded with technology, improved security, and increased consumer acceptance.

Financial institutions offer convenient services through technology.

DEBIT CARD TRANSACTIONS Nearly every store and online retailer processes debit card transactions, with the amount of the purchase deducted from your checking or other bank account. Most debit cards can be used two ways: (1) with your signature, like a credit card, and (2) with your personal identification number (PIN), like an ATM card. When the debit card is processed like a credit card, you have more security in case of a fraudulent transaction or a purchase dispute. But when using a debit card to check into a hotel, buy gas, or rent a car, a merchant may *freeze* an amount in your bank account above what you actually spend. This hold on your funds could result in an overdrawn account.

Use a Credit Card to	Use a Debit Card to
Delay the payment for a purchase.	Limit your spending to available money.
Build a credit history with wise buying.	Avoid bills that will be paid in the future.
Buy online or for major purchases.	Avoid interest payment or an annual fee.
Earn more generous rewards points for spending.	Obtain better protection if you process a transaction as a credit card.

Exhibit 5-9 Payment alternatives

Electronic Payments	Checking Accounts	Other Payment Methods
• Debit (cash, check) cards • Online payments, mobile transfers • Stored-value (prepaid) cards • Smart cards ("electronic wallet")	• Regular checking account • Activity checking account • Interest-earning checking account	• Certified check • Cashier's check • Money order • Traveler's checks

ONLINE PAYMENTS Banks and Internet companies serve as third parties to facilitate online bill payments. These organizations include www.paypal.com, www.mycheckfree.com, www.paytrust.com, and Google Wallet (previously Google Checkout). Some online payment services give you a choice of using a credit card or a bank account, while others require one or the other. Being linked to your checking account, rather than to a credit card, may not give you as much leverage when disputing a transaction.

People without a credit or debit card can use PayNearMe for online buying and other transactions. This service allows buyers to make a purchase and then pay cash at a local store, The consumer receives a receipt and the seller is notified of the payment. This cash transaction network may be used for online purchases, telephone orders, loan repayments, money transfers, and other transactions that might require a credit card. PayNearMe has partnerships with several major online and storefront retailers.

Another payment alternative with no disclosure of credit card information is eBillme, which only requires an email address to establish an account for making purchases. Then, you make your payment to eBillme through online banking or at a local walk-in site. When using these services, be sure to consider all fees, online security, and customer service availability.

MOBILE TRANSFERS Apps for mobile payment systems through smart phones, tablets, and other wireless devices are expanding. The *near-field communications* (NFC) technology stores credit card and bank account information. These wireless devices replace debit and credit cards for processing financial and purchasing transactions. A tap or wave of your phone at the point-of-sale terminal sensor completes the purchase. While these mobile transactions usually occur through a bank account, in the future these payments may bypass banks with charges directly on your phone bill.

Mobile banking is increasing the availability of "person-to-person" payments with the transfer of funds by email or to a mobile phone number. The opportunity to send and receive money through links to bank accounts and cards may also occur with online payment services.

STORED-VALUE CARDS Prepaid cards for telephone service, transit fares, highway tolls, laundry service, and school lunches are common. While some of these stored-value cards are disposable, others can be reloaded with an additional amount. Also called *prepaid debit cards,* some stored-value cards may have activation charges, ATM fees, and other transaction costs. Recipients of government benefits may receive Social Security and other payments on a prepaid debit card, which is practical for people without a bank account.

SMART CARDS These "electronic wallets" are similar to other ATM cards with an embedded microchip. In addition to banking activities, the card may also store past purchases, insurance information, and your medical history. Recent developments in smart cards include an option that allows you to pay with reward points.

TYPES OF CHECKING ACCOUNTS

Checking accounts fall into three major categories: regular checking accounts, activity accounts, and interest-earning checking accounts.

REGULAR CHECKING ACCOUNTS *Regular checking accounts* usually have a monthly service charge that you may avoid by keeping a minimum balance in the account. Some financial institutions will waive the monthly fee if you keep a certain amount in savings. Avoiding the monthly service charge can be beneficial. For example, a monthly fee of $7.50 results in $90 a year. However, you lose interest on the minimum-balance amount in a non-interest-earning account.

ACTIVITY ACCOUNTS *Activity accounts* charge a fee for each check written and sometimes a fee for each deposit, in addition to a monthly service charge. However, you do not have to maintain a minimum balance. An activity account is most appropriate for people who write only a few checks each month and are unable to maintain the required minimum balance.

INTEREST-EARNING CHECKING ACCOUNTS *Interest-earning checking accounts,* sometimes called *NOW accounts* (NOW stands for *negotiable order of withdrawal*), usually require a minimum balance. If the account balance goes below this amount, you may not earn interest and will likely incur a service charge.

share draft account An interest-bearing checking account at a credit union.

The **share draft account** is an interest-earning checking account at a credit union. Credit union members write checks, called *share drafts,* against their account balances.

EVALUATING CHECKING ACCOUNTS

DID YOU KNOW?

An extensive number of fake check scams occur each year. Information and videos are available at www.fakechecks.org.

Would you rather have a checking account that pays interest and requires a $1,000 minimum balance or an account that doesn't pay interest and requires a $300 minimum balance? This decision requires evaluating factors such as restrictions, fees and charges, interest, and special services (see Exhibit 5-10).

RESTRICTIONS The most common limitation on checking accounts is the amount you must keep on deposit to earn interest or avoid a service charge. Until recently, financial institutions also placed various restrictions on the holding period for deposited checks; that is, they required a period of time for checks to clear before you were allowed to use the funds. The Expedited Funds Availability Act requires that funds from local checks be available

Exhibit 5-10

Checking account selection factors

CHECKING ACCOUNT SELECTION FACTORS

Restrictions
- Minimum balance
- Federal deposit insurance
- Hours and location of branch offices
- Holding period for deposited checks

Fees and Charges
- Monthly fee
- Fees for each check or deposit
- Printing of checks
- Fee to obtain canceled check copy
- Overdraft, stop-payment order, certified check fee
- Fees for preauthorized bill payment, fund transfer, or home banking activity

Special Services
- Direct deposit of payroll and government checks
- 24-hour teller machines
- Overdraft protection
- Banking at home
- Discounts or free checking for certain groups (students, senior citizens, employees of certain companies)
- Free or discounted services, such as traveler's checks

Interest
- Interest rate
- Minimum deposit to earn interest
- Method of compounding
- Portion of balance used to compute interest
- Fee charged for falling below necessary balance to earn interest

HOW TO ...

Avoid Identity Theft

People who put their Social Security and driver's license numbers on their checks are making identity theft fairly easy. With one check, a con artist could know your Social Security, driver's license, and bank account numbers as well as your address, phone number, and perhaps even a sample of your signature. Identity fraud can range from passing bad checks and using stolen credit cards to theft of another person's total financial existence. To avoid identity theft, take these actions:

1. Use only your initials and last name on checks so a person will not know how you sign checks.
2. Do not put the full account number on checks when paying a bill; use only the last four numbers.
3. If possible, use your work phone and a post office box on checks instead of your home address.
4. Do not put your Social Security number on any document unless it is legally required. Do not carry your Social Security card in your wallet.
5. Shred or burn financial information containing account or Social Security numbers.
6. Use passwords involving both letters and numbers.
7. Do not mail bills from your home mailbox, especially if it is out by the street.
8. Check your credit report each year to make sure it is correct with all three major credit reporting agencies.
9. Ask to have your name removed from mailing lists operated by credit agencies and companies offering credit promotions.
10. Keep a photocopy of the contents of your wallet (both sides of each item) as a record to cancel accounts if necessary.
11. Use only secure websites of reputable organizations when making online purchases or when providing sensitive personal information.
12. Maintain up-to-date anti-virus software with anti-spam features and a personal firewall.

If you are a victim of identity theft, take the following actions:

- File a police report immediately in the area where the item was stolen. This proves you were diligent and is a first step toward an investigation (if there ever is one).
- Call the three national credit reporting organizations *immediately* to place a fraud alert on your name and Social Security number. The numbers are: Equifax, 1-800-525-6285; Experian, 1-888-397-3742; and TransUnion, 1-800-680-7289.
- Contact the Social Security Administration fraud line at 1-800-269-0271.

Additional information on financial privacy and identity theft is available at www.myidscore.com, www.identitytheft.org, www.idfraud.org, www.privacyrights.org, and www.idtheftcenter.org.

within two business days and funds from out-of-town checks be withheld for no more than five business days.

FEES AND CHARGES Nearly all financial institutions require a minimum balance or impose service charges for checking accounts. When using an interest-bearing checking account, compare your earnings with any service charge or fee. Also, consider the cost of lost or reduced interest due to the need to maintain the minimum balance.

Checking account fees have increased in recent years. Items such as check printing, overdraft fees, and stop-payment orders have doubled or tripled in price at some financial institutions. Some institutions will "bait" you with fancy checks at a low price and then charge a much higher price when you reorder. You may be able to purchase checks at a lower cost from a mail-order or online company.

INTEREST As discussed earlier, the interest rate, the frequency of compounding, and the interest computation method will affect the earnings on your checking account.

SPECIAL SERVICES As financial institutions attempted to reduce paper and postage costs, canceled checks are no longer returned. Bank customers are provided with more detailed monthly statements and usually have online access to view and print checks that have been paid.

overdraft protection An automatic loan made to checking account customers to cover the amount of checks written in excess of the available balance in the checking account.

Overdraft protection is an automatic loan made to checking account customers for checks written in excess of the available balance. This service is convenient but costly. Most overdraft plans make loans based on $50 or $100 increments. An overdraft of just $1 might trigger a $50 loan and corresponding finance charges of perhaps 18 percent. But overdraft protection can be less costly than the fee charged for a check you write when you do not have enough money on deposit to cover it. That fee may be $20 or more. Many financial institutions will allow you to cover checking account overdrafts with an automatic transfer from a savings account for a nominal fee. If so, take advantage of this service.

Beware of checking accounts that offer several services (safe deposit box, traveler's checks, low-rate loans, and travel insurance) for a single monthly fee. This may sound like a good value; however, such accounts benefit only a small group of people who make use of all the services in the package.

my life 5

I regularly maintain a record of my checking account balance.

Each year, fewer and fewer checks are written. However, most debit cards and online payments are still connected to traditional checking accounts. Contact several financial institutions to determine the features and fees associated with various payment accounts.

MANAGING YOUR CHECKING ACCOUNT

Obtaining and using a checking account involves several activities.

OPENING A CHECKING ACCOUNT First, decide the owner of the account. Only one person is allowed to write checks on an *individual account.* A *joint account* has two or more owners. Both an individual account and a joint account require a signature card. This document is a record of the official signatures of the person or persons authorized to write checks on the account.

MAKING DEPOSITS A *deposit ticket* is used for adding funds to your checking account. On this document, you list the amounts of cash and checks being deposited. Each check you deposit requires an *endorsement*—your signature on the back of the check—to authorize the transfer of the funds into your account. The three common endorsement forms are:

- A *blank endorsement* is just your signature, which should only be used when you are actually depositing or cashing a check, since a check could be cashed by anyone once it has been signed.
- A *restrictive endorsement* consists of the words *for deposit only,* followed by your signature, which is especially useful when you are depositing checks.
- A *special endorsement* allows you to transfer a check to someone else with the words *pay to the order of,* followed by the name of the other person and then your signature.

RECONCILING YOUR CHECKING ACCOUNT

The process of comparing your checkbook balance to the bank statement is vital for determining any errors that may have occurred. Use the following steps to reconcile your account.

At this point, the revised balances for both the checkbook and the bank statement should be the same. If the two do not match, check your math; make sure every check and deposit was recorded correctly.

The Bank Statement			Your Checkbook	
Balance on current bank statement	$	643.96	Current balance in your checkbook	$ 295.91
Step 1.	*Date*	*Amount*	**Step 3.**	
Add up outstanding checks (checks that you have written but have not yet cleared the banking system) and withdrawals still outstanding.	10-4	70.00	Subtract total of fees or other charges listed on bank statement	
	10-6	130.00		
	10-7	111.62		
				$ −15.75
			Subtract ATM withdrawals, debit card payments, and other automatic payments	$ −100.00
Subtract the total	$	−311.62	**Step 4.**	
			Add interest earned.	$ +2.18
Step 2.	*Date*	*Amount*		
Add up deposits in transit (deposits that have been made but are not reported on the current statement).	10-2	60.00	Add direct deposits.	$ +300.00
	10-5	90.00		
Add the total.	$	+150.00		
Adjusted bank balance	$	482.34	**Adjusted checkbook balance**	$ 482.34

WRITING CHECKS Before writing a check, record the information in your check register and deduct the amount of the check from your balance. Many checking account customers use duplicate checks to maintain a record of their current balance.

The procedure for proper check writing has the following steps: (1) record the date; (2) write the name of the person or organization receiving the payment; (3) record the amount of the check in figures; (4) write the amount of the check in words (checks for less than a dollar should be written as "only 79 cents," for example, and cross out the word *dollars* on the check); (5) sign the check; (6) note the reason for payment.

A *stop-payment order* may be necessary if a check is lost or stolen. Most banks do not honor checks with "stale" dates, usually six months old or older. The fee for a stop-payment commonly ranges from $10 to $20. If several checks are missing or you lose your checkbook, closing the account and opening a new one is likely to be less costly than paying several stop-payment fees.

DID YOU KNOW?

In recent years, the Federal Reserve reported that over $900 billion was being held in low- or no-interest checking accounts. Consumers are encouraged to consider high-yield checking accounts, available online or at a credit union, or move some of these funds into long-term investments.

RECONCILING YOUR CHECKING ACCOUNT Each month you will receive a *bank statement* summarizing deposits, checks paid, interest earned, and fees such as service charges and printing of checks. The balance reported on the statement will usually differ from the balance in your checkbook. Reasons for a difference include checks that have not yet cleared, deposits not received by the bank, and interest earned.

To determine the correct balance, prepare a *bank reconciliation* to account for differences between the bank statement and your checkbook balance. See the Financial Planning Calculations box on page 179 for details of the bank reconciliation process.

A failure to reconcile your bank account each month can result in not knowing

- Your exact spending habits for wise money management.
- If the correct deposit amounts have been credited to your account.
- Any unauthorized ATM withdrawals.
- If you have been overcharged for fees.
- Errors that your bank may have made in your account.

OTHER PAYMENT METHODS

While personal checks are a very common payment form, other methods are available. A *certified check* is a personal check with guaranteed payment. The amount of the check is deducted from your balance when the financial institution certifies the check. A *cashier's check* is a check of a financial institution. You may purchase one by paying the amount of the check plus a fee. You may purchase a *money order* in a similar manner from financial institutions, post offices, and stores. Certified checks, cashier's checks, and money orders allow you to make a payment that the recipient knows is valid.

Traveler's checks allow you to make payments when you are away from home. This payment form requires you to sign each check twice. First, you sign the traveler's checks when you purchase them. Then, to identify you as the authorized person, you sign them again as you cash them. Electronic traveler's checks, in the form of a prepaid travel card, are also available. The card allows travelers visiting other nations to get local currency from an ATM.

Payment account comparison

Checking/payment account cost analysis

Checking account reconciliation

PRACTICE QUIZ 5-5

1 What factors are commonly considered when selecting a checking account?
2 Are checking accounts that earn interest preferable to regular checking accounts? Why or why not?

my life stages for using financial services . . .

YOUR PERSONAL FINANCE DASHBOARD

A key indicator of your future financial success is the percentage of income saved each month. Various financial institutions and savings instruments can be used to implement this element of your financial plan.

While most people in our society save nothing or very little, financial experts recommend a saving rate of between 5 and 10 percent. These funds might be used for emergencies, unexpected expenses, or short-term financial goals as well as long-term financial security.

YOUR SITUATION Are you able to set aside an amount for savings each month? Are there expenses you can reduce, or sources of increased income that could add to the amount you save each month? An improving savings rate is the foundation for progress toward financial independence. Other financial services actions you might consider during various stages of your life include. . .

. . . in college

- Establish account with a bank or credit union (seek special student accounts)
- Maintain proper spending to avoid overdraft charges
- Monitor ATM fees and other account charges

. . . in my 20s

- Use online payments for convenience
- Increase savings amount in your emergency fund
- Compare fees and charges among various financial institutions

. . . in my 30s and 40s

- Evaluate the use of other financial services such as an asset management account and a trust account
- Expand savings and investment program for funding future needs

. . . in my 50s and beyond

- Consider special "senior" accounts with lower fees and other features
- Coordinate ownership of bank accounts in relation to estate planning activities

SUMMARY OF LEARNING OBJECTIVES

LO5-1

Analyze factors that affect the selection and use of financial services.

Your understanding of financial services should include knowledge of savings plans, payment accounts, loans, trust services, and electronic banking, which are used for managing daily financial activities. Technology, opportunity costs, and economic conditions are some of the factors that affect the selection and use of financial services.

LO5-2

Compare the types of financial institutions.

When selecting a primary financial service provider, your choices include commercial banks, savings and loan associations, mutual savings banks, credit unions, life insurance companies, investment companies, and online banks. These financial institutions should be assessed on the basis of services offered, rates and fees, safety, convenience, and special programs available to customers.

LO5-3

Compare the costs and benefits of various savings plans.
The most common savings plans available to consumers are regular savings accounts, certificates of deposit, money market accounts, money market funds, and U.S. savings bonds.

LO5-4

Identify the factors used to evaluate different savings plans.
Evaluate a savings plan on the basis of rate of return, inflation, tax considerations, liquidity, safety, restrictions, and fees.

LO5-5

Compare the costs and benefits of different types of payment accounts.
When considering various payment alternatives, electronic methods include debit cards, mobile and online payment systems, stored-value cards, and smart cards. Regular checking accounts, activity accounts, and interest-earning checking accounts can be compared with regard to restrictions (such as a minimum balance), fees and charges, interest, and special services. Other payment alternatives include certified checks, cashier's checks, money orders, and traveler's checks.

KEY TERMS

annual percentage yield (APY) 170
asset management account 158
automatic teller machine (ATM) 159
certificate of deposit (CD) 166
commercial bank 161
compounding 170
credit union 162
debit card 159
money market account 167
money market fund 164
mutual savings bank 161
overdraft protection 178
rate of return 170
savings and loan association 161
share account 166
share draft account 176
trust 157

KEY FORMULAS

Page	Topic	Formula
171	Annual percentage yield (APY)	$\text{APY} = 100[(1 + \text{Interest/Principal})^{365/\text{days in term}} - 1]$ Principal = The amount of funds on deposit Interest = The total dollar amount earned on the principal Days in term = The actual number of days in the term of the account
	When the number of days in the term is 365 or where the account does not have a stated maturity, the APY formula is simply	$\text{APY} = 100\ (\text{Interest/Principal})$ *Example:* $100\left[\left(1 + \frac{\$56.20}{\$1{,}000}\right)^{\frac{365}{365}} - 1\right] = 0.0562 = 5.62\%$
173	After-tax rate of return	Interest rate × (1 − Tax rate) *Example:* $0.05 \times (1 - 0.28) = 0.036 = 3.6\%$

SELF-TEST PROBLEMS

1. What would be the annual percentage yield (APY) for a savings account that earned $174 on a balance of $3,250 over the past 365 days?
2. If you earned a 4.2 percent return on your savings, with a 15 percent tax rate, what is the after-tax rate of return?

Answers to Self-Test Problems

1. To calculate the APY when the number of days in the term is 365, use this formula:

   APY = 100 (Interest/Principal)

   APY = 100 (174/3250)

   APY = 100 (.0535) = 5.35 percent

2. To calculate the after-tax rate of return use:

   Interest rate × (1 − Tax rate)

   $0.042 \times (1 - 0.15) = 0.042\ (0.85) = 0.0357 = 3.57\%$

FINANCIAL PLANNING PROBLEMS

1. *Calculating the Cost of ATM Fees.* If a person has ATM fees each month of $18 for 6 years, what would be the total cost of those banking fees? L05-1
2. *Determining an Annual Interest Rate.* A payday loan company charges 4 percent interest for a two-week period. What would be the annual interest rate from that company? L05-2
3. *Computing CD Interest.* A certificate of deposit will often result in a penalty for withdrawing funds before the maturity date. If the penalty involves two months of interest, what would be the amount for early withdrawal on a $20,000, 6 percent CD? L05-4
4. *Computing Future Value.* What would be the value of a savings account started with $1,200, earning 3 percent (compounded annually) after 10 years? L05-4
5. *Calculating Present Value.* Brenda Young desires to have $20,000 eight years from now for her daughter's college fund. If she will earn 4 percent (compounded annually) on her money, what amount should she deposit now? Use the present value of a single amount calculation. L05-4
6. *Computing Future Value of Annual Deposits.* What amount would you have if you deposited $2,500 a year for 30 years at 8 percent (compounded annually)? (Use the Chapter 1 appendix.) L05-4
7. *Comparing Taxable and Tax-Free Yields.* With a 28 percent marginal tax rate, would a tax-free yield of 7 percent or a taxable yield of 9.5 percent give you a better return on your savings? Why? L05-4
8. *Computing APY.* What would be the annual percentage yield for a savings account that earned $56 in interest on $800 over the past 365 days? L05-4
9. *Calculating Opportunity Cost.* What is the annual opportunity cost of a checking account that requires a $400 minimum balance to avoid service charges? Assume an interest rate of 3 percent. L05-4
10. *Comparing Costs of Checking Accounts.* What would be the net *annual* cost of the following checking accounts? L05-5

    a. Monthly fee, $3.75; processing fee, $0.25 cents per check; checks written, an average of 22 a month.

    b. Interest earnings of 6 percent with a $500 minimum balance; average monthly balance, $600; monthly service charge of $15 for falling below the minimum balance, which occurs three times a year (no interest earned in these months).
11. *Computing Checking Account Balance.* Based on the following information, determine the true balance in your checking account. (See page 179) L05-5

Balance in your checkbook, $356	Interest earned on the account, $4
Balance on bank statement, $472	Total of outstanding checks, $187
Service charge and other fees, $15	Deposits in transit, $60

FINANCIAL PLANNING ACTIVITIES

1. *Researching Banking Services.* Talk to several people regarding their experiences with mobile banking and prepaid debit cards. What benefits and concerns have they experienced with these services? LO 5-1
2. *Comparing Financial Institutions.* Conduct a study of services offered by various financial institutions. How has technology influenced the types of services and costs of these services? LO 5-2

LO 5-2 3. *Researching Alternative Financial Services.* Conduct research (online and by talking with people) about pawnshops, payday loans, check-cashing outlets, rent-to-own purchases, and car title loans. What actions might a person take to avoid these high-cost financial services?

LO 5-3, 5-4 4. *Comparing Savings Plans.* Collect information from varied financial institutions (national bank, local bank, credit union, online bank) about the savings plans they offer. Using Sheet 25 in the Personal Financial Planner, compare the features and potential earnings of two or three savings plans.

LO 5-5 5. *Comparing Payment Accounts.* Using Sheets 26 and 27 in the Personal Financial Planner, compare the features and costs of checking accounts at two financial institutions. Online searches for this information may be useful.

FINANCIAL PLANNING CASE

Evaluating Banking Services

"Wow! My account balance is a little lower than I expected," commented Melanie Harper as she reviewed her bank statement. "Wait a minute! There's nearly $20 in fees for ATM withdrawals and other service charges."

"Oh no! I also went below the minimum balance required for my *free* checking account," Melanie groaned. "That cost me $7.50!" Melanie is not alone in her frustration with fees paid for financial services. While careless money management caused many of these charges, others could have been reduced or eliminated by comparing costs at various financial institutions.

Melanie has decided to investigate various alternatives to her current banking services. Her preliminary research provided the following:

Mobile banking – allows faster access to account information, to quickly transfer funds, make payments and purchases. May include access to expanded financial services, such as low-cost, online investment trading and instant loan approval.

Prepaid debit card – would prevent overspending, staying within the budgeted amount loaded to the card. Cards are usually accepted in most retail locations and online. A variety of fees might be associated with the card.

Check-cashing outlet – would result in fees only when services are used, such as money orders, cashing a check, obtaining a prepaid cash card, or paying bills online.

Many people do not realize the amount they pay each month for various bank fees. Some basic research can result in saving several hundred dollars a year.

Questions

1. What benefits and drawbacks might Melanie encounter when using each of these financial services?

Mobile banking	Prepaid debit card	Check-cashing outlet

2. What factors should Melanie consider when selecting among these various banking services?
3. What actions might you take to better understand the concerns associated with using various banking services?

PERSONAL FINANCIAL PLANNER IN ACTION

Selecting Savings and Payment Services

The use of payment services and savings programs influences other aspects of financial planning. Minimizing banking fees and maximizing earnings on funds are common objectives.

Your Short-Term Financial Planning Activities	*Resources*
1. Identify various financial services needed for savings, payment, and money management activities. Identify financial institutions that you might use to obtain these services.	PFP Sheet 23 www.bankrate.com www.creditunion.coop www.wachovia.com
2. Compare the rates of return, fees, and other factors for different savings plans that you might use to meet your financial goals.	PFP Sheets 24, 25 www.fdic.gov www.savingsbonds.gov
3. Compare the features and costs of checking and check card services at various financial institutions.	PFP Sheets 26, 27 www.bankrate.com www.mycheckfree.com

Your Long-Term Financial Planning Activities	*Resources*
1. Identify savings decisions that would best help you achieve long-term financial goals.	www.clevelandsaves.org www.asec.org
2. List the economic conditions (inflation, current interest rates) and personal factors related to the costs and benefits of financial services that you should monitor as your personal life situation changes over time.	Text page 160 www.federalreserve.gov www.bls.gov

CONTINUING CASE

Banking Services

Life Situation	*Financial Data*
Single	Monthly Income $1,750
Age 21	Living Expenses $1,210
No dependents	Personal property $7,300
College student	Savings $1,000
	Student loan $3,000
	Credit card debt $2,400

Shelby Johnson has been working at a local pet store, trying to save money so that she can open up her own business some day. She is nearing graduation; however, she recently lost some of her savings due to an unexpected illness and medical expenses. She knows that this may affect when she will be able to open her Pet Salon. She and her parents, Matt and Madison Johnson (ages 49 and 47), are close and Shelby frequently seeks out their financial advice. They warn her that she may need to make some life changes in order to build back up her savings. They also advise her to establish an emergency fund so that she can avoid having to dip into her savings in case something happens in the future.

Questions

1. Given her current situation, list some suggestions on what Shelby should do to increase her emergency fund.
2. Based on her current and future life situation, what other money management and financial planning activities would you recommend for Shelby?
3. Describe how Shelby might use the Personal Financial Planner sheets 26 and 28 (Payment Account Comparison and Checking Account Reconciliation).

DAILY SPENDING DIARY

"My cash withdrawals have resulted in ATM fees that take away money from other budget items."

Directions

Start (or continue) your "Daily Spending Diary" to record and monitor spending in various categories using the sheets provided at the end of the book. Or you may create your own format to monitor your spending. Your comments should reflect what you have learned about your spending patterns and help you consider possible changes you might want to make in your spending habits.

Questions

1. What banking fees do you pay each month? What actions might you take to reduce or eliminate these cash outflows?
2. What other areas of your daily spending might be reduced or revised?

The Daily Spending Diary sheets are located in Appendix D at the end of the book and on the student website at www.mhhe.com/kdh.

chapter 6

Introduction to Consumer Credit

Learning Objectives

LO6-1 Define *consumer credit* and analyze its advantages and disadvantages.

LO6-2 Differentiate among various types of credit.

LO6-3 Assess your credit capacity and build your credit rating.

LO6-4 Describe the information creditors look for when you apply for credit.

LO6-5 Identify the steps you can take to avoid and correct credit mistakes.

LO6-6 Describe the laws that protect you if you have a complaint about consumer credit.

What will this mean for me?

Understanding the advantages and disadvantages of consumer credit as well as the types of credit that are available will enable you to make wise decisions regarding credit, now and in the future.

my life

CASH, CREDIT, OR DEBIT—WALKING A TIGHTROPE

Remember how thrilled you were when you graduated from high school and received an offer for a credit card? Soon afterward, you were excited when you made your first charge for some new clothes. After making a few more purchases, you reached your card limit. So you applied for two more credit cards, each with an annual interest rate of 23 percent. Then you began to charge groceries and furniture, because it was easier than paying cash. Do you know how to use credit wisely?

As you start or expand your use of credit, consider the following statements. For each of the following statements, select the letter to indicate your answers regarding these statements:

1. If I need more money for my expenses, I borrow it _____.
   a. never.
   b. sometimes.
   c. often.
2. I pay any bills I have when they are due _____.
   a. always.
   b. most of the time.
   c. sometimes.
3. If I want to see a copy of my credit report, I can contact _____.
   a. a credit reporting agency.
   b. a bank.
   c. the dean of my economics department.

(continued)

4. If I default (do not repay) on a loan, it will stay on my credit report for _____.
   a. 7 years.
   b. 2 years.
   c. 6 months.
5. I can begin building a good rating by _____.
   a. opening a savings account and making regular monthly deposits.
   b. paying most of my bills on time.
   c. opening a checking account and bouncing checks.
6. If I have serious credit problems, I should _____.
   a. contact my creditors to explain the problem.
   b. contact only the most persistent creditors.
   c. not contact my creditors and hope they will forget about me.

SCORING: **Give yourself 3 points for each "a," 2 points for each "b," and 1 point for each "c." Add up the number of points.**

If you scored 6–9 points, you might want to take a closer look at how credit works before you get over your head in debt.

If you scored 10–13 points, you are off to a good start, but be sure you know the pitfalls of opening a credit account.

Source: *How to Be Credit Smart* (Washington, DC: Consumer Education Foundation, 1994).

As you study this chapter, you will encounter "My Life" boxes with additional information and resources related to these items.

What Is Consumer Credit?

LO6-1

Define *consumer credit* and analyze its advantages and disadvantages.

"Charge it!" "Cash or credit?" "Put it on my account." As these phrases indicate, the use of credit is a fact of life in personal and family financial planning. When you use credit, you satisfy needs today and pay for this satisfaction in the future. While the use of credit is often necessary and even advantageous, responsibilities and disadvantages are associated with its use.

Credit is an arrangement to receive cash, goods, or services now and pay for them in the future. **Consumer credit** refers to the use of credit for personal needs (except a home mortgage) by individuals and families, in contrast to credit used for business purposes. Many people use credit to live beyond their means, largely because of a change in perception about credit. Past generations viewed credit as a negative and used it very sparingly. Society today has popularized credit with phrases such as "Life takes Visa," "Priceless" campaigns, and even references to a "Plunk factor" when using a sought-after credit card. That said, when used appropriately, credit can be a very useful tool.

credit An arrangement to receive cash, goods, or services now and pay for them in the future.

consumer credit The use of credit for personal needs (except a home mortgage).

Although Polonius cautioned, "Neither a borrower nor a lender be," using and providing credit have become a way of life for many people and businesses in today's economy. In January, you pay a bill for electricity that you used in December. A statement arrives in the mail for medical services that you received last month. You write a check for $40, a minimum payment on a $300 department store bill. With a bank loan, you purchase a new car. These are all examples of using credit: paying later for goods and services obtained now.

Most consumers have three alternatives in financing current purchases: They can draw on their savings, use their present earnings, or borrow against their expected future income. Each of these alternatives has trade-offs. If you continually deplete your savings, little will be left for emergencies or retirement income. If you spend your current income on luxuries instead of necessities, your well-being will eventually suffer. And if you pledge your future income to make current credit purchases, you will have little or no spendable income in the future.

Consumer credit is based on trust in people's ability and willingness to pay bills when due. It works because people by and large are honest and responsible. But how does consumer credit affect our economy, and how is it affected by our economy?

THE IMPORTANCE OF CONSUMER CREDIT IN OUR ECONOMY

Consumer credit dates back to colonial times. While credit was originally a privilege of the affluent, farmers came to use it extensively. No direct finance charges were imposed; instead, the cost of credit was added to the prices of goods. With the advent of the automobile in the early 1900s, installment credit, in which the debt is repaid in equal installments over a specified period of time, exploded on the American scene.

All economists now recognize consumer credit as a major force in the American economy. Any forecast or evaluation of the economy includes consumer spending trends and consumer credit as a sustaining force. To paraphrase an old political expression, as the consumer goes, so goes the U.S. economy.

The aging of the baby boom generation has added to the growth of consumer credit. This generation currently represents about 30 percent of the population but holds nearly 60 percent of the outstanding debt. The people in this age group have always been disproportionate users of credit, since consumption is highest as families are formed and homes are purchased and furnished. Thus, while the extensive use of debt by this generation is nothing new, the fact that it has grown rapidly has added to overall debt use.

USES AND MISUSES OF CREDIT

Using credit to purchase goods and services may allow consumers to be more efficient or more productive or to lead more satisfying lives. There are many valid reasons for using credit. A medical emergency may leave a person strapped for funds. A homemaker returning to the workforce may need a car. It may be possible to buy an item now for less money than it will cost later. Borrowing for a college education is another valid reason. But it probably is not reasonable to borrow for everyday living expenses or finance a Ford Thunderbird on credit when a Ford Fusion is all your budget allows.

"Shopaholics" and young adults are most vulnerable to misusing credit. College students are a prime target for credit card issuers, and issuers make it very easy for students to get credit cards. Wendy Leright, a 25-year-old teacher in Detroit, knows this all too well. As a college freshman, she applied for and got seven credit cards, all bearing at least an 18.9 percent interest rate and a $20 annual fee. Although unemployed, she used the cards freely, buying expensive clothes for herself, extravagant Christmas presents for friends and family, and even a one-week vacation in the Bahamas. "It got to a point where I didn't even look at the price tag," she said. By her senior year, Wendy had amassed $9,000 in credit card debt and couldn't make the monthly payments of nearly $200. She eventually turned to her parents to bail her out. "Until my mother sat me down and showed me how much interest I had to pay, I hadn't even given it a thought. I was shocked," Wendy said. "I would have had to pay it off for years."[1]

Using credit increases the amount of money a person can spend to purchase goods and services now. But the trade-off is that it decreases the amount of money that will be available to spend in the future. However, many people expect their incomes to increase and therefore expect to be able to make payments on past credit purchases and still make new purchases.

Here are some questions you should consider before you decide how and when to make a major purchase, for example, a car:

- Do I have the cash I need for the down payment?
- Do I want to use my savings for this purchase?
- Does the purchase fit my budget?
- Could I use the credit I need for this purchase in some better way?
- Could I postpone the purchase?
- What are the opportunity costs of postponing the purchase (alternative transportation costs, a possible increase in the price of the car)?
- What are the dollar costs and the psychological costs of using credit (interest, other finance charges, being in debt and responsible for making a monthly payment)?

If you decide to use credit, make sure the benefits of making the purchase now (increased efficiency or productivity, a more satisfying life, etc.) outweigh the costs (financial and psychological) of using credit. Thus, credit, when effectively used, can help you have more and enjoy more. When misused, credit can result in default, bankruptcy, and loss of creditworthiness.

ADVANTAGES OF CREDIT

Consumer credit enables people to enjoy goods and services now—a car, a home, an education, help in emergencies—and pay for them through payment plans based on future income.

Credit cards permit the purchase of goods even when funds are low. Customers with previously approved credit may receive other extras, such as advance notice of sales and the right to order by phone or to buy on approval. In addition, many shoppers believe it is easier to return merchandise they have purchased on account. Credit cards also provide shopping convenience and the efficiency of paying for several purchases with one monthly payment.

It is safer to use credit, since charge accounts and credit cards let you shop and travel without carrying a large amount of cash. You need a credit card to make a hotel reservation, rent a car, and shop by phone. You may also use credit cards for identification when cashing checks, and the use of credit provides you with a record of expenses.

The use of credit cards can provide up to a 50-day "float," the time lag between when you make the purchase and when the lender deducts the balance from your checking account when the payment is due. This float, offered by many credit card issuers, includes a grace period of 21 to 25 days. During the grace period, no finance charges are assessed on current purchases if the balance is paid in full each month within 25 days after billing.

Some large corporations, such as General Electric Company and General Motors Corporation, issue their own Visa and MasterCard and offer rebates on purchases. For example, every time you make a purchase with the GM MasterCard, 5 percent of the purchase price is set aside for you in a special GM Card Rebate account. When you are ready to buy or lease a GM car or truck, you just cash in your rebate at the GM dealership. Similarly, with an AT&T MasterCard, you can earn a cash bonus of up to 5 percent based on your total purchases during the year. In the late 1990s, however, some corporations began to eliminate these cards.

Some credit cards, including gold and platinum MasterCards and Visa Signature cards, extend the manufacturer's warranty by up to one year when you buy products with their cards. American Express and Citi's Thank You Premiere cards pay up to $1,000 per claim to repair broken items or replace lost purchases within 90 days.

Platinum credit cards offered by American Express provide emergency medical evacuation for travelers. When Stephen Bradley of New York was vacationing in tiny, isolated Coruripe, Brazil, he ate something that made him gravely ill. With no doctor nearby, a friend frantically called American Express about its guarantee to arrange emergency medical evacuation and treatment for Platinum Card users. AmEx moved fast: It lined up a car to rush Bradley to the nearest large town, managed to book a room in a sold-out hotel, and sent a doctor there to make a house call. The physician even accompanied Bradley's travel partner, Richard Laermer, to a local pharmacy for medicine. "When we went home to see our doctor, he told us she had saved Steve's life," recalls Laermer. "For the last five years we have been indebted to Platinum."

In addition, many major credit cards provide the following benefits to their customers at no extra cost:

- Accidental death and dismemberment insurance when you travel on a common carrier (train, plane, bus, or ship), up to $250,000.
- Auto rental collision damage waiver (CDW) for damage due to collision or theft for $50,000 or more.
- Roadside dispatch referral service for emergency roadside assistance, such as towing, locksmith services, and more.
- Redeem your points or miles for gift cards, cash, or to book travel—from airfare, hotels, and rental cars to vacation packages.
- Some cards, such as CapitalOne, don't charge foreign transaction fees.

Finally, credit indicates stability. The fact that lenders consider you a good risk usually means you are a responsible individual. However, if you do not repay your debts in a timely manner, you will find that credit has many disadvantages.

DISADVANTAGES OF CREDIT

Perhaps the greatest disadvantage of using credit is the temptation to overspend, especially during periods of inflation. It seems easy to buy today and pay tomorrow using cheaper dollars. But continual overspending can lead to serious trouble.

Whether or not credit involves security (something of value to back the loan), failure to repay a loan may result in loss of income, valuable property, and your good reputation. It can even lead to court action and bankruptcy. Misuse of credit can create serious long-term financial problems, damage to family relationships, and a slowing of progress toward financial goals. Therefore, you should approach credit with caution and avoid using it more extensively than your budget permits.

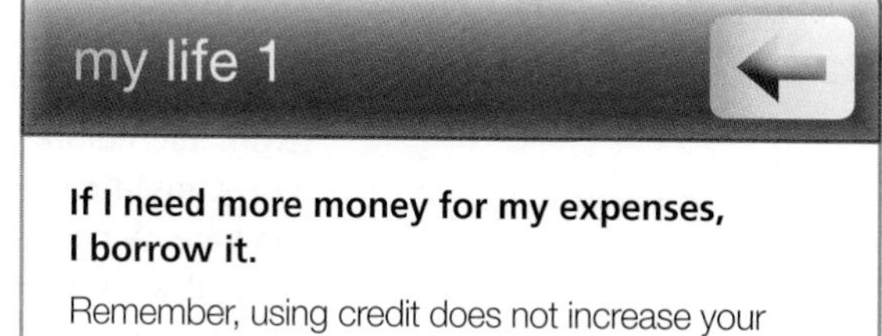

If I need more money for my expenses, I borrow it.

Remember, using credit does not increase your total purchasing power, nor does it mean that you have more money. It just allows you to buy things now for which you must pay later. Conduct an online search to locate suggestions for wise uses of credit.

Although credit allows more immediate satisfaction of needs and desires, it does not increase total purchasing power. Credit purchases must be paid for out of future income; therefore, credit ties up the use of future income. Furthermore, if your income does not increase to cover rising costs, your ability to repay credit commitments will diminish. Before buying goods and services on credit, consider whether they will have lasting value, whether they will increase your personal satisfaction during present and future income periods, and whether your current income will continue or increase.

Finally, credit costs money. It is a service for which you must pay. Paying for purchases over a period of time is more costly than paying for them with cash. Purchasing with credit rather than cash involves one very obvious trade-off: the fact that it will cost more due to monthly finance charges and the compounding effect of interest on interest. Just think of it! Suppose you are 18 and charge $1,500 worth of clothes and DVDs on a credit card with a 19 percent interest rate. If your minimum payment is 2.5 percent of your outstanding balance, you will make 208 monthly payments of $37.50. You will be over 35 years old when you pay off the debt, and will have paid more than $2,138 in interest, even if you charge nothing else on the account and have no other fees.

SUMMARY: ADVANTAGES AND DISADVANTAGES OF CREDIT

The use of credit provides immediate access to goods and services, flexibility in money management, safety and convenience, a cushion in emergencies, a means of increasing resources, and a good credit rating if you pay your debts back in a timely manner. But remember, the use of credit is a two-sided coin. An intelligent decision as to its use demands careful evaluation of your current debt, your future income, the added cost, and the consequences of overspending.

PRACTICE QUIZ 6-1

1 What is consumer credit?
2 Why is consumer credit important to our economy?
3 What are the uses and misuses of credit?
4 What are the advantages and disadvantages of credit?

Types of Credit

LO6-2

Differentiate among various types of credit.

Two basic types of consumer credit exist: closed-end credit and open-end credit. With **closed-end credit,** you pay back one-time loans in a specified period of time and in payments of equal amounts. With **open-end credit,** loans are made on a continuous basis and you are billed periodically for at least partial payment. Exhibit 6-1 shows examples of closed-end and open-end credit.

closed-end credit One-time loans that the borrower pays back in a specified period of time and in payments of equal amounts.

open-end credit A line of credit in which loans are made on a continuous basis and the borrower is billed periodically for at least partial payment.

CLOSED-END CREDIT

Closed-end credit is used for a specific purpose and involves a specified amount. Mortgage loans, automobile loans, and installment loans for purchasing furniture or appliances are examples of closed-end credit. An agreement, or contract, lists the repayment terms: the number of payments, the payment amount, and how much the credit will cost. Closed-end payment plans usually involve a written agreement for each credit purchase. A down payment or trade-in may be required, with the balance to be repaid in equal weekly or monthly payments over a period of time. Generally, the seller holds title to the merchandise until the payments have been completed.

The three most common types of closed-end credit are installment sales credit, installment cash credit, and single lump-sum credit. *Installment sales credit* is a loan that allows you to receive merchandise, usually high-priced items such as large appliances or furniture. You make a down payment and usually sign a contract to repay the balance, plus interest and service charges, in equal installments over a specified period.

Installment cash credit is a direct loan of money for personal purposes, home improvements, or vacation expenses. You make no down payment and make payments in specified amounts over a set period.

Exhibit 6-1

Examples of closed-end and open-end credit

Closed-End Credit	Open-End Credit
• Mortgage loans • Automobile loans • Installment loans (installment sales contract, installment cash credit, single lump-sum credit)	• Cards issued by department stores, bank cards (Visa, MasterCard) • Travel and entertainment cards (Diners Club, American Express) • Overdraft protection

Single lump-sum credit is a loan that must be repaid in total on a specified day, usually within 30 to 90 days. Lump-sum credit is generally, but not always, used to purchase a single item. As Exhibit 6-2 shows, consumer credit reached over $2.7 trillion in 2013.

OPEN-END CREDIT

Using a credit card issued by a department store, using a bank credit card (Visa, MasterCard) to make purchases at different stores, charging a meal at a restaurant, and using overdraft protection are examples of open-end credit. As you will soon see, you do not apply for open-end credit to make a single purchase, as you do with closed-end credit. Rather, you can use open-end credit to make any purchases you wish if you do not exceed your **line of credit,** the maximum dollar amount of credit the lender has made available to you. You may have to pay **interest,** a periodic charge for the use of credit, or other finance charges.

line of credit The dollar amount, which may or may not be borrowed, that a lender makes available to a borrower.

interest A periodic charge for the use of credit.

You may have had an appointment with a doctor or a dentist that you did not pay for until later. Professionals and small businesses often do not demand immediate payment

Exhibit 6-2 Volume of consumer credit (Not seasonally adjusted)

All economists now recognize consumer credit as a major force in the American economy.

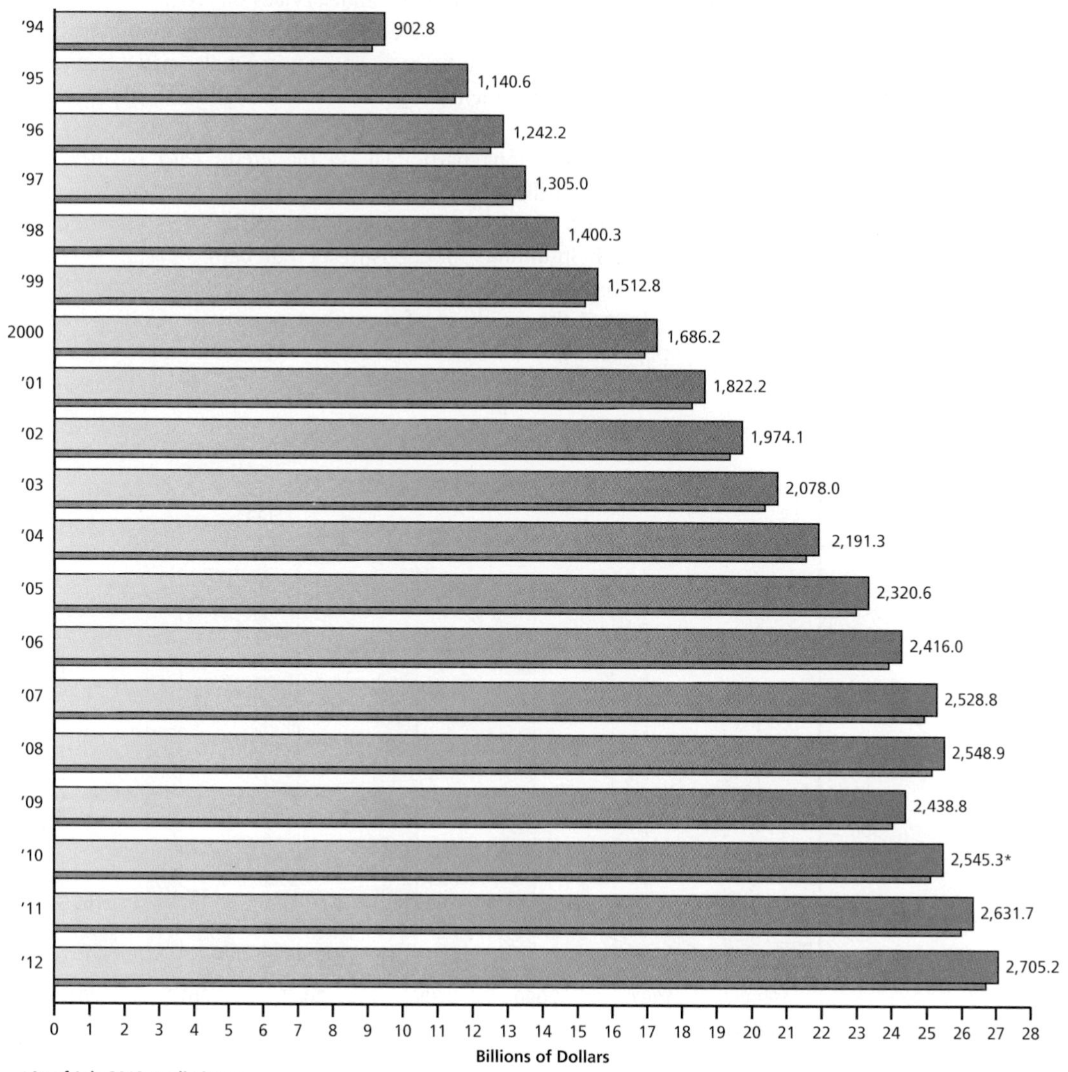

*As of July 2012, preliminary

Source: http://www.federalreserve.gov/RELEASES/g19/current/g19.htm table 1, accessed March 12, 2013.

but will charge interest if you do not pay the bill in full within 30 days. *Incidental credit* is a credit arrangement that has no extra costs and no specific repayment plan.

Many retailers use open-end credit. Customers can purchase goods or services up to a fixed dollar limit at any time. Usually you have the option to pay the bill in full within 30 days without interest charges or to make set monthly installments based on the account balance plus interest.

revolving check credit A prearranged loan from a bank for a specified amount; also called a *bank line of credit.*

Many banks extend **revolving check credit.** Also called a *bank line of credit,* this is a prearranged loan for a specified amount that you can use by writing a special check. Repayment is made in installments over a set period. The finance charges are based on the amount of credit used during the month and on the outstanding balance.

CREDIT CARDS Credit cards are extremely popular. According to a recent *American Banker* survey, 8 out of 10 U.S. households carry one or more credit cards. Two out of three households have at least one retail credit card, 56 percent have one or more Visa cards, and 47 percent have at least one MasterCard.

One-third of all credit card users generally pay off their balances in full each month. These cardholders are often known as *convenience users.* Others are borrowers; they carry balances beyond the grace period and pay finance charges. As Exhibit 6-3 illustrates, consumers use almost 1.2 billion credit cards to buy clothing, meals, vacations, gasoline, groceries, doctor visits, and other goods and services on credit.

While cash advances on credit cards can look attractive, remember that interest usually accrues from the moment you accept the cash, and you must also pay a transaction fee. One cash advance could cost you the money you were saving for a birthday gift for that special someone.

About 25,000 financial institutions participate in the credit card business, and the vast majority of them are affiliated with Visa International or the Interbank Card Association, which issues MasterCard. The Financial Planning for Life's Situations box on page 195 provides a few helpful hints for choosing a credit card.

Cobranding is the linking of a credit card with a business trade name offering "points" or premiums toward the purchase of a product or service. Cobranding has become increasingly popular since the success of General Motors Corporation's credit

Exhibit 6-3

Credit card holders and credit cards held

About 160 million people use almost 1.2 billion credit cards to buy goods and services.

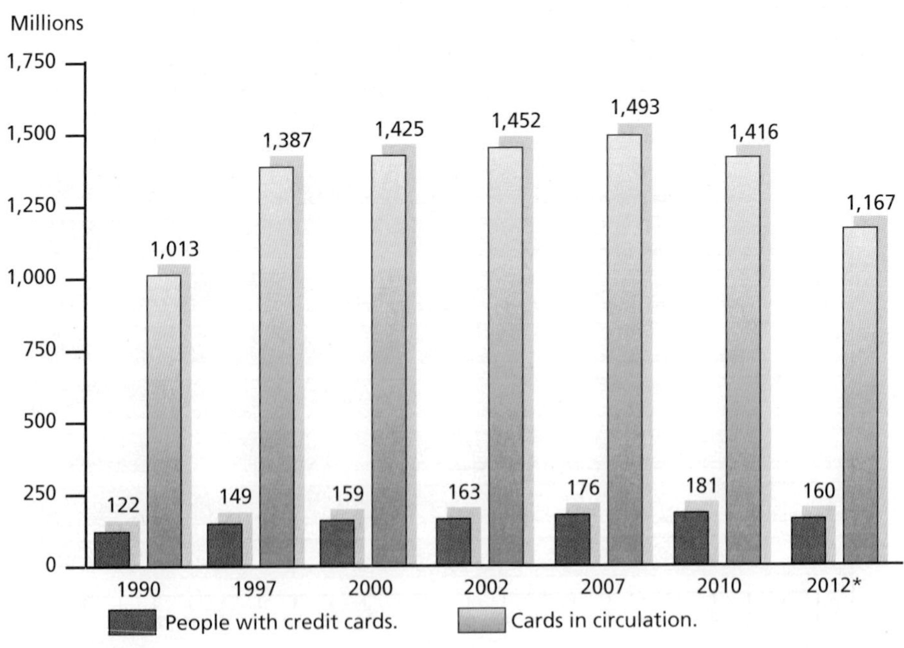

*Estimated.

Source: *Statistical Abstract of the United States 2012,* Table 1181, www.census.gov/compendia/statab/2012/tables/12s 1187.pdf accessed March 3, 2013.

CHOOSING A CREDIT CARD?

When choosing a credit card, it pays to shop around. Follow these suggestions to select the card that best meets your needs.

1. Department stores and gasoline companies are good places to obtain your first credit card. Pay your bills in full and on time, and you will begin to establish a good credit history.
2. Bank cards are offered through banks and savings and loan associations. Fees and finance charges vary considerably (from 8 to 21.6 percent), so shop around.
3. If you usually pay your bills in full, try to deal with a financial institution with an interest-free grace period, which is the time after a purchase has been made and before a finance charge is imposed, typically 21 to 30 days.
4. If you're used to paying monthly installments, look for a card with a low monthly finance charge. Be sure you understand how that finance charge is calculated.
5. Consider obtaining a card from an out-of-state financial institution if it offers better terms than those offered locally.
6. Be aware of some credit cards that offer "no fee" or low interest but start charging interest from the day you purchase an item.
7. Watch out for credit cards that do not charge annual fees but instead charge a "transaction fee" each time you use the card.
8. If you're paying only the minimum amounts on your monthly statement, you need to plan your budget more carefully. The longer it takes for you to pay off a bill, the more interest you pay. The finance charges you pay on an item could end up being more than the item is worth.
9. With a grace period of 25 days, you actually get a free loan when you pay bills in full each month.
10. To avoid delays that may result in finance charges, follow the card issuer's instructions as to where, how, and when to make bill payments.
11. If you have a bad credit history and problems getting a credit card, look for a savings institution that will give you a secured credit card if you open a savings account. Your line of credit will be determined by the amount you have on deposit.
12. Beware of offers of easy credit. No one can guarantee to get you credit.
13. Think twice before making a 900 number telephone call for a credit card. You will pay from $2 to $50 for the 900 call and may never receive a credit card.
14. Be aware of credit cards offered by "credit repair" companies or "credit clinics." These firms may also offer to clean up your credit history for a fee. But remember, only time and good credit habits will repair your credit report if you have a poor credit history.
15. If you don't have a list of your credit issuers' telephone numbers, you may be able to obtain them by calling the 800 number directory assistance at 1-800-555-1212.
16. Travel and entertainment (T&E) cards often charge higher annual fees than most credit cards. Usually you must make payment in full within 30 days of receiving your bill or typically no further purchases will be approved on the account.
17. Often additional credit cards on your account for a spouse or child (over 18) are available with a minimum additional fee or no fee at all.
18. Be aware that debit cards are not credit cards but simply a substitute for a check or cash. The amount of the sale is subtracted from your checking account.

Sources: American Institute of Certified Public Accountants; U.S. Office of Consumer Affairs; Federal Trade Commission.

card, launched in 1992. Cobranded credit cards offer rebates on products and services such as health clubs, tax preparation services from H&R Block, and gasoline purchases. Banks are realizing that cobranded credit cards help build customer loyalty.

SMART CARDS The ultimate plastic, smart cards, are embedded with a computer chip that can store 500 times the data of a credit card. Smart cards may ultimately combine credit cards, a driver's license, a health care ID with your medical history and insurance information, frequent-flier miles, and telephone cards. A single smart card, for example, could be used to buy an airline ticket, store it digitally, and track frequent-flier miles.

At Florida State University, smart cards have become practically indispensable. Students use smart cards to pay tuition, buy meals in the cafeteria, borrow library books, rent videos, and gain access to dormitories and online study groups.

DID YOU KNOW?

In 2012, an estimated 191 million debit card holders used 530 million cards for 52.6 billion transactions amounting to over $2.1 trillion.

Source: Statistical Abstract of the United States 2012, Table 1187.

debit card Electronically subtracts the amount of a purchase from the buyer's account at the moment the purchase is made.

DEBIT CARDS Don't confuse credit cards with debit cards. Debit cards are often called *bank cards, ATM cards, cash cards,* and *check cards.* Although they may look alike, the **debit card,** as the name implies, electronically subtracts from your account at the moment you buy goods or services, while the credit card extends credit and delays your payment. Debit cards are most commonly used at automatic teller machines, but they are increasingly being used to purchase goods at point-of-sale terminals in stores and service stations. It is estimated that in 2012, over 52.6 *billion transactions worth* $2.1 trillion will take place with 530 million debit cards.[2]

You are never responsible for charges on a debit card you haven't accepted. If you report a lost or stolen debit card within two days, federal regulations limit your liability to $50. After two days, your liability is limited to $50 plus any amount resulting from your failure to notify the issuer. If your debit card is lost or stolen, you must work directly with the issuer.

STORED VALUE (OR GIFT) CARDS Stored-value cards, gift cards or prepaid cards, resemble a typical debit card, using magnetic stripe technology to store information and track funds. However, unlike traditional debit cards, stored value cards are prepaid, providing you with immediate money. By the mid-1990s, large retailers began issuing stored-value cards instead of traditional paper gift certificates. Over the past decade, the stored-value cards have grown rapidly. Today, gift cards are being used for many purposes, including payroll, general spending, travel expenses, government benefit payments, and employee benefit and reward payments.

One market research firm estimates that holders of gift cards recently lost more than $75 million when the number of retailer bankruptcies increased sharply. Bankruptcy courts, treat gift cards the same way they handle unsecured debt: If a retailer goes bankrupt, holders get pennies on the dollar at most—and in many cases nothing. Recently, American shoppers spent over $35 billion on retailers' gift cards.

my life 2

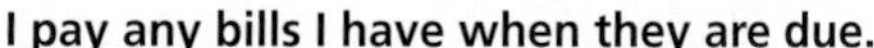

I pay any bills I have when they are due.

If you are having trouble paying your bills and need help, contact your creditors and try to work out an adjusted repayment plan. Before taking out a loan, make sure you can afford to repay it. Exhibit 6-4 on page 201 can help you determine your debt payments–to–income ratio.

TRAVEL AND ENTERTAINMENT (T&E) CARDS T&E cards are really not credit cards, because the monthly balance is due in full. However, most people think of Diners Club or American Express cards as credit cards because they don't pay the moment they purchase goods or services. Diners Club card, owned by Discover Financial Services, is accepted by millions of merchants in more than 185 countries and provides cash access at over 845,000 locations worldwide. American Express now issues credit cards also.

SMART PHONES Some phones are now equipped to make purchases. This concept, called *mobile commerce,* has seen a significant increase in interest from consumers, retailers, and finance companies. For example, some credit card companies, instead of providing a physical credit card, provide stickers that attach to a phone that will allow the customer to scan the code. In addition, retailers such as Starbucks have apps that are scannable barcodes to quickly pay using a mobile phone.

home equity loan A loan based on the current market value of a home less the amount still owed on the mortgage.

HOME EQUITY LOANS A **home equity loan** is based on the difference between the current market value of your home and the amount you still owe on your mortgage. With such a loan, you can borrow up to $100,000 or more on your home. Depending on the value of the home, you can borrow up to 85 percent of its appraised

Financial Planning Calculations

HOW MUCH CAN YOU BORROW WITH A HOME EQUITY LOAN?

Depending on your income and the equity in your home, you can apply for a line of credit for anywhere from $10,000 to $250,000 or more.

Some lenders let you borrow only up to 75 percent of the value of your home, less the amount of your first mortgage. At some banks you may qualify to borrow up to 85 percent! This higher lending limit may make the difference in your ability to get the money you need for home improvements, education, or other expenses.

Use the following chart to calculate your home loan value, which is the approximate amount of your home equity line of credit.

	Example	Your Home
Approximate market value of your home	$100,000	$ ____
Multiply by .75	× .75	× .75
Approximate loan value	75,000	____
Subtract balance due on mortgage(s)	50,000	____
Approximate credit limit available	$25,000	$ ____

In the above example, your "credit limit available" home loan value see table above (the amount for which you could establish your account) is $25,000. Once your account is established, you can write a check for any amount you need up to $25,000.

In choosing a home equity loan,

1. Find out if your lending institution protects you against rising interest rates.
2. Compare the size of your lender's fee with those of other institutions.
3. Find out if your lender charges an inactivity fee.
4. Make sure high annual fees and other costs do not outweigh the tax advantage of a home equity loan, especially if you are borrowing only a small amount.
5. Be careful of interest-only payments on home equity loans.
6. Find out whether your lender has the right to change the terms and conditions of your loan or to terminate your loan.
7. Make sure that all of the interest you hope to finally deduct on your home equity loan is in fact deductible.
8. Carefully evaluate your reasons for using the equity in your home for loans.
9. Know the full costs and risks of home equity loans before you make a commitment to a lending institution.

Sources: Household Bank, F.S.B., *Home Equity Loan Guide*, August 1991, p. 3; American Institute of CPAs, *Home Equity Loans: A Consumer's Guide*, n.d.

value, less the amount you still owe on your mortgage. The interest you pay on a home equity loan is tax deductible, unlike interest on other types of loans.

A home equity loan is usually set up as a revolving line of credit, typically with a variable interest rate. A *revolving line of credit* is an arrangement whereby borrowings are permitted up to a specified limit and for a stated period, usually 5 to 10 years. Once the line of credit has been established, you draw from it only the amount you need at any one time (see the Financial Planning Calculations box). Today many lenders offer home equity lines of credit. But your home is probably your largest asset. You should use the home equity loan only for major items such as education, home improvements, or medical bills and not for daily expenses or to buy a boat, new car, or to pay for a cruise. *Remember, if you miss payments on a home equity loan, you can lose your home.* Furthermore, when you sell your home, you probably will be required to pay off your equity line in full. If you plan to sell your house in the near future, consider whether annual fees to maintain the account and other costs of setting up an equity credit line make sense.

PROTECTING YOURSELF AGAINST DEBIT/CREDIT CARD FRAUD *Dead Man Walking* is the title of a movie, but it's also the nickname for a man arrested by postal inspectors. Using a bizarre twist on mail fraud and credit card fraud, Michael Dantorio was accused of using personal information from at least 17 deceased persons across the

Credit card companies spend hundreds of millions of dollars to promote their credit cards. The average cardholder has more than nine credit cards.

country to acquire credit cards in their names, resulting in fraudulent charges of over $60,000. Hence his nickname, "Dead Man Walking."

Dantorio relied on the use of several private mailboxes. He filed false changes of address for the deceased individuals and directed the credit cards to his private mailboxes. Once he received the cards, he lost no time in running up huge charges. If you have recently lost a loved one, be on the lookout for crooks who try to take advantage when you are most vulnerable.

In a country where consumers owe more than $2.7 trillion on their credit cards, estimates of a few billion dollars in credit fraud losses—just two to three one-thousandths of 1 percent—may not seem all that terrible. But it *is* terrible for victims of fraud. Though they may be protected financially, they are forced to endure major inconvenience. Many fraud victims are devastated emotionally. The negative effects can linger for years. Moreover, all of us pay the costs of credit card fraud through higher prices, higher interest rates, and increased inconvenience.

How can you protect yourself against credit card fraud? You can take several measures:

- Sign your new cards as soon as they arrive.
- Treat your cards like money. Store them in a secure place.
- Shred anything with your account number before throwing it away.
- Don't give your card number over the phone or online unless you initiate the call.
- Don't write your card number on a postcard or the outside of an envelope.
- Remember to get your card and receipt after a transaction, and double-check to be sure it's yours.
- If your billing statement is incorrect or your credit cards are lost or stolen, notify your card issuers immediately.
- If you don't receive your billing statement, notify the company immediately.

New technology is making it more difficult to use, alter, or counterfeit credit and debit cards. The security features being added to major credit cards include a holograph—a three dimensional, laser-produced optical device that changes its color and image as the card is tilted. Another feature is the use of ultra-violet ink that is visible only under ultra-violet light, which displays the credit card company logo.

The Internet has joined the telephone and television as an important part of our lives. Every day, more consumers use the Internet for financial activities like investing, banking, and shopping.

When you make purchases online, make sure your transactions are secure, your personal information is protected, and your fraud sensors are sharpened. Although you can't control fraud or deception on the Internet, you can take steps to recognize it, avoid it, and report if it does occur. Here's how:

- *Use a secure browser,* software that encrypts or scrambles the purchase information you send over the Internet, to guard the security of your online transactions. Most computers come with a secure browser already installed. You can also download some browsers for free over the Internet.
- *Keep records of your online transactions.* Read your e-mail. Merchants may send you important information about your purchases.
- *Review your monthly bank and credit card statements* for any billing errors or unauthorized purchases. Notify your credit card issuer or bank immediately if your credit card or checkbook is lost or stolen.
- *Read the policies of websites you visit,* especially the disclosures about a site's security, its refund policies, and its privacy policy on collecting and using your

WHAT'S "PHISHING"?

You open an e-mail and see messages like these: "We suspect an unauthorized transaction on your account. To ensure that your account is not compromised, please click the link below and confirm your identity." "During our regular verification of accounts, we could not verify your information. Please click here to update and verify your information." "Our records indicate that your account was overcharged. You must call us within 7 days to receive your refund." These senders are "phishing" for your information to commit fraud.

Regulatory agencies have published a brochure, *Internet Pirates Are Trying to Steal Your Information,* to assist you in identifying and preventing a new type of Internet fraud known as "phishing." With this type of scam, you receive fraudulent e-mail messages that appear to be from your financial institution. The messages often appear authentic and may include the institution's logo and marketing slogans.

These messages usually describe a situation that requires immediate attention and state that your accounts will be terminated unless you verify your personal information by clicking on a provided Web link. The Web link then takes you to a screen that asks for confidential information, including:

- Account numbers.
- Social Security numbers.
- Passwords.
- Place of birth.
- Other information used to identify you.

Those perpetrating the fraud then use this information to access your accounts or assume your identity.

The brochure advises consumers:

- If you're not sure the e-mail is legitimate, go to the company's site by typing in a Web address that you know is authentic.
- If you think the e-mail message might be fraudulent, *do not* click on any embedded link within the e-mail. The link may contain a virus.
- Do not be intimidated by e-mails that warn of dire consequences for not following the sender's instructions.
- If you do you fall victim to a phishing scam, act immediately to protect yourself by alerting your financial institution, placing fraud alerts on your credit files, and monitoring your account statements closely.
- Report suspicious e-mails or calls from third parties to the Federal Trade Commission, either through the Internet at www.consumer.gov/idtheft or by calling 1-877-IDTHEFT.

The brochure is on the Office of the Comptroller of the Currency's website, www.occ.gov/consumer/phishing.htm.

Source: Federal Trade Commission, www.consumer.ftc.gov/articles/0003-phishing, March 6, 2013.

personal information. Some websites' disclosures are easier to find than others; look at the bottom of the home page, on order forms, or in the "About" or "FAQs" section of a site. If you can't find a privacy policy, consider shopping elsewhere.

- *Keep your personal information private.* Don't disclose personal information—your address, telephone number, Social Security number, or e-mail address—unless you know who's collecting the information, why they're collecting it, and how they'll use it.
- *Give payment information only to businesses you know and trust* and only in appropriate places such as electronic order forms.
- *Never give your password to anyone online,* even your Internet service provider.
- *Do not download files sent to you by strangers or click on hyperlinks from people you don't know.* Opening a file could expose your computer system to a virus.[3]

DID YOU KNOW?

OPTING OUT

You can stop preapproved credit card offers by calling 1-888-567-8688.

The accompanying Financial Planning for Life's Situations box describes what *phishing* is and what you can do to protect yourself.

PRACTICE QUIZ 6-2

1 What are the two main types of consumer credit?
2 What is a debit card?
3 What is a home equity loan?

Measuring Your Credit Capacity

LO6-3

Assess your credit capacity and build your credit rating.

The only way to determine how much credit you can assume is to first learn how to make an accurate and sensible personal or family budget. Budgets, as you learned in Chapter 3, are simple, carefully considered spending plans. With budgets, you first provide for basic necessities such as rent or mortgage, food, and clothing. Then you provide for items such as home furnishings and other heavy, more durable goods.

CAN YOU AFFORD A LOAN?

Before you take out a loan, ask yourself whether you can meet all of your essential expenses and still afford the monthly loan payments. You can make this calculation in two ways. One is to add up all of your basic monthly expenses and then subtract this total from your take-home pay. If the difference will not cover the monthly payment and still leave funds for other expenses, you cannot afford the loan.

A second and more reliable method is to ask yourself what you plan to give up to make the monthly loan payment. If you currently save a portion of your income that is greater than the monthly payment, you can use these savings to pay off the loan. But if you do not, you will have to forgo spending on entertainment, new appliances, or perhaps even necessities. Are you prepared to make this trade-off? Although it is difficult to precisely measure your credit capacity, you can follow certain rules of thumb.

GENERAL RULES OF CREDIT CAPACITY

DEBT PAYMENTS–TO–INCOME RATIO The debt payments–to–income ratio is calculated by dividing your monthly debt payments (not including house payment, which is a long-term liability) by your net monthly income. Experts suggest that you spend no more than 20 percent of your net (after-tax) income on consumer credit payments. Thus, as Exhibit 6-4 shows, a person making $2,136 per month after taxes should spend no more than $426 on credit payments per month.

The 20 percent estimate is the maximum; however, 15 percent is much better. The 20 percent estimate is based on the average family, with average expenses; it does not take major emergencies into account. If you are just beginning to use credit, you should not consider yourself safe if you are spending 20 percent of your net income on credit payments.

DEBT-TO-EQUITY RATIO The debt-to-equity ratio is calculated by dividing your total liabilities by your net worth. In calculating this ratio, do not include the value of your home and the amount of its mortgage. If your debt-to-equity ratio is about 1—that is, if your consumer installment debt roughly equals your net worth

Monthly gross income	$3,000
Less:	
All taxes	540
Social Security	224
Monthly IRA contribution	− 100
Monthly net income	$2,136
Monthly installment credit payments:	
Visa	50
MasterCard	40
Discover card	30
Education loan	—
Personal bank loan	—
Auto loan	+ 306
Total monthly payments	$ 426
Debt payments–to–income ratio ($426/$2,136)	19.94%

Exhibit 6-4

How to calculate debt payments–to–income ratio

Spend no more than 20 percent of your net (after-tax) income on credit payments.

(not including your home or the mortgage)—you have probably reached the upper limit of debt obligations.

EXAMPLE: Calculating the Debt-to-Equity Ratio

Shayna's net worth is $150,000. Her liabilities of $60,000 include medical bills; charge account and credit card balances; balance due on auto loan and a home improvement loan. Her home has a market value of $210,000 and she owes $180,000 to the mortgage company. What is Shayna's ratio?

In calculating the debt-to-equity ratio, simply divide Shayna's total liabilities by her net worth (do not include the value of her home and the amount of its mortgage).

$$\text{ratio} = \frac{\text{Liabilities}}{\text{Net worth}} = \frac{\$60{,}000}{\$150{,}000} = 0.4$$

The ratio for business firms in general ranges between 0.33 and 0.50. The larger this ratio, the riskier the situation for lenders and borrowers. Of course, you can lower the ratio by paying off debts.

None of the above methods is perfect for everyone; the limits given are only guidelines. Only you, based on the money you earn, your current obligations, and your financial plans for the future, can determine the exact amount of credit you need and can afford. You must be your own credit manager.

Keep in mind that you adversely affect your credit capacity if you cosign a loan for a friend or a relative.

COSIGNING A LOAN

What would you do if a friend or a relative asked you to cosign a loan? Before you give your answer, make sure you understand what cosigning involves. Under a Federal Trade Commission rule, creditors are required to give you a notice to help explain your obligations. The cosigner's notice says,

> You are being asked to guarantee this debt. Think carefully before you do. If the borrower doesn't pay the debt, you will have to. Be sure you can afford to pay if you have to, and that you want to accept this responsibility.
>
> You may have to pay up to the full amount of the debt if the borrower does not pay. You may also have to pay late fees or collection costs, which increase this amount.
>
> The creditor can collect this debt from you without first trying to collect from the borrower. The creditor can use the same collection methods against you that can be used against the borrower, such as suing you, garnishing your wages, etc. If this debt is ever in default, that fact may become a part of *your* credit record.

COSIGNERS OFTEN PAY Some studies of certain types of lenders show that as many as three of four cosigners are asked to wholly or partially repay the loan. That statistic should not surprise you. When you are asked to cosign, you are being asked to take a risk that a professional lender will not take. The lender would not require a cosigner if the borrower met the lender's criteria for making a loan.

In most states, if you do cosign and your friend or relative misses a payment, the lender can collect the entire debt from you immediately without pursuing the borrower first. Also, the amount you owe may increase if the lender decides to sue to collect. If the lender wins the case, it may be able to take your wages and property.

IF YOU DO COSIGN Despite the risks, at times you may decide to cosign. Perhaps your child needs a first loan or a close friend needs help. Here are a few things to consider before you cosign:

1. Be sure you can afford to pay the loan. If you are asked to pay and cannot, you could be sued or your credit rating could be damaged.
2. Consider that even if you are not asked to repay the debt, your liability for this loan may keep you from getting other credit you want.
3. Before you pledge property such as your automobile or furniture to secure the loan, make sure you understand the consequences. If the borrower defaults, you could lose the property you pledge.
4. Check your state law. Some states have laws giving you additional rights as a cosigner.
5. Request that a copy of overdue-payment notices be sent to you so that you can take action to protect your credit history.

BUILDING AND MAINTAINING YOUR CREDIT RATING

If you apply for a charge account, credit card, car loan, personal loan, or mortgage, your credit experience, or lack of it, will be a major consideration for the creditor. Your credit experience may even affect your ability to get a job or buy life insurance. A good credit rating is a valuable asset that should be nurtured and protected. If you want a good rating, you must use credit with discretion: Limit your borrowing to your capacity to repay, and live up to the terms of your contracts. The quality of your credit rating is entirely up to you.

credit bureau A reporting agency that assembles credit and other information about consumers.

In reviewing your creditworthiness, a creditor seeks information from a credit bureau. Most creditors rely heavily on credit reports in considering loan applications.

CREDIT BUREAUS

Credit bureaus or Consumer Reporting Agencies (CRAs) collect credit and other information about consumers. There are three major credit bureaus: Experian Information Solutions (formerly TRW, Inc.), TransUnion Credit Information Company, and Equifax Services, Inc. Each bureau maintains over 200 million credit files on individuals based on over 2½ billion items of information received each month from lenders. In addition, several thousand regional credit bureaus collect credit information about consumers. These firms sell the data to creditors that evaluate credit applications.

The Federal Trade Commission receives more consumer complaints about credit bureaus than about any other industry, on average 12,000 a year. A common complaint involves mixups between people with identical surnames. However, the accuracy of credit reports has improved recently, due primarily to public outcry and the threat of stricter federal laws.

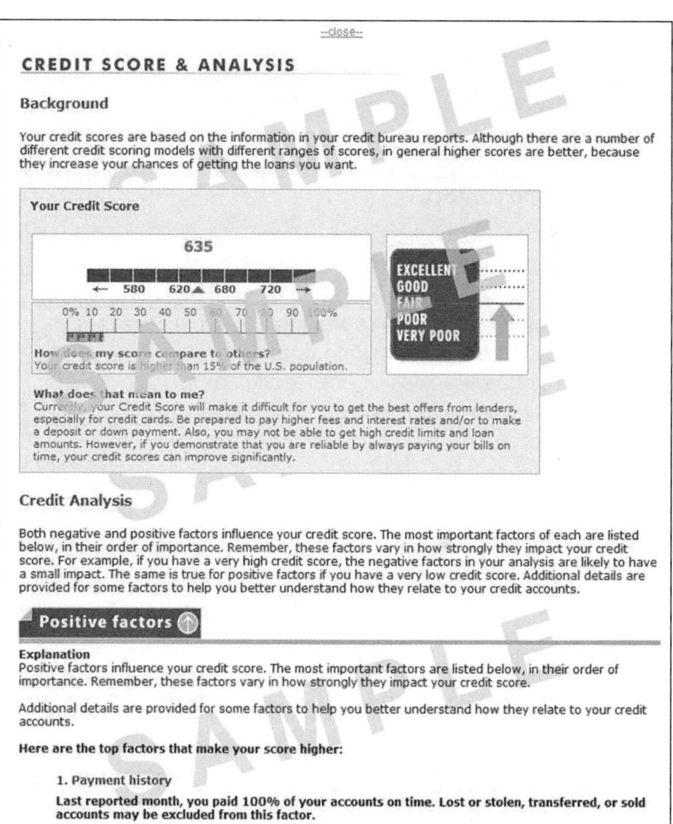

Before taking out a loan, a consumer needs to examine his or her credit report.

WHO PROVIDES DATA TO CREDIT BUREAUS?

Credit bureaus obtain their data from banks, finance companies, merchants, credit card companies, and other creditors. These sources regularly send reports to credit bureaus containing information about the kinds of credit they extend to customers, the amounts and terms of that credit, and customers' paying habits. Credit bureaus also collect some information from other sources, such as court records.

WHAT IS IN YOUR CREDIT FILES?

The credit bureau file contains your name, address, Social Security number, and birth date. It may also include the following information:

- Your employer, position, and income.
- Your former address.
- Your former employer.
- Your spouse's name, Social Security number, employer, and income.
- Whether you own your home, rent, or board.
- Checks returned for insufficient funds.

Your credit file may also contain detailed credit information. Each time you buy from a reporting store on credit or take out a loan at a bank, a finance company, or some other reporting creditor, a credit bureau is informed of your account number and the date, amount, terms, and type of credit. As you make payments, your file is updated to show the outstanding balance, the number and amounts of payments past due, and the frequency of 30-, 60-, or 90-day delinquencies. Any suits, judgments, or tax liens against you may appear as well. However, a federal law protects your rights if the information in your credit file is erroneous.

Fair Credit Reporting Act Regulates the use of credit reports, requires the deletion of obsolete information, and gives consumers access to their files and the right to have erroneous data corrected.

FAIR CREDIT REPORTING You can see that fair and accurate credit reporting is vital to both creditors and consumers. In 1971 Congress enacted the **Fair Credit Reporting Act,** which regulates the use of credit reports, requires the deletion of obsolete information, and gives consumers access to their files and the right to have erroneous data corrected. Furthermore, the act allows only authorized persons to obtain credit reports.

Credit bureaus provide lists of creditworthy consumers for companies to offer credit. These are called prescreened lists. You can remove your name from all Experian generated mail and telephone lists by sending your full name and addresses for the past five years to Experian, Consumer Opt Out, P.O. Box 919, Allen, TX 75013. Your name will be shared with Equifax and TransUnion, the other two national credit reporting systems.

my life 3

If I want to see a copy of my credit report, I know who to contact.

In 2005 all consumers became eligible to receive a free credit report from each of the three major credit reporting agencies (CRAs). Call 1-877-322-8228 or visit **www.annualcreditreport.com**. Your FICO® score is available from **www.myfico.com** for a fee. A good strategy is to ask for one report from a different agency every four months. That makes it easier to spot suspicious activity over the course of a year.

WHO MAY OBTAIN A CREDIT REPORT? Your credit report may be issued only to properly identified persons for approved purposes. It may be furnished to prospective employers in response to a court order or in accordance with your own written request. A credit report may also be provided to someone who will use it in connection with a credit transaction, underwriting of insurance, or some other legitimate business need or in determining eligibility for a license or other benefit granted by a government agency. Your friends and neighbors may not obtain credit information about you. If they request such information, they may be subject to fine and imprisonment.

The credit bureaus contend that current laws protect consumers' privacy, but many consumer organizations believe that anyone with a personal computer and a modem can easily access credit bureau files.

TIME LIMITS ON ADVERSE DATA Most of the information in your credit file may be reported for only seven years. If you have declared personal bankruptcy, however, that fact may be reported for 10 years. After 7 or 10 years, a credit reporting agency can't disclose the information in your credit file unless you are being investigated for a credit application of $75,000 or more or for an application to purchase life insurance of $150,000 or more.

If there is inaccurate or incomplete information in your credit report, contact both the credit reporting agency and the company that provided the information to the credit bureau.

INCORRECT INFORMATION IN YOUR CREDIT FILE Credit bureaus are required to follow reasonable procedures to ensure that subscribing creditors report information accurately. However, mistakes may occur. Your file may contain erroneous data or records of someone with a name similar to yours. When you notify the credit bureau that you dispute the accuracy of its information, it must reinvestigate and modify or remove inaccurate data. You should give the credit bureau any pertinent data you have concerning an error. If you contest an item on your credit report, the reporting agency must remove the item unless the creditor verifies that the information is accurate (see Exhibit 6-5).

If you are denied credit, insurance, employment, or rental housing based on the information in the report, you can get a copy of your credit report free within 60 days of your request. You should review your credit files every year even if you are not planning to apply for a big loan. Married women and young adults should make sure that all accounts for which they are individually and jointly liable are listed in their credit files.

WHAT ARE THE LEGAL REMEDIES? Any consumer reporting agency or user of reported information that willfully or through negligence fails to comply with the provisions of the Fair Credit Reporting Act may be sued by the affected consumer.

Date

Your Name
Your Address
Your City, State, Zip Code

Complaint Department
Name of Credit Reporting Agency
Address
City, State, Zip Code

Dear Sir or Madam:

I am writing to dispute the following information in my file. The items I dispute are also encircled on the attached copy of the report I received. (Identify item(s) disputed by name of source, such as creditor or tax court, and identify type of item, such as credit account, judgment, etc.)

This item is (inaccurate or incomplete) because (describe what is inaccurate or incomplete and why). I am requesting that the item be deleted (or request another specific change) to correct the information.

Enclosed are copies of (use this sentence if applicable and describe any enclosed documentation, such as payment records, court documents) supporting my position. Please reinvestigate this (these) matter(s) and (delete or correct) the disputed item(s) as soon as possible.

Sincerely,
Your name
Enclosures: (List what you are enclosing)

Source: Federal Trade Commission, http://www.consumer.ftc.gov/topics/resolving-consumer-problems, March 6, 2013.

Exhibit 6-5

Sample dispute letter

The law requires credit card companies to correct inaccurate or incomplete information in your credit report.

If the agency or the user is found guilty, the consumer may be awarded actual damages, court costs, and attorneys' fees and, in the case of willful noncompliance, punitive damages as allowed by the court. The action must be brought within two years of the occurrence or within two years after the discovery of material and willful misrepresentation of information. An unauthorized person who obtains a credit report under false pretenses may be fined up to $5,000, imprisoned for one year, or both. The same penalties apply to anyone who willfully provides credit information to someone not authorized to receive it.

Exhibit 6-6 on page 206 outlines the steps you can take if you are denied credit.

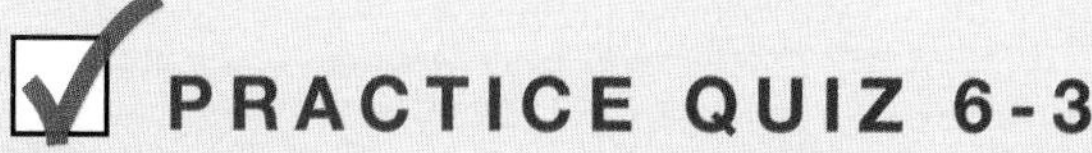

1 What are the general rules for measuring credit capacity?
2 What can happen if you cosign a loan?
3 What can you do to build and maintain your credit rating?
4 What is the Fair Credit Reporting Act?
5 How do you correct erroneous information in your credit file?
6 What are your legal remedies if a credit reporting agency engages in unfair reporting practices?

Consumer credit usage patterns

Exhibit 6-6 What if you are denied credit?

Steps you can take if you are denied credit.

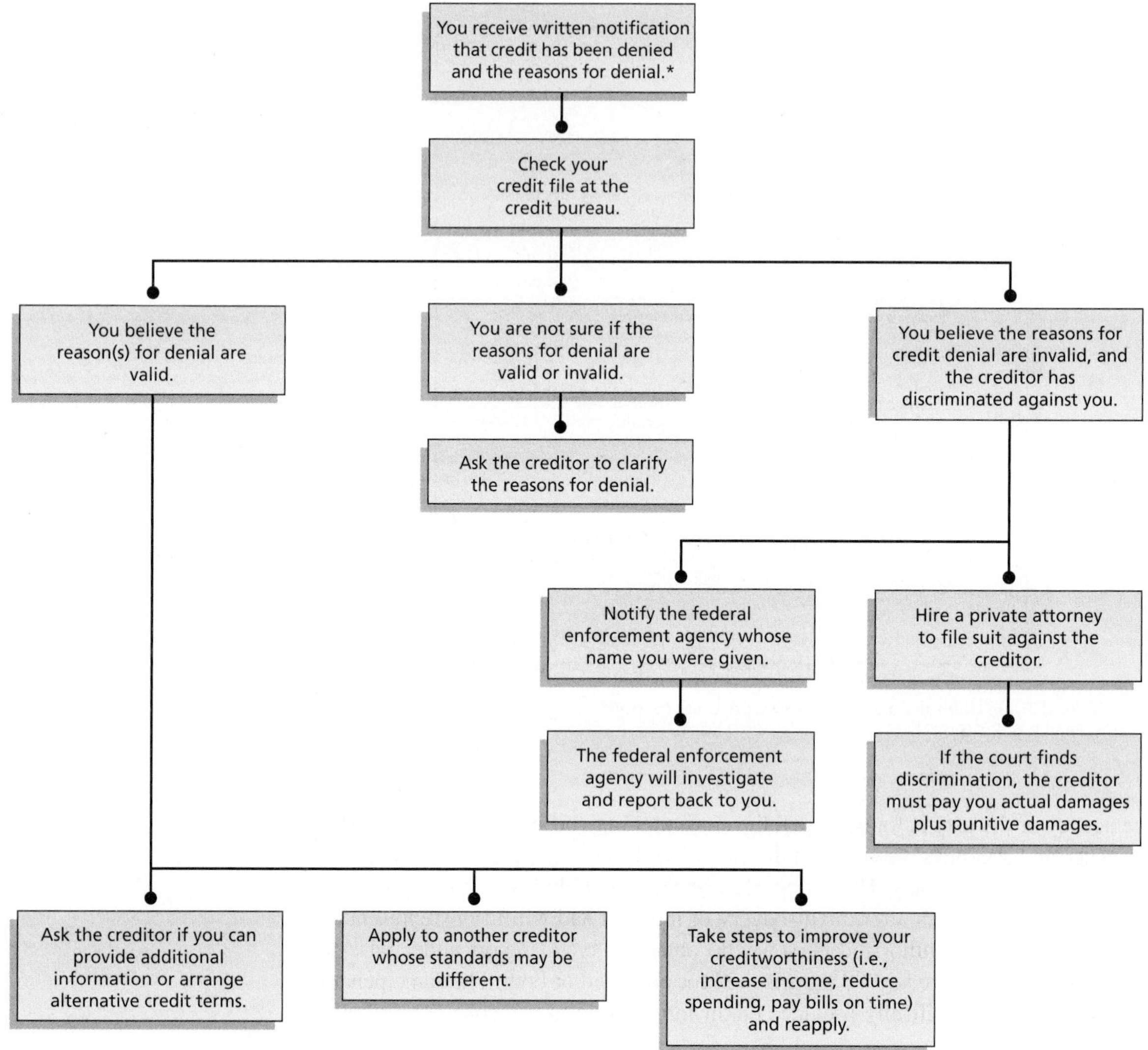

Source: Reprinted courtesy of Office of Public Information, Federal Reserve Bank of Minneapolis, Minneapolis, MN 55480.

Applying for Credit

LO6-4

Describe the information creditors look for when you apply for credit.

A SCENARIO FROM THE PAST

Mary and John Jones have a joint income that is more than enough for them to make payments on their dream house. Yet they are turned down for a mortgage loan. The lender says Mary might become pregnant and leave her job.

In fact, however, it is illegal for a creditor to ask or assume anything about a woman's childbearing plans. It is even illegal to discourage the Joneses from applying for a loan because Mary is of childbearing age. Also, the lender must fully acknowledge Mary's income.

THE FIVE Cs OF CREDIT

Here is what lenders look for in determining your creditworthiness.

1. Character: Will you repay the loan? **Yes** **No**

CREDIT HISTORY

Do you have a good attitude toward credit obligations? ___ ___

Have you used credit before? ___ ___

Do you pay your bills on time? ___ ___

Have you ever filed for bankruptcy? ___ ___

Do you live within your means? ___ ___

STABILITY ___ ___

How long have you lived at your present address? ___ yrs.

Do you own your home? ___ ___

How long have you been employed by your present employer? ___ yrs.

2. Capacity: Can you repay the loan?

INCOME

Your salary and occupation? $ ___________;

Place of occupation? ___________

How reliable is your income? Reliable ___ Not reliable ___

Any other sources of income? $ ___________

EXPENSES

Number of dependents? ___________

Do you pay any alimony or child support? Yes ___ No ___

Current debts? $ ___________

3. Capital: What are your assets and net worth?

NET WORTH

What are your assets? $ ___________

What are your liabilities? $ ___________

What is your net worth? $ ___________

4. Collateral: What if you don't repay the loan?

LOAN SECURITY

What assets do you have to secure the loan? (Car, home, furniture?) ___________

What sources do you have besides income? (Savings, stocks, bonds, insurance?) ___________

5. Conditions: What general economic conditions can affect your repayment of the loan?

JOB SECURITY

How secure is your job? Secure ___ Not secure ___

How secure is the firm you work for? Secure ___ Not secure ___

Source: Adapted from William M. Pride, Robert J. Hughes, and Jack R. Kapoor, *Business,* 12th ed. (Mason, OH; Cengage Learning, 2014) p. 541.

When you are ready to apply for credit, you should know what creditors think is important in deciding whether you are creditworthy. You should also know what they cannot legally consider in their decisions. The **Equal Credit Opportunity Act (ECOA)** starts all credit applicants off on the same footing. It states that race, color, age, sex, marital status, and certain other factors may not be used to discriminate against you in any part of a credit dealing. Credit rights of women are protected under the ECOA. Women should build and protect their own credit histories.

Equal Credit Opportunity Act (ECOA) Bans discrimination in the extension of credit on the basis of race, color, age, sex, marital status, and other factors.

character The borrower's attitude toward his or her credit obligations.

capacity The borrower's financial ability to meet credit obligations.

capital The borrower's assets or net worth.

collateral A valuable asset that is pledged to ensure loan payments.

conditions The general economic conditions that can affect a borrower's ability to repay a loan.

WHAT CREDITORS LOOK FOR: THE FIVE Cs OF CREDIT MANAGEMENT[4]

When a lender extends credit to its customers, it recognizes that some customers will be unable or unwilling to pay for their purchases. Therefore, lenders must establish policies for determining who will receive credit. Most lenders build their credit policies around the *five Cs of credit:* **character, capacity, capital, collateral,** and **conditions** (see the Financial Planning for Life's Situations box, the Five Cs of Credit).

Character is the borrower's attitude toward credit obligations. Most credit managers consider character the most important factor in predicting whether you will make timely payments and ultimately repay your loan.

Capacity is your financial ability to meet credit obligations, that is, to make regular loan payments as scheduled in the credit agreement. Therefore, the lender checks your salary statements and other sources of income, such as dividends and interest. Your other financial obligations and monthly expenses are also considered before credit is approved.

Capital refers to your assets or net worth. Generally, the greater your capital, the greater your ability to repay a loan. The lender determines your net worth by requiring you to complete certain credit application questions (see Exhibit 6-7). You must authorize your employer and financial institutions to release information to confirm the claims made in the credit application.

Collateral is an asset that you pledge to a financial institution to obtain a loan. If you fail to honor the terms of the credit agreement, the lender can repossess the collateral and then sell it to satisfy the debt.

Conditions refer to general economic conditions that can affect your ability to repay a loan. The basic question focuses on security—of both your job and the firm that employs you.

Creditors use different combinations of the five Cs to reach their decisions. Some creditors set unusually high standards, and others simply do not make certain kinds of loans. Creditors also use different kinds of rating systems. Some rely strictly on their own instinct and experience. Others use a credit-scoring or statistical system to predict whether an applicant is a good credit risk. They assign a certain number of points to each characteristic that has proven to be a reliable sign that a borrower will repay. Then they rate the applicant on this scale.

my life 4

Most of the information in your credit file may be reported for seven years. Several websites can provide current information about credit files. Visit ftc.gov, equifax.com, or experian.com for more information.

DID YOU KNOW?

WHAT'S IN YOUR FICO® SCORE?
The data from your credit report is generally grouped into five categories. The percentages in the pie diagram reflect how important each of the categories is in determining your FICO® score.

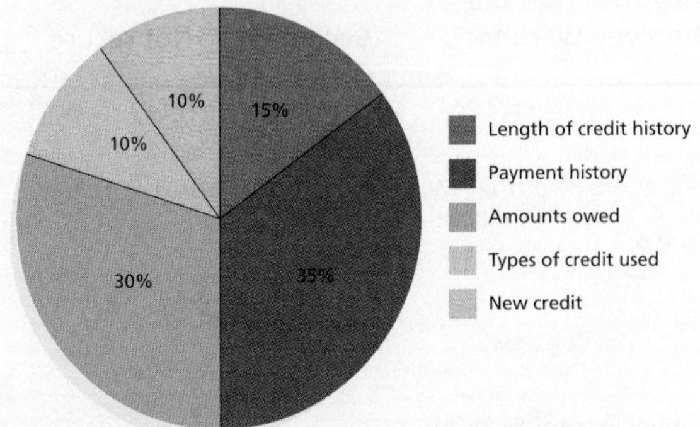

Source: How Your FICO Credit Score is Calculated, FICO website at http://www.myfico.com/CreditEducation/

FICO® AND VANTAGESCORE Typical questions in a credit application appear in Exhibit 6-7. The information in your credit report is used to calculate your FICO® credit score—a number generally between 300 and 850 that rates how risky a borrower is. The higher the score, the less risk you pose to creditors. You need about 760 score to get the best mortgage rate, and a score of 720 to get the best deal on an auto loan. Your FICO® score is available from www.myfico.com for a fee. Free credit reports do not contain your credit score. Exhibit 6-8 shows a numerical depiction of your creditworthiness and how you can improve your credit score.

VantageScore, launched in 2006, is a new scoring technique, the first to be developed collaboratively by the three credit reporting companies. This model allows for a more predictive score for consumers, even

- Amount of loan requested.
- Proposed use of the loan.
- Your name and birth date.
- Social Security and driver's license numbers.
- Present and previous street addresses.
- Present and previous employers and their addresses.
- Present salary.
- Number and ages of dependents.
- Other income and sources of other income.
- Have you ever received credit from us?
- If so, when and at which office?
- Checking account number, institution, and branch.
- Savings account number, institution, and branch.
- Name of nearest relative not living with you.
- Relative's address and telephone number.
- Your marital status.
- Information regarding joint applicant: same questions as above.

Exhibit 6-7 Sample credit application questions

Exhibit 6-8 TransUnion personal credit score

The higher your score, the less risk you pose to creditors.

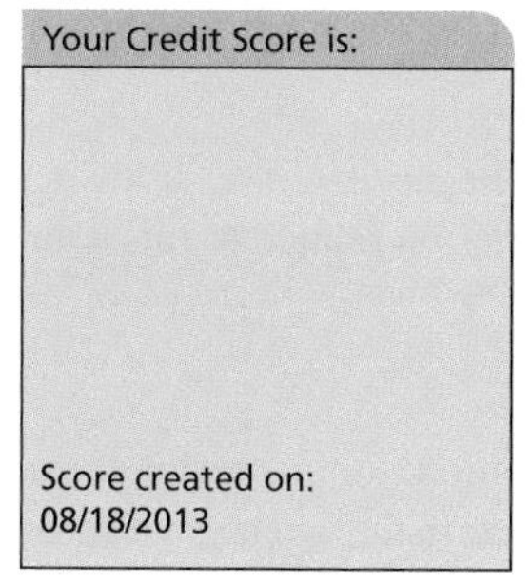

You can purchase your credit score for $7.95 by calling 1-866-SCORE-TU or 1-866-726-7388.

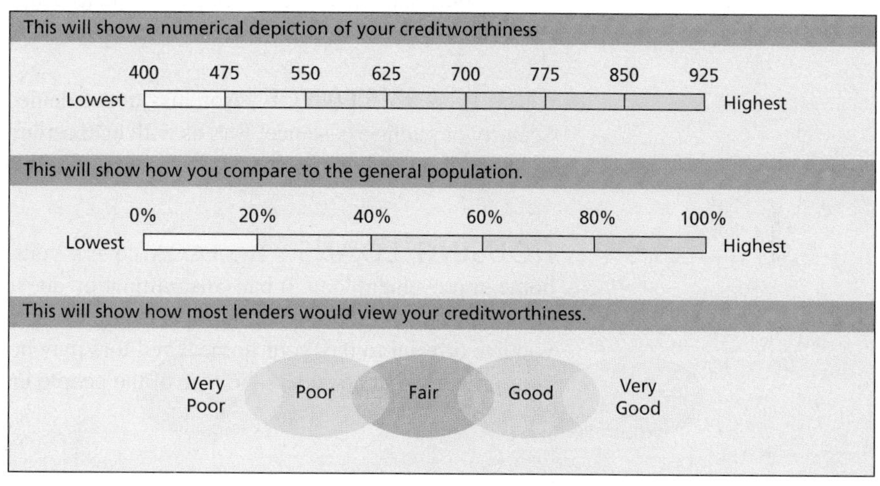

for those with limited credit histories, reducing the need for creditors to manually review credit information. Introduced in 2013, the new VantageScore 3.0:

- Features a common score range of 300–850 (higher scores represent lower likelihood of risks).
- Does not count debt collections that have been paid off.
- Makes up to 30 million additional consumers with short credit histories eligible for credit reports.
- Ignores negative credit history if you are impacted by natural disasters, such as Hurricane Sandy.

A key benefit of VantageScore is that as long as the three major credit bureaus have the same information regarding your

my life 5

I can improve my credit score.

A credit score is a snapshot of the contents of your credit report at the time it is calculated. The first step in improving your score is to review your credit report to ensure it is accurate. Long-term, responsible credit behavior is the most effective way to improve future scores. Open a savings account and make regular monthly deposits. Pay bills on time, lower balances, and use credit wisely to improve your score over time. Read the "How To. . . ." box on page 211.

credit history, you will receive the same score from each of them. A different score alerts you that there are discrepancies in your report.

In addition, during the loan application process, the lender may evaluate many of the following criteria to determine whether you are a good credit risk.

DID YOU KNOW?

YOU CAN GET FREE CREDIT REPORT UPDATES Sign up for credit monitoring with Credit Sesame (www.creditsesame.com/credit-monitoring) for e-mail alerts. Credit Karma (www.creditkarma.com/credit-monitoring) provides free daily monitoring of your TransUnion report.

AGE Retired couples and many older people have complained that they were denied credit because they were over a certain age or that, when they retired, their credit was suddenly cut off or reduced.

The ECOA is very specific about how a person's age may be used in credit decisions. A creditor may ask about your age, but if you're old enough to sign a binding contract (usually 18 or 21 years old, depending on state law), a creditor may not

- Turn you down or decrease your credit because of your age.
- Ignore your retirement income in rating your application.
- Close your credit account or require you to reapply for it because you have reached a certain age or retired.
- Deny you credit or close your account because credit life insurance or other credit-related insurance is not available to people of your age.

PUBLIC ASSISTANCE You may not be denied credit because you receive Social Security or public assistance. But, as with age, certain information related to this source of income could have a bearing on your creditworthiness.

HOUSING LOANS The ECOA covers your application for a mortgage or a home improvement loan. It bans discrimination due to characteristics such as your race, color, or sex or to the race or national origin of the people in the neighborhood where you live or want to buy your home. Creditors may not use any appraisal of the value of your property that considers the race of the people in your neighborhood.

WHAT IF YOUR APPLICATION IS DENIED?

ASK QUESTIONS IF YOUR APPLICATION IS DENIED If you receive a notice that your application has been denied, the ECOA gives you the right to know the specific reasons for denial. If the denial is based on a credit report, you are entitled to know the specific information in the credit report that led to it. After you receive this information from the creditor, you should contact the local credit bureau to find out what information it reported. The bureau cannot charge you a disclosure fee if you ask for a copy of your credit report within 60 days of being notified of a denial based on a credit report. You may ask the bureau to investigate any inaccurate or incomplete information and correct its records.

How Can I Improve My Credit Score? A credit score is a snapshot of the contents of your credit report at the time it is calculated. The first step in improving your score is to review your credit report to ensure it is accurate. Long-term, responsible credit behavior is the most effective way to improve future scores. Pay bills on time, lower balances and use credit wisely to improve your score over time. (Read the accompanying How to . . . feature on page 211).

HOW TO ...

Improve Your Credit Score

1. **Get copies of your credit report—then make sure information is correct.** Go to www.annualcreditreport.com. This is the only authorized online source for a free credit report. Under federal law, you can get a free report from each of the three national credit reporting companies every 12 months.

   You can also call 877-322-8228 or complete the *Annual Credit Report Request Form* and mail it to Annual Credit Report Request Service, P.O. Box 105281, Atlanta, GA 30348-5281.

2. **Pay your bills on time.** One of the most important steps you can take to improve your credit score is to pay your bills by the due date. You can set up automatic payments from your bank account to help you pay on time, but be sure you have enough money in your account to avoid overdraft fees.
3. **Understand how your credit score is determined.** Your credit score is usually based on the answers to these questions.
   - **Do you pay your bills on time?** The answer to this question is very important. If you have paid bills late, had an account referred to a collection agency, or have ever declared bankruptcy, this history will show up in your credit report.
   - **What is your outstanding debt?** Many scoring models compare the amount of debt you have and your credit limits. If the amount you owe is close to your credit limit, it is likely to have a negative effect on your score.
   - **How long is your credit history?** A short credit history may have a negative effect on your score, but a short history can be offset by other factors, such as timely payments and low balances.
   - **Have you applied for new credit recently?** If you have applied for too many new accounts recently, that may negatively affect your score. However, if you request a copy of your own credit report, or if creditors are monitoring your account or looking at credit reports to make prescreened credit offers, these inquiries about your credit history are not counted as applications for credit.
   - **How many and what types of credit accounts do you have?** Many credit-scoring models consider the number and type of credit accounts you have. A mix of installment loans and credit cards may improve your score. However, too many finance company accounts or credit cards might hurt your score.

   To learn more about credit scoring, see the Federal Trade Commission's website, *Facts for Consumers* at www.ftc.gov.

4. **Learn the legal steps to take to improve your credit report.** The Federal Trade Commission's *"Building a Better Credit Report"* has information on correcting errors in your report, tips on dealing with debt and avoiding scams—and more.
5. **Beware of credit-repair scams.** Sometimes doing it yourself is the best way to repair your credit. The Federal Trade Commission's *"Credit Repair, How to Help Yourself"* explains how you can improve your creditworthiness and lists legitimate resources for low-cost or no-cost help.

Source: Board of Governors of the Federal Reserve System, http://www.federalreserve.gov/consumerinfo/fivetips_creditscore.htm, accessed March 6, 2013.

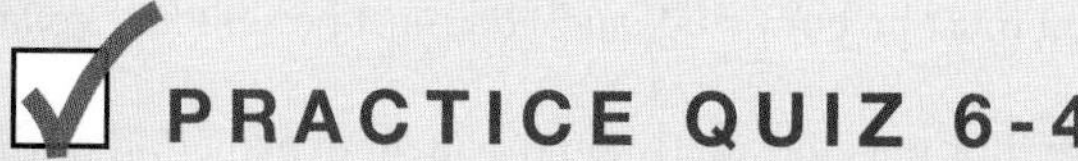

PRACTICE QUIZ 6-4

1 What is the Equal Credit Opportunity Act?
2 What are the five Cs of credit?
3 What can you do if your credit application is denied?

Avoiding and Correcting Credit Mistakes

LO6-5

Identify the steps you can take to avoid and correct credit mistakes.

Has a department store's computer ever billed you for merchandise that you returned to the store or never received? Has a credit company ever charged you for the same item twice or failed to properly credit a payment on your account?

The best way to maintain your credit standing is to repay your debts on time. But complications may still occur. To protect your credit and save your time, money, and future credit rating, you should learn how to correct any mistakes and misunderstandings that crop up in your credit accounts. If a snag occurs, first try to deal directly with the creditor. The credit laws can help you settle your complaints.

DID YOU KNOW?

The Federal Trade Commission estimates that in 2013 one out of five consumers has an inaccurate credit report—that's 42 million mistakes!

The **Fair Credit Billing Act (FCBA),** passed in 1975, sets procedures for promptly correcting billing mistakes, refusing to make credit card or revolving credit payments on defective goods, and promptly crediting your payments.

Fair Credit Billing Act (FCBA) Sets procedures for promptly correcting billing mistakes, refusing to make credit card payments on defective goods, and promptly crediting payments.

The act defines a billing error as any charge for something you did not buy or for something bought by a person not authorized to use your account. Also included among billing errors is any charge that is not properly identified on your bill (that is, for an amount different from the actual purchase price) or that was entered on a date other than the purchase date. A billing error may also be a charge for something you did not accept on delivery or was not delivered according to agreement.

Billing errors also include errors in arithmetic; failure to reflect a payment or other credit to your account; failure to mail the statement to your current address, provided you notified the creditor of an address change at least 20 days before the end of the billing period; and questionable items, or items about which you need additional information.

IN CASE OF A BILLING ERROR

If you think your bill is wrong or you want more information about it, follow these steps. First, notify the creditor *in writing* within 60 days after the bill was mailed. A telephone call will not protect your rights. Be sure to write to the address the creditor lists for billing inquiries. Give the creditor your name and account number, say that you believe the bill contains an error, and explain what you believe the error to be. State the suspected amount of the error or the item you want explained. Then pay all the parts of the bill that are not in dispute. While waiting for an answer, you do not have to pay the disputed amount or any minimum payments or finance charges that apply to it.

The creditor must acknowledge your letter within 30 days, unless it can correct your bill sooner. Within two billing periods, but in no case longer than 90 days, either your account must be corrected or you must be told why the creditor believes the bill is correct. If the creditor made a mistake, you need not pay any finance charges on the disputed amount. Your account must be corrected, and you must be sent an explanation of any amount you still owe.

If no error is found, the creditor must promptly send you an explanation of the reasons for that determination and a statement of what you owe, which may include any finance charges that have accumulated and any minimum payments you missed while you were questioning the bill. Exhibit 6-9 summarizes the steps in resolving a billing dispute, and Exhibit 6-9A shows a sample letter to dispute a billing error.

Exhibit 6-9 Steps in the process of resolving a billing dispute

A creditor may not threaten your credit rating while you are resolving a billing dispute.

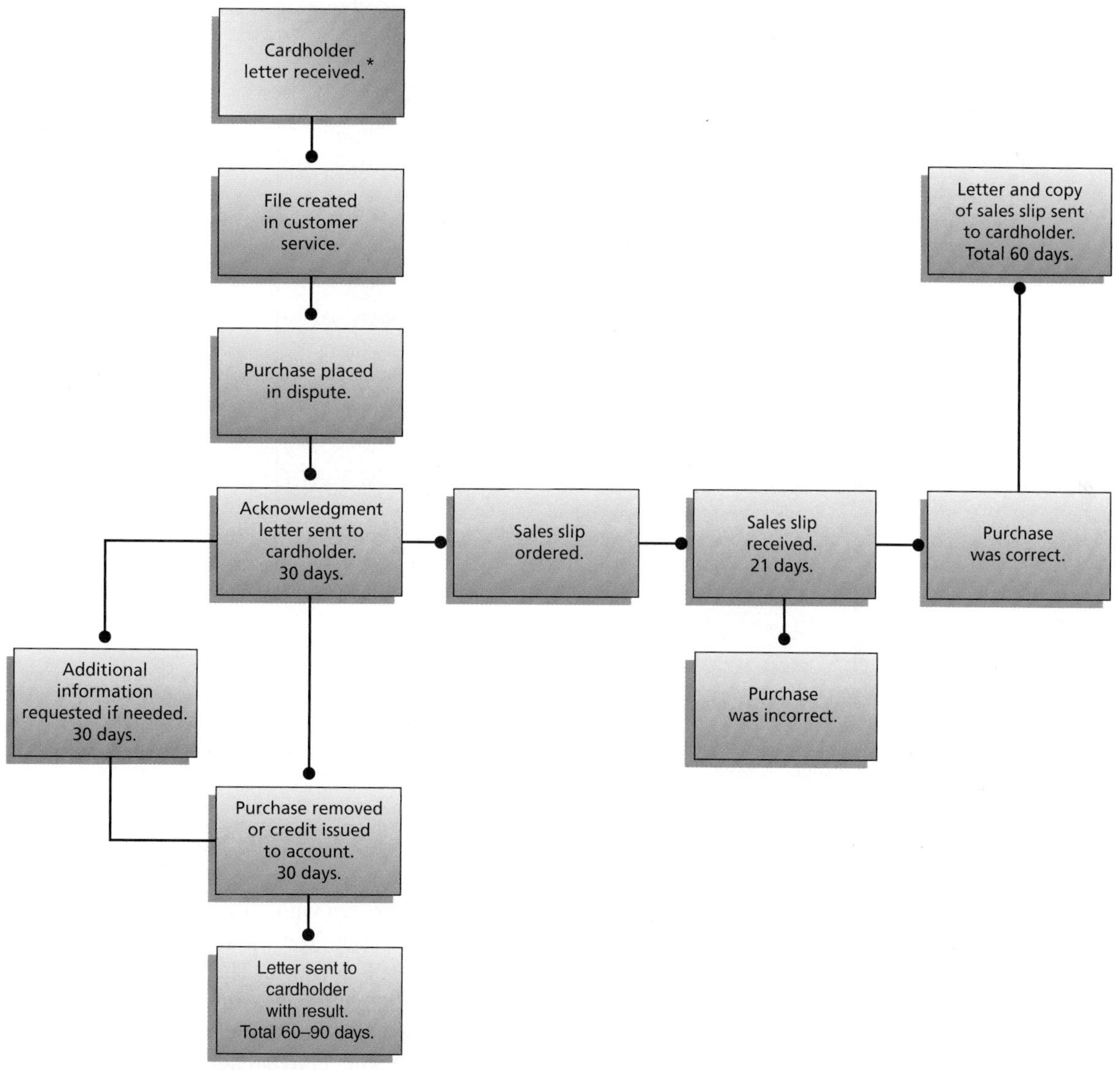

*Exhibit 6-9A shows a sample letter to dispute a billing error.

Source: Courtesy of Charge-It-System, Billing Errors Section, *Cardholder Tips,* March 1992, n.p.

YOUR CREDIT RATING DURING THE DISPUTE

A creditor may not threaten your credit rating while you are resolving a billing dispute. Once you have written about a possible error, a creditor is prohibited from giving out information that would damage your credit reputation to other creditors or credit bureaus. And until your complaint has been answered, the creditor may not take any action to collect the disputed amount.

After explaining the bill, the creditor may report you as delinquent on the amount in dispute and take action to collect if you do not pay in the time allowed. Even so, you can still disagree in writing. Then the creditor and the credit bureau must report that you have challenged your bill and give you the name and address of each recipient of information about your account. When the matter has been settled, the creditor must report the outcome to each recipient of the information. Remember, you may also place your version of the dispute in your credit record.

Exhibit 6-9A

A sample letter to dispute a billing error

Write to the creditor at the address given for "billing inquiries," not the address for sending your payments.

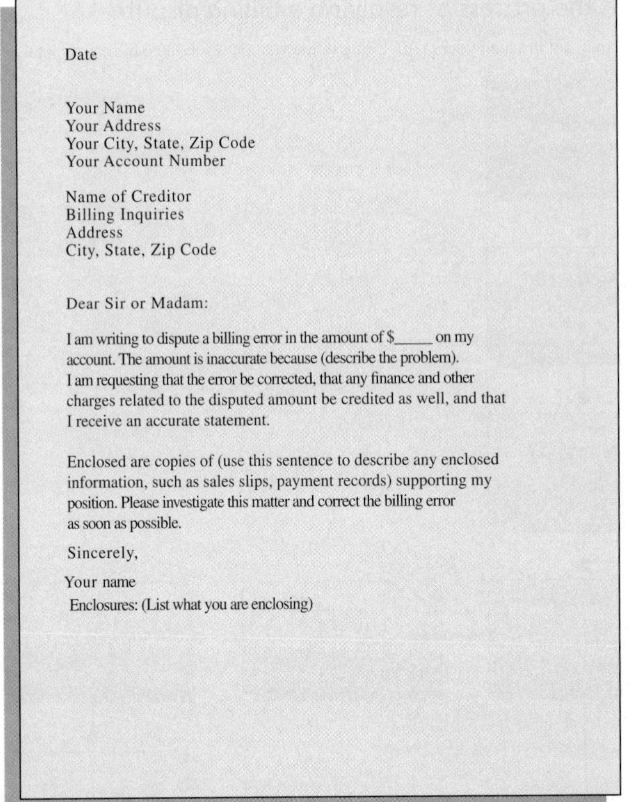

Date

Your Name
Your Address
Your City, State, Zip Code
Your Account Number

Name of Creditor
Billing Inquiries
Address
City, State, Zip Code

Dear Sir or Madam:

I am writing to dispute a billing error in the amount of $_____ on my account. The amount is inaccurate because (describe the problem). I am requesting that the error be corrected, that any finance and other charges related to the disputed amount be credited as well, and that I receive an accurate statement.

Enclosed are copies of (use this sentence to describe any enclosed information, such as sales slips, payment records) supporting my position. Please investigate this matter and correct the billing error as soon as possible.

Sincerely,

Your name

Enclosures: (List what you are enclosing)

Source: Federal Trade Commission, http//.www.consumer.ftc.gov/topics/resolving-consumer-problems, accessed March 7, 2013.

DID YOU KNOW?

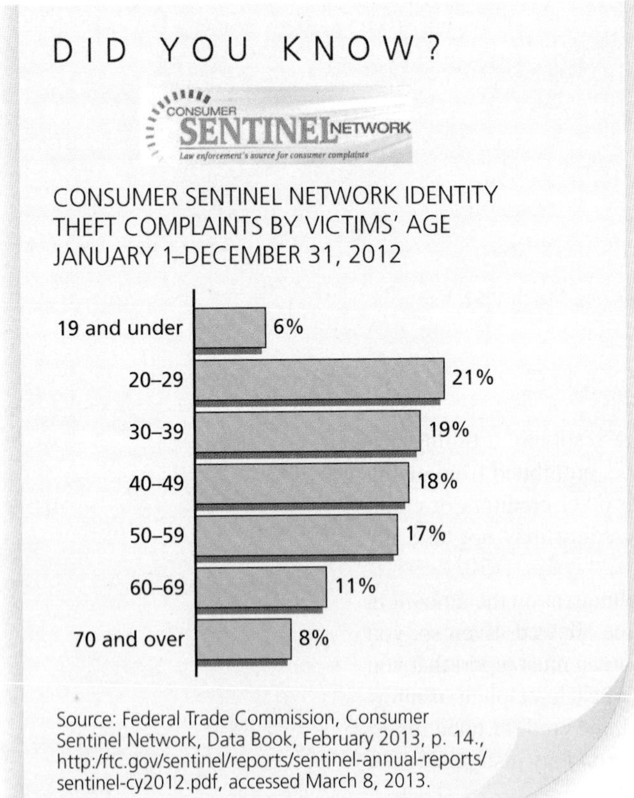

Source: Federal Trade Commission, Consumer Sentinel Network, Data Book, February 2013, p. 14., http:/ftc.gov/sentinel/reports/sentinel-annual-reports/sentinel-cy2012.pdf, accessed March 8, 2013.

DEFECTIVE GOODS OR SERVICES

Your new sofa arrives with only three legs. You try to return it, but no luck. You ask the merchant to repair or replace it; still no luck. The Fair Credit Billing Act provides that you may withhold payment on any damaged or shoddy goods or poor services that you have purchased with a credit card as long as you have made a sincere attempt to resolve the problem with the merchant.

IDENTITY CRISIS: WHAT TO DO IF YOUR IDENTITY IS STOLEN

"I don't remember charging those items. I've never even been in that store." Maybe you never charged those goods and services, but someone else did—someone who used your name and personal information to commit fraud. When impostors take your name, Social Security number, credit card number, or some other piece of your personal information for their use, they are committing a crime.

The biggest problem is that you may not know your identity has been stolen until you notice that something is amiss: You may get bills for a credit card account you never opened, your credit report may include debts you never knew you had, a billing cycle may pass without you receiving a statement, or you may see charges on your bills that you didn't sign for, didn't authorize, and know nothing about.

If someone has stolen your identity, the Federal Trade Commission recommends that you take three actions immediately:

1. *Contact the fraud departments of each of the three major credit bureaus* (see the table that follows). Tell them to flag your file with a fraud alert, including a statement that creditors should call you for permission before they open any new accounts in your name.

	To Report Fraud	To Order Credit Report	Website
Equifax	1-800-525-6285	1-800-685-1111	www.equifax.com
Experian	1-888-397-3742	1-888-EXPERIAN	www.experian.com
Trans Union	1-800-680-7289	1-800-916-8800	www.transunion.com

2. *Contact the creditors for any accounts that have been tampered with or opened fraudulently.* Ask to speak with someone in the security or fraud department, and follow up in writing.
3. *File a police report.* Keep a copy in case your creditors need proof of the crime.

If someone steals your identity, contact credit bureaus, the creditors, and file a police report immediately.

To prevent an identity thief from picking up your trash to capture your personal information, tear or shred your charge receipts, copies of credit applications, insurance forms, bank checks and statements, expired charge cards, and credit offers you get in the mail.

If you believe an identity thief has accessed your bank accounts, checking account, or ATM card, close the accounts immediately. When you open new accounts, insist on password-only access. If your checks have been stolen or misused, stop payment. If your ATM card has been lost, stolen, or otherwise compromised, cancel the card and get another with a new personal identification number (PIN).

If, after taking all these steps, you are still having identity problems, stay alert to new instances of identity theft. Notify the company or creditor immediately, and follow up in writing. Also, contact the Privacy Rights Clearinghouse, which provides information on how to network with other identity theft victims. Call 619-298-3396 or visit www.privacyrights.org.

The U.S. Secret Service has jurisdiction over financial fraud cases. Although the service generally investigates cases where the dollar loss is substantial, your information may provide evidence of a larger pattern of fraud that requires its involvement. Contact your local field office.

The Social Security Administration may issue you a new Social Security number if you still have difficulties after trying to resolve problems resulting from identity theft. Unfortunately, however, there is no guarantee that a new Social Security number will resolve your problems. Call the Social Security Administration at 1-800-772-1213.

DID YOU KNOW?

The Federal Trade Commission maintains the Identity Theft Data Clearinghouse and provides information to identify theft victims. You can call toll-free 1-877-ID-THEFT or visit **www.consumer.gov/idtheft**.

Finally, you can file a complaint with the Federal Trade Commission (FTC) through a toll-free consumer help line at 1-877-FTC-HELP; by mail at

Consumer Response Center, Federal Trade Commission, 600 Pennsylvania Ave., NW, Washington, DC 20580; or at its website, www.ftc.gov, using the online complaint form. Although the FTC cannot resolve individual problems for consumers, it can act against a company if it sees a pattern of possible law violations.

PRACTICE QUIZ 6-5

1 What is the Fair Credit Billing Act?
2 What must you do to protect your rights if a billing error occurs?
3 What happens to your credit rating during the billing dispute?
4 What can you do if your identity is stolen?

Complaining about Consumer Credit

LO6-6

Describe the laws that protect you if you have a complaint about consumer credit.

If you have a complaint about credit, first try to solve your problem directly with the creditor. Only if that fails should you use more formal complaint procedures. This section describes how to file a complaint with the federal agencies responsible for administering consumer credit protection laws.

COMPLAINTS ABOUT BANKS

If you have a complaint about a bank in connection with any of the federal credit laws, or if you think any part of your business with a bank has been handled in an unfair or deceptive way, you may get advice and help from the Federal Reserve System. You don't need to have an account at the bank to file a complaint. (See Exhibit 6-10.)

my life 6

I know what to do if I have serious credit problems.

First, try to solve your problems directly with your creditors. Debt Counselors of America (dca.org), National Center for Financial Education (ncfe.org), and National Foundation for Consumer Credit (nfcc.org) are good Internet sources of further information.

PROTECTION UNDER CONSUMER CREDIT LAWS

You may also take legal action against a creditor. If you decide to file a lawsuit, there are important consumer credit laws you should know about.

TRUTH IN LENDING AND CONSUMER LEASING ACTS If a creditor fails to disclose information required under the Truth in Lending Act or the Consumer Leasing Act, gives inaccurate information, or does not comply with the rules regarding credit cards or the right to cancel them, you may sue for actual damages, that is, any money loss you suffer. Class action suits are also permitted. A class action suit is a suit filed on behalf of a group of people with similar claims.

EQUAL CREDIT OPPORTUNITY ACT If you think you can prove that a creditor has discriminated against you for any reason prohibited by the ECOA, you may sue for actual damages plus punitive damages (that is, damages for the fact that the law has been violated) of up to $10,000.

COMPLAINT FORM

Federal Reserve System

Name ______ Name of Bank ______

Address ______ Address ______

Street City State Zip

City State Zip

Daytime telephone ______ (include area code) Account number (if applicable) ______

The complaint involves the following service: Checking Account ☐ Savings Account ☐ Loan ☐

Other: Please specify ______

I have attempted to resolve this complaint directly with the bank: No ☐ Yes ☐

If "No," an attempt should be made to contact the bank and resolve the complaint.

If "Yes," name of person or department contacted is ______ Date

MY COMPLAINT IS AS FOLLOWS (Briefly describe the events in the order in which they happened, including specific dates and the bank's actions to which you object. Enclose copies of any pertinent information or correspondence that may be helpful. Do not send us your only copy of any document):

This information is solicited under the Federal Trade Commission Improvement Act. Providing the information is voluntary, complete information is necessary to expedite investigation of your complaint. Routine use of the information may include disclosing it to bank(s) or others involved or to other governmental agencies as deemed appropriate.

Date ______ Signatures ______

Exhibit 6-10

Complaint form to report violations of federal credit laws

Source: Board of Governors of the Federal Reserve System, http://www.federalreserveconsumerhelp.gov/ComplaintForm.pdf, accessed March 7, 2013.

FAIR CREDIT BILLING ACT A creditor that fails to comply with the rules applying to the correction of billing errors automatically forfeits the amount owed on the item in question and any finance charges on it, up to a combined total of $50, even if the bill was correct. You may also sue for actual damages plus twice the amount of any finance charges.

FAIR CREDIT REPORTING ACT You may sue any credit reporting agency or creditor for violating the rules regarding access to your credit records and correction of errors in your credit file. You are entitled to actual damages plus any punitive damages the court allows if the violation is proven to have been intentional.

CONSUMER CREDIT REPORTING REFORM ACT An unfavorable credit report can force you to pay a higher interest rate on a loan or cost you a loan, an insurance policy, an apartment rental, or even a job offer. The **Consumer Credit Reporting Reform Act** of 1997 places the burden of proof for accurate credit information on the credit reporting agency rather than on you. Under this law, the creditor must certify that disputed data are accurate. If a creditor or the credit bureau verifies incorrect data, you can sue for damages. The federal government and state attorneys general can also sue creditors for civil damages.

Consumer Credit Reporting Reform Act Places the burden of proof for accurate credit information on the credit reporting agency.

CREDIT CARD ACCOUNTABILITY, RESPONSIBILITY, AND DISCLOSURE ACT OF 2009 Also known as the Credit CARD Act, this law provides the most sweeping changes in credit card protections for you since the Truth in Lending Act of 1968. The **Credit Card Accountability, Responsibility, and Disclosure Act** places new restrictions on credit card lending and eliminates certain fees. The accompanying Financial Planning for Life's Situations feature summarizes new credit card rules which began on February 22, 2010.

Credit Card Accountability, Responsibility and Disclosure Act Places new restrictions on credit card lending and eliminates certain fees.

NEW CREDIT CARD RULES

The Federal Reserve's *new rules for credit card companies* mean new credit card protections for you. Here are some key changes you should expect from your credit card company beginning on February 22, 2010.

What your credit card company has to tell you.

1. **When they plan to increase your rate or other fees.** Your credit card company must send you a notice 45 days before they can

- increase your interest rate;
- change certain fees (such as annual fees, cash advance fees, and late fees) that apply to your account; or
- make other significant changes to the terms of your card.

If your credit card company plans to make changes to the terms of your card, it must give you the option to cancel the card before certain fee increases take effect.

For example, the credit card company can require you to pay off the balance in five years, or it can double the percentage of your balance used to calculate your minimum payment (which will result in faster repayment than under the terms of your account).

The company does **not** have to send you a 45-day advance notice if

- you have a variable interest rate tied to an index; if the index goes up, the company does not provide notice before your rate goes up;
- your introductory rate expires and reverts to the previously disclosed "go-to" rate;
- your rate increases because you haven't made your payments as agreed.

2. **How long it will take to pay off your balance.** Your monthly credit card bill will include information on how long it will take you to pay off your balance if you only make minimum payments. It will also tell you how much you would need to pay each month in order to pay off your balance in three years. For example, suppose you owe $3,000 and your interest rate is 14.4%—your bill might look like this:

New balance		$3,000.00
Minimum payment due		$ 90.00
Payment due date		4/20/14
Late Payment Warning: If we do not receive your minimum payment by the date listed above, you may have to pay a $35 late fee and your APRs may be increased up to the Penalty of 28.99%.		
Minimum Payment Warning: If you make only the minimum payment each period, you will pay more interest and it will take you longer to pay off your balance. For example:		
If you make no additional charges using this card and each month you pay . . .	You will pay off the balance shown on this statement in about . . .	And you will end up paying an estimated total of . . .
Only the minimum payment	11 years	$4,745
$103	3 years	$3,712
		(Savings = $1,033)

Source: Board of Governors of the Federal Reserve System, http://wwwfederalreserve.gov/consummerinfo/wyntk_creditcardrules.htm, accessed March 7, 2013.

Exhibit 6-11 summarizes the major federal consumer credit laws. The Federal Reserve System has set up a separate office, the Division of Consumer and Community Affairs, in Washington to handle consumer complaints. Contact the director of this division in Washington, DC 20551. This division also writes regulations to carry out the consumer credit laws, enforces these laws for state-chartered banks that are members of the Federal Reserve System, and helps banks comply with these laws.

YOUR RIGHTS UNDER CONSUMER CREDIT LAWS

If you believe you have been refused credit due to discrimination, you can do one or more of the following:

1. Complain to the creditor. Let the creditor know you are aware of the law.
2. File a complaint with the government. You can report any violations to the appropriate government enforcement agency (see Exhibit 6-12). Although the agencies

Exhibit 6-11 Summary of federal consumer credit laws

Act (effective date)	Major Provisions
Truth in Lending Act (July 1, 1969)	Provides specific cost disclosure requirements for the annual percentage rate and the finance charges as a dollar amount. Requires disclosure of other loan terms and conditions. Regulates the advertising of credit terms. Provides the right to cancel a contract when certain real estate is used as security.
(January 25, 1971)	Prohibits credit card issuers from sending unrequested cards; limits a cardholder's liability for unauthorized use of a card to $50.
(October 1, 1982)	Requires that disclosures for closed-end credit (installment credit) be written in plain English and appear apart from all other information. Allows a credit customer to request an itemization of the amount financed if the creditor does not automatically provide it.
Fair Credit Reporting Act (April 24, 1971)	Requires disclosure to consumers of the name and address of any consumer reporting agency that supplied reports used to deny credit, insurance, or employment. Gives consumers the right to know what is in their files, have incorrect information reinvestigated and removed, and include their versions of a disputed item in the file. Requires credit reporting agencies to send the consumer's version of a disputed item to certain businesses or creditors. Sets forth identification requirements for consumers wishing to inspect their files. Requires that consumers be notified when an investigative report is being made. Limits the amount of time certain information can be kept in a credit file.
Fair Credit Billing Act (October 28, 1975)	Establishes procedures for consumers and creditors to follow when billing errors occur on periodic statements for revolving credit accounts. Requires creditors to send a statement setting forth these procedures to consumers periodically. Allows consumers to withhold payment for faulty or defective goods or services (within certain limitations) when purchased with a credit card. Requires creditors to promptly credit customers' accounts and to return overpayments if requested.
Equal Credit Opportunity Act (October 28, 1975)	Prohibits credit discrimination based on sex and marital status. Prohibits creditors from requiring women to reapply for credit upon a change in marital status. Requires creditors to inform applicants of acceptance or rejection of their credit application within 30 days of receiving a completed application. Requires creditors to provide a written statement of the reasons for adverse action.
(March 23, 1977)	Prohibits credit discrimination based on race, national origin, religion, age, or the receipt of public assistance.
(June 1, 1977)	Requires creditors to report information on an account to credit bureaus in the names of both husband and wife if both use the account and both are liable for it.
Fair Debt Collection Practices Act (March 20, 1978)	Prohibits abusive, deceptive, and unfair practices by debt collectors. Establishes procedures for debt collectors contacting a credit user. Restricts debt collector contacts with a third party. Specifies that payment for several debts be applied as the consumer wishes and that no money be applied to a debt in dispute.
Consumer Credit Reporting Reform Act (September 30, 1997)	Places the burden of proof for accurate credit information on credit issuers rather than on consumers. Requires creditors to certify that disputed credit information is accurate. Requires "credit repair" companies to give consumers a written contract that can be canceled within three business days. Requires the big three credit bureaus (Experian, Equifax, and TransUnion) to establish a joint toll-free system that allows consumers to call and remove their names permanently from all prescreened lists. Places the maximum cost of a credit report at $8; however, indigent persons, welfare recipients, unemployed persons, and job hunters can get one free report annually.

(continued)

Exhibit 6-11 (concluded)

Act (effective date)	Major Provisions
Fair and Accurate Credit Transactions Act (April 28, 2003)	Requires the Federal Trade Commission to issue proposed rules to address identity theft concerns. Defines identity theft as a fraud committed or attempted using the identifying information of another person without lawful authority. Requires credit reporting agencies to develop and implement reasonable requirements for what information can be considered a consumer's proof of identity.
Credit Card Accountability, Responsibility, and Disclosure (CARD) Act (February 22, 2010)	Bans unfair rate increases on existing balances and restricts retroactive increases due to late payment. Ends late fee traps such as weekend deadlines, due dates that change every month, and deadlines that fall in the middle of the day. Requires issuers to display on monthly statement how long it would take to pay off the existing balance—and the total interest cost—if the consumer paid only the minimum due. Contains new protections for college students and young adults. Requires issuers extending credit to people under 21 to obtain signature of a parent, guardian, or other individual 21 years or older who will take responsibility for the debt, or proof that the applicant has an independent means of repaying the debt.

Sources: *Managing Your Credit,* rev. ed. (Prospect Heights, IL: Money Management Institute, Household Financial Services, 1988), p. 36, © Household Financial Services, Prospect Heights, IL; *Banking Legislation & Policy,* Federal Reserve Bank of Philadelphia, April–June 1997, pp. 3–4; Federal Trade Commission, www.ftc.gov, March 2005; Board of Governors of the Federal Reserve System, http://www.federalreserve.gov/consumerinfo/wyntk_creditcardrules.htm, March 7, 2013.

Exhibit 6-12 Federal government agencies that enforce consumer credit laws

If you think you've been discriminated against by:	You may file a complaint with the following agency:
Consumer reporting agencies, creditors and others not listed below.	Federal Trade Commission Consumer Response Center—FCRA Washington, DC 20580 877-382-4357
National banks, federal branches/agencies of foreign banks (word "National" or initials "N.A." appear in or after bank's name).	Office of the Comptroller of the Currency Compliance Management, Mail Stop 6-6 Washington, DC 20219 800-613-6743
Federal Reserve System member banks (except national banks, and federal branches/agencies of foreign banks).	Federal Reserve Board Division of Consumer & Community Affairs Washington, DC 20551 202-452-3693
Savings associations and federally chartered savings banks (word "Federal" or initials "F.S.B." appear in federal institution's name).	Office of Thrift Supervision Consumer Complaints Washington, DC 20552 800-842-6929
Federal credit unions (words "Federal Credit Union" appear in institution's name).	National Credit Union Administration 1775 Duke Street Alexandria, VA 22314 800-755-1030
State-chartered banks that are not members of the Federal Reserve System.	Federal Deposit Insurance Corporation Consumer Response Center, 2345 Grand Avenue, Suite 100, Kansas City, Missouri 64108-2638 877-275-3342
Air, surface, or rail common carriers regulated by former Civil Aeronautics Board or Interstate Commerce Commission.	Department of Transportation Office of Financial Management Washington, DC 20590 202-366-4000

Source: Federal Trade Commission, www.ftc.gov, March 3, 2013.

use complaints to decide which companies to investigate, they cannot handle private cases. When you are denied credit, the creditor must give you the name and address of the appropriate agency to contact.

3. If all else fails, sue the creditor. You have the right to bring a case in a federal district court. If you win, you can recover your actual damages and punitive damages of up to $10,000. You can also recover reasonable attorneys' fees and court costs. A private attorney can advise you on how to proceed.

1 What federal laws protect you if you have a complaint regarding consumer credit?
2 What are your rights under the consumer credit laws?

my life stages for managing my credit

YOUR PERSONAL FINANCE DASHBOARD

A key indicator of your creditworthiness is your capacity to handle a certain level of debt. Lenders will review your current debt payments-to-income ratio. Based on this, they will determine how much credit they will extend and at what interest rate. Lenders will be more reluctant to lend to individuals who are near the top of the acceptable range of 20 percent.

YOUR SITUATION Are you able to pay your credit cards off each month when the bill is due? If you carry a balance, is it steadily increasing? Are there debts that you can eliminate to reduce the amount of your overall debt payments? An improving debt payments-to-income ratio is the foundation for progress toward financial independence. Other personal financial planning actions you might consider during various stages of your life include . . .

. . . in college

- If possible, become an authorized user on your parent's credit card
- Monitor your current spending
- Be aware of the risks of credit card fraud
- Set credit card limit and review monthly statements

. . . in my 20s

- Get a secured credit card in your own name when you are 21
- Build your own positive credit file
- Set up a budget for credit use and pay in full when the bill arrives

. . . in my 30s and 40s

- Qualify and get an unsecured credit card
- Shop around for the best card
- Avoid maxing out your credit card
- Continue to monitor your credit card spending

. . . in my 50s and beyond

- Maintain good credit rating
- Know what is in your credit files
- Become a cautious guardian of your credit
- Be debt-free

SUMMARY OF LEARNING OBJECTIVES

LO6-1

Define *consumer credit* and analyze its advantages and disadvantages.

Consumer credit is the use of credit by individuals and families for personal needs. Among the advantages of using credit are the ability to purchase goods when needed and pay for them gradually, the ability to meet financial emergencies, convenience in shopping, and establishment of a credit rating. Disadvantages are that credit costs money, encourages overspending, and ties up future income.

LO6-2

Differentiate among various types of credit.

Closed-end and open-end credit are two types of consumer credit. With closed-end credit, the borrower pays back a one-time loan in a stated period of time and with a specified number of payments. With open-end credit, the borrower is permitted to take loans on a continuous basis and is billed for partial payments periodically.

LO6-3

Assess your credit capacity and build your credit rating.

Two general rules for measuring credit capacity are the debt payments–to–income ratio and the debt-to-equity ratio. In reviewing your creditworthiness, a creditor seeks information from one of the three national credit bureaus or a regional credit bureau.

LO6-4

Describe the information creditors look for when you apply for credit.

Creditors determine creditworthiness on the basis of the five Cs: character, capacity, capital, collateral, and conditions.

LO6-5

Identify the steps you can take to avoid and correct credit mistakes.

If a billing error occurs on your account, notify the creditor in writing within 60 days. If the dispute is not settled in your favor, you can place your version of it in your credit file. You may also withhold payment on any defective goods or services you have purchased with a credit card as long as you have attempted to resolve the problem with the merchant.

LO6-6

Describe the laws that protect you if you have a complaint about consumer credit.

If you have a complaint about credit, first try to deal directly with the creditor. If that fails, you can turn to the appropriate consumer credit law. These laws include the Truth in Lending Act, the Consumer Leasing Act, the Equal Credit Opportunity Act, the Fair Credit Billing Act, the Fair Credit Reporting Act, the Consumer Credit Reporting Reform Act, and the Fair and Accurate Credit Transactions Act.

KEY TERMS

capacity 208
capital 208
character 208
closed-end credit 192
collateral 208
conditions 208
consumer credit 188
Consumer Credit Reporting Reform Act 217
credit 188
credit bureau 203
Credit Card Accountability, Responsibility, and Disclosure Act 217
debit card 196
Equal Credit Opportunity Act (ECOA) 207
Fair Credit Billing Act (FCBA) 212
Fair Credit Reporting Act 204
home equity loan 196
interest 193
line of credit 193
open-end credit 192
revolving check credit 194

SELF-TEST PROBLEMS

1. Current approximate value of Joshua's home is about $180,000. He still has a $100,000 balance on his mortgage. His bank has agreed to let him borrow 80 percent of the value of his home. What is the maximum home equity line of credit available to Josh?
2. Audra has a monthly net income of $2,100. She has a house payment of $900 per month, a car loan with payments of $500 per month, a Visa card with payments of $100 per month and a credit card with a local department store with payments of $200 per month. What is Audra's debt payment–to–income ratio?
3. Hannah has determined that her net worth is $60,000. She has also determined that the face value of her mortgage is $160,000. She has determined that the face value of the rest of her debt is $30,000. What is Hannah's debt-to-equity ratio?

Solutions to Self-Test Problems

1. Approximate market value of Joshua's house $180,000

Approximate market value of Joshua's house	$180,000
Multiply by .80	144,000
Approximate loan value	144,000
Subtract balance due on mortgage	100,000
Approximate credit limit available	$ 44,000

2. Audra's net monthly income = $2,100

Audra's monthly expenses:

House payment	900
Car loan	500
Visa card	100
Store card	200
Total expenses	1,700

$$\text{Debt payments–to–income} = \frac{\$1{,}700-\$900}{\$2{,}100} = .38 \text{ or } 38 \text{ percent}$$

3. Hannah's net worth = $60,000

Face value of her mortgage	$160,000
Remainder of her debt	30,000
Hannah's debt-to-equity ratio	$\frac{30{,}000}{\$\ 60{,}000} = .5$

FINANCIAL PLANNING PROBLEMS

1. *Calculating the Amount for a Home Equity Loan.* A few years ago, Michael Tucker purchased a home for $100,000. Today the home is worth $150,000. His remaining mortgage balance is $50,000. Assuming Michael can borrow up to 80 percent of the market value of his home, what is the maximum amount he can borrow? LO6-2

2. *Determining the Debt Payments–to–Income Ratio.* Louise McIntyre's monthly gross income is $2,000. Her employer withholds $400 in federal, state, and local income taxes and $160 in Social Security taxes per month. Louise contributes $80 per month for her IRA. Her monthly credit payments for Visa, MasterCard, and Discover cards are $35, $30, and $20, respectively. Her monthly payment on an automobile loan is $285. What is Louise's debt payments–to–income ratio? Is Louise living within her means? Explain. LO6-3

3. *Calculating the Debt-to-Equity Ratio.* Robert Thumme owns a $140,000 townhouse and still has an unpaid mortgage of $110,000. In addition to his mortgage, he has the following liabilities: LO6-3

Visa	$ 565
MasterCard	480
Discover card	395
Education loan	920
Personal bank loan	800
Auto loan	4,250
Total	$7,410

Robert's net worth (not including his home) is about $21,000. This equity is in mutual funds, an automobile, a coin collection, furniture, and other personal property. What is Robert's debt-to-equity ratio? Has he reached the upper limit of debt obligations? Explain.

LO6-3 **4.** *Calculating Net Worth and Determining a Safe Credit Limit.*

a. Calculate your net worth based on your present assets and liabilities.

b. Refer to your net worth statement and determine your safe credit limit. Use the debt payments–to–income and debt-to-equity formulas.

LO6-3 **5.** *Calculating the Debt Payments–to–Income Ratio.* Kim Lee is trying to decide whether she can afford a loan she needs in order to go to chiropractic school. Right now Kim is living at home and works in a shoe store, earning a gross income of $820 per month. Her employer deducts $145 for taxes from her monthly pay. Kim also pays $95 on several credit card debts each month. The loan she needs for chiropractic school will cost an additional $120 per month. Help Kim make her decision by calculating her debt payments–to–income ratio with and without the college loan. (Remember the 20 percent rule.)

LO6-3 **6.** *Calculating the Debt Payments–to–Income Ratio.* Suppose that your monthly net income is $2,400. Your monthly debt payments include your student loan payment and a gas credit card. They total $360. What is your debt payments–to–income ratio?

LO6-3 **7.** *Calculating the Debt Payments–to–Income Ratio.* What is your debt payments–to–income ratio if your debt payments total $684 and your net income is $2,000 per month?

LO6-3 **8.** *Calculating a Safe Credit Limit.* Drew's monthly net income is $1,600. What is the maximum he should use on debt payments?

LO6-3 **9.** *Credit Reduces Future Income.* The disposable income from your part-time job in 2010 and 2011 is $12,000. In 2010, you borrow $500 at 18 percent interest. You repay your loan with interest in 2011. How much would you have available for spending in 2011?

LO6-4 **10.** *Analyzing the Feasibility of a Loan.* Fred Reinero has had a student loan, two auto loans, and three credit cards. He has always made timely payments on all obligations. He has a savings account of $2,400 and an annual income of $25,000. His current payments for rent, insurance, and utilities are about $1,100 per month. Fred has accumulated $12,800 in an individual retirement account. Fred's loan application asks for $10,000 to start up a small restaurant with some friends. Fred will not be an active manager; his partner will run the restaurant. Will he get the loan? Explain your answer.

LO6-4 **11.** *Analyzing a Spending Plan.* Carl's house payment is $1,050 per month and his car payment is $385 per month. If Carl's take-home pay is $2,800 per month, what percentage does Carl spend on his home and car?

FINANCIAL PLANNING ACTIVITIES

LO6-1 **1.** *Determining Whether or Not to Use Credit.* Survey friends and relatives to determine the process they used in deciding whether or not to use credit to purchase an automobile or a major appliance. What risks and opportunity costs did they consider?

LO6-1 **2.** *Analyzing Opportunity Costs Using Credit.* Think about the last three major purchases you made.

a. Did you pay cash? If so, why?

b. If you paid cash, what opportunity costs were associated with the purchase?

c. Did you use credit? If so, why?

d. What were the financial and psychological opportunity costs of using credit?

LO6-2 **3.** *Comparing Reasons for Using Credit.* Prepare a list of similarities and differences in the reasons the following individuals might have for using credit.

a. A teenager.

b. A young adult.

c. A growing family of four.

d. A retired couple.

LO6-2 **4.** *Using the Internet to Obtain Information about Credit Cards.* Choose one of the following organizations and visit its website. Then prepare a report that summarizes the information the organization provides. How could this information help you in choosing your credit card?

a. Credit Card Network—provides information on credit card rates. (www.creditnet.com)

b. Federal Trade Commission—provides information on how to regain financial health, uses and misuses of credit cards, and many other related topics. (www.ftc.gov)

5. *Using Your Home Equity to Obtain a Loan.* Visit your local financial institutions, such as commercial banks, federal savings banks, and credit unions, to obtain information about getting a home equity loan. Compare their requirements for the loan. L06-2

6. *Determining Whether to Cosign a Loan.* Talk to a person who has cosigned a loan. What experiences did this person have as a cosigner? L06-3

7. *Determining Net Worth and Credit Capacity.* What changes might take place in your personal net worth during different stages of your life? How might these changes affect your credit capacity? L06-4

8. *Assessing How Lenders Determine Creditworthiness.* Survey credit representatives such as bankers, managers of credit departments in retail stores, managers of finance companies, credit union officers, managers of credit bureaus, and savings and loan officers. Ask what procedures they follow in granting or refusing a loan. Write a report of your survey. L06-4

9. *Analyzing Credit-Related Problems.* Bring to class examples of credit-related problems of individuals or families. Suggest ways in which these problems might be solved. L06-5

10. *Evaluating Creditors and Seeking Help with Credit-Related Problems.* Compile a list of places a person can call to report dishonest credit practices, get advice and help with credit problems, and check out a creditor's reputation before signing a contract. L06-6

FINANCIAL PLANNING CASE

Don't Let Crooks Steal Your Identity: How to Protect Yourself—and Your Credit Rating

In 2009 Consumer Sentinel, the complaint database developed and maintained by the Federal Trade Commission, received over 1.3 million consumer fraud and identity theft complaints. Consumers reported losses from fraud of more than $1.7 billion.

Identity theft is the fastest-growing financial crime. One of the first things the FBI discovered about the September 11 hijackers was that as many as half a dozen were using credit cards and driver's licenses with identities lifted from stolen or forged passports.

If you care at all about the privacy of your financial information—your credit history, your portfolio, your charge card numbers—you can protect yourself from criminals determined to exploit that information. The theft can be as simple as someone pilfering your credit card number and charging merchandise to your account. Or it can be as elaborate as a crook using your name, birth date, and Social Security number to take over your credit card and bank accounts, or set up new ones.

If your identity has been snatched, you're first likely to learn about it when checks start bouncing or a collection agency begins calling. The damage isn't so much in dollars, since the financial institutions are liable for the unauthorized charges. Rather, the fallout includes a checkered credit history, which could prevent you from getting a mortgage or a job, and the countless phone calls and piles of paperwork you'll need to go through to set the records straight. Guarding against identity theft is much like locking the door and activating the burglar alarm when you leave your home. By and large, the crime is a low-tech operation, despite well-publicized instances of hackers breaking into websites and stealing millions of credit card numbers. Usually, someone fishes a bank statement or credit card offer out of your trash, or a dishonest employee peeks at your personnel file.

To protect yourself, keep your Social Security number in a secure place and never carry it around with you. Provide your Social Security number only when necessary. Instead, try to use other forms of identification. Ignore e-mail requests for your personal financial information. Shred your discarded financial records and any preapproved credit card applications. And check your credit report regularly, because credit card companies don't have to honor fraud alerts.

Finally, protect your identity by giving it a lower profile. For example, remove your name from junk mail and telemarketing lists by going to the Direct Marketing association's website at www.thedma.org/consumers/privacy.html. Call 1-888-567-8688 to stop receiving preapproved credit card offers.

Questions

1. What are several methods that crooks use to steal your identity?
2. How do you discover that someone has stolen your identity?
3. What steps can you take to thwart identity thieves?
4. What actions might you take to ensure that your credit cards and other financial information are secure?

Source: Federal Trade Commission, *National and State Trends in Fraud and Identity Theft,* February 1, 2005, p. 2, Federal Trade Commission, *Consumer Sentinel Network Data Book,* February 2013, www.ftc.gov/sentinel/reports/sentinel-annual-reports/sentinel-cy2012.pdf, accessed March 8, 2013.

PERSONAL FINANCIAL PLANNER IN ACTION

Establishing and Maintaining a Credit Record

The wise use of credit requires knowing the process for establishing credit. In addition, you should develop an awareness of credit reports and the legal rights associated with using consumer credit.

Your Short-Term Financial Planning Activities	*Resources*
1. Prepare an inventory of current credit balances and monthly payments.	PFP Sheet 29 http://credit.about.com www.bankrate.com www.banx.com
2. Review your credit file for current accuracy of information.	www.myfico.com www.equifax.com www.experian.com www.transunion.com
3. Become familiar with consumer credit laws that may relate to various aspects of your use of credit.	www.ftc.gov www.federalreserve.gov
Your Long-Term Financial Planning Activities	
1. Describe actions you may take to reduce your credit balances (if applicable).	www.ncfe.org www.profina.org
2. Create a plan for spending that provides for using credit at an appropriate level.	Text pages 189–192 www.mymoney.gov

CONTINUING CASE

Getting Started

Life Situation	*Financial Data*
Single	Monthly Income $1,750
Age 21	Living Expenses $1,210
No dependents	Personal property $7,300
Graduate and engaged	Savings $5,000
	Student loan $4,200
	Credit card debt $4,600

Shelby has been out of college for about a year and has continued to work at the pet store full time. She recently got engaged to Mark Lawrence. After the last year of saving, she now has an adequate emergency fund. However, in the last year, she and Mark have used credit cards to make many of their purchases. They used cards (they each have several) when they ran out of money near the end of each month. They also used credit to fund a vacation to the beach. Shelby justified the trip and many of her purchases because both of the cards she uses have rewards programs. Both Shelby and Mark almost always make their payments on time but have been unable to pay off more than the minimum balance every month, leaving them with credit card debt.

Shelby and Mark would like to get married soon and possibly even buy a condo, but are not sure how to finance these things while also starting Shelby's pet salon.

Questions

1. Given her current situation, list some suggestions on how Shelby can reduce her credit card debt.
2. What is the best way for Shelby and Mark to become more aware of the effect of credit card debt on their current and long-term financial situation?
3. Explain how the Personal Financial Planner sheet (Consumer Credit Usage Patterns) might be useful for Shelby and Mark.

"I admire people who are able to pay off their credit cards each month."

Directions

Your ability to monitor spending and credit use is a fundamental success for wise money management and long-term financial security. The Daily Spending Diary can help in this process. Use the "Daily Spending Diary" sheets provided at the end of the book to record all of your spending in the categories provided. Be sure to indicate the use of a credit card with (CR).

Analysis Questions

1. What do your spending habits indicate about your use of credit?

2. How might your Daily Spending Diary provide information for wise use of credit?

The Daily Spending Diary Sheets are located in Appendix D at the end of the book and on the student website at www.mhhe.com/kdh.

chapter 7

Choosing a Source of Credit: The Costs of Credit Alternatives

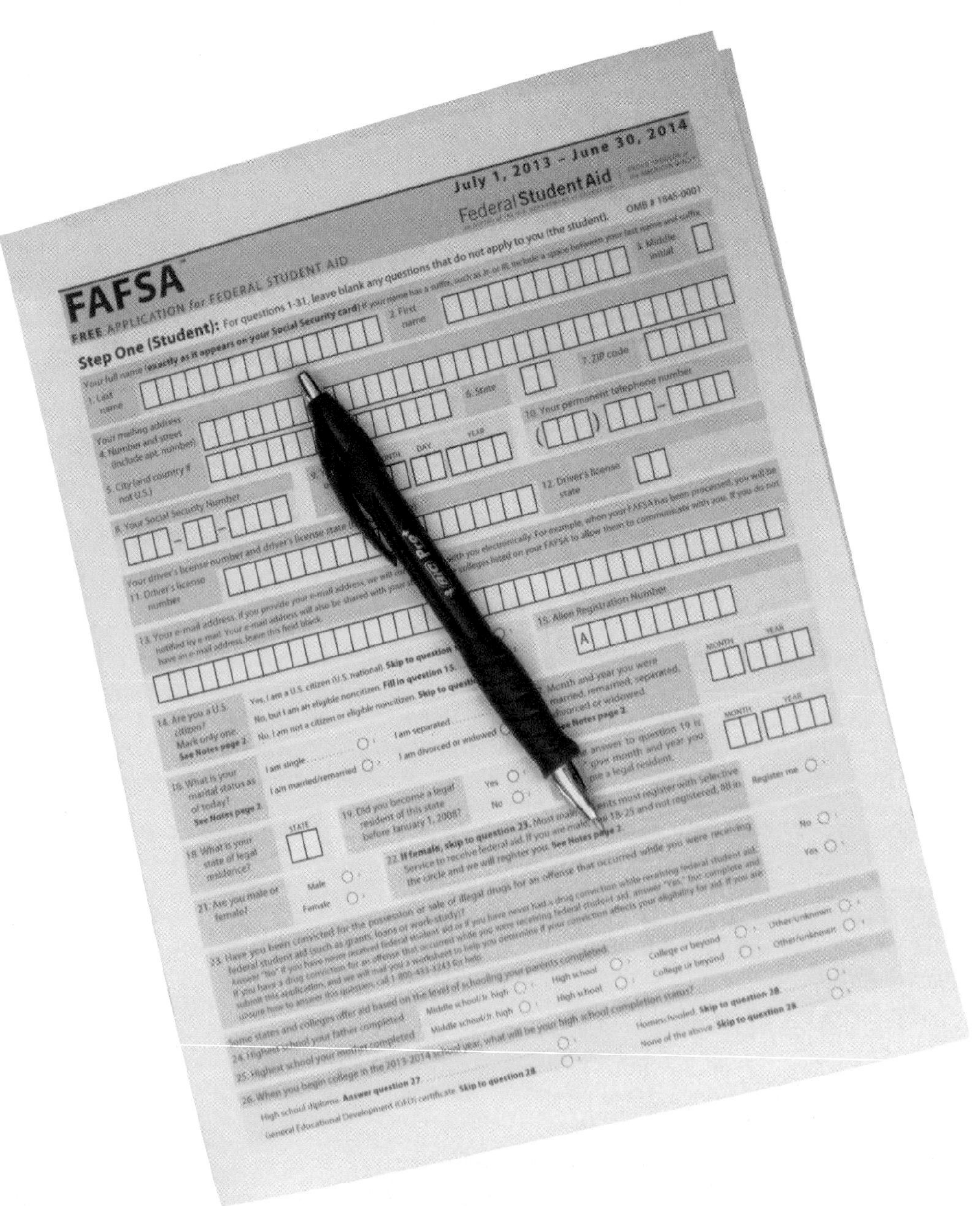

Learning Objectives	What will this mean for me?

LO7-1 Analyze the major sources of consumer credit.

LO7-2 Determine the cost of credit by calculating interest using various interest formulas.

LO7-3 Develop a plan to manage your debts.

LO7-4 Evaluate various private and governmental sources that assist consumers with debt problems.

LO7-5 Assess the choices in declaring personal bankruptcy.

Like everything else you buy, credit has a price tag and it pays to comparison shop. Understanding the cost involved in obtaining credit will give you the tools to acquire the best source of credit. If you experience the warning signs of debt problems, there are several options available to manage your finances.

my life

CAN I AFFORD A LOAN AND REPAY IT ON TIME?

If you are thinking of taking out a loan or applying for a credit card, your first step should be to figure out how much the loan will cost you and whether you can afford it. Then you should shop for the best credit terms. But what if you are having trouble paying your bills and need help? Do you know your options? The main focus is to keep the cost of credit low, and avoid the warning signs of debt problems.

For each of the following statements, select "yes," "no," or "uncertain" to indicate your personal response regarding these situations.

1. If I need to borrow money, my parents or family members are often the source of the least expensive loans	Yes	No	Uncertain
2. I am aware of the two most common methods of calculating interest.	Yes	No	Uncertain
3. If my household is experiencing problems in paying bills, it is time to examine the family budget for ways to reduce expenses.	Yes	No	Uncertain
4. I am aware that everyone who is overburdened with credit obligations can phone, write, or visit the Consumer Credit Counseling Service.	Yes	No	Uncertain
5. I realize that the Bankruptcy Abuse Prevention and Consumer Protection Act of 2005 made it more difficult for consumers to file a Chapter 7 bankruptcy.	Yes	No	Uncertain

As you study this chapter, you will encounter "My Life" boxes with additional information and resources related to these items.

Sources of Consumer Credit

LO7-1

Analyze the major sources of consumer credit.

Credit costs got you down? Well, you are not alone. Credit costs money; therefore, always weigh the benefits of buying an item on credit now versus waiting until you have saved enough money to pay cash. We can all get into credit difficulties if we do not understand how and when to use credit.

Financial and other institutions, the sources of credit, come in all shapes and sizes. They play an important role in our economy, and they offer a broad range of financial services. By evaluating your credit options, you can reduce your finance charges. You can reconsider your decision to borrow money, discover a less expensive type of loan, or find a lender that charges a lower interest rate.

Before deciding whether to borrow money, ask yourself these three questions: Do I need a loan? Can I afford a loan? Can I qualify for a loan? We discussed the affordability of loans and the qualifications required to obtain loans in the last chapter. Here we wrestle with the first question.

my life 1

If I need to borrow money, my parents or family members are often the source of the least expensive loans.

Borrowing from relatives and friends is usually the least expensive, but make sure the loan agreement is in writing. It should state the interest rate, repayment schedule, and the final payment date. Information on various sources of loans and costs is available at www.consumerworld.org and www.ftc.gov/credit.

You should avoid credit in two situations. The first situation is one in which you do not need or really want a product that will require financing. Easy access to installment loans or possession of credit cards sometimes encourages consumers to make expensive purchases they later regret. The solution to this problem is simple: After you have selected a product, resist any sales pressure to buy immediately and take a day to think it over.

The second situation is one in which you can afford to pay cash. Consider the trade-offs and opportunity costs involved. Paying cash is almost always cheaper than using credit. In fact, some stores even offer a discount for payment in cash.

WHAT KIND OF LOAN SHOULD YOU SEEK?

As discussed in the last chapter, two types of credit exist: closed-end and open-end credit. Because installment loans may carry a lower interest rate, they are the less expensive credit option for loans that are repaid over a period of many months or years. However, because credit cards usually provide a float period—a certain number of days during which no interest is charged—they represent the cheaper way to make credit purchases that are paid off in a month or two. Also, once you have a credit card, using it is always easier than taking out an installment loan. An alternative to a credit card is a travel and entertainment (T&E) card, such as an American Express or Diners Club card. A T&E card requires full payment of the balance due each month but does not impose a finance charge. Annual fees, however, can be high.

In seeking an installment loan, you may think first of borrowing from a bank or a credit union. However, less expensive credit sources are available.

Parents may often loan their children money. If you are the recepient of such a loan, make sure to come to an agreement regarding repayment.

INEXPENSIVE LOANS Parents or family members are often the source of the least expensive loans. They may charge you only the interest they would have earned had they not made the loan—as little as the 1 percent they would have earned on a passbook account. Such loans, however, can complicate family relationships. All loans to or from family members should be in writing and state the interest rate, if any, repayment schedule, and the final payment date.

Also relatively inexpensive is money borrowed on financial assets held by a lending institution, for example, a bank certificate of deposit or the cash value of a whole life

Financial Planning Calculations

CASH ADVANCES

A cash advance is a loan billed to your credit card. You can obtain a cash advance with your credit card at a bank or an automated teller machine (ATM) or by using checks linked to your credit card account.

Most cards charge a special fee when a cash advance is taken out. The fee is based on a percentage of the amount borrowed, usually about 2 or 3 percent.

Some credit cards charge a minimum cash advance fee, as high as $5. You could get $20 in cash and be charged $5, a fee equal to 25 percent of the amount you borrowed.

Most cards do not have a grace period on cash advances. This means you pay interest every day until you repay the cash advance, even if you do not have an outstanding balance from the previous statement.

On some cards, the interest rate on cash advances is higher than the rate on purchases. Be sure you check the details on the contract sent to you by the card issuer.

Here is an example of charges that could be imposed for a $200 cash advance that you pay off when the bill arrives:

Cash advance fee = $4 (2% of $200)

Interest for one month = $3 (1.5% APR on $200)

Total cost for one month = $7 ($4 + $3)

In comparison, a $200 purchase on a card with a grace period could cost $0 if paid off promptly in full.

The bottom line: It is usually much more expensive to take out a cash advance than to charge a purchase to your credit card. Use cash advances only for real emergencies.

Source: A pamphlet provided by the office of Public Responsibility, American Express Company and Consumer Action, San Francisco, CA 94105. (n.p; n.d.)

insurance policy. The interest rate on such loans typically ranges from 5 to 7 percent. But the trade-off is that your assets are tied up until you have repaid the loan.

MEDIUM-PRICED LOANS Often you can obtain medium-priced loans from commercial banks, federal savings banks (savings and loan associations), and credit unions. New-car loans, for example, may cost 6 to 8 percent; used-car loans and home improvement loans may cost slightly more.

Borrowing from credit unions has several advantages. These institutions provide free credit life insurance, are generally sympathetic to borrowers with legitimate payment problems, and provide personalized service. Credit unions can now offer the same range of consumer loans that banks and other financial institutions do. Over 92 million Americans belong to credit unions, and the number of credit union members has been growing steadily. About 6,800 credit unions exist in the United States today.[1]

EXPENSIVE LOANS Though convenient to obtain, the most expensive loans available are from finance companies, retailers, and banks through credit cards. Finance companies often lend to people who cannot obtain credit from banks or credit unions. Typically, the interest ranges from 8 to 20 percent. If you are denied credit by a bank or a credit union, you should question your ability to afford the higher rate a loan company charges.

While there are no legal definitions of predatory lending, it is the unfair, deceptive, or fraudulent practices of some lenders. These lenders exploit lower-income and minority borrowers and elderly homeowners. Before you sign a loan contract, make sure to

- Explore other financing options.
- Do your homework: contact several lenders, compare interest rates, payments, terms of the loan, other fees, and costs of the loan.
- Know your rights under the law.

Check cashers, finance companies, and others make small, short-term, high-rate loans called payday loans, cash advance loans, check advance loans, postdated check loans, or deferred deposit check loans. Such loans secured by a personal check are extremely expensive. Suppose you write a personal check for $115 to borrow $100 for 14 days. The lender agrees to hold the check until your next payday, when you redeem the check by paying the $115 in cash. Your cost of this loan is a $15 finance charge that amounts to a whopping 391 percent annual percentage rate (APR).

Another expensive way to borrow money is a tax refund loan. This type of credit lets you get an advance on a tax refund. APRs as high as 774 percent have been reported. If you are short of cash, avoid these loans by asking for more time to pay a bill or seek a traditional loan. Even a cash advance on your credit card may cost less.

Borrowing from car dealers, appliance stores, department stores, and other retailers is also relatively expensive. The interest rates retailers charge are usually similar to those charged by finance companies, frequently 15 percent or more.

Banks lend funds not only through installment loans but also through cash advances on MasterCard or Visa cards. (See the Financial Planning Calculations box on page 231.) According to Stephen Brobeck, executive director of the Consumer Federation of America in Washington, DC, the average household has more than 9 credit cards and owes about $15,400 on them. Credit card cobranding has become increasingly popular with banks and industries. Cobranded credit cards, such as the Yahoo! Visa card will make shopping over the Internet easier and faster. Yahoo! will designate Visa as its "preferred card" and will promote Visa throughout its websites and to online merchants worldwide.

One type of loan from finance companies is currently less expensive than most other credit. Loans of this kind, which often can be obtained at a rate of under 4 percent, are available from the finance companies of major automakers—General Motors Acceptance Corporation, Ford Motor Credit Corporation, and others. In early 2013, Toyota was offering zero percent financing for up to 5 years. But a car dealer that offers you such a rate may be less willing to discount the price of the car or throw in free options.

Exhibit 7-1 summarizes the major sources of consumer credit: commercial banks, consumer finance companies, credit unions, life insurance companies, and savings and loan associations. This exhibit attempts to generalize the information and give an average picture of each source regarding the type of credit available, lending policies, and customer services. Due to the dramatic fluctuations in interest rates in recent years, it is no longer possible to provide a common range of annual percentage rates for each source of credit. Check with your local lender for current interest rates. Study and compare the differences to determine which source can best meet your needs and requirements.

Today borrowing and credit are more complex than ever. As more and more types of financial institutions offer financial services, your choices of what and where to borrow will widen. The Internet may be used to compare interest rates for different loan sources and credit cards. Shopping for credit is just as important as shopping for an automobile, furniture, or major appliances.

PRACTICE QUIZ 7-1

1 What are the major sources of consumer credit?
2 What are some advantages and disadvantages of securing a loan from a credit union? From a finance company?

Exhibit 7-1 Sources of consumer credit

Credit Source	Type of Loan	Lending Policies
Commercial banks	Single-payment loans Personal installment loans Passbook loans Check-credit loans Credit card loans Second mortgages	• Seek customers with established credit history. • Often require collateral or security. • Prefer to deal in large loans, such as vehicle, home improvement, and home modernization, with the exception of credit card and check-credit plans. • Determine repayment schedules according to the purpose of the loan. • Vary credit rates according to the type of credit, time period, customer's credit history, and the security offered. • May require several days to process a new credit application.
Consumer finance companies	Personal installment loans Second mortgages	• Often lend to consumers without established credit history. • Often make unsecured loans. • Often vary rates according to the size of the loan balance. • Offer a variety of repayment schedules. • Make a higher percentage of small loans than other lenders. • Maximum loan size limited by law. • Process applications quickly, frequently on the same day the application is made.
Credit unions	Personal installment loans Share draft–credit plans Credit card loans Second mortgages	• Lend to members only. • Make unsecured loans. • May require collateral or cosigner for loans over a specified amount. • May require payroll deductions to pay off loan. • May submit large loan applications to a committee of members for approval. • Offer a variety of repayment schedules.
Life insurance companies	Single-payment or partial-payment loans	• Lend on cash value of life insurance policy. • No date or penalty on repayment. • Deduct amount owed from the value of policy benefit if death or other maturity occurs before repayment.
Federal savings banks (savings and loan associations)	Personal installment loans (generally permitted by state-chartered savings associations) Home improvement loans Education loans Savings account loans Second mortgages	• Will lend to all creditworthy individuals. • Often require collateral. • Loan rates vary depending on size of loan, length of payment, and security involved.

Consumer credit is available from several types of sources. *Which sources seem to offer the widest variety of loans?*

The Cost of Credit

LO7-2

Determine the cost of credit by calculating interest using various interest formulas.

Truth in Lending law A federal law that requires creditors to disclose the annual percentage rate (APR) and the finance charge as a dollar amount.

The **Truth in Lending law** of 1969 was a landmark piece of legislation. For the first time, creditors were required to state the cost of borrowing as a dollar amount so that consumers would know exactly what the credit charges were and thus could compare credit costs and shop for credit.

If you are thinking of borrowing money or opening a credit account, your first step should be to figure out how much it will cost you and whether you can afford it. Then you should shop for the best terms. Two key concepts that you should remember are the finance charge and the annual percentage rate.

FINANCE CHARGE AND ANNUAL PERCENTAGE RATE (APR)

Credit costs vary. If you know the finance charge and the annual percentage rate (APR), you can compare credit prices from different sources. Under the Truth in Lending law, the creditor must inform you, in writing and before you sign any agreement, of the finance charge and the APR.

DID YOU KNOW?

Most every time you use a credit card in a foreign country, Visa or Mastercard charges a 1% fee for converting the purchase or cash advance into U.S. dollars. If you travel frequently, you should investigate your credit card's policies; there are some cards on the market that may waive or absorb the fee, and those can save you a great deal of money if you plan to spend much on your travels.

The **finance charge** is the total dollar amount you pay to use credit. It includes interest costs and sometimes other costs such as service charges, credit-related insurance premiums, or appraisal fees. For example, borrowing $100 for a year might cost you $10 in interest. If there is also a service charge of $1, the finance charge will be $11.

The **annual percentage rate (APR)** is the percentage cost (or relative cost) of credit on a yearly basis. The APR is your key to comparing costs, regardless of the amount of credit or how much time you have to repay it. Suppose you borrow $100 for one year and pay a finance charge of $10. If you can keep the entire $100 for the whole year and then pay it all back at once, you are paying an APR of 10 percent:

finance charge The total dollar amount paid to use credit.

annual percentage rate (APR) The percentage cost (or relative cost) of credit on a yearly basis. The APR yields a true rate of interest for comparison with other sources of credit.

Amount Borrowed	Month Number	Payment Made	Loan Balance
$100	1	$0	$100
	2	0	100
	3	0	100
	.	.	.
	.	.	.
	.	.	.
	.	.	.
	12	100	0
		(plus $10 interest)	

On average, you had full use of $100 throughout the year. To calculate the average use, add the loan balance during the first and last month, then divide by 2:

$$\text{Average balance} = \frac{\$100 + \$100}{2} = \$100$$

But if you repay the $100 in 12 equal monthly payments, you don't get use of the $100 for the whole year. In fact, as shown next, you get use of less and less of that $100 each month. In this case, the $10 charge for credit amounts to an APR of 18.5 percent.

Note that you are paying 10 percent interest on $100 even though you had use of only $91.67 during the second month, not $100. During the last month, you owed only $8.37

Amount Borrowed	Month Number	Payment Made	Loan Balance
$100	1	$0	$100.00
	2	8.33	91.67
	3	8.33	83.34
	4	8.33	75.01
	5	8.33	66.68
	6	8.33	58.35
	7	8.33	50.02
	8	8.33	41.69
	9	8.33	33.36
	10	8.33	25.03
	11	8.33	16.70
	12	8.33	8.37

(and had use of $8.37), but the $10 interest is for the entire $100. As calculated in the previous example, the average use of the money during the year is $100 + $8.37 ÷ 2, or $54.18.

The Financial Planning Calculations box The Arithmetic of the Annual Percentage Rate, shows how to calculate the APR. All creditors—banks, stores, car dealers, credit card companies, and finance companies—must state the cost of their credit in terms of the finance charge and the APR. The law does not set interest rates or other credit charges, but it does require their disclosure so that you can compare credit costs and tackle the trade-offs.

TACKLING THE TRADE-OFFS

When you choose your financing, there are trade-offs between the features you prefer (term, size of payments, fixed or variable interest, or payment plan) and the cost of your loan. Here are some of the major trade-offs you should consider.

TERM VERSUS INTEREST COSTS Many people choose longer-term financing because they want smaller monthly payments. But the longer the term for a loan at a given interest rate, the greater the amount you must pay in interest charges. Consider the following analysis of the relationship between the term and interest costs.

Financial Planning Calculations

THE ARITHMETIC OF THE ANNUAL PERCENTAGE RATE (APR)

There are two ways to calculate the APR: using an APR formula and using the APR tables. The APR tables are more precise than the formula. The formula, given below, only approximates the APR:

$$r = \frac{2 \times n \times I}{P(N + 1)}$$

where

r = Approximate APR

n = Number of payment periods in one year (12, if payments are monthly; 52, if weekly)

I = Total dollar cost of credit

P = Principal, or net amount of loan

N = Total number of payments scheduled to pay off the loan

Let us compare the APR when the $100 loan is paid off in one lump sum at the end of the year and when the same loan is paid off in 12 equal monthly payments. The stated annual interest rate is 10 percent for both loans.

Using the formula, the APR for the lump-sum loan is

$$r = \frac{2 \times 1 \times \$10}{\$100(1 + 1)} = \frac{\$20}{\$100(2)} = \frac{\$20}{\$200} = 0.10$$

or 10 percent.

Using the formula, the APR for the monthly payment loan is

$$r = \frac{2 \times 12 \times \$10}{\$100(12 + 1)} = \frac{\$240}{\$100(13)} = \frac{\$240}{\$1,300}$$

$= 0.1846$, or 18.46 percent (rounded to 18.5 percent).

A COMPARISON Even when you understand the terms a creditor is offering, it's easy to underestimate the difference in dollars that different terms can make. Suppose you're buying a $7,500 used car. You put $1,500 down, and you need to borrow $6,000. Compare the following three credit arrangements:

	APR	Length of Loan	Monthly Payment	Total Finance Charge	Total Cost
Creditor A	15%	3 years	$205.07	$1,382.52	$7,382.52
Creditor B	15	4 years	163.96	1,870.08	7,870.08
Creditor C	16	4 years	166.98	2,015.04	8,015.04

How do these choices compare? The answer depends partly on what you need. The lowest-cost loan is available from creditor A. If you are looking for lower monthly payments, you could repay the loan over a longer period of time. However, you would have to pay more in total costs. A loan from creditor B—also at a 15 percent APR, but for four years—would add about $488 to your finance charge.

If that four-year loan were available only from creditor C, the APR of 16 percent would add another $145 to your finance charges. Other terms, such as the size of the down payment, will also make a difference. Be sure to look at all the terms before you make your choice.

LENDER RISK VERSUS INTEREST RATE You may prefer financing that requires low fixed payments with a large final payment or only a minimum of up-front cash. But both of these requirements can increase your cost of borrowing because they create more risk for your lender.

If you want to minimize your borrowing costs, you may need to accept conditions that reduce your lender's risk. Here are a few possibilities.

Variable Interest Rate A variable interest rate is based on fluctuating rates in the banking system, such as the prime rate. With this type of loan, you share the interest rate risks with the lender. Therefore, the lender may offer you a lower initial interest rate than it would with a fixed-rate loan.

A Secured Loan If you pledge property or other assets as collateral, you'll probably receive a lower interest rate on your loan.

Up-Front Cash Many lenders believe you have a higher stake in repaying a loan if you pay cash for a large portion of what you are financing. Doing so may give you a better chance of getting the other terms you want. Of course, by making a large down payment, you forgo interest that you might earn in a savings account.

A Shorter Term As you have learned, the shorter the period of time for which you borrow, the smaller the chance that something will prevent you from repaying and the lower the risk to the lender. Therefore, you may be able to borrow at a lower interest rate if you accept a shorter-term loan, but your payments will be higher.

In the next section, you will see how the above-mentioned trade-offs can affect the cost of closed-end and open-end credit.

my life 2

I am aware of the two most common methods of calculating interest.

The two most common methods of calculating interest are compound and simple interest formulas. For examples of calculating interest, be sure to read the Financial Planning Calculations boxes in this chapter.

CALCULATING THE COST OF CREDIT

The two most common methods of calculating interest are compound and simple interest formulas. Perhaps the most basic method is the simple interest calculation. Simple interest on the declining balance, add-on interest, bank discount, and compound interest are variations of simple interest.

SIMPLE INTEREST **Simple interest** is the interest computed on principal only and without compounding; it is the dollar cost of borrowing money. This cost is based on three elements: the amount borrowed, which is called the *principal;* the rate of interest; and the amount of time for which the principal is borrowed.

simple interest Interest computed on principal only and without compounding.

You can use the following formula to find simple interest:

$$\text{Interest} = \text{Principal} \times \text{Rate of interest} \times \text{Time}$$

or

$$I = P \times r \times T$$

EXAMPLE: Using the Simple Interest Formula

Suppose you have persuaded a relative to lend you $1,000 to purchase a laptop computer. Your relative agreed to charge only 5 percent interest, and you agreed to repay the loan at the end of one year. Using the simple interest formula, the interest will be 5 percent of $1,000 for one year, or $50, since you have the use of $1,000 for the entire year:

$$I = \$1{,}000 \times 0.05 \times 1$$
$$= \$50$$

Using the APR formula discussed earlier,

$$\text{APR} = \frac{2 \times n \times I}{P(N + 1)} = \frac{2 \times 1 \times \$50}{\$1{,}000(1 + 1)} = \frac{\$100}{\$2{,}000} = 0.05\text{, or 5 percent}$$

Note that the stated rate, 5 percent, is also the annual percentage rate.

declining balance method A method of computing interest when more than one payment is made on a simple interest loan.

SIMPLE INTEREST ON THE DECLINING BALANCE When more than one payment is made on a simple interest loan, the method of computing interest is known as the **declining balance method.** Since you pay interest only on the amount of the original principal that you have not yet repaid, the more frequent the payments, the lower the interest you will pay. Most credit unions use this method for their loans.

EXAMPLE: Using the Simple Interest Formula on the Declining Balance

Using simple interest on the declining balance to compute interest charges, the interest on a 5 percent, $1,000 loan repaid in two payments, one at the end of the first half-year and another at the end of the second half-year, would be $37.50, as follows:

First payment:

$$I = P \times r \times T$$
$$= \$1{,}000 \times 0.05 \times \tfrac{1}{2}$$
$$= \$25 \text{ interest plus } \$500\text{, or } \$525$$

Second payment:

$$I = P \times r \times T$$
$$= \$500 \times 0.05 \times \tfrac{1}{2}$$
$$= \$12.50 \text{ interest plus the remaining balance of } \$500\text{, or } \$512.50$$

Total payment on the loan:

$$\$525 + \$512.50 = \$1{,}037.50$$

Using the APR formula,

$$\text{APR} = \frac{2 \times n \times I}{P(N+1)} = \frac{2 \times 2 \times \$37.50}{\$1{,}000(2+1)} = \frac{\$150}{\$3{,}000} = 0.05\text{, or 5 percent}$$

Note that using simple interest under the declining balance method, the stated rate, 5 percent, is also the annual percentage rate. The add-on interest, bank discount, and compound interest calculation methods differ from the simple interest method as to when, how, and on what balance interest is paid. For these methods, the real annual rate, or the annual percentage rate, differs from the stated rate.

add-on interest method A method of computing interest in which interest is calculated on the full amount of the original principal.

ADD-ON INTEREST With the **add-on interest method,** interest is calculated on the full amount of the original principal. The interest amount is immediately added to the original principal, and payments are determined by dividing principal plus interest by the number of payments to be made. When only one payment is required, this method produces the same APR as the simple interest method. However, when two or more payments are to be made, the add-on method results in an effective rate of interest that is higher than the stated rate.

Note that using the add-on interest method means that no matter how many payments you are to make, the interest will always be $50. As the number of payments increases, you have use of less and less credit over the year. For example, if you make four quarterly payments of $262.50, you have use of $1,000 during the first quarter, about $750 during the second quarter, about $500 during the third quarter, and about $250 during

EXAMPLE: Using the Add-on Method

Consider again the two-payment loan in the previous example. Using the add-on method, interest of $50 (5 percent of $1,000 for one year) is added to the $1,000 borrowed, giving $1,050 to be repaid—half (or $525) at the end of the first half-year and the other half at the end of the second half-year.

Even though your relative's stated interest rate is 5 percent, the real interest rate is

$$\text{APR} = \frac{2 \times n \times I}{P(N + 1)} = \frac{2 \times 2 \times \$50}{\$1{,}000(2 + 1)} = \frac{\$200}{\$3{,}000} = 0.066\text{, or 6.6 percent}$$

the fourth and final quarter. Therefore, as the number of payments increases, the true interest rate, or APR, also increases.

COST OF OPEN-END CREDIT As discussed earlier, open-end credit includes credit cards, department store charge cards, and check overdraft accounts that allow you to write checks for more than your actual balance. You can use open-end credit again and again until you reach a prearranged borrowing limit. The Truth in Lending law requires that open-end creditors let you know how the finance charge and the APR will affect your costs.

First, creditors must tell you how they calculate the finance charge. Creditors use various systems to calculate the balance on which they assess finance charges. Some creditors add finance charges after subtracting payments made during the billing period; this is called the **adjusted balance method.** Other creditors give you no credit for payments made during the billing period; this is called the **previous balance method.** Under the third—and the fairest—method, the **average daily balance method,** creditors add your balances for each day in the billing period and then divide by the number of days in the period. The average daily balance may include or exclude new purchases during the billing period.

adjusted balance method The assessment of finance charges after payments made during the billing period have been subtracted.

previous balance method A method of computing finance charges that gives no credit for payments made during the billing period.

average daily balance method A method of computing finance charges that uses a weighted average of the account balance throughout the current billing period.

Here is how some different methods of calculating finance charges affect the cost of credit:

	Average Daily Balance (*including* new purchases)	Average Daily Balance (*excluding* new purchases)
Monthly rate	1½%	1½%
APR	18%	18%
Previous balance	$400	$400
New purchases	$50 on 18th day	$50 on 18th day
Payments	$300 on 15th day (new balance = $100)	$300 on 15th day (new balance = $100)
Average daily balance	$270*	$250**
Finance charge	$4.05 (1½% × $270)	$3.75 (1½% × $250)

*To figure average daily balance (*including* new purchases):
[($400 × 15 days) + ($100 × 3 days) + ($150 × 12 days)] ÷ 30 days =
($6,000 + $300 + $1,800) ÷ 30 = $8,100 ÷ 30 days = $270

**To figure average daily balance (*excluding* new purchases):
[($400 × 15 days) + ($100 × 15 days)] ÷ 30 days =
($6,000 + $1,500) ÷ 30 = $7,500 ÷ 30 days = $250

	Adjusted Balance	Previous Balance
Monthly rate	1½%	1½%
APR	18%	18%
Previous balance	$400	$400
Payments	$300	$300
Average daily balance	N/A	N/A
Finance charge	$1.50 (1½% × $100)	$6.00 (1½% × $400)

As the example shows, the finance charge varies for the same pattern of purchases and payments. Furthermore, some creditors used a *two-cycle average daily balance* method, which may *include* or *exclude* new purchases. Instead of using the average daily balance for one billing cycle, as described above, these creditors use the average daily balance for *two* consecutive billing cycles. The new Credit CARD Act of 2009 bans a two-cycle average daily balance method.

Second, creditors must tell you when finance charges on your credit account begin, so that you know how much time you have to pay your bills before a finance charge is added. Some creditors, for example, give you a 21- to 25-day grace period to pay your balance in full before imposing a finance charge. But in most cases, the grace period applies only if you have no outstanding balance on your card. Therefore, if you want to take advantage of the interest-free period on your card, you must pay your bill in full every month.

All credit card issuers must include the following key pieces of information with their applications for credit cards. Look for a box similar to the one below for information about interest rates, fees, and other terms for the card you are considering.

Interest Rates and Interest Charges	
Annual Percentage Rate (APR) for Purchases ①	**8.99%, 10.99%, or 12.99%** introductory APR for one year, based on your creditworthiness. After that, your APR will be **14.99%**. This APR will vary with the market based on the Prime Rate.
APR for Balance Transfers ②	**15.99%** This APR will vary with the market based on the Prime Rate
APR for Cash Advances ③	**21.99%** This APR will vary with the market based on the Prime Rate.
Penalty APR and When It Applies ④	**28.99%** This APR may be applied to your account if you: 1. Make a late payment; 2. Go over your credit limit; 3. Make a payment that is returned; or 4. Do any of the above on another account that you have with us. **How Long Will the Penalty APR Apply?:** If your APRs are increased for any of these reasons, the Penalty APR will apply until you make six consecutive minimum payments when due.

How to Avoid Paying Interest on Purchases ⑤	Your due date is at least 25 days after the close of each billing cycle. We will not charge you any interest on purchases if you pay your entire balance by the due date each month.
Minimum Interest Charge ⑥	If you are charged interest, the charge will be no less than $1.50.
For Credit Card Tips from the Federal Reserve Board	To learn more about factors to consider when applying for or using a credit card, visit the website of the Federal Reserve Board at http://www.federalreserve.gov/creditcard.
Fees	
Set-up and Maintenance Fees ⑦	NOTICE: Some of these set-up and maintenance fees will be assessed before you begin using your card and will reduce the amount of credit you initially have available. For example, if you are assigned the minimum credit limit of $250, your initial available credit will be only about $209 (or about $204 if you choose to have an additional card).
• Annual Fee	$20
• Account Set-up Fee	$20 (one-time fee)
• Participation Fee	$12 annually ($1 per month)
• Additional Card Fee	$5 annually (if applicable)
Transaction Fees ⑧	
• Balance Transfer	Either $5 or 3% of the amount of each transfer, whichever is greater (maximum fee: $100).
• Cash Advance	Either $5 or 3% of the amount of each cash advance, whichever is greater.
• Foreign Transaction	2% of each transaction in U.S. dollars.
Penalty Fees ⑨	
• Late Payment	$29 if balance is less than or equal to $1,000; $35 if balance is more than $1,000
• Over-the-Credit Limit	$29
• Returned Payment	$35
Other Fees ⑩	Credit insurance, or debt cancellation, or debt suspension coverage

⑪

How We Will Calculate Your Balance: We use a method called "average daily balance (including new purchases)."

⑫

Loss of Introductory APR: We may end your introductory APR and apply the Penalty APR if you become more than 60 days late in paying your bill.

Source: http://www.federalreserve.gov/creditcard/flash/offerflash.html, accessed March 5, 2013.

The Truth in Lending law does not set rates or tell the creditor how to make interest calculations. It requires only that the creditor tell you the method that will be used. You should ask for an explanation of any terms you don't understand.

COST OF CREDIT AND EXPECTED INFLATION Borrowers and lenders are less concerned about dollars, present or future, than about the goods and services those dollars can buy—that is, their purchasing power.

Inflation erodes the purchasing power of money. Each percentage point increase in inflation means a decrease of approximately 1 percent in the quantity of goods and services you can purchase with a given quantity of dollars. As a result, lenders, seeking to protect their purchasing power, add the expected rate of inflation to the interest rate they charge. You are willing to pay this higher rate because you expect inflation to enable you to repay the loan with cheaper dollars.

For example, if a lender expects a 3 percent inflation rate for the coming year and desires an 6 percent return on its loan, it will probably charge you a 9 percent nominal or stated rate (a 3 percent inflation premium plus an 6 percent "real" rate).

Return to the example on page 237 in which you borrowed $1,000 from your relative at the bargain rate of 5 percent for one year. If the inflation rate was 4 percent during that year, your relative's real rate of return was only 1 percent (5 percent stated interest minus 4 percent inflation rate) and your "real" cost was not $50 but only $10 ($50 minus $40 inflation premium).

DID YOU KNOW?

BEWARE: OFFERS TO SKIP A PAYMENT
If your credit company invites you to skip a monthly payment without a penalty, it is not doing you a favor. You will still owe finance charges on your unpaid balance. And interest could be adding up on any purchases you make after the due date you skipped.

COST OF CREDIT AND TAX CONSIDERATIONS Before the Tax Reform Act of 1986, the interest you paid on consumer credit reduced your taxable income. The new law did not affect the deductibility of home mortgage interest, but now you can no longer deduct interest paid on consumer loans.

AVOID THE MINIMUM MONTHLY PAYMENT TRAP The "minimum monthly payment" is the smallest amount you can pay and still be a cardholder in good standing. Banks often encourage you to make the minimum payment, such as 2 percent of your outstanding balance or $20, whichever is greater. Some statements refer to the minimum as the "cardholder amount due." But that is not the total amount you owe.

Consider the following examples. In each example, the minimum payment is based on 1/36 of the outstanding balance or $20, whichever is greater.

EXAMPLE: Minimum Monthly Payment Trap

You are buying new books for college. If you spend $500 on textbooks using a credit card charging 19.8 percent interest and make only the minimum payment, it will take you more than 2½ years to pay off the loan, adding $150 in interest charges to the cost of your purchase. The same purchase on a credit card charging 12 percent interest will cost only $78 extra.

EXAMPLE: Minimum Monthly Payment Trap

You purchase a $2,000 stereo system using a credit card with 19 percent interest and a 2 percent minimum payment. If you pay just the minimum every month, it will take you 265 months—over 22 years—to pay off the debt and will cost you nearly $4,800 in interest payments. Doubling the amount paid each month to 4 percent of the balance owed would allow you to shorten the payment time to 88 months from 265 months—or 7 years as opposed to 22 years—and save you about $3,680.

EXAMPLE: Minimum Monthly Payment Trap

You charge $2,000 in tuition and fees on a credit card charging 18.5 percent interest. If you pay off the balance by making the minimum payment each month, it will take you more than 11 years to repay the debt. By the time you have paid off the loan, you will have spent an extra $1,934 in interest alone—almost the actual cost of your tuition and fees. Again, to be prudent, pay off the balance as quickly as possible.

The new Credit CARD law requires creditors to include the minimum payment warning in their monthly statements. Here is an example:

Minimum Payment Warning: If you make only the minimum payment each period, you will pay more in interest and it will take you longer to pay off your balance. For example:

If you make no additional charges using this card and each month you pay . . .	You will pay off the balance shown on this statement in about . . .	And you will end up paying an estimated total of . . .
Only the minimum payment	10 years	$3,284
$62	3 years	$2,232 (*Savings* = $1,052)

If you would like information about credit counseling services, call 1-800-388-CCCS.

WHEN THE REPAYMENT IS EARLY: THE RULE OF 78S

Creditors sometimes use tables based on a mathematical formula called the **rule of 78s,** also called *the sum of the digits,* to determine how much interest you have paid at any point in a loan. This formula favors lenders and dictates that you pay more interest at the beginning of a loan, when you have the use of more of the money, and pay less and less interest as the debt is reduced. Because all of the payments are the same in size, the part going to pay back the amount borrowed increases as the part representing interest decreases.

rule of 78s A mathematical formula to determine how much interest has been paid at any point in a loan term.

OTHER METHODS OF DETERMINING THE COST OF CREDIT

BANK DISCOUNT METHOD

When the *bank discount rate* method is used, interest is calculated on the amount to be paid back and you receive the difference between the amount to be paid back and the interest amount. For instance, if your relative lends you $1,000 less $50 (interest at 5 percent), you receive $950.

Example 1. Using the APR formula, you find the true interest rate, or the annual percentage rate, is 5.263 percent, not the stated 5 percent:

$$\text{APR} = \frac{2 \times n \times I}{P(N+1)} = \frac{2 \times 1 \times \$50}{\$950(1+1)} = \frac{\$100}{\$1{,}900}$$

$$= 0.05263, \text{ or } 5.263 \text{ percent}$$

COMPOUND INTEREST

Unlike simple interest, *compound interest* is the interest paid on the original principal *plus* the accumulated interest. With interest compounding, the greater the number of periods for which interest is calculated, the more rapidly the amount of interest on interest and interest on principal builds.

Annual compounding means there is only *one* period annually for the calculation of interest. With such compounding, interest charges on a *one-year* loan are identical whether they are figured on a simple interest basis or on an annual compound basis. However, a new interest formula, based on the simple interest formula, must be used if there is annual compounding for two or more years or compounding with more than one compound period per year.

A compact formula that describes compound interest calculations is

$$F = P(1 + r)^T$$

where

F = Total future repayment value of a loan (principal *plus* total accumulated or compound interest)

P = Principal

r = Rate of interest per year, or annual interest rate

T = Time in years

Before the compound interest formula can be used for *multiple*-period compounding, two important adjustments must be made.

First, adjust the *annual* interest rate (r) to reflect the number of compounding periods per year. For example, a 5 percent annual rate of interest, compounded half-yearly, works out to 2.5 percent (5 percent divided by 2) per half-year.

Second, adjust the time factor (T), which is measured in years, to reflect the *total* number of compounding periods. For example, your loan for one year compounded half-yearly works out to two compound periods (1 year multiplied by 2 compounding periods per year) over the length of the loan.

Example 2. Suppose your relative compounds interest semiannually and you make two payments, six months apart. Using the compound interest formula, here is the annual percentage rate:

$$F = P(1 + r)^T$$

$$F = \$1{,}000[1 + (0.05/2)]^{1 \times 2}$$

$$= \$1{,}000(1 + 0.025)^2$$

$$= \$1{,}000(1.050625)$$

$$= \$1{,}050.625$$

That is, you are paying $50.63 in interest for a one-year, $1,000 loan. Now, using the APR formula, you find the APR is 6.75 percent:

$$\text{APR} = \frac{2 \times n \times I}{P(N+1)}$$

$$= \frac{2 \times 2 \times \$50.63}{\$1{,}000(2+1)}$$

$$= \frac{\$202.52}{\$3{,}000}$$

$$= 0.0675, \text{ or } 6.75 \text{ percent}$$

If your relative chose to compound interest daily (365 compounding periods per year), the solution to this problem would be quite complicated. A calculator or a compound interest table can make interest calculations more manageable.

The following table summarizes the effects on the APR when the interest on a one-year, $1,000 loan is calculated using the simple interest, declining balance, add-on interest, bank discount, and compound interest methods:

Method	Amount Borrowed	Stated Interest	Total Interest	Number of Payments	APR
Simple interest*	$1,000	5%	$50.00	1	5.00%
Declining balance*	1,000	5	37.50	2	5.00
Add-on*	1,000	5	50.00	2	6.60
Bank discount	1,000(–50)	5	50.00	1	5.26
Compound interest	1,000	5	50.63	2	6.75

*Discussed in the chapter.

The laws of several states authorize the use of the rule of 78s as a means of calculating finance charge rebates when you pay off a loan early. The Truth in Lending law requires that your creditor disclose whether or not you are entitled to a rebate of the finance charge if you pay off the loan early. Loans for a year or less, however, usually do not allow for a finance charge rebate. Read the accompanying Financial Planning Calculations box to learn about other methods of determining the cost of credit.

DID YOU KNOW?

It would take 61 years to pay off a $5,000 credit card balance if you make only the minimum monthly payment. You'd pay almost $16,000 in interest. (Assuming a 14% interest rate and minimum payment of 1.5% of the outstanding balance.)

CREDIT INSURANCE

Credit insurance ensures the repayment of your loan in the event of death, disability, or loss of property. The lender is named the beneficiary and directly receives any payments made on submitted claims.

credit insurance Any type of insurance that ensures repayment of a loan in the event the borrower is unable to repay it.

There are three types of credit insurance: credit life, credit accident and health, and credit property. The most commonly purchased type of credit insurance is credit life insurance, which provides for the repayment of the loan if the borrower dies. According to the Consumer Federation of America and the National Insurance Consumer Organization, most borrowers don't need credit life insurance. Those who don't have life insurance can buy term life insurance for less. Term life insurance is discussed in Chapter 12.

Credit accident and health insurance, also called *credit disability insurance,* repays your loan in the event of a loss of income due to illness or injury. Credit property insurance provides coverage for personal property purchased with a loan. It may also insure collateral property, such as a car or furniture. However, premiums for such coverages are quite high.

COST OF CREDIT AND THE CREDIT CARD ACCOUNTABILITY, RESPONSIBILITY, AND DISCLOSURE ACT OF 2009 (THE CREDIT CARD ACT)

The Credit CARD Act has a sweeping effect on annual percentage rates, fees, and disclosures. The law:

- Limits card issuers' ability to increase the APR on transferred balances during the first year that the account is opened.
- Restricts card issuers from applying new (higher) interest rates to the existing card balances.
- Requires companies to inform consumers of rate increases or other significant changes at least 45 days in advance.
- States that teaser rates must stay in effect for at least 6 months.
- Requires issuers to mail monthly statements at least 21 days before payment is due.
- Makes new disclosure statements clear and more timely.
- Mandates that monthly credit card statements must prominently display the due date and potential late fees, as well as the interest you have paid during the current year, the monthly payment required to pay off the existing balance, and warn consumers about the costs of making only the minimum payments.
- Requires credit card issuers to post their standard card agreements on the Internet.
- Sets a consistent due date for card payments each month. If the due date falls on a holiday or weekend, the deadline is considered the next business day.
- Restricts the penalties that card issuers can charge for going over the credit limit.
- Prohibits card issuers from issuing cards to consumers under 21 unless they have a co-signer or can demonstrate that they have independent means to repay the card debt.

Credit card/charge account comparison

Consumer loan comparison

PRACTICE QUIZ 7-2

1 Distinguish between the finance charge and the annual percentage rate.
2 What are the three variations of the simple interest formula?
3 Distinguish among the adjusted balance, previous balance, and average daily balance methods of calculating the cost of open-end credit.
4 What is the rule of 78s?

Managing Your Debts

LO7-3

Develop a plan to manage your debts.

A sudden illness or the loss of your job may make it impossible for you to pay your bills on time. If you find you cannot make your payments, contact your creditors at once and try to work out a modified payment plan with them. If you have paid your bills promptly in the past, they may be willing to work with you. Do not wait until your account is turned over to a debt collector. At that point, the creditor has given up on you.

Automobile loans present special problems. Most automobile financing agreements permit your creditor to repossess your car anytime you are in default on your payments. No advance notice is required. If your car is repossessed and sold, you will still owe the difference between the selling price and the unpaid debt, plus any legal, towing, and storage charges. Try to solve the problem with your creditor when you realize you will not be able to meet your payments. It may be better to sell the car yourself and pay off your debt than to incur the added costs of repossession.

If you are having trouble paying your bills, you may be tempted to turn to a company that claims to offer assistance in solving debt problems. Such companies may offer debt consolidation loans, debt counseling, or debt reorganization plans that are "guaranteed" to stop creditors' collection efforts. Before signing with such a company, investigate it. Be sure you understand what services the company provides and what they will cost you. Do not rely on verbal promises that do not appear in your contract. Also, check with the Better Business Bureau and your state or local consumer protection office. They may be able to tell you whether other consumers have registered complaints about the company.

DID YOU KNOW?

Collection agencies can't:

- contact you before 8 a.m. or after 9 p.m.
- contact you at your place of employment.
- harass you.
- threaten harm.
- make false claims, such as representing that they work for credit reporting companies or misrepresent the amount you owe.
- say that you will be arrested if you don't pay the debt.
- state that they are taking legal action if they don't intend to do so.

For more information about your rights or to file a complaint, contact your state's attorney general or the Federal Trade Commission.

A constant worry for a debtor who is behind in payments is the fear of debt collection agencies. However, as you will see in the next section, a federal agency protects certain legal rights that you possess in your dealings with such agencies.

DEBT COLLECTION PRACTICES

Fair Debt Collection Practices Act (FDCPA) A federal law, enacted in 1978, that regulates debt collection activities.

The Federal Trade Commission enforces the **Fair Debt Collection Practices Act (FDCPA),** which prohibits certain practices by agencies that collect debts for creditors. The act does not apply to creditors that collect debts themselves. While the act does not erase the legitimate debts consumers owe, it does regulate the ways debt collection agencies do business. Exhibit 7-2 summarizes the steps you may take if a debt collector calls.

Exhibit 7-2 What to do if a debt collector calls

The Federal Trade Commission enforces the Fair Debt Collection Practices Act. The law dictates how and when a debt collector may contact you.

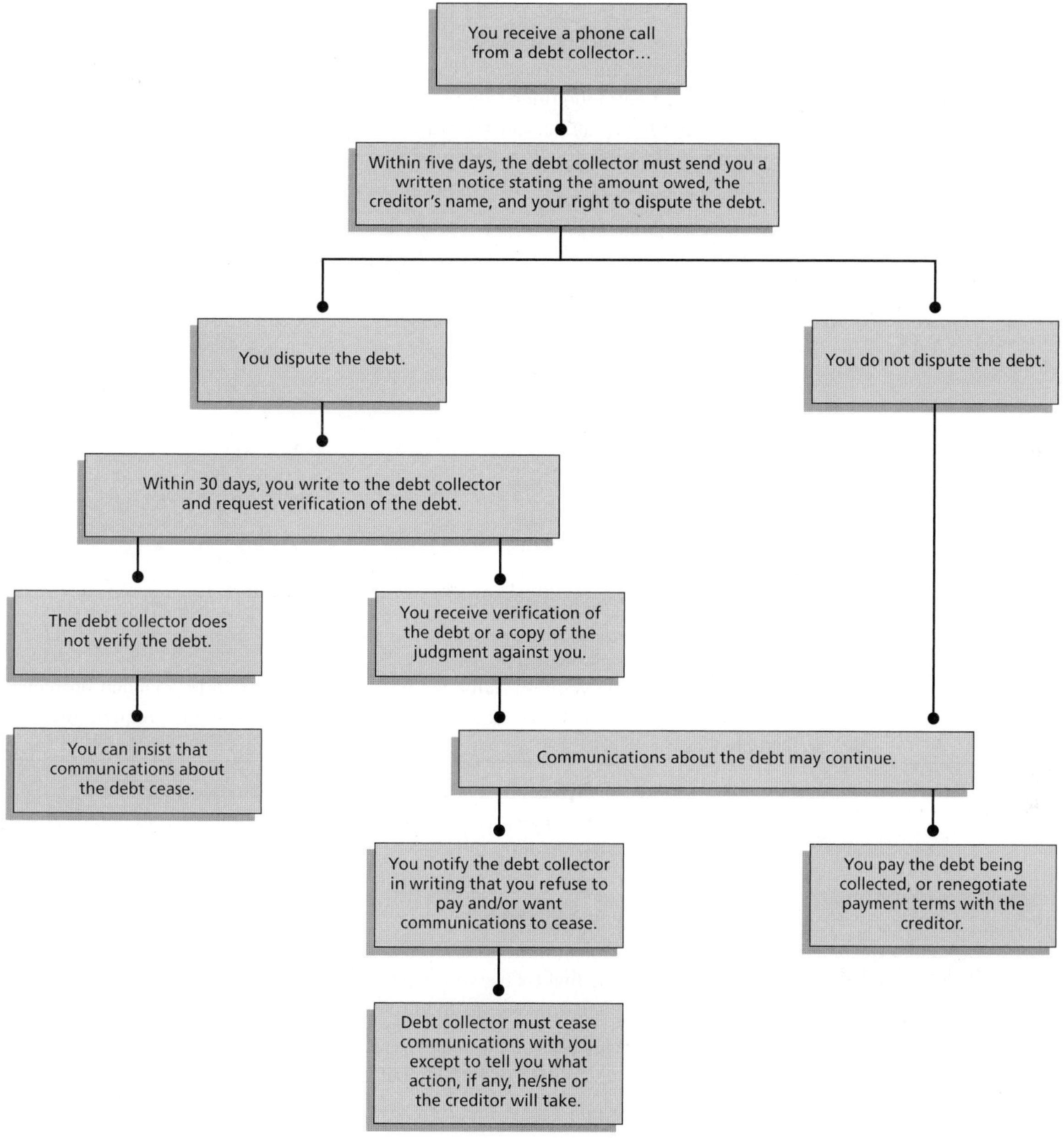

Source: Reprinted courtesy of Office of Public Information, Federal Reserve Bank of Minneapolis, Minneapolis, MN 55480.

WARNING SIGNS OF DEBT PROBLEMS

Bill Kenney, in his early 30s, has a steady job with an annual income of $55,000. Bill, his wife, and their two children enjoy a comfortable life. A new car is parked in the driveway of their home, which is furnished with such amenities as a six-burner gourmet stove, a subzero freezer, and a large-screen 3-D television set.

However, Bill Kenney is in debt. He is drowning in a sea of bills, with most of his income tied up in repaying debts. Foreclosure proceedings on his home have been instituted, and several stores have court orders to repossess practically every major appliance in it. His current car payment is overdue, and three charge accounts at local stores are several months delinquent.

This case is neither exaggerated nor isolated. Unfortunately, a large number of people are in the same floundering state. These people's problem is immaturity. Mature consumers have certain information; they demonstrate self-discipline, control their impulses, and use sound judgment; they accept responsibility for money management; and they are able to postpone and govern expenditures when overextension of credit appears likely. As Exhibit 7-3 shows, excessive use of credit is the most common reason consumers are unable to pay their bills on time.

Exhibit 7-3

Why consumers don't pay

Excessive use of credit and loss of income due to unemployment are the major reasons consumers don't pay.

Reason for Default	Primary or Contributing Cause of Default (percent of cases)
Excessive use of credit	39
Unemployment/reduced income	24
Poor money management	15
Divorce/separation	8
Medical expenses	7
Other	7

Source: Consumer Credit Counseling Service of the Gulf Coast Area, www.nfcc.org, April 12, 2005.

Referring to overindebtedness as the nation's number one family financial problem, a nationally noted columnist on consumer affairs lists the following as frequent reasons for indebtedness:

1. *Emotional problems,* such as the need for instant gratification, as in the case of a man who can't resist buying a costly suit or a woman who impulsively purchases an expensive dress in a trendy department store.
2. *The use of money to punish,* such as a husband who buys a new car without consulting his wife, who in turn buys a diamond watch to get even.
3. *The expectation of instant comfort* among young couples who assume that by use of the installment plan, they can have immediately the possessions their parents acquired after years of work.
4. *Keeping up with the Joneses,* which is more apparent than ever, not only among prosperous families but among limited-income families too.
5. *Overindulgence of children,* often because of the parents' own emotional needs, competition with each other, or inadequate communication regarding expenditures for the children.
6. *Misunderstanding or lack of communication among family members.* For example, a salesperson visited a Memphis family to sell them an expensive freezer. Although the freezer was beyond the means of this already overindebted family and too large for their needs anyway, the husband thought his wife wanted it. Not until later, in an interview with a debt counselor, did the wife relate her concern when she signed the contract; she had wanted her husband to say no.
7. *The amount of the finance charges,* which can push a family over the edge of their ability to pay, especially when they borrow from one company to pay another and these charges pyramid.

Drowning in a sea of debt can turn your American dream into a nightmare.

Exhibit 7-4 lists the danger signals of potential debt problems.

Exhibit 7-4

Danger signals of potential debt problems

Seek help from your local Consumer Credit Counseling Service if you experience these danger signals.

1. Paying only the minimum balance on credit card bills each month.
2. Increasing the total balance due on credit accounts each month.
3. Missing payments, paying late, or paying some bills this month and others next month.
4. Intentionally using the overdraft or automatic loan features on checking accounts or taking frequent cash advances on credit cards.
5. Using savings to pay routine bills such as groceries or utilities.
6. Receiving second or third payment notices from creditors.
7. Not talking to your spouse about money or talking *only* about money.
8. Depending on overtime, moonlighting, or bonuses to meet everyday expenses.
9. Using up your savings.
10. Borrowing money to pay old debts.
11. Not knowing how much you owe until the bills arrive.
12. Going over your credit limit on credit cards.
13. Having little or nothing in savings to handle unexpected expenses.
14. Being denied credit because of a negative credit bureau report.
15. Getting a credit card revoked by the issuer.
16. Putting off medical or dental visits because you can't afford them right now.

If your household is experiencing more than two of these warning signals, it's time to examine your budget for ways to reduce expenses.

Sources: *Advice for Consumers Who Use Credit* (Silver Springs, MD: Consumer Credit Counseling Service of Maryland, Inc.); *How to Be Credit Smart* (Washington, DC: Consumer Credit Education Foundation).

THE SERIOUS CONSEQUENCES OF DEBT

Just as the causes of indebtedness vary, so too do the other personal and family problems that frequently result from overextension of credit. Loss of a job because of garnishment proceedings may occur in a family that has a disproportionate amount of income tied up in debts. Another possibility is that such a family is forced to neglect vital areas. In the frantic effort to rob Peter to pay Paul, skimping may seriously affect the family's health and neglect the educational needs of children. Excessive indebtedness may also result in heavy drinking, neglect of children, marital difficulties, and drug abuse. Paying only the minimum balance on credit card bills each month can lead you to a bankruptcy.

But help is available to those debtors who seek it. See the Financial Planning for Life's Situations feature, Money Management in Cyberspace, to obtain free credit information on the Internet.

If my household is experiencing problems in paying bills, it is time to examine the family budget for ways to reduce expenses.

Over indebtedness is the nation's number one family financial problem. Refer to Exhibit 7-4 for 16 danger signals of potential debt problems. For additional information, visit www.moneymanagement.org or call 1-866-899-9347.

MONEY MANAGEMENT IN CYBERSPACE

Whether you're developing a plan for reaching your financial goals or searching for a low-interest credit card, you can look to the Internet for a world of free information. Many websites provide interactive worksheets that allow you to plug in personal information and obtain customized reports. Here are some suggestions.

www.bankrate.com (Bank Rate Monitor). Looking for the best credit card rates available or up-to-the- minute news on the credit industry? Then log on here. This site posts a survey of card rates and even lets you apply online for some cards.

www.ramresearch.com (RAM Research). Created by this independent bank research organization, the site contains everything you ever wanted to know about credit cards. It includes a database of 10,000 financial institutions, and news and statistics on the credit industry.

www.aaii.org (American Association of Individual Investors). The AAII website covers the fundamentals of investing, with an array of subjects that will interest both the novice and the advanced investor.

www.napfa.org (National Association of Personal Financial Advisors). NAPFA offers consumer information on what to expect from a financial planner, as well as how and why to choose one. A handy search tool lets you pinpoint an adviser close to home.

www.iafp.org (International Association for Financial Planning). Check here to learn how to assess your financial situation and ways to set budget goals. The site also features a section on determining whether or not you need a financial planner.

www.money.com (*Money* magazine). This site covers virtually all topics related to money, including credit information, current money indexes, and a financial calculator.

www.consumercredit.com (American Consumer Credit Counseling, Inc.). This site is a good place to go if you have a credit problem or are heading that way.

www.nfcc.org (National Foundation for Consumer Credit). This is the home page for a network of local nonprofit organizations that provide consumer credit education and services.

PRACTICE QUIZ 7-3

1 What is the Fair Debt Collection Practices Act?
2 What are the most frequent reasons for indebtedness?
3 What are common danger signals of potential debt problems?

Consumer Credit Counseling Services

LO7-4

Evaluate various private and governmental sources that assist consumers with debt problems.

If you are having problems paying your bills and need help, you have several options. You can contact your creditors and try to work out an adjusted repayment plan yourself, or you can check your telephone directory for a nonprofit financial counseling program to get help.

The **Consumer Credit Counseling Service (CCCS)** is a local, nonprofit organization affiliated with the National Foundation for Consumer Credit (NFCC). Branches of the CCCS provide debt counseling services for families and individuals with serious financial problems. It is not a charity, a lending institution, or a governmental or legal agency. The Consumer Credit Counseling Service is supported by contributions from banks, consumer finance companies, credit unions, merchants, and other community-minded organizations and individuals.

According to the NFCC, every year millions of consumers contact CCCS offices for help with their personal financial problems. More than 90 percent of the U.S. population has convenient access to CCCS services. To find an office near you, check the white pages of your local telephone directory under Consumer Credit Counseling Service, or call 1-800-388-CCCS. All information is kept strictly confidential. Exhibit 7-5 reveals the characteristics of the typical CCCS client.

Consumer Credit Counseling Service (CCCS) A local, nonprofit organization that provides debt counseling services for families and individuals with serious financial problems.

Exhibit 7-5

Profile of a CCCS Client

Characteristics of the Typical Client of the Consumer Credit Counseling Service	
Age:	38
Sex:	Male 43%, female 57%
Marital status:	Single 31%, married 48%
	Separated, divorced, or widowed 21%
Number in family:	3.3
Buying or own home:	38%
Average monthly gross income:	$2,562
Average total debt:	$20,045
Average number of creditors:	10.5

Source: Consumer Credit Counseling Service (Houston), www.cccsintl.org/info/stats.html, February 28, 2005.

WHAT THE CCCS DOES

Credit counselors are aware that most people who are in debt over their heads are basically honest people who want to clear up their indebtedness. Too often, the problems of such people arise from a lack of planning or a miscalculation of what they earn. Therefore, the CCCS is as concerned with preventing the problems as with solving them. As a result, its activities are divided into two parts:

Being forced to pawn your belongings for some cash is just one of the serious consequences of debt.

1. Aiding families with serious debt problems by helping them manage their money better and setting up a realistic budget and plan for expenditures.
2. Helping people prevent debt problems by teaching them the necessity of family budget planning, providing education to people of all ages regarding the pitfalls of unwise credit buying, suggesting techniques for family budgeting, and encouraging credit institutions to provide full information about the costs and terms of credit and to withhold credit from those who cannot afford to repay it.

Anyone who is overburdened by credit obligations can phone, write, or visit a CCCS office. The CCCS requires that an applicant complete an application for credit counseling and then arranges an appointment for a personal interview with the applicant.

CCCS counseling is usually free. However, when the CCCS administers a debt repayment plan, it sometimes charges a nominal fee to help defray administrative costs.

CREDIT COUNSELING IN CRISIS

The National Consumer Law Center and Consumer Federation of America's comprehensive report recently indicated that a new generation of credit counseling agencies is a serious threat to debt-burdened consumers. The study found that, unlike the previous creditor-funded counseling services, these new agencies often harm debtors with improper advice, deceptive practices, excessive fees, and abuse of their nonprofit status. "Nonprofit" credit counseling agencies are increasingly performing like profit-making enterprises and pay their executives lavishly. For example, recently American Consumer Credit Counseling paid its president $462,350 in annual salary plus over $130,000 in benefits. According to Thomas Leary, a member of the Federal Trade Commission (FTC), "some companies use their nonprofit status as a badge of trustworthiness to attract customers, who are then duped into paying large fees." For example, Mr. Leary testified that the commission filed a lawsuit against AmeriDebt, a large, Maryland-based credit-counseling firm. According to the FTC complaint, the firm "aggressively advertises itself as a nonprofit and dedicated to assisting consumers with their finances. AmeriDebt advertises its services as 'free' when in fact the company retains a consumer's first payment as a 'contribution.' "

Traditional credit-counseling agencies offer financial and budget counseling, debt counseling, and community education as well as debt-management plans (DMP). Newer agencies, however, force consumers only into DMPs (also known as debt consolidation plans) and charge high monthly maintenance fees. Some agencies charge as much as a full month's consolidated payment, usually hundreds of dollars, simply to establish an account.

The report recommends that Congress and the states enact laws to curb abuses by credit counseling agencies. The law should:

- Prohibit false or misleading advertising and referral fees.
- Require credit-counseling agencies to better inform consumers about fees, the sources of agency funding, suitability of DMPs for many consumers, and other options that consumers should consider, such as bankruptcy.
- Prohibit agencies from receiving a fee for service from a consumer until all her/his creditors have approved a DMP.
- Give consumers three days to cancel an agreement with a credit-counseling agency without obligation.
- Cap fees charged by agencies at $50 for enrollment or set-up. Allow only reasonable monthly charges.
- Require agencies to prominently disclose all financial arrangements with lenders or financial service providers.
- Provide consumers with the right to enforce the law in court.

Finally, the Internal Revenue Service should aggressively enforce existing standards for nonprofit credit counseling organizations, and credit counseling trade associations should set strong "best practice standards."

my life 4

I am aware that everyone who is overburdened with credit obligations can phone, write, or visit the Consumer Credit Counseling Service.

In addition to the services provided by Consumer Credit Counseling Service, universities, military bases, credit unions, local county extension agents, and state and federal housing authorities provide debt counseling services. For additional information, visit Money Management International at www.moneymanagement.org (1-866-899-9347) or InCharge Institute of America at www.incharge.org (1-800-565-8953).

ALTERNATIVE COUNSELING SERVICES

In addition to the CCCS, universities, military bases, credit unions, local county extension agents, and state and federal housing authorities sometimes provide nonprofit counseling services. These organizations usually charge little or nothing for such assistance. You can also check with your local bank or consumer protection office to see whether it has a listing of reputable, low-cost financial counseling services.

Several national nonprofit organizations provide information and assist people with debt problems by phone and Internet.

- American Consumer Credit Counseling. Visit www.consumercredit.com or call 1-800-769-3571.
- Association of Independent Consumer Credit Counseling Agencies, www.aiccca.org or call 1-866-703-8787.
- InCharge Institute of America. Visit www.incharge.org or call 1-800-565-8953.

HOW TO...

Choose a Credit Counselor

Credit counseling organizations provide valuable assistance to financially distressed consumers. However, some firms may be misleading you about who they are, what they do, or how much they charge. Experts advise that you ask the following questions to find the best credit counselor:

- *What services do you offer?* Look for an organization that offers budget counseling and money management classes as well as a debt-management plan.
- *Do you offer free information?* Avoid organizations that charge for information or demand details about your problem first.
- *What are your fees?* Are there set-up and/or monthly fees? A typical set-up fee is $10. If you're paying a lot more, you may be the one who's being set up.
- *How will the debt-management plan work?* What debts can be included in the plan, and will you get regular reports on your accounts?
- *Can you get my creditors to lower or eliminate my interest and fees?* If the answer is yes, contact your creditors to verify this.
- *What if I can't afford to pay you?* If an organization won't help you because you can't afford to pay, go somewhere else for help.
- *Will you help me avoid future problems?* Getting a plan for avoiding future debt is as important as solving the immediate debt problem.
- *Will we have a contract?* All verbal promises should be in writing before you pay any money.
- *Are your counselors accredited or certified?* Legitimate credit counseling firms are affiliated with the National Foundation for Credit Counseling or the Association of Independent Consumer Credit Counseling Agencies.

Check with your local consumer protection agency and the Better Business Bureau to see if any complaints have been filed about the company.

- Money Management International. Visit www.moneymanagement.org or call 1-866-899-9347.

Typically, a counseling service will negotiate lower payments with your creditors, then make the payments using money you send to them each month. The creditor, not you, pays the cost of setting up this debt management plan (DMP). Read the How To . . . feature on how to find the best credit counselor. Also, read the Financial Planning for Life's Situations box, Credit Counseling in Crisis, on page 252, to be aware of deceptive credit counseling organizations.

PRACTICE QUIZ 7-4

1 What is the Consumer Credit Counseling Service?
2 What are the two major activities of the Consumer Credit Counseling Service?
3 What options other than the CCCS do consumers have for financial counseling?

Declaring Personal Bankruptcy

LO7-5

Assess the choices in declaring personal bankruptcy.

What if a debtor suffers from an extreme case of financial woes? Can there be any relief? The answer is bankruptcy proceedings. *Bankruptcy* is a legal process in which some or all of the assets of a debtor are distributed among the creditors because the debtor is unable to pay his or her debts. Bankruptcy may also include a plan for the debtor to repay creditors on an installment basis. Declaring bankruptcy is a last resort because it severely damages your credit rating.

Jan Watson illustrates the new face of bankruptcy. A 43-year-old freelance commercial photographer from Point Reyes, California, she was never in serious financial trouble until she began incurring big medical costs last year and reached for her credit cards to pay the bills. Since Jan didn't have health insurance, her debt quickly mounted and soon reached $17,000. It was too much for her to pay off with her $40,000-a-year freelance income. Her solution: Declare personal bankruptcy and the immediate freedom it would bring from creditors' demands.

Ms. Watson's move put her in familiar company, demographically speaking. An increasing number of bankruptcy filers are well-educated, middle-class baby boomers with an overwhelming level of credit card debt. These baby boomers make up 45 percent of the adult population, but they account for 60 percent of personal bankruptcies. In that group, the people most likely to be in bankruptcy are between 35 and 44 years old (average age is 38), an age group that is usually assumed to be economically established. Increasingly, too, the bankruptcy debtor is likely to be female. Women now account for 36 percent of bankruptcy filers, up from 17 percent twenty-five years ago.

In 1994, the U.S. Senate unanimously passed a bill that reduced the time and cost of bankruptcy proceedings. The bill strengthened creditor rights and enabled more individuals to weather bankruptcy proceedings without selling their assets.

Unfortunately, for some debtors, bankruptcy had become an acceptable tool of credit management. According to the American Bankruptcy Institute, a record 2 million people declared bankruptcy in 2005, the highest rate since the U.S. bankruptcy code took effect in 1979 (see Exhibit 7-6). Bankruptcy courts had turned to regular

Exhibit 7-6 U.S. Consumer Bankruptcy Filings, 1980–2012

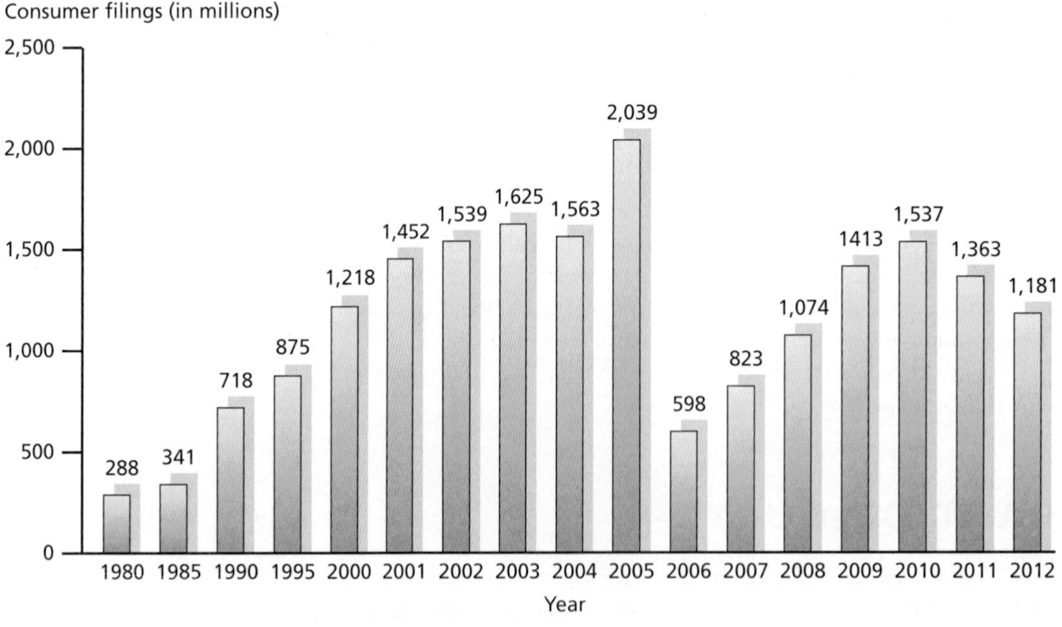

Source: Administrative Office of the U.S. Courts, http://www.uscourts.gov/uscourts/Statistics/Bankruptcy Statistics/BankruptcyFilings/2012/, accessed March 14, 2013.

Saturday sessions to handle the overflow. This drastic increase in personal bankruptcy filing led to the Bankruptcy Abuse Prevention and Consumer Protection Act of 2005.

my life 5

I realize that the Bankruptcy Abuse Prevention and Consumer Protection Act of 2005 made it more difficult for consumers to file a Chapter 7 bankruptcy.

The filing process is now more difficult for debtors:

- Debtors must file more documents, including itemized statements of monthly net income, proof of income (pay stubs) for the last 60 days, and tax returns for the preceding year (four years for Chapter 13).
- Debtors must take a prefiling credit counseling and postfiling education course to have debts discharged.
- Debtors face increased filing fees, plus fees for credit counseling/education.
- The bankruptcy petition and process are more complicated, so it's very difficult to file without an attorney.

THE BANKRUPTCY ABUSE PREVENTION AND CONSUMER PROTECTION ACT OF 2005

On April 20, 2005, President Bush signed the Bankruptcy Abuse Prevention and Consumer Protection Act, which is perhaps the largest overhaul of the Bankruptcy Code since it was enacted in 1978. Signing the bill, the president declared, "Bankruptcy should always be the last resort in our legal system. In recent years too many people have abused the bankruptcy laws. Under the new law, Americans who have the ability to pay will be required to pay back at least a portion of their debts. The law will help make credit more affordable, because when bankruptcy is less common, credit can be extended to more people at better rates. Debtors seeking to erase all debts will now have to wait eight years from their last bankruptcy before they can file again. The law will also allow us to clamp down on bankruptcy mills that make their money by advising abusers on how to game the system."

Among other provisions, the law requires that:

- The director of the Executive Office for U.S. Trustees develop a financial management training curriculum to educate individual debtors on how to better manage their finances; and test, evaluate, and report to Congress on the curriculum's effectiveness.
- Debtors complete an approved instructional course in personal financial management.
- The clerk of each bankruptcy district maintains a list of credit counseling agencies and instructional courses on personal financial management.

Furthermore, the law may require that states should develop personal finance curricula designed for use in elementary and secondary schools.

At first the new law seemed to slow bankruptcy filings. According to the American Bankruptcy Institute, only 597,965 personal bankruptcies were filed in the first year after the law passed. But as the economy worsened, bankruptcies rose to 822,590 in 2007; and 1.181 million in 2012.

The bottom line: the new law made it more difficult for consumers to file a Chapter 7 bankruptcy and forces them into a Chapter 13 repayment plan. You have two choices in declaring personal bankruptcy: Chapter 7 (a straight bankruptcy) and Chapter 13 (a wage earner plan) bankruptcy. Both choices are undesirable, and neither should be considered an easy way out.

CHAPTER 7 BANKRUPTCY In a **Chapter 7 bankruptcy,** a debtor is required to draw up a petition listing his or her assets and liabilities. The debtor submits the petition to a U.S. district court and pays a filing fee. A person filing for relief under the bankruptcy code is called a *debtor;* the term *bankrupt* is not used.

Chapter 7 bankruptcy One type of personal (or straight) bankruptcy in which many debts are forgiven.

Chapter 7 is a straight bankruptcy in which many, but not all, debts are forgiven. Most of the debtor's assets are sold to pay off creditors. However, certain assets of the debtor are protected to some extent. For example, Social Security payments; unemployment compensation; limited values of your equity in a home, car, or truck; household goods and appliances; trade tools; books; and so forth are protected.

The courts must charge a $306 case filing fee, a $46 miscellaneous administrative fee, and a $15 trustee fee. If the debtor is unable to pay the fees even in installments, the court may waive the fees.

In filing a petition, a debtor must provide the following information:

- A list of all creditors and the amount and nature of their claims.
- The source, amount, and frequency of the debtor's income.
- A list of all the debtor's property.
- A detailed list of the debtor's monthly expenses.

The discharge of debts in Chapter 7 does not affect alimony, child support, certain taxes, fines, certain debts arising from educational loans, or debts that you fail to properly disclose to the bankruptcy court. At the request of a creditor, the bankruptcy judge may also exclude from the discharge debts resulting from loans you received by giving the lender a false financial statement. Furthermore, debts arising from fraud, embezzlement, driving while intoxicated, larceny, or certain other willful or malicious acts may also be *excluded.*

Chapter 13 bankruptcy A voluntary plan that a debtor with regular income develops and proposes to a bankruptcy court.

CHAPTER 13 BANKRUPTCY In a **Chapter 13 bankruptcy,** (also called a wage-earner's plan) a debtor with a regular income proposes to a bankruptcy court a plan for extinguishing his or her debts from future earnings or other property over a period of time. In such a bankruptcy, the debtor normally keeps all or most of the property.

During the period the plan is in effect, which can be as long as five years, the debtor makes regular payments to a Chapter 13 trustee. The trustee, in turn, distributes the money to the creditors. Under certain circumstances, the bankruptcy court may approve a plan permitting the debtor to keep all property even though the debtor repays less than the full amount of the debts. Certain debts not dischargeable in Chapter 7, such as those based on fraud, may be discharged in Chapter 13 if the debtor successfully completes the plan.

According to two recent studies, Chapter 13 bankruptcy is an effective collection method. Some creditors receive almost nothing after discharge and nearly half of debtors do not get their debt discharged. "This suggests that the rationale for the new bankruptcy act must be sought in its other effects, such as deterring bankruptcy altogether among those who have the capacity to repay."[2]

EFFECT OF BANKRUPTCY ON YOUR JOB AND YOUR FUTURE CREDIT

Different people have different experiences in obtaining credit after they file bankruptcy. Some find obtaining credit more difficult. Others find obtaining credit easier because they have relieved themselves of their prior debts or because creditors know they cannot file another bankruptcy case for a period of time. Obtaining credit may be easier for people who file a Chapter 13 bankruptcy and repay some of their debts than for people who file a Chapter 7 bankruptcy and make no effort to repay. The bankruptcy law prohibits your employer from discharging you simply because you have filed a bankruptcy case.

One caution: Don't confuse a personal bankruptcy with a business (or Chapter 11) bankruptcy. The Chapter 11 bankruptcy is a reorganization requested by a business and ordered by the court because a business is unable to pay its debts.

SHOULD A LAWYER REPRESENT YOU IN A BANKRUPTCY CASE?

When 29-year-old Lynn Jensen of San Gabriel, California, lost her $35,000-a-year job, she ended up filing for bankruptcy using a "how to file for bankruptcy" book because she could not afford a lawyer. Like Lynn, you have the right to file your own bankruptcy case and to represent yourself at all court hearings. In any bankruptcy case, however, you must complete and file with a bankruptcy court several detailed forms concerning your property, debts, and financial condition. Many people find it easier to complete these forms with the assistance of experienced bankruptcy counsel. In addition, you may discover that your case will develop complications, especially if you own a substantial amount of property or your creditors object to the discharge of your debts. Then you will require the advice and assistance of a lawyer.

Choosing a bankruptcy lawyer may be difficult. Some of the least reputable lawyers make easy money by handling hundreds of bankruptcy cases without adequately considering individual needs. Recommendations from those you know and trust and from employee assistance programs are most useful.

DID YOU KNOW?

ALERT: "DEBT RELIEF" MAY BE CODE FOR BANKRUPTCY

The Federal Trade Commission cautions you to read between the lines when faced with ads in newspapers or telephone directories that promise debt relief. This relief may actually be bankruptcy. The following catch phrases are commonly used:

"Consolidate your bills into one monthly payment without borrowing."

"Keep your property."

"Stop credit harassment, foreclosures, repossessions, and garnishments."

"Wipe out your debts! Consolidate your bills!"

"Use the protection and assistance provided by federal law. For once let the law work for you."

WHAT ARE THE COSTS? The monetary costs to the debtor under Chapter 13 bankruptcy include the following:

1. *Court costs.* The debtor must pay a filing fee to the clerk of the court at the time of filing his or her petition. The filing fee may be paid in up to four installments if the court grants authorization.
2. *Attorneys' fees.* These fees are usually the largest single item of cost. Often the attorney does not require them to be paid in advance at the time of filing but agrees to be paid in installments after receipt of a down payment. Fees range between $2,000 and $4,000.
3. *Trustees' fees and costs.* The trustees' fees are established by the bankruptcy judge in most districts and by a U.S. trustee in certain other districts.

Although it is possible to reduce these costs by purchasing the legal forms in a local office supplies store and completing them yourself, an attorney is strongly recommended.

There are also intangible costs to bankruptcy. For example, obtaining credit in the future may be difficult, since bankruptcy reports are retained in credit bureaus for 10 years. Therefore, you should take the extreme step of declaring personal bankruptcy only when no other options for solving your financial problems exist.

Since you now know everything you ever wanted to know about consumer credit, read the Financial Planning for Life's Situations feature on page 258 to test your credit IQ.

DID YOU KNOW?

According to Fair Isaac Corporation (FICO), a personal bankruptcy can cause an immediate drop of up to 260 points on your credit report. This damage is serious, harmful and long lasting.

WHAT'S YOUR CREDIT IQ?

CREDIT-ABILITY SCORECARD

Test your credit IQ. For each question, circle the letter that best describes your credit habits.

1. **I pay my bills when they are due.**
   (A) Always (B) Almost Always (C) Sometimes
2. **After paying my regular bills each month, I have money left from my income.**
   (A) Yes (B) Sometimes (C) Never
3. **I know how much I owe on my credit cards each month before I receive my bills.**
   (A) Yes (B) Sometimes (C) No
4. **When I get behind in my payments, I ignore the past-due notices.**
   (A) Never or Not Applicable (B) Sometimes (C) Always
5. **When I need more money for my regular living expenses, I take out a loan or use my line of credit on my credit card or checking account.**
   (A) Never (B) Sometimes (C) Often
6. **If I want to see a copy of my credit report, I would contact . . .**
   (A) A credit reporting agency (B) My lenders (C) My lawyer
7. **My credit record shows that I am current on all my loans and charge accounts.**
   (A) Yes (B) Don't know (C) No
8. **I pay more than the minimum balance due on my credit card accounts.**
   (A) Always (B) Sometimes (C) Never
9. **To pay off my current credit and charge card accounts, it would take me . . .**
   (A) 4 months or less (B) 5 to 8 months (C) Over 8 months
10. **My consumer loans (including auto loans, but not mortgage payment) and credit card bills each month average more than 20% of my take-home pay.**
    (A) No (B) Sometimes (C) Always
11. **If I had serious credit problems, I would contact my creditors to explain the problem.**
    (A) Yes (B) Probably (C) No
12. **If I default (don't repay) on a loan, that fact can stay on my credit report for . . .**
    (A) 7 years (B) 3 years (C) 1 year

Assign a score of 3 for each "A" answer, 2 for each "B" answer, and 1 for each "C" response. Total the score.

If you scored:	
31–36	You have an excellent knowledge of credit and its responsible use.
24–30	You should take steps toward better understanding your personal finances and the credit process.
18–23	You probably need to take a serious look at your personal finances; consider controlling your spending and keeping on a tight budget.
12–17	You may be heading for serious trouble; consider seeking help, such as nonprofit consumer credit counseling services.

Source: AFSA Education Foundation, *How to Be Credit Smart,* 1997.

PRACTICE QUIZ 7-5

1 What is the purpose of Chapter 7 bankruptcy?
2 What is the difference between Chapter 7 and Chapter 13 bankruptcy?
3 How does bankruptcy affect your job and future credit?
4 What are the costs of declaring bankruptcy?

my life stages for credit

YOUR PERSONAL FINANCE DASHBOARD

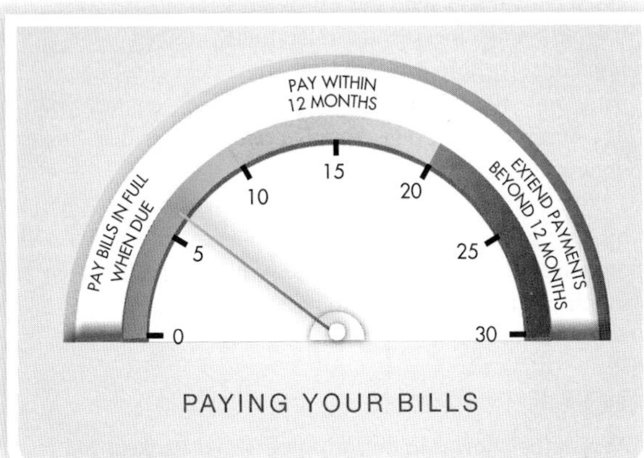

One indicator of your sound financial health is your ability to pay your bills in a timely manner. Not only should you figure out how much the loan will cost you, but whether you can pay it on time without incurring excessive interest.

YOUR SITUATION If you need to borrow money, do you know where you can get the least expensive loan? Can you calculate interest on your loan? Do you know the consequences and costs of paying the minimum amount due on your credit card balances?

Paying your bills on time is the foundation for progress toward good financial health. Other personal financial planning actions you might consider during various stages of your life include:

. . . in college

- Reassess the use of your parent's credit card
- Shop around for the best credit card (visit www.billshrink.com)
- Look for a low interest rate card and no annual fees
- Don't charge if you can't pay the full balance within one month
- Consider contacting a credit counseling agency if you need help in managing your credit
- Don't miss or be late on your payments and avoid late fees
- Check the online tools and resources at www.federalreserve.gov to make well-informed decisions about the use and sources of credit

. . . in my 20s

- Create a realistic budget and stick to it
- Boost your credit score
- Pay bills on time and pay down the balances to boost your credit score
- Build your emergency fund.
- Spend within your means
- Don't go over your credit limit on credit cards
- Keep your own credit account after you change your name or marital status
- Request a free credit report every year from each of the three credit reporting agencies

. . . in my 30s and 40s

- Check your credit report for accuracy and continue monitoring your credit score
- Decrease the total balance due on credit accounts each month
- Use your savings to purchase big ticket items
- Contact your lenders immediately if you have problems making payments
- Remain diligent about managing your credit and become familiar with the provisions of the CARD Act

. . . in my 50s and beyond

- Avoid any negative entry on your credit report and maintain an excellent credit rating
- Don't depend on overtime, a part-time job, or bonuses to meet expenses
- Keep balances low on credit cards and other revolving credit
- Lower your cost of credit by consolidating your debt through a second mortgage or a home equity line of credit
- Consider carefully before taking out a home equity loan

SUMMARY OF LEARNING OBJECTIVES

LO7-1

Analyze the major sources of consumer credit.

The major sources of consumer credit are commercial banks, savings and loan associations, credit unions, finance companies, life insurance companies, and family and friends. Each of these sources has unique advantages and disadvantages.

Parents or family members are often the source of the least expensive loans. They may charge you only the interest they would have earned had they not made the loan. Such loans, however, can complicate family relationships.

LO7-2

Determine the cost of credit by calculating interest using various interest formulas.

Compare the finance charge and the annual percentage rate (APR) as you shop for credit. Under the Truth in Lending law, creditors are required to state the cost of borrowing so that you can compare credit costs and shop for credit.

For a borrower, the most favorable method of calculating the cost of open-end credit is the adjusted balance method. In this method, creditors add finance charges after subtracting payments made during the billing period. The rule of 78s favors lenders. This formula dictates that you pay more interest at the beginning of a loan, when you have the use of more money, and pay less and less interest as the debt is reduced. Because all the payments are the same size, the part going to pay back the amount borrowed increases as the part representing interest decreases.

LO7-3

Develop a plan to manage your debts.

The Fair Debt Collection Practices Act prohibits certain practices by debt collection agencies. Debt has serious consequences if a proper plan for managing it is not implemented.

Most people agree that emotional problems, the use of money to punish, the expectation of instant comfort, keeping up with the Joneses, overindulgence of children, misunderstanding or lack of communication among family members, and the amount of finance charges are common reasons for indebtedness.

LO7-4

Evaluate various private and governmental sources that assist consumers with debt problems.

If you cannot meet your obligations, contact your creditors immediately. Before signing up with a debt consolidation company, investigate it thoroughly. Better yet, contact your local Consumer Credit Counseling Service or other debt counseling organizations.

Such organizations help people manage their money better by setting up a realistic budget and plan for expenditures. These organizations also help people prevent debt problems by teaching them the necessity of family budget planning and providing education to people of all ages.

LO7-5

Assess the choices in declaring personal bankruptcy.

A debtor's last resort is to declare bankruptcy, permitted by the U.S. Bankruptcy Act of 1978. Consider the financial and other costs of bankruptcy before taking this extreme step. A debtor can declare Chapter 7 (straight) bankruptcy or Chapter 13 (wage earner plan) bankruptcy.

Some people find obtaining credit more difficult after filing bankruptcy. Others find obtaining credit easier because they have relieved themselves of their prior debts or because creditors know they cannot file another bankruptcy case for a period of time. Obtaining credit may be easier for people who file a Chapter 13 bankruptcy and repay some of their debts than for people who file a Chapter 7 bankruptcy and make no effort to repay their debts.

The Bankruptcy Abuse Prevention and Consumer Protection Act of 2005 overhauls the Bankruptcy Code. The Act makes it more difficult for consumers to file Chapter 7 bankruptcy, often forcing them into a Chapter 13 repayment plan instead.

KEY TERMS

add-on interest method 238
adjusted balance method 239
annual percentage rate (APR) 234
average daily balance method 239
Chapter 7 bankruptcy 255
Chapter 13 bankruptcy 256
Consumer Credit Counseling Service (CCCS) 250
credit insurance 245
declining balance method 238
Fair Debt Collection Practices Act (FDCPA) 246
finance charge 234
previous balance method 239
rule of 78s 243
simple interest 237
Truth in Lending law 234

KEY FORMULAS

Page	Topic	Formula
236	Calculating annual percentage rate (APR)	$\text{APR} = \frac{2 \times \text{Number of payment periods in one year} \times \text{Dollar cost of credit}}{\text{Loan amount (Total number of payments to pay off the loan + 1)}}$ $= \frac{2 \times n \times I}{P(N + 1)}$ *Example:* $P =$ Principal borrowed, \$100 $n =$ number of payments in one year, 1 $I =$ Dollar cost of credit, \$8 $\text{APR} = \frac{2 \times 1 \times \$8}{\$100(1 + 1)} = \frac{\$16}{\$200} = 0.08$, or 8 percent For 12 equal monthly payments, $\text{APR} = \frac{2 \times 12 \times \$8}{\$100(12 + 1)} = \frac{\$192}{\$1{,}300} = 0.1476$, or 14.76 percent
237	Calculating simple interest	Interest (in dollars) = Principal borrowed × Interest rate × Length of loan in years $I = P \times r \times T$ *Example:* From above: $P = \$100$; $r = 0.08$; $T = 1$ $I = \$100 \times 0.08 \times 1 = \$8$
244	Calculating compound interest	Total future value of a loan = Principal $(1 + \text{Rate of interest})^{\text{Time in years}}$ $F = P(1 + r)^T$ *Example:* From above: $P = \$100$; $r = 0.08$; $T = 1$ $F = \$100(1 + 0.08)^1 = \$100(1.08) = \$108$

SELF-TEST PROBLEMS

1. Your bankcard has an APR of 18 percent and there is a 2 percent fee for cash advances. The bank starts charging you interest on cash advances immediately. You get a cash advance of \$600 on the first day of the month. You get your credit card bill at the end of the month. What is the total finance charge you will pay on this cash advance for the month?
2. You borrowed \$1,000 at the stated interest rate of 8 percent. You pay off the loan in one lump sum at the end of the year. What is the approximate annual percentage rate?

Solutions

1. Cash advance fee = 2 percent of \$600 = \$12

Interest for one month = \$600 × .18 × 1 = \$108 ÷ 12 = \$9

(Using $I = P \times r \times T$ formula)

Total cost for one month = \$12 + \$9 = \$21

2. Using the formula, the APR for the lump-sum loan is

$$r = \frac{2 \times n \times 1}{P\,(N + 1)} = \frac{2 \times 1 \times \$8}{\$1{,}000(1 + 1)} = \frac{\$16}{\$2{,}000} = .008 \text{ or 8 percent or 8 percent}$$

FINANCIAL PLANNING PROBLEMS

LO7-2 1. *Calculating the Finance Charge on a Loan.* Dave borrowed $500 for one year and paid $50 in interest. The bank charged him a $5 service charge. What is the finance charge on this loan?

LO7-2 2. *Calculating the Annual Percentage Rate.* In problem 1, Dave borrowed $500 on January 1, 2006, and paid it all back at once on December 31, 2006. What was the APR?

LO7-2 3. *Calculating the Annual Percentage Rate.* If Dave paid the $500 in 12 equal monthly payments, what was the APR?

LO7-2 4. *Comparing the Costs of Credit Cards.* Bobby is trying to decide between two credit cards. One has no annual fee and an 18 percent interest rate, and the other has a $40 annual fee and an 8.9 percent interest rate. Should he take the card that's free or the one that costs $40?

LO7-2 5. *Calculating the Cash Advance Fee and the Dollar Amount of Interest.* Sidney took a $200 cash advance by using checks linked to her credit card account. The bank charges a 2 percent cash advance fee on the amount borrowed and offers no grace period on cash advances. Sidney paid the balance in full when the bill arrived. What was the cash advance fee? What was the interest for one month at an 18 percent APR? What was the total amount she paid? What if she had made the purchase with her credit card and promptly paid off the bill in full?

LO7-2 6. *Comparing the Cost of Credit during Inflationary Periods.* Dorothy lacks cash to pay for a $600 dishwasher. She could buy it from the store on credit by making 12 monthly payments of $52.74. The total cost would then be $632.88. Instead, Dorothy decides to deposit $50 a month in the bank until she has saved enough money to pay cash for the dishwasher. One year later, she has saved $642—$600 in deposits plus interest. When she goes back to the store, she finds the dishwasher now costs $660. Its price has gone up 10 percent. Was postponing her purchase a good trade-off for Dorothy?

LO7-2 7. *Comparing Costs of Credit Using Three Calculation Methods.* You have been pricing a compact disk player in several stores. Three stores have the identical price of $300. Each store charges 18 percent APR, has a 30-day grace period, and sends out bills on the first of the month. On further investigation, you find that store A calculates the finance charge by using the average daily balance method, store B uses the adjusted balance method, and store C uses the previous balance method. Assume you purchased the disk player on May 5 and made a $100 payment on June 15. What will the finance charge be if you made your purchase from store A? From store B? From store C?

LO7-2 8. *Determining Interest Cost Using the Simple Interest Formula.* What are the interest cost and the total amount due on a six-month loan of $1,500 at 13.2 percent simple annual interest?

LO7-2 9. *Calculating the Total Cost of a Purchase, the Monthly Payment, and an APR.* After visiting several automobile dealerships, Richard selects the used car he wants. He likes its $10,000 price, but financing through the dealer is no bargain. He has $2,000 cash for a down payment, so he needs an $8,000 loan. In shopping at several banks for an installment loan, he learns that interest on most automobile loans is quoted at add-on rates. That is, during the life of the loan, interest is paid on the full amount borrowed even though a portion of the principal has been paid back. Richard borrows $8,000 for a period of four years at an add-on interest rate of 11 percent. What is the total interest on Richard's loan? What is the total cost of the car? What is the monthly payment? What is the annual percentage rate (APR)?

LO7-2 10. *Calculating Simple Interest on a Loan.* Damon convinced his aunt to lend him $2,000 to purchase a plasma digital TV. She has agreed to charge only 6 percent simple interest, and he has agreed to repay the loan at the end of one year. How much interest will he pay for the year?

LO7-2 11. *Calculating Simple Interest on a Loan.* You can buy an item for $100 on a charge with the promise to pay $100 in 90 days. Suppose you can buy an identical item for $95 cash. If you buy the item for $100, you are in effect paying $5 for the use of $95 for three months. What is the effective annual rate of interest?

LO7-2 12. *Calculating Interest Using the Simple Interest Formula.* Rebecca wants to buy a new saddle for her horse. The one she wants usually costs $500, but this week it is on sale for $400. She does not have $400, but she could buy it with $50 down and pay the rest in 6 months with 10 percent interest. Does Rebecca save any money buying the saddle this way?

LO7-2 13. *Calculating Interest Using the Simple Interest Formula.* You just bought a used car for $3,500 from your cousin. He agreed to let you make payments for 3 years with simple interest at 7 percent. How much interest will you pay?

LO7-2 14. *Calculating Interest Using the Bank Discount Method.* Your uncle lends you $2,000 less $100 (interest at 5 percent), and you receive $1,900. Use the APR formula to find the true annual percentage rate.

LO7-2 15. *Calculating the Annual Percentage Rate Using the Compound Interest Formula.* A $1,000 loan is paid off in 12 equal monthly payments. The stated annual interest rate is 10 percent. What is the annual percentage rate?

FINANCIAL PLANNING ACTIVITIES

1. *Determining Whether a Loan Is Needed.* Survey friends and relatives to find out what criteria they used to determine the need for credit. L07-1

2. *Comparing Costs of Loans from Various Lenders.* Prepare a list of sources of inexpensive loans, medium-priced loans, and expensive loans in your area. What are the trade-offs in obtaining a loan from an "easy" lender? L07-1

3. *Using Current Information on Obtaining the Best Credit Terms.* Choose a current issue of *Worth, Money, Kiplinger's Personal Finance Magazine,* or *BusinessWeek* and summarize an article that provides suggestions on how you can choose the best, yet least expensive, source of credit. L07-2

4. *Using the Internet to Obtain Information about the Costs of Credit.* As pointed out at the beginning of this chapter, credit costs money; therefore, you must conduct a cost/benefit analysis before making any major purchase. While most people consider credit costs, others simply ignore them and eventually find themselves in financial difficulties. To help consumers avoid this problem, each of the following organizations has a home page on the Internet: L07-2

   Finance Center Inc. helps consumers save money when purchasing, financing, or refinancing a new home or a car, or making a credit card transaction. (www.financenter.com)

   Debtors Anonymous offers financial counseling to debt-ridden consumers. (www.debtorsanonymous.org)

   Bank Rate Monitor provides rate information for mortgages, credit cards, auto loans, home equity loans, and personal loans. (www.bankrate.com)

   Choose one of the above organizations and visit its website. Then prepare a report that summarizes the information the organization provides. Finally, decide how this information could help you better manage your credit and its costs.

5. *Calculating the Cost of Credit Using Three APR Formulas.* How are the simple interest, simple interest on the declining balance, and add-on interest formulas used in determining the cost of credit? L07-2

6. *Handling Harassment from Debt Collection Agencies.* Your friend is drowning in a sea of overdue bills and is being harassed by a debt collection agency. Prepare a list of the steps your friend should take if the harassment continues. L07-3

7. *Seeking Assistance from the Consumer Credit Counseling Service.* Visit a local office of the Consumer Credit Counseling Service. What assistance can debtors obtain from this office? What is the cost of this assistance, if any? L07-4

8. *Assessing the Choices in Declaring Personal Bankruptcy.* What factors would you consider in assessing the choices in declaring personal bankruptcy? Why should personal bankruptcy be the choice of last resort? L07-5

FINANCIAL PLANNING CASE

Financing Sue's Hyundai Excel

After shopping around, Sue Wallace decided on the car of her choice, a used Hyundai Excel. The dealer quoted her a total price of $8,000. Sue decided to use $2,000 of her savings as a down payment and borrow $6,000. The salesperson wrote this information on a sales contract that Sue took with her when she set out to find financing.

When Sue applied for a loan, she discussed loan terms with the bank lending officer. The officer told her that the bank's policy was to lend only 80 percent of the total price of a used car. Sue showed the officer her copy of the sales contract, indicating that she had agreed to make a $2,000, or 25 percent, down payment on the $8,000 car, so this requirement caused her no problem. Although the bank was willing to make 48-month loans at an annual percentage rate of 15 percent on used cars, Sue chose a 36-month repayment schedule. She believed she could afford the higher payments, and she knew she would not have to pay as much interest if she paid off the loan at a faster rate. The bank lending officer provided Sue with a copy of the Truth-in-Lending Disclosure Statement shown here.

Truth-in-Lending Disclosure Statement (Loans)

Annual Percentage Rate	Finance Charge	Amount Financed	Total of Payments, 36
The cost of your credit as a yearly rate.	The dollar amount the credit will cost you.	The amount of credit provided to you or on your behalf.	The amount you will have paid after you have made all payments as scheduled.
15%	$1,487.64	$6,000.00	$7,487.64

You have the right to receive at this time an itemization of the Amount Financed.

☒ I want an itemization. ☐ I do not want an itemization.

Your payment schedule will be:

Number of Payments	Amount of Payments	When Payments Are Due
36	$207.99	1st of each month

Sue decided to compare the APR she had been offered with the APR offered by another bank, but the 20 percent APR of the second bank (bank B) was more expensive than the 15 percent APR of the first bank (bank A). Here is her comparison of the two loans:

	Bank A 15% APR	Bank B 20% APR
Amount financed	$6,000.00	$6,000.00
Finance charge	1,487.64	2,027.28
Total of payments	7,487.64	8,027.28
Monthly payments	207.99	222.98

The 5 percent difference in the APRs of the two banks meant Sue would have to pay $15 extra every month if she got her loan from the second bank. Of course, she got the loan from the first bank.

Questions

1. What is perhaps the most important item shown on the disclosure statement? Why?
2. What is included in the finance charge?
3. What amount will Sue receive from the bank?
4. Should Sue borrow from bank A or bank B? Why?

PERSONAL FINANCIAL PLANNER IN ACTION

Comparing Credit Sources and Costs

Credit is available from many sources. Becoming aware of the differences among financial institutions related to borrowing costs and other factors while wisely managing your debt will help you avoid financial difficulties.

Your Short-Term Financial Planning Activities	*Resources*
1. Evaluate your current use of credit cards. Compare various credit card offers related to APR, annual fee, grace period, and other fees.	PFP Sheet 30 www.bankrate.com www.consumer-action.org
2. Compare various credit sources for loans related to various financial needs.	PFP Sheet 31 www.eloan.com www.lendingtree.com www.finance-center.com
Your Long-Term Financial Planning Activities	*Resources*
1. Investigate various actions commonly taken to avoid debt problems.	www.moneymanagement.org www.nfcc.org www.dca.org
2. Prepare a spending plan to minimize the use of credit.	Text pages 246–250 www.debtadvice.org www.kiplinger.com/tools

CONTINUING CASE

Managing Credit

Life Situation	*Financial Data*	
Single	Monthly Income	$1,750
Age 24	Living Expenses	$1,210
No dependents	Personal property	$7,300
Graduate and engaged	Savings	$5,000
	Student loan	$4,200
	Credit card debt	$4,600

Shelby and Mark are making plans to get married, open her pet salon, and possibly buy a condo, but they realize that they must manage their credit situation better. They have made a budget so that they can reduce their individual credit card balances. However, they are looking for other ways to help them achieve their goals more quickly.

Questions

1. Given their current situation, list some suggestions on how Shelby and Mark can reduce the cost of using credit. What are some alternative sources of credit they might consider?
2. What is the best way for Shelby and Mark to compare the cost of credit from different sources?
3. Explain how Shelby and Mark might use the Personal Financial Planner sheets (Credit Card/Charge Account Comparison and Consumer Loan Comparison).

DAILY SPENDING DIARY

"Tracking my spending has helped me avoid credit problems."

Directions

Continue (or start) your "Daily Spending Diary" to record and monitor your spending in various categories. Also record comments to reflect what you have learned about your spending patterns and help you consider possible changes you might want to make in your spending habits.

Analysis Questions

1. Describe any aspects of your spending habits that might indicate an overuse of credit.
2. How might your Daily Spending Diary information help you avoid credit problems?

The Daily Spending Diary Sheets are located in Appendix D at the end of the book and on the student website at www.mhhe.com/kdh.

chapter 8

Consumer Purchasing Strategies and Legal Protection

Learning Objectives

LO8-1 Identify strategies for effective consumer buying.

LO8-2 Implement a process for making consumer purchases.

LO8-3 Identify steps to take to resolve consumer problems.

LO8-4 Evaluate legal alternatives available to consumers.

What will this mean for me?

In times of economic uncertainly and financial difficulty, the number of unwise buying decisions often increases. People are tempted into scams that promise they will "earn easy money" or "get out of debt fast." Unplanned and careless buying will reduce your potential for long-term financial security. Impulse buying activities of a few dollars a week can cost you thousands in just a couple of years. Many wise buying strategies are available to avoid poor purchasing choices.

my life

DON'T DROP WHEN YOU SHOP

Recreational shopping and impulse buying are major causes of financial trouble. In contrast, wise consumer decisions can result in lower spending and better long-term financial security.

For each of the following shopping behaviors, circle "agree," "neutral," or "disagree" to indicate your attitude toward this action.

1. Buying famous brand name items is usually the best strategy for my personal situation.	Agree	Neutral	Disagree
2. The use of a buying process with various stages is useful for me when planning purchases.	Agree	Neutral	Disagree
3. I know what actions to take when complaining about a consumer purchase.	Agree	Neutral	Disagree
4. The legal actions available to consumers may be of value to me in the future.	Agree	Neutral	Disagree

As you study this chapter, you will encounter "My Life" boxes with additional information and resources related to these items.

Consumer Buying Activities

LO8-1

Identify strategies for effective consumer buying.

FINANCIAL IMPLICATIONS OF CONSUMER DECISIONS

Every person making personal financial decisions is a consumer. Regardless of age, income, or household situation, we all use goods and services. Daily buying decisions involve a trade-off between current spending and saving for the future.

Various economic, social, and personal factors affect daily buying habits (see Exhibit 8-1). These factors influence your spending, saving, and investing choices, and when combined with wise buying activities can contribute to your long-term financial security.

Throughout your life, your buying decisions reflect many influences. You should consider opportunity costs to maximize the satisfaction you obtain from available financial resources. Commonly overlooked trade-offs when buying include

- Paying a higher price over time by using credit to buy items that you need now.
- Buying unknown, possibly poor-quality brands that are less expensive.
- Selecting brands that may be difficult to service or repair.

Exhibit 8-1 Buying influences and wise spending strategies

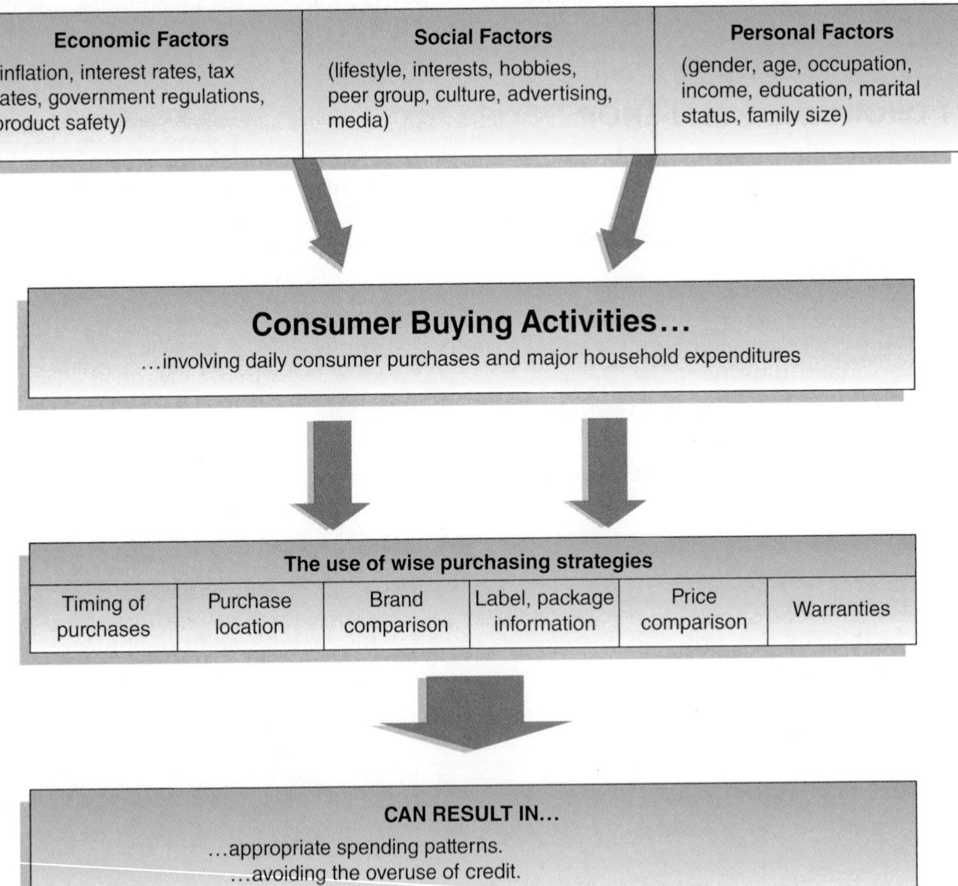

- Ordering online, which saves time and money but may make it harder to return, replace, or repair purchases.
- Taking time and effort to comparison-shop to save money and obtain better after-sale service.

Your buying decisions reflect many aspects of your personality, life situation, values, and goals. Combine this fact with the complexity of the marketplace, and you can see that most purchase decisions require analysis.

WISE PURCHASING STRATEGIES

Comparison shopping is the process of considering alternative stores, brands, and prices. In contrast, **impulse buying** is unplanned purchasing, which can result in financial problems. Several buying techniques are commonly suggested for wise buying.

impulse buying Unplanned buying.

TIMING PURCHASES Certain items go on sale the same time each year. You can obtain bargains by buying winter clothing in mid- or late winter, or summer clothing in mid- or late summer. Many people save by buying holiday items and other products at reduced prices in late December and early January.

Weather reports and other news can also help you plan your purchasing. A crop failure can quickly result in higher prices for certain food products. Changing economic conditions and political difficulties around the world may result in higher prices and reduced supplies of certain products. Awareness of such situations can help you buy when prices are relatively low.

DID YOU KNOW?

Psychological factors affecting compulsive shopping can be revealed by these questions: Do you have an overwhelming desire to buy things? Do you buy to change your mood? Do your shopping habits hurt your relationships? Does overshopping damage your finances?

cooperative A nonprofit organization whose member-owners may save money on certain products or services.

PURCHASE LOCATION Your decision to use a particular retailer is probably influenced by location, price, product selection, and services available. Competition and technology have changed retailing with superstores, specialty shops, and online buying. This expanded shopping environment provides consumers with greater choice, potentially lower prices, and the need to carefully consider buying alternatives.

One alternative is the **cooperative,** a nonprofit organization whose member-owners may save money on certain products or services. As discussed in Chapter 5, a credit union is an example of a financial services cooperative. Food cooperatives, usually based in a community group or church, buy grocery items in large quantities. The savings on these bulk purchases are passed on to the co-op's members in the form of lower food prices. Cooperatives have also been organized to provide less expensive child care, recreational equipment, health care, cable television, and burial services.

Buying at "dollar stores" can result in bargains on many basic needs. However, avoid expired food products, "look-alikes" posing as famous brands, items that might be more expensive when compared to the sales price at other stores, and potentially unsafe imported products such as extension cords, toys, vitamins, and jewelry.

Consumers have a wide variety of shopping alternatives from which to choose.

ANALYZING CONSUMER PURCHASES

NET PRESENT VALUE OF A CONSUMER PURCHASE: Is a Hybrid Car Worth the Cost?

The time value of money (explained in Chapter 1) may be used to evaluate the financial benefits of a consumer purchase. For example, when deciding to buy a hybrid car, the money saved on gas would be considered a cash *inflow* (since money not going out is like money coming in). The cost difference between a hybrid and a fuel-version vehicle would be the current cash *outflow.* If the car has an expected life of 8 years, the *net present value* calculations might be as shown here:

Step 1: Estimate the annual savings on gas (for example, 2,000 miles at $4 a gallon), with a vehicle getting 50 miles per gallon rather than 25 miles per gallon.

Step 2: Calculate the present value (PV) of a series using either the time value of money tables (Chapter 1 Appendix) or a financial calculator. Assume a 2 percent interest rate, 8 years.

Step 3: Subtract the difference in cost of hybrid car (compared with a gasoline-powered car)

Annual gas savings $2,400 → PV of annual savings $7,032 − Vehicle cost difference $ 6,000

The result: $1,032 is a positive (favorable) net present value of the savings from a hybrid car compared to a gasoline-powered car. A negative net present value would indicate that the financial aspects of the purchase are not desirable.

This analysis for buying a hybrid car can vary based on other factors, such as vehicle maintenance costs, miles driven per year, and gas prices. Hybrid car cost calculators are also available online. Remember that this decision will also be influenced by personal attitudes and social factors. This calculation format may be used to assess the financial benefits of other consumer purchases by comparing the present value of the cost savings over time with the price of the item.

(continued)

BRAND COMPARISON Food and other products come in various brands. *National-brand* products are highly advertised items available in many stores. You are probably familiar with brands such as Green Giant, Nabisco, Del Monte, Kellogg's, Kraft, Apple, Samsung, LG, Banana Republic, and Gap. Brand-name products are usually more expensive than nonbrand products, but they offer a consistency of quality for which people are willing to pay.

Store-brand and *private-label* products, sold by one chain of stores, are low-cost alternatives to famous-name products. These products have labels that identify them with a specific retail chain, such as Safeway, Kroger, Walgreen's, and Walmart. Since store-brand products are frequently manufactured by the same companies that produce brand-name counterparts, these lower-cost alternatives allow consumers to save money. Private-label and store-brand items can result in great savings over time.

CONSUMER BUYING MATRIX

Buying alternatives may be evaluated based on personal values and goals, available time and money, and specific needs with regard to product size, quality, quantity, and features. Presented here is a buying matrix that may be used to evaluate alternatives.

Item Notebook Computer

Information Sources/Comments Consumer magazine/brand C slow compared to others tested; Friend/brand B performs well

Attribute	Weight	Alternatives: Brand A, Price $1,100		Brand B, Price $950		Brand C, Price $875	
		Rating (1-10)	Weighted Score	Rating (1-10)	Weighted Score	Rating (1-10)	Weighted Score
Features	.3	6	1.8	8	2.4	10	3
Performance	.4	9	3.6	7	2.8	5	2
Design	.1	8	.8	8	.8	7	.7
Warranty	.2	9	1.8	6	1.2	4	.8
■ Totals	1.0		8.0		7.2		6.5

Step 1 (Attributes and weights) · Step 2 (Brands) · Step 3 (Ratings) · Step 4 (Totals)

In this example, a consumer is using the following steps to evaluate the purchase of one of three brands of notebook computers.

Step 1. Identify attributes such as features, performance, design, and warranty; assign a weight based on the importance of each attribute.

Step 2. Select the brands to be evaluated.

Step 3. Rate (from 1 to 10) each brand based on the attributes identified in step 1. Multiply the rating number by the weight. For example, in this example, brand A received a rating of 6 for "features," giving a weighted score of 1.8 (6 × .3).

Step 4. Total and assess the results. Besides the numeric evaluation, consider factors such as price, store reputation, and your needs.

As you research a consumer purchase, identify the attributes that are important to you. Helpful sources are friends who own the product, salespeople, periodicals such as *Consumer Reports,* and various websites. The specific attributes will vary depending on the product or service. When selecting a provider of services, instead of products, you will likely consider training, experience, and reputation.

LABEL INFORMATION Certain label information is helpful; however, other information is nothing more than advertising. Federal law requires that food labels contain the company name and address, ingredients, nutrients, and food allergy warnings. Product labeling for appliances includes information about operating costs, to assist you in selecting the most energy-efficient models. **Open dating** describes the freshness or shelf life of a perishable product. Phrases such as "Use before May 6, 2015" or "Not to be sold after October 8" appear on most grocery items.

open dating Information about freshness or shelf life found on the package of a perishable product.

unit pricing The use of a standard unit of measurement to compare the prices of packages of different sizes.

PRICE COMPARISON **Unit pricing** uses a standard unit of measurement to compare the prices of packages of different sizes. To calculate the unit price, divide the price by the number of units of measurement, such as ounces, pounds, gallons, or number of sheets (for items such as paper towels and facial tissues). Then, compare the unit prices for various sizes, brands, and stores.

EXAMPLE: Unit Pricing

To calculate the unit price of an item, divide the cost by the number of units. For example, a 64-ounce product costing $8.32 would be calculated in this manner:

Unit price = $8.32 ÷ 64
= $0.13, or 13 cents an ounce

rebate A partial refund of the price of a product.

Coupons and rebates also provide better pricing for wise consumers. A family saving about $8 a week on their groceries by using coupons will save $416 over a year and $2,080 over five years (not counting interest). A **rebate** is a partial refund of the price of a product.

When comparing prices, remember that

- More store convenience (location, hours, sales staff) usually means higher prices.
- Ready-to-use products have higher prices.
- Large packages are usually the best buy; however, compare using unit pricing.
- "Sale" may not always mean saving money.

Exhibit 8-2 provides a summary of wise online buying.

WARRANTIES

warranty A written guarantee from the manufacturer or distributor of a product that specifies the conditions under which the product can be returned, replaced, or repaired.

Most products come with some guarantee of quality. A **warranty** is a written guarantee from the manufacturer or distributor that specifies the conditions under which the product can be returned, replaced, or repaired. An *express warranty,* usually in written form, is created by the seller or manufacturer and has two forms: the full warranty and the limited warranty. A *full warranty* states that a defective product can be fixed or replaced during a reasonable amount of time. A *limited warranty* covers only certain aspects of the product, such as parts, or requires the buyer to incur part of the costs for shipping or repairs. An *implied warranty* covers a product's intended use or other basic understandings that are not in writing. For example, an implied *warranty of title* indicates that the seller has the right to sell the product. An implied *warranty of merchantability* guarantees that the product is fit for the ordinary uses for which it is intended: A toaster must toast bread, and an MP3 player must play music. Implied warranties vary from state to state.

my life 1

Buying famous brand name items is usually the best strategy for my personal situation.

Experienced shoppers are an excellent source of effective buying tips. Talk with friends, relatives, and other people you know about wise buying habits that save time and money.

USED-CAR WARRANTIES The Federal Trade Commission (FTC) requires businesses that sell used cars to place a buyer's guide sticker in the windows of cars for sale. This disclosure must state whether the car comes with a warranty and, if so, what protection the dealer will provide. If no warranty is offered, the car is sold "as is" and the dealer assumes no responsibility for any repairs, regardless of any oral claims.

Exhibit 8-2 Wise Online Buying Activities

1. Conduct online research
- Compare brands and features
- Use label and warranty information
- Use product testing reports to assess quality, safety, nutrition

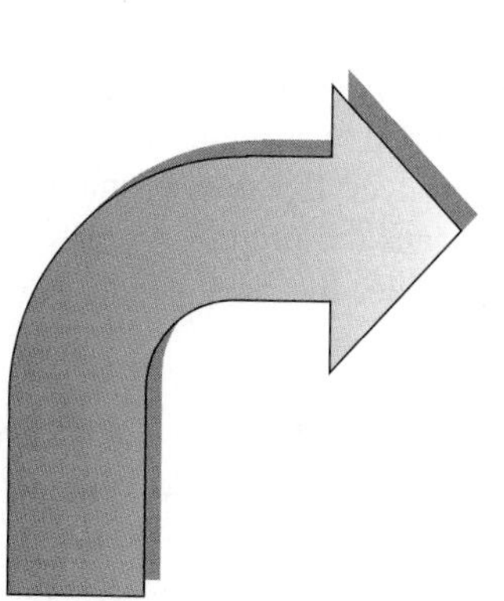

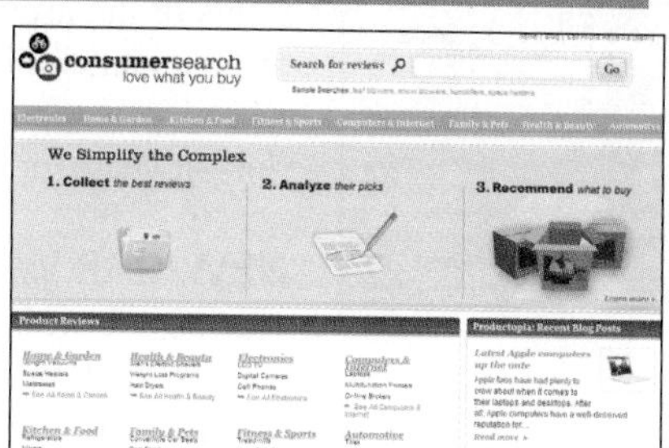

2. Compare stores
- Consider both stores and online
- Evaluate price, service, product quality, warranties, shipping cost and time, return policy
- Determine reputation, location

3. Make Purchase
- Use secure buying website
- Seek discounts, coupons
- Select payment method based on security, fees, other factors

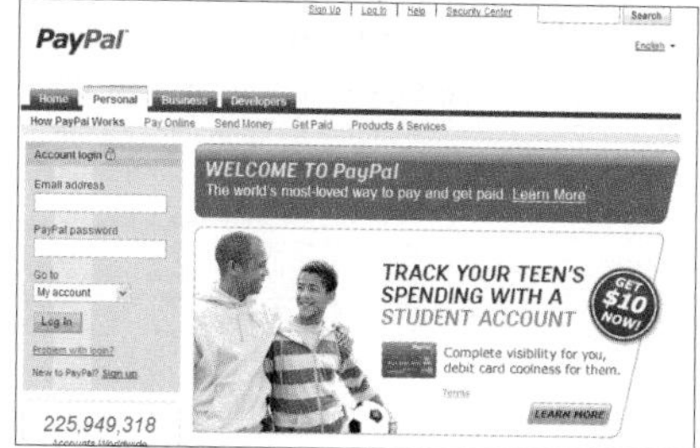

4. Plan for future purchases
- Keep receipts, other documents
- Know return, complaint process
- Watch e-mails for special offers
- Evaluate time, effort involved

About one-half of all the used cars sold by dealers come without a warranty, and if you buy such a car, you must pay for any repairs needed to correct problems. Be sure to get in writing any promises made by the salesperson.

The buyer's guide required by the FTC encourages you to have the used car inspected by a mechanic and to get all promises in writing. You also receive a list of the 14 major

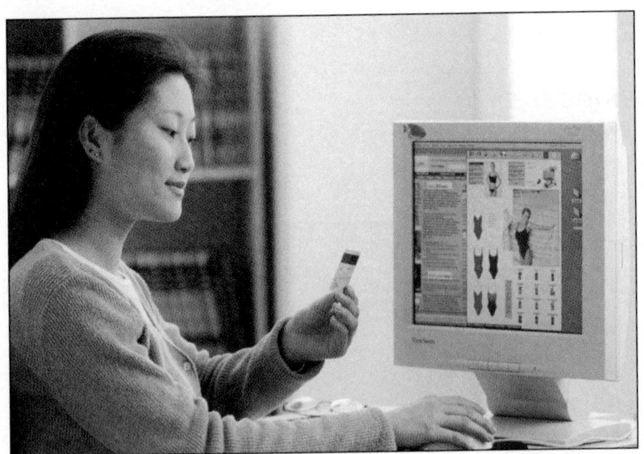

Online shopping and information sources provide consumers with convenience.

systems of an automobile and some of the major problems that may occur in these systems. This list can be helpful in comparing the vehicles and warranties offered by different dealers. FTC used-car regulations do not apply to vehicles purchased from private owners.

While a used car may not have an express warranty, most states have implied warranties that protect basic rights of the used-car buyer. Because an implied warranty of merchantability means the product is guaranteed to do what it is supposed to do, the used car is guaranteed to run—at least for awhile!

NEW-CAR WARRANTIES New-car warranties provide buyers with an assurance of quality. These warranties vary in the time, mileage, and parts they cover. The main conditions of a new-car warranty are (1) coverage of basic parts against defects; (2) power train coverage for the engine, transmission, and drive train; and (3) the corrosion warranty, which usually applies only to holes due to rust, not to surface rust. Other important conditions include whether the warranty is transferable to other owners of the car and details about the charges, if any, that will be incurred for major repairs, in the form of a *deductible*.

DID YOU KNOW?

Near-field communications (NFC) allows consumers to make purchases by waving their smartphones in front of a sensor when paying. Technology companies, financial service providers, and retailers are combining to become a part of this mobile-payments network. NFC also offers coupons and other deals that can result in people spending more than they might otherwise.

SERVICE CONTRACTS **Service contracts** are agreements between a business and a consumer to cover the repair costs of a product. Frequently called *extended warranties,* they are not warranties. For a fee, these agreements protect the buyer from high servicing costs resulting from certain repairs and other losses. Beware of service contracts that offer coverage for three years but really only cover two since the item has a manufacturer's one-year warranty.

service contract An agreement between a business and a consumer to cover the repair costs of a product.

Automotive service contracts can cover repairs not included in the manufacturer's warranty. Service contracts range from $400 to over $1,000; however, they do not always include everything you might expect. These contracts usually cover failure of the engine cooling system; however, some contracts exclude coverage of such failures if caused by overheating.

Because of costs and exclusions, some service contracts may not be a wise financial decision. You can minimize your concern about expensive repairs by setting aside money to cover those costs. Then, if you need repairs, the funds will be available.

Unit pricing worksheet

PRACTICE QUIZ 8-1

1 What factors commonly influence a person's daily buying choices?
2 How are daily buying decisions related to overall financial planning?
3 What types of brands are commonly available to consumers?
4 In what situations can comparing prices help in purchasing decisions?
5 How does a service contract differ from a warranty? What rights do purchasers of products have even if no written warranty exists?

COMMON CONSUMER MYTHS

The National Association of Consumer Agency Administrators has identified a list of misconceptions among consumers. These common myths include:

- "I can return my car within three days of purchase." While many people believe this (including many lawyers), there is no cooling-off period for motor vehicles.
- "My credit report information is confidential." Although wrongfully obtaining another person's credit report is a crime, there are many ways the information can be legally distributed.
- "My creditors can't call me at work." In most states, creditors (but not third-party debt collectors) can call—days, nights, weekends, and holidays—and contact you until the debts are repaid.
- "You can't repossess my car; it's on private property." While state laws differ, the general rule is that repossession cannot occur if it involves force, a breach of the peace, or entry into a dwelling. Vehicles in driveways and unlocked garages are usually fair game.
- "An auto lease is like a rental; if I have problems with the car or problems paying, I can just bring it back." Most leases require payments for the duration of the contract. Early termination often results in various additional charges.
- "If I lose my credit cards, I'm liable for purchases." Federal laws limit charges on lost or stolen cards to $50. Most national credit card companies will not charge the $50 if the consumer makes a good-faith effort to notify the lender quickly of lost or stolen cards.
- "It says right here that I've won; it must be true." Fake prize notifications continue to become more convincing. Some consumers actually go to the company office to try to pick up their prizes.

Source: "Ten Top Consumer Law 'Urban Myths,'" National Association of Consumer Agency Administrators.

Major Consumer Purchases: Buying Motor Vehicles

Shopping decisions should be based on a specific decision-making process. Exhibit 8-3 presents effective steps for purchasing a motor vehicle.

LO8-2

Implement a process for making consumer purchases.

PHASE 1—PRESHOPPING ACTIVITIES

First, define your needs and obtain relevant product information. These activities are the foundation for buying decisions to help you achieve your goals.

PROBLEM IDENTIFICATION Effective decision making should start with an open mind. Some people always buy the same brand, although another brand at a lower price would also serve their needs or another brand at the same price may provide better quality. A narrow view of the problem can be a weakness in your initial analysis. You may think the problem is "I need to have a car," when the real problem is "I need transportation."

INFORMATION GATHERING Information is power. The better informed you are, the better buying decisions you will make. Some people spend little time gathering and evaluating buying information. At the other extreme are people who spend

Exhibit 8-3

A research-based approach for purchasing a motor vehicle

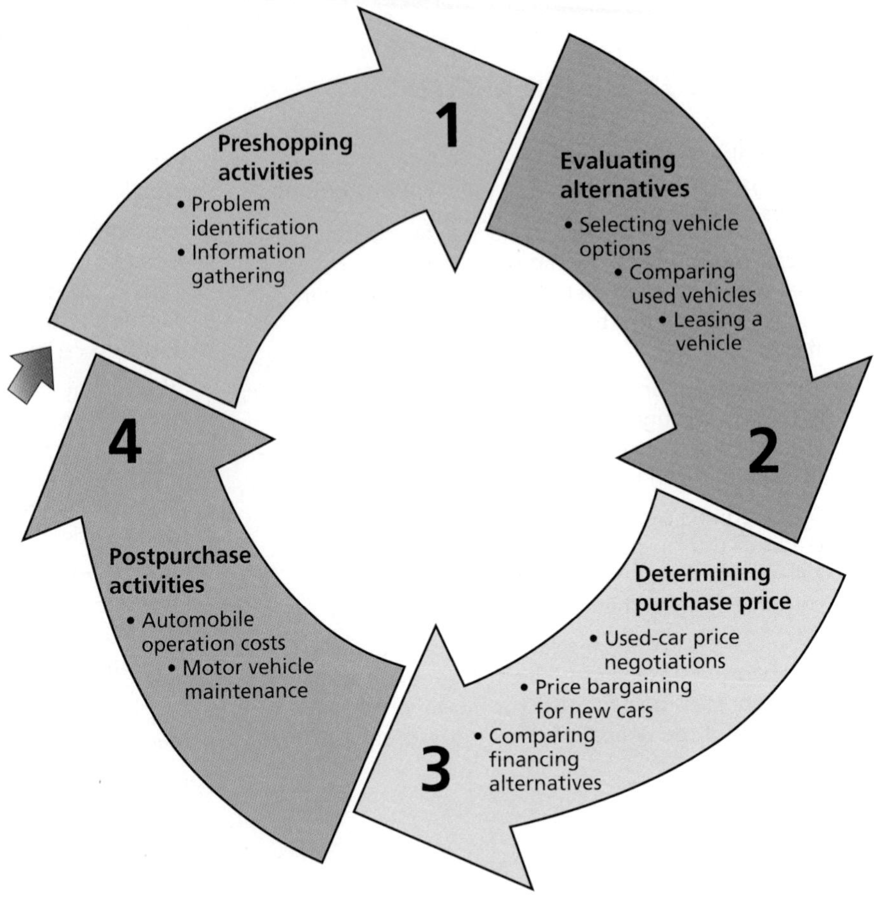

much time obtaining consumer information. While information is necessary for wise purchasing, too much information can create confusion and frustration. Following are some common information sources:

- *Personal contacts* can provide information about product performance, brand quality, and prices from family, friends, and others.
- *Business organizations* offer advertising, product labels, and packaging with basic facts about price, ingredients, quality, and availability.
- *Media sources* (television, radio, newspapers, magazines, websites) offer purchase location availability, prices, shopping suggestions, and product reviews from other consumers.
- *Independent testing organizations,* such as Consumers Union (publisher of *Consumer Reports*) report the quality of products and services. Underwriters Laboratories (UL) tests products for electrical and fire safety to assure items meet safety standards.
- *Government agencies,* at the local, state, and federal levels, provide information sources, complaint hotlines, and educational programs.

Basic information about car buying may be obtained at www.edmunds.com, www.caranddriver.com, www.autoweb.com, www.autotrader.com, and autos.msn.com. Consumers Union (www.ConsumerReports.org) offers a computerized car cost data service. Car-buying services, such as www.acscorp.com and www.autobytel.com, allow you to order your vehicle online.

PHASE 2—EVALUATING ALTERNATIVES

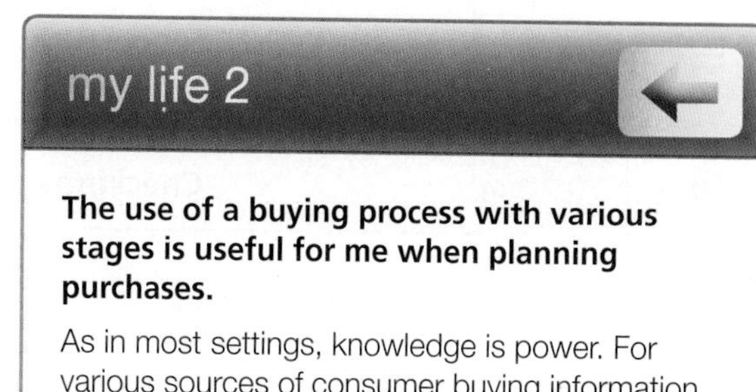

The use of a buying process with various stages is useful for me when planning purchases.

As in most settings, knowledge is power. For various sources of consumer buying information, government agencies, and consumer organizations, see Appendixes B and C.

Most purchasing decisions have several acceptable alternatives. Ask yourself: Is it possible to delay the purchase or to do without the item? Should I pay for the item with cash or buy it on credit? Which brands should I consider? How do the price, quality, and service compare at different stores? Is it possible to rent the item instead of buying it? Considering such alternatives will result in more effective purchasing decisions.

Research shows that prices can vary for all types of products. For a camera, prices may range from under $100 to well over $500. The price of aspirin may range from less than $1 to over $3 for 100 five-grain tablets. While differences in quality and attributes may exist among the cameras, the aspirin are equivalent in quantity and quality.

Many people view comparison shopping as a waste of time. While this may be true in some situations, comparison shopping can be beneficial when (1) buying expensive or complex items; (2) buying items that you purchase often; (3) comparison shopping can be done easily, such as with advertisements, catalogs, or online; (4) different sellers offer different prices and services; and (5) product quality or prices vary greatly.

SELECTING VEHICLE OPTIONS Optional equipment for cars may be viewed in three categories: (1) *mechanical devices* to improve performance, such as a larger engine, the transmission, power steering, power brakes, and cruise control; (2) *convenience options,* including power seats, air conditioning, stereo systems, power locks, rear window defoggers, and tinted glass; and (3) *aesthetic features* that add to the vehicle's visual appeal, such as metallic paint, special trim, and upholstery.

COMPARING USED VEHICLES The average used car costs about $10,000 less than the average new car. Common sources of used vehicles include:

- New-car dealers offer late-model vehicles and may give you a warranty, which usually means higher prices than at other sources.
- Used-car dealers usually have older vehicles. Warranties, if offered, will be limited. However, lower prices may be available.
- Individuals selling their own cars. These cars can be a bargain if the vehicle was well maintained. Few consumer protection regulations apply to private-party sales. Caution is suggested.
- Auctions and dealers sell automobiles previously owned by businesses, auto rental companies, and government agencies.
- Used-car superstores, such as CarMax, offer a large inventory of previously-owned vehicles.
- Online used-car businesses, such as www.dealernet.com and www.autotrader.com.

Certified, preowned (CPO) vehicles are nearly new cars that come with the original manufacturer's guarantee of quality. The rigorous inspection and repair process means a higher price than other used vehicles. CPO programs were originally created to create demand for the many low-mileage vehicles returned at the end of a lease.

The appearance of a used car can be deceptive. A well-maintained engine may be inside a body with rust; a clean, shiny exterior may conceal major operational problems. Therefore, conduct a used-car inspection as outlined in Exhibit 8-4. Have a trained and trusted mechanic of *your* choice check the car to estimate the costs of potential repairs. This service will help you avoid surprises. Every year, more than 450,000 people buy

Exhibit 8-4 Checking out a used car

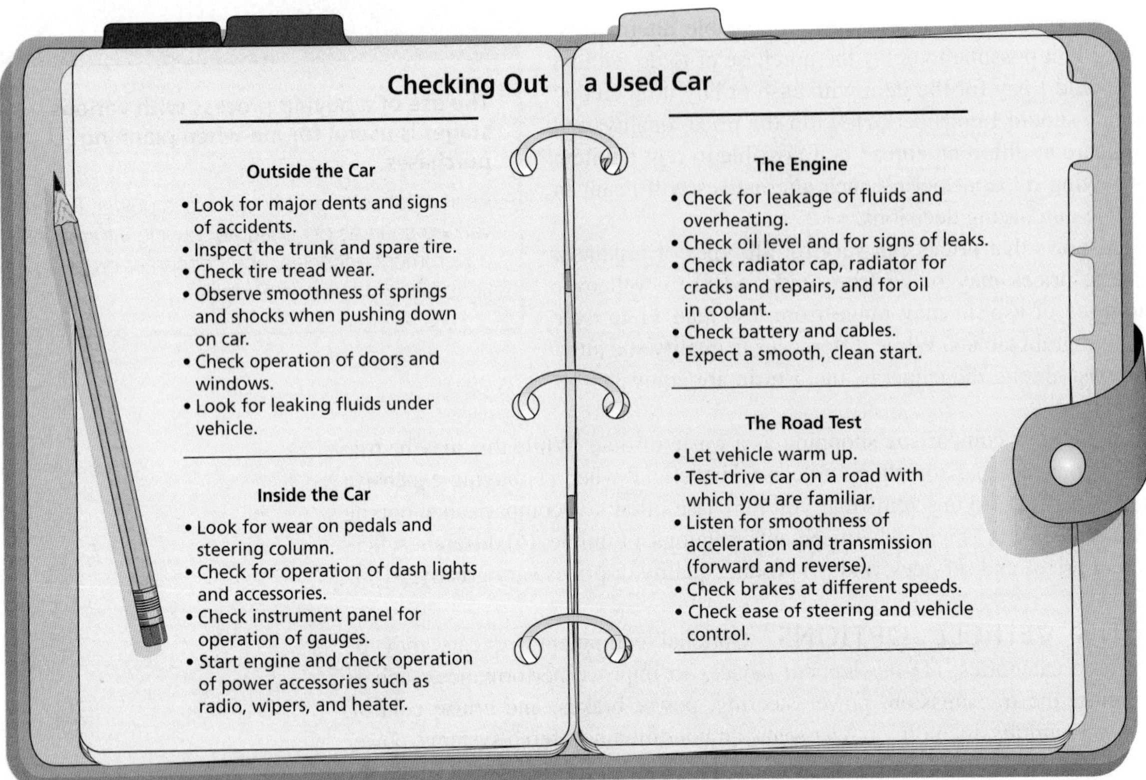

used vehicles with mileage gauges rolled back. According to the National Highway Traffic Safety Administration, consumers pay an average of $2,336 more than they should for vehicles with fraudulent mileage totals.

LEASING A MOTOR VEHICLE *Leasing* is a contractual agreement with monthly payments for the use of an automobile over a set time period, typically three, four, or five years. At the end of the lease term, the vehicle is usually returned to the leasing company.

The main advantages of leasing include (1) only a small cash outflow may be required for the security deposit, whereas buying can require a large down payment; (2) monthly lease payments are usually lower than monthly financing payments; (3) the lease agreement provides detailed records for business purposes; and (4) you are usually able to obtain a more expensive vehicle, more often.

Major drawbacks of leasing include (1) no ownership interest in the vehicle; (2) a need to meet requirements similar to qualifying for credit; and (3) possible additional costs incurred for extra mileage, certain repairs, turning the car in early, or even a move to another state.

When leasing, you arrange for the dealer to sell the vehicle through a financing company. As a result, be sure you know the true cost, including

1. The *capitalized cost,* which is the price of the vehicle. The average car buyer pays about 92 percent of the list price for a vehicle; the average leasing arrangement has a capitalized cost of 96 percent of the list price.
2. The *money factor,* which is the interest rate being paid on the capitalized cost.

Financial Planning Calculations

BUYING VERSUS LEASING AN AUTOMOBILE

To compare the costs of purchasing and leasing a vehicle, use the following framework. This analysis involves two situations based on comparable payment amounts.

Purchase Costs	Example	Your Figures
Total vehicle cost, including sales tax ($20,000)		
Down payment (or full amount if paying cash)	$ 2,000	$ ____
Monthly loan payment: $385 × 48-month length of financing (this item is zero if vehicle is not financed)	18,480	____
Opportunity cost of down payment (or total cost of the vehicle if it is bought for cash): $2,000 × 4 years of financing/ownership × 3 percent	240	____
Less: Estimated value of vehicle at end of loan term/ ownership period	−6,000	____
Total cost to buy	$14,720	____

Leasing Costs	Example	Your Figures
Security deposit ($300)		
Monthly lease payments: $385 × 36-month length of lease	$13,860	$ ____
Opportunity cost of security deposit: $300 security deposit × 3 years × 3 percent	27	____
End-of-lease charges* (if applicable)	800	____
Total cost to lease	$14,687	____

*Such as charges for extra mileage.

AVOIDING LEASE TRAPS

When considering a lease agreement for a motor vehicle, beware of the following common pitfalls:

- Not knowing the total cost of the agreement, including the cost of the vehicle, not just the monthly payment.
- Making a larger up-front payment than is required or paying unnecessary add-on costs.
- Negotiating the monthly payment rather than the capitalized cost of the vehicle.
- Not having the value of any trade-in vehicle reflected in the lease.
- Signing a contract you don't understand.

Compare monthly payments and other terms among several leasing companies. People have been known to pay over $24,000 to lease a vehicle worth only $20,000 at the start of the lease agreement. Comparison of leasing terms is available at websites such as www.leasesource.com, www.leaseguide.com, and www.carinfo.com.

3. The monthly payment and number of payments.

4. The *residual value,* which is the expected value of the vehicle at the end of the lease.

After the final payment, you may choose to return, keep, or sell the vehicle. If the current market value is greater than the residual value, you may be able to sell it for a profit. If the residual value is greater than the market value (which is the typical case), returning the vehicle to the leasing company is usually the best decision.

PHASE 3—DETERMINING PURCHASE PRICE

Once you've done your research and evaluations, other activities and decisions will be necessary. Products such as real estate or automobiles may be purchased using price negotiation. Negotiation may also be used in other buying situations to obtain a lower price or additional features. Two vital factors in negotiation are (1) having all the necessary information about the product and buying situation and (2) dealing with a person who has the authority to give you a lower price or additional features, such as the owner or store manager.

USED-CAR PRICE NEGOTIATION Begin to determine a fair price by checking newspaper ads for the prices of comparable vehicles. Other sources of current used-car prices are *Edmund's Used Car Prices* (www.edmunds.com) and the *Kelley Blue Book* (www.kbb.com).

A number of factors influence the basic price of a used car, including the number of miles the car has been driven and the car's features and options. A low-mileage car will have a higher price than a comparable car with high mileage. The condition of the vehicle and the demand for the model also affect price.

PRICE BARGAINING FOR NEW CARS An important new-car price information source is the *sticker price,* which is the suggested retail price printed on a label affixed to the vehicle. This label presents the base price of the car with costs of added features. The dealer's cost, or *invoice price,* is an amount less than the sticker price. The difference between the sticker price and the dealer's cost is the range available for negotiation. This range is larger for full-size, luxury cars with more options; subcompacts usually do not have a wide negotiation range. Information about dealer's cost is available from sources such as *Edmund's New Car Prices* (www.edmunds.com) and *Consumer Reports* (www.ConsumerReports.org).

Set-price dealers use no-haggling car selling, with prices presented to be accepted or rejected as stated. *Car-buying services* are businesses that help buyers obtain a specific new car at a reasonable price. Also referred to as an *auto broker,* these businesses offer desired models with options for prices ranging between $50 and $200 over the dealer's cost. First, the auto broker charges a small fee for price information on desired models. Then, if you decide to buy a car, the auto broker arranges the purchase with a dealer near your home.

To prevent confusion in determining the true price of the new car, do not mention a trade-in vehicle until the cost of the new car has been settled. Then ask how much the dealer is willing to pay for your old car. If the offer price is not acceptable, sell the old car on your own.

A typical negotiating conversation when buying a car might go like this:

Customer: "I'm willing to give you $15,600 for the car. That's my top offer."
Auto salesperson: "Let me check with my manager." After returning, "My manager says $16,200 is the best we can do."
Customer (who should be willing to walk out at this point): "I can go to $15,650."
Auto salesperson: "We have the car you want, ready to go. How about $15,700?"

If the customer agrees, the dealer has gotten $100 more than the customer's "top offer!"

DID YOU KNOW?

According to bankrate.com, negotiating a lower price requires a psychological strategy that starts by: (1) determining exactly what you want; (2) researching a fair price for the item; and (3) figuring out what's most important to you and to the seller. This information will put you in a better position for bargaining.

Other questionable sales techniques used in the past include:

- *Lowballing,* when quoted a very low price that increases when add-on costs are included at the last moment.
- *Highballing,* when offered a very high amount for a trade-in vehicle, with the extra amount made up by increasing the new-car price.

- When asked "How much can you afford per month?" be sure to also ask how many months.
- "A small deposit will hold this vehicle for you." Never leave a deposit unless you are ready to buy a vehicle or are willing to lose that amount.
- "Your price is only $100 above our cost." However, many hidden costs may have been added in to get the dealer's cost.
- Beware of sales agreements with preprinted amounts. Cross out numbers you believe are not appropriate for your purchase.

COMPARING FINANCING ALTERNATIVES You may pay cash; however, most people buy cars on credit. Auto loans are available from banks, credit unions, consumer finance companies, and other financial institutions. Many lenders will *preapprove* you for a certain loan amount, which separates financing from negotiating the price of the car. Until the new-car price is set, you should not indicate that you intend to use the dealer's credit plan.

The lowest interest rate or the lowest payment does not necessarily mean the best credit plan. Also consider the loan length. Otherwise, after two or three years, the value of your car may be less than the amount you still owe; this situation is referred to as *upside-down* or *negative equity*. If you default on your loan or sell the car at this time, you will have to pay the difference.

EXAMPLE: Upside Down

A $26,000 vehicle is purchased with an initial loan of $18,000. After a period of time, the vehicle may only be worth $12,000 while still owing $15,000. To avoid this situation, make a large down payment, have a short-term loan (less than five years), and pay off the loan faster than the decline in value of the vehicle.

Over the years, automobile manufacturers offered low-interest financing. On occasion, at the same time, they may also offer rebates, giving buyers a choice between a rebate and a low-interest loan. Carefully compare financing at various financial institutions and the rebate (see Exhibit 8-5). Special rebates are sometimes offered to students, teachers, credit union members, real estate agents, and other groups.

The annual percentage rate (APR) is the best indicator of the true cost of credit. The federal Truth in Lending law requires that the APR be clearly stated in advertising and other communications. Low payments may seem to be a good deal, but they mean you will be paying longer and your total finance charges will be higher. Consider both the APR

	AUTO MANUFACTURER FINANCING	FINANCIAL INSTITUTION FINANCING (BANK, CREDIT UNION)
ANNUAL PERCENTAGE RATE	2.9%	6.0%
VEHICLE PRICE	$17,500	$17,500
DOWN PAYMENT	$ 2,500	$ 2,500
MANUFACTURER'S REBATE	$ 1,500	$ 1,500
LOAN AMOUNT	$13,500	$13,500
TERM OF LOAN	60 MONTHS	60 MONTHS
MONTHLY PAYMENT	$ 242.00	$ 262.00
TOTAL PAYMENT (NOT INCLUDING DOWN PAYMENT)	$14,520	$15,720

TOTAL SAVINGS USING AUTO MANUFACTURER: $1,200

Exhibit 8-5

Comparing rebates and special financing: an example

and the finance charge when comparing credit terms of different lenders. Additional auto financing information may be obtained at www.bankrate.com and www.carfinance.com.

PHASE 4—POSTPURCHASE ACTIVITIES

Maintenance and ownership costs are associated with most purchases. Correct use can result in improved performance and fewer repairs. When you need repairs not covered by a warranty, follow a pattern similar to that used when making the original purchase. Investigate, evaluate, and negotiate a variety of servicing options.

In the past, when major problems occurred with a new car and the warranty didn't solve the difficulty, many consumers lacked a course of action. As a result, all 50 states and the District of Columbia enacted *lemon laws* that require a refund for the vehicle after the owner has made repeated attempts to obtain servicing. These laws apply when four attempts and made to get the same problem corrected or when the vehicle has been out of service for more than 30 days within 12 months of purchase or the first 12,000 miles. The terms of the state laws vary; for details go to www.lemonlawamerica.com.

AUTOMOBILE OPERATION COSTS Over your lifetime, you can expect to spend more than $200,000 on automobile-related expenses. Your driving costs will vary based on two main factors: the size of your automobile and the number of miles you drive. These costs involve two categories:

Fixed Ownership Costs	Variable Operating Costs
Depreciation	Gasoline and oil
Interest on auto loan	Tires
Insurance	Maintenance and repairs
License, registration, taxes, and fees	Parking and tolls

The largest fixed expense associated with a new automobile is *depreciation,* the loss in the vehicle's value due to time and use. Since money is not paid out for depreciation, many people do not consider it an expense. However, this decreased value is a cost that owners incur. Well-maintained vehicles and certain high-quality, expensive models, such as BMW and Lexus, depreciate at a slower rate.

Costs such as gasoline, oil, and tires increase with the number of miles driven. Planning expenses is easier if the number of miles you drive is fairly constant. Unexpected trips and vehicle age will increase such costs.

Awareness of the total cost of owning and operating an automobile can help your overall financial planning. An automobile expense record should include the dates of odometer readings. Recording your mileage each time you buy gas will allow you to compute fuel efficiency. For tax-deductible travel, the Internal Revenue Service requires specific information about the mileage, locations, dates, and purposes of trips. Use a notebook to keep records of regular operating expenses such as gas, oil, parking, and tolls. Also, consider keeping files on maintenance, repair, and replacement part costs. Finally, keep a record of infrequent expenditures such as insurance payments and license and registration fees.

MOTOR VEHICLE MAINTENANCE People who sell, repair, or drive automobiles for a living stress the importance of regular care. While owner's manuals and articles suggest mileage or time intervals for certain servicing, more frequent oil changes or tune-ups can minimize major repairs and maximize vehicle life. Exhibit 8-6 offers suggested maintenance areas to consider.

Exhibit 8-6

Extend vehicle life with proper maintenance

- Get regular oil changes (every 3 months or 3,000 miles).
- Check fluids (brake, power steering, transmission).
- Inspect hoses and belts for wear.
- Get a tune-up (new spark plugs, fuel filter, air filter) 12,000–15,000 miles.
- Check and clean battery cables and terminals.
- Check tire pressures regularly.
- Check spark plug wires after 50,000 miles.
- Flush radiator and service transmission every 25,000 miles.
- Keep lights, turn signals, and horn in good working condition.
- Check muffler and exhaust pipes.
- Check tires for wear; rotate tires every 7,500 miles.
- Check condition of brakes.

AUTOMOBILE SERVICING SOURCES The various businesses that offer automobile maintenance and repair service include

- Car dealers, which provide a service department with a wide range of car care services. Service charges at a car dealer may be higher than those of other repair businesses.
- Service stations, which can provide convenience and reasonable prices for routine maintenance and repairs. However, the number of full-service stations has declined in recent years.
- Independent auto repair shops, which can service your vehicle at fairly competitive prices. Since the quality of these repair shops can vary, talk with previous customers.
- Mass merchandise retailers, such as Sears and Walmart, which may emphasize the sale of tires and batteries, as well as brakes, oil changes, and tune-ups.
- Specialty shops that offer brakes, tires, automatic transmissions, and oil changes at a reasonable price with fast service.

Regular maintenance can reduce future repair costs and increase your vehicle's life.

To avoid unnecessary expenses, be aware of the common repair frauds presented in Exhibit 8-7 and deal only with reputable auto service businesses. Be sure to get a

Exhibit 8-7

Common auto repair scams

The majority of automobile servicing sources are fair and honest. Sometimes, however, consumers waste dollars when they fall prey to the following tricks:

- When checking the oil, the attendant puts the dipstick only partway down and then shows you that you need oil.
- An attendant cuts a fan belt or punctures a hose. Watch carefully when someone checks under your hood.
- A garage employee puts some liquid on your battery and then tries to convince you that it is leaking and you need a new battery.
- Removing air from a tire instead of adding air to it can make an unwary driver open to buying a new tire or paying for an unneeded patch on a tire that is in perfect condition.
- The attendant puts grease near a shock absorber or on the ground and then tells you your present shocks are dangerous and you need new ones.
- You are charged for two gallons of antifreeze with a radiator flush when only one gallon was put in.

Dealing with reputable businesses and a basic knowledge of your automobile are the best methods of avoiding deceptive repair practices.

written, detailed estimate in advance as well as a detailed, paid receipt for the service completed. Studies of consumer problems consistently rank auto repairs as one of the top consumer ripoffs. Some people avoid problems and minimize costs by working on their own vehicles.

Consumer purchase comparison

eXcel PFP Sheet 34

Current and future transportation needs

Used-car purchase comparison

PRACTICE QUIZ 8-2

1 What are the major sources of consumer information?
2 What actions are appropriate when buying a used car?
3 When might leasing a motor vehicle be appropriate?
4 What maintenance activities could increase the life of your vehicle?

eXcel PFP Sheet 36

Buying vs. leasing an automobile

eXcel PFP Sheet 37

Comparing cash and credit for major purchases

eXcel PFP Sheet 38

Auto ownership and operation costs

Resolving Consumer Complaints

LO8-3

Identify steps to take to resolve consumer problems.

Most customer complaints result from defective products, low quality, short product lives, unexpected costs, deceptive pricing, and fraudulent business practices. These problems are most commonly associated with motor vehicles, online purchases, work-at-home businesses, landlord–tenant relations, investment scams, telemarketing, electronics, health clubs, diet plans, mortgages, home repairs, credit cards, debt collection, phony contests, travel services, rent-to-own companies, employment opportunities, and deceptive charities.

Federal consumer agencies estimate annual consumer losses from fraudulent business activities at $10 billion to $40 billion for telemarketing and mail order, $3 billion for credit card fraud and credit "repair" scams, and $10 billion for investment swindles.

To minimize consumer problems, before making a purchase: (1) obtain recommendations from friends, family members, and online reviews; (2) verify company affiliations, certifications, and licenses; and (3) understand the sale terms, return policies, and warranty provisions. Most people do not anticipate or have problems with their purchases. However, since problems do arise, it's best to be prepared for them. The process for resolving differences between buyers and sellers includes the steps presented in Exhibit 8-8.

I know what actions to take when complaining about a consumer purchase.

Consumer scams are a frequent source of complaints. These deceptions can be very creative. For examples of these cons, see Financial Planning for Life's Situations: Beware of These Common (and Not So Common) Frauds on page 286.

Step 1—Initial Communication

- Return to place of purchase or contact online retailer.
- Provide a detailed explanation and the action you desire.
- Be pleasant yet persistent in your efforts to obtain a resolution.

Step 2—Communication with the Company

- Send an e-mail with the details of the situation (Exhibit 8-9).
- Post your concerns on the company's online social media sites.
- Comment on a blog or a consumer review website.

Step 3—Consumer Agency Assistance

- Seek guidance from a local, state, or federal consumer agency.
- Determine if any laws have been violated in the situation.
- Consider the use of mediation or arbitration.

Step 4—Legal Action

- Consider bringing your case to small claims court.
- Determine if a class action suit is appropriate.
- Seek assistance from a lawyer or legal aid organization.

Exhibit 8-8

Resolving consumer complaints

Before starting this process, know your rights and the laws that apply to your situation. Information on consumer rights is available online and through phone apps, such as the one that allows airline passengers to monitor the status of their flights. Information on delays, cancellations, and other situations can be submitted to keep airlines accountable.

To help ensure success when you make a complaint, keep a file of receipts, names of people you talked to, dates of attempted repairs, copies of letters you wrote, and costs incurred. Written documents can help to resolve a problem in your favor. An automobile owner kept detailed records and receipts for all gasoline purchases, oil changes, and repairs. When a warranty dispute occurred, the owner was able to prove proper maintenance and received a refund for the defective vehicle. Your perseverance is vital since companies might ignore your request or delay their response.

STEP 1: INITIAL COMMUNICATION

Most consumer complaints are resolved at the original sales location. Since most business firms are concerned about their reputations, they usually honor legitimate complaints. As you talk with the salesperson, customer service person, or store manager, avoid yelling, threatening a lawsuit, or demanding unreasonable action. In general, a calm, rational, yet persistent approach is recommended.

BEWARE OF THESE COMMON (AND NOT SO COMMON) FRAUDS

Foreign Scams. Many people have received a letter or e-mail from a Nigerian bank or other foreign source promising all or part of $30 million. The letter requested the recipient's bank account number so the money could be transferred. There can be another catch: To receive the fortune, the recipient would have to pay between $15,000 and $1 million in taxes—in advance!

Disaster-Related Fraud. A variety of scams surface after tragedies and natural disasters. Phony charities solicit funds for families of the victims.

Credit Repair. Companies offer to clean up the credit reports of consumers with poor credit histories. After paying hundreds of dollars, consumers find out these companies can do nothing to improve their credit reports.

Employment Scams. Unemployed workers are often the target of fraudulent opportunities for résumé preparation that guarantee a job, work-at-home schemes, assistance to obtain "special" unemployment benefits, and fees for specialized training or employment services that assure employment.

Automatic Debit Scams. Automatic debiting of your checking account can be a legitimate payment method. However, many fraudulent telemarketers use this technique to take money from a person's checking account. Do not give out checking account information unless you are familiar with the company.

Fraudulent Diet Products and Health Claims. Americans spend an estimated $6 billion a year on fraudulent diet products such as "The Amazing Skin Patch Melts Away Body Fat," "Lose Weight While You Sleep," and "Lose All the Weight You Can for Just $99." Spotting false health claims may be as easy as being cautious of phrases such as "scientific breakthrough," "miraculous cure," "exclusive product," "secret ingredient," or "ancient remedy." Common health fraud schemes occur in the areas of cancer, HIV-AIDS, and arthritis.

Toll-Free Scams. Calls to 800, 888, and 877 numbers are almost always free. However, there are some exceptions. Companies that provide audio entertainment or information services may charge for calls to toll-free numbers, but only if they follow the Federal Trade Commission's 900-number rule.

Bogus "Campus Card." Consumer protection offices in 20 states warned about "campus cards" available for a $25 fee. These prepaid debit cards were being promoted as "required" for many services and privileges at whichever college or university the student decided to attend. While the company appeared to be affiliated with the school, it was actually a for-profit business.

Internet Pyramid Scheme. The Council of Better Business Bureaus issued an alert about an "international program of wealth distribution" called "Pentagono" or "Future Strategies International." The plan, based in Italy and promoted on the Internet, advertised that consumers could receive up to $116,000 for an initial investment of about $120. Participants were asked to purchase three certificates and sell those to three other people. For everyone to profit in the scheme, there had to be a never-ending supply of potential and willing participants.

Phishing. This high-tech scam uses e-mail spam or pop-up messages to deceive you into revealing your credit card number, bank account information, Social Security number, passwords, or other private information. These e-mails usually look official, like they are coming from a legitimate financial institution or government agency. This fraud also occurs by phone (live or automated calls), referred to as "vishing," and by cell phone text message, called "smishing." Never click on the link in these e-mails or disclose personal data by phone to a questionable source.

Pharming. Pharming involves computer viruses or worms. Malicious software or an e-mail attachment plants the virus or worm in the user's computer or in a server that directs traffic on the Internet. Even if you type in the correct address of a website, the software sends you to a bogus one. Computer users are encouraged to keep antivirus and anti-spyware programs up to date.

Fraudulent Hotline. The attorney general in Missouri obtained a court order to shut down a fraudulent consumer telemarketing "hotline" that was being used to divert inquiries and complaints about a vacation company from legitimate consumer protection agencies.

Further information about various frauds and deceptive business practices is available at www.fraud.org and www.ftc.gov.

STEP 2: COMMUNICATION WITH THE COMPANY

Express your dissatisfaction to the corporate level if a problem is not resolved at the local store. A e-mail like the one in Exhibit 8-9 may be appropriate. You can obtain addresses of companies you wish to contact from the *Consumer Action Handbook* (www.consumeraction.gov), published by the federal government, or other reference books available at your library. The websites of major companies also offer a method to communicate with these organizations.

You can obtain a company's consumer hotline number by using a directory of toll-free numbers or calling 1-800-555-1212, the toll-free information number. Many companies print the toll-free hotline number and website address on product packages. Studies reveal that most consumer complaints made to a company are resolved on the first contact.

Exhibit 8-9 Sample complaint e-mail

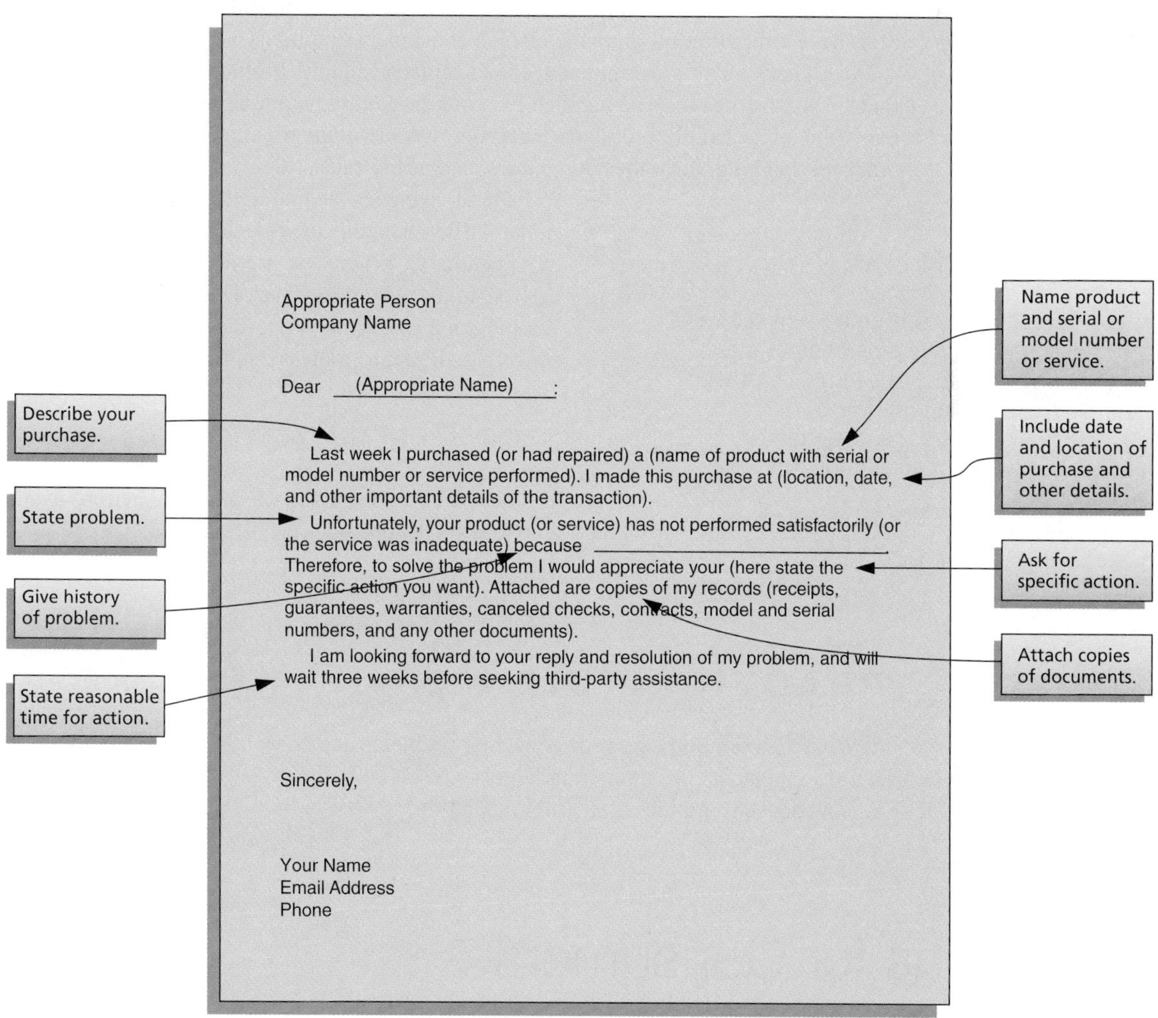

Appropriate Person
Company Name

Dear (Appropriate Name):

Last week I purchased (or had repaired) a (name of product with serial or model number or service performed). I made this purchase at (location, date, and other important details of the transaction).

Unfortunately, your product (or service) has not performed satisfactorily (or the service was inadequate) because __________________________________.
Therefore, to solve the problem I would appreciate your (here state the specific action you want). Attached are copies of my records (receipts, guarantees, warranties, canceled checks, contracts, model and serial numbers, and any other documents).

I am looking forward to your reply and resolution of my problem, and will wait three weeks before seeking third-party assistance.

Sincerely,

Your Name
Email Address
Phone

Note: Keep copies of your letter and all related documents and information.
Source: *Consumer Action Handbook* (www.pueblo.gsa.gov).

STEP 3: CONSUMER AGENCY ASSISTANCE

If you do not receive satisfaction from the company, several consumer, business, and government organizations are available. These include national organizations specializing in issues such as automobile safety, health care, and nutrition, and local organizations that handle complaints, conduct surveys, and provide legal assistance.

The Better Business Bureaus are a network of offices that resolve complaints against local merchants. Better Business Bureaus are sponsored by local business organizations, and companies are not obligated to respond to the complaints. The Better Business Bureau in your area can be of value before you make a purchase. They can tell you about the experiences of others with a firm with which you are planning to do business.

mediation The attempt by an impartial third party to resolve a difference between two parties through discussion and negotiation.

arbitration The settlement of a difference by a third party whose decision is legally binding.

Mediation involves the use of a third party to settle grievances. In mediation, an impartial person—the *mediator*—tries to resolve a conflict between a customer and a business through discussion and negotiation. Mediation is a nonbinding process. It can save time and money compared to other dispute settlement methods.

Arbitration is the settlement of a difference by a third party—the *arbitrator*—whose decision is legally binding. After both sides agree to the arbitration process, each side presents its case to the arbitrator. Arbitrators are selected from volunteers trained for this purpose. Most major automobile manufacturers and many industry organizations have arbitration programs to resolve consumer complaints.

A vast network of government agencies is also available. Problems with local restaurants or food stores may be handled by a city or county health department. Every state has agencies to handle problems involving deceptive advertising, fraudulent business practices, banking, insurance companies, and utility rates.

Federal agencies available to help resolve consumer difficulties and provide information are listed in Appendix C. When you are uncertain about which agency to use, contact your U.S. representative in Washington, DC. This office can help channel your concern to the appropriate consumer protection agency.

DID YOU KNOW?

Without realizing it, many consumers sign contracts with provisions that stipulate arbitration as the method to resolve disputes. As a result, consumers face various risks, including rules vastly different from a jury trial, higher costs for the arbitrator's time, and selection of an arbitrator by the defendant.

STEP 4: LEGAL ACTION

The next section discusses various legal actions available to resolve consumer problems.

PRACTICE QUIZ 8-3

1 What are common causes of consumer problems and complaints?
2 How can most consumer complaints be resolved?
3 How does arbitration differ from mediation?

Legal Options for Consumers

LO8-4

Evaluate the legal alternatives available to consumers.

What should you do if all of the previously mentioned avenues of action fail to bring about a resolution of a consumer complaint? One of the following legal actions may be appropriate.

SMALL CLAIMS COURT

Every state has a court system to settle minor disagreements. In **small claims court,** a person may file a claim involving amounts below a set dollar limit. The maximum varies from state to state, ranging from $500 to $10,000; most states have a limit of between $1,500 and $3,000. The process usually takes place without a lawyer, although in many states attorneys are allowed in small claims court. To make best use of small claims court, experts suggest observing other cases to learn more about the process. For additional information on "How to File a Suit in Small Claims Court," see the "How to . . ." feature on page 290.

A variety of legal alternatives are available to consumers.

CLASS-ACTION SUITS

Occasionally a number of people have the same complaint—for example, people who were injured by a defective product, customers who were overcharged by a utility company, or travelers who were cheated by a tour business. Such people may qualify for a class-action suit. A **class-action suit** is a legal action taken by a few individuals on behalf of all the people who have suffered the same alleged injustice. These people, called a *class,* are represented by one lawyer or by a group of lawyers working together.

Once a situation qualifies as a class-action suit, all of the affected parties must be notified of the suit. At this point, a person may decide not to participate in the class-action suit and instead file an individual lawsuit. If the court ruling is favorable to the class, the funds awarded may be divided among all the people involved, used to reduce rates in the future, or assigned to public funds for government use. Recent class-action suits included auto owners who were sold unneeded replacement parts for their vehicles and a group of investors who sued a brokerage company for unauthorized buy-and-sell transactions that resulted in high commission charges.

small claims court A court that settles legal differences involving amounts below a set limit and employs a process in which the litigants usually do not use a lawyer.

class-action suit A legal action taken by a few individuals on behalf of all the people who have suffered the same alleged injustice.

USING A LAWYER

When small claims court or a class-action suit is not appropriate, you may seek the services of an attorney. The most common sources of available lawyers are referrals from people you know, the local branch of the American Bar Association, and telephone directory listings. Lawyers advertise in newspapers, on television, and in other media. Be aware that impressive advertising does not mean competent legal counsel.

Deciding when to use a lawyer is difficult. In general, straightforward legal situations such as appearing in small claims court, renting an apartment, or defending yourself on a minor traffic violation usually do not require legal counsel. But for more complicated matters, such as writing a will, settling a real estate purchase, or suing for injury damages caused by a product, obtaining the services of an attorney is probably wise.

When selecting a lawyer, you should consider several questions. Is the lawyer experienced in your type of case? Will you be charged on a flat fee basis, at an hourly rate, or on a contingency basis? Is there a fee for the initial consultation? How and when will you be required to make payment for services?

DID YOU KNOW?

A class-action suit can be expensive. After winning $2.19 in back interest, Dexter J. Kamilewicz also noted a $91.33 "miscellaneous deduction" on his mortgage escrow account. This charge was his portion for lawyers he never knew he hired to win a class-action suit.

HOW TO...

File a Suit in Small Claims Court

In every state, small claims courts are available to handle legal disputes involving minor amounts. While specific procedures vary from state to state, these actions are usually involved:

Step 1. Notify the defendant to request a payment for damages with a deadline, such as within 30 days. Note in your letter that you will initiate legal action after that point in time.

Step 2. Determine the appropriate location for filing the case. Also, decide if your type of case is allowed in small claims court in your state, and if the amount is within the state limit. (Information on state limits is available at www.nolo.com/legal-encyclopedia/article-30031.html.)

Step 3. Obtain and complete the required filing documents. These forms can be obtained at the courthouse or may be available online. The petition will include the plaintiff's name (you), the defendant (person or organization being sued), the amount being requested, a detailed and clear description of the claim with dates of various actions, and copies of any pertinent documents (contracts, receipts).

Step 4. File the documents and pay the required fee. The petition will be served to the defendant notifying that person of the suit. After being served, the defendant is usually required to file a written response, denying or not contesting the claim. If the defendant does not respond, a default judgment will most likely be entered.

Step 5. Next, a hearing date will be set. Prepare evidence with a clear and concise presentation of: (a) the details of what happened and when; (b) evidence, such as contracts, leases, receipts, cancelled checks, credit card statements or photographs; and (c) the testimony of people who witnessed aspects of the dispute or who are knowledgeable about the type of situation. If both parties decide to settle before the hearing, be sure that you receive payment before the case is dismissed.

Step 6. At the hearing, be clear and concise, and bring supporting documentation with you. Witnesses whom you wish present at the hearing may involve a subpoena requiring them to appear in court.

Step 7. Once you receive a favorable judgment, you still have to collect the funds. While the court does not collect the money for you, the party may pay when the judgment is rendered. If not, a letter from you or an attorney may result in payment. Or, more formal debt collection actions might be necessary.

Every state has different procedures and regulations related to small claims court. Conduct a Web search to obtain information for your specific location. Careful and detailed preparation of your case is the key to success in small claims court.

OTHER LEGAL ALTERNATIVES

legal aid society One of a network of publicly supported community law offices that provide legal assistance to consumers who cannot afford their own attorney.

The cost of legal services can be a problem, especially for low-income consumers. A **legal aid society** is one of a network of publicly supported community law offices that provide legal assistance to people who cannot afford their own attorney. These community agencies provide this assistance at a minimal cost or without charge.

Prepaid legal services provide unlimited or reduced-fee legal assistance for a set fee. Some of these programs provide certain basic services, such as telephone consultation and preparation of a simple will, for an annual fee ranging from $50 to $150 or more. More complicated legal assistance requires an additional fee, usually at a reduced rate. Other programs do not charge an advance fee but allow members to obtain legal services at discount rates. In general, prepaid legal programs are designed to prevent minor troubles from becoming complicated legal problems. Legal questions may be researched online at www.nolo.com.

IS IT LEGAL?

The following situations are common problems for consumers. How would you respond to the question at the end of each situation?

	Yes	No
1. You purchase a stereo system for $650. Two days later, the same store offers the same item for $425. Is this legal?	____	____
2. You receive an unordered sample of flower seeds in the mail. You decide to plant them to see how well they will grow in your yard. A couple of days later, you receive a bill for the seeds. Do you have to pay for the seeds?	____	____
3. A 16-year-old injured while playing ball at a local park is taken to a hospital for medical care. The parents refuse to pay the hospital since they didn't request the service. Can the parents be held legally responsible for the charges?	____	____
4. You purchase a shirt for a friend. The shirt doesn't fit, but when you return it to the store, you are offered an exchange since the store policy is no cash refunds. Is this legal?	____	____
5. A manufacturer refuses to repair a motorcycle that is still under warranty. The manufacturer can prove that the motorcycle was used improperly. If this is true, must the manufacturer honor the warranty?	____	____
6. An employee of a store incorrectly marks the price of an item at a lower amount. Is the store obligated to sell the item at the lower price?	____	____

Circumstances, interpretations of the law, and store policies, as well as state and local laws, can affect the above situations. The generally accepted answers are *no* for 2, 5, and 6; *yes* for 1, 3, and 4.

PERSONAL CONSUMER PROTECTION

While many laws, agencies, and legal tools are available to protect your rights, none will be of value unless you use them. (See Financial Planning for Life's Situations: Is It Legal? on this page.) Consumer protection experts suggest that to prevent being taken in by deceptive business practices, you should

1. Do business only with reputable companies with a record of satisfying customers.
2. Avoid signing contracts and other documents you do not understand.
3. Be cautious about offerings that seem too good to be true—they probably are!
4. Compare the cost of buying on credit with the cost of paying cash; also, compare the interest rates the seller offers with those offered by a bank or a credit union.
5. Avoid rushing to get a good deal; successful con artists depend on impulse buying.

The legal actions available to consumers may be of value to me in the future.

At some point in your life, going to small claims court may be an appropriate action for a consumer complaint situation. To learn more, conduct an Internet search for small claims court procedures for your state.

DID YOU KNOW?

Websites such as LegalZoom, Nolo, and Rocket Lawyer are available to assist with basic legal documents, such as creating a will. Beyond this minimal document preparation, consumers are encouraged to consult a lawyer.

Legal services cost comparison

PRACTICE QUIZ 8-4

1 In what types of situations would small claims court and class-action suits be helpful?
2 Describe some situations in which you might use the services of a lawyer.

my life stages for consumer buying ...

YOUR PERSONAL FINANCE DASHBOARD

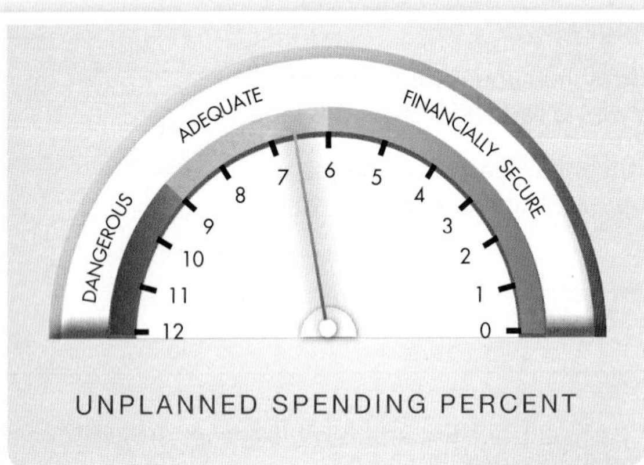

Unplanned spending, often called *impulse buying,* is a common danger in preventing effective financial planning. While people may spend to feel good about themselves, that action often results in budget problems, higher debt levels, and greater financial stress.

Measuring the key performance indicator of unplanned spending as part of your personal finance dashboard can contribute to your financial progress. Careful spending will result in lower debt, increased savings, and achieving your financial goals.

YOUR SITUATION Are you able to minimize the amount you spend on unplanned purchases? Are there areas of spending you might reduce? A low unplanned spending ratio can result in improved financial security. Other consumer buying actions you might consider during various stages of your life include:

. . . in college

- Maintain spending diary to monitor daily spending activities
- Develop research skills for making consumer purchases
- Learn wise buying techniques and comparison shopping strategies

. . . in my 20s

- Create a spending plan that allows for saving and avoids unnecessary spending
- Save funds for the purchase of expensive items to avoid credit costs
- Assess your needs for major consumer items

. . . in my 30s and 40s

- Update your spending activities based on changing household situations
- Teach other household members about wise buying strategies
- Save to replace major purchases, as needed

. . . in my 50s and beyond

- Determine spending needs in relation to current and future household situation
- Plan for changing in spending activities that might occur during retirement
- Consider the sale or donation of unneeded consumer items

SUMMARY OF LEARNING OBJECTIVES

LO8-1

Identify strategies for effective consumer buying.

An attraction to famous brand-name items can result in wasteful expenses. Various economic, social, and personal factors influence daily buying decisions. Overspending and poor money management are frequent causes of overuse of credit and other financial difficulties. Timing purchases, comparing buying sources and brands, using label information, computing unit prices, and evaluating warranties are common strategies for effective purchasing.

LO8-2

Implement a process for making consumer purchases.

A buying process with various stages can be useful when planning purchases. A research-based approach to consumer buying involves (1) preshopping activities, such as problem identification and information gathering; (2) evaluating alternatives; (3) determining the purchase price; and (4) postpurchase activities, such as proper operation and maintenance.

LO8-3

Identify steps to take to resolve consumer problems.

Knowing what actions to take when complaining about a consumer purchase can effectively resolve a situation. This process should involve these steps: (1) return to the place of purchase; (2) contact the company's main office; (3) obtain assistance from a consumer agency; and (4) take legal action.

LO8-4

Evaluate legal alternatives available to consumers.

The legal actions available to consumers include small claims court, class-action suits, the services of a lawyer, legal aid societies, and prepaid legal services. These legal means for handling consumer problems should be considered when a situation cannot be resolved through communication with the company or through the help of a consumer protection agency.

KEY TERMS

SELF-TEST PROBLEMS

1. An item bought on credit with a $60 down payment, and monthly payments of $70 for 36 months, would have a total cost of what amount?
2. A food package with 32 ounces costing $1.76, would have a unit cost of what amount?

Solutions

1. 36 × $70 = $2,520 plus the $60 down payment for a total of $2,580
2. $1.76 ÷ 32 = 5.5 cents an ounce

FINANCIAL PLANNING PROBLEMS

1. *Calculating Future Value.* You can purchase a service contract for all of your major appliances for $180 a year. If the appliances are expected to last for 10 years and you earn 5 percent on your savings, what would be the future value of the amount you will pay for the service contract? LO8-1
2. *Future Value of Wise Buying.* If a person saves $63 a month by using coupons and doing comparison shopping, (*a*) what is the amount for a year? (*b*) What would be the future value of this annual amount over 10 years, assuming an interest rate of 4 percent? LO8-1

LO8-2 **3.** *Comparing Buying Alternatives.* Tammy Monahan is considering the purchase of a home entertainment center. The product attributes she plans to consider and the weights she gives to them are as follows:

Portability	.1
Sound projection	.6
Warranty	.3

Tammy related the brands as follows:

	Portability	Sound Projection	Warranty
Brand A	6	8	7
Brand B	9	6	8
Brand C	5	9	6

Using the consumer buying matrix (p. 271), conduct a quantitative product evaluation rating for each brand. What other factors is Tammy likely to consider when making her purchase?

LO8-2 **4.** *Calculating the Cost of Credit.* John Walters is comparing the cost of credit to the cash price of an item. If John makes a $80 down payment and pays $34 a month for 24 months, how much more will that amount be than the cash price of $695?

LO8-2 **5.** *Computing Unit Prices.* Calculate the unit price of each of the following items:

Item	Price	Size	Unit Price
Motor oil	$1.95	2.5 quarts	_____ cents/quart
Cereal	2.17	15 ounces	_____ cents/ounces
Canned fruit	0.89	13 ounces	_____ cents/ounces
Facial tissue	2.25	300 tissues	_____ cents/100 tissues
Shampoo	3.96	17 ounces	_____ cents/ounces

LO8-2 **6.** *Calculating the Present Value of a Consumer Purchase.* What would be the net present value of a microwave oven that costs $159 and will save you $68 a year in time and food away from home? Assume an average return on your savings of 4 percent for five years.

LO8-2 **7.** *Comparing Automobile Purchases.* Based on financial and opportunity costs, which of the following do you believe would be the wiser purchase?

Vehicle 1: A three-year-old car with 45,000 miles, costing $8,700, and requiring $585 of immediate repairs.

Vehicle 2: A five-year-old car with 62,000 miles, costing $6,500, and requiring $960 of immediate repairs.

LO8-2 **8.** *Calculating Motor Vehicle Operating Costs.* Using Sheet 38 in the Personal Financial Planner, calculate the approximate yearly operating cost of the following vehicle.

Annual depreciation, $2,500

Annual mileage, 13,200

Current year's loan interest, $650

Miles per gallon, 24

Insurance, $680

License and registration fees, $65

Average gasoline price, $3.68 per gallon

Oil changes/repairs, $370

Parking/tolls, $420

9. *Buying* versus *Leasing a Motor Vehicle.* Based on the following, calculate the costs of buying and of leasing a motor vehicle. LO8-2

Purchase Costs		Leasing Costs	
Down payment	$1,500	Security deposit	$500
Loan payment	$450 for 48 months	Lease payment	$450 for 36 months
Estimated value at end of loan	$4,000	End of lease charges	$600
Opportunity cost interest rate:	4%		

FINANCIAL PLANNING ACTIVITIES

1. *Analyzing Influences on Consumer Buying.* Use advertisements, online articles, and personal observations to describe the economic, social, and personal factors influencing purchases of people in the following life situations: (a) a retired person; (b) a single parent with children ages 5 and 9; (c) a dual-income couple with no children; (d) a person with a dependent child and a dependent parent. LO8-1
2. *Comparing Consumer Information Sources.* Obtain online reviews to evaluate and compare different brands of a product. Also obtain information on the product from people who sell the item and those who have recently purchased it. Compare the information received from these sources. LO8-2
3. *Researching Consumer Purchases.* Using the consumer buying matrix (p. 271), analyze a consumer purchase you plan to make sometime in the future. What factors affected the selection of the attributes and weights you chose for this purchase analysis? LO8-2
4. *Comparing Used Cars.* Use Sheet 35 in the Personal Financial Planner to compare different sources of used motor vehicles. LO8-2
5. *Evaluating Motor Vehicle Leases.* Use Sheet 36 in the Personal Financial Planner to compare the costs of buying and leasing a motor vehicle. LO8-2
6. *Identifying and Solving Consumer Problems.* Conduct online research to determine the most common sources of consumer complaints. Interview someone who has had a consumer complaint. What was the basis of the complaint? What actions did the person take? Was the complaint resolved in a satisfactory manner? LO8-3
7. *Comparing Legal Services.* Prepare a survey of legal services available to students and others in your community. Use Sheet 39 in the Personal Financial Planner to compare the fees and services provided by lawyers and other sources of legal assistance. LO8-4

FINANCIAL PLANNING CASE

Online Car Buying

With a click of the mouse, Mackenzie enters the auto "showroom." In the past few months she had realized that the repair costs for her 11-year-old car were accelerating. She thought it was time to start shopping for a new car online and decided to start her Internet search for a vehicle by looking at small and mid-sized SUVs.

Her friends suggested that Mackenzie research more than one type of vehicle. They reminded her that comparable models were available from various auto manufacturers.

In her online car-buying process, Mackenzie next did a price comparison. She obtained more than one price quote by using various online sources. She then prepared an overview of her online car buying experiences.

Online Car-Buying Action	Online Activities	Websites Consulted
Information gathering	• Review available vehicle models and options • Evaluate operating costs and safety features	http://autos.msn.com www.consumerreports.org www.caranddriver.com www.motortrend.com
Comparing prices	• Identify specific make, model, and features desired • Locate availability and specific price in your geographic area.	www.autosite.com www.edmunds.com www.kbb.com www.nada.com
Finalize purchase	• Make payment or financing arrangements • Conduct in-person inspection • Arrange for delivery	www.autobytel.com www.autonation.com www.autoweb.com www.carsdirect.com

Mackenzie's next step was to make her final decision. After selecting what she planned to buy, she finalized the purchase online and decided to take delivery at a local dealer.

In recent years, less than 5 percent of car buyers have actually purchased vehicles over the Internet. That number is increasing; however, car buying experts strongly recommend that you make a personal examination of the vehicle before taking delivery.

Questions

1. Based on Mackenzie's experience, what benefits and drawbacks are associated with online car buying?
2. What additional actions might Mackenzie consider before buying a motor vehicle?
3. What do you consider to be the benefits and drawbacks of shopping online for motor vehicles and other items?

PERSONAL FINANCIAL PLANNER IN ACTION

Comparison Shopping and Buying Motor Vehicles

Daily buying actions such as comparing prices, evaluating brands, and avoiding fraud allow you to wisely use resources for both current living expenses and long-term financial security.

Your Short-Term Financial Planning Activities	*Resources*
1. Compare the use of cash and credit, and various brands, for the purchase of a major consumer item you may need in the near future.	PFP Sheets 33, 37 www.ConsumerReports.org www.pricescan.com www.bbbonline.org
2. Conduct a unit pricing comparison at several stores.	PFP Sheet 32 www.consumer.gov
3. Determine current transportation needs related to new and used motor vehicles and compare buying and leasing options.	PFP Sheets, 34, 35, 36 http://autoadvice.about.com www.leaseguide.com www.kbb.com www.leasesource.com
Your Long-Term Financial Planning Activities	*Resources*
1. Determine buying guidelines for major purchases (appliances, furniture, home entertainment equipment). Identify brands, store locations, and savings plans to avoid buying on credit.	www.consumer.gov www.pueblo.gsa.gov www.consumerworld.org

2. Identify and compare various legal services available for use.	PFP Sheet 39 www.ftc.gov www.fraud.org www.nolo.com
3. Identify motor vehicles that would provide the lowest operating and insurance costs.	PFP Sheet 38 www.consumerreports.org www.autobytel.com www.carsafety.org

CONTINUING CASE

Making Purchase Decisions

Life Situation

Single
Age 24
No dependents
Graduate and engaged

Financial Data

Monthly Income	$1,750
Living Expenses	$1,210
Personal property	$7,300
Savings	$5,000
Student loan	$4,200
Credit card debt	$1,500

Shelby and Mark have been preparing for their wedding, which is now three months away. In addition, they have been discussing what furniture and other items each of them will bring into the relationship. They realize that some of the items are worn out and will need to be replaced such as the sofa. Further, they are planning to replace Shelby's car as it is old, unreliable, and requires frequent repairs. They need a second car and while they love the idea of owning a new car, they realize that a used car would be a better option for them so that they can reach their goals of owning a condo and opening Shelby's pet salon within the next two years.

Questions

1. What strategies should they use to research and purchase a used car and other high dollar items such as furniture?
2. What items should Shelby and Mark consider a part of the real cost of owning a car?
3. Explain how Shelby and Mark might use the Personal Financial Planner sheets (Used-Car Purchase Comparison and Buying versus Leasing an Automobile).

DAILY SPENDING DIARY

"Using the daily spending diary has helped me control impulse buying. When I have to write down every amount, I'm more careful in my spending. I can now put more in savings."

Directions

Consider continuing (or starting) the use of a "Daily Spending Diary" to record and monitor your cash outflows. Sheets are provided for you to record *every cent* of your spending in various categories. Most people who have participated in this activity have found it beneficial for monitoring and controlling their spending habits.

Analysis Questions

1. What daily spending items are amounts that might be reduced or eliminated to allow for higher savings amounts?
2. How might a "Daily Spending Diary" result in wiser consumer buying and more saving for the future?

The Daily Spending Diary Sheets are located in Appendix D at the end of the book and on the student website at www.mhhe.com/kdh.

chapter 9

The Housing Decision: Factors and Finances

Learning Objectives

LO9-1 Evaluate available housing alternatives.

LO9-2 Analyze the costs and benefits associated with renting.

LO9-3 Implement the home-buying process.

LO9-4 Calculate the costs associated with purchasing a home.

LO9-5 Develop a strategy for selling a home.

What will this mean for me?

Deciding whether to rent or buy housing is a fundamental personal finance decision. Balancing costs of a place to live with available resources requires research, analysis, and trade-offs between what you would like and what you can afford. An ability to know yourself and the housing market is the foundation of your home choice. At the same time, you must be aware of various rental, housing, and mortgage deceptions attempting to con renters and home buyers.

my life

PLANNING WHERE TO LIVE

Housing represents the largest expenditure most people will encounter. Your choice of a place to live will require an extensive use of your resources, both time and money.

To assess your attitudes and behaviors related to housing, for each of the following statements, select the choice that best describes your current situation.

1. When selecting a place to live, what is most important for you?
   a. Being close to work or school.
   b. The costs involved.
   c. Flexibility for moving in the future.
2. A benefit of renting for me would be
   a. ease of mobility.
   b. low initial costs.
   c. There are no benefits of renting for me.
3. The housing type I would purchase that would be best for me is
   a. a house.
   b. a condominium or townhouse.
   c. a mobile home.

(continued)

4. The type of mortgage I am most likely to use is
   a. a fixed-rate, 30-year mortgage.
   b. an adjustable rate mortgage.
   c. an FHA or VA mortgage.
5. When planning to sell my home, I would most likely
   a. sell it on my own.
   b. use the services of a real estate agent.
   c. attempt to sell it using an online service.

As you study this chapter, you will encounter "My Life" boxes with additional information and resources related to these items.

Housing Alternatives

LO9-1

Evaluate available housing alternatives.

As you travel through various neighborhoods, you will see a variety of housing types. When you assess housing alternatives, you need to identify the factors that will influence your choice.

YOUR LIFESTYLE AND YOUR CHOICE OF HOUSING

While the concept of *lifestyle*—how you spend your time and money—may seem intangible, it materializes in consumer purchases. Every buying decision is a statement about your lifestyle. Your lifestyle, needs, desires, and attitudes are reflected in your choice of a place to live. For example, some people want a kitchen large enough for family gatherings. Career-oriented people may want a lavish bathroom or a home spa where they can escape the pressures of work. As you select housing, you might consider the alternatives in Exhibit 9-1.

While personal preferences are the foundation of a housing decision, financial factors will modify the final choice. A budget and other financial records discussed in Chapter 3 can help you evaluate your income, living costs, and other financial obligations to determine an appropriate amount for your housing expenses.

my life 1

I consider various factors when selecting a place to live.

Use various information sources when making your housing decisions. These may range from discussions with people you know to using websites such as http://homebuying.about.com, http://realestate.msn.com, www.hud.gov/buying, and www.homefair.com.

OPPORTUNITY COSTS OF HOUSING CHOICES

Although the selection of housing is usually based on life situation and financial factors, you should also consider what you might have to give up. While the opportunity costs of your housing decision will vary, some common trade-offs include

- The interest earnings lost on the money used for a down payment on a home or the security deposit for an apartment.

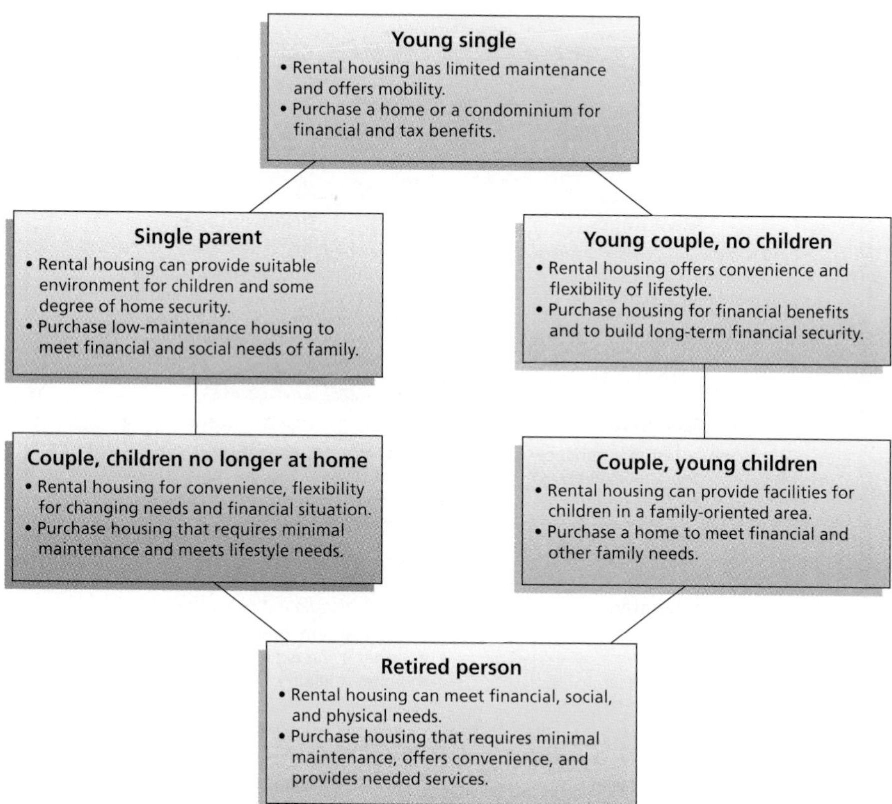

Exhibit 9-1

Housing for different life situations

- The time and cost of commuting to work when you live in an area that offers less expensive housing or more living space.
- The loss of tax advantages and equity growth when you rent a city apartment to be close to your work.
- The time and money you spend when you repair and improve a lower-priced home.
- The time and effort involved when you have a home built to your personal specifications.

Like every other financial choice, a housing decision requires consideration of what you give up in time, effort, and money.

Renting versus Buying Housing

Living in a mobile society affects the decision as to whether to rent or buy your housing. Your choice of residence should be analyzed based on lifestyle and financial factors. Exhibit 9-2 can help you assess various housing alternatives.

For many young people, renting may be preferable for now. However, if you plan to live in the same area for several years and believe real estate prices will increase, you should consider owning your home.

Some people who are financially able to buy a home may choose to rent to avoid the time and money commitment required to maintain a house. If you continue

Exhibit 9-2

Evaluating housing alternatives

EVALUATING HOUSING ALTERNATIVES

Renting
Apartment

Advantages	Disadvantages
• Easy to move • Fewer responsibilities for maintenance • Minimal financial commitment	• No tax benefits • Limitations regarding remodeling • May have restrictions regarding pets, other activities

Renting
House

Advantages	Disadvantages
• Easy to move; less maintenance • More room than apartment • Minimal financial commitment	• Higher utility expenses than apartment • Limitations regarding remodeling

Owning
New house

Advantages	Disadvantages
• No previous owner • Pride of ownership • Tax benefits	• Financial commitment • Higher living expenses than renting • Limited mobility

Owning
Previously owned house

Advantages	Disadvantages
• Pride of ownership • Established neighborhood • Tax benefits	• Financial commitment • Possibility of repairs or replacements • Limited mobility

Owning
Condominium

Advantages	Disadvantages
• Tax benefits • Fewer maintenance responsibilities than house • Usually good accessibility to recreation and business districts	• Less privacy than house • Financial commitment • Uncertain demand affecting property value • Potential disagreements with condominium association regarding rules • Assessment fees

Owning
Cooperative

Advantages	Disadvantages
• Ownership in form of nonprofit organization • Stable property values	• Frequently difficult to sell • Potential disagreements among members • Other members may have to cover costs of unrented units

Owning
Manufactured home (mobile home)

Advantages	Disadvantages
• Less expensive than other ownership options • Flexibility in selection of home features and appliances	• May be difficult to sell in future • Financing may be difficult to obtain • Construction quality may be poor

to rent, be sure to invest your savings so you can easily buy a home should the situation arise. Long-term renting may also be appropriate for people not able to maintain a home because of physical limitations.

As you can see in the Financial Planning Calculations feature on page 304 the choice between renting and buying usually is not obvious. In general, renting is less costly in the short run, but home ownership usually has long-term financial advantages.

Online sources are very useful for buying, selling, or renting a home.

Housing Information Sources

As with other consumer purchases, housing information is available. Start your data search with basic resources such as this book and other information sources. Consult online sources for information about renting, buying, financing, remodeling, and other housing topics. Other helpful information sources are friends, real estate agents, and government agencies (see Appendix C).

PRACTICE QUIZ 9-1

1 How does a person's employment and household situation influence the selection of housing?
2 What are some common opportunity costs associated with the selection of housing?

PFP Sheet 40
Current and future housing needs

PFP Sheet 41
Renting versus buying housing

Renting Your Residence

LO9-2
Analyze the costs and benefits associated with renting.

Are you interested in a "2-bd. garden apt, a/c, crptg, mod bath, lndry, sec $850"? Not sure? Translated, this means a two-bedroom garden apartment (at or below ground level) with air conditioning, carpeting, a modern bath, and laundry facilities. An $850 security deposit is required.

At some point in your life, you are likely to rent your place of residence. You may rent when you are first on your own or later in life when you want to avoid the activities required to maintain your own home. About 35 percent of U.S. households live in rental units.

RENTING VERSUS BUYING YOUR PLACE OF RESIDENCE

Comparing the costs of renting and buying involves consideration of a variety of factors. The following framework and example provide a basis for assessing these two housing alternatives. The apartment in the example has a monthly rent of $1,250, and the home costs $200,000. A 28 percent tax rate is assumed.

Although the numbers in this example favor buying, remember that in any financial decision, calculations provide only part of the answer. You should also consider your needs and values, and assess the opportunity costs associated with renting and buying.

	Example	Your Figures
RENTAL COSTS		
Annual rent payments	$ 15,000	$ ______
Renter's insurance	210	______
Interest lost on security deposit (amount of security deposit times after-tax savings account interest rate)	36	______
Total annual cost of renting	$ 15,246	
BUYING COSTS		
Annual mortgage payments	$ 15,168	______
Property taxes (annual costs)	4,800	______
Homeowner's insurance (annual premium)	600	______
Estimated maintenance and repairs (1%)	2,000	______
After-tax interest lost on down payment and closing costs	750	______
Less (financial benefits of home ownership):		______
Growth in equity	−1,120	− ______
Tax savings for mortgage interest (annual mortgage interest times tax rate)	−3,048	− ______
Tax savings for property taxes (annual property taxes times tax rate)	−1,344	− ______
Estimated annual appreciation (1.5%)*	−3,000	− ______
Total annual cost of buying	$ 14,806	

*This is a nationwide average; actual appreciation of property will vary by geographic area and economic conditions.

As a tenant, you pay for the right to live in a residence owned by someone else. Exhibit 9-3 presents the activities involved in finding and living in a rental unit.

SELECTING A RENTAL UNIT

An apartment is the most common type of rental housing. Apartments range from modern, luxury units with extensive recreational facilities to simple one- and two-bedroom units in quiet neighborhoods.

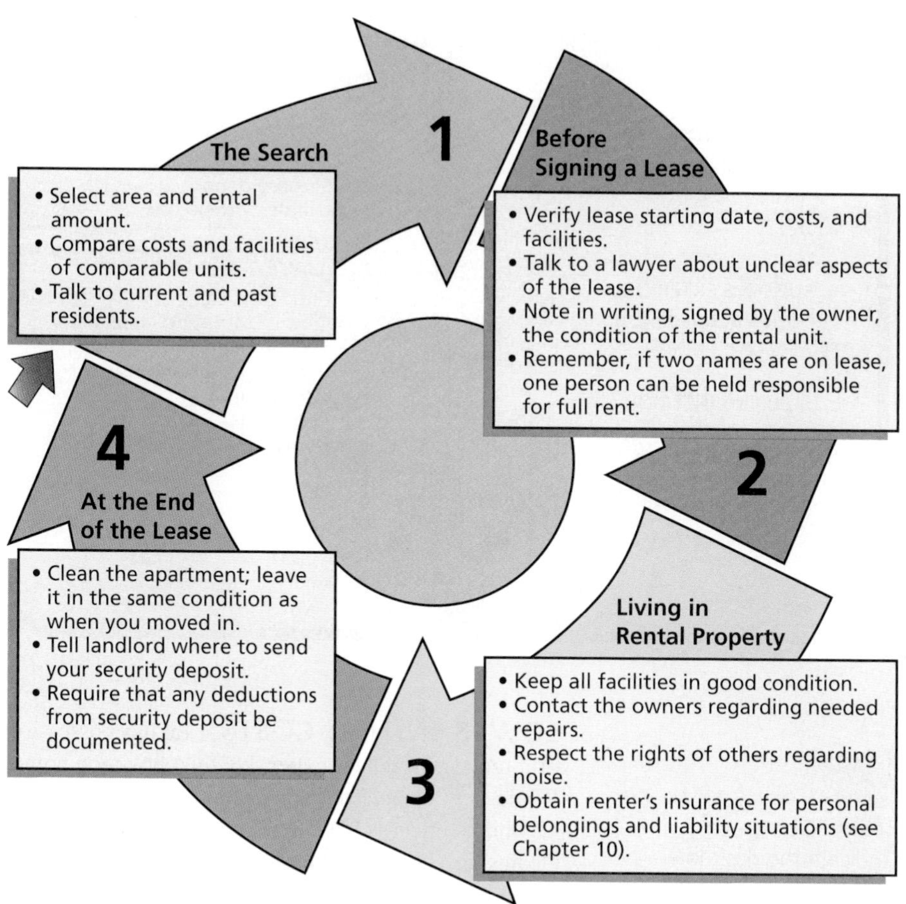

Exhibit 9-3

Housing rental activities

If you need more room, you should consider renting a house. The increased space will cost more, and you will probably have some responsibility for maintaining the property. If you need less space, you may rent a room in a private house.

The main sources of information on available rental units are newspaper ads, real estate and rental offices, and people you know. When comparing rental units, consider the factors presented in Exhibit 9-4.

ADVANTAGES OF RENTING

The three main advantages of renting are mobility, fewer responsibilities, and lower initial costs.

MOBILITY Renting offers mobility when a location change is necessary or desirable. A new job, a rent increase, the need for a larger apartment, or the desire to live in a different community can make relocation necessary. Moving is easier when you are renting than when you own a home. After you have completed school and started your career, renting makes job transfers easier.

FEWER RESPONSIBILITIES Renters have fewer responsibilities than homeowners since they usually do not have to be concerned with maintenance and repairs. However, they are expected to do regular household cleaning. Renters also have fewer financial concerns. Their main housing costs are rent and utilities, while homeowners incur expenses related to property taxes, property insurance, and upkeep.

Exhibit 9-4

Selecting an apartment

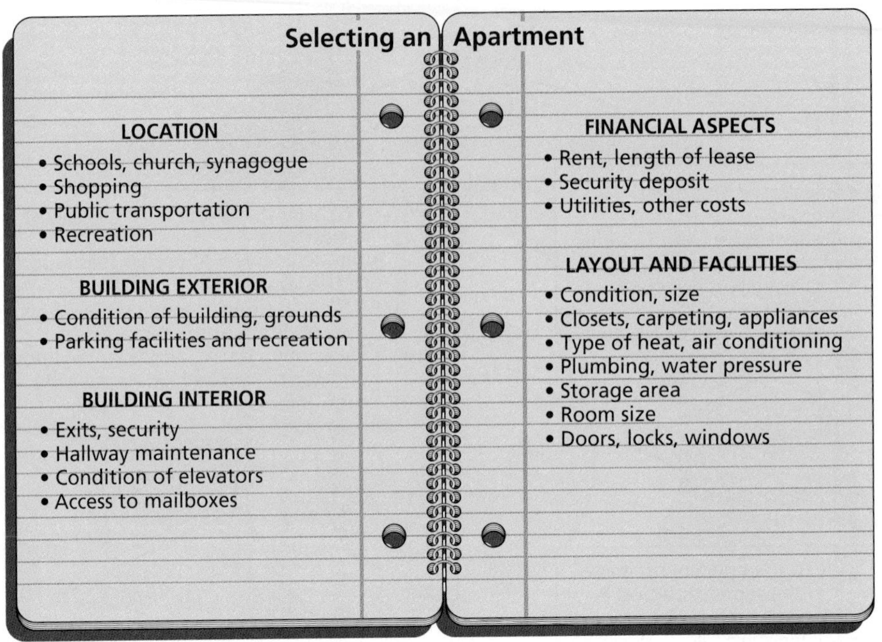

DID YOU KNOW?

The *price-to-rent ratio,* the relationship between home prices annual rents, can indicate the desirability of owning over renting. During the past 20 years, the average ratio has been about 15. When home prices rose, the number was 20 or more in some areas. More recently, the number has lowered. Real estate advisors suggest a ratio of 18 or lower when you buy to possibly avoid a lower home value after your purchase.

LOWER INITIAL COSTS Taking possession of a rental unit is less expensive than buying a home. While new tenants usually pay a security deposit, a new home buyer is likely to have a down payment and closing costs of several thousand dollars.

DISADVANTAGES OF RENTING

Renting has few financial benefits, may impose a restricted lifestyle, and involves legal details.

FEW FINANCIAL BENEFITS Renters do not enjoy the financial advantages homeowners do. Tenants cannot take tax deductions for mortgage interest and property taxes or benefit from the increased value of real estate. They are subject to rent increases over which they have little control.

RESTRICTED LIFESTYLE Renters are generally limited in the types of activities they can pursue in their place of residence. Sound from a home entertainment system or parties may be monitored closely. Tenants are often subject to restrictions regarding pets and decorating the rental unit.

lease A legal document that defines the conditions of a rental agreement.

LEGAL DETAILS Most tenants sign a **lease,** a legal document that defines the conditions of a rental agreement. This document provides the following information:

- A description of the property, including the address.
- The name and address of the owner/landlord (the *lessor*).
- The name of the tenant (the *lessee*).
- The effective date of the lease.

- The length of the lease.
- The amount of the security deposit.
- The amount and due date of the monthly rent.
- The location at which the rent must be paid.
- The date and amount due of charges for late rent payments.
- A list of the utilities, appliances, furniture, or other facilities that are included in the rental amount.
- The restrictions regarding certain activities (pets, remodeling).
- The tenant's right to sublet the rental unit.
- The charges for damages or for moving out of the rental unit later (or earlier) than the lease expiration date.
- The conditions under which the landlord may enter the apartment.

Standard lease forms include conditions you may not want to accept. The fact that a lease is printed does not mean you must accept it as is. If you have a high credit score, you may be able to negotiate a lower rent or a reduced security deposit. Also, discuss with the landlord any lease terms you consider unacceptable.

Some leases give you the right to *sublet* the rental unit. Subletting may be necessary if you must vacate the premises before the lease expires. Subletting allows you to have another person take over rent payments and live in the rental unit.

Most leases are written, but oral leases are also valid. With an oral lease, one party must give a 30-day written notice to the other party before terminating the lease or imposing a rent increase.

A lease provides protection to both landlord and tenant. The tenant is protected from rent increases during the lease term unless the lease contains a provision allowing an increase. In most states, the tenant cannot be locked out or evicted without a court hearing. The lease gives the landlord the right to take legal action against a tenant for nonpayment of rent or destruction of property.

my life 2

I am aware of the benefits of leasing.

Before signing a lease, be sure that you understand the various elements of this legal document. For additional information on leases, and the potential benefits and drawbacks of renting, go to http://apartments.about.com.

DID YOU KNOW?

Lease-to-purchase and *rent-with-option* allow renters to become homeowners; however, problems can occur. Beware of offers that may seem beneficial but can turn into financial disasters. For example, an upfront deposit and other purchase funds could be lost if a late rent payment is made.

COSTS OF RENTING

A *security deposit* is usually required when you sign a lease. This money is held by the landlord to cover the cost of any damages done to the rental unit during the lease period. The security deposit is usually one month's rent.

Several state and local governments require that the landlord pay interest on a security deposit. After you vacate the rental unit, your security deposit should be refunded within a reasonable time. Many states require that it be returned within 30 days of the end of the lease. If money is deducted from your security deposit, you have the right to an itemized list of the cost of repairs.

As a renter, you will incur other living expenses besides monthly rent. For many apartments, water is covered by the rent; however, other utilities may not be covered. If you rent a house, you will probably pay for heat, electricity, water, and telephone. When you rent, you should obtain insurance coverage for your personal property. Renter's insurance is discussed in Chapter 10.

Apartment rental comparison

PRACTICE QUIZ 9-2

1 What are the main benefits and drawbacks of renting a place of residence?
2 Which components of a lease are likely to be most negotiable?

The Home-Buying Process

LO9-3

Implement the home-buying process.

Many people dream of having a place of residence they can call their own. Home ownership is a common financial goal. Exhibit 9-5 presents the process for achieving this goal.

STEP 1: DETERMINE HOME OWNERSHIP NEEDS

In the first phase of the home-buying process, you should consider the benefits and drawbacks of this major financial commitment. Also, evaluate different types of housing units and determine the amount you can afford.

EVALUATE OWNING YOUR PLACE OF RESIDENCE

What Are the Benefits of Home Ownership? Whether you purchase a house, a condominium, or a manufactured home, you can enjoy the pride of ownership, financial benefits, and lifestyle flexibility of home ownership.

Exhibit 9-5

The home-buying process

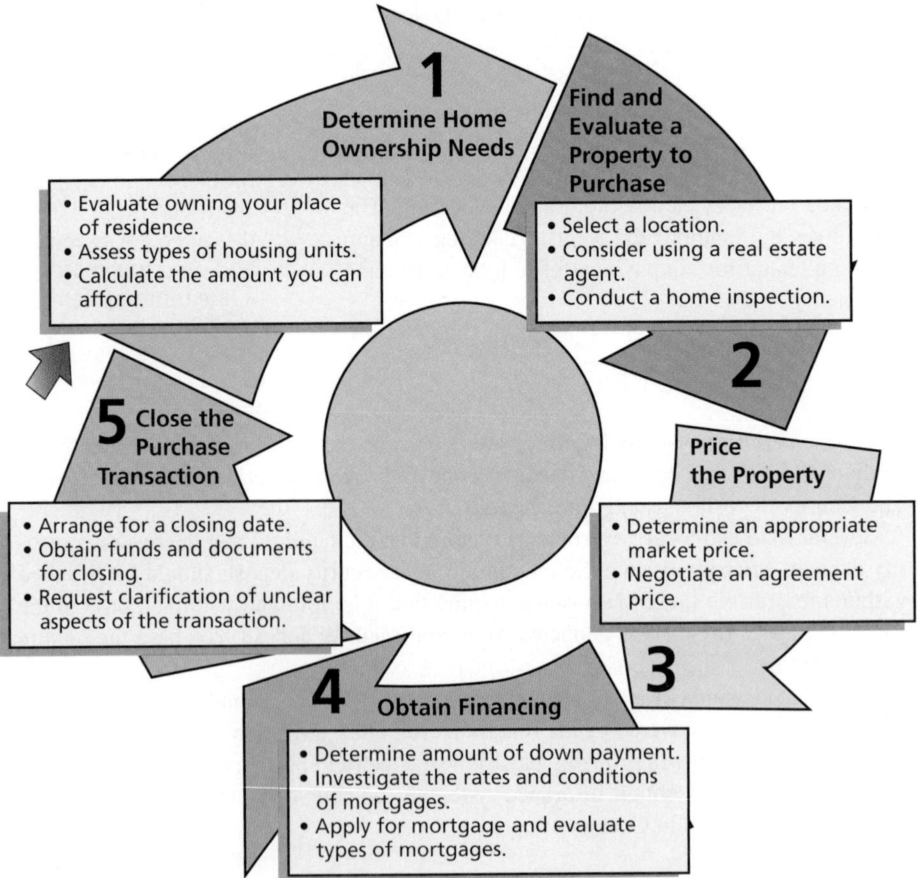

1. *Pride of ownership.* Having a place to call their own is a primary motive of many home buyers. Stability of residence and a personalized living location can be important.
2. *Financial benefits.* One financial benefit is the deductibility of mortgage interest and real estate tax payments for federal income taxes. A potential benefit is increases in the value of the property. Finally, homeowners in most states may be able to borrow against the equity in their homes. *Equity* is the home value less the amount owed on the mortgage.
3. *Lifestyle flexibility.* While renting gives you mobility, home ownership gives you more opportunity to express individuality. Homeowners have greater freedom than renters in decorating their dwellings and entertaining guests.

What Are the Drawbacks of Home Ownership? The American dream of buying one's own home does not guarantee a glamorous existence. This investment can result in financial uncertainty, limited mobility, and higher living costs.

1. *Financial uncertainty.* Among the financial uncertainties associated with buying a home is obtaining money for a down payment. Obtaining mortgage financing may be a problem due to your personal situation or current economic conditions. Finally, changing property values in an area can affect your financial investment.
2. *Limited mobility.* Home ownership does not provide ease of changing living location as does renting. If changes in your situation make it necessary to sell your home, doing so may be difficult. High interest rates and other factors can result in a weak demand for housing.
3. *Higher living costs.* Owning your place of residence can be expensive. The homeowner is responsible for maintenance and costs of repainting, repairs, and home improvements.

Real estate taxes are a major expense of homeowners. Higher property values and higher tax rates mean higher real estate taxes. Higher taxes affect homeowners more directly than renters, who pay them in the form of higher rent. It is harder for homeowners to counter the effects of high taxes by moving to less expensive housing.

Home ownership allows you the flexibility to decorate as you desire.

ASSESS TYPES OF HOUSING AVAILABLE

Seven housing options are commonly available to home buyers:

1. *Single-family dwellings* are the most popular form of housing. These residences include previously owned houses, new houses, and custom-built houses. Older houses may be preferred by people who want a certain style and quality of housing.
2. *Multiunit dwellings,* dwellings with more than one living unit, include duplexes and townhouses. A *duplex* is a building that contains two separate homes. A *townhouse* contains two, four, or six single-family living units.
3. **Condominiums** are individually owned housing units in a building with several units. Individual ownership does not include the common areas, such as hallways, outside grounds, and recreational facilities. These areas are owned by the condominium association, which is run by the people who own the housing units. The condominium association oversees the management and operation of the housing complex. Condominium owners are charged a monthly fee to cover the maintenance, repairs, improvements, and insurance for the building and common areas. A condominium is not a type of building structure; it is a legal form of home ownership.

condominium An individually owned housing unit in a building with several such units.

HOW TO ...

Appeal Your Property Taxes

Property taxes vary from area to area and usually range from 2 to 4 percent of the market value of the home. Taxes are based on the *assessed value,* the amount that your local government determines your property to be worth for tax purposes. Assessed values are normally lower than the market value, often about half. A home with a market value of $180,000 may be assessed at $90,000. If the tax rate is $60 per $1,000 of assessed value, this would result in annual taxes of $5,400 ($90,000 divided by $1,000 times $60). This rate is 6 percent of the assessed value but only 3 percent of the market value.

Although higher home values are desirable, this increase means higher property assessments. Quickly increasing property taxes are frustrating, but there are actions you can take:

Step 1: Know the appeal deadline. Call the local assessor's office. You will usually have between 14 and 90 days to initiate your appeal. Late requests will most likely not be accepted. Send your appeal by certified mail to have proof that you met the deadline; keep copies of all documents.

Step 2: Check for mistakes. The assessment office may have incorrect information. Obvious mistakes may include incorrect square footage or an assessment may report a home with four bedrooms when there are only three.

Step 3: Determine the issues to emphasize. A property tax appeal can be based on a mistake in the assessment or a higher assessment than comparable homes. Note items that negatively affect the value of your home. For example, a bridge is no longer in operation near your home, making your house much less accessible—and less valuable. Or if a garage has been taken down to increase garden space, the home's value likely would be less. Compare your assessment with homes of the same size, age, and general location. Obtain comparisons for 5 to 10 homes.

Step 4: Prepare for the hearing. Gather evidence and prepare an organized presentation. Use photos of comparable properties. A spreadsheet can make it easy for the hearing officials to view your evidence. Suggest a specific corrected assessment, and give your reasons. Observe the hearing of another person to become familiar with the process.

cooperative housing A form of housing in which a building containing a number of housing units is owned by a nonprofit organization whose members rent the units.

manufactured home A housing unit that is fully or partially assembled in a factory before being moved to the living site.

4. **Cooperative housing** is a form of housing in which the units in a building are owned by a nonprofit organization. The shareholders purchase stock to obtain the right to live in a unit in the building. While the residents do not own the units, they have the legal right to occupy a unit for as long as they own stock in the cooperative association. The title for the property belongs to the co-op. This ownership arrangement is different from condominiums, in which residents own the individual living unit.
5. **Manufactured homes** are housing units that are fully or partially assembled in a factory and then moved to the living site. There are two basic types of manufactured homes. One type is the *prefabricated home,* with components built in a factory and then assembled at the housing site. With this type of housing, mass production can keep building costs lower.
6. *Mobile homes* are a second type of manufactured home. Since very few mobile homes are moved from their original sites, the term is not completely accurate. These housing units are typically less than 1,000 square feet in size; however, they usually

offer the same features as a conventional house—fully equipped kitchens, fireplaces, cathedral ceilings, and whirlpool baths. The site for a mobile home may be either purchased or leased in a development specifically designed for such housing units.

The safety of mobile homes is often debated. Fires occur no more frequently in these housing units than in other types of homes. But due to the construction of mobile homes, a fire may spread faster than in conventional houses. Manufacturers' standards for the fire safety of mobile homes are higher than in the past. Still, when a fire occurs in a mobile home, the unit is often completely destroyed. This type of housing is also vulnerable to wind damage.

Another common concern about mobile homes is their tendency to depreciate in value. When this occurs, an important benefit of home ownership is eliminated. Depreciation may make it difficult to obtain financing to purchase a mobile home.

7. *Building a home* is another option. Some people want a home built to their specifications. Before you begin such a project, be sure you possess the necessary knowledge, money, and perseverance. When choosing a contractor to coordinate the project, consider the following:

   - Does the contractor have the experience needed to handle the type of building project you require?
   - Does the contractor have a good working relationship with the architect, materials suppliers, electricians, plumbers, carpenters, and other personnel needed to complete the project?
   - What assurance do you have about the quality of materials?
   - What arrangements must be made for payments during construction?
   - What delays in the construction process will be considered legitimate?
   - Is the contractor licensed and insured?
   - Is the contractor willing to provide names, addresses, and phone numbers of satisfied customers?
   - Have local consumer agencies received any complaints about this contractor?

Your written contract should include a time schedule, cost estimates, a description of the work, and a payment schedule.

DETERMINE HOW MUCH YOU CAN AFFORD

As you determine how much of your budget you will spend on a home, consider the price of the house along with its size and quality.

I know how to research which housing type would be best for me.

As you start the home-buying process, you need to consider what you can afford to spend. You can prequalify for a mortgage online at www.mortgage101.com or www.erate.com.

Price and Down Payment The amount you can spend is affected by funds available for a down payment, your income, and your current living expenses. Other factors you should consider are current mortgage rates, the potential future value of the property, and your ability to make monthly mortgage, tax, and insurance payments. To determine how much you can afford to spend on a home, have a loan officer at a mortgage company or other financial institution *prequalify* you. This service is provided without charge.

DID YOU KNOW?

A second-story addition, a remodeled bathroom, an updated kitchen, addition of a deck, and a finished basement are the home upgrades most likely to add value to a home.

Size and Quality You may not get all the features you want in your first home, but financial advisors suggest you get into the housing market

Before buying a home, be sure to inspect all aspects of the property you are considering.

by purchasing what you can afford. As you move up in the housing market, your second or third home can include more of the features you want.

Ideally, the home you buy will be in good condition. In certain circumstances, you may be willing to buy a *handyman's special,* a home that needs work and that you are able to get at a lower price because of its condition. You will then need to put more money into the house for repairs and improvements or to invest *sweat equity* by doing some of the work yourself. Home improvement information and assistance are available from hardware stores and other home product retailers.

STEP 2: FIND AND EVALUATE A PROPERTY TO PURCHASE

Next, you should select a location, consider using the services of a real estate agent, and conduct a home inspection.

SELECTING A LOCATION An old adage among real estate professionals is that the three most important factors to consider when buying a home are *location, location,* and *location!* Perhaps you prefer an urban, a suburban, or a rural setting. Or perhaps you want to live in a small town or in a resort area. In selecting a neighborhood, compare your values and lifestyle with those of current residents.

zoning laws Restrictions on how the property in an area can be used.

Be aware of **zoning laws,** restrictions on how the property in an area can be used. The location of businesses and the anticipated construction of industrial buildings or a highway may influence your buying decision.

If you have or plan to have a family, you should assess the school system. Educators recommend that schools be evaluated on program variety, achievement level of students, percentage of students who go to college, dedication of faculty members, facilities, school funding, and involvement of parents. Homeowners without children also benefit from strong schools, since the educational advantages of a community help maintain property values.

USING A REAL ESTATE AGENT A real estate agent can help you assess your housing needs and determine the amount you can afford to spend. Real estate agents have information about areas of interest and what housing is available to buy.

DID YOU KNOW?

The CLUE® (Comprehensive Loss Underwriting Exchange) report provides a five-year history of insurance losses at a property that a home buyer is considering for purchase. This disclosure report is an independent source of information. Further information is at www.choicetrust.com.

The main services a real estate agent provides include (1) presenting your offer to the seller, based on current market conditions, (2) negotiating a settlement price, (3) assisting you in obtaining financing, and (4) representing you at the closing. A real estate agent will also recommend lawyers, insurance agents, home inspectors, and mortgage companies to serve your needs.

Since the seller of the home usually pays the real estate agent's commission, the buyer may not incur a direct cost. However, this expense is reflected in the price paid for the home. In some states, the agent could be working for the seller. In others, the agent may be working for the buyer, the seller, or as a *dual agent,* working for both the buyer and the seller. When dual agency exists, some states require that buyers sign a disclosure acknowledging that they are aware the agent is working for both buyer and seller. This agreement, however, can limit the information provided to each party.

Many states now have *buyer agents* who represent the buyer's interests. In these situations, the buyer agent may be paid by either the seller or the buyer.

CONDUCTING A HOME INSPECTION Before reaching your decision about a specific home, conduct a complete evaluation of the property. An evaluation by a trained home inspector can minimize future problems. Do not assume everything is in proper working condition just because someone lives there now. Being cautious and determined will save you headaches and unplanned expenses. Exhibit 9-6 presents a suggested format for inspecting a home. A home purchase agreement may include the right to have various professionals (roofer, plumber, electrician) inspect the property.

Some states, cities, and lenders require inspection documents. The mortgage company will usually conduct an *appraisal* to determine the fair market value of the property. An appraisal is not a detailed inspection.

STEP 3: PRICE THE PROPERTY

After you have selected a home, determine an offer price and negotiate a final buying price.

Exhibit 9-6 Conducting a home inspection

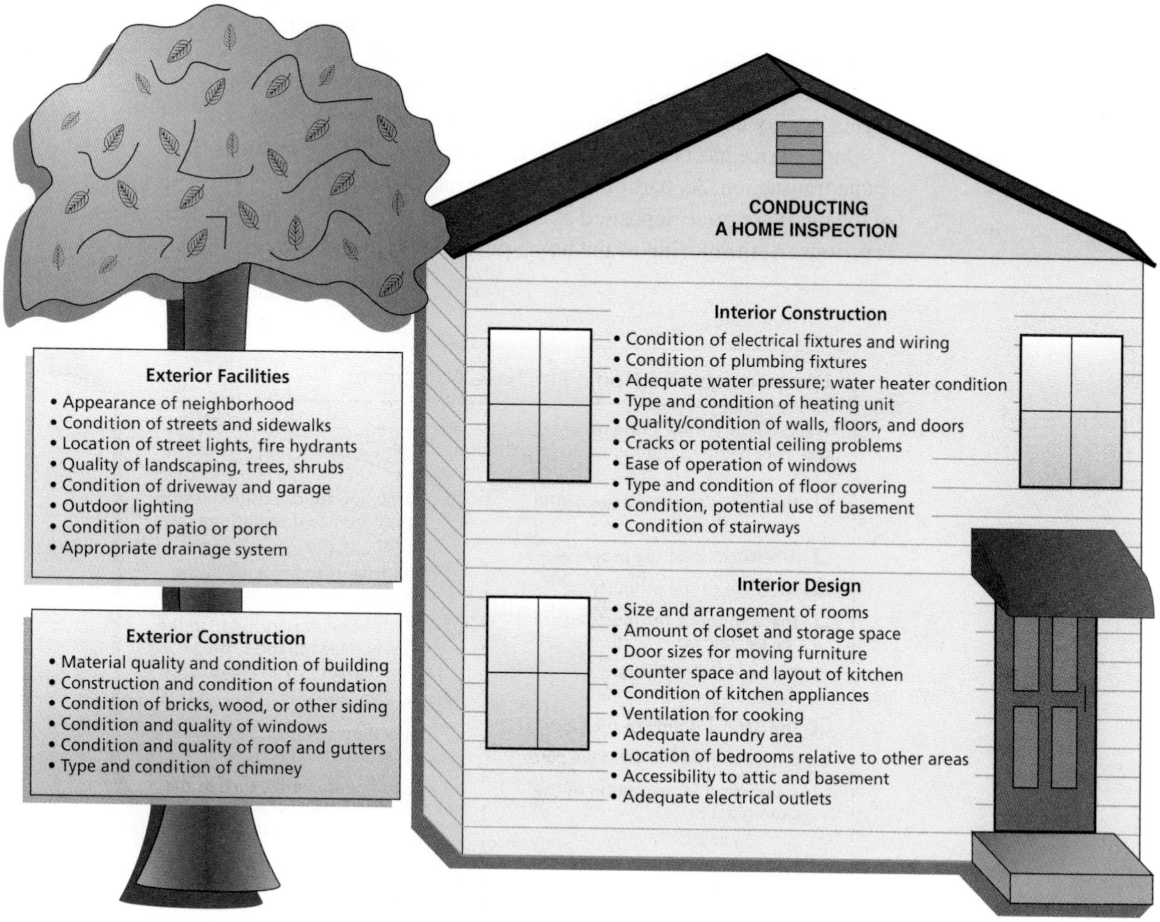

DETERMINING THE HOME PRICE What price should you offer for the home? The main factors to consider are recent selling prices in the area, current demand for housing, the length of time the home has been on the market, the owner's need to sell, financing options, and features and condition of the home. Each of these factors can affect your offer price. For example, you will have to offer a higher price in times of low interest rates and high demand for homes. On the other hand, a home that has been on the market for over a year could mean an opportunity to offer a lower price. The services of a real estate agent or an appraiser can assist you in assessing the current value of the home.

Your offer will be in the form of a *purchase agreement,* or contract (see Exhibit 9-7). This document constitutes your legal offer to purchase the home. Your first offer price usually will not be accepted.

NEGOTIATING THE PURCHASE PRICE If your initial offer is accepted, you have a valid contract. If your offer is rejected, you have several options, depending on the seller. A *counteroffer* from the owner indicates a willingness to negotiate a price settlement. If the counteroffer is only slightly lower than the asking price, you are expected to move closer to that price with your next offer. If the counteroffer is quite a bit off the asking price, you are closer to the point where you might split the difference to arrive at the purchase price. If no counteroffer is forthcoming, you may wish to make another offer to determine whether the seller is willing to negotiate.

In times of high demand for housing, negotiating may be minimized; this situation is referred to as a *seller's market,* since the current homeowner is likely to have several offers for the property. In contrast, when home sales are slow, a *buyer's market* exists and a lower price is likely.

When you buy a previously owned home, your negotiating power is based on current market demand and the current owner's need to sell. When you buy a new home, a slow market may mean lower prices or an opportunity to obtain various amenities (fireplace, higher quality carpeting) from the builder at a lower cost.

earnest money A portion of the price of a home that the buyer deposits as evidence of good faith to indicate a serious purchase offer.

Once a price has been agreed on, the purchase contract becomes the basis for the real estate transaction. As part of the offer, the buyer must submit **earnest money,** a portion of the purchase price deposited as evidence of good faith to show that the purchase offer is serious. At the closing of the home purchase, the earnest money is applied toward the

Exhibit 9-7

The components of a home purchase agreement

Components of a Home Purchase Agreement

In a real estate transaction, the contract between buyer and seller contains the following information:

- ❑ The names and addresses of the buyer and seller
- ❑ A description of the property
- ❑ The price of the property
- ❑ The amount of the mortgage that will be needed
- ❑ The amount of the earnest money deposit
- ❑ The date and time of the closing
- ❑ Where the closing will take place
- ❑ A provision for extension of the closing date
- ❑ A provision for disposition of the deposit money if something goes wrong
- ❑ Adjustments to be made at the closing
- ❑ Details of what is included in the sale—home appliances, drapes, carpeting, and other items
- ❑ Special conditions of the sale
- ❑ Inspections the buyer can make before the closing
- ❑ Property easements, such as the use of an area of the property for utility lines or poles

Source: *Homeownership: Guidelines for Buying and Owning a Home* (Richmond, VA: Federal Reserve Bank of Richmond).

down payment. This money is usually returned if the sale cannot be completed due to circumstances beyond the buyer's control.

Home purchase agreements often contain a *contingency clause*. This contract condition states that the agreement is binding only if a certain event occurs. For example, a real estate contract may stipulate that the contract will not be valid unless the buyer obtains financing for the purchase within a certain period of time, or it may make the purchase of a home contingent on the sale of the buyer's current home.

PRACTICE QUIZ 9-3

1 What are the advantages and disadvantages of owning a home?
2 What guidelines can be used to determine the amount to spend for a home purchase?
3 How can the quality of a school system benefit even homeowners in a community who do not have school-age children?
4 What services are available to home buyers from real estate agents?
5 How does a *seller's* market differ from a *buyer's* market?

The Finances of Home Buying

LO9-4

Calculate the costs associated with purchasing a home.

While looking for a place to buy, also consider your financing options. Most homebuyers will meet with a banker or mortgage broker early in the process to determine the amount they can afford for their home. Financing a home purchase requires obtaining a mortgage, an awareness of types of mortgages, and settling the real estate transaction.

STEP 4: OBTAIN FINANCING

DETERMINE DOWN PAYMENT The amount of cash available for a down payment will affect the size of the mortgage loan you require. A large down payment, such as 20 percent or more, will make it easier for you to obtain a mortgage.

Personal savings, pension plan funds, sales of investments or other assets, and assistance from relatives are the most common sources of a down payment. Parents can help their children purchase a home by giving them a cash gift or a loan.

Private mortgage insurance (PMI) is usually required if the down payment is less than 20 percent. This coverage protects the lender from financial loss due to default. PMI charges, which the borrower pays, vary depending on the amount of the down payment and the credit score. These costs may be paid in full at closing or are sometimes financed over the life of the mortgage, through a monthly fee, depending on the type of financing.

After building up 20 percent equity in a home, a home buyer should contact the lender to cancel PMI. The Homeowners Protection Act requires that a PMI policy be terminated automatically when a homeowner's equity reaches 22 percent of the property value at the time the mortgage was executed. Homeowners can request termination earlier if they can provide proof that the equity in the home has grown to 20 percent of the current market value. Additional information is available at www.privatemi.com.

DID YOU KNOW?

Today, with a strong credit score (700 or higher), a person can obtain home financing without a down payment. This high credit score will also likely result in a lower mortgage rate and less required paperwork to process the loan.

mortgage A long-term loan on a specific piece of property such as a home or other real estate.

QUALIFYING FOR A MORTGAGE Do you have funds for a down payment? Do you earn enough to make mortgage payments while covering other living expenses? Do you have a good credit rating? Unless you pay cash for a home, a favorable response to these questions is necessary.

A **mortgage** is a long-term loan on a specific piece of property such as a home or other real estate. Payments on a mortgage are usually made over 10, 15, 20, 25, or 30 years. Banks, savings and loan associations, credit unions, and mortgage companies are the most common home financing sources. *Mortgage brokers* can help home buyers obtain financing, since they are in contact with several financial institutions. A mortgage broker may charge higher fees than a lending institution with which you deal directly.

DID YOU KNOW?

By taking out a 15-year instead of a 30-year mortgage, a home buyer borrowing $200,000 can save more than $150,000 in interest over the life of the loan. The faster equity growth with the shorter mortgage is also a benefit.

To qualify for a mortgage, you must meet criteria similar to those for other loans. The home you buy serves as security, or *collateral,* for the mortgage. The major factors that affect the affordability of your mortgage are your income, other debts, the amount available for a down payment, the length of the loan, and current mortgage rates.

The recent subprime crisis, when many mortgages were issued to borrowers with poor credit histories, resulted in numerous loan defaults. As a result, lenders are facing new regulations. To ensure your creditworthiness for a home loan, pay down your credit cards, make payments on time to existing loan accounts, and accumulate funds for a down payment. This process can improve the mortgage amount for which you qualify. The results calculated in Exhibit 9-8 are (*a*) the

Exhibit 9-8 Housing affordability and mortgage qualification amounts

	Example A	Example B
Step 1: Determine your monthly gross income (annual income divided by 12).	$48,000 ÷ 12	$48,000 ÷ 12
Step 2: With a down payment of at least 5 percent, lenders use 33 percent of monthly gross income as a guideline for PITI (principal, interest, taxes, and insurance) and 38 percent of monthly gross income as a guideline for PITI plus other debt payments.	$ 4,000 × .38 $ 1,520	$ 4,000 × .33 $ 1,320
Step 3: Subtract other debt payments (e.g., payments on an auto loan) and an estimate of the monthly costs of property taxes and homeowner's insurance.	−380 −300	— −300
(a) Affordable monthly mortgage payment	$ 840	$1,020
Step 4: Divide this amount by the monthly mortgage payment per $1,000 based on current mortgage rates—an 8 percent, 30-year loan, for example (see Exhibit 9-9)—and multiply by $1,000.	÷ $ 7.34 × $1,000	÷ $ 7.34 × $1,000
(b) Affordable mortgage amount	$114,441	$138,965
Step 5: Divide your affordable mortgage amount by 1 minus the fractional portion of your down payment (e.g., 1 – .1 with a 10 percent down payment).	÷ .9	÷ .9
(c) Affordable home purchase price	$127,157	$154,405

Note: The two ratios lending institutions use (step 2) and other loan requirements may vary based on a variety of factors, including the type of mortgage, the amount of the down payment, your income level, and current interest rates. For example, with a down payment of 10 percent or more and a credit score exceeding 720, the ratios might increase to 40/45 or 45/50 percent in the above exhibit.

monthly mortgage payment you can afford, (*b*) the mortgage amount you can afford, and (*c*) the home purchase price you can afford.

The procedures in Exhibit 9-8 include the following:

1. Indicate your monthly gross income.
2. Multiply your monthly gross income by 0.33 (or 0.38 if you have other debts, such as an auto loan). Lenders commonly use 33 and 38 percent as guidelines to determine the amount most people can comfortably afford for housing.
3. After subtracting the monthly debt payments and an estimate of the monthly cost for property taxes and homeowner's insurance, you arrive at your *affordable monthly mortgage payment (a).*
4. Divide (*a*) by the factor from Exhibit 9-9, based on your mortgage term (in years) and rate. Then multiply your answer by $1,000 to convert your figure to thousands of dollars. This gives you your *affordable mortgage amount (b).* Exhibit 9-9 provides the factors for determining the amount you need to pay back $1,000 over 15, 20, 25, or 30 years based on various interest rates.
5. To obtain your *affordable home purchase price (c),* divide (*b*) by the amount you will be financing, such as 0.9 when you make a 10 percent down payment.

These sample calculations are typical of those most financial institutions use; the actual qualifications for a mortgage may vary by lender and by the type of mortgage. Your credit record, job stability, and assets, along with current mortgage interest rates, will affect the amount of the mortgage loan for which you qualify.

The mortgage loan amount for which you can qualify will usually be larger when interest rates are lower. As interest rates rise, fewer people will be able to afford the cost of an average-priced home. For example, a person who can make a monthly mortgage payment of $700 will qualify for a 30-year loan of:

$130,354 at 5 percent	$95,368 at 8 percent
$116,667 at 6 percent	$86,956 at 9 percent
$105,263 at 7 percent	$79,726 at 10 percent

Exhibit 9-9

Mortgage payment factors (principal and interest factors per $1,000 of loan amount)

Term Rate	30 Years	25 Years	20 Years	15 Years
3.0%	$4.22	$4.74	$5.55	$6.91
3.5	4.49	5.01	5.80	7.15
4.0	4.77	5.28	6.06	7.40
4.5	5.07	5.56	6.33	7.65
5.0	5.37	5.85	6.60	7.91
5.5	5.68	6.14	6.88	8.17
6.0	6.00	6.44	7.16	8.43
6.5	6.32	6.67	7.45	8.71
7.0	6.65	7.06	7.75	8.98
7.5	6.99	7.39	8.06	9.27
8.0	7.34	7.72	8.36	9.56
8.5	7.69	8.05	8.68	9.85

EXAMPLE: Calculate Mortgage Payment

To determine the amount of your monthly mortgage payment, multiply the factor from Exhibit 9-9 by the number of thousands of the loan amount. For a 30-year, 7 percent, $223,000 mortgage:

Monthly payment amount = 223 × $6.65
= $1,482.95

In addition to using the mortgage payment factors from Exhibit 9-9, the monthly payment may be calculated using a formula, a financial calculator, Excel spreadsheet, website, or app. Loan payment amounts may also be determined using these methods:

Formula	Financial Calculator		Excel®
$M = P[i(1 + i)n]/[(1 + i)n - 1]$	(payments a year)	12 P/YR	= PMT (rate/12,30*12,loan amount)
M = mortgage payment (monthly)	(total loan payments)	360 N	= denotes a formula
P = principal of the loan (loan amount)	(interest rate)	6 I/YR	rate/12 provides monthly rate
i = interest rate divided by 12	(loan amount)	180000 PV	total number of payments, such as 12 a year for 30 years
n = number of months of the loan	(calculate monthly payment)	PMT	loan amount – beginning mortgage balance

points Prepaid interest charged by a lending institution for the mortgage; each discount point is equal to 1 percent of the loan amount.

EVALUATING POINTS When you compare costs at several mortgage companies, the interest rate you are quoted is not the only factor to consider. The required down payment and the points charged will affect the interest rate. **Points** are prepaid interest charged by the lender. Each *discount point* is equal to 1 percent of the loan amount and should be viewed as a premium you pay for obtaining a lower mortgage rate. In deciding whether to take a lower rate with more points or a higher rate with fewer points, do the following:

1. Determine the dollar difference between the monthly payments you will make for the two different situations.
2. Determine the difference between the points charged for the two different rates or at two different lenders.
3. Divide the result in step 2 by the result in step 1. This will tell you the break-even point of how many months it will take for the lower monthly payment to offset the higher cost of the points.

If you plan to live in your home longer than the time calculated in step 3, paying the points and taking the lower mortgage rate is probably the best action. This decision will, however, be affected by the amount of funds available to pay the points at the time of closing. If you plan to sell your home sooner than the time calculated in step 3, the higher mortgage rate with fewer discount points may be better.

DID YOU KNOW?

By taking out a 15-year instead of a 30-year mortgage, a home buyer borrowing $200,000 can save more than $150,000 in interest over the life of the loan. The faster equity growth and savings on interest with the shorter mortgage will also occur if a homebuyer pays an additional amount toward principal each month.

THE APPLICATION PROCESS Applying for a mortgage involves three main phases:

1. *Prequalification,* which involves completing the mortgage application. The borrower presents evidence of employment, income, ownership of assets, and amounts of existing debts. The lender obtains a credit report and verifies other aspects of the borrower's application and financial status. A decision to approve or deny the mortgage is made, indicating the maximum mortgage for which you qualify.
2. *Fee payment and obtain commitment,* at this point, lenders will likely charge a fee of between $400 and $500. The loan commitment is the financial institution's decision to provide the funds to purchase the home, which is when the purchase contract becomes legally binding. You decide whether to *lock in* an interest rate for 30–90 days, or if you believe rates may drop, you may *float,* locking in your rate at a later point in time.
3. *Finding a property* that you desire to purchase. An *appraisal* of the home occurs to determine the value based on location, features, and condition.

FIXED-RATE, FIXED-PAYMENT MORTGAGES As Exhibit 9-10 shows, fixed-rate, fixed-payment mortgages are one of the two major types of mortgages.

Conventional Mortgages The **conventional mortgage** usually has equal payments over 15, 20, or 30 years based on a fixed interest rate. This mortgage offers home buyers certainty about future loan payments. The mortgage payments are set at a level that allows **amortization** of the loan; that is, the balance owed is reduced with each payment. Since the amount borrowed is large, the payments made during the early years of the mortgage are applied mainly to interest, with only small reductions in the principal of the loan. As the amount owed declines, the monthly payments have an increasing impact on the loan balance. Near the end of the mortgage term, nearly all of each payment is applied to the balance.

conventional mortgage A fixed-rate, fixed-payment home loan with equal payments over 10, 15, 20, 25, or 30 years.

amortization The reduction of a loan balance through payments made over a period of time.

Exhibit 9-10 Types of mortgage loans

Loan Type	Benefits	Drawbacks
1. Conventional 30-year mortgage.	• Fixed monthly payments for 30 years provide certainty of principal and interest payments.	• Higher initial rates than adjustables.
2. Conventional 15- or 20-year mortgage.	• Lower rate than 30-year fixed; faster equity buildup and quicker payoff of loan.	• Higher monthly payments.
3. FHA/VA fixed-rate mortgage (30-year and 15-year).	• Low down payment requirements and fully assumable with no prepayment penalties.	• May require additional processing time.
4. Adjustable-rate mortgage (ARM)—payment changes on 1-, 3-, 5-, 7-, or 10-year schedules.	• Lower initial rates than fixed-rate loans, particularly on the 1-year adjustable. Offers possibility of future rate and payment decreases. Loans with rate "caps" may protect borrowers against increases in rates.	• Shifts far greater interest rate risk onto borrowers than fixed-rate loans. May push up monthly payments in future years.
5. Interest-only mortgage	• Lower payments; more easily affordable.	• No decrease in amount owed; no building equity unless home value increases.

For example, a $125,000, 30-year, 6 percent mortgage would have monthly payments of $749.44. The payments would be divided as follows:

	Interest	Principal	Remaining Balance
For the first month	$625.00 ($125,000 × 0.06 × 1/12)	$124.44	$124,875.56 ($125,000 − $124.44)
For the second month	624.72 ($124,966.82 × 0.06 × 1/12)	125.06	124,750.50 ($124,875.56 − $125.06)
For the 360th month	3.73	745.71	–0–

my life 4

I understand the various types of mortgages.

What are the current mortgage rates in your area? The information may be obtained at www.bankrate.com, www.hsh.com, and www.interest.com as well as from local financial institutions.

In the past, many conventional mortgages were *assumable.* This feature allowed a home buyer to continue with the seller's original agreement. Assumable mortgages were especially attractive if the mortgage rate was lower than market interest rates at the time of the sale. Today, due to volatile interest rates, few assumable mortgages are offered.

Government Financing Programs *Government financing programs* include loans insured by the Federal Housing Authority (FHA) and loans guaranteed by the Veterans Administration (VA). These government agencies do not provide the mortgage money; rather, they help home buyers obtain low-interest, low-down-payment loans.

To qualify for an FHA-insured loan, a person must meet certain conditions related to the down payment and fees. Most low- and middle-income people can qualify for the FHA loan program. The minimum down payment starts at 3.5 percent and varies depending on the loan size. This lower down payment makes it easier for a person to purchase a home. The borrower is required to pay a fee for insurance that protects the lender from financial loss due to default.

The VA-guaranteed loan program assists eligible armed services veterans with home purchases. As with the FHA program, the funds for VA loans come from a financial institution or a mortgage company, with the risk reduced by government participation. A VA loan can be obtained without a down payment, with the rate based on the borrower's credit score.

Both FHA-insured loans and VA-guaranteed loans can be attractive financing alternatives and are assumable by future owners when the house is sold to qualifying buyers. Both impose limits on the amount one can borrow, and a backlog of processing applications and approving loans may occur during periods of high demand.

adjustable-rate mortgage (ARM) A home loan with an interest rate that can change during the mortgage term due to changes in market interest rates; also called a *flexible-rate mortgage* or a *variable-rate mortgage.*

rate cap A limit on the increases and decreases in the interest rate charged on an adjustable-rate mortgage.

payment cap A limit on the payment increases for an adjustable-rate mortgage.

ADJUSTABLE-RATE, VARIABLE-PAYMENT MORTGAGES As noted in Exhibit 9-10, The **adjustable-rate mortgage (ARM),** also referred to as a *flexible-rate mortgage* or a *variable-rate mortgage,* has an interest rate that increases or decreases during the life of the loan. When mortgage rates were at record highs, many people took out variable-rate home loans, expecting rates would eventually go down. ARMs usually have a lower initial interest rate than fixed-rate mortgages; however, the borrower, not the lender, bears the risk of future interest rate increases.

A **rate cap** restricts the amount by which the interest rate can increase or decrease during the ARM term. This limit prevents the borrower from having to pay an interest rate significantly higher than the one in the original agreement. Most rate caps limit increases (or decreases) in the mortgage rate to one or two percentage points in a year and to no more than five points over the life of the loan.

A **payment cap** keeps the payments on an adjustable-rate mortgage at a given level or limits the amount to which those payments can rise. When payment amounts do not rise but interest rates do, the amount owed can increase in months in which the mortgage payment does not cover the interest owed. This increased loan balance, called *negative amortization,* means the amount of the home equity is decreasing instead of increasing. As a result of these increases in the amount owed, the borrower usually has to make payments for a period longer than planned. Beware: Some adjustable-rate mortgages may stretch out as long as 40 years.

Consider several factors when you evaluate adjustable-rate mortgages: (1) determine the frequency of and restrictions on allowed changes in interest rates; (2) consider the frequency of and restrictions on changes in the monthly payment; (3) investigate the possibility that the loan will be extended due to negative amortization, and find out whether the mortgage agreement limits the amount of negative amortization; (4) find out what index the lending institution will use to set the mortgage interest rate over the term of the loan.

A lending institution will revise the rate for an adjustable-rate mortgage based on changes in interest rates. The London Interbank Offered Rate (LIBOR) is most commonly used as a base index for setting rates for adjustable rate mortgages. Studies reveal that an ARM can be less costly over the life of a mortgage as long as interest rates remain fairly stable.

DID YOU KNOW?

Housing phone apps are available to make the home buying process easier. These include programs to identify nearby homes available for sale, along with price information and other data. Other apps provide estimates of home values, community crime data, open-house information, and mortgage calculators.

INTEREST-ONLY MORTGAGE An *interest-only mortgage* allows a homebuyer to have lower payments for the first few years of the loan. During that time, none of the mortgage payment goes toward the loan amount. Once the initial period ends, the mortgage adjusts to be interest only at the new payment rate. Or, a borrower may obtain a different type of mortgage to start building equity.

Remember, with an interest-only mortgage, higher payments will occur later in the loan. The payment will be based on the amount of the original loan since no principal has been paid. Interest-only mortgages can be especially dangerous if the value of the property declines.

A variety of mortgage companies are available to finance your home purchase.

OTHER FINANCING METHODS To assist first-time home buyers, builders and financial institutions offer financing plans to make the purchase easier.

Buy-Downs A **buy-down** is an interest rate subsidy from a home builder or a real estate developer that reduces the mortgage payments during the first few years of the loan. This assistance is intended to stimulate sales among home buyers who cannot afford conventional financing. After the buy-down period, the mortgage payments increase to the level that would have existed without the financial assistance. A buy-down can also be purchased with a buyer's own funds.

buy-down An interest rate subsidy from a home builder or a real estate developer purchased by the buyer that reduces a home buyer's mortgage payments during the first few years of the loan.

Second Mortgages A **second mortgage,** more commonly called a *home equity loan,* allows a homeowner to borrow on the paid-up value of the property. Traditional second mortgages allow a homeowner to borrow a lump sum against the equity and repay it in monthly installments. Recently, lending institutions have offered a variety of home equity loans, including a line of credit program that allows the borrower to obtain additional funds. You need to be careful when using a home equity line of credit. This revolving credit plan can keep you continually in debt as you request new cash advances.

second mortgage A cash advance based on the paid-up value of a home; also called a *home equity loan.*

A home equity loan makes it possible to deduct the interest on consumer purchases on your federal income tax return. However, it creates the risk of losing the home if

ARE YOU AWARE OF . . .?

Buying a Home Online. Technology makes it possible to purchase a home without ever meeting in person with a mortgage broker or the title insurance representative. Financing activities will include (a) online mortgage prequalification, (b) comparing mortgage rates with various lenders, and (c) a Web-based mortgage application. Price negotiation involves e-mail, and the online *closing* is conducted with the mortgage provider sending the settlement documents electronically. Documents are "signed" on a specially formatted screen. The Electronic Signature in Global and National (ESIGN) Commerce Act allows this process to take place. This law recognizes an *electronic signature* as "an electronic sound, symbol, or process, attached to or logically associated with a contract or other record and executed or adopted by a person with the intent to sign the record." Traditionally, the recording of documents and issuing of the title insurance policy takes up to 45 days. Online, the process is completed in three hours.

Co-op College Housing. Students are saving thousands of dollars for their housing by living in an off-campus co-op. This living arrangement does require you to do various chores as part of your "payment." However, the few hours a week can result in reducing housing costs by several thousands of dollars. In recent years, the North American Students of Cooperation (www.nasco.coop) has helped students organize housing cooperatives near the University of Virginia, Penn State, the University of Rochester, and Western Michigan University.

Tenant Rights. When you sign a lease, you are assured of (a) *habitability*—a building with minimum health and safety standards that is free of serious defects and has running water, heat, and electricity; (b) prompt return of your security deposit, including interest when required by state law; and (c) an advance notice of rent increases and eviction, as prescribed in the lease. For additional information on tenant rights, check your lease or conduct a Web search.

Mortgage Fraud. Each year, mortgage fraud costs lenders more than $1 billion. These scams most often occur when a person misrepresents income or the home value in an effort to obtain a loan. While banks and mortgage lenders are usually the victims, individual investors may also face losses. Communities are affected when the deception results in vacant buildings that are in disrepair. To avoid participating in mortgage fraud, be sure to verify that a mortgage company is properly licensed and report any incorrect information in the lending process.

required payments on both the first and second mortgages are not made. To help prevent financial difficulties, home equity loans for amounts that exceed 70 percent of your equity are not allowed in many states.

reverse mortgage A loan based on the equity in a home, that provides elderly homeowners with tax-free income and is paid back with interest when the home is sold or the homeowner dies.

refinancing The process of obtaining a new mortgage on a home to get a lower interest rate.

Reverse Mortgages Programs are available to assist people who have a high equity in their homes and need cash. **Reverse mortgages** provide elderly homeowners with tax-free income in the form of a loan that is paid back (with interest) when the home is sold or the homeowner dies. You must be 62 to qualify. These financing plans, also called *home equity conversion mortgages,* allow a person to access funds in several ways. A person may take a lump sum, a line of credit, monthly payments, or a combination of a credit line and regular payments. As with any financial decision, obtain reliable information and consider alternatives, such as a home equity loan. Beware of dishonest reverse mortgage providers that charge exorbitant fees.

Refinancing During the term of a mortgage, you may want to **refinance,** that is, obtain a new mortgage at a lower rate. Before taking this action, consider the refinancing costs in relation to the savings with a lower monthly payment, and how long you plan to be in the home. Refinancing is often advantageous when you can get at least a one percent lower rate than your current rate. To assess the situation, divide the costs of refinancing by the amount saved each month to determine the number of months to cover your costs. Refinancing benefits will occur more quickly with larger mortgages.

Another financing decision involves making extra payments on your mortgage (see the Financial Planning for Life's Situations feature on page 324).

STEP 5: CLOSE THE PURCHASE TRANSACTION

Before finalizing the transaction, do a *walk-through* to inspect the condition and facilities of the home you plan to buy. You can use a digital camera to collect evidence for any last-minute items you may need to negotiate.

The *closing* involves a meeting among the buyer, seller, and lender of funds, or representatives of each party, to complete the transaction. Documents are signed, last-minute details are settled, and appropriate amounts are paid. A number of expenses are incurred at the closing. The **closing costs,** also referred to as *settlement costs,* are the fees and charges paid when a real estate transaction is completed (see Exhibit 9-11).

Title insurance is one closing cost. This coverage has two phases. First, the title company defines the boundaries of the property being purchased and conducts a search to determine whether the property is free of claims such as unpaid real estate taxes. Second, during the mortgage term, the title company protects the owner and the lender against financial loss resulting from future defects in the title and from other unforeseen property claims not excluded by the policy.

Also due at closing time is the deed recording fee. The **deed** is the document that transfers ownership of property from one party to another. With a *warranty deed,* the

closing costs Fees and charges paid when a real estate transaction is completed; also called *settlement costs.*

title insurance Insurance that, during the mortgage term, protects the owner and lender against financial loss resulting from future defects in the title and from other unforeseen property claims not excluded by the policy.

deed A document that transfers ownership of property from one party to another.

Exhibit 9-11 Common closing costs

At the transaction settlement of a real estate purchase and sale, the buyer and seller will encounter a variety of expenses that are commonly referred to as *closing costs.*

	Cost Range Encountered	
	By the Buyer	**By the Seller**
Title search fee	\$150–\$375	—
Title insurance	\$700–\$1500	\$800–\$1800
Attorney's fee	\$400–\$700	\$50–\$700
Property survey	—	\$100–\$400
Appraisal fee (or nonrefundable application fee)	\$400–\$600	—
Recording fees; transfer taxes	\$ 95–\$130	\$15–\$30
Settlement fee	\$500–\$1000+	—
Termite inspection	\$ 70–\$150	—
Lender's origination fee	1–3% of loan amount	—
Reserves for home insurance and property taxes	Varies	—
Interest paid in advance (from the closing date to the end of the month) and "points"	Varies	—
Real estate broker's commission	—	4–7% of purchase price

Note: The amounts paid by the buyer are in addition to the down payment.

SHOULD YOU PAY OFF YOUR MORTGAGE EARLY?

If you have a mortgage, you might consider paying it off early. Make sure the mortgage does not include a *prepayment penalty,* a fee you pay for the privilege of retiring a loan early. Most mortgages do not include this penalty. Before paying off your mortgage early, however, consider the tax deductions you may lose and your lost earnings on the money you use to retire this debt.

Instead of paying off your entire mortgage early, consider paying an additional amount each month—for example, $25. Since this amount will be applied to the loan principal, you will save interest and pay off the mortgage in a shorter time than the contracted period.

Paying an additional amount each month can save you tens of thousands of dollars in interest. However, financial advisors warn that before paying an additional amount on your mortgage, be sure to pay off your credit card balances and other high-interest debt.

Beware of organizations that promise to help you make additional payments on your mortgage. This is something you could do on your own, and they are likely to charge you a fee for doing it. In addition, these organizations frequently collect money from you every two weeks but make a payment only once a month, which gives them the use of thousands of *your* dollars to invest for their gain.

seller guarantees the title is good. This document certifies that the seller is the true owner of the property, there are no claims against the title, and the seller has the right to sell the property.

Mortgage insurance is another possible closing cost. If required, mortgage insurance protects the lender from loss resulting from a mortgage default.

The Real Estate Settlement Procedures Act (RESPA) helps home buyers understand the closing process and closing costs. This legislation requires that loan applicants be given certain information, including an estimate of the closing costs, before the actual closing. Obtaining this information as early as possible will allow you to plan for the closing costs. Information on RESPA is available online at www.hud.gov.

escrow account Money, usually deposited with the lending financial institution, for the payment of property taxes and homeowner's insurance.

At the closing and when you make your monthly payments, you will probably deposit money to be used for home expenses. For example, the lender will require that you have property insurance. An **escrow account** is money, usually deposited with the lending institution, for the payment of property taxes, homeowner's insurance, and private mortgage insurance. This account protects the lender from financial loss due to unpaid real estate taxes or damage from fire or other hazards.

As a new home buyer, you might also consider purchasing an agreement that gives you protection against defects in the home. *Implied warranties* created by state laws may cover some problem areas; other repair costs can occur. Home builders and real estate sales companies offer warranties to buyers. Coverage offered commonly provides protection against structural, wiring, plumbing, heating, and other mechanical defects. Most home warranty programs have many limitations.

In addition, a new homeowner may purchase a service contract from a real estate company such as Century 21 or Remax. This agreement warrants appliances, plumbing, air conditioning and heating systems, and other items for one year. As with any service contract, you must decide whether the coverage provided and the chances of repair expenses justify the cost.

HOME BUYING: A SUMMARY

For most people, buying a home is the most expensive decision they will undertake. As a reminder, Exhibit 9-12 on page 325 provides an overview of the major elements to consider when making this critical financial decision.

Exhibit 9-12

The main elements of buying a home

- **Location.** Consider the community and geographic region. A $250,000 home in one area may be an average-priced house, while in another part of the country it may be fairly expensive real estate. The demand for homes is largely affected by the economy and the availability of jobs.
- **Down payment.** While making a large down payment reduces your mortgage payments, you will also need the funds for closing costs, moving expenses, repairs, or furniture.
- **Mortgage application.** When applying for a home loan, you will usually be required to provide copies of recent tax returns, pay stubs, w–2 forms, a residence and employment history,information about bank and investment accounts, a listing of debts, and evidence of auto and any real estate ownership.
- **Points.** You may need to select between a higher rate with no discount points and a lower rate requiring points paid at closing.
- **Closing costs.** Settlement costs can range from 2 to 6 percent of the loan amount. This means you could need as much as $6,000 to finalize a $100,000 mortgage; this amount is in addition to your down payment.*
- **PITI.** Your monthly payment for principal, interest, taxes, and insurance is an important budget item. Beware of buying "too much house" and not having enough for other living expenses.
- **Maintenance costs.** As any homeowner will tell you, owning a home can be expensive. Set aside funds for repair and remodeling expenses.

*Some states limit the amount of closing costs.

PRACTICE QUIZ 9-4

1 What are the main sources of money for a down payment?
2 What factors affect a person's ability to qualify for a mortgage?
3 How do changing interest rates affect the amount of mortgage a person can afford?
4 How do discount points affect the cost of a mortgage?
5 Under what conditions might an adjustable-rate mortgage be appropriate?
6 When might refinancing a mortgage be advisable?
7 How do closing costs affect a person's ability to afford a home purchase?

Housing affordability and mortgage qualification

Mortgage company comparison

Mortgage refinance analysis

Selling Your Home

LO9-5

Develop a strategy for selling a home.

Most people who buy a home will eventually be on the other side of a real estate transaction. Selling your home requires preparing it for selling, setting a price, and deciding whether to sell it yourself or use a real estate agent.

PREPARING YOUR HOME FOR SELLING

The effective presentation of your home can result in a fast and financially favorable sale. Real estate salespeople recommend that you make needed repairs and paint worn exterior and interior areas. Clear the garage and exterior areas of toys, debris, and old vehicles, and keep the lawn cut and the leaves raked. Keep the kitchen and bathroom clean. Avoid offensive odors by removing garbage and keeping pets and their areas clean. Remove excess furniture and dispose of unneeded items to make the house, closets, and storage areas look larger. When showing your home, open drapes and turn on lights to give it a pleasant atmosphere. Consider environmentally friendly features such as energy-saving lightbulbs and water-saving faucets. This effort will give your property a positive image and make it attractive to potential buyers.

DETERMINING THE SELLING PRICE

Putting a price on your home can be difficult. You risk not selling it quickly if the price is too high, and you may not get a fair amount if the price is too low. An **appraisal,** an estimate of the current value of the property, can provide a good indication of the price you should set.

appraisal An estimate of the current value of a property.

An appraisal is likely to cost between $200 and $300. This expense can help people selling a home on their own to get a realistic view of the property's value. An asking price is influenced by recent selling prices of comparable homes in your area, demand in the housing market, and available financing based on current mortgage rates.

The home improvements you have made may or may not increase the selling price. A hot tub or an exercise room may have no value for potential buyers. Among the most desirable improvements are energy-efficient features, a remodeled kitchen, an additional or remodeled bathroom, added rooms and storage space, a finished basement, a fireplace, and an outdoor deck or patio.

The time to think about selling your home is when you buy it and every day you live there. Daily maintenance, timely repairs, and home improvements will increase the future sales price.

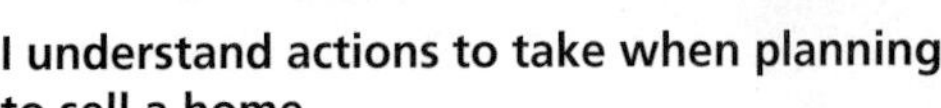

I understand actions to take when planning to sell a home.

When selling a home on your own, various information sources are available. You can find assistance at www.owners.com. Talking with people who have sold their home on their own is also valuable.

SALE BY OWNER

Each year, over 10 percent of home sales are made by the home's owners. If you decide to sell your home without using a real estate professional, price the home and advertise it through local newspapers, a detailed information sheet, and online. Obtain a listing sheet from a real estate office as an example of the information to include in your property description. Distribute information at stores, in other public areas, and online.

When selling your home on your own, obtain information about the availability of financing and financing requirements. This information will help you and potential buyers to determine whether a sale is possible. Use the services of a lawyer or title company to assist you with the contract, the closing, and other legal matters.

Require potential buyers to provide their names, addresses, telephone numbers, and background information, and show your home only by appointment. As a security measure, show it only when two or more adults are at home. Selling your own home can save you several thousand dollars in commission, but it requires an investment of time and effort.

LISTING WITH A REAL ESTATE AGENT

You may decide to sell your home with the assistance of a real estate agent. These businesses range from firms owned by one person to nationally franchised companies. Primary selection factors should be the real estate agent's knowledge of the community and the agent's willingness to actively market your home.

Your real estate agent will provide you with various services. These services include suggesting a selling price, making potential buyers and other agents aware of your home, providing advice on features to highlight, conducting showings of your home, and handling the financial aspects of the sale. A real estate agent can also help screen potential buyers to determine whether they will qualify for a mortgage.

Discount real estate brokers are available to assist sellers who are willing to take on certain duties and want to reduce selling costs. Companies such as Save More Real Estate and Help-U-Sell Real Estate charge a flat fee or 1 to 2 percent of the selling price instead of the customary 6 percent.

DID YOU KNOW?

A real estate *short sale* occurs when the new selling price is less than the amount owed on a previous mortgage. This alternative to foreclosure can result in a "bargain" for a homebuyer. However, beware that it may take a long time before the lender accepts the offer, if the offer is accepted at all. Also, the home is usually sold "as is," which means some items expected to be in the home may be missing or damaged. When doing a short sale, be sure to use a lawyer and a negotiator, and obtain a release from any deficiencies for previous loan amounts.

1. What actions are recommended when planning to sell your home?
2. What factors affect the selling price of a home?
3. What should you consider when deciding whether to sell your home on your own or use the services of a real estate agent?

my life stages for housing...

YOUR PERSONAL FINANCE DASHBOARD

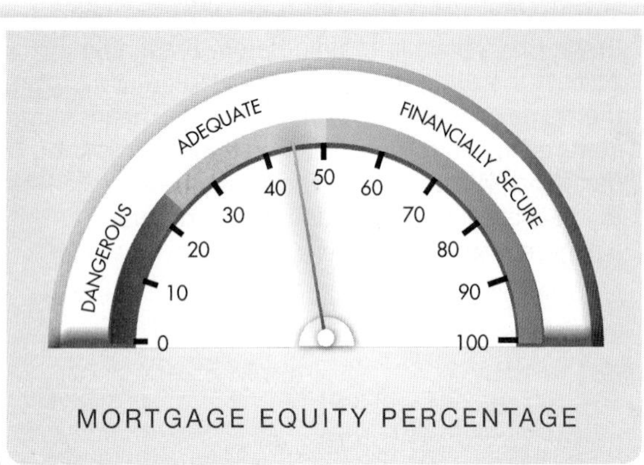

For homebuyers, *home equity,* the amount of your ownership in the property, can be an indicator of financial progress. Equity is calculated by subtracting the mortgage amount owed from the current market value of the home. For example, a home worth $200,000 with $80,000 still owed on the mortgage would have equity of $120,000, which is 60 percent of the home's value.

In recent years, as the market value of many homes declined, home equity became lower for many homeowners. Building equity through shorter mortgages and additional principal payments can be a key financial strategy.

YOUR SITUATION Are you able to make additional mortgage payments toward the loan principal to build the equity in your home? What budget areas might be reduced to be able to pay down your mortgage? Are there home improvements you might make to increase the market value of your home? Increased equity in your home is a vital component for building long-term financial security. Other housing actions you might consider during various stages of your life include

. . . in college

- Develop a positive renting reputation with the property owner
- Obtain an understanding of leases and rental activities
- Learn about the advantages and disadvantages of owning a home

. . . in my 20s

- Compare renting and buying your housing based on your finances and life situation
- Consider a savings fund that might be used for a down payment to buy a house
- Assess various types of mortgages

. . . in my 30s and 40s

- Make additional principal payments to reduce your mortgage balance
- Consider refinancing your mortgage based on lower interest rates
- Adapt your housing budget and situation based on changing family needs

. . . in my 50s and beyond

- Determine changes in housing needs resulting from changing life and household situations
- Consider various housing situations and locations for retirement

SUMMARY OF LEARNING OBJECTIVES

LO9-1

Evaluate available housing alternatives.

When selecting a place to live consider your needs, life situation, and financial resources. These major factors influence your selection of housing. Also, assess renting and buying alternatives in terms of their financial and opportunity costs.

LO9-2

Analyze the costs and benefits associated with renting.

The main benefits of renting are mobility, fewer responsibilities, and lower initial costs. The main disadvantages of renting are few financial benefits, a restricted lifestyle, and legal concerns.

LO9-3

Implement the home-buying process.

When assessing the type of housing that would be best for you to purchase, use the home-buying process: (1) determine home ownership needs, (2) find and evaluate a property to purchase, (3) price the property, (4) finance the purchase, and (5) close the real estate transaction.

LO9-4

Calculate the costs associated with purchasing a home.

The costs associated with purchasing a home include the down payment; mortgage origination costs; closing costs such as a deed fee, prepaid interest, attorney's fees, payment for title insurance, and a property survey; and an escrow account for homeowner's insurance and property taxes.

LO9-5

Develop a strategy for selling a home.

When planning to sell a home, you must decide whether to make certain repairs and improvements, determine a selling price, and choose between selling the home yourself and using the services of a real estate agent.

KEY TERMS

adjustable-rate mortgage (ARM) 320
amortization 319
appraisal 326
buy-down 321
closing costs 323
condominium 309
conventional mortgage 319
cooperative housing 310
deed 323
earnest money 314
escrow account 324
lease 306
manufactured home 310
mortgage 316
payment cap 320
points 318
rate cap 320
refinancing 322
reverse mortgage 322
second mortgage 321
title insurance 323
zoning laws 312

SELF-TEST PROBLEMS

1. What would be the monthly payment for an $180,000, 20-year mortgage at 6 percent?
2. What is the total amount of a 30-year mortgage with monthly payments of $850?

Solutions

1. Using Table 9-9 (p. 317), multiple 180 times $7.16 to determine the monthly payment of $1,288.80.
2. 360 payments (30 years × 12 months) are multiplied by $850 for a total of $306,000.

FINANCIAL PLANNING PROBLEMS

LO9-2 **1.** *Comparing Renting and Buying.* Based on the following data, would you recommend buying or renting?

Rental Costs	Buying Costs
Annual rent, $7,380	Annual mortgage payments, $9,800 ($9,575 is interest)
Insurance, $145	Property taxes, $1,780
Security deposit, $650	Insurance/maintenance, $1,050
	Down payment/closing costs, $4,500
	Growth in equity, $225
	Estimated annual appreciation, $1,700

Assume an after-tax savings interest rate of 6 percent and a tax rate of 28 percent.

LO9-4 **2.** *Estimating a Monthly Mortgage Payment.* Estimate the affordable monthly mortgage payment, the affordable mortgage amount, and the affordable home purchase price for the following situation (see Exhibit 9-8).

Monthly gross income, $2,950

Down payment to be made—15 percent of purchase price

Other debt (monthly payment), $160

Monthly estimate for property taxes and insurance, $210

30-year loan at 8 percent.

LO9-4 **3.** *Calculating Monthly Mortgage Payments.* Based on Exhibit 9-9, what would be the monthly mortgage payments for each of the following situations?

a. $40,000, 15-year loan at 4.5 percent.

b. $76,000, 30-year loan at 5 percent.

c. $65,000, 20-year loan at 6 percent.

What relationship exists between the length of the loan and the monthly payment? How does the mortgage rate affect the monthly payment?

LO9-4 **4.** *Comparing Total Mortgage Payments.* Which mortgage would result in higher total payments?

Mortgage A: $970 a month for 30 years

Mortgage B: $760 a month for 5 years and $1005 for 25 years

LO9-4 **5.** *Evaluating a Refinance Decision.* Kelly and Tim Browne plan to refinance their mortgage to obtain a lower interest rate. They will reduce their mortgage payments by $83 a month. Their closing costs for refinancing will be $1,670. How long will it take them to recover the cost of refinancing?

LO9-4 **6.** *Saving for a Down Payment.* In an attempt to have funds for a down payment, Jan Carlson plans to save $3,500 a year for the next five years. With an interest rate of 3 percent, what amount will Jan have available for a down payment after the five years?

LO9-4 **7.** *Calculating the Monthly Housing Payment.* Ben and Carla Manchester plan to buy a condominium. They will obtain a $150,000, 30-year mortgage at 6 percent. Their annual property taxes are expected to be $1,800. Property insurance is $480 a year, and the condo association fee is $220 a month. Based on these items, determine the total monthly housing payment for the Manchesters.

LO9-5 **8.** *Future Value of an Amount Saved.* You estimate that you can save $3,800 by selling your home yourself rather than using a real estate agent. What would be the future value of that amount if invested for five years at 9 percent?

FINANCIAL PLANNING ACTIVITIES

LO9-1 **1.** *Comparing Housing Alternatives.* Interview several people about the factors that influenced the select of their current residence.

LO9-1 **2.** *Determining Appropriate Housing.* What type of housing would you suggest for people in the following life situations? (a) A single parent with two school-age children; (b) A two-income couple without children; (c) A person with both dependent children and a dependent parent; (d) A couple near retirement with grown children.

3. *Researching Rental Situations.* Using Sheet 42 in the Personal Financial Planner, compare the costs, facilities, and features of apartments and other rental housing in your area. You may obtain this information through newspaper advertisements, rental offices, or online searches. LO9-2

4. *Analyzing the Buy-versus-Rent Decision.* Use the buy-versus-rent analysis on page 304 to compare two residences you might consider. LO9-2

5. *Contrasting Rental Perspectives.* Talk to a tenant and a landlord to obtain their views about potential problems associated with renting. How do their views on tenant–landlord relations differ? LO9-2

6. *Assessing Home-Buying Alternatives.* Talk with a real estate agent about the process involved in selecting and buying a home. Obtain information about housing prices in your area and the services the agent provides. LO9-3

7. *Comparing Mortgage Sources.* Using Sheet 44 in the Personal Financial Planner, contact several mortgage companies and other financial institutions to obtain information about current mortgage rates, application fees, and the process for obtaining a mortgage. LO9-4

8. *Researching Home for Sale.* Conduct online research of homes for sale in your area. What features do you believe would appeal to potential buyers? What efforts were made to attract potential buyers to these properties? LO9-5

FINANCIAL PLANNING CASE

Housing Decisions

When Mark and Valerie Bowman first saw the house, they didn't like it. However, it was a dark, rainy day. They viewed the house more favorably on their second visit, which they had expected to be a waste of time. Despite cracked ceilings, the need for a paint job, and a kitchen built in the 1980s, the Bowmans saw a potential to create a place they could call their own.

Beth Young purchased her condominium several years ago. She obtained a mortgage rate of 6.75 percent, a very good rate then. Recently, when interest rates dropped, Beth was considering refinancing her mortgage at a lower rate.

Matt and Peggy Zoran had been married for five years and were still living in an apartment. Several of the Zorans' friends had purchased homes recently. However, Matt and Peggy were not sure they wanted to follow this example. Although they liked their friends' homes and had viewed photographs of homes currently on the market, they also liked the freedom from maintenance responsibility they enjoyed as renters.

Questions

1. How could the Bowmans benefit from buying a home that needed improvements?
2. How might Beth Young have found out when mortgage rates were at a level that would make refinancing her condominium more affordable?
3. Although the Zorans had good reasons for continuing to rent, what factors might make it desirable for an individual or a family to buy a home?

PERSONAL FINANCIAL PLANNER IN ACTION

Selecting and Financing Housing

Housing represents a major budget expenditure. This area of financial planning requires careful analysis of needs along with a comparison of the costs and benefits of housing alternatives.

Your Short-Term Financial Planning Activities	*Resources*
1. Compare your current housing situation with your housing needs and financial situation.	PFP Sheet 40 http://homebuying.about.com http://realestate.msn.com www.mymoney.gov www.hud.gov
2. Conduct an analysis to compare renting and buying of housing.	PFP Sheet 41 www.homefair.com www.newbuyer.com http://homes.yahoo.com

3. Compare various rental alternatives as needed.	PFP Sheet 42 http://apartments.about.com
4. Determine your housing and mortgage affordability, and compare various sources of mortgages.	PFP Sheet 43, 44 www.mortgage101.com www.bankrate.com www.hsh.com
Your Long-Term Financial Planning Activities	*Resources*
1. Monitor changing interest rates and assess refinancing alternatives.	PFP Sheet 45 www.interest.com www.mortgage-net.com
2. Develop a plan for assessing housing needs and costs in the future.	Text pages 308–325 www.realestatejournal.com www.hud.gov/buying/rvrsmort.cfm

CONTINUING CASE

Home Buying Decisions

Life Situation	*Financial Data*	
Young married couple	Monthly Gross Income	$ 3,600
Shelby, age 26	Living Expenses	$ 3,100
Mark, age 2	Assets	$25,000
	Liabilities	$ 3,000

Shelby and Mark Lawrence were married a year ago and are planning to purchase a condo as their first home together. Rent for a two-bedroom apartment costs them around $800. They want to stay as close to this amount as possible, since they are preparing to open Shelby's pet salon within the next year. They need help in evaluating all of the elements of home ownership.

Questions

1. Let's assume the Lawrences will qualify for a 6%, 30-year loan and will make a down payment of 10%. They are currently paying $300 on a used car auto loan for Shelby and will pay $220 per month for property taxes and homeowners' insurance. Using the "Housing affordability and mortgage qualification amounts" exhibit within the chapter, calculate the following:

a. the amount of their affordable monthly mortgage payment

b. the amount of their affordable mortgage loan amount and

c. the amount they can afford to pay for a home.

2. What are the tax advantages for the Lawrences of owning a home rather than renting?

3. Explain how Shelby and Mark might use these Personal Financial Planner sheets when deciding to purchase a home:

a. Renting versus Buying Housing

b. Housing Affordability and Mortgage Qualification

"After I pay my rent, utilities, and renter's insurance, I have very little for other expenses."

Directions

Your "Daily Spending Diary" will help you manage your housing expenses to create a better overall spending plan. As you record daily spending, your comments should reflect what you have learned about your spending patterns and help you consider possible changes you might want to make.

Analysis Questions

1. What portion of your daily spending involves expenses associated with housing?
2. What types of housing expenses might be reduced with more careful spending habits?

The Daily Spending Diary Sheets are located in Appendix D at the end of the book and on the student website at www.mhhe.com/kdh.

chapter 10

Property and Motor Vehicle Insurance

Learning Objectives

LO10-1 Develop a risk management plan using insurance.

LO10-2 Discuss the importance of property and liability insurance.

LO10-3 Explain the insurance coverages and policy types available to homeowners and renters.

LO10-4 Analyze factors that influence the amount of coverage and the cost of home insurance.

LO10-5 Identify the important types of automobile insurance coverages.

LO10-6 Evaluate factors that affect the cost of automobile insurance.

What will this mean for me?

While hurricanes, tornadoes, ice storms, and wildfires are the most visual disasters faced by people, losses from other hazards are much more common. Your insurance coverage for losses due to property damage and liability should be considered carefully. Planning your home and auto insurance program is a vital element for your overall financial planning activities.

my life

INSURING YOUR STUFF

We all have items with a financial value that require protection. While several risk management actions are available, most people purchase insurance.

The main focus when making insurance decisions is to avoid major financial losses. Do you take wise planning actions related to property and liability insurance? For each of the following statements, select "yes," "no," or "uncertain" to indicate your personal response regarding these insurance activities.

1. I use various risk management actions to reduce the chance of financial loss.	Yes	No	Uncertain
2. I have knowledge of property and liability insurance coverages.	Yes	No	Uncertain
3. I have appropriate home or renter's insurance coverage.	Yes	No	Uncertain
4. I understand methods to reduce my home or renter's insurance costs.	Yes	No	Uncertain
5. I understand the main types of auto insurance coverages.	Yes	No	Uncertain
6. I take various actions to reduce my auto insurance costs.	Yes	No	Uncertain

As you study this chapter, you will encounter "My Life" boxes with additional information and resources related to these items.

Insurance and Risk Management: An Introduction

LO10-1

Develop a risk management plan using insurance.

Insurance involves property and people. By providing protection against the risks of financial uncertainty and unexpected losses, insurance makes it possible to plan for the future.

WHAT IS INSURANCE?

insurance Protection against possible financial loss.

insurance company A risk-sharing firm that assumes financial responsibility for losses that may result from an insured risk.

insurer An insurance company.

policy A written contract for insurance.

premium The amount of money a policyholder is charged for an insurance policy.

insured A person covered by an insurance policy.

policyholder A person who owns an insurance policy.

risk Chance or uncertainty of loss; also used to mean "the insured."

peril The cause of a possible loss.

hazard A factor that increases the likelihood of loss through some peril.

Insurance is protection against possible financial loss. Although many types of insurance exist, they all have one thing in common: They give you the peace of mind that comes from knowing that money will be available to meet the needs of your survivors, pay medical expenses, protect your home and belongings, and cover personal or property damage caused by you when driving.

Life insurance replaces income that would be lost if the policyholder died. Health insurance helps meet medical expenses when the policyholder becomes ill. Automobile insurance helps cover property and personal damage caused by the policyholder's car. Home insurance covers the policyholder's place of residence and its associated financial risks, such as damage to personal property and injuries to others.

Insurance is based on the principle of *pooling risks,* in which thousands of policyholders pay a small sum of money (*premium*) into a central pool. The pool is then large enough to meet the expenses of the small number of people who actually suffer a loss.

An **insurance company,** or **insurer,** is a risk-sharing firm that agrees to assume financial responsibility for losses that may result from an insured risk. A person joins the risk-sharing group (the insurance company) by purchasing a **policy** (a contract). Under the policy, the insurance company agrees to assume the risk for a fee (the **premium**) that the person (the **insured** or the **policyholder**) pays periodically.

Insurance can provide protection against many risks of financial uncertainty and unexpected losses. The financial consequences of failing to obtain the right amount and type of insurance can be disastrous.

TYPES OF RISKS

You face risks every day. You cross the street with some danger that you'll be hit by a car. You can't own property without taking the chance that it will be lost, stolen, damaged, or destroyed. Insurance companies offer financial protection against such dangers and losses by promising to compensate the insured for a relatively large loss in return for the payment of a much smaller but certain expense called the *premium.*

Risk, peril, and *hazard* are important terms in insurance. While in popular use these terms tend to be interchangeable, each has a distinct, technical meaning in insurance terminology.

Basically, **risk** is uncertainty or lack of predictability. In this instance, it refers to the uncertainty as to loss that a person or a property covered by insurance faces. Insurance companies frequently refer to the insured person or property as the *risk.*

Peril is the cause of a possible loss. It is the contingency that causes someone to take out insurance. People buy policies for financial protection against perils such as fire, windstorms, explosions, robbery, accidents, and premature death.

Hazard increases the likelihood of loss through some peril. For example, defective house wiring is a hazard that increases the likelihood of the peril of fire.

The most common risks are classified as personal risks, property risks, and liability risks. *Personal risks* are the uncertainties surrounding loss of income or life due to premature death, illness, disability, old age, or unemployment. *Property risks* are the uncertainties of direct or indirect losses to personal or real property due to fire, windstorms, accidents, theft, and other hazards. *Liability risks* are possible losses due to negligence resulting in bodily injury or property damage to others. Such harm or damage could be caused by an automobile, professional misconduct, injury suffered on one's property, and so on.

Personal risks, property risks, and liability risks are types of **pure risk,** or *insurable risk,* since there would be a chance of loss only if the specified events occurred. Pure risks are accidental and unintentional risks for which the nature and financial cost of the loss can be predicted.

A **speculative risk** is a risk that carries a chance of either loss or gain. Starting a small business that may or may not succeed is an example of speculative risk. So is gambling. Most speculative risks are considered to be uninsurable.

DID YOU KNOW?

The Institute for Business and Home Safety (IBHS) created a six-story "disaster blaster" with 105 fans to simulate a category 3 hurricane. This chamber tests the wind resistance of structural modifications. Metal joint straps, a second roof water barrier, fortified decks, and siding attached with specialized fasteners can save more than $20 billion in home insurance claims a year. IBHS testing has resulted in life-saving features for motor vehicles, helping to reduce auto insurance rates.

RISK MANAGEMENT METHODS

Risk management is an organized strategy for protecting assets and people. It helps reduce financial losses caused by destructive events. Risk management is a long-range planning process. People's risk management needs change at various points in their lives. If you understand risks and how to manage them, you can provide better protection for yourself and your family. In this way, you can reduce your financial losses and thereby improve your chances for economic, social, physical, and emotional well-being. Since you will probably be unable to afford to cover all risks, you need to understand how to obtain the best protection you can afford.

Most people think of risk management as buying insurance. However, insurance is not the only method of dealing with risk; in certain situations, other methods may be less costly. Four risk management techniques are commonly used.

pure risk A risk in which there is only a chance of loss; also called *insurable risk.*

speculative risk A risk in which there is a chance of either loss or gain.

1. RISK AVOIDANCE You can avoid the risk of being in an automobile accident by not driving or being a passenger. McDonald's can avoid the risk of product failure by not introducing new products. Risk avoidance would be practiced in both instances, but at a very high cost. You might have to give up your job, and McDonald's might lose out to competitors that introduce new products.

In some situations, however, risk avoidance is practical. At the personal level, people avoid risks by not smoking or by not walking through high-crime neighborhoods. At the business level, jewelry stores avoid losses through robbery by locking their merchandise in vaults. Obviously, no person or business can avoid all risks.

Taking thoughtful actions can reduce the risks you face in your daily life.

2. RISK REDUCTION While avoiding risks completely may not be possible, reducing risks may be a cause of action. You can reduce the risk of injury in an auto accident by wearing a seat belt. You can install smoke alarms and fire extinguishers to protect life and reduce potential fire damage. You can reduce the risk of illness by eating a balanced diet and exercising.

3. RISK ASSUMPTION Risk assumption means taking on responsibility for the loss or injury that may result from a risk. Generally, it makes sense to assume a risk when the potential loss is small, when risk management has reduced the risk, when insurance coverage is expensive, and when there is no other way to obtain protection. For instance, you might decide not to purchase collision insurance on an older car. Then, if an accident occurs, you will bear the costs of fixing the car.

self-insurance The process of establishing a monetary fund to cover the cost of a loss.

deductible The set amount a policyholder must pay per loss on an insurance policy.

Self-insurance is the process of establishing a monetary fund to cover the cost of a loss. Self-insurance does not eliminate risks; it only provides means for covering losses. Many people self-insure by default, not by choice, by not obtaining insurance.

4. RISK SHIFTING The most common method of dealing with risk is to shift it. That simply means to transfer it to an insurance company or some other organization. In exchange for the fee you pay, the insurance company agrees to pay for your losses.

Most insurance policies include deductibles, which are a combination of risk assumption and risk shifting. A **deductible** is the set amount that the policyholder must pay per loss on an insurance policy. For example, if a falling tree damages your car, you may have to pay $200 toward the repairs. Your insurance company will pay the remaining amount.

Exhibit 10-1 summarizes various risks and appropriate strategies for managing them.

DID YOU KNOW?

Deductibles are a combination of risk assumption and risk shifting. The insured person assumes part of the risk, paying the first $250, $500, or $1,000 of a claim. The majority of the risk for a large claim is shifted to another party, the insurance company.

PLANNING AN INSURANCE PROGRAM

Because all people have their own needs and goals, many of which change over the years, a personal insurance program should be tailored to those changes.

Exhibit **10-1** Examples of risks and risk management strategies

Risks		Possible Strategies for Reducing Financial Impact		
Personal Events	**Financial Impact**	**Personal Resources**	**Private Sector**	**Public Sector**
Disability	Loss of one's income Loss of services Increased expenses	Savings, investments Family observing safety precautions	Disability insurance	Disability insurance Social Security
Illness	Loss of one's income Catastrophic hospital expenses	Health-enhancing behavior	Health insurance Health maintenance organizations	Military health care Medicare, Medicaid
Death	Loss of one's income Loss of services Final expenses	Estate planning Risk reduction	Life insurance	Veteran's life insurance Social Security survivor's benefits
Retirement	Decreased income Unplanned living expenses	Savings Investments Hobbies, skills Part-time work	Retirement and/or pensions	Social Security Pension plan for government employees
Property loss	Cost to repair damage to property Repair or replacement cost of theft	Property repair and upkeep Security plans	Automobile insurance Homeowner's insurance Flood insurance (joint program with government)	Flood insurance (joint program with business)
Liability	Claims and settlement costs Lawsuits and legal expenses Loss of personal assets and income	Observing safety precautions Maintaining property	Homeowner's insurance Automobile insurance Malpractice insurance	State-operated insurance plans

In the early years of marriage, when the family is growing, most families need certain kinds of insurance protection. This protection may include property insurance on an apartment or a house, life and disability insurance for wage earners and caretakers of dependents, and adequate health insurance for all family members.

Later, when the family has a higher income and a different financial situation, protection needs will change. There might be a long-range provision for the children's education, more life insurance to match higher income and living standards, and revised health insurance protection. Still later, when the children have grown and are on their own, retirement benefits will be a consideration, further changing the family's personal insurance program.

The Financial Planning for Life's Situations feature on page 340 suggests several guidelines to follow in planning your insurance program. Exhibit 10-2 outlines the steps in developing a personal insurance program.

Various risk management actions may be used to reduce the chance of financial loss.

A wide range of insurance coverages exist in our society. Talk with an insurance agent or financial planner to obtain recommendations about the types of insurance you may need.

STEP 1: SET INSURANCE GOALS In managing risks, your goals are to minimize personal, property, and liability risks. Your insurance goals should define what to do to cover the basic risks present in your life situation. Covering the basic risks means providing a financial resource to cover costs resulting from a loss.

Suppose your goal is to buy a new car. You must plan to make the purchase and to protect yourself against financial losses from accidents. Auto insurance on the car lets you enjoy the car without worrying that an auto accident might leave you worse off, financially and physically, than before.

Exhibit 10-2

Creating a personal insurance program

HOW CAN YOU PLAN AN INSURANCE PROGRAM?

Did you:	Yes	No
1. Seek advice from a competent and reliable insurance adviser?	☐	☐
2. Determine what insurance you need to provide your family with sufficient protection if you die?	☐	☐
3. Consider what portion of the family protection is met by Social Security and by group insurance?	☐	☐
4. Decide what other needs insurance must meet (funeral expenses, savings, retirement annuities, etc.)?	☐	☐
5. Decide what types of insurance best meet your needs?	☐	☐
6. Plan an insurance program and implement it except for periodic reviews of changing needs and changing conditions?	☐	☐
7. Avoid buying more insurance than you need or can afford?	☐	☐
8. Consider dropping one policy for another that provides the same coverage for less money?	☐	☐

Note: Yes answers reflect wise actions for insurance planning.

Each individual has unique goals. Income, age, family size, lifestyle, experience, and responsibilities influence the goals you set, and the insurance you buy must reflect those goals. In general, financial advisers say that a basic risk management plan must set goals to reduce

- Potential loss of income due to the premature death, illness, accident, or unemployment of a wage earner.
- Potential loss of income and extra expense resulting from the illness, disability, or death of a spouse.
- Additional expenses due to the injury, illness, or death of other family members.
- Potential loss of real or personal property due to fire, theft, or other hazards.
- Potential loss of income, savings, and property due to personal liability.

STEP 2: DEVELOP A PLAN TO REACH YOUR GOALS Planning is a sign of maturity, a way of taking control of life instead of letting life happen to you. What risks do you face? Which risks can you afford to take without having to back away from your goals? What resources—public programs, personal assets, family, church, or private risk-sharing plans—are available to you?

To understand and use the resources at your command, you need good information. In terms of insurance, this means a clear picture of the available insurance, the reliability of different insurers, and the comparative costs of the coverage needed.

STEP 3: PUT YOUR PLAN INTO ACTION As you carry out your plan, obtain financial and personal resources, budget them, and use them to reach risk management goals. If, for example, you find the insurance protection you have is not enough to cover your basic risks, you may purchase additional coverage, change the kind of insurance coverage, restructure your budget to cover additional insurance costs, and strengthen your savings or investment programs to reduce long-term risk.

The best risk management plans have flexibility. Savings accounts or other cash, for example, should be available as emergency funds for unexpected financial problems. The best plans are also flexible enough to allow you to respond to changing life situations. Your goal should be an insurance program that expands (or contracts) with changing protection needs.

To put your risk management plan to work, you must answer these questions: What should be insured? For how much? What kind of insurance should I buy? From whom? What amount can I afford?

STEP 4: REVIEW YOUR RESULTS Evaluate your insurance plan periodically, at least every two or three years or whenever your family circumstances change. Among the questions you should ask yourself are: Does it work? Does it adequately protect my plans and goals? An effective risk manager consistently checks the outcomes of decisions and is alert to changes that may reduce the effectiveness of the current risk management plan.

A young working couple may be entirely happy with their life and health insurance coverage. When they add an infant to the family, a review of protection is appropriate. Suddenly the risk of financial catastrophe to the family (should one or both parents die or become disabled) is much greater.

The needs of a single person differ from those of a family, a single parent, a couple, or a group of unrelated adults living in the same household. While these people face similar risks, their financial responsibility to others differs greatly. In each case, the vital question is: Have I provided the financial resources and risk management strategy needed to take care of my basic responsibilities for my own well-being and the well-being of others?

1 What is the purpose of insurance?
2 How are the most common risks classified?
3 What is the difference between pure risk and speculative risk?
4 What are the methods of managing risk?
5 What are the steps in planning your personal insurance coverage?

Current insurance policies and needs

Property and Liability Insurance

LO10-2

Discuss the importance of property and liability insurance.

Major disasters have caused catastrophic amounts of property loss in the United States. In recent years, hurricanes, tornadoes, and floods in various areas have caused billions of dollars of damage.

Property owners face a variety of risks including fire and smoke damage.

Since most people invest large amounts of money in their homes and motor vehicles, protecting these assets from loss is a great concern. Each year, homeowners and renters lose billions of dollars from more than 3 million burglaries, 500,000 fires, and 200,000 instances of damage from other hazards. The cost of injuries and property damage caused by automobiles is also very great. Most people use insurance to reduce their chances of economic loss from these risks.

The price you pay for home and automobile insurance may be viewed as an investment in financial protection against these losses. Although the costs of home and automobile insurance may seem high, the financial losses from which insurance protects you are much higher. Property and liability insurance offer protection from financial losses that may arise from a wide variety of situations.

The main types of risks related to a home and an automobile are (1) property damage or loss and (2) your responsibility for injuries or damage to the property of others.

my life 2

Knowledge of property and liability insurance coverages is a fundamental element of personal financial planning.

We each face various legal responsibilities in our daily lives. Conduct an online search about various types of liability insurance protection.

POTENTIAL PROPERTY LOSSES

Houses, automobiles, furniture, clothing, and other personal belongings are a substantial financial commitment. Property owners face two basic types of risks. The first is *physical damage* caused by hazards such as fire, wind, water, and smoke. These hazards can cause destruction of your property or temporary loss of its use. For example, if a windstorm causes a large tree branch to break your automobile windshield, you lose the use of the vehicle while it is being repaired. The second type of risk property owners face is *loss of use* due to robbery, burglary, vandalism, or arson.

LIABILITY PROTECTION

liability Legal responsibility for the financial cost of another person's losses or injuries.

negligence Failure to take ordinary or reasonable care in a situation.

strict liability A situation in which a person is held responsible for intentional or unintentional actions.

vicarious liability A situation in which a person is held legally responsible for the actions of another person.

In a wide variety of circumstances, a person may be judged legally responsible for bodily injuries or property damages. For example, if a child walks across your property, falls, and sustains severe injuries, the child's family may be able to recover substantial damages from you as a result of the injuries. If you accidentally damage a rare painting while assisting a friend with home repairs, the friend may take legal action against you to recover the cost of the painting.

Liability is legal responsibility for the financial cost of another person's losses or injuries. Your legal responsibility is commonly caused by **negligence,** failure to take ordinary or reasonable care. Doing something in a careless manner, such as improperly supervising children at a swimming pool or failing to remove items from a frequently used staircase, may be ruled as negligence in a liability lawsuit.

Despite taking great care, a person may still be held liable in a situation. **Strict liability** is present when a person is held responsible for intentional or unintentional actions. **Vicarious liability** occurs when a person is held responsible for the actions of another person. If the behavior of a child causes financial or physical harm to others, the parent may be held responsible; if the activities of an employee cause damage, the employer may be held responsible.

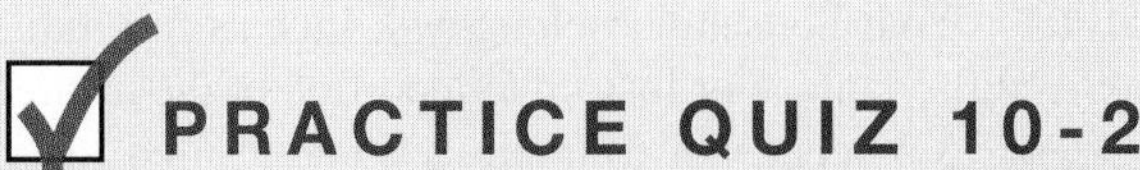

1 What property and liability risks might some people overlook?
2 How could a person's life situation influence the need for certain types of property and liability insurance?

Home and Property Insurance

LO10-3

Explain the insurance coverages and policy types available to homeowners and renters.

Your home and personal belongings are probably a major portion of your assets. Whether you rent your dwelling or own a home, property insurance is vital. **Homeowner's insurance** is coverage for your place of residence and its associated financial risks, such as damage to personal property and injuries to others (see Exhibit 10-3).

homeowner's insurance Coverage for a place of residence and its associated financial risks.

HOMEOWNER'S INSURANCE COVERAGES

A homeowner's policy provides coverages for the house and other structures, additional living expenses, personal property, personal liability and related coverages, and specialized coverages.

HOUSE AND OTHER STRUCTURES The main component of homeowner's insurance is protection against financial loss due to damage or destruction to a house or other structures. Your dwelling and attached structures are covered for fire and other hazards. Detached structures on the property, such as a garage, toolshed, or gazebo, are also protected. The coverage will usually also include trees, shrubs, and plants.

ADDITIONAL LIVING EXPENSES If damage from a fire or other event prevents the use of your home, *additional living expense coverage* pays for the cost of living in a temporary location while your home is being repaired. Some policies limit additional living expense coverage to 10 to 20 percent of the home's coverage and limit payments to a maximum of six to nine months; other policies pay the full cost incurred for up to a year.

Exhibit 10-3 Home insurance coverage

House and other structures

Personal property

Loss of use/additional living expenses while home is uninhabitable

Personal liability and related coverages

PERSONAL PROPERTY Your household belongings, such as furniture, appliances, and clothing, are covered for damage or loss up to a portion of the insured value of the home, usually 55, 70, or 75 percent. For example, a home insured for $80,000 might have $56,000 (70 percent) of coverage for household belongings.

Personal property coverage commonly has limits for the theft of certain items, such as $1,000 for jewelry, $2,000 for firearms, and $2,500 for silverware. Items with a value exceeding these limits can be protected with a **personal property floater,** which covers the damage or loss of a specific item of high value. A floater requires a detailed description of the item and periodic appraisals to verify the current value. This coverage protects the item regardless of location; thus, the item is insured while you are traveling or transporting it.

personal property floater Additional property insurance to cover the damage or loss of a specific item of high value.

Floaters to protect home computers and other electronic equipment are recommended. This additional coverage can prevent financial loss due to damage or loss of your computer. Contact your insurance agent to determine whether the equipment is covered against damage from mischievous pets, spilled drinks, dropping, or power surges.

Personal property coverage usually provides protection against the loss or damage of articles taken with you when away from home. For example, possessions taken on vacation or used while at school are usually covered up to a policy limit. Property that you rent, such as some power tools or a rug shampoo machine, is insured while in your possession.

In the event of damage or loss of property, you must be able to prove both ownership and value. A **household inventory** is a list or other documentation of personal belongings, with purchase dates and cost information. You can get a form for such an inventory from an insurance agent or online. Exhibit 10-4 provides a reminder of the items you should include in the inventory. For items of special value, you should have receipts, serial numbers, brand names, model names, and written appraisals of value.

household inventory A list or other documentation of personal belongings, with purchase dates and cost information.

A household inventory can be a list, photographs, or a video of your home and contents. Photograph closets and storage areas open to see all items. Indicate the date and the value of property. Regularly update your inventory, photos, and appraisal documents. Keep information in a waterproof bag in a fireproof box with a copy in a safe-deposit box. Online inventory tools and phone apps are also available.

PERSONAL LIABILITY AND RELATED COVERAGES Each day, you face the risk of financial loss due to injuries to others or damage to property for which you are responsible. The following are examples of this risk:

- A neighbor or guest falls on your property, resulting in permanent disability.
- A spark from burning leaves on your property starts a fire that damages a neighbor's roof.
- A member of your family accidentally breaks an expensive glass statue while at another person's house.

In each of these situations, you could be held responsible for the costs incurred. The personal liability component of a homeowner's policy protects you from financial losses resulting from legal action or claims against you or family members due to damages to the property of others. This coverage includes the cost of legal defense.

Not all individuals who come to your property are covered by your liability insurance. While a babysitter or others who assist you occasionally are probably covered, regular employees, such as a housekeeper or a gardener, may require worker's compensation coverage.

DID YOU KNOW?

Errors and omissions (E&O) is liability insurance to protect service professionals from claims if a client holds them responsible for errors or if they fail to perform as promised. E&O coverage is used by doctors, lawyers, accountants, architects, engineers, printers, wedding planners, and others.

Exhibit 10-4 Household inventory contents

Most homeowner's policies provide a basic personal liability coverage of $100,000, but additional amounts are frequently recommended. An **umbrella policy,** also called a *personal catastrophe policy,* supplements your basic personal liability coverage. This added protection covers you for personal injury claims such as libel, slander, defamation of character, and invasion of property. An umbrella policy also increases bodily injury and property damage coverages. Extended liability policies are sold in amounts of $1 million or more and are useful for individuals with substantial net worth. If you are a business owner, you may need other types of liability coverage.

umbrella policy Supplementary personal liability coverage; also called a *personal catastrophe policy.*

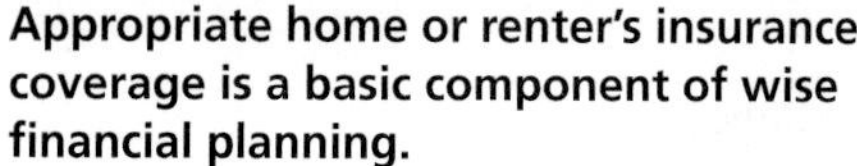

Appropriate home or renter's insurance coverage is a basic component of wise financial planning.

To determine the value of your property for planning insurance coverage, you should prepare a household inventory. For information about conducting a household inventory, go to www.iii.org or conduct a Web search for "household inventory."

Medical payments coverage pays the costs of minor accidental injuries on your property and minor injuries caused by you, family members, or pets. Settlements under medical payments coverage are made without determining fault. This protection allows fast processing of small claims, generally up to $5,000. Suits for more severe personal injuries are covered by the personal liability portion of the homeowner's policy. Medical payments coverage does not cover the people who live in the home being insured.

Should you or a family member accidentally damage another person's property, the *supplementary coverage* of homeowner's insurance will pay for these minor mishaps. This protection is usually limited to $500 or $1,000. Again, payments are made regardless of fault. Any property damage claims for greater amounts would require action under the personal liability coverage.

medical payments coverage Home insurance that pays the cost of minor accidental injuries on one's property.

endorsement An addition of coverage to a standard insurance policy.

SPECIALIZED COVERAGES Homeowner's insurance usually does not cover losses from floods and earthquakes. People living in areas with these two risks need special coverage. In various communities, the National Flood Insurance Program makes flood insurance available. This protection is separate from the homeowner's policy. An insurance agent or the Federal Emergency Management Agency of the Federal Insurance Administration (see Appendix C) can give you additional information about this coverage. Fewer than half of the people who live in flood-prone areas have this coverage.

Earthquake insurance can be obtained as an **endorsement,** or addition of coverage, to the homeowner's policy. Since the most severe earthquakes occur in the Pacific Coast region, most insurance against this risk is bought in that region. Remember, however, that every state is vulnerable to earthquakes and this insurance coverage is available in all areas. Lenders frequently require insurance against both floods and earthquakes for a mortgage to buy a home in areas with these risks.

DID YOU KNOW?

For $50 to $80 a year, homeowners can obtain $10,000 for sewage and drain backup damage. Heavy rains that clog a sewer line can cause damage to furniture and other items in a finished basement. Information on flood insurance is available at www.floodsmart.gov.

RENTER'S INSURANCE

While more than 9 out of 10 homeowners have property insurance, only about 4 out of 10 renters are covered. For people who rent, home insurance coverages include personal property protection, additional living expenses coverage, and personal liability and related coverages. Protection against financial loss due to damage or loss of personal property is the main component of renter's insurance. Often renters believe they are covered under the insurance policy of the building owner. In fact, the building owner's property insurance does not cover tenants' personal property unless the building owner can be proven liable. For example, faulty wiring causes a fire and damages a tenant's property, the renter may be able to collect for damages from the building owner.

The personal belongings of students in college housing are usually covered (up to certain amount) on the home insurance policies of their parents. However, if living off campus or owning many expensive items, a separate policy should be considered. Renter's

DID YOU KNOW?

Computers and other equipment used in a home-based business may not be covered by a home insurance policy. Contact your insurance agent to obtain needed business coverage.

insurance is relatively inexpensive and provides protection from financial loss due to many of the same risks covered in homeowner's policies.

HOME INSURANCE POLICY FORMS

Until the mid-1950s, a homeowner had to buy separate coverage for fire, theft, and other risks. Then the insurance industry developed a series of package policies as shown in Exhibit 10-5. Some property is excluded from most home insurance (see Exhibit 10-6).

Manufactured housing units and mobile homes usually qualify for insurance coverage with conventional policies. However, certain mobile homes may require a special arrangement and higher rates since their construction makes them more prone to fire and wind damage. The cost of mobile home insurance coverage is most heavily affected

Exhibit 10-5 Types of home insurance policies

Each of the policies below covers these perils, in addition to the items noted:

- Fire, lightning
- Windstorm, hail
- Explosion
- Riot or civil commotion
- Aircraft
- Vehicles
- Discharge of water
- Freezing
- Accidental damage from steam or electrical current
- Smoke
- Vandalism or malicious mischief
- Theft
- Glass breakage
- Volcanic eruption
- Falling objects
- Tearing apart of heating system or appliance
- Weight of ice, snow, or sleet

Special Form (All risk) (HO-3)	Covers all above perils, plus any other perils except those specifically excluded from the policy, such as • Flood • War • Earthquake • Nuclear accidents
Tenants Form (HO-4)	Covers personal belongings against the perils in the top section.
Comprehensive Form (HO-5)	Expands coverage of HO-3 to include endorsements for items such as replacement cost coverage on contents and guaranteed replacement cost coverage on buildings.
Condominium Form (HO-6)	Covers personal belongings and additions to the living unit.
Country Home Form (HO-7)	For nonfarm business rural residents with coverage on agricultural buildings and equipment.

The other major coverages of each policy are

- Personal liability
- Medical payments for guests on the property
- Additional living expenses

Note: HO-1 (Basic Form), HO-2 (Broad Form), and HO-8 (Modified Coverage Form for older homes with a high replacement value) are no longer being offered by most companies.

Exhibit 10-6

Not everything is covered

Certain personal property is specifically excluded from the coverage provided by homeowner's insurance:

- Articles separately described and specifically insured, such as jewelry, furs, boats, or expensive electronic equipment.
- Animals, birds, or fish.
- Motorized land vehicles, except those used to service an insured's residence, that are not licensed for road use.
- Any device or instrument for the transmission and recording of sound, including any accessories or antennas, while in or on motor vehicles.
- Aircraft and parts.
- Property of roomers, boarders, and other tenants who are not related to any insured.
- Property contained in an apartment regularly rented or held for rental to others by any insured.
- Property rented or held for rental to others away from the residence premises.
- Business property in storage, or held as a sample, or for sale, or for delivery after sale.
- Business property pertaining to business actually conducted on the residence premises.
- Business property away from the residence premises.

by location and by the method used to attach the housing unit to the ground. This type of property insurance is quite expensive; a $20,000 mobile home can cost as much to insure as a $60,000 house.

In addition to the property and liability risks previously discussed, home insurance policies include coverage for

- Credit card fraud, check forgery, and counterfeit money.
- The cost of removing damaged property.
- Emergency removal of property to protect it from damage.
- Temporary repairs after a loss to prevent further damage.
- Fire department charges in areas with such fees.

Home inventory

PRACTICE QUIZ 10-3

1 What main coverages are included in home insurance policies?
2 What is the purpose of personal liability coverage?
3 How does renter's insurance differ from other home insurance policies?

Home Insurance Cost Factors

LO10-4

Analyze factors that influence the amount of coverage and the cost of home insurance.

Studies reveal that as many as two-thirds of homes in the United States are not insured or are underinsured. Financial losses caused by fire, theft, wind, and other risks amount to billions of dollars each year. Since most homeowners have a mortgage on their property, their lending institutions usually require insurance. When purchasing insurance, you can get the best value by selecting the appropriate coverage amount and being aware of factors that affect insurance costs.

HOW MUCH COVERAGE DO YOU NEED?

Insurance premiums are affected by claims in your area.

Several factors affect the insurance coverage needed for your home and property (see Exhibit 10-7). Your insurance protection should be based on the amount needed to rebuild or repair your house, not the amount you paid for it. As construction costs rise, you should increase the amount of coverage. In recent years, most insurance policies have had a built-in inflation clause that increases coverage as property values increase.

In the past, most homeowner's policies contained a provision requiring that the building be insured for at least 80 percent of the replacement value. Under this **coinsurance clause,** the homeowner would have to pay for part of the losses if the property was not insured for the specified percentage of the replacement value. Few companies still use coinsurance, most require full coverage.

coinsurance clause A policy provision that requires a homeowner to pay for part of the losses if the property is not insured for the specified percentage of the replacement value.

If you are financing a home, the lending institution will require you to have property insurance in an amount that covers its financial investment. Remember, too, that the amount of insurance on your home will determine the coverage on the contents. Personal belongings are generally covered up to an amount ranging from 55 to 75 percent of the insurance amount on the dwelling.

Insurance companies base claim settlements on one of two methods. Under the **actual cash value (ACV)** method, the payment you receive is based on the current replacement cost of a damaged or lost item less depreciation. This means you would get $180 for a five-year-old television set that cost you $400 and had an estimated life

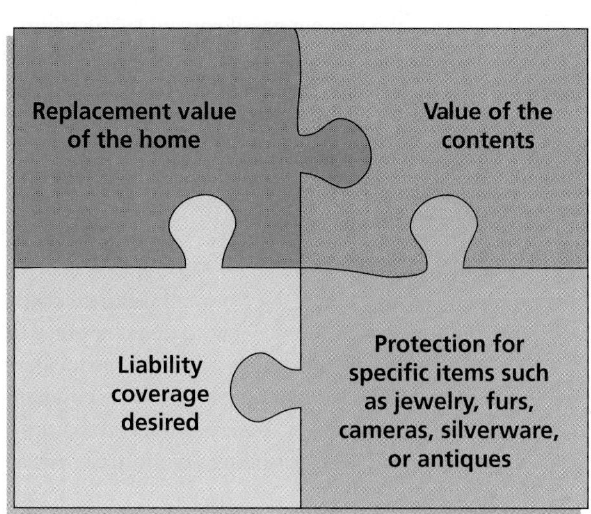

Exhibit 10-7

Determining the amount of home insurance you need

of eight years if the same set now costs $480. Your settlement amount is determined by taking the current cost of $480 and subtracting five years of depreciation from it—$300 for five years at $60 a year.

Under the **replacement value** method for settling claims, you receive the full cost of repairing or replacing a damaged or lost item; depreciation is not considered. However, many companies limit the replacement cost to 400 percent of the item's actual cash value. Replacement value coverage costs about 10 to 20 percent more than ACV coverage.

actual cash value (ACV) A claim settlement method in which the insured receives payment based on the current replacement cost of a damaged or lost item, less depreciation.

replacement value A claim settlement method in which the insured receives the full cost of repairing or replacing a damaged or lost item.

FACTORS THAT AFFECT HOME INSURANCE COSTS

The main influences on the premium paid for home and property insurance are the location of the home, the type of structure, the coverage amount and policy type, discounts, and differences among insurance companies.

LOCATION OF HOME The location of the residence affects insurance rates. If more claims have been filed in an area, home insurance rates for people living there will be higher. Weather events such as a hailstorm or a hurricane also affect insurance costs.

TYPE OF STRUCTURE The type of home and the construction materials influence the costs of insurance coverage. A brick house, for example, would cost less to insure than a similar house made of wood. However, earthquake coverage is more expensive for a brick home than for a wood dwelling. Stronger, more wind-resistant home construction can reduce insurance costs in Florida and provide greater protection against hurricane damage. Also, the age and style of the house can create potential risks and increase insurance costs.

COVERAGE AMOUNT AND POLICY TYPE The policy you select and the financial limits of coverage affect the premium you pay. It costs more to insure a $150,000 home than a $100,000 home. The comprehensive form of homeowner's policy costs more than a tenant's policy.

The *deductible* amount in your policy also affects the cost of your insurance. If you increase the amount of your deductible, your premium will be lower since the company will pay out less in claims. The most common deductible amounts are $500 or $1,000 or higher, which can reduce the premium 15 percent or more.

DID YOU KNOW?

In some areas, a home could be automatically rejected for insurance coverage if it has had two or three claims of any sort in the past three years. Homes that have encountered water damage, storm damage, and burglaries are most vulnerable to rejection.

REDUCING HOME INSURANCE COSTS

HOME INSURANCE DISCOUNTS Most companies offer incentives that reduce home insurance costs. Your premium may be lower if you have smoke detectors or a fire extinguisher. Deterrents to burglars, such as dead bolt locks or an alarm system, can also save you money. Some companies offer home insurance discounts to policy-holders who are nonsmokers or may give a discount for being "claim free" for a certain number of years.

my life 4

Understanding methods to reduce home or renter's insurance costs can save you money.

To identify options that you might take to reduce home insurance costs, talk to various people you know about actions of which they are aware.

COMPANY DIFFERENCES Studies show that you can save more than 30 percent on homeowner's insurance by comparing companies. Contact both insurance agents who work for one company and independent agents who represent several. The information you obtain will enable you to compare rates. Home insurance rates may be compared using information from websites such as www.netquote.com.

Don't select a company on the basis of price alone. Also consider service and coverage. Not all companies settle claims in the same way. For example, a number of homeowners had two sides of their houses dented by hail. Since the type of siding used in these houses was no longer available, all of the siding had to be replaced. Some insurance companies paid for complete replacement of the siding, while others paid only for replacement of the damaged areas. State insurance commissions, other government agencies, and consumer organizations can provide information about the reputations of insurance companies. *Consumer Reports* (www.Consumer Reports.org) regularly publishes a satisfaction index of property insurance companies.

1 What major factors influence the cost of home insurance?
2 What actions can a person take to reduce the cost of home insurance?

Automobile Insurance Coverages

LO10-5

Identify the important types of automobile insurance coverages.

Each year, motor vehicle crashes cost over $150 billion in lost wages and medical costs. The National Traffic Safety Administration estimates that alcohol use, texting, and cell phone use are factors in more than half of all automobile accidents. Such accidents result in thousands of highway deaths and injuries and over $30 billion in costs. These automobile accidents create a risk that affects many people financially and emotionally. Automobile insurance cannot eliminate the costs of automobile accidents; however, it does reduce the financial impact.

A **financial responsibility law** is state legislation that requires drivers to prove their ability to cover the cost of damage or injury caused by an automobile accident. All states have such laws to protect the public from physical harm and property damage losses caused by drivers. When injuries or significant property damage occur in an accident, the drivers involved are required to file a report with the state and to show financial responsibility. Nearly all states have compulsory automobile insurance laws. In other states, most people meet the financial responsibility requirement by buying insurance, since very few have the financial resources to meet this legal requirement on their own. Exhibit 10-8 presents each state's minimum limits (in thousands of dollars) for financial responsibility. These amounts represent the minimum state requirement; higher coverage is recommended to protect the financial assets of individuals.

financial responsibility law State legislation that requires drivers to prove their ability to cover the cost of damage or injury caused by an automobile accident.

The main coverages provided by automobile insurance fall into two categories: bodily injury coverages and property damage coverages (see Exhibit 10-9). Other coverages include wage loss insurance, towing service, accidental death, and car rental when a vehicle is undergoing repairs due to an accident or other damage.

Exhibit **10-8**

Automobile financial responsibility/compulsory insurance minimum limits, in thousands of dollars (as of 2013)

State	Liability Limits	State	Liability Limits
Alabama	25/50/25	Montana	25/50/10
Alaska	50/100/25	Nebraska	25/50/25
Arizona	15/30/10	Nevada	15/30/10
Arkansas	25/50/25	New Hampshire	25/50/25
California	15/30/5	New Jersey	15/30/5
Colorado	25/50/15	New Mexico	25/50/10
Connecticut	20/40/10	New York*	25/50/10
Delaware	15/30/10	North Carolina	30/60/25
District of Columbia	25/50/10	North Dakota	25/50/25
Florida	10/20/10	Ohio	12.5/25/7.5
Georgia	25/50/25	Oklahoma	25/50/25
Hawaii	20/40/10	Oregon	25/50/20
Idaho	20/50/15	Pennsylvania	15/30/5
Illinois	20/40/15	Rhode Island	25/50/25
Indiana	25/50/10	South Carolina	25/50/25
Iowa	20/40/15	South Dakota	25/50/25
Kansas	25/50/10	Tennessee	25/50/15
Kentucky	25/50/10	Texas	30/60/25
Louisiana	15/30/25	Utah	25/65/15
Maine	50/100/25	Vermont	25/50/10
Maryland	30/60/15	Virginia	25/50/20
Massachusetts	20/40/5	Washington	25/50/10
Michigan	20/40/10	West Virginia	20/40/10
Minnesota	30/60/10	Wisconsin	25/50/10
Mississippi	25/50/25	Wyoming	25/50/20
Missouri	25/50/10		

Source: © Insurance Information Institute. Used with permission.
*50/100 in cases where injury results in death.

MOTOR VEHICLE BODILY INJURY COVERAGES

Most money automobile insurance companies pay in claims goes for the cost of injury lawsuits, medical expenses, and related legal costs. The main bodily injury coverages are bodily injury liability, medical payments coverage, and uninsured motorist's protection. No-fault systems in a number of states have influenced the process of settling bodily injury claims.

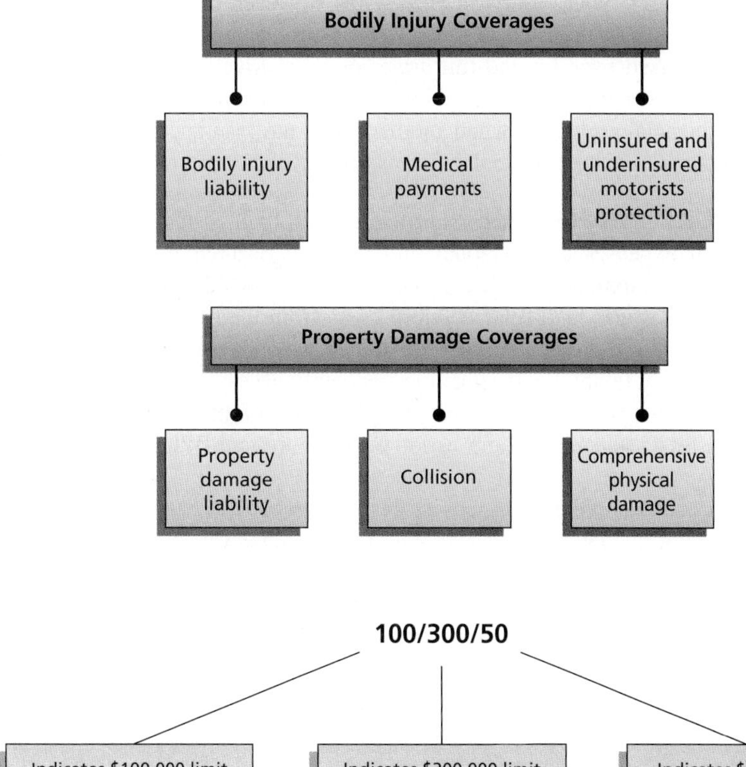

Exhibit 10-9

Two major categories of automobile insurance

100/300/50

Indicates $100,000 limit that will be paid to one person in an accident

Indicates $300,000 limit that will be paid to all persons in an accident

Indicates $50,000 limit for payment for damage of property of others

Bodily Injury Liability

Property Damage Liability

Exhibit 10-10

Automobile liability insurance coverage

BODILY INJURY LIABILITY **Bodily injury liability** covers the risk of financial loss due to legal expenses, medical expenses, lost wages, and other expenses associated with injuries caused by an automobile accident for which you were responsible. This insurance protects you from extensive financial loss.

Bodily injury liability is usually expressed as a split limit, such as 50/100 or 100/300. These amounts represent thousands of dollars of coverage. The first number (see Exhibit 10-10) is the limit for claims that can be paid to one person; the second number is the limit for each accident; the third number is discussed in the section on property damage coverages. With 100/300 bodily injury coverage, for example, a driver would have a limit of $100,000 for claims that could be paid to one person in an accident. In addition, there would be a $300,000 limit for all bodily injury claims from a single accident.

bodily injury liability Coverage for the risk of financial loss due to legal expenses, medical costs, lost wages, and other expenses associated with injuries caused by an automobile accident for which the insured was responsible.

medical payments coverage Automobile insurance that covers medical expenses for people injured in one's car or as a pedestrian.

uninsured motorist's protection Automobile insurance coverage for the cost of injuries to a person and members of his or her family caused by a driver with inadequate insurance or by a hit-and-run driver.

MEDICAL PAYMENTS COVERAGE While bodily injury liability pays for the costs of injuries to persons who were not in your automobile, **medical payments coverage** covers the costs of health care for people who were injured in your automobile, including yourself. This protection covers friends, carpool members, and others who ride in your vehicle. Medical payments insurance also provides medical benefits if you or a member of your family is struck by an automobile or injured while riding in another person's automobile.

UNINSURED MOTORIST'S PROTECTION If you are in an accident caused by a person without insurance, **uninsured motorist's protection** covers the cost of

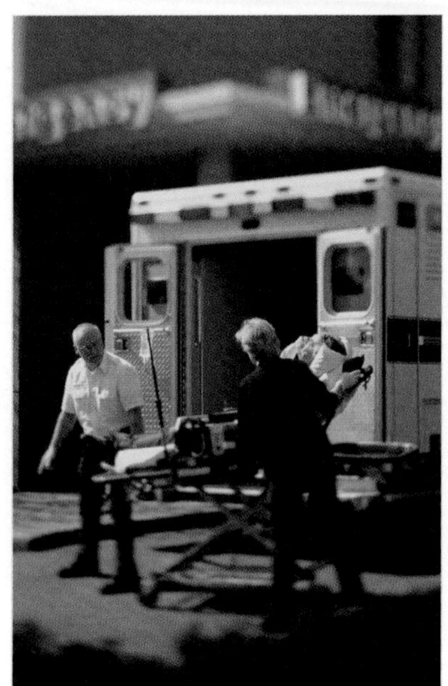

Bodily injuries contribute to the major portion of costs for auto insurance claims.

injuries to you and your family; in most states, however, it does not cover property damage. This insurance also provides protection against financial losses due to injuries caused by a hit-and-run driver or by a driver who has insufficient coverage to cover the cost of your injuries. *Underinsured motorists coverage* provides financial protection when another driver has insurance coverage below the amount to cover the financial damages you have encountered.

NO-FAULT INSURANCE Difficulties and high costs of settling claims for medical expenses and personal injuries have resulted in the creation of the **no-fault system,** in which drivers involved in accidents collect medical expenses, lost wages, and related injury costs from their own insurance companies. The system is intended to provide fast, smooth methods of paying for damages without taking the legal action frequently necessary to determine fault.

Massachusetts was the first state to implement no-fault insurance. In recent years, nearly 30 states had some variation of the system. While no-fault automobile insurance was intended to reduce the time and cost associated with the settlement of automobile injury cases, this has not always been the result. One reason for continued difficulties is that no-fault systems vary from state to state. Some no-fault states set limits on medical expenses, lost wages, and other claim settlements, while other states allow lawsuits under certain conditions, such as permanent paralysis or death. Some states include property damage in no-fault insurance. Drivers should investigate the coverages and implications of no-fault insurance in their states.

no-fault system An automobile insurance program in which drivers involved in accidents collect medical expenses, lost wages, and related injury costs from their own insurance companies.

property damage liability Automobile insurance coverage that protects a person against financial loss when that person damages the property of others.

collision Automobile insurance that pays for damage to the insured's car when it is involved in an accident.

MOTOR VEHICLE PROPERTY DAMAGE COVERAGES

Three coverages protect you from financial loss due to damage of property of others and damage to your vehicle: (1) property damage liability, (2) collision, and (3) comprehensive physical damage. (See the Financial Planning for Life's Situation: Are You Covered? on page 355)

PROPERTY DAMAGE LIABILITY When you damage the property of others, **property damage liability** protects you against financial loss. This coverage applies mainly to other vehicles; however, it also includes damage to street signs, lampposts, buildings, and other property. Property damage liability protects you and others covered by your policy when driving another person's automobile with permission. The policy limit for property damage liability is commonly stated with your bodily injury coverages. The last number in 50/100/25 and 100/300/50, for example, is for property damage liability ($25,000 and $50,000, respectively).

COLLISION When your automobile is involved in an accident, **collision** insurance pays for the damage to the automobile regardless of fault. However, if another driver caused the accident, your insurance company may attempt to recover the repair costs for your vehicle through the other driver's property damage liability. The insurance company's right to recover the amount it pays for the loss from the person responsible for the loss is called *subrogation.*

The amount you can collect with collision insurance is limited to the actual cash value of the automobile at the time of the accident. This amount is usually based on the figures provided by some appraisal service such as the *Official Used Car Guide* of the National Automobile Dealers Association (www.nada.org). If you have an automobile with many add-on

DID YOU KNOW?

Global positioning systems (GPSs) and other technology are being used to encourage safer driving and reduce auto insurance costs. In Britain, one insurance company adjusts premiums each month based on a driver's braking and acceleration habits. The Car Chip (www.carchip.com) allows parents to monitor the speed and braking actions of young drivers.

ARE YOU COVERED?

Often people believe their insurance will cover various financial losses. For each of the following situations, name the type of home or automobile insurance that would protect you.

1. While you are on vacation, clothing and other personal belongings are stolen. ______________
2. Your home is damaged by fire, and you have to live in a hotel for several weeks. ______________
3. You and members of your family suffer injuries in an automobile accident caused by a hit-and-run driver. ______________
4. A delivery person is injured on your property and takes legal action against you. ______________
5. Your automobile is accidentally damaged by some people playing baseball. ______________
6. A person takes legal action against you for injuries you caused in an automobile accident. ______________
7. Water from a local lake rises and damages your furniture and carpeting. ______________
8. Your automobile needs repairs because you hit a tree. ______________
9. You damaged a valuable tree when your automobile hit it, and you want to pay for the damage. ______________
10. While riding with you in your automobile, your nephew is injured in an accident and incurs various medical expenses. ______________

Answers: (1) Personal property coverage of home insurance; (2) additional living expenses of home insurance; (3) uninsured motorist's protection; (4) personal liability coverage of home insurance; (5) comprehensive physical damage; (6) bodily injury liability; (7) flood insurance—requires coverage separate from home insurance; (8) collision; (9) property damage liability of automobile insurance; (10) medical payments.

features or one that is several years old and has been restored, you should obtain a documented statement of its condition and value before an accident occurs.

my life 5 

Knowing the main types of auto insurance coverages is vital for reduced financial risk.

Auto insurance coverages are not completely understood by many people. In an attempt to increase your knowledge and to inform others, conduct a series of informal discussions with various people about the purpose of the main types of auto insurance coverages.

COMPREHENSIVE PHYSICAL DAMAGE

Another protection for your automobile involves financial losses from damage caused by a risk other than a collision. **Comprehensive physical damage** covers you for risks such as fire, theft, glass breakage, falling objects, vandalism, wind, hail, flood, tornado, lightning, earthquake, avalanche, or damage caused by hitting an animal. Certain articles in your vehicle, such as some radios and stereo systems, may be excluded from this insurance. These articles may be protected by the personal property coverage of your home insurance. Like collision insurance, comprehensive coverage applies only to your car, and claims are paid without considering fault. Both collision and comprehensive coverage are commonly sold with a *deductible* to help reduce insurance costs. Deductibles keep insurance premiums lower by reducing the number of small claims companies pay. Going from full-coverage comprehensive insurance to a $100 deductible may reduce the cost of that coverage by as much as 40 percent.

comprehensive physical damage Automobile insurance that covers financial loss from damage to a vehicle caused by a risk other than a collision, such as fire, theft, glass breakage, hail, or vandalism.

EXAMPLE: Deductible

If a broken windshield costs $250 to replace and you have a $100 deductible on your comprehensive coverage, the insurance company will pay $150 of the damages.

OTHER AUTOMOBILE INSURANCE COVERAGES

In addition to basic bodily injury and property damage coverages, other protection is available. *Wage loss insurance* will reimburse you for any salary or income lost due to injury in an automobile accident. Wage loss insurance is usually required in states with a no-fault insurance system; in other states, it is available on an optional basis.

Towing and emergency road service coverage pays for the cost of breakdowns and mechanical assistance. This coverage can be especially beneficial on long trips or during inclement weather. Towing and road service coverage pays for the cost of getting the vehicle to a service station or starting it when it breaks down on the highway, not for the cost of repairs. If you belong to an automobile club, your membership may include towing coverage. Purchasing duplicate coverage as part of your automobile insurance could be a waste of money. Rental reimbursement coverage pays for a rental car if your vehicle is stolen or is in the shop for repairs from an accident or for other covered damages.

PRACTICE QUIZ 10-5

1 What is the purpose of financial responsibility laws?
2 What are the main coverages included in most automobile insurance policies?
3 What is no-fault insurance?
4 How does collision coverage differ from comprehensive physical damage coverage?

Automobile Insurance Costs

LO10-6

Evaluate factors that affect the cost of automobile insurance.

Most households spend more than $1,200 for auto insurance each year. Automobile insurance premiums reflect the amounts insurance companies pay for injury and property damage claims. Your automobile insurance is directly related to coverage amounts and factors such as the vehicle, your place of residence, and your driving record.

DID YOU KNOW?

The foods and drinks that were reported as the most common distractions in auto accidents: coffee, hot soup, tacos, chili-covered foods, hamburgers, chicken, jelly- or cream-filled doughnuts, and soft drinks. These are in addition to other common driving disruptions such as cell phones and other electronic devices, shaving, cosmetics, and reading.

AMOUNT OF COVERAGE

"How much coverage do I need?" This question affects the amount you pay for insurance. Our legal environment and increasing property values influence coverage amounts.

LEGAL CONCERNS As discussed earlier, every state has laws that require or encourage automobile liability insurance coverage. Since very few people can afford to pay an expensive court settlement with personal assets, most drivers buy automobile liability insurance.

In the past, bodily injury liability coverage of 10/20 was considered adequate. In fact, most states have only recently increased their minimum limits for financial responsibility above 10/20. However, in recent injury cases, some people have been awarded millions of dollars; thus, legal and insurance advisers now recommend 100/300. As discussed earlier in this chapter, an umbrella policy can provide additional liability coverage of $1 million or more.

PROPERTY VALUES Just as medical expenses and legal settlements have increased, so has the cost of vehicles. Therefore, a policy limit of more than $10,000 for property damage liability is appropriate; $50,000 or $100,000 is usually suggested.

AUTOMOBILE INSURANCE PREMIUM FACTORS

Several factors influence the premium you pay for automobile insurance. The main factors are vehicle type, rating territory, and driver classification.

AUTOMOBILE TYPE The year, make, and model of your motor vehicle strongly influence automobile insurance costs. Expensive replacement parts and complicated repairs due to body style contribute to higher rates. Also, certain makes and models are stolen more often than others.

DID YOU KNOW?

While larger cars are usually safer than smaller ones in a crash, bigger vehicles often cause more damage to other cars. Certain models of pickups, sport utility vehicles, and sedans resulted in the greatest property damage liability claims, according to the Highway Data Loss Institute.

RATING TERRITORY In most states, your **rating territory** is the place of residence used to determine your automobile insurance premium. Various geographic locations have different costs due to differences in the number of claims made. For example, fewer accidents and less vandalism occur in rural areas than in large cities. New York City, Los Angeles, and Chicago have the highest incidence of automobile theft.

rating territory The place of residence used to determine a person's automobile insurance premium.

DRIVER CLASSIFICATION You are compared with other drivers to set your automobile insurance premium. **Driver classification** is a category based on the driver's age, sex, marital status, driving record, and driving habits; drivers' categories are used to determine automobile insurance rates. In general, young drivers (under 25) and those over 70 have more frequent and severe accidents. As a result, they pay higher premiums.

driver classification A category based on the driver's age, sex, marital status, driving record, and driving habits; used to determine automobile insurance rates.

Accidents and traffic violations influence your driver classification. A poor driving record increases your insurance costs. Finally, you pay less for insurance if you do not drive to work than if you use your automobile for business. Belonging to a carpool instead of driving to work alone can reduce insurance costs.

Your credit history may also be considered when applying for auto insurance. While some states limit the use of credit scoring in auto insurance, the practice is common in other areas.

The number of claims you file with your insurance company also affects your premiums. Expensive liability settlements or extensive property damage will increase your rates. If you have many expensive claims or a poor driving record, your company may cancel your policy, making it difficult for you to obtain coverage from another company. To deal with this problem, every state has an **assigned risk pool** consisting of people who are unable to obtain automobile insurance. Some of these people are assigned to each insurance company operating in the state. They pay several times the normal rates, but do get coverage. Once a good driving record is established, the driver can reapply for insurance with a lower premium.

assigned risk pool Consists of people who are unable to obtain automobile insurance due to poor driving or accident records and must obtain coverage at high rates through a state program that requires insurance companies to accept some of them.

HOW TO...

Decide Whether to File an Auto Insurance Claim

You quickly back out of your driveway, late for a meeting. A short mental lapse and BANG . . . you hit a post at the end of your driveway. The damage seems minor. Should you report it to your insurance company? As you answer this question, consider the following:

1. *Are you required to file all damages?* Some insurance companies require that all accidents be reported. This policy condition prevents a driver from missing hidden damages.
2. *Was someone else involved?* Insurance companies strongly encourage filing a claim when others are involved. Reporting the incident is especially crucial when a person appears to be injured.
3. *How much is your deductible?* If your collision deductible is $500 and you have $600 of damage, not reporting the claim might be appropriate. Remember, higher deductibles will reduce your insurance costs, but will also increase the amount you have to pay when a claim is filed. Be sure to set aside money for those situations.
4. *What recent claims have you had?* If you have an accident-free record for several years, a claim may be an appropriate action. However, several claims in a short time period may increase your rates or make it difficult to obtain future coverage.

While no one plans to have an auto accident, more than 6 million occur each year. If you are involved in an auto accident, take the following actions:

- Stop your vehicle. Turn off the engine. Stay at the accident scene. Remain calm.
- Seek medical assistance for anyone with injuries; **do not move** an injured person.
- Obtain names and contact information of others in the accident and witnesses. Take notes and photos to document the circumstances of the accident.
- File an accident report with the police; obtain a copy of the accident report. Also, file any necessary reports with state agencies.
- Discuss the accident only with the police; do not admit any fault or liability.

Source: Excerpted in part from Mark Solheim, "When to Phone in a Fender Bender: Filing a Claim for Minor Damage Could be a Second Accident," Kiplinger's Personal Finance, March 2005. Used with permission.

my life 6

Various actions are available to reduce auto insurance costs.

People take various actions to reduce their auto insurance costs. Locate a blog about auto insurance coverage and costs. What advice is offered that you might consider?

REDUCING AUTOMOBILE INSURANCE PREMIUMS

Methods for lowering automobile insurance costs include comparing companies and taking advantage of commonly offered discounts.

COMPARING COMPANIES Rates and service vary among automobile insurance companies. Among companies in the same area, premiums can vary as much as 100 percent. If you relocate, don't assume your present company will offer the best rates in your new living area. Rates may be compared online at www.netquote.com.

Also consider the service the local insurance agent provides. Will this company representative be available to answer questions, change coverages, and handle claims as needed? You can check a company's reputation for handling automobile insurance claims and other matters with sources such as *Consumer Reports* or your state insurance department. Several states publish information with sample auto insurance rates for different companies to help consumers save money. The address and contact information of your state insurance regulator may be found online.

DID YOU KNOW?

To reduce driving accidents among teens, some parents have installed an in-car monitoring device that records seat belt use, engine speed, and tire traction. The device also beeps when preset limits for speed, braking, or sharp turns are violated.

PREMIUM DISCOUNTS The best way to keep your rates down is to establish and maintain a safe driving record. Taking steps to avoid accidents and traffic violations will mean lower automobile insurance premiums. In addition, most insurance companies offer various discounts. Drivers under 25 can qualify for reduced rates by completing a driver training program or maintaining good grades in school. When young drivers are away at school without a car, families are likely to get reduced premiums since the student will not be using the vehicle on a regular basis.

Installing security devices such as a fuel shutoff switch, a second ignition switch, or an alarm system will decrease your chances of theft and lower your insurance costs. Being a nonsmoker can qualify you for lower automobile insurance premiums. Discounts are also offered for participating in a carpool and insuring two or more vehicles with the same company. Ask your insurance agent about other methods for lowering your automobile insurance rates.

Increasing the amount of deductibles will result in a lower premium. Also, some people believe an old car is not worth the amount paid for collision and comprehensive coverages and therefore dispense with them. However, before doing this, be sure to compare the value of your car for getting you to school or work with the cost of these coverages.

If you change your driving habits, get married, or alter your driving status in other ways, be sure to notify the insurance company. Premium savings can result. Also, some employers make group automobile insurance available to workers. Before you buy a motor vehicle, find out which makes and models have the lowest insurance costs. This information can result in a purchasing decision with many financial benefits.

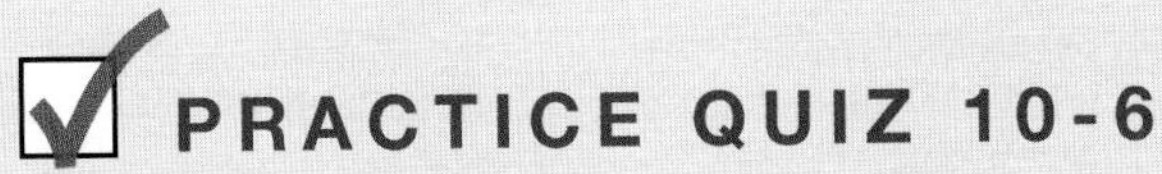

1 What factors influence how much a person pays for automobile insurance?
2 What actions can a person take to reduce the cost of automobile insurance?

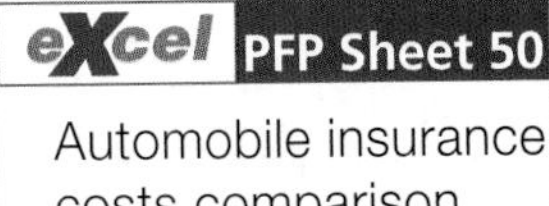

Automobile insurance costs comparison

my life stages for home and auto insurance...

YOUR PERSONAL FINANCE DASHBOARD

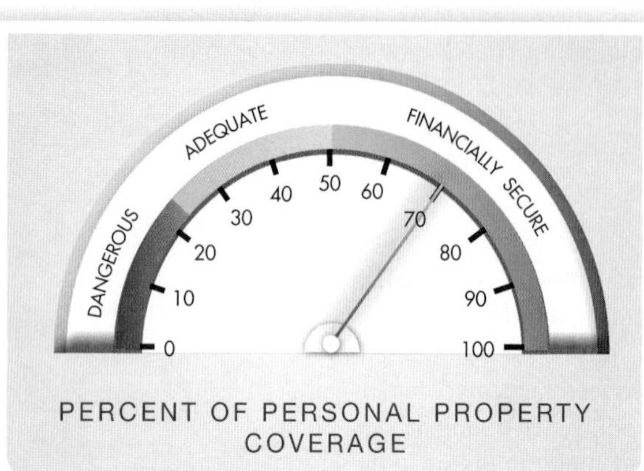

A personal finance dashboard can help you determine if you have proper coverage for household belongings. Homeowner's insurance protects you against financial loss in case your home is damaged or destroyed.

Your household belongings, such as furniture, appliances, and clothing, are covered by the personal property portion of a homeowners insurance policy up to a portion of the insured value of the home. That portion may range from 55 to 75 percent.

YOUR SITUATION Have you established a specific and measurable portion of coverage for your household belongings? Do you have adequate additional living expense coverage if a fire or other event damages your home? Some policies limit additional living expense coverage to 10 to 20 percent of the home's total coverage amount. Have you considered a personal property floater for additional property insurance that covers the damage or loss of a specific item of high value? Other insurance actions you might consider during various stages of your life include. . . .

. . . in college

- Obtain appropriate auto insurance coverage based on vehicle value, driving habits, and financial situation
- Consider renters insurance to cover personal property and liability risks

. . . in my 20s

- Determine additional home property and motor vehicle insurance coverage based on current life situation
- Prepare inventory (list, receipts, photos, video) of personal belongings

. . . in my 30s and 40s

- Review home insurance policy to determine possible coverage changes and discounts
- Assess auto insurance coverage based on changes in household and vehicle situation

. . . in my 50s and beyond

- Determine potential changes in driving habits that might affect auto insurance costs
- Update home and property insurance coverage based on housing situation

SUMMARY OF LEARNING OBJECTIVES

LO10-1

Develop a risk management plan using insurance.

An understanding of various risk management actions can reduce the chance of financial loss. The four general risk management techniques are risk avoidance, risk reduction, risk assumption, and risk shifting. In planning a personal insurance program, set your goals, make a plan to reach your goals, put your plan into action, and review your results.

LO10-2

Discuss the importance of property and liability insurance.

Your knowledge of property and liability insurance coverages should include awareness that owners of homes and automobiles face the risks of (1) property damage or loss and (2) legal actions by others for the costs of injuries or property damage. Property and liability insurance offer protection from financial losses that may arise from a wide variety of situations faced by owners of homes and users of automobiles.

LO10-3

Explain the insurance coverages and policy types available to homeowners and renters.

Appropriate homeowner's or renter's insurance coverage is a fundamental aspect of personal financial planning. Homeowner's insurance includes protection for the building and other structures, additional living expenses, personal property, and personal liability. Renter's insurance includes the same coverages excluding protection for the building and other structures, which is the concern of the building owner.

LO10-4

Analyze factors that influence the amount of coverage and the cost of home insurance.

Awareness of methods to reduce homeowner's or renter's insurance costs can result in big savings. The amount of home insurance coverage is determined by the replacement cost of your dwelling and personal belongings. The cost of home insurance is influenced by the location of the home, the type of structure, the coverage amount, the policy type, discounts, and insurance company differences.

LO10-5

Identify the important types of automobile insurance coverages.

Your understanding of the main types of auto insurance coverages is vital for successful financial planning. Automobile insurance is used to meet states' financial responsibility laws and to protect drivers against financial losses associated with bodily injury and property damage. The major types of automobile insurance coverages are bodily injury liability, medical payments, uninsured motorists, property damage liability, collision, and comprehensive physical damage.

LO10-6

Evaluate factors that affect the cost of automobile insurance.

Various actions can be taken to reduce auto insurance costs. The cost of automobile insurance is affected by the amount of coverage, automobile type, rating territory, driver classification, differences among insurance companies, and premium discounts.

KEY TERMS

SELF-TEST PROBLEMS

1. A person with homeowner's insurance incurs roof damage of $17,000. The policy has a $500 deductible. What amount would the insurance pay for the claim?
2. A person lost control of the vehicle that was being driven and hit a parked car, and damaged a storefront. The damage to the parked car was $4,300 and the damage to the store was $15,400. If the driver has 50/100/15 vehicle insurance coverage, what amount will the insurance company pay? Is the driver responsible for any of the damages?

Solutions

1. The claim would be settled for $16,500 ($17,000 minus the $500 deductible)
2. Of the total damages of $19,700, the insurance company would pay $15,000. The driver would be responsible for $4,700 (19,700 − $15,000).

FINANCIAL PLANNING PROBLEMS

LO10-2 1. *Calculating Property Loss Claim Coverage.* Most home insurance policies cover jewelry for $1,000 and silverware for $2,500 unless items are covered with additional insurance. If $3,800 worth of jewelry and $2,800 worth of silverware were stolen from a family, what amount of the claim would not be covered by insurance?

LO10-3 2. *Computing Actual Cash Value Coverage.* What amount would a person with actual cash value (ACV) coverage receive for two-year-old furniture destroyed by a fire? The furniture would cost $1,000 to replace today and had an estimated life of five years.

LO10-3 3. *Determining Replacement Cost.* What would it cost an insurance company to replace a family's personal property that originally cost $42,000? The replacement costs for the items have increased 15 percent.

LO10-4 4. *Calculating a Coinsurance Claim.* If Carissa Dalton has a $130,000 home insured for $100,000, based on the 80 percent coinsurance provision, how much would the insurance company pay on a $5,000 claim?

LO10-3 5. *Determining the Claim Amount (with Deductibles).* For each of the following situations, what amount would the insurance company pay?

a. Wind damage of $835; the insured has a $500 deductible.

b. Theft of a home entertainment system worth $1,150; the insured has a $250 deductible.

c. Vandalism that does $425 of damage to a home; the insured has a $500 deductible.

LO10-3 6. *Computing Claims.* When Carolina's house burned down, she lost household items worth a total of $50,000. Her house was insured for $160,000 and her homeowner's policy provided coverage for personal belongings up to 55 percent of the insured value of the house. Calculate how much insurance coverage Carolina's policy provides for her personal possessions and whether she will receive payment for all of the items destroyed in the fire.

LO10-3 7. *Calculating Insurance Discounts.* Matt and Kristin are newly married and living in their first house. The yearly premium on their homeowner's insurance policy is $450 for the coverage they need. Their insurance company offers a 5 percent discount if they install dead-bolt locks on all exterior doors. The couple can also receive a 2 percent discount if they install smoke detectors on each floor. They have contacted a locksmith, who will provide and install dead-bolt locks on the two exterior doors for $60 each. At the local hardware store, smoke detectors cost $8 each, and the new house has two floors. Kristin and Matt can install them themselves. What discount will Matt and Kristin receive if they install the dead-bolt locks? If they install smoke detectors?

LO10-3 8. *Computing Discount Payback.* In the preceding problem, assuming their insurance rates remain the same, how many years will it take Matt and Kristin to earn back in discounts the cost of the dead-bolts? The cost of the smoke detectors?

LO10-5 9. *Calculating Auto Liability Claim Coverage.* Becky Fenton has 25/50/10 automobile insurance coverage. If two other people are awarded $35,000 each for injuries in an auto accident in which Becky was judged at fault, how much of this judgment would the insurance cover?

LO10-5 10. *Determining a Property Damage Liability Claim.* Kurt Simmons has 50/100/15 auto insurance coverage. One evening he lost control of his vehicle, hitting a parked car and damaging a storefront along the street. Damage to the parked car was $5,400, and damage to the store was $12,650. What amount will the insurance company pay for the damages? What amount will Kurt have to pay?

LO10-6 11. *Calculating Future Value of Insurance Savings.* Beverly and Kyle Nelson currently insure their cars with separate companies, paying $650 and $575 a year. If they insured both cars with the same company, they would save 10 percent on the annual premiums. What would be the future value of the annual savings over 10 years based on an annual interest rate of 6 percent?

FINANCIAL PLANNING ACTIVITIES

1. *Determining Insurance Coverages.* Survey friends and relatives to determine the types of insurance coverages they have. Also, ask them about the process they followed when selecting and comparing various insurance coverages. L010-1
2. *Analyzing Insurance Coverages.* Talk to a financial planner or an insurance agent about the financial difficulties faced by people who lack adequate home and auto insurance. What common coverages do many people overlook? L010-2
3. *Maintaining a Household Inventory.* Survey several people about their household inventory methods. In the event of damage or loss, would they be able to prove the value of their personal property and other belongings? L010-3
4. *Comparing Homeowner's Insurance Costs.* Contact two or three insurance agents to obtain information about homeowner's or renter's insurance. Use Sheet 49 in the Personal Financial Planner to compare the coverages and costs. L010-4
5. *Reducing Homeowner's Insurance Costs.* Talk to several homeowners about the actions they take to reduce the cost of their homeowner's insurance. Locate websites that offer information about reducing homeowner's insurance costs. Prepare a video or other visual presentation to communicate your findings. L010-4
6. *Assessing Property Risks.* Conduct Web research or contact an insurance agent to determine the natural disasters that occur most frequently in your geographic area. What actions could a renter or homeowner take to reduce the financial risk of these natural disasters? L010-4
7. *Comparing Auto Insurance Costs.* Contact two or three insurance agents to obtain information about automobile insurance. Use Sheet 50 in the Personal Financial Planner to compare costs and coverages for various insurance companies. L010-6

FINANCIAL PLANNING CASE

We Rent, So Why Do We Need Insurance?

"Have you been down in the basement?" Nathan asked his wife, Erin, as he entered their apartment.

"No, what's up?" responded Erin.

"It's flooded because of all that rain we got last weekend!" he exclaimed.

"Oh no! We have the extra furniture my mom gave us stored down there. Is everything ruined?" Erin asked.

"The couch and coffee table are in a foot of water; the loveseat was the only thing that looked OK. Boy, I didn't realize the basement of this building wasn't waterproof. I'm going to call our landlady to complain."

As Erin thought about the situation, she remembered that when they moved in last fall, Kathy, their landlady, had informed them that her insurance policy covered the building but not the property belonging to each tenant. Because of this, they had purchased renter's insurance. "Nathan, I think our renter's insurance will cover the damage. Let me give our agent a call."

When Erin and Nathan purchased their insurance, they had to decide whether they wanted to be insured for cash value or for replacement costs. Replacement was more expensive, but it meant they would collect enough to go out and buy new household items at today's prices. If they had opted for cash value, the couch Erin's mother had paid $1,000 for five years ago would be worth less than $500 today.

Erin made the call and found out their insurance did cover the furniture in the basement, and at replacement value after they paid the deductible. The $300 they had invested in renter's insurance last year was well worth it!

Not every renter has as much foresight as Erin and Nathan. Fewer than 4 in 10 renters have renter's insurance. Some aren't even aware they need it. They may assume they are covered by the landlord's insurance, but they aren't. This mistake can be costly.

Think about how much you have invested in your possessions and how much it would cost to replace them. Start with your home entertainment system that you bought last year. Experts suggest that people who rent start thinking about these things as soon as they move into their first apartment. Your policy should cover your personal belongings and provide funds for living expenses if you are dispossessed by a fire or other disaster.

Questions

1. Why is it important for people who rent to have insurance?
2. Does the building owner's property insurance ever cover the tenant's personal property?
3. What is the difference between cash value and replacement value?
4. When shopping for renter's insurance, what coverage features should you look for?

PERSONAL FINANCIAL PLANNER IN ACTION

Obtaining Home and Auto Insurance

Creating an insurance plan, including appropriate coverage for your home, personal property, and motor vehicles, helps to avoid financial difficulties.

Your Short-Term Financial Planning Activities	*Resources*
1. List current and needed insurance coverages.	PFP Sheet 46, 48 www.smartmoney.com/insurance www.insure.com www.iii.org
2. (a) Prepare an inventory of personal belongings. (b) Compare the cost of homeowner's or renter's insurance from two or more companies.	PFP Sheet 47, 49 www.netquote.com www.insweb.com
3. Compare the cost of auto insurance from two or more companies	PFP Sheet 50 http://personalinsure.about.com www.insquote
Your Long-Term Financial Planning Activities	*Resources*
1. Identify buying decisions that could reduce your future home and auto insurance costs.	Text pages 350–351, 358–359 www.iiaa.com
2. Develop a plan to monitor changes in your life situation that would affect the need to change home or auto insurance coverages.	www.ircweb.org www.nqic.org

CONTINUING CASE

Property Insurance

Life Situation	*Financial Data*	
Young married couple	Monthly Gross Income	$4,000
Shelby, age 26	Living Expenses	$3,500
Mark, age 27	Assets	$180,000
	Liabilities	$123,000

Shelby and Mark Lawrence recently purchased a condo as their first home together. They have been advised by their parents, Matthew and Madison, to obtain homeowner's insurance from a reliable company and to analyze their situation to determine the appropriate coverage. At the same time, they need to review the components of their automobile insurance on their vehicles to make sure their coverage is appropriate and adequate. They admit that they could use some help in understanding both types of insurance.

Questions

1. When obtaining homeowner's insurance for their condo, what factors should the Lawrences consider in determining the amount of home insurance coverage they will need?

2. What are the two categories of automobile insurance coverage that Shelby and Mark should consider when purchasing automobile insurance and what do they include?

3. Explain how Shelby and Mark might use these Personal Financial Planner sheets as they assess property insurance:

a. Determining Needed Property Insurance

b. Automobile Insurance Cost Comparison

"My spending takes most of my money. So after adding car insurance payments, my budget is really tight."

Directions

As you continue (or start using) the "Daily Spending Diary" sheets, you should be able to make better choices for your spending priorities. The financial data you develop will help you better understand your spending patterns and help you plan for achieving financial goals.

Analysis Questions

1. What information from your Daily Spending Diary might encourage you to use your money differently?
2. How can your spending habits be developed to assure that you will be able to afford appropriate home and auto insurance coverage?

The Daily Spending Diary Sheets are located in Appendix D at the end of the book and on the student website at www.mhhe.com/kdh.

chapter 11

Health, Disability, and Long-Term Care Insurance

Learning Objectives

LO11-1 Explain why the costs of health insurance and health care have been increasing.

LO11-2 Define *health insurance* and *disability income insurance* and explain their importance in financial planning.

LO11-3 Analyze the benefits and limitations of the various types of health care coverage.

LO11-4 Evaluate private sources of health insurance and health care.

LO11-5 Appraise the sources of government health care programs.

LO11-6 Recognize the need for disability income insurance.

What will this mean for me?

Knowing how to determine the type of health, disability, and long-term care insurance that you need can help you meet your financial goals even when dealing with unexpected medical costs or the inability to work.

my life

KEEP FIT AND HEALTHY FOREVER?

You are young. You are healthy. And it's easy to take good health for granted. However, as you get older, staying healthy can become a challenge. Because health insurance premiums have outpaced inflation for more than a decade, you are paying more for your health insurance premiums and copayments every time you visit a doctor. Health, disability, and long-term care insurance are an important part of your financial planning. How can you best plan for your health, disability, and long-term care insurance as you grow older?

For each of the following statements, select "agree," "neutral," or "disagree" to indicate your personal response regarding these health and disability income insurance topics.

1. The best way to avoid the high cost of illness for me and my family is to stay well.	Agree	Neutral	Disagree
2. To safeguard my family's economic security, medical expense insurance and disability income insurance should be a part of my overall insurance program.	Agree	Neutral	Disagree
3. With today's high cost of health care, it makes sense for me to be as fully insured as I can afford.	Agree	Neutral	Disagree
4. My membership in an HMO should cover office visits, routine checkups, hospital and surgical care, eye exams, laboratory and x-ray service, and mental health services.	Agree	Neutral	Disagree
5. I am aware of various state and federal health care programs.	Agree	Neutral	Disagree
6. I realize that for all age groups, disability is more likely than death.	Agree	Neutral	Disagree

As you study this chapter, you will encounter "My Life" boxes with additional information and resources related to these items.

Health Care Costs

LO11-1

Explain why the costs of health insurance and health care have been increasing.

Health insurance is one way people protect themselves against economic losses due to illness, accident, or disability. Health coverage is available through private insurance companies, service plans, health maintenance organizations, and government programs. Employers often offer health insurance, called *group health insurance,* as part of an employee benefits package, and health care providers sell it to individuals.

Affordable health care has become one of the most important social issues of our time. News broadcasts abound with special reports on "America's health care crisis" or politicians demanding "universal health insurance." "Unless we fix our health care system—in both the public and private sectors—rising health care costs will have severe, adverse consequences for the federal budget as well as the U.S. economy in the future." This is one of the key messages that politicians have been delivering across the country in town-hall style meetings, in speeches, and on radio and television programs.

Consequently, on March 23, 2010, President Obama signed the Patient Protection and Affordable Care Act, and the Health Care and Education Reconciliation Act on March 30, 2010. The Obama Administration believes that this comprehensive health care reform should:

- Reduce long-term growth of health care costs for businesses and government.
- Protect families from bankruptcy or debt because of health care costs.
- Guarantee choice of doctors and health plans.
- Invest in prevention and wellness.
- Improve patient safety and quality of care.
- Assure affordable, quality health coverage for all Americans.
- Maintain coverage when you change or lose your job.
- End barriers to coverage for people with pre-existing medical conditions.

However, the health care debate still continues even though the U.S. Supreme Court upheld the law on June 28, 2012. Polls suggest that the public has been opposed to reform as passed, and opponents have vowed that the debate will continue into the future. The Republicans labeled the Act as "a fiscal Frankenstein," "a decisive step in the weakening of the United States," and "one of the worst offenses of social engineering legislation in the history of the United States," while the Democrats hailed the law as "a new day in America," and that it would "improve the quality of life for millions of American families." Let us stay tuned!

HIGH MEDICAL COSTS

What do an aging and overweight population, the cost of prescription drugs, the growing number of uninsured, and advancements in medical technology have in common? These and other factors all add up to rising health costs. The United States has the highest per capita medical expenditures of any country in the world. We spend twice as much on health care as the average for the 24 industrialized countries in Europe and North America. The average per capita cost for health care was $9,767 in 2013. It seems that, year after year, there is a third sure thing for U.S. citizens besides death and taxes: higher health costs.

Health care costs were estimated at $3.111 trillion in 2013 (see Exhibit 11-1). Since 1993, health care spending as a percentage of gross domestic product (GDP) has remained relatively constant at 13.6 percent, except in 1997, when it fell to 13.4 percent, and in 2005, when it increased to 16 percent. Despite the recession, health care spending rose approximately 3.9 percent to $2.77 trillion in 2011. Furthermore, the percentage of GDP spent on health care jumped to 17.9 percent from 16.2 percent in 2008. The latest projections from The Centers for Medicare and Medicaid Services show that over the next 5 years annual health care spending is expected to grow to $4.35 trillion, or almost 20 percent of GDP.

Exhibit 11-1 U.S. national health expenditures, 1960–2018

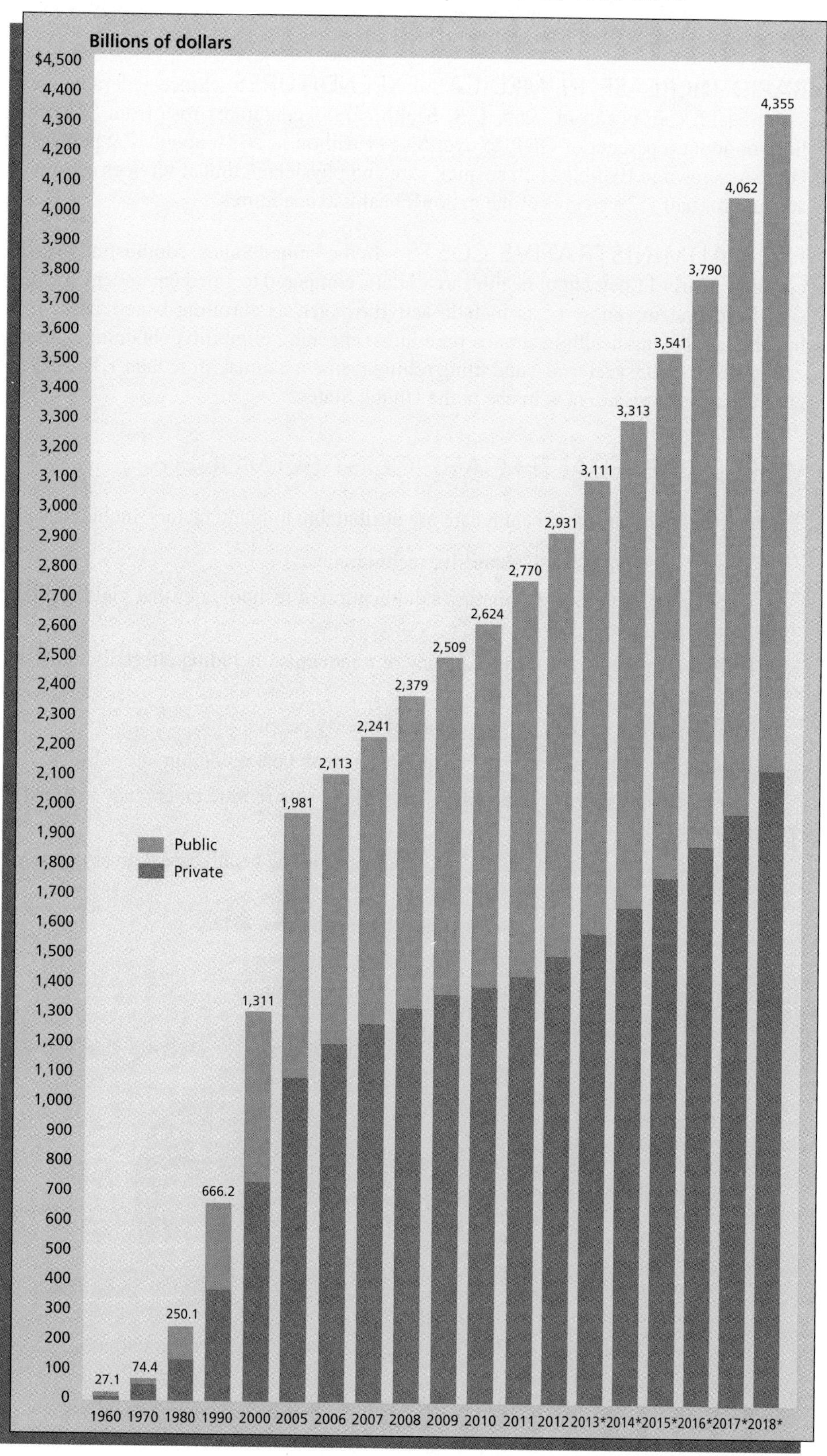

* Projected

Source: http://www.census.gov/compendia/statab/2010/tables/10s0127.pdf, accessed March 18, 2013.

Yet about 50 million people under the age of 65, or 15 percent of our population, have no health insurance.[1] While national health care reform will extend coverage to many of these people, most will remain uninsured until 2014.

RAPID INCREASE IN MEDICAL EXPENDITURES Since federally sponsored health care began in 1965, U.S. health care expenditures rose from $41.6 billion, or about 6 percent of GDP, to over $3.111 trillion in 2013, about 17.9 percent of GDP. As shown in Exhibit 11-2, hospital care and physician/clinical services combined account for half (52 percent) of the nation's health expenditures.

HIGH ADMINISTRATIVE COSTS In the United States, administrative costs consume nearly 11 percent of health care dollars, compared to 1 percent under Canada's socialized system. These costs include activities such as enrolling beneficiaries in a health plan, paying health insurance premiums, checking eligibility, obtaining authorizations for specialist referrals, and filing reimbursement claims. More than 1,100 different insurance forms are now in use in the United States.

WHY DOES HEALTH CARE COST SO MUCH?

The high and rising costs of health care are attributable to many factors, including

- The use of sophisticated, expensive technologies.
- Duplication of tests and sometimes duplication of technologies that yield similar results.
- Increases in the variety and frequency of treatments, including allegedly unnecessary tests.
- The increasing number and longevity of elderly people.
- Regulations that result in cost shifting rather than cost reduction.
- The increasing number of accidents and crimes that require emergency medical services.
- Limited competition and restrictive work rules in the health care delivery system.

Exhibit 11-2

How is the U.S. health care dollar spent?

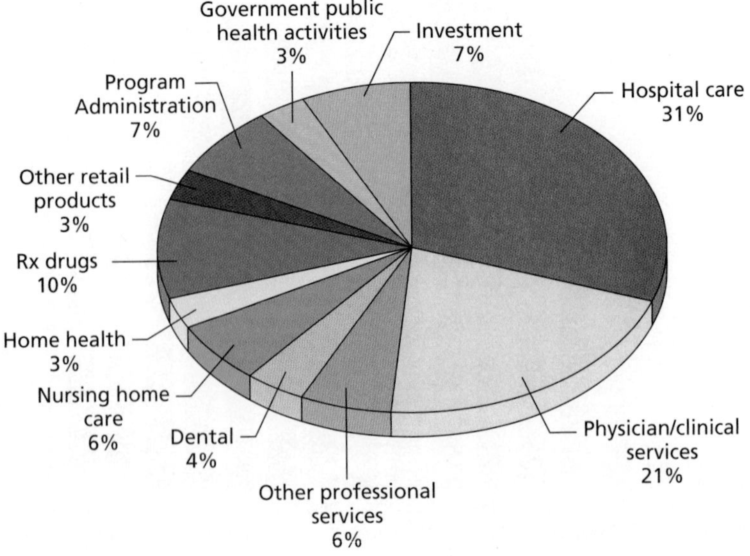

Source: Centers for Medicare and Medicaid Services, Office of the Actuary, National Health Statistics Group, March 2013.

- Labor intensiveness and rapid average earnings growth for health care professionals and executives.
- Using more expensive medical care than necessary, such as going to an emergency room with a bad cold.
- Built-in inflation in the health care delivery system.
- Aging baby boomers' use of more health care services, whether they're going to the doctor more often or snapping up pricier drugs, from Celebrex to Viagra.
- Other major factors that cost billions of dollars each year, including fraud, administrative waste, malpractice insurance, excessive surgical procedures, a wide range of prices for similar services, and double health coverage.

According to the Government Accountability Office, fraud and abuse account for nearly 10 percent of all dollars spent on health care.

Because third parties—private health insurers and government—pay such a large part of the nation's health care bill, hospitals, doctors, and patients often lack the incentive to make the most economical use of health care services.

WHAT IS BEING DONE ABOUT THE HIGH COSTS OF HEALTH CARE?

In the private sector, concerned groups such as employers, labor unions, health insurers, health care professionals, and consumers have undertaken a wide range of innovative activities to contain the costs of health care. These activities include

- Programs to carefully review health care fees and charges and the use of health care services.
- The establishment of incentives to encourage preventive care and provide more services out of hospitals, where this is medically acceptable.
- Involvement in community health planning to help achieve a better balance between health needs and health care resources.
- The encouragement of prepaid group practices and other alternatives to fee-for-service arrangements.
- Community health education programs that motivate people to take better care of themselves.
- Physicians encouraging patients to pay cash for routine medical care and lab tests.

President Barack Obama maintains that improving health information technology could lower costs, setting up electronic health records would be a "smart" investment and could reduce medical errors. According to Karen Davis, president of Commonwealth Fund, a health policy research organization, "improvements in health information technology could save $88 billion over 10 years, though no gains will be realized in the first few years."

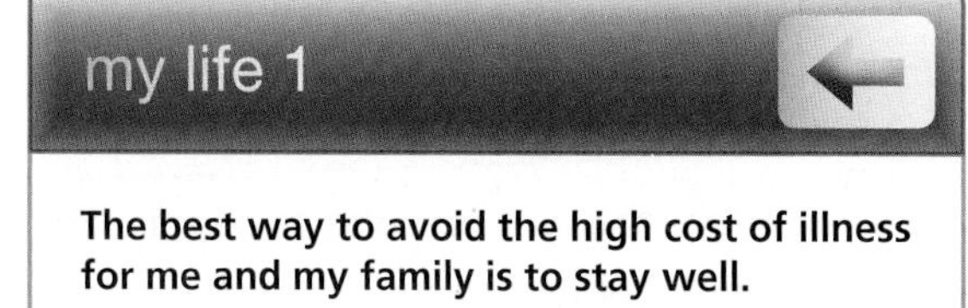

The best way to avoid the high cost of illness for me and my family is to stay well.

You can reduce personal health care costs by eating well, avoiding tobacco, getting sufficient rest, and driving carefully. For additional information visit the Office of Disease Prevention and Health Promotion at www.healthfinder.gov.

WHAT CAN YOU DO TO REDUCE PERSONAL HEALTH CARE COSTS?

As health care costs continue to rise, there are a few steps that you can take to reduce your own medical costs.

- Consider participating in a flexible spending account if your employer offers it.
- Consider a high-deductible health plan which provides medical insurance coverage and a tax-free opportunity to save for future medical needs.

- Ask your physician and pharmacist if a less expensive generic drug is available.
- Consider using a mail-order or legitimate on-line pharmacy, especially if you will take a drug for a long period.
- Most states offer free or low-cost coverage for children under 19 who do not have health insurance. Visit www.insurekidsnow.gov or call 1-877-KIDS-NOW for more information.
- Many states offer State Pharmacy Assistance Programs that help pay for prescription drugs based on financial need, age, or medical condition.
- If your doctor wants you to return for a follow-up visit, ask if it is really necessary, or can you follow up by phone.
- If your doctor suggests a non-urgent procedure, ask for information and some time to think about it. Research the suggested treatment on Web MD (www.WebMD.com), compare costs on Health Care Blue Book (www.healthcarebluebook.com) or New Choice Health (www.newchoicehealth.com).
- Review billing statements from medical providers for billing errors.
- Appeal unfair decisions by your health plan (Read the accompanying "How to. . ." feature).
- Practice preventative care and stay well.

The best way to avoid the high cost of illness is to stay well. The prescription is the same as it has always been:

1. Eat a balanced diet and keep your weight under control.
2. Avoid smoking and don't drink to excess.
3. Get sufficient rest, relaxation, and exercise.
4. Drive carefully and watch out for accident and fire hazards in the home.

HOW TO...

Appeal Health Insurance Claim Decisions

If your health insurer has denied coverage for medical care you received, you have a right to appeal the claim and ask that the company reverse that decision. You can be your own health care advocate. Here's what you can do:

Step 1: Review your policy and explanation of benefits.

Step 2: Contact your insurer and keep detailed records of your contacts (copies of letters, time and date of conversations).

Step 3: Request documentation from your doctor or employer to support your case.

Step 4: Write a formal complaint letter explaining what care was denied and why you are appealing through use of the company's internal review process.

Step 5: If the internal appeal is not granted through step 4, file a claim with your state's insurance department. For more information visit nclnet.org or statehealthfacts.org.

PRACTICE QUIZ 11-1

1 What are the reasons for rising health care expenditures?
2 What are various groups doing to curb the high costs of health care?
3 What can individuals do to reduce health care costs?

Health Insurance and Financial Planning

LO11-2

Define *health insurance* and *disability income insurance* and explain their importance in financial planning.

Although the United States spent over $3.1 trillion on health care in 2013 (see Exhibit 11-1), the number of Americans without basic health insurance has been growing. In this wealthy country of over 315.5 million people, about 50 million citizens have no health insurance. Two-thirds of uninsured persons are either full-time workers or family members of full-time employees.

According to recent government reports, two-thirds of uninsured pregnant women fail to receive adequate prenatal care. Among children, 40 percent fail to receive basic childhood vaccinations, 25 percent don't see a doctor even once a year, and 31 percent in low-income families lack health coverage.

A growing number of college students have been uninsured due to the growth of an older student population not covered by family policies. Today 40 percent of college students are older than 25.

WHAT IS HEALTH INSURANCE?

Health insurance is a form of protection to alleviate the financial burdens individuals suffer from illness or injury. According to The Centers for Medicare and Medicaid Services, health insurance includes both medical expense insurance and disability income insurance.

To safeguard my family's economic security, medical expense insurance and disability income insurance should be a part of my overall insurance program.

Your overall insurance program should include a comprehensive health care coverage. Many families go into debt because they did not have medical insurance or they did not have savings to pay the expenses that were not covered by their health plan.

HEALTH INSURANCE Health insurance, like other forms of insurance, reduces the financial burden of risk by dividing losses among many individuals. It works in the same way as life insurance, homeowner's insurance, and automobile insurance. You pay the insurance company a specified premium, and the company guarantees you some degree of financial protection. Like the premiums and benefits of other types of insurance, the premiums and benefits of health insurance are figured on the basis of average experience. To establish rates and benefits, insurance company actuaries rely on general statistics that tell them how many people in a certain population group will become ill and how much their illnesses will cost.

Medical expense insurance and disability income insurance, discussed in this chapter's last section, are an important part of your financial planning. To safeguard your family's economic security, both protections should be a part of your overall insurance program.

There are many ways individuals or groups of individuals can obtain health insurance protection. Planning a health insurance program takes careful study because the protection should be shaped to the needs of the individual or family. For many families, the task is simplified because the group health insurance they obtain at work already provides a foundation for their coverage.

GROUP HEALTH INSURANCE Group plans comprise about 90 percent of all the health insurance issued by health and life insurance companies. Most of these plans are employer sponsored, and the employer often pays part or most of their cost. Because insurance premiums have outpaced inflation for more than a decade, employers are increasing the share paid by employees and offering cheaper plans. Group insurance will cover you and your immediate family. Group insurance seldom requires evidence that you are insurable, if you enroll when you first become eligible for coverage.

The *Health Insurance Portability and Accountability Act of 1996 (HIPAA)* legislates new federal standards for health insurance portability, nondiscrimination in health insurance, and guaranteed renewability. The law provides tax breaks for long-term care insurance and authorizes various government agencies to investigate Medicare/Medicaid fraud and abuses.

This landmark legislation gives millions of workers the comfort of knowing that if they change jobs, they need not lose their health insurance. For example, a parent with a sick child can move from one group plan to another without lapses in health insurance and without paying more than other employees for coverage. In addition to providing health care portability, this law created a stable source of funding for fraud control activities.

The protection group insurance provides varies from plan to plan. The plan may not cover all of your health insurance needs; therefore, you will have to consider supplementing it with individual health insurance.

INDIVIDUAL HEALTH INSURANCE Individual health insurance covers either one person or a family. If the kind of health insurance you need is not available through a group or if you need coverage in addition to the coverage a group provides, you should obtain an individual policy—a policy tailored to your particular needs—from the company of your choice. This requires careful shopping, because coverage and cost vary from company to company. For example, the premiums for similar coverage can vary up to 50 percent for the same person, according to Mark Gurda, president of Castle Group Health in Northbrook, Illinois. Moreover, the rules and regulations vary from state to state.

Find out what your group insurance will pay for and what it won't. Make sure you have enough insurance, but don't waste money by overinsuring. Remember the opportunity cost of not being adequately insured can be extremely high.

SUPPLEMENTING YOUR GROUP INSURANCE A sign that your group coverage needs supplementing would be its failure to provide benefits for the major portion of your medical care bills, mainly hospital, doctor, and surgical charges. If, for example, your group policy will pay only $1,000 per day toward a hospital room and the cost in your area is $1,500, you should look for an individual policy that covers most of the remaining amount. Similarly, if your group policy will pay only about half the going rate for surgical procedures in your area, you need individual coverage for the other half.

In supplementing your group health insurance, consider the health insurance benefits your employer-sponsored plan provides for family members. Most group policy contracts have a **coordination of benefits (COB)** provision. The COB is a method of integrating the benefits payable under more than one health insurance plan so that the benefits received from all sources are limited to 100 percent of allowable medical expenses.

coordination of benefits (COB) A method of integrating the benefits payable under more than one health insurance plan.

If you have any questions about your group plan, you should be able to get answers from your employer, union, or association. If you have questions about an individual policy, talk with your insurance company representative. Since the cost of not being insured is very high, make sure to maintain your health insurance if you lose your job.

ALL YOU NEED TO KNOW ABOUT COBRA

Here's what you need to know about COBRA's continuation coverage. Remember, since your employer does not pay for COBRA coverage, you will pay the monthly premiums:

- In general, COBRA coverage requirements only apply to employers with 20 or more employees.
- If your family was covered under your employer coverage, they may also qualify for COBRA coverage.
- In most situations, you should get a notice from your employer's benefits administrator or the health plan telling you that your coverage is ending and offering you the right to take COBRA coverage.
- You have limited time to sign up for COBRA coverage. In most cases, you have 60 days after your last day of coverage to sign up for COBRA.
- COBRA coverage usually lasts for 18 months but could last up to 36 months. If you recently lost your employer health coverage, you may be eligible for a 65 percent reduction of your COBRA premium for up to 15 months.

WHERE CAN I GET MORE INFORMATION ABOUT COBRA COVERAGE?

- Call your employer's benefit administrator for questions about your specific COBRA coverage options.
- If your health plan coverage was from a private employer, you can visit the Department of Labor's website or call 1-866-444-3272.
- If your health plan coverage was from a state or local government employer, you can call 1-877-267-2323 extension 61565.
- If your coverage was with the Federal government, you can visit the Office of Personnel Management's website at www.opm.gov.

STATE COVERAGE SIMILAR TO COBRA COVERAGE

- Many states have laws similar to COBRA that apply to insurance bought by employers with fewer than 20 employees. Contact your State Department of Insurance to ensure that "state continuation coverage" applies to you.

Source: HealthCare.gov website at http://finder.healthcare.gov/more_info/cobra?age=3&audience=fam&no_afford=y&nojs=n, accessed March 16, 2013.

MEDICAL COVERAGE AND DIVORCE

Medical coverage of nonworking spouses is a concern when couples divorce. Under federal law, coverage under a former spouse's medical plan can be continued for 36 months if the former spouse works for a company with 20 or more employees.

Premiums will be totally paid by the individual and can run as high as $12,000 annually. If there are children and the custodial parent doesn't work, the working parent usually can still cover the children under an employer's group plan.

The federal *Consolidated Omnibus Budget Reconciliation Act of 1986 (COBRA)* requires many employers to offer employees and dependents who would otherwise lose group health insurance the option to continue their group coverage for a set period of time. Employees of private companies and state and local governments are covered by this law; employees of the federal government and religious institutions are not. Read the Financial Planning for Life's Situations box, "All You Need to Know about COBRA," to learn about COBRA's continuation coverage.

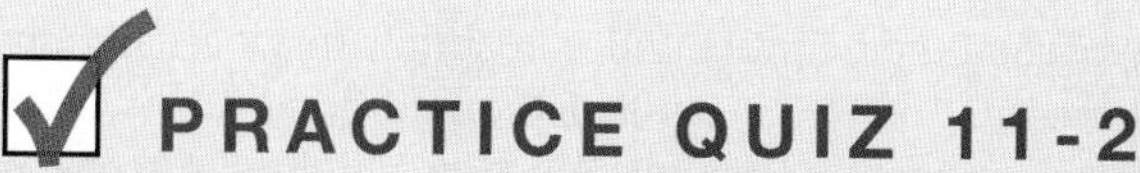

PRACTICE QUIZ 11-2

1 What is health insurance, and what is its purpose?
2 What are group health and individual health insurance?
3 What is a coordination of benefits provision?

Types of Health Insurance Coverage

LO11-3

Analyze the benefits and limitations of the various types of health care coverage.

With today's high cost of health care, it makes sense to be as fully insured as you can afford. Combining the group plan available where you work with the individual policies insurance companies offer will enable you to put together enough coverage to give you peace of mind. A good health insurance plan should

- Offer basic coverage for hospital and doctor bills.
- Provide at least 120 days' hospital room and board in full.
- Provide at least a $1 million lifetime maximum for each family member.
- Pay at least 80 percent for out-of-hospital expenses after a yearly deductible of $1,000 per person or $2,000 per family.
- Impose no unreasonable exclusions.
- Limit your out-of-pocket expenses to no more than $4,000 to $6,000 a year, excluding dental, optical, and prescription costs.

my life 3

With today's high cost of health care, it makes sense for me to be as fully insured as I can afford.

Premiums are lower on employer-provided health insurance plans because risk is spread over a large group of employees. Take advantage of the lower costs that employer-sponsored plans offer, but expect to pay part of the premium out of your paycheck.

Several types of health insurance coverage are available under group and individual policies.

TYPES OF MEDICAL COVERAGE

hospital expense insurance Pays part or all of hospital bills for room, board, and other charges.

surgical expense insurance Pays part or all of the surgeon's fees for an operation.

physician expense insurance Provides benefits for doctors' fees for nonsurgical care, x-rays, and lab tests.

basic health insurance coverage Combination of hospital expense insurance, surgical expense insurance, and physician expense insurance.

major medical expense insurance Pays most of the costs exceeding those covered by the hospital, surgical, and physician expense policies.

deductible An amount the insured must pay before benefits become payable by the insurance company.

HOSPITAL EXPENSE INSURANCE

Hospital expense insurance pays part or the full amount of hospital bills for room, board, and other charges. Frequently, a maximum amount is allowed for each day in the hospital, up to a maximum number of days. More people have hospital insurance than any other kind of health insurance.

SURGICAL EXPENSE INSURANCE

Surgical expense insurance pays part or the full amount of the surgeon's fees for an operation. A policy of this kind usually lists a number of specific operations and the maximum fee allowed for each. The higher the maximum fee allowed in the policy, the higher the premium charged. People often buy surgical expense insurance in combination with hospital expense insurance.

PHYSICIAN EXPENSE INSURANCE

Physician expense insurance helps pay for physician's care that does not involve surgery. Like surgical expense insurance, it lists maximum benefits for specific services. Its coverage may include visits to the doctor's office, x-rays, and lab tests. This type of insurance is usually bought in combination with hospital and surgical insurance. The three types of insurance combined are called **basic health insurance coverage.**

MAJOR MEDICAL EXPENSE INSURANCE

Major medical expense insurance protects against the large expenses of a serious injury or a long illness. It adds to the protection offered by basic health insurance coverage. The costs of a serious illness can easily exceed the benefits under hospital, surgical, and physician expense policies. Major medical pays the bulk of the additional costs. The maximum benefits payable under major medical insurance are high—up to $1 million. Because major medical insurance offers such a wide range of benefits and provides high maximums, it contains two features to help keep the premium within the policyholder's means.

One of these features is a **deductible** provision that requires the policyholder to pay a basic amount before the policy benefits begin—for example, the first $500 per year under an individual plan and a lesser amount under a group plan. (Sometimes part or all of the deductible amount is covered by the benefits of a basic hospital and surgical plan.) The other feature is a **coinsurance** provision that requires the policyholder to share expenses beyond the deductible amount. Many policies pay 75 or 80 percent of expenses above the deductible amount; the policyholder pays the rest.

coinsurance A provision under which both the insured and the insurer share the covered losses.

EXAMPLE: Deductibles and Coinsurance

Ariana's policy includes an $800 deductible and a coinsurance provision requiring her to pay 20 percent of all bills. If her total is $3,800, for instance, the company will first exclude $800 from coverage, which is Ariana's deductible. It will then pay 80 percent of the remaining $3,000, or $2,400. Therefore, Ariana's total costs are $1,400 ($800 for the deductible and $600 for the coinsurance).

Some major medical policies contain a **stop-loss,** or out-of-pocket limit, provision. This requires the policyholder to pay up to a certain amount, after which the insurance company pays 100 percent of all remaining covered expenses. Typically, the out-of-pocket payment is between $4,000 and $6,000. (See Exhibit 11-3)

stop-loss A provision under which an insured pays a certain amount, after which the insurance company pays 100 percent of the remaining covered expenses.

COMPREHENSIVE MAJOR MEDICAL INSURANCE **Comprehensive major medical insurance** is a type of major medical insurance that has a very low deductible amount, often $400 or $500, and is offered without a separate basic plan. This all-inclusive health insurance helps pay hospital, surgical, medical, and other bills. Many major medical policies have specific maximum benefits for certain expenses, such as hospital room and board and the cost of surgery.

comprehensive major medical insurance A type of major medical insurance that has a very low deductible and is offered without a separate basic plan.

Exhibit 11-3 How You and Your Insurer Share Costs

Jane's Plan: Deductible: $1,500 Co-insurance: 20% Out-of-pocket Limit: $5,000

January 1st
Beginning of coverage period

December 31st
End of coverage period

Jane pays 100% Her plan pays 0%

Jane hasn't reached her $1,500 deductible yet
Her plan doesn't pay any of the costs.

Office visit costs: $125
Jane pays: $125
Her plan pays: $0

more costs

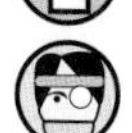

Jane pays 20% Her plan pays 80%

Jane reaches her $1,500 deductible, co-insurance begins
Jane has seen a doctor several times and paid $1,500 in total. Her plan pays some of the costs for her next visit,

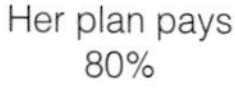

Office visit costs: $75
Jane pays: 20% of $75 = $15

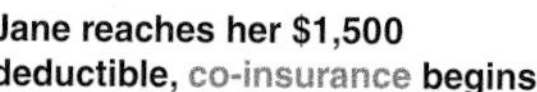

Her plan pays: 80% of $75 = $60

more costs

Jane pays 0% Her plan pays 100%

Jane reaches her $5,000 out-of-pocket limit
Jane has seen the doctor often and paid $5,000 in total. Her plan pays the full cost of her coverd health care services for the rest of the year.

Office visit costs: $200
Jane pays: $0
Her plan pays = $200

SOURCE: Glossary of Health Coverage and Medical Terms, HealthCare.gov, accessed March 19, 2013.

hospital indemnity policy Pays stipulated daily, weekly, or monthly cash benefits during hospital confinement.

HOSPITAL INDEMNITY POLICIES A **hospital indemnity policy** pays benefits only when you are hospitalized, but these benefits, stipulated in the policy, are paid to you in cash and you can use the money for medical, nonmedical, or supplementary expenses. While such policies have limited coverage, their benefits can have wide use. The hospital indemnity policy is not a substitute for basic or major medical protection but a supplement to it. Many people buy hospital indemnity policies in the hope that they will make money if they get sick, but the average benefit return does not justify the premium cost.

DENTAL EXPENSE INSURANCE *Dental expense insurance* provides reimbursement for the expenses of dental services and supplies and encourages preventive dental care. The coverage normally provides for oral examinations (including x-rays and cleanings), fillings, extractions, inlays, bridgework, and dentures, as well as oral surgery, root canal therapy, and orthodontics.

VISION CARE INSURANCE A recent development in health insurance coverage is *vision care insurance.* An increasing number of insurance companies and prepayment plans are offering this insurance, usually to groups.

Vision and eye health problems are second among the most prevalent chronic health care concerns, affecting more than 140 million Americans. Good vision care insurance should cover diagnosing and treating eye diseases such as glaucoma, periodic eye examinations, eyeglasses, contact lenses, and eye surgery.

In considering vision and dental coverages, you should analyze their costs and benefits. Sometimes these coverages cost more than they are worth.

long-term care insurance (LTC) Provides day-in, day-out care for long-term illness or disability.

OTHER INSURANCE POLICIES Dread disease, trip accident, death insurance, and cancer policies, which are usually sold through the mail, in newspapers and magazines, or by door-to-door salespeople working on commission, are notoriously poor values. Their appeal is based on unrealistic fears, and a number of states have prohibited their sale. Such policies provide coverage only for specific conditions and are no substitute for comprehensive insurance.

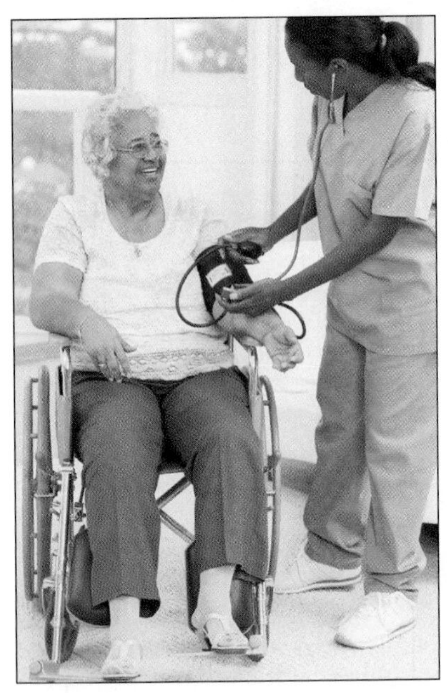

Long-term care insurance provides coverage for the expense of daily help that you may need if you become seriously ill or disabled and are unable to care for yourself.

LONG-TERM CARE INSURANCE

Long-term care insurance (LTC), virtually unknown 40 years ago, is growing faster than any other form of insurance in the country. *Long-term care* is day-in, day-out assistance that you might need if you ever have an illness or a disability that lasts a long time and leaves you unable to care for yourself. You may or may not need lengthy care in a nursing home, but you may need help at home with daily activities such as dressing, bathing, and doing household chores.

In 2012, more than 9 million men and women over age 65 were estimated to need long-term care. The number is expected to increase to 12 million by the year 2020. Most of these older Americans will be cared for at home; family members and friends are the sole caregivers for 70 percent of the elderly population. A recent study by Americans for Long-Term Care Security (ALTCS) found that one out of five Americans over age 50 is at risk of needing some form of long-term care within the next 12 months. The same study revealed that more than half of the U.S. population will need long-term care during their lives.[2] While older people are more likely to need long-term care, your need for long-term care can come at any age. In fact, the U.S. Government Accountability Office estimates that 40 percent of the 13 million people receiving long-term care services are between the ages of 18 and 64.

Long-term care can be very expensive. As a national average, a year in a nursing home can cost $88,000. In some regions, it can cost as much as $100,000. Bringing an aide into your home just three times a week to help with dressing, bathing, preparing meals, and similar household chores can easily cost $2,500 a month.

The annual premium for LTC policies can range from under $2,000 up to $16,000, depending on your age and the choices you make. The older you are when you enroll, the higher your annual premium. Typically, individual insurance plans are sold to the 50-to-80 age group, pay benefits for a maximum of two to six years, and carry a dollar limit on the total benefits they will pay.

The number of policies in effect has more than doubled since 1990, to about 9 million. About 120 insurance companies cover 12 percent of people age 65 and over. But long-term care insurance is not for everyone; it is rarely recommended for people under 60. If you are over 60, you may consider it if you wish to protect your assets, but if you have substantial wealth ($1 million or more), or very little (less than $150,000), the premium can be a waste of money.[3] However, if your employer pays the premium, the Health Insurance Portability and Accountability Act of 1996 treats a long-term care premium as a tax-deductible expense for the employer.

Explore services available in your community to help meet long-term care needs. Care given by family members can be supplemented by visiting nurses, home health aides, friendly visitor programs, home-delivered meals, chore services, adult day care centers, and respite services for caregivers who need a break from daily responsibilities.

These services are becoming more widely available. Some or all of them may be found in your community. Your local area Agency on Aging or Office on Aging can help you locate the services you need. Call the Eldercare Locator at 1-800-677-1116 to locate your local office.

DID YOU KNOW?

The average costs in the United States (in 2012) were:

- $205/day for a semi-private room in a nursing home.
- $229/day for a private room in a nursing home.
- $3,293/month for care in an Assisted Living Facility (for a one-bedroom unit).
- $21/hour for a Home Health Aide.
- $20/hour for Homemaker services.
- $72/day for care in an Adult Day Health Care Center.

Source: www.longtermcare.gov/LTC/Main_Site/Paying/Costs/Index.aspx, and http://www.keiro.org/longtermcare, accessed March 19, 2013.

MAJOR PROVISIONS IN A HEALTH INSURANCE POLICY

All health insurance policies have certain provisions in common. Be sure you understand what your policy covers. Even the most comprehensive policy may be of little value if a provision in small print limits or denies benefits.

An insurance company usually allows you a minimum of 10 days to review your health insurance policy, so be sure to check the major provisions that affect your coverage. Deductible, coinsurance, and stop-loss provisions were discussed under major medical expense insurance. Other major provisions are described in the following sections.

ELIGIBILITY The eligibility provision defines who is entitled to benefits under the policy. Age, marital status, and dependency requirements are usually specified in this provision. For example, foster children usually are not automatically covered under the family contract, but stepchildren may be. Check with your insurance company to be sure.

ASSIGNED BENEFITS When you assign benefits, you sign a paper allowing your insurance company to make payments to your hospital or doctor. Otherwise, the payments will be made to you when you turn in your bills and claim forms to the company.

INTERNAL LIMITS A policy with internal limits will pay only a fixed amount for your hospital room no matter what the actual rate is, or it will cover your surgical expenses only to a fixed limit no matter what the actual charges are. For example, if your policy has an internal limit of $600 per hospital day and you are in a $1,000-a-day hospital room, you will have to pay the difference.

copayment A provision under which the insured pays a flat dollar amount each time a covered medical service is received after the deductible has been met.

COPAYMENT **Copayment** is a type of cost sharing. Most major medical plans define *copayment* as the amount the patient must pay for medical services after the deductible has been met. You pay a flat dollar amount each time you receive a covered medical service. Copayments of $15 to $30 for prescriptions and $20 to $30 for doctors' office visits are common. The amount of copayment does not vary with the cost of service.

SERVICE BENEFITS In a service benefits provision, insurance benefits are expressed in terms of entitlement to receive specified hospital or medical care rather than entitlement to receive a fixed dollar amount for each procedure. Service benefits are always preferable to a coverage stated in dollar amounts.

BENEFIT LIMITS The benefit limits provision defines the maximum benefits possible, in terms of either a dollar amount or a number of days in the hospital. Many policies today have benefit limits ranging from $250,000 to unlimited payments.

EXCLUSIONS AND LIMITATIONS The exclusions and limitations provision specifies the conditions or circumstances for which the policy does not provide benefits. For example, the policy may exclude coverage for preexisting conditions, cosmetic surgery, or routine checkups.

COORDINATION OF BENEFITS As discussed earlier, the coordination-of-benefits provision prevents you from collecting benefits from two or more group policies that would in total exceed the actual charges. Under this provision, the benefits from your own and your spouse's policies are coordinated to allow you up to 100 percent payment of your covered charges.

GUARANTEED RENEWABLE With this policy provision, the insurance company cannot cancel a policy unless you fail to pay premiums when due. Also, it cannot raise premiums unless a rate increase occurs for all policyholders in that group.

CANCELLATION AND TERMINATION This provision explains the circumstances under which the insurance company can terminate your health insurance policy. It also explains your right to convert a group contract into an individual contract.

The medical costs of giving birth can be high. However, most people have the basic health insurance coverage to minimize out-of-pocket costs.

WHICH COVERAGE SHOULD YOU CHOOSE?

Now that you are familiar with the types of health insurance available and some of their major provisions, how do you choose one? The most important thing to understand is that the more money you can pay for health insurance, the more coverage you can get.

For medical insurance, you have three choices. You can buy (1) basic, (2) major medical, or (3) both basic and major medical. If your budget is very limited, it is a toss-up between choosing a basic plan or a major medical plan. In many cases, either plan will handle a major share of your hospital and doctor bills. In the event of an illness involving catastrophic costs, however, you will need the protection a major medical policy offers. Ideally, you should get a basic plan and a major medical supplementary plan or a comprehensive major medical policy that combines the values of both these plans in a single policy.

HEALTH INSURANCE TRADE-OFFS

The benefits of health insurance policies differ, and the differences can have a significant impact on your premiums. Consider the following trade-offs.

REIMBURSEMENT VERSUS INDEMNITY A reimbursement policy provides benefits based on the actual expenses you incur. An indemnity policy provides specified benefits, regardless of whether the actual expenses are greater or less than the benefits.

INTERNAL LIMITS VERSUS AGGREGATE LIMITS A policy with internal limits stipulates maximum benefits for specific expenses, such as the maximum reimbursement for daily hospital room and board. Other policies may limit only the total amount of coverage, such as $1 million major expense benefits, or may have no limits.

DEDUCTIBLES AND COINSURANCE The cost of a health insurance policy can be greatly affected by the size of the deductible (the amount you must pay toward medical expenses before the insurance company pays), the degree of coinsurance, and the share of medical expenses you must pay (for example, 20 percent).

OUT-OF-POCKET LIMIT A policy that limits the total of the coinsurance and deductibles you must pay (for example, $5,000) will limit or eliminate your financial risk, but it will also increase the premium.

BENEFITS BASED ON REASONABLE AND CUSTOMARY CHARGES A policy that covers "reasonable and customary" medical expenses limits reimbursement to the usual charges of medical providers in an area and helps prevent overcharging.

HEALTH INFORMATION ONLINE

Recent studies indicate that consumers are seeking information on health and health care online to supplement traditional medical counsel. Many legitimate providers of reliable health and medical information, including the federal Food and Drug Administration, are taking advantage of the Web's popularity by offering brochures and in-depth information on specific topics at their websites.

1 What are several types of health insurance coverage available under group and individual policies?
2 What are the major provisions of a health insurance policy?
3 How do you decide which coverage to choose?
4 How can you analyze the costs and benefits of your health insurance policy?

eXcel PFP Sheet 51
Assessing current and needed health care insurance

Private Sources of Health Insurance and Health Care

LO11-4

Evaluate private sources of health insurance and health care.

Health insurance is available from more than 800 private insurance companies. Moreover, service plans such as Blue Cross/Blue Shield, health maintenance organizations, preferred provider organizations, government programs such as Medicare, fraternal organizations, and trade unions provide health insurance.

PRIVATE INSURANCE COMPANIES

Insurance companies sell health insurance through either group or individual policies. Of these two types, group health insurance represents about 90 percent of all medical expense insurance and 80 percent of all disability income insurance.

The policies insurance companies issue provide for payment either directly to the insured for reimbursement of expenses incurred or, if assigned by the insured, to the provider of services.

Most private insurance companies sell health insurance policies to employers, who in turn offer them as fringe benefits to employees and employees' dependents. The premiums may be partially paid by employers. The Health Insurance Portability and Accountability Act, as discussed earlier, requires employers to keep detailed records of all employees and dependents covered by the company's health plan.

As of September 23, 2012, all health insurance companies and group health plans are required to give you a summary of health plan's benefits and coverage. See Exhibit 11-4 for a uniform Summary of Benefits and Coverage (SBC).

HOSPITAL AND MEDICAL SERVICE PLANS

Blue Cross and Blue Shield are statewide organizations similar to commercial health insurance companies. Each state has its own Blue Cross and Blue Shield. The Blues plans play an important role in providing private health insurance to millions of Americans.

Blue Cross An independent, nonprofit membership corporation that provides protection against the cost of hospital care.

Blue Shield An independent, nonprofit membership corporation that provides protection against the cost of surgical and medical care.

Blue Cross plans provide *hospital care benefits* on essentially a "service-type" basis. Through a separate contract with each member hospital, Blue Cross reimburses the hospital for covered services provided to the insured.

Blue Shield plans provide benefits for *surgical and medical services* performed by physicians. The typical Blue Shield plan provides benefits similar to those provided under the benefit provisions of hospital-surgical policies issued by insurance companies.

HEALTH MAINTENANCE ORGANIZATIONS (HMOs)

managed care Prepaid health plans that provide comprehensive health care to members.

During the 1970s and 1980s, increasing health care costs spurred the growth of managed care. **Managed care** refers to prepaid health plans that provide comprehensive health care to members. Managed care is offered by health maintenance organizations, preferred provider organizations, exclusive provider organizations, point-of-service plans, and traditional indemnity insurance companies.

A recent industry survey estimated that 85 percent of employed Americans are enrolled in some form of managed care. Managed care companies now provide information that helps you better manage your health care needs. Health plans have launched Internet programs that allow you to access medical research, support groups, and professional advice, and to exchange e-mail with health care providers. The best-known managed care plans are health maintenance organizations (HMOs) and preferred provider organizations (PPOs), which offer a wide range of preventive services.

health maintenance organization (HMO) A health insurance plan that provides a wide range of health care services for a fixed, prepaid monthly premium.

Prepaid managed care is designed to make the provision of health care services cost-effective by controlling their use. Health maintenance organizations are an alternative to basic and major medical insurance plans. A **health maintenance organization (HMO)** is a health insurance plan that directly employs or contracts with selected physicians, surgeons, dentists, and optometrists to provide health care services in exchange for a fixed, prepaid monthly premium. HMOs operate on the premise that maintaining health through preventive care will minimize future medical problems.

Exhibit 11-4 Sample Summary of Benefits and Coverage (SBC)

Insurance Company 1: Plan Option 1 **Coverage Period: 01/01/2014–12/31/2014**
Summary of Benefits and Coverage: What This Plan Covers and What It Costs:
Coverage for Individual + Spouse/Type: PPO

This is only a summary. If you want more detail about your coverage and costs, contact your insurance company for complete terms in the policy or plan document.

Important Questions	Answers	Why This Matters
What is the overall deductible?	$500 person/$1,000 family. Doesn't apply to preventive care.	You must pay all the costs up to the deductible amount before this plan begins to pay for covered services you use. Check your policy or plan document to see when the deductible starts over (usually, but not always. January 1). See how much you pay for covered services after you meet the deductible.
Are there other deductibles for specific services?	Yes. $300 for prescription drug coverage. There are no other specific deductibles.	You must pay all the costs for the services up to the specific deductible amount before this plan begins to pay for these services.
Is there an out-of-pocket limit on my expenses?	Yes. For participating providers $2,500 person/$5,000 family. For non-participating providers $4,000 person/$8,000 family.	The out-of-pocket limit is the most you could pay during a coverage period (usually one year) for your share of the cost of covered services. This limit helps you plan for health care expenses.
What is not included in the out-of-pocket limit?	Premiums, balance-billed charges, and health care this plan doesn't cover.	Even though you pay these expenses, they don't count toward the out-of-pocket limit.
Is there an overall annual limit on what the plan pays?	No	The plan document describes any limits on what the plan will pay for specific covered services, such as office visits.
Does this plan use a network of providers?	Yes. Ask for a list of participating providers.	If you use an in-network doctor or other health care provider, this plan will pay some or all of the costs of covered services. Be aware, your in-network doctor or hospital may use an out-of-network provider for some services. Plans use the term in-network, preferred, or participating for providers in their network.
Do I need a referral to see a specialist?	No	You can see the specialist you choose without permission from this plan.
Are there services this plan doesn't cover?	Yes	Some of the services are not covered. See your policy or plan document for additional information about excluded services.

Source: Centers for Medicare and Medicaid Services website at http;//cciio.cms.gov/resources/files/sbc-sample.PDF, accessed March 10, 2013.

my life 4

My membership in an HMO should cover office visits, routine checkups, hospital and surgical care, eye exams, laboratory and x-ray service, and mental health services.

Conduct a brief interview with some families you know about what is covered in their HMO plan. Also read the Financial Planning for Life's Situations feature for tips on using and choosing an HMO.

The preventive care HMOs provide includes periodic checkups, screening programs, diagnostic testing, and immunizations. HMOs also provide a comprehensive range of other health care services. These services are divided into two categories: basic and supplemental. *Basic health services* include inpatient, outpatient, maternity, mental health, substance abuse, and emergency care. *Supplemental services* include vision, hearing, and pharmaceutical care, which are usually available for an additional fee.

Your membership in a typical HMO should cover office visits, routine checkups, hospital and surgical care, eye exams, laboratory and x-ray services, hemodialysis for kidney failure, and mental health services. See the "How To . . ." feature, "Tips on Using and Choosing an HMO."

PREFERRED PROVIDER ORGANIZATIONS (PPOs)

preferred provider organization (PPO) A group of doctors and hospitals that agree to provide health care at rates approved by the insurer.

A **preferred provider organization (PPO)** is a group of doctors and hospitals that agree to provide health care at rates approved by the insurer. In return, PPOs expect prompt payment and the opportunity to serve an increased volume of patients. The premiums for PPOs are slightly higher than those for HMOs. An insurance company or your employer contracts with a PPO to provide specified services at predetermined fees to PPO members.

Preferred provider organizations combine the best elements of the fee-for-service and HMO systems. PPOs offer the services of doctors and hospitals at discount rates or give breaks in copayments and deductibles. PPOs provide their members with essentially the same benefits HMOs offer. However, while HMOs require members to seek care from HMO providers only (except for emergency treatment), PPOs allow members to use a preferred provider—or another provider for a higher copayment—each time a medical need arises. This combination of allowing free choice of physicians and low-cost care makes PPOs popular.

exclusive provider organization (EPO) Renders medical care from affiliated health care providers.

point-of-service plan (POS) A network of selected contracted, participating providers; also called an *HMO-PPO hybrid* or *open-ended HMO.*

The **exclusive provider organization (EPO)** is the extreme form of the PPO. Services rendered by nonaffiliated providers are not reimbursed. Therefore, if you belong to an EPO, you must receive your care from affiliated providers or pay the entire cost yourself. Providers typically are reimbursed on a fee-for-service basis according to a negotiated discount or fee schedule.

A **point-of-service plan (POS),** sometimes called an *HMO-PPO hybrid* or *open-ended HMO,* combines characteristics of both HMOs and PPOs. POSs use a network of selected, contracted, participating providers. Employees select a primary care physician, who controls referrals for medical specialists. If you receive care from a plan provider, you pay little or nothing, as in an HMO, and do not file claims. Medical care provided by out-of-plan providers will be reimbursed, but you must pay significantly higher copayments and deductibles. Hybrid plans are useful if you want to try managed care but don't want to be locked into a network of doctors. A drawback is that they cost more than HMOs.

The distinction among HMOs, PPOs, EPOs, and POSs is becoming blurred. PPOs and POS plans combine features from both fee-for-service and HMOs. PPOs and POS plans offer more flexibility than HMOs in choosing physicians and other providers. POS plans have primary care physicians who coordinate patient care, but, in most cases, PPOs do not. Premiums tend to be somewhat higher in PPOs and POS plans than in traditional HMOs. As cost reduction pressures mount and these alternative delivery systems try to increase their market share, each tries to make its system more attractive. The evolution of health care plans will likely continue so that it will become increasingly difficult to characterize a particular managed care delivery system as adhering to any particular model.

HOW TO...

Tips on Using and Choosing an HMO

HOW TO USE AN HMO

When you first enroll in an HMO, you must choose a plan physician (family practitioner, internist, pediatrician, or obstetrician-gynecologist) who provides or arranges for all of your health care services. It is extremely important that you receive your care through the plan physician. If you don't, you are responsible for the cost of the service rendered.

The only exceptions to the requirement that care be received through the plan physician are medical emergencies. A medical emergency is a sudden onset of illness or a sudden injury that would jeopardize your life or health if not treated immediately. In such instances, you may use the facilities of the nearest hospital emergency room. All other care must be provided by hospitals and doctors under contract with the HMO.

HOW TO CHOOSE AN HMO

If you decide to enroll in an HMO, you should consider these additional factors:

1. *Accessibility.* Since you must use plan providers, it is extremely important that they be easily accessible from your home or office.
2. *Convenient office hours.* Your plan physician should have convenient office hours.
3. *Alternative physicians.* Should you become dissatisfied with your first choice of a physician, the HMO should allow you the option to change physicians.
4. *Second opinions.* You should be able to obtain second opinions.
5. *Type of coverage.* You should compare the health care services offered by various HMOs, paying particular attention to whether you will incur out-of-pocket expenses or copayments.
6. *Appeal procedures.* The HMO should have a convenient and prompt system for resolving problems and disputes.
7. *Price.* You should compare the prices various HMOs charge, to ensure that you are getting the most services for your health care dollar.

WHAT TO DO WHEN AN HMO DENIES TREATMENT OR COVERAGE

- *Get it in writing.* To better defend your case, ask for a letter detailing the clinical reasons your claim was denied and the name and medical expertise of the HMO staff member responsible.
- *Know your rights.* The plan document or your HMO's member services department will tell you how experimental treatments are defined and covered and how the appeals process works.
- *Keep records.* Make copies of any correspondence, including payments and any reimbursements. Also, keep a written log of all conversations relevant to your claim.
- *Find advocates.* Enlist the help of your doctor, employer, and state insurance department to lobby your case before the HMO.

Source: Reprinted from *BusinessWeek,* May 19, 1997, by special permission.

Starting in 2014, you may be able to buy from a new type of nonprofit, consumer-run health insurer, called Consumer Operated and Oriented Plan (CO-OP).

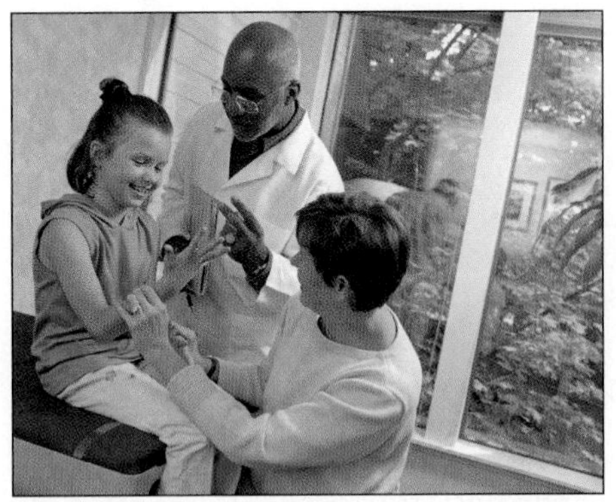

HMOs are based on the premise that preventive medical services will minimize future medical problems.

HOME HEALTH CARE AGENCIES

Home health care providers furnish and are responsible for the supervision and management of preventive medical care in a home setting in accordance with a medical order. Rising hospital care costs, new medical technology, and the increasing number of elderly and infirm people have helped make home care one of the fastest-growing areas of the health care industry.

Spending on home health care has been growing at an annual rate of about 20 percent over the past few years. This rapid growth reflects (1) the increasing proportion of older people in the U.S. population, (2) the lower costs of home health care compared to the costs of institutional health care, (3) insurers' active support of home health care, and (4) Medicare's promotion of home health care as an alternative to institutionalization. Home health care consists of home health agencies; home care aide organizations, and hospices, facilities that care for the terminally ill.

THE HEALTH INSURANCE MARKETPLACES

The Health Insurance Marketplace makes buying health care coverage easier and more affordable. Starting in 2014, the Marketplace will allow you to compare health plans, get answers to questions, find out if you are eligible for tax credits for private insurance, and enroll in a health plan that meets your needs. Open enrollment began in October 2013; however, many people were unable to access the government website. Read the accompanying Financial Planning for Life's Situations feature, "Checklist for You and Your Family," to get ready for these Marketplaces.

EMPLOYER SELF-FUNDED HEALTH PLANS

Certain types of health insurance coverage are made available by plans that employers, labor unions, fraternal societies, or communities administer. Usually these groups provide the amount of protection a specific group of people desires and can afford.

Self-funded groups must assume the financial burden if medical bills are greater than the amount covered by premium income. While private insurance companies have the assets needed in such situations, self-funded plans often do not. The results can be disastrous.

NEW HEALTH CARE ACCOUNTS

Health savings accounts (HSAs), which Congress authorized in 2003, are the newest addition to the alphabet soup of health insurance available to American workers. Now you and your employer must sort through HSAs, health reimbursement accounts (HRAs), and flexible spending accounts (FSAs). Each has its own rules about how money is spent, how it can be saved, and how it is taxed.

How do FSAs, HRAs, and HSAs differ? FSAs allow you to contribute pretax dollars to an account managed by your employer. You use the money for health care spending but forfeit anything left over at the end of the year.

HRAs are tied to high-deductible policies. They are funded *solely* by your employer and give you a pot of money to spend on health care. You can carry over unspent money from year to year, but you lose the balance if you switch jobs. Premiums tend to be

CHECKLIST FOR YOU AND YOUR FAMILY

Whether you are uninsured, or just want to explore new options, the Health Insurance Marketplace will give you and your family more choice and selection in health plans.

SEVEN STEPS YOU CAN TAKE TO GET READY NOW

1. **Learn about different types of health insurance.** Through the Marketplace, you'll be able to choose a health plan that gives you the right balance of costs and coverage.
2. **Make a list of questions before it's time to choose your health plan.** For example, "Can I stay with my current doctor?" or "Will this plan cover my health costs when I'm traveling?"
3. **Make sure you understand how insurance works, including deductibles, out-of-pocket maximums, copayments, etc.** Consider these details while you're shopping around. Visit the HealthCare.gov website to learn more about how insurance works.
4. **Start gathering basic information about your household income.** Most people will qualify to get a break on costs, and you'll need income information to find out how much.
5. **Set your budget.** There will be different types of health plans to meet a variety of needs and budgets, and breaking them down by cost can help narrow your choices.
6. **Ask your employers whether they plan to offer health insurance, especially if you work for a small business.**
7. **Explore current options.** You will be able to get help with insurance now, through existing programs or changes that are in effect already from the new health care law. Use HealthCare.gov resources to get information about health insurance for adults up to age 26, children in families with limited incomes, and Medicare for people who are over 65 or are disabled.

Source: HealthCare.gov website at http://www.healthcare.gov/marketplace/get-ready/consumer-checklist/index.html, accessed March 16, 2013.

lower than for traditional insurance but higher than for HSAs. With HSAs, you can invest the funds in stocks, bonds, and mutual funds. The money grows tax-free but can be spent only on health care. And it's your money. Any unspent funds stay in your account year to year, and you take it all with you if you leave the company.

HSAs allow you to contribute money to a tax-free account that can be used for out-of-pocket health care expenses if you buy high-deductible health insurance policies to cover catastrophic expenses. Read the accompanying Financial Planning for Life's Situations feature to learn how HSAs will work in 2013.

In addition to the private sources of health insurance and health care discussed in this section, government health care programs cover over 50 million people. The next section discusses these programs.

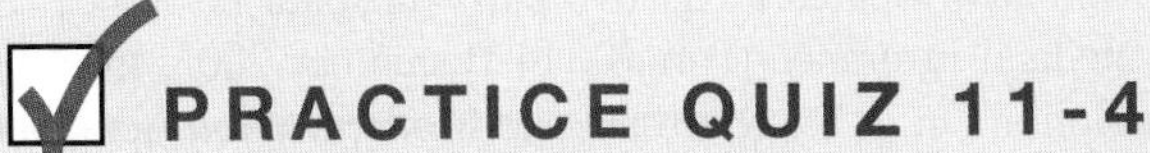

1 What are the major sources of health insurance and health care?
2 What are Blue Cross and Blue Shield plans? What benefits does each plan provide?
3 What are the differences among HMOs, PPOs, EPOs, and POSs?
4 What are home health care agencies?
5 What are employer self-funded health plans?

HSAs: HOW THEY WORK IN 2013

1. Your company offers a health insurance policy with an *annual deductible* of at least $1,250 for individual coverage or $2,500 for family coverage.
2. You can put *pretax dollars* into an HSA each year, up to the amount of the deductible—but no more than $6,450 for family coverage or $3,250 for individual coverage.
3. You withdraw the money from your HSA tax-free, but it can only go for your *family's medical expenses.* After the deductible and copays are met, insurance still typically *covers 80 percent* of health costs.
4. HSA plans are required to have maximum *out-of-pocket spending limits,* $6,250 for individuals, $12,500 for families. That's when your company's insurance kicks in again at 100 percent coverage.
5. Your *company can match* part or all of your HSA contributions if it wishes, just as it does with 401(k)s.
6. You can invest your HSA in stocks, bonds, or mutual funds. *Unused money remains* in your account at the end of the year and *grows tax free.*
7. You can also take your HSA with you if you *change jobs or retire.*
8. To help you *shop for health care* now that you're spending your own money, employers say they will give you detailed information about prices and quality of doctors and hospitals in your area.

Source: Internal Revenue Service, www.treas.gov, accessed March 19, 2013.

Government Health Care Programs

LO11-5

Appraise the sources of government health care programs.

Federal and state governments offer health coverage in accordance with laws that define the premiums and benefits they can offer. Specific requirements as to age, occupation, length of service, and family income may be used to determine eligibility for coverage. Two sources of government health insurance are Medicare and Medicaid.

my life 5

I am aware of various state and federal health care programs.

Two sources of state and federal health care programs are Medicaid and Medicare. For a brief summary of Medicare Parts A, B, C, and D, examine Exhibit 11-3. For additional information, visit medicare.gov or call 1-800-Medicare (1-800-633-4227).

MEDICARE

Medicare, established in 1965, is a federal health insurance program for people 65 or older, people of any age with permanent kidney failure, and people with certain disabilities. The program is administered by The Centers for Medicare and Medicaid Services (formerly known as the Health Care Financing Administration). Local Social Security Administration offices take applications for Medicare, assist beneficiaries in filing claims, and provide information about the program.

Originally, Medicare had two parts: hospital insurance (Part A) and medical insurance (Part B). In December 2003, the Medicare Prescription Drug, Improvement and Modernization Act created the Medicare Advantage program (Part C) and Medicare prescription drug benefit program (Part D).

Medicare *hospital insurance* (Part A) helps pay for inpatient hospital care, inpatient care in a skilled nursing facility, home health care, and hospice care. Hospital insurance is financed from a portion of the Social Security tax. Part A pays for all covered services for inpatient hospital care after you pay a single annual deductible. Most people over 65 are eligible for free Medicare hospital insurance.

Medicare *medical insurance* (Part B) helps pay for doctors' services and a variety of other medical services and supplies not covered by hospital insurance. Each year, as soon as you meet the annual medical insurance deductible, medical insurance will pay 80 percent of the approved charges for the covered services that you receive during the rest of the year. Voluntary medical insurance is financed from the monthly premiums paid by people who have enrolled in it and from general federal revenues. You must sign up for Part B coverage.

The Balanced Budget Act of 1997 created the new Medicare + Choice program. The act expands managed care options by encouraging wider availability of HMOs and allows other types of health plans to participate in Medicare. It gives you the option to remain in the original Medicare (Parts A and B) or to enroll in a Medicare Advantage Plan. The Medicare Prescription, Drug Improvement and Modernization Act of 2003 renamed the Medicare + Choice program as Medicare Advantage (Part C). This new plan may be less expensive than the original Medicare and offers extra benefits. The plan is run by private health care providers who receive a set amount from Medicare for your health care regardless of how many or how few services you use.

The law also provides Medicare beneficiaries with prescription drug discounts (Part D). This voluntary, comprehensive Medicare drug coverage became effective on January 1, 2006. Most seniors pay about $35 per month for this new drug benefit and pay a copayment or coinsurance for each prescription. As with Medicare Part B enrollment, there is a penalty for not enrolling in the Medicare drug benefit in the first six months that you are eligible. People with the lowest incomes will pay no premiums or deductibles and small or no copayments. For a brief summary of Medicare Parts A, B, C, and D, see Exhibit 11-5.

While Medicare enjoys broad support among seniors and the American people, it faces many policy challenges. These challenges include addressing the affordability of health and long-term care for the beneficiaries, financing the program over the long term, and examining the role of government versus the private sector in the Medicare program.

WHAT IS NOT COVERED BY MEDICARE? Although Medicare is very helpful for meeting medical costs, it does not cover everything. In addition to the deductibles and coinsurance mentioned earlier, Medicare does not cover some medical expenses at all, including

- Accupuncture.
- Care in a skilled nursing facility (SNF) beyond 100 days per benefit period.
- Skilled nursing care in facilities not approved by Medicare.
- Intermediate and custodial nursing care (the kind many nursing home residents need).
- Most screening tests, vaccinations, and some diabetic supplies.
- Private-duty nursing.
- Routine checkups, dental care, most immunizations, cosmetic surgery, routine foot care, eyeglasses, and hearing aids.

DID YOU KNOW?

MEDICARE—BEFORE AND AFTER

1965: Medicare enacted into law. By 1969, Medicare represents about 0.7 percent of gross domestic product.

2004: Medicare provides benefits to 41.7 million elderly and disabled. Total cost of $308.9 billion. Represents 2.6 percent of gross domestic product.

2006: Prescription drug coverage (Medicare Part D) takes full effect (results from Medicare Modernization Act of 2003).

2020: Part A Hospital Insurance trust fund reserves projected to be depleted. (Program will be able to pay 79 percent of benefits.)

2035: Total Medicare costs (including prescription drug coverage) projected to represent 7.5 percent of gross domestic product.

DID YOU KNOW?

Medicare enrollment has increased from 19 million in 1966 to over 50 million in 2012.

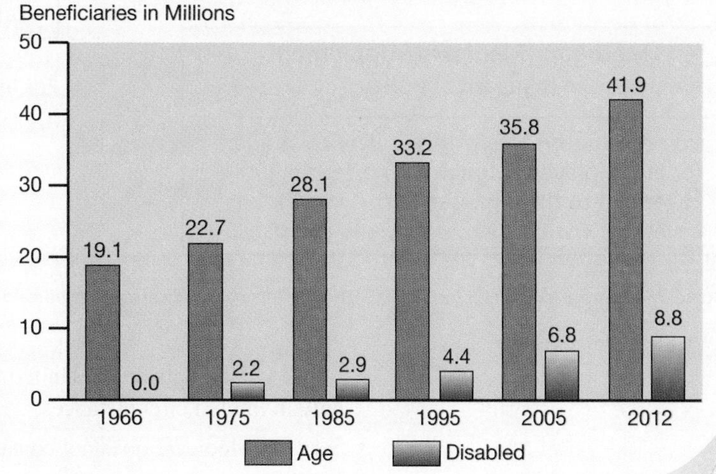

Source: The Centers for Medicare and Medicaid Services, 2012. Financial Report, 2012.

Exhibit 11-5 A Brief Look at Medicare

Medicare is health insurance for people age 65 or older, under age 65 with certain disabilities, and any age with end-stage renal disease (permanent kidney failure requiring dialysis or a kidney transplant).

Most people get their Medicare health care coverage in one of two ways. Your costs vary depending on your plan's coverage, and the services you use.

Original Medicare Plan

Part A (Hospital)	Part B (Medical)

Medicare provides this coverage. Part B is optional. You have your choice of doctors. Your costs may be higher than in Medicare Advantage Plans.

+

Part D (Prescription Drug Coverage)

You can choose this coverage. Private companies approved by Medicare run these plans. Plans cover different drugs. Medically necessary drugs must be covered.

+

Medigap (Medicare Supplement Insurance) Policy

You can choose to buy this private coverage (or an employer or union may offer similar coverage) to fill in gaps in Part A and Part B coverage. Costs vary by policy and company.

or

Medicare Advantage Plans (Like HMOs and PPOs)

Called "Part C," this option combines your Part A (Hospital) and Part B (Medical)

Private insurance companies approved by Medicare provide this coverage. Generally, you must see doctors in the plan. Your costs may be lower than in the Original Medicare Plan, and you may get extra benefits.

+

Part D (Prescription Drug Coverage)

Most Part C plans cover prescription drugs. If they don't, you may be able to choose this coverage. Plans cover different drugs. Medically necessary drugs must be covered.

For information about Medicare, visit www.medicare.gov or call 1-800-MEDICARE (1-800-633-4227).

Source: *Medicare & You* (Washington, DC: The Centers for Medicare and Medicaid Services, 2013), p.55.

- Care received outside the United States except in Canada and Mexico, and then only in limited circumstances.
- Services Medicare does not consider medically necessary.
- Physician charges above Medicare's approved amount. The government has a fee schedule for physician charges and places limits on charges in excess of the Medicare-approved amount when the physician does not accept Medicare's approved amount as payment in full.

Exhibit 11-6 compares features of different medicare options. For a more complete description of Medicare coverage and costs, ask your local Social Security Administration office for a copy of *The Medicare Handbook*. For more information, call the Medicare Hotline at 1-800-633-4227.

medigap (MedSup) insurance Supplements Medicare by filling the gap between Medicare payments and medical costs not covered by Medicare.

MEDIGAP Medicare was never intended to pay all medical costs. To fill the gap between Medicare payments and medical costs not covered by Medicare, many companies sell medigap insurance policies. **Medigap** or **MedSup insurance** is not sold or serviced by the federal government or state governments. Contrary to the claims

Exhibit 11-6 A comparison of various Medicare plans

	Current Options	New Options (Medicare and Advantage)	Plan Description
Original Medicare	√	√	• You choose your health care providers. • Medicare pays your providers for covered services. • Most beneficiaries choose Medicare supplemental insurance to cover deductible and copayments.
Medicare health maintenance organization (HMO)	√	√	• You must live in the plan's service area. • You agree to use the plan's network of doctors, hospitals, and other health providers, except in an emergency. • Medicare pays the HMO to provide all medical services.
Preferred provider organization (PPO)		√	• Works like an HMO, except you have the choice to see a health provider out of the network. • If you do see an out-of-network provider, you will pay a higher cost.
Provider-sponsored organization (PSO)		√	• Works like a Medicare HMO, except the networks are managed by health care providers (doctors and hospitals) rather than an insurance company.
Private fee for service		√	• Medicare pays a lump sum to a private insurance health plan. • Providers can bill more than what the plan pays; you are responsible for paying the balance. • The plan may offer more benefits than original Medicare.
Medical savings account (MSA)		√	• Medicare MSAs are a special type of savings account that can be used to pay medical bills. • Centers for Medicare and Medicaid Services (CMS) will make an annual lump-sum deposit into enrollee's account (only Medicare can deposit funds into this account). • MSAs work with a special private insurance company and carry a very high deductible. • Funds withdrawn for nonmedical purposes are taxable and subject to a penalty.

Source: *Medicare & You* (Washington, DC: The Centers for Medicare and Medicaid Services, 2013).

made by some advertising and insurance agents, Medicare supplement insurance is not a government-sponsored program.

Most states now have 10 standardized Medicare supplement policies, designated by the letters *A* through *N*. These standardized policies make it easier to compare the costs of policies issued by different insurers. All Medicare policies must cover certain gaps in Medicare coverage, such as the daily coinsurance amount for hospitalization. In addition to the basic benefits that must now be included in all newly issued Medicare supplement policies in most states, you should consider other policy features. For more information, visit www.medicare.gov/publications to view the booklet "Choosing a Medigap Policy: A Guide to Health Insurance for people with Medicare", or Call 1-800-633-4227.

MEDICAID

Title XIX of the Social Security Act provides for a program of medical assistance to certain low-income individuals and families. In 1965 the program, known as *Medicaid,* became federal law.

Medicaid is administered by each state within certain broad federal requirements and guidelines. Financed by both state and federal funds, it is designed to provide medical assistance to groups or categories of persons who are eligible to receive payments under one of the cash assistance programs such as Aid to Families with Dependent Children and Supplemental Security Income. The states may also provide Medicaid to medically needy individuals, that is, to persons who fit into one of the categories eligible for public assistance.

Many members of the Medicaid population are also covered by Medicare. Where such dual coverage exists, most state Medicaid programs pay for the Medicare premiums, deductibles, and copayments and for services not covered by Medicare. Medicaid differs from Medicare because eligibility for Medicaid depends on having very low income and assets. Once a person is eligible, Medicaid provides more benefits than does Medicare. Because Medicaid coverage is so comprehensive, people using it do not need to purchase supplemental insurance.

To qualify for federal matching funds, state programs must include inpatient hospital services; outpatient hospital services; laboratory and x-ray services; skilled nursing and home health services for individuals age 21 and older; family planning services; early and periodic screening, diagnosis, and treatment for individuals under 21; and physicians' services in the home, office, hospital, nursing home, or elsewhere. Under the Affordable Care Act, Medicaid eligibility expands in 2014 to reach millions more poor Americans, mostly uninsured adults.

HEALTH INSURANCE AND THE PATIENT PROTECTION AND AFFORDABLE CARE ACT OF 2010

Americans have been debating for years that the nation needs health care reform to ensure that we get high quality, affordable health care. The Patient Protection and Affordable Care Act of 2010, sets aside $635 billion over the next 10 years to help finance this reform. Here are the key provisions of the Act that will take effect now and in the years to come. The Act:

- Offers tax credits for small businesses to make employee coverage more affordable.
- Prohibits denying coverage to children with pre-existing medical conditions.
- Provides access to affordable insurance for those who are uninsured because of a pre-existing condition through a temporary subsidized high-risk pool.
- Bans insurance companies from dropping people from coverage when they get sick.
- Eliminates co-payments for preventive services and exempts preventive services from deductibles under the Medicare program.
- Requires new health plans to allow young people up to their 26th birthday to remain on their parents' insurance policy.
- Prohibits health insurance companies from placing lifetime caps on coverage.
- Restricts the use of annual limits to ensure access to needed care in all plans.

- Requires new private plans to cover preventive services with no co-payment and with preventive services being exempt from deductibles.
- Ensures consumers in new plans have access to an effective internal and external appeals process to appeal decisions by their health insurance plans.
- Provides aid to states in establishing offices of health insurance consumer assistance to help individuals with the filing of complaints and appeals.
- Increases funds for Community Health Centers to allow for nearly a doubling of the number of patients seen by the centers over the next five years.
- Provides new investments to increase the number of primary care practitioners, including doctors, nurses, nurse practitioners, and physician assistants.
- Requires health insurance companies to submit justification for all requested premium increases.
- Requires that most Americans purchase health insurance by 2014.
- Creates state-based health insurance marketplaces (also called *insurance exchanges*) through which individuals can purchase coverage, with subsidies available to lower-income individuals.
- Expands Medicaid program for the nation's poorest individuals.
- Requires employers with more than 20 employees to provide health insurance to their employees or pay penalties.[4]

The law is expansive and will be implemented over several years, but all major provisions take effect by January 2014. On June 28, 2012, the Supreme Court, in a 5 to 4 vote, upheld the majority of the landmark Affordable Care Act. Under the law, if you don't have health insurance, you will have to pay 1 percent of your income to the IRS starting in 2014. However, there are some exceptions for religious beliefs and financial hardship.

According to the Health and Human Services secretary, "Three years ago, the Affordable Care Act ushered in a new day for health care. Since then, more than 6.3 million seniors and people with disabilities with Medicare have saved more than $6.1 billion dollars on prescription drugs. Nearly 71 million Americans got expanded access to preventive services at no charge through their private insurance plans, and 47 million women now have guaranteed access to additional preventive services without cost sharing. More than 3.1 million young adults who were uninsured were able to gain coverage by being able to stay on their parents' insurance policies until they turned 26. And, parents no longer have to worry about insurers denying coverage to their children because of a pre-existing condition.

Americans are getting more value for their health care dollars due to the health care law. Affordable Care Act initiatives are promoting coordinated care; paying for quality, not quantity; and dramatically reducing fraud and waste, contributing to the slowest growth in national health spending in 50 years."[5]

The opponents, however, claim that "Three years later, the Act has failed to live up to its name, leaving a trail of broken promises in its wake. Instead of lowering costs as promised and making the system simpler for patients, the law has added a litany of new rules, regulations and fines. The pledge that, 'If you like your current health care plan, you'll be able to keep it' is already broken. In fact, the Congressional Budget Office estimated that 7 million people will lose their coverage, no matter how much they like it. Even though the law promised that families could save $2,500 in health care premiums, the average family premium has, in fact, increased by more than $3,000 since 2008. Moreover, the House Ways and Means Committee reported that the law includes about $1.1 trillion in new taxes that will hit Americans at all income levels. And, a recent Government Accountability Office report shows that the law will add $6.2 trillion to the primary deficit. Nothing is free; it's being paid with higher taxes and insurance premiums."[6]

DID YOU KNOW?

FIGHTING FRAUD CAN PAY

You may get a reward of up to $1,000 if you meet **all** these conditions:

- You report suspected Medicare fraud.
- The Inspector General's Office reviews your suspicion.
- The suspected fraud you report isn't already being investigated.
- Your report leads directly to the recovery of at least $100 of Medicare money.

For more information, call 1-800-MEDICARE (1-800-633-4227).

An ethical dilemma: is a government-run health care system that provides universal health care to all the most ethical? The current health care issues and the health care reform will have long-term effects on federal and state governments, insurance companies, health care providers, pharmaceutical companies, and, most important, patients. Most Americans believe that an ethical health care system should provide high, if not the highest, quality of health care, freedom of choice, and it must be affordable and available to all citizens. Will "Obamacare" have long-term positive or negative effects on the general population? Only time will tell!

The Affordable Care Act is intended to make our health insurance system work better for families. It also contains some of the strongest anti–health care fraud provisions in American history.

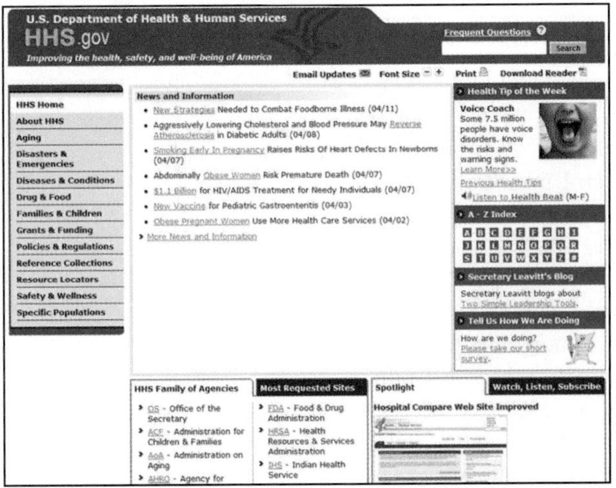

The Department of Health and Human Services maintains one of the richest and most reliable sources of information on the Internet.

FIGHT AGAINST MEDICARE/MEDICAID FRAUD AND ABUSE

Nearly 70 percent of consumers believe the Medicare program would not go broke if fraud and abuse were eliminated. Moreover, nearly 80 percent are not aware of any efforts to reduce health care fraud and abuse. In 1997 President Clinton introduced the Medicare/Medicaid Anti-Waste, Fraud and Abuse Act, which established tough new requirements for health care providers that wish to participate in the Medicare/Medicaid program.

The Financial Planning for Life's Situations feature on the next page provides some consumer tips on health and disability insurance.

GOVERNMENT CONSUMER HEALTH INFORMATION WEBSITES

With more than 60 central websites on eight separate Web domains, the Department of Health and Human Services (HHS) maintains one of the richest and most reliable sources of information on the Internet (www.hhs.gov). HHS documents on the Web include information on health issues, research-related data, and access to HHS services, including interactive sites. Major HHS health information websites include the following:

HEALTHFINDER Healthfinder includes links to more than 1,600 websites, including over 250 federal sites and 1,000 state, local, not-for-profit, university, and other consumer health resources. Topics are organized in a subject index. With more than 7 million hits in its first two months of operation, Healthfinder is currently rated 21st among consumers' favorite websites on the "Web 100" list (www.hhs.gov).

MEDLINEPLUS MEDLINEplus, the world's most extensive collection of published medical information, is coordinated by the National Library of Medicine. Originally designed for health professionals and researchers, MEDLINEplus is also valuable for students and for those seeking more specific information about health care (www.nlm.nih.gov).

CONSUMER TIPS ON HEALTH AND DISABILITY INSURANCE

1. If you pay your own premiums directly, try to arrange to pay them on an annual or quarterly basis rather than a monthly basis. It is cheaper.
2. Policies should be delivered to you within 30 days. If not, contact your insurer and find out, in writing, why. If a policy is not delivered in 60 days, contact the state department of insurance.
3. When you receive a policy, take advantage of the free-look provision. You have 10 days to look it over and obtain a refund if you decide it is not for you.
4. Unless you have a policy with no internal limits, read over your contract every year to see whether its benefits are still in line with medical costs.
5. Don't replace a policy because you think it is out of date. Switching may subject you to new waiting periods and new exclusions. Rather, add to what you have if necessary.
6. On the other hand, don't keep a policy because you've had it a long time. You don't get any special credit from the company for being an old customer.
7. Don't try to make a profit on your insurance by carrying overlapping coverages. Duplicate coverage is expensive. Besides, most group policies now contain a coordination-of-benefits clause limiting benefits to 100 percent.
8. Use your health emergency fund to cover small expenses.
9. If you're considering the purchase of a dread disease policy such as cancer insurance, understand that it is supplementary and will pay for only one disease. You should have full coverage before you consider it. Otherwise, it's a gamble.
10. Don't lie on your insurance application. If you fail to mention a preexisting condition, you may not get paid. You can usually get paid even for that condition after one or two years have elapsed if you have had no treatment for the condition during that period.
11. Keep your insurance up to date. Some policies adjust to inflation better than others. Some insurers check that benefits have not been outdistanced by inflation. Review your policies annually.
12. Never sign a health insurance application (such applications are lengthy and detailed for individually written policies) until you have recorded full and complete answers to every question.

Source: Health Insurance Association of America.

NIH HEALTH INFORMATION PAGE This website provides a single access point to the consumer health information resources of the National Institutes of Health, including the NIH Health Information Index, NIH publications and clearinghouses, and the Combined Health Information Database (www.nih.gov).

FDA: THE FOOD AND DRUG ADMINISTRATION (FDA) The FDA also runs a website. This consumer protection agency's site provides information about the safety of various foods, drugs, cosmetics, and medical devices (www.fda.gov).

In addition, you can visit www.YouTube.com/cmshhsgov to see videos covering different health care topics on Medicare's YouTube channel. For Messages/Tweets, follow official Medicare information at CMSGov and the Children's Health Insurance Program at @IKNGov. For latest news and activity information from Medicare's websites, visit http://blog.medicare.gov/feed/ or http://blog.cms.gov/feed/.

1 What are the two sources of government health insurance?
2 What benefits do Part A and Part B of Medicare provide?
3 What is medigap, or MedSup, insurance?

Disability Income Insurance

LO11-6

Recognize the need for disability income insurance.

Because you feel young and healthy now, you may overlook the very real need for disability income insurance. Disability income insurance protects your most valuable asset: your ability to earn income. People are more likely to lose their incomes due to disability than to death. The fact is, for all age groups, disability is more likely than death.

disability income insurance Provides payments to replace income when an insured person is unable to work.

Disability income insurance provides regular cash income lost by employees as the result of an accident or illness. Disability income insurance is probably the most neglected form of available insurance protection. Many people who insure their houses, cars, and other property fail to insure their most valuable resource: their earning power. Disability can cause even greater financial problems than death. In fact, disability is often called "the living death." Disabled persons lose their earning power while continuing to incur normal family expenses. In addition, they often face huge expenses for the medical treatment and special care their disabilities require.

Every year, 12 percent of the adult U.S. population suffers a long-term disability. One out of every seven workers will suffer a five-year or longer period of disability before age 65, and if you are 35 now, your chances of experiencing a three-month or longer disability before you reach age 65 are 50 percent, according to the National Association of Insurance Commissioners. If you have no disability income protection, you are betting that you will not become disabled, and that could be a very costly bet.

my life 6

I realize that for all age groups, disability is more likely than death.

People are more likely to lose their incomes due to disability than death. What would happen if your paychecks suddenly stopped because you were too sick or injured to work? What if you could not work for months or years? For additional information, visit America's Health Insurance Plans website at www.aahp.org.

DEFINITION OF DISABILITY

Disability has several definitions. Some policies define it simply as the inability to do your regular work. Others have stricter definitions. For example, a dentist who is unable to do his or her regular work because of a hand injury but can earn income through related duties, such as teaching dentistry, would not be considered permanently disabled under certain policies.

Good disability plans pay when you are unable to work at your regular job; poor disability plans pay only when you are unable to work at any job. A good disability plan will also make partial disability payments when you return to work on a part-time basis.

DID YOU KNOW?

- One in three working Americans will become disabled for 90 days or more before age 65.
- The average disability absence is 2½ years.
- More than 80 percent of working Americans don't have disability income insurance or aren't covered adequately.

DISABILITY INSURANCE TRADE-OFFS

Following are some important trade-offs you should consider in purchasing disability income insurance.

WAITING OR ELIMINATION PERIOD

Benefits don't begin on the first day you become disabled. Usually there is a waiting or elimination period of between 30 and 90 days. Some waiting periods may be as long as 180 days. Generally, disability income policies with longer waiting periods have lower premiums. If you have substantial savings to cover three to six months of expenses, the reduced premiums of a policy with a long waiting period may be attractive. But if you need every paycheck to cover your bills, you are probably better off paying the higher premium for a short waiting period. Short waiting periods, however, are very expensive.

DURATION OF BENEFITS The maximum time a disability income policy will pay benefits may be a few years, to age 65, or for life. You should seek a policy that pays benefits for life. If you became permanently disabled, it would be financially disastrous if your benefits ended at age 55 or 65.

AMOUNT OF BENEFITS You should aim for a benefit amount that, when added to your other income, will equal 60 to 70 percent of your gross pay. Of course, the greater the benefits, the greater the cost.

ACCIDENT AND SICKNESS COVERAGE Consider both accident and sickness coverage. Some disability income policies will pay only for accidents, but you want to be insured for illness, too.

GUARANTEED RENEWABILITY Ask for noncancelable and guaranteed renewable coverage. Either coverage will protect you against your insurance company dropping you if your health becomes poor. The premium for these coverages is higher, but the coverages are well worth the extra cost. Furthermore, look for a disability income policy that waives premium payments while you are disabled.

See whether you qualify for a lower premium if you agree to forgo part of your monthly benefit when Social Security, company retirement benefits, or worker's compensation benefits begin. Most disability income policies coordinate their benefits with these programs.

SOURCES OF DISABILITY INCOME

Before you buy disability income insurance, remember that you may already have some form of such insurance. This coverage may come to you through your employer, Social Security, or worker's compensation.

EMPLOYER Many, but not all, employers provide disability income protection for their employees through group insurance plans. Your employer may have some form of wage continuation policy that lasts a few months or an employee group disability plan that provides long-term protection. In most cases, your employer will pay part or all of the cost of this plan.

SOCIAL SECURITY Most salaried workers in the United States participate in the Social Security program. In this program, your benefits are determined by your salary and by the number of years you have been covered under Social Security. Your dependents also qualify for certain benefits. However, Social Security has strict rules. You must be totally disabled for 12 months or more, and you must be unable to do *any* work.

WORKER'S COMPENSATION If your accident or illness occurred at your place of work or resulted from your type of employment, you could be entitled to worker's compensation benefits in your state. Like Social Security benefits, these benefits are determined by your earnings and work history.

Other possible sources of disability income include Veterans Administration

An individual's chances of disability are 2 to 3 times greater than death during their working years.

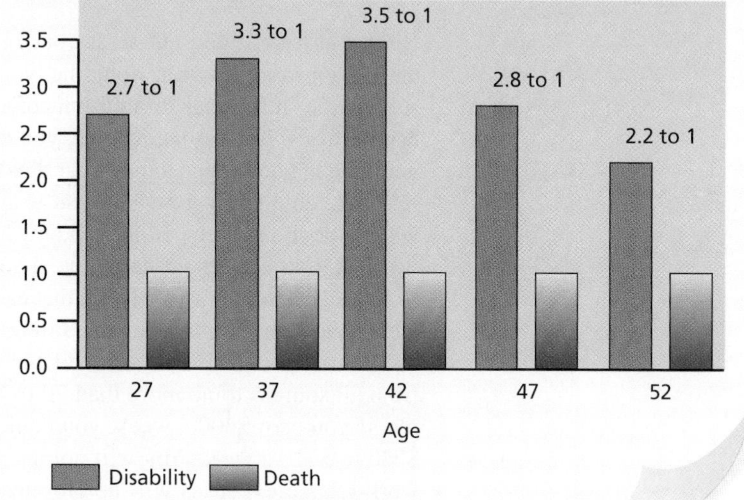

Source: Commissioner's Individual Disability Table A, n.d.

Exhibit 11-7

Disability income worksheet

How much income will you have available if you become disabled?	Monthly Amount	After Waiting:	For a Period of:
Sick leave or short-term disability	____	____	____
Group long-term disability	____	____	____
Social Security	____	____	____
Other government programs	____	____	____
Individual disability insurance	____	____	____
Credit disability insurance	____	____	____
Other income:	____	____	____
Savings	____	____	____
Spouse's income	____	____	____
Total monthly income while disabled:	$ ____		____

pension disability benefits, civil service disability benefits for government workers, state vocational rehabilitation benefits, state welfare benefits for low income people, Aid to Families with Dependent Children, group union disability benefits, automobile insurance that provides benefits for disability from an auto accident, and private insurances. Programs such as credit disability insurance, which covers loan payments when you are disabled. Exhibit 11-7 will help you identify the sources and amount of income available to you if you become disabled.

The availability and extent of these and other disability income sources vary widely in different parts of the country. Be sure to look into such sources carefully before calculating your need for additional disability income insurance.

DETERMINING YOUR DISABILITY INCOME INSURANCE REQUIREMENTS

Once you have found out what your benefits from the numerous public and private disability income sources would be, you should determine whether those benefits are sufficient to meet your disability income needs. If the sum of your disability benefits approaches your after-tax income, you can safely assume that should disability strike, you'll be in good shape to pay your day-to-day bills while recuperating.

You should know how long you would have to wait before the benefits begin (the waiting or elimination period) and how long they would be paid (the benefit period).

What if, as is often the case, Social Security and other disability benefits are not sufficient to support your family? In that case, you may want to consider buying disability income insurance to make up the difference.

Don't expect to insure yourself for your full salary. Most insurers limit benefits from all sources to no more than 70 to 80 percent of your take-home pay. For example, if you earn $400 a week, you could be eligible for disability insurance of about $280 to $320 a week. You will not need $400, because while you are disabled, your work-related expenses will be eliminated and your taxes will be far lower or may even be zero.

The Financial Planning for Life's Situations box "Disability Income Policy Checklist" shows you how to compare different features among disability income policies.

DISABILITY INCOME POLICY CHECKLIST

Every disability income policy may have different features. The following checklist will help you compare policies you may be considering.

	Policy A	Policy B
1. How is disability defined?		
Inability to perform your own job?	____	____
Inability to perform any job?	____	____
2. Does the policy cover		
Accident?	____	____
Illness?	____	____
3. Are benefits available		
For total disability?	____	____
For partial disability?	____	____
Only after total disability?	____	____
Without a prior period of total disability?	____	____
4. Are full benefits paid, whether or not you are able to work, for loss of		
Sight?	____	____
Speech?	____	____
Hearing?	____	____
Use of limbs?	____	____
5. What percentage of your income will the maximum benefit replace?	____	____
6. Is the policy noncancelable, guaranteed renewable, or conditionally renewable?	____	____
7. How long must you be disabled before premiums are waived?	____	____
8. Is there an option to buy additional coverage, without evidence of insurability, at a later date?	____	____
9. Does the policy offer an inflation adjustment feature?	____	____
If so, what is the rate of increase?	____	____
How often is it applied?	____	____
For how long?	____	____

	Policy A		**Policy B**	
10. What does the policy cost?	**With Inflation Feature**	**Without Inflation Feature**	**With Inflation Feature**	**Without Inflation Feature**
For a waiting period of ______ days and (30–180)	____	____	____	____
For a benefit period of ______ 1 yr.–lifetime?	____	____	____	____
Total	____	____	____	____

Source: Health Insurance Association of America, Washington, DC.

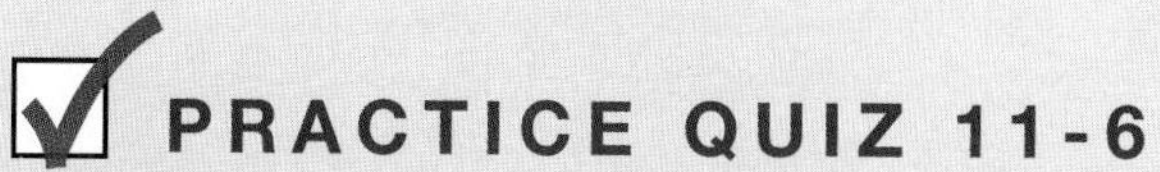

PRACTICE QUIZ 11-6

Disability income insurance needs

1 What is disability income insurance?
2 What are the three main sources of disability income?
3 How can you determine the amount of disability income insurance you need?

my life stages for health, disability and long-term care insurance...

YOUR PERSONAL FINANCE DASHBOARD

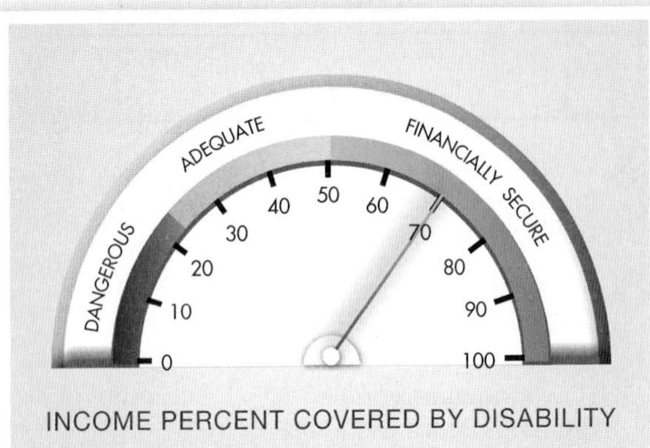

A personal finance dashboard with key performance indicators can help you monitor your financial situation and guide you toward financial independence. Disability can be more disastrous financially than death. If you are disabled, you lose your earning power, but you still have living expenses and often huge expenses for medical care.

YOUR SITUATION: Do you know how disability is defined? When do your benefits begin? How long do your benefits last? What is the amount of your benefits? Can benefits be reduced by Social Security disability and workers' compensation payments? Are the benefits adjusted for inflation? You should aim for benefit amounts that, when added to your other income, equal 70 or 80 percent of your gross pay. Other personal financial planning actions you might consider during various stages of your life include:

. . . in college

- Stay on your parents' health care insurance plan
- Most states offer free or low cost coverage for children who do not have health insurance. Call 1-877-543-7669 for more information
- Take meaningful action to ensure your own good health. Stay healthy: avoid smoking, drinking, bad nutrition, and lack of exercise

. . . in my 20s

- Get health care coverage from your employer
- Consider HMOs for lower co-payments and deductibles
- Don't give your insurance identification numbers to companies you don't know
- Consider purchasing disability income insurance
- Consider participating in a flexible spending account if your employer offers it

. . . in my 30s and 40s

- If you lose your group coverage from an employer due to unemployment, or divorce, continue your coverage through COBRA Act
- Consider PPOs that offer lower co-payments like HMOs, but give you more flexibility
- Consider purchasing long-term care insurance

. . . in my 50s and beyond

- Consider enrolling in Part D drug plan when you are first eligible
- Only give your Medicare number to your physician or other approved Medicare providers
- Review your Medicare statements to ensure that your account is not billed for services you did not receive

SUMMARY OF LEARNING OBJECTIVES

LO11-1

Explain why the costs of health insurance and health care have been increasing.

Your health care costs, except during 1994–1996, have gone up faster than the rate of inflation. Among the reasons for high and rising health care costs are the use of expensive technologies, duplication of tests and sometimes technologies, increases in the variety and frequency of treatments, unnecessary tests, the increasing number and longevity of elderly people, regulations that shift rather than reduce costs, the increasing number of accidents and crimes requiring emergency services, limited competition and restrictive work rules in the health care delivery system, rapid earnings growth among health care professionals, built-in inflation in the health care delivery system, and other factors.

LO11-2

Define *health insurance* and *disability income insurance* and explain their importance in financial planning.

Health insurance is protection that provides payment of benefits for a covered sickness or injury. Disability income insurance protects your most valuable asset: the ability to earn income. Health insurance and disability income insurance are two protections against economic losses due to illness, accident, or disability. Both protections should be a part of your overall insurance program to safeguard your family's economic security.

Disability can cause even greater financial problems than death. In fact, disability is often called "the living death." Disabled persons lose their earning power while continuing to incur normal family expenses. In addition, they often face huge expenses for the medical treatment and special care their disabilities require.

LO11-3

Analyze the benefits and limitations of the various types of health care coverage.

Five basic types of health insurance are available to you under group and individual policies: hospital expense insurance, surgical expense insurance, physician's expense insurance, major medical expense insurance, and comprehensive major medical insurance. The benefits and limitations of each policy differ. Ideally, you should get a basic plan and a major medical supplementary plan, or a comprehensive major medical policy that combines the values of both of these plans in a single policy.

Major provisions of a health insurance policy include eligibility requirements, assigned benefits, inside limits, copayment, service benefits, benefit limits, exclusions and limitation, coordination of benefits, guaranteed renewability, and cancellation and termination.

LO11-4

Evaluate private sources of health insurance and health care.

Health insurance and health care are available from private insurance companies, hospital and medical service plans such as Blue Cross/Blue Shield, health maintenance organizations (HMOs), preferred provider organizations (PPOs), exclusive provider organizations (EPOs), point-of-service plans (POSs), home health care agencies, and employer self-funded health plans.

LO11-5

Appraise the sources of government health care programs.

The federal and state governments offer health coverage in accordance with laws that define the premiums and benefits. Two well-known government health programs are Medicare and Medicaid.

LO11-6

Recognize the need for disability income insurance.

Disability income insurance provides regular cash income you lose as the result of an accident or illness. Sources of disability income insurance include the employer, Social Security, worker's compensation, the Veterans Administration, the federal and state governments, unions, and private insurance.

KEY TERMS

SELF-TEST PROBLEMS

1. The MacDonald family has health insurance coverage that pays 75 percent of out-of-hospital expenses after a $600 deductible per person. Mrs. MacDonald incurred doctor and prescription medication expenses of $1,380. What amount would the insurance company pay?
2. Under Rose's PPO, emergency room care at a network hospital is 80 percent covered after the member has met a $300 annual deductible. Assume that Rose went to a hospital within her PPO network and that she has not met her annual deductible yet. Her total emergency room bill was $850. What amount did Rose have to pay? What amount did the PPO cover?
3. Gene, an assembly line worker at an automobile manufacturing plant, has take-home pay of $900 a week. He is injured in an accident that kept him off work for 18 weeks. His disability insurance coverage replaces 65 percent of his earnings after a six-week waiting period. What amount would he receive in disability benefits?

Answers to Self-Test Problems

1.

Total expenses	=	$1,380
Deductible	=	− 600
		$ 780

Insurance company will pay 75 percent of $780 or $780 × .75 = $585.

2.

Total bill	$ 850
Deductible	− 300
	$ 550

Rose pays $550 × .20 = $110 + $300 = $410.

PPO pays $550 × .80 = $440.

3. Insurance will replace 65 percent of $900 or $900 × .65 = $585 per week. Insurance will pay for 18 − 6, or 12 weeks or $585 × 12 = $7,020.

FINANCIAL PLANNING PROBLEMS

LO11-1 1. *Calculating the Effect of Inflation on Health Care Costs.* As of 2008, per capita spending on health care in the United States was about $8,000. If this amount increased by 5 percent a year, what would be the amount of per capita spending for health care in 10 years?

LO11-3 2. *Calculating the Amount of Reimbursement from an Insurance Company.* The Kelleher family has health insurance coverage that pays 80 percent of out-of-hospital expenses after a $500 deductible per person. If one family member has doctor and prescription medication expenses of $1,100, what amount would the insurance company pay?

LO11-3 3. *Comparing the Costs of a Regular Health Insurance Policy and an HMO.* A health insurance policy pays 65 percent of physical therapy costs after a $200 deductible. In contrast, an HMO charges $15 per visit for physical therapy. How much would a person save with the HMO if he or she had 10 physical therapy sessions costing $50 each?

LO11-3 4. *Calculating the Cost of Health Care Coverage with and without a Stop-Loss Policy.* Sarah's comprehensive major medical health insurance plan at work has a deductible of $750. The policy pays 85 percent of any amount above the deductible. While on a hiking trip, she contracted a rare bacterial disease. Her medical costs for treatment, including medicines, tests, and a six-day hospital stay, totaled $8,893. A friend told her that she would have paid less if she had a policy with a stop-loss feature that capped her out-of-pocket expenses at $3,000. Was her friend correct? Show your computations. Then determine which policy would have cost Sarah less and by how much.

LO11-6 5. *Calculating the Amount of Disability Benefits.* Georgia Braxton, a widow, has take-home pay of $600 a week. Her disability insurance coverage replaces 70 percent of her earnings after a four-week waiting period. What amount would she receive in disability benefits if an illness kept Georgia off work for 16 weeks?

LO11-3 6. *Calculating the Cost of In-Network Care with a PPO.* Stephanie was injured in a car accident and was rushed to the emergency room. She received stitches for a facial wound and treatment for a broken finger. Under Stephanie's PPO plan, emergency room care at a network hospital is 80 percent covered after the member has met a $300 annual deductible. Assume that Stephanie went to a hospital within her PPO network. Her total emergency room bill was $850. What amount did Stephanie have to pay? What amount did the PPO cover?

Problems 7, 8, and 9 are based on the following scenario:

Evaluating Health Insurance Options. Ronald Roth started his new job as controller with Aerosystems today. Carole, the employee benefits clerk, gave Ronald a packet that contains information on the company's health insurance options. Aerosystems offers its employees the choice between a private insurance company plan (Blue Cross/Blue Shield), an HMO, and a PPO. Ronald needs to review the packet and make a decision on which health care program fits his needs. The following is an overview of that information. LO11-4

a. The monthly premium cost to Ronald for the *Blue Cross/Blue Shield plan* will be $42.32. For all doctor office visits, prescriptions, and major medical charges, Ronald will be responsible for 20 percent and the insurance company will cover 80 percent of covered charges. The annual deductible is $500.

b. The *HMO* is provided to employees free of charge. The copayment for doctors' office visits and major medical charges is $10. Prescription copayments are $5. The HMO pays 100 percent after Ronald's copayment. There is no annual deductible.

c. The *POS* requires that the employee pay $24.44 per month to supplement the cost of the program with the company's payment. If Ron uses health care providers within the plan, he pays the copayments as described above for the HMO. He can also choose to use a health care provider out of the service and pay 20 percent of all charges after he pays a $500 deductible. The POS will pay for 80 percent of those covered visits. There is no annual deductible.

Ronald decided to review his medical bills from the previous year to see what costs he had incurred and to help him evaluate his choices. He visited his general physician four times during the year at a cost of $125 for each visit. He also spent $65 and $89 on prescriptions during the year. Using these costs as an example, what would Ron pay for each of the plans described above? (For the purposes of the POS computation, assume that Ron visited a physician outside of the network plan. Assume he had his prescriptions filled at a network-approved pharmacy.

7. *Evaluating Health Insurance Options.* What annual medical costs will Ronald pay using the sample medical expenses provided if he were to enroll in the Blue Cross/Blue Shield plan? LO11-4

8. *Evaluating Health Insurance Options.* What total costs will Ronald pay if he enrolls in the HMO plan? LO11-4

9. *Evaluating Health Insurance Options.* If Ronald selects the POS plan, what would annual medical costs be? LO11-4

10. *Calculating Out-of-Pocket Costs.* Ariana's health insurance policy includes an $800 deductible and a coinsurance provision requiring her to pay 20 percent of all bills. Her total bill is $3,800. What is Ariana's total cost? LO11-3

11. *Comparing Health Care Plan Costs.* Richard is 35, single, and in reasonably good health. He works for a construction company that offers three health insurance plans. The first has a lifetime benefit of $1 million for all covered expenses, an annual deductible of $500, and a 15 percent coinsurance provision up to the first $2,000 in covered charges. The second requires a monthly premium of $50 and sets a $500,000 lifetime limit on benefits, has no annual deductible, and requires a $15 co-payment per office visit. The third has an annual deductible of $250 and a 25 percent coinsurance provision up to the first $1,500 in covered charges, with a lifetime limit on benefits of $700,000. Which plan should he choose? LO11-3

12. *Calculating Health Care Costs over Time.* In 2009, Mark spent $9,500 on his health care. If this amount increased by 6 percent per year, what would be the amount Mark will spend in 2019? (*Hint:* Use the compounded sum future value table in Chapter 1.) LO11-4

FINANCIAL PLANNING ACTIVITIES

1. *Identifying Financial Resources Needed to Pay for Health Care Services.* List health care services that you and other members of your family have used during the past year. Assign an approximate dollar cost to each of these services, and identify the financial resources (savings, health insurance, government sources, etc.) you used to pay for them. LO11-1

2. *Using Current Information to Obtain Costs of Health Care.* Choose a current issue of *Consumer Reports, Money, BusinessWeek,* or *Kiplinger's Personal Finance* and summarize an article that updates the costs of health care. How might you use this information to reduce your health care costs? LO11-1

3. *Comparing Major Provisions in a Health Care Insurance Policy.* Obtain sample health insurance policies from insurance agents or brokers, and analyze the policies for definitions, coverages, exclusions, limitations on coverage, and amounts of coverage. In what ways are the policies similar? In what ways do they differ? LO11-3

4. *Using the Internet to Obtain Information about Various Types of Health Insurance Coverages.* Visit the following Department of Health and Human Services websites to gather information about various types of health insurance coverages. Prepare a summary report on how this information may be useful to you. LO11-5

   a. Healthfinder (www.healthfinder.gov)

   b. MEDLINE (www.medline.gov)

5. *Learning about Social Security Benefits.* Visit the Social Security Administration's Web page to determine your approximate monthly Social Security disability benefits should you become disabled in the current year. Or call your Social Security office to request the latest edition of *Social Security: Understanding the Benefits.* LO11-6

FINANCIAL PLANNING CASE

Making Sense of Medicare

Eugenio Costa, 65, received a 148-page booklet from Uncle Sam called *Medicare and You 2013.* It doesn't have much of a plot, but it might be the most important reading he does this year.

For seniors or their adult children, the booklet outlines the choices Medicare recipients face in the fast-changing world of health care. But Medicare is mind-numbingly complicated, and it is too easy to get lost in a maze of options.

Eugenio is fully aware, however, that Medicare, Medicare HMO (Medicare + Choice), or medigap do not cover long-term nursing home or at-home care. For that, he will have to buy private insurance, which can cost thousands of dollars a year if he signs up now.

All of these choices allow seniors to tailor a plan to their needs. But it also makes picking insurance much more complicated. Eugenio knows that a mistake can be costly in terms of both health and money.

Questions

1. What factors should Eugenio Costa consider in making the choice among various types of Medicare, medigap, or HMO health care insurance policies?
2. Visit the following websites for Medicare resources to obtain general information, guides on buying medigap or HMO coverage, and price quotations with insurance company ratings on medigap insurance carriers.

General Information

Medicare
1-800-633-4227
www.medicare.gov
ElderCare Locator
1-800-677-1116

Guides on Buying Medigap or HMO Coverage

Medicare Rights Center
www.medicarerights.org
United Seniors Health Cooperative
www.ushc-online.org

Quotes and Ratings on Medigap Carriers

The Street, Com Ratings
1-800-289-9222
www.TheStreet.com
Insure.com
1-800-324-6370
www.insure.com

PERSONAL FINANCIAL PLANNER IN ACTION

Comparing Health Insurance Plans

Changing programs and regulations influence your ability to be properly covered for health care and disability insurance coverage. Awareness of policy types, coverages, and limitations will help you plan this phase of your financial plan.

Short-Term Financial Planning Activities	*Resources*
1. Assess your current habits that could improve your health and reduce medical costs.	www.webmd.com www.healthfinder.gov www.healthseek.com
2. Analyze current health insurance coverage in relation to family and household needs.	PFP Sheet 51 www.quicken.com/insurance www.healthchoices.org www.ncqa.org
3. Compare the cost of health insurance programs available from various sources.	http://personalinsure.about.com www.insure.com
4. Evaluate your need for expanded disability insurance.	PFP Sheet 52 www.life-line.org www.disability-insurance-center.com
Long-Term Financial Planning Activities	*Resources*
1. Identify possible future needs for supplemental Medicare and long-term care insurance coverages.	www.longtermcareinsurance.org www.ssa.gov www.medicare.gov www.naic.org
2. Develop a plan for reducing health care and medical insurance costs.	Text pages 368–372 www.ahip.org www.mib.com

CONTINUING CASE

Health Insurance

Life Situation	*Financial Data*	
Young married couple	Monthly Gross Income	$4,400
Shelby, age 27	Living Expenses	$3,500
Mark, age 28	Assets	$180,000
	Liabilities	$121,000

The Lawrences are assessing their health insurance coverage. Since Mark's current employer offers him only two weeks of sick leave per year, they need to consider this factor when assessing disability insurance plans. In addition, Shelby realized her dream this year and opened her pet salon. Since she is self-employed, they are dependent on Mark's health insurance. In recent weeks, his company has been considering several types of plans including traditional health insurance plans and an HMO. These plans offer a wide variety of coverage and differences in costs so they could use some help in finding the right one especially since they are considering having a baby in the near future.

Questions

1. In evaluating the various health insurance plans, what factors should the Lawrences look for in a good health insurance plan?
2. When considering disability income insurance, what are the trade-offs of purchasing this type of insurance and how does this affect the Lawrences?
3. Explain how Shelby and Mark might use the following Personal Financial Planner sheets when figuring out their health insurance needs.
   a. Assessing Current and Needed Health Care Insurance
   b. Disability Income Insurance Needs

DAILY SPENDING DIARY

"Some of my eating habits not only waste money but are also not best for my health."

Directions

Continue your "Daily Spending Diary" to record and monitor your spending in various categories. Your comments should reflect what you have learned about your spending patterns and help you consider possible changes you might want to make in your spending habits.

Analysis Questions

1. What spending actions might directly or indirectly affect your health and physical well-being?
2. What amounts (if any) are currently required from your spending for the cost of health and disability insurance?

The Daily Spending Diary Sheets are located in Appendix D at the end of the book and on the student website at www.mhhe.com/kdh.

chapter 12

Life Insurance

Learning Objectives

LO12-1 Define *life insurance* and describe its purpose and principle.

LO12-2 Determine your life insurance needs.

LO12-3 Distinguish between the two types of life insurance companies and analyze various types of life insurance policies these companies issue.

LO12-4 Select important provisions in life insurance contracts.

LO12-5 Create a plan to buy life insurance.

LO12-6 Evaluate the payout options for life insurance.

What will this mean for me?

Life insurance helps to provide for the people who depend on you. Deciding whether you need it and choosing the right policy takes time, research, and careful thought.

my life

WHO NEEDS LIFE INSURANCE?

Life insurance helps to provide for the people who depend on you for financial support by replacing some or all of your lost income when you die. It can help pay expenses that your income would have covered, including mortgage payments, bills, and a dependent's child care or college tuition. If you don't have anyone depending on you for financial support, you may not need life insurance. Some people may need only enough to cover funeral expenses or other financial obligations.

Should you be covered with life insurance? How will you best plan for life insurance needs? You can start now by assessing your life insurance needs. For each of the following statements, indicate if you "agree," are "neutral," or "disagree."

1. I need life insurance because someone depends on me for financial support.	Agree	Neutral	Disagree
2. I am aware of several general methods for determining the amount of life insurance I may need now or in the future.	Agree	Neutral	Disagree
3. Although term life insurance premiums increase as I get older, I can reduce my coverage as my children grow up and my assets increase.	Agree	Neutral	Disagree
4. An important provision in every life insurance policy is the right to name my beneficiary.	Agree	Neutral	Disagree
5. The life insurance company I choose is essential to my beneficiaries' financial future.	Agree	Neutral	Disagree
6. I am aware of the different payout options in a life insurance policy.	Agree	Neutral	Disagree

As you study this chapter, you will encounter "My Life" boxes with additional information and resources related to these items.

Life Insurance: An Introduction

LO12-1

Define *life insurance* and describe its purpose and principle.

Even though it is impossible to put a price on your life, you probably own some life insurance—through a group plan where you work, as a veteran, or through a policy you bought. Perhaps you are considering the purchase of additional life insurance to keep pace with inflation or to provide for your growing family. If so, you should prepare for that purchase by learning as much as possible about life insurance and how it can help you meet your needs.

Most American families face a substantial loss when one spouse dies unexpectedly. Unfortunately, 45 percent of widows and 37 percent of widowers say their spouse had been inadequately insured. Life for the surviving spouse becomes a financial struggle.

Life insurance is one of the most important and expensive purchases you may ever make. Deciding whether you need it and choosing the right policy from dozens of options take time, research, and careful thought. This chapter will help you make decisions about life insurance. It describes what life insurance is and how it works, the major types of life insurance coverage, and how you can use life insurance to protect your family.

Consumer awareness of life insurance has changed little over the years. Life insurance is still more often sold than bought. In other words, while most people actively seek to buy insurance for their property and health, they avoid a life insurance purchase until an agent approaches them. Still, recently, over 39.3 million policies, with face value of about $2.9 trillion, were sold in one year. Eight out of ten households now have life insurance. At the beginning of 2012, 286 million policies were in force, with a total value of $19.2 trillion.[1]

my life 1

I need life insurance because someone depends on me for financial support.

Most Americans need life insurance, and many who already have it may need to update their coverage. If you are providing financial support for a spouse, children, aging parents, or siblings, or if you have significant debt, you should consider buying life insurance.

WHAT IS LIFE INSURANCE?

Life insurance is neither mysterious nor difficult to understand. It works in the following manner. A person joins a risk-sharing group (an insurance company) by purchasing a contract (a policy). Under the policy, the insurance company promises to pay a sum of money at the time of the policyholder's death to the person or persons (the beneficiaries) selected by him or her. In the case of an endowment policy, the money is paid to the policyholder (the insured) if he or she is alive on the future date (the maturity date) named in the policy. The insurance company makes this promise in return for the insured's agreement to pay it a sum of money (the premium) periodically.

DID YOU KNOW?

You can receive a free *Life Insurance Buyer's Guide* from the National Association of Insurance Commissioners. Visit their website at www.naic.org. The guide helps you get the most for your money and answers questions about buying life insurance, deciding how much is needed, and finding the right kind of insurance.

THE PURPOSE OF LIFE INSURANCE

Most people buy life insurance to protect someone who depends on them from financial losses caused by their death. That someone could be the nonworking spouse and children of a single-income family. It could be the wife or husband of a two-income family. It could be an aging parent. It could be a business partner or a corporation.

Life insurance proceeds may be used to

- Pay off a home mortgage or other debts at the time of death.
- Provide lump-sum payments through an endowment to children when they reach a specified age.
- Provide an education or income for children.
- Cover medical expenses and funeral costs.
- Make charitable bequests after death.
- Provide a retirement income.
- Accumulate savings.
- Establish a regular income for survivors.
- Set up an estate plan.
- Make estate and death tax payments.

Life insurance is one of the few ways to provide liquidity at the time of death.

Most people buy life insurance to protect someone who depends on them from financial losses caused by their death.

THE PRINCIPLE OF LIFE INSURANCE

The principle of home insurance, discussed in Chapter 10, can be applied to the lives of persons. From records covering many years and including millions of lives, mortality tables have been prepared to show the number of deaths among various age groups during any year. In the 1950s, the life insurance industry developed and the National Association of Insurance Commissioners (NAIC) approved a mortality table known as the Commissioners 1958 Standard Ordinary (CSO) Mortality Table. In 2001 the NAIC approved a new Standard Ordinary Mortality Table. Unlike the 1958 CSO table, which combined the mortality experience of males and females, the 2001 CSO table separates the experience by gender.

HOW LONG WILL YOU LIVE?

No one really knows how long a particular individual will live. But life expectancy in the United States has been steadily increasing since 1900. One major reason for the increase is constantly improving medical care as well as overall knowledge of ways to have a healthier lifestyle. The fact remains, however, that the number of years that you have already lived is the biggest factor of determining how many years you have remaining. Historically, women have outlived men. For example, in 1900 the life expectancy of a man was 46.3 years and of a woman 48.3 years. By 2010, life expectancy had increased to 76.2 years for males and 81 for females. Further, projections now indicate that by 2020, life expectancy will increase to 77.1 for males and 81.9 for females. Exhibit 12-1 shows the most recent life expectancy table, issued in 2010 by the National Center for Health Statistics. The life expectancy shown does not indicate the age at which a person has the highest probability of dying. For example, the exhibit shows that the life expectancy of a male at age 30 is 47.8 years. This does not mean 30-year-old males will probably die at age 77.8 years. It means 47.8 is the average number of additional years males alive at age 30 may expect to live.

LIFE EXPECTANCY AND EDUCATION

The education level that you attain has also been linked to life expectancy. Exhibit 12-2 shows how life expectancy differs based upon education obtained. There are many factors that could explain this trend: (1) knowledge of healthier eating habits; (2) financial means to acquire healthier food; (3) housing locations and options; (4) education level of ancestors (parents and prior generations).

Exhibit 12-1 Life expectancy tables, all races, 2010

This table helps insurance companies determine insurance premiums. *Use the table to find the average number of additional years a 25-year-old male and female are expected to live.*

Expectation of Life in Years		
Age	**Male**	**Female**
0	76.2	81
1	75.7	80.5
5	71.8	76.6
10	66.8	71.6
15	61.9	66.6
20	57.1	61.7
25	52.4	56.9
30	47.8	52
35	43.1	47.2
40	38.5	42.4
45	33.9	37.7

Expectation of Life in Years		
Age	**Male**	**Female**
50	29.6	33.2
55	25.4	28.8
60	21.5	24.5
65	17.7	20.3
70	14.2	16.5
75	11.0	12.9
80	8.2	9.7
85	5.8	6.9
90	4.1	4.8
95	2.9	3.3
100	2.1	2.3

Source: The U.S. Census Bureau (www.census.gov/compendia/statb/cats/births_deaths-mar), accessed March 16, 2013.

Exhibit 12-2 Life expectancy at age 25, by gender and education level: United States 2006

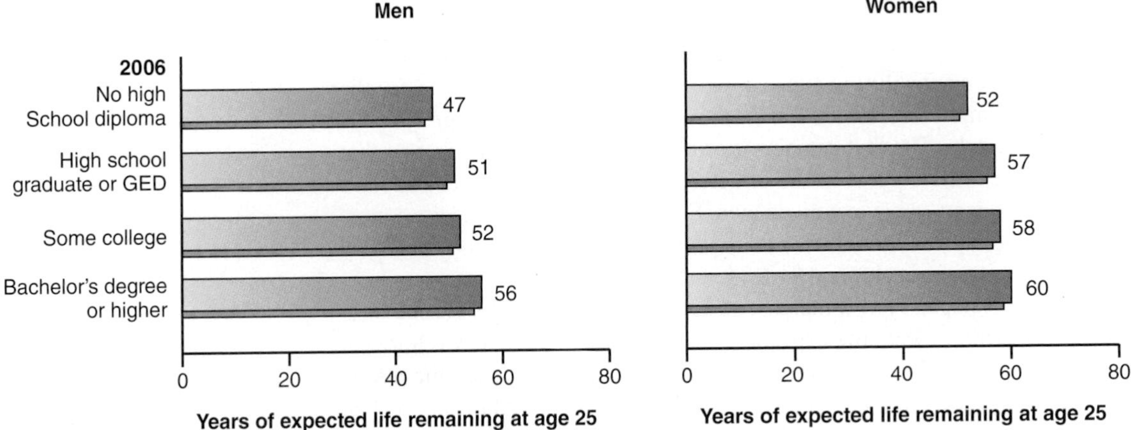

Note: GED is General Educational Development high school equivalency diploma.

Source: CDC/NCHS, National Health Interview Survery Linked Mortality File. See Appendix I, National Health Interview Survey (NHIS) Linked Mortality File.

PRACTICE QUIZ 12-1

1 How can the Internet help you create a life insurance plan?
2 What is the purpose of life insurance?
3 What is the principle of life insurance?
4 What do life expectancy tables indicate?

Determining Your Life Insurance Needs

LO12-2

Determine your life insurance needs.

You should consider a number of factors before you buy life insurance. These factors include your present and future sources of income, other savings and income protection, group life insurance, group annuities (or other pension benefits), net worth, and Social Security. First, however, you should determine whether you *need* life insurance.

DO YOU NEED LIFE INSURANCE?

If your death would cause financial stress for your spouse, children, parents, or anyone else you want to protect, you should consider purchasing life insurance. Your stage in the life cycle and the type of household you live in will influence this decision. Single persons living alone or with their parents usually have little or no need for life insurance. Consider Brian Brickman, 28, a bachelor who does not smoke, is in excellent health, and has no dependents. Brian owns a $100,000 condominium with a $90,000 mortgage. Since his employer provides a $100,000 group term life policy, he needs no additional life insurance. Larry Lucas, 32, and his wife, Liz, 30, are professionals, each earning $45,000 a year. The Lucases have no dependents. This two-earner couple may have a moderate need for life insurance, especially if they have a mortgage or other large debts. Households with small children usually have the greatest need for life insurance.

DETERMINING YOUR LIFE INSURANCE OBJECTIVES

Before you consider types of life insurance policies, you must decide what you want your life insurance to do for you and your dependents.

First, how much money do you want to leave to your dependents should you die today? Will you require more or less insurance protection to meet their needs as time goes on?

Second, when would you like to be able to retire? What amount of income do you believe you and your spouse would need then?

Third, how much will you be able to pay for your insurance program? Are the demands on your family budget for other living expenses likely to be greater or lower as time goes on?

When you have considered these questions and developed some approximate answers, you are ready to select the types and amounts of life insurance policies that will help you accomplish your objectives.

Once you have decided what you want your life insurance to accomplish, the next important decision is how much to buy.

I am aware of several general methods for determining the amount of life insurance I may need now or in the future.

The most difficult part of buying life insurance is determining how much you need. But with some effort you can come up with a good estimate that takes into account your specific financial situation. Visit various insurance needs calculators on the Internet, including the nonprofit Life and Health Insurance Foundation at www.lifehappens.org. The average insured adult American has about $162,000 in life insurance coverage, or about three times his or her gross annual income.[2]

ESTIMATING YOUR LIFE INSURANCE REQUIREMENTS

How much life insurance should you carry? This question is important for every person who owns or intends to buy life insurance. Because of the various factors involved, the question cannot be answered by mathematics alone. Nevertheless, an insurance policy puts a price on the life of the insured person. Therefore, methods are needed to estimate what that price should be.

There are five general methods for determining the amount of insurance you may need: the easy method, the DINK method, the "nonworking" spouse method, the "family need" method, and online calculators.

THE EASY METHOD The easy method is based on the earnings multiple method that has been used in the insurance industry for many years. Simple as this method is, it is remarkably useful. It uses the insurance agent's rule of thumb that a "typical family" will need approximately 70 percent of your salary for seven years before they adjust to the financial consequences of your death. In other words, for a simple estimate of your life insurance needs, just multiply your current gross income by 7 (7 years) and 0.70 (70 percent). For example:

EXAMPLE: The Easy Method

$30,000 current income × 7 = $210,000; $210,000 × 0.70 = $147,000

Your figures:

$________ current income × 7 = $________ × 0.70 = $________

This method assumes your family is "typical." You may need more insurance if you have four or more children, if you have above-average family debt, if any member of your family suffers from poor health, or if your spouse has poor employment potential. On the other hand, you may need less insurance if your family is smaller.

THE DINK (DUAL INCOME, NO KIDS) METHOD If you have no dependents and your spouse earns as much as or more than you do, you have simple insurance needs. All you need to do is ensure that your spouse will not be unduly burdened by debts should you die. Here is an example of the DINK method:

EXAMPLE: The DINK Method

	Example	Your Figures
Funeral expenses (Estimated)	$ 5,000	$________
One-half of mortgage	60,000	________
One-half of auto loan	7,000	________
One-half of credit card balance	1,500	________
One-half of personal debt	1,500	________
Other debts	1,000	________
	________	________
Total insurance needs	$76,000	$________

This method assumes your spouse will continue to work after your death. If your spouse suffers poor health or is employed in an occupation with an uncertain future, you should consider adding an insurance cushion to see him or her through hard times.

THE "NONWORKING" SPOUSE METHOD Insurance experts have estimated that extra costs of up to $10,000 a year may be required to replace the services of a homemaker in a family with small children. These extra costs may include the cost of a housekeeper, child care, more meals out, transportation, laundry services, and so on. They do not include the lost potential earnings of the surviving spouse, who often must take time away from the job to care for the family.

To estimate how much life insurance a homemaker should carry, multiply the number of years before the youngest child reaches age 18 by $10,000. For example:

EXAMPLE: The "Nonworking" Spouse Method

10 years (years before the youngest child is 18) × $10,000 = $100,000

Your figures:

_______ years × $10,000 = $_______

If there are teenage children, the $10,000 figure can be reduced. If there are more than two children under age 13, or anyone in the family suffers poor health or has special needs, the $10,000 figure should be adjusted upward. Also, be aware that the $10,000 figure can vary greatly based upon recent estimates of nonworking spouse's duties and proposed wages as reported in the nearby Did You Know? box.

DID YOU KNOW?

According to a survey by Salary.com, stay-at-home moms work 94.7 hours per week and would have an equivalent wage of $112,962.

Source: Salary.com (http://www.salary.com/stay-at-home-mom-infographic/), accessed March 16, 2013.

THE "FAMILY NEED" METHOD The first three methods assume you and your family are "typical" and ignore important factors such as Social Security and your liquid assets. Exhibit 12-3 provides a detailed worksheet for making a thorough estimation of your life insurance needs.

Although this method is quite thorough, you may believe it does not address all of your special needs. If so, you should obtain further advice from an insurance expert or a financial planner.

As you determine your life insurance needs, don't forget to consider the life insurance you may already have. You may have ample coverage through your employer and through any mortgage and credit life insurance you have purchased.

In our dynamic economy, inflation and interest rates change often. Therefore, experts recommend that you reevaluate your insurance coverage every two years. Be sure to update your insurance whenever your situation changes substantially. For example, the birth of another child, an increase in your home mortgage, or the needs of an aging parent can boost your insurance needs.

ONLINE CALCULATORS AND APPLICATIONS (APPS)

There are numerous online calculators that can provide estimates of insurance needs.

Many of the premier financial magazines and websites also offer life insurance estimators. These may provide a slightly more impartial view of your insurance needs versus using an online calculator via an insurance company website.

Exhibit 12-3

The "family need" method worksheet to calculate your life insurance needs

1. Five times your personal yearly income		_________ (1)
2. Total approximate expenses above and beyond your daily living costs for you and your dependents (e.g., tuition, care for a disabled child or parent) amount to		_________ (2)
3. Your emergency fund (3 to 6 months of living expenses) amounts to		_________ (3)
4. Estimated amount for your funeral expenses (U.S. average is $5,000 to $10,000)	+	_________ (4)
5. Total estimate of your family's financial needs (add lines 1 through 4)	=	_________ (5)
6. Your total liquid assets (e.g., savings accounts, CDs, money market funds, existing life insurance both individual and group, pension plan death benefits, and Social Security benefits	−	_________ (6)
7. Subtract line 6 from line 5 and enter the difference here.	=	_________ (7)

The net result (line 7) is an estimate of the shortfall your family would face upon your death. Remember, these are just rules of thumb. For a complete analysis of your needs, consult a professional.

Sources: Metropolitan Life Insurance Company, *About Life Insurance,* February 1997, p. 3; *The TIAA Guide to Life Insurance Planning for People in Education* (New York: Teachers Insurance and Annuity Association, January 1997), p. 3.

Here are some helpful websites with online calculators:

www.kiplingers.com

http://money.msn.com

www.smartmoney.com

Life insurance estimators on insurance company websites can also be used as a comparison. However, remember that these will typically provide a higher estimate of insurance needs. Thus, the higher the estimate, the higher the premium and commission for the agent.

Apps can also be handy for calculating insurance needs. There are many Apps on the market and more are being added each day.

Here are some of the more popular Apps today.

Life Happens

Human Life Value Calculator

Life Calculate

Determining life insurance needs

PRACTICE QUIZ 12-2

1 How do you determine the need for life insurance?
2 What determines your life insurance objectives?
3 What are the five methods of estimating your life insurance requirements?

Types of Life Insurance Companies and Policies

TYPES OF LIFE INSURANCE COMPANIES

LO12-3

Distinguish between the two types of life insurance companies and analyze various types of life insurance policies these companies issue.

You can purchase the new or extra life insurance you need from two types of life insurance companies: stock life insurance companies, owned by shareholders, and mutual life insurance companies, owned by their policyholders. About 76 percent of U.S. life insurance companies are stock companies, and about 24 percent are mutuals.[3]

Stock companies generally sell **nonparticipating** (or *nonpar*) policies, while mutual companies specialize in the sale of **participating** (or *par*) policies. A participating policy has a somewhat higher premium than a nonparticipating policy, but a part of the premium is refunded to the policyholder annually. This refund is called the *policy dividend.*

nonparticipating policy Life insurance that does not provide policy dividends; also called a *nonpar policy.*

participating policy Life insurance that provides policy dividends; also called a *par policy.*

There has been long and inconclusive debate about whether stock companies or mutual companies offer less expensive life insurance. You should check with both stock and mutual companies to determine which type offers the best policy for your particular needs at the lowest price.

If you wish to pay exactly the same premium each year, you should choose a nonparticipating policy with its guaranteed premiums. Indeed, about 80 percent of individual life insurance policies purchased recently were nonparticipating. However, you may prefer life insurance whose annual price reflects the company's experience with its investments, the health of its policyholders, and its general operating costs, that is, a participating policy.

Nevertheless, as with other forms of insurance, price should not be your only consideration in choosing a life insurance policy. You should consider the financial stability, reliability, and service the insurance company provides. Currently about 900 insurance companies in the United States sell life insurance.[4]

TYPES OF LIFE INSURANCE POLICIES

Both mutual insurance companies and stock insurance companies sell two basic types of life insurance: temporary and permanent insurance. Temporary insurance can be term, renewable term, convertible term, or decreasing term insurance. Permanent insurance is known by different names, including *whole life, straight life, ordinary life,* and *cash value life insurance.* As you will learn in the next section, permanent insurance can be limited payment, variable, adjustable, or universal life insurance. Other types of insurance policies—group life and credit life insurance—are generally temporary forms of insurance. Exhibit 12-4 shows major types and subtypes of life insurance.

Exhibit 12-4

Major types and subtypes of life insurance

Term (temporary)	Whole, Straight, or Ordinary Life	Other Types
• Renewable term	• Limited payment	• Group life
• Multiyear level term	• Single premium	• Credit life
• Convertible term	• Modified life	• Endowment life
• Decreasing term	• Variable life	
• Return of premium	• Adjustable life	
	• Universal life	
	• Variable universal life	

TERM LIFE INSURANCE

term insurance Life insurance protection for a specified period of time; sometimes called *temporary life insurance.*

Term insurance is protection for a specified period of time, usually 1, 5, 10, or 20 years or up to age 70. A term insurance policy pays a benefit only if you die during the period it covers. If you stop paying the premiums, the insurance stops. Term insurance is therefore sometimes called *temporary life insurance.*

Term insurance is a basic, "no frills" form of life insurance and is the best value for most consumers. The premiums for people in their 20s and 30s are less expensive than those for whole life insurance, discussed in the next section.

You need insurance coverage most while you are raising young children. Although term life insurance premiums increase as you get older, you can reduce your coverage as your children grow up and your assets (the value of your savings, investments, home, autos, etc.) increase.

Here are various options in choosing your term insurance.

DID YOU KNOW?

An excellent source of information about all types of topics in life insurance is available on the CNN/Money website at money.cnn.com/pf/101/lessons.

my life 3

Although term life insurance premiums increase as I get older, I can reduce my coverage as my children grow up and my assets increase.

Term insurance makes the most sense when your need for it is going to diminish in the future, such as when your children graduate from college or when a debt is paid off. Typically, term insurance offers the greatest amount of coverage for the lowest initial premium and is a good choice for young families on a tight budget.

RENEWABILITY OPTION The coverage of term insurance ends at the conclusion of the term, but you can continue it for another term if you have a renewability option. For example, the term insurance of the Teachers Insurance and Annuity Association is renewable at your option for successive five-year periods to age 70 without medical reexamination. Level premiums are paid during each five-year period. The premiums increase every five years.

MULTIYEAR LEVEL TERM (OR STRAIGHT TERM) *Multiyear term life* is a relatively new policy. This type of policy continues to grow in popularity. The growth is primarily because the policyholder pays the same premium amount for the life of the policy. This makes it much easier to budget for insurance needs. Most recently, 35 percent of the Individual life insurance policies issued were level term.[5]

CONVERSION OPTION If you have convertible term insurance, you can exchange it for a whole life policy without a medical examination and at a higher premium. The premium for the whole life policy stays the same for the rest of your life. Consider this option if you want cash-value life insurance and can't afford it now but expect to do so in the future.

DECREASING TERM INSURANCE Term insurance is also available in a form that pays less to the beneficiary as time passes. The premiums will typically remain constant while the payout amount of the insurance will decrease. This type of insurance was originally designed to be paired with a debt repayment, such as a mortgage on a home. For example, a decreasing term contract for 30 years might be appropriate as coverage of a mortgage loan balance on a house, because the coverage will decrease as the balance on the mortgage decreases. The insurance period you select might depend on your age, the term of the debt, or other assets that you currently own. Decreasing term insurance will help keep the premiums at a constant amount and therefore, not be subjected to dramatic increases due to the age of the policyholder. You could get the same result by purchasing annual renewable term policies of diminishing amounts during the period of the mortgage loan. Additionally, an annual renewable policy would offer more flexibility to change coverage if you were to sell or remortgage the house.

RETURN-OF-PREMIUM POLICIES

For those who see term life insurance as a losing proposition—live and you lose the money you paid in, die and, well, you're dead—an old insurance product is back. Called return of premium (ROP) or money-back term, these policies refund every penny paid in premiums if you outlive the 15-, 20-, or 30-year term of the policy.

There is a catch. The policies cost more—perhaps 30 percent to 50 percent more for a 30-year policy—than traditional term life. A healthy 35-year-old man might pay $550 annually for a basic $500,000, 30-year term policy versus $810 for one with the ROP feature. You can get policies for a shorter term, but they cost so much more—sometimes six or seven times as much as simple term—that Byron Udell, CEO of insurance brokerage AccuQuote, advises against them. American General Life & Accident Insurance is the biggest player in this field, but ROPs are also offered by Fidelity & Guaranty Life Insurance, United of Omaha Life Insurance, and Federal Kemper Life Assurance.

Does an ROP policy make sense? That depends on your answer to two questions: Would you earn more buying a cheaper term policy and investing the savings? Are you likely to cancel before the 30 (or however many) years are up?

In the example above, the ROP would cost $260 more each year than regular term insurance but would return $24,300 in premiums at the end of 30 years. That amounts to an annualized return of 6.6 percent, and it's tax-free because you're just getting back your own money. For someone looking for a conservative investment, such a policy could make sense, says Charles Hais, manager of the insurance department at Brecek & Young Advisors, a Cincinnati brokerage.

But remember, you get that return only if you pay the premiums for the entire 30 years. If you drop the policy before (most buyers of term life do), you'll get less, or perhaps nothing, in return for those higher premiums. "A company generally counts on people dropping the policies—in order to pay the money to those who don't," says James Hunt, a life insurance actuary for the Consumer Federation of America.

If you've decided to use insurance as an investment vehicle, you ought to check out universal, variable universal, and whole life policies as well. These other types of insurance usually cost even more. But because they pay interest or dividends or allow you to invest in mutual funds, they have the potential for higher returns.

Source: Carol Marie Cropper, "Premiums You Can Retrieve," *BusinessWeek*, May 10, 2004, p. 114.

RETURN OF PREMIUM Return-of-premium (ROP), or money-back term policies refund every penny you paid in premiums if you outlive the 15-, 20-, or 30-year term of the policy. However, ROP policies cost 30 percent to 50 percent more than traditional term life. Does an ROP policy make sense for you? Read the accompanying Financial Planning for Life's Situations feature, "Return-of-Premium Policies."

If you want to compare rates and avoid a high-pressure pitch for permanent insurance, contact a low-load, no-commission insurer. One life insurance adviser recommends either USAA Life & Health Insurance Company (1-800-531-8000) or Ameritas Life Insurance Corporation (1-800-552-3553); both give quotes over the phone.

WHOLE LIFE INSURANCE

The most common type of permanent life insurance is the **whole life policy** (also called a *straight life policy,* a *cash-value life policy,* or an *ordinary life policy*), for which you pay a specified premium each year for as long as you live. In return, the insurance company promises to pay a stipulated sum to the beneficiary when you die. The amount of your premium depends primarily on the age at which you purchase the insurance.

One important feature of the whole life policy is its cash value. **Cash value** (or *cash surrender value*) is an amount, which increases each year, that you receive if you give up the insurance. Hence, cash-value policies provide a death benefit *and* a savings account. Insurance salespeople often emphasize the "forced savings" aspect of cash-value insurance. A table in the whole life policy enables you to tell exactly how much cash value the policy has at any given time (see Exhibit 12-5).

whole life policy An insurance plan in which the policyholder pays a specified premium each year for as long as he or she lives; also called a *straight life policy, cash-value life policy,* or *ordinary life policy.*

cash value The amount received after giving up a life insurance policy.

Exhibit 12-5

An example of guaranteed cash value

Plan and Additional Benefits	Amount	Premium	Years Payable
Whole life (premiums payable to age 90)	$10,000	$229.50	55
Waiver of premium (to age 65)		4.30	30
Accidental death (to age 70)	10,000	7.80	35

A premium is payable on the policy date and every 12 policy months thereafter. The first premium is $241.60.

Explanation for Table of Guaranteed Values: To cancel the policy in the 10th year, the insured would get $1,719 in savings (cash value). He or she could use the $1,719 to purchase a $3,690 paid-up life policy or purchase an extended term policy that would be in effect for 19 years and 78 days.

Table of Guaranteed Values

End of Policy Year	Cash or Loan Value	Paid-up Insurance	Extended Term Insurance	
			Years	Days
1	$14	$30	0	152
2	174	450	4	182
3	338	860	8	65
4	506	1,250	10	344
5	676	1,640	12	360
6	879	2,070	14	335
7	1,084	2,500	16	147
8	1,293	2,910	17	207
9	1,504	3,300	18	177
10	1,719	3,690	19	78
11	1,908	4,000	19	209
12	2,099	4,300	19	306
13	2,294	4,590	20	8
14	2,490	4,870	20	47
15	2,690	5,140	20	65
16	2,891	5,410	20	66
17	3,095	5,660	20	52
18	3,301	5,910	20	27
19	3,508	6,150	19	358
20	3,718	6,390	19	317
Age 60	4,620	7,200	18	111
Age 65	5,504	7,860	16	147

Paid-up additions and dividend accumulations increase the cash values; indebtedness decreases them.

Direct Beneficiary: Helen M. Benson, wife of the insured
Owner: Thomas A. Benson, the insured
Insured: Thomas A. Benson **Age and Sex:** 37 Male
Policy Date: November 1, 2011 **Policy Number:** 000/00
Date of Issue: November 1, 2011

Source: *Sample Life Insurance Policy* (Washington, DC: American Council of Life Insurance, n.d.), p. 2.

GUIDELINES FOR PREFERRED RATES

Do you qualify for preferred rates? These guidelines are used to determine preferred rates; standard rates are higher.

Blood Profile. All favorable values for cholesterol, triglycerides, and lipids.

Blood Pressure. May not exceed 140/90.

Urinalysis. No abnormal findings. Presence of nicotine will disqualify the applicant for no-tobacco rates.

Personal History. No history of or current treatment for high blood pressure, cancer, diabetes, mental or nervous disorders, or disorders of the heart, lungs, liver, or kidneys.

Build. Weight may not exceed 115 percent of average for height.

Driving. No convictions for reckless driving or driving under the influence of alcohol or drugs in the past five years; no more than three moving violations in the past three years; no more than one moving violation in the past six months.

Family History. No family history (natural parents and siblings) of death from heart disease, cardiovascular impairments, cancer, or diabetes prior to age 60.

Source: Ameritas Life Insurance Corporation.

Cash-value policies may make sense for people who intend to keep the policies for the long term or for people who must be forced to save. But you should not have too low a death benefit just because you would like the savings component of a cash-value life policy. Experts suggest that you explore other savings and investment strategies before investing your money in a permanent life insurance policy.

The insurance company accumulates a substantial reserve during the early years of the whole life policy to pay the benefits in the later years, when your chances of dying are greater. At first, the annual premium for whole life insurance is higher than that for term insurance. However, the premium for a whole life policy remains constant throughout your lifetime, whereas the premium for a term policy increases with each renewal.

Several types of whole life insurance have been developed to meet different objectives. A few of the more popular types are discussed next.

LIMITED PAYMENT POLICY

One type of whole life policy is called the *limited payment policy.* With this plan, you pay premiums for a stipulated period, usually 20 or 30 years, or until you reach a specified age, such as 60 or 65 (unless your death occurs earlier). Your policy then becomes "paid up," and you remain insured for life. The company will pay the face amount of the policy at your death. Because the premium payment period for a limited payment policy is shorter than that for a whole life policy, the annual premium is higher. For example, recently a 35-year-old person buying a $25,000, 20-payment life policy at a preferred risk rate from the Teachers Insurance and Annuity Association (TIAA) would pay a $236.25 premium during the first year. In contrast, the premium for an ordinary life policy would be $183.50 for the same coverage. How do you qualify for preferred risk rates? See the accompanying Financial Planning for Life's Situations feature, "Guidelines for Preferred Rates," above.

A special form of the limited payment plan is the single-premium policy. In this type of contract, you make only one very large premium payment.

VARIABLE LIFE INSURANCE POLICY

The cash values of a *variable life* insurance policy fluctuate according to the yields earned by a separate fund, which can be a stock fund, a money market fund, or a bond fund. A minimum death benefit is guaranteed, but the death benefit can rise above that minimum depending on the earnings of the dollars invested in the separate fund. Hence, policyholders, not insurance companies, assume the investment risk. The premium payments for a variable life policy are fixed.

When you purchase a variable life policy, you assume the risk of poor investment performance. Therefore, the cash value of a variable life policy is not guaranteed. Life insurance agents selling variable life policies must be registered representatives of a broker-dealer licensed by the National Association of Securities Dealers and registered with the Securities and Exchange Commission. If you are interested in a variable life policy, be sure your agent gives you a prospectus that includes an extensive disclosure about the policy.

ADJUSTABLE LIFE INSURANCE POLICY (OR FLEXIBLE PREMIUM ADJUSTABLE LIFE INSURANCE) The *adjustable life* insurance policy is another relatively recent type of whole life insurance. You can change such a policy as your needs change. For example, if you want to increase or decrease your coverage, you can change either the premium payments or the period of coverage.

universal life A whole life policy that combines term insurance and investment elements.

UNIVERSAL LIFE Subject to certain minimums, **universal life** insurance, first introduced in 1979, is designed to let you pay premiums at any time in virtually any amount. The amount of insurance can be changed more easily in a universal life policy than in a traditional policy. The increase in the cash value of a universal life policy reflects the interest earned on short-term investments. Thus, the universal life policy clearly combines term insurance and investment elements.

Like the details of other types of policies, the details of universal life policies vary from company to company. The key distinguishing features of universal life policies are explicit, separate accounting reports to policyholders of (1) the charges for the insurance element, (2) the charges for company expenses (commissions, policy fees, etc.), and (3) the rate of return on the investment (cash value) of the policy. The rate of return is flexible; it is guaranteed to be not less than a certain amount (usually 4 percent), but it may be more, depending on the insurance company's decision.

What are the differences between universal life and whole life insurance? While both policy types have cash value, universal life gives you more direct control. With universal life, you control your outlay and can change your premium without changing your coverage. Whole life, in contrast, requires you to pay a specific premium every year, or the policy will lapse. Universal life allows you access to your cash value by a policy loan or withdrawal. Whole life allows only for policy loans.

Since your primary reason for buying a life insurance policy is the insurance component, the cost of that component should be your main consideration. Thus, universal life policies that offer a high rate of return on the cash value but charge a high price for the insurance element generally should be avoided.

Over the years, many variations on term and whole life insurance have been developed. The details of these policies may differ among companies. Therefore, check with individual companies to determine the best policy for your needs. Exhibit 12-6 compares some important features of term, whole life, universal life, and variable life policies.

OTHER TYPES OF LIFE INSURANCE POLICIES

GROUP LIFE INSURANCE In recent decades, *group life insurance* has grown in popularity. A group insurance plan insures a large number of persons under the terms of a single policy without requiring medical examinations. In general, the principles that apply to other forms of insurance also apply to group insurance.

Fundamentally, group insurance is term insurance, which was described earlier. Usually the cost of group insurance is split between an employer and the employees so that the cost of insurance per $1,000 is the same for each employee, regardless of age. For older employees, the employer pays a larger portion of the costs of the group policy.

Exhibit 12-6 Comparing the major types of life insurance

	Term Life	Whole Life	Universal Life
Premium	Lower initially, increasing with each renewal.	Higher initially than term; normally doesn't increase.	Flexible premiums.
Protects for	A specified period.	Entire life if you keep the policy.	A flexible time period.
Policy benefits	Death benefits only.	Death benefits and eventually a cash and loan value.	Flexible death benefits and eventually a cash and loan value.
Advantages	Low outlay. Initially, you can purchase a larger amount of coverage for a lower premium.	Helps you with financial discipline. Generally fixed premium amount. Cash value accumulation. You can take loan against policy.	More flexibility. Takes advantages of current interest rates. Offers the possibility of improved mortality rates (increased life expectancy because of advancements in medicine, which may lower policy costs).
Disadvantages	Premium increases with age. No cash value.	Costly if you surrender early. Usually no cash value for at least three to five years. May not meet short-term needs.	Same as whole life. Greater risks due to program flexibility. Low interest rates can affect cash value and premiums.
Options	May be renewable or convertible to a whole life policy.	May pay dividends. May provide a reduced paid-up policy. Partial cash surrenders permitted.	May pay dividends. Minimum death benefit. Partial cash surrenders permitted.

However, group life insurance is not always a good deal. Insurance advisers offer countless stories about employer-sponsored plans, or group plans offered through professional associations, offering coverage that costs 20, 50, or even 100 percent more than policies their clients could buy on the open market.

ENDOWMENT LIFE INSURANCE *Endowment life insurance* provides coverage from the beginning of the contract to maturity and guarantees payment of a specified sum to the insured, even if he or she is still living at the end of the endowment period. The face value of the policy is paid to beneficiaries upon the death of the insured. The endowment period typically has a duration of 10 to 20 years or the attainment of a specified age. Recently, these types of insurance policies have been used as a way to save for college for beneficiaries. The guaranteed payout will be paid at a specified time as determined at the start of the policy. Should the insured die, the beneficiary will receive a death benefit for the face value of the policy. Either way, the beneficiary will have money for college.

CREDIT LIFE INSURANCE *Credit life insurance* is used to repay a personal debt should the borrower die before doing so. It is based on the belief that "no person's debts should live after him or her." It was introduced in the United States in 1917, when installment financing and purchasing became popular.

Credit life insurance policies for auto loans and home mortgages are not the best buy for the protection they offer. Instead, buy less expensive decreasing term insurance,

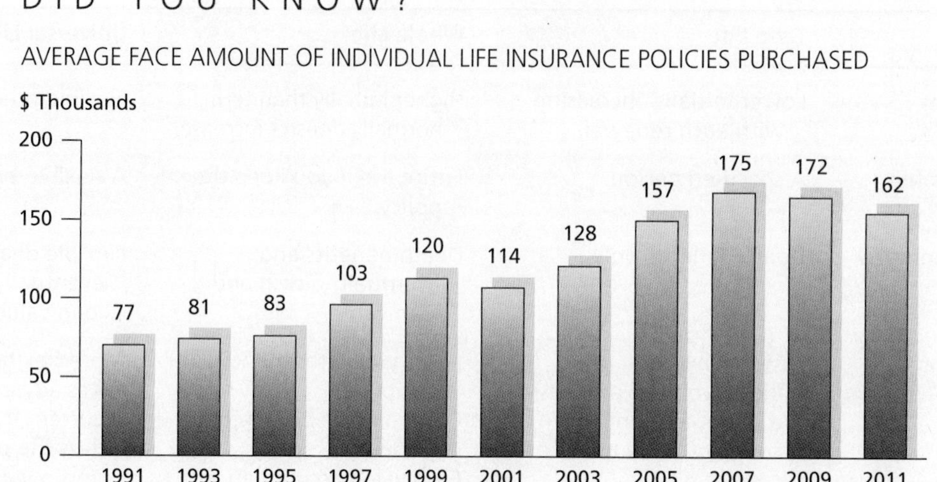

Note: NAIC does not endorse any analysis or conclusions based on use of its data. Data represent U.S. life insurers, and, as of 2003, fraternal benefit societies.

Source: ACLI tabulations of National Association of Insurance Commissioners (NAIC) data, used with permission. American Council of Life Insurers, *2009 Life Insurance Fact Book,* p. 67, www.acli.com/ACLI/Templates, accessed March 16, 2013.

discussed earlier. In fact, some experts claim that credit life insurance policies are the nation's biggest ripoff.

Exhibit 12-7 shows the growth of individual and group life insurance in the United States.

INDUSTRIAL LIFE INSURANCE With industrial life insurance policies, also known as home service or debit insurance, agents collect weekly, bimonthly, or monthly premiums at the insured's home. Industrial life insurance is the least popular form, and its appeal continues to drop rapidly.

Exhibit 12-7

Growth of individual, group, and credit life insurance in force in the United States

By the end of 2011, total life insurance coverage in the United States reached $19.2 trillion. Most group life insurance contracts are issued to employers, though many are issued to unions, professional associations, and other groups.

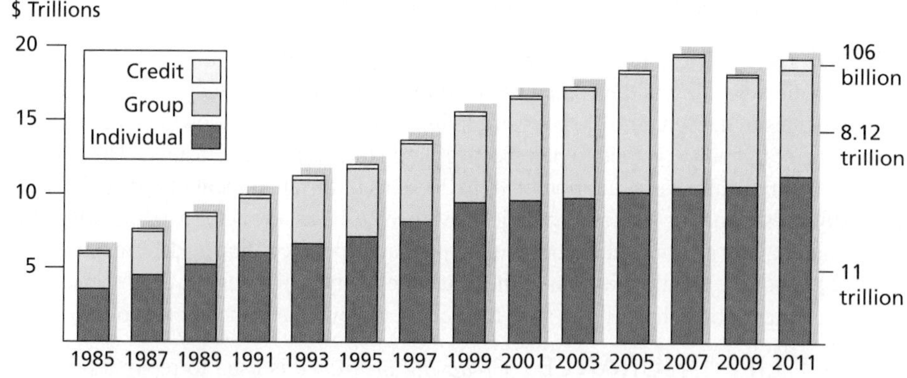

Note: NAIC does not endorse any analysis or conclusions based on use of its data. Data represent U.S. life insurers and, as of 2003, fraternal benefit societies.

Source: ACLI tabulations of National Association of Insurance Commissioners (NAIC) data, used with permission. American Council of Life Insurers, *2009 Life Insurers Fact Book,* p. 67, www.acli.com/ACLI/Templates, accessed March 16, 2013.

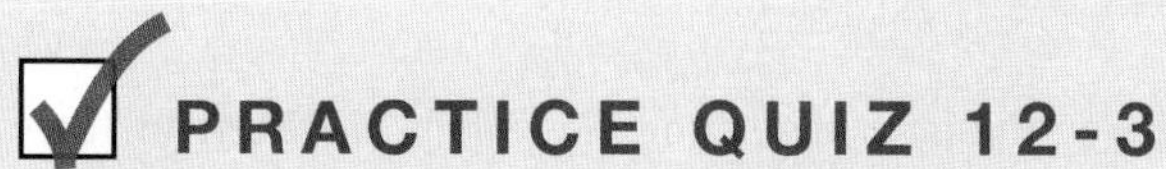

1 What are the two types of life insurance companies?
2 What are the major types and subtypes of life insurance?
3 What are the main differences between whole life and term policies?

Important Provisions in a Life Insurance Contract

LO12-4

Select important provisions in life insurance contracts.

Life insurance policies today contain numerous provisions whose terminology can be confusing. Therefore, an understanding of these provisions is very important for the insurance buyer.

Your life insurance policy is valuable only if it meets your objectives. When your objectives change, however, it may not be necessary to change or give up the policy. Instead, study the policy carefully and discuss its provisions with your agent. Following are some of the most common provisions.

NAMING YOUR BENEFICIARY

An important provision in every life insurance policy is the right to name your beneficiary. A **beneficiary** is a person who is designated to receive something, such as life insurance proceeds, from the insured. In your policy, you can name one or more persons as contingent beneficiaries who will receive your policy proceeds if the primary beneficiary dies at the same time or before you do.

An important provision in every life insurance policy is the right to name my beneficiary.

You decide who receives the benefits of your life insurance policy: your spouse, your child, or even your business partner. You can also name one or more contingent beneficiaries.

THE GRACE PERIOD

When you buy a life insurance policy, the insurance company agrees to pay a certain sum of money under specified circumstances and you agree to pay a certain premium regularly. The *grace period* allows 28 to 31 days to elapse, during which time you may pay the premium without penalty. After that time, the policy lapses if you have not paid the premium.

POLICY REINSTATEMENT

A lapsed policy can be put back in force, or reinstated, if it has not been turned in for cash. To reinstate the policy, you must again qualify as an acceptable risk, and you must pay overdue premiums with interest. There is a time limit on reinstatement, usually one or two years.

beneficiary A person designated to receive something, such as life insurance proceeds, from the insured.

nonforfeiture clause A provision that allows the insured not to forfeit all accrued benefits.

NONFORFEITURE CLAUSE

One important feature of a whole life policy is the **nonforfeiture clause.** This provision prevents the forfeiture of accrued benefits if you choose to drop the policy. For example, if you decide not to continue paying premiums, you can exercise specified options with your cash value. (See Exhibit 12-5 for cash value example)

INCONTESTABILITY CLAUSE

incontestability clause A provision stating that the insurer cannot dispute the validity of a policy after a specified period.

suicide clause A provision stating that if the insured dies by suicide during the first two years the policy is in force, the death benefit will equal the amount of the premium paid.

The **incontestability clause** stipulates that after the policy has been in force for a specified period (usually two years), the insurance company cannot dispute its validity during the lifetime of the insured for any reason, including fraud. One reason for this provision is that the beneficiaries, who cannot defend the company's contesting of the claim, should not be forced to suffer because of the acts of the insured.

SUICIDE CLAUSE

The **suicide clause** provides that if the insured dies by suicide during the first two years the policy is in force, the death benefit will equal the amount of the premium paid. Generally, after two years, the suicide becomes a risk covered by the policy and the beneficiaries of a suicide receive the same benefit that is payable for death from any other cause.

AUTOMATIC PREMIUM LOANS

With an automatic premium loan option, if you do not pay the premium within the grace period, the insurance company automatically pays it out of the policy's cash value if that cash value is sufficient in your whole life policy. This prevents you from inadvertently allowing the policy to lapse.

MISSTATEMENT OF AGE PROVISION

The misstatement of age provision says that if the company finds out that your age was incorrectly stated, it will pay the benefits your premiums would have bought if your age had been correctly stated. The provision sets forth a simple procedure to resolve what could otherwise be a complicated legal matter.

POLICY LOAN PROVISION

A loan from the insurance company is available on a whole life policy after the policy has been in force for one, two, or three years, as stated in the policy. This feature, known as the *policy loan provision,* permits you to borrow any amount up to the cash value of the policy. However, a policy loan reduces the death benefit by the amount of the loan plus interest if the loan is not repaid.

RIDERS TO LIFE INSURANCE POLICIES

rider A document attached to a policy that modifies its coverage.

An insurance company can change the provisions of a policy by attaching a rider to it. A **rider** is any document attached to the policy that modifies its coverage by adding or excluding specified conditions or altering its benefits. For instance, whole life insurance policy may include a waiver of premium disability benefit, an accidental death benefit, or both.

DID YOU KNOW?

The most common rider is waiver of premium. Nearly 98 percent of individual policies provide this option.

WAIVER OF PREMIUM DISABILITY BENEFIT Under this provision, the company waives any premiums that are due after the onset of total and permanent disability. In effect, the company pays the premiums. The disability must occur before you reach a certain age, usually 60.

The waiver of premium rider is sometimes desirable. Don't buy it, however, if the added cost will prevent you from carrying needed basic life insurance. Some insurance companies include this rider automatically in all policies issued through age 55.

ACCIDENTAL DEATH BENEFIT Under this provision, the insurance company pays twice the face amount of the policy if the insured's death results from an accident. The accidental death benefit is often called **double indemnity.** Accidental death must occur within a certain time period after the injury, usually 90 days, and before the insured reaches a certain age, usually 60 or 65.

double indemnity A benefit under which the company pays twice the face value of the policy if the insured's death results from an accident.

The accidental death benefit is expensive. Moreover, your chances of dying in the exact manner stated in the policy are very small, so the chances that your beneficiary will collect the double payment are also small.

GUARANTEED INSURABILITY OPTION This option allows you to buy specified additional amounts of life insurance at stated intervals without proof of insurability. Thus, even if you do not remain in good health, you can increase the amount of your insurance as your income rises. This option is desirable if you anticipate the need for additional life insurance in the future.

COST-OF-LIVING PROTECTION This special rider is designed to help prevent inflation from eroding the purchasing power of the protection your policy provides. A *loss, reduction,* or *erosion of purchasing power* refers to the impact inflation has on a fixed amount of money. As inflation increases the costs of goods and services, that fixed amount will not buy as much in the future as it does today. The Financial Planning Calculations Feature on Page 426 shows the effects of inflation on a $100,000 life insurance policy. However, your insurance needs are likely to be smaller in later years.

ACCELERATED BENEFITS *Accelerated benefits,* also known as *living benefits,* are life insurance policy proceeds paid to the terminally ill policyholder *before* he or she dies. The benefits may be provided for directly in the policies, but more often they are added by riders or attachments to new or existing policies. In most cases, the amount of the payout ranges between 25 and 95 percent of the death benefit. Any amounts paid out will reduce the death benefit that the beneficiary will receive upon the death of the insured. A representative list of insurers that offer accelerated benefits is available from the National Insurance Consumer Helpline (NICH) at 1-800-942-4242. Although more than 150 companies offer some form of accelerated benefits, not all plans are approved in all states. NICH cannot tell you whether a particular plan is approved in any given state. For more information, check with your insurance agent or your state department of insurance.

National Life Insurance, John Hancock, and Columbus Life Insurance now sell a new life insurance policy with an accelerated benefits rider that promises to pay out all or part of the death benefit should you need it for long-term care.

SECOND-TO-DIE OPTION A *second-to-die life insurance* policy, also called *survivorship life,* insures two lives, usually husband and wife. The death benefit is paid when the second spouse dies. Usually a second-to-die policy is intended to pay estate taxes when both spouses die. However, some attorneys claim that with the right legal advice, you can minimize or avoid estate taxes completely.

Now that you know the various types of life insurance policies and the major provisions of and riders to such policies, you are ready to make your buying decisions.

Financial Planning Calculations

CALCULATING THE EFFECT OF INFLATION ON A LIFE INSURANCE POLICY

Inflation can be described as an increase in the cost of a variety of goods and services. This has the effect of reducing the amount of goods and services that we can buy in the future. Therefore, inflation reduces the purchasing power of a fixed amount of money. The chart below shows the effect that inflation at different percentages could have on $100,000. For example, if you were to purchase a $100,000 life insurance policy today and inflation averaged 3 percent over 10 years. The value of the goods and services your beneficiary would be able to purchase is $74,409.

Note: the calculations for time value of money can be used to calculate the amounts presented above.

Follow these steps to determine the effect that 2 percent inflation would have after five years:

1. Review Exhibit 1-A (page 42), Future Value of $1 after a Given Number of Time Periods.
2. Locate the table factor for 2 percent and five years. The factor is 1.104.
3. Divide the $100,000 original amount by the 1.104 table factor:

$100,000/1.104 = $90,580

Now, it's Your Turn. Using Exhibit 1-A (page 42), Future Value of $1 after a Given Number of Time Periods, calculate the purchasing power of $100,000 after 10 years assuming 2% inflation.

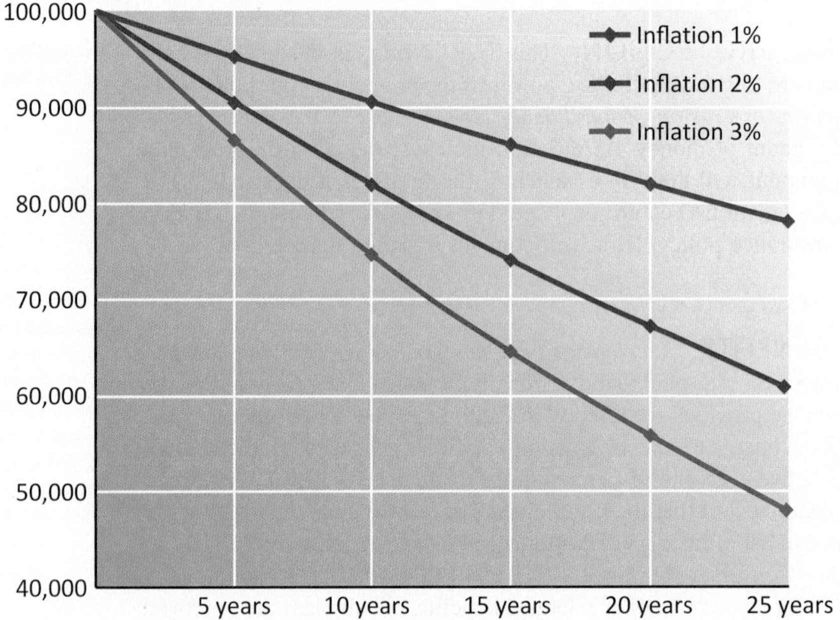

Answer: $82,034 ($100,000 / 1.219)

PRACTICE QUIZ 12-4

1 What are the most common provisions in life insurance contracts?
2 What is a beneficiary?
3 What is a rider?
4 What is the concept of double indemnity?

Buying Life Insurance

LO12-5

Create a plan to buy life insurance.

You should consider a number of factors before buying life insurance. As discussed earlier in this chapter, these factors include your present and future sources of income, other savings and income protection, group life insurance, group annuities (or other pension benefits), Social Security, and, of course, the financial strength of the company.

FROM WHOM TO BUY?

Look for insurance coverage from financially strong companies with professionally qualified representatives. It is not unusual for a relationship with an insurance company to extend over a period of 20, 30, or even 50 years. For that reason alone, you should choose carefully when deciding on an insurance company or an insurance agent. Fortunately, you have a choice of sources.

SOURCES Protection is available from a wide range of private and public sources, including insurance companies and their representatives; private groups such as employers, labor unions, and professional or fraternal organizations; and financial institutions and manufacturers offer credit insurance.

With life expectancies going up, life insurance rates should be coming down, right? That has been the case for over a decade, as term life premiums dropped by about half. But now the industry is tightening its guidelines, and that could spell a hike of 5–25 percent for many applicants. Some insurers are raising rates outright, says Bob Barney, president of Compulife Software, which provides rate comparisons. Others are simply making it harder to qualify for their best rate. Insurers are also getting pickier about cholesterol levels, family history of disease, even driving records, says Byron Udell, CEO of AccuQuote.

my life 5

The life insurance company I choose is essential to my beneficiaries' financial future.

Make sure that your insurance company and its agents are licensed in your state. Contact the National Association of Insurance Commissioners (NAIC) at 444 North Capitol St., NW, Washington, DC 20001, or visit www.naic.org. You can request several consumer protection and life insurance publications from the NAIC.

RATING INSURANCE COMPANIES Some of the strongest, most reputable insurance companies in the nation provide excellent insurance coverage at reasonable costs. In fact, the financial strength of an insurance company may be a major factor in holding down premium costs for consumers.

Locate an insurance company by checking the reputations of local agencies. Ask members of your family, friends, or colleagues about the insurers they prefer.

For a more official review, consult *Best's Agents Guide* or *Best's Insurance Reports* at your public library or online at www.ambest.com. Exhibit 12-8 describes the rating systems used by A. M. Best and the other big four rating agencies. As a rule, you should deal with companies rated superior or excellent. In addition, *Consumer Reports, Kiplinger's Personal Finance,* and *Money* periodically provide satisfaction ratings on various types of insurance and insurance companies.

CHOOSING YOUR INSURANCE AGENT An insurance agent handles the technical side of insurance. However, that's only the beginning. The really important part of the agent's job is to apply his or her knowledge of insurance to help you select the proper kind of protection within your financial boundaries.

Not all agents are paid the same way. Some insurance companies, such as GEICO and USAA, use salaried agents. Firms such as Allstate and State Farm use primarily "captive agents," who may be salaried or paid on commission. Either way, they sell only those companies' policies. Independent agents represent multiple carriers and can offer more choices. They collect conventional commissions from insurance companies. Is one kind of agent better than another? In theory, independent agents have an edge

Exhibit 12-8

Rating systems of major rating agencies

You should deal with companies rated superior or excellent.

	A. M. Best	Standard & Poor's, Duff & Phelps	Moody's	Weiss Research	Fitch Ratings
Superior	A + + A +	AAA	Aaa	A +	AAA
Excellent	A A−	AA + AA AA−	Aa1 Aa2 Aa3	A A− B +	AA + AA AA−
Good	B + + B +	A + A A−	A1 A2 A3	B B− C +	A + A A−
Adequate	B B−	BBB + BBB BBB−	Baa1 Baa2 Baa3	C C− D +	BBB + BBB BBB−
Below average	C + + C +	BB + BB BB−	Ba1 Ba2 Ba3	D D− E +	BB + BB BB−
Weak	C C− D	B + B B−	B1 B2 B3	E E−	B + B B−
Nonviable	E F	CCC CC C, D	Caa Ca C	F	CCC DD SR*

* Suspended Rating

because they're not limited to just one insurance company's products. But they may be tempted to direct consumers to companies that pay them the most. Truth is, you can get a good policy from any of the different types of insurance agents.

Choosing a good agent is among the most important steps in building your insurance program. How do you find an agent? One of the best ways to begin is by asking your parents, friends, neighbors, and others for their recommendations. However, note that you will seldom have the same agent all your life. The accompanying How to . . . feature, "Choosing an Insurance Agent," offers guidelines for choosing an insurance agent.

chartered life underwriter (CLU) A life insurance agent who has passed a series of college-level examinations on insurance and related subjects.

You may also want to investigate an agent's membership in professional groups. Agents who belong to a local Life Underwriters Association are often among the more experienced agents in their communities. A **chartered life underwriter (CLU)** is a life insurance agent who has passed a series of college-level examinations on insurance and related subjects. Such agents are entitled to use the designation CLU after their names. Other professional designations that life insurance agents may earn include life underwriter training council fellow (LUTCF), chartered financial consultant (ChFC), certified financial planner (CFP), financial services specialist (FSS) or member of The Registry of Financial Planning Practitioners. Agents who have passed a series of examinations on property and casualty insurance are designated as *chartered property and casualty underwriters (CPCUs).*

Once you have found an agent, you must decide which policy is right for you. The best way to do this is to talk to your agent, which does not obligate you to buy insurance.

HOW TO...

Choose an Insurance Agent

	Yes	No
1. Is your agent available when needed? Clients sometimes have problems that need immediate answers.	☐	☐
2. Does your agent advise you to have a financial plan? Each part of the plan should be necessary to your overall financial protection.	☐	☐
3. Does your agent pressure you? You should be free to make your own decisions about insurance coverage.	☐	☐
4. Does your agent keep up with changes in the insurance field? Agents often attend special classes or study on their own so that they can serve their clients better.	☐	☐
5. Is your agent happy to answer questions? Does he or she want you to know exactly what you are paying for with an insurance policy?	☐	☐

COMPARING POLICY COSTS

DID YOU KNOW?

Insure.com has quotes from multiple life insurance companies and details on policies available from them. It also provides ratings for the insurance companies from the major rating agencies.

Each life insurance company designs the policies it sells to make them attractive and useful to many policyholders. One policy may have features another policy doesn't; one company may be more selective than another company; one company may get a better return on its investments than another company. These and other factors affect the prices of life insurance policies.

In brief, five factors affect the price a company charges for a life insurance policy: the company's cost of doing business, the return on its investments, the mortality rate it expects among its policyholders, the features the policy contains, and competition among companies with comparable policies.

underwriting The process that insurance companies use to determine the premiums that will be charged and whom they will insure.

Underwriting uses many attributes of individuals such as age, gender, health, and even occupation to determine the appropriate premiums to charge for insurance. The work of underwriting is completed by actuaries. Actuaries help determine who will be a higher risk and whether they want to charge higher premiums or deny coverage. Actuaries use sophisticated statistical models to help them determine the chance of loss for the insurers.

The prices of life insurance policies therefore vary considerably among life insurance companies. Moreover, a particular company will not be equally competitive for all

Financial Planning Calculations

DETERMINING THE COST OF INSURANCE

In determining the cost of insurance, don't overlook the time value of money. You must include as part of your cost the interest (opportunity cost) you would earn on money if you did not use it to pay insurance premiums. For many years, insurers did not assign a time value to money while making their sales presentations. Only recently has the insurance industry widely adopted interest-adjusted cost estimates.

If you fail to consider the time value of money, you may get the false impression that the insurance company is giving you something for nothing.

For example, suppose you are 35 and have a $10,000 face amount, 20-year, limited-payment, participating policy:

Annual premium	$210, or $4,200 over the 20-year period ($210 × 20)
Dividends	$1,700 (used to build up cash value) over the 20-year period
Net premium	$2,500 ($4,200 − $1,700).
Cash value of policy	$4,600 at the end of 20 years
Excess value	$2,100 ($4,600 − $2,500)

If you disregard the interest your premiums could otherwise have earned, you might get the impression that the insurance company is giving you $2,100 more than you paid ($4,600 − $2,500). But if you consider the time value of money (or its opportunity cost), the insurance company is not giving you $2,100. What if you had invested the annual premiums in a conservative stock mutual fund?

At an 8 percent annual yield, your account would have accumulated to $9,610 in 20 years (See Exhibit 1-B on page 43). Therefore, instead of having received $2,100 from the insurance company, you have paid $5,010 for 20 years of insurance protection:

Annual premium (20 years)	$4,200
Time value of money	+ $5,410 ($9,610 − $4,200)
Total cost of policy	$9,610
Cash value (end of 20 years)	− $4,600
Net cost of insurance	$5,010 ($9,610 − $4,600)

Be sure to request interest-adjusted indexes from your agent. If he or she doesn't give them to you, look for another agent. As you have seen in the example, you can compare the costs among insurance companies by combining premium payments, dividends, cash value buildup, and present value analysis into an index number.

policies. Thus, one company might have a competitively priced policy for 24-year-olds but not for 35-year-olds.

interest-adjusted index A method of evaluating the cost of life insurance by taking into account the time value of money.

Ask your agent to give you interest-adjusted indexes. An **interest-adjusted index** is a method of evaluating the cost of life insurance by taking into account the time value of money. Highly complex mathematical calculations and formulas combine premium payments, dividends, cash-value buildup, and present value analysis into an index number that makes possible a fairly accurate cost comparison among insurance companies. The lower the index number, the lower the cost of the policy. The Consumer Federation of America Insurance Group offers a computerized service for comparing policy costs. Visit them at www.consumerfed.org.

Price quote services offer convenient and free, no-obligation premium comparisons. Many life insurance companies provide free price quotes for term insurance. An agent will run your age, health status, and occupation through computer data banks covering about 650 different policies and send you the names of the five policies suitable for you and sold in your state. TermQuote in Dayton, Ohio, represents about 100 insurance companies, and Select Quote in San Francisco represents about

20 insurance companies. Here are the Web addresses and telephone numbers of some price quote services:

- AccuQuote (www.accuquote.com) 1-800-442-9899
- InsuranceQuote Services (www.iquote.com) 1-800-352-9742
- InstantQuote (www.instantquote.com) 1-888-223-2220
- QuickQuote (www.quickquote.com) 1-800-867-2404
- SelectQuote (www.selectquote.com) 1-800-676-2928

These services are not always unbiased, since most sell life insurance themselves; they may recommend more coverage than you need. Ask them to quote you the rate each insurer charges most of its policyholders, not the best rate, for which few persons qualify.

The accompanying Financial Planning Calculations feature above shows how to use an interest-adjusted index to compare the costs of insurance.

OBTAINING A POLICY

A life insurance policy is issued after you submit an application for insurance and the insurance company accepts the application. The application usually has two parts. In the first part, you state your name, age, and gender, what type of policy you desire, how much insurance you want, your occupation, and so forth. In the second part, you give your medical history. While a medical examination is frequently required for ordinary policies, usually no examination is required for group insurance.

The company determines your insurability by means of the information in your application, the results of the medical examination, and the inspection report. Of all applicants, 98 percent are found to be insurable, though some may have to pay higher premiums because of an existing medical condition.

DID YOU KNOW?

THE "FREE LOOK" RULE

- When you receive your new policy, read it carefully.
- Every new life insurance policy is issued with a 10-day "free look" period. (Some states now provide a longer time period)
- If you are not satisfied for any reason, you may return the new policy within 10 days after you receive it.
- Mail it to the company's home office or give it back to the agent who sold it to you.
- Be sure to get a dated receipt from the post office or the agent.
- The company must return your premium within 30 days from the date you returned the policy. If the insurance company keeps your money longer, legally it is responsible for a 10 percent penalty—payable to you.

EXAMINING A POLICY

BEFORE THE PURCHASE When you buy a life insurance policy, read every word of the contract and, if necessary, ask your agent for a point-by-point explanation of the language. Many insurance companies have rewritten their contracts to make them more understandable. These are legal documents, and you should be familiar with what they promise, even though they use technical terms.

AFTER THE PURCHASE After you buy new life insurance, you have a 10-day "free-look" period during which you can change your mind. *Note:* Some states now offer a longer "free-look" period. If you change your mind, the company will return your premium without penalty.

It's a good idea to give your beneficiaries and your lawyer a photocopy of your policy. Your beneficiaries should know where the policy is kept, because to obtain the insurance proceeds, they will have to send it to the company upon your death, along with a copy of the death certificate.

Life insurance policy comparison

PRACTICE QUIZ 12-5

1 Why is it important to know the ratings of the insurance company?
2 How do insurance companies price their products?
3 How do insurance companies determine your insurability?
4 What should you do in examining a policy before and after the purchase?

Life Insurance Proceeds

LO12-6

Evaluate the payout options for life insurance.

A well-planned life insurance program can serve two purposes: (1) to provide a financial death benefit to those who depend on upon them and (2) to provide funds to the insured while they are still living. Typically, the insured will have to choose between these two options because taking money from the insurance policy will usually reduce the death benefit paid out.

DEATH (OR SURVIVOR BENEFITS)

The two main objectives of a death (or survivor) benefit are (1) to cover the immediate expenses resulting from the death of the insured and (2) to protect dependents against a loss of income resulting from the premature death of the primary wage earner. Thus, selecting the appropriate settlement option is an important part of designing a life insurance program. The most common settlement options are lump-sum payment, proceeds left with the company, limited installment payment, and life income option.

LUMP-SUM PAYMENT The insurance company pays the face amount of the policy in one installment to the beneficiary or to the estate of the insured. This form of settlement is the most widely used option.

PROCEEDS LEFT WITH THE COMPANY The life insurance proceeds are left with the insurance company at a specified rate of interest. The company acts as trustee and pays the interest to the beneficiary. The guaranteed minimum interest rate paid on the proceeds varies among companies.

LIMITED INSTALLMENT PAYMENT This option provides for payment of the life insurance proceeds in equal periodic installments for a specified number of years after your death.

annuity A contract that provides a regular income typically for as long as the person lives.

LIFE INCOME OPTION Under the life income option, payments are made to the beneficiary for as long as she or he lives. An **annuity** is the basis for this option. An annuity is a financial contract written by an insurance company that provides a regular income. Generally, the payments are received monthly. The payments may begin at once (immediate annuity) or at some future date (deferred annuity). The amount of each payment is based primarily on the gender and attained age of the beneficiary at the time of the insured's death. As with the life insurance principle discussed earlier, the predictable mortality experience of a large group of individuals is fundamental to the annuity principle.

TEN GOLDEN RULES FOR BUYING LIFE INSURANCE

Remember that your need for life insurance coverage will change over time. Your income may go up or down, or your family size might change. Therefore, it is wise to review your coverage periodically to ensure that it keeps up with your changing needs.

Follow these rules when buying life insurance:	Done
1. Understand and know what your life insurance needs are before you make any purchase, and make sure the company you choose can meet those needs.	☐
2. Buy your life insurance from a company that is licensed in your state.	☐
3. Select an agent who is competent, knowledgeable, and trustworthy.	☐
4. Shop around and compare costs.	☐
5. Buy only the amount of life insurance you need and can afford.	☐
6. Ask about lower premium rates for nonsmokers.	☐
7. Read your policy and make sure you understand it.	☐
8. Inform your beneficiaries about the kinds and amount of life insurance you own.	☐
9. Keep your policy in a safe place at home, and keep your insurance company's name and your policy number in a safe deposit box.	☐
10. Check your coverage periodically, or whenever your situation changes, to ensure that it meets your current needs.	☐

Source: American Council of Life Insurance, 1001 Pennsylvania Avenue, NW, Washington, DC 20004-2599.

INCOME FROM LIFE INSURANCE POLICIES

As you have seen so far, life insurance can provide a sum of money at death to a named beneficiary. There are times when the insured may need money for expenses such as college, retirement, or medical needs. Whole life policies have a cash value balance. The insured may either take a loan on this balance or surrender the policy and receive the amount of the cash value. If a loan is taken and not paid back, it will typically reduce the death benefit paid to the beneficiary.

Variable life insurance policies were designed to be an insurance policy combined with a separate investment product. Many people choose to supplement their retirement income by withdrawing some of the investment portion as an annuity to provide regular income. The appeal of variable annuities increased during the mid-1990s due to a rising stock market. A fixed annuity states that the annuitant (the person who is to receive the annuity) will receive a fixed amount of income over a certain period or for life. With a variable annuity, the monthly payments vary because they are based on the income received from stocks or other investments.

Variable annuities offer many optional features including a stepped-up death benefit, a guaranteed minimum income benefit, or long-term care insurance. The features often come with additional fees and charges. Read the accompanying Financial Planning for Life's Situation feature, "Variable Annuity Charges," on page 434 to understand these charges.

VARIABLE ANNUITY CHARGES

You will pay several charges when you invest in a variable annuity. Be sure you understand all the charges before you invest. *These charges will reduce the value of your account and the return on your investment.* Often, they will include the following:

Surrender Charges. If you withdraw money from a variable annuity within a certain period after a purchase payment (typically within 6 to 8 years, but sometimes as long as 10 years), the insurance company usually will assess a "surrender" charge, which is a type of sales charge. This charge is used to pay your insurance agent a commission for selling the variable annuity to you. Generally, the surrender charge is a percentage of the amount withdrawn, and declines gradually over a period of several years, known as the *"surrender period."* For example, a 7 percent charge might apply in the first year after a purchase payment, 6 percent in the second year, 5 percent in the third year, and so on until the eighth year, when the surrender charge no longer applies. Often, contracts will allow you to withdraw part of your account value each year—10 percent or 15 percent of your account value, for example—without paying a surrender charge.

Mortality and Expense Risk Charge. This charge is equal to a certain percentage of your account value, typically in the range of 1.25 percent per year. This charge compensates the insurance company for insurance risks it assumes under the annuity contract. Profit from the mortality and expense risk charge is sometimes used to pay the insurer's costs of selling the variable annuity, such as a commission paid to your insurance agent for selling the variable annuity to you.

Administrative Fees. The insurer may deduct charges to cover record-keeping and other administrative expenses. This may be charged as a flat account maintenance fee (perhaps $25 or $30 per year) or as a percentage of your account value (typically in the range of 0.15 percent per year).

Underlying Fund Expenses. You will also indirectly pay the fees and expenses imposed by the mutual funds that are the underlying investment options for your variable annuity.

Fees and Charges for Other Features. Special features offered by some variable annuities, such as a stepped-up death benefit, a guaranteed minimum income benefit, or long-term care insurance, often carry additional fees and charges.

Other charges, such as initial sales loads or fees for transferring part of your account from one investment option to another, may also apply. You should ask your insurance agent to explain to you all charges that may apply. You can also find a description of the charges in the prospectus for any variable annuity that you are considering.

As a consumer, the best way to arm yourself against the pressures of annuity marketers is to know the common sales pitches and how to respond to them. In the end, you still might want a variable annuity. But make that decision after careful consideration of the product and alternative solutions—not because someone pressured you into it.

my life 6

I am aware of the different payout options in a life insurance policy.

The choice of determining how insurance proceeds will be paid is typically a factor of how you believe the beneficiary will be able to financially handle the payout.

SWITCHING POLICIES

Think twice if your agent suggests that you replace the whole life or universal life insurance you already own. According to a recent study by the Consumer Federation of America, consumers lose billions of dollars each year because they don't hold their cash-value life insurance policies long enough or because they purchase the wrong policies. The author of the study, James Hunt, Vermont's former insurance commissioner, notes that half of those who buy whole or universal life policies drop them within 10 years.

Before you give up this protection, make sure you are still insurable (check medical and any other qualification requirements).

Remember that you are now older than you were when you purchased your policy, and a new policy will therefore cost more. Moreover, the older policy may have provisions that are not duplicated in some of the new policies. This does not mean you should reject the idea of replacing your present policy; rather, you should proceed with caution. We recommend that you ask your agent or company for an opinion about the new proposal to get both sides of the argument.

The insurance industry is regulated by state insurance commissioners. Recently many states passed new laws to protect consumers from overzealous sales agents. The National Association of Insurance Commissioners, state regulators, and insurance companies plan to develop new standards to protect consumers.

The Financial Planning for Life's Situations feature, "Ten Golden Rules for Buying Life Insurance" on page 433, presents 10 important guidelines for purchasing life insurance.

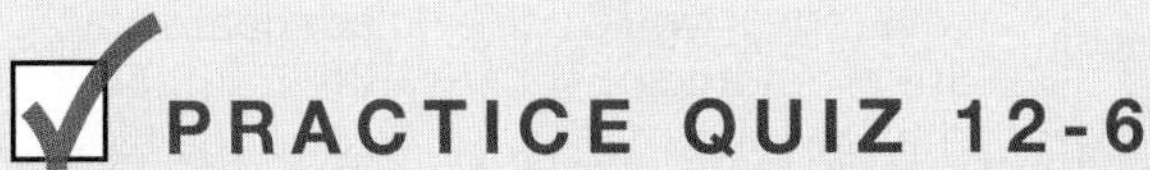

1 What are the four most common settlement options?
2 Should you switch life insurance policies?
3 What is an annuity?
4 What makes a variable annuity different?

my life stages for life insurance...

YOUR PERSONAL FINANCIAL DASHBOARD

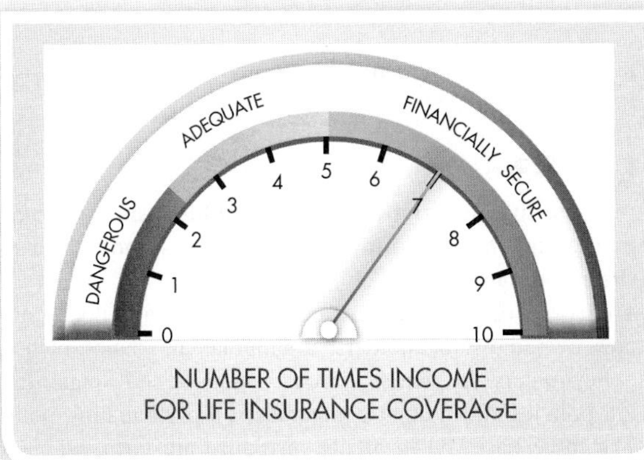

A personal finance dashboard with key performance indicators can help you monitor your financial situation and guide you toward financial independence.

Your need for life insurance will change with your stage in life. For example, if you are single or live with your parents, you may not need life insurance, unless you have a debt or want to provide for your parents, a friend, a relative, or charity. However, as children are born, your need for life insurance will increase. As children grow older and leave the nest, you will probably need less insurance.

YOUR SITUATION Do you know if you need life insurance? Have you taken time to consider why you need life insurance and to find a sales agent who is knowledgeable and trustworthy? Have you evaluated the advantages and disadvantages of term life, whole life, and other life insurance options available to you? Personal financial planning actions you might consider depending upon your stage in life include:

(continued)

my life stages for life insurance...

. . . in college

- Generally, young single people with no dependents don't need life insurance
- Buy term insurance if you have debts or dependents who need financial support from you

. . . in my 20s

- If your spouse can live on his/her income alone and you don't have a mortgage, your only insurance need may be to cover final expenses at your death
- Buy term insurance if you have any dependents who need your financial support

. . . in my 30s and 40s

- As children arrive, you'll need more life insurance
- Reevaluate your life insurance coverage if you are promoted or change jobs
- If you are providing financial support for aging parents or siblings, keep adequate life insurance coverage

. . . in my 50s and beyond

- As children grow older and leave, you'll probably need less insurance
- Maintain adequate life insurance coverage to protect the widow or widower
- If you have dependents and have enough assets to provide for them, then you don't need life insurance

SUMMARY OF LEARNING OBJECTIVES

LO12-1

Define *life insurance* and describe its purpose and principle.

Life insurance is a contract between an insurance company and a policyholder under which the company agrees to pay a specified sum to a beneficiary upon the insured's death. Most people buy life insurance to protect someone who depends on them from financial losses caused by their death. Fundamental to the life insurance principle is the predictable mortality experience of a large group of individuals.

LO12-2

Determine your life insurance needs.

In determining your life insurance needs, you must first determine your insurance objectives and then use the easy method, the DINK method, the "nonworking" spouse method, or the "family need" method. The "family need" method is recommended. You should consider a number of factors before you buy insurance, including your present and future sources of income, other savings and income protection, group life insurance, group annuities (or other pension benefits), and Social Security.

LO12-3

Distinguish between the two types of life insurance companies and analyze various types of life insurance policies these companies issue.

The two types of life insurance companies are stock companies, owned by stockholders, and mutual companies, owned by policyholders. In general, stock companies sell nonparticipating policies and mutual companies sell participating policies. The three basic types of life insurance are term, whole life, and endowment policies. Many variations and combinations of these types are available. You should check with both stock and mutual companies to determine which type offers the best policy for your particular needs at the lowest price.

Nevertheless, as with other forms of insurance, price should not be your only consideration in choosing a life insurance policy. You should also consider the financial stability, reliability, and service the insurance company provides.

LO12-4

Select important provisions in life insurance contracts.

The naming of the beneficiary, the grace period, policy reinstatement, the incontestability clause, the suicide clause, automatic premium loans, the misstatement of age provision, and the policy loan provision are important provisions in most life insurance policies. Common riders in life insurance policies are the waiver of premium disability benefit, the accidental death benefit, the guaranteed insurability option, cost of living protection, and accelerated benefits.

LO12-5

Create a plan to buy life insurance.

Before buying life insurance, consider your present and future sources of income, group life insurance, group annuities (or other pension benefits), and Social Security. Then compare the costs of several life insurance policies. Examine your policy before and after the purchase.

LO12-6

Evaluate the payout options for life insurance.

Choose appropriate settlement options based on the needs of your beneficiary. The most common settlement options are lump-sum payment, proceeds left with the company, limited installment payment, and life income option. Online computer services provide a wealth of information about all topics related to life insurance. An annuity can provide regular payments to your beneficiaries with the life income option. An annuity can also be used to provide you with a regular income for expenses in later years.

KEY TERMS

annuity 432
beneficiary 423
cash value 417
chartered life underwriter (CLU) 428
double indemnity 425
incontestability clause 424
interest-adjusted index 430
nonforfeiture clause 423
nonparticipating policy 415
participating policy 415
rider 424
suicide clause 424
term insurance 416
underwriting 429
universal life 420
whole life policy 417

SELF-TEST PROBLEMS

1. Suppose that yours is a typical family. Your annual income is $70,000. Use the easy method to determine your need for life insurance.
2. Using the "nonworking" spouse method, what should be the life insurance needs for a family whose youngest child is three years old?
3. Suppose your annual premium for a $20,000, 20-year limited-payment policy is $450 over the 20-year period. The cash value of your policy at the end of 20 years is $8,500. Assume that you could have invested the annual premium in a mutual fund yielding seven percent annually. What is the net cost of your insurance for the 20-year period?

Solutions

1. Current gross income	=	$70,000
Multiply gross income by 7 years	=	$490,000
Take 70 percent of $490,000	=	$490,000 × .70
Approximate insurance needed	=	$343,000
2. Youngest child's age	=	3 years
15 years before the child is 18 years old		
Insurance needed 15 × $10,000	=	$150,000
3. Premiums paid over 20 years	=	$450 × 20 = $9,000
Time value of 20-year annual payments of $420 at 7 percent yield.		
(See Exhibit 1-B, use a factor of 40.995)	=	40.995 × $450 = $18,448
Cash Value	=	$8,500
Net cost of insurance	=	$18,448 − $8,500 = $9,948

FINANCIAL PLANNING PROBLEMS

LO12-1 **1.** *Calculating Life Expectancy.* Using Exhibit 12-1, determine the life expectancy of a 40-year-old male.

LO12-1 **2.** *Calculating Life Expectancy.* Using Exhibit 12-1, determine the average numbers of additional years males alive at age 35 may expect to live.

LO12-1 **3.** *Calculating Life Expectancy.* Using Exhibit 12-1 determine the life expectancy of a 60-year-old female.

LO12-2 **4.** *Calculating the Amount of Life Insurance Needed Using the Easy Method.* You are the wage earner in a "typical family," with $50,000 gross annual income. Use the easy method to determine how much life insurance you should carry.

LO12-2 **5.** *Calculating the Amount of Life Insurance Needed Using the Easy Method.* Suppose that yours is a typical family. Your annual income is $45,000. Using the easy method, what should be your need for life insurance?

LO12-2 **6.** *Estimating Life Insurance Needs Using the DINK Method.* You and your spouse are in good health and have reasonably secure jobs. Each of you makes about $38,000 annually. You own a home with an $80,000 mortgage, and you owe $15,000 on car loans, $5,000 in personal debt, and $2,000 in credit card loans. You have no other debt. You have no plans to increase the size of your family in the near future. You estimate that funeral expenses will be $5,000. Estimate your total insurance needs using the DINK method.

LO12-2 **7.** *Estimating Life Insurance Needs Using the DINK Method.* You are a dual income, no kids family. You and your spouse have the following debts:

Mortgage = $190,000; Auto loan = $10,000; Credit card balance = $2,000, and other debts of $4,000. Further, you estimate that your funeral will cost $6,000. Your spouse expects to continue to work after your death. Using the DINK method, what should be your need for life insurance?

LO12-2 **8.** *Using the "Nonworking" Spouse Method to Determine Life Insurance Needs.* Tim and Allison are married and have two children, ages 2 and 6. Allison is a "nonworking" spouse who devotes all of her time to household activities. Estimate how much life insurance Tim and Allison should carry.

LO12-2 **9.** *Using the "Non-working" Spouse Method to Determine Life Insurance Needs.* Using the "non-working" spouse method, what should be the life insurance needs for a family whose youngest child is 5 years old?

LO12-2 **10.** *Using the "Non-working" Spouse Method to Determine Life Insurance Needs.* Using the "non-working" spouse method, what should be the life insurance needs for a family whose youngest child is 4 years old?

LO12-4 **11.** *Calculating the Effect of Inflation on a Life Insurance Policy.* Susan has purchased a whole life policy with a death benefit of $200,000. Assuming that she dies in 10 years and the average inflation has been 3 percent, what is the value of the purchasing power of the proceeds?

LO12-4 **12.** *Calculating the Effect of Inflation on a Life Insurance Policy.* Allen has purchased a whole life policy with a death benefit of $150,000. Assuming that he dies in 8 years and the average inflation has been 2 percent, what is the value of the purchasing power of the proceeds?

LO12-5 **13.** *Determining the Cost of Insurance.* Suppose you are 45 and have a $10,000 face amount, 15-year, limited-payment, participating policy (dividends will be used to build up the cash value of the policy). Your annual premium is $350. The cash value of the policy is expected to be $4,000 in 15 years. Using time value of money and assuming you could invest your money elsewhere for a 7 percent annual yield, calculate the net cost of insurance.

LO12-5 **14.** *Determining the Cost of Insurance.* Suppose you are 30 and have a $25,000 face amount, 20-year, limited-payment, participating policy (dividends will be used to build up the cash value of the policy). Your annual premium is $225. The cash value of the policy is expected to be $3,000 in 20 years. Using time value of money and assuming you could invest your money elsewhere for a 5 percent annual yield, calculate the net cost of insurance.

LO12-6 **15.** *Calculating a Mortality and Expense Risk Charge.* Your variable annuity has a mortality and expense risk charge at an annual rate of 1.25 percent of account value. Your average account value during the year is $20,000. What are your mortality and expense risk charges for the year?

LO12-6 **16.** *Calculating Administrative Fees.* Your variable annuity charges administrative fees at an annual rate of 0.15 percent of account value. Your average account value during the year is $50,000. What is the administrative fee for the year?

FINANCIAL PLANNING ACTIVITIES

1. *Planning for Life Insurance.* Choose a current issue of *Money, Kiplinger's Personal Finance, Consumer Reports,* or *Worth* and summarize an article that provides information on human life expectancy and how life insurance may provide financial security. LO12-1
2. *Assessing the Need for Life Insurance.* Interview relatives and friends to determine why they purchased life insurance. Summarize your findings. LO12-1
3. *Comparing the Methods of Determining Life Insurance Requirements.* Analyze the five methods of determining life insurance requirements. Which method is best for you and why? LO12-2
4. *Determining the Need for Life Insurance.* Jake is a 27-year-old single man with no children. He has a younger sister who has a developmental disability. Both his parents are living, though neither parent is in good health. Jake has an auto loan, a $50,000 mortgage on his condominium, and no consumer debt. Is Jake a good candidate for life insurance? If so, what kind and how much life insurance should he buy? LO12-2
5. *Calculating Your Life Insurance Needs.* Use Exhibit 12-3 to calculate your insurance needs. LO12-2
6. *Comparing Premiums for Life Insurance Policies.* Choose one stock and one mutual life insurance company. Obtain and compare premiums for LO12-3

   a. Term life insurance for $50,000.

   b. Whole life insurance for $50,000.

   c. Universal life insurance for $50,000.

   Prepare a summary table indicating which policy you would consider and why.
7. *Using the Internet to Obtain Information about Various Types of Life Insurance.* Visit a few websites of companies such as Metropolitan Life, New York Life, Transamerica Life, Lincoln Benefit Life, or others of your choice. Then prepare a report that summarizes the various types of insurance coverages available from these companies. LO12-4
8. *Comparing the Provisions of Life Insurance Policies.* Examine your life insurance policies and the policies of other members of your family. Note the contractual provisions of each policy. What does the company promise to do in return for premiums? LO12-4
9. *Using the Services Provided by State Insurance Departments.* Contact your state insurance department to get information about whether your state requires interest-adjusted cost disclosure. Prepare a summary report of your findings. LO12-5
10. *Evaluating the Financial Strength of Insurance Companies.* Look up the ratings of at least three insurance companies that you are familiar with. LO12-5
11. *Comparing Insurance Payout Options.* List the factors that would influence you in selecting the type of settlement option. LO12-6

FINANCIAL PLANNING CASE

Life Insurance for Young Married People

Jeff and Ann are both 28 years old. They have been married for three years, and they have a son who is almost two. They expect their second child in a few months.

Jeff is a teller in a local bank. He has just received a $60-a-week raise. His income is $960 a week, which, after taxes, leaves him with $3,200 a month. His company provides $50,000 of life insurance, a medical/hospital/surgical plan, and a major medical plan. All of these group plans protect him as long as he stays with the bank.

When Jeff received his raise, he decided that part of it should be used to add to his family's protection. Jeff and Ann talked to their insurance agent, who reviewed the insurance Jeff obtained through his job. Under Social Security, they also had some basic protection against the loss of Jeff's income if he became totally disabled or if he died before the children were 18.

But most of this protection was only basic, a kind of floor for Jeff and Ann to build on. For example, monthly Social Security payments to Ann would be approximately $1,550 if Jeff died leaving two children under age 18. Yet the family's total expenses would soon be higher after the birth of the second baby. Although the family's expenses would be lowered if Jeff died, they would be at least $500 a month more than Social Security would provide.

Questions

1. In your opinion, do Jeff and Ann need additional insurance? Why or why not?
2. What type of policy would you suggest for Jeff and Ann? Why?

PERSONAL FINANCIAL PLANNER IN ACTION

Determining Life Insurance Needs

Providing for the financial needs of dependents is the primary goal of a life insurance program. Comparing policy types, coverage amounts, and other provisions will help you meet this financial purpose.

Your Short-Term Financial Planning Activities	*Resources*
1. Determine life insurance needs for your current life situation.	PFP Sheet 53 www.lifehappens.org www.bankrate.com/calculators http://money.msn.com www.finaid.org/calculators/
2. Compare rates and coverages for different life insurance policies and companies.	PFP Sheet 54 http://personalinsure.about.com www.quickquote.com www.insure.com www.accuquote.com
3. Evaluate the various payout options from life insurance in your financial plan.	www.lifeinsurancehub.net www.reliaquote.com www.annuities.com http://invest-faq.com www.sec.gov
Your Long-Term Financial Planning Activities	*Resources*
1. Identify information sources to monitor changes in life insurance coverages and costs offered by life insurance companies.	www.lifehappens.org
2. Develop a plan for reassessing life insurance needs as family and household situations change.	Text pages 411–414 www.insurance.com

CONTINUING CASE

Life Insurance

Life Situation	*Financial Data*	
Young married couple	Monthly Gross Income	$4,600
Shelby, age 28	Living Expenses	$3,500
Mark, age 29	Assets	$182,000
	Liabilities	$118,000

The Lawrences recently had a baby named Blair and are concerned about their life insurance needs. Shelby has $5,000 of coverage while Mark has life insurance coverage equal to approximately six times his annual salary. They need help in determining the appropriate life insurance amount for their family.

Questions

1. What are the four general methods for estimating the amount of life insurance that the Lawrences need?
2. Explain how Shelby and Mark might use the Personal Financial Planner sheet for figuring out their life insurance needs.
   a. Determining Life Insurance Needs

"I'm not sure spending for life insurance is necessary for my life situation."

Directions

As you continue to record and monitor spending in various categories, be sure to consider how various decisions will affect your long-term financial security. Various comments you record might remind you to consider possible changes you might want to make in your spending habits.

Analysis Questions

1. Are there any spending amounts or items that you might consider reducing or eliminating?
2. What actions might you consider now or in the future regarding spending on life insurance?

The Daily Spending Diary Sheets are located in Appendix D at the end of the book and on the student website at www.mhhe.com/kdh.

chapter 13

Investing Fundamentals

Learning Objectives

LO13-1 Describe why you should establish an investment program.

LO13-2 Assess how safety, risk, income, growth, and liquidity affect your investment decisions.

LO13-3 Explain how asset allocation and different investment alternatives affect your investment plan.

LO13-4 Recognize the importance of your role in a personal investment program.

LO13-5 Use various sources of financial information to reduce risks and increase investment returns.

What will this mean for me?

The investment principles presented in this chapter, along with the information on stocks, bonds, mutual funds, real estate, and other alternatives in the remaining investment chapters, will enable you to create an investment plan that is custom-made for you.

my life

WHY INVEST?

Should you worry about investing for retirement? You bet! There is no better time to begin an investment program than now. The reason is quite simple. If you start an investment program now and let the earnings from your investments compound, you probably won't have to worry about finances when you reach retirement age.

While reading this chapter won't magically make you a millionaire, it does provide some of the tools you need to begin investing. For each of the following statements, select "yes," "no," or "maybe."

1. My investment goals are written down.	Yes	No	Maybe
2. I understand how the factors of safety and risk affect an investment decision.	Yes	No	Maybe
3. I use asset allocation to minimize risks when investing.	Yes	No	Maybe
4. I am actively involved in my investment program.	Yes	No	Maybe
5. I know how to evaluate different investment alternatives.	Yes	No	Maybe

As you study this chapter, you will encounter "My Life" boxes with additional information and resources related to these items.

Preparing for an Investment Program

LO13-1

Describe why you should establish an investment program.

The old saying goes "I've been rich and I've been poor, and believe me, rich is better." While being rich doesn't guarantee happiness, the creation of wealth does provide financial security. The creation of wealth can also provide a safety net for the unexpected emergencies you may experience as you travel life's uncertain road. Finally, the act of saving and investing money will allow you to retire on your terms when and where you choose. Regardless of the reason, the creation of wealth is a worthy goal. And yet, just dreaming of being rich doesn't make it happen.

By studying the basic investment principles presented in this chapter, along with the information on stocks, bonds, mutual funds, real estate, and other alternatives in the remaining investment chapters, you can create an investment plan that is custom-made for you.

ESTABLISHING INVESTMENT GOALS

For most people, the first step is to establish investment goals. Without investment goals, you cannot know what you want to accomplish. To be useful, investment goals must be *written, specific,* and *measurable.* They must also be tailored to your particular financial needs. The following questions will help you establish valid investment goals:

1. How much money do you need to satisfy your investment goals?
2. How will you obtain the money?
3. How long will it take you to obtain the money?
4. How much risk are you willing to assume in an investment program?
5. What possible economic or personal conditions could alter your investment goals?
6. Are you willing to make the sacrifices necessary to reach your investment goals?
7. What will the consequences be if you don't reach your investment goals?
8. Considering your economic circumstances, are your investment goals reasonable?

Your investment goals are always oriented toward the future. In Chapter 1, we classified goals as *short term* (within the next year), *intermediate* (one to five years), or *long term* (more than five years). These same classifications are also useful in planning your investment program. For example, you may establish a short-term goal of accumulating $5,000 in a savings account over the next 12 months. You may then use the $5,000 to purchase stocks or mutual funds to help you obtain your intermediate or long-term investment goals.

my life 1

My investment goals are written down.

If you answered yes to this question at the beginning of the chapter, that's good. If not, Personal Financial Planner sheet 55 can help you develop investment goals that will help you achieve financial security both now and in the future.

PERFORMING A FINANCIAL CHECKUP

Before beginning an investment program, your personal financial affairs should be in good shape. In this section, we examine several factors you should consider before making your first investment.

ETHICAL CONCERNS: PAYING YOUR BILLS ON TIME While there are many reasons why people can't pay their bills on time, the problem often starts with people wanting more than they can afford. From both legal and ethical standpoints, you have an obligation to pay for credit purchases. Moreover, business firms that extend credit expect you to pay for a product or service purchased using credit.

Serious repercussions occur if you don't pay for products or services purchased on credit.

For example

- Merchandise can be repossessed.
- A business can sue to recover the cost of the product or service.
- Your credit score can be lowered to reflect late or missed payments.
- The cost of additional credit, if available, may be higher because of lower credit scores or late or missed payments.

WORK TO BALANCE YOUR BUDGET To avoid the problems just described, you can work to balance your budget. Many individuals regularly spend more than they make. They purchase items on credit and then must make monthly installment payments and pay finance charges often over 20 percent. With this situation, it makes no sense to start an investment program until credit and installment purchases, along with the accompanying finance charges, are reduced or eliminated. A good rule of thumb is to limit consumer credit payments to no more than 20 percent of your net (after tax) income. Eventually, the amount of cash remaining after the bills are paid will increase and can be used to start a savings program or finance investments. For help with budgeting, you may want to review the material in Chapter 3—Money Management Strategies: Financial Statements and Budgeting.

MANAGE YOUR CREDIT CARD DEBT While all cardholders have reasons for using their credit cards, the important point to remember is that it is *very* easy to get in trouble by using your credit cards. Consider the following statistics:

- By the end of 2012, it was projected that 191 million Americans will possess at least one credit card.[1]
- For U.S. families, the average credit card debt was $15,422 at the beginning of 2013.[2]
- For college students, the average credit card debt is $2,200.[3]

Pretty frightening statistics! And the problem becomes worse if you just pay the minimum payment each month. For example, it will take over 9 years to pay off a $1,000 credit card debt. This figure is based on an 18 percent annual percentage interest rate, the average for credit cards used by college students, and a $25 minimum payment.[4]

Things to consider when applying for a credit card include the annual percentage rate. Obviously, the lower the annual percentage rate, the better. Also, consider if there is an annual fee or not. Again an obvious conclusion: A credit card with no annual fee is better than a card with an annual fee.

To avoid the financial problems associated with excessive credit card debt, experts suggest that you take control of your personal finances. Helpful hints include

- Pay your credit card balance in full each month.
- Don't use your credit cards to pay for many small purchases during the month.
- Don't use the cash advance provision that accompanies most credit cards.
- For most people, one or two cards are enough.
- If you think you are in trouble, get help.

The material in Chapter 6—Introduction to Consumer Credit—will help you manage your credit card debt. Also organizations like the Consumer Credit Counseling Service (www.cccs.net) can often help you work out a plan to pay down your credit card debt.

START AN EMERGENCY FUND As suggested in Chapter 3, an investment program should begin with the accumulation of an emergency fund. An **emergency fund** is an amount of money you can obtain quickly in case of immediate need. The amount

emergency fund An amount of money you can obtain quickly in case of immediate need.

of money to be put away in the emergency fund varies from person to person. However, most financial planners agree that an amount equal to three to six months' living expenses is reasonable. For example, Debbie Martin's monthly expenses total $1,600. Before Debbie can begin investing, she must save at least $4,800 ($1,600 × 3 months = $4,800) in a savings account or other near-cash investments to meet emergencies. And while any emergency fund is better than no emergency fund, there are times when you may want to increase the amount. For example, in the recent economic crisis, many unemployed individuals found that an emergency fund equal to three months living expenses was not enough to tide them over until they found new employment.

line of credit A short-term loan that is approved before the money is actually needed.

HAVE ACCESS TO OTHER SOURCES OF CASH FOR EMERGENCY NEEDS You may also want to establish a line of credit at a bank, savings and loan association, or credit union. A **line of credit** is a short-term loan that is approved before you actually need the money. Because the paperwork has already been completed and the loan has been preapproved, you can later obtain the money as soon as you need it. The cash advance provision offered by major credit card companies can also be used in an emergency. However, both lines of credit and credit cards have a ceiling, or maximum dollar amount, that limits the amount of available credit. If you have already exhausted both of these sources of credit on everyday expenses, they will not be available in an emergency.

MANAGING A FINANCIAL CRISIS

DID YOU KNOW?

CONSUMER DEBT!!!

At the beginning of 2013, American consumer debt totaled $11.38 trillion, a staggering amount although actually 2.95 percent lower than the total consumer debt for 2011. For individuals, average amounts for home mortgages decreased—a sure sign that consumers were taking control of their personal finances as a result of the recent economic crisis.

Source: The CreditExaminer website at www.creditexaminer.com, accessed February 2, 2013.

While the typical personal finance course is not an economics course, it does help to have a basic understanding of how the nation's economy affects your personal financial situation. Let's begin with a basic definition for economics. **Economics** is the study of how wealth is created and distributed. By *wealth,* we mean *anything* of value. *How wealth is distributed* means who gets what. Experts often use economics to explain the choices the government, businesses, and individuals make and what is important to each group. For example, assume you want to save money to pay off your credit card debt, and you also want to take a weekend trip to New York City. Because you can't afford to do both, you must decide what is the most important. The decision you make is an example of the concept of opportunity costs—what a person gives up by making a choice—defined in Chapter 1.

economics The study of how wealth is created and distributed.

business cycle The increase and decrease in a nation's economic activity.

A nation's business cycle also affects your personal finances. Many economists define a **business cycle** as the increase and decrease in a nation's economic activity. While all industrialized nations seek sustained conomic growth, full employment, and price stability, the fact is that a nation's economy fluctuates from year to year. If you were to graph the economic growth rate for a country like the United States, it would resemble a roller coaster ride with peaks (strong economy) and low points (weak economy). For example, the stock market as measured by the Dow Jones Industrial Average reached an all-time high at 14,000 in fall 2007. By March 2009, the same average had declined to 6,600. What happened? The simple answer is that the United States (and most of the world) experienced an economic meltdown. This economic crisis had many causes, including banking and investor crises, a downturn in home sales, lower consumer spending, and high unemployment rates. Although the economy shows signs of improving at the time of publication, and the Dow Jones Industrial Average is at record levels, it could happen again.

The recent economic crisis underscores the importance of managing your personal finances *and* your investment program. Here are six steps you can take:

1. *Establish a larger than usual emergency fund.* Under normal circumstances, an emergency fund of three to six months' living expenses is considered adequate, but you may want to increase your fund in anticipation of a crisis.
2. *Know what you owe.* Make a list of all your debts and the amount of the required monthly payments, and then identify the debts that *must* be paid. Typically these include the mortgage or rent, medicine, utilities, food, and transportation.
3. *Reduce spending.* Cut back to the basics and reduce the amount of money spent on entertainment, dining at restaurants, and vacations. Although this is not pleasant, the money saved from reduced spending can be used to increase your emergency fund or pay for everyday necessities.
4. *Notify credit card companies and lenders if you are unable to make payments.* Although not all lenders are willing to help, many will work with you and lower your interest rate, reduce your monthly payment, or extend the time for repayment.
5. *Monitor the value of your investment and retirement accounts.* Tracking the value of your stock, mutual fund, and retirement accounts, for example, will help you decide which investments to sell if you need cash for emergencies. Continued evaluation of your investments can also help you reallocate your investments to reduce investment risk.
6. *Consider converting investments to cash to preserve value.* According to personal finance experts, most investors accumulate more money when they use a buy-and-hold approach over a long period of time. Still, there may be times when you could sell some of your investments and place the cash in a savings account to weather an economic crisis. For this strategy to work, you must be able to sell when the economy is beginning a downturn and then repurchase quality investments before the economy begins to rebound.

Above all, don't panic. While financial problems are stressful, staying calm and considering all the options may help reduce the stress.

GETTING THE MONEY NEEDED TO START AN INVESTMENT PROGRAM

Once you have established your investment goals and completed your financial checkup, it's time to start investing—assuming you have enough money to finance your investments. Unfortunately, the money doesn't automatically appear.

PRIORITY OF INVESTMENT GOALS How badly do you want to achieve your investment goals? Are you willing to sacrifice some purchases to provide financing for your investments? The answers to both questions are extremely important. Take Rita Johnson, a 32-year-old nurse in a large St. Louis hospital. As part of a divorce settlement in 2005, she received a cash payment of almost $55,000. At first, she was tempted to spend this money on a trip to Europe, a new BMW, and new furniture. But after some careful planning, she decided to save $35,000 in a certificate of deposit and invest the remainder in a conservative mutual fund. On May 31, 2013, these investments were valued at $79,000.

What is important to you? What do you value? Each of these questions affects your investment goals. At one extreme are people who save or invest as much of each paycheck as they can. At the other extreme are people who spend everything they make and run out of money before their next paycheck. Most people find either extreme unacceptable and take a more middle-of-the-road approach. These people often spend money on the items that make their lives more enjoyable and still save enough to fund an investment program.

HOW TO...

Obtain the Money Needed to Establish an Investment Program!

Ever feel like it's hard to save money? Well, you're not alone. In fact, most people—especially younger savers—often find it difficult to save money. Below are some suggestions for obtaining the money you need to begin investing.

Suggestion	Suggested Action
1. Pay yourself first.	Each month, pay your monthly bills, save or invest a reasonable amount of money, and use whatever money is left over for personal expenses.
2. Take advantage of employer-sponsored retirement programs.	Sign up for a retirement program at work because many employers will match part or all of the contributions.
3. Participate in an elective savings program.	Elect to have money withheld from your paycheck each payday and automatically deposited in a savings or investment account.
4. Make a special savings effort one or two months each year.	Many financial planners recommend that you cut back to the basics for one or two months each year.

For many people, the easiest way to begin an investment program is to participate in an employer-sponsored retirement account—often referred to as a 401(k) or a 403(b) account. Many employers will match part or all of your contributions to a retirement account. For example, an employer may contribute $0.25 for every $1.00 the employee contributes. And while the amount of the "match" varies, some employers still match $1.00 for every $1.00 employees contribute up to a certain percentage of their annual salary. *Be warned:* many employers reduced or eliminated the matching provisions in their employee's retirement plans during the economic crisis.

Some additional suggestions to help you obtain the money you need to establish an investment program are described in the How To . . . Obtain the Money Needed to Establish an Investment Program feature on this page.

HOW THE TIME VALUE OF MONEY AFFECTS YOUR INVESTMENTS

Many people never start an investment program, because they have only small sums of money. But even small sums grow over a long period of time. For example, if you invest $2,000 *each year* for 40 years at a 3 percent annual rate of return, your investment will grow to $150,802. Notice that the value of your investments increases each year because of two factors. First, it is assumed you will invest another $2,000 each year. At the end of 40 years, you will have invested a total of $80,000 ($2,000 × 40 years = $80,000). Second, all investment earnings are allowed to accumulate and are added to your yearly deposits. In the above example, you earned $70,802 ($150,802 total return − $80,000 yearly contributions = $70,802 accumulated earnings).

Also, the rate of return makes a difference. As noted above, a $2,000 annual investment that earns 3 percent is worth $150,802 at the end of 40 years. But if the same $2,000 annual investment earns 11 percent each year, your investment is worth $1,163,660 at the end of the same 40-year period. The search for higher returns is one reason many investors choose stocks and mutual funds, which offer higher potential returns compared to certificates of deposit or savings accounts. Be warned: investments with higher returns are not guaranteed. In order to obtain higher returns, you must be willing to accept more risk and sacrifice some safety. The material in the next section will help you understand the relationship between safety and risk when choosing an investment.

The information in the Financial Planning Calculations feature on page 450 illustrates one way of calculating the time value of money when you make a series of deposits.

EXAMPLE: Calculating the Time Value of Money Using a Table

Assume you invest $1,200 each year for 25 years. Also, assume that your investment earns 6 percent each year. To determine the future value of your investments at the end of 25 years, use the table in the Financial Planning Calculations feature and follow these steps.

1. Locate the table factor for 6 percent and 25 years.
2. The table factor is 54.865.
3. Multiply the $1,200 yearly investment by the 54.865 table factor.

$$\$1{,}200 \times 54.865 = \$65{,}838$$

In this example, your yearly investments total $30,000 ($1,200 × 25 years = $30,000). At the end of 25 years, your investment earnings are $35,838 ($65,838 total return − $30,000 yearly contributions = $35,838 accumulated earnings). While you can determine the answer to this and similar problems by using the formula presented in the appendix that follows Chapter 1 or by using a financial calculator, most people find that it is easier to use a table factor from a future value table like the one illustrated in the nearby Financial Planning Calculations feature. For more practice, you may want to review the material and work the tryout problem in this Financial Planning Calculations feature.

The investment earnings illustrated in this section are taxable under current Internal Revenue Service guidelines. To avoid or postpone taxation, you may want to invest your money in a traditional individual retirement account (IRA), a Roth IRA, a 401(k) or 403(b) retirement account offered through your employer, or one of the tax-free investments described later in the text. The details about different types of retirement accounts are presented in Chapter 18.

Investment Objectives

PRACTICE QUIZ 13-1

1 Why should an investor develop specific investment goals?
2 What factors should you consider when performing a financial checkup?
3 Explain the time value of money concept and how it affects your investment program.
4 Using the information in the Financial Planning Calculations feature, calculate the future value of your investments if you invest $3,000 each year for 20 years. Assume your investments earn 5 percent each year.

Financial Planning Calculations

USING THE TIME VALUE OF MONEY TO CALCULATE INVESTMENT RETURNS

$2,000 invested each year at 4 percent for 40 years equals $190,052.

Question: How do you calculate this amount? *Answer:* The calculation was based on the time value of money concept presented in the appendix that follows Chapter 1. The fact is that this type of calculation is so important to your investment program that it makes sense to review the concept.

To work this problem, follow these steps:

1. Locate the table factor for 4 percent and 40 years.
2. The table factor is 95.026.
3. Multiply the $2,000 yearly deposit by the 95.026 table factor.

$2,000 × 95.026 = $190,052.

Now, It's Your Turn. Using the table below, calculate the future value of a $1,500 annual investment that earns 10 percent a year for 20 years.

FUTURE VALUE (COMPOUNDED SUM) OF $1 PAID IN AT THE END OF EACH PERIOD OF A GIVEN NUMBER OF TIME PERIODS (AN ANNUITY)

Period	1%	2%	3%	4%	5%	6%	7%	8%	9%	10%	11%
1	1.000	1.000	1.000	1.000	1.000	1.000	1.000	1.000	1.000	1.000	1.000
5	5.101	5.204	5.309	5.416	5.526	5.637	5.751	5.867	5.985	6.105	6.228
10	10.462	10.950	11.464	12.006	12.578	13.181	13.816	14.487	15.193	15.937	16.722
15	16.097	17.293	18.599	20.024	21.579	23.276	25.129	27.152	29.361	31.772	34.405
20	22.019	24.297	26.870	29.778	33.066	36.786	40.995	45.762	51.160	57.275	64.203
25	28.243	32.030	36.459	41.646	47.727	54.865	63.249	73.106	84.701	98.347	114.410
30	34.785	40.588	47.575	56.085	66.439	79.058	94.461	113.280	136.310	164.490	199.020
40	48.886	60.402	75.401	95.026	120.800	154.760	199.640	259.060	337.890	442.590	581.830

Tryout problem answer: $85,912.50

Factors Affecting the Choice of Investments

LO13-2

Assess how safety, risk, income, growth, and liquidity affect your investment decisions.

Millions of Americans buy stocks, bonds, or mutual funds, purchase real estate, or make similar investments. And they all have reasons for investing their money. Some people want to supplement their retirement income when they reach age 65, while others want to become millionaires before age 40. Although each investor may have specific, individual goals for investing, all investors must consider a number of factors before choosing an investment alternative.

SAFETY AND RISK

How do you define a perfect investment? For most people, the perfect investment is one with no risk and above average returns. Unfortunately, the perfect investment does not exist, because of the relationship between safety and risk. The safety and risk factors are two sides of the same coin. *Safety* in an investment means minimal risk of loss. On the other hand, *risk* in an investment means a measure of uncertainty about the outcome.

Investments range from very safe to very risky. At one end of the investment spectrum are very safe investments that attract conservative investors. Investments in this category include government bonds, certificates of deposit, and certain stocks, mutual funds, and corporate bonds. Real estate may also sometimes be a very safe investment. At the other end of the investment spectrum are speculative investments. A **speculative investment** is a high-risk investment made in the hope of earning a relatively large profit in a short time. Such investments offer the possibility of larger dollar returns, but if they are unsuccessful, you may lose most or all of your initial investment. Speculative stocks, certain bonds, some mutual funds, some real estate, commodities, options, precious metals, precious stones, and collectibles are high-risk investments.

speculative investment A high-risk investment made in the hope of earning a relatively large profit in a short time.

THE RISK–RETURN TRADE-OFF

You invest your money and your investments earn money. That's the way investing is supposed to work, but there is some risk associated with all investments. In fact, you may experience two types of risks with many investments.

- First, investors often choose some investments because they provide a predictable source of income. For example, you may choose to purchase a corporate bond because the bond pays a predictable amount of interest every six months. If the corporation experiences financial difficulties, it may default on interest payments. In other words, there is a risk that you will not receive periodic income payments.
- A second type of risk associated with many investments is that an investment will decrease in value. For example, the value of Apple stock decreased on January 24, 2013, when executives for this large technology company known for computers, tablets, and iPhones suggested that sales and profit growth may slow in the future. As a result, the stock decreased 12 percent in just one day.[5] In fact, many investments decreased in value during the recent economic crisis.

Exhibit 13-1 lists a number of factors related to safety and risk that can affect an investor's choice of investments.

EVALUATING YOUR TOLERANCE FOR RISK

When investing, not everyone has the same tolerance for risk. In fact, some people will seek investments that offer the least risk. For example, Ana Luna was injured in a work-related accident three years ago. After a lengthy lawsuit, she received a legal settlement totaling $420,000. When she thought about the future, she knew she needed to get a job, but realized she

Exhibit 13-1

Factors that can affect your tolerance for risk and your investment choices

Conservative Investments with Less Risk	Speculative Investments with Higher Risks
People with no financial training or investment background	Investors with financial training and investment background
Older investors	Younger investors
Lower-income investors	Higher-income investors
Families with children	Married couples with no children or single individuals
Employees worried about job loss	Employees with secure employment positions

would be forced to acquire new employment skills. She also realized she had received a great deal of money that could be invested to provide a steady source of income not only for the next two years while she obtained job training but also for the remainder of her life. Having never invested before, she quickly realized her tolerance for risk was minimal.

When people choose investments that have a higher degree of risk, they expect larger returns. Simply put, one basic rule sums up the relationship between the factors of safety and risk: *The potential return on any investment should be directly related to the risk the investor assumes.* To help you determine how much risk you are willing to assume, take the test for risk tolerance presented in the Financial Planning for Life's Situations feature on page 454.

CALCULATING RETURN ON AN INVESTMENT When you invest, you expect a return on your investment. For example, if you purchase a one-year certificate of deposit (CD) *guaranteed* by the FDIC (Federal Deposit Insurance Corporation), your CD may earn 2 percent a year. At the end of one year, you receive your initial investment plus 2 percent interest. Another investment alternative like a mutual fund may earn 7 percent a year. In this case, you receive an additional 5 percent return when compared to the CD because you chose to invest in a mutual fund that increased in value. While most investors don't like to think about it, an investor must assume more risk because the fund could decrease in value for a number of reasons and your original investment or any possible returns are *not guaranteed.*

rate of return The total income you receive on an investment over a specific period of time divided by the original amount invested.

To determine how much you actually earn on an investment over a specific period of time, you can calculate your rate of return. To calculate **rate of return**, the total income you receive on an investment over a specific period of time is divided by the original amount invested.

EXAMPLE: Rate of Return

Assume that you invest $3,000 in a mutual fund. Also assume the mutual fund pays you $25 in dividends this year and that the mutual fund is worth $3,275 at the end of one year. Your rate of return is 10 percent, as illustrated below.

$$\text{Rate of return} = \frac{\text{Increase or decrease in value} + \text{Annual income}}{\text{Original investment}}$$

$$\text{Rate of return} = \frac{\$275 + \$25}{\$3{,}000}$$

$$= \frac{\$300}{\$3{,}000}$$

$$= 0.10$$

$$= 10 \text{ percent}$$

Note: If an investment decreases in value, the formula used to calculate the rate of return is the same, but the answer is a negative number.

With these same steps, it is possible to compare the projected rate of return for different investment alternatives that offer more or less risk. If based on projections, the rate of return you calculate is only as good as the projections used in the calculations.

Often, beginning investors are afraid of the risk associated with many investments. But it helps to remember that without risk, it is impossible to obtain larger returns that really make an investment program grow. The key is to determine how much risk you are willing to assume, and then choose quality investments that offer higher returns without an unacceptably high risk.

I understand how the factors of safety and risk affect an investment decision.

While some people are afraid of investment risk, the fact is that you must choose investments with acceptable risk in order to generate higher returns.

To help determine the amount of risk you are comfortable with, why not take a second look at your answers to the questions in the Quick Test to Measure Investment Risk Tolerance that is presented in the following Financial Planning for Life's Situations feature.

COMPONENTS OF THE RISK FACTOR

When choosing an investment, you must carefully evaluate changes in the risk factor. In fact, the overall risk factor can be broken down into five components.

INFLATION RISK As defined in Chapter 1, inflation is a rise in the general level of prices. During periods of high inflation, there is a risk that the financial return on an investment will not keep pace with the inflation rate. To see how inflation reduces your buying power, let's assume you have deposited \$10,000 in the bank at 2 percent interest. At the end of one year, your money will have earned \$200 in interest (\$10,000 × 2% = \$200). Assuming an inflation rate of 3 percent, it will cost you an additional \$300 (\$10,000 × 3% = \$300), or a total of \$10,300, to purchase the same amount of goods you could have purchased for \$10,000 a year earlier. Thus, even though you earned \$200, you lost \$100 in purchasing power. And after paying taxes on the \$200 interest, your loss of purchasing power is even greater.

INTEREST RATE RISK The interest rate risk associated with government or corporate bonds or preferred stock is the result of changes in the interest rates in the economy. The value of these investments with a fixed rate of return decreases when overall interest rates increase. In contrast, the value of these same investments rises when overall interest rates decrease. When interest rates in the economy change, you can calculate the approximate value of a bond. The first step is to calculate the dollar amount of annual interest for a bond.

EXAMPLE: Bond Interest Calculation

Suppose you purchase a corporate bond with a face value of \$1,000 issued by J.M. Smucker Company, that matures in 2021 and pays 3.5 percent interest until maturity. Using the following formula, you can calculate the dollar amount of annual interest for the Smucker bond.

$$\begin{aligned}\text{Dollar amount of annual interest} &= \text{Face value} \times \text{Interest rate} \\ &= \$1{,}000 \times 3.5\% \\ &= \$1{,}000 \times 0.035 \\ &= \$35\end{aligned}$$

If bond interest rates for comparable bonds increase to 4 percent, the market value of your 3.5 percent bond will decrease. No one will be willing to purchase your bond at the price you paid for it, since a comparable bond that pays 4 percent can be purchased for \$1,000. As a result, you will have to sell your bond for less than \$1,000 or hold it until maturity. The second step to determine the approximate market value is to divide the bond's annual interest amount by the comparable interest rate.

A QUICK TEST TO MEASURE INVESTMENT RISK TOLERANCE

The following quiz, adapted from one prepared by the T. Rowe Price group of mutual funds, can help you discover how comfortable you are with varying degrees of risk. Other things being equal, your risk tolerance score is a useful guide in deciding how heavily you should weight your portfolio toward safe investments versus more risk-oriented, speculative investments.

1. You're the winner on a TV game show. Which prize would you choose?
   - ☐ $2,000 in cash (1 point).
   - ☐ A 50 percent chance to win $4,000 (3 points).
   - ☐ A 20 percent chance to win $10,000 (5 points).
   - ☐ A 2 percent chance to win $100,000 (9 points).
2. You're down $500 in a poker game. How much more would you be willing to put up to win the $500 back?
   - ☐ More than $500 (8 points).
   - ☐ $500 (6 points).
   - ☐ $250 (4 points).
   - ☐ $100 (2 points).
   - ☐ Nothing—you'll cut your losses now (1 point).
3. A month after you invest in a stock, it suddenly goes up 15 percent. With no further information, what would you do?
   - ☐ Hold it, hoping for further gains (3 points).
   - ☐ Sell it and take your gains (1 point).
   - ☐ Buy more—it will probably go higher (4 points).
4. Your investment suddenly goes down 15 percent one month after you invest. Its fundamentals still look good. What would you do?
   - ☐ Buy more. If it looked good at the original price, it looks even better now (4 points).
   - ☐ Hold on and wait for it to come back (3 points).
   - ☐ Sell it to avoid losing even more (1 point).
5. You're a key employee in a start-up company. You can choose one of two ways to take your year-end bonus. Which would you pick?
   - ☐ $1,500 in cash (1 point).
   - ☐ Company stock options that could bring you $15,000 next year if the company succeeds, but will be worthless if it fails (5 points).

Your total score: _____

SCORING

5–18 Points. You are a more conservative investor. You prefer to minimize financial risks. The lower your score, the more cautious you are. When you choose investments, look for high credit ratings, stability, and an orientation toward safety. In stocks, bonds, and real estate, look for a focus on income.

19–30 Points. You are a less conservative investor. You are willing to take more chances in pursuit of greater rewards. The higher your score, the bolder you are. When you invest, look for high overall returns. You may want to consider bonds with higher yields and lower credit ratings, the stocks of newer, smaller companies, and real estate investments that use mortgage debt.

A primer on the ABCs of investing is available from T. Rowe Price, 100 E. Pratt St., Baltimore, MD 21202 (1-800-638-5660).

EXAMPLE: Approximate Market Value

If interest rates for comparable bonds increase to 4 percent, and you decide to sell your Smucker bond that pays 3.5 percent annual interest, the approximate price you could sell it for would be $875, as follows:

$$\text{Approximate market value} = \frac{\text{Dollar amount of annual interest}}{\text{Comparable interest rate}}$$

$$= \frac{\$35}{4\%} = \frac{\$35}{.04} = \$875$$

The price calculated in the above example would provide the purchaser with a 4 percent return, and you would lose $125 ($1,000 − $875 = $125) because you owned a bond with a fixed interest rate during a period when overall interest rates in the economy increased. Of course, if overall interest rates declined, your bond would increase in value.

BUSINESS FAILURE RISK The risk of business failure is associated with investments in stock, corporate bonds, and mutual funds that invest in stocks or bonds. With each of these investments, you face the possibility that bad management, unsuccessful products, competition, or a host of other factors will cause the business to be less profitable than originally anticipated. Lower profits usually mean lower dividends or no dividends at all. If the business continues to operate at a loss, even interest payments and repayment of bonds may be questionable. The business may even fail and be forced to file for bankruptcy, in which case your investment may become totally worthless. Before ignoring the possibility of business failure, consider the plight of employees and investors who owned stock in Borders Books and Blockbuster Video. Of course, the best way to protect yourself against such losses is to carefully evaluate the companies that issue the stocks and bonds you purchase. It also helps to purchase different types of investments. Business failure risk can also affect the value of mutual funds that invest in stocks and bonds or municipal bonds issued by local and state governments.

MARKET RISK Two different types of risk—systematic and unsystematic—can affect the market value of stocks, bonds, mutual funds, real estate, and other investments. *Systematic* risk occurs because of overall risks in the market and the economy. Factors such as an economic crisis, increasing interest rates, changes in consumer purchasing power, and wars all represent sources of systematic risk. Because this type of risk affects the entire market, it is not possible to eliminate the risk through diversification. On the other hand, *unsystematic* risk affects a specific company or a specific industry. Because this type of risk affects one company or one industry, unsystematic risk can be reduced by diversifying an investment portfolio. For example, an investor who owns 30 different stocks in different industries can reduce unsystematic risk because she or he is well diversified. Anything that happens to one company in the investor's portfolio is not likely to wipe out the value of the entire portfolio.

The prices of stocks, bonds, mutual funds, and other investments may also fluctuate because of the behavior of investors in the marketplace. During 2008 and most of 2009, for example, many investors could not sell real estate because of the nation's depressed housing market. Fluctuations in the market price for stocks, bonds, and mutual funds may have nothing to do with the fundamental changes in the financial health of corporations or the corporations that issue the stocks contained in a mutual fund. Such fluctuations may be caused by political or social conditions. The price of petroleum stocks, for instance, may increase or decrease as a result of political activity in the Middle East.

GLOBAL INVESTMENT RISK Today more investors are investing in stocks and bonds issued by foreign firms and in global mutual funds because investing in global securities can diversify your portfolio. For example, when the U.S. markets are in decline, other markets around the globe may be increasing. An investor can purchase stocks or bonds issued by individual foreign firms or purchase shares in a global mutual fund. For the small investor who has less than $200,000 to invest and is unaccustomed to the risks in foreign investments, global or international mutual funds offer more safety. Before investing in global investments remember that *global investments must be evaluated just like domestic investments.* But evaluating foreign firms and global mutual funds may be difficult because reliable accounting and financial information on foreign firms is often scarce.

INVESTMENT INCOME

Investors sometimes purchase certain investments because they want a predictable source of income. The safest investments—passbook savings accounts, certificates of deposit, and securities issued by the United States government—are also the most predictable sources of income. With these investments, you know exactly how much income will be paid on a specific date.

If investment income is a primary objective, you can also choose municipal bonds, corporate bonds, preferred stocks, utility stocks, or selected common stock issues. When purchasing these investments, most investors are concerned about the issuer's ability to continue making periodic interest or dividend payments. For example, some corporations, such as ExxonMobil and General Electric, are very proud of their long record of consecutive dividend payments and will maintain that policy if at all possible.

Other investments that may provide income potential are mutual funds and real estate rental property. Although the income from mutual funds is not guaranteed, you can choose funds whose primary objective is income. Income from rental property is not guaranteed, because the possibility of either vacancies or unexpected repair bills always exists.

INVESTMENT GROWTH

To investors, *growth* means their investments will increase in value. Often the greatest opportunity for growth is an investment in common stock. Companies with better than average earnings potential, sales revenues that are increasing, and managers who can solve the problems associated with rapid expansion are often considered to be growth companies. Both Shutterfly (technology) and Biogen Idec (biotechnology) are considered growth stocks. These same companies generally pay little or no dividends. Thus, investors often sacrifice immediate cash dividends in return for greater dollar value in the future.

For most growth companies, profits that would normally be paid to stockholders in the form of dividends are reinvested in the companies. The money the companies keep can provide at least part of the financing they need for future growth and expansion and control the cost of borrowing money. As a result, they grow at an even faster pace. Growth financed by profits reinvested in the company normally increases the dollar value of a share of stock for the investor.

Other investments that may offer growth potential include selected mutual funds and real estate. For example, many mutual funds are referred to as growth funds or aggressive growth funds because of the growth potential of the individual securities included in the fund.

INVESTMENT LIQUIDITY

liquidity The ability to buy or sell an investment quickly without substantially affecting the investment's value.

Liquidity is the ability to buy or sell an investment quickly without substantially affecting the investment's value. Investments range from near-cash investments to frozen investments from which it is impossible to get your money. Checking and savings accounts are very liquid because they can be quickly converted to cash. Certificates of deposit impose penalties for withdrawing money before the maturity date.

With other investments, you may be able to sell quickly, but market conditions, economic conditions, or many other factors may prevent you from regaining the amount you originally invested. For example, the owner of real estate may have to lower the asking price to find a buyer. And it may be difficult to find a buyer for investments in collectibles such as antiques and paintings.

PRACTICE QUIZ 13-2

1 In your own words, describe the risk–return trade-off.
2 What are the five components of the risk factor?
3 How do income, growth, and liquidity affect the choice of an investment?

Asset Allocation and Investment Alternatives

LO13-3

Explain how asset allocation and different investment alternatives affect your investment plan.

By now, you are probably thinking, How can I choose the right investment for me? Good question. To help answer that question, consider the following:

- Since 1926, stocks, as measured by the Standard & Poor's 500 Stock Index, have returned 9.8 percent.[6]
- By comparison, long-term government bonds have returned just over 5 percent.[7]
- Since 1926, stocks had positive gains in 63 years.[8]
- Since 1926, stocks lost money in 25 years.[9]

Based on the above facts, it would seem that everyone should invest in stocks because they offer the largest returns. And yet, as indicated by the last bulleted item, stocks can lose money or decline in value. In fact, in 2009—during the recent economic crisis—stocks lost a staggering 37 percent.[10] In reality, stocks may have a place in every investment portfolio, but there is more to establishing a long-term, investment program than just picking a bunch of stocks. Before making the decision to purchase stocks, consider the factors of asset allocation, the time period that your investments will work for you, and your age.

ASSET ALLOCATION AND DIVERSIFICATION

asset allocation The process of spreading your assets among several different types of investments (sometimes referred to as asset classes) to lessen risk.

Asset allocation is the process of spreading your assets among several different types of investments (sometimes referred to as asset classes) to lessen risk. While the term *asset allocation* is a fancy way of saying it, simply put, it really means that you need to diversify and avoid the pitfall of putting all your eggs in one basket—a common mistake made by investors. The diversification provided by investing in *different* asset classes provides a measure of safety and reduces risk, because a loss in one investment is usually offset by gains from other types of investments. Typical asset classes include

- Stocks issued by large corporations (large cap).
- Stocks issued by medium-size corporations (midcap).
- Stocks issued by small, rapidly growing companies (small cap).
- Foreign stocks.
- Bonds.
- Cash.

Note: Mutual funds can also be included as an asset class, but the typical mutual fund will invest in the above securities or a combination of the above securities.

How difficult is it to find the right mix of asset classes? Surprisingly easy! According to noted financial expert and author William Bernstein, if you had invested your investment portfolio in the stocks and bonds that make up the widely quoted averages for large-cap U.S. stocks, small-cap U.S. stocks, foreign stocks, and high-quality U.S. bonds (25 percent in each of these asset classes), you would have beaten over 90 percent of all professional money managers and with considerably less risk over a 10- to 20-year period.[11] And Bernstein is not alone. Today, most financial experts recommend asset allocation as a valued tool that can reduce the risk associated with long-term investment programs.

The percentage of your investments that should be invested in each asset class is determined by

- Your age.
- Investment goals.
- Ability to tolerate risk.
- How much you can save and invest each year.
- The dollar value of your current investments.
- The economic outlook for the economy.
- And several other factors.

DID YOU KNOW?

The more you make, the more challenging your investment goals can be. Here are household income levels for U.S. families.

Over $100,000	20 percent
$75,000 to $99,999	12 percent
$50,000 to $74,999	18 percent
$25,000 to $49,999	25 percent
Under $25,000	25 percent

Source: The U.S. Bureau of the Census, *Statistical Abstract of the United States 2012* (Washington, DC: U.S. Government Printing Office). Table 692 (www.census.gov).

Given these factors, a typical asset allocation for a 31-year-old investor is illustrated in Exhibit 13-2. Typically, the asset allocation will change and become more conservative as you get older.

Now the big questions! What percentage of your assets do you want to invest in stocks and bonds? What percentage of your assets do you want to put in certificates of deposit and other investment alternatives? The answers to these questions are often tied to your tolerance for risk. Remember the basic rule presented earlier in this chapter: *The potential return on any investment should be directly related to the risk the investor assumes.*

my life 3

I use asset allocation to minimize risks when investing.

You may want to use one of the asset allocation calculators that are available on the Internet to determine what percentage of your assets should be in different investment alternatives. To find an asset allocation calculator, use a search engine like Google (www.google.com) or Yahoo! (www.yahoo.com) and enter "asset allocation calculator" in the search box.

To help you decide how much risk is appropriate for your investment program, many financial planners suggest that you think of your investment program as a pyramid consisting of four levels, as illustrated in Exhibit 13-3. In Exhibit 13-3, the cash, CDs, and other conservative investments provide the foundation for your financial security. After the foundation is established in level 1, most investors choose from the investments in levels 2 and 3. Be warned: Many investors may decide

Exhibit 13-2

Suggested asset allocation for a young investor

Asset Allocation by Investment Category

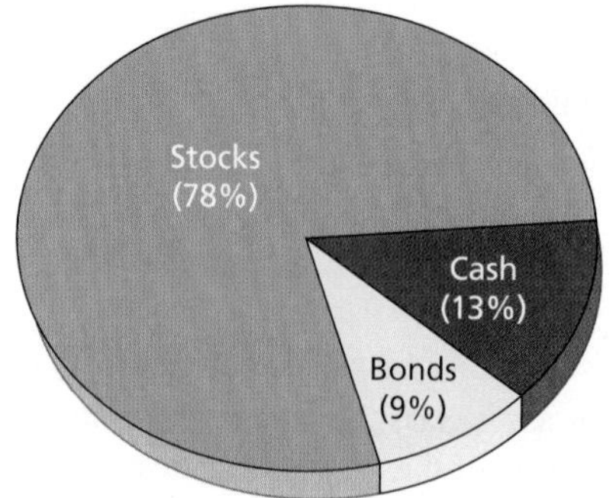

The suggested investments are for an investor who is 31 years old, has current investments valued at $50,000, is committed to saving $2,000 a year, and has an average tolerance for risk.

Source: Bankrate.com (http://www.bankrate.com/calculators/retirement/asset-allocation.aspx), accessed November 15, 2013.

Exhibit 13-3 Typical investments for financial security, safety and income, growth, and speculation

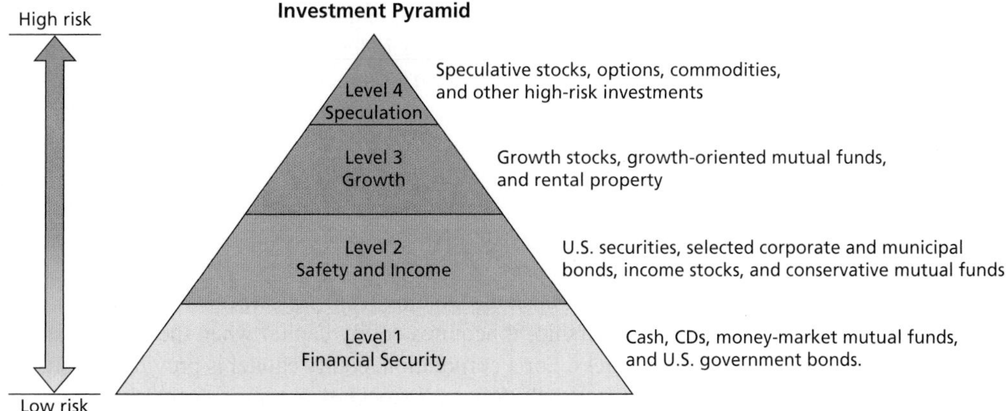

the investments in level 4 are too speculative for their investment program. While the investments at this level may provide high dollar returns, they also have an unacceptable level of risk for many investors.

It may be necessary to adjust your asset allocation from time to time. Often, the main reasons for making changes are because of the amount of time that your investments have to work for you and your age.

THE TIME FACTOR The amount of time that your investments have to work for you is another important factor when managing your investment portfolio. Review the investment returns presented earlier in this section. For over 85 years, stocks have returned 9.8 percent a year and returned more than other investment alternatives. And yet, during the same period, there were years when stocks decreased in value.[12] The point is that if you invested at the wrong time and then couldn't wait for the investment to recover, you would lose money.

The amount of time you have before you need your investment money is crucial. If you can leave your investments alone and let them work for 5 to 10 years or more, then you can invest in stocks and mutual funds. On the other hand, if you need your investment money in two years, you should probably invest in short-term government bonds, highly rated corporate bonds, or certificates of deposit. By taking a more conservative approach for short-term investments, you reduce the possibility of having to sell your investments at a loss because of depressed market value or a staggering economy.

YOUR AGE A final factor to consider when choosing an investment is your age. Younger investors tend to invest a large percentage of their nest egg in growth-oriented investments. If their investments take a nosedive, they have time to recover. On the other hand, older investors tend to be more conservative and invest in government bonds, high-quality corporate bonds, and very safe corporate stocks or mutual funds. As a result, a smaller percentage of their nest egg is placed in growth-oriented investments.

How much of your portfolio should be in growth-oriented investments? Well-known personal financial expert Suze Orman suggests that you subtract your age from 110, and the difference is the percentage of your assets that should be invested in growth investments. For example, if you are 40 years old, subtract 40 from 110, which gives you 70. Therefore, 70 percent of your assets should be invested in growth-oriented investments, while the remaining 30 percent should be kept in safer, conservative investments.[13]

AN OVERVIEW OF INVESTMENT ALTERNATIVES

Once you have considered the risks involved when investing, asset allocation, the length of time your investments can work for you, and your age, it's time to consider which investment alternative is right for you. The remainder of this section provides a brief overview of different investment alternatives. The remaining investment chapters provide more detailed information on stocks, bonds, mutual funds, real estate, and other investment alternatives.

STOCK OR EQUITY FINANCING

equity capital Money that a business obtains from its owners.

Equity capital is money that a business obtains from its owners. If a business is a sole proprietorship or a partnership, it acquires equity capital when the owners invest their own money in the business. For a corporation, equity capital is provided by stockholders, who buy shares of its stock. Since all stockholders are owners, they share in the success of the corporation. This can make buying stock an attractive investment opportunity.

However, you should consider at least two factors before investing in stock. First, a corporation is not required to repay the money obtained from the sale of stock or to repurchase the stock at a later date. Assume you purchased 100 shares of Southwest Airlines stock. Later you decide to sell your Southwest stock. Your stock is sold to another investor, not back to the company. In many cases, a stockholder sells a stock because he or she thinks its price is going to decrease in value. The purchaser, on the other hand, buys that stock because he or she thinks its price is going to increase. This creates a situation in which either the seller or the buyer earns a profit while the other party to the transaction experiences a loss.

dividend A distribution of money, stock, or other property that a corporation pays to stockholders.

Second, a corporation is under no legal obligation to pay dividends to stockholders. A **dividend** is a distribution of money, stock, or other property that a corporation pays to stockholders. Dividends are paid out of earnings, but if a corporation that usually pays dividends has a bad year, its board of directors can vote to omit dividend payments to help pay necessary business expenses. Corporations may also retain earnings to make additional financing available for expansion, research and product development, or other business activities.

There are two basic types of stock: *common stock* and *preferred stock.* A share of common stock represents the most basic form of corporate ownership. People often purchase common stock because this type of investment can provide (1) a source of income if the company pays dividends, (2) growth potential if the dollar value of the stock increases, and (3) profit potential if the company splits its common stock. *Be warned: There are no guarantees that a stock's value will go up after a split.*

The most important priority an investor in preferred stock enjoys is receiving cash dividends before common stockholders are paid any cash dividends. This factor is especially important when a corporation is experiencing financial problems and cannot pay cash dividends to both preferred and common stockholders. Other factors you should consider before purchasing either common or preferred stock are discussed in Chapter 14.

corporate bond A corporation's written pledge to repay a specified amount of money, along with interest.

government bond The written pledge of a government or a municipality to repay a specified sum of money, along with interest.

CORPORATE AND GOVERNMENT BONDS

There are two types of bonds an investor should consider. A **corporate bond** is a corporation's written pledge to repay a specified amount of money, along with interest. A **government bond** is the written pledge of a government or a municipality to repay a specified sum of money, along with interest. Thus, when you buy a bond, you are loaning a corporation or government entity money for a period of time. Regardless of who issues the bond, you need to consider two major questions before investing in bonds. First, will the bond be repaid at maturity? The **maturity date** is the date on which a corporation, government, or municipality will repay the borrowed money. For example, assume you purchase an AT&T corporate bond that pays 5.6 percent interest. The maturity date is May 15, 2018—the date the corporation will repay your investment. The maturity dates for most bonds range between 1 and 30 years. An investor who purchases a bond has two options: keep the bond until maturity and then redeem it, or sell the bond to another investor before maturity. In either case, the value of the bond is closely tied to the ability of the corporation or government agency to repay the bond at maturity. Also, keep in mind, that the value of a bond may increase or decrease in value before it reaches maturity because of changes in interest rates in the economy. To review how interest rates affect the value of a bond, review the material on interest rate risk discussed on page 453.

maturity date The date on which a corporation, government, or municipality will repay the borrowed money.

Second, will the corporation or government entity be able to maintain interest payments to bondholders until maturity? Bondholders normally receive interest payments every six months. For example, investors who purchase the AT&T bond in the previous example earn 5.6 percent or $56 each year until maturity. Because interest payments on bonds are paid every six months, investors would receive a check for $28 every six months for each bond they own.

Receiving periodic interest payments until maturity is one method of making money on a bond investment. Investors also use two other methods that can provide more liberal returns on bond investments. Chapter 15 discusses each of these methods.

MUTUAL FUNDS

A **mutual fund** pools the money from many investors—its shareholders—to invest in a variety of securities.[14] When choosing a mutual fund, *professional management* is an especially important factor for investors with little or no previous experience in financial matters. Another reason investors choose mutual funds is *diversification.* Since mutual funds invest in a number of different securities, an occasional loss in one security is often offset by gains in other securities. As a result, the diversification provided by a mutual fund reduces risk.

mutual fund Pools the money from many investors—its shareholders—to invest in a variety of securities.

The goals of one investor often differ from those of another. The managers of mutual funds realize this and tailor their funds to meet their clients' needs and objectives. As a result of all the different investment alternatives, mutual funds range from very conservative to extremely speculative investments.

In many cases, mutual funds can also be used for retirement accounts, including traditional individual retirement accounts, Roth IRAs, and retirement plans sponsored by your employer. As mentioned earlier in this chapter, many employees contribute a portion of their salary to a retirement account. And in many cases, the employer matches the employee's contribution.

Although investing money in a mutual fund provides professional management, even the best managers can make errors in judgment. The responsibility for choosing the right mutual fund is still based on your evaluation of a mutual fund investment. Chapter 16 presents more information on the different types of mutual funds, the costs involved, and techniques for evaluating mutual fund investments.

REAL ESTATE

As a rule, real estate increases in value and eventually sells at a profit, but there are no guarantees. Although many beginning investors believe real estate values increase by 10 or 15 percent a year, in reality the nationwide average annual increase is about 2 to

3 percent a year over a long time period. This growth rate makes real estate a long-term investment and not a get-rich-quick scheme. It also helps to remember that real estate values can decrease because of an economic crisis or recession.

Success in real estate investments depends on how well you evaluate alternatives. Experts often tell would-be investors that the three most important factors when evaluating a potential real estate investment are *location, location,* and *location.* Other factors may also determine whether or not a piece of real estate is a good investment. For example, you should answer the following questions before making a decision to purchase any property:

1. Is the property priced competitively with similar properties?
2. What type of financing is available, if any?
3. How much are the taxes?
4. What is the condition of the buildings and houses in the immediate area?
5. Why are the present owners selling the property?
6. Is there a chance that the property will decrease in value?

Chapter 17 presents additional information on how to evaluate a real estate investment.

OTHER INVESTMENT ALTERNATIVES

As defined earlier in this chapter, a speculative investment is a high-risk investment made in the hope of earning a relatively large profit in a short time. By its very nature, any investment may be speculative; that is, it may be quite risky. However, a true speculative investment is speculative because of the methods investors use to earn a quick profit. Typical speculative investments include

- Options
- Commodities
- Derivatives
- Precious metals and gemstones
- Coins and stamps
- Antiques and collectibles

Without exception, investments of this kind are normally referred to as speculative for one reason or another. For example, the gold market has many unscrupulous dealers who sell worthless gold-plated lead coins to unsuspecting, uninformed investors. With any speculative investment, it is extremely important to deal with reputable dealers and recognized investment firms. It pays to be careful. While investments in this category can lead to large dollar gains, they should not be used by anyone who does not fully understand the risks involved. Chapter 14 presents information on options. Chapter 17 discusses precious metals, gemstones, and collectibles.

DID YOU KNOW?

When it comes to planning your financial future, take nothing for granted—ask questions, demand answers, and make sure you understand the consequences of your choices before you commit your hard-earned money.

A PERSONAL PLAN FOR INVESTING

Earlier in this chapter, we examined how safety, risk, income, growth, and liquidity affect your investment choices. In the preceding section we looked at investment alternatives. Now let's

Exhibit 13-4

Factors used to evaluate typical investment alternatives

	Type of Investment	Safety	Risk	Income	Growth	Liquidity
		Factors to Be Evaluated				
Traditional Investments	Common stock	Average	Average	Average	High	Average
	Preferred stock	Average	Average	High	Average	Average
	Corporate bonds	Average	Average	High	Low	Average
	Government bonds	High	Low	Low	Low	High
	Mutual funds	Average	Average	Average	Average	Average
	Real estate	Average	Average	Average	Average	Low
Speculative Investments	Options	Low	High	N/A	Low	Average
	Commodities	Low	High	N/A	Low	Average
	Derivatives	Low	High	N/A	Low	Average
	Precious metals, gemstones, antiques, and collectibles	Low	High	N/A	Low	Low

N/A = Not applicable.

compare the factors that affect the choice of investments with each alternative. Exhibit 13-4 ranks the alternatives in terms of safety, risk, income, growth, and liquidity.

With this type of information, it is now possible to begin building a personal plan for investing. Most people use a series of steps like those listed in Exhibit 13-5. And while each step is important, establishing investment goals (step 1), evaluating risk and potential return for each investment alternative (step 5), and continued evaluation (step 8) may be the most important. Although your investment plan may be quite different from someone else's plan, the steps in Exhibit 13-5 will help you follow through and obtain your investment goals.

Exhibit 13-5

Steps for effective investment planning

1. Establish your investment goals.
2. Determine the amount of money you need to obtain your goals.
3. Specify the amount of money you currently have available to fund your investments.
4. List different investments that you want to evaluate.
5. Evaluate (*a*) the risk factor and (*b*) the potential return for all investments.
6. Reduce possible investments to a reasonable number.
7. Choose at least two different investments.
8. Continue to evaluate your investment program.

Investment Risk

PRACTICE QUIZ 13-3

1 How can asset allocation help you build an investment program to reach your financial goals?
2 How do the time your investments have to work for you and your age affect your investment program?
3 Of all the investment alternatives presented in this chapter, which one do you think would help you obtain your investment goals? Explain your answer.
4 Using the Suze Orman method described on page 459, determine how much of your investments should be growth oriented. Does this seem like a reasonable amount?

Factors That Reduce Investment Risk

LO13-4

Recognize the importance of your role in a personal investment program.

In this section, we examine the factors that can spell the difference between success and failure for an investor. We begin by considering your role in the investment process.

YOUR ROLE IN THE INVESTMENT PROCESS

An informed investor has a much better chance of choosing the types of investments that will increase in value. But you have to be willing to work and learn if you want to be an informed investor.

EVALUATE POTENTIAL INVESTMENTS Let's assume you have $25,000 to invest. Also assume your investment will earn a 10 percent return the first year. At the end of one year, you will have earned $2,500 and your investment will be worth $27,500. Not a bad return on your original investment! Now ask yourself: How long would it take to earn $2,500 if I had to work for this amount of money at a job? For some people it might take a month; for others, it might take longer. The point is that if you want this type of return, you should be willing to work for it. When choosing an investment, the work is the time needed to research different investments so that you can make an informed decision. In fact, much of the information in the remaining investment chapters will help you learn how to evaluate different investment opportunities. Keep in mind that successful investors evaluate their investments, but the most successful investors continue to evaluate their investments.

MONITOR THE VALUE OF YOUR INVESTMENTS Would you believe that some people invest large sums of money and don't know what their investments are worth? They don't know if their investments have increased or decreased in value. They don't know if they should sell their investments or continue to hold them. A much better approach is to monitor the value of your investments.

Regardless of which type of investment you choose, close surveillance will keep you informed of whether your investment increases or decreases in value. The nearby

Financial Planning Calculations

MONITORING THE VALUE OF YOUR INVESTMENT

To monitor the value of their investments, many investors use a simple chart like the one illustrated here. To construct a chart like this one, place the original purchase price of your investment on the side of the chart. Then use price increments of a logical amount to show increases and decreases in dollar value.

Place individual dates along the bottom of the chart. For stocks, bonds, mutual funds, and similar investments, you may want to graph every two weeks and chart current values on, say, a Friday. For longer-term investments like real estate, you can chart current values every six months. It is also possible to use computer software to chart the value of your investments.

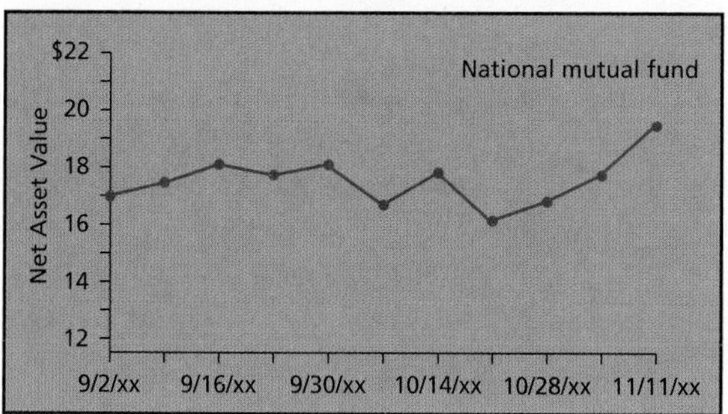

A WORD OF CAUTION

If an investment is beginning to have a large increase or decrease in value, you should watch that investment more closely. You can still continue to chart at regular intervals, but you may want to check dollar values more frequently—in some cases, daily. You may also want to calculate the rate of return on your investment.

NOW IT'S YOUR TURN!

Using the dates and the dollar amounts below, construct a graph to illustrate the price movements for a share of stock issued by Chesapeake Manufacturing.

Date	Price
June 1	$19
June 15	$17
June 29	$18
July 13	$20
July 27	$22
August 10	$24
August 24	$22

Financial Planning Calculations feature presents further information on monitoring the value of your investments.

I am actively involved in my investment program.

You should be involved in and informed about your investment program. Read up on companies you've invested in and stay current by reading economic and financial news. Develop a list of activities, such as these, to stay active in your investment plan.

KEEP ACCURATE AND CURRENT RECORDS

Accurate recordkeeping can help you spot opportunities to maximize profits or reduce dollar losses when you sell your investments. Accurate recordkeeping can also help you decide whether you want to invest additional funds in a particular investment. At the very least, you should keep purchase records for each of your investments that include the actual dollar cost of the investment, plus any commissions or fees you paid, along with records of income (dividends, interest payments, rental income, etc.) you receive from your investment holdings. It is also useful to keep a list of the sources of information (Internet addresses, business periodicals, research publications, etc.), along with copies of the material you used to evaluate each investment. Then, when it is time to reevaluate an existing investment, you will know where to begin your search for current information. Accurate recordkeeping is also necessary for tax purposes.

OTHER FACTORS THAT IMPROVE INVESTMENT DECISIONS

To achieve their financial goals, many people seek professional help. In many cases, they turn to stockbrokers, lawyers, accountants, bankers, or insurance agents. However, these professionals are specialists in one specific field and may not be qualified to provide the type of advice required to develop a thorough financial plan. *Be warned: Some of the above professionals earn commissions on the investments they recommend. The fact they are receiving commissions may influence which investments they recommend for their clients.*

Another source of investment help is a financial planner who has had training in securities, insurance, taxes, real estate, and estate planning. Because financial planners have knowledge, expertise, and experience that you don't possess, they can help you make decisions and establish an investment program. While financial planners can receive commissions for the investment products they recommend, many charge consulting fees that range from $75 to $200 an hour. For more information on the type of services financial planners provide, you may want to review the material in Appendix B at the end of the text.

If you choose to use a financial planner or other professional, keep in mind you are the one who must make the final decisions with the help of the professional. After all, it is your money *and* your financial future.

Regardless of whether you are making your own decisions or have professional help, you must consider the tax consequences of selling your investments. Taxes were covered in Chapter 4, and it is not our intention to cover them again. And yet, it is your responsibility to determine how taxes affect your investment decisions. You may also want to read the material on tax-deferred investment income and retirement planning presented in Chapter 18.

PRACTICE QUIZ 13-4

1 What is your role in the investment process?
2 Why should you monitor the value of your investment?
3 Assume that you have $10,000 that can be invested. Would you make your own decisions or seek professional help? Explain your answer.

Sources of Investment Information

LO13-5

Use various sources of financial information to reduce risks and increase investment returns.

With most investments, more information is available than you can read and comprehend. Therefore, you must be selective in the type of information you use for evaluation purposes. Regardless of the number or availability of sources, always determine how reliable and accurate the information is. Following are sources of information you can use to evaluate present and future investments.

THE INTERNET

Today more people have access to personal finance and investment information provided by Internet sites than ever before. For example, you can obtain interest rates for certificates of deposit; current price information for stocks, bonds, and mutual funds; and brokers' recommendations to buy, hold, or sell a corporation's securities. You can even trade securities online with a click of your computer's mouse. You can also use financial planning software and financial calculators available on many personal finance websites to develop a personal financial plan.

To use your computer to generate information you really need, you must be selective. Search engines like Yahoo! and Google allow you to do a word search for either the personal finance topic or investment alternative that you want to explore. Why not take a look at the type of information available on the Internet? Here's how:

1. Go to www.yahoo.com or www.google.com.
2. Enter a topic that you want to research in the search window and then click the search button. For example, topics of interest might include "financial planning," "asset allocation," or "growth stocks."
3. When the results are displayed, click on one of the individual websites that you want to explore.

Federal, state, and local governments; brokerage firms and investment companies; banks and other financial institutions; and most corporations also have a home page where you can obtain valuable investment information.

While it is impossible to list all the Internet sites related to personal finance, those listed in Exhibit 13-6 will get you started. We will examine other specific Internet sites in the remaining investment chapters. Also, read Appendix B at the end of the text for information on how to use the Internet and software for personal financial planning.

DID YOU KNOW?

With any investment, whether promoted in person, by mail, telephone, or on the Internet, a wise investor should always slow down, ask questions, and get written information. Take notes so you have a record of what you were told, and do your own research.

Source: The Securities and Exchange Commision (SEC) website at www.sec.gov, accessed February 6, 2013.

NEWSPAPERS AND NEWS PROGRAMS

One of the most readily available sources of information for the average investor is the financial pages of a metropolitan newspaper or *The Wall Street Journal*. In addition to limited stock coverage, newspapers may provide information on mutual funds, corporate and government bonds, other investment alternatives,

Exhibit 13-6

Useful Internet sites for personal financial planning

These websites provide information that you can use to establish a financial plan and begin an investment program.

Sponsor and Description	Web Address
The **CNN/Money** website provides current financial news and material that can help investors sharpen their investment skills.	money.cnn.com
The **Kiplinger** website contains a number of tools to help beginners become better investors. You may also want to study the information in the "Personal Finance Basics" section of the site.	kiplinger.com
The **Money Café** website provides a large number of links to valuable personal finance and investment websites.	moneycafe.com
The **Motley Fool** website provides lighthearted but excellent educational materials.	fool.com
The **Quicken** website provides information about software products that help you track your finances.	quicken.com
The **Securities and Exchange Commission** provides investment and financial information for both beginning and experienced investors. You can also check to see if a broker or salesperson is licensed.	sec.gov

and general economic news. Detailed information on how to read price quotations for stocks, bonds, mutual funds, and other investments is presented in the remaining investment chapters.

It is also possible to obtain economic and investment information on radio or television. Many stations broadcast investment market summaries and economic information as part of their regular news programs. For example, CNBC provides ongoing market coverage, investment information, and economic news. See Exhibit 13-7 for publications and news programs used by successful investors.

BUSINESS PERIODICALS AND GOVERNMENT PUBLICATIONS

Most business periodicals are published weekly, twice a month, or monthly. *Barron's, Bloomberg BusinessWeek, Fortune, Forbes,* and similar business periodicals provide not only general news about the overall economy but detailed financial information about individual corporations. Some business periodicals—for example, *Advertising Age*—focus on information about the firms in a specific industry. In addition to business periodicals, more general magazines such as *Time* and *Newsweek* provide investment information as a regular feature. Finally, *Money, Kiplinger's Personal Finance, Worth,* and similar periodicals provide information and advice designed to improve your investment skills. In addition to print versions, most of the above magazines also have an online version. Many magazines may also be available in college or public libraries.

The U.S. government is the world's largest provider of information. Much of this information is of value to investors and is either free or available at minimal cost. U.S. government publications that investors may find useful include the *Federal Reserve Bulletin,* published by the Federal Reserve System, and the *Survey of Current Business,* published by the Department of Commerce.

CORPORATE REPORTS

The federal government requires corporations selling new issues of securities to disclose information about corporate earnings, assets and liabilities, products or services, and the qualifications of top management in a *prospectus* that they must give to investors.

Exhibit 13-7

A personal reading list for successful investing

While individual investors have their favorite sources for investment information, it is quite likely that most successful investors use some of the following newspapers, periodicals, and news programs on a regular basis.

Newspapers	***Business and General Periodicals***
• Metropolitan newspapers	• *Barron's*
• *The Wall Street Journal*	• *Bloomberg BusinessWeek*
• *USA Today*	• *Fortune*
• *The New York Times*	• *Forbes*
	• *Newsweek*
Television	***Personal Financial Publications***
• CNN	• *Kiplinger's Personal Finance Magazine*
• CNBC	• *Money*
	• *Worth*

In addition to the prospectus, publicly owned corporations send their stockholders an annual report that contains detailed financial data. Annual reports contain a statement of financial position, which describes changes in assets, liabilities, and owners' equity. These reports also include an income statement, which provides dollar amounts for sales, expenses, and profits or losses. Finally, annual reports contain a statement of cash flows to report corporate operating, investing, and financing activities. A wealth of information about a corporation can be obtained by contacting the investor relations department of a corporation. Either a written request or a telephone call is usually all it takes. And most corporate financial information is also available on the corporation's website.

INVESTOR SERVICES AND NEWSLETTERS

Investors can subscribe to services that provide investment information. The fees for investor services generally range from $30 to $1,000 or more a year.

Five widely used services are available for investors who specialize in stocks, bonds, and mutual funds:

1. *Standard & Poor's Stock Reports* (www.standardandpoors.com). These up-to-date reports on corporations cover such topics as analysis and commentary, prospects, recent developments, and detailed financial information. Standard & Poor's also provides information about mutual funds.
2. *Value Line* (www.valueline.com). These reports supply detailed information about major corporations—earnings, sales, cash, liabilities, total returns, and other financial data. Like Standard & Poor's, Value Line also provides detailed information about mutual funds.
3. *Mergent* (www.mergent.com). Mergent's reports help investors evaluate potential investments in corporate securities and provide information similar to that contained in Standard & Poor's and Value Line reports.
4. *Morningstar Investment Reports* (www.morningstar.com). Morningstar tracks thousands of mutual funds and issues reports on safety, financial performance, and other important information that investors can use to evaluate a corporate stock or a mutual fund.
5. *Lipper Reports* (www.lipperweb.com). The mutual fund information provided by Lipper is similar to Morningstar's detailed reports.

In addition to the preceding publications, each of the following securities exchanges provides information about investing:

- New York Stock Exchange Euronext (www.nyse.com).
- Nasdaq over-the-counter market (www.nasdaq.com).

Each of these websites provides basic information about the exchange, offers educational material and a glossary of important terms, provides detailed information about investment alternatives, and describes how investors can profit from transactions through the exchange.

This discussion of investment information is not exhaustive, but it gives you some idea of the amount and scope of the information available to serious investors. Although most small investors find many of the services and newsletters described here too expensive for personal subscriptions, this information may be available from stockbrokers or financial planners. This type of information is also available at many public libraries. More detailed information about sources of investment information is provided in the remaining investment chapters.

I know how to evaluate different investment alternatives.

Once you identify the sources of information that are most useful for evaluating a specific investment, make photocopies of the information. That way, you can refer back to the information when needed. Also, you can go back to those same sources when it's time to reevaluate your investment choices. To help sort through the wealth of information available, use Personal Financial Planner sheet 57.

Investment Information Sources

PRACTICE QUIZ 13-5

1 What do you think is the most readily available source of information for the average investor? Explain your answer.
2 What type of information can you obtain using the Internet?
3 Briefly describe the additional sources of information you can use to evaluate a potential investment and lessen risk.

my life stages for investing...

YOUR PERSONAL FINANCIAL DASHBOARD

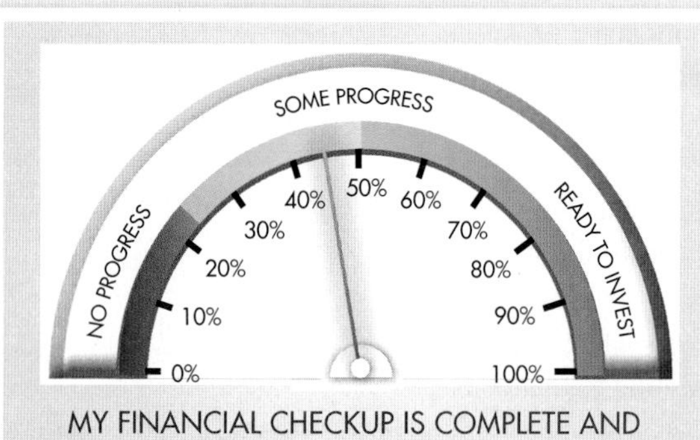

A personal finance dashboard allows you to assess your financial situation.

Once you have established your investment goals and completed your financial checkup, it's time to start investing—assuming you have enough money to finance your investments. Unfortunately, the money doesn't automatically appear.

YOUR SITUATION Have you established specific and measurable investment goals? Have you performed a financial checkup to see if you are ready to begin investing? Do you have any money to invest? All three questions are imporant and should be answered before you begin to invest. Other personal financial planning actions you might consider during various stages of your life include:

. . . in college

- Establish investment and financial goals
- Work to balance your budget
- Start an emergency fund
- Save a reasonable amount of money from each paycheck

. . . in my 20s

- Revise investment and financial goals
- Pay off any college loans and other debts
- Explore different retirement plans
- Begin investing after careful evaluation of different types of investments

. . . in my 30s and 40s

- Revise investment and financial goals
- Continue to evaluate new and current investments
- Increase your amount of savings and investments

. . . in my 50s and beyond

- Revise investment and financial goals
- Begin planning for retirement within a specific number of years
- Increase your amount of savings and investments
- Consider conservative investment options
- Continue to evaluate current investments

LO13-1

Describe why you should establish an investment program.

As pointed out in the My Life opening scenario for this chapter, there is no better time for college students to begin planning for retirement than now. The reason is quite simple: If you start an investment program when you are young, let the time value of money work for you, and make sound investments, you won't have to worry about finances when you reach retirement age. It all begins with creating the investment goals that are right for you.

Investment goals must be written, specific, and measurable and should be classified as short term, intermediate, and long term. Before beginning an investment program, you must then make sure your personal financial affairs are in order. This process begins with learning to live within your means including managing your credit card debt. The next step is the accumulation of an emergency fund equal to three to six months' living expenses or more. Then, and only then, is it time to save the money needed to establish an investment program. Because of the time value of money, even small investments can grow to substantial amounts over a long period of time.

LO13-2

Assess how safety, risk, income, growth, and liquidity affect your investment decisions.

All investors must consider the factors of safety, risk, income, growth, and liquidity. Especially important is the relationship between safety and risk. Keep in mind that there is risk associated with all investments. Often, investors may experience two types of risk: a risk you will not receive periodic income payments; and a risk that an investment will decrease in value. As a result, all investors must evaluate their tolerance for risk. Basically, this concept can be summarized as follows: *The potential return for any investment should be directly related to the risk the investor assumes.* In fact, some investors base their investment decisions on projections for rate of return. You can also use the same calculation to determine how much you actually earn on an investment over a specific period of time.

The risk factor can be broken down into five components: inflation risk, interest rate risk, business failure risk, market risk, and global investment risk. Income, growth, and liquidity may also affect your choice of investments.

LO13-3

Explain how asset allocation and different investment alternatives affect your investment plan.

Asset allocation is the process of spreading your assets among several different types of investments to lessen risk. Typical asset classes include large-cap stocks, midcap stocks, small-cap stocks, foreign stocks, bonds, and cash. The percentage of your investments that should be invested in each asset class is determined by your age, investment objectives, ability to tolerate risk, how much you can save and invest each year, the dollar value of your current investments, the economic outlook for the economy, and several other factors.

Typical long-term investment alternatives include stocks, bonds, mutual funds, and real estate. More speculative investment alternatives include options, commodities, derivatives, precious metals, gemstones, and collectibles. Before choosing a specific investment, you should evaluate all potential investments on the basis of safety, risk, income, growth, and liquidity. With all of these factors in mind, the next step is to develop a specific, personal investment plan to help you accomplish your goals.

LO13-4

Recognize the importance of your role in a personal investment program.

It is your responsibility to evaluate and to monitor the value of your investments. Accurate recordkeeping can also help you spot opportunities to maximize profits or reduce losses when you sell your investments. These same detailed records can help you decide whether you want to invest additional funds in a particular investment. To achieve their financial goals, many people seek professional help. In many cases, they turn to stockbrokers, lawyers, accountants, bankers, insurance agents, or financial planners. If you choose to use a financial planner or other professional, keep in mind you are the one who must make the final decisions with the help of the professionals. Finally, it is your responsibility to determine how taxes affect your investment decisions.

LO13-5

Use various sources of financial information to reduce risks and increase investment returns.

Because more information on investments is available than most investors can read and comprehend, you must be selective in the type of information you use for evaluation purposes. Sources of information include the Internet, newspapers and news programs, business periodicals, government publications, corporate reports, investor services, and newsletters.

KEY TERMS

asset allocation 457
business cycle 446
corporate bond 460
dividend 460
economics 446
emergency fund 445
equity capital 460
government bond 460
line of credit 446
liquidity 456
maturity date 461
mutual fund 461
rate of return 452
speculative investment 451

KEY FORMULAS

Page	Topic	Formula
452	Rate of return	$\text{Rate of return} = \dfrac{\text{Increase or decrease in value} + \text{Annual income}}{\text{Original investment}}$
	Example:	$\text{Rate of return} = \dfrac{\$200 + \$50}{\$4{,}000}$ $= \dfrac{\$250}{\$4{,}000}$ $= 0.063$ $= 6.3\%$
453	Interest calculation for a corporate bond	$\text{Dollar amount of annual interest} = \text{Face value} \times \text{Interest rate}$
	Example:	$\text{Dollar amount of annual interest} = \$1{,}000 \times 7\%$ $= \$1{,}000 \times 0.07$ $= \$70$
454	Approximate market value	$\text{Approximate market value} = \dfrac{\text{Dollar amount of annual interest}}{\text{Comparable interest rate}}$
	Example:	$\text{Approximate market value} = \dfrac{\$80}{9\%} \quad \dfrac{\$80}{0.09}$ $= \$888.89$

1. For Alicia Thompson, the last few years have been a financial nightmare. It all started when she lost her job. Because she had no income and no emergency fund, she began using her credit cards to obtain the cash needed to pay everyday living expenses. Finally, after an exhaustive job search, she has a new job that pays \$51,000 a year. While her monthly take-home pay is \$2,975, she must now establish an emergency fund, pay off her \$7,300 credit card debt, and start saving the money needed to begin an investment program.
   a. If monthly expenses are \$2,150, what is the minimum amount of money should Alicia save for an emergency fund?
   b. What steps should Alicia take to pay the \$7,300 credit card debt?
   c. Alicia has decided that she will save and invest \$2,000 a year for the next five years. If her savings and investments earn 3 percent each year, how much money will she have at the end of five years? (Use the table in the Financial Planning Calculations feature—see page 450).
2. Matt Jackson purchased a \$1,000 corporate bond issued by Chevron Corporation. The annual interest rate for the bond is 2.36 percent.
   a. What is the annual interest amount for the Chevron bond?
   b. Since the annual interest for this bond is paid every six months or semiannually, how much will Matt receive for his Chevron bond each six months?
   c. If comparable, new bonds pay 3 percent interest, what is the approximate market value for this bond?

Solutions

1. a. The minimum emergency fund is \$6,450. *Note:* This is the minimum emergency fund, and the amount can be increased because of personal or economic circumstances.

$$\begin{aligned}\text{Minimum emergency fund} &= \text{Monthly expenses} \times 3 \text{ months}\\ &= \$2{,}150 \times 3\\ &= \$6{,}450\end{aligned}$$

   b. To pay her \$7,300 credit card debt, Alicia should take the following actions: (1) talk to the credit card companies and ask if they will lower the interest rate she is paying; (2) pay at least the minimum balance on all credit cards to ensure that she does not get behind on any payments; and (3) pay off the credit card with the highest interest rate first, then work on the remaining credit cards.

   c. Alicia will have saved \$10,000 at the end of five years. If her savings and investments earn 3 percent each year, she will have accumulated \$10,618 based on the information in the table in the Financial Planning Calculations feature.

2. a. The annual interest amount for the Chevron bond is \$23.60.

$$\begin{aligned}\text{Amount of annual interest} &= \text{Face value} \times \text{Interest rate}\\ &= \$1{,}000 \times 2.36\%\\ &= \$1{,}000 \times 0.0236\\ &= \$23.60\end{aligned}$$

   b. Every six months Matt will receive \$11.80 for each Chevron bond he owns.

$$\begin{aligned}\text{Semi Annual Payment} &= \text{Annual interest amount per bond} \div 2\\ &= \$23.60 \div 2\\ &= \$11.80\end{aligned}$$

   c. If comparable, new bonds pay 3 percent interest, the approximate market value of Matt's Chevron bond is \$787.

$$\begin{aligned}\text{Approximate market value} &= \text{Dollar amount of annual interest} \div \text{Comparable interest rate}\\ &= \$23.60 \div 3\%\\ &= \$23.60 \div .03\\ &= \$787\end{aligned}$$

FINANCIAL PLANNING PROBLEMS

LO13-1 **1.** *Calculating the Amount for an Emergency Fund.* Beth and Bob Martin have total take-home pay of $4,000 a month. Their monthly expenses total $2,900. Calculate the minimum amount this couple needs to establish an emergency fund. How did you calculate this amount?

LO13-1 **2.** *Planning for an Investment Program.* Assume you are 29 years old, your take-home pay totals $2,400 a month, your monthly living expenses total $1,400, your monthly car payment is $400, and your credit card debts total $3,500. Using the information presented in this chapter, develop a three-part plan to (*a*) reduce your monthly expense, (*b*) establish an emergency fund, and (*c*) save $6,000 to establish an investment program.

LO13-1 **3.** *Determining Profit or Loss from an Investment.* Three years ago, you purchased 150 shares of IBM stock for $92 a share. Today, you sold your IBM stock for $183 a share. For this problem, ignore commissions that would be charged to buy and sell your IBM shares and dividends you might have received as a shareholder.

a. What is the amount of profit you earned on each share of IBM stock?

b. What is the total amount of profit for your IBM investment?

LO13-1 **4.** *Determining the Time Value of Money.* Using the table in the Financial Planning Calculations feature on page 450, complete the following table. Then answer the questions that follow the table. *Hint:* To calculate the total amount of interest or earnings, subtract the amount of your total investment from the value at the end of the time period.

Annual Deposit	Rate of Return	Number of Years	Investment Value at the End of Time Period	Total Amount of Investment	Total Amount of Interest or Earnings
$2,000	5%	10			
$2,000	9%	10			
$2,000	5%	20			
$2,000	9%	20			

a. In the above situations, describe the effect that the rate of return has on the investment value at the end of the selected time period.

b. In the above situations, describe the effect that the number of years has on the investment value at the end of the selected time period.

LO13-2 **5.** *Calculating Rate of Return.* Assume that at the beginning of the year, you purchase an investment for $5,500 that pays $110 annual income. Also assume the investment's value has increased to $6,400 by the end of the year.

a. What is the rate of return for this investment?

b. Is the rate of return a positive or negative number?

LO13-2 **6.** *Calculating Rate of Return.* Assume that at the beginning of the year, you purchase an investment for $7,100 that pays $80 annual income. Also assume that the investment's value has increased to $7,590 at the end of the year.

a. What is the rate of return for this investment?

b. Is the rate of return a positive or negative number?

LO13-2 **7.** *Calculating Rate of Return.* Assume that at the beginning of the year, you purchase an investment for $7,000 that pays $100 annual income. Also assume the investment's value has decreased to $6,600 by the end of the year.

a. What is the rate of return for this investment?

b. Is the rate of return a positive or negative number?

LO13-2 **8.** *Determining Interest.* Assume that you purchased a corporate bond with a face value of $1,000. The interest rate is 4.10 percent. What is the dollar amount of annual interest you will receive each year?

LO13-2 **9.** *Determining Interest.* Three years ago you purchased a Heinz corporate bond that pays 3.125 percent annual interest. The face value of the bond is $1,000. What is the total dollar amount of interest that you received from your bond investment over the three-year period?

10. *Determining Interest.* Jackie Martin purchased three $1,000 corporate bonds issued by J. C. Penney. The bonds pay 5.65 percent and mature in 2020. What is the total dollar amount of interest Jackie will receive for her three bonds each year? LO13-2

11. *Determining Interest and Approximate Bond Value.* Assume that three years ago, you purchased a corporate bond that pays 6.10 percent. The purchase price was $1,000. Also assume that three years after your bond investment, comparable bonds are paying 7.20 percent. LO13-2

a. What is the annual dollar amount of interest that you receive from your bond investment?

b. Assuming that comparable bonds are paying 7.20 percent, what is the approximate dollar price for which you could sell your bond?

c. In your own words, explain why your bond increased or decreased in value.

12. *Determining Interest and Approximate Bond Value.* Eight years ago, Burt Brownlee purchased a U.S. government bond that pays 3.80 percent interest. The face value of the bond was $1,000. LO13-2

a. What is the dollar amount of annual interest that Burt received from his bond investment each year?

b. Assume that comparable bonds are now paying 2.9 percent. What is the approximate dollar price for which Burt could sell his bond?

c. In your own words, explain why Burt's bond increased or decreased in value.

13. *Using Asset Allocation to Diversify Risk.* Assume you are 59 years old, want to retire in 6 years, and currently have an investment portfolio valued at $550,000 invested in technology stocks. After talking with friends and relatives, you have decided that you have "too many eggs in one basket." Based on this information, use the asset allocation method described in this chapter and the table below to diversify your investment portfolio. Then answer the questions below. LO13-3

Investment Alternative	Percentage You Would Like in This Category
Large-cap stocks	
Midcap stocks	
Small-cap stocks	
Foreign stocks	
Government bonds	
Corporate bonds	
Cash	
Other investments (specify type)	
	100%

a. What are the advantages of asset allocation?

b. How could the time your investments have to work for you and your age affect your asset allocation?

14. *Monitoring an Investment's Financial Performance.* Based on the following information, construct a graph that illustrates price movement for a share of the Davis New York Venture Mutual Fund. *Note:* You may want to review the material presented in the Financial Planning Calculations feature on page 465. LO13-4

January	$28.70	July	$26.10
February	28.00	August	25.50
March	30.30	September	26.40
April	31.35	October	26.90
May	29.50	November	28.40
June	27.80	December	27.20

FINANCIAL PLANNING ACTIVITIES

1. *Using Investment Information.* Choose a current issue of *Kiplinger's Personal Finance* or *Money* and summarize an article that provides suggestions on how you could use your money more effectively. L013-1

2. *Using the Internet to Obtain Information about Money Management.* As pointed out at the beginning of this chapter, it doesn't make sense to establish an investment program until credit card and installment purchases are reduced or eliminated. While most people are responsible and make payments when they're supposed to, some people get in trouble. To help avoid this problem, each of the following organizations has a home page on the Internet: L013-1

   Consumer Credit Counseling Service provides information about how to manage consumer debt (cccs.net).

   Green Path Debt Solutions provides counseling for people with debt problems. (greenpath.com).

   Choose one of the above organizations and visit its home page. Then prepare a report that summarizes the information provided by the organization. Finally, indicate if this information could help you manage your consumer debt.

3. *Choosing Investment Alternatives.* From the investment alternatives described in this chapter, choose two specific investments you believe would help an individual who is 35 years old, is divorced, and earns $27,000 a year begin an investment program. Assume this person has $30,000 to invest at this time. As part of your recommendation, compare each of your investment suggestions on safety, risk, income, growth, and liquidity. L013-2

4. *Developing a Financial Plan.* Assume you are single and have graduated from college. Your monthly take-home pay is $2,500, and your monthly expenses total $2,300, leaving you with a monthly surplus of $200. Develop a personal plan of action for investing using the steps listed in Exhibit 13-5. L013-3

5. *Using Financial Information to Track the Value of an Investment.* Choose one stock and one mutual fund investment. Using the Internet, *The Wall Street Journal,* or your local newspaper, track the value of both investments on a daily basis for a two-week period. Then construct a graph that illustrates the changes in each investment's value over the two-week period. In a one-page report, indicate whether either of the two investments would have been a good investment over the two-week time period. Explain your answer. L013-5

6. *Using Investment Information.* Assume you have established an emergency fund and have saved an additional $12,000 to fund an investment in common stock issued by AT&T Corporation. Using the sources of information discussed in this chapter, go to the library or use the Internet to obtain information about this company. Summarize your findings in a three-page report describing AT&T's current operations and the firm's past and present financial performance. Finally, indicate whether you would purchase AT&T common stock based on the information in your report. L013-5

FINANCIAL PLANNING CASE

First Budget, Then Invest for Success!

Joe and Mary Garner, married 12 years, have an eight-year-old child. Six years ago, they purchased a home on which they owe about $110,000. They also owe $6,000 on their two-year-old automobile. All of their furniture is paid for, but they owe a total of $4,120 on two credit cards. Joe is employed as an engineer and makes $60,000 a year. Mary works as a part-time computer analyst and earns about $16,000 a year. Their combined monthly income after deductions is $4,520.

About six months ago, the Garners had what they now describe as a "financial meltdown." It all started one Monday afternoon when their air conditioner stopped cooling. Since their home was only six years old, they thought the repair ought to be a simple one—until the repair technician diagnosed their problem as a defective compressor. Unfortunately, the warranty on the compressor had run out about three months before the compressor broke down. According to the technician, it would cost over $1,200 to replace the compressor. At the time, they had about $2,000 in their savings account, which they had been saving for their summer vacation, and now they had to use their vacation money to fix the air conditioner.

For the Garners, the fact that they didn't have enough money to take a vacation was like a wake-up call. They realized they were now in their mid-30s and had serious cash problems. According to Joe, "We don't waste money, but there just never seems to be enough money to do the things we want to do." But according to Mary, "The big problem is that we never have enough money to start an investment program that could pay for our daughter's college education or fund our retirement."

They decided to take a "big" first step in an attempt to solve their financial problems. They began by examining their monthly expenses for the past month. Here's what they found:

Income (cash inflow)		
Joe's take-home salary	$3,500	
Mary's take-home salary	$1,020	
Total income		$4,520
Cash outflows		
Monthly fixed expenses:		
Home mortgage payment, including taxes and insurance	$ 890	
Automobile loan	315	
Automobile insurance	130	
Life insurance premium	50	
Total fixed expenses		$1,385
Monthly variable expenses:		
Food and household necessities	$ 680	
Electricity	240	
Natural gas	175	
Water	35	
Telephone	80	
Family clothing allowance	230	
Gasoline and automobile repairs	195	
Personal and health care	150	
Recreation and entertainment	700	
Gifts and donations	350	
Minimum payment on credit cards	80	
Total variable expenses		$2,915
Total monthly expenses		$4,300
Surplus for savings or investments		$ 220

Once the Garners realized they had a $220 surplus each month, they began to replace the $1,200 they had taken from their savings account to pay for repairing the air conditioner. Now it was time to take the next step.

Questions

1. How would you rate the financial status of the Garners before the air conditioner broke down?
2. The Garners' take-home pay is over $4,500 a month. Yet, after all expenses are paid, there is only a $220 surplus each month. Based on the information presented in this case, what expenses, if any, seem out of line and could be reduced to increase the surplus at the end of each month?
3. Given that both Joe and Mary Garner are in their mid-30s and want to retire when they reach age 65, what type of investment goals would be most appropriate for them?
4. How does the time value of money and the asset allocation concept affect the types of long-term goals and the investments that a couple like the Garners might use to build their financial nest egg?
5. Based on the different investments described in this chapter, what specific types of investments (stocks, mutual funds, real estate, etc.) would you recommend for the Garners? Why?

PERSONAL FINANCIAL PLANNER IN ACTION

Developing an Investment Plan

An investment program should consider safety, risk, current income, growth potential, liquidity, and taxes. Your ability to set financial goals and select investment vehicles is crucial to long-term financial prosperity.

Your Short-Term Financial Planning Activities	*Resources*
1. Set investment goals for various financial needs.	PFP Sheet 55 http://beginnersinvest.about.com www.investopedia.com www.fool.com www.aaii.org
2. Assess various types of investments for market risk, inflation, interest rate risk, and liquidity.	PFP Sheet 56 http://finance.yahoo.com www.marketwatch.com

3. Identify and evaluate investment information sources.	PFP Sheet 57 www.invest-faq.com www.sec.gov
Your Long-Term Financial Planning Activities	*Resources*
1. Identify saving and investing decisions that would serve your changing life situations.	www.betterinvesting.org www.money.cnn.com
2. Develop a plan for revising investments as family and household situations change.	Text pages 464–466 www.quicken.com

CONTINUING CASE

Starting an Investment Program

Life Situation	*Financial Data*	
Shelby, age 30	Monthly Gross Income	$7,000
Mark, age 31	Living Expenses	$4,500
One child, age 4	Assets	$180,000
	Liabilities	$123,000

Shelby and her family have been living in their condo for five years. Shelby's pet salon has been successful but her income fluctuates with the economy. Mark, on the other hand, is continuing to work for the same company and has been participating in its 401(k) matching program. He has been able to accumulate $35,000, since his company matches his contributions up to 5%. Shelby's parents are encouraging her and Mark to begin planning for their daughter, Blair's college fund and for their future retirement. Shelby and Mark have been really busy with work and their toddler but are ready to make some investment decisions. They are wondering how to get started.

Questions

1. What are the steps that Shelby and Mark should take to prepare for an Investment Program?
2. Explain how Shelby and Mark might obtain money to start an Investment Program?
3. Explain how Shelby and Mark might use the Personal Financial Planner sheets Investment Objectives and Investment Information Sources.

"While I have a fairly large amount in a savings account, I should think about investing some of this money in other ways."

Directions

The use of your "Daily Spending Diary" can provide an important foundation for monitoring and controlling spending. This will enable you to use money more wisely now and in the future.

Analysis Questions

1. Explain how the use of a Daily Spending Diary could result in starting an investment program.
2. Based on your Daily Spending Diary, describe actions that you might take to identify and achieve various investment goals.

The Daily Spending Diary sheets are located in Appendix D at the end of the book and on the student website at www.mhhe.com/kdh.

chapter 14

Investing in Stocks

Learning Objectives

LO14-1 Identify the most important features of common and preferred stocks.

LO14-2 Explain how you can evaluate stock investments.

LO14-3 Analyze the numerical measures that cause a stock to increase or decrease in value.

LO14-4 Describe how stocks are bought and sold.

LO14-5 Explain the trading techniques used by long-term investors and short-term speculators.

What will this mean for me?

Investors who want their investments to grow often choose stocks because of the historically high returns. To help you evaluate this investment alternative, this chapter provides the information you need to know before investing in stocks.

my life

WHY STOCKS?

There is more to investing in stocks than just luck. In fact, the best investors are the ones that "invest" the time to research a stock investment before they invest their money. And they continue to evaluate their investment after they have made their decision to purchase a specific stock.

This chapter provides valuable information that can help you become a "best" investor. Before beginning this chapter, respond to the statements below.

1. I know how to make money with stock investments.	Yes	No	Maybe
2. I can evaluate stock investments.	Yes	No	Maybe
3. I appreciate the relationship between a corporation's earnings and the value of a corporation's stock.	Yes	No	Maybe
4. I know what factors to consider when choosing an account executive and a brokerage firm.	Yes	No	Maybe
5. I can explain the difference between long-term and short-term investment techniques.	Yes	No	Maybe

As you study this chapter, you will encounter "My Life" boxes with additional information and resources related to these statements.

Common and Preferred Stocks

LO14-1

Identify the most important features of common and preferred stocks.

Today, investors—especially beginning investors—face two concerns when they begin an investment program. First, they don't know where to get the information they need to evaluate potential investments. In reality, more information is available than most investors can read.

Second, beginning investors sometimes worry that they won't know what the information means when they do find it. Yet common sense goes a long way when evaluating potential investments. For example, consider the following questions:

1. Is an increase in sales revenues a healthy sign for a corporation? (Answer: yes)
2. Should a firm's net income increase or decrease over time? (Answer: increase)
3. Should a corporation's earnings per share increase or decrease over time? (Answer: increase)

Although the answers to these questions are obvious, you will find more detailed answers to these and other questions in this chapter. In fact, that's what this chapter is all about. We want you to learn how to evaluate a stock and to make money from your investment decisions.

But before investing your money, it helps to understand why corporations issue common stock and why investors purchase that stock.

common stock The most basic form of ownership for a corporation.

equity financing Money received from the sale of shares of ownership in a business.

dividend A distribution of money, stock, or other property that a corporation pays to stockholders.

WHY CORPORATIONS ISSUE COMMON STOCK

Common stock is the most basic form of ownership for a corporation. Corporations issue common stock to finance their business start-up costs and help pay for expansion and their ongoing business activities. Corporate managers prefer selling common stock as a method of financing for several reasons.

A FORM OF EQUITY *Important point:* Corporations prefer selling stock because the money doesn't have to be repaid, and the company doesn't have to buy back shares from stockholders. Stock is equity financing. **Equity financing** is money received from the sale of shares of ownership in a business. A stockholder who buys common stock may sell his or her stock to another individual. The selling price is determined by how much a buyer is willing to pay for the stock. The price for a share of stock changes when information about the firm or its future prospects is released to the general public. For example, information about future sales revenues, earnings, expansion or mergers, or other important developments within the firm can increase or decrease the price for a share of the firm's stock.

DIVIDENDS NOT MANDATORY *Important point:* Dividends are paid out of profits, and dividend payments must be approved by the corporation's board of directors. A **dividend** is a distribution of money, stock, or other property that a corporation pays to stockholders. Dividend policies vary among corporations, but most firms distribute between 30 and 70 percent of their earnings to stockholders. However, some corporations follow a policy of smaller or no dividend distributions to stockholders. In general, these are rapidly growing firms, like eBay (online auctions), Medifast (weight management), and Google (Internet search engine) that retain a large share of their earnings for research and development, expansion, acquistions, or major projects. On the other hand, utility companies, such as Duke Energy and CenterPoint Energy, and other financially secure corporations, may distribute 70 to 90 percent of their earnings. Always remember that the board of directors may vote to reduce or omit dividend payments because the corporation had a bad year or for any other reason.

VOTING RIGHTS AND CONTROL OF THE COMPANY In return for the financing provided by selling common stock, management must make concessions to stockholders that may restrict corporate policies. For example, the common stockholders elect the board of directors and must approve major changes in corporate policies. Stockholders may vote in person at the corporation's annual meeting or by proxy. A **proxy** is a legal form that lists the issues to be decided at a stockholders' meeting and requests that stockholders transfer their voting rights to some individual or individuals.

proxy A legal form that lists the issues to be decided at a stockholders' meeting and requests that stockholders transfer their voting rights to some individual or individuals.

WHY INVESTORS PURCHASE COMMON STOCK

In the search for investments that offered larger returns, Patricia Nelson invested $10,000 in McDonald's Corporation on January 3, 2005. In February 2013, Nelson's investment had increased to $29,494.[1] What happened? Well, three factors account for her investment's increase in value. First, Nelson made the decision to look at McDonald's stock as an investment alternative when she noticed that the local McDonald's where she often had breakfast and lunch was always busy. People were buying sausage biscuits, hamburgers, chicken tenders, salads, and the firm's other food products. Second, she took the next step and evaluated the firm and its financial performance. She also looked at what stock advisory services said about the company. In all, she spent over 20 hours on the Internet and in the library learning all she could about McDonald's. Finally, McDonald's Corporation did its part. The fast-food chain continued to sell fast-food items in record numbers while managing to improve its operating and marketing activities. Will Nelson's investment continue to increase in value? Will McDonald's stock continue to increase in value? Both good questions, but that's why successful investors like Nelson continue to evaluate their stock investments—even if they are enjoying above average returns.

THE PSYCHOLOGY OF STOCK INVESTING Why do people invest in stocks? Good question—especially when stories about people losing money during the recent economic crisis abound. The simple answer is that investors want the larger returns that stocks offer, even though they are aware of the potential for losses. Just for a moment review the statistics that were presented in Chapter 13.

- Since 1926, stocks, as measured by the Standard & Poor's 500 Stock Index, have averaged an annual return of 9.8 percent.[2]
- Since 1926, stocks had positive gains in 63 years.[3]
- Since 1926, stocks lost money in 25 years.[4]

While the first two items are pretty impressive, investors sometimes forget that stocks can decrease in value. Before you invest in stock, consider the last item one more time: *Since 1926, stocks lost money in 25 years.* For more proof that stocks can decrease in value, just ask a stock investor what happened to the value of their investments during the economic crisis that began in the fall of 2007. In fact, stocks, lost a staggering 37 percent in 2009—in the middle of the economic crisis.[5] Fortunately, at the time of publication, stocks and some other investment alternatives are once again approaching record high values. Still, it is important to remember how important your role is when picking just the right investments to help you obtain your investment goals.

The key to success with any investment program is often the opportunity to allow your investments to work for you over a long period of time. That's why it is so important for people in their 20s and 30s to begin an investment program. The sooner you start investing, the more time your investments have to work for you. In addition to holding stocks for a long period of time, the speculative methods—buying stock on margin, selling short, and trading in options—described at the end of this chapter can also be used to earn returns on stock investments. Be warned: Both long-term and short-term methods should not be used by anyone who doesn't understand the risks involved and the possibility of larger losses.

From a psychological standpoint, many investors have trouble making the decision to buy or sell a stock. Regardless of whether you choose a long-term or short-term method, the following suggestions can be used to reduce anxiety when you make stock investment decisions:

- *Evaluate each investment.* Too often, investors purchase or sell a stock without doing their homework. A much better approach is to become an expert and learn all that you can about the company (and its stock).
- *Analyze the firm's finances.* Look at the company's financial information, which is available in the firm's annual report or on many investment websites. Examine trends for sales, profits, dividends, and other important financial information. More specific information on how to evaluate a firm's finances is provided later in the chapter.
- *Track the firm's product line.* If the firm's products become obsolete and the company fails to introduce new products, its sales—and ultimately, profits—may take a nosedive.
- *Monitor economic developments.* An economic recovery or an economic recession may cause the value of a stock investment to increase or decrease. Also, watch the unemployment rate, inflation rate, interest rates, and similar economic indicators.
- *Be patient.* The secret of success for making money with stocks is often time. If you choose quality stocks based on quality research and in some cases hold on to the stocks before selling, eventually your stock investments will provide average or even above-average returns. And remember: There are no guarantees. Increased returns are always accompanied by increased risk when investing in stocks.

DID YOU KNOW?

Percentage of people in each age group that own stocks.

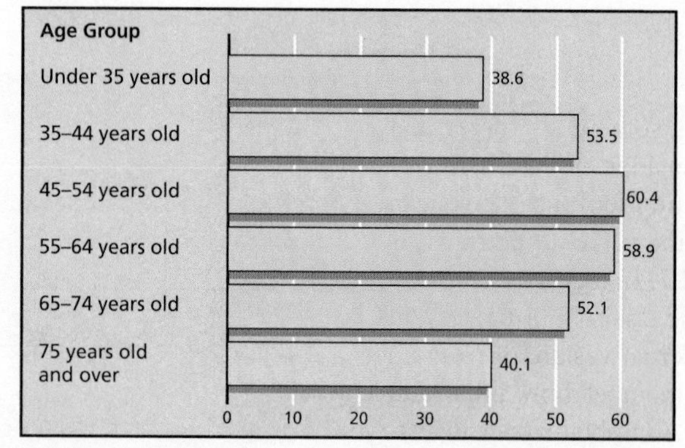

Source: U.S. Bureau of the Census, *Statistical Abstract of the United States* 2012. Website at www.census.gov, accessed February 19, 2013, Table 1211.

How do you make money by buying common stock? Basically, there are two ways: income from dividends and dollar appreciation of stock value. In addition to dividend income and dollar appreciation, a stock split may affect the value of a corporation's stock.

INCOME FROM DIVIDENDS Investors must be concerned about the corporation's ability to earn profits and pay dividends in the future. Keep in mind that if a corporation isn't profitable, it is unlikely that stockholders will continue to receive income from dividends. Also, remember that the board of directors for a corporation must approve all dividend distributions to stockholders. While the corporation's board members are under no legal obligation to pay dividends, most board members like to keep stockholders happy (and prosperous). Therefore, board members usually declare dividends if the corporation's after-tax profits are sufficient for them to do so.

Corporate dividends for common stock may take the form of cash, additional stock, or company products. However, the last type of dividend is extremely unusual. If the board of directors declares a cash dividend, each common stockholder receives an equal amount per share. Although dividend policies vary, most corporations pay dividends on a quarterly basis.

Notice in Exhibit 14-1 that Chevron corporation declared a quarterly dividend of $0.90 per share to stockholders who own the stock on the record date of February 15. The **record date** is the date on which a stockholder must be registered on the corporation's books in order to receive dividend payments. When a stock is traded around the record date, the company must determine whether the buyer or the seller is entitled to the dividend. To solve this problem, this rule is followed: *Dividends remain with the stock until two business days before the record date.* On the second day before the record date, the stock begins selling *ex-dividend.* The term **ex-dividend** describes a situation when a stock trades "without dividend," and the seller—not the buyer—is entitled to a declared dividend payment.

record date The date on which a stockholder must be registered on the corporation's books in order to receive dividend payments.

ex-dividend A situation when a stock trades "without dividend," and the seller—not the buyer—is entitled to a declared dividend payment.

For example, Chevron declared a quarterly dividend of $0.90 per share to stockholders who owned its stock on Friday, February 15. The stock went ex-dividend on Wednesday, February 13, *two business days* before the February 15 date. A stockholder who purchased the stock on Wednesday, February 13, or after was not entitled to this quarterly dividend payment. Chevron made the actual dividend payment on Monday, March 11 to stockholders who owned the stock on the record date. Investors are generally very conscious of the date on which a stock goes ex-dividend, and the dollar value of the stock may go down by the value of the quarterly dividend.

DOLLAR APPRECIATION OF STOCK VALUE In most cases, you purchase stock and then hold onto that stock for a period of time. If the market value of the stock increases, you must decide whether to sell the stock at the higher price or continue to hold it. If you decide to sell the stock, the dollar amount of difference between the purchase price and the selling price represents your profit.

Let's assume that on January 4, 2007, you purchased 100 shares of Walt Disney stock at a cost of $34 a share. Your cost for the stock was $3,400 plus $25 in commission charges, for a total investment of $3,425. (*Note:* Commissions, a topic covered later in this chapter, are charged when you buy stock and when you sell stock.) Let's also assume you held your 100 shares until January 4, 2013, and then sold them for $52 a share. During the six-year period you owned Disney stock, the company paid

1	2	3	4
Company	Amount of Dividend	Record Date	Payable Date
Chevron	$0.90	Fri., February 15	Mon., March 11

1. Name of the company that will pay the dividend: Chevron
2. The dollar amount of the dividend: $0.90 per share
3. The record date: Friday, February 15. Stockholders must be registered on the corporate books by the record date in order to receive this quarterly dividend. The stock begins selling "ex-dividend" Wednesday, February 13—two days before the record date.
4. The payable date: Monday, March 11. The quarterly dividend is actually paid to stockholders of record on this date.

Source: The Chevron Corporation website at www.chevron.com, accessed February 19, 2013.

Exhibit 14-1

Information about corporate dividends is available by using the Internet to access a corporation's website or other investment sites. The numbers above each of the columns correspond to the numbered entries in the list of explanations.

HOW TO...

Open an Account with a Brokerage Firm

Often people never begin investing because they don't know how to open a brokerage account. In reality, it's easier than you think if you follow the steps below.

Take This Step	Suggested Action
1. Develop investment goals and establish an emergency fund.	You may want to review both topics in Chapter 13. In a nutshell, you should establish an emergency fund equal to at least three months' of living expenses. Your goals must be specific, measurable, and tailored to your particular financial needs. Don't skip this step—it's important.
2. Choose the type of brokerage account that meets your needs.	Before making this decision, research the following three types of accounts:• A taxable account with no immediate or deferred tax benefits.• A traditional IRA account with immediate tax benefits, but requires you to pay taxes when money is withdrawn when you reach age 59.5 or older.• A Roth IRA with no immediate tax benefits, but tax-free withdrawals of earnings when you reach age 59.5 or older.
3. Save some money.	While the amount varies, most brokerage firms require an initial deposit of $500 to $2,000 to open an account. The minimum amount also may depend on if you are opening a taxable, traditional IRA, or Roth IRA account.
4. Research different brokerage firms.	All brokerage firms have a website where you can get information about commissions, fees, available research, financial advice, and other important topics. Don't just choose the last company you saw advertised on TV. Do the research.
5. Do the paperwork.	Once you have made the choice, you can go online and follow the steps required to open an account. You can also talk to the firm's representative by going to a branch office or by telephone.

dividends totaling $2.80 per share. Exhibit 14-2 shows your return on the investment.[6] In this case, you made money because of dividend payments and because the value of a share of Disney stock increased from $34 to $52 a share. Of course, if the stock's value had decreased, or if the firm's board of directors had reduced or voted to omit dividends, your return might have been less than the original investment.

WHAT HAPPENS WHEN A CORPORATION SPLITS ITS STOCK?

A **stock split** is a procedure in which the shares of stock owned by existing stockholders are divided into a larger number of shares. In late December 2012, for example, the board of directors of Nike approved a 2-for-1 stock split. After the stock split, a stockholder who had previously owned 100 shares now owned 200 shares. Most common stock splits are 2-for-1, 3-for-1, and 3-for-2.

stock split A procedure in which the shares of stock owned by existing stockholders are divided into a larger number of shares.

Why do corporations split their stock? In many cases, a firm's management has a theoretical ideal price range for the firm's stock. If the market value of the stock rises above the ideal range, a stock split brings the market value back in line. In the case of Nike, the 2-for-1 stock split reduced the market value to one-half of the stock's value on the day prior to the split. The lower market value for each share of stock was the result of dividing the dollar value of the company by a larger number of shares of common stock. Also, a decision to split a company's stock and the resulting lower market value may make the stock more attractive to the investing public. This attraction is based on the belief that most corporations split their stock only when their financial future is improving and revenues and profits are on the upswing.

Be warned: There are no guarantees that a stock's market value will go up after a split. It is important to understand this warning, because investors often think that a stock split leads to long-term profits. Nothing could be further from the truth. Here's why. The total market *capitalization*—the value of the company's stock and other securities—does not change because a corporation splits its stock. Notice the effect of a 2-for-1 stock split on common stock issued by Martin & Martin Inc., illustrated in Exhibit 14-3. Total capitalization ($100 million) and annual earnings ($4 million) are unaffected by the stock split. The earnings per share declines to $1 per share because annual earnings are divided by twice as many shares. In simple terms, the earnings "pie" is the same size but has been sliced up into more pieces.

I know how to make money with stock investments.

Basically, there are three methods investors can use to earn a financial return on stock investments: (1) income from dividends, (2) dollar appreciation of stock value; and (3) possible gains from stock splits.

Keep in mind, that while you can make money on a short-term basis with stock investments, a better approach is to invest in quality stocks for a long period of time. If you start early when you are in your twenties or thirties, your stock investments have more time to grow and appreciate in value.

Exhibit 14-2

Sample stock transaction for Walt Disney

Assumptions

100 shares of common stock purchased January 4, 2007, sold January 4, 2013; total dividends of $2.80 per share for the investment period.

Costs when purchased		***Return when sold***	
100 shares @ $34	= $3,400	100 shares @ $52	= $5,200
Plus commission	+ 25	Minus commission	− 25
Total investment	$3,425	Total return	$5,175

Transaction summary	
Total return	$5,175
Minus total investment	−3,425
Profit from stock sale	$1,750
Plus dividends	+ 280
Total return for the transaction	$2,030

Exhibit 14-3

Effect of a 2-for-1 stock split on capitalization and earnings per share for common stock issued by Martin & Martin Inc.

Assume that the firm has two million shares before the split and four million shares after the split.

	Total Capitalization	Annual Earnings	Number of Shares	Earnings per Share
Before the split	$100,000,000	$4,000,000	2,000,000	$2
After the split	$100,000,000	$4,000,000	4,000,000	$1

Although there is often a lot of frenzy, with brokers pushing investors to purchase a stock before a stock is split in order to make short-term profits, keep in mind that a stock's long-term value is always determined by the firm's ability to generate sales, earn profits, and introduce new products.

PREFERRED STOCK

preferred stock A type of stock that gives the owner the advantage of receiving cash dividends before common stockholders are paid any dividends.

In addition to, or instead of, purchasing common stock, you may purchase preferred stock. **Preferred stock** is a type of stock that gives the owner the advantage of receiving cash dividends before common stockholders are paid any dividends. This is the most important priority an investor in preferred stock enjoys. Unlike the amount of the dividend on common stock, the dollar amount of the dividend on preferred stock is known before the stock is purchased.

Preferred stocks are often referred to as "middle" investments because they represent an investment midway between common stock (an ownership position for the stockholder) and corporate bonds (a creditor position for the bondholder). When compared to corporate bonds, the yield on preferred stocks is often higher than the yield on bonds but less secure than corporate bonds. When compared to common stocks, preferred stocks are safer investments that offer more secure dividends. They are often purchased by individuals who need a predictable source of income greater than offered by common stock investments. They are also purchased by other corporations, because corporations receive a tax break on the dividend income from stock investments. For all other investors, preferred stocks lack the growth potential that common stocks offer and the safety of many corporate bond issues.

While preferred stock does not represent a legal debt that must be repaid, if the firm is dissolved or declares bankruptcy, preferred stockholders do have first claim to the corporation's assets after creditors (including bondholders). In reality, preferred stockholders don't receive anything in most bankruptcies, because creditors have a priority claim and must be paid before preferred stockholders receive anything.

Preferred stock, like common stock, is equity financing that does not have to be repaid. And dividends on preferred stock, as on common stock, may be omitted by action of the board of directors.

PRACTICE QUIZ 14-1

1 Why do corporations issue common stock?
2 Describe the two reasons why investors purchase common stock.
3 Why do corporations split their stock? Is a stock split good or bad for investors?
4 What is the most important priority a preferred stockholder has compared to common stockholders?

Evaluating a Stock Issue

LO14-2

Explain how you can evaluate stock investments.

Many investors are unwilling to spend the time required to become a good investor. They wouldn't buy a car without a test drive, but for some unknown reason they invest without doing their homework. The truth is that there is no substitute for a few hours of detective work when choosing an investment. A wealth of information is available to stock investors, and a logical place to start the evaluation process for stock is with the classification of different types of stock investments.

CLASSIFICATION OF STOCK INVESTMENTS

When evaluating a stock investment, stockbrokers, financial planners, and investors often classify stocks into different categories (See Exhibit 14-4). *Be warned:* Regardless of a stock's classification, a stock is a speculative investment because there are no guarantees. Before investing in stocks, it may be useful to review the risk–return trade-off that was discussed in Chapter 13. You may also want to review the concept of asset allocation that was discussed in Chapter 13 because some of the 10 stock classifications described in Exhibit 14-4 may help you diversify your stock portfolio.

THE INTERNET

In this section, we examine some websites that are logical starting points when evaluating a stock investment, but there are many more than those described. Let's begin with information about the corporation that is available on the Internet.

Exhibit 14-4

Classification of stock investments

Investors often classify stock into the following 10 categories.

Type of Stock	Characteristics of This Type of Investment
Blue chip	A safe investment that generally attracts conservative investors.
Cyclical	A stock that follows the business cycle of advances and declines in the economy.
Defensive	A stock that provides consistent dividends and stable earnings during declines in the economy.
Growth	A stock issued by a corporation that has the potential of earning profits above the average profits of all firms in the economy.
Income	An investment that pays higher-than-average dividends.
Large cap	A stock issued by a corporation that has a large market capitalization, in excess of $10 billion.
Midcap	A stock issued by a corporation that has market capitalization of between $2 and $10 billion.
Small cap	A stock issued by a company that has a market capitalization of between $300 million and $2 billion.
Micro cap	A stock issued by a company that has a market capitalization of $300 million or less.
Penny stock	A penny stock is often defined as a stock that sells for $1 or less per share (or in some cases, less than $5 per share).

Today most corporations have a website, and the information these sites provide is especially useful. First, it is easily accessible. All you have to do is type in the corporation's URL address or use a search engine to locate the corporation's home page. Second, the information on the corporate website may be more up to date and thorough than printed material obtained from the corporation or outside sources. By clicking on a button, like the Investor Relations button, you can access information on the firm's earnings and other financial factors that could affect the value of the company's stock.

You can also use websites like Yahoo!, Google, MSN, and other search engines to obtain information about stock investments. For example, the Yahoo! Finance website (http://finance.yahoo.com) provides a wealth of information. Under the Stock Investing category, there is a stock screener that will help you pick stock investments. You can also get current market values by entering a corporation's stock symbol and clicking on the Quote Lookup button. If you don't know the symbol, just begin entering the corporation's name and the symbol will be displayed. Notice in Exhibit 14-5, you can obtain price information for the last trade for a share of the Gap common stock, the high and low price for the day, and a 52-week price range for the Gap common stock with a click of a computer's mouse. You can also obtain information about the firm's P-E ratio, earnings per share, dividends, and dividend yield—all topics discussed later in this chapter.

In addition to the current market value, the Yahoo! Finance site provides even more specific information about a particular company. By clicking on the Chart, Financials, Profile, Analyst Opinion, Analyst Estimates, Headlines, SEC Filings, Insider Transactions, or other buttons, which are part of the screen for each corporation, it is possible to obtain even more information.

See Exhibit 14-6 for additional websites that provide detailed information about corporate stocks. How about picking a company like Coca-Cola (symbol KO) or Home Depot (symbol HD) and going exploring on the Internet? To begin, enter the Web address for Yahoo! Finance or one of the websites listed in Exhibit 14-6. Then enter the name or the symbol for one of the above corporations. You'll be surprised at the amount of information you can obtain with a click of your mouse.

In addition, you can use the Internet to access professional advisory services like Standard & Poor's Financial Information Services (www.netadvantage.standardandpoors.com), Morningstar (www.morningstar.com), and Value Line (www.valueline.com). While some of the information provided by these services is free, there may be a charge for the more detailed information you may need to evaluate a stock investment. For more information about professional advisory services and the type of information they provide, read the next section.

Exhibit 14-5

Stock price information available on the Internet

Current information about the price for a share of the Gap common stock is presented below.

Gap Inc. (GPS) - NYSE
32.08 ↑0.12(0.38%) 9:30AM EST - Nasdaq Real Time Price

Prev Close:	31.96	Day's Range:	32.01–32.16
Open:	N/A	52wk Range:	22.53–37.85
Bid:	31.96 × 300	Volume:	5,400
Ask:	32.34 × 500	Avg Vol (3m):	5,938,370
1y Target Est:	39.11	Market Cap:	15,328
Beta:	1.26	P-E (ttm):	15.62
Next Earnings Date:	28-Feb-13	EPS (ttm):	2.05
		Div & Yield:	0.50 (1.00%)

Source: The Yahoo! Finance website at http://finance.yahoo.com, accessed February 24, 2013.

Website and Description	Web Address
Market Watch: Current price information, news, corporate profiles, analyst estimates, and detailed analysis about individual corporate stock issues.	www.marketwatch.com
Reuters: News site that provides detailed information about individual stocks including overview, charts, key developments, financial statements, ratios, sales and earnings estimates, and recommendations. All information is free with the exception of the detailed Research reports.	www.reuters .com/finance/stocks
Standard & Poor's: Many experienced investors rely on S&P's Stock Reports to provide a snapshot of a corporation's activities, performance, and investment outlook. Individual reports are available for purchase.	www.netadvantage. standardandpoors.com
Morningstar: Detailed research that can be used to sort, screen, graph, and report on individual common stocks. Some free information, but a subscription is required for more detailed information.	www.morningstar.com

Exhibit 14-6

Four websites that can help you evaluate a corporation's stock.

STOCK ADVISORY SERVICES

In addition to using online stock advisory services, you can use their printed materials to evaluate potential stock investments. In choosing among the hundreds of stock advisory services that charge fees for their information, you must consider both the quality and the quantity of the information they provide. The information ranges from simple alphabetical listings to newsletters to detailed financial reports.

Value Line, Standard and Poor's, and Morningstar were briefly described in the last section. Here we will examine a detailed report for Dollar Tree that is published in the Value Line Investment Survey (see Exhibit 14-7).

While there is a lot of information about Dollar Tree in Exhibit 14-7, it helps to break down the entire Value Line report into different sections. For example:

- Overall ratings for timeliness, safety, and technical along with price information and projections for the price of a share of stock are included at the top of the report.
- Detailed Information about sales per share, earnings per share, dividends, book value, total sales, net profit, capital structure, and other important financial information is included in the middle and along the left side of the report.
- Information about the type of business and prospects for the future is provided toward the bottom in the right-hand corner.

DID YOU KNOW?

One of the oldest and most recognized measures of stock market activity is The Dow Jones Industrial Average (DJIA). This measure is a price-weighted average of 30 stocks that are considered leaders in the economy. As shown below, the DJIA looks more like a roller coaster ride than most investors would like.

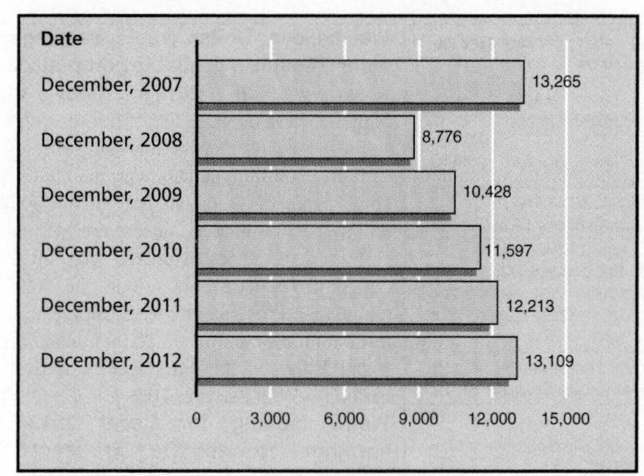

Source: The MarketWatch website at www.marketwatch.com, accessed February 24, 2013.

Exhibit 14-7 Value Line report for the Dollar Tree Corporation

DOLLAR TREE NDQ-DLTR

RECENT PRICE 39.53 | P/E RATIO 15.0 (Trailing: 17.0 Median: 16.0) | RELATIVE P/E RATIO 0.91 | DIV'D YLD Nil | VALUE LINE 2141

TIMELINESS 3 Lowered 3/2/12

SAFETY 1 Raised 5/4/12

TECHNICAL 5 Lowered 1/25/13

BETA .55 (1.00 = Market)

	2001	2002	2003	2004	2005	2006	2007	2008	2009	2010	2011	2012	Target Price Range 2015	2016	2017
High:	11.7	13.7	13.3	11.3	9.8	10.7	15.3	14.7	17.4	29.0	42.3	56.8			
Low:	5.2	6.4	5.8	7.4	6.9	7.8	8.4	6.9	11.0	15.7	24.3	37.1			

LEGENDS
— 12.5 x "Cash Flow" p sh
..... Relative Price Strength
3-for-2 split 6/00
3-for-2 split 6/10
2-for-1 split 6/12
Options. Yes
Shaded area: indicate recession

2015–17 PROJECTIONS

	Price	Gain	Ann'l Total Return
High	85	(+115%)	21%
Low	70	(+75%)	15%

Insider Decisions

	M	A	M	J	J	A	S	O	N
to Buy	0	0	0	0	0	0	0	0	1
Options	2	0	0	0	1	0	1	0	0
to Sell	6	2	2	4	1	2	1	0	0

Institutional Decisions

	1Q2012	2Q2012	3Q2012
to Buy	185	188	218
to sell	271	282	258
Hld's(000)	202584	195230	191452

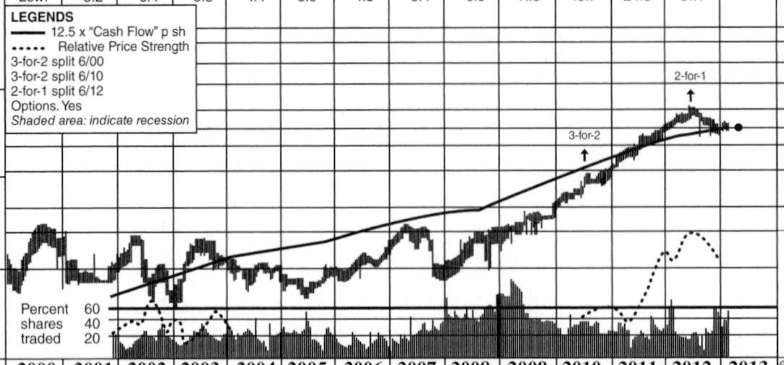

% TOT. RETURN 12/12

	THIS STOCK	VL ARITH INDEX
1 yr.	-2.4	17.4
3 yr.	151.9	40.1
5 yr.	369.4	40.9

1996	1997	1998	1999	2000	2001	2002	2003	2004	2005	2006	2007	2008	2009	2010	2011	2012	2013	© VALUE LINE PUB., LLC.	15–17
1.88	2.41	3.35	4.29	5.02	5.89	6.80	8.18	9.22	10.62	13.28	15.75	17.06	19.92	23.84	28.68	*32.65*	*35.45*	Sales per sh A	*48.55*
.17	.23	.34	.46	.50	.52	.66	.82	.91	.98	1.17	1.34	1.44	1.82	2.26	2.82	*3.25*	*3.60*	"Cash Flow" per sh	*5.80*
.12	.17	.24	.32	.37	.36	.45	.51	.53	.53	.62	.70	.84	1.19	1.55	2.02	*2.50*	*2.80*	Earnings per sh AB	*4.30*
--	--	--	--	--	--	--	--	--	--	--	--	--	--	--	--	--	*Nil*	Div'ds Decl'd per sh	*Nil*
.39	.59	.89	1.29	1.54	1.93	2.50	2.96	3.43	3.67	3.91	3.67	4.60	5.44	5.91	5.82	*7.50*	*9.45*	Book Value per sh C	*17.50*
262.78	264.21	273.95	279.50	336.14	337.52	342.56	342.25	339.06	319.66	298.99	269.35	272.31	262.57	246.79	231.16	*226.00*	*222.00*	Common Shs Outst'g D	*210.00*
26.8	30.1	32.8	27.2	32.8	22.8	22.4	19.7	17.7	15.3	15.4	17.3	13.9	12.7	14.5	17.0	*18.6*		Avg Ann'l P/E Ratio	*17.5*
1.68	1.73	1.71	1.55	2.13	1.17	1.22	1.12	.94	.81	.83	.92	.84	.85	.92	1.07	*1.15*		Relative P/E Ratio	*1.15*
--	--	--	--	--	--	--	--	--	--	--	--	--	--	--	--	--		Avg Ann'l Div'd Yield	*Nil*
						2329.2	2799.9	3126.0	3393.9	3969.4	4242.6	4644.9	5231. 2	5882.4	6630.5	*7380*	*7870*	Sales ($mill) A	*10200*
						39.5%	39.8%	39.7%	38.7%	38.2%	38.2%	37.8%	38.5%	38.2%	38.3%	*38.3%*	*38.3%*	Gross Margin	*38.5%*
						14.0%	14.1%	13.5%	12.5%	11.8%	11.5%	11.4%	12.8	13.4%	14.3%	*15.0%*	*15.0%*	Operating Margin	*15.0%*
						2263	2513	2735	2914	3219	3411	3591	3806	4101	4351	*4625*	*4950*	Number of stores	*6080*
						154.6	177.6	180.3	173.9	192.0	201.3	229.5	320.5	397.3%	488.3	*560*	*640*	Net Profit ($mill)	*915*
						38.5%	38.5%	37.5%	36.8%	36.6%	37.1%	36.1%	36.9%	36.9%	37.4	*37.2%*	*37.5%*	Income Tax Rate	*37.0%*
						6.6%	6.3%	5.8%	5.1%	4.8%	4.7%	4.9%	6.1%	6.8%	7.4%	*7.6%*	*8.1%*	Net Profit Margin	*8.2%*
						509.6	457.5	675.5	648.2	575.7	382.9	663.3	829.7	800.5	628.4	*700*	*900*	Working Cap ($mill)	*1200*
						23.6	154.8	250.5	250.6	250.0	250.0	250.0	250.0	250.0	250.0	*250*	*250*	Long-Term Debt ($mill)	*Nil*
						855.4	1014.5	1164.2	1172.3	1167.3	988.4	1253.2	1429.2	1459.0	1344.6	*1700*	*2100*	Shr.Equity($mill)	*3680*
						17.7%	15.5%	13.0%	12.7%	14.1%	16.9%	15.6%	19.3%	23.4%	30.07%	*29.0%*	*27.5%*	Return on Total Cap'l	*25.0%*
						18.1%	17.5%	15.5%	14.8%	16.4%	20.4%	18.3%	22.4%	27.2%	36.3%	*33.0%*	*30.5%*	Return on Shr. Equity	*25.0%*
						18.1%	17.5%	15.5%	14.8%	16.4%	20.4%	18.3%	22.4%	27.2%	36.3%	*33.0%*	*30.5%*	Retained to Com Eq	*25.0%*
						--	--	--	--	--	--	--	--	--	--	Nil	Nil	All Div'ds to Net Prof.	*Nil*

CAPITAL STRUCTURE as of 10/27/12
Total Debt $264.3 mill. **Due in 5 Yrs** $264.3 mill.
LT Debt $250.0 mill. **LT Interest** $7.0 mill.
(Total int. coverage: over 25x) (14% of Cap'l)
Leases, Uncapitalized Annual rentals $452.9 mill.
No Defined Benefit Pension plan
Pfd Stock None

Common Stock 227,206,335 shs.
as of 11/9/12

MARKET CAP: $9.0 billion (Large Cap)

CURRENT POSITION ($MILL.)	**2010**	**2011**	**10/27/12**
Cash Assets	486.0	288.3	222.4
Receivables	--	--	--
Inventory(FIFO)	803.1	867.4	1133.2
Other	44.2	53.7	52.9
Current Assets	1333.3	1209.4	1408.5
Accts Payable	261.4	286.7	420.0
Debt Due	16.5	15.5	14.3
Other	254.9	276.8	266.7
Current Liab	532.8	581.0	701.0

ANNUAL RATES of change (per sh)	**Past** 10 Yrs	**Past** 5 Yrs	**Est'd '09-'11** to '15–'17
Sales	17.0%	17.0%	12.5%
"Cash Flow"	16.5%	17.5%	16.5%
Earnings	16.0%	23.0%	18.0%
Dividends	--	--	Nil
Book Value	13.5%	9.5%	20.5%

Fiscal Year Begins	QUARTERLY SALES ($ mill.)A Apr.Per	Jul.Per	Oct.Per	Jan.per	Full Fiscal Year
2009	1201.1	1222.8	1248.7	1558.6	5231.2
2010	1352.6	1377.9	1426.6	1725.3	5882.4
2011	1545.9	1542.4	1596.6	1945.6	6630.5
2012	1723.6	1704.6	1720.5	2231.3	*7380*
2013	*1845*	*1840*	*1885*	*2300*	*7870*

Fiscal Year Begins	EARNINGS PER SHARE ABE Apr.Per	Jul.Per	Oct.Per	Jan.per	Full Fiscal Year
2009	.22	.21	.25	.51	1.19
2010	.24	.31	.37	.65	1.55
2011	.41	.39	.44	.80	2.02
2012	.50	.51	.51	*.98*	*2.50*
2013	*.57*	*.57*	*.58*	*1.68*	*2.80*

Calendar	QUARTERLY DIVIDENDS PAID B Mar.31	Jun.30	Sep.30	Dec.31	Full Year
2009	NO CASH DIVIDENDS BEING PAID				
2010					
2011					
2012					
2013					

BUSINESS: Dollar Tree, Inc, operates discount variety stores offering merchandise at the $1.00 price point. Its stores offer a wide assortment of everyday general merchandise: housewares, toys, food, health and beauty aids, gifts, party goods, stationary, closeouts and seasonal items. Dollar Tree operates 4,630 stores in 48 states and Canada. About 190 Deals stores sell some terms at prices greater than $1.00. Acq, Dollar Express, 5/00: Greenbacks. 6/03; Deal$, 3/06; Dollar Giant, 11/10. Has 72,700 employees, officers & directors own 3.1% of stock; BlackRock, 6.6%, FMR, 13.3% (5/12 Proxy) chairman: Macon F, Block, Jr, Pres, & CEO, Bob Sasser, Inc: VA Addr: 500 Volvo Parkway, Chesapeake, VA 23320. Tel: 757-321-5000. Internet www.dollartree.com.

We believe Dollar Tree's earnings rose nicely despite a probable comp-store sales slowdown in 2012's final quarter. Same-store sales were likely flat to up by a low single digit. It appears that stressed low- and middle-income consumers were purchasing fewer consumable items (about half of the company's volume). Discretionary lines were also modestly softer. Management estimated that 2012 final-period share net would fall in the $0.97-$1.02 range, helped by an extra week adding about $120 million to sales and $0.07-$0.08 a share in profits. Even deducting the extra week's impact, share earnings would rise over 10%.

We're looking for fiscal 2013 share earnings to rise to at least $2.80. We believe lackluster conditions will continue for a few quarters, with the company's strongest same-store sales comparisons coming in the second half (versus modest year-earlier figures). Several ideas implemented in the fiscal 2012 might help increase the average $8 transaction size. These include more stationary and candy items, a better selection of impulse items near the cash register, most locations accepting Master Card (credit card users are much bigger spenders than cash purchasers), The company will continue to add freezers and coolers to 300-400 stores (which could lift these locations' sales 5%-10%).

Finances are first-rate. At the end of October, the company had $222.4 million in cash. And that's after purchasing $149.8 million (3.3 million shares) during the third quarter. Dollar Tree typically generates substantial amounts of free cash during the January period, suggesting cash may have at least doubled by fiscal year end. We believe that sum will have been reduced as the company probably bought back more of its shares ($965 million remains under a share repurchase authorization). Note: The share count has been trimmed by one-third since 2003.

Patient buyers will likely be well rewarded over the next 3 to 5 years. Slowing comp-store sales are giving investors a chance to purchase this historically well-run, financially solid chain at 14 times anticipated fiscal 2013 earnings. Moreover, we project future share earnings will grow at a mid-teens pace.

Jerome H. Kaplan *February 1, 2013*

(A) Through 2002, year ended Dec: 31st Afterward, fiscal year ends on Saturday nearest to Jan 31st of the following calendar year.
(B) Diluted earnings. Excludes acquisition costs: '98, $0, 04; '99, $0, 03; '00, $0, 02 incl inventory accounting changes Q1'10, $0.06 Next earning report due February 27th. (C) intang As of 1/28/12: $173.1 mill, $75a stare.
(D) 'in mill., adjusted for stock splits.
(E) Qtrly egs, may not add to total due to change in shares outstanding.

Company's Financial Strength	A++
Stock's Price Stability	80
Price Growth Persistence	75
Earnings Predictability	100

Source: "Dollar Tree" *The Value Line Investment Survey,* (New York: The Value Line Publishing, Inc., 2013), p. 2141.

Other stock advisory services, like Morningstar and Standard & Poor's, provide the same types of information as that in Exhibit 14-7. It is the investor's job to interpret such information and decide whether the company's stock is a good investment. You may want to use the information in Exhibit 14-7 to complete the Financial Planning Case on page 517.

NEWSPAPER COVERAGE AND CORPORATE NEWS

Although some newspapers have eliminated or reduced the amount of financial coverage, *The Wall Street Journal* and some metropolitan newspapers still contain some information about corporate stocks. Although not all newspapers print exactly the same information, they usually provide the basic information. Stocks are listed alphabetically, so your first task is to move down the table to find the stock you're interested in. Then, to read the stock quotation, you simply read across the table. Typical information provided by newspapers includes the name of the company, stock symbol, and price informaion.

I can evaluate stock investments.

In most cases, the search for a quality stock investment begins with a specific company. It may be a company that produces a product or provides a service that you purchased and really like. Then most good investors begin to "dig" for facts about the company and its financial outlook. To practice your skills at evaluating a potential stock investment, complete Personal Financial Planner Sheet No. 58—Corporate Stock Evaluation.

As mentioned in Chapter 13, the federal government requires corporations selling new issues of securities to disclose information about corporate earnings, assets and liabilities, products or services, and the qualifications of top management in a prospectus that they must give to investors. After stock is sold to the public, the federal government also requires that corporations report financial information to the Securities and Exchange Commission (SEC). By accessing the SEC website (www.sec.gov), you can view this information. In addition to the prospectus and the information reported to the SEC, all publicly owned corporations send their stockholders an annual report that contains detailed financial data. Even if you're not a stockholder, you can obtain an annual report from the corporation. For most corporations, all it takes is a call to an 800 number. You can also write to the company or visit their website to obtain an annual report. An annual report can be an excellent tool to learn about a company, its management, its past performance, and its goals.

In addition to newspapers, corporate publications, and government information, many business and personal finance periodicals can help you evaluate a corporation and its stock issues.

1 How would you define (*a*) a blue-chip stock, (*b*) a cyclical stock, (*c*) a defensive stock, (*d*) a growth stock, (*e*) an income stock, (*f*) a large-cap stock, (*g*) a mid cap stock, (*h*) a small-cap stock, (*i*) a micro-cap stock, and (*j*) a penny stock.
2 Which type of stock could help you obtain your investment and financial goals? Justify your choice.
3 What sources of information would you use to evaluate a stock issue?

Numerical Measures That Influence Investment Decisions

LO14-3

Analyze the numerical measures that cause a stock to increase or decrease in value.

In addition to the material in the last section, Evaluating a Stock Issue, many investors rely on numerical measures and different calculations to decide if it is the right time to buy or sell a stock. We begin this section by examining the relationship between a stock's price and a corporation's earnings.

WHY CORPORATE EARNINGS ARE IMPORTANT

Many analysts believe that a corporation's ability or inability to generate earnings in the future is one of the most significant factors that account for an increase or decrease in the price of a stock. Simply put, higher earnings generally equate to higher stock prices. Unfortunately, the reverse is also true. If a corporation's earnings decline, generally the stock's price will also decline. It also helps to remember that the price for a share of stock is determined by what another investor is willing to pay for it. While most successful investors use investment research and financial calculations to choose stock investments, there are times when investors may pay a high, inflated price for a share of stock. For example, the term **stock market bubble** is used to describe a situation when stocks are trading at prices above their actual worth. Often the high stock prices are driven by investor optimism and irrational expectations. Unfortunately, stock market bubbles may burst because of an economic slowdown, high unemployment rates, higher interest rates, and other factors that affect the economy. The bubble for a specific stock can also burst when a company reduces or omits dividend payments to stockholders, lowers earnings expectations, or stockholders begin to sell the stock for any other reason.

stock market bubble A situation in which stocks are trading at prices above their actual worth.

earnings per share A corporation's after-tax income divided by the number of outstanding shares of a firm's common stock.

Many investors consider earnings per share when evaluating the financial health of a corporation. **Earnings per share** is a corporation's after-tax income divided by the number of outstanding shares of a firm's common stock.

EXAMPLE: Earnings Per Share

Assume that in 2012, Great Exploration Corporation has after-tax earnings of $25,000,000. Also assume that Great Exploration has 10,000,000 shares of common stock. This means Great Exploration earnings per share are $2.50, as illustrated below.

$$\text{Earnings per share} = \frac{\text{After-tax income}}{\text{Number of shares outstanding}}$$

$$= \frac{\$25{,}000{,}000}{10{,}000{,}000}$$

$$= \$2.50$$

No meaningful average for this measure exists, mainly because the number of shares of a firm's stock is subject to change via stock splits and stock dividends. *As a general rule, however, an increase in earnings per share is a healthy sign for any corporation and its stockholders.*

price-earnings ratio The price of a share of stock divided by the corporation's earnings per share of stock.

Another calculation, the price-earnings (P-E) ratio can be used to evaluate a potential stock investment. The **price-earnings ratio** is the price of a share of stock divided by the corporation's earnings per share of stock.

EXAMPLE: Price-Earnings (P-E) Ratio

Assume Great Exploration Corporation's common stock is selling for $50 a share. As determined earlier, the corporation's earnings per share are $2.50. Great Exploration's price-earnings ratio is 20, as illustrated below.

$$\text{Price-Earnings (P-E) ratio} = \frac{\text{Price per share}}{\text{Earnings per share}}$$

$$= \frac{\$50.00}{\$\ 2.50}$$

$$= 20$$

The price-earnings ratio is a key calculation that serious investors use to evaluate stock investments. Generally, a price-earnings ratio gives investors an idea of how much they are paying for a company's earning power. The higher the price-earnings ratio, the more investors are paying for earnings. For example, if eBay has a P-E ratio of 27, investors are paying $27 for each dollar the firm earns. Stocks with high price-earnings ratios are often issued by young, fast-growing corporations. For these stocks, a high price-earnings ratio (above 20) often indicates investor optimism because of the expectation of higher earnings in the future. Always remember the relationship between earnings and stock value. If earnings do increase, the stock usually becomes more valuable in the future. On the other hand, stocks with low price-earnings ratios (under 20) tend to be issued by large, established, mature corporations or corporations in mature industries. In these situations, investors have lower earnings expectations. If future earnings don't maintain the same level of growth or decrease, the stock will become less valuable in the future. Like earnings per share, a corporation's P-E ratio is often reported on investment websites. When researching a stock, comparing the P-E ratios of one company to other companies in the *same* industry, to the market in general, or against the company's own historical P-E ratios is usually helpful. Keep in mind that the P-E ratio calculation is just another piece of the puzzle when researching a stock for investment purposes.

PROJECTED EARNINGS

Both earnings per share and the price-earnings ratio are based on *historical* numbers. In other words, this is what the company has done in the past. With this fact in mind, many investors will access investment websites that provide earnings estimates for major corporations. At the time of publication, for example, the MSN money website provided the following earnings estimates for Boeing, a world leader in the aerospace industry.[7]

Boeing	2013	2014
Yearly earnings estimates	$6.38 per share	$7.29 per share

From an investor's standpoint, a projected increase in earnings from $6.38 per share to $7.29 per share is a good sign. In the case of Boeing, these estimates were determined by surveying over 10 different analysts who track the Boeing Corporation. By using the same projected earnings amount, it is possible to calculate a price/earnings to growth (PEG) ratio. For more information about the price/earnings to growth ratio, read the Financial Planning Calculations boxed feature on page 496. Always keep in mind that changes that affect the economy or the company's sales and profit amounts could cause analysts to revise their estimates.

THE PRICE/EARNINGS TO GROWTH RATIO: A LOOK TO THE FUTURE

When evaluating a corporate stock, you may want to calculate a price/earnings-to-growth (PEG) ratio if you want to determine whether a stock is undervalued or not. Unlike the price-earnings ratio based on historical data, the PEG ratio includes a future projection for earnings per share in the calculation. If you use the earnings estimates for Boeing from page 495, the first step is to determine the earnings per share growth stated as a percentage. This percentage is calculated below:

$7.29 (2014) − $6.38 (2013) =
$0.91 (projected change)

$0.91 (projected change) ÷ $6.38 (this year) =
0.14 = 14 percent

Then, the following formula can be used to calculate the PEG ratio:

$$\textbf{PEG ratio} = \frac{\text{Price-earnings ratio}}{\text{Annual EPS growth}}$$

$$= \frac{15}{14\%}$$

$$= 1.07$$

(*Note:* For the above calculation, the 15 represents the current P-E ratio for Boeing. Also, the percent sign (%) is ignored in the above calculation.)

Generally, a PEG value less than 1 implies that a stock may be undervalued based on its projected growth rate. And a PEG value greater than 1 indicates that a stock may be overvalued based on its projected growth rate. With a PEG ratio of 1.07 (15 ÷ 14 = 1.07), Boeing may be overvalued. *Caution: Your answer for the PEG ratio is only as good as the projection for earnings per share growth. If the projections are too high or too low, then the PEG ratio calculation can be an inaccurate predictor of a stock's value.*

Source: Values for Boeing's stock were obtained from the MSN money website, www.money.msn.com, February 24, 2013.

OTHER FACTORS THAT INFLUENCE THE PRICE OF A STOCK

dividend payout The percentage of a firm's earnings paid to stockholders in cash.

Today, many investors purchase stocks for dividend income. Because dividends are a distribution of a corporation's earnings, these same investors must be concerned about the firm's future earnings and the dividend payout. The **dividend payout** is the percentage of a firm's earnings paid to stockholders in cash. This ratio is calculated by dividing the annual dividend amount by the earnings per share.

EXAMPLE: Dividend Payout

Assume you own stock issued by Caterpillar Corporation, and the construction equipment manufacturer pays an annual dividend of $2.08. Also, assume that Caterpillar earns $8.48 a share. The dividend payout is 25 percent, calculated as follows:

$$\text{Dividend payout} = \frac{\text{Annual dividend amount}}{\text{Earnings per share}}$$

$$= \frac{\$2.08}{\$8.48}$$

$$= 0.25 = 25 \text{ percent}$$

dividend yield The annual dividend amount generated by an investment divided by the investment's current price per share.

For Caterpillar, the dividend payout ratio indicates the company is paying 25 percent of earnings to its stockholder. Caterpillar should be able to continue to pay dividends even if earnings should decline. One of the most common calculations investors use to monitor the value of their investments is the dividend yield. The **dividend yield** is the annual dividend amount generated by an investment divided by the investment's current price per share.

EXAMPLE: Dividend Yield

Assume Caterpillar is currently selling for $85 a share and the annual dividend is $2.08 a share. The dividend yield is 2.4 percent, calculated as follows:

$$\text{Dividend yield} = \frac{\text{Annual dividend amount}}{\text{Price per share}}$$

$$= \frac{\$2.08}{\$85}$$

$$= 0.024 = 2.4 \text{ percent}$$

As a general rule, an increase in dividend yield is a healthy sign for any investment. A dividend yield of 4 percent is better than a 2.4 percent dividend yield.

Although the dividend yield calculation is useful, you should also consider whether the investment is increasing or decreasing in dollar value. **Total return** is a calculation that includes not only the yearly dollar amount of dividends but also any increase or decrease in the original purchase price of the investment. The following formula is used to calculate total return:

total return A calculation that includes the annual dollar amount of dividends as well as any increase or decrease in the original purchase price of the investment.

$$\text{Total return} = \text{Dividends} + \text{Capital gain}$$

While this concept may be used for any investment, let's illustrate it by using the assumptions for Caterpillar stock presented in the preceding example.

EXAMPLE: Total Return

Assume that you own 100 shares of Caterpillar stock that you purchased for $78 a share and that you hold your stock for two years before deciding to sell it at the current market price of $85 a share. Also, assume that during the two-year period, Caterpillar paid total dividends of $3.68. Your total return for this investment would be $1,068 calculated as follows:

$$\text{Total Return} = \text{Dividends} + \text{Capital gain}$$

$$= \$368 + \$700$$

$$= \$1{,}068$$

In this example, the dividends total $368 ($3.68 per-share dividend × 100 shares = $368). The capital gain of $700 results from the increase in the stock price from $78 a share to $85 a share ($7.00 per share increase × 100 shares = $700). (Of course, commissions to buy and sell your stock, a topic covered in the next section, would reduce your total return.)

In this example, the investment increased in value and dividends were paid for each of the two years. And while it may be obvious, we should point out that the larger the dollar amount of total return, the better.

The **annualized holding period yield** calculation takes into account the total return, the original investment, and the time the investment is held. The following formula is used to calculate the annualized holding period yield:

annualized holding period yield A yield calculation that takes into account the total return, the original investment, and the time the investment is held.

$$\text{Annualized holding period yield} = \frac{\text{Total return}}{\text{Original investment}} \times \frac{1}{N}$$

where

$$N = \text{Number of years investment is held}$$

TIME VALUE OF MONEY CAN HELP YOU EVALUATE YOUR INVESTMENTS!

Many investors spend substantially more time initially selecting an investment than ensuring that it continues to perform and meet their investment objectives.

Assume that you purchase a *growth* stock that does not pay dividends. In this situation, you plan to make money based upon an increase in the value of the stock over a long period of time. Your investment objective is to make at least 6 percent on your investment each year.

When you initially purchased the stock, you invested $2,400. Three years have passed and the value of your investment is now $2,700. You want to evaluate whether you are meeting your investment objective of 6 percent each year. In this situation, you can use the annualized holding period yield formula to evaluate the performance of your investment.

Step 1: Subtract the value of the investment at the end of three years from your original investment. $2,700 Value at the end of 3 years − $2,400 Original investment = $300 Total Return

Step 2: Use the Annualized Holding Period Yield calculation to determine the annual return.

$$\text{Annualized Holding Period Yield} = \frac{\text{Total return}}{\text{Original investment}} \times \frac{1}{N}$$

(Where N = Number of years the investment is held)

$$= \frac{\$300}{\$2{,}400} \times \frac{1}{3}$$

$$= 0.0417 = 4.17 \text{ percent}$$

CONCLUSION

Based upon the above calculations, the stock is not meeting the objective of earning at least 6 percent a year. You may want to revaluate this investment or possibly sell this investment. Then, you could search for another investment that could help you obtain your objective of a 6 percent annual return.

To illustrate this concept, let's return to your Caterpillar investment, for which the total return was $1,068.

EXAMPLE: Annualized Holding Period Yield

Assume that two years ago you invested $7,800 to purchase 100 shares of Caterpillar stock and that your total return when you sold your stock was $1,068. The annualized holding period yield is 6.8 percent for each of the two years you held the investment, as illustrated below:

$$\text{Annualized holding period yield} = \frac{\text{Total return}}{\text{Original investment}} \times \frac{1}{2}$$

$$= \frac{\$1{,}068}{\$7{,}800} \times \frac{1}{2}$$

$$= 0.068 = 6.8 \text{ percent}$$

There is no meaningful average for annualized holding period yield, because individual investments vary. But an increase in annualized holding period yield is a healthy sign. For instance, an annualized holding period yield of 8 percent is better than one of 6.8 percent.

beta A measure that compares the volatility associated with a specific stock issue with the volatility of the Standard & Poor's 500 Stock Index.

The **beta** is a measure reported in many financial publications that compares the volatility associated with a specific stock issue with the volatility of the Standard & Poor's 500 Stock Index. The beta for the S&P 500 is 1.0. The majority of stocks have betas between 0.5 and 2.0. Generally, conservative stocks have low betas while more speculative stocks have betas greater than one.

EXAMPLE: Beta Calculation (Google)

Assume that the overall stock market increases by 10 percent and that Google has a beta of 1.20. Based on the calculation below, Google is 20 percent more volatile than the stock market and will increase 12 percent when the market increases 10 percent.

$$\text{Volatility for a stock} = \text{Increase in overall market} \times \text{Beta for a specific stock}$$
$$= 10 \text{ percent} \times 1.20$$
$$= 12 \text{ percent}$$

Because individual stocks generally move in the same direction as the stock market, most betas are positive, but it is possible for a stock to have a negative beta. A negative beta occurs when a corporation's stock moves in the opposite direction compared to the stock market in general.

Although little correlation may exist between the market value of a stock and its book value, book value is widely reported in financial publications. Therefore, it deserves mention. The **book value** for a share of stock is determined by deducting all liabilities from the corporation's assets and dividing the remainder by the number of outstanding shares of common stock.

book value Determined by deducting all liabilities from the corporation's assets and dividing the remainder by the number of outstanding shares of common stock.

EXAMPLE: Book Value

If First National Corporation has assets of $60 million and liabilities of $30 million and has issued 1,000,000 shares of common stock, the book value for one share of First National stock is $30, as follows:

$$\text{Book value} = \frac{\text{Assets} - \text{Liabilities}}{\text{Shares outstanding}}$$
$$= \frac{\$60{,}000{,}000 - \$30{,}000{,}000}{1{,}000{,}000 \text{ shares of stock}}$$
$$= \$30 \text{ per share}$$

Investors can also calculate a market-to-book ratio (sometimes called a price-to-book ratio). The **market-to-book ratio** is the current market value of one share of stock divided by the book value for one share of stock.

market-to-book ratio The current market value of one share of stock divided by the book value for one share of stock.

EXAMPLE: Market-to-Book Ratio

Using First National's $30 per share book value and assuming the stock has a current market price of $36 a share, the market-to-book ratio would be 1.20 as follows:

$$\text{Market-to-book ratio} = \frac{\text{Market value per share}}{\text{Book value per share}}$$
$$= \frac{\$36}{\$30}$$
$$= 1.20$$

A low market-to-book ratio (less than 1) could mean that the stock is undervalued, and a high market-to-book (greater than 1) ratio could mean that a stock is overvalued. And yet, it is a mistake to look at just this ratio to make an investment decision. A better approach is to examine *all* of the available information described in the last section and the numerical calculations in this section before making an investment decision.

Some investors believe they have found a bargain when a stock's market value is about the same as or lower than its book value. *Be warned:* Book value and market-to-book ratio calculations may be misleading, because the dollar amount of assets used in the above formula may be understated or overstated on the firm's financial statements.

fundamental analysis An investment practice based on the assumption that a stock's intrinsic or real value is determined by the company's future earnings.

technical analysis An investment practice based on the assumption that a stock's market value is determined by the forces of supply and demand in the stock market as a whole.

efficient market hypothesis (EMH) An investment theory based on the assumption that stock price movements are purely random.

INVESTMENT THEORIES

Investors sometimes use three different investment theories to determine a stock's value. **Fundamental analysis** is based on the assumption that a stock's intrinsic or real value is determined by the company's future earnings. If a corporation's expected earnings are higher than its present earnings, the corporation's stock should increase in value. If its expected earnings are lower than its present earnings, the stock should decrease in value. In addition to expected earnings, fundamentalists consider (1) the financial strength of the company, (2) the type of industry the company is in, (3) new-product development, and (4) the economic growth of the overall economy. The goal of fundamental analysis is to find a stock's intrinsic value, which is a fancy way of trying to determine what you think a stock is really worth instead of what the stock is actually trading for in the marketplace. If you find a stock with an intrinsic value that is more than the current market price, it makes sense to buy the stock. One of the most famous and successful users of fundamental analysis is Warren Buffett, the chairman and CEO of Berkshire Hathaway. Mr. Buffett is well known for successfully employing fundamental analysis to identify both stocks and corporations that are undervalued. His ability to use fundamental analysis has turned him into a billionaire.[8]

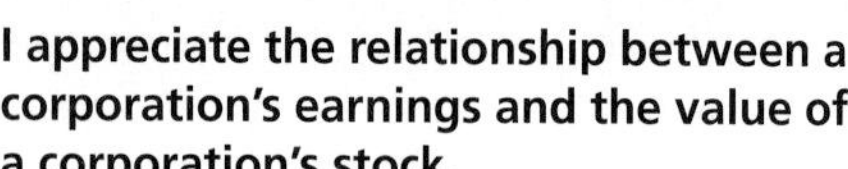

I appreciate the relationship between a corporation's earnings and the value of a corporation's stock.

Numbers, formulas, ratios! What do they all mean? For an investor, they could mean the difference between a profit and loss on a stock investment. To provide more practice on these important calculations, complete the financial problems at the end of this chapter.

Technical analysis is based on the assumption that a stock's market value is determined by the forces of supply and demand in the stock market as a whole, *not* on the expected earnings or the intrinsic value of an individual corporation's stock. Technical analysis is also based on the assumption that past market trends can predict the future direction for the market as a whole. Typical technical factors are price movements, the total number of shares traded, the number of buy orders, and the number of sell orders over a period of time. Technical analysts, sometimes called *chartists,* construct charts or use computer programs to plot past price movements and other market averages. These charts allow them to observe trends and patterns for the market as a whole that enable them to predict the effect that changes in supply and demand will have on different securities.

The **efficient market hypothesis (EMH)** is based on the assumption that stock price movements are purely random. Advocates of the efficient market hypothesis assume the stock market is completely efficient and buyers and sellers have considered all of the available information about an individual stock. According to this theory, it is impossible for an investor to outperform the average for the stock market as a whole over a long period of time. Advocates of the efficient market hypothesis believe it is useless to identify undervalued or overvalued stocks and the only way to achieve superior results is to pick riskier investments. Most investors reject the efficient market hypothesis on the assumption that, by means of the fundamental theory, technical analysis, or a combination of the two theories, they can improve their performance (and ultimately their financial returns) in the stock market.

PRACTICE QUIZ 14-3

1 Explain the relationship between earnings and a stock's market value.
2 Why are earnings per share and price-earnings calculations important?
3 What are the formulas for dividend payout, dividend yield, total return, annualized holding period yield, book value, and market-to-book ratio?
4 Explain how fundamental analysis, technical analysis, or the efficient market hypothesis can be used to describe price movements for the stock market.

Corporate Stock Evaluation

Buying and Selling Stocks

LO14-4

Describe how stocks are bought and sold.

To purchase common or preferred stock, you generally have to work through a brokerage firm. In turn, your brokerage firm must buy the stock in either the primary or secondary market. In the **primary market,** you purchase financial securities, via an investment bank or other representative, from the issuer of those securities. An **investment bank** is a financial firm that assists corporations in raising funds, usually by helping to sell new security issues.

New security issues sold through an investment bank can be issued by corporations that have sold stocks and bonds before and need to sell new issues to raise additional financing. The new securities can also be initial public offerings. An **initial public offering (IPO)** occurs when a corporation sells stock to the general public for the first time. For example, Xoom, a corporation that enables customers to wire cash to friends and relatives in 30 different countries, used an IPO to raise approximately $100 million in 2013. The company used the money to fund business expansion and other business activities.[9] *Be warned:* The promise of quick profits often lures investors to purchase IPOs. An IPO is generally classified as a high-risk investment—one made in the hope of earning a relatively large profit in a short time. Depending on the corporation selling the new security, IPOs are usually too speculative for most people.

After a stock has been sold through the primary market, it is traded through the secondary market. The **secondary market** is a market for existing financial securities that are currently traded among investors. Once stocks are sold in the primary market, they can be sold time and again in the secondary market.

primary market A market in which an investor purchases financial securities, via an investment bank or other representative, from the issuer of those securities.

investment bank A financial firm that assists corporations in raising funds, usually by helping to sell new security issues.

initial public offering (IPO) Occurs when a corporation sells stock to the general public for the first time.

secondary market A market for existing financial securities that are currently traded among investors.

securities exchange A marketplace where member brokers who represent investors meet to buy and sell securities.

SECONDARY MARKETS FOR STOCKS

When you purchase stock in the secondary market, the transaction is completed on a securities exchange or through the over-the-counter market.

SECURITIES EXCHANGES A **securities exchange** is a marketplace where member brokers who represent investors meet to buy and sell securities. The securities sold at a particular exchange must first be listed, or accepted for trading, at that exchange. Generally, the securities issued by nationwide corporations are traded at either the New York Stock Exchange or regional exchanges. The securities of very large corporations may be traded at more than one exchange. American firms that do business abroad may also be listed on foreign securities exchanges—in Tokyo, London, or Paris, for example.

The New York Stock Exchange (now owned by the NYSE Euronext holding company) is one of the largest securities exchanges in the world. The NYSE Euronext exchange lists stocks for more than 8,000 corporations.[10] Most of NYSE members represent brokerage firms that charge commissions on security trades made by their representatives for their customers. Other members are called *specialists* or *specialist firms.* A **specialist** buys *or* sells a particular stock in an effort to maintain an orderly market.

The stock of corporations that cannot meet the NYSE requirements, find it too expensive to be listed on the NYSE, or choose not to be listed on the NYSE is often traded on one of the regional exchanges or through the over-the-counter market.

specialist Buys or sells a particular stock in an effort to maintain an orderly market.

over-the-counter (OTC) market A network of dealers who buy and sell the stocks of corporations that are not listed on a securities exchange.

Nasdaq An electronic marketplace for approximately 3,200 different stocks.

account executive A licensed individual who buys or sells securities for clients; also called a *stockbroker.*

THE OVER-THE-COUNTER MARKET Not all securities are traded on organized exchanges. Stocks issued by several thousand companies are traded in the over-the-counter market. The **over-the-counter (OTC) market** is a network of dealers who buy and sell the stocks of corporations that are not listed on a securities exchange. Today these stocks are not really traded over the counter. The term was coined more than 100 years ago when securities were sold "over the counter" in stores and banks.

Many stocks are traded through Nasdaq (pronounced "nazzdack"). **Nasdaq** is an electronic marketplace for approximately 3,300 different stocks.[11] In addition to providing price information, this computerized system allows investors to buy and sell shares of companies listed on Nasdaq. When you want to buy or sell shares of a company that trades on Nasdaq—say, Microsoft—your account executive sends your order into the Nasdaq computer system, where it shows up on the screen with all the other orders from people who want to buy or sell Microsoft. Then a Nasdaq dealer (sometimes referred to as a *market maker*) matches buy and sell orders for Microsoft. Once a match is found, your order is completed.

Nasdaq is known for its innovative, forward-looking growth companies. Although many securities are issued by smaller companies, some large firms, including Intel, Microsoft, and Cisco Systems, also trade on Nasdaq.

BROKERAGE FIRMS AND ACCOUNT EXECUTIVES

An **account executive,** or *stockbroker,* is a licensed individual who buys or sells securities for his or her clients. Before choosing an account executive, you should have already determined your financial objectives. Then you must be careful to communicate those objectives to the account executive so that he or she can do a better job of advising you. Needless to say, account executives may err in their investment recommendations. To help avoid a situation in which your account executive's recommendations are automatically implemented, you should be *actively* involved in your investment program and you should never allow your account executive to use his or her discretion without your approval. *Finally, keep in mind that account executives generally are not liable for client losses that result from their recommendations.* In fact, most brokerage firms require new clients to sign a statement in which they promise to submit any complaints to an arbitration board. This arbitration clause generally prevents a client from suing an account executive or a brokerage firm.

DID YOU KNOW?

The Securities Investor Protection Corporation (SIPC) protects customers as long as their brokerage firm is an SIPC member.

- If your brokerage firm fails, you get back all securities that are already registered in your name or are in the process of being registered.
- You could get up to $500,000 that includes a maximum of $250,000 for cash claims if a failed brokerage firm doesn't have enough funds or securities to satisfy claims.

Source: The Securities Investor Protection Corporation website at www.sipc.org, accessed February 27, 2013.

SHOULD YOU USE A FULL-SERVICE, DISCOUNT, OR ONLINE BROKERAGE FIRM?

Today a healthy competition exists between full-service, discount, and online brokerage firms. While the most obvious difference between firms is the amount of the commissions they charge when you buy or sell stock and other securities, there are other factors to consider. For example, consider how much research information is available and how much it costs. Most brokerage firms offer excellent research materials, but you are more likely to pay extra for detailed information if you choose a discount or online brokerage firm.

Also, consider how much help you need when making an investment decision. Although there are many exceptions, the information below may help you decide whether to use a full-service, discount, or online brokerage firm.

• Full service	Beginning investors with little or no experience.Individuals who are uncomfortable making investment decisions.
• Discount	People who understand the "how to" of researching stocks and prefer to make their own decisions. Individuals who are uncomfortable trading stocks online.
• Online	People who understand the "how to" of researching stocks and prefer to make their own decisions. Individuals who are comfortable trading stocks online.

Finally, consider how easy it is to buy and sell stock and other securities when using a full-service, discount, or online brokerage firm. Questions to ask include:

1. Can I buy or sell stocks online or over the phone?
2. Where is your nearest office located?
3. Do you have a toll-free telephone number for customer use?
4. Is there a charge for statements, research reports, and other financial reports?
5. Are there any fees in addition to the commissions I pay when I buy or sell stocks?

my life 4

I know what factors to consider when choosing an account executive and a brokerage firm.

While all brokerage firms can buy and sell stocks and other securities for you, there are important differences. For help making the right choice, go to the brokerage firm's website. Take a look at the information contained on the websites for at least three different brokerage firms. You can use Personal Financial Planner Sheet No. 59 to compare account executives and brokerage firms.

COMMISSION CHARGES

Most brokerage firms have a minimum commission ranging from $5 to $25 for buying *and* selling stock. Additional commission charges are based on the number of shares and the value of stock bought and sold. Exhibit 14-8 shows the minimum amount to open an account and typical commissions charged by online brokerage firms.

Generally, full-service and discount brokerage firms charge higher commissions than those charged by online brokerage firms. As a rule of thumb, full-service brokers may charge approximately 1 percent of the transaction amount.

Exhibit 14-8

Typical commission charges for online stock transactions.

	Minimum to Open an Account	Internet Trades	Broker-Assisted Trades
E*Trade	$ 500	$9.99	$54.99
Schwab	1,000	8.95	33.95
Scottrade	500	7.00	27.00
TD Ameritrade	0	9.99	44.99

Source: The BrokerStance website at www.brokerstance.com, accessed February 27, 2013.

For example, if you use a full-service brokerage firm to purchase Verizon stock valued at $10,000, and the brokerage firm charges 1 percent, you will pay commissions totaling $100 ($10,000 × 0.01 = $100). In return for charging higher commissions, full-service brokers usually spend more time with each client, help make investment decisions, and provide free research information.

While full-service brokerage firms usually charge higher commissions, on some occasions a discount brokerage firm may charge higher commissions. This generally occurs when the transaction is small, involving a total dollar amount of less than $1,000, and the investor is charged the discount brokerage firm's minimum commission charge. Also, many brokerage firms—especially online firms—will offer a specific number of free trades to attract new customers.

COMPLETING STOCK TRANSACTIONS

Once you and your account executive have decided on a particular stock investment, it is time to execute an order to buy or sell. Today most investors either trade online or telephone their account executives. Let's begin by examining three types of orders used to trade stocks.

market order A request to buy or sell a stock at the current market value.

A **market order** is a request to buy or sell a stock at the current market value. Since the stock exchange is an auction market, the account executive's representative will try to get the best price available and the transaction will be completed as soon as possible. Payment for stocks is generally required within three business days after the transaction. Then, in about four to six weeks, a stock certificate is sent to the purchaser of the stock, unless the securities are left with the brokerage firm for safekeeping. Today it is common practice for investors to leave stock certificates with a brokerage firm. Because the stock certificates are in the broker's care, transfers when the stock is sold are much easier. The phrase "left in the street name" is used to describe investor-owned securities held by a brokerage firm.

limit order A request to buy or sell a stock at a specified price or better.

A **limit order** is a request to buy or sell a stock at a specified price or better. When you purchase stock, a limit order ensures that you will buy at the best possible price but not above a specified dollar amount. When you sell stock, a limit order ensures that you will sell at the best possible price, but not below a specified dollar amount. For example, if you place a limit order to buy Macy's common stock for $40 a share, the stock will not be purchased until the price drops to $40 a share or lower. Likewise, if your limit order is to sell Macy's for $40 a share, the stock will not be sold until the price rises to $40 a share or higher. *Be warned:* Limit orders are executed if and when the specified price or better is reached and *all* other previously received orders have been fulfilled.

stop-loss order An order to sell a particular stock at the next available opportunity after its market price reaches a specified amount.

Many stockholders are certain they want to sell their stock if it reaches a specified price. A limit order does not guarantee this will be done. With a limit order, as mentioned above, orders by other investors may be placed ahead of your order. If you want to guarantee that your order will be executed, you place a special type of order known as a stop-loss order. A **stop-loss order** is an order to sell a particular stock at the next available opportunity after its market price reaches a specified amount. This type of order is used to protect an investor against a sharp drop in price and thus stop the dollar loss on a stock investment. For example, assume you purchased Ford common stock at $14 a share. Two weeks after making your investment, Ford is facing multiple product liability lawsuits. Fearing that the market value of your stock will decrease, you enter a stop-loss order to sell your Ford stock at $10. This means that if the price of the stock decreases to $10 or lower, the account executive will sell it. While a stop order does not guarantee that your stock will be sold at the price you specified, it does guarantee that it will be sold at the next available opportunity. Both limit and stop-loss orders may be good for one day, one week, one month, good until canceled (GTC), or a specified date.

PRACTICE QUIZ 14-4

1 What is the difference between the primary market and the secondary market?
2 Describe the types of orders that are used to buy or sell stocks in the secondary market.
3 Assume you want to purchase stock. Would you use a full-service broker or a discount broker? Would you ever trade stocks online?

eXcel PFP Sheet 59
Investment broker comparison

Long-Term and Short-Term Investment Strategies

LO14-5

Explain the trading techniques used by long-term investors and short-term speculators.

One of the facts we have stressed throughout this text is the need to start a savings and investment program as soon as possible. Long-term stock investments are a very effective option that allows you to take advantage of the time value of money concept. As mentioned in the first part of this chapter, stocks have returned on average 9.8 percent a year—substantially more than other investment alternatives—since 1926. And while there have been years when stocks didn't earn 9.8 percent or possibly went down in value, investing for the long term allows you to "get through the rough years" and "enjoy the good years" when your investments are earning 9.8 percent or even more.

Once you purchase stock, the investment may be classified as either long term or short term. Generally, individuals who hold an investment for a long period of time are referred to as *investors*. Typically, long-term investors hold their investments for at least a year or longer. Individuals who routinely buy and then sell stocks within a short period of time are called *speculators* or *traders*.

DID YOU KNOW?

Wall Street is a street name of historical significance. Here's the story. Back in the 17th century, Dutch settlers on the southern tip of Manhattan Island erected a wall to protect their colony. Even though the wall was never used for defensive purposes, the name remains and is now recognized as one of the most famous streets in the financial world.

LONG-TERM TECHNIQUES

In this section, we discuss the long-term techniques of buy and hold, dollar cost averaging, direct investment programs, and dividend reinvestment programs.

BUY-AND-HOLD TECHNIQUE Many long-term investors purchase stock and hold onto it for a number of years. When they do this, their investment can increase in value two ways. First, they are entitled to dividends if the board of directors approves dividend payments to stockholders. While stockholders can use dividends for immediate needs, another option is to reinvest the dividends in either the same stock or a different investment alternative. By reinvesting the dividends, even small amounts can increase over a long period of time. Second, the price of the stock may go up. To see the effect of an increase in stock value over a long period of time, you may want to review the sample stock transaction for The Walt Disney Company illustrated in Exhibit 14-2. Over a six-year period, both dividends *and* increase in value contributed to total profits for this investment. Finally, keep in mind that corporations do split their stock for

HOW DO I PICK A WINNING STOCK?

Good question! Now for some answers. Stock investors who are willing to do their homework can make sense out of all the information and numbers that are available. Below are some suggestions for pulling it all together.

1. LEARN WHY THE INFORMATION AND NUMBERS ARE IMPORTANT.

There are many sources—this chapter, self-help investing books, and Internet investment sites—that will help you learn the "how to" of researching a stock investment.

2. DEVELOP A PLAN OR A SYSTEM TO HELP ORGANIZE THE DATA.

With so much information available, you need to organize the information so that it makes sense. One suggestion is to use the Personal Financial Planner sheet 58, "Corporate Stock Evaluation," as a starting point. You can customize this sheet by adding or deleting questions that help you to establish a database of information for each potential stock investment.

3. USE SOFTWARE AND FINANCIAL CALCULATORS TO FINE TUNE YOUR INVESTMENT SELECTIONS.

Many investment websites have both software and financial calculators that will help you evaluate a corporate stock. For example, a financial calculator that provides detailed information is MSN Money's StockScouter Report (http://money.msn.com).

A FINAL WORD OF CAUTION!

Making informed investment decisions takes hard work and time. While each of the above suggestions will help you accumulate the information you need to make a more informed decision, a better approach is to use all three suggestions *and* any other available information to get a more complete picture of a corporation and the investment potential for its stock.

various reasons. Although there are no guarantees that a stock split will increase the value of your stock over a long period of time, it is a factor that should be considered when choosing stocks that have a history of stock splits or stocks that may split in the future.

dollar cost averaging A long-term technique used by investors who purchase an equal dollar amount of the same stock at equal intervals.

direct investment plan A plan that allows stockholders to purchase stock directly from a corporation without having to use an account executive or a brokerage firm.

dividend reinvestment plan A plan that allows current stockholders the option to reinvest or use their cash dividends to purchase stock of the corporation.

DOLLAR COST AVERAGING

Dollar cost averaging is a long-term technique used by investors who purchase an equal dollar amount of the same stock at equal intervals. Assume you invest $2,000 in Johnson & Johnson's common stock each year for a period of seven years. The results of your investment program are illustrated in Exhibit 14-9. The average cost for a share of stock, determined by dividing the total investment ($14,000) by the total number of shares, is $61.57 ($14,000 ÷ 227.4 = $61.57). Other applications of dollar cost averaging occur when employees purchase shares of their company's stock through a payroll deduction plan or as part of an employer-sponsored retirement plan over an extended period of time.

Investors use dollar cost averaging to avoid the common pitfall of buying high and selling low. In the situation shown in Exhibit 14-9, you would lose money only if you sold your stock at less than the average cost of $61.57. Thus, with dollar cost averaging, you can make money if the stock is sold at a price higher than the average cost for a share of stock.

DIRECT INVESTMENT AND DIVIDEND REINVESTMENT PLANS

Today a large number of corporations offer direct investment plans. A **direct investment plan** allows you to purchase stock directly from a corporation without having to use an account executive or a brokerage firm. For example, McDonalds, Procter & Gamble, and ExxonMobil allow investors to purchase stock from the corporation. Similarly, a **dividend reinvestment plan** (sometimes called a DRIP) allows you the option to reinvest your cash dividends to purchase stock of the corporation. For stockholders, the chief advantage of both types

Year	Investment	Stock Price	Shares Purchased
2007	$2,000	$60	33.3
2008	2,000	65	30.8
2009	2,000	50	40.0
2010	2,000	60	33.3
2011	2,000	66	30.3
2012	2,000	62	32.3
2013	2,000	73	27.4
Total	$14,000		227.4

Average cost = Total investment ÷ Total shares
= $14,000 ÷ 227.4
= $61.57

Exhibit 14-9

Dollar cost averaging for Johnson & Johnson

of plans is that these plans enable them to purchase stock without paying a commission charge to a brokerage firm. The fees (if any), minimum investment amounts, rules, and features for both direct investment and dividend reinvestment do vary from one corporation to the next.

In addition to saving the commissions that would be paid to account executives, both types of plans enable investors to purchase a small number of shares of stock. Both plans also allow you to purchase fractional shares of stock and are practical applications of dollar cost averaging—a topic discussed in the last section. For corporations, the chief advantage of both types of plans is that they provide an additional source of capital. As an added bonus, they are providing a service to their stockholders. A number of websites provide information about direct investment or dividend reinvestment plans.

my life 5

I can explain the difference between long-term and short-term investment techniques.

Sooner or later, you will hear stories about people who have made a great deal of money in the stock market in a very short period of time. While there's nothing wrong with short-term investing, keep in mind that for most people the odds of making quick profits on a continual basis are against you. On the other hand, long-term *quality* stock investments provide the continued growth needed to obtain your financial goals. To start investing for the long term.

- Read this chapter a second time.
- Participate in an employer-sponsored retirement account.
- Open a Roth IRA or traditional individual retirement account—See Chapter 18.
- Save the money needed to purchase your first stock.

SHORT-TERM TECHNIQUES

Investors sometimes use more speculative, short-term techniques. In this section, we discuss day traders, buying stock on margin, selling short, and trading in options. *Be warned: The methods presented in this section are quite risky; do not use them unless you fully understand the underlying risks.*

DAY TRADING A **day trader** is an individual who buys and then later sells stocks and other securities in a very short period of time. What could be easier? Buy a stock in the morning that has a great deal of momentum because of a projected revenues jump or an increase in earnings and then sell it a few hours later the same day or in just a few days? Sounds simple! Here's the problem—*most day traders lose money!* Be warned: This is one of the most speculative techniques used today—much like going to Las Vegas and gambling. And yet, the lure of quick profits and the success stories of a few cause people to try their luck at day trading. Individuals should never use day trading if they don't fully understand the risks involved and cannot afford to lose money if the strategy doesn't work.

day trader An individual who buys and then later sells stocks and other securities in a very short period of time.

margin A speculative technique whereby an investor borrows part of the money needed to buy a particular stock.

BUYING STOCK ON MARGIN When buying stock on **margin,** you borrow part of the money needed to buy a particular stock. The margin requirement is set by the Federal Reserve Board and is subject to periodic change. The current margin requirement is 50 percent. This requirement means you may borrow up to half of the total stock purchase price. Although margin is regulated by the Federal Reserve, specific requirements and the interest charged on the loans used to fund margin transactions may vary among brokerage firms. Usually the brokerage firm either lends the money or arranges the loan with another financial institution.

Investors buy on margin because the financial leverage created by borrowing money can increase the return on an investment. Because they can buy up to twice as much stock by buying on margin, they can earn larger returns. Suppose you expect the market price for a share of Microsoft to *increase* in the next three to four months. Let's say you have enough money to purchase 100 shares of the stock. However, if you buy on margin, you can purchase an additional 100 shares for a total of 200 shares.

EXAMPLE: Margin Transaction

If the price of Microsoft's stock increases by $4 a share, your profit will be

Without margin:	$400 = $4 increase per share × 100 shares
With margin:	$800 = $4 increase per share × 200 shares

In this example, the Microsoft stock did exactly what it was supposed to do: It increased in market value. Because the stock increased $4 per share, you made $800 because you owned 200 shares. Your actual profit would be reduced by commissions and the amount of interest your broker would charge for the margin transaction. Had the value of microsoft stock gone down, buying on margin would have increased your loss.

If the value of a margined stock decreases to approximately 65 percent of the original purchase price, you may receive a *margin call* from the brokerage firm. After the margin call, you must pledge additional cash or securities to serve as collateral for the loan. If you don't have acceptable collateral or cash, the margined stock is sold and the proceeds are used to repay the loan. The exact price at which the brokerage firm issues the margin call is determined by the amount of money you borrowed when you purchased the stock and the rules established by the brokerage firm. Generally, the more money you borrow, the sooner you will receive a margin call if the price of the margined stock drops.

In addition to facing the possibility of larger dollar losses, you must pay interest on the money borrowed to purchase stock on margin. Interest charges can absorb the potential profits if the price of margined stock does not increase rapidly enough and the margined stocks must be held for long periods of time.

selling short Selling stock that has been borrowed from a brokerage firm and must be replaced at a later date.

SELLING SHORT Normally, you buy stocks and assume they will increase in value, a procedure referred to as *buying long.* But not all stocks increase in value. In fact, the value of a stock may decrease for many reasons, including lower sales, lower profits, reduced dividends, product failures, increased competition, and product liability lawsuits. With this fact in mind, you may use a procedure called *selling short* to make money when the value of a stock is expected to decrease in value. **Selling short** is selling stock that has been borrowed from a brokerage firm and must be replaced at a later date. When you sell short, you sell today, knowing you must buy, or *cover* your short transaction, at a later date. To make money in a short transaction, you must take these steps:

1. Arrange to *borrow a stock certificate* for a certain number of shares of a particular stock from a brokerage firm.
2. *Sell the borrowed stock,* assuming it will drop in value in a reasonably short period of time.

3. *Buy the stock at a lower price* than the price it sold for in step 2.
4. Use the stock purchased in step 3 to *replace the stock borrowed from the brokerage firm* in step 1.

When selling short, your profit is the difference between the amount received when the stock is sold in step 2 and the amount paid for the stock in step 3. For example, assume that you think J. C. Penney is overvalued at $17 a share. You also believe the stock will *decrease* in value over the next four to six months because of declining sales and increased competition from other retailers. You call your broker and arrange to borrow 100 shares of J. C. Penney stock (step 1). The broker then sells the borrowed stock for you at the current market price of $17 a share (step 2). Also assume that four months later J. C. Penney stock drops to $12 a share. You instruct your broker to purchase 100 shares of J. C. Penney stock at the current lower price (step 3). The newly purchased stock is given to the brokerage firm to repay the borrowed stock (step 4).

EXAMPLE: Selling Short

Your profit from the J. C. Penney short transaction was $500 because the price declined from $17 to $12.

$1,700 selling price = $17 price per share × 100 shares (Step 2)

$1,200 purchase price = $12 price per share × 100 shares (Step 3)

$500 Profit from selling short

Note: For illustration purposes, no commission was included in the above example. In reality, the profits for this transaction would be reduced by the commissions to buy and sell the stock.

Before selling short, consider two factors. First, since the stock you borrow from your broker is actually owned by another investor, you must pay any dividends the stock earns before you replace the stock. After all, you borrowed the stock and then sold the borrowed stock. Eventually, dividends can absorb the profits from your short transaction if the price of the stock does not decrease rapidly enough. Second, to make money selling short, you must be correct in predicting that a stock will decrease in value. If the value of the stock increases, you lose because you must replace the borrowed stock with stock purchased at a higher price.

TRADING IN OPTIONS An **option** gives you the right to buy or sell a stock at a predetermined price during a specified period of time. If you think the market price of a stock will increase during a short period of time, you may decide to purchase a call option. A *call option* is sold by a stockholder and gives the purchaser the right to *buy* 100 shares of a stock at a guaranteed price before a specified expiration date. With a call option, the purchaser is betting that the price of the stock will increase in value before the expiration date.

option The right to buy or sell a stock at a predetermined price during a specified period of time.

It is also possible to purchase a put option. A *put option* is the right to sell 100 shares of a stock at a guaranteed price before a specified expiration date. With a put option, the purchaser is betting that the stock will decrease in value before the expiration date. With both call and put options, the price movement must occur before the expiration date, or you lose the money you paid for your option.

Because of the increased risk involved in option trading, a more detailed discussion of how you profit or lose money with options is beyond the scope of this book. *Be warned:* Amateurs and beginning investors should stay away from options unless they fully understand all of the risks involved. For the rookie, the lure of large profits over a short period of time may be tempting, but the risks are real.

PRACTICE QUIZ 14-5

1 How can an investor make money using the buy-and-hold technique?
2 What is the advantage of using dollar cost averaging?
3 Explain the difference between direct investment plans and dividend reinvestment plans.
4 Why would an investor buy stock on margin?
5 Why would an investor use the selling-short technique?

my life stages for managing my stock investments . . .

YOUR PERSONAL FINANCE DASHBOARD

HAVE YOU SAVED ENOUGH MONEY TO OPEN A BROKERAGE ACCOUNT AND PURCHASE YOUR FIRST STOCK?

A dashboard is a tool used by organizations to monitor key performance indicators, such as delivery time, product defects, or customer complaints. As an individual, a personal finance dashboard allows you to assess your financial situation.

Beginning investors are often reluctant to begin investing because of two factors. First, they don't have the money to establish an investment program. Second, they don't know how to research different investment alternatives.

YOUR SITUATION Have you saved enough money to open a brokerage account? Depending on the brokerage firm, you will typically need between $500 and $2,000 to open an account. Next, you should research any potential investment. The material in this chapter along with information available on Internet websites and material in the library will help.

. . . in college

- Establish investment and financial goals
- Work to balance your budget
- Start an emergency fund
- Save the money needed to begin investing
- Open a brokerage account and begin investing

. . . in my 20s

- Revise investment and financial goals
- Participate in an employer sponsored 401(k) retirement accounts
- Consider investing in a Roth IRA or traditional IRA
- Invest in growth-oriented investments

. . . in my 30s and 40s

- Revise investment and financial goals
- Continue to save money and invest in growth-oriented investments
- Evaluate new investments before purchase
- Evaluate all existing investments on a regular basis

. . . in my 50s and beyond

- Revise investment and financial goals
- Begin planning for retirement within a specific number of years
- Evaluate existing and new investments
- Use asset allocation to make sure that there is a balance between growth and conservative investments

SUMMARY OF LEARNING OBJECTIVES

LO14-1

Identify the most important features of common and preferred stocks.

Both common and preferred stock are equity financing. Corporations sell common stock to finance their business start-up costs and help pay for business expansion and ongoing business activities. People invest in common stock because of dividend income and appreciation of value. There is also the *possibility* of gain through stock splits. Dividend payments to common stockholders must be approved by a corporation's board of directors. In return for providing the money needed to finance the corporation, stockholders have the right to elect the board of directors. They must also approve changes to corporate policies. The most important priority an investor in preferred stock enjoys is receiving cash dividends before any cash dividends are paid to common stockholders. Still, dividend distributions to both preferred and common stockholders must be approved by the board of directors.

LO14-2

Explain how you can evaluate stock investments.

A number of factors can make a share of stock increase or decrease in value. Depending on specific characteristics associated with a stock investment, account executives, financial planners, and investors often classify a particular stock as blue chip, cyclical, defensive, growth, income, large cap, midcap, small cap, micro cap, or penny stock. When evaluating a particular stock issue, most investors begin with the information contained on the Internet. Stock advisory services, annual reports, and information contained on the SEC website and in newspapers and business periodicals can all be used to help evaluate a stock investment.

LO14-3

Analyze the numerical measures that cause a stock to increase or decrease in value.

Many analysts believe that a corporation's ability or inability to generate earnings in the future may be one of the most significant factors that account for an increase or decrease in the value of a stock. Generally, higher earnings equate to higher stock value, and lower earnings equate to lower stock value. It is also possible to calculate earnings per share and price-earnings ratio to evaluate a stock investment. While both earnings per share and price-earnings ratio are historical numbers based on what a corporation has already done, it is possible to obtain earnings estimates for most corporations. Other calculations that help evaluate stock investments include dividend payout, dividend yield, total return, annualized holding period yield, beta, book value, and market-to-book ratio. Fundamental analysis, technical analysis, and the efficient market hypothesis can also be used to explain the price movements that occur in the stock market.

LO14-4

Describe how stocks are bought and sold.

A corporation may sell a new stock issue in the primary market with the help of an investment bank. Once the stock has been sold in the primary market, it can be sold time and again in the secondary market. In the secondary market, investors buy or sell stock listed on a securities exchange or traded in the over-the-counter market. Most securities transactions are made through an account executive who works for a brokerage firm. A growing number of investors are using discount brokerage firms or online firms to complete security transactions. Most brokerage firms charge a minimum commission for buying or selling stock. Additional commission charges are generally based on the number and value of the stock shares bought or sold and if you use a full-service or discount broker or trade stocks online. To purchase stocks you can use a market, limit, or stop-loss order.

LO14-5

Explain the trading techniques used by long-term investors and short-term speculators.

Purchased stock may be classified as either a long-term investment or a speculative investment. Long-term investors typically hold their investments for at least a year or longer; speculators (sometimes referred to as *traders*) usually sell their investments within a shorter time period. Traditional trading techniques long-term investors use include the buy-and-hold technique, dollar cost averaging, direct investment plans, and dividend reinvestment plans. More speculative techniques include day trading, buying on margin, selling short, and trading in options.

KEY TERMS

account executive 502
annualized holding period yield 497
beta 498
book value 499
common stock 482
day trader 507
direct investment plan 506
dividend 482
dividend payout 496
dividend reinvestment plan 506
dividend yield 496
dollar cost averaging 506
earnings per share 494
efficient market hypothesis (EMH) 500
equity financing 482
ex-dividend 485
fundamental analysis 500
initial public offering (IPO) 501
investment bank 501

KEY FORMULAS

Page	Topic	Formula
494	Earnings per share	$\text{Earnings per share} = \dfrac{\text{After-tax income}}{\text{Number of shares outstanding}}$
	Example:	$\text{Earnings per share} = \dfrac{\$11{,}250{,}000}{3{,}750{,}000} = \$3.00 \text{ per share}$
495	Price-earnings (P-E) ratio	$\text{P-E ratio} = \dfrac{\text{Price per share}}{\text{Earnings per share}}$
	Example:	$\text{Price-earnings ratio} = \dfrac{\$54}{\$3.00} = 18$
496	Dividend payout	$\text{Dividend payout} = \dfrac{\text{Annual dividend amount}}{\text{Earnings per share}}$
	Example:	$\text{Dividend payout} = \dfrac{\$0.90}{\$1.28} = 0.70 = 70\%$
497	Dividend yield	$\text{Dividend yield} = \dfrac{\text{Annual dividend amount}}{\text{Price per share}}$
	Example:	$\text{Dividend yield} = \dfrac{\$2.00}{\$50.00} = 0.04 = 4 \text{ percent}$
497	Total return	$\text{Total return} = \text{Dividends} + \text{Capital gain}$
	Example:	$\text{Total return} = \$120 + \$710 = \$830$
497	Annualized holding period yield	$\text{Annualized holding period yield} = \dfrac{\text{Total return}}{\text{Original investment}} \times \dfrac{1}{N}$ N = Number of years investment is held
	Example:	$\text{Annualized holding period yield} = \dfrac{\$830}{\$2{,}600} \times \dfrac{1}{4} = 0.08 = 8 \text{ percent}$

Page	Topic	Formula
496	Price/earnings to growth ratio (PEG)	$\text{Price/earnings to growth ratio} = \dfrac{\text{Price-earnings ratio}}{\text{Annual EPS growth}}$
	Example:	$\text{Price/earnings to growth ratio} = \dfrac{20}{24\%} = 0.83$
	Note: The percent sign (%) is ignored in the above calculation.	
499	Beta calculation	$\text{Volatility for a stock} = \text{Increase in overall market} \times \text{Beta for a specific stock} = 8 \text{ percent} \times 1.25 = 10 \text{ percent}$
499	Book value	$\text{Book value} = \dfrac{\text{Assets} - \text{Liabilities}}{\text{Shares outstanding}}$
	Example:	$\text{Book value} = \dfrac{\$135{,}000{,}000 - \$60{,}000{,}000}{3{,}750{,}000} = \$20 \text{ per share}$
499	Market-to-book ratio	$\text{Market-to-book ratio} = \dfrac{\text{Market value per share}}{\text{Book value per share}} = \dfrac{\$40}{\$32} = 1.25$

SELF-TEST PROBLEMS

1. Kristy Nguyen is trying to decide between two different stock investments, and she asks for your help. Information about each investment is below.

Company	Price per share	Annual Dividend	After-Tax Income This Year	Projected Earnings Next Year	Number of Shares Outstanding
One Source Manufacturing	$24	$0.40	$35 million	$39 million	20 million shares
Down South Homes	$40	$0.56	$122 million	$90 million	140 million shares

a. Calculate the dividend yield for each company.

b. Calculate the earnings per share for each company.

c. Calculate the price-earnings (P-E) ratio for each company.

d. Based on this information, which company would you recommend?

2. Last year, Shanna Young purchased 100 shares of Iowa Farm Implement. During the last 12 months, she received dividends totaling $1.20 a share. During the 12-month period, the company earned $4.00 a share.

a. For the 12-month period, what is the amount of total dividends that Ms. Young received?

b. If a share of Iowa Farm Implement is selling for $52, what is the dividend yield?

c. What is the dividend payout during this 12-month period?

3. Four years ago, David Robertson purchased 200 shares of Harrison Microchips. At the time, each share of Harrison Microchips was selling for $40. He also paid a $22 commission when the shares were purchased. Now, four years later, he has decided it's time to sell his investment. Harrison Microchips share price when sold was $52.50. In addition, he paid a $34 commission to sell his shares. He also received dividends of $2.20 per share over the four-year investment period.

   a. What was the total return for Mr. Robertson's investment?

   b. What is the annualized holding yield for his investment?

Solutions

1. a. Calculate the dividend yield for each company.

One Source Manufacturing	Dividend yield = Annual dividend amount ÷ Price per share = $0.40 ÷ $24 = 0.017 = 1.7 percent
Down South Homes	Dividend yield = Annual dividend ÷ Price per share = $0.56 ÷ $40 = 0.014 = 1.4 percent

   b. Calculate the earnings per share for each company.

One Source Manufacturing	Earnings per share = After-tax income ÷ Number of shares outstanding = $35,000,000 ÷ 20,000,000 = $1.75 per share
Down South Homes	Earnings per share = After-tax income ÷ Number of Shares outstanding = $122,000,000 ÷ $140,000,000 = $0.87 per share

   c. Calculate the price-earnings (P-E) ratio for each company.

One Source Manufacturing	P-E Ratio = Price per share ÷ Earnings per share = $24 ÷ $1.75 = 13.7 = 14
Down South Homes	P-E Ratio = Price per share ÷ Earnings per share = $40 ÷ $0.87 = 45.9 = 46

   d. Based on this information, which company would you recommend?

Based on the calculations, One Source Manufacturing is a better investment because it has a higher dividend yield and higher earnings per share—both good signs. While a lower P-E ratio usually indicates slower earnings growth, it does indicate that One Source Manufacturing is earning quite a lot when compared to its current share price. Also, looking ahead, One Source is projected to have higher earnings next year. During the same period, Down South Homes' earnings are projected to decline.

2. a. For the 12-month period, what is the amount of total dividends that Ms. Young received?

   Total dividends = Dividend per share × number of shares
   = $1.20 × 100
   = $120

   b. If a share of Iowa Farm Implement is selling for $52 a share, what is the dividend yield?

   Dividend yield = Annual dividend amount ÷ Price per share
   = $1.20 × $52
   = 0.023 = 2.3 percent

   c. What is the dividend payout during this 12-month period?

   Dividend payout = Annual dividend amount ÷ Earnings per share
   = $1.20 ÷ $4.00
   = 0.30 = 30 percent

3. **a.** What was the total return for Mr. Robertson's investment?

Total Dividends = Annual dividends ÷ number of shares
= $2.20 × 200 shares
= $440

Purchase price = $40 × 200 Shares = $8,000 + $22 Commission = $8,022
Selling price = $52.50 × 200 shares = $10,500 − $34 Commission = $10,466
Capital Gain = $10,466 Selling price − $8,022 Purchase price = $2,444
Total return = $440 Total dividends + $2,444 Capital gain = $2,884

b. What is the annualized holding yield for his investment? *Note:* In the formula below, *N* is the number of years investment is held

$$\text{Annualized holding period yield} = \frac{\text{Total Return}}{\text{Original investment}} \times \frac{1}{N}$$

$$= \frac{\$2{,}884}{\$8{,}022} \times \frac{1}{4}$$

$$= 0.09 = 9 \text{ percent}$$

FINANCIAL PLANNING PROBLEMS

1. *Calculating Dividend Amounts.* Betty and John Martinez own 220 shares of ExxonMobil common stock. ExxonMobil's annual dividend is $2.28 per share. What is the amount of the dividend check the Martinez couple will receive for this year? L014-1
2. *Determining the Number of Shares after a Stock Split.* In March, stockholders of 3D Systems Corporation approved a 2-for-1 stock split. After the split, how many shares of 3D Systems stock will an investor have if she or he owned 230 shares before the split? L014-1
3. *Calculating Total Return.* Tammy Jackson purchased 100 shares of All-American Manufacturing Company stock at $31.50 a share. One year later, she sold the stock for $38 a share. She paid her broker a $15 commission when she purchased the stock and a $29 commission when she sold it. During the 12 months she owned the stock, she received $160 in dividends. Calculate Tammy's total return on this investment. L014-1
4. *Calculating Total Return.* Marie and Bob Houmas purchased 200 shares of General Electric stock for $23 a share. One year later, they sold the stock for $31 a share. They paid their broker a $32 commission when they purchased the stock and a $41 commission when they sold it. During the 12 months they owned the stock, they received $152 in dividends. Calculate the total return on this investment. L014-1
5. *Determining a Preferred Dividend Amount.* James Hayes owns 370 shares of Ohio Utility preferred stock. If this preferred stock issue pays $2.80 per share, what is the total dollar amount Mr. Hayes will receive in one year? L014-1
6. *Calculating Dividend Payout.* Assume you own shares in Honeywell Inc. and that the company currently earns $3.69 per share and pays annual dividend payments that total $1.64 a share each year. Calculate the dividend payout for Honeywell. L014-3
7. *Compounding Investment Returns.* Nancy Cardoza invested $2,450 in ExxonMobil stock because her research indicated the company should average an 8 percent return over the next four years. If ExxonMobil does earn 8 percent each year, what will her $2,450 investment be worth at the end of four years. (To solve this problem, you may want to use Exhibit 1-A in the appendix that follows Chapter 1.) L014-3
8. *Compounding Dividend Amounts.* Carl Patterson likes investing in stocks that pay dividends. Carl owns 25 shares of a local utility company. The stock pays a regular annual dividend in the amount of $3 per share and the company has indicated that the dividend will stay the same for a long time. If Carl reinvests his dividends each year and the dividends earn a return of 6 percent each year, how much will Carl accumulate in 15 years? (To solve this problem, you may want to use Exhibit 1-B in the appendix that follows Chapter 1.) L014-3
9. *Calculating Return on Investment.* Two years ago, you purchased 100 shares of Coca-Cola Company. Your purchase price was $33 a share, plus a total commission of $29 to purchase the stock. During the last two years, you have received the following dividend amounts: $0.94 per share for the first year and $1.12 per share the second year. Also, assume that at the end of two years, you sold your Coca-Cola stock for $40 a share minus a total commission of $34 to sell the stock. L014-3

   a. Calculate the dividend yield for your Coca-Cola stock at the time you purchased it.

   b. Calculate the dividend yield for your Coca-Cola stock at the time you sold it.

c. Calculate the total return for your Coca-Cola investment when you sold the stock at the end of two years.

d. Calculate the annualized holding period yield for your Coca-Cola investment at the end of the two-year period.

LO14-3 **10.** *Calculating Earnings per Share, Price-Earnings Ratio, and Book Value.* As a stockholder of Bozo Oil Company, you receive its annual report. In the financial statements, the firm has reported assets of $9 million, liabilities of $5 million, after-tax earnings of $2 million, and 750,000 outstanding shares of common stock.

a. Calculate the earnings per share of Bozo Oil's common stock.

b. Assuming a share of Bozo Oil's common stock has a market value of $40, what is the firm's price-earnings ratio?

c. Calculate the book value of a share of Bozo Oil's common stock.

LO14-3 **11.** *Calculating Beta.* Thompson Home Remodeling has a 1.40 beta. If the overall stock market increases by 7 percent, how much will Thompson Remodeling change?

LO14-3 **12.** *Calculating Ratios.* According to the financial statements for Samson Electronics, Inc., the firm has total assets valued at $310 million. It also has total liabilities of $190 million. Company records indicate that the firm has issued 2 million shares of stock.

a. Based on the above information, calculate the book value for a share of Samson Electronics.

b. If a share of Samson Electronics, Inc., currently has a market value of $50 a share, what is the market-to-book ratio?

c. Based on the market-to-book ratio, is a share of Samson Electronics overpriced or underpriced? Explain your answer.

LO14-5 **13.** *Using Dollar Cost Averaging.* For four years, Mary Nations invested $4,000 each year in America Bank stock. The stock was selling for $34 in 2010, for $48 in 2011, $37 in 2012, and for $52 in 2013.

a. What is Mary's total investment in America Bank?

b. After four years, how many shares does Mary own?

c. What is the average cost per share of Mary's investment?

LO14-5 **14.** *Using Margin.* Bill Campbell invested $4,000 and borrowed $4,000 to purchase shares in Walmart. At the time of his investment, Walmart stock was selling for $70 a share.

a. If Bill paid a $30 commission, how many shares could he buy if he used *only* his own money and did not use margin?

b. If Bill paid a $50 commission, how many shares could he buy if he used his $4,000 and borrowed $4,000 on margin to buy Walmart stock?

c. Assuming Bill did use margin, paid a $90 total commission to sell his Walmart stock, and sold his stock for $77 a share, how much profit did he make on his Walmart investment?

LO14-5 **15.** *Selling Short.* After researching Best Buy common stock, Sally Jackson is convinced the stock is overpriced. She contacts her account executive and arranges to sell short 200 shares of Best Buy. At the time of the sale, a share of common stock had a value of $27. Three months later, Best Buy is selling for $18 a share, and Sally instructs her broker to cover her short transaction. Total commissions to buy and sell the stock were $74. What is her profit for this short transaction?

FINANCIAL PLANNING ACTIVITIES

LO14-1 **1.** *Surveying Investors.* Survey investors who own stock. Then explain, in a short paragraph, their reasons for owning stock.

LO14-2 **2.** *Researching Stocks.* Use the Internet to find the following information for the four stocks listed below in the chart.

Date _____
Website _____

Stock	Stock Symbol	52-Week High	52-Week Low	Dividend	Dividend Yield %	Close Price
Microsoft						
Clorox						
IBM						
Pfizer						

3. *Using Stock Advisory Services.* Pick a stock of interest to you and research the company at the library by examining the information contained in reports published by Value Line, Standard & Poor's, or Morningstar, or business periodicals like *BusinessWeek, Money,* or *Kiplinger's Personal Finance.* Then write a one- or two-page summary of your findings. Based on your research, would you still want to invest in this stock? Why or why not? LO14-2

4. *Using the Yahoo! Finance Website.* Visit the Yahoo! Finance Website and evaluate one of the corporations listed below. To complete this activity, follow these steps: LO14-2

   a. Go to finance.yahoo.com.

   b. Choose one of the following three corporations, enter its stock ticker symbol, and click on the Quote Lookup button: General Electric (GE), Facebook (FB), Abbott Laboratories (ABT).

   c. For your corporation, print out the information for the profile, 2-year chart, and analyst opinion.

   d. Based on the information included in this research report, would you invest in this corporation? Explain your answer.

5. *Using Long-Term Investment Techniques.* Interview people who have used the long-term investment techniques of buy and hold, dollar cost averaging, direct investment plan, or dividend reinvestment plan. Describe your findings. LO14-5

6. *Analyzing Short-Term Investments.* Prepare a chart that describes the similarities and differences among day trading, buying stock on margin, and selling short. LO14-5

7. *Practicing Your Investments Skills.* Today, you can practice your investing skills by playing a virtual stock game. To complete this activity, use an Internet search engine like Google or Yahoo!. Begin by entering "virtual stock game" in the search box. Select one of the virtual stock games and then play the game for a specific time period. At the end of the time period, prepare a two-page report that describes what you learned by playing the virtual stock game. LO14-5

FINANCIAL PLANNING CASE

Research Information Available from Value Line

This chapter stressed the importance of evaluating potential investments. Now it's your turn to try your skill at evaluating a potential investment in the Dollar Tree Corporation. Assume you could invest $10,000 in the common stock of this company. To help you evaluate this potential investment, carefully examine Exhibit 14-7, which reproduces the research report on Dollar Tree from Value Line. The report was published in February of 2013.

Questions

1. Based on the research provided by Value Line, would you buy Dollar Tree's stock? Justify your answer.
2. What other investment information would you need to evaluate Dollar Tree's common stock? Where would you obtain this information?
3. On Monday, February 25, 2013, Dollar Tree's common stock was selling for $41 a share. Using the Internet, determine the current price for a share of Dollar Tree's common stock. Based on this information, would your investment have been profitable if you had purchased the common stock for $41 a share? (*Hint:* Dollar Tree's stock symbol is DLTR.)
4. Assuming you purchased Dollar Tree's stock on February 25, 2013, and based on your answer to question 3, would you want to hold or sell your Dollar Tree stock? Explain your answer.

PERSONAL FINANCIAL PLANNER IN ACTION

Investing in Stocks

For many investors, selection of stocks for their portfolios is an important element that helps achieve various investment goals.

Your Short-Term Financial Planning Activities	*Resources*
1. Identify investment goals that might be appropriate for investing in stocks for your life situation.	www.fool.com www.money.cnn.com
2. Research a potential stock investment. Consider risk, potential growth, income, and recent market performance.	PFP Sheet 58 finance.yahoo.com www.quote.com
3. Monitor current economic conditions that may affect the value of individual stocks as well as the stock market as a whole.	www.wsj.com www.federalreserve.gov www.bea.gov
4. Compare the cost of various investment broker services.	PFP Sheet 59 www.scottrade.com www.schwab.com www.etrade.com
Your Long-Term Financial Planning Activities	*Resources*
1. Identify stock investing strategies that might be used for achieving long-term financial goals.	www.morningstar.com www.marketwatch.com
2. Develop a plan for investing in stocks as family and household situations change.	Text pages 501–505 www.kiplinger.com

CONTINUING CASE

Investing in Stocks

Life Situation

Shelby, age 34
Mark, age 35
Two children, ages 8 and 2

Financial Data

Monthly Gross Income	$7,000
Living Expenses	$4,500
Assets	$205,000
Liabilities	$115,000

Over the past four years, Shelby and Mark have had another baby but have managed to set aside money for investing. They have accumulated $5,000 for this purpose. They are considering stock investments but are not sure how to get started. They have heard that stock investments can grow quickly but that there is great risk in this type of investment. Therefore, they definitely want more information before they begin.

Questions

1. What are the ways that Shelby and Mark might earn money from stock investments? What are the risks involved?
2. If Shelby and Mark want to use the Internet to evaluate stocks, what are four websites that can help them and what information do they provide?
3. Explain how Shelby and Mark might use the Personal Financial Planner sheet Number 58, Corporate Stocks Evaluation.

"Investing in stock is not possible. I'm barely able to pay my various living expenses."

Directions

Your "Daily Spending Diary" will help you manage your expenses to create a better overall spending plan. Once you try to control your spending, you will be able to save the money needed to fund various types of investments.

Analysis Questions

1. What information from your daily spending records can help you better achieve financial goals?
2. Based on your observations of our society and the economy, what types of stocks might you consider for investing in now or in the near future?

The Daily Spending Diary sheets are located in Appendix D at the end of the book and on the student website at www.mhhe.com/kdh.

chapter 15

Investing in Bonds

Learning Objectives

LO15-1 Describe the characteristics of corporate bonds.

LO15-2 Discuss why corporations issue bonds.

LO15-3 Explain why investors purchase corporate bonds.

LO15-4 Discuss why federal, state, and local governments issue bonds and why investors purchase government bonds.

LO15-5 Evaluate bonds when making an investment.

What will this mean for me?

By choosing corporate or government bonds, investors can use the principle of asset allocation and diversify their investment holdings. Although most bonds are conservative investments, there is still risk. This chapter provides the information you need to evaluate bond investments.

my life

WHY BONDS?

While most beginning investors think bonds are for "old folks afraid of losing their money," there are valid reasons why you might want to invest in corporate or government bonds—regardless of your age. The fact is that bonds can provide a measure of safety and allow you to use asset allocation to diversify your investment portfolio. To begin, answer the questions below.

1. I understand the basics of corporate bonds.	Agree	Neutral	Disagree
2. I understand why corporations issue bonds.	Agree	Neutral	Disagree
3. I appreciate the advantages of investing in corporate bonds.	Agree	Neutral	Disagree
4. I sometimes think about investing in government and tax-free municipal bonds.	Agree	Neutral	Disagree
5. I know how to evaluate bond investments.	Agree	Neutral	Disagree

As you study this chapter, you will encounter "My Life" boxes with additional information and resources related to these items.

When it comes to investing, how do bonds fit in the "big picture"? Good question. Many people believe that the best investments are always stock investments. And while stocks have traditionally returned more than other investment alternatives, bonds are often considered a safer investment when compared to stocks or mutual funds that invest in stocks.

Assuming you thought the stock market was headed for a long period of decline, you could sell some or all of your stocks and use asset allocation to diversify your investment portfolio by purchasing corporate and government bonds. That's exactly what Joe Goode, a 30-year-old marketing manager for a sports equipment company, did in October 2007—about the time the stock market began to decline. Although his friends thought he was crazy for taking such a conservative approach, he actually avoided the deep downturn in the stock market. According to Joe, he earned interest on his bond investments while preserving his investment funds for a return to the stock market when the economy turned around. Sure enough, in the spring of 2010, he sold his corporate and government bonds and used the money to purchase many of the same stocks he had sold at the beginning of the economic crisis at much lower prices. At the time of publication, his strategy of using asset allocation to diversify his investment portfolio was working, and he had earned an average of 9 percent each year since October 2007—during a time when many investors were losing money.

corporate bond A corporation's written pledge to repay a specified amount of money with interest.

face value The dollar amount the bondholder will receive at the bond's maturity.

maturity date For a corporate bond, the date on which the corporation is to repay the borrowed money.

bond indenture A legal document that details all of the conditions relating to a bond issue.

In addition to asset allocation, investors often choose bonds because they need current income provided by bond interest payments, and they expect to be repaid when the bonds mature. Some investors even choose specific bonds because the bond's maturity date coincides with their expected future expenses. For example, you may want to pick bonds that mature when your first child begins college. Then, when the bonds are repaid at maturity, the money can be used to pay college tuition. We begin this chapter by describing the basic characteristics of corporate bonds that define the relationship between investors and corporations that sell bonds to obtain financing.

Characteristics of Corporate Bonds

LO15-1

Describe the characteristics of corporate bonds.

A **corporate bond** is a corporation's written pledge to repay a specified amount of money with interest. The **face value** (sometimes referred to as par value) is the dollar amount the bondholder will receive at the bond's maturity. The usual face value of a corporate bond is $1,000, but the face value of some corporate bonds may be as high as $50,000. The total face value of all the bonds in an issue usually runs into millions of dollars. Between the time of purchase and the maturity date, the corporation pays interest to the bondholder, usually every six months, at the stated interest rate. *Note:* The interest rate is sometimes referred to as the coupon rate in some financial publications.

trustee A financially independent firm that acts as the bondholders' representative.

The **maturity date** of a corporate bond is the date on which the corporation is to repay the borrowed money. At the maturity date, the bondholder returns the bond to the corporation and receives cash equal to the bond's face value. Maturity dates for bonds generally range from 1 to 30 years after the date of issue. Maturities for corporate bonds may also be classified as short term (under 5 years), intermediate term (5 to 10 years), and long term (over 10 years).

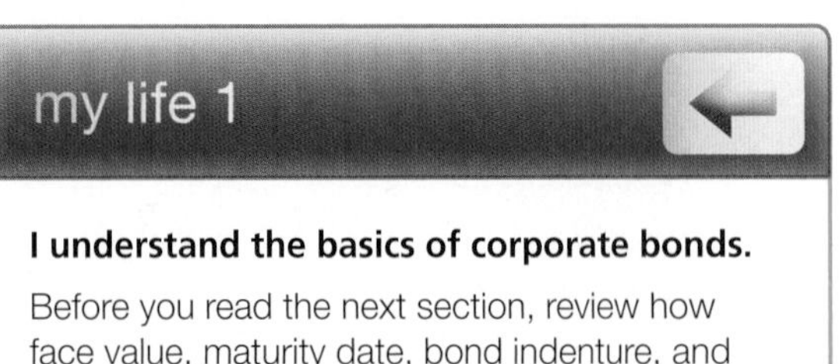

I understand the basics of corporate bonds.

Before you read the next section, review how face value, maturity date, bond indenture, and the trustee affect an investment in corporate bonds.

The actual legal conditions for a corporate bond are described in a bond indenture. A **bond indenture** is a legal document that details all of the conditions relating to a bond issue. Since corporate bond indentures are difficult for the average person to read and understand, a corporation issuing bonds appoints a trustee. The **trustee** is a financially independent firm that acts as the bondholders' representative. Usually the trustee is a commercial bank or some other financial institution. The corporation must report to the trustee periodically regarding its ability to make interest payments and eventually redeem the bonds. In turn, the trustee transmits this information to the bondholders along with its own evaluation of the corporation's ability to pay. If the corporation fails to live up to all the provisions in the indenture agreement, the trustee may bring legal action to protect the bondholders' interests.

1 What is the usual face value for a corporate bond?
2 In your own words, define *maturity date* and *bond indenture.*
3 How does a trustee evaluate the provisions contained in a bond indenture?

Why Corporations Sell Corporate Bonds

LO15-2

Discuss why corporations issue bonds.

Let's begin this section with some basics of why corporations sell bonds. Corporations sell bonds to obtain borrowed money when they

- Don't have enough money to pay for major purchases.
- Need to finance ongoing business activities.
- Find it is difficult or impossible to sell stock.
- Want to improve a corporation's financial leverage—the use of borrowed funds to increase the firm's return on investment.
- Use the interest paid to bond owners as a tax-deductible expense that reduces the taxes the corporation pays to federal and state governments.

Corporate bonds are often referred to as the "workhorse" of corporate finance. They are used by many corporations to raise capital because it often costs less to issue bonds than to sell a new stock issue. While a corporation may use both bonds and stocks to finance its activities, there are important distinctions between the two. Corporate bonds are a form of *debt financing,* whereas stock is a form of *equity financing.* Bond owners must be repaid at a future date; stockholders do not have to be repaid. Interest payments on bonds are required; dividends are paid to stockholders at the discretion of the board of directors. In the event of bankruptcy, bondholders have a claim to the assets of the corporation prior to that of stockholders. Finally, many financial managers prefer selling bonds because they retain control of the corporation since bondholders generally do not have a right to vote. On the other hand, stockholders do have a right to vote on many corporate issues, including the right to elect the board of directors. Before issuing bonds, a corporation must decide what type of bond to issue and how the bond issue will be repaid.

TYPES OF BONDS

Most corporate bonds are debentures. A **debenture** is a bond that is backed only by the reputation of the issuing corporation. If the corporation fails to make either interest payments or repayment at maturity, debenture bondholders become general creditors, much like the firm's suppliers. In the event of corporate bankruptcy, general creditors, including debenture bondholders, can claim any asset not specifically used as collateral for a loan or other financial obligation.

To make a bond issue more appealing to conservative investors, a corporation may issue a mortgage bond. A **mortgage bond** (sometimes referred to as a *secured bond*) is

debenture A bond that is backed only by the reputation of the issuing corporation.

mortgage bond A corporate bond secured by various assets of the issuing firm.

DID YOU KNOW?

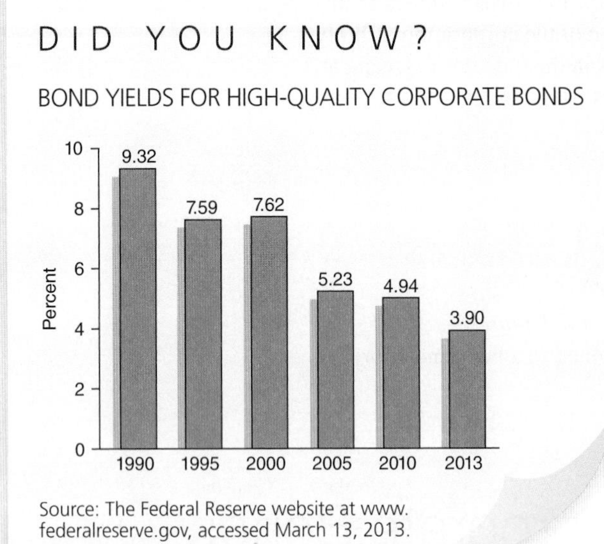

Source: The Federal Reserve website at www.federalreserve.gov, accessed March 13, 2013.

a corporate bond secured by various assets of the issuing firm. A mortgage bond is safer than a debenture because corporate assets or collateral may be sold to repay the bondholders if the corporation defaults on interest or repayment. Because of this added security, interest rates on mortgage bonds are usually lower than interest rates on unsecured debentures.

A third type of bond a corporation may issue is called a *subordinated* debenture. A **subordinated debenture** is an unsecured bond that gives bond holders a claim secondary to that of mortgage or debenture bondholders with respect to interest payments, repayment, and assets. Investors who purchase subordinated debentures usually enjoy higher interest rates than other bondholders because of the increased risk associated with this type of bond.

subordinated debenture An unsecured bond that gives bondholders a claim secondary to that of other designated bondholders with respect to interest payments, repayment, and assets.

convertible bond A bond that can be exchanged, at the owner's option, for a specified number of shares of the corporation's common stock.

convertible corporate note Legal debt that is convertible to shares of common stock at the investor's option.

high-yield bonds Corporate bonds that pay higher interest, but also have a higher risk of default.

CONVERTIBLE BONDS AND NOTES A special type of bond a corporation may issue is a convertible bond. A **convertible bond** can be exchanged, at the owner's option, for a specified number of shares of the corporation's common stock. A **convertible corporate note** is a legal debt that is convertible to shares of common stock at the investors option. This conversion feature allows investors to enjoy the lower risk of a corporate bond or note but also take advantage of the speculative nature of common stock. For example, Ford Motor Company's $1,000 note with a 2036 maturity date is convertible. Each note can be converted to 108.6957 shares of the corporation's common stock. This means you could convert the note to common stock whenever the price of the company's common stock is $9.20 ($1,000 ÷ 108.6957 = $9.20) or higher.[1]

In reality, there is no guarantee that Ford investors will convert to common stock even if the market value of the common stock does increase to $9.20 or higher. The reason for choosing not to exercise the conversion feature in this example is quite simple. As the market value of the common stock increases, the market value of the convertible note *also* increases. By not converting to common stock, investors enjoy the added safety of the bond or note and interest income in addition to the increased market value caused by the price movement of the common stock.

The corporation gains three advantages by issuing convertible bonds or notes. First, the interest rate on a convertible bond or note is often 1 to 2 percent lower. Second, the conversion feature attracts investors who are interested in the speculative gain that conversion to common stock may provide. Third, if the investor converts to common stock, the corporation no longer has to redeem the bond or note at maturity.

Convertible bonds, like all potential investments, must be carefully evaluated. Remember, not all convertible bonds are quality investments.

HIGH-YIELD BOND **High-yield bonds** are corporate bonds that pay higher interest but also have a higher risk of default. Before investing in high-yield bonds, keep in mind these investments are often referred to as "junk bonds" in the financial world. High-yield (junk) bonds are sold by companies with a poor earnings history, companies with a questionable credit record, or newer companies with the unproven ability to increase sales and earn profits. They are also frequently used in connection with leveraged buyouts—a situation where investors acquire a company and sell high-yield bonds to pay for the company.

While high-yield bonds do pay more interest than safer corporate bond issues, the corporation issuing high-yield bonds may not be able to pay interest each year and the risks of default and nonpayment at maturity are real. So, why do investors purchase high-yield bonds? The answer is simple: Corporations issuing high-yield bonds must offer investors interest rates that are three to four percentage points higher than safer bond issues. *Caution:* You should not invest in high-yield (junk) bonds unless you fully understand all of the risks associated with this type of investment.

PROVISIONS FOR REPAYMENT

Today most corporate bonds are callable. A **call feature** allows the corporation to call in or buy outstanding bonds from current bondholders before the maturity date. For bondholders who purchased bonds for income, a problem is often created when a bond paying high interest is called. For example, if your bond that pays 8 percent annual interest is called, it may be difficult for you to replace the bond with a new bond of the same quality that also pays the same 8 percent interest rate. This is especially true when overall interest rates in the economy are declining. If you choose to replace your bond, you may have to purchase a bond with a lower interest rate (and ultimately lower income from your new bond investment) or a bond with lower quality to obtain an 8 percent interest rate. The money needed to call a bond may come from the firm's profits, the sale of additional stock, or the sale of a new bond issue that has a lower interest rate.

call feature A feature that allows the corporation to call in or buy outstanding bonds from current bondholders before the maturity date.

sinking fund A fund to which annual or semiannual deposits are made for the purpose of redeeming a bond issue.

In most cases, corporations issuing callable bonds agree not to call them for the first 5 to 10 years after the bonds have been issued. When a call feature is used, the corporation may have to pay the bondholders a *premium,* an additional amount above the face value of the bond. The amount of the premium is specified in the bond indenture; a $10 to $25 premium over the bond's face value is common.

A corporation may use one of two methods to ensure that it has sufficient funds available to redeem a bond issue. First, the corporation may establish a sinking fund. A **sinking fund** is a fund to which annual or semiannual deposits are made for the purpose of redeeming a bond issue. To retire a $275 million bond issue, Union Pacific Corporation agreed to establish a sinking fund and make annual payments in order to retire 95 percent of the bonds in the issue prior to the maturity date.

A sinking fund provision in the bond indenture is generally advantageous to bondholders. Such a provision forces the corporation to make arrangements for bond repayment before the maturity date. If the terms of the provision are not met, the trustee or bondholders may take legal action against the company.

Second, a corporation may issue serial bonds. **Serial bonds** are bonds of a single issue that mature on different dates. For example, Seaside Productions used a 20-year, $100 million bond issue to finance its expansion. None of the bonds mature during the first 10 years. Thereafter, 10 percent of the bonds mature each year until all the bonds are retired at the end of the 20-year period. A call provision can also be used to buy back bonds before the maturity date.

my life 2

I understand why corporations issue bonds.

To be an educated bond investor, you must understand that corporate bonds

- Are sold for many reasons including paying for major purchases and ongoing business activities, when it is impossible to sell stock, or to improve the firm's financial leverage.
- Can be debentures, mortgage bonds, subordinated debentures, convertible bonds, or high-yield bonds.
- May be callable before maturity.
- May be repaid by using a sinking fund or issued as serial bonds.

serial bonds Bonds of a single issue that mature on different dates.

Detailed information about provisions for repayment, along with other vital information (including maturity date, interest rate, bond rating, call provisions, trustee, and details about security), is available from Moody's Investors Service, Standard & Poor's Corporation, Fitch Ratings Service, Mergent, Inc. and other financial service companies. More information about evaluating bonds is provided in the last section of this chapter.

PRACTICE QUIZ 15-2

1 Why do corporations sell bonds?
2 What are the differences among a debenture, a mortgage bond, and a subordinated debenture?
3 Why would an investor purchase a convertible bond or a high-yield bond?
4 Describe three reasons a corporation would sell convertible bonds.
5 Explain the methods corporations can use to repay a bond issue.

Why Investors Purchase Corporate Bonds

LO15-3

Explain why investors purchase corporate bonds.

Over many years, stocks have returned more than corporate bonds. With this fact in mind, you may be wondering why you should consider bonds as an investment alternative. Why not just choose stocks or mutual funds that invest in stocks because they provide the highest possible return of the different investment alternatives? To answer that question, read the next section.

DID YOU KNOW?

The Securities and Exchange Commission website has information about bonds. For example, the brochure on *Saving and Investing: A Roadmap to Your Financial Security Through Saving and Investing* is an excellent publication that encourages people to begin saving and investing sooner rather than later. This same article also provides information about different investment alternatives—including corporate and municipal bonds.

Source: The Securities and Exchange Commission website at www.sec.gov, accessed March 13, 2013.

THE PSYCHOLOGY OF INVESTING IN BONDS

In reality, there are at least three reasons why you as an investor would choose bonds in place of stocks. First, bonds are another way to use asset allocation to diversify your investment portfolio. You may want to review the concept of asset allocation that was explained in Chapter 13. *Asset allocation* is the process of spreading your money among several different types of investments to lessen risk. And if diversification is your goal, you may also purchase bond funds. Bond funds are an indirect way of owning bonds issued by the U.S. Treasury, state and local governments, and corporations. Many financial experts recommend bond funds for small investors because they offer diversification and professional management. The advantages and disadvantages of bond funds are discussed in more detail in Chapter 16, "Investing in Mutual Funds."

Second, investors consider government and corporate bonds a safer investment when compared to stocks, mutual funds that invest in stocks, or other investments because bonds represent a debt that must be repaid at maturity. Many investors believe that bonds are a "safe harbor" in troubled economic times. For example, many stock investors lost money during the recent economic crisis. Susan and Brandon Davidson, a couple in their early 40s, had an investment portfolio valued at more than $270,000 in October 2007. Yet, they lost almost $100,000 over the next two years during the worst part of the economic crisis. If they had been diversified, used the principle of asset allocation, and invested some of their money in bonds, they would have reduced their losses or even made some money depending on the investments they chose.

Finally, bonds may provide more growth and income potential than other conservative options. Savings accounts, certificates of deposit, money market accounts, and savings bonds—all discussed in Chapter 5—provide a safe place to invest your money. Unfortunately, they don't offer a lot of growth or income potential. Other conservative

Exhibit 15-1

Financial suggestions for bond investors

Financial Need	Suggestion
1. Asset allocation	Bonds are an excellent way to diversify your portfolio and lessen risk.
2. Income for current financial needs	Generally, bonds pay interest (income) semiannually (every six months).
3. Long-term financial needs	Bonds can be purchased with staggered maturity dates that match future financial needs.
4. Conservative investment in an economic downturn	Buy quality bonds to lock in higher income and avoid potential losses in other types of investments.

investments that may offer more potential return include bonds and debt securities issued by the U.S. government, state and local governments, and corporations.

For specific suggestions to help determine whether bonds will help you achieve your financial goals, see Exhibit 15-1. Basically, investors purchase corporate bonds for three reasons: (1) interest income, (2) possible increase in value, and (3) repayment at maturity.

INTEREST INCOME

As mentioned earlier in this chapter, bondholders normally receive interest payments every six months. The dollar amount of interest is determined by multiplying the face value of the bond by the interest rate.

EXAMPLE: Interest Calculation (AT&T)

Assume you purchase a $1,000 corporate bond issued by AT&T Corporation. The interest rate for this bond is 5.50 percent. The annual interest is $55, as shown below.

$$\begin{aligned}\text{Dollar amount of annual interest} &= \text{Face value} \times \text{Interest rate}\\ &= \$1{,}000 \times 5.50 \text{ percent}\\ &= \$1{,}000 \times 0.0550\\ &= \$55\end{aligned}$$

The investor will receive $55 a year, paid in installments of $27.50 at the end of each six-month period.

The method used to pay bondholders their interest depends on whether they own registered bonds, registered coupon bonds, or bearer bonds. A **registered bond** is registered in the owner's name by the issuing company. Generally, interest checks for registered bonds are mailed directly to the bondholder of record. Today, almost all ownership records for bonds are maintained by a process called *book entry.* With book entry, ownership of bonds is recorded electronically by a central depository or custodian. When book entry is used, brokerage firms are usually listed as the owners of bonds instead of individual investors. As a result, it is the brokerage firm's responsibility to maintain accurate ownership records for its individual clients.

registered bond A bond that is registered in the owner's name by the issuing company.

registered coupon bond A bond registered for principal only and not for interest.

A second type of bond is a registered coupon bond. A **registered coupon bond** is registered for principal only, not for interest. While only the registered owner can collect the principal at maturity, interest payments can be made to anyone. To collect interest

Financial Planning Calculations

TIME VALUE OF MONEY: REINVESTING INTEREST CAN MAKE A DIFFERENCE!

How can the time value of money help you achieve your financial goals? Here's how Joe and Audrey Johnson used this simple concept to increase the dollar value of their investments.

The Facts: Ten years ago, the Johnsons purchased 10 Procter & Gamble bonds. They chose this investment because:

- The corporate bonds were issued by Procter & Gamble (P&G) and each bond paid 8.0 percent or $80 each year until maturity in 2029.
- The bonds were rated AA by Fitch Ratings Service.
- They could take advantage of the time value of money concept if they chose to reinvest their interest from the P&G bonds.

Conclusion: The Johnsons received $800 interest each year from their P&G bonds. They also committed to reinvesting the $800 annual income they received each year. They used a time value of money table like Exhibit 1-B in the appendix after Chapter 1 of your text to estimate that if they earned 6 percent each year on their reinvested interest, they would accumulate $10,544.80 at the end of 10 years, as shown below.

Step 1: Locate the table factor for 6 percent and 10 years in Exhibit 1-B.

The table factor is 13.181

Step 2: Multiply the annual interest from their 10 P&G bonds by the table factor.

$\$800 \times 13.181 = \$10.544.80$

Ten years later, the Johnsons still have the Procter & Gamble bonds that are still paying 8 percent interest. They also have an additional $10,544.80 because they reinvested their interest income.

Tryout Problem: Assume you invest in a bond that pays $64 interest each year. Also assume you choose to reinvest your interest income in an investment that earns 5 percent. What is the value of your reinvested income at the end of 12 years? (Use Exhibit 1-B in the appendix after Chapter 1 for this calculation.)

Answer: $64 annual interest × 15.917 table factor = $1,018.69 total of reinvested interest

bearer bond A bond that is not registered in the investor's name.

payments on a registered coupon bond, the owner must present one of the detachable coupons to the issuing corporation or the paying agent.

A third type of bond is a **bearer bond,** which is not registered in the investor's name. While U.S. corporations no longer issue them, bearer bonds are generally issued by corporations in foreign countries. *Be warned:* If you own a bearer bond, anyone—the rightful owner or a thief—can collect interest payments and the face value at maturity if he or she has physical possession of the bearer bond.

DOLLAR APPRECIATION OF BOND VALUE

Most beginning investors think that a $1,000 bond is always worth $1,000. In reality, the price of a corporate bond may fluctuate until the maturity date. Changes in overall interest rates in the economy are the primary cause of most bond price fluctuations.

yield The rate of return earned by an investor who holds a bond for a stated period of time—usually a 12-month period.

Changing bond prices that result from these changes in overall interest rates are an example of interest rate risk and market risk, discussed in Chapter 13. *In fact, there is an inverse relationship between a bond's market value and overall interest rates in the economy.* When AT&T issued the bond mentioned earlier, the 5.50 percent interest rate was competitive with the interest rates offered by other corporations issuing bonds at that time. If overall interest rates fall, the AT&T bond will go up in market value due to its higher, 5.50 percent, interest rate. Because your AT&T bond has increased in value, you may want to sell your bond at the current higher price. Or, if you prefer, you can hold your bond until maturity and receive the bond's face value. *Note:* While the interest rate for corporate bonds is fixed, the market value and the yield for your AT&T bond are not. In this case, **yield** is the rate of return earned by an investor who holds a bond for a stated period of time—usually a 12-month period. Changes in the yield for a bond are caused by an increase *or* decrease in market value. The actual steps required to calculate yield are described later in this chapter.

On the other hand, this inverse relationship also affects a bond's market value if overall interest rates in the economy rise. For example, if overall interest rates for comparable bonds rise, the market value of your AT&T bond will decrease due to its fixed 5.50 percent stated interest rate. Keep in mind, you can always sell your bond, but if the price has decreased below the price you paid, you will incur a loss. In this situation, many investors choose to hold the bond until maturity and collect the face value. It is possible to calculate a bond's approximate market value using the following formula:

$$\text{Approximate market value} = \frac{\text{Dollar amount of annual interest}}{\text{Comparable interest rate}}$$

EXAMPLE: Approximate Market Value

Assume you purchase an AT&T bond that pays 5.50 percent interest based on a face value of $1,000 until the bond's maturity in 2018. Also assume new corporate bond issues of comparable quality are currently paying 7 percent. The approximate market value of your AT&T bond is $786, as follows:

$$\begin{aligned}\text{Dollar amount of annual interest} &= \$1{,}000 \times 5.50 \text{ percent}\\ &= \$1{,}000 \times 0.055\\ &= \$55\end{aligned}$$

$$\text{Approximate market value} = \frac{\text{Dollar amount of annual interest}}{\text{Comparable interest rate}} = \frac{\$55}{7\%}$$

$$= \$786$$

If you purchase the AT&T bond for $786, you will receive $55 interest each year until the bond's maturity. You will also be repaid the $1,000 face value at maturity, which results in a $214 profit because the bond's value increased from $786 to $1,000 between the time of purchase and the maturity date.

The value of a bond may also be affected by the financial condition of the company or government unit issuing the bond, the factors of supply and demand, an upturn or downturn in the economy, and the proximity of the bond's maturity date.

BOND REPAYMENT AT MATURITY

Corporate bonds are repaid at maturity. After you purchase a bond, you have two options: You may keep the bond until maturity and then redeem it, or you may sell the bond at any time to another investor. In either case, the value of your bond is closely tied to the corporation's ability to repay its bond indebtedness. The risk of business failure and how it affects bond repayment was discussed in Chapter 13. For example, bonds issued by American Airlines immediately dropped in value due to questions concerning continued interest payments and the prospects for bond repayment at maturity when American filed for bankruptcy in late 2011.

To help diversify their bond investments, some investors use a concept called "bond laddering." A **bond ladder** is a strategy where investors divide their investment dollars among bonds that mature at regular intervals in order to balance risk and return. To start your bond ladder, you purchase different bonds with maturities spread out over a number of years. For example, you might purchase bonds that mature in 1, 2, 3, 4, 5, 6, 7, 8, 9, and 10 years. When the first bond matures, you purchase a new bond that matures in 10 years. This new purchase continues the bond ladder. The short-term bonds

bond ladder A strategy where investors divide their investment dollars among bonds that mature at regular intervals in order to balance risk and return.

provide a high degree of stability because the bonds are not very sensitive to changing interest rates. The long-term bonds provide a higher yield, but you must accept the risk that the prices of the bonds might change. By choosing bonds with different maturities, you realize greater returns than from holding only short-term bonds, but with lower risk than holding only long-term bonds. With a bond ladder, you can also take advantage of the concept of dollar-cost averaging that was discussed in Chapter 14.

I appreciate the advantages of investing in corporate bonds.

Investors purchase corporate bonds for many different reasons, but basically there are three ways to make money with a bond investment: (1) interest income, (2) possible dollar appreciation of bond value, and (3) bond repayment at maturity. To learn more about why investors purchase bonds, use a Web search engine like Google or Yahoo! to search for the phrase "reasons to purchase bonds."

A TYPICAL BOND TRANSACTION

Assume that on January 16, 2007, you purchased a 5.25 percent corporate bond issued by E. I. du Pont de Nemours (DuPont). Your cost for the bond was $980 plus a $10 commission charge, for a total investment of $990. Also, assume you held the bond until January 16, 2013, when you sold it at its current market value of $1,190. Exhibit 15-2 shows the return on your investment.

After paying commissions for buying and selling your DuPont bond, you experienced a profit of $190 because the value of the bond increased from $990 to $1,180. The increase in the value of the bond resulted because overall interest rates in the economy declined during the 6-year period in which you owned the bond. Also, bonds will generally increase in value the closer they get to the maturity date in 2016.

You also made money on your DuPont bond because of interest payments. For each of the six years you owned the bond, DuPont paid you $52.50 ($1,000 × 5.25% = $52.50) interest. Thus, you received interest payments totaling $315. In this example, you made a total return of $505, as follows:

$$\begin{aligned}\text{Total return} &= \text{Current return} + \text{Capital gain}\\ &= \$315 + \$190\\ &= \$505\end{aligned}$$

Before investing in bonds, you should remember that the price of a corporate bond can decrease and that interest payments and eventual repayment may be a problem for

Exhibit 15-2

Sample corporate bond transaction for DuPont.

Assumptions

Interest, 5.25 percent; maturity date, 2016; purchased January 16, 2007; sold January 16, 2013.

Costs when purchased		**Return when sold**	
1 bond @ $980	$980	1 bond @ $1,080	$1,190
Plus commission	+ 10	Minus commission	− 10
Total investment	$990	Dollar return	$1,180

Transaction summary

Dollar return	$1,180
Minus total investment	− 990
Profit from bond sale	$ 190
Plus interest ($52.50 for 6 years)	+ 315
Total return on the transaction	$ 505

ARE BOND FUNDS RIGHT FOR YOU?

Bond funds are an indirect way of owning bonds issued by the U.S. Treasury, corporations, or state, city, and local governments. Many financial experts recommend bond funds for small investors because these investments offer two advantages: diversification and professional management. Diversification spells safety because an occasional loss incurred with one bond issue is usually offset by gains from other bond issues in the fund. Also, professional managers should be able to do a better job of picking bonds than individual investors.

Before investing, consider three factors. First, even the best managers make mistakes. Second, it may cost more to purchase bond funds than individual bonds. Finally, rising interest rates can cause the value of an individual bond with a fixed interest rate to decline. And since bond funds are made up of individual bonds, the share value for a bond fund is likely to decline if interest rates rise. Of course, the reverse is also true: if interest rates fall, the value of an individual bond with a fixed interest rate can increase. Thus, lower interest rates can cause shares in a bond fund to increase in value. As with most investments, the key to making money with funds is evaluation.

EVALUATING BOND FUNDS

Martha Hernandez, a working mother with one child, received $45,000 following the death of her grandmother. After some careful planning, she decided to invest $35,000 in two high-quality corporate bond funds. She used the remaining $10,000 to pay off some credit card debts and establish an emergency fund. During the next two years, she earned over 7 percent on her bond investments each year—not bad during a period when CDs were paying between 0.50 and 2 percent.

Martha's 7 percent return wasn't just luck. She began by establishing an investment goal: Find a safe investment with minimal risk. After establishing her goal, she talked with an account executive at Merrill Lynch and asked for five suggestions that would enable her to attain her goal. Of the five original suggestions, three were bond funds.

Next, Martha took a crucial step that many investors forget: She did her own research and didn't just rely on the account executive's suggestions. She used the Internet to obtain both a prospectus and an annual report for each fund. Then she made a trip to the library, where she analyzed the performance of each bond fund using business and personal finance periodicals. Based on the account executive's suggestions and her own research, she chose the "top" two bond funds.

Martha spent almost 25 hours researching her investments, but believes the time was well spent. When you consider the amount of money she made on her bond fund investments during the first two years—about $5,000—she made $200 an hour.

a corporation that encounters financial difficulties or enters bankruptcy. Also, both the annual interest and profits from bond transactions are taxable. For more information on how taxation affects a bond investment, see Chapter 4 of this text or visit the IRS website at www.irs.gov. Instead of purchasing individual bonds, some investors prefer to purchase bond funds. To help you decide whether you should purchase individual bonds or bond funds, read the Financial Planning for Life's Situations box on this page.

THE MECHANICS OF A BOND TRANSACTION

Most bonds are sold through full-service brokerage firms, discount brokerage firms, or the Internet. If you use a full-service brokerage firm, your account executive should provide both information and advice about bond investments. As with stock investments, the chief advantage of using a discount brokerage firm or trading online is lower commissions, but you must do your own research. As you will see later in this chapter, many sources of information can be used to evaluate bond investments.

Generally, if you purchase a $1,000 bond through an account executive or brokerage firm, you should expect to pay a minimum commission of between $5 and $25. If you purchase more bonds, the commission usually drops to $1 to $10 per bond. You should also expect to pay commissions when you sell bonds. Some brokerage firms have begun charging a flat commission charge regardless of how many bonds you buy or sell. Commissions to buy and sell bonds are generally less if you use a discount brokerage firm or the Internet.

PRACTICE QUIZ 15-3

1 Describe the three reasons investors purchase bonds.
2 What are the differences among a registered bond, registered coupon bond, and a bearer bond?
3 In what ways can interest rates in the economy affect the price of a corporate bond?
4 Why is the value of a bond closely tied to the issuing corporation's ability to repay its bond indebtedness?
5 How are corporate bonds bought and sold?

Government Bonds and Debt Securities

LO15-4

Discuss why federal, state, and local governments issue bonds and why investors purchase government bonds.

In addition to corporations, the U.S. government and state and local governments issue bonds to obtain financing. A **government bond** is a written pledge of a government or a municipality to repay a specified sum of money, along with interest. In this section, we discuss bonds issued by these three levels of government and look at why investors purchase these bonds.

government bond A written pledge of a government or a municipality to repay a specified sum of money, along with interest.

TREASURY BILLS, NOTES, AND BONDS

Traditionally, investors chose U.S. government securities because they were backed by the full faith and credit of the U.S. government and carried a decreased risk of default. Today, as a result of the economic crisis, concerns about the national debt, the debt crisis in some European nations, and downgrades or threats of downgrades by U.S. rating agencies, many investors are beginning to worry about what were once considered risk-free investments. Even with concerns about default and the nation's economic problems, many investors in the United States and from around the globe still regard securities issued by the U.S. as a very conservative and safe investment.

Today, the U.S. Treasury Department issues five principal types of securities: Treasury bills, Treasury notes, Treasury bonds, Treasury Inflation-Protected Securities (TIPS), and U.S. government savings bonds. *Note:* Refer to Chapter 5 for a review of different types of U.S. savings bonds. Treasury bills, notes, bonds, TIPS, and savings bonds can be purchased through Treasury Direct at www.treasurydirect.gov. For more information about the Treasury Direct website, see Exhibit 15-3.

Treasury Direct conducts auctions to sell Treasury securities. Buyers interested in purchasing these securities at such auctions may bid competitively or noncompetitively. Most individual investors use noncompetitive bids once they have visited the website and opened an account. If they bid competitively, they must specify the rate or interest yield they are willing to accept. If they bid noncompetitively, they are willing to accept the interest rate or yield determined at auction. Treasury securities may also be purchased directly from banks or brokers, which charge a commission. *Be warned:* Interest rates for securities issued by the U.S. Treasury are at record low levels. And yet, investors often choose these securities because of the decreased risk of default. U.S. Treasury securities are also used by some investors as part of their efforts to use asset allocation to lessen overall risk.

Interest paid on U.S. government securities is taxable for federal income tax purposes but is exempt from state and local taxation. Current information on prices and interest rates appears on the Internet and in *The Wall Street Journal* and other financial publications.

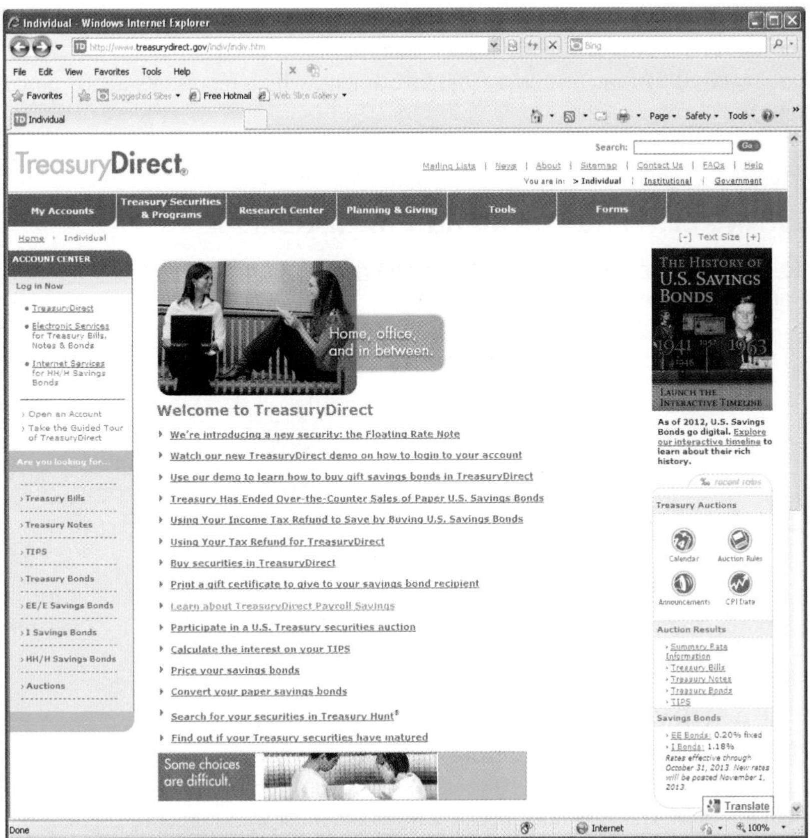

Source: www.treasurydirect.gov, March 14, 2013.

Exhibit 15-3

The Treasury Direct website provides information regarding United States Treasury securities.

TREASURY BILLS A *Treasury bill,* sometimes called a *T-bill,* is sold in a minimum unit of \$100 with additional increments of \$100 above the minimum. The maturity for T-bills may be short as a few days or as long as 1 year. The Treasury Department currently only sells T-bills with 4-week, 13-week, 26-week, and 52-week maturities. Another type of bill, the cash management bill, is issued in terms usually shorter than those of other T-bills.

T-bills are discounted securities, and the actual purchase price you pay is less than the maturity value of the T-bill. At maturity, you receive the maturity value often referred to as the face value.

EXAMPLE: Discount Amount for a T-Bill

Assume you purchase a 52-week \$1,000 T-bill with a stated interest rate of 1 percent. The discount amount (\$10) is calculated in Step 1. The purchase price (\$990) is calculated in Step 2.

Step 1: Discount amount = Maturity value × interest rate
= \$1,000 × 1 percent
= \$1,000 × 0.01
= \$10

Step 2: Purchase price = Maturity value − Discount amount
= \$1,000 − \$10
= \$990

When T-bills reach maturity, you are paid the maturity value or face amount. In reality, the yield on T-bills is slightly higher than the stated interest rate. In the above example, you received $10 interest on a $990 investment, which represents a 1.01 percent annual return.

EXAMPLE: Yield Calculation for a T-Bill

To calculate the annual yield, divide the discount amount by the purchase price. For the above example,

$$\text{Current yield for a T-bill} = \frac{\text{Discount amount}}{\text{Purchase price}} = \frac{\$10}{\$990} = 0.0101 = 1.01 \text{ percent}$$

The stated interest rate for the T-bill in the above examples is only for illustration purposes. In reality, the actual interest rate paid by the U.S. Treasury for T-bills is quite a bit less at the time of publication of your text.

TREASURY NOTES A *Treasury note* (sometimes called a *T-note*) is issued in $100 units with a maturity of more than 1 year but not more than 10 years. Typical maturities are 2, 3, 5, 7, and 10 years. Interest rates for Treasury notes are slightly higher than those for Treasury bills, because investors must wait longer to get their money back and therefore demand a higher interest rate. Interest for Treasury notes is paid every six months until maturity. At maturity the face value of the note is paid to the owner. Notes can also be sold before maturity.

TREASURY BONDS A *Treasury bond* is issued in minimum units of $100 that have a 30-year maturity. Interest rates for Treasury bonds are generally higher than those for either Treasury bills or Treasury notes. Again, the primary reason for the higher interest rates is the length of time investors must hold Treasury bonds. Like interest on Treasury notes, interest on Treasury bonds is paid every six months until maturity. When a bond matures, the owner is paid the face value of the bond. Bonds can also be sold before maturity.

TREASURY INFLATION-PROTECTED SECURITIES (TIPS) *Treasury inflation-protected securities (TIPS)* are sold in minimum units of $100 with additional increments of $100 above the minimum. Currently, TIPS are sold with 5-, 10-, or 30-year maturities. The principal of TIPS securities increases with inflation and decreases with deflation, as measured by the consumer price index. When TIPS mature, you are paid the adjusted principal or original principal, whichever is greater. TIPS also pay interest twice a year, at a fixed rate. The rate is applied to the adjusted principal; so, like the principal, interest payments rise with inflation and fall with deflation. Interest income and growth in principal are exempt from state and local income taxes but are subject to federal income tax. Like other Treasury securities, TIPS can be held until maturity or sold before maturity.

DID YOU KNOW?

YIELDS FOR U.S. GOVERNMENT 10-YEAR TREASURY NOTES

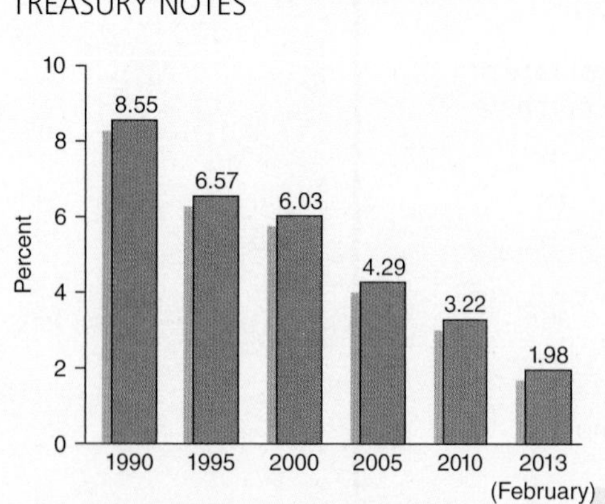

Source: The Federal Reserve website at www.federalreserve.gov, accessed March 17, 2013.

FEDERAL AGENCY DEBT ISSUES

In addition to the bonds and securities issued by the Treasury Department, debt securities are issued by federal agencies or government sponsored enterprises, which include the Federal National Mortgage Association (sometimes referred to as Fannie Mae), the Government National Mortgage Association (sometimes referred to as Ginnie Mae), and the Federal Home Loan Mortgage Corporation (which somehow became known as Freddie Mac).

While some federal agencies or enterprises may be government sponsored, strictly speaking they are not actually part of the U.S. government, and the securities they issue do not have the same guarantee that the bills, notes, and bonds issued by the United States Treasury have. As a result, agency debt issues often have a slightly higher interest rate than securities issued by the Treasury Department. Still, these debt issues are considered safe investments by most financial planners because of the relationship between the government and the agency or enterprise. In many cases, the agencies or enterprises are considered too large or too important to the nation's economy to be allowed to fail. Both Fannie Mae and Freddie Mac, for instance, were chartered by the U.S. Congress. And both Fannie Mae and Freddie Mac received federal monies to avoid failure during the recent economic crisis. The loan programs they provide were needed to help consumers obtain home mortgages. In addition to the slightly increased risk associated with agency debt issues, there are other factors that should be considered before investing in agency debt. For example, their minimum denomination may be as high as $5,000 to $25,000. Also, securities issued by federal agencies have maturities ranging up to 30 years, with an average life of 5 to 12 years.

Often brokers and account executives recommend federal agency debt instruments because the interest rate is 0.50 to 1.0 percent higher than Treasury securities. However, you should know that there are differences in how interest is paid when compared to Treasury securities and that most agency debt is also callable before the maturity date. Simply put, investing in agency debt is more complicated than buying and selling Treasury securities.

STATE AND LOCAL GOVERNMENT SECURITIES

A **municipal bond,** sometimes called a *muni,* is a debt security issued by a state or local government. In the United States, there are 50 state governments. In addition, cities, counties, school districts, and special taxing districts may sell municipal bonds. Such securities are used to finance the ongoing activities of state and local governments and major projects such as airports, schools, toll roads, and toll bridges. They may be purchased directly from the government entity that issued them or through account executives or brokerage firms.

municipal bond A debt security issued by a state or local government.

State and local securities are classified as either general obligation bonds or revenue bonds. A **general obligation bond** is backed by the full faith, credit, and unlimited taxing power of the government that issued it. A **revenue bond** is repaid from the income generated by the project it is designed to finance. Although both general obligation and revenue bonds are relatively safe, defaults have occurred in recent years.

general obligation bond A bond backed by the full faith, credit, and unlimited taxing power of the government that issued it.

revenue bond A bond that is repaid from the income generated by the project it is designed to finance.

If the risk of default worries you, you can purchase insured municipal bonds. A number of states offer to guarantee payments on selected securities. Also, there are two large private insurers: MBIA Inc.(Municipal Bond Insurance Association), and the Assured Guaranty Municipal Corporation. Even if a municipal bond issue is insured, however, financial experts worry about the insurer's ability to pay off in the event of default on a large bond issue. Most experts advise investors to determine the underlying quality of a bond whether or not it is insured. Also, guaranteed municipal securities usually carry a slightly lower interest rate than uninsured bonds because of the reduced risk of default. While many investors think that municipal bonds are as safe as securities offered by the U.S. Treasury or federal agency debt issues, they are not because there

I sometimes think about investing in government and tax-free municipal bonds.

U.S. Treasury and municipal bonds are conservative investments, but there may be reasons why they may be the right choice for your investment portfolio. One important reason for choosing government and municipal bonds may be asset allocation. Other reasons might include the outlook for the economy, your age, your tolerance for risk and possible tax advantages.

have been defaults. *Caution:* The majority of municipal bonds are safe investments, but it is your responsibility to evaluate different bond issues before investing your money.

Like a corporate bond, a municipal bond may be callable by the government unit that issued it. *Be warned:* Your municipal bond may be called if interest rates fall and the government entity that issued the bond can sell new bonds with lower rates. For example, since 2000 thousands of bondholders who purchased high-yielding municipal bonds in the late 1980s and 1990s were shocked to have their bonds called. Many were counting on another 5 to 10 years of high yields to finance their retirement. Although they were repaid the principal invested in the bond that was called, they faced the challenge of reinvesting their money when interest rates were at record lows. If the bond is not called, the investor has two options. First, the bond may be held until maturity, in which case the investor will be repaid its face value. Second, the bond may be sold to another investor before maturity.

One of the most important features of municipal bonds is that the interest on them may be exempt from federal taxes—a factor especially important for wealthy investors. Whether or not the interest on municipal bonds is tax exempt often depends on how the funds obtained from their sale are used. *It is your responsibility, as an investor, to determine whether or not interest on municipal bonds is taxable.* Municipal bonds exempt from federal taxation are generally exempt from state and local taxes only in the state where they are issued. Furthermore, although the interest income on municipal bonds may be exempt from taxation, a *capital gain* that results when you sell a municipal bond before maturity and at a profit may be taxable just like capital gains on other investments sold at a profit.

Because of their tax-exempt status, the interest rates on municipal bonds are lower than those on taxable bonds. By using the following formula, you can calculate the *taxable equivalent yield* for a municipal security:

$$\text{Taxable equivalent yield} = \frac{\text{Tax-exempt yield}}{1.0 - \text{Your tax rate}}$$

EXAMPLE: Tax Equivalent Yield

The taxable equivalent yield on a 3 percent tax-exempt municipal bond for a person in the 28 percent tax bracket is 4.17 percent, as follows:

$$\begin{aligned}\text{Taxable equivalent yield} &= \frac{\text{Tax-exempt yield}}{1.0 - \text{Your tax rate}}\\ &= \frac{3\%}{1.0 - 0.28}\\ &= \frac{0.03}{0.72}\\ &= 0.0417 = 4.17 \text{ percent}\end{aligned}$$

Once you have calculated the taxable equivalent yield, you can compare the return on tax-exempt securities with the return on taxable investments that include certificates of deposit, corporate bonds, stocks, mutual funds, and other investment alternatives. Exhibit 15-4 illustrates the yields for tax-exempt investments and their taxable equivalent yields.

Exhibit 15-4

Yields for tax-exempt investments

The following information can be used to compare the return on tax-exempt investments with the returns offered by taxable investments.

	Equivalent Yields for Taxable Investments					
Tax-Exempt Yield	15% Tax Rate	25% Tax Rate	28% Tax Rate	33% Tax Rate	35% Tax Rate	39.6% Tax Rate
2%	2.35%	2.67%	2.78%	2.99%	3.08%	3.31%
3	3.53	4.00	4.17	4.48	4.62	4.97
4	4.71	5.33	5.56	5.97	6.15	6.62
5	5.88	6.67	6.94	7.46	7.69	8.28
6	7.06	8.00	8.33	8.96	9.23	9.93

1 What are the maturities for a Treasury bill, a Treasury note, a Treasury bond, and Treasury Inflation-Protected Securities?
2 What is the difference between a general obligation bond and a revenue bond?
3 What risks are involved when investing in municipal bonds?

The Decision to Buy or Sell Bonds

LO15-5

Evaluate bonds when making an investment.

One basic principle we have stressed throughout this text is the need to evaluate any potential investment. Certainly corporate *and* government bonds are no exception. Only after you have completed your evaluation should you purchase bonds. In this section, we examine methods you can use to evaluate bond investments.

THE INTERNET

Just as you can use the Internet to evaluate a stock investment, you can use much of the same financial information to evaluate a bond investment. By accessing a corporation's website and locating the topics "financial information," "annual report," or "investor relations," you can find a great deal of information about the firm and its current financial condition. As an added bonus, a corporation may provide more than one year's annual report on its website, so you can make comparisons from one year to another.

When investing in bonds, you can use the Internet in three other ways. First, you can obtain price information on specific bond issues to track the value of your investments. Second, it is possible to trade bonds online and pay lower commissions than you would pay a full-service or discount brokerage firm. Third, you can get research about corporate and government bond issues (including recommendations to buy or sell) by accessing specific bond websites. *Be warned:* Bond websites are not as numerous as websites that provide information on stocks, mutual funds, or personal financial planning. And many of the better bond websites charge an annual subscription fee or you must register to access their research and recommendations. The following websites provide basic and detailed information designed to make you a better bond investor:

www.shop4bonds.com
www.bonds-online.com
www.buysellbonds.com
www.investinginbonds.com
www.bondsearch123.com
http://finance.yahoo.com/bonds

While many of the above websites provide information for government bonds and debt securities, the websites below provide specific information about government securities issued by the United States government or state and local governments.

www.emuni.com
www.fmsbonds.com
www.municipalbonds.com
www.treasurydirect.gov

You may also want to visit the Moody's website (www.moodys.com), the Standard & Poor's website (www.standardandpoors.com), the Mergent website (www.mergent.com), and Fitch Ratings (www.fitchratings.com) to obtain detailed information about both corporate and government bonds. While you may be asked to pay a fee to access the information on these Internet sites, much of the same information may be available in printed form at a college or public library.

FINANCIAL COVERAGE FOR BOND TRANSACTIONS

Detailed information obtained from the Yahoo! Finance website (http://finance.yahoo.com/bonds) for a $1,000 American Express corporate bond that pays 6.150 percent interest and matures in 2017 is provided in Exhibit 15-5. In addition to Internet coverage of bond transactions, *The Wall Street Journal, Barron's,* and some metropolitan newspapers publish information on bonds. *Note:* Most bonds are traded in the over-the-counter market by bond dealers and brokers around the country who trade bonds over the phone or electronically. Thus, the bonds whose prices are reported in the newspaper make up only a small portion of the bonds actually bought and sold each day.

In bond quotations, prices are given as a percentage of the face value, which is usually $1,000. Thus, to find the actual price for a bond, you must multiply the face value (usually $1,000) by the bond quotation.

EXAMPLE: Bond Price Calculation

Assume that a bond has a price quote of 84. The actual price for the bond is $840, as calculated below.

$$\begin{aligned}\text{Bond price} &= \text{Face value} \times \text{bond quote}\\ &= \$1{,}000 \times 84 \text{ percent}\\ &= \$1{,}000 \times 0.84\\ &= \$840\end{aligned}$$

In the United States bond price quotations are based on the *clean price.* The clean price represents the price of a bond with no accrued or earned interest. On the other hand, the *dirty price* of a bond represents the price of the bond *plus* accrued interest

Exhibit 15-5

Bond information available by accessing the Yahoo! bond site

AMERICAN EXPRESS CO

OVERVIEW

1. Price:	115.64
2. Coupon (%):	6.150
3. Maturity Date:	28-Aug-2017
4. Yield to Maturity (%):	3.151
5. Current Yield (%):	5.318
6. Fitch Ratings:	A
7. Coupon Payment Frequency:	Semi-Annual
8. First Coupon Date:	28-Feb-2008
9. Type:	Corporate
10. Callable:	No

1. *Price* is quoted as a percentage of the face value: $1,000 × 115.64% = $1,156.40
2. *Coupon (%)* is the rate of interest: 6.150 percent
3. *Maturity Date* is the date when bondholders will receive repayment of the face value: August 28, 2017
4. *Yield to Maturity (%)* takes into account the relationship among a bond's maturity value, the time to maturity, the current price, and the annual amount of interest: 3.151 percent
5. *Current Yield (%)* is determined by dividing the dollar amount of annual interest by the current price of the bond: $61.50 ÷ 1,156.40 = 5.318 percent
6. *Fitch Ratings* shows the rating issued by Fitch Bond Ratings. This rating is used to assess the risk associated with this bond: A
7. *Coupon Payment Frequency* tells bondholders how often they will receive interest payments: Semi-annual
8. *First Coupon Date* tells bondholders when the first interest payment will be paid: February 28, 2008
9. *Type:* Corporate
10. *Callable* tells the bondholder if the bond is callable or not: No

Source: The Yahoo! Finance bond website, http://finance.yahoo.com/bonds, March 18, 2013.

earned by the bond owner since the last interest payment date. The dirty price is different from the clean price because bond owners earn interest for every day that they own a bond issue. For example, assume that Samantha Karlee owns a $1,000 corporate bond that pays 6.0 percent interest. She receives her regular semiannual interest payment on June 1. Two months later, she decides to sell her bond. In this case, the buyer will pay Samantha the dirty price, which includes the quoted price of the bond *plus* interest for the two-month period since Samantha's last interest payment. When the next semiannual interest payment date arrives, the buyer will receive the full interest payment.

For government bonds, most financial publications include two price quotations. The first price quotation, or the *bid price,* is the price a dealer or buyer is willing to pay for a government security. The bid price represents the amount that a seller could receive for a government bond. The second price quotation, or the *asked price,* represents the price at which a dealer or seller is willing to sell a government security. The asked price represents the amount for which a buyer could purchase the security.

ANNUAL REPORTS

As pointed out earlier in this chapter, bondholders must be concerned about the financial health of the corporation or government unit that issues bonds. To understand how important financial information is when evaluating a bond issue, consider the following two questions:

1. Will the bond be repaid at maturity?
2. Will you receive interest payments until maturity?

While it may be difficult to answer these questions with 100 percent accuracy, the information contained in a firm's annual report is the logical starting point. Today there are two ways to obtain a corporation's annual report. First, you can either write or telephone the corporation and request an annual report. (Many corporations have 800 telephone numbers for your use.) Second, as mentioned in an earlier section, most corporations maintain a website that provides access to annual reports and detailed information about their financial performance.

Regardless of how you obtain an annual report, you should look for signs of financial strength or weakness. Is the firm profitable? Are sales revenues increasing? Are the firm's long-term liabilities increasing? In fact, there are many questions you should ask before making a decision to buy a bond. To help you determine the right questions to ask when evaluating a bond issue, examine the How To . . . feature on page 542. Also, you may want to examine the bond's rating and perform the calculations described on pages 540–544 before investing your money.

BOND RATINGS

To determine the quality and risk associated with bond issues, investors rely on the bond ratings provided by Moody's Investors Service Inc., Standard & Poor's Corporation, and Fitch Ratings. These companies rank thousands of corporate and municipal bonds.

As Exhibit 15-6 illustrates, bond ratings generally range from AAA (the highest) to D (the lowest) for Standard Poor's and Aaa (the highest) to C (the lowest) for Moody's. For both Moody's and Standard & Poor's, the first two categories (high-grade and medium-grade) represent investment-grade securities. Investment-grade securities are suitable for conservative investors who want a safe investment that provides a predictable source of income. Bonds in the speculative category are considered speculative in nature and are often referred to as high-yield or "junk" bonds. Finally, the C and D categories are used to rank bonds where there are poor prospects of repayment or even continued payment of interest. Bonds in these categories may be in default.

Generally, U.S. government securities issued by the Treasury Department and various federal agencies are not graded because they are risk free for practical purposes. The rating of municipal bonds is similar to that of corporate bonds.

BOND YIELD CALCULATIONS

Earlier in this chapter the *yield* for a bond investment was defined as the rate of return earned by an investor who holds a bond for a stated period of time. Two methods are used to measure the yield on a bond investment: the current yield and the yield to maturity.

Exhibit 15-6 Description of bond ratings provided by Moody's Investors Service and Standard & Poor's Corporation

Quality	Moody's	Standard & Poor's	Description
High-grade	Aaa	AAA	Bonds that are judged to be of the best quality.
	Aa	AA	Bonds that are judged to be of high quality by all standards. Together with the first group, they comprise what are generally known as *high-grade* bonds.
Medium-grade	A	A	Bonds that possess many favorable investment attributes and are to be considered upper-medium-grade obligations.
	Baa	BBB	Bonds that are considered medium-grade obligations. They may be subject to moderate credit risk.
Speculative	Ba	BB	Bonds that are judged to have speculative elements; their future cannot be considered well assured.
	B	B	Bonds that generally lack characteristics of a safe investment and are subject to high credit risk.
Default	Caa	CCC	Bonds that are of poor standing and vulnerable.
	Ca	CC	Bonds that represent obligations that are highly speculative and very near default.
	C		Moody's rating given to bonds that are typically in default and regarded as having extremely poor prospects for recovery of principal or interest.
		C	Standard & Poor's rating given to bonds that are highly vulnerable.
		D	Bond issues in default.

Sources: The Standard & Poor's website at www.standardandpoors.com, accessed March 18, 2013, and Moody's Investors Service website at www.moodys.com, accessed March 18, 2013.

The **current yield** is determined by dividing the annual income amount generated by an investment by the investment's current market value. For bonds, the following formula may help you complete this calculation:

$$\text{Current yield on a corporate bond} = \frac{\text{Annual income amount}}{\text{Current market value}}$$

current yield Determined by dividing the annual dollar amount of income generated by an investment by the investment's current market value.

EXAMPLE: Current Yield Calculation

Assume you own a General Motors Acceptance Corporation (GMAC) corporate bond that pays 6.75 percent interest ($67.50) each year until the bond's maturity in 2018. Also assume the current market price of the GMAC bond is $900.

Because the current market value is less than the bond's face value, the current yield increases to 7.5, as shown below.

$$\text{Current yield} = \frac{\text{Annual income amount}}{\text{Current market value}}$$

$$= \frac{\$67.50}{\$900}$$

$$= 0.075 = 7.5 \text{ percent}$$

HOW TO . . .

Evaluate Corporate, Government, and Municipal Bonds

When investing in bonds, there are a lot of factors to consider. To help you decide if a bond is a good investment that will help you reach your financial goals, use the suggestions contained in this How To . . . feature.

Take This Step	Suggested Action
☑ 1. Determine what type of bond you want.	Bonds are issued by the federal government, state and local governments, and corporations. Regardless of who issues the bond, you should always evaluate a potential bond investment.
☑ 2. To help narrow the field of potential bond investments, use a bond screener.	While there are many available, the bond screener at http://finance.yahoo.com/bonds is an excellent place to begin your search. By entering the type of bond you want and other criteria like acceptable interest rate, current yield, and other factors, the Yahoo! Screener will display bonds that match your criteria.
☑ 3. Dig in deeper to find more information.	Many of the sources of bond information discussed in this chapter can be used to gather important information about the financial health of the issuer of a specific bond issue. *Hint:* You can use Personal Financial Planner sheet 60 to record the information you find.
☑ 4. Use a financial calculator to determine if a bond is a good investment or not.	You can use a bond calculator to help evaluate your bond. For example, the Morningstar bond calculator at http://screen.morningstar.com/bondcalc/BondCalculator_YTM.html can be used to calculate yield to maturity and the tax-equivalent yield for different bond issues. You can find other bond calculators by using an Internet search engine like Google or Yahoo! and entering the term "bond calculator" in the search window.

This calculation allows you to compare the current yield on a bond investment with the yields of other investment alternatives, which include savings accounts, certificates of deposit, common stock, preferred stock, and mutual funds. Naturally, the higher the current yield, the better! A current yield of 9 percent is better than a current yield of 7.5 percent. Before choosing a bond because of a high current yield, keep in mind there are other factors to consider. One very important factor to consider is the risk associated with a potential bond investment. For example, the GMAC bond in the above example is rated B by Fitch ratings. The "B" rating indicates that this investment is a speculative bond issue and may not be suitable for investors interested in conservative investments with minimal risk. On the other hand, a more risk-oriented investor may choose this bond because of the higher yield.

The **yield to maturity** takes into account the relationship among a bond's maturity value, the time to maturity, the current price, and the dollar amount of interest. This calculation is often reported in financial publications and on the Internet, but you can approximate a bond's yield to maturity using the formula below.

yield to maturity A yield calculation that takes into account the relationship among a bond's maturity value, the time to maturity, the current price, and the dollar amount of interest.

$$\text{Yield to maturity} = \frac{\text{Dollar amount of annual interest} + \dfrac{\text{Face value} - \text{Market value}}{\text{Number of periods}}}{\dfrac{\text{Market value} + \text{Face value}}{2}}$$

EXAMPLE: Yield to Maturity

Assume you purchased the GMAC bond in the above example on September 15, 2013 for $900 and held the bond for five years until its maturity on September 15, 2018. The yield to maturity is 9.21 percent, as illustrated below:

$$\text{Yield to maturity} = \frac{\text{Dollar amount of annual interest} + \dfrac{\text{Face value} - \text{Market value}}{\text{Number of periods}}}{\dfrac{\text{Market value} + \text{Face value}}{2}}$$

$$= \frac{\$67.50 + \dfrac{\$1{,}000 - \$900}{5}}{\dfrac{\$900 + \$1{,}000}{2}}$$

$$= \frac{\$87.50}{\$950}$$

$$= 0.0921 = 9.21 \text{ percent}$$

Note: It is also possible to calculate yield to maturity using a financial calculator.

In this situation, the yield to maturity takes into account two types of return on the bond. First, you will receive interest income from your purchase date until the maturity date. Second, at maturity you will receive a payment for the face value of the bond. If you purchased the bond at a price below the face value, the yield to maturity will be greater than the stated interest rate. If you purchased the bond at a price above the face value, the yield to maturity will be less than the stated interest rate. Remember, the actual price you pay for a bond may be higher or lower than the face value because of many factors, including changes in the economy, increases or decreases in comparable interest rates on similar investments, and the financial condition of the company. At least part of the reason the GMAC bond in this example is priced below the $1,000 face value is because of the corporation's B rating issued by Fitch—a major bond rating service.

The yield to maturity calculation is an annualized rate of return if the bond is held until maturity. If the bond is sold before maturity, the yield to maturity for the investor may be higher or lower, depending on the price the bond is sold for and the length of time the bond is held. Like the current yield, the yield to maturity allows you to compare returns on a bond investment with similar investments. Also, like the current yield, the higher the yield to maturity, the better. A yield to maturity of 10 percent is better than a yield to maturity of 9.21 percent.

DID YOU KNOW?

The U.S. Treasury provides a number of bond calculators to help you determine if securities issued by the federal government are the right investment to help you achieve your investment goals. To begin using the different calculators on this site, go to www.treasurydirect.gov and enter "calculators" in the search box.

my life 5

I know how to evaluate bond investments.

How do you choose the right bond to help you meet your investment objectives? Although there are many sources of information about bond investments, most serious investors use the Internet to obtain current price information, bond ratings, and other important information about bond issues.

Financial Planning Calculations

THE TIMES INTEREST EARNED RATIO: ONE TOOL TO HELP YOU EVALUATE BOND ISSUES

After evaluating AT&T Corporation, Shira and Mathew Matson wanted to purchase the firm's corporate debentures. But she was concerned about the corporation's ability to make future interest payments. To determine AT&T's ability to pay interest, she used a formula called the *times interest earned ratio,* illustrated below:

$$\text{Times interest earned} = \frac{\text{Operating income before interest and taxes}}{\text{Interest expense}}$$

For example, AT&T Corporation had interest expense of $3,444 million and operating income before interest and taxes of $12,997 million in 2012 (the latest year for which actual figures are available at the time of this publication). The times interest earned ratio for AT&T Corporation is 3.77 to 1, as follows:

$$\text{Times interest earned} = \frac{\$12{,}997 \text{ million}}{\$3{,}444 \text{ million}}$$

$$= 3.77 \text{ to } 1$$

Although the average for the times interest earned ratio varies from industry to industry, a higher number is better than a lower number. AT&T Corporation is earning slightly over 3.77 times the amount required to pay the annual interest on its notes, bonds, and other financial obligations. With a times interest earned ratio of 3.77 to 1, AT&T could experience a drop in earnings and still meet its financial obligations.

Source: Based on information contained in AT&T Corporation's 2012 annual report.

OTHER SOURCES OF INFORMATION

Investors can use two additional sources of information to evaluate potential bond investments. First, business periodicals can provide information about the economy and interest rates and detailed financial information about a corporation or government entity that issues bonds. You can locate many of these periodicals at your college or public library or on the Internet.

Second, a number of federal agencies provide information that may be useful to bond investors in either printed form or on the Internet. Reports and research published by the Federal Reserve System (www.federalreserve.gov), the U.S. Treasury (www.treasury.gov), and the Bureau of Economic Analysis (www.bea.gov) may be used to assess the nation's economy. You can also obtain information that corporations have reported to the Securities and Exchange Commission by accessing the SEC website (www.sec.gov). Finally, state and local governments will provide information about specific municipal bond issues.

Corporate Bond Evaluation

PRACTICE QUIZ 15-5

1 What type of information is contained on a corporation's website? How could this information be used to evaluate a bond issue?
2 What is the market value for a bond with a face value of $1,000 and a newspaper quotation of 77?
3 How important are bond ratings when evaluating a bond issue?
4 Why should you calculate the current yield and yield to maturity on a bond investment?
5 How can business periodicals and government publications help you evaluate a bond issue?

my life stages for investing in bonds . . .

YOUR PERSONAL FINANCE DASHBOARD

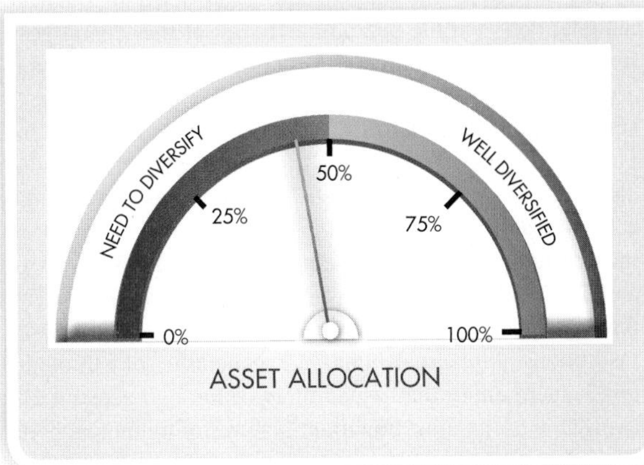

BONDS AND ASSET ALLOCATION

A personal finance dashboard allows you to assess your financial situation.

While some investors think of bonds as an investment for "older folks," there are other valid reasons to choose bonds for your investment portfolio. In fact, many investors use bonds to diversify their investment portfolio.

YOUR SITUATION: Bonds are an excellent way to use asset allocation to diversify your investments—especially if you think your investments may decline in value because of current or future economic conditions. Do you need to diversify your investments? Other personal financial planning actions you might consider during various stages of your life include:

. . . in college

- Establish investment and financial goals
- Work to balance your budget
- Start an emergency fund
- Save a reasonable amount of money from each paycheck
- Open a brokerage account and begin investing

. . . in my 20s

- Revise investment and financial goals
- Participate in an employer sponsored 401(k) retirement account and/or open a Roth IRA or Traditional IRA
- After careful evaluation, continue investing in growth investments including stocks and mutual funds
- Begin using asset allocation to diversify your investments

. . . in my 30s and 40s

- Revise investment and financial goals
- Continue to save money and invest
- Begin to plan for retirement in 20 to 30 years
- Choose investments that match your tolerance for risk
- Use asset allocation to diversity your investments in stocks, bonds, and mutual funds
- Evaluate all existing investments on a regular basis

. . . in my 50s and beyond

- Revise investment and financial goals
- Determine current financial status and the number of years until retirement
- Begin to increase the amount of money invested in bonds and other conservative investments and decrease the amount invested in growth investments
- Use asset allocation to diversify all your investments
- Evaluate all existing investments on a regular basis

SUMMARY OF LEARNING OBJECTIVES

LO15-1

Describe the characteristics of corporate bonds.

A corporate bond is a corporation's written pledge to repay a specified amount of money with interest. All of the details about a bond (face value, interest rate, maturity date, repayment, etc.) are contained in the bond indenture. The trustee is the bondholder's representative.

LO15-2

Discuss why corporations issue bonds.

Corporations issue bonds and other securities to pay for major purchases and to help finance their ongoing activities. Firms also issue bonds when it is difficult or impossible to sell stock to improve a corporation's financial leverage, and to reduce taxes paid to federal and state governments. Bonds may be debentures, mortgage bonds, subordinated debentures, convertible bonds, or high-yield (junk) bonds. Most bonds are callable. A call provision can be used to buy back bonds before the maturity date. To ensure that the money will be available when needed to repay bonds, many corporations establish a sinking fund. Corporations can also issue serial bonds that mature on different dates.

LO15-3

Explain why investors purchase corporate bonds.

Investors purchase corporate bonds for three reasons: (1) interest income, (2) possible increase in value, and (3) repayment at maturity. They are also an excellent way to use asset allocation to diversify your investment portfolio. The method used to pay bondholders their interest depends on whether they own registered bonds, registered coupon bonds, or bearer bonds. Because bonds can increase or decrease in value, it is possible to purchase a bond at a discount and hold the bond until it appreciates in value. Changes in overall interest rates in the economy and changes in the financial condition of the corporation are the primary causes of most bond price fluctuations. You can lose money on your investment if your bond decreases in value. You can also choose to hold the bond until maturity, when the corporation will repay the bond's face value. Corporate bonds are sold by full-service and discount brokerage firms and online.

LO15-4

Discuss why federal, state, and local governments issue bonds and why investors purchase government bonds.

Bonds issued by the U.S. Treasury are used to finance the national debt and the ongoing activities of the federal government. Currently, the U.S. Treasury issues five principal types of securities: Treasury bills, Treasury notes, Treasury bonds, Treasury Inflation-Protected Securities (TIPS), and savings bonds. Federal agencies, government-sponsored enterprises, and state and local governments also issue bonds to finance their ongoing activities and special projects. Typical activities and projects include home mortage financing, airports, schools, toll roads, and toll bridges. U.S. Treasury securities can be purchased through Treasury Direct, brokerage firms, and other financial institutions. Municipal bonds are generally sold through the government entity that issued them or through account executives. One of the most important features of municipal bonds is that interest on them may be exempt from federal taxes.

LO15-5

Evaluate bonds when making an investment.

Today it is possible to trade bonds online and obtain research information via the Internet. Some local newspapers, *The Wall Street Journal,* and *Barron's* provide bond investors with information they need to evaluate a bond issue. Detailed financial information can also be obtained by requesting a printed copy of the corporation's annual report or accessing its website. To determine the quality of a bond issue, most investors study the ratings provided by Standard & Poor's, Moody's, and Fitch Bond Ratings. Investors can also calculate a current yield and a yield to maturity to evaluate a decision to buy or sell bond issues.

The current yield is determined by dividing the annual income amount by a bond's current market value. The yield to maturity takes into account the relationship among a bond's maturity value, the time to maturity, the current price, and the dollar amount of interest.

KEY TERMS

bearer bond 528
bond indenture 522
bond ladder 529
call feature 525
convertible bond 524
convertible corporate note 524
corporate bond 522
current yield 541
debenture 523
face value 522
general obligation bond 535
government bond 532
high-yield bonds 524
maturity date 522
mortgage bond 523
municipal bond 535
registered bond 527
registered coupon bond 527
revenue bond 535
serial bonds 525
sinking fund 525
subordinated debenture 524
trustee 522
yield 528
yield to maturity 543

Page	Topic	Formula
527	Annual interest	Dollar amount of annual interest = Face value × Interest rate
	Example:	= \$1,000 × 6.75 percent
		= \$1,000 × 0.0675
		= \$67.50
529	Approximate market value	$\text{Approximate market value} = \frac{\text{Dollar amount of annual interest}}{\text{Comparable interest rate}}$
	Example:	$\text{Approximate market value} = \frac{\$65}{0.07}$
		= \$928.57
533	Purchase price for a Treasury bill	Step 1: Discount amount = Maturity value × interest rate
		= \$1,000 × 0.50 percent
		= \$1,000 × 0.005
		= \$5
		Step 2: Purchase price = Maturity value − Discount amount
		= \$1,000 − \$5
		= \$995
534	Current yield for a 52-week T-bill	$\text{Current yield} = \frac{\text{Discount amount}}{\text{Purchase price}}$
	Example:	$\text{Current yield} = \frac{\$5}{\$995}$
		= 0.00503 = 0.503 percent
536	Taxable equivalent yield (25% tax rate)	$\text{Taxable equivalent yield} = \frac{\text{Tax-exempt yield}}{1.0 - \text{Your tax rate}}$
	Example:	$\text{Taxable equivalent yield} = \frac{0.04}{1.0 - 0.25}$
		= 0.0533 = 5.33 percent
538	Bond price	Bond price = Face value × bond quote
		= \$1,000 × 92 percent
		= \$1,000 × 0.92
		= \$920
541	Current yield on a corporate bond	$\text{Current yield} = \frac{\text{Annual income amount}}{\text{Current market value}}$
	Example:	$\text{Current yield} = \frac{\$75}{\$900}$
		= 0.0833 = 8.33 percent

Page	Topic	Formula
543	Yield to maturity	$\text{Yield to maturity} = \dfrac{\text{Dollar amount of annual interest} + \dfrac{\text{Face value} - \text{Market value}}{\text{Number of periods}}}{\dfrac{\text{Market value} + \text{Face value}}{2}}$
	Example:	$\text{Yield to maturity} = \dfrac{\$60 + \dfrac{\$1{,}000 - \$900}{10}}{\dfrac{\$900 + \$1{,}000}{2}}$ $= 0.074 = 7.4 \text{ percent}$
544	Times interest earned	$\text{Times interest earned} = \dfrac{\text{Operating income before interest and taxes}}{\text{Interest expense}}$ $= \dfrac{\$4{,}800 \text{ million}}{\$1{,}066 \text{ million}}$ $= 4.50 \text{ to } 1$

SELF-TEST PROBLEMS

1. Charlie Nelson is 50 years old and wants to diversify her investment portfolio and must decide if she should invest in tax-free municipal bonds or corporate bonds. The tax-free bonds are highly rated and pay 4.25 percent. The corporate bonds are more speculative and pay 6.5 percent.

a. If Ms. Nelson is in the 33 percent tax bracket, what is the taxable equivalent yield for the municipal bond?

b. If you were Ms. Nelson, would you choose the municipal bonds or corporate bonds? Justify your answer.

2. James Gomez purchased ten $1,000 corporate bonds issued by Kohls. The annual interest rate for the bonds is 4.00 percent.

a. What is the annual interest amount for each Kohl's bond?

b. If the bonds have a current price quotation of 106, what is the current price of this bond?

c. Given the above information, what is the current yield for a Kohl's bond?

d. If comparable bonds are paying 3.80 percent, what is the approximate market value for the Kohl's bonds?

3. Matt Redburn has decided to invest $1,000 and purchase 52-week T-bills with some excess cash he doesn't need for the next year. He knows that T-bills are discounted securities, but he is confused about the purchase price and current yield and asks for your help.

a. If the T-bill has a stated interest rate of 0.40 percent, what is the purchase price?

b. What is the current yield for the T-bill?

Solutions

1. a. The taxable equivalent yield is 6.34 percent for the municipal bond.

$$\text{Taxable equivalent yield} = \frac{\text{Tax-exempt yield}}{1.0 - \text{Your tax rate}}$$

$$= \frac{.0425}{0.67}$$

$$= 0.0634 = 6.34 \text{ percent}$$

b. The taxable equivalent yield for the municipal bond (6.34 percent) is only slightly lower than the current yield on the corporate bond (6.5 percent). Because Ms. Nelson is 50 years old and will probably retire in 10 to 15 years, the highly rated municipal bond is a better choice than the more speculative corporate bond.

2. a. The annual interest amount is $40 for each Kohl's bond.

$$\text{Dollar amount of annual interest} = \text{Face value} \times \text{Interest rate}$$
$$= \$1{,}000 \times 4.00 \text{ percent}$$
$$= \$40$$

b. The current bond price for the Kohl's bond is $1,060.

$$\text{Bond price} = \text{Face value} \times \text{bond quote}$$
$$= \$1{,}000 \times 106 \text{ percent}$$
$$= \$1{,}060$$

c. The current yield for the Kohl's bond is 3.77 percent.

$$\text{Current yield} = \frac{\text{Annual income amount}}{\text{Current market value}}$$
$$= \frac{\$40}{\$1{,}060}$$
$$= 0.0377 = 3.77 \text{ percent}$$

d. The approximate market value for the Kohl's bond is $1,052.63.

$$\text{Approximate market value} = \frac{\text{Dollar amount of annual interest}}{\text{Comparable interest rate}}$$
$$= \frac{\$40}{3.80\%}$$
$$= \$1{,}052.63$$

3. a. The purchase price for the 52-week T-bill is $996.

$$\text{Step 1: Discount amount} = \text{Maturity value} \times \text{interest rate}$$
$$= \$1{,}000 \times 0.40 \text{ percent}$$
$$= \$1{,}000 \times 0.0040$$
$$= \$4$$

$$\text{Step 2: Purchase price} = \text{Maturity value} - \text{Discount amount}$$
$$= \$1{,}000 - \$4$$
$$= \$996$$

b. The current yield for the T-bill is

$$\text{Current yield} = \frac{\text{Discount amount}}{\text{Purchase price}}$$
$$= \frac{\$4}{\$996}$$
$$= 0.00402 = 0.402 \text{ percent}$$

FINANCIAL PLANNING PROBLEMS

1. *Calculating Interest.* Calculate the annual interest and the semiannual interest payment for the following corporate bond issues with a face value of $1,000. LO15-1

Annual Interest Rate	Annual Interest Amount	Semiannual Interest Payment
4.20%		
5.10%		
5.00%		
4.70%		

LO15-2 **2.** *Analyzing Convertible Bonds.* Jackson Metals, Inc., issued a $1,000 convertible corporate bond. Each bond is convertible to 40 shares of the firm's common stock.

a. What price must the common stock reach before investors would consider converting their bond to common stock?

b. If you owned a bond in Jackson Metals, would you convert your bond to common stock if the stock's price did reach the conversion price? Explain your answer.

LO15-3 **3.** *Determining the Approximate Market Value for a Bond.* Approximate the market value for the following $1,000 bonds.

Interest Rate When Issued	Dollar Amount of Interest for the Existing Bond	Interest Rate for Comparable Bonds Issued Today	Approximate Market Value
5%		4%	
5.1%		6.2%	
7%		6%	

LO15-3 **4.** *Calculating Total Return.* Jean Miller purchased a $1,000 corporate bond for $910. The bond paid 5 percent annual interest. Three years later, she sold the bond for $1,010. Calculate the total return for Ms. Miller's bond investment.

LO15-3 **5.** *Calculating Total Return.* Mark Crane purchased a $1,000 corporate bond five years ago for $1,060. The bond pays 4.5 percent annual interest. Five years later, he sold the bond for $950. Calculate the total return for Mr. Crane's bond investment.

LO15-4 **6.** *Calculating Bond Yield for a T-Bill.* Sandra Waterman purchased a 52-week, $1,000 T-bill issued by the U.S. Treasury. The purchase price was $996.

a. What is the amount of the discount?

b. What is the amount Ms. Waterman will receive when the T-bill matures?

c. What is the current yield for the 52-week T-bill?

LO15-4 **7.** *Calculating Total Return.* James McCulloch purchased a 30-year U.S. Treasury bond four years ago for $1,000. The bond paid 3.125 percent annual interest. Four years later he sold the bond for $1,040.

a. What is the annual interest amount for the bond?

b. What is the total interest Mr. McCulloch earned during the four-year period?

c. What is the total return for Mr. McCulloch's bond investment?

LO15-4 **8.** *Calculating the Purchase Price for a T-Bill.* Calculate the purchase price for a 52-week, $1,000 treasury bill with a stated interest rate of 0.60 percent.

LO15-4 **9.** *Calculating Tax-Equivalent Yield.* Assume you are in the 39.6 percent tax bracket and purchase a 3.35 percent, tax-exempt municipal bond. Use the formula presented in this chapter to calculate the taxable equivalent yield for this investment.

LO15-4 **10.** *Calculating Tax-Equivalent Yield.* Assume you are in the 33 percent tax bracket and purchase a 4.20 percent, tax-exempt municipal bond. Use the formula presented in this chapter to calculate the taxable equivalent yield for this investment.

LO15-5 **11.** *Determining Bond Prices.* What is the current price for a $1,000 bond that has a price quote of 87?

LO15-5 **12.** *Calculating Current Yields.* Calculate the interest amount and current yield for the following $1,000 bonds.

Interest Rate	Interest Amount	Current Market Value	Current Yield
6%		$1,020	
5.3%		$1,170	
5.10%		$930	

LO15-5 **13.** *Calculating Yields.* Assume you purchased a high-yield corporate bond at its current market price of $850 on January 2, 2004. It pays 9 percent interest and will mature on December 31, 2013, at which time the corporation will pay you the face value of $1,000.

a. Determine the current yield on your bond investment at the time of purchase.

b. Determine the yield to maturity on your bond investment.

LO15-5 **14.** *Calculating Yields.* Assume that 10 years ago you purchased a $1,000 bond for $820. The bond pays 6.75 percent interest and will mature this year.

a. Calculate the current yield on your bond investment at the time of the purchase.

b. Determine the yield to maturity on your bond investment.

FINANCIAL PLANNING ACTIVITIES

1. *Explaining Why Corporations Sell Bonds.* Prepare a two-minute oral presentation that describes why corporations sell bonds. LO15-1
2. *Analyzing Why Investors Purchase Bonds.* In your own words, explain how each of the following factors is a reason to invest in bonds. LO15-3
   a. Interest income.
   b. Possible increase in value.
   c. Repayment at maturity.
3. *Using the Internet to Obtain Investment Information.* Use the Internet to locate the website for Treasury Direct (www.treasurydirect.gov). Then prepare a report that summarizes how one of the securities issued by the U.S. Treasury could help you obtain your financial goals. LO15-4
4. *Using the Internet.* Use the information at the bond site on Yahoo! Finance lo answer the following questions about a corporate bond. To complete this activity, follow these steps. LO15-5
   a. Go to http://finance.yahoo.com/bonds and click on Bond Screener.
   b. Click on Corporate and enter the information requested in the section "Select Bond Criteria." Then click Find Bonds.
   c. Choose one of the issues listed.
   d. Using the information on the Yahoo! bond website, determine the current yield for this bond issue. What does the current yield calculation measure?
   e. Using the information on the Yahoo! bond website, what is the yield to maturity for this bond issue? What does the yield to maturity calculation measure?
   f. What is the rating for this bond? What does this rating mean?
   g. Based on your answer to the above questions, would you choose this bond for your investment portfolio? Explain your answer.
5. *Evaluating a Bond Transaction.* Choose a corporate bond that you would consider purchasing. Then, using information obtained in the library or on the Internet, answer the questions on the evaluation form presented in the Personal Financial Planner Sheet 60, "Corporate Bond Evaluation," at the end of the text. Based on your research, would you still purchase this bond? Explain your answer. LO15-5

FINANCIAL PLANNING CASE

A Lesson from the Past

Back in 2000, Mary Goldberg, a 34-year-old widow, got a telephone call from a Wall Street account executive who said that one of his other clients had given him her name. Then he told her his brokerage firm was selling a new corporate bond issue in New World Explorations, a company heavily engaged in oil exploration in the western United States. The bonds in this issue paid investors 8.9 percent a year. He then said that the minimum investment was $10,000 and that if she wanted to take advantage of this "once in a lifetime" opportunity, she had to move fast. To Mary, it was an opportunity that was too good to pass up, and she bit hook, line, and sinker. She sent the account executive a check—and never heard from him again. When she went to the library to research her bond investment, she found there was no such company as New World Explorations. She lost her $10,000 and quickly vowed she would never invest in bonds again. From now on, she would put her money in the bank, where it was guaranteed.

Over the years, she continued to deposit money in the bank and accumulated more than $42,000. Things seemed to be pretty much on track until her certificate of deposit (CD) matured. When she went to renew the CD, the bank officer told her interest rates had fallen and current CD interest rates ranged between 1 and 2 percent. To make matters worse, the banker told Mary that only the bank's 60-month CD offered the 2 percent interest rate. CDs with shorter maturities paid lower interest rates.

Faced with the prospects of lower interest rates, Mary decided to shop around for higher rates. She called several local banks and got pretty much the same answer. Then a friend suggested that she talk to Peter Manning, an account executive for Fidelity Investments. Manning told her there were conservative corporate bonds and quality stock issues that offered higher returns. But, he warned her, these investments were *not* guaranteed. If she wanted higher returns, she would have to take some risks.

While Mary wanted higher returns, she also remembered how she had lost $10,000 investing in corporate bonds. When she told Peter Manning about her bond investment in the fictitious New World Explorations, he pointed out that she made some pretty serious mistakes. For starters, she bought the bonds over the phone from someone she didn't know, and she bought them without doing any research. He assured her that the bonds and stocks he would recommend would be issued by real companies, and she would be able to find a lot of information on each of his recommendations at the library or on the Internet. For starters, he suggested the following three investments:

1. AT&T Broadband corporate bond that pays 9.455 percent annual interest and matures on November 15, 2022. This bond has a current market value of $1,530 and is rated BBB.
2. John Deere Capital corporate note that pays 5.35 percent annual interest and matures on April 13, 2018. This bond has a current market value of $1,190 and is rated A.
3. Procter & Gamble common stock (listed on the New York Stock Exchange and selling for $76 a share with annual dividends of $2.25 per share).

Questions

1. According to Mary Goldberg, the chance to invest in New World Explorations was "too good to pass up." Unfortunately, it was too good to be true, and she lost $10,000. Why do you think so many people are taken in by get-rich-quick schemes?
2. Over the past 5 to 8 years, investors have been forced to look for ways to squeeze additional income from their investment portfolios. Do you think investing in corporate bonds or quality stocks is the best way to increase income? Why or why not?
3. Using information obtained in the library or on the Internet, answer the following questions about Peter Manning's investment suggestions.
   a. What does the rating for the AT&T Broadband bond mean?
   b. What does the rating for the Deere corporate note mean?
   c. How would you describe the common stock issued by Procter & Gamble?
4. Based on your research, which investment would you recommend to Mary Goldberg? Why?
5. Using a current newspaper, *The Wall Street Journal, Barron's,* or the Internet, determine the current market value for each of the three investments suggested in this case. Based on this information, would these investments have been profitable if Mary had purchased the AT&T Broadband bond for $1,530, the Deere corporate note for $1,190, or General Electric stock for $76 a share?

PERSONAL FINANCIAL PLANNER IN ACTION

Investing in Bonds

Including bonds in an investment portfolio can be useful for achieving various financial goals when certain life situations, business conditions, and economic trends arise.

Your Short-Term Financial Planning Activities	*Resources*
1. Evaluate a bond investment that might be appropriate for your various financial goals and life situation.	PFP Sheet 60 www.investinginbonds.com www.invest-faq.com
2. Compare various corporate bonds that could be appropriate investments for you.	http://finance.yahoo.com/bonds
3. Research federal government and municipal bonds. Determine how these might be used in your investment portfolio.	www.treasurydirect.gov www.emuni.com www.fmsbonds.com
Your Long-Term Financial Planning Activities	*Resources*
1. Identify bond investing situations that could help minimize risk.	PFP Sheet 60
2. Develop a plan for selecting bond investments in the future.	Text pages 537–544 www.kiplinger.com

CONTINUING CASE

Investing in Bonds

Life Situation	*Financial Data*	
Shelby, age 37	Monthly Gross Income	$7,000
Mark, age 38	Living Expenses	$4,500
Two children, ages 11 and 5	Assets	$205,000
	Liabilities	$115,000

Shelby and Mark Lawrence have been talking with her parents about investments. Her parents have recommended that they include bonds as part of their portfolio. Shelby and Mark understand that the mix of a portfolio is based on your age and investment goals. Therefore, they would like to know how and when bonds might fit into their portfolio.

Questions

1. What types of financial goals might include an investment in bonds for the Lawrences?
2. If the Lawrences were interested in a particular bond, describe the bond ratings that would help them evaluate its quality and risk.
3. Explain how Shelby and Mark might use the Personal Financial Planner sheet Corporate Bond Evaluation.

DAILY SPENDING DIARY

"How do I know if investing in bonds would be the right action for me?"

Directions

Your "Daily Spending Diary" will help you maintain a record of your expenses to better understand your spending habits. As you record daily spending, your comments should reflect what you have learned about your spending patterns and help you consider possible changes you might want to make.

Analysis Questions

1. How might changes in your spending activities allow you to increase funds available for investing?
2. In what types of situations might investing in bonds be appropriate?

The Daily Spending Diary sheets are located in Appendix D at the end of the book and on the student website at www.mhhe.com/kdh.

chapter 16

Investing in Mutual Funds

Learning Objectives

LO16-1 Describe the characteristics of mutual fund investments.

LO16-2 Classify mutual funds by investment objective.

LO16-3 Evaluate mutual funds for investment purposes.

LO16-4 Describe how and why mutual funds are bought and sold.

What will this mean for me?

For many investors, mutual funds have become the investment of choice. Yet even though mutual funds offer professional management and diversification, investors still need to evaluate mutual funds before investing their money.

my life

WHY MUTUAL FUNDS?

Why do almost half of U.S. households invest in mutual funds? Here are three reasons: (1) it's an easy way to invest, (2) mutual funds offer professional management, and (3) funds can help you diversify your investment dollars. And yet, you must still evaluate specific funds to make sure you choose the right one that can help you obtain your investment objectives. Before beginning this chapter, respond to the questions below.

	Yes	No
1. I understand the reasons investors choose fund investments.	____	____
2. I can identify the types of funds that will help me achieve my investment goals.	____	____
3. I know how to evaluate a fund investment.	____	____
4. I know how I can make money with fund investments.	____	____

As you study this chapter, you will encounter "My Life" boxes with additional information and resources related to these items.

mutual fund Pools the money of many investors—its shareholders—to invest in a variety of securities.

Consider this! Karen Southworth, a single mother, had always worked hard for her money. And when it came time to invest, she did her homework. After accumulating a $5,000 emergency fund and an additional $9,000 for investment purposes, she purchased shares in the Janus Enterprise fund based on research information available on the Morningstar and Value Line websites. According to research information, the fund manager chose corporations that have the potential to increase in value. Although she researched other funds that were more aggressive, she felt comfortable with the companies in this Janus fund. Did her research efforts pay off? You bet! Over the last five years, she earned an average return of just over 12 percent each year. Not a bad investment—especially when you consider that many fund investments lost money in 2009 because of a downturn in the economy.

If you ever thought about buying stocks or bonds but decided not to, your reasons were probably like most other people's: You didn't know enough to make a good decision, and you lacked enough money to diversify your investments among several choices. These same two reasons explain why people invest in mutual funds. By pooling your money with money from other investors, a mutual fund can do for you what you can't do on your own. According to the Mutual Fund Education Alliance (www.mfea.com), a **mutual fund** pools the money of many investors—its shareholders—to invest in a variety of securities.[1] Because of professional management and diversification, mutual funds are an excellent choice for many individuals.

In many cases, they can also be used for retirement accounts, including, traditional individual retirement accounts, Roth IRAs, and employer-sponsored 401(k) accounts and 403(b) retirement accounts. For example, many employees contribute a portion of their salary to a 401(k) retirement account. And in many cases, the employer matches the employee's contribution. A common match would work like this: For every $1 the employee invests, the employer contributes an additional $0.25. All monies—both the employee's and employer's contributions—are often invested in mutual funds that are selected by the employee. *Be warned:* Although some employers reduced or eliminated matching provisions during the recent economic crisis, some employers still match employee contributions. In fact, during a job interview you may want to ask about the employers' matching provisions for a 401(k) or 403(b) retirement account.

Regardless, whether you are investing in an account subject to immediate taxation or in a retirement-type account with deferred taxation, you must be able to select the funds that will help you obtain your investment goals.

Why Investors Purchase Mutual Funds

LO16-1

Describe the characteristics of mutual fund investments.

Today, the notion of investing money in a mutual fund may be a new idea, but mutual funds have been around for a long time. Fund investing began in Europe in the late 1700s and became popular in the United States before the Great Depression in 1929. After the depression, government regulations increased, the number of funds grew, and the amount invested in funds continued to increase. New types of funds including index funds, aggressive growth funds, and social responsibility and green funds were created to meet the needs of a larger and more demanding group of investors. During this same time period, the cost of investing in funds decreased while the popularity of fund investing increased.

No one invests money to lose money. But during the recent economic crisis, many people gained firsthand knowledge that the value of fund shares can decline. In fact, the financial gains Karen Southworth obtained during the last five years were an exception. Despite the nation's economic problems and the poor performance of some funds over the last few years, the following statistics illustrate how important mutual fund investments are to both individuals and the nation's economy:

1. In the United States, an estimated 90.4 million individuals in nearly forty-five percent of all U.S. households own mutual funds.

2. The number of funds grew from 361 in 1970 to almost 13,000 in late 2011.
3. At the end of 2011, the last year for which complete totals are available, the combined value of assets owned by mutual funds in the United States totaled $13 trillion. This amount is expected to continue to increase based on long-term performance.[2]

THE PSYCHOLOGY OF INVESTING IN FUNDS

The major reasons investors purchase mutual funds are *professional management* and *diversification.* Most investment companies do everything possible to convince you that they can do a better job of picking securities than you can. Sometimes these claims are true, and sometimes they are just so much hot air. Still, investment companies do have professional fund managers with years of experience who devote large amounts of time to picking just the "right" securities for their funds' portfolios. *Be warned:* Even the best portfolio managers make mistakes. So you, the investor, must be careful!

The diversification mutual funds offer spells safety because an occasional loss incurred with one investment contained in a mutual fund is usually offset by gains from other investments in the fund. For example, consider the diversification provided in the portfolio of the Invesco Growth and Income Fund, shown in Exhibit 16-1. An investment in the $7.4 billion Invesco Growth and Income Fund represents ownership in at least 10 different industries. In addition, the companies in the fund's portfolio are often market leaders, as seen by the fund's top holdings. With over 70 different companies included in the fund's investment portfolio, investors enjoy diversification coupled with Invesco's stock selection expertise.

For beginning investors or investors without a great deal of money to invest, the diversification offered by funds is especially important because there is no other practical way to purchase the individual stocks issued by a large number of corporations. A fund like the Invesco Growth and Income Fund, on the other hand, can provide a practical way for investors to obtain diversification because the fund can use the pooled money of a large number of investors to purchase shares of many different companies.

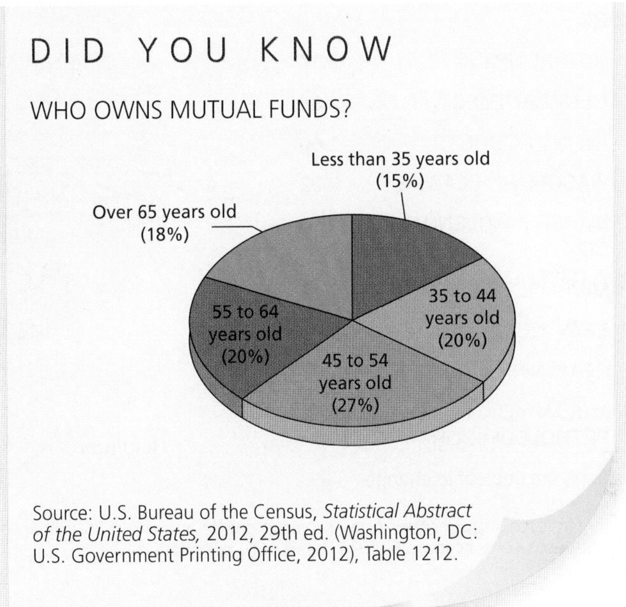

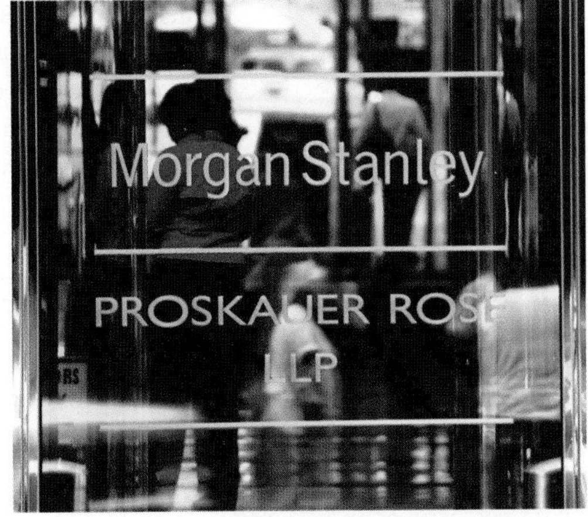

Today, many investors use firms like Morgan Stanley to create a financial plan to generate the income needed to satisfy their long-term goals.

CHARACTERISTICS OF MUTUAL FUNDS

Today mutual funds may be classified as either closed-end funds, exchange-traded funds, or open-end funds.

CLOSED-END FUNDS Closed-end funds are one of three types of fund investments, along with exchange-traded funds, and open-end funds. Approximately 2 percent, or about 240, of all funds are closed-end funds offered by investment companies.[3] A **closed-end fund** is a fund whose shares are issued by an investment company only when the fund is organized. As a result, only a certain number of shares are available to investors. After all the shares originally issued have been sold, an investor can

closed-end fund A fund whose shares are issued by an investment company only when the fund is organized.

Exhibit 16-1 Invesco Growth and Income Fund top holdings

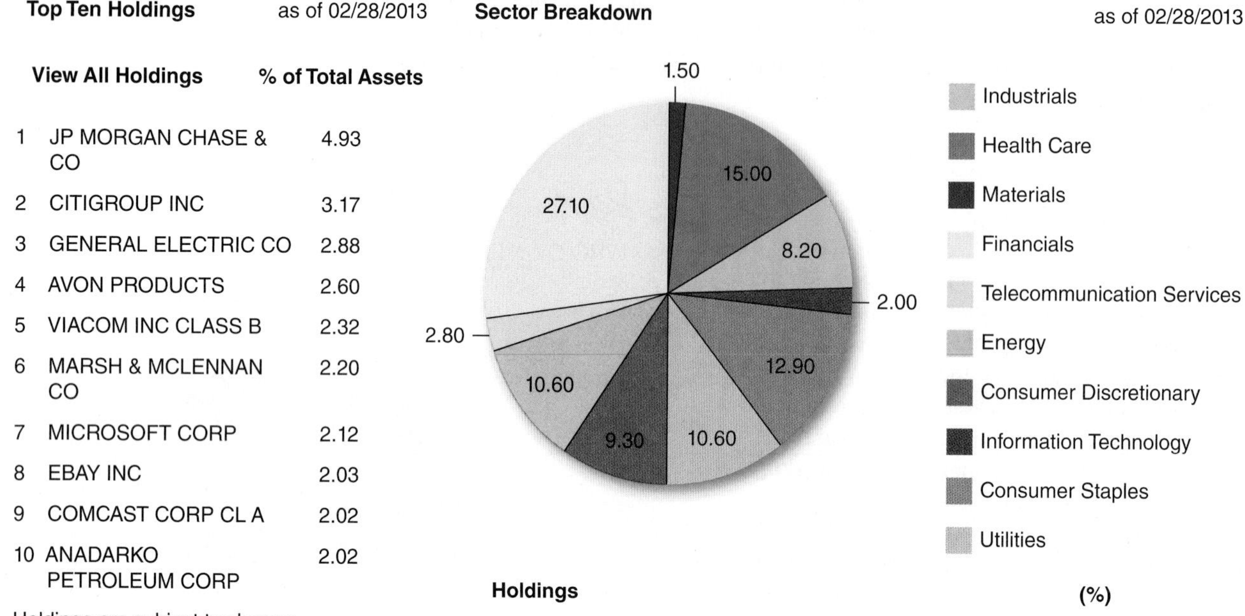

Top Ten Holdings as of 02/28/2013

View All Holdings	% of Total Assets
1 JP MORGAN CHASE & CO	4.93
2 CITIGROUP INC	3.17
3 GENERAL ELECTRIC CO	2.88
4 AVON PRODUCTS	2.60
5 VIACOM INC CLASS B	2.32
6 MARSH & MCLENNAN CO	2.20
7 MICROSOFT CORP	2.12
8 EBAY INC	2.03
9 COMCAST CORP CL A	2.02
10 ANADARKO PETROLEUM CORP	2.02

Holdings are subject to change.

Source: Invesco supplies this data as example only and is not to be construed as an offer to buy or sell any financial instruments. www.invesco.com, March 26, 2013. Used with permission.

purchase shares only from another investor who is willing to sell. Closed-end funds are actively managed by professional fund managers, in accordance with the fund's investment objective and policies, and may be invested in stocks, bonds, and other securities. Shares are traded on the floors of securities exchanges or in the over-the-counter market during the day like individual corporate stocks. Like the prices of stocks, the prices of shares for closed-end funds are determined by the factors of supply and demand, by the value of stocks and other investments contained in the fund's portfolio, and by investor expectations.

exchange-traded fund (ETF) A fund that generally invests in the stocks or other securities contained in a specific stock or securities index.

EXCHANGE-TRADED FUNDS An **exchange-traded fund (ETF)** is a fund that generally invests in the stocks or other securities contained *in a specific stock or securities index.* While most investors think of an ETF as investing in the stocks contained in the Standard & Poor's 500 stock index, the Dow Jones Industrial Average, or the Nasdaq 100 index, today there are many different types of ETFs available that attempt to track all kinds of indexes that include

- Midcap stocks.
- Small-cap stocks.
- Fixed-income securities.
- Stocks issued by companies in specific industries.
- Stocks issued by corporations in different countries.
- Commodities.

Like a closed-end fund, shares of an exchange-traded fund are traded on a securities exchange or in the over-the-counter market at any time during the business day. Like the price for shares in closed-end funds, the price for shares in ETFs is determined on a stock exchange or in the over-the-counter market. Consequently, two investors buying or selling shares in the same ETF fund at different times on the same day may pay or receive different prices for their shares. Share prices for ETFs are determined by supply and demand, by the value of stocks and other investments contained in the fund's portfolio, and by investor expectations. With both closed-end funds and ETFs, an investor can purchase as little as one share of a fund, because both types are traded on a securities exchange like individual corporate stock issues.

Although exchange-traded funds are similar to closed-end funds, there is an important difference. Most closed-end funds are actively managed, with portfolio managers making the selection of stocks and other securities contained in a closed-end fund. Almost all exchange-traded funds, on the other hand, normally invest in the stocks, bonds, or securities included in a specific index. *Note:* There are a *few* ETFs that are actively managed with portfolio managers buying stocks, bonds, and securities. The vast majority of exchange-traded funds tend to mirror the performance of the index, moving up or down as the individual stocks or securities contained in the index move up or down. Therefore, there is less need for a portfolio manager to make investment decisions. Because of passive management, fees associated with owning shares are generally less when compared to both closed-end and open-end funds. In addition to lower fees, there are other advantages to investing in ETFs, which include

- No minimum investment amount, because shares are traded on an exchange and not purchased from an investment company, which often requires a minimum investment of $500, $1,000, or more.
- You can use limit orders and the more speculative techniques of selling short and margin—all discussed in Chapter 14—to buy and sell ETF shares.

The major disadvantage of exchange-traded funds is the cost of buying and selling shares. Because they are traded like stocks, investors must pay commissions when they buy *and* sell shares. Although increasing in popularity, there are only about 1,000 exchange-traded funds, or about 8 percent of all funds.[4]

open-end fund A mutual fund whose shares are issued and redeemed by the investment company at the request of investors.

net asset value (NAV) The current market value of the securities contained in the mutual fund's portfolio minus the mutual fund's liabilities divided by the number of shares outstanding.

OPEN-END FUNDS Approximately 90 percent—over 11,600 funds—are open-end funds.[5] An **open-end fund** is a mutual fund whose shares are issued and redeemed by the investment company at the request of investors. Investors are free to buy and sell shares at the net asset value. The **net asset value (NAV)** per share is equal to the current market value of securities contained in the mutual fund's portfolio minus the mutual fund's liabilities divided by the number of shares outstanding:

$$\text{Net asset value} = \frac{\text{Value of the fund's portfolio} - \text{Liabilities}}{\text{Number of shares outstanding}}$$

EXAMPLE: Net Asset Value

Assume the portfolio of stocks, bonds, and other securities contained in the New American Frontiers mutual fund has a current market value of $655 million. The fund also has liabilities totaling $5 million. If this mutual fund has 30 million shares outstanding, the net asset value per share is $21.67, as illustrated below:

$$\begin{aligned}\text{Net asset value} &= \frac{\text{Value of the fund's portfolio} - \text{Liabilities}}{\text{Number of shares outstanding}}\\ &= \frac{\$655\text{ million} - \$5\text{ million}}{30\text{ million shares}}\\ &= \$21.67\text{ per share}\end{aligned}$$

For most mutual funds, the net asset value is calculated at the close of trading each day. From a practical standpoint, this means that you can place an order to buy or sell shares

HOW TO...

Open an Investment Account and Begin Investing in Funds

You may want to use the seven suggestions contained in this How To . . . feature to open an investment account and begin investing in funds.

Take This Step	Suggested Action
1. Determine your investment goals and perform a financial checkup.	Without investment goals, you don't know what you want to accomplish. For more information on establishing goals, review the material in Chapter 13. Also, make sure your budget is balanced and you have an emergency fund.
2. Save the money you need to purchase mutual funds.	Although the amount will vary, $250 to $3,000 is usually required to open an account with a brokerage firm or an investment company.
3. Research different brokerage firms and investment companies.	Many experienced investors buy and sell closed-end, exchange-traded, and open-end funds through a brokerage firm. You can also contact an investment company to buy and sell shares in an open-end fund. When choosing a brokerage firm or investment company, use the Internet to find information about available funds, fees, available research information, and requirements to open an account.
4. Find a fund with an objective that matches your objective.	Use the Internet, *The Wall Street Journal,* professional advisory services, and investment publications to identify funds with objectives that match your objectives.
5. Once you identify two to five possible fund investments, evaluate each alternative before buying shares.	Sources of detailed information include the Internet, professional advisory services, the fund's annual report and prospectus, and financial publications—all sources described in this chapter.
6. Learn about the fund.	Look for basic information about minimum investing requirements, sales fees, expense ratio, performance, and portfolio holdings.
7. After all your research and evaluation, purchase shares in a fund that will help you obtain your investment goals.	Evaluate your investments on a regular basis. If necessary, sell funds that no longer are helping you achieve your financial goals.

in an open-end fund during the day, *but* your shares will not be bought or sold until the end of the trading day. Assume you want to sell shares in an open-end fund that is heavily invested in financial stocks because the government announces that it will be investigating the trading practices of the nation's largest banks. Because your fund has a large portion of its portfolio invested in bank stocks, the value of shares in your fund will decrease. Since you own shares in an open-end fund, your order to sell will not be executed until the end of the day. Thus, you are locked in and cannot reduce your dollar loss. By contrast, if you owned shares in either a closed-end fund or an exchange-traded fund you could sell your shares during the day because both closed-end funds and ETFs are traded on an exchange or in the over-the-counter market at any time during the day.

In addition to buying and selling shares on request, most open-end funds provide their investors with a wide variety of services, including payroll deduction programs, automatic reinvestment programs, automatic withdrawal programs, and the option to change shares in one fund to another fund within the same fund family—all topics discussed later in this chapter.

LOAD FUNDS AND NO-LOAD FUNDS Before investing in mutual funds, you should compare the cost of this type of investment with the cost of other investment alternatives, such as stocks or bonds. With regard to cost, mutual funds are classified as load funds or no-load funds. A **load fund** (sometimes referred to as an *"A" fund*) is a mutual fund in which investors pay a commission every time they purchase shares. The commission, sometimes referred to as the *sales charge,* may be as high as 8½ percent of the purchase price.

load fund A mutual fund in which investors pay a commission (as high as 8½ percent) every time they purchase shares.

While many exceptions exist, the average load charge for mutual funds is between 3 and 5 percent.

EXAMPLE: Sales Load Calculation

Let's assume you decide to invest $10,000 in the Davis New York Venture fund. This fund charges a sales load of 4.75 percent that you must pay when you purchase shares. The dollar amount of the sales charge on your $10,000 investment is $475, as calculated below:

Dollar amount of sales load = Original investment × Sales load stated as a percentage
= $10,000 × 4.75 percent
= $10,000 × 0.0475
= $475

After paying the $475, the amount available for investment is reduced to $9,525 ($10,000 − $475 = $9,525). The "stated" advantage of a load fund is that the fund's sales force (account executives, financial planners, or brokerage divisions of banks and other financial institutions) will explain the mutual fund to investors and offer advice as to when shares of the fund should be bought or sold.

A **no-load fund** is a mutual fund for which the individual investor pays no sales charge. No-load funds don't charge commissions when you buy shares because they have no salespeople. If you want to buy shares of a no-load fund, you must deal directly with the investment company. The usual means of contact is by telephone, the Internet, or mail. You can also purchase shares in a no-load fund from many discount brokers, including Charles Schwab, TD Ameritrade, and E*Trade.

no-load fund A mutual fund for which the individual investor pays no sales charge.

As an investor, you must decide whether to invest in a load fund or a no-load fund. Some investment salespeople have claimed that load funds outperform no-load funds. But many financial analysts suggest there is no significant performance difference between mutual funds that charge commissions and those that do not.[6]

Since no-load funds offer the same investment opportunities load funds offer, you should investigate them further before deciding which type of mutual fund is best for you. The chief reason why no-load funds may be a better choice is because of the amount of sales fees and the commissions paid to salespeople that are deducted from your investment when you purchase shares in a load fund. Although the sales commission should not be the decisive factor, the possibility of saving a load charge of up to 8½ percent is a factor to consider. For example, suppose Barbara Harrington invests $10,000 in a mutual fund that charges a 5.50 percent sales fee. Since this fee is deducted in advance, her initial $10,000 investment is reduced by $550. Simply put, she now has $9,450 that she can use to buy shares in this load fund. By comparison, Mary Hernandez decides to invest $10,000 in a no-load mutual fund. Since there is no sales fee, she can use the entire $10,000 to purchase shares in this no-load fund. Depending on the load fund's performance, it may take Barbara a year or more just to "catch up" and cover the cost of the sales fee. Does the above information imply that all no-load funds are superior to all load funds? No. Which is better depends on which fund you choose. A mutual fund that charges a 4 percent load fee but has above average annual returns over a long period of time may provide better returns than a no-load fund that has average performance.

contingent deferred sales load A 1 to 5 percent charge that shareholders pay when they withdraw their investment from a mutual fund.

Instead of charging investors a fee when they purchase shares in a mutual fund, some mutual funds charge a **contingent deferred sales load** (sometimes referred to as a *back-end load* or a *"B" fund*) on withdrawals. These fees range from 1 to 5 percent, depending on how long you own the mutual fund before making a withdrawal.

EXAMPLE: Contingent Deferred Sales Load

Assume you withdraw $5,000 from B shares that you own in the Alger Capital Appreciation fund within a year of your original purchase date. You must pay a 5 percent contingent deferred sales fee. Your fee is $250, as illustrated below:

Contingent deferred sales load = Withdrawal amount × Contingent deferred sales load as a percentage

= $5,000 × 5 percent

= $5,000 × 0.05

= $250

After the fee is deducted from your $5,000 withdrawal, you will receive $4,750 ($5,000 − $250 = $4,750). *Generally,* the deferred charge declines until there is no withdrawal charge if you own the shares in the fund for more than five to seven years. It is also common for some fund investment companies to convert B shares to A shares after a specified number of years. This type of conversion usually results in lower ongoing expenses for the shareholder.

MANAGEMENT FEES AND OTHER CHARGES In evaluating a specific mutual fund, you should consider different fees you will pay as an investor. For example, investment companies that sponsor mutual funds charge *management fees.* This fee, which is disclosed in the fund's prospectus, is a fixed percentage of the fund's asset value. Typically annual management fees range between 0.25 and 1.5 percent of the fund's asset value. While fees vary considerably, the average is 0.5 to 1 percent of the fund's assets.

12b-1 fee A fee that an investment company levies to defray the costs of distribution and marketing a mutual fund and commissions paid to a broker who sold you shares in the mutual fund.

The investment company may also levy a **12b-1 fee** (sometimes referred to as a *distribution fee*) to defray the costs of distribution and marketing a mutual fund and commissions paid to a brokerage firm that sold you shares in the mutual fund. Approved by the Securities and Exchange Commission, annual 12b-1 fees are calculated on the value of a fund's assets and cannot exceed 1 percent of the fund's assets per year. *Note:* For a fund to be called a "no-load" fund, its 12b-1 fee must not exceed 0.25 percent of its assets.

Unlike the one-time sales load fees that some mutual funds charge to purchase or sell shares, the 12b-1 fee is an ongoing fee that is charged on an annual basis. Note that 12b-1 fees can cost you a lot of money over a period of years. Assuming there is no difference in performance offered by two different mutual funds, one of which charges a 12b-1 fee while the other doesn't, choose the latter fund. The 12b-1 fee is so lucrative for investment companies that a number of them have begun selling Class C shares that often charge a higher 12b-1 fee but no sales load or contingent deferred sales fee to attract new investors. (*Note:* Some investment companies may charge a small contingent deferred sales fee for class C shares if withdrawals are made within a short time—usually one year). When compared to Class A shares (commissions charged when shares are purchased) and Class B shares (commissions charged when withdrawals are made over the first five to seven years), Class C shares, with their ongoing, higher 12b-1 fees, may be more expensive than Class A shares over a long period of time.

Together, all the different management fees, 12b-1 fees, if any, and additional operating costs for a specific fund are referred to as an **expense ratio.** Since it is important to keep fees and costs as low as possible, you should examine a fund's expense ratio as one more factor to consider when evaluating a mutual fund. *As a guideline, many financial planners recommend that you choose a mutual fund with an expense ratio of 1 percent or less.*

expense ratio All the different management fees, 12b-1 fees, if any, and additional fund operating costs for a specific mutual fund.

By now, you are probably asking yourself, "Should I purchase Class A shares, Class B shares, or Class C shares?" There are no easy answers, but your professional financial adviser or broker can help you determine which class of shares of a particular mutual fund best suits your financial needs. You can also do your own research to determine which fund is right for you. Factors to consider include whether you want to invest in a load fund or no-load fund, management fees, expense ratios, and how long you plan to own the fund. As you will see later in this chapter, a number of sources of information can help you make your investment decisions.

The investment company's prospectus must provide all details relating to management fees, sales fees, 12b-1 fees, and other expenses. Exhibit 16-2 reproduces the summary of expenses (sometimes called a *fee table*) for the Davis New York Venture fund. Notice that this exhibit has two separate parts. The first part describes shareholder transaction expenses. For this fund, the maximum sales charge is 4.75 percent. The second part describes the fund's annual operating expenses. For this fund, the expense ratio is 0.90 percent for Class A shares.

Exhibit 16-3 summarizes information for load charges, no-load charges, and Class A, Class B, and Class C shares. In addition, it reports typical contingent deferred sales loads, management fees, 12b-1 charges, and expense ratios.

I understand the reasons investors choose fund investments.

While investors choose mutual funds because of professional management and diversification, these same investors often complain about fees and charges. As you can tell from reading this section, there are a lot of different fees that can take away from your profits on fund investments. To make sure you know the amount of fees you will be expected to pay, review the fee table contained in a fund's prospectus. Also, take a second look at the fee information summarized in Exhibit 16-3.

PRACTICE QUIZ 16-1

1 What are two major reasons investors purchase mutual funds?
2 How do a closed-end fund, an open-end fund, and an exchange-traded fund differ?
3 What are the typical sales fees charged for load and no-load mutual funds?
4 What is the difference among Class A, B, and C shares?
5 What are the typical management fees, 12b-1 fees, and expense ratios?

Exhibit 16-2 Summary of expenses paid to invest in the Davis New York Venture mutual fund

Shareholder Fees *(fees paid directly from your investment)*			
	Class A shares	**Class B shares**	**Class C shares**
Maximum sales charge (load) imposed on purchases *(as a percentage of offering price.)*	4.75%	None	None
Maximum deferred sales charge (load) imposed on redemptions *(as a percentage of the lesser of the net asset value of the shares redeemed or the total cost of such shares. Only applies to Class A shares if you buy shares valued at $1 million or more without a sales charge and sell the shares within one year of purchase.)*	0.50%	4.00%	1.00%
Redemption fee *(as a percentage of total redemption proceeds.)*	None	None	None
Annual Fund Operating Expenses *(expenses that you pay each year as a percentage of the value of your investment)*			
	Class A shares	**Class B shares**	**Class C shares**
Management fees	0.50%	0.50%	0.50%
Distribution and/or service (12b-l) fees	0.24%	1.00%	1.00%
Other expenses	0.16%	0.32%	0.18%
Total annual operating expenses	0.90%	1.82%	1.68%

Source: Excerpted from page 8 of *Davis New York Venture Fund Prospectus*, 2012. Copyright © 2012. Used with permission.

Exhibit 16-3 Typical fees associated with mutual fund investments

Type of Fee or Charge	**Customary Amount**
Load fund	Up to 8½ percent of the purchase.
No-load fund	No sales charge.
Contingent deferred sales load	1 to 5 percent of withdrawals, depending on how long you own the fund before making a withdrawal.
Management fee	0.25 to 1.5 percent per year of the fund's total assets.
12b-1 fee	Cannot exceed 1 percent of the fund's assets per year.
Expense ratio	The amount investors pay for all fees and operating costs.
Class A shares	Commission charge when shares are purchased.
Class B shares	Commission charge when money is withdrawn during the first five to seven years.
Class C shares	No commission to buy or sell shares of a fund, but may have higher, ongoing 12b-1 fees.

TIME VALUE OF MONEY: SHOULD YOU CHOOSE A MUTUAL FUND OR A SAVINGS ACCOUNT?

Choosing an appropriate investment vehicle can be a difficult decision. Of course, there are many factors to consider, but two deserve special attention. First, you need to evaluate your tolerance for risk. One basic rule that was discussed in Chapter 13, is worth remembering: Simply put: *The potential return on any investment should be directly related to the risk the investor assumes.*

Second, your time horizon for investing should also be considered. If you need your money in a short period of time, you should consider conservative investments with less risk. If you can leave your investments alone and let them work for 5 to 10 years, you can invest in stocks or mutual funds.

THE TIME VALUE OF MONEY CONCEPT

Assume you have just received an inheritance of $50,000. The $50,000 is currently in a savings account earning 1 percent. It is expected that it will earn 1 percent for the next 20 years. Also, assume you could average about an 8 percent return for the next 20 years if you invested in an index fund. How much additional earnings would you receive by choosing the index fund instead of the savings account?

THE SOLUTION

To solve the problem, you need to use Exhibit 1-A (Future Value Table) in the appendix that follows Chapter 1.

Step 1: $50,000 invested at 1 percent for 20 years has increased to $61,000, as shown below.

$50,000 investment × 1.220 (Table Factor for 1 percent) = $61,000

Step 2: $50,000 invested at 8 percent for 20 years has increased to $233.050, as shown below.

$50,000 initial investment × 4.661 (Table Factor for 8 percent) = $233,050

CONCLUSION

You earned an additional $172,050 ($233,050 − $61,000 = $172,050) by investing in the index fund. While the earnings for the index fund are substantially more than the earnings for the savings account, keep in mind the index fund is not guaranteed, and therefore more speculative.

Classifications of Mutual Funds

LO16-2

Classify mutual funds by investment objective.

The managers of mutual funds tailor their investment portfolios in order to achieve specific investment objectives. Usually a fund's objectives are plainly disclosed in its prospectus. For example, the objectives of the Vanguard Growth Equity fund are described as follows:

> This fund seeks to invest in large U.S. companies that have the potential to grow consistently at a faster-than-average pace. The fund's managers tend to focus on a company's earnings growth, rather than its dividend or yield. One of the key risks is that, at certain times, the fund's strategy of investing in growth-oriented stocks may underperform the broader stock market. Long-term investors with a tolerance for volatility may wish to consider this fund complementary to a well-balanced portfolio.[7]

While it may be helpful to categorize the almost 13,000 mutual funds into different categories, different sources of investment information may use different categories for the same mutual fund. In most cases, the name of the category gives a pretty good clue to the types of investments included within the category. The *major* fund categories are described below in alphabetical order.

STOCK FUNDS

- *Aggressive growth funds* seek rapid growth by purchasing stocks whose prices are expected to increase dramatically in a short period of time. Turnover within an aggressive growth fund is high because managers are buying and selling individual

my life 2

I can identify the types of funds that will help me achieve my investment goals.

Often investors begin the search for a mutual fund by attempting to match their financial objectives with a specific fund's objective. The fund's objective is always contained in the prospectus available by accessing the Internet, making a phone call, or requesting a prospectus by mail. In addition, many websites and financial publications provide information about a fund's objective (along with a lot of other useful information).

stocks of small, growth companies. Investors in these funds experience wide price swings because of the underlying speculative nature of the stocks in the fund's portfolio.

- *Equity income funds* invest in stocks issued by companies with a long history of paying dividends. The major objective of these funds is to provide income to shareholders. These funds are attractive investment choices for conservative or retired investors.
- *Global stock funds* invest in stocks of companies throughout the world, including the United States.
- *Growth funds* invest in companies expecting higher-than-average revenue and earnings growth. While similar to aggressive growth funds, growth funds tend to invest in larger, well-established companies. As a result, the prices for shares in a growth fund are less volatile compared to aggressive growth funds.
- *Index funds* invest in the same companies included in an index like the Standard & Poor's 500 Stock Index or Nasdaq 100 Index. Since fund managers pick the stocks issued by the companies included in the index, an index fund should provide approximately the same performance as the index. Also, since index funds are cheaper to manage, they often have lower management fees and expense ratios.
- *International funds* invest in foreign stocks sold in securities markets throughout the world; thus, if the economy in one region or nation is in a slump, profits can still be earned in others. Unlike global funds, which invest in stocks issued by companies in both foreign nations and the United States, a true international fund invests outside the United States.
- *Large-cap funds* invest in the stocks of companies with total capitalization of $10 billion or more. Large-capitalization stocks are generally stable, well-established companies and likely to have minimal fluctuation in their value.
- *Midcap funds* invest in companies with total capitalization of $2 to $10 billion whose stocks offer more security than small-cap funds and more growth potential than funds that invest in large corporations.
- *Regional funds* seek to invest in stock traded within one specific region of the world, such as the European region, the Latin American region, or the Pacific region.
- *Sector funds* invest in companies within the same industry. Examples of sectors include health and biotechnology, science and technology, and natural resources.
- *Small-cap funds* invest in smaller, lesser-known companies with a total capitalization of less than $2 billion. Because these companies are small and innovative, these funds offer higher growth potential. They are more speculative than funds that invest in larger, more established companies.
- *Socially responsible funds* avoid investing in companies that may cause harm to people, animals, and the environment. Typically, these funds do not invest in companies that produce tobacco, nuclear energy, or weapons or in companies

DID YOU KNOW?

WHY DO PEOPLE INVEST IN MUTUAL FUNDS? Often the 90.4 million Americans who own funds, invest for multiple reasons that include

Why Do People Invest in Funds?	Percentage of Fund Owners
Saving for someone's education	26
Saving for emergencies	48
Using funds to reduce taxable income	49
Saving for retirement	94

Source: Table from Investment Company Institute website at: A15, p. 45, http://www.ici.org/pdf/per19-09.pdf, accessed March 25, 2013.

that have a history of discrimination. These funds invest in companies that have a history of making ethical decisions, establishing efforts to reduce pollution and other socially responsible activities.

BOND FUNDS

- *High-yield (junk) bond funds* invest in high-yield, high-risk corporate bonds.
- *Intermediate corporate bond funds* invest in investment-grade corporate debt with maturities between 5 and 10 years.
- *Intermediate U.S. bond funds* invest in U.S. Treasury securities with maturities between 5 and 10 years.
- *Long-term corporate bond funds* invest in investment-grade corporate bond issues with maturities in excess of 10 years.
- *Long-term (U.S.) bond funds* invest in U.S. Treasury securities with maturities in excess of 10 years.
- *Municipal bond funds* invest in municipal bonds that provide investors with tax-free interest income.
- *Short-term corporate bond funds* invest in investment-grade corporate bond issues with maturities between 1 and 5 years.
- *Short-term (U.S.) government bond funds* invest in U.S. Treasury securities with maturities between 1 and 5 years.
- *World bond funds* invest in bonds and other debt securities offered by foreign companies and governments.

OTHER FUNDS

- *Asset allocation funds* invest in various asset classes, including, but not limited to, stocks, bonds, fixed-income securities, and money market instruments. These funds seek high total return by maintaining precise amounts within each type of asset.
- *Balanced funds* invest in both stocks and bonds with the primary objectives of conserving principal, providing income, and long-term growth. Often the percentage of stocks and bonds is stated in the fund's prospectus.
- *Funds of funds* invest in shares of other mutual funds. The main advantage of a fund of funds is increased diversification and asset allocation, because this type of fund purchases shares in many different funds. Expenses and higher fees are quite common with this type of fund.
- *Lifecycle funds* (sometimes referred to as lifestyle or target-date funds) are popular with investors planning for retirement by a specific date. Typically, these funds initially invest in more risk-oriented securities (stocks) and become increasingly conservative and income oriented (bonds and CDs) as the specified date approaches and investors are closer to retirement.
- *Money market funds* invest in certificates of deposit, government securities, and other safe and highly liquid investments.

A **family of funds** exists when one investment company manages a group of mutual funds. Each fund within the family has a different financial objective. For instance, one fund may be a long-term government bond fund and another a growth stock fund. Most investment companies offer exchange privileges that enable shareholders to switch among the mutual funds in a fund family. For example, if you own shares in the Fidelity Disciplined Equity Fund, you may, at your discretion, switch to the Fidelity Capital and Income Fund. Generally, investors may give instructions to switch from one fund

family of funds A group of mutual funds managed by one investment company.

to another within the same family either in writing, over the telephone, or by using the Internet. The family-of-funds concept makes it convenient for shareholders to switch their investments among funds as different funds offer more potential, financial reward, or security. Charges for exchanges, if any, generally are small for each transaction. For funds that do charge, the fee may be as low as $5 per transaction.

PRACTICE QUIZ 16-2 

1 How important is the investment objective as stated in a fund's prospectus?
2 Why do you think fund managers offer so many different kinds of funds?
3 What is a family of funds? How is it related to shareholder exchanges?

How to Decide to Buy or Sell Mutual Funds

LO16-3

Evaluate mutual funds for investment purposes.

Often the decision to buy or sell shares in mutual funds is "too easy" because investors assume they do not need to evaluate these investments. Why question what the professional portfolio managers decide to do? Yet professionals do make mistakes. The responsibility for choosing the right mutual fund rests with *you.* After all, you are the only one who knows how much risk you are willing to assume and how a particular mutual fund can help you achieve your goals.

Fortunately, a lot of information is available to help you evaluate a specific mutual fund. Let's begin with one basic question: Do you want a managed fund or an index fund?

MANAGED FUNDS VERSUS INDEXED FUNDS

Most mutual funds are managed funds. In other words, there is a professional fund manager (or team of managers) that chooses the securities that are contained in the fund. The fund manager also decides when to buy and sell securities in the fund. *Caution: Don't forget the role of the fund manager in determining a fund's success.* One important question is how long the present fund manager has been managing the fund. To help evaluate a fund, you may want to determine how well a fund manager manages during both good and bad economic times. The benchmark for a good fund manager is the ability to increase share value when the economy is good and retain that value when the economy is bad. For example, most funds increased in value during the first part of 2007. Yet, only a few funds were able to retain those gains during the recent economic crisis. While there are no guarantees, if a fund has performed well under its present manager over a 5-year, 10-year, or longer period, there is a strong likelihood that it will continue to perform well under that manager in the future. On the other hand, if the fund has a new manager, his or her decisions may affect the performance of the fund. Ultimately, the fund manager is responsible for the fund's success. Managed funds may be open-end funds or closed-end funds. As mentioned earlier in this chapter, there are even a *few* exchange-traded funds that are actively managed.

Instead of investing in a managed fund, some investors choose to invest in an index fund. Why? The answer to that question is simple: Over many years, the majority of managed mutual funds fail to outperform the Standard & Poor's 500 stock index. The exact statistics vary depending on the year and the specific fund, but on average the Standard & Poor's 500 stock index outperforms 50 to 80 percent of actively managed funds over a long period of time.[8] The major reason why index funds outperform managed funds is because index funds have lower fees when compared to managed funds. And while lower fees may not sound significant, don't be fooled. Even a small difference can make a huge difference over a long period of time. For example, assume two different investors each invest $10,000. One investor chooses an index fund that has annual expenses of 0.20 percent; the other chooses a managed fund that has annual expenses of 1.22 percent. Both funds earn 10 percent a year. At the end of 35 years, the index fund is worth $263,683 while the managed fund is worth $190,203. That's a difference of $73,480.[9] Thus, even though the two funds earned the same 10 percent a year, the difference in annual expenses made a substantial difference in the amount of money each investor had at the end of 35 years.

Over a long period of time, it's hard to beat an index like the Standard & Poor's 500. If the individual securities included in an index increase in value, the index goes up. Because an index mutual fund is a mirror image of a specific index, the dollar value of a share in an index fund also increases when the index increases. Unfortunately, the reverse is true. If the index goes down, the value of a share in an index fund goes down.

The concept behind index funds is based on the efficient market hypothesis discussed in Chapter 14, which states that it is impossible to consistently beat the market without raising your risk level. John Bogle, founder of the Vanguard mutual funds, created the first index fund in 1975 as a low-cost alternative to managed mutual funds. Today, the Vanguard 500 Index fund is one of the largest mutual funds in the world.[10] Index funds, sometimes called "passive" funds, do have managers, but they simply buy the stocks or bonds contained in the index.

As mentioned earlier, investors choose index funds because they have a lower expense ratio when compared to managed funds. As defined earlier in this chapter, the total fees charged by a mutual fund is called the *expense ratio.* (Remember, financial planners recommend that you choose a mutual fund with an expense rate of 1 percent or less.) If a fund's expense ratio is 1.25 percent, then the fund has to earn at least that amount on its investment holdings each year just to break even. With very few exceptions, the expense ratios for index funds are lower than the expense ratios for managed funds. Typical expense ratios for an index fund are 0.50 percent or less. Index funds may be open-end funds, closed-end funds, or exchange-traded funds.

Which type of fund is best? The answer depends on which managed mutual fund you choose. If you pick a managed fund that has significantly better performance than an index, then you made the right choice. If, on the other hand, the index (and the index fund) outperforms the managed fund—which happens most of the time—an index fund is a better choice. With both investments, the key is how well you can research a specific investment alternative using the sources of information that are described in the remainder of this section.

THE INTERNET

Many investors have found a wealth of information about mutual fund investments on the Internet. Basically, there are three ways to access information. First, you can obtain current market values for mutual funds by using one of the websites, such as Yahoo! The Yahoo! finance page (finance.yahoo.com) has a box where you can enter the symbol of the mutual fund you want to research. If you don't know the symbol, just begin entering the mutual fund's name in the "Quote Lookup" box and the symbol will be displayed. In addition to current market values, you can obtain a price history for a mutual fund and a profile including specific holdings that the fund owns, performance data, comparative data, morningstar rating, and research reports.

Second, most investment companies that sponsor mutual funds have a website. To obtain information,

DID YOU KNOW?

MORNINGSTAR "STAR" RATINGS

Morningstar rates mutual funds from 1 (the lowest rating) to 5 (the highest rating) stars on how well they've performed in comparison with similar funds.

Within each Morningstar category, only the top 10 percent of funds receive the 5-star rating. And the bottom 10 percent of all funds receive the 1-star rating. All the other funds within each category are given ratings of 2, 3, or 4 stars depending on past performance.

Source: The Morningstar, Inc. website at www.morningstar.com, accessed March 28, 2013.

all you have to do is access one of the Internet search engines and type in the name of the fund. Generally, statistical information about individual funds, procedures for opening an account, promotional literature, and different investor services are provided. How about picking one of the fund families listed in Exhibit 16-4 and going exploring on the Internet. While the three investment companies listed in Exhibit 16-4 are quite large, there are many smaller firms that also sell funds. Regardless if an investment company is large or small, you can obtain a great deal of information about each company's funds, the forms required to open an account, and how much money is required to open an account with just a click of your mouse. A word of caution: Investment companies want you to become a shareholder. As a result, the websites for *some* investment companies read like a sales pitch. Read between the glowing descriptions and look at the facts before investing your money.

Finally, professional advisory services, covered in the next section, offer online research reports for mutual funds. Professional advisory services provide some of the most detailed information that can be used to evaluate mutual funds. Some investors also use their services as a first step to identify potential mutual fund investments. For example, Morningstar, one of the most recognized mutual fund websites, has a fund screener to help investors choose mutual funds. To begin the search process, investors enter criteria including the type of fund, desired expense ratio, performance returns, risk, etc. Then the Morningstar computer matches the criteria with different potential fund investments. If you would like to use this fund screener go to www.morningstar.com and click on Funds. Then click on Fund Screener.[11]

PROFESSIONAL ADVISORY SERVICES

As pointed out in the last section, a number of subscription services provide detailed information on mutual funds. Standard and Poor's Corporation, Lipper Analytical Services, Morningstar Inc. and Value Line are four widely used sources of such information.

Exhibit 16-4 Information about three of the world's largest mutual fund investment companies

Mutual Fund Company	Website Information	Assets under Management	Basic Information
The Vanguard Group	www.vanguard.com	$2.1 trillion	The Vanguard group has always been known as the leader in low-cost investing and has over 240 different funds. Many investors choose Vanguard because of its index funds and low expense ratios.
Fidelity Investments	www.fidelity.com	$1.7 trillion	In addition to more than 500 Fidelity mutual funds, Fidelity is both a fund supermarket that provides access to most available funds and a discount brokerage firm.
American Funds	www.americanfunds.com	$900 billion	Because this company believes in the value of professional advice, American Funds are often sold through account executives and financial advisors and may also charge higher fees.

Source: The Vanguard Group website at www.vanguard.com, accessed March 29, 2013; the Fidelity Investments website at www.fidelity.com, accessed March 29, 2013; and, the American Funds website at www.americanfunds.com, accessed March 29, 2013.

While in the past, much of the research information for mutual funds was available in printed materials and available in libraries, today most professional advisory services are using the Internet to provide research information online. And in many cases, you may be required to register and a fee may be charged for more detailed information you may need to research a fund investment. Still, many investors have found that the research reports provided by Standard & Poor's, Lipper, Morningstar, and Value Line are well worth the cost.

Today investors can obtain a wealth of information by using a computer to access the website for a professional advisory service. For example, Exhibit 16-5 illustrates research information about the Vanguard 500 Index Fund provided by Morningstar. Just by entering the fund's symbol (VFINX) in the Quote box at the top, you can obtain information including current price, changes in the NAV, yield, total assets, expenses, turnover, minimum investment, performance, and a graph that displays the growth of a $10,000 investment over a period of time.

I know how to evaluate a fund investment.

Where do you start with so much information available about fund investments? For many investors, the answer is a professional advisory service like Morningstar, Lipper, Standard & Poor's, or Value Line. Research information for each of these professional advisory services is available at many libraries and on the Internet. *Note:* You may be required to register or pay a charge for accessing information available on the Internet.

Even more detailed information is available by clicking on the different tabs at the top of this Morningstar report. The descriptions below provide basic information for some of the more important tabs:

Fund analysis tab	Provides in-depth information reported by professional analysts. To access this premium content, you will need to subscribe or take advantage of a free-trial offer.
Performance tab	Provides detailed information about how this fund has performed over selected time period and also compares the fund's performance with selected benchmarks including other large-blend funds and the Standard & Poor's 500 index.
Ratings and Risk tab	Describes the current Morningstar ratings for both performance and risk. Notice that this Vanguard fund received a 4-star rating from Morningstar. While not a 5-star fund, it is consistently rated above average for return and average for risk.
Management tab	Describes the current fund manager (or team of managers) and how long he or she has managed the fund.
Portfolio tab	Provides information about the type of securities included in the fund.
Expense tab	Provides information about fees and the expense ratio for this fund.
Purchase tab	Indicates this fund is open to new investors. Indicates the minimum initial investment is $3,000 for new investors. Additional investments can be as small as $100.

While Exhibit 16-5 provides detailed information about the Vanguard 500 Index Fund, you can obtain the same type of information for many more funds with a click of your computer's mouse. Why not take a look at the type of research information available for a fund you think would help you obtain your personal financial goals? To begin the search, go to www.morningstar.com and enter the symbol for a specific fund. If you don't know the symbol, you can enter the name of the fund, and the symbol will be

Exhibit 16-5 Information about the Vanguard 500 Index Fund available from the Morningstar website

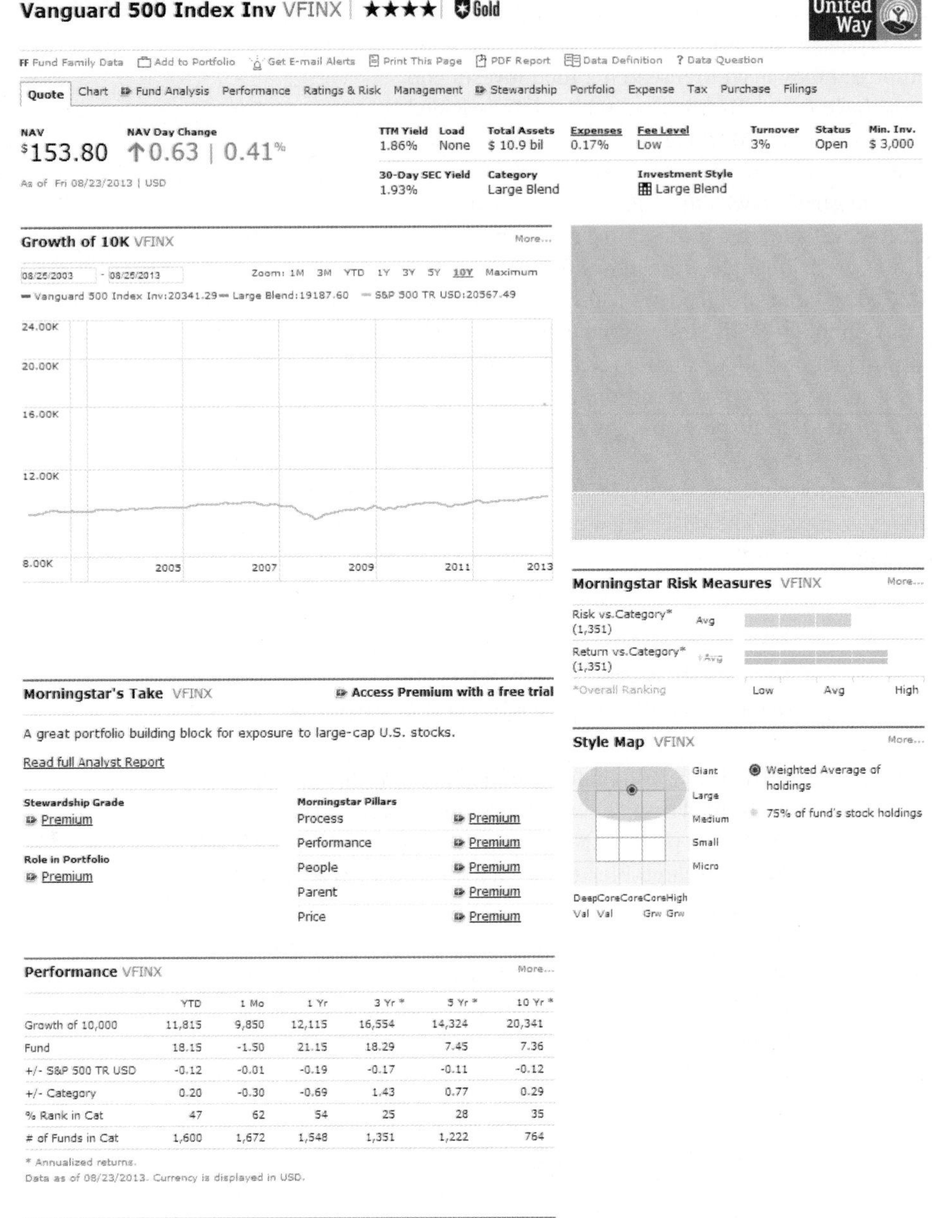

	YTD	1 Mo	1 Yr	3 Yr *	5 Yr *	10 Yr *
Growth of 10,000	11,815	9,850	12,115	16,554	14,324	20,341
Fund	18.15	-1.50	21.15	18.29	7.45	7.36
+/- S&P 500 TR USD	-0.12	-0.01	-0.19	-0.17	-0.11	-0.12
+/- Category	0.20	-0.30	-0.69	1.43	0.77	0.29
% Rank in Cat	47	62	54	25	28	35
# of Funds in Cat	1,600	1,672	1,548	1,351	1,222	764

* Annualized returns.
Data as of 08/23/2013. Currency is displayed in USD.

Source: The Morningstar website at www.morningstar.com, accessed August 23, 2013.

displayed. Then click on the quote button and read the available information about your potential investment. It's that easy.

As you can see, the research information for this fund is pretty upbeat. However, other research firms like Standard & Poor's, Lipper Analytical Services, and Value Line, as well as Morningstar Inc. will also tell you if a fund is a poor performer that offers poor investment potential.

In addition, various mutual fund newsletters provide financial information to subscribers for a fee. All of the professional advisory services are rather expensive, but some reports may be available from brokerage firms or libraries.

MUTUAL FUND PROSPECTUS AND ANNUAL REPORT

An investment company sponsoring a mutual fund must give potential investors a prospectus. You can also request a prospectus by mail, by calling a toll-free number, or by accessing the investment company's website.

According to financial experts, investors should read the prospectus completely before investing. Although it may look foreboding, a commonsense approach to reading a fund's prospectus can provide valuable insights. As pointed out earlier, the prospectus summarizes the fund's objective. Also, the fee table provides a summary of the fees a fund charges. In addition to information about objectives and fees, the prospectus should provide the following:

- A statement describing the risk factors associated with the fund.
- A description of the fund's past performance.
- A statement describing the type of investments contained in the fund's portfolio.
- Information about dividends and capital gain distributions.
- Information about the fund's management.
- Information on limitations or requirements the fund must honor when choosing investments.
- The process investors can use to buy or sell shares in the fund.
- A description of services provided to investors and fees for services, if any.
- Information about how often the fund's investment portfolio changes and tax consequences of a fund's trading activities.

Finally, the prospectus provides information about how to open a mutual fund account with the investment company.

If you are a prospective investor, you can request an annual report by mail, through an 800 telephone number, or on the Internet. Once you are a shareholder, the investment company will send you an annual report. As an alternative, many investors access a fund's annual report by using the Internet. A fund's annual report contains a letter from the president of the investment company, from the fund manager, or both. The annual report also contains detailed financial information about the fund's assets and liabilities, performance, statement of operations, and statement of changes in net assets. Next, the annual report includes a schedule of investments. Finally, the fund's annual report should include a letter from the fund's independent auditors that provides an opinion as to the accuracy of the fund's financial statements.

NEWSPAPERS AND FINANCIAL PUBLICATIONS

Although many newspapers have reduced or eliminated mutual fund coverage, many large, metropolitan newspapers and *The Wall Street Journal* often provide news and information about mutual fund investments. In addition, these same publications may provide basic information for current prices and performance. Typical coverage includes the name of a fund family and names of specific funds within the family, current net asset value for a fund, and percentage of year-to-date (YTD) return. Much of this same information (along with more detailed information) is available on the Internet.

Investment-oriented magazines such as *Bloomberg Businessweek, Forbes, Fortune, Kiplinger's Personal Finance,* and *Money* provide information about mutual funds and investing. Depending on the publication, coverage ranges from detailed articles that provide in-depth information to simple listings of which funds to buy or sell. And many investment oriented magazines have websites that provide information about mutual funds.

Exhibit 16-6 A portion of *Money Magazine's* 2013 list of high quality funds and ETFs

Fund	YTD Return	5 yr Return	Expense Ratio	Type
Large Cap Actively Managed Funds				
AMRMX American Funds American Mutual Fund	+10.01%	+5.80%	0.63%	Value
SSHFX Sound Shore Fund	+11.60%	+3.02%	0.94%	Value
PRFDX T Rowe Price Equity Income Fund	+10.70%	+4.65%	0.68%	Value
VWNFX Vanguard Windsor II Fund Investor S	+10.31%	+4.21%	0.35%	Value
FMIHX FMI Large Cap Fund	+11.40%	+7.02%	0.96%	Blend
SLASX Selected American Shares Fund Class	+10.41%	+2.25%	0.94%	Blend
AMCPX American Funds AMCAP Fund Class A	+10.37%	+5.98%	0.73%	Growth
JENSX Jensen Quality Growth Fund Class J	+10.62%	+6.34%	0.91%	Growth
TRBCX T Rowe Price Blue Chip Growth Fund	+8.15%	+6.59%	0.77%	Growth

Source: "Money 70: Best Mutual Funds and ETFs," *Money Magazine: Investor's Guide 2013,* CNNMoney website, www.money.cnn.com, March 29, 2013.

The material in Exhibit 16-6 was obtained from the *Money Magazine: Investor's Guide 2013* and provides basic information for each of the funds recommended in the exhibit. For example, information is provided about the

- Size and general type of fund.
- Actual fund name.
- Year-to-date (YTD) return.
- Five-year average annual return.
- Expense ratio stated as a percentage of assets.
- Type of fund.

The point of the Money 70: Best Mutual Funds and ETFs article is to give you a menu of high-quality funds and ETFs that can be used to construct a well-diversified portfolio. For each fund selected, four criteria were used: fees, stewardship, experience, and performance.[12] Even though these funds are recommended, investors still need to dig deeper and examine more detailed research information to determine whether the funds described in this article could help them achieve their investment goals.

In addition to mutual fund information in financial publications, a number of mutual fund guidebooks are available at your local bookstore or public library.

Mutual Fund Investment Information

Mutual Fund Evaluation

PRACTICE QUIZ 16-3

1 Many financial experts say that purchasing a mutual fund is "too easy." Do you think this statement is true or false? Explain.

2 In your own words, describe the difference between a managed fund and an index fund. Which fund would you choose for your investment program?

3 How can the following help you evaluate a mutual fund?

a. The Internet

b. Professional advisory services

c. The prospectus

d. The annual report

e. Newspapers and financial publications

The Mechanics of a Mutual Fund Transaction

LO16-4

Describe how and why mutual funds are bought and sold.

For many investors, mutual funds have become the investment of choice. In fact, you probably either own shares or know someone who owns shares in a mutual fund—they're that popular! They may be part of a 401(k) or 403(b) retirement account, a SEP-IRA, a Roth IRA, or a traditional IRA retirement account, all topics discussed in Chapter 18. They can also be owned outright by purchasing shares through account executives or salespeople who work for a brokerage firm or directly from an investment company that sponsors a mutual fund. As you will see later in this section, it's easy to purchase shares in a mutual fund. For $250 to $3,000 or more, you can open an account and begin investing. And there are other advantages that encourage investors to purchase shares in funds. Unfortunately, there are also disadvantages. Exhibit 16-7 summarizes the advantages and disadvantages of mutual fund investments.

One advantage of any investment is the opportunity to make money on it. In the next section, we examine how you can make money by investing in closed-end funds, exchange-traded funds, or open-end funds. We consider how taxes affect your mutual fund investments. Then we look at the options used to purchase shares in a mutual fund. Finally, we examine the options used to withdraw money from a mutual fund.

RETURN ON INVESTMENT

income dividends The earnings a fund pays to shareholders from its dividend and interest income.

capital gain distributions The payments made to a fund's shareholders that result from the sale of securities in the fund's portfolio.

As with other investments, the purpose of investing in a closed-end fund, exchange-traded fund, or open-end fund is to earn a financial return. Shareholders in such funds can receive a return in one of three ways. First, all three types of funds pay income dividends. **Income dividends** are the earnings a fund pays to shareholders from its dividend and interest income. Second, investors may receive capital gain distributions. **Capital gain distributions** are the payments made to a fund's shareholders that result from the sale of securities in the fund's portfolio. These amounts generally are paid once a year. *Note:* The majority of exchange-traded funds don't usually pay end-of-the-year capital gain distributions.

Exhibit 16-7

Advantages and disadvantages of investing in mutual funds

Advantages
• Diversification. • Professional management. • Ease of buying and selling shares. • Multiple withdrawal options. • Distribution or reinvestment of income and capital gain distributions. • Switching privileges within the same fund family. • Services that include toll-free telephone numbers, complete records of all transactions, and savings and checking accounts.
Disadvantages
• Purchase/withdrawal costs. • Ongoing management fees and 12b-1 fees. • Poor performance that may not match the Standard & Poor's 500 stock index or some other index. • Inability to control when capital gain distributions occur and complicated tax-reporting issues. • Potential market risk associated with all investments. • Some sales personnel are aggressive and/or unethical.

DID YOU KNOW?

A COMMON MISTAKE MADE BY FUND INVESTORS
A fund usually pays income dividends and capital gain distributions at the end of the calendar year. For investors that own shares in a taxable account, this creates a taxing problem. When they receive dividend income and/or a capital gain distribution, they immediately receive taxable income that must be reported on their tax return. To make matters worse, the net asset value per share usually decreases by the amount of the dividend and distribution.

my life 4

I know how I can make money with fund investments.

As crazy as it may sound, some people invest money in mutual funds without really knowing how to make money from mutual funds. As pointed out in this section, there are three ways: (1) income dividends; (2) capital gains distributions that result from the fund selling securities contained in the fund, and (3) capital gains that result when you sell shares for more than you pay for them. Why not review the material in this section one more time? It's that important!

Third, as with stock and bond investments, you can buy shares in funds at a low price and then sell them after the price has increased. For example, assume you purchased shares in the Fidelity Stock Selector Fund at $26 per share and sold your shares two years later at $31 per share. In this case, you made $5 ($31 selling price minus $26 purchase price) per share. With this financial information along with the dollar amounts for income dividends and capital gain distributions, you can calculate a total return for your mutual fund investment. Before completing this section, you may want to examine the actual procedure used to calculate the dollar amount of total return and percentage of total return in the Financial Planning Calculations box on page 577.

When shares in a mutual fund are sold, the profit that results from an increase in value is referred to as a *capital gain.* Note the difference between a capital gain distribution and a capital gain. A capital gain distribution occurs when *the fund* distributes profits that result from *the fund* selling securities in the portfolio at a profit. On the other hand, a capital gain is the profit that results when *you* sell your shares in the fund for more than you paid for them. Of course, if the price of a fund's shares goes down between the time of your purchase and the time of sale, you incur a loss.

TAXES AND MUTUAL FUNDS

Income dividends, capital gain distributions, and financial gains and losses from the sale of closed-end, exchange-traded, or open-end funds are subject to taxation. When you pay taxes is determined by the type of account you own. For example, if your mutual fund shares are part of a 401(k) retirement account or traditional IRA account, taxation is postponed until you begin making withdrawals. On the other hand, if your shares are part of a taxable account, then taxes must be paid each year. For taxable accounts, investment companies are required to send each shareholder a statement specifying how much he or she received in dividends and capital gain distributions at the end of each calendar year. Although investment companies may provide this information as part of their year-end statement, most funds also use IRS Form 1099 DIV.

The following information provides general guidelines on how mutual fund transactions are taxed:

- Income dividends are reported on your federal tax return and are taxed as income.
- Capital gain distributions that result from the fund selling securities in its portfolio at a profit are reported on your federal tax return. Capital gain distributions are taxed as long-term capital gains regardless of how long you own shares in the mutual fund.
- Capital gains or losses that result from your selling shares in a mutual fund are reported on your federal tax return. How long you hold the shares determines whether your gains or losses are taxed as a short-term or long-term capital gain. (See Chapter 4 for more information on capital gains and capital losses or visit the IRS website at www.irs.gov.)

Financial Planning Calculations

CALCULATING TOTAL RETURN FOR MUTUAL FUNDS

In Chapter 14, we defined *total return* as a value that includes not only the yearly dollar amount of income but also any increase or decrease in market value from the original purchase price of an investment. For mutual funds, you can use the following calculation to determine the dollar amount of total return:

Income dividends
+ Capital gain distributions
+ Change in share market value when sold
Dollar amount of total return

For example, assume you purchased 100 shares of Majestic Growth Fund for $12.20 per share for a total investment of $1,220. During the next 12 months, you received income dividends of $0.20 a share and capital gain distributions of $0.30. Also, assume you sold your investment at the end of 12 months for $13.40 a share. As illustrated below, the dollar amount for total return is $170:

Income dividends = 100 × $0.20 =	$ 20
Capital gain distributions = 100 × $0.30 =	+ 30
Change in share value = $13.40 − $12.20	
= $1.20 × 100 =	+ 120
Dollar amount of total return	$170

To calculate the percentage of total return, divide the dollar amount of total return by the original cost of your mutual fund investment. The percentage of total return for the above example is 13.9 percent, as follows:

$$\text{Percent of total return} = \frac{\text{Dollar amount of total return}}{\text{Original cost of your investment}}$$

$$= \frac{\$170}{\$1{,}220}$$

$$= 0.139, \text{ or } 13.9\%$$

Now it's your turn. Use the following information for the New Frontiers Natural Resources fund to calculate the dollar amount of total return and percent of total return over a 12-month period:

Number of shares: 100
Purchase price: $16.00 a share
Income dividends: $0.25 a share
Capital gain distribution: $0.15 a share
Sale price: $18.00 a share

What is your total return on your fund investment and what is the percentage of total return?

Answer: The total return is $240 and the percentage of total return is 15 percent.

Two specific problems develop with taxation of mutual funds. First, almost all investment companies allow you to reinvest dividend income and capital gain distributions from the fund in additional shares instead of receiving cash. Even though you didn't receive cash because you chose to reinvest such distributions, they are still taxable and must be reported on your federal tax return as current income.

Second, when you purchase shares of stock, corporate bonds, or other investments and use the buy-and-hold technique described in Chapter 14, you decide when you sell. Thus, you can pick the tax year when you pay tax on capital gains or deduct capital losses. Mutual funds, on the other hand, buy and sell securities within the fund's portfolio on a regular basis during any 12-month period. At the end of the year, profits that result from the mutual fund's buying and selling activities are paid to shareholders in the form of capital gain distributions. Because capital gain distributions are taxable, one factor to consider when choosing a mutual fund is its turnover. For a mutual fund, the **turnover ratio** measures the percentage of a fund's holdings that have changed or "been replaced" during a 12-month period.

turnover ratio The percentage of a fund's holdings that have changed or "been replaced" during a 12-month period.

Simply put, it is a measure of a fund's trading activity. *Caution:* Unless you are using the fund in a 401(k) or 403(b) retirement account or some type of individual retirement account, a mutual fund with a high turnover ratio can result in higher income tax bills. A higher turnover ratio can also result in higher transaction costs and fund expenses. Unlike the investments that you manage, you have no control over when the mutual fund sells securities and when you will be taxed on capital gain distributions.

To ensure having all of the documentation you need for tax reporting purposes, it is essential that *you* keep accurate records. The same records will help you monitor the value of your mutual fund investments and make more intelligent decisions with regard to buying and selling these investments.

PURCHASE OPTIONS

You can buy shares of a closed-end fund or exchange-traded fund through a securities exchange or in the over-the-counter market. You can purchase shares of an open-end, no-load fund by contacting the investment company that sponsors the fund. You can purchase shares of an open-end, load fund through an account executive or salesperson who is authorized to sell them or directly from the investment company that sponsors the fund.

You can also purchase both no-load and load funds from mutual fund supermarkets available through most brokerage firms. A mutual fund supermarket offers at least two advantages. First, instead of dealing with numerous investment companies that sponsor mutual funds, you can make one toll-free phone call or use the Internet to obtain information, purchase shares, and sell shares in a large number of mutual funds. Second, you receive one statement from the brokerage firm instead of receiving a statement from each investment company you deal with. One statement can be a real plus, because it provides the information you need to monitor the value of your investments in one place and in the same format.

Because of the unique nature of open-end fund transactions, we will examine how investors buy and sell shares in this type of mutual fund. To purchase shares in an open-end mutual fund from an investment company, you may use four options:

- Regular account transactions.
- Voluntary savings plans.
- Contractual savings plans.
- Reinvestment plans.

The most popular and least complicated method of purchasing shares in an open-end fund is through a regular account transaction. When you use a regular account transaction, you decide how much money you want to invest and when you want to invest, and simply buy as many shares as possible.

The chief advantage of the voluntary savings plan is that it allows you to make smaller purchases than the minimum purchases required by the regular account method described above. At the time of the initial purchase, you declare an intent to make regular minimum purchases of the fund's shares. Also, many investors can choose mutual funds as a vehicle to invest money that is contributed to a 401(k), 403(b), or individual retirement account. As mentioned earlier, Chapter 18 provides more information on the tax advantages of different types of retirement accounts. Although there is no penalty for not making purchases, most investors feel an "obligation" to make purchases on a periodic basis, and, as pointed out throughout this text, small monthly investments are a great way to save for long-term financial goals. For most voluntary savings plans, the minimum purchase ranges from $25 to $100 for each purchase after the initial investment required to open the account. Funds try to make investing as easy as possible. Most offer payroll deduction plans, and many will deduct, upon proper shareholder authorization, a specified amount from a shareholder's bank account.

Not as popular as they once were, contractual savings plans (sometimes referred to as *periodic payment plans*) require you to make regular purchases over a specified period of time, usually 10 to 20 years. These plans are sometimes referred to as *front-end load plans* because almost all of the commissions are paid in the first few years of the contract period. You will incur penalties if you do not fulfill the purchase requirements. For example, if you drop out of a contractual savings plan before completing the purchase requirements, you may sacrifice the prepaid commissions. In some cases, contractual savings plans combine mutual fund shares and life insurance to make these plans more attractive. Many financial experts and government regulatory agencies are critical of contractual savings plans. As a result, the Securities and Exchange Commission and many states have imposed new disclosure rules on investment companies offering contractual savings plans.

You may also purchase shares in an open-end fund by using the fund's reinvestment plan. A **reinvestment plan** is a service provided by an investment company in which income dividends and capital gain distributions are automatically reinvested to purchase additional shares of the fund. Most reinvestment plans allow shareholders to use reinvested money to purchase shares without having to pay additional sales charges or commissions. *Reminder:* When your dividends or capital gain distributions are reinvested, you must still report these transactions as taxable income.

reinvestment plan A service provided by an investment company in which income dividends and capital gain distributions are automatically reinvested to purchase additional shares of the fund.

All four purchase options allow you to buy shares over a long period of time. As a result, you can use the principle of *dollar cost averaging,* which was explained in Chapter 14. Dollar cost averaging allows you to average many individual purchase prices over a long period of time. This method helps you avoid the problem of buying high and selling low. With dollar cost averaging, you can make money if you sell your mutual fund shares at a price higher than their *average* purchase price.

WITHDRAWAL OPTIONS

Because closed-end funds and exchange-traded funds are listed on securities exchanges or traded in the over-the-counter market, it is possible to sell shares in such a fund to another investor. Shares in an open-end fund can be sold on any business day to the investment company that sponsors the fund. In this case, the shares are redeemed at their net asset value. All you have to do is give proper notification and the investment company will send you a check. With some funds, you can even write checks to withdraw money from the fund.

In addition, most funds have provisions that allow investors with shares that have a minimum net asset value (usually at least $5,000) to use four options to systematically withdraw money. First, you may withdraw a specified, fixed dollar amount each investment period. Normally, an investment period is three months.

A second option allows you to liquidate or "sell off" a certain number of shares each investment period. Since the net asset value of shares in a fund varies from one period to the next, the amount of money you receive will also vary.

A third option allows you to withdraw a fixed percentage of asset growth. Under this option, your principal remains untouched and, assuming you withdraw less than 100 percent of asset growth, your fund continues to grow.

EXAMPLE: Withdrawal Calculation

You arrange to receive 60 percent of the asset growth from your fund investment and the asset growth amounts to $800 in a particular investment period. For that period, you will receive a check for $480, as shown below.

Amount you receive = Investment growth × Percentage of growth withdrawn
= $800 × 60 percent
= $800 × 0.60
= $480

A final option allows you to withdraw all asset growth earned by the fund during an investment period. Under this option, your principal remains untouched.

PRACTICE QUIZ 16-4

1 How can you make money when investing in mutual funds?
2 What are the differences among income dividends, capital gain distributions, and capital gains?
3 How would you purchase a closed-end fund? An exchange-traded fund?
4 What options can you use to purchase shares in an open-end mutual fund from an investment company?
5 What options can you use to withdraw money from an open-end mutual fund?

my life stages for investing in mutual funds . . .

YOUR PERSONAL FINANCE DASHBOARD

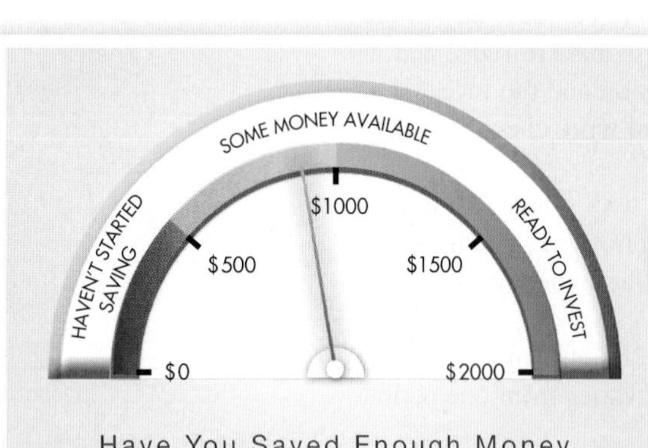

A personal finance dashboard allows you to assess your financial situation.

Because of professional management and diversification, beginning investors often choose mutual funds. Still you must choose the right fund that will help you achieve your financial objectives. Then you must evaluate each fund alternative before investing your money.

YOUR SITUATION Are you ready to invest in mutual funds? A very important step is to save the money you need to begin investing. Typically most brokerage firms and investment companies require investors to have $250 to $3,000 to open an account. Other personal financial planning actions you might consider during various stages of your life include:

(continued)

my life stages for investing in mutual funds *(concluded)*

. . . in college	. . . in my 20s	. . . in my 30s and 40s	. . . in my 50s and beyond
• Establish investment and financial goals • Work to balance your budget • Start an emergency fund • Save the money needed to begin investing • Open an account with a brokerage firm or an investment company • Evaluate different fund investments that offer a potential for growth • Begin investing	• Revise investment and financial goals • Participate in an employer sponsored 401(k) retirement account • Consider investing in a Roth IRA or Traditional IRA • Continue to evaluate all existing investments • Evaluate different funds that offer growth opportunities for new investments	• Revise investment and financial goals • Continue to save money and participate in retirement and IRA accounts • Continue to evaluate all existing investments • Use asset allocation to diversify investments in stocks, bonds, and funds with different objectives	• Revise investment and financial goals • Evaluate all existing investments on a regular basis • Determine current financial status and the number of years until retirement • Continue to save and begin increasing the amount of money invested in conservative funds • Use asset allocation to make sure that there is a balance between growth oriented investments and conservative investments

SUMMARY OF LEARNING OBJECTIVES

LO16-1

Describe the characteristics of mutual fund investments.

The major reasons investors choose mutual funds are professional management and diversification. Mutual funds are also a convenient way to invest money. There are three types of mutual funds. A closed-end fund is a mutual fund whose shares are issued only when the fund is organized. An exchange-traded fund (ETF) is a fund that invests in the stocks and securities contained in a specific stock or securities index. Both closed-end funds and exchange-traded funds are traded on a securities exchange or in the over-the-counter market. An open-end fund is a mutual fund whose shares are sold and redeemed by the investment company at the net asset value (NAV) at the request of investors. Mutual funds are also classified as load or no-load funds. A load fund charges a commission every time you purchase shares. No commission is charged to purchase shares in a no-load fund. Mutual funds can also be classified as A shares (commissions charged when shares are purchased), B shares (commissions charged when money is withdrawn during the first five to seven years), and C shares (no commission to buy or sell shares, but higher, ongoing 12b-1 fees). Other possible fees include management fees, contingent deferred fees, and 12b-1 fees. Together all the different fees are reported as an expense ratio.

LO16-2

Classify mutual funds by investment objective.

The major categories of stock mutual funds, in terms of the types of securities in which they invest, are aggressive growth, equity income, global, growth, index, international, large-cap, midcap, regional, sector, small-cap, and socially responsible. There are also bond funds that include high-yield, intermediate corporate, intermediate U.S. government, long-term corporate, long-term U.S. government, municipal, short-term corporate, short-term U.S. government, and world. Finally, other funds invest in a mix of different stocks, bonds, and other investment securities that include asset allocation funds, balanced funds, funds of funds, lifecycle, and money market funds. Today many investment companies use a family-of-funds concept, which allows shareholders to switch their investments among funds as different funds offer more potential, financial reward, or security.

LO16-3

Evaluate mutual funds for investment purposes.

The responsibility for choosing the "right" mutual fund rests with you, the investor. One of the first questions you must answer is whether you want a managed fund or an index fund. Most mutual funds are managed funds, with a professional fund manager (or team of managers) who chooses the securities contained in the fund. An index fund invests in the securities that are contained in an index such as the Standard & Poor's 500 stock index. Statistically, the majority of managed mutual funds have failed to outperform the Standard & Poor's 500 stock index over a long period of time. The information on the Internet, from professional advisory services, in the fund prospectus and annual report, and in newspapers and financial publications can all help you evaluate a mutual fund.

LO16-4

Describe how and why mutual funds are bought and sold.

The advantages and disadvantages of mutual funds have made mutual funds the investment of choice for many investors. For $250 to $3,000 or more, you can open an account and begin investing. The shares of a closed-end fund or exchange-traded fund are bought and sold on organized securities exchanges or the over-the-counter market. The shares of an open-end fund may be purchased through an account executive or salesperson who is authorized to sell them, from a mutual fund supermarket, or from the investment company that sponsors the fund. The shares in an open-end fund can be sold to the investment company that sponsors the fund. Shareholders in mutual funds can receive a return in one of three ways: income dividends, capital gain distributions when the *fund* buys and sells securities in the fund's portfolio at a profit, and capital gains when the *shareholder* sells shares in the mutual fund at a higher price than the price paid. Unless your mutual fund account is part of an individual retirement account, or 401k or 403(b) retirement account, income dividends, capital gain distributions, and capital gains are subject to taxation. A number of purchase and withdrawal options are available.

KEY TERMS

capital gain distributions 575
closed-end fund 557
contingent deferred sales load 562
exchange-traded fund (ETF) 558
expense ratio 563
family of funds 567
income dividends 575
load fund 561
mutual fund 556
net asset value (NAV) 559
no-load fund 561
open-end fund 559
reinvestment plan 579
turnover ratio 577
12b-1 fee 562

KEY FORMULAS

Page	Topic	Formula
559	Net asset value	$\text{Net asset value} = \dfrac{\text{Value of the fund's portfolio} - \text{Liabilities}}{\text{Number of shares outstanding}}$
	Example:	$\text{Net asset value} = \dfrac{\$245\text{ million} - \$5\text{ million}}{8\text{ million}}$
		$= \$30\text{ per share}$

Page	Topic	Formula
561	Dollar amount of sales load	Dollar amount of sales load = Original investment × Sales load stated as a percentage
	Example:	Dollar amount of sales load = \$20,000 × 5 percent = \$20,000 × 0.05 = \$1,000
562	Contingent deferred sales load	Contingent deferred sales load = Withdrawal amount × Contingent deferred sales load as a percentage
	Example:	Contingent deferred sales load = \$12,000 × 4 percent = \$12,000 × 0.04 = \$480
577	Total return	Income dividends + Capital gain distributions + Change in market value Dollar amount of total return
	Example:	Dollar amount of total return: \$120 Income dividends + 80 Capital gain distributions + 320 Change in market value \$520 Dollar amount of total return
577	Percent of total return	Percent of total return = $\frac{\text{Dollar amount of total return}}{\text{Original cost of your investment}}$
	Example:	Percent of total return = $\frac{\$520}{\$4{,}500}$ = 0.116, or 11.6%
580	Withdrawal calculation	Amount you receive = Investment growth × Percentage of growth withdrawn
	Example:	Amount you receive = \$2,000 × 30 percent = \$2,000 × 0.30 = \$600

SELF-TEST PROBLEMS

1. Three years ago, Dorothy Schwartz's mutual fund portfolio was worth \$320,000. Now, because of a downturn in the economy, the total of her investment portfolio has decreased to \$243,000. Even though she has lost a significant amount of money, she has not changed her investment holdings, which consist of either aggressive growth funds or growth funds.
   a. How much money has Ms. Schwartz lost in the last three years?
   b. Given the above information, calculate the percentage of lost value.
   c. What actions would you take to get her investments back in shape if you were Dorothy Schwartz?

2. Twelve months ago, Bill Crandall purchased 500 shares in the BlackRock Equity Dividend B fund—a Morningstar 4-star fund that seeks long-term total return and current income. His rationale for choosing this fund was that he wanted a fund that was conservative and highly rated. Each share in the fund cost $18.30. At the end of the year, he received income dividends of $0.13 a share. There were no capital gain distributions. At the end of 12 months, the shares in the fund were selling for $21.55.

   a. How much did Mr. Crandall invest in this fund?

   b. At the end of 12 months, what is the total return for this fund?

   c. What is the percentage of total return?

Solutions

1. a. Dollar lost = $320,000 Value three years ago − $243,000 Current value

   = $77,000

   b. Percent of dollar lost = $77,000 Dollar lost ÷ $320,000 Value three years ago

   = 0.24 = 24 percent

   c. While Ms. Schwartz has several options, any decision should be based on careful research and evaluation. First, she could do nothing. While she has lost a substantial portion of her investment portfolio ($77,000, or 24 percent), it may be time to hold on to her investments if she believes the economy is improving and the value of her funds will increase. Second, she could sell (or exchange) some or all of her shares in the aggressive growth or growth funds and move her money into more conservative funds, or even certificates of deposit. Finally, she could buy more shares if she believes the economy is beginning to improve. Because of depressed prices for quality funds, this may be a real buying opportunity. Deciding which option for Ms. Schwartz to take may depend on the economic conditions at the time you answer this question.

2. a. Total investment = Price per share × Number of shares

   = $18.30 × 500

   = $9,150

   b. Income dividends = $0.13 × 500 = $65

   Change in share value = $21.55 − $18.30 = $3.25 gain per share

   Total increase in value = $3.25 gain per share × 500 = $1,625 gain in value

   Total return = $65 Income dividends

   $1,625 Gain in value

   $1,690 Dollar amount of total return

   c. Percent of dollar loss = $\frac{\$1{,}690}{\$9{,}150 \text{ Investment}}$

   = 0.185 = 18.5 percent

FINANCIAL PLANNING PROBLEMS

L016-1 1. *Calculating Net Asset Value.* Given the following information, calculate the net asset value for the Boston Equity mutual fund.

Total assets	$240,000,000
Total liabilities	$8,000,000
Total number of shares	5,000,000

2. *Calculating Net Asset Value.* Given the following information, calculate the net asset value for the New Empire small-cap mutual fund. LO16-1

Total assets	$380,000,000
Total liabilities	$15,000,000
Total number of shares	25,000,000

3. *Calculating Sales Fees.* Jan Throng invested $31,000 in the Invesco Charter mutual fund. The fund charges a 5.50 percent commission when shares are purchased. Calculate the amount of commission Jan must pay. LO16-1

4. *Calculating Sales Fees.* Bill Matthews invested $9,500 in the John Hancock Government Income fund. The fund charges a 4.50 percent commission when shares are purchased. Calculate the amount of commission Bill must pay. LO16-1

5. *Calculating Contingent Deferred Sales Loads.* Ted Paulson needed money to pay for unexpected medical bills. To obtain $6,000, he decided to sell some of his shares in the Ridgemoor Capital Appreciation Fund. When he called the investment company, he was told that the following fees would be charged to sell his B shares: LO16-1

First year	5 percent withdrawal fee
Second year	4 percent withdrawal fee
Third year	3 percent withdrawal fee
Fourth year	2 percent withdrawal fee
Fifth year	1 percent withdrawal fee

If he has owned the fund for 21 months and withdraws $6,000 to pay medical bills, what is the amount of the contingent deferred sales load?

6. *Calculating Contingent Deferred Sales Loads.* Mary Canfield purchased the New Dimensions bond fund. While this fund doesn't charge a front-end load, it does charge a contingent deferred sales load of 4 percent for any withdrawals in the first five years. If Mary withdraws $7,500 during the second year, how much is the contingent deferred sales load? LO16-1

7. *Determining Management Fees.* Mike Jackson invested a total of $22,000 in the New Colony Pacific Region mutual fund. The management fee for this particular fund is 0.80 percent of the total asset value. Calculate the management fee Mike must pay this year. LO16-1

8. *Calculating 12b-1 Fees.* Jane Ramirez owns shares in the Touchstone Health and Biotechnology Fund that have a current value of $13,150. The fund charges an annual 12b-1 fee of 0.25 percent. What is the amount of the 12b-1 fee Ms. Ramirez must pay? LO16-1

9. *Calculating Mutual Fund Fees.* In the prospectus for the Brazos Small Cap Fund, the fee table indicates that the fund has a 12b-1 fee of 0.35 percent and an expense ratio of 1.65 percent that is collected once a year on December 1. If Joan and Don Norwood have shares valued at $31,000 on December 1: LO16-1

a. What is the amount of the 12b-1 fee this year?

b. What is the amount they will pay for expenses this year?

10. *Finding Total Return.* Assume that one year ago, you bought 100 shares of a mutual fund for $13.50 per share, you received a $0.42 per-share capital gain distribution during the past 12 months, and the market value of the fund is now $17. Calculate the total return for this investment if you were to sell it now. LO16-4

11. *Finding Percent of Total Return.* Given the information in question 10, calculate the percent of total return for your $1,350 investment. LO16-4

12. *Finding Total Return.* Assume that one year ago, you bought 200 shares of a mutual fund for $21 per share, you received an income distribution of $0.11 cents per share and a capital gain distribution of $0.32 cents per share during the past 12 months. Also assume the market value of the fund is now $23 a share. Calculate the total return for this investment if you were to sell it now. LO16-4

13. *Finding Percent of Total Return.* Given the information in question 12, calculate the percent of total return for your $4,200 investment. LO16-4

LO16-4 **14.** *Using Dollar Cost Averaging.* Over a four-year period, Matt Ewing purchased shares in the Oakmark I Fund. Using the following information, answer the questions below. You may want to review the concept of dollar cost averaging in Chapter 14 before completing this problem.

Year	Investment Amount	Price per Share
2010	$3,000	$40 per share
2011	$3,000	$45 per share
2012	$3,000	$42 per share
2013	$3,000	$50 per share

a. At the end of four years, what is the total amount invested?

b. At the end of four years, what is the total number of mutual fund shares purchased?

c. At the end of four years, what is the average cost for each mutual fund share?

LO16-4 **15.** *Calculating Withdrawal Amounts.* Since Tanya Martin retired, she has used income from her investment in the Alger Mid Cap Growth fund to supplement her other retirement income. During one three-month period, the fund grew by $4,000. If she withdraws 65 percent of the growth, how much will she receive?

FINANCIAL PLANNING ACTIVITIES

LO16-1 **1.** *Deciding Whether Mutual Funds Are Right for You.* Assume you are 35, are divorced, and have just received a $120,000 legal settlement. Prepare a one-page report on the major reasons you want to invest in mutual funds.

LO16-1 **2.** *Applying Terms to Mutual Fund Investments.* Using the Internet or recent newspapers, magazines, or mutual fund reports, find examples of the following concepts.

a. The net asset value for a mutual fund.

b. An example of a load fund.

c. An example of a no-load fund.

d. The management fee for a specific mutual fund.

e. A fund that charges a contingent deferred sales load.

f. A fund that charges a 12b-1 fee.

g. An expense ratio.

LO16-2 **3.** *Matching Mutual Funds with Investor Needs.* This chapter classified mutual funds into different categories based on the nature of the fund's investments. Using the following information, pick a mutual fund category that you consider suitable for each investor described and justify your choice.

a. A 25-year old single investor with a new job that pays $30,000 a year?

Mutual fund category: ____________________

Why? ____________________________

b. A single parent with two children who has just received a $300,000 divorce settlement, has no job, and has not worked outside the home for the past five years.

Mutual fund category: ____________________

Why? ____________________________

c. A husband and wife who are both in their early 60s and retired.

Mutual fund category ________________

Why? ____________________________

4. *Matching Mutual Funds with Investor Needs.* This chapter explored a number of different classifications of mutual funds. LO16-2

a. Based on your age and current financial situation, which type of mutual fund seems appropriate for your investment needs? Explain your answer.

b. As people get closer to retirement, their investment goals often change. Assume you are now 45 and have accumulated $110,000 in a retirement account. In this situation, what type of mutual funds would you choose? Why?

c. Assume you are now 60 years of age and have accumulated $400,000 in a retirement account. Also, assume you would like to retire when you are 65. What type of mutual funds would you choose to help you reach your investment goals? Why?

5. *Using the Internet to Obtain a Prospectus.* Use the Internet to obtain a prospectus for a specific mutual fund that you believe would be a quality long-term investment. Then describe the purchase and withdrawal options described in the fund's prospectus. LO16-3

6. *Using the Yahoo! Finance Website.* Visit the Yahoo! Finance website and evaluate one of the following mutual funds. To complete this activity, follow these steps. LO16-3

a. Go to finance.yahoo.com.

b. Choose one of the following three funds, enter its symbol, and click on the "Quote Lookup" button: Fidelity Select Energy (FSENX), Templeton Global Bond A (TPINX), and Washington Mutual Investors Fund/A (AWSHX).

c. Print out the information for the mutual fund that you chose to evaluate.

d. Based on the information included in this research report, would you invest in this fund? Explain your answer.

FINANCIAL PLANNING CASE

Mutual Fund Research Can Make a "Big" Difference

This chapter stressed the importance of evaluating potential mutual fund investments. Now it's your turn to try your skill at evaluating a potential fund investment. To complete this case assignment, you need to begin by picking a specific fund. You can choose any type of fund that you think will help you achieve your personal financial goals. For help choosing a fund, you may want to use the fund screener at the Yahoo! Finance website (http://screener.finance.yahoo.com/funds.html). Once you have selected your fund, use information from the Internet, professional advisory services, newspapers, or financial publications to research your fund. *Hint:* Before completing this assignment, you may want to review the material in the section "How to Decide to Buy or Sell Mutual Funds" in this chapter. Then complete the assignment below.

Assignment

1. Describe the process you used to choose your fund.
2. Describe the specific sources of information you used to evaluate your fund. Were the sources of information helpful or not?
3. Based on your research, answer all of the questions on Your Personal Financial Planner Sheet 62—Mutual Fund Evaluation that is located at the end of your text.
4. In a one to two-page report, explain your decision to buy or not buy the fund you chose to research. Be sure to indicate if this fund could help you obtain your personal financial goals and what you have learned about evaluating a mutual fund.

PERSONAL FINANCIAL PLANNER IN ACTION

Investing in Mutual Funds

Diversification and asset allocation through the use of mutual funds provides investors with convenience and professional management. The variety of mutual funds contributes to your ability to achieve various long-term and short-term financial goals.

Your Short-Term Financial Planning Activities	*Resources*
1. Identify types of information that could help you choose a mutual fund.	PFP Sheet 61 www.mutualfunds.about.com http://finance.yahoo.com/funds www.mfea.com
2. Research the recent performance and costs of a mutual fund that could be an appropriate investment for you.	PFP Sheet 62 www.money.cnn.com www.morningstar.com
Your Long-Term Financial Planning Activities	*Resources*
1. Identify types of mutual funds that you might use for your long-term financial goals.	www.money.cnn.com www.kiplinger.com
2. Develop a plan for selecting and monitoring your mutual fund portfolio.	Text pages 568–574

CONTINUING CASE

Investing in Mutual Funds

Life Situation

Shelby, age 39
Mark, age 40
Two children, ages 13 and 7

Financial Data

Monthly Gross Income	$8,000
Living Expenses	$6,500
Assets	$205,000
Liabilities	$105,000

Shelby and Mark Lawrence have become very busy. Shelby's pet salon is continuing to grow while Mark's responsibilities at work have been increasing. In addition, they share the burden of transporting Blair to cheerleading practice and Travis to soccer practice. They are concerned that they do not have much time to monitor their investments and are looking for other alternatives to manage them. Some of their friends have recommended mutual funds. Shelby and Mark plan to meet with a Financial Advisor to learn the ins and outs of these types of investments.

Questions

1. What are the major reasons investors purchase mutual funds as reported to the Lawrences by the Financial Advisor?

2. The Lawrences are concerned about the costs associated with mutual funds. Describe how the Financial Advisor is likely to explain the differences between load funds and no-load funds.

3. Explain how Shelby and Mark might use the Personal Financial Planner sheet Mutual Fund Evaluation.

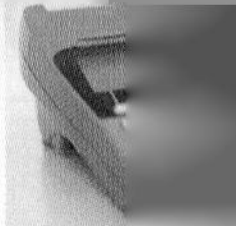

"I must choose between spending money on something now or investing for the future."

Directions

Monitoring your daily spending will allow you to better consider financial planning alternatives. You will have better information and the potential for better control if you use your spending information for making wiser choices.

Analysis Questions

1. Are there any spending items that you might consider revising to allow you to increase the amount you invest?
2. Based on your investment goals and the amount of money you have available to invest, what types of mutual funds would you consider?

The Daily Spending Diary sheets are located in Appendix D at the end of the book and on the student website at www.mhhe.com/kdh.

chapter 17

Investing in Real Estate and Other Investment Alternatives

Learning Objectives	What will this mean for me?
LO17-1 Identify types of real estate investments. **LO17-2** Evaluate the advantages of real estate investments. **LO17-3** Assess the disadvantages of real estate investments. **LO17-4** Analyze the risks and rewards of investing in precious metals, gems, and collectibles.	Real estate investment opportunities vary widely. In order to invest your money wisely, you'll need to consider the advantages and disadvantages of each type. The risks and rewards of investing in precious metals, gems, and collectibles may help you build a diversified portfolio.

my life

ALL THAT GLOWS AND GLITTERS!

Real estate has always been a favorite investment for Americans. Unlike stocks and bonds, a piece of property is something you can see and touch and take pride in. However, if you are new to the real estate market, you may be confused by all the different choices you have. On the other hand, if you are interested in antiques or other collectibles, you have to buy items at the right price. To better understand what objects sell for and what makes something valuable, you can visit the website of an auction house and view collectible objects and their suggested prices.

You can now start to assess your investment knowledge and skills. For each of following statements, indicate your choice.

1. An example of a direct real estate investment is:
   a. a home mortgage.
   b. a real estate syndicate.
   c. a real estate investment trust.
2. Generally, an indirect investment in real estate is
   a. only for the wealthy.
   b. a hedge against inflation.
   c. a good tax shelter.
3. One of the disadvantages of investing in real estate is that
   a. it is illiquid.
   b. it provides no financial leverage.
   c. it almost always declines in value.
4. Drawbacks of finding collectibles on the Internet include the
   a. inability to comparison shop.
   b. lack of wide range of sellers.
   c. inability to examine items for flaws.

As you study this chapter, you will encounter "My Life" boxes with additional information and resources related to these items.

Investing in Real Estate

LO17-1

Identify types of real estate investments.

Traditionally, Americans have invested in real estate. It is an asset that we can see, touch, and smell, and it is generally a good hedge against inflation. However, as you will see, the choices in real estate investment can be bewildering for the new investor. Furthermore, the Tax Reform Act of 1986 has lessened the appeal of investing in real estate.

Real estate investments are classified as direct or indirect. In a **direct investment,** the investor holds legal title to the property. Direct real estate investments include single-family dwellings, duplexes, apartments, land, and commercial property.

With an **indirect investment,** investors appoint a trustee to hold legal title on behalf of all the investors in the group. Limited partnerships and syndicates, real estate investment trusts, mortgages, and mortgage pools are examples of indirect real estate investments.

Exhibit 17-1 summarizes the advantages and disadvantages of the two types of investments.

direct investment Investment in which the investor holds legal title to property.

indirect investment Investment in which a trustee holds legal title to property on behalf of the investors.

DIRECT REAL ESTATE INVESTMENTS

DID YOU KNOW?

Home ownership in the United States soared to a historic high of 69.1 percent in 2005, up from 65.4 percent in 1997, but it dropped again to 65.4 percent in 2012.

Source: U.S. Bureau of the Census, http://www.census.gov/housing/hvs/files/qtr412/q412press.pdf, accessed March 22, 2013.

YOUR HOME AS AN INVESTMENT

Your home is, first, a place to live; second, it is an income tax shelter if you have a mortgage on it; finally, it is a possible hedge against inflation. In addition, according to National Association of REALTORS® (NAR) president Cathy Whatley, "Home ownership brings about a sense of belonging, an emotional connection not just to the home itself but also to the neighborhood and community in which homeowners live and work."

The tax deductions you can take for mortgage interest and property taxes greatly increase the financial benefits of home ownership.

EXAMPLE: Tax Benefits of Home Ownership

Assessed value of your home	= $180,000
Amount of loan	= $150,000
Term of loan	= 30 years
Interest rate	= 7 percent
Property tax rate	= 1.5 percent of assessed value
Mortgage interest paid in Year 5	= $9,877
Property tax paid in Year 5 (1.5% on $180,000)	= $2,700
Total deduction on your federal income tax ($9,877 + $2,700)	= $12,577
Assumed tax bracket	= 28 percent
Federal income tax lowered by ($12,577 × .28)	= $3,521.56

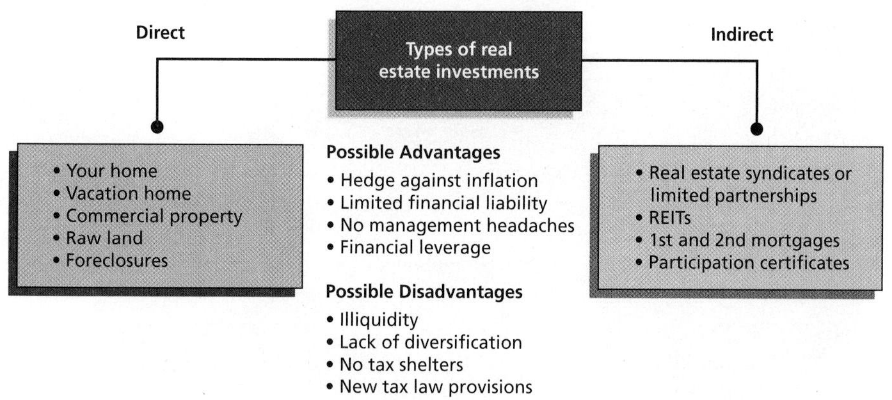

Exhibit 17-1

Types, advantages, and disadvantages of real estate investments

Is your home a hedge against inflation? Yes, according to the National Association of REALTORS. Over the past 30 years, the median price of existing homes has increased an average of more than 6 percent every year, and home values nearly double every 10 years, according to historical data from NAR's existing-home sales series. A Federal Reserve study has shown that the average homeowner's net worth is 46 times the net worth of the average renter.

But let the homebuyer beware: due to the recent economic downturn, housing prices had tumbled across the country over the past five years. Indeed, about $7 *trillion* in household wealth was lost as average house prices decreased by nearly 33 percent from their peak in 2007. However, recent economic indicators suggest that the worst of the housing crisis is over, with home sales and prices reaching bottom in 2011.[1] (See Exhibit 17-2).

Exhibit 17-3A displays the peak-to-trough house price declines for each state during the housing bust. The red states (shown in red) suffered the largest declines while green states were mildly affected during the crisis. The declines were concentrated on the coasts, especially in the Southwest and Florida. Many of the red states are now showing the greatest house price gains as their housing markets recover. Exhibit 17-3B shows the increase in house prices since prices bottomed out in each state through June 2012. Indeed, U.S. house prices increased 5.45 percent in 2012, and almost 10 percent in 2013.

While near-term increases aren't expected to match the gains of the past, economists say demographics should then hold prices roughly in line with disposable-income gains during the coming decade. That's expected to be 5.5 percent to 6 percent, says David

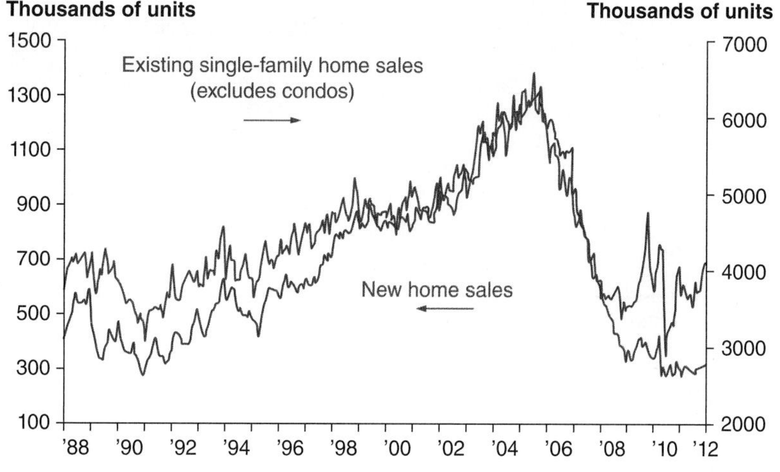

Exhibit 17-2

U.S. Home Sales of Existing and New Homes

Note: Data are seasonally adjusted, annualized rates.

Sources: Census Bureau; National Association of REALTORS®, 2013.

Exhibit 17-3A

House Price Declines (in percent)

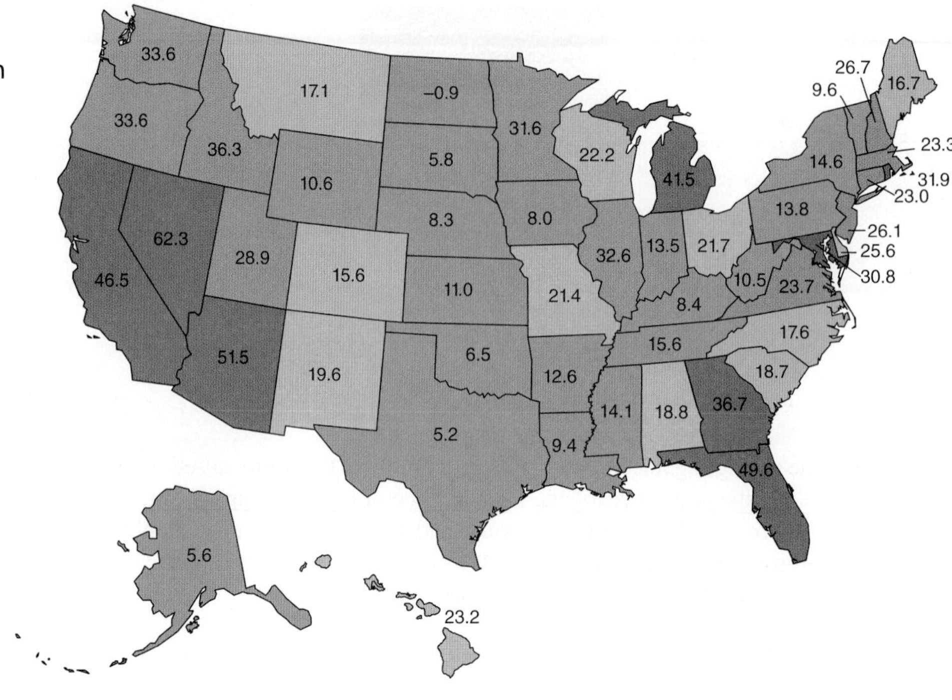

Exhibit 17-3B

House Price Rebounds (in percent)

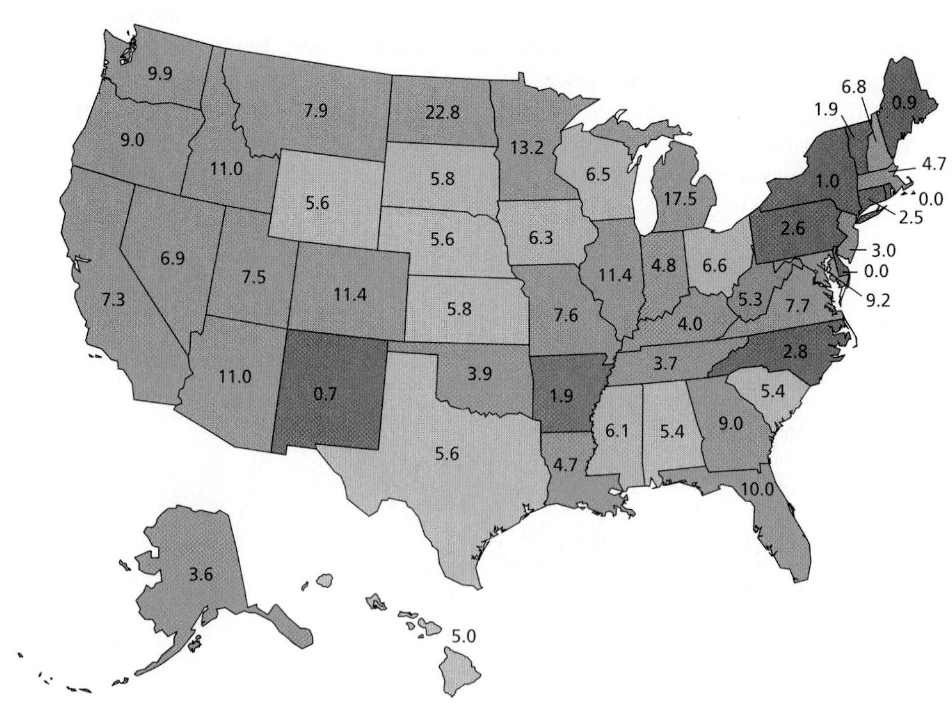

Sources: Federal Home Loan Mortgage Corporation, Federal Reserve Bank of Dallas, http://www.dallasfed.ord/research/update/us/2012/1206.cfm, accessed March 25, 2013.

Berson, chief economist at Fannie Mae. Over time, prices have risen at a rate 1 percent above inflation, notes Doug Duncan, chief economist at the Mortgage Bankers Association.

Housing will continue to be a not-so-liquid investment that promises steady returns over time. Just how much depends on your timing—and location, location, location.

YOUR VACATION HOME If you have a vacation home, the after-tax cost of owning it has risen since 1987. How much depends largely on whether the Internal Revenue Service views the property as your second home or as a rental property. It is deemed a second home as long as you don't rent it for more than 14 days a year. In that case, you can write off your mortgage interest and property tax. If you rent the vacation home regularly, the size of your deductions is determined by whether you actively manage it and by the size of your income. According to one certified public accountant, "The primary reason you buy a vacation home is because you want to use it. Tax reasons . . . are way down on the list."

More second-home buyers today are blurring the line between vacation and rental properties, justifying the purchase by planning to rent it out and figuring it's sure to appreciate. But if you're really looking for an investment property, do the math.

The National Association of REALTORS (NAR) reports that the typical vacation-home owner is 47 years old, while the median age of investment property owners is 45. While 80 percent of vacation-home owners purchased their home to use for vacations, other owners reported that it was a good investment opportunity as well.

DID YOU KNOW?

Home ownership is very low for people under 35, but it rises sharply as people enter their mid-30s.

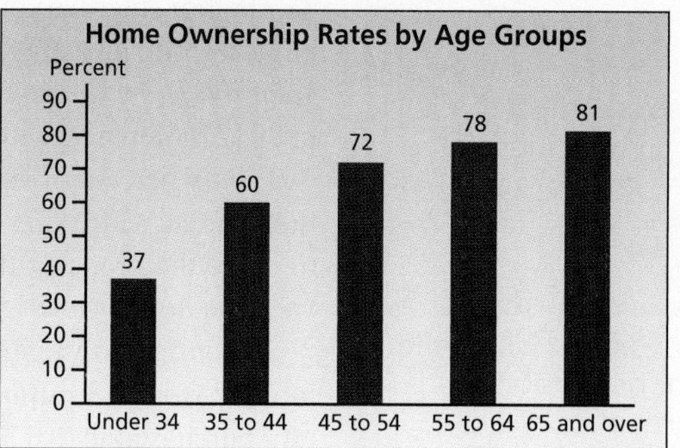

Source: U.S. Bureau of the Census, www.census.gov/housing/hvs/data/q412ind.html, accessed March 22, 2013.

my life 1

An example of a direct real estate investment is . . .

In a direct real estate investment, you hold the legal title to the property. Direct investments include single-family houses, duplexes, apartments, land, and commercial property.

DID YOU KNOW?

REAL ESTATE DROPS BELOW STOCKS AS A SHARE OF HOUSEHOLD NET WORTH

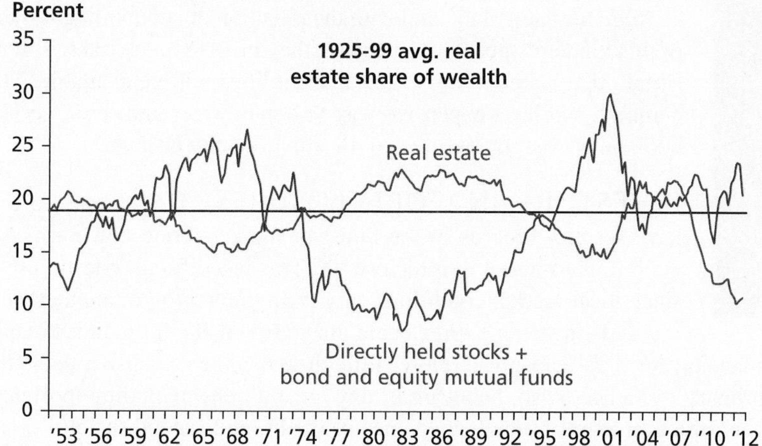

Sources: *Flow of Funds,* Federal Reserve Board; calculations by FRB Dallas. http://www.dallasfed.org/microsites/research/econdata/housing-charts.pdf, accessed March 25, 2013.

The typical vacation home is located 435 miles from the owner's primary residence, and owners spend a median of 39 nights in their vacation home each year. On the other hand, investment property owners reported that their rental property was a median of 21 miles from their primary residence. Half of investment properties are detached single-family homes, and the typical rental property is 1,520 square feet in size.[2]

The housing market may be facing economic challenges, but that didn't stop many buyers from investing in vacation properties in 2012. NAR's *2013 Investment and Vacation Home Buyers Survey* shows vacation home sales rose 10.1 percent to 553,000 in 2012, compared with 502,000 in 2011.

commercial property Land and buildings that produce lease or rental income.

passive activity A business or trade in which the investor does not materially participate.

passive loss The total amount of losses from a passive activity minus the total income from the passive activity.

Eighty percent of survey respondents plan to use their second home as a family vacation retreat. Only one in four plan to rent it to tenants. Twenty-seven percent intend to make the property their primary residence in the future. The median sale price of a vacation home was $150,000 in 2012, compared with $100,000 in 2011.

In contrast to vacation homes, investment home sales fell 2.1 percent to 1.2 million in 2012 from 2.3 million in 2011. The median transaction price of an investment property purchased in 2012 was $115,000 compared with $100,000 in 2011.[3]

COMMERCIAL PROPERTY The term **commercial property** refers to land and buildings that produce lease or rental income. Such property includes duplexes, apartments, hotels, office buildings, stores, and many other types of commercial establishments. After a home, the real property investment most widely favored by small investors is the duplex, fourplex, or small apartment building. Many investors have acquired sizable commercial properties by first investing in a duplex and then "trading up" to larger units as equity in the original property increases.

Under current tax laws, deductions such as mortgage interest, depreciation, property taxes, and other expenses of rental property are limited to the amount of rental income you receive. Any excess deductions are considered a passive loss and, with some exceptions, can be used only to offset income from a similar investment such as another rental property. A **passive activity** is a business or trade in which you do not materially participate, such as rental activity. **Passive loss** is the total amount of losses from a passive activity minus the total income from the passive activity.

Do you want to invest in a tangible asset?

UNDEVELOPED LAND If land investments have promised tremendous gains, they have also posed enormous risks. With their money riding on a single parcel, investors could end up owning overpriced cropland in the event of a building slowdown or an economic downturn. Furthermore, land usually does not produce any cash flow.

Many investors buy land with the intention of subdividing it. Purchases of this kind are speculative because they involve many risks. You must be certain that water, sewers, and other utilities will be available. The most common and least expensive way to obtain water and sewer service is to hook onto existing facilities of an adjoining city or town.

INVESTING IN FORECLOSURES U.S. home foreclosures have set new records in the midst of the economic downturn. Is now a good time to invest in foreclosures? This is a difficult question to answer since local market conditions vary from one region to another. However, if you do invest in a foreclosure, make sure that your loan is preapproved. The financing for a foreclosure is more difficult and more expensive than financing your primary residence. Also, be aware of any unpaid liens, including mortgage debt, taxes, construction loans, home equity lines of credit, and second or third mortgages. Any outstanding foreclosure liens and fees will become your financial responsibility.

If you want a clean and clear title to the property, buy it after the property has been repossessed by the creditor. According to John T. Reed, editor of Real Estate Investor's Monthly Newsletter, "You can buy foreclosures for as cheap as 30 percent or 40 percent

5 TIPS FOR PROTECTING YOUR HOME FROM FORECLOSURE

1. **Don't ignore your mortgage problem.** If you are unable to pay—or haven't paid—your mortgage, contact your lender or the company that collects your mortgage payment as soon as possible. Mortgage lenders want to work with you to resolve the problem, and you may have more options if you contact them early. Call the phone number on your monthly mortgage statement or payment coupon book. Explain your financial situation and offer to work with your lender to find the right payment solution for you. If your lender won't talk with you, contact a housing counseling agency. You can find a list of counseling resources at NeighborWorks (www.nw.org/network/home.asp) and on the U.S. Department of Housing and Urban Development's (HUD) website (www.hud.gov/offices/hsg/sfh/hcc/hccprof14.cfm) or by calling (800) 569-4287.
2. **Do your homework before you talk to your lender or housing counselor.** Find your original mortgage loan documents and review them. Review your income and budget. Gather information on your expenses, including food, utilities, car payment, insurance, cable, phone, and other bills. If you don't feel comfortable talking to your lender, contact a housing or credit counseling agency. Counselors can help you examine your budget and determine the options available to you. They may also advise you about ways to work with your lender or offer to negotiate with your lender on your behalf.
3. **Know your options.** Some options provide short-term solutions/help, while others provide long-term or permanent solutions. You may be able to work out a temporary plan for making up missed payments, or you may be able to modify the loan terms. Sometimes, the best option may be to sell the house. For information on different options, visit HUD's website (www.hud.gov/foreclosure/index.cfm) or Foreclosure Resources for Consumers (www.federalreserve.gov/consumerinfo/foreclosure.htm) for links to local resources.
4. **Stick to your plan.** Protect your credit score by making timely payments. Prioritize bills and pay those that are most necessary, such as your new mortgage payment. Consider cutting optional expenses such as eating out and premium cable TV services. If your situation changes and you can no longer meet your new payment schedule, call your lender or housing counselor immediately.
5. **Beware of foreclosure rescue scams.** Con artists take advantage of people who have fallen behind on their mortgage payments and who face foreclosure. These con artists may even call themselves *"counselors." Your mortgage lender or a legitimate* housing counselor can best help you decide which option is best for you. For tips on spotting scam artists, visit the Federal Trade Commission's website, Foreclosure Rescue Scams (www.ftc.gov/bcp/edu/pubs/consumer/credit/cre42.shtm). Report suspicious schemes to your state and local consumer protection agencies, which you can find on the Consumer Action website (www.consumeraction.gov/caw_state_resources.shtml).

Source: The Board of Governors of the Federal Reserve System, www.federalreserve.gov/consumerinfo. 0109, accessed May 1, 2013.

below market, but most foreclosures sell for 5 percent below market." So forget about buying foreclosed properties for pennies on the dollar. Remember, too, that real estate laws for each state are different, therefore, you should understand the laws and procedures before you invest your money in foreclosed properties.

Investing in a foreclosure may be profitable, but make sure to protect your own property from being foreclosed. Read the accompanying Financial Planning for Life's Situations feature: Five Tips for Protecting Your Home From Foreclosure.

INDIRECT REAL ESTATE INVESTMENTS

Indirect real estate investments include investing in real estate syndicates, real estate investment trusts, and participation certificates.

Bernice R. Hecker, a Seattle anesthesiologist, made her first real estate investment in 1985. She joined a partnership that bought an office building in Midland, Texas.

"Why real estate? Probably superstition," she said. "I wanted a tangible asset. I felt I could evaluate a piece of property much more readily" than stocks, bonds, or a cattle ranch.

syndicate A temporary association of individuals or firms organized to perform a specific task that requires a large amount of capital.

real estate investment trust (REIT) A firm that pools investor funds and invests them in real estate or uses them to make construction or mortgage loans.

Dr. Hecker used a real estate syndicate, one of the three basic indirect methods of investing in real estate: (1) real estate syndicates, partnerships that buy properties; (2) real estate investment trusts (REITs), stockholder-owned real estate companies; and (3) participation certificates sold by federal and state agencies. Indirect real estate investments are sold by most brokerage firms, such as Merrill Lynch.

REAL ESTATE SYNDICATES OR LIMITED PARTNERSHIPS

A **syndicate** is a temporary association of individuals or firms organized to perform a specific task that requires a large amount of capital. The syndicate may be organized as a corporation, as a trust, or, most commonly, as a limited partnership.

The limited partnership works as follows. It is formed by a general partner, who has unlimited liability for its liabilities. The general partner then sells participation units to the limited partners, whose liability is generally limited to the extent of their initial investment, say, $5,000 or $10,000. Limited liability is particularly important in real estate syndicates, because their mortgage debt obligations may exceed the net worth of the participants.

In addition to limited liability, a real estate syndicate provides professional management for its members. A syndicate that owns several properties may also provide diversification.

DID YOU KNOW?

Most frequently asked questions about REITs, such as, Who invests in REITs? Why should you invest in REITs? and What should you look for before investing in a REIT? are answered on the National Association of Real Estate Investment Trusts website at www.reit.com, or call 1-800-3NAREIT.

REAL ESTATE INVESTMENT TRUSTS (REITs)

Another way to invest in real estate is the **real estate investment trust (REIT),** which is similar to a mutual fund or an investment company, and trades on stock exchanges or over the counter.

DID YOU KNOW?

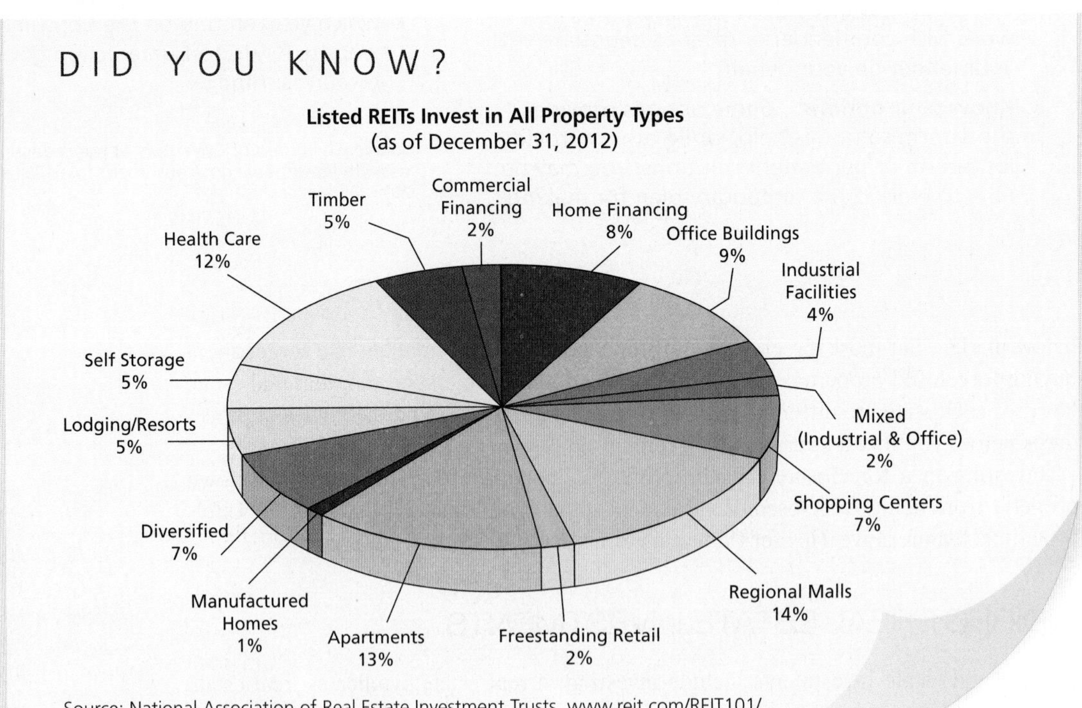

Source: National Association of Real Estate Investment Trusts, www.reit.com/REIT101/REITFAQs/BasicsOfREIT.aspx, accessed April 23, 2013.

Like mutual funds, REITs pool investor funds. These funds, along with borrowed funds, are invested in real estate or used to make construction or mortgage loans.

The REIT story is an economic success story. Investing in commercial real estate is a reality for all investors.

There are three types of REITs: Equity REITs, mortgage REITs, and hybrid REITs. *Equity REITs* own and operate income-producing real estate. They increasingly have become real estate operating companies engaged in leasing, maintenance, and development of real property and tenant services. About 90 percent of REITs are equity REITs and their revenues mostly come from rents. *Mortgage REITs,* about seven percent of all REITs, loan money to real estate owners or invest in existing mortgages. *Hybrid REITs* are combinations of mortgage and equity REITs.

You can buy or sell shares in REITs as easily as you buy or sell shares in any other publicly-traded company. REIT shares are traded on all of the major stock exchanges, including the New York Stock Exchange and NASDAQ. As in the case of equity investments in other publicly traded companies, you have no personal liability for the debts of the REITs in which you invest.

Federal law requires REITs to

- Distribute at least 90 percent of their taxable annual earnings to shareholders.
- Refrain from engaging in speculative, short-term holding of real estate to sell for quick profits.
- Hire independent real estate professionals to carry out certain management activities.
- Have at least 100 shareholders; no more than half the shares may be owned by five or fewer people.
- Invest at least 75 percent of the total assets in real estate.

Today, REITs invest in apartment buildings, hospitals, hotels, industrial facilities, nursing homes, office buildings, shopping malls, storage centers, student housing, and timberlands. Most REITs specialize in one property type only, such as shopping malls, timberlands, or self storage facilities. In 2012, 166 REITs traded on the New York Stock Exchange. Since 1991, the industry's market value has soared from $13 billion to $579 billion.

You may choose from among more than 1,100 REITs. Further information on REITs is available from the National Association of Real Estate Investment Trusts, 1875 I Street, N.W., Suite 600, Washington, DC 20006-5413.

INVESTING IN FIRST AND SECOND MORTGAGES Mortgages and other debt contracts are commonly purchased by more well-to-do investors. The purchaser of a mortgage may take on some sort of risk that is unacceptable to the financial institutions from which mortgage financing is ordinarily obtained. Perhaps the mortgage is on a property for which there is no ready market. The title to the property may not be legally clear, or the title may not be insurable. Nevertheless, many people purchase such mortgages. These investments may provide relatively high rates of return due to their special risk characteristics.

PARTICIPATION CERTIFICATES If you want a risk-proof real estate investment, participation certificates (PCs) are for you. A **participation certificate (PC)** is an equity investment in a pool of mortgages that have been purchased by one of several government agencies. Participation certificates are sold by federal agencies such as the Government National Mortgage Association (Ginnie Mae), the Federal Home Loan Mortgage Corporation (Freddie Mac), the Federal National Mortgage Association (Fannie Mae), and the Student Loan Marketing Association (Sallie Mae). A few states issue "little siblings," such as the State of New York Mortgage Agency (Sonny Mae) and the New England Education Loan Marketing Corporation (Nellie Mae).

participation certificate (PC) An equity investment in a pool of mortgages that have been purchased by a government agency, such as Ginnie Mae.

Maes and Macs are guaranteed by agencies closely tied to the federal government, making them as secure as U.S. Treasury bonds and notes. At one time, you needed a minimum of $25,000 to invest in PCs. Thanks to Maes and Macs mutual funds, you now need as little as $1,000 to buy shares in a unit trust or a mutual fund whose portfolio consists entirely of these securities. Either way, you assume the role of a mortgage lender. Each month, as payments are made on the mortgages, you receive interest and principal by check, or, if you wish, the mutual fund will reinvest the amount for you.

Financial Planning for Life's Situations: Uncle Sam and His Family on page 601 describes various types of participation certificates sold by federal and state agencies.

PRACTICE QUIZ 17-1

1 What are four examples of direct investments in real estate?
2 What are four examples of indirect investments in real estate?
3 What is a syndicate? An REIT? A participation certificate (PC)?

Advantages of Real Estate Investments

LO17-2

Evaluate the advantages of real estate investments.

For many types of real estate investments, blanket statements about their investment advantages and disadvantages are not possible. However, certain types of real estate investments may possess some of the advantages discussed in this section.

A POSSIBLE HEDGE AGAINST INFLATION

Real property equity investments usually (but not always) provide protection against purchasing power risk. In some areas, the prices of homes have increased consistently. For example, prices are rising modestly in the Midwest and in some western areas, such as Colorado and Texas.

my life 2

Generally, an indirect investment in real estate is . . .

Before you invest in real estate, you should weigh the advantages and disadvantages. Real estate investments provide some protection against inflation. Historically, real estate continues to increase in value or at least holds its value, thus protecting you from declining purchasing power.

EASY ENTRY

You can gain entry to a shopping center or a large apartment building investment by investing $5,000 as a limited partner. (A limited partner's liability is restricted by the amount of his or her investment. A limited partner cannot take part in the management of the partnership.) The minimum capital requirements for the total venture may be as high as $1 million or more, which is beyond the limits of a typical real estate investor.

LIMITED FINANCIAL LIABILITY

If you are a limited partner, you are not liable for losses beyond your initial investment. This can be important if the venture is speculative and rewards are not assured. General partners, however, must bear all financial risks.

UNCLE SAM AND HIS FAMILY

The government securities named Maes and Macs can offer safety and relatively high yields.

1. **Ginnie Mae—Government National Mortgage Association (GNMA).** Introduced the first mortgage-backed securities in 1970 and still dominates this market. The residential mortgage-backed securities are packaged in pools and then resold to investors as certificates ($25,000) or as shares by mutual funds. Regular payments to investors are guaranteed by the GNMA, an agency of the Department of Housing and Urban Development. Ginnie Maes are backed by the full faith and credit of the federal government. The average life of mortgages is 12 years.
2. **Freddie Mac—Federal Home Loan Mortgage Corporation (FHLMC).** Created by Congress in 1970, the agency issues mortgage-backed securities similar to Ginnie Maes. The pools of fixed-rate home mortgages are made up of conventional home loans rather than mortgages insured by the FHA or the VA. The timely payment of interest and the *ultimate* payment of principal are guaranteed.
3. **Fannie Mae—Federal National Mortgage Association (FNMA).** Created in 1938, the agency issues mortgage-backed securities similar to Ginnie Maes and Freddie Macs. The pools of fixed-rate home mortgages are similar to Freddie Macs but not to Ginnie Maes. Like Ginnie Maes, Fannie Maes guarantee a fair share of interest and principal *every month.* Like Ginnie Maes and Freddie Macs, newly issued Fannie Mae certificates require a minimum investment of $25,000; the older certificates (whose principal has been partially paid off) require an investment of as little as $10,000.
4. **Sallie Mae—Student Loan Marketing Association, (SLM Corporation)** Created by Congress in 1972 to provide a national secondary market for government-guaranteed student loans. Issues bonds, each backed by Sallie Mae as a whole rather than as specific pools of loans. Sallie Mae bonds are considered as safe as government Treasuries. Brokers sell bonds having minimum denominations of $10,000. You can also buy shares of Sallie Mae *stock;* the corporation is government chartered but publicly owned, and its shares are traded on the New York Stock Exchange.
5. **Sonny Mae (SONYMA)—State of New York Mortgage Agency.** Issues bonds backed by fixed-rate, single-family home mortgages and uses proceeds to subsidize below-market-rate mortgages for first-time home buyers. As with ordinary bonds, interest on Sonny Maes is paid only until the bonds mature. Sonny Maes are exempt from federal income tax, and New York State residents do not pay state income tax on them.
6. **Nellie Mae—New England Education Loan Marketing Corporation.** A nonprofit corporation created by the Commonwealth of Massachusetts. Provides a secondary market for federally guaranteed student loans issued in Massachusetts and New Hampshire. It has been a wholly owned subsdiary of Sallie Mae since 1999. The AAA-rated Nellie Mae bonds mature in three years and are sold in minimum denominations of $5,000.

NO MANAGEMENT CONCERNS

If you have invested in limited partnerships, REITs, mortgages, or participation certificates, you need not worry about paperwork and accounting, maintenance chores, and other administrative duties.

FINANCIAL LEVERAGE

Financial leverage is the use of borrowed funds for investment purposes. It enables you to acquire a more expensive property than you could on your own. This is an advantage when property values and incomes are rising. Assume you buy a $100,000 property with no loan and then sell it for $120,000. The $20,000 gain represents a 20 percent return on your $100,000 investment. Now assume you invest only $10,000 of your own money and borrow the other $90,000 (90 percent financing). Now you have made $20,000 on your $10,000 investment, or a 200 percent return. Of course, you will have to deduct the interest paid on the borrowed money.

PRACTICE QUIZ 17-2

1 What are the advantages of real estate investments?
2 How is financial leverage calculated?

Disadvantages of Real Estate Investments

LO17-3

Assess the disadvantages of real estate investments.

Real estate investments have several disadvantages. However, these disadvantages do not affect all kinds of real estate investments to the same extent.

ILLIQUIDITY

Perhaps the largest drawback of direct real estate investments is the absence of large, liquid, and relatively efficient markets for them. Whereas stocks or bonds generally can be sold in a few minutes at the market price, this is not the case for real estate. It may take months to sell commercial property or limited partnership shares.

my life 3

One of the disadvantages of investing in real estate is . . .

Unfortunately, there are several possible disadvantages to real estate investments. Real estate is an illiquid investment, which means that it cannot be easily converted into cash without a loss in value. It may take months or even years to sell real property or shares in a limited partnership.

DECLINING PROPERTY VALUES

As discussed earlier, real property investments usually provide a hedge against inflation. But during deflationary and recessionary periods, the value of such investments may decline. For example, thousands of developers, lenders, and investors were victims of a deflation in commercial real estate in the 1980s and in 2007–2009.

LACK OF DIVERSIFICATION

Diversification in direct real estate investments is difficult because of the large size of most real estate projects. REITs, Ginnie Maes, Freddie Macs, and other syndicates, however, do provide various levels of diversification.

LACK OF A TAX SHELTER

The Tax Reform Act of 1986 limits taxpayers' ability to use losses generated by real estate investments to offset income gained from other sources. Thus, investors cannot deduct their real estate losses from income generated by wages, salaries, dividends, and interest. In short, the tax shelter aspect of real estate syndicates no longer exists.

Beginning in 2013, a new 3.8 percent tax on some investment income generates about $210 billion over the next 10 years to fund the Affordable Care Act. The new law imposes this tax on some, but not all income from interest, dividends, net rents, and capital gains. You will pay the tax if your adjusted gross income is over $200,000 ($250,000 if you file a joint return).

LONG DEPRECIATION PERIOD

Before the Tax Reform Act of 1986 went into effect, commercial real estate could be depreciated within 18 years. Under the accelerated cost recovery system (ACRS), adopted in 1980, an investor was allowed to use accelerated depreciation methods to recover the costs. Now investors must use the straight-line depreciation method over 27½ years for residential real estate and over 31½ years for all other types of real estate.

Other provisions of the 1986 act affect real estate investments, and all reduce the value of the tax credits for such investments. Investors are not allowed to take losses in excess of the actual amounts they invest. Furthermore, the investment tax credit has been eliminated entirely for all types of real estate except low-income housing projects.

MANAGEMENT PROBLEMS

Although investments in limited partnerships, REITs, mortgages, and participation certificates do not create management problems, buying individual properties does. Along with the buildings come the responsibilities of management: finding reliable tenants, buying new carpeting, fixing the furnace when it breaks down in the middle of the night, and so on. Many people aren't willing to take on these responsibilities. "This is one reason I dislike small real estate investments," says one financial planner. "There should be a large enough amount of money that it is very important to you and you pay a lot of attention to it. Otherwise it won't work."

If you believe investing in real estate is too risky or too complicated, you might want to consider other tangible investments such as gold and other precious metals, gems, and collectibles. But remember, these investments entail both risk and reward.

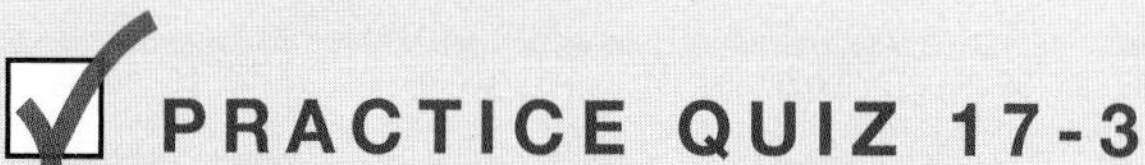

1 What are the disadvantages of real estate investments?
2 What depreciation method is used for residential real estate?

Investing in Precious Metals, Gems, and Collectibles

LO17-4

Analyze the risks and rewards of investing in precious metals, gems, and collectibles.

When the economy picks up, some investors predict higher inflation. Therefore, many think precious metals such as gold, platinum, and silver will regain some of their glitter. In this section, we discuss several methods for buying precious metals.

GOLD

Gold prices tend to be driven up by factors such as fear of war, political instability, and inflation. On the other hand, easing of international tensions or disinflation causes a decline in gold prices. High interest rates also depress gold prices, because they make it very expensive to carry gold as an investment.

Many people have acquired gold directly. Many others have invested in gold through a number of other kinds of investments that serve a variety of purposes. Some of these investments promise quick profits at high risk, others preserve capital, and still others provide income from dividends or interest. But all of them are subject to daily gold price fluctuations. Exhibit 17-4 shows gold price fluctuations between 1976 and July 2013. Gold soared to $1,908 an ounce in midday trading on August 22, 2011, and dropped to $1,307 on November 7, 2013. But consider this: in 2007 gold rose less than corn or oil. It's still below its inflation-adjusted peak of about $2,200, which it hit in 1980. More gold is in jewelry than in government reserves.

GOLD BULLION Gold bullion includes gold bars and wafers. The basic unit of gold bullion is 1 kilogram (32.15 troy ounces) of 0.995 fine gold. Coin dealers, precious

Exhibit 17-4 Fluctuations in the price of gold since 1976

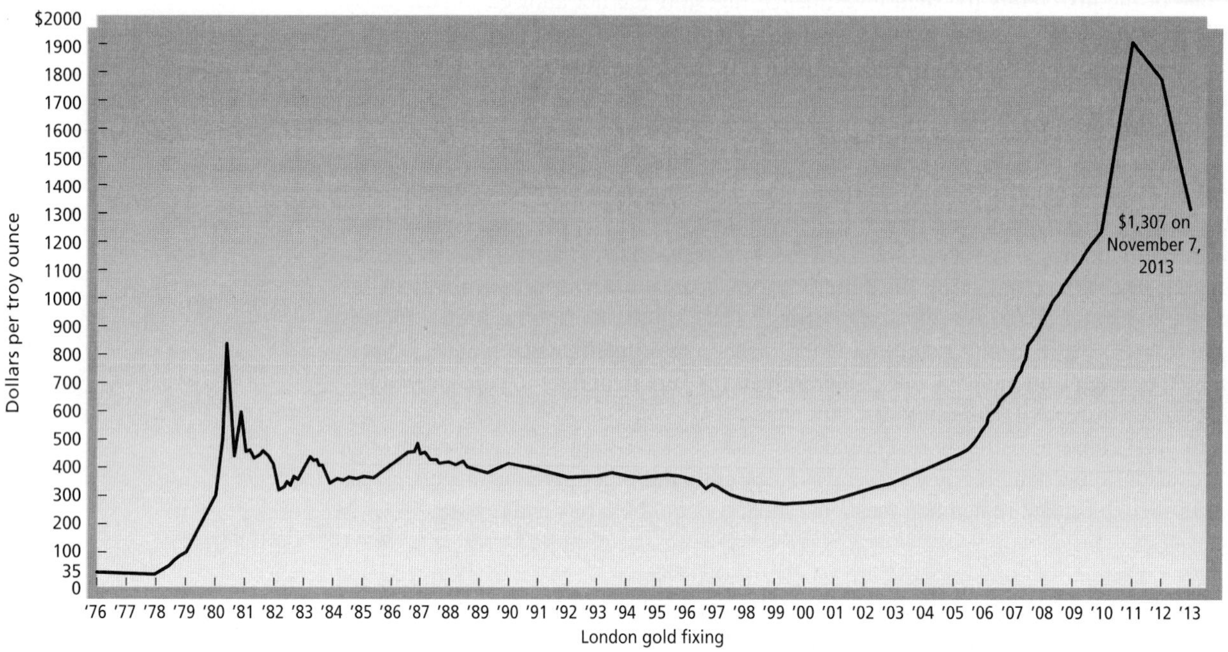

metals dealers, and some banks sell gold bullion in amounts ranging from 5 grams (16/100 of a troy ounce) to 500 ounces or more. According to industry specialists, Gold Bars Worldwide, there are 94 accredited bar manufacturers and brands in 26 countries, producing a total of more than 400 types of standard gold bars. They normally contain 99.5 percent fine gold. The Gold Bars Worldwide website, www.gold.org, provides a wealth of information about international gold bar market.[4] On small bars, dealers and banks add a 5 to 8 percent premium over the pure gold bullion value; on larger bars, the premium is usually 1 to 2 percent. Gold bullion poses storage and insurance problems, and unless the gold bar or wafer remains in the custody of the bank or dealer that sells it initially, it must be reassayed (retested for fineness) before being sold.

GOLD BULLION COINS You can avoid storage and assaying problems by investing in gold bullion coins. In the early 1980s, before South Africa's political problems intensified, South African krugerrands were the most popular gold bullion coins in the United States. Popular gold bullion coins today include Australia's kangaroo nugget, the Canadian gold maple leaf, the Mexican 50 peso, the Austrian 100 koronas, the British sovereign, Chinese Panda, and Austria's Vienna Philharmonic. The American eagle gold coin, the first gold bullion coin ever produced by the U.S. government, was first issued in late 1986. Most brokers require a minimum order of 10 coins and charge a commission of at least 2 percent. Don't confuse bullion coins with commemorative or numismatic coins, whose value depends on their rarity, design, and finish rather than on their fine gold content. Many dealers sell both.

GOLD STOCKS In addition to investing in gold bullion and gold bullion coins, you may invest in gold by purchasing the common stocks of gold mining companies. Over 300 gold mining companies are listed on the U.S. stock exchanges. Among the gold

DID YOU KNOW

THE BIGGEST GOLD PRODUCERS

China was the world's largest gold producer in 2011. The U.S. was third after China and Australia.

Total Worldwide Production in 2011:
About 2,700 metric tons, which is almost the weight of 1,100 Cadillac Escalade SUVs.

South Africa (7%)
U.S (8.3%)
China (13.2%)
Australia (9.2%)
Peru (6.7%)
Russia (7.5%)
Indonesia (4%)
Canada (3.8%)
Rest of the world (40%)

mining stocks listed on U.S. stock exchanges are those of Barrick Gold Corp. (based in the United States) and Campbell Red Lake and Dome Mines (based in Canada). Because such stocks often move in a direction opposite to that of the stock market as a whole, they may provide excellent portfolio diversification. You may also wish to examine exchange traded funds (ETFs) for precious metals.

Investing in mining stocks, like that of Dome Mines, can be a way to invest in gold or other valuable ores.

GOLD CERTIFICATES Historically, gold certificates were issued by the U.S. Treasury from the civil war until 1933. Denominated in dollars, these certificates were used as part of the gold standard and could be exchanged for an equal value of gold. These U.S. Treasury gold certificates have been out of circulation for many years, and they have become collectibles. They were initially replaced by silver certificates, and later by Federal Reserve notes.

Nowadays, gold certificates offer you a method of holding gold without taking physical delivery. Issued by individual banks, particularly in countries like Germany and Switzerland, they confirm your ownership while the bank holds the metal on your behalf. You save on storage and personal security problems and gain liquidity because you can sell portions of the holdings (if need be) by simply telephoning the custodian bank. The Perth Mint in Australia also runs a certificate program that is guaranteed by the government of Western Australia and is distributed in a number of countries.

SILVER, PLATINUM, PALLADIUM, AND RHODIUM

Investments in silver, platinum, palladium, and rhodium, like investments in gold, are used as a hedge against inflation and as a safe haven during political or economic upheavals. During the last 81 years, silver prices ranged from a historic low of 24.25 cents an ounce in 1932, to over $50 an ounce in early 1980, and then back to less than $22 an ounce in November 2013.

Three lesser-known precious metals, platinum, palladium, and rhodium, are also popular investments. All have industrial uses as catalysts, particularly in automobile production. Some investors think increased car sales worldwide could mean higher prices for these metals. Platinum currently sells for about $1,450 an ounce and palladium for about $760 an ounce. The rhodium price in June 2008 was about $9,750 per ounce, but it dropped to only $992 in January 2009, and to $975 on November 7, 2013.

As discussed earlier, finding storage for your precious metals can be tricky. While $20,000 in gold, for example, occupies only as much space as a paperback book, $20,000 in silver weighs more than 75 pounds and could require a few safe-deposit boxes. Such boxes, moreover, are not insured against fire and theft.

You should remember too that, unlike stocks, bonds, and other interest-bearing investments, precious metals sit in vaults earning nothing. And whether you profit on an eventual sale depends entirely on how well you call the market. Read the accompanying Financial Planning for Life's Situations feature. Is Gold a Solid Investment?

PRECIOUS STONES

Precious stones include diamonds, sapphires, rubies, and emeralds. Precious stones appeal to investors because of their small size, ease of concealment, great durability, and potential as a hedge against inflation. Inflation and investor interest in tangible assets helped increase diamond prices 40-fold between 1970 and 1980. A few lucky investors made fortunes, and brokerage and diamond firms took up the investment diamond business.

Whether you are buying precious stones to store in a safe-deposit box or to wear around your neck, there are a few risks to keep in mind. Diamonds and other precious stones are not easily turned into cash. It is difficult to determine whether you are getting a good stone. Diamond prices can be affected by the whims of De Beers Consolidated Mines of South Africa Ltd., which controls 85 percent of the world's supply of rough

IS GOLD A SOLID INVESTMENT?

It's true that people sometimes use gold to diversify their investment portfolio: It helps hedge against inflation and economic uncertainty. How much gold to buy, in what form, at what price, and from whom, are important questions to answer before you make that investment. Some gold promoters don't deliver what they promise and may push you into an investment that isn't right for you.

ALL GOLD IS NOT CREATED EQUAL

There are several ways to invest in gold:

1. Gold Stocks and Funds—You can buy stock in a gold mining firm or purchase a mutual fund that invests in gold bullion. Gold stocks and mutual funds may offer more liquidity than actual gold, and there is no need for you to store or insure gold. However, any gold stock or mutual fund may carry inherent risk and may drop in value regardless of the price of gold.

   Gold stocks and funds should only be purchased from licensed commodity brokers. You can check the registration status and disciplinary history of any futures firm or broker by contacting the National Futures Association (NFA).

2. Bullion and Bullion Coins—Bullion is a bulk quantity of precious metal, usually gold, platinum, or silver, assessed by weight and typically cast as ingots or bars. Dealers and some banks and brokerage firms sell bullion. Bullion coins are struck from precious metal—usually gold, platinum, or silver—and kept as an investment. The value of bullion coins is determined mostly by their precious metals content rather than by rarity and condition. Prices may change throughout the day, depending on the prices for precious metals in the world markets. Coin dealers and some banks, brokerage firms, and precious metal dealers buy and sell bullion coins. The U.S. Mint has produced gold and silver bullion coins for investment purposes since 1986 and began producing platinum bullion coins in 1997. The U.S. Mint guarantees the precious metal weight, content, and purity of the coins.

3. Collectible Coins—These coins have some historic or aesthetic value to coin collectors. Most collectible coins have a market value that exceeds their face value or their metal content. This collectible value is often called numismatic value. The coin dealers who sell collectible coins often have valuable coins graded by professional services, but grading can be subjective.

INVESTIGATE BEFORE YOU INVEST

Whether you are buying gold stocks and funds, bullion and bullion coins, or collectible coins, the Federal Trade Commission cautions that:

- If you are buying bullion coins or collectible coins, ask for the coin's melt value—the basic intrinsic bullion value of a coin if it were melted and sold. The melt value for virtually all bullion coins and collectible coins is widely available.
- Consult with a reputable dealer or financial advisor you trust who has specialized knowledge.
- Get an independent appraisal of the specific gold product you're considering. The seller's appraisal might be inflated.
- Consider additional costs. You may need to buy insurance, a safe deposit box, or rent offsite storage to safeguard bullion. These costs will reduce the investment potential of bullion.
- Some sellers deliver bullion or bars to a secured facility rather than to a consumer. When you buy metals without taking delivery, take extra precautions to ensure that the metal exists, is of the quality described, and is properly insured.
- Walk away from sales pitches that minimize risk or sales representatives who claim that risk disclosures are mere formalities. Reputable sales reps are honest about the risk of particular investments. Always get a receipt for your transaction.
- Refuse to "act now." Any sales pitch that urges you to buy immediately is a signal to walk away and hold on to your money.
- Check out the seller by entering the company's name in a search engine online. Read about other investors' experiences with the company. In addition, contact your state attorney general and local consumer protection agency. This research is prudent, although it isn't fool-proof.

To summarize, before you invest, investigate: take your time, do some research, get details, be skeptical, find out who you are dealing with, and ask if the investment has a track record.

Source: The Federal Trade Commission, ftc.gov, accessed May 2, 2013.

diamonds, and by political instability in diamond-producing countries. Moreover, you should expect to buy at retail and sell at wholesale, a difference of at least 10 to 15 percent and perhaps as much as 50 percent.

The best way to know exactly what you are getting, especially if you are planning to spend more than $5,000, is to insist that your stone be certified by an independent geological laboratory, one not connected with a diamond-selling organization. (The acknowledged industry leader in this area is the Gemological Institute of America.) The certificate should list the stone's characteristics, including its weight, color, clarity, and quality of cut. The grading of diamonds, however, is not an exact science, and recent experiments have shown that when the same diamond is submitted twice to the same institute, it can get two different ratings.

Michael Roman, former chairman of the Jewelers of America, a trade group representing 12,000 retailers, stated that his group did not recommend diamonds as an investment and scoffed at the notion that local retail jewelers were realizing huge profits on diamond sales to misguided customers. He also did not believe in certification unless the stone in question was a high-grade diamond weighing at least one carat.

collectibles Rare coins, works of art, antiques, stamps, rare books, and other items that appeal to collectors and investors.

Drawbacks of finding collectibles on the Internet include . . .

Before the era of the World Wide Web, finding items to add to your collections could be very time-consuming. The Internet has made buying and selling collectibles efficient and convenient, and the number of websites for collectors has exploded. Unfortunately, as an online buyer, you cannot assess a dealer face-to-face or examine the objects for flaws or trademarks.

COLLECTIBLES

Collectibles include rare coins, works of art, antiques, stamps, rare books, sports memorabilia, rugs, Chinese ceramics, paintings, and other items that appeal to collectors and investors. Each of these items offers the knowledgeable collector/investor both pleasure and the opportunity for profit. Many collectors have discovered only incidentally that items they bought for their own pleasure had gained greatly in value while they owned them.

COLLECTIBLES ON THE WEB Before the era of the World Wide Web, author and antiques collector David Maloney had to search far and wide to find a 1950s cut crystal Val St. Lambert pitcher. No one in his hometown of Frederick, Maryland, carries fancy glassware, he says, "and I would spend days driving around to yard sales and little shops." Recently, though, Maloney logged on to the Net and, in only 15 seconds, found a store in Pennsylvania that carries 40 styles of his prized crystal.

Whether you collect glassware, home-run baseballs, or Ming vases, you no longer need to travel to far-flung antiques fairs or pore over trade magazines to add to your collection. The world of collectibles has expanded onto the Web, bringing unprecedented efficiency and convenience to an art collector's market. The explosion of online collecting and the success of the biggest auction site, eBay, prompted Guernsey's Auction House to open the bidding for Mark McGwire's 70th home-run baseball to online buyers as well as those in the salesroom (it went for $3 million to an anonymous phone bidder).

Many collectors have been surprised to learn that their old belongings have attained considerable value over the years.

It's easy to see why the Web has such appeal. Buyers can target obscure items with a few keystrokes, and sellers can reach a much larger, more varied market. Of course, online buyers can't kick the tires or size up dealers face to face. But so far, fraud is rare, and preventive measures are increasing.

PREVENTING FRAUD

Looking for an online investment opportunity that is "unaffected by the volatile stock market," guarantees "virtually unlimited profits," "minimizes or eliminates risk factors," and is "IRA approved"?

"Forget it," advises Jodie Bernstein, director of the Federal Trade Commission's Bureau of Consumer Protection. "Claims that an investment is IRA approved are a tip-off to a rip-off. You must be just as careful when investing in opportunities touted on the Net as you are when you make other investments. You should check out these with state securities regulators and other investment professionals." For more information about investing on the Internet, Bernstein suggests that you contact the following organizations:

- Federal Trade Commission (www.ftc.gov)
- North American Securities Administrators Association Inc. (www.nasaa.org)
- Commodity Futures Trading Commission (www.cftc.gov)
- National Association of Securities Dealers (www.nasd.com)
- Securities and Exchange Commission (www.sec.gov)
- National Association of Investors Corporation (www.better-investing.org)
- InvestorGuide (www.investorguide.com)
- InvestorWords (www.investorwords.com)
- The Motley Fool (www.fool.com)
- Alliance for Investor Education (www.investoreducation.org)
- The Online Investor (www.investhelp.com)
- National Fraud Information Center (www.fraud.org)

Although you can find antique armoires and vintage cars, dealers say the Net is best suited to smaller items, such as books, coins, stamps, buttons, and textiles, that can be easily scanned for viewing and shipped by mail.

Prices aren't necessarily cheaper on the Web, but it's much easier to compare them, and most sites don't charge a buyer's commission. To purchase an early edition of Mark Twain's *The Adventures of Tom Sawyer,* for example, use a search engine, such as www.amazon.com, to view descriptions of dealers' inventories. The site will provide details on the condition, publisher, and price of the book. Most editions of Tom Sawyer published in the 20th century sell for about $10, but a first British edition from 1898 lists for $350. Since the Net has opened up a wider market, items that probably wouldn't sell at a local antiques show can find an appropriate home.

Still, virtual collecting has drawbacks. Buyers can't examine objects for flaws or trademarks. Many knowledgeable old-time dealers aren't computer literate, while some collectors prefer the thrill of hunting in out-of-the-way junk shops. "The average person still wants to see and feel the antiques," says Terry Kovel, author of *Kovel's Antiques & Collectibles Price List.* "An awful lot of antiques purchases are emotional, because someone walks into a store and sees an object they had as a kid."[5]

A more serious concern, perhaps, is the security risk of buying online when you don't know who's getting your cash or credit card number. But while the security risks of online collecting grab headlines, Kovel says fraud has been negligible. Collectors do take gambles, but for many happy hunters, the increased selection and convenience of shopping on the Web is far outweighs its dangers.

CAVEAT EMPTOR Collecting can be a good investment and a satisfying hobby, but for many Americans it has recently become a financial disaster. For example, as the market for paintings by Pablo Picasso and Andy Warhol has exploded, forgeries have become a significant problem. Art experts and law enforcement officials say that a new generation of collectors is being victimized by forgeries more sophisticated, more expensive, and more difficult to detect than ever before.

HOW TO...

Buy Authentic Indian Arts and Crafts for Fun or Investment

Whether you're drawn to the beauty of turquoise and silver jewelry or the earth-toned colors of Indian pottery, having some knowledge about American Indian arts and crafts can help you get the most for your money. Be aware also that because Indian arts and crafts are prized and often command higher prices, a few unscrupulous sellers misrepresent imitation arts and crafts as genuine.

Buying Tips. American Indian arts and crafts are sold through many outlets, including tourist stores, gift shops and art galleries. Here are some tips to help you shop wisely:

Buying Tips	Why is this important?
Familiarize yourself with the Indian Art Act of 1990.	The Indian Arts and Crafts Act of 1990 helps ensure that buyers of Indian arts and crafts products get what they pay for by making it illegal to misrepresent that a product is made by an Indian. You can obtain more information about the Indian Arts and Crafts Act and related regulations by visiting the website of the Indian Arts and Crafts Board, www.iacb.doi.gov, or by calling the Board's toll-free number, 1-888-ART-FAKE.
Buy from an established dealer	Well established and reputable dealers should always be able to give you a written guarantee or written verification of authenticity.
Get a receipt that includes all the vital information about the value of your purchase, including any verbal representations.	Your receipt will help protect you and your investment. If the salesperson told you that the piece of jewelry you're buying is sterling silver and natural turquoise and was handmade by an American Indian artisan, insist that this information appears on your receipt as proof of what you have been told.
Before buying Indian arts and crafts at powwows, annual fairs, juried competitions, and other events, check the event requirements for information about the authenticity of the products being offered for sale.	Many legitimate events list the requirements in newspaper ads, promotional flyers and printed programs. If the event organizers make no statements about the authenticity of Indian arts and crafts being offered for sale, get written verification of authenticity for any item you purchase that claims to be authentic.
Know your recourse if you have a complaint.	Even in specialized markets, there are associations that protect consumers. The Indian Arts and Crafts Board receives and refers valid complaints about variations of the Indian Arts and Crafts Act to the FBI for investigation and to the Department of Justice for legal action. To file a complaint under the Act, or to get free information about the Act, call the Indian Arts and Crafts Board, U.S. Department of the Interior, toll free at 1-888-278-3253 or use the online complaint form at www.iacb.doi.gov.

Forgeries or not, art prices are booming. For example, Damien Hirst's *The Lovers,* four jars filled with cow organs in formaldehyde, sold for $229,350, and a plaster cast of the underside of a sink by Rachel Whiteread fetched $220,275. However, a single painting, a van Gogh called *Portrait of Dr. Gachnet,* which sold for an all-time record of $82.5 million in 1990, had been up for sale privately for months. The minimum asking price: $80 million. An 1889 self-portrait believed to be the last painted by van Gogh sold for $71.5 million.

Nostalgia and limited availability will also fuel certain markets. With failed airlines and railroads becoming distant memories, count on Pan Am wing pins and Pullman porter badges to go up in value. Fanaticism, combined with a dwindling supply, will also push up prices of rock-and-roll record albums.

Collecting for investment purposes is very different from collecting as a hobby. Like investing in real estate or the stock market, investing in collectibles should be approached with care. Don't consider collectibles as your savings plan for retirement, and be especially careful if you buy from online auctions.

Investment counselors caution that collectibles do not provide interest or dividends, that it may be difficult to sell them at the right price on short notice, and that if they become valuable enough, they must be appraised periodically and insured against loss or theft.

Summary for Investment Activities

PRACTICE QUIZ 17-4

1 What are several methods for buying precious metals?
2 Why do precious stones appeal to investors?
3 What are collectibles?
4 How can you protect yourself from fraudulent practices in the collectibles market?

my life stages for investing . . .

YOUR PERSONAL FINANCE DASHBOARD

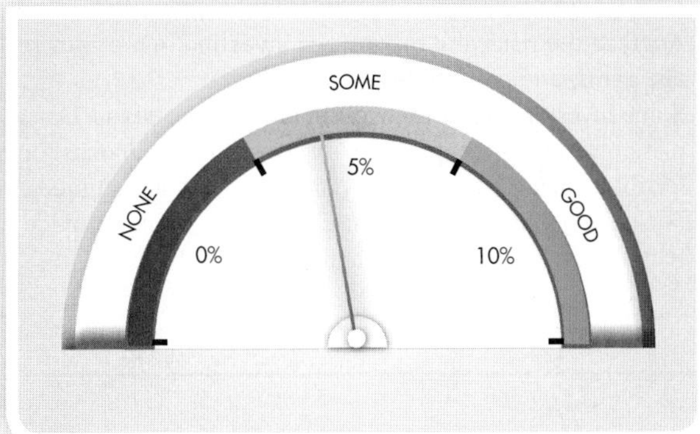

PORTFOLIO DIVERSIFICATION: PRECIOUS METALS, GEMS, AND COLLECTIBLES

A personal finance dashboard with key performance indicators can help you monitor your financial situation and guide you toward financial independence. You can achieve investment diversification by including a variety of assets in your portfolio—for example, stocks, bonds, mutual funds, real estate, collectibles, and precious metals. Financial experts recommend placing about 10 percent of your investment portfolio in precious metals and other collectibles.

YOUR SITUATION: Are all of your investment eggs in one basket? Do you know that spreading your assets among several different types of investments lessens risk? Are you reducing investment risk by investing in a variety of assets? Is your portfolio properly diversified? What percentage of your assets do you want to invest in stocks, bonds, real estate, and precious metals? Other personal financial planning actions you might consider during various stages of your life include:

. . . in college

- Establish investment and financial goals
- Work to balance your budget.
- Start an emergency fund
- Save a reasonable amount of money from each paycheck

. . . in my 20s

- Revise investment and financial goals
- Pay off any college loans and other debts
- Explore different retirement plans
- Begin investing after careful evaluation of different types of investments

. . . in my 30s and 40s

- Revise investment and financial goals
- Continue to evaluate new and current investments
- Increase your amount of savings and investments

. . . in my 50s and beyond

- Revise investment and financial goals
- Begin planning for retirement within a specific number of years
- Increase your amount of savings and investments
- Consider conservative investment options
- Continue to evaluate current investments

SUMMARY OF LEARNING OBJECTIVES

LO17-1

Identify types of real estate investments.

Real estate investments are classified as direct or indirect. Direct real estate investments, in which you hold legal title to the property, include a home, a vacation home, commercial property, and undeveloped land. Indirect real estate investments include real estate syndicates, REITs, mortgages, and participation certificates.

LO17-2

Evaluate the advantages of real estate investments.

Real estate investments offer a hedge against inflation, easy entry, limited financial liability, no management headaches, and financial leverage.

LO17-3

Assess the disadvantages of real estate investments.

Real estate investments may have the disadvantages of illiquidity, declining values, lack of diversification, lack of a tax shelter, a long depreciation period, and management problems.

LO17-4

Analyze the risks and rewards of investing in precious metals, gems, and collectibles.

Some investors prefer to invest in precious metals such as gold, platinum, and silver; precious stones such as diamonds; or collectibles such as stamps, rare coins, works of art, antiques, rare books, and Chinese ceramics. Collectibles do not provide current income, and they may be difficult to sell quickly.

KEY TERMS

collectibles 607
commercial property 596
direct investment 592
indirect investment 592
participation certificate (PC) 599
passive activity 596
passive loss 596
real estate investment trust (REIT) 598
syndicate 598

SELF-TEST PROBLEMS

1. You bought a rental property for $150,000 cash. Later you sell the property for $180,000. What was your return on investment?
2. Suppose you invested just $20,000 of your own money and had a $130,000 mortgage with an interest rate of 7.5 percent. After one year you sell the property for $180,000. a) What is your gross profit? b) What is your net profit? c) What is your percent rate of return on investment?
3. Assume your home is assessed at $200,000. You have a $150,000 loan for 15 years at five percent. Your property tax rate is two percent of the assessed value. Assume you are in a 28 percent federal income tax bracket. By what amount your federal income tax is lowered?

Self-Test Solutions

1. Selling price = $180,000

   Purchase price = $150,000

   Profit = $30,000

   $$\text{Return on investment} = \frac{\text{Profit}}{\text{Purchase price}} = \frac{\$30{,}000}{\$150{,}000} = .20 \text{ or } 20 \text{ percent}$$

2. a. Gross profit = Selling price − Purchase price

   $180,000 − $150,000 = $30,000

   b. Net profit = Gross profit − Interest paid in one year

   = $30,000 − ($130,000 × .075 × 1)

   = $30,000 − $9,750 = $20,250

   c. $$\text{Percent of return on investment} = \frac{\$20{,}250}{\$20{,}000} = \frac{\text{Net profit}}{\text{Amount invested}} = 1.01 \text{ percent}$$

3. Assessed value of your home	= \$200,000
Amount of loan	= \$150,000
Term of loan	= 15 years
Interest rate	= 5 percent
Property tax rate	= 2 percent of assessed value
Mortgage interest for one year	= (\$150,000 × .05 × 1)
	= \$7,500
Property tax paid for one year	= \$200,000 × .02
	= \$4,000
Total deduction on your federal income tax	= \$7,500 + \$4,000
	= \$11,500
Assumed tax bracket	= 28 percent
Federal income tax lowered by (\$11,500 × .28)	= \$3,220

FINANCIAL PLANNING PROBLEMS

1. *Calculating the Return on Investment.* Dave bought a rental property for \$200,000 cash. One year later, he sold it for \$240,000. What was the return on his \$200,000 investment? L017-1

2. *Calculating the Return on Investment Using Financial Leverage.* Suppose Dave invested only \$20,000 of his own money and borrowed \$180,000 interest-free from his rich father. What was his return on investment? L017-1

3. *Calculating the Rate of Return on Investment.* Rani bought a rental property for \$100,000 with no borrowed funds. Later, she sold the building for \$120,000. What was her return on investment? L017-1

4. *Calculating the Rate of Return on Investment Using Financial Leverage.* Suppose Shaan invested just \$10,000 of his own money and had a \$90,000 mortgage with an interest rate of 8.5 percent. After three years, he sold the property for \$120,000. L017-1

a. What is his gross profit?

b. What is his net profit or loss?

c. What is the rate of return on investment?

Problems 5 and 6 are based on the following scenario: Felice bought a duplex apartment at a cost of \$150,000. Her mortgage payments on the property are \$940 per month, \$121 of which can be deducted from her income taxes. Her real estate taxes total \$1,440 per year, and insurance costs \$900 per year. She estimates that she will spend \$1,000 each year per apartment for maintenance, replacing appliances, and other costs. The tenants will pay for all utilities. L017-1

5. *Calculating Profit or Loss on a Rental Property.* What monthly rent must she charge for each apartment to break even?

6. *Calculating Profit or Loss on a Rental Property.* What must she charge to make \$2,000 in profit each year? L017-1

Problems 7 and 8 are based on the following scenario: Assume your home is assessed at \$200,000. You have a \$150,000 loan for 30 years at 6 percent. Your property tax rate is 1.5 percent of the assessed value. In year one, you would pay \$9,000 in mortgage interest and \$3,000 in property tax (1.5 percent on \$200,000 assessed value).

7. *Calculating Net Profit after Taxes.* What is the total deduction you can take on your federal income tax return?

8. *Calculating Net Profit after Taxes.* Assuming you are in a 28 percent tax bracket, by what amount would you have lowered your federal income tax? L017-1

Problems 9 and 10 are based on the following scenario: Audra owns a rental house. She makes mortgage payments of \$600 per month, which include insurance, and pays \$1,800 per year in property taxes and maintenance. Utilities are paid by the renter.

9. *Determining the Monthly Rent.* How much should Audra charge for monthly rent to cover her costs?

10. *Determining the Monthly Rent.* What should Audra charge for monthly rent to make \$1,000 profit each year?

Problems 11 and 12 are based on the following scenario: In 1978 Juan bought 50 ounces of gold for \$1,750 as protection against rising inflation. He sold half the gold in 1980 at a price of \$800 an ounce. Juan sold the other half in 1982 when the price was \$400 an ounce. L017-4

11. *Calculating a Return on Investment.* What was Juan's profit in 1980 and in 1982?

12. *Calculating a Return on Investment.* What would Juan's profit have been if he had sold all of his gold in 1980?

FINANCIAL PLANNING ACTIVITIES

LO17-1 **1.** *Using the Internet to Obtain Information about Various Types of REITs.* Many REITs now maintain websites. Visit a few websites of REIT companies discussed in this chapter and of the National Association of Real Estate Investment Trusts (NAREIT) at www.nareit.com. Then prepare a report that summarizes the various types of REITs available to investors.

LO17-1 **2.** *Assessing the Prices of Single-Family Dwellings.* Interview local real estate brokers and research current business magazines and the business section of the local newspaper to determine if the prices of single-family dwellings in your area have been increasing during the last 10 years. Prepare a written report indicating the reasons for the increase or decrease.

LO17-1 **3.** *Assessing the Investment Potential of Commercial Real Estate.* Research current commercial real estate sections of local newspapers. How many listings do you find for duplexes? For fourplexes and small apartment buildings? Prepare an analysis of the investment potential of these properties.

LO17-2 **4.** *Checking the Availability of Real Estate Limited Partnerships.* Call a few real estate and stockbrokerage firms in your area to find out if any real estate limited partnerships are available for investors.

LO17-3 **5.** *Comparing Mortgage Rates and Terms of a Loan.* Obtain duplex mortgage rates from your local commercial bank, a savings and loan association, and a credit union. Compare these rates and terms such as the down payment, loan costs (points), loan length, and maximum amount available to determine which of the three lenders offers the best financing.

LO17-4 **6.** *Checking Current Prices of Precious Metals.* Listen to business news on radio or television. What are the current quotes for an ounce of gold and an ounce of silver? Are the prices of precious metals going up or down? How do the latest prices compare with the prices quoted in the chapter? What might be some reasons for fluctuations in the prices of precious metals?

FINANCIAL PLANNING CASE

Bogus Brushstroke: Art Fraud

Richard received a letter inviting him to participate in a drawing for a free original lithograph by a famous artist. He was asked to return a postcard with his name, address, and phone number. After he returned the postcard, he was telephoned for more information, including his credit card number.

At some point, the caller asked Richard to buy a print, using such glowing terms as "fabulous opportunity," "one-time offer," "limited edition," and "excellent work of a famous artist." The artist, the caller said, was near death and the print's value would increase after the artist's death. He was assured that when the artist died, the company that the caller represented would gladly buy back the print at two to three times what he paid for it and that he could always resell the print elsewhere at a substantial profit. He was told that he would receive a certificate to the "authenticity" of the print. And he was promised a trial examination period with a 30-day money-back guarantee.

Questions

1. Does the offer seem genuine to you? Explain your answer.
2. How can Richard protect himself against a phony offer? List at least five suggestions that you would give him.
3. If Richard bought the work of art and discovered fraud, how should he try to resolve his dispute with the company that sold it to him? Where should he complain if the dispute is not resolved?

PERSONAL FINANCIAL PLANNER IN ACTION

Comparing Other Types of Investments

Real estate and collectibles allow investors to achieve greater potential returns, However, these sometimes speculative ventures must be considered carefully in relation to your personal financial situation.

Your Short-Term Financial Planning Activities	*Resources*
1. Identify types of real estate and other investments that might serve your various financial goals and life situation.	www.hud.com www.nreionline.com www.creonline.com
2. Compare the cost of buying and operating various types of real estate investments.	www.quotes.ino.com www.kiplinger.com www.worth.com

Your Long-Term Financial Planning Activities	*Resources*
1. Identify real estate and other investments that might serve you in the future.	www.ft.com www.cbot.com www.cme.com www.antiquecast.com
2. Develop a plan for selecting and monitoring real estate.	Text pages 592–600 www.nareit.com

CONTINUING CASE

Investing in Real Estate

Life Situation	*Financial Data*	
Shelby, age 44	Monthly Gross Income	$8,000
Mark, age 45	Living Expenses	$6,500
Two children, ages 18 and 12	Assets	$230,000
	Liabilities	$80,000

Shelby and Mark Lawrence are about 20 years away from retirement. They worry that they have not been aggressive enough in their investment decisions. While they have already established an investment program, they are aware of the need for long-range retirement planning. Some friends have recommended supplementing their investment program with highly speculative investments such as real estate. Since the Lawrences live a busy life style, they realize that a direct investment in real estate would require too much of their time. They are also worried about the housing market. Therefore, they are considering an indirect investment. They would like to evaluate whether this would fit into their portfolio.

Questions

1. What are the advantages of investing in real estate as a limited partner for the Lawrences?
2. What are the disadvantages of investing in real estate as a limited partner for the Lawrences?

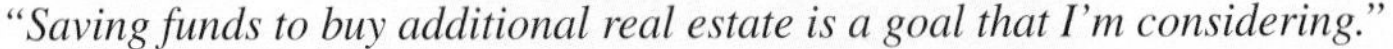

DAILY SPENDING DIARY

"Saving funds to buy additional real estate is a goal that I'm considering."

Directions

Maintaining a "Daily Spending Diary" can provide important information for monitoring and controlling spending. Taking time to reconsider your spending habits can result in achieving better long-term satisfaction from your finances.

Analysis Questions

1. What changes in your daily spending patterns could help you increase the amount you have available for investing?
2. When might you consider investing in real estate, precious metals, or collectibles?

The Daily Spending Diary Sheets are located in Appendix D at the end of the book and on the student website at www.mhhe.com/kdh.

chapter 18

Starting Early: Retirement Planning

Learning Objectives

LO18-1 Recognize the importance of retirement planning.

LO18-2 Analyze your current assets and liabilities for retirement.

LO18-3 Estimate your retirement spending needs.

LO18-4 Identify your retirement housing needs.

LO18-5 Determine your planned retirement income.

LO18-6 Develop a balanced budget based on your retirement income.

What will this mean for me?

Retirement planning is important because you'll probably spend many years in retirement. Properly estimating your retirement living costs and housing needs will enable you to save or invest enough money to live comfortably during retirement.

my life

STARTING NOW FOR A SECURE RETIREMENT?

Most of us know it is smart to save money for those big-ticket items we really want to buy—a new television or car or home. Yet you may not realize that probably the most expensive thing you will ever buy in your lifetime is your retirement. Perhaps you've never thought of "buying" your retirement. Yet that is exactly what you do when you put money into a retirement nest egg. You are paying today for the cost of your retirement tomorrow. The cost of those future years is getting more expensive for most Americans, for two reasons. First, we live longer after we retire. Many of us will spend 15, 20, even 30 years in retirement—and we are more active. Second, you may have to provide a greater share of the cost of your retirement, because fewer employers are providing traditional pension plans and they are contributing less to those plans. Many retirement plans today, such as the popular 401(k), are paid for primarily by you, not the employer. You may not have a retirement plan at work or you may be self-employed. This makes you responsible for choosing retirement investments.

For every 10 years you delay before starting to save for retirement, you will need to save three times as much each month to catch up. That's why, no matter how young you are, the sooner you begin saving for retirement the better. Whether you are 18 or 58, you can take steps toward a better, more secure future.

As you start (or expand) your retirement planning activities, consider the following statements. For each, select "yes," "no," or "uncertain" to indicate your personal response regarding these retirement planning activities.

1. I can depend on Social Security and my company pension to pay for my basic living expenses.	Yes	No	Uncertain
2. Reviewing my assets to ensure they are sufficient for retirement is a sound idea.	Yes	No	Uncertain
3. My spending patterns during retirement will probably not change that much.	Yes	No	Uncertain
4. The place where I live during retirement can have a significant impact on my financial needs.	Yes	No	Uncertain
5. My Social Security benefits will be reduced if I retire before age 65.	Yes	No	Uncertain
6. To supplement my retirement income, I may want to work part-time or start a new part-time career after I retire.	Yes	No	Uncertain

As you study this chapter, you will encounter "My Life" boxes with additional information and resources related to these items.

Why Retirement Planning?

LO18-1

Recognize the importance of retirement planning.

"As 79 million Baby Boomers near and enter their retirement years, they will encounter a unique set of challenges unlike those any previous generation has faced," said Cathy Weatherford, Insured Retirement Institute president and chief executive officer. "These challenges—including changes in employee benefits, longer life spans, uncertainty with Social Security and Medicare, as well as rising cost of health care—have made preparing for retirement more difficult and could put their future financial security at risk. As a result, many Boomers lack confidence in their ability to meet their retirement goals."

Retirement can be a rewarding phase of your life. However, a successful, happy retirement doesn't just happen; it takes planning and continual evaluation. Thinking about retirement in advance can help you anticipate future changes and gain a sense of control over the future.

The ground rules for retirement planning are changing rapidly. Reexamine your retirement plans if you hold any of these misconceptions:

- My expenses will drop when I retire.
- My retirement will last only 15 years.
- I can depend on Social Security and my company pension to pay for my basic living expenses.
- My pension benefits will increase to keep pace with inflation.
- My employer's health insurance plan and Medicare will cover my medical expenses.
- There's plenty of time for me to start saving for retirement.
- Saving just a little bit won't help.

my life 1

I can depend on Social Security and my company pension to pay for my basic living expenses.

While Social Security replaces about 40 percent of the average worker's preretirement earnings, most financial advisors suggest that you will need 70 to 90 percent of preretirement earnings to live comfortably. Even if you are lucky enough to have a company pension, you will still need to save.

It is vital to engage in basic retirement planning activities throughout your working years and to update your retirement plans periodically. While it is never too late to begin sound financial planning, you can avoid many unnecessary and serious difficulties by starting this planning early. Saving now for the future requires tackling the trade-offs between spending and saving.

TACKLING THE TRADE-OFFS

Although exceptions exist, the old adage "You can't have your cake and eat it too" is particularly true in planning for retirement. For example, if you buy state-of-the-art home entertainment systems, drive expensive cars, and take extravagant vacations now, don't expect to retire with plenty of money.

Only by saving now and curtailing current spending can you ensure a comfortable retirement later. Yet saving money doesn't come naturally to many young people. Ironically, although the time to begin saving is when you are young, the people who are in the best position to save are middle-aged.

Seventy-five percent of workers expect to live as well as, if not better than, they do now when they retire, but only 20 percent of those surveyed have begun to save seriously for retirement.

With more free time, many retirees spend more money on leisure activities.

THE IMPORTANCE OF STARTING EARLY

Consider this: If from age 25 to 65 you invest $300 per month and earn an average of 9 percent return a year, you'll have $1.4 million in your retirement fund. Waiting just 10 years until age 35 to begin your $300-a-month investing

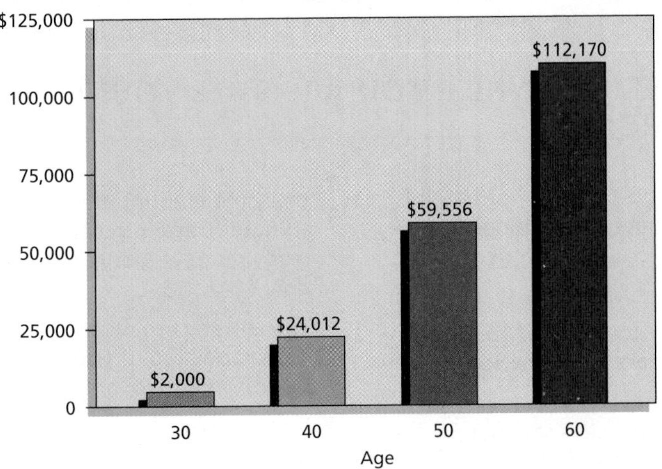

Exhibit 18-1

It's never too early to start planning for retirement

Start young. A look at the performance of $2,000 per year of retirement plan investments over time, even at 4 percent, shows the value of starting early.

will yield about $550,000, while if you wait 20 years to begin this investment, you will have only $201,000 at age 65. Exhibit 18-1 shows how even a $2,000 annual investment earning just 4 percent will grow.

For 40 years your life, and probably your family's life, revolves around your job. One day you retire, and practically every aspect of your life changes. There's less money, more time, and no daily structure.

You can expect to spend about 16 to 30 years in retirement—too many years to be bored, lonely, and broke. You want your retirement years to be rewarding, active, and rich in new experiences. It's never too early to begin planning for retirement; some experts even suggest starting while you are in school. Be certain you don't let your 45th birthday roll by without a comprehensive retirement plan. Remember, the longer you wait, the less you will be able to shape your life in retirement.

Consider this: centenarians are the fastest-growing segment of our population. The second fastest is the age group 85+. Currently, there are about 53,400 centenarians in the United States, or a little more than two centenarians per 10,000 in population; 83 percent of them are women, 17 percent men.

Retirement planning has both emotional and financial components. Emotional planning for retirement involves identifying your personal goals and setting out to meet them. Financial planning for retirement involves assessing your postretirement needs and income and plugging any gaps you find. Financial planning for retirement is critical for several reasons:

1. You can expect to live in retirement for 16 to 30 years. At age 65, the average life expectancy is 17 years for a man and almost 20 years for a woman.
2. Social Security and a private pension, if you have one, are most often insufficient to cover the cost of living.
3. Inflation may diminish the purchasing power of your retirement savings. Even a 3 percent rate of inflation will cause prices to double every 24 years.

You should anticipate your retirement years by analyzing your long-range goals. What does retirement mean to you? Does it mean an opportunity to stop work and relax, or does it mean time to travel, develop a hobby, or start a second career? Where and how do you want to live during your retirement? Once you have considered your retirement goals, you are ready to evaluate their cost and assess whether you can afford them.

THE POWER OF COMPOUNDING

No matter where you choose to invest your money—cash, mutual funds, stocks, bonds, or real estate—the key to saving for retirement is to make your money work for you. It does this through the power of compounding. Compounding investment earnings is what can make even small investments become larger given enough time.

PLANNING FOR RETIREMENT WHILE YOU ARE STILL YOUNG: THE TIME VALUE OF MONEY

Retirement probably seems vague and far off at this stage of your life. Besides, you have other things to buy right now. Yet there are some crucial reasons to start preparing now for retirement.

- You'll probably have to pay for more of your own retirement than earlier generations. The sooner you get started, the better.
- You have one huge ally—time. Let's say that you put $1,000 at the beginning of each year into an IRA from age 20 through age 30 (11 years) and then never put in another dime. The account earns 7 percent annually. When you retire at age 65 you'll have $168,514 in the account. A friend doesn't start until age 30, but saves the same amount annually for 35 years straight. Despite putting in three times as much money, your friend's account grows to only $147,913.
- You can start small and grow. Even setting aside a small portion of your paycheck each month will pay off in big dollars later.
- You can afford to invest more aggressively. You have years to overcome the inevitable ups and downs of the market.

Developing the habit of saving for retirement is easier when you are young.

Source: U.S. Department of Labor, www.dol.gov/ebsa, May 2, 2013.

You already know the principle of compounding. Money you put into a savings account earns interest. Then you earn interest on the money you originally put in, plus on the interest you've accumulated. As the size of your savings account grows, you can earn interest on a bigger and bigger pool of money.

The following example shows how investment grows at different annual rates of return over different time periods. Notice how the amount of gain gets bigger each 10-year period. That's because money is being earned on a bigger and bigger pool of money.

EXAMPLE: Power of Compounding: The Time Value of Money

The value of $1,000 compounded at various rates of return over time:

Years	4 Percent	6 Percent	8 Percent	10 Percent
10	$1,481	$1,791	$2,159	$2,594
20	2,191	3,207	4,661	6,728
30	3,243	5,743	10,063	17,449

Also notice that when you double your rate of return from 4 percent to 8 percent, the result after 30 years is over three times what you would have accumulated with a 4 percent return. That's the power of compounding!

The real power of compounding comes with time. The earlier you start saving, the more your money can work for you. Look at it another way. For every 10 years you delay before starting to save for retirement, you will need to save three times as much each month to catch up. That's why no matter how young you are, the sooner you begin saving for retirement, the better.

THE BASICS OF RETIREMENT PLANNING

Before you decide where you want to be financially, you have to find out where you are. Your first step, therefore, is to analyze your current assets and liabilities. Then estimate your spending needs and adjust them for inflation. Next, evaluate your planned retirement income. Finally, increase your income by working part-time, if necessary. An attorney, for example, might teach some law courses. Recent articles and other retirement information may be accessed through online computer services. For further information, see Appendix B. Exhibit 18-2 shows some good online sources for retirement planning using a personal computer. Also, read the Financial Planning for Life's Situations feature "Planning for Retirement While You Are Still Young."

1 How can the Internet assist you in retirement planning?
2 Why is retirement planning important?
3 What are the four basic steps in retirement planning?

Exhibit 18-2

Using a personal computer for retirement planning

It's never too early to start planning for retirement.

General Websites
American Savings Education Council (www.asec.org) Diversified Investment Advisors (www.divinvest.com) 401KAFE (www.401kafe.com) InvestorGuide (www.investorguide.com/retirement.htm) Longevity Game (www.northwesternmutual.com/games/longevity) Roth IRA website (www.rothira.com)
Online Planning Software
Financial Engines (www.financialengines.com) FinancialPlanAuditors.com (www.fplanauditors.com) Vanguard (https://personal.vanguard.com/us/home)
Financial Calcuator Websites
www.kiplinger.com—Click on Your Retirement www.moneymag.com—Click on Personal Finance and then Retirement www.aarp.org—Click on Retirement Calculator www.asec.org—Click on Ballpark Estimate Worksheet www.finra.org—Click on Investor Services, then Financial Calculators

Source: U.S. Department of Labor, www.dol.gov/ebsa, May 3, 2013.

Conducting a Financial Analysis

LO18-2

Analyze your current assets and liabilities for retirement.

As you learned in Chapter 3, your assets include everything you own that has value: cash on hand and in checking and savings accounts; the current value of your stocks, bonds, and other investments; the current value of your house, car, jewelry, and furnishings; and the current value of your life insurance and pensions. Your liabilities are everything you owe: your mortgage, car payments, credit card balances, taxes due, and so forth. The difference between the two totals is your *net worth,* a figure you should increase each year as you move toward retirement. Use Exhibit 18-3 to calculate your net worth now and at retirement.

Exhibit 18-3

Review your assets, liabilities, and net worth

Reviewing your assets to ensure they are sufficient for retirement is a sound idea.

Net worth: Assets of $108,800 minus liabilities of $16,300 equals $92,500.

	Sample Figures	Your Figures
Assets: What We Own		
Cash:		
Checking account	$ 800	________
Savings account	4,500	________
Investments:		
U.S. savings bonds (current cash-in value)	5,000	________
Stocks, mutual funds	4,500	________
Life insurance:		
Cash value, accumulated dividends	10,000	________
Company pension rights:		
Accrued pension benefit	20,000	________
Property:		
House (equity)	50,000	________
Furniture and appliances	8,000	________
Collections and jewelry	2,000	________
Automobile	3,000	________
Other:		
Loan to brother	1,000	________
Gross assets	$108,800	________
Liabilities: What We Owe		
Current unpaid bills	$ 600	________
Home mortgage (remaining balance)	9,700	________
Auto loan	1,200	________
Property taxes	1,100	________
Home improvement loan	3,700	________
Total liabilities	$ 16,300	________

REVIEW YOUR ASSETS

Reviewing my assets to ensure they are sufficient for retirement is a sound idea.

It is a good idea to review your assets on a regular basis. You may need to make adjustments in your saving, spending, and investing in order to stay on track. As you review your assets, consider your housing, life insurance, and other investments. Each will have an important effect on your retirement income.

Reviewing your assets to ensure they are sufficient for retirement is a sound idea. Make any necessary adjustments in your investments and holdings to fit your circumstances. In reviewing your assets, consider the following factors.

HOUSING If you own your house, it is probably your biggest single asset. The amount tied up in your house, however, may be out of line with your retirement income. You might consider selling your house and buying a less expensive one. The selection of a smaller, more easily maintained house can also decrease your maintenance costs. The difference saved can be put into a savings account or certificates of deposit or into other income-producing investments. If your mortgage is largely or completely paid off, you may be able to get an annuity to provide you with extra income during retirement. In this arrangement, a lender uses your house as collateral to buy an annuity for you from a life insurance company. Each month, the lender pays you (the homeowner) from the annuity after deducting the mortgage interest payment. The mortgage principal, which was used to obtain the annuity, is repaid to the lender by probate after your death. This special annuity is known as a **reverse annuity mortgage (RAM)** or *equity conversion.*

reverse annuity mortgage (RAM) A mortgage in which the lender uses the borrower's house as collateral to buy an annuity for the borrower from a life insurance company; also called an *equity conversion.*

The amount of money available depends on your age, the value of your home, and interest rates. For example, a 75-year-old couple with a $150,000 condominium in Chicago or the suburbs could receive a monthly check of about $900 for the next 10 years or $599 for as long as either partner lives in the home.

For more information about reverse mortgages, go to www.aarp.org/revmort. AARP's booklet *Home Made Money: A Consumer's Guide to Reverse Mortgages* is available online or by calling (888) 687-2277 and asking for publication D 15601.

LIFE INSURANCE You may have set up your life insurance to provide support and education for your children. Now you may want to convert some of this asset into cash or income (an annuity). Another possibility is to reduce premium payments by decreasing the face value of your insurance. This will give you extra money to spend on living expenses or invest for additional income.

OTHER INVESTMENTS Evaluate any other investments you have. When you chose them, you may have been more interested in making your money grow than in getting an early return. Has the time come to take the income from your investments? You may now want to take dividends rather than reinvest them.

After thoroughly reviewing your assets, estimate your spending needs during your retirement years.

YOUR ASSETS AFTER DIVORCE

Any divorce is difficult, particularly when it comes to a division of marital assets. Your pension benefits are considered marital property, which must be divided in a divorce. "Even if a person is not ready to retire, pension benefits are considered a marital asset subject to the division of property," says Howard Sharfstein, a partner in Schulte Roth & Zabel of New York. Any retirement fund money, including a 401(k) plan or a profit-sharing plan, set aside during a marriage and the dollar growth of a pension plan during a marriage are considered marital property.

MAKE DIVORCE A LESS TAXING TIME

Suppose you and your spouse are calling it quits. You've got two jointly owned assets—a house and a retirement account—each worth $500,000. Would it make a difference which one you walked away with? You bet. Equal division of the assets does not mean equal tax bills. "If the tax implications of a divorce settlement are not taken into account, a spouse can unwittingly end up with less, sometimes substantially less, than he or she bargained for," says Cindy Wofford, a tax attorney in Washington.

Divorcing couples should pay attention to the tax implications of retirement benefits. If the transfer of assets from one spouse to another is not done properly, the monies withdrawn from the retirement account will be subject to taxes and early withdrawal penalties.

To correctly divide retirement benefits, the couple needs to create a legal document called a qualified domestic relations order (QDRO), which is a judgment, decree, or order for a retirement plan to pay child support, alimony, or marital property rights to a spouse, former spouse, child, or other dependent of the participant. A QDRO helps a former spouse get his or her fair share of a retirement account accumulated during the marriage. With a QDRO, a husband or wife can transfer some of the assets from his or her retirement account into a separate IRA account for the ex-spouse without incurring taxes and penalties. Also, remember to account for the taxes that must be paid when the retirement account is drawn down. The best way, says Ginita Wall, an accountant in San Diego who specializes in divorce settlements, is to use a 27 percent tax bracket to estimate the amount of taxes owed at retirement.

There is no single best way to divide retirement benefits in a QDRO. What will be best in your case depends on many factors, including:

- The type or kind of retirement plan.
- The benefits available to the retirement plan participant.
- Why the parties want to divide the benefits.

The judge considers several factors in dividing marital property and debt to make sure the division is fair and equitable.

Equitably dividing assets in divorce is never easy, but you can make sure the financial nightmare doesn't continue long after the divorce is final.

Source: Condensed from Toddi Gutner, "Make Divorce a Less Taxing Time," *BusinessWeek*, April 15, 2002, p. 118, updated May 3, 2013.

Division of pension benefits generally depends on the length of the marriage. "In a five-year marriage the percentage of one person's assets given to the spouse is usually small," says Sharfstein. "In an eight-year marriage about 25 percent of the monetary assets earned by one partner may be given to the other partner. In a marriage that lasts more than 15 years there's generally a 50–50 split of the marital assets."

Be warned: Many retirement-planning strategies accommodate the traditional husband-wife-kids family unit. But millions of nontraditional households have unique retirement needs. Nearly half of all American marriages end in divorce, creating difficulties for millions of adults thinking about their retirement years. Likewise, single parents, gays and lesbians, and individuals who choose to live together outside of marriage all have formidable retirement-planning challenges. See Financial Planning for Life's Situations: Make Divorce a Less Taxing Time, on this page, for suggestions regarding retirement accounts and divorce.

PRACTICE QUIZ 18-2

1 How can you calculate your net worth today and at retirement?
2 What assets are considered marital assets?

Retirement Living Expenses

LO18-3

Estimate your retirement spending needs.

The exact amount of money you will need in retirement is impossible to predict. However, you can estimate the amount you will need by considering the changes you anticipate in your spending patterns and in where and how you live.

Your spending patterns will probably change. A study conducted by the Bureau of Labor Statistics on how families spend money shows that retired families use a greater share for food, housing, and medical care than nonretired families. Although no two families adjust their spending patterns to changes in the life cycle in the same manner, the tabulation in Exhibit 18-4 can guide you in anticipating your own future spending patterns.

The following expenses may be lowered or eliminated:

- *Work expenses.* You will no longer make payments into your retirement fund. You will not be buying gas and oil for the drive back and forth to work or for train or bus fares. You may be buying fewer lunches away from home.
- *Clothing expenses.* You will probably need fewer clothes after you retire, and your dress may be more casual.
- *Housing expenses.* If you have paid off your house mortgage by the time you retire, your cost of housing may decrease (although increases in property taxes and insurance may offset this gain).
- *Federal income taxes.* Your federal income taxes will probably be lower. No federal tax has to be paid on some forms of income, such as railroad retirement benefits and certain veterans' benefits. Under the U.S. Civil Service Retirement System, your retirement income is not taxed until you have received the amount you have invested in the retirement fund. After that, your retirement income is taxable. A retirement credit is allowed for some sources of income, such as annuities. You will probably pay taxes at a lower rate because your taxable income will be lower.

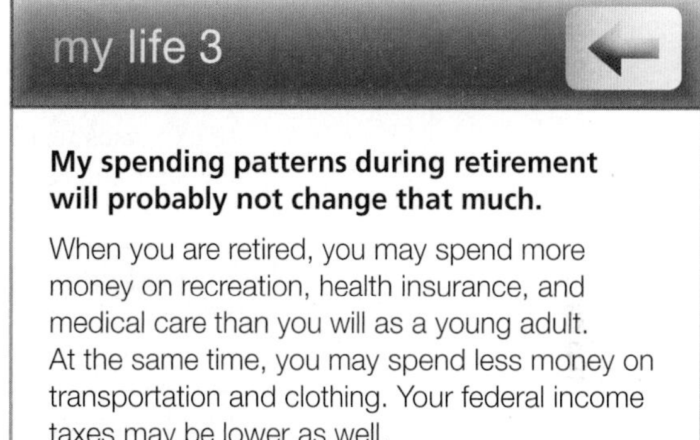

my life 3

My spending patterns during retirement will probably not change that much.

When you are retired, you may spend more money on recreation, health insurance, and medical care than you will as a young adult. At the same time, you may spend less money on transportation and clothing. Your federal income taxes may be lower as well.

Exhibit 18-4

How an "average" older (65+) household spends its money

Retired families spend a greater share of their income for food, housing, and medical care than nonretired families.

Reading, education, entertainment 6.1%
Personal insurance and pensions 7.5%
Contributions 6.1%
Housing 35.0%
Clothing and personal care 4.4%
Healthcare 12.2%
Food 13.9%
Transportation 14.7%

Approximately $39,173 = 100 percent in 2011
25,873,000 households

Source: U.S. Bureau of Labor Statistics, *Consumer Expenditure Survey,* Consumer Expenditures in 2011, April 2013, Table 4, www.bls.gov/cex/csxann11,pdf, accessed May 2, 2013.

You can also estimate which of the following expenses may increase:

- *Insurance.* The loss of your employer's contribution to health and life insurance will increase your own payments. Medicare, however, may offset part of this increased expense.
- *Medical expenses.* Although medical expenses vary from person to person, they tend to increase with age.
- *Expenses for leisure activities.* With more free time, many retirees spend more money on leisure activities. You may want to put aside extra money for a retirement trip or other large recreational expenses.
- *Gifts and contributions.* Many retirees who continue to spend the same amount of money on gifts and contributions find their spending in this area takes a larger share of their smaller income. Therefore, you may want to reevaluate such spending.

Using the worksheet in Exhibit 18-5, list your present expenses and estimate what these expenses would be if you were retired. To make a realistic comparison, list your major spending categories, starting with fixed expenses such as rent or mortgage

Exhibit 18-5

Your monthly present expenses and your estimated monthly retirement expenses

Don't forget inflation in calculating the prices of goods and services in retirement.

Monthly Expenses

Item	Present	Retirement
Fixed expenses:		
Rent or mortgage payment	$ ______	$ ______
Taxes	______	______
Insurance	______	______
Savings	______	______
Debt payment	______	______
Other	______	______
Total fixed expenses	______	______
Variable expenses:		
Food and beverages	______	______
Household operation and maintenance	______	______
Furnishings and equipment	______	______
Clothing	______	______
Personal	______	______
Transportation	______	______
Medical care	______	______
Recreation and education	______	______
Gifts and contributions	______	______
Other	______	______
Total variable expenses	______	______
Total expenses	______	______

payments, utilities, insurance premiums, and taxes. Then list variable expenses—food, clothing, transportation, and so on, as well as miscellaneous expenditures such as medical expenses, entertainment, vacations, gifts, contributions, and unforeseen expenses.

Be sure you have an emergency fund for unforeseen expenses. Even when you are living a tranquil life, unexpected events can occur. Build a cushion to cope with inflation. Estimate high in calculating how much the prices of goods and services will rise.

ADJUST YOUR EXPENSES FOR INFLATION

You now have a list of your likely monthly (and annual) expenses if you were to retire today. With inflation, however, those expenses will not be fixed. The potential loss of buying power due to inflation is what makes planning ahead so important. (See Exhibit 18-6.) During the 1970s and the early 1980s, the cost of living increased an average of 6.1 percent a year, though the annual increase slowed to less than 3 percent between 1983 and 2013.

To help you plan for this likely increase in your expenses, use the inflation factor table in the accompanying Financial Planning Calculations feature, How Much Inflation Is in Your Future.

DID YOU KNOW?

THE EFFECTS OF INFLATION
This chart shows you what $10,000 will be worth in 10, 20, and 30 years, assuming a fairly conservative 4 percent rate of inflation.

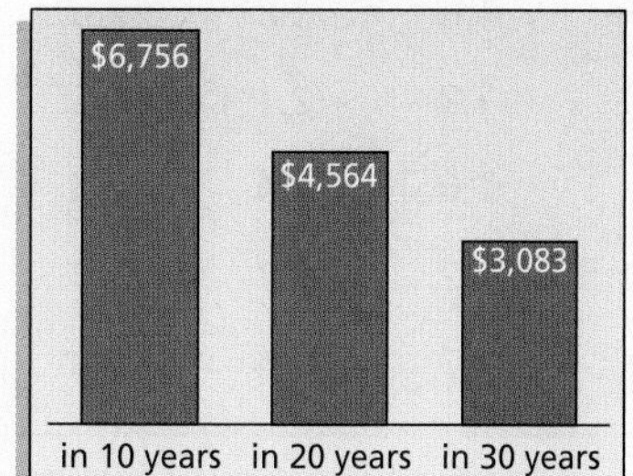

Source: TIAA-CREF.

PRACTICE QUIZ 18-3

1 How can you estimate the amount of money you will need during retirement?
2 What expenses are likely to increase or decrease during retirement?
3 How might you adjust your expenses for inflation?

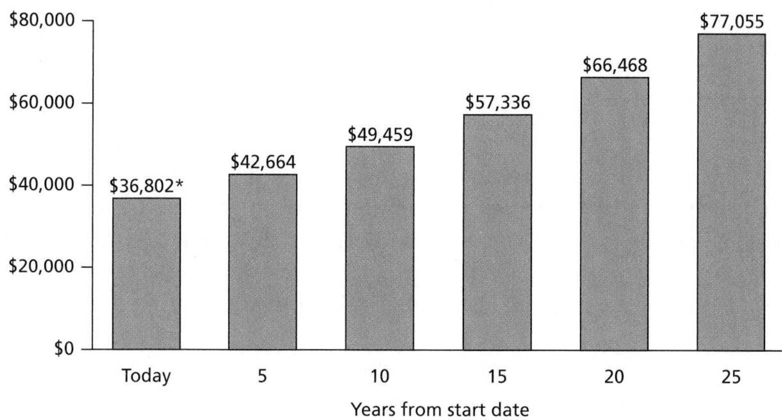

*The initial expense number, $36,802, is pulled from 2010 U.S. Census data as the average annual expenditure for individuals over age 65. The rest of the numbers were calculated based on an annual rate of 3% inflation, which is close to U.S. historical rates of inflation over the last 30 years.

Source: U.S. Department of Labor, Bureau of Labor Statistics, Consumer Expenditures in 2010.

Exhibit 18-6

Even low inflation can damage purchasing power

Even at relatively low annual rates of inflation, your cost of living could more than double over time.

Financial Planning Calculations

HOW MUCH INFLATION IS IN YOUR FUTURE?

ESTIMATED ANNUAL RATE OF INFLATION BETWEEN NOW AND RETIREMENT										
Years to Retirement	3%	4%	5%	6%	7%	8%	9%	10%	11%	12%
5	1.2	1.2	1.3	1.3	1.4	1.5	1.5	1.6	1.7	1.8
8	1.3	1.4	1.5	1.6	1.7	1.8	2.0	2.1	2.3	2.5
10	1.4	1.5	1.6	1.8	2.0	2.2	2.4	2.6	2.8	3.1
12	1.5	1.6	1.8	2.0	2.3	2.5	2.8	3.1	3.5	3.9
15	1.6	1.8	2.1	2.4	2.8	3.2	3.6	4.2	4.8	5.5
18	1.8	2.0	2.4	2.8	3.4	4.0	4.7	5.6	6.5	7.7
20	2.0	2.2	2.7	3.2	3.9	4.7	5.6	6.7	8.1	9.6
25	2.1	2.7	3.4	4.3	5.4	6.8	8.6	10.8	13.6	17.0

1. Choose from the first column the approximate number of years until your retirement.
2. Choose an estimated annual rate of inflation. The rate of inflation cannot be predicted accurately and will vary from year to year. The 2007 inflation rate was less than 3 percent.
3. Find the inflation factor corresponding to the number of years until your retirement and the estimated annual inflation rate. (Example: 10 years to retirement combined with a 4 percent estimated annual inflation rate yields a 1.5 inflation factor.)
4. Multiply the inflation factor by your estimated retirement income and your estimated retirement expenses. (Example: $6,000 × 1.5 = $9,000.)

Total annual inflated retirement income: $ _____.

Total annual inflated retirement expenses: $ _____.

Sources: The above figures are from a compound interest table showing the effective yield of lump-sum investments after inflation that appeared in Charles D. Hodgman, ed., *Mathematical Tables from the Handbook of Chemistry and Physics* (Cleveland: Chemical Rubber Publishing, 1959); *Citicorp Consumer Views,* July 1985, pp. 2–3, © Citicorp, 1985; *Financial Planning Tables,* A. G. Edwards, August 1991.

Planning Your Retirement Housing

LO18-4

Identify your retirement housing needs.

Think about where you will want to live. If you think you will want to live in another city, it's a good idea to plan vacations now in areas you might enjoy later. When you find one that appeals to you, visit that area during various times of the year to experience the year-round climate. Meet the people. Check into available activities, transportation, and taxes. Be realistic about what you will have to give up and what you will gain.

Where you live in retirement can influence your financial needs. You must make some important decisions about whether or not to stay in your present community and in your current home. Everyone has unique needs and preferences; only you can determine the location and housing that are best for you.

Consider what moving involves. Moving is expensive, and if you are not satisfied with your new location, returning to your former home may be impossible. Consider the social aspects of moving. Will you want to be near your children, other relatives, and good friends? Are you prepared for new circumstances?

my life 4

The place where I live during retirement can have a significant impact on my financial needs.

Even if you do not move to a new location, housing needs may change during retirement. Many retirees want a home that is easy and inexpensive to maintain, such as a smaller house, condominium or an apartment.

TYPE OF HOUSING

Housing needs often change as people grow older. The ease and cost of maintenance and nearness to public transportation, shopping, church/synagogue, and entertainment often become more important to people when they retire.

Many housing alternatives exist, several of which were discussed in Chapter 9. Staying in their present home, whether a single-family dwelling, a condominium, or an apartment, is the alternative preferred by most people approaching retirement. That's what John and Virginia Wolf decided to do after John took early retirement at age 47 from his job as a service manager of a Van Nuys, California, Ford dealership in the late 1970s. Even though the couple had already paid off the mortgage on their small, three-bedroom ranch house and could have moved up into a bigger or fancier place, all John wanted to do was tinker in the garage and dabble in the stock market.[1] A recent survey of over 5,000 men and women revealed that 92 percent wanted to own their homes in retirement.

DeLoma Foster of Greenville, South Carolina, has seen the future, and she wants to be prepared. DeLoma, 69, has osteoporosis, just as her mother did. Although she's not having difficulty now, she knows the debilitating bone condition eventually could make it difficult, if not impossible, to navigate steep stairs, cramped bathrooms, and narrow doorways. So two years ago, she and her husband, Clyde, a 72-year-old retired textile executive, moved into a novel type of home, one that can comfortably accommodate them no matter what disabilities old age may bring. Called a "universal design home," their residence is on the cutting edge of an architectural concept that an aging population may well embrace. The only house of its kind in the neighborhood, it has wide doors, pull-out cabinet shelves, easy-to-reach electrical switches, and dozens of other features useful for elderly persons or those with disabilities. Yet these features are incorporated into the design unobtrusively.

During retirement, will you want to be near your children, grandchildren, other relatives, and good friends?

Apart from aesthetics, universal design is appealing because it allows people to stay in their homes as they grow older and more frail. "The overwhelming majority of people would prefer to grow old in their own homes in their own communities," says Jon Pynoos, a gerontologist at the University of Southern California in Los Angeles. Recognizing this trend, building suppliers now offer everything from lever door handles to faucets that turn on automatically when you put your hand beneath the spigot. Remodeling so far is creating the biggest demand for these products. But increasingly, contractors are building universal design homes from scratch, which generally costs less than completely retro-fitting an existing house. Philip Stephen Companies in St. Paul, Minnesota, has built six universal design homes in the Southeast, ranging from a 1,240-square-foot ranch in Greer, South Carolina, that sold for $90,000 to the 2,200-square-foot home that DeLoma and Clyde bought for $190,000.

With the many choices available, determining where to live in retirement is itself turning into a time-consuming job. But whether you want to race cars, go on a safari, or stay home to paint, the goal is to end up like Edna Cohen. "Don't feel bad if I die tomorrow," she says. "I've had a wonderful life." Who could ask for more?

Whatever retirement housing alternative you choose, make sure you know what you are signing and understand what you are buying.

AVOIDING RETIREMENT HOUSING TRAPS

Too many people make the move without doing enough research, and often it's a huge mistake. How can retirees avoid being surprised by hidden tax and financial traps when they move? Here are some tips from retirement specialists on how to uncover hidden taxes and other costs of a retirement area before moving:

- Write or call the local chamber of commerce to get an economic profile and details on area property taxes.
- Contact the state's tax department to find out state income, sales, and inheritance taxes and special exemptions for retirees. If your pension will be taxed by the state you're leaving, check whether the new state will give you credit for those taxes.
- Subscribe to the Sunday edition of a local newspaper.
- Call a local CPA to find out which taxes are rising.
- Check with local utilities to estimate your energy costs. Visit the area in as many seasons as possible. Talk to retirees and other local residents about costs of health care, auto insurance, food, and clothing.
- Rent for a while instead of buying immediately.

Retirement housing and lifestyle planning

PRACTICE QUIZ 18-4

1 What are some housing options for retirees?
2 How can retirees avoid retirement housing traps?

Planning Your Retirement Income

LO18-5

Determine your planned retirement income.

Once you have determined your approximate future expenses, you must evaluate the sources and amounts of your retirement income. Possible sources of income for many retirees are Social Security, other public pension plans, employer pension plans, personal retirement plans, and annuities.

SOCIAL SECURITY

Social Security is the most widely used source of retirement income; it covers almost 97 percent of U.S. workers. Many Americans think of Social Security as benefiting only retired people. But it is actually a package of protection, providing retirement, survivors', and disability benefits. The package protects you and your family while you work and after you retire. Today more than 58 million people, almost one out of every six Americans, collect over $821 billion in some kind of Social Security benefit.[2]

The Social Security Administration estimates that 47 percent of individuals age 65 and older would live in poverty without Social Security benefits, four times as many as live in poverty today.

Social Security should not be the only source of your retirement income, however. It should be only a small part of your plan, or you won't live a very exciting retired life. Even the Social Security Administration cautions that Social Security was never intended to provide 100 percent of retirement income.

DID YOU KNOW?

For a worker with average income, a spouse, and two small children, Social Security's survivor protection is equivalent to a life insurance policy with a value of $433,000. For the same worker, Social Security's disability benefits are worth a $414,000 disability policy.

Who Receives Social Security Benefits?

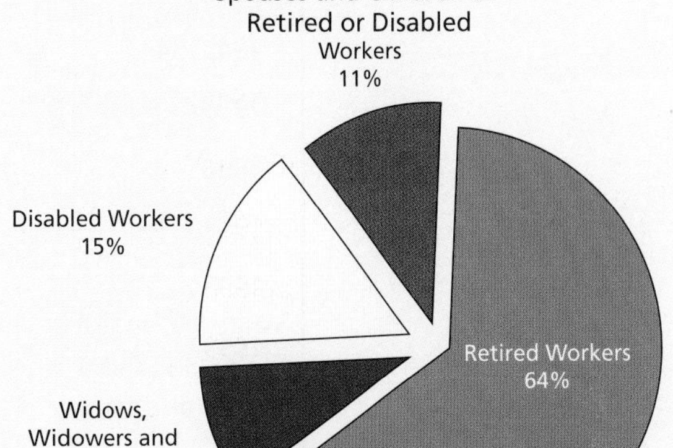

Note: The chart does not add up to 100% due to rounding.

Source: Social Security Administration, *Fast Facts and Figures About Social Security,* 2012, p. 19, ssa.gov/policy/docs/chartbooks/fast_facts/2012/fast_facts12.pdf, accessed May 3, 2013.

WHEN AND WHERE TO APPLY Most people qualify for reduced Social Security retirement benefits at age 62; widows or widowers can begin collecting Social Security benefits earlier.

Three months before you retire, apply for Social Security benefits by telephoning the Social Security office at 1-800-772-1213. The payments will not start unless you apply for them. If you apply late, you risk losing benefits.

WHAT INFORMATION WILL YOU NEED? The Social Security office will tell you what proof you need to establish your particular case. Generally, you will be asked to provide the following:

- Proof of your age.
- Your Social Security card or Social Security number.
- Your W-2 withholding forms for the past two years.
- Your marriage license if you are applying for your spouse's benefits.
- The birth certificates of your children if you are applying for their benefits.

WHAT IF YOU RETIRE AT 62 INSTEAD OF 65? Your Social Security benefits will be reduced if you retire before age 65. Currently there is a permanent reduction of five-ninths of 1 percent for each month you receive payments before age 65. Thus, if you retire at 62, your monthly payments will be permanently reduced by 20 percent of what they would be if you waited until 65 to retire. However, if you wait until 65 to collect Social Security, your benefits will not decrease. If you work after 65, your benefits will increase by one-fourth of 1 percent for each month past age 65 that you delay retirement, but only up to age 70.

Because of longer life expectancies, the full retirement age will be increased in gradual steps until it reaches 67. This change started in 2003 and affects people born in 1938 and later. Look at Exhibit 18-7 to determine your full retirement age.

ESTIMATING YOUR RETIREMENT BENEFITS Beginning in 2012, the Social Security Administration provides a history of your earnings and an estimate of your future monthly benefits online. To create your personal and confidential account, visit socialsecurity.gov/myaccount. The statement includes an estimate, in today's dollars, of how much you will get each month from Social Security when you retire—

Exhibit 18-7

Age to receive full Social Security benefits

Because of longer life expectancies, the full retirement age will be increased in gradual steps until it reaches 67.

Year of Birth	Full Retirement Age
1937 or earlier	65
1938	65 and 2 months
1939	65 and 4 months
1940	65 and 6 months
1941	65 and 8 months
1942	65 and 10 months
1943–54	66
1955	66 and 2 months
1956	66 and 4 months
1957	66 and 6 months
1958	66 and 8 months
1959	66 and 10 months
1960 and later	67
Although the full retirement age is rising, you should still apply for Medicare benefits within three months of your 65th birthday.	

Source: Social Security Administration, *Social Security: Understanding the Benefits* (Washington, D.C., February 2013), p. 9.

My Social Security benefits will be reduced if I retire before age 65.

Most people can begin collecting Social Security retirement benefits at age 62. However, the monthly amount at age 62 is less than it would be if you waited until full retirement age. The full retirement age is being increased in gradual steps. For people born in 1960 and later, the full retirement age is 67.

at age 62, 65, or 70—based on your earnings to date and your projected future earnings. Use the accompanying Financial Planning for Life's Situations feature, Choosing a Social Security Benefit Calculator, to estimate your potential monthly benefits.

HOW TO BECOME ELIGIBLE To qualify for Social Security retirement benefits, you must have the required number of quarters of coverage. The number of quarters you need depends on your year of birth. People born after 1928 need 40 quarters to qualify for benefits.

TAXABILITY OF SOCIAL SECURITY BENEFITS Up to 85 percent of your Social Security benefits may be subject to federal income tax for any year in which your adjusted gross income plus your nontaxable interest income and one-half of your Social Security benefits exceed a base amount. For current information, telephone the Internal Revenue Service at 1-800-829-3676 for Publication 554, *Tax Benefits for Older Americans,* and Publication 915, *Tax Information on Social Security.*

IF YOU WORK AFTER YOU RETIRE Your Social Security benefits may be reduced if you earn above a certain amount a year, depending on your age and the amount you earn. You will receive all of your benefits for the year if your employment earnings do not exceed the annual exempted amount.

BENEFITS INCREASE AUTOMATICALLY Social Security benefits increase automatically each January if the cost of living increased during the preceding year. Each year, the cost of living is compared with that of the year before. If it

CHOOSING A SOCIAL SECURITY BENEFIT CALCULATOR

Use any of the three calculators below to estimate your potential benefit amounts using different retirement dates and different levels of potential future earnings. The calculators will show your retirement benefits as well as disability and survivor benefit amounts on your record if you should become disabled or die today.

- The Quick and Online calculators can be used from the screen. Mac users can use the Online Calculator.
- The Detailed Calculator must be downloaded. You can download the Mac version of the Detailed Calculator from ftp.ssa.gov/pub/oact/anypiamac.sea.hqx.
- Calculator estimates will differ from those on your Social Security Statement if you use different assumptions.
- If you are eligible for a pension based on work that was not covered by Social Security, your benefit amount may be reduced.

1. **Quick Calculator.** Simple, rough estimate calculator. You input your date of birth and this year's earnings. (You must be over age 21 to use this calculator.)
2. **Online Calculator.** You input your date of birth and your complete earnings history. You may project your future earnings. (This calculation is similar to that shown on your Social Security Statement.)
3. **Detailed Calculator.** This program provides the most precise estimates. It must be downloaded and installed on your computer. (Includes reduction for Government Pension Offset).

Source: www.ssa.gov/OACT/anypia/index.html, accessed May 2, 2013.

has increased, Social Security benefits increase by the same percentage.

SPOUSE'S BENEFITS The full benefit for a spouse is one-half of the retired worker's full benefit. If your spouse takes benefits before age 65, the amount of the spouse's benefit is reduced to a low of 37.5 percent at age 62. However, a spouse who is taking care of a child who is under 16 or has a disability gets full (50 percent) benefits, regardless of age.

If you are eligible for both your own retirement benefits and for benefits as a spouse, Social Security pays your own benefit first. If your benefit as a spouse is higher than your retirement benefit, you'll get a combination of benefits equal to the higher spouse benefit.

DID YOU KNOW?

AVERAGE 2013 MONTHLY SOCIAL SECURITY BENEFITS:

- Retired worker: $1,261
- Retired couple: $2,048
- Disabled worker: $1,132
- Disabled worker with a spouse and child: $1,919
- Widow or widower: $1,214
- Young widow or widower with two children: $2,592

Source: *Social Security: Understanding the Benefits* (Washington, D.C., Social Security Administration, January 2013), p. 22.

INTERNET ACCESS To view and print the Social Security Administration's publications, forms, reports, and program history, with links to information for employers, employees, children, parents, and teachers, visit the agency at www.ssa.gov.

THE FUTURE OF SOCIAL SECURITY According to the 2012 Trustees Report, "Social Security is not sustainable over the long term at current benefit and tax rates." Beginning in 2010 and continuing in 2011, Social Security paid more in benefits and expenses than it collected in taxes and other income. The report projects this pattern to continue for the next 75 years. The trustees estimate that the trust funds will be exhausted by 2033. At that point, payroll taxes and other income will flow into the fund but will be sufficient to pay only 75 percent of program costs.

Exhibit 18-8

The number of workers per beneficiary has plummeted

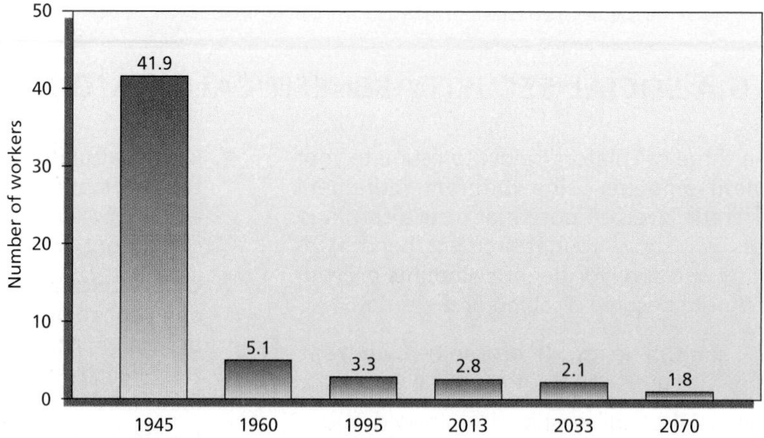

Source: *2012 Annual Report of the Board of Trustees of the Federal Old-Age and Survivors Insurance and Disability Insurance Trust Funds,* Table IV.B2, ssa.gov/policy/docs/chartbooks/fast_facts/2012/fast_facts12.pdf, accessed May 1, 2013.

However, many people are concerned about the future of Social Security. They contend that enormous changes since Social Security started over 78 years ago have led to promises that are impossible to keep. Longer life expectancies mean retirees collect benefits over a greater number of years. More workers are retiring early, thus entering the system sooner and staying longer. The flood of baby boomers who began retiring early in the 21st century will mean fewer workers to contribute to the system. In 1945, 42 workers supported every recipient. By 2013, that number had dropped to 2.8. The Social Security Administration estimates the number will drop to 2.1 workers by 2033 and 1.8 workers by 2070. (see Exhibit 18-8).

In early 2005 President George W. Bush suggested the most sweeping change to the Social Security program since its inception: Let the stock market help fix it. Is he right? Are private accounts really a good idea? Are there other options to fix Social Security?

OTHER PUBLIC PENSION PLANS

Besides Social Security, the federal government administers several other retirement plans (for federal government and railroad employees). Employees covered under these plans are not covered by Social Security. The Veterans Administration provides pensions for many survivors of men and women who died while in the armed forces and disability pensions for eligible veterans. The Railroad Retirement System is the only retirement system administered by the federal government that covers a single private industry. Many state, county, and city governments operate retirement plans for their employees.

EMPLOYER PENSION PLANS

Another possible source of retirement income is the pension plan your company offers. With employer plans, your employer contributes to your retirement benefits, and sometimes you contribute too. Contributions and earnings on those contributions accumulate tax free until you receive them.

Since private pension plans vary, you should find out (1) when you become eligible for pension benefits and (2) what benefits you will be entitled to. Most employer plans are defined-contribution or defined-benefit plans.

DEFINED-CONTRIBUTION PLAN Over the last two decades, the defined-contribution plan has grown rapidly, while the number of defined-benefit plans has generally dropped. A **defined-contribution plan** has an individual account for each employee; therefore, these plans are sometimes called *individual account plans.* The plan document describes the amount the employer will contribute, but it does not promise any particular benefit. When a plan participant retires or otherwise becomes eligible for benefits, the benefit is the total amount in the participant's account, including past investment earnings on amounts put into the account.

defined-contribution plan A plan—profit sharing, money purchase, Keogh, or 401(k)—that provides an individual account for each participant; also called an *individual account plan.*

401(k) (TSA) plan A plan under which employees can defer current taxation on a portion of their salary.

Defined-contribution plans include the following:

1. *Money-purchase pension plans.* Your employer promises to set aside a certain amount for you each year, generally a percentage of your earnings.
2. *Stock bonus plans.* Your employer's contribution is used to buy stock in your company for you. The stock is usually held in trust until you retire, at which time you can receive your shares or sell them at their fair market value.
3. *Profit-sharing plans.* Your employer's contribution depends on the company's profits.
4. *Salary reduction or 401(k) plans.* Under a **401(k) plan,** your employer makes nontaxable contributions to the plan for your benefit and reduces your salary by the same amounts. Sometimes your employer matches a portion of the funds contributed by you. If your employer is a tax-exempt institution such as a hospital, university, or museum, the salary reduction plan is called a *Section 403(b) plan.* Or, if you are a government employee, you may have a *Section 457 plan.* These plans are often referred to as *tax-sheltered annuity (TSA) plans.*

The Economic Growth and Tax Relief Reconciliation Act (the EGTRRA) was passed by Congress in 2001. The Act increased the employee contribution limit for 401(k) and other employer-sponsored retirement plans. For example, you can contribute $17,500 to your 401(k), 403(b), or Section 457(b) plan in 2013 ($23,000 if you are 50 or older). This new provision is intended to allow older workers to make up for lost time and catch up on their contributions.

An Example: How Funds Accumulate All earnings in a tax-sheltered annuity grow without current federal taxation. Dollars saved on a pretax basis while your earnings grow tax deferred will enhance the growth of your funds (see Exhibit 18-9).

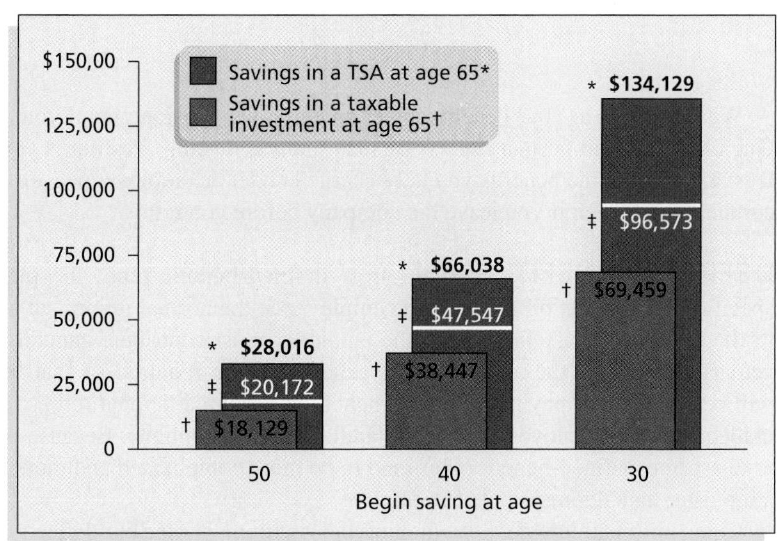

Exhibit 18-9

An early start + tax-deferred growth = greater savings

All earnings in a tax-sheltered annuity grow without current federal taxation.

Source: Massachusetts Mutual Life Insurance Company.

*Tax-deferred growth: Assumes a 28 percent tax bracket, a $100 contribution per month, and a 6 percent tax-deferred annual return.

†Taxable growth: Assumes a 28 percent tax bracket, a $72 contribution ($100 − $28 paid in taxes) per month, and a 6 percent taxable annual return (a 4.32 percent after-tax earnings rate). A 10 percent federal tax penalty may be due on amounts withdrawn before age 59½.

‡Net after 28 percent tax at retirement.

One caution! Don't overlook your 401(k) plan fees. Your account balance will determine the amount of retirement income you will receive from the plan. Fees and expenses paid by your plan may substantially reduce the growth in your account. For example, assume you are a 30-year-old with $25,000 in a 401(k) plan. If your account earns 7 percent and incurs fees of 0.5 percent a year, without another contribution, your payout at age 65 will be $227,000. But if the same account incurs fees of 1.5 percent, your payout at age 65 will be only $163,000. *That extra 1 percent per year reduces your payout by 28 percent.*

Tax Benefits of a TSA With a TSA, your investment earnings are tax deferred. Your savings compound at a faster rate and provide you with a greater sum than in an account without this advantage. Ordinary income taxes will be due when you receive the income. The following table illustrates the difference between saving in a conventional savings plan and a tax-deferred TSA for a single person earning $28,000 a year. Notice how you can increase your take-home pay with a TSA.

EXAMPLE: Tax Benefits of a TSA

	Without a TSA	With a TSA
Your income	$28,000	$28,000
TSA contribution	−0	− 2,400
Taxable income	$28,000	$25,600
Estimated federal income taxes	−5,319	−4,647
Gross take-home pay	$22,681	$20,953
After-tax savings contributions	−2,400	−0
Net take-home pay	$20,281	$20,953
Increase in take-home pay with a TSA		$672

vesting An employee's right to at least a portion of the benefits accrued under an employer pension plan, even if the employee leaves the company before retiring.

defined-benefit plan A plan that specifies the benefits the employee will receive at the normal retirement age.

What happens to your benefits under an employer pension plan if you change jobs? One of the most important aspects of such plans is vesting. **Vesting** is your right to at least a portion of the benefits you have accrued under an employer pension plan (within certain limits), even if you leave the company before you retire.

DEFINED-BENEFIT PLAN In a **defined-benefit plan,** the plan document specifies the benefits promised to the employee at the normal retirement age. The plan itself does not specify how much the employer must contribute annually. The plan's actuary determines the annual employer contribution required so that the plan fund will be sufficient to pay the promised benefits as each participant retires. If the fund is inadequate, the employer must make additional contributions. Because of their actuarial aspects, defined-benefit plans tend to be more complicated and more expensive to administer than defined-contribution plans.

Companies nationwide are switching their retirement plans to defined contributions from defined benefits. "Paternalistic employers are dying fast—if they're not already dead," says an actuary with an international consulting firm. The result is that "the shift to defined contributions has forced employees to take more responsibility for retirement. They have discretion as to how to invest the money and must make substantive decisions about their own financial futures."[3] Exhibit 18-10 compares important features of defined-benefit and defined-contribution plans.

Exhibit 18-10 Comparison of defined-benefit and defined-contribution plans

	Defined Benefit Plan	Defined Contribution Plan
Employer Contributions and/or Matching Contributions	Employer funded. Federal rules set amounts that employers must contribute to plans in an effort to ensure that plans have enough money to pay benefits when due. There are penalties for failing to meet these requirements.	There is no requirement that the employer contribute, except in the SIMPLE 401(k) and Safe Harbor 401(k)s, money purchase plans, SIMPLE IRA and SEP plans. The employer may choose to match a portion of the employee's contributions or to contribute without employee contributions. In some plans, employer contributions may be in the form of employer stock.
Employee Contributions	Generally, employees do not contribute to these plans.	Many plans require the employee to contribute in order for an account to be established.
Managing the Investment	Plan officials manage the investment and the employer is responsible for ensuring that the amount it has put in the plan plus investment earnings will be enough to pay the promised benefit.	The employee often is responsible for managing the investment of his or her account, choosing from investment options offered by the plan. In some plans, plan officials are responsible for investing all the plan's assets.
Amount of Benefits Paid Upon Retirement	A promised benefit is based on a formula in the plan, often using a combination of the employee's age, years worked for the employer, and/or salary.	The benefit depends on contributions made by the employee and/or the employer, performance of the account's investments, and fees charged to the account.
Type of Retirement Benefit Payments	Traditionally, these plans pay the retiree monthly annuity payments that continue for life. Plans may offer other payment options.	The retiree may transfer the account balance into an individual retirement account (IRA) from which the retiree withdraws money, or may receive it as a lump sum payment. Some plans also offer monthly payments through an annuity.
Guarantee of Benefits	The federal government, through the Pension Benefit Guaranty Corporation (PBGC), guarantees some amount of benefits.	No federal guarantee of benefits.
Leaving the Company Before Retirement Age	If an employee leaves after vesting in a benefit but before the plan's retirement age, the benefit generally stays with the plan until the employee files a claim for it at retirement. Some defined benefit plans offer early retirement options.	The employee may transfer the account balance to an individual retirement account (IRA) or, in some cases, another employer plan, where it can continue to grow based on investment earnings. The employee also may take the balance out of the plan, but will owe taxes and possibly penalties, thus reducing retirement income. Plans may cash out small accounts.

PLAN PORTABILITY AND PROTECTION Some pension plans allow portability. This feature enables you to carry earned benefits from one employer's pension plan to another's when you change jobs.

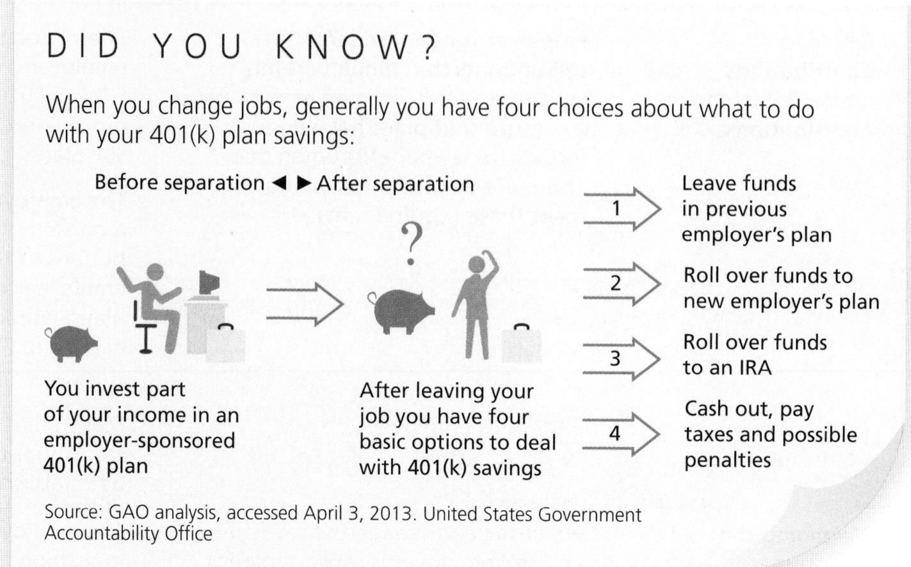

The Employee Retirement Income Security Act of 1974 (ERISA) sets minimum standards for pension plans in private industry and protects more than 50 million workers. Under this act, the federal government has insured part of the payments promised to retirees from private defined-benefit pensions. ERISA established the Pension Benefit Guaranty Corporation (PBGC), a quasi-governmental agency, to provide pension insurance. The PBGC protects employees' pensions to some degree if a firm defaults. For example, in 2005 United Airlines and U.S. Airways terminated their defined-benefit plans in bankruptcy. The PBGC will pay workers and retirees with high-paying jobs at airlines with reduced pension benefits. The PBGC's board of directors includes the secretaries of the U.S. Departments of Labor, the Treasury, and Commerce.

PERSONAL RETIREMENT PLANS

In addition to the retirement plans offered by Social Security, other public pension plans, and employer pension plans, many individuals have set up personal retirement plans. The two most popular personal retirement plans are individual retirement accounts (IRAs) and Keogh accounts.

individual retirement account (IRA) A special account in which the employee sets aside a portion of his or her income; taxes are not paid on the principal or interest until money is withdrawn from the account.

INDIVIDUAL RETIREMENT ACCOUNTS (IRAs) The **individual retirement account (IRA),** which entails the establishment of a trust or a custodial account, is a retirement savings plan created for an individual. The Taxpayer Relief Act of 1997 included several provisions designed to help you save for retirement. The act expanded rules on traditional (classic) IRAs and created several new types of IRAs.

Furthermore, the EGTRRA of 2001 increased the amount of money you can contribute to an IRA from $2,000 in 2001 to $5,500 in 2013. If you are 50 or older, you can contribute $1,000 more than the regular limits in 2013.

Whether or not you are covered by a pension plan, you can still make nondeductible IRA contributions, and all of the income your IRA earns will compound tax deferred until you withdraw money from the IRA. Remember, the biggest benefit of an IRA lies in its tax-deferred earnings growth; the longer the money accumulates tax deferred, the bigger the benefit.

Exhibit 18-11 shows the power of tax-deferred compounding of earnings, an important advantage offered by an IRA. Consider how compounded earnings transformed the lives of two savers, Abe and Ben. As the exhibit shows, Abe regularly invested $2,000 a year in an IRA for 10 years, from ages 25 to 35. Then Abe sat back and let compounding work its magic. Ben started making regular $2,000 annual contributions at age 35 and contributed for 30 years until age 65. As you can see, Abe retired with a much larger nest egg—over $192,000 more than Ben's. Moral? Get an early start on your plan for retirement.

Your investment opportunities for IRA funds are not limited to savings accounts and certificates of deposit. You can put your IRA funds in many kinds of investments—mutual funds, annuities, stocks, bonds, U.S.-minted gold and silver coins, real estate, and so forth. Only investments in life insurance, precious metals, collectibles, and securities bought on margin are prohibited.

Regular (Traditional or Classic) IRA This arrangement lets you contribute up to $5,500 in 2013 ($6,500 if over 50). Whether the contribution is tax deductible depends on your tax filing status, your income, and your participation in an employer-provided retirement plan.

Roth IRA With a *Roth IRA,* contributions are not tax deductible, but earnings accumulate tax free. You may contribute up to the amounts shown in the above paragraph (reduced by the amount contributed to a traditional IRA). You can make contributions even after age 70½. Five years after you establish your Roth IRA, you can take tax-free, penalty-free distributions if you are at least 59½ or will use the fund for first-time home buyer expenses.

Your Roth IRA is exclusively for you. Your interest in the account is nonforfeitable. You can't borrow from your Roth IRA. If you use your Roth IRA as collateral for a loan, the part you pledge as collateral will be taxed as a withdrawal.

In 2013, if you are a single taxpayer, your Roth IRA contribution limit is reduced when your adjusted gross income (AGI) is more than $112,000. You can not contribute when your AGI reaches $127,000. If you are filing jointly, the amounts are $178,000 and $188,000, respectively.

You may convert your traditional IRA to a Roth IRA. Depending on your current age and your anticipated tax bracket in retirement, it may be a good idea to convert. Is a tax-deductible IRA or a Roth IRA better for you? If you are saving for a first-time home purchase or retirement at age 59½, and these events are at least five years away, the Roth IRA allows for penalty-free withdrawals as well as tax-free distributions.

Spousal IRA A *spousal IRA* lets you contribute up to the amounts shown above on behalf of your nonworking spouse if you file a joint tax return. As in the traditional IRA, whether or not this contribution is tax deductible depends on your income and on whether you or your spouse participates in an employer-provided retirement plan.

Rollover IRA A *rollover IRA* is a traditional IRA that accepts rollovers of all or a portion of your taxable distribution from a retirement plan or from another IRA. A rollover IRA may also let you roll over to a Roth IRA. To avoid a mandatory 20 percent federal income tax withholding, the rollover must be made directly to a similar employer-provided retirement plan or to an IRA. If you receive the money yourself, you must roll it over within 60 days. However, you will receive only 80 percent of the amount you request as a distribution (distribution minus the mandatory 20 percent withholding tax). Unless you add additional money to the rollover accumulation to equal the 20 percent withheld, the IRS will consider the 20 percent withheld to be taxable income. If you are under 59½, the 20 percent withholding will be considered an early distribution subject to a 10 percent penalty tax. The 80 percent you roll over will not be taxed until you take it out of the IRA.

The 2001 law made retirement savings more portable, permitting workers to roll money between 401(k)s, 403(b)s, and governmental 457s. That's especially good now for those with a 457. Before, you could not even transfer savings into an IRA when you left a job. You can now also roll regular deductible IRA savings into a 401(k).

Exhibit **18-11** Tackling the trade-offs (saving now versus saving later): The time value of money

Get an early start on your plan for retirement.

Saver Abe				Saver Ben			
Age	**Years**	**Contributions**	**Year-End Value**	**Age**	**Years**	**Contributions**	**Year-End Value**
25	1	$ 2,000	$ 2,188	25	1	$ 0	$ 0
26	2	2,000	4,580	26	2	0	0
27	3	2,000	7,198	27	3	0	0
28	4	2,000	10,061	28	4	0	0
29	5	2,000	13,192	29	5	0	0
30	6	2,000	16,617	30	6	0	0
31	7	2,000	20,363	31	7	0	0
32	8	2,000	24,461	32	8	0	0
33	9	2,000	28,944	33	9	0	0
34	10	2,000	33,846	34	10	0	0
35	11	0	37,021	35	11	2,000	2,188
36	12	0	40,494	36	12	2,000	4,580
37	13	0	44,293	37	13	2,000	7,198
38	14	0	48,448	38	14	2,000	10,061
39	15	0	52,992	39	15	2,000	13,192
40	16	0	57,963	40	16	2,000	16,617
41	17	0	63,401	41	17	2,000	20,363
42	18	0	69,348	42	18	2,000	24,461
43	19	0	75,854	43	19	2,000	28,944
44	20	0	82,969	44	20	2,000	33,846
45	21	0	90,752	45	21	2,000	39,209
46	22	0	99,265	46	22	2,000	45,075
47	23	0	108,577	47	23	2,000	51,490
48	24	0	118,763	48	24	2,000	58,508
49	25	0	129,903	49	25	2,000	66,184
50	26	0	142,089	50	26	2,000	74,580
51	27	0	155,418	51	27	2,000	83,764
52	28	0	169,997	52	28	2,000	93,809
53	29	0	185,944	53	29	2,000	104,797
54	30	0	203,387	54	30	2,000	116,815
55	31	0	222,466	55	31	2,000	129,961
56	32	0	243,335	56	32	2,000	144,340
57	33	0	266,162	57	33	2,000	160,068
58	34	0	291,129	58	34	2,000	177,271
59	35	0	318,439	59	35	2,000	196,088
60	36	0	348,311	60	36	2,000	216,670
61	37	0	380,985	61	37	2,000	239,182
62	38	0	416,724	62	38	2,000	263,807
63	39	0	455,816	63	39	2,000	290,741
64	40	0	498,574	64	40	2,000	320,202
65	41	0	545,344	65	41	2,000	352,427
		$20,000				$62,000	
Value at retirement*			$545,344	Value at retirement*			$352,427
Less total contributions			−20,000	Less total contributions			−62,000
Net earnings			$525,344	Net earnings			$290,427

*The table assumes a 9 percent fixed rate of return, compounded monthly, and no fluctuation of the principal. Distributions from an IRA are subject to ordinary income taxes when withdrawn and may be subject to other limitations under IRA rules.

Source: *The Franklin Investor* (San Mateo, CA: Franklin Distributors Inc., January 1989).

Education IRA The Education IRA, renamed the *Coverdell Education Savings Account* after the late Senator Paul Coverdell, has also been enhanced. You can now give $2,000 a year to each child—up from $500—for the Education IRA. These accounts grow tax-free and can be invested any way you choose. Coverdells can now be used for elementary and secondary school costs, including books, tuition, and tutoring.

Simplified Employee Pension Plans–IRA (SEP–IRA) A *SEP–IRA plan* is simply an individual retirement account funded by the employer. Each employee sets up an IRA account at a bank or a brokerage house. Then the employer makes an annual contribution of up to $51,000 in 2013 (indexed to cost-of-living adjustments in the future).

The SEP–IRA is the simplest type of retirement plan if you are fully or partially self-employed. Your contributions, which can vary from year to year, are tax deductible, and earnings accumulate on a tax-deferred basis. A SEP–IRA has no IRS filing requirements, so paperwork is minimal.

Exhibit 18-12 summarizes various IRA options.

Exhibit 18-12

Summary of IRA options

Type of Plan	Plan Features
Regular or Traditional IRA	• Tax-deferred interest and earnings. • Annual limit on individual contributions. • Limited eligibility for tax-deductible contributions.
Roth IRA	• Tax-deferred interest and earnings. • Annual limit on individual contributions. • Withdrawals are tax free in specific cases. • Contributions do not reduce current taxes.
Spousal IRA	• Tax-deferred interest and earnings. • Both working spouse and nonworking spouse can contribute up to the annual limit. • Limited eligibility for tax-deductible contributions.
Rollover IRA	• Traditional IRA that accepts rollovers of all or a portion of your taxable distribution from a retirement plan. • You can roll over to a Roth IRA.
Education IRA (Coverdell Education Savings Account)	• Tax-deferred interest and earnings. • 10% early withdrawal penalty is waived when money is used for higher-education expenses. • Annual limit on individual contributions. • Contributions do not reduce current taxes.
Employer-sponsored retirement plan (SEP–IRA)	• "Pay yourself first" payroll reduction contributions. • Pretax contributions. • Tax-deferred interest and earnings.

Sources: Adapted from "12 Easy Retirement Planning Tips for Women," VALIC, An American General Company, April 1998, p. 20; and *BusinessWeek*, January 28, 2002, p. 111.

HOW TO...

Dodge IRA Pitfalls

For years, you've been stashing money in 401(k)s and individual retirement accounts. But soon after you turn 70½, the Internal Revenue Service requires you to start taking it out. The rules are complex, and penalties can be stiff. To help you avoid costly mistakes, here's some advice from IRA expert Ed Slott.

WHAT ARE SOME COMMON MISTAKES?

For most people, the date you're required to begin taking withdrawals is April 1 of the year following the year in which you turn 70½. So if you turn 70½ in 2013, the IRS gives you until April 1 of 2014 to start. But it's a mistake to wait, because you'll have to take two distributions in 2014—one covering your first year of required distributions and the other covering your second. It's better to take your first distribution in 2013. That way you separate the distributions into two tax years and generally lower your income—and your tax bill—in each year.

CAN YOU DELAY DISTRIBUTIONS IF YOU'RE STILL WORKING AT 70½?

You don't have to take distributions from your employer's 401(k) plan until you stop working. But when it comes to IRAs and 401(k)s from past employers, you can't escape.

IF YOU HAVE SEVERAL ACCOUNTS, DO YOU HAVE TO TAKE WITHDRAWALS FROM EACH?

If you have more than one IRA, add their balances. You can take a distribution from one account that covers all of them. Be careful not to mix 401(k)s and IRAs this way, though, since the rules require you to take money from each. Likewise, a married couple can't take money out of one spouse's account to cover the other spouse's distribution. And with more than one 401(k), you've got to take separate withdrawals from each.

ARE THERE ANY PROBLEMATIC INVESTMENTS?

Some people tie all their money up in certificates of deposit. As a result, they have to break into a CD early just to take their distribution and incur a penalty.

ANYTHING ELSE WE SHOULD KNOW?

You don't have to take distributions in cash. Say your required distribution is $10,000. If you own IBM stock in your IRA but want to hang onto it, you can transfer shares worth $10,000 to a taxable account and pay income tax on it. But when you sell the stock, remember that you already paid this tax, or you might accidentally pay the IRS twice.

Source: *BusinessWeek,* July 26, 2004, p. 84; updated May 4, 2013.

IRA Withdrawals When you retire, you will be able to withdraw your IRA in a lump sum, withdraw it in installments over your life expectancy, or place it in an annuity that guarantees payments over your lifetime. If you take the lump sum, the entire amount will be taxable as ordinary income and the only tax break you will have is standard five-year income averaging. IRA withdrawals made before age 59½ are subject to a 10 percent tax in addition to ordinary income tax, unless the participant dies or becomes disabled. You can avoid this tax if you roll over your IRA. Read the accompanying How to . . . feature to avoid pitfalls in taking IRA distributions.

You cannot keep money in most retirement plans indefinitely. Except for Roth IRAs, most tax-qualified retirement plans, including 403(b), 401(k), and other IRAs, are required by the IRS to begin what is known as "minimum lifetime distributions" at age 70½. If you have retired, you must either receive the entire balance of your tax-qualified plan or start receiving periodic distributions by April 1 of the year following the year in which you reach 70½ or retire, if later.

The amount of the minimum required distribution is based on your life expectancy at the time of the distribution. The IRS provides single- and joint-life expectancy tables for calculating required distribution amounts. The penalties for noncompliance in this case are severe. Insufficient distributions may be subject to an excise tax of 50 percent on the amount not withdrawn as required.

KEOGH PLANS The new tax package of 2001 did not forget the self-employed. A **Keogh plan,** named for U.S. Representative Engene James Keogh of New York also known as an HR10 or a *self-employed retirement plan,* is a qualified pension plan developed for self-employed people and their employees. Generally, Keogh plans cannot discriminate in favor of a self-employed person or any employee. Both defined-contribution and defined-benefit Keogh plans have tax-deductible contribution limits, and other restrictions also apply to Keogh plans. These plans are more complicated to set up and maintain, but offer more advantages than SEP–IRAs. Therefore, you should obtain professional tax advice before using this type of retirement plan. Whether you have an employer pension plan or a personal retirement plan, you must start withdrawing at age 70½ or the IRS will charge you a penalty.

Keogh plan A plan in which tax-deductible contributions fund the retirement of self-employed people and their employees; also called a *self-employed retirement plan.*

ANNUITIES

In Chapter 12, you learned what an annuity is and how annuities provide lifelong security. You can outlive the proceeds of your IRA, your Keogh plan, or your investments, but an **annuity** provides guaranteed income for life. Who should consider an annuity? One financial planner uses them for clients who have fully funded all other retirement plan options, including 401(k), 403(b), Keogh, and profit-sharing plans, but still want more money for retirement.

annuity A contract that provides an income for life.

You can buy an annuity with the proceeds of an IRA or a company pension, or as supplemental retirement income. You can buy an annuity with a single payment or with periodic payments. You can buy an annuity that will begin payouts immediately, or, as is more common, you can buy one that will begin payouts at a later date.

To the extent that annuity payments exceed your premiums, these payments are taxed as ordinary income as you receive them, but earned interest on annuities accumulates tax free until the payments begin. Annuities may be fixed, providing a specific income for life, or variable, with payouts above a guaranteed minimum level dependent on investment return. Either way, the rate of return on annuities is often pegged to market rates.

TYPES OF ANNUITIES *Immediate annuities* are generally purchased by people of retirement age. Such annuities provide income payments at once. They are usually purchased with a lump-sum payment.

With *deferred annuities,* income payments start at some future date. Interest builds up on the money you deposit. Younger people often use such annuities to save money toward retirement. If you are buying a deferred annuity, you may wish to obtain a contract that permits flexible premiums. With such an annuity, your contributions may vary from year to year.

A deferred annuity purchased with a lump sum is known as a *single-premium deferred annuity.* In recent years, such annuities have been popular because of the tax-free buildup during the accumulation period.

The cash value of your life insurance policy may be converted to an annuity. If you are over 65 and your children have completed their education and are financially self-sufficient, you may no longer need all of your life insurance coverage. An option in your life insurance policy lets you convert its cash value to a lifetime income.

OPTIONS IN ANNUITIES You can decide on the terms under which your annuity pays you and your family. Exhibit 18-13 summarizes the major options and their uses.

Exhibit 18-13 Annuity income options

This exhibit gives you an approximate idea of how different income options compare. The amount of income you actually receive is based on factors such as how you invest, your age, your sex, and the income option you choose. Market conditions at any given time, especially interest rates, influence income amounts.

Income Option	Description	Common Uses	Typical Monthly Income*
Lifetime income. Also called *life income* or *life only.*	You receive income payments for the rest of your life. The income ceases upon your death.	Provides the most income per dollar invested of any lifetime option. Frequently used by single people with limited sources of additional income.	$923.71 per month for life.
Lifetime income with a minimum number of payments guaranteed. Also called *life with period certain.*	You receive income for the rest of your life. If you die before you receive a specific number of payments, your beneficiary will receive the balance of the number of income payments you choose.	Appropriate if you want a life income but dislike the risk of lost income in the event of premature death. People with heirs often consider this option.	$791.49 per month for life, 240-month minimum.
Lifetime income for two people. Also called *joint* and *survivor.*	Income payments are received for as long as either of the two people are alive. Upon the death of either person, income continues as a percentage of the original amount. Common percentages chosen for the survivor are 50, 66⅔, and 100%.	Often chosen by couples, who may choose the 100% option when there is little other income, or 50% or 66⅔% when there is other income. Lifetime income with period certain and installment refund† options are also available for joint-income plans.	$774.06 per month for as long as at least one of the people is alive, assuming the 100% option.

Note: The numbers above are hypothetical, and your actual income may differ. Only a portion of each payment would be taxable.
*Assumes a 65-year-old male with a 65-year-old spouse who invests $100,000 and begins receiving income immediately.
†In an installment refund annuity, you receive an income for the rest of your life. However, if you die before receiving as much money as you paid in, your beneficiary receives regular income until the total payments equal that amount.

Source: *Building Your Future with Annuities: A Consumer Guide* (Fidelity Investments and U.S. Department of Agriculture, August 1991), p. 12.

WHICH ANNUITY OPTION IS THE BEST? The straight life annuity gives more income per dollar of outlay than any other type. But payments stop when you die, whether a month or many years after the payout begins.

Should you get an annuity with a guaranteed return? Opinions differ. Some experts argue that it is a mistake to diminish your monthly income just to make sure your money is returned to your survivors. Some suggest that if you want to ensure that your spouse or someone else continues to receive annuity income after your death, you might choose the joint-and-survivor annuity. Such an annuity pays its installments until the death of the last designated survivor.

You have still another choice to make: how your annuity premiums are to be invested. With a fixed-dollar annuity, the money you pay is invested in bonds and mortgages that

	Variable	Fixed
Tax-deferred earnings	Yes	Yes
Variety of income options	Yes	Yes
Annual investment ceiling	No	No
Investment flexibility	Yes	No
Potential for higher returns	Yes	No
Increased investment risk	Yes	No
Hedge against inflation	Yes	No
Security of principal and earnings	No	Yes
Guaranteed interest rate	No	Yes
Control over type of investment in the annuity	Yes	No

Exhibit 18-14

A comparison of variable and fixed annuities

The costs, fees, and other features of annuities differ from policy to policy.

have a guaranteed return. Such an annuity guarantees you a fixed amount each payout period. With a variable annuity, the money you pay is generally invested in common stocks or other equities. The income you receive will depend on the investment results. Exhibit 18-14 compares variable and fixed annuities.

An annuity guarantees lifetime income, but you have a choice regarding the form it will take. Discuss all of the possible options with your insurance agent. The costs, fees, and other features of annuities differ from policy to policy. Ask about sales and administrative charges, purchase and withdrawal fees, and interest rate guarantees. Also, as explained in Chapter 12, be sure to check the financial health of the insurance company.

WILL YOU HAVE ENOUGH MONEY DURING RETIREMENT?

Now that you have reviewed all the possible sources of your retirement income, estimate what your annual retirement income will be. Don't forget to inflate incomes or investments that increase with the cost of living (such as Social Security) to what they will be when you retire. (Use the inflation factor table in the Financial Planning Calculations box on page 628.) Remember, inflation is a major uncontrollable variable for retirees.

Now compare your total estimated retirement income with your total inflated retirement expenses. If your estimated income exceeds your estimated expenses and a large portion of your planned income will automatically increase with the cost of living during your retirement, you are in good shape. (You should evaluate your plans every few years between now and retirement to be sure your planned income is still adequate to meet your planned expenses.)

If, however, your planned retirement income is less than your estimated retirement expenses, now is the time to take action to increase your retirement income. Also, if a large portion of your retirement income is fixed and will not increase with inflation, you should make plans for a much larger retirement income to meet your rising expenses during retirement.

Exhibit 18-15 summarizes the government and private sources of retirement income.

Exhibit 18-15 Sources of retirement income

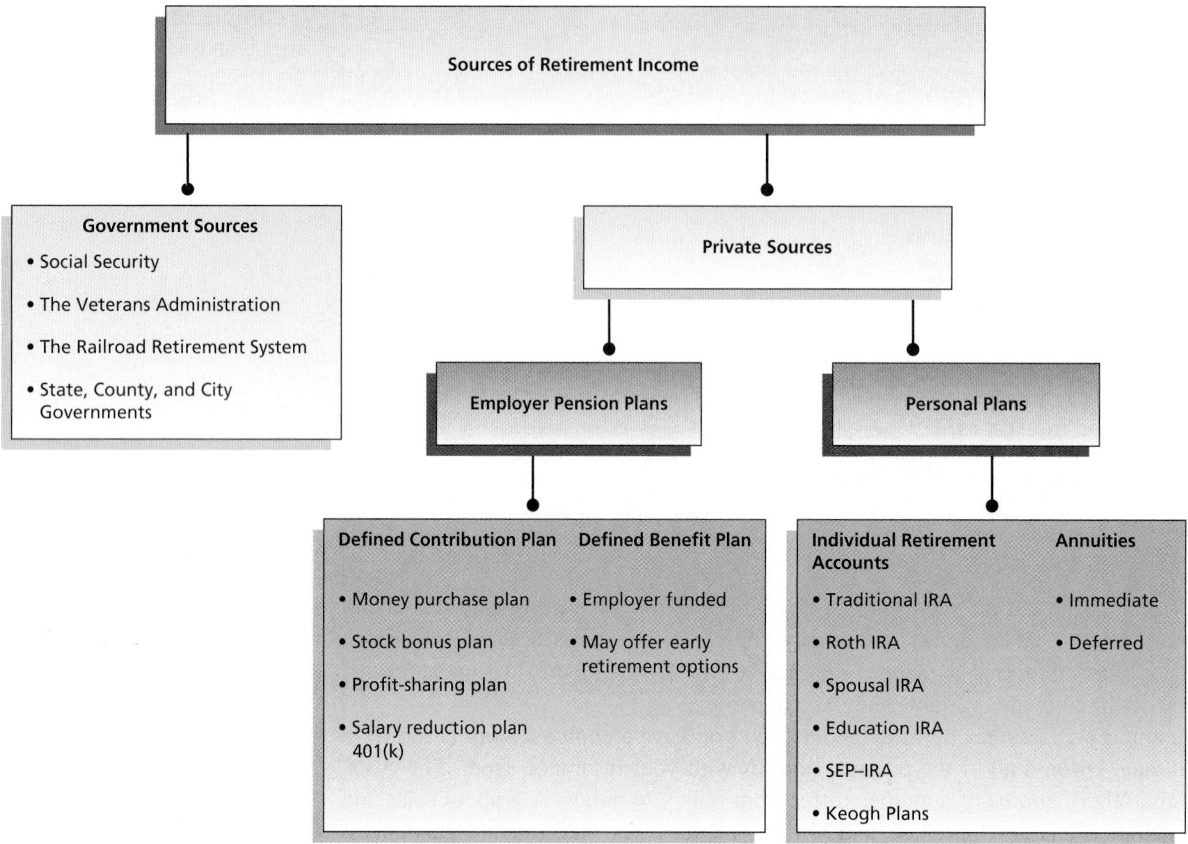

PFP Sheet 64

Retirement plan comparison

PFP Sheet 65

Forecasting retirement income

PRACTICE QUIZ 18-5

1 What are possible sources of income for retirees?
2 What are examples of defined-contribution plans? How do they differ from defined-benefit plans?
3 What are the two most popular personal retirement plans?
4 What are annuities? What options are available in annuities? Which option is best?

Living on Your Retirement Income

LO18-6

Develop a balanced budget based on your retirement income.

As you planned retirement, you estimated a budget or spending plan, but you may find your actual expenses at retirement are higher than anticipated.

The first step in stretching your retirement income is to make sure you are receiving all of the income to which you are entitled. Examine the possible sources of retirement income mentioned earlier to see whether you could qualify for more programs or additional benefits. What assets or valuables could you use as a cash or income source?

To stay within your income, you may also need to make some changes in your spending plans. For example, you can use your skills and time instead of your money. There are probably many things you can do yourself instead of paying someone else to do them. Take advantage of free and low-cost recreation such as walks, picnics, public parks, lectures, museums, libraries, art galleries, art fairs, gardening, and church and club programs.

TAX ADVANTAGES

Be sure to take advantage of all the tax savings retirees receive. For more information, ask your local IRS office for a free copy of *Tax Benefits for Older Americans.* If you have any questions about your taxes, get free help from someone at the IRS. You may need to file a quarterly estimated income tax return beginning with the first quarter of your first year of retirement or arrange for withholdings on Social Security and pension payments.

Pursuing a personal interest or hobby during retirement can keep your mind and body active and healthy.

WORKING DURING RETIREMENT

You may want to work part-time or start a new part-time career after you retire. Work can provide you with a greater sense of usefulness, involvement, and self-worth and may be the ideal way to add to your retirement income. You may want to pursue a personal interest or hobby, or you can contact your state or local agency on aging for information about employment opportunities for retirees.

If you decide to work part-time after you retire, you should be aware of how your earnings will affect your Social Security income. As long as you do not earn more than the annually exempt amount, your Social Security payments will not be affected. But if you earn more than the annual exempt amount, your Social Security payments will be reduced. Check with your local Social Security office for the latest information.

my life 6 

To supplement my retirement income, I may want to work part-time or start a new part-time career after I retire.

Retirees can use their skills and time instead of spending money. Some people decide to work part-time after they retire; some even take new part-time or new full-time jobs. Many people prefer to keep active and pursue new careers.

INVESTING FOR RETIREMENT

The guaranteed-income part of your retirement fund consists of money paid into lower-yield, very safe investments. This part of your fund may already be taken care of through Social Security and retirement plans, as discussed earlier. To offset inflation, your retirement assets must earn enough to keep up with, and even exceed, the rate of inflation.

DIPPING INTO YOUR NEST EGG

When should you draw on your savings? The answer depends on your financial circumstances, your age, and how much you want to leave to your heirs. Your savings may be large enough to allow you to live comfortably on the interest alone. Or you may need to make regular withdrawals to help finance your retirement. Dipping into savings isn't wrong, but you must do so with caution.

How long would your savings last if you withdrew monthly income? If you have $10,000 in savings that earns 5.5 percent interest, compounded quarterly, you could take out $68 every month for 20 years before reducing this nest egg to zero. If you have $40,000, you could collect $224 every month for 30 years before exhausting your nest egg. For different possibilities, see Exhibit 18-16 on page 649.

DID YOU KNOW?

More than half of Americans ages 65 to 74 are still in the workforce.

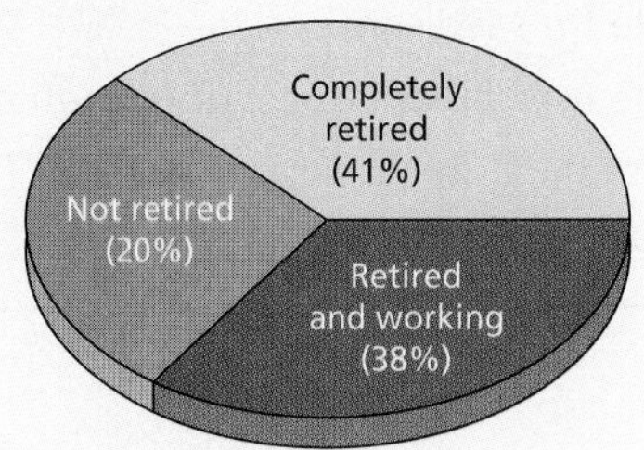

Note: The chart does not add up to 100% due to rounding.
Source: National Council on Aging, 2008.

RETIREMENT CHECKLIST

As you approach retirement, assess your financial condition using the following checklist. Don't wait too long, or you will miss one or more opportunities to maximize your future financial independence.

	Yes	No
1. Do you talk regularly and frankly to family members about finances and agree on your goals and the lifestyle you will prefer as you get older?	☐	☐
2. Do you know what your sources of income will be after retirement, how much to expect from each source, and when?	☐	☐
3. Do you save according to your plan, shifting from growth-producing to safe, income-producing investments?	☐	☐
4. Do you know where your health insurance will come from after retirement and what it will cover?	☐	☐
5. Do you review your health insurance and consider options such as converting to cash or investments?	☐	☐
6. Do you have your own credit history?	☐	☐
7. Do you have a current will or a living trust?	☐	☐
8. Do you know where you plan to live in retirement?	☐	☐
9. Do you anticipate the tax consequences of your retirement plans and of passing assets on to your heirs?	☐	☐
10. Do your children or other responsible family members know where your important documents are and whom to contact if questions arise?	☐	☐
11. Do you have legal documents, such as a living will or a power of attorney, specifying your instructions in the event of your death or incapacitating illness?	☐	☐

TIMELINE FOR RETIREMENT

At age 50 Begin making catch-up contributions, an extra amount that those over 50 can add, to 401(k) and other retirement accounts.

At 59½ No more tax penalties on early withdrawals from retirement accounts, but leaving money in means more time for it to grow.

At 62 The minimum age to receive Social Security benefits, but delaying means a bigger monthly benefit.

At 65 Eligible for Medicare.

At 66 Eligible for full Social Security benefits if born between 1943 and 1954.

At 70½ Start taking minimum withdrawals from most retirement accounts by this age; otherwise, you may be charged heavy tax penalties in the future.

Exhibit 18-17 on page 650, summarizes major sources of retirement income and their advantages and disadvantages. Finally, use Financial Planning for Life's Situations: Retirement Checklist (above) to assess your financial condition as you approach retirement.

Exhibit 18-16 Dipping into your nest egg

Dipping into savings isn't wrong; however, you must do so with caution.

Starting Amount of Nest Egg	You Can Reduce Your Nest Egg to Zero by Withdrawing This Much Each Month for the Stated Number of Years . . .					Or You Can Withdraw This Much Each Month and Leave Your Nest Egg Intact
	10 Years	15 Years	20 Years	25 Years	30 Years	
$ 10,000	$ 107	$ 81	$ 68	$ 61	$ 56	$ 46
15,000	161	121	102	91	84	69
20,000	215	162	136	121	112	92
25,000	269	202	170	152	140	115
30,000	322	243	204	182	168	138
40,000	430	323	272	243	224	184
50,000	537	404	340	304	281	230
60,000	645	485	408	364	337	276
80,000	859	647	544	486	449	368
100,000	1,074	808	680	607	561	460

Note: Based on an interest rate of 5.5 percent per year, compounded quarterly.
Source: Select Committee on Aging, U.S. House of Representatives.

1 What is the first step in stretching your retirement income?
2 How should you invest to obtain retirement income?

Exhibit 18-17 Major sources of retirement income: advantages and disadvantages

The income needed to live during retirement can come from various sources.

Source	Advantages	Disadvantages
Social Security		
In planning	Forced savings. Portable from job to job. Cost shared with employer.	Increasing economic pressure on the system as U.S. population ages.
At retirement	Inflation-adjusted survivorship rights.	Minimum retirement age specified.
		Earned income may partially offset benefits.
Employee Pension Plans		
In planning	Forced savings.	May not be portable.
	Cost shared or fully covered by employer.	No control over how funds are managed.
At retirement	Survivorship rights.	Cost-of-living increases may not be provided on a regular basis.
Individual Saving and Investing (including housing, IRA, and Keogh plans)		
In planning	Current tax savings (e.g., IRAs).	Current needs compete with future needs.
	Easily incorporated into family (home equity).	Penalty for early withdrawal (IRAs and Keoghs).
	Portable.	
	Control over management of funds.	
At retirement	Inflation resistant.	Some sources taxable.
	Can usually use as much of the funds as you wish, when you wish (within certain requirements).	Mandatory minimum withdrawal restrictions (IRAs and Keoghs).
Postretirement Employment		
In planning	Special earning skills can be used as they are developed.	Technology and skills needed to keep up may change rapidly.
At retirement	Inflation resistant.	Ill health can mean loss of this income source.

my life stages for retirement planning . . .

YOUR PERSONAL FINANCE DASHBOARD

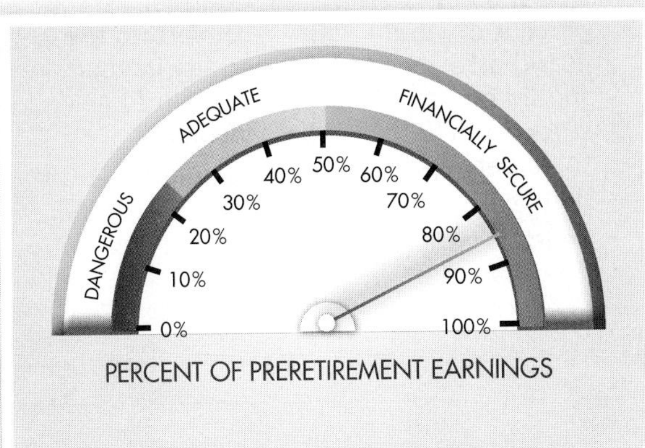

PERCENT OF PRERETIREMENT EARNINGS

A dashboard is a tool used by organizations to monitor key performance indicators, such as delivery time, product defects, or customer complaints. As an individual, you can use a personal finance dashboard to assess your own financial situation.

You have several retirement savings opportunities available to you—from IRAs and SEPs to 401(k)s and 403(b)s. These options are especially important now that traditional pensions and other employer-funded retirement plans have become increasingly rare.

YOUR SITUATION: Have you figured out how much money you should save for retirement? Most financial advisers suggest that you will need 70 to 90 percent of preretirement earnings to live comfortably. Are you taking advantage of retirement savings programs at work, especially those where your employer matches contributions? Have you made sure that your investments are diversified? Other personal financial planning actions you might consider during various stages of your life include:

. . . in college

- Stop procrastinating and start planning for retirement now
- Starting savings small is better than not starting at all
- Work part-time and start your Roth IRA account
- If you begin saving later, you'll have to save and invest more each month
- You can typically afford to take a little more risk with your investments

. . . in my 20s

- If you are putting off retirement planning because you don't know how, speak to a professional who does
- Take full responsibility of your financial future
- Put together a retirement plan and save more
- Try to put aside 10 percent of your income for retirement (If your employer matches three percent, then you should be saving seven percent, for a total of 10 percent

. . . in my 30s and 40s

- You've been diligent about contributing to a savings account, but is it enough?
- Are you sure your money is invested properly? Are there better options for you?
- Make your retirement a priority and determine how much you'll need during retirement
- Try to put aside 15 to 20 percent of your income for retirement

. . . in my 50s and beyond

- If you are already near or past your retirement date, it is still not too late
- Consider how you are receiving your income and how long it will last
- Revise your income distribution strategy
- Consider the impact of inflation, taxes and long-term care expense
- Try to extend your working years and work at least part-time during retirement

(continued)

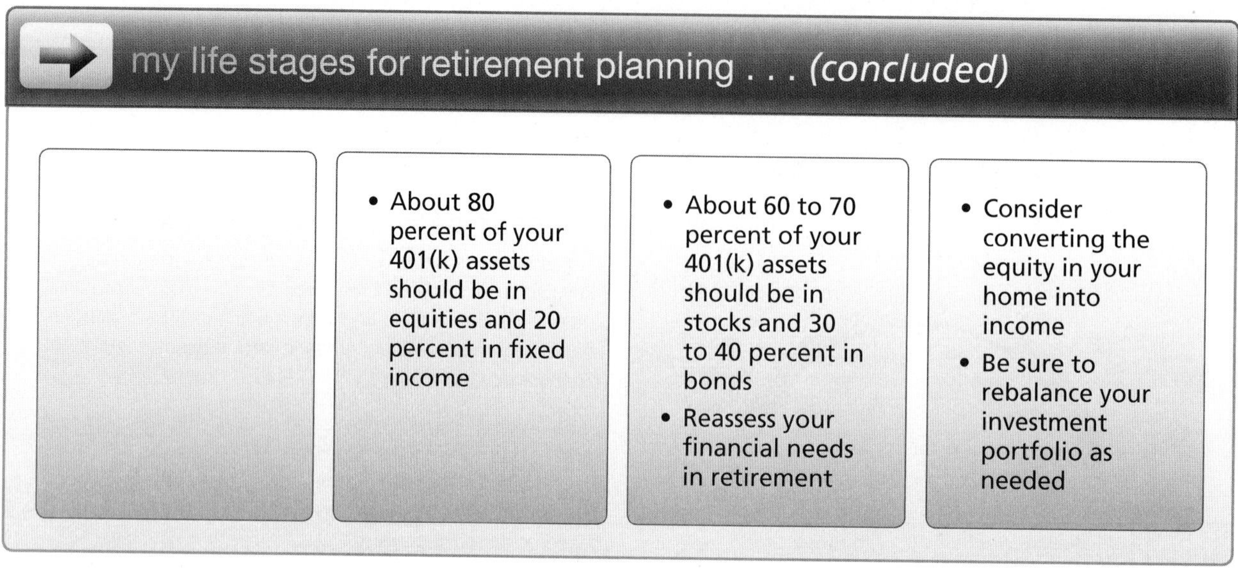

SUMMARY OF LEARNING OBJECTIVES

LO18-1

Recognize the importance of retirement planning.

Retirement planning is important because you will probably spend many years in retirement, Social Security and a private pension may be insufficient to cover the cost of living, and inflation may erode the purchasing power of your retirement savings. Many young people are reluctant to think about retirement, but they should start retirement planning now, before they reach age 45.

LO18-2

Analyze your current assets and liabilities for retirement.

Analyze your current assets (everything you own) and your current liabilities (everything you owe). The difference between your assets and your liabilities is your net worth. Review your assets to ensure they are sufficient for retirement.

LO18-3

Estimate your retirement spending needs.

Since the spending patterns of retirees change, it is impossible to predict the exact amount of money you will need in retirement. However, you can estimate your expenses. Some of those expenses will increase; others will decrease. The expenses that are likely to be lower or eliminated are work-related expenses, clothing, housing expenses, federal income taxes, and commuting expenses.

LO18-4

Identify your retirement housing needs.

Where you live in retirement can influence your financial needs. You are the only one who can determine the location and housing that are best for you. Would you like to live in your present home or move to a new location? Consider the social aspects of moving.

LO18-5

Determine your planned retirement income.

Estimate your retirement expenses and adjust those expenses for inflation using the appropriate inflation factor. Your possible sources of income during retirement include Social Security, other public pension plans, employer pension plans, personal retirement plans, and annuities.

LO18-6

Develop a balanced budget based on your retirement income.

Compare your total estimated retirement income with your total inflated retirement expenses. If your income approximates your expenses, you are in good shape; if not, determine additional income needs and sources.

KEY TERMS

annuity 643
defined-benefit plan 636
defined-contribution plan 635
401(k) (TSA) plan 635
individual retirement account (IRA) 638
Keogh plan 643
reverse annuity mortgage (RAM) 623
vesting 636

SELF-TEST PROBLEMS

1. Beverly Foster is planning for her retirement. She has determined that her car is worth $10,000, her home is worth $150,000, her personal belongings are worth $100,000, and her stocks and bonds are worth $300,000. She owes $50,000 on her home and $5,000 on her car. Calculate her net worth.
2. Calculate how much money an average older (65+) household with an annual income of $39,173 spends on food each year. (*Hint:* Use Exhibit 18-4)
3. You have $100,000 in your retirement fund that is earning 5.5 percent per year, compounding quarterly. How many dollars in withdrawals per month would keep your nest egg intact forever? (*Hint:* Use Exhibit 18-16)

Solutions

1.

Assets				*Liabilities*	
Car	$ 10,000			Mortgage	$50,000
Home	$150,000			Car	$ 5,000
Personal belongings	$100,000			Total Liabilities	$55,000
Stocks and bonds	$300,000				
Total assets	$560,000				
Net worth	=	Assets	−	Liabilities	
	=	$560,000	−	$55,000 =	$505,000

2. Average older household with an annual income of $39,173 spends about 13.9 percent of their income on food. Thus $39,173 × 13.9 percent = $5,445.
3. Referring to Exhibit 18-16, students will find that at a withdrawal rate of $460 a month, the nest egg of $100,000 would stay intact forever.

FINANCIAL PLANNING PROBLEMS

1. *Calculating Net Worth.* Shelly's assets include money in checking and savings accounts, investments in stocks and mutual funds, and personal property, including furniture, appliances, an automobile, a coin collection, and jewelry. Shelly calculates that her total assets are $108,800. Her current unpaid bills, including an auto loan, credit card balances, and taxes total $16,300. Calculate Shelly's net worth. LO18-2
2. *Preparing a Net Worth Statement.* Prepare your net worth statement using the guidelines presented in Exhibit 18-3. LO18-2
3. *Calculating Living Expenses.* Calculate how much money an older household with an annual income of $40,000 spends on transportation each year. (*Hint:* Use Exhibit 18-4.) LO18-3

LO18-3 **4.** *Calculating Living Expenses.* Using Exhibit 18-4, calculate how much money the household from Problem 3 spends on housing.

LO18-5 **5.** *Calculating an IRA Accumulation.* When Jamal graduated from college recently, his parents gave him $1,000 and told him to use it wisely. Jamal decided to use the money to start a retirement account. After doing some research about different options, he put the entire amount into a tax-deferred IRA that pays 11 percent interest, compounded annually. Calculate how much money Jamal will have in his IRA at the end of 10 years, assuming that the interest rate remains the same and that he does not deposit any additional money. Show your calculations in the form of a chart.

LO18-5 **6.** *Calculating an IRA Accumulation.* Janine is 25 and has a good job at a biotechnology company. She currently has $5,000 in an IRA, an important part of her retirement nest egg. She believes her IRA will grow at an annual rate of 8 percent, and she plans to leave it untouched until she retires at age 65. Janine estimates that she will need $875,000 in her *total* retirement nest egg by the time she is 65 in order to have retirement income of $20,000 a year (she expects that Social Security will pay her an additional $15,000 a year). How much will Janine's IRA be worth when she needs to start withdrawing money from it when she retires? (*Hint:* Use Exhibit A–1 in the appendix to Chapter 1.)

LO18-5 **7.** *Calculating an IRA Accumulation.* In the above problem, how much money will Janine have to accumulate in her company's 401(k) plan over the next 40 years in order to reach her retirement income goal?

LO18-5 **8.** *Calculating Retirement Amount.* Calculate how much you would have in 10 years if you saved $2,000 a year at an annual rate of 10 percent with the company contributing $500 a year.

LO18-5 **9.** *Calculating an IRA Contribution.* Gene and Dixie, husband and wife (ages 35 and 32), both work. They have an adjusted gross income of $50,000, and they are filing a joint income tax return. What is the maximum IRA contribution they can make? How much of that contribution is tax deductible?

LO18-5 **10.** *Calculating Net Pay and Spendable Income.* Assume your gross pay per pay period is $2,000 and you are in the 33 percent tax bracket. Calculate your net pay and spendable income if you save $200 per pay period after paying income tax on $2,000.

LO18-5 **11.** *Calculating Net Pay and Spendable Income.* In the above example, calculate your net pay and spendable income if you save $200 per pay period in a tax-sheltered annuity.

LO18-6 **12.** *Dipping into Your Nest Egg.* You have $50,000 in your retirement fund that is earning 5.5 percent per year, compounded quarterly. How many dollars in withdrawals per month would reduce this nest egg to zero in 20 years?

LO18-6 **13.** *Dipping into Your Nest Egg.* In the above example, how many dollars per month can you withdraw for as long as you live and still leave this nest egg intact?

FINANCIAL PLANNING ACTIVITIES

LO18-1 1. *Conducting Interviews.* Survey friends, relatives, and other people to get their views on retirement planning. Prepare a written report of your findings.

LO18-2 2. *Obtaining Information about Reverse Mortgages.* Obtain a consumer information kit from Senior Income Reverse Mortgage Corporation in Chicago (1-800-774-6266). Examine and evaluate the kit. How might a reverse mortgage help you or a family member?

LO18-1 3. *Using the Internet to Obtain Reverse Mortgage Information.*

a. Visit the website of the American Association of Retired Persons (AARP) at www.aarp.org. Locate the AARP Home Equity Information Center, which presents basic facts about reverse mortgages. Then prepare a report on how reverse mortgages work, who is eligible, what you get, what you pay, and what other choices are available to borrowers.

b. Visit Fannie Mae's website at www.fanniemae.com/Homebuyer to find out about its reverse mortgage program.

LO18-3 4. *Determining Expenses during Retirement.* Read newspaper or magazine articles to determine what expenses are likely to increase and decrease during retirement. How might this information affect your retirement-planning decisions?

LO18-4 5. *Evaluating Retirement Housing Options.* Which type of housing will best meet your retirement needs? Is such housing available in your community? Make a checklist of the advantages and disadvantages of your housing choice.

6. *Writing Letters to Representatives in Congress.* Write a letter urging your Representative in Congress to introduce or support legislation repealing the provisions of the present Social Security law that limit the earnings of Americans ages 65 to 69 who must work to provide for their needs. LO18-5

7. *Requesting Personal Earnings and Benefits Statement.* Obtain Form SSA-7004 from your local Social Security office. Complete and mail the form to receive a personal earnings and benefits statement. Use the information in this statement to plan your retirement. LO18-5

FINANCIAL PLANNING CASE

Planning for Retirement

Is a bad day fishing better than a good day at the office? Yes, according to a retired dad, Chuck. With his company pension, at least he didn't have to worry about money. In the good old days, if you had a decent job, you'd hang on to it, and then your company's pension combined with Social Security payments would be enough to live comfortably. Chuck's son, Rob, does not have a company pension and is not sure whether Social Security will even exist when he retires. So when it comes to retirement, the sooner you start saving, the better.

Take Maureen, a salesperson for a computer company, and Therese, an accountant for a lighting manufacturer. Both start their jobs at age 25. Maureen starts saving for retirement right away by investing $300 a month at 9 percent until age 65. But Therese does nothing until age 35. At 35 she begins investing the same $300 a month at 9 percent until age 65. What a shocking difference! Maureen has accumulated $1.4 million, while Therese has only $553,000 in her retirement fund. The moral? The sooner you start, the more you'll have for your retirement. Women especially need to start sooner, because they typically enter the workforce later, have lower salaries, and, ultimately, lower pensions.

Laura Tarbox, owner and president of Tarbox Equity, explains how to determine your retirement needs and how your budget might change when you retire. Tarbox advises that the old rule of thumb that you need 60 to 70 percent of preretirement income is too low an estimate. She cautions that most people will want to spend very close to what they were spending before retiring. There are some expenses that might be lower, however, such as clothing for work, dry cleaning, commuting expenses, and so forth. Other expenses, though, such as insurance, travel, and recreation, may increase during retirement.

Questions

1. In the past, many workers chose to stay with their employers until retirement. What was the major reason for employees' loyalty?
2. How did Maureen amass $1.4 million for retirement, while Therese could only accumulate $553,000?
3. Why do women need to start early to save for retirement?
4. How is net worth determined?
5. What expenses may increase or decrease during retirement?

PERSONAL FINANCIAL PLANNER IN ACTION

Planning for Retirement

Long-term financial security is a common goal of most people. Retirement planning should consider both personal decisions (location, housing, activities) and financial factors (investments, pensions, living expenses).

Your Short-Term Financial Planning Activities	*Resources*
1. Identify personal and financial retirement needs for various stages of your life.	http://retireplan.about.com www.aarp.org www.mymoney.gov www.ssa.gov
2. Compare the benefits and costs of a traditional IRA, a Roth IRA, and other pension plans.	PFP Sheet 64 www.rothira.com www.pensionplanners.com www.401k.com www.403bwise.com

Your Short-Term Financial Planning Activities	*Resources*
1. Research costs and benefits of various housing alternatives.	PFP Sheet 63 www.virtual-retirement.com
2. Estimate future retirement income needs and identify appropriate investments to meet those needs.	PFP Sheet 65 www.kiplinger.com/tools www.centura.com/tools
3. Develop a plan for expanding personal interests and increasing contributions to retirement accounts.	www.asec.org

CONTINUING CASE

Retirement Planning

Life Situation	*Financial Data*	
Shelby, age 45	Monthly Gross Income	$8,000
Mark, age 46	Living Expenses	$6,500
Two children, ages 19 and 13	Assets	$230,000
	Liabilities	$85,000

Shelby and Mark Lawrence are less than 20 years away from retirement. They have one child in college and one in high school. Their primary goals are to help their children with their college expenses and plan for their retirement.

Currently, the balance in Mark's pension plan at work is $102,000. This balance is smaller than he would have liked due to fluctuations in the stock market. In addition, the investment plan that he and Shelby started many years ago is now worth $35,000 (includes mostly bond investments and mutual funds). Last year, they had considered an investment in a limited real estate partnership but decided the timing was not right since Blair had begun college. At this point, Shelby and Mark want to evaluate their retirement plans and determine whether they will have enough to fund their retirement.

Questions

1. How would you assess the strengths and weaknesses of the Lawrence's financial condition at this stage in their lives?
2. At their current ages, what should their major priorities be as they continue to plan for retirement?
3. Explain how Shelby and Mark might use the Personal Financial Planner sheets on Retirement Housing and Lifestyle Planning & Forecasting Retirement Income.

"Keeping track of my daily spending gets me to start thinking about saving and investing for retirement."

Directions

The consistent use of a "Daily Spending Diary" can provide you with ongoing information that will help you manage your spending, saving, and investing activities. Taking time to reconsider your spending habits can result in achieving better satisfaction from your available finances.

Analysis Questions

1. What portion of your net income is set aside for saving or investing for long-term financial security?
2. What types of retirement planning activities might you start to consider at this point of your life?

The Daily Spending Diary sheets are located in Appendix D at the end of the book and on the student website at www.mhhe.com/kdh.

chapter 19

Estate Planning

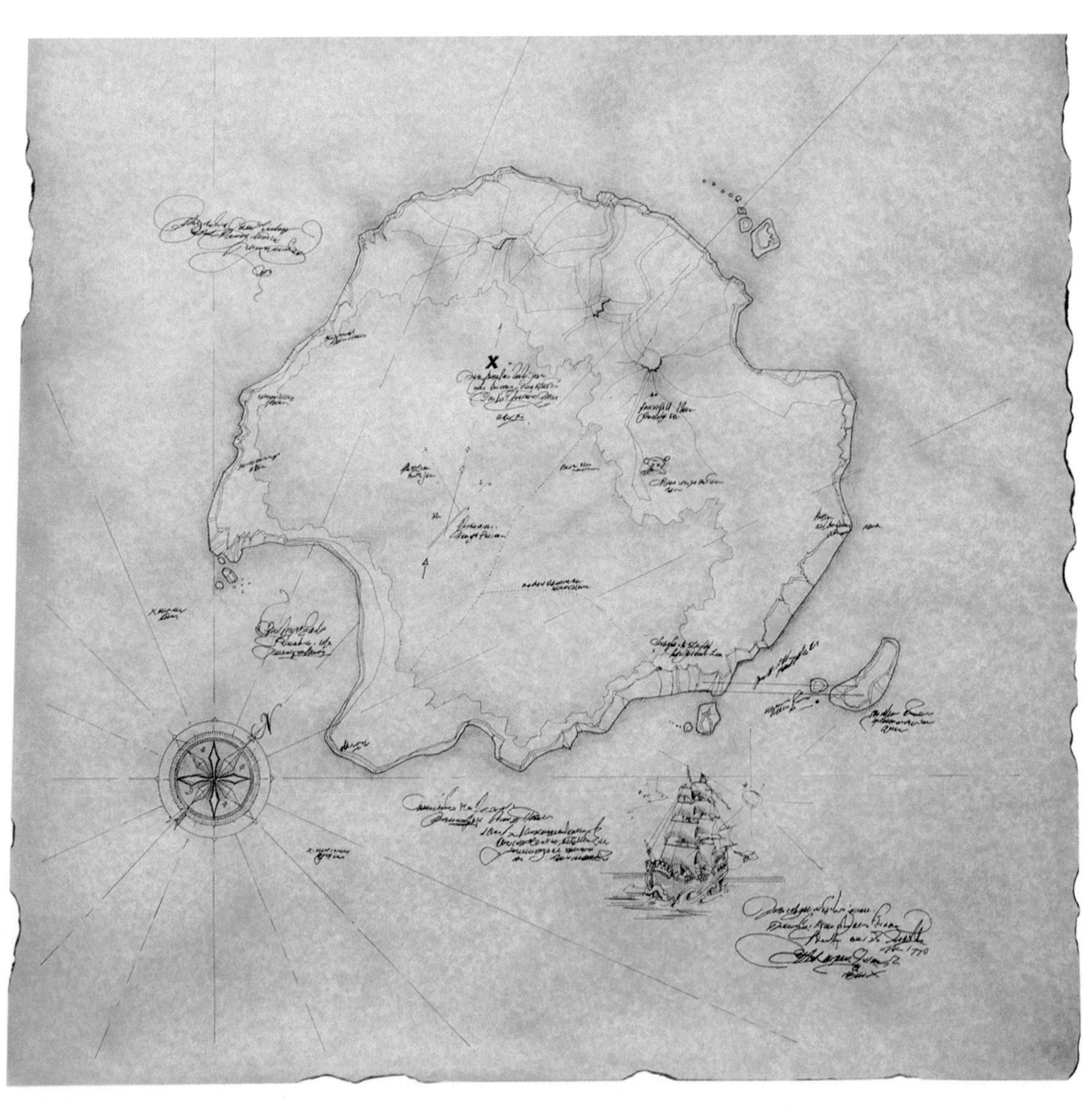

Learning Objectives

LO19-1 Analyze the personal aspects of estate planning.

LO19-2 Assess the legal aspects of estate planning.

LO19-3 Distinguish among various types and formats of wills.

LO19-4 Appraise various types of trusts and estates.

LO19-5 Evaluate the effects of federal and state taxes on estate planning.

What will this mean for me?

Identifying various kinds of wills and trusts will help you devise an estate plan that protects your interests as well as those of your family. Creating an effective estate plan will allow you to prosper during retirement and provide for your loved ones when you die.

my life

WHERE THERE IS A WILL!

Do you think of estates belonging only to the rich or elderly? The fact is, however, everyone has an estate. During your working years, your financial goal is to build your estate by acquiring and accumulating money for your current and future needs. However, as you grow older, your point of view will change. Instead of working to acquire assets, you will start to think about what will happen to your hard-earned wealth after you die.

What are your current attitudes toward estate planning? For each of the following statements, select "agree," "neutral," or "disagree" to indicate your personal response regarding these estate planning situations.

1. I believe estate planning is only for the rich and famous.	Agree	Neutral	Disagree
2. If I die intestate (without a valid will), my legal state of residence will control the distribution of my estate.	Agree	Neutral	Disagree
3. In addition to my will, I should prepare a letter of last instruction.	Agree	Neutral	Disagree
4. If I establish a trust, it will avoid probate and transfer my assets immediately to my beneficiaries.	Agree	Neutral	Disagree
5. I can reduce my taxable estate by giving away assets to ***anyone*** during my lifetime.	Agree	Neutral	Disagree

As you study this chapter, you will encounter "My Life" boxes with additional information and resources related to these items.

Why Estate Planning?

LO19-1

Analyze the personal aspects of estate planning.

Your **estate** consists of everything you own including bank accounts, stocks, bonds, real estate, and personal property. While you work, your objective is to accumulate funds for your future and for your dependents. As you grow older, your point of view will change. The emphasis in your financial planning will shift from accumulating assets to distributing them wisely. Your hard-earned wealth should go to those whom you wish to support and not to the various taxing agencies.

Contrary to widely held notions, estate planning, which includes wills and trusts, is useful not only to rich and elderly people. Trusts can be used for purposes other than tax advantages, such as choosing a guardian for children and avoiding family fights over personal belongings. Furthermore, most people can afford the expense of using them.

my life 1

I believe estate planning is only for the rich and famous.

Contrary to popular belief, estate planning is useful not only to the rich, famous, and elderly. Because everyone has an estate (owns something), estate planning is important. The National Association of Financial and Estate Planning website at www.nafep.com includes free, useful information to help you with estate planning.

This chapter discusses a subject most people would rather avoid: death—your own or that of your spouse. Many people give little or no thought to setting their personal and financial affairs in order.

As you learned in the previous chapter, most people today live longer than those of previous generations and have ample time to think about and plan for the future. Yet a large percentage of people do little or nothing to provide for those who will survive them.

estate Everything one owns.

Planning for your family's financial security in the event of your death or the death of your spouse is not easy. Therefore, the objective of this chapter is to help you initiate discussions about questions you should ask before that happens. Does your spouse, for instance, know what all of the family's resources and debts are? Does your family have enough insurance protection?

The question of whether your family can cope financially without your or your spouse's income and support is a difficult one. This chapter can't provide all of the answers, but it supplies a basis for sound estate planning for you and your family.

WHAT IS ESTATE PLANNING?

estate planning A definite plan for the administration and disposition of one's property during one's lifetime and at one's death.

Estate planning is a definite plan for the administration and disposition of one's property during one's lifetime and at one's death. Thus, it involves both handling your property while you are alive and dealing with what happens to that property after your death.

Estate planning is an essential part of retirement planning and an integral part of financial planning. It has two components. The first consists of building your estate through savings, investments, and insurance. The second involves transferring your estate, at your death, in the manner you have specified. As this chapter explains, an estate plan is usually implemented by a will and one or more trust agreements.

Nearly every adult engages in financial decision making and must keep important records. Whatever your status—single or married, male or female, taxi driver or corporate executive—you must make financial decisions that are important to you. Those decisions may be even more important to others in your family. Knowledge in certain areas and good recordkeeping can simplify those decisions.

At first, planning for financial security and estate planning may seem complicated. Although many money matters require legal and technical advice, if you and your spouse learn the necessary skills, you will find yourselves managing your money affairs more efficiently and wisely. Begin by answering the questionnaire in Financial Planning for Life's Situations: Estate Planning Checklist to see how much you and your family know about your own money affairs. You and your family should be able to answer some of these questions. The questions can be bewildering

ESTATE PLANNING CHECKLIST

Do you and your family members know the answers to the following questions?

1. Where are your previous years' income tax returns?
2. Where is your safe-deposit box located? Where is the key to it kept?
3. What kinds and amounts of life insurance protection do you have?
4. Can you locate your insurance policies—life, health, property, casualty, and auto?
5. Who are the beneficiaries and contingent beneficiaries of your life insurance policies?
6. What type of health insurance protection do you have, and what are the provisions of your health insurance policy?
7. Do you and your spouse have current wills? Who was the attorney who drafted them? Where are they kept?
8. Do you have a separate record of the important papers you keep in your safe-deposit box? Where is this record located?
9. Do you have a record of your spouse's and children's Social Security numbers?
10. Where is your marriage certificate and the birth certificates of all members of your family?
11. Do you know the name and address of your life insurance agent?
12. Do you know the principal financial resources and liabilities of your estate?
13. Are you knowledgeable about simple, daily, and compound interest rates? About retirement funds and property ownership?
14. Have you given any thought to funerals and burial arrangements?
15. What papers and records will be important to other people when you die?
16. Do you understand the functions of a bank trust department and the meaning of joint ownership?

Source: *Planning with Your Beneficiaries* (Washington, DC: American Council of Life Insurance, Education, and Community Services, n.d.), p. 2.

if the subjects are unfamiliar to you, but after reading this chapter, you'll be able to answer most of them.

IF YOU ARE MARRIED

If you are married, your estate planning involves the interests of at least two people, and more if you have children. Legal requirements and responsibilities can create problems for married people that are entirely different from those of single people. Situations become more complex. Possessions accumulate. The need for orderliness and clarity increases.

Your death will mean a new lifestyle for your spouse. If you have no children or if the children are grown and lead separate lives, your spouse will once again be single. The surviving spouse must confront problems of grief and adjustment. Daily life must continue. At the same time, the estate must be settled. If not, catastrophic financial consequences may result.

If children survive you, making sure that your estate can be readily analyzed and distributed may be even more critical. If relatives or friends are beneficiaries, bequests have to be made known quickly and clearly.

Your desires and information about your estate have to be accessible, understandable, and legally documented. Otherwise, your beneficiaries may encounter problems and your intentions may not be carried out.

Most people have various assets and many possessions that make up their estate.

IF YOU NEVER MARRIED

Never having been married does not eliminate the need to organize your financial affairs. For people who live alone, as for married people, it is essential that important documents and personal information be consolidated and accessible.

Remember that in the event of your death, difficult questions and situations will confront some person at a time of severe emotional strain. That person may not be prepared to face them objectively. Probably the single most important thing you can do is take steps to see that your beneficiaries have the information and the knowledge they need to survive emotionally and financially when you die.

Everyone should take such steps. However, the need to take them is especially great if you are only 5 or 10 years away from retirement. By then, your possessions will probably be of considerable value. Your savings and checking account balances will probably be substantial. Your investment plans will have materialized. If you stop and take a look at where you are, you may be pleasantly surprised at the value of your estate.

NEW LIFESTYLES

Millions of nontraditional households have unique estate planning problems. Nearly half of all American marriages end in divorce, creating difficulties for millions of adults contemplating estate planning. Single parents and other single persons all have formidable estate planning challenges. Financial planners and estate attorneys universally offer such households the following smart advice: Plan early, and get expert help. The law provides plenty of protection for married couples, but it is rife with pitfalls for almost everyone else.

Single parents, divorced or not, must plan for their own death as part of retirement and estate planning. David Scott Sloan, chairman of trusts and estates at Sherburne, Powers & Needham, a law firm in Boston, says that simply leaving money to your children can result in a huge estate tax bill, sharply decreasing the funds available if your estate is worth more than $5.25 million in 2013. Sloan recommends setting up a trust for the children's benefit.

Unmarried couples face formidable retirement and estate planning challenges. A partner lacks any legal right to the companion's assets upon the companion's disability or death or upon the breakup of the partnership. Unmarried couples also cannot use the so-called marital deduction, which allows spouses to pass on everything they own to their surviving spouse tax free. Estate planning is even more important for unmarried couples. For example, if no beneficiary is named on your pension plan, the plan sponsor is required to give the proceeds to your closest blood relative. If you want your partner to receive the plan proceeds after you die, make sure he or she is named the beneficiary. Also, check to see whether the plan allows unmarried partners to receive joint-and-survivor benefits.

THE OPPORTUNITY COST OF RATIONALIZING

Daily living often gets in the way of thinking about death. You mean to organize things that others need to know in case you die, but you haven't done this yet. One of your rationalizations may be that you are not sure what information you need to provide.

Think about the outcome of your delay. Your beneficiary will meet people who offer specific types of assistance—morticians, clergy, lawyers, insurance agents, clerks of federal government agencies, and so on. These people will probably be strangers—sympathetic, courteous, and helpful, but disinterested. Also, your bereaved beneficiary may find it difficult to reveal confidences to them. Today, however, the information survivors need is as close as the telephone. Call LIMRA

International, a financial services research organization, at 1-800-235-4672 to order their booklet, *What Do You Do Now?*

The moral is to plan your estate while you are in good health and think through the provisions carefully. Last-minute "death-bed" estate planning may fail to carry out your wishes.

1 If you needed information about estate planning, would you go to the library or the Internet? Why?
2 Why is estate planning an important component of financial planning?
3 Why is estate planning important for single as well as married individuals? For "new" lifestyle individuals?

eXcel PFP Sheet 66
Estate planning activities

Legal Aspects of Estate Planning

LO19-2
Assess the legal aspects of estate planning.

When death occurs, proof of claims must be produced or the claims will not be processed. If no thought was given to gathering the necessary documents beforehand (with a sufficient number of copies), a period of financial hardship may follow until proof is obtained. If needed documentation cannot be located, irretrievable loss of funds may occur. Your heirs may experience emotionally painful delays until their rights have been established.

Important papers include the following:

1. Birth certificates—yours, your spouse's, and your children's.
2. Marriage certificates—always important, but especially important if you or your spouse were married previously—and divorce papers.
3. Legal name changes—judgment of court documents pertaining to any legal changes in the names that appear on birth certificates (especially important to protect the adopted children of a previous marriage or children who have been adopted through adoption agencies).
4. Military service records—the standard DD–214 (Armed Forces of the United States Report of Transfer or Discharge) or any other official statement of your military service details, if appropriate.

If I die intestate (without a valid will), my legal state of residence will control the distribution of my estate.

A will is the most practical first step in estate planning; it makes clear how you want your property to be distributed after you die. If you die intestate, your estate could be distributed differently than what you would like.

Here is a list of additional important documents:

- Social Security documents.
- Veteran documents.
- Insurance policies.
- Transfer records of joint bank accounts.
- Safe-deposit box records.
- Registration of automobiles.
- Title to stock and bond certificates.

Preparing a will can make things easier for your family after your death and ensure that your estate is distributed according to your wishes.

You should have several copies of certain documents because when you submit a claim, the accompanying proof often becomes a permanent part of the claim file and is not returned. Remember too that in some circumstances, children may be required to furnish proof of their parents' birth, marriage, or divorce.

WILLS

One of the most vital documents every adult should have is a written will. A **will** is the legal declaration of a person's mind as to the disposition of his or her property after death. Thus, a will is a way to transfer your property according to your wishes after you die. Although wills are simple to create, about half of all Americans die without one.

Whether you prepare a will before you die or neglect to take that sensible step, you still have a will. If you fail to prepare your own will, the state in which you legally reside steps in and controls the distribution of your estate without regard for wishes you may have had but failed to define in legal form. Thus, if you die **intestate**—without a valid will—the state's law of descent and distribution becomes your copy of the will, as shown in Exhibit 19-1.

Consider the opportunity cost of a husband and father who died without a will. By default, he has authorized his estate to be disposed of according to the provisions of the fictitious document in Exhibit 19-1. The wording in this exhibit represents a pattern of distribution that could occur unless you prepare a valid will specifying otherwise.

This does not happen only to a husband. It could happen to anyone. To avoid such consequences, make a will! Consulting an attorney for this purpose can spare your heirs many difficulties, especially since the passage of the Economic Recovery Tax Act of 1981. This act created estate planning opportunities and problems for many people. It also created some difficult choices as to types of wills.

DID YOU KNOW?

RULES TO REMEMBER WHEN WRITING A WILL

In most states, you must be 18 years of age or older.

- A will must be written in sound judgment and mental capacity to be valid.
- The document must clearly state that it is your will.
- The will must name an executor, who ensures your estate is distributed according to your wishes.
- It is not necessary to notarize or record your will, but these can safeguard against any claims that your will is invalid. To be valid, you must sign a will in the presence of at least two witnesses.

THE EFFECT OF MARRIAGE OR DIVORCE ON YOUR WILL

If you already have a will and are about to be married or divorced, review your will with an attorney for necessary changes. Upon divorce, only provisions favoring a former spouse are automatically revoked; provisions favoring family members of your ex-spouse, such as stepchildren, nieces, nephews, or in-laws, are not affected.

If you marry after you have made a will, the will is revoked automatically unless certain conditions are met. For example, marriage does not revoke a will if

- The will indicates an intent that it not be revoked by a subsequent marriage.
- The will was drafted under circumstances indicating that it was in contemplation of marriage.

Because your existing will's legal status may be uncertain, you are better off drawing a new will to fit your new circumstances.

will The legal declaration of a person's mind as to the disposition of his or her property after death.

intestate Without a valid will.

Exhibit 19-1

Your Will: If You Don't Write One

If you die without a will, the state's law of descent and distribution becomes your will.

My Last Will and Testament

Being of sound mind and memory, I, _____, do hereby publish this as my last Will and Testament.

FIRST

I give my wife only one-third of my possessions, and I give my children the remaining two-thirds.

A. I appoint my wife as guardian of my children, but as a safeguard I require that she report to the Probate Court each year and render an accounting of how, why, and where she spent the money necessary for the proper care of my children.

B. As a further safeguard, I direct my wife to produce to the Probate Court a Performance Bond to guarantee that she exercise proper judgment in the handling, investing, and spending of the children's money.

C. As a final safeguard, my children shall have the right to demand and receive a complete accounting from their mother of all of her financial actions with their money as soon as they reach legal age.

D. When my children reach age 18, they shall have full rights to withdraw and spend their shares of my estate. No one shall have any right to question my children's actions on how they decide to spend their respective shares.

SECOND

Should my wife remarry, her second husband shall be entitled to one-third of everything my wife possesses. Should my children need some of this share for their support, the second husband shall not be bound to spend any part of his share on my children's behalf.

A. The second husband shall have the sole right to decide who is to get his share, even to the exclusion of my children.

THIRD

Should my wife predecease me or die while any of my children are minors, I do not wish to exercise my right to nominate the guardian of my children.

A. Rather than nominating a guardian of my preference, I direct my relatives and friends to get together and select a guardian by mutual agreement.

B. In the event that they fail to agree on a guardian, I direct the Probate Court to make the selection. If the court wishes, it may appoint a stranger acceptable to it.

FOURTH

Under existing tax law, certain legitimate avenues are open to me to lower estate and inheritance taxes rates. Since I prefer to have my money used for government purposes rather than for the benefit of my wife and children, I direct that no effort be made to lower taxes.

IN WITNESS WHEREOF, I have set my hand to this, my LAST WILL AND TESTAMENT, this _______ day of _______________ 20 _______.

COST OF A WILL Legal fees for drafting a will vary with the complexities of your estate and family situation. A standard will costs between $300 and $400. The price varies from place to place, but generally the cost of writing a will is less than that for writing a living trust (to be discussed later in the chapter). Look for an attorney experienced in drafting wills and in estate planning.

probate The legal procedure of proving a valid or invalid will.

Probate is the legal procedure of proving a valid or invalid will. It is the process by which an executor manages and distributes your property after you die according to your will's provisions. A probate court generally validates wills and makes sure debts are paid. You should avoid probate because it is expensive, lengthy, and public. As you'll read later, a living trust avoids probate and is less expensive, quicker, and private.

PRACTICE QUIZ 19-2

1 What are the legal aspects of estate planning?
2 What is a will? Why is it an important estate planning tool?
3 How does marriage or divorce affect a will?

Types and Formats of Wills

LO19-3

Distinguish among various types and formats of wills.

TYPES OF WILLS

A brief review of the types of wills will be helpful, since the tax effects of these wills differ. The four types of wills are the simple will, the traditional marital share will, the exemption trust will, and the stated dollar amount will.

simple will A will that leaves everything to the spouse; also called an *I love you will.*

SIMPLE WILL A **simple will,** sometimes called an *I love you will,* leaves everything to the spouse. Such a will is sufficient for most smaller estates. However, if you have a large or complex estate, especially one involving business interests that you want to pass on to your children, a simple will may not meet your objectives. It may also create higher overall taxation, because everything would be taxed in your spouse's subsequent estate.

TRADITIONAL MARITAL SHARE WILL The **traditional marital share will** leaves one-half of the **adjusted gross estate** (the gross estate minus debts and costs) to the spouse outright as a marital share. The other half of the adjusted gross estate might go to children or other heirs or be held in trust for the family. A trust can provide the spouse with a lifelong income and would not be taxed at the spouse's death.

Under this type of will, half of your estate is taxed at your death and half at your spouse's death. This results in the lowest overall amount of federal estate taxes on estates above a certain size (twice the exemption amount). However, there are other considerations. State inheritance taxes may be greater, especially at the first death, due to conflicting federal and state exemption and beneficiary classifications. Also, under this type of will, unlike a simple will or an exemption trust, federal estate taxes may have to be paid up front at the first death that will involve the loss of use of money. If your spouse has considerable assets in his or her own right, it might not be prudent to increase your spouse's estate by any amount. In such a situation, a will that equalizes estates might be better. Finally, the nine community-property states severely limit your options as to how to allocate your money.

traditional marital share will A will in which the grantor leaves one-half of the adjusted gross estate to the spouse.

adjusted gross estate The gross estate minus debts and costs.

exemption trust will A will in which everything passes to the spouse except the exemption ($2,000,000 in 2008 and $3,500,000 in 2009).

EXEMPTION TRUST WILL The **exemption trust will** has been gaining in popularity due to its increased exemption. Under this type of will, everything passes to your spouse with the exception of an amount equal to the exemption, which would pass into trust. The amount passed to your spouse can be by will, trust, or other means. The exemption trust can provide your spouse with a lifelong income.

There would be little or no tax at your death due to the combination of the exemption and the marital deduction. The main advantage of the exemption trust will is that it eliminates future taxation of the exemption amount and any growth in it, which may be important if property values appreciate considerably.

STATED DOLLAR AMOUNT WILL The **stated dollar amount will** allows you to pass on to your spouse any amount that satisfies your family objectives. These objectives may or may not include tax considerations. For example, you could pass on the stated amount of $5.25 million (in 2013). However, the stated amount might instead be related to anticipated income needs or to the value of personal items.

stated dollar amount will A will that allows you to pass on to your spouse any amount that satisfies your family objectives.

State law may dictate how much you must leave your spouse. Most states require that your spouse receive a certain amount, usually one-half or one-third. Some states require that such interests pass outright, and others permit life interests. The stated dollar amount will may satisfy such requirements and pass the balance to others. You may, for example, decide to pass most of your estate to your children, thereby avoiding subsequent taxation of your spouse's estate. It may also make sense to pass interests in a business to children who are involved in the business.

Such plans may increase taxes at your death, since not all of your property passes to your spouse. However, the taxes at your spouse's subsequent death would be lower. You can also leave your spouse an outright amount equal to the exemption with a life estate in the balance, or a life estate in trust.

The stated dollar amount has one major shortcoming: The will may leave specific dollar amounts to listed heirs and the balance to the surviving spouse. Although these amounts may be reasonable when the will is drafted, they can soon become obsolete. What if estate values suddenly decrease due to a business setback or a drop in the stock market? Consider an individual with an extensive equities portfolio who drafted a will in 2007. After two years of bear markets, the value of the portfolio may have shrunk by one-third. None of that decrease will be borne by those who were left specific dollar amounts. The entire decrease will be borne by the surviving spouse. Therefore, you should use percentages instead of designated amounts.

WHICH TYPE OF WILL IS BEST FOR YOU? The four types of wills just discussed are your basic choices. Which one is best for you?

Prior to the Economic Recovery Tax Act of 1981, many experts advocated the traditional marital share will. Today many attorneys believe the exemption trust will is best. However, there is no one ideal will. Which will is best for you depends on factors such as the size of your estate, the future appreciation of your estate, inflation, the respective ages of you and your spouse, cash on hand, and—most important—your objectives.

DID YOU KNOW?

According to a recent American Association of Retired Persons (AARP) survey, over 40 percent of Americans age 45 or older have not drawn up a will.

FORMATS OF WILLS

Wills may be holographic or formal. A **holographic will** is a handwritten will that you prepare yourself. It should be written, dated, and signed entirely in your handwriting; no printed or typed information should be on its pages. Some states, however, may not recognize a holographic will.

holographic will A handwritten will.

A **formal will** is usually prepared with an attorney's assistance. It may be either typed or on a preprinted form. You must sign the will and acknowledge it as your will in the presence of two witnesses, neither of whom is a **beneficiary** (a person you have named to receive property under the will). The witnesses must then sign the will in your presence.

formal will A will that is usually prepared with an attorney's assistance.

beneficiary A person who has been named to receive property under a will.

A **statutory will** is one type of formal will. It is a preprinted form that may be obtained from lawyers and stationery stores. There are serious risks in using this or any other preprinted form. One risk is that such a form usually requires you to conform to rigid provisions, some of which may not be in the best interests of your beneficiaries.

statutory will A formal will on a preprinted form.

THE 10 COMMANDMENTS OF MAKING YOUR WILL

1. Work closely with your spouse as you prepare your will. Seek professional help so that your family objectives can be met regardless of who dies first.
2. Write your will to conform with your current wishes. When your circumstances change (for example, when you retire or move to another state), review your will and, if appropriate, write a new one.
3. Do not choose a beneficiary as a witness. If such a person is called on to validate your will, he or she may not be able to collect an inheritance.
4. If you are remarrying, consider signing a pre-nuptial agreement to protect your children. If you sign such an agreement before the wedding, you and your intended spouse can legally agree that neither of you will make any claim on the other's estate. The agreement can be revoked later, if you both agree.
5. Consider using percentages rather than dollar amounts when you divide your estate. For example, if you leave $15,000 to a friend and the rest to your spouse, your spouse will suffer if your estate shrinks to $17,000.
6. Both you and your spouse should have a will, and those wills should be separate documents.
7. Be flexible. Don't insist that your heirs keep stock or run a cattle ranch. If you do so, they may suffer if economic conditions change.
8. Sign the original copy of your will and keep it in a safe place; keep an unsigned copy at home for reference.
9. Alter your will by preparing a new will or adding a codicil. Don't change beneficiaries by writing on the will itself; this may invalidate the will.
10. Select an executor or executrix who is both willing and able to carry out the complicated tasks associated with the job.

Also, if you change the preprinted wording, you may violate the law regarding wills, which may cause the changed sections or even the entire will to be declared invalid. There is also a risk that the form is out of date with respect to current law. It is always prudent to seek legal assistance in developing these documents.

WRITING YOUR WILL

The way to transfer your property according to your wishes is to write a will specifying those wishes. Joint ownership is no substitute for a will. Although jointly owned property passes directly to the joint owner and may be appropriate for some assets, such as your home, only a will allows you to distribute your property as a whole exactly as you wish. Select a person who will follow your instructions (your *executor* or *executrix*). By naming your own executor, you will eliminate the need for a court-appointed administrator, prevent unnecessary delay in the distribution of your property, and minimize estate taxes and settlement costs. See Financial Planning for Life's Situations: The 10 Commandments of Making Your Will for guidance on important aspects of making a will.

If you have a will drawn, you are testate in the eyes of the law, and an executor (named in your will) will carry out your wishes in due time.

SELECTING AN EXECUTOR Select an executor or executrix who is both willing and able to carry out the complicated tasks associated with executing a will. These tasks are preparing an inventory of assets, collecting any money due, paying off any debts, preparing and filing all income and estate tax returns, liquidating and reinvesting other assets to pay off debts and provide income for your family while the estate is being administered, distributing the estate, and making a final accounting to your beneficiaries and to the probate court.

Who can be an executor? Any U.S. citizen over 18 who has not been convicted of a felony can be named the executor of a will. Your executor can be a family member, a friend, an attorney, an accountant, or the trust department of a bank. Fees for executors, whether professionals or friends, are set by state law. Exhibit 19-2 summarizes typical duties of an executor.

SELECTING A GUARDIAN In addition to disposing of your estate, your will should name a guardian and/or trustee to care for minor children if both parents die at the same time, such as in an automobile accident or a plane crash. A **guardian** is a person who assumes the responsibilities of providing the children with personal care and of managing the estate for them. A **trustee,** on the other hand, is a person or an institution that holds or generally manages property for the benefit of someone else under a trust agreement.

guardian A person who assumes responsibility for providing children with personal care and managing the deceased's estate for them.

trustee A person or an institution that holds or manages property for the benefit of someone else under a trust agreement.

You should take great care in selecting a guardian for your children. You want a guardian whose philosophy on raising children is similar to yours and who is willing to accept the responsibility.

Most states require a guardian to post a bond with the probate court. The bonding company promises to reimburse the minor's estate up to the amount of the bond if the guardian uses the property of the minor for his or her own gain. The bonding fee (usually several hundred dollars) is paid from the estate. However, you can waive the bonding requirement in your will.

Through your will, you may want to provide funds to raise your children. You could, for instance, leave a lump sum for an addition to the guardian's house and establish monthly payments to cover your children's living expenses.

The guardian of the minor's estate manages the property you leave behind for your children. This guardian can be a person or the trust department of a financial institution, such as a bank. Property that you place in trust for your children can be managed by the trustee rather than by the guardian of the minor's estate.

Exhibit 19-2

Major responsibilities of an executor

An executor is someone who is willing and able to perform the complicated tasks involved in carrying out your will.

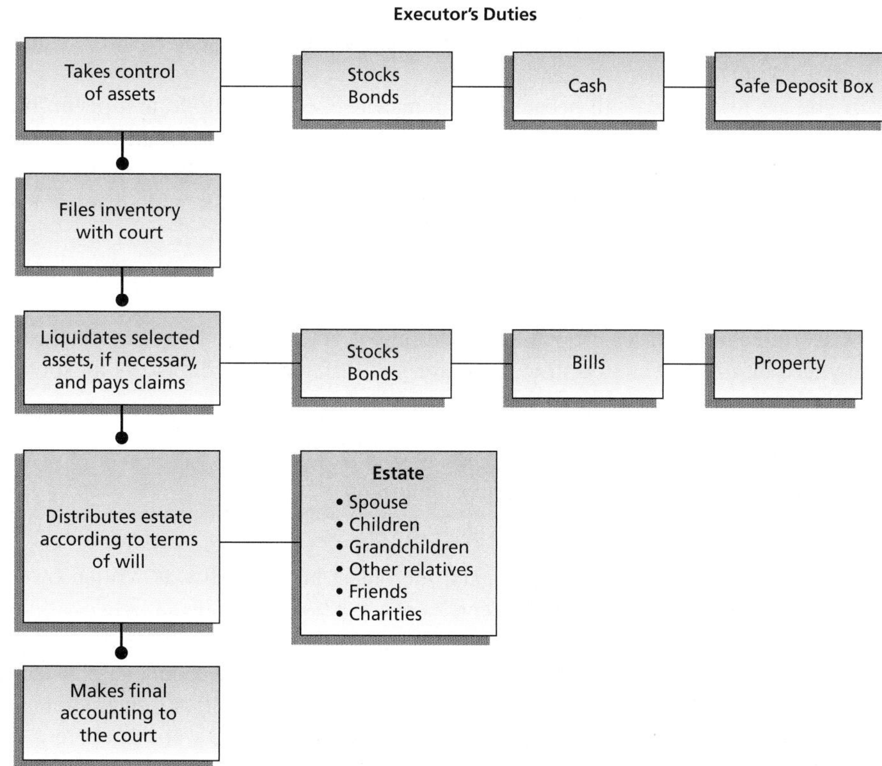

Source: American Bankers Association, *Trust Services from Your Bank,* rev. ed. (Washington, DC: American Bankers Association, 1978), p. 9.

Each executor or a trustee has a fiduciary relationship to the beneficiaries of the will. This relationship dictates that beneficiaries' interests are paramount. The executor or trustee must not take advantage of his or her position.

ALTERING OR REWRITING YOUR WILL

Sometimes you will need to change provisions of your will. Consider one change involving the marital deduction. The old law limited the amount you could pass to your spouse tax free to one-half of your adjusted gross estate. But the Economic Recovery Tax Act of 1981 created an unlimited marital deduction. You can now pass any amount to your spouse tax free.

If you do have a will, you should review it. This is necessary even if you have already done some planning and your will refers to the old 50 percent marital deduction. Why? The new 100 percent marital deduction is not automatic. Congress would not alter or rewrite your will; this task was left to you. Therefore, unless you change your will or unless your state passes a law making the new definition applicable, you will have to rewrite your will to make the unlimited marital deduction apply. Because many choices are of a personal nature, few, if any, states will get involved. For example, some people may not want to leave the entire estate to their spouse, perhaps for valid tax reasons.

You should review your will if you move to a different state; if you have sold property mentioned in the will; if the size and composition of your estate have changed; if you have married, divorced, or remarried; or if new potential heirs have died or been born.

Don't make any changes on the face of your will. Additions, deletions, or erasures on a will that has been signed and witnessed can invalidate the will.

codicil A document that modifies provisions in an existing will.

prenuptial agreement A documentary agreement between spouses before marriage.

If only a few changes are needed in your will, adding a codicil may be the best choice. A **codicil** is a document that explains, adds, or deletes provisions in your existing will. It identifies the will being amended and confirms the unchanged sections of the will. To be valid, it must conform to the legal requirements for a will.

If you wish to make major changes in your will or if you have already added a codicil, preparing a new will is preferable to adding a new codicil. In the new will, include a clause revoking all earlier wills and codicils.

If you are rewriting a will because of a remarriage, consider drafting a **prenuptial agreement.** This is a documentary agreement between spouses before marriage. In such agreements, one or both parties often waive a right to receive property under the other's will or under state law. Be sure to consult an attorney in drafting a prenuptial agreement.

LIVING WILL AND ADVANCE DIRECTIVES

Advance directives are legal documents that allow you to state what kind of health care you want if you were too ill to speak for yourself. Advance directives most often include the following:

- A living will.
- A health care proxy (durable power of attorney).
- Letter of last instructions (after-death wishes).

Wills have existed for thousands of years; the oldest known will was written by the Egyptian pharaoh Uah in 2448 BC. Recently a new type of will, called a living will, has emerged.

living will A document that enables an individual, while well, to express the intention that life be allowed to end if he or she becomes terminally ill.

A **living will** provides for your wishes to be followed if you become so physically or mentally disabled that you are unable to act on your own behalf. A living will is not a substitute for a traditional will. It enables an individual, while well, to express the intention that life be allowed to end if he or she becomes terminally ill. Many states recognize living wills, and you may consider writing one when you draw a conventional will. Exhibit 19-3 is an example of a typical living will.

Exhibit 19-3

A living will

Many states recognize living wills.

To My Family, My Physician, My Lawyer, My Clergyman;
To Any Medical Facility in Whose Care I Happen to Be;
To Any Individual Who May Become Responsible for My Health or Welfare;

Living Will Declaration

Declaration made this _____ day of _______________ (month, year)

I, ______________________, being of sound mind, willfully and voluntarily make known my desire that my dying shall not be artifically prolonged under the circumstances set forth below, do hereby declare

If at any time I should have an incurable injury, disease, or illness regarded as a terminal condition by my physician and if my physician has determined that the application of life-sustaining procedures would serve only to artificially prolong the dying process and that my death will occur whether or not life-sustaining procedures are utilized, I direct that such procedures be withheld or withdrawn and that I be permitted to die with only the administration of medication or the performance of any medical procedure deemed necessary to provide me with comfort care.

In the absence of my ability to give directions regarding the use of such life-sustaining procedures, it is my intention that this declaration shall be honored by my family and physician as the final expression of my legal right to refuse medical or surgical treatment and accept the consequences from such refusal.

I understand the full import of this declaration, and I am emotionally and mentally competent to make this declaration.

Signed ________________

City, County, and State of Residence ________________

The declarant has been personally known to me, and I believe him or her to be of sound mind.

Witness ________________

Witness ________________

Source: *Don't Wait until Tomorrow* (Hartford, CT: Aetna Life and Casualty Company, n.d.), p. 11.

To ensure the effectiveness of a living will, discuss your intention of preparing such a will with the people closest to you. You should also discuss this with your family doctor. Sign and date your document before two witnesses. Witnessing shows that you signed of your own free will.

Give copies of your living will to those closest to you, and have your family doctor place a copy in your medical file. Keep the original document readily accessible, and look it over periodically—preferably once a year—to be sure your wishes have remained unchanged. To verify your intent, redate and initial each subsequent endorsement.

Most lawyers will do the paperwork for a living will at no cost if they are already preparing your estate plan. You can also get the necessary forms from nonprofit advocacy groups. Aging With Dignity (www.agingwithdignity.org) lets you download a free, plain-English version called Five Wishes that's valid in 33 states. Partnership for Caring: America's Voices for the Dying is a national nonprofit organization that operates the only national crisis and information hotline dealing with end-of-life issues. It also provides documents, such as living wills and medical powers of attorney, geared to specific states. You may download these documents free at www.partnershipforcaring.org. Working through end-of-life issues is difficult, but it can help avoid forcing your family to make a decision in a hospital waiting room—or worse, having your last wishes ignored.

A living will can become a problem. A once-healthy person may have a change of heart and prefer to remain alive even as death seems imminent. Living wills call for careful thought, but they do provide you with a choice as to the manner of your death.

ETHICAL WILL

ethical will A document that dispenses emotional and spiritual wealth to heirs.

Renewed interest in another type of will has emerged since the September 11, 2001, terrorist attacks. An **ethical will** is a way to pass on your values and beliefs to your heirs. Even though it is not a legally binding document, ethical wills help with estate planning.

Before taking a trip to California shortly after September 11, 2001, Kim Payfrock, 42, wrote letters to her two sons and two stepsons, ages 11 to 17. The letters expressed her love for them as well as her joys and regrets in life. "I was nervous about flying and wanted them to open the letters if anything happened to me," says Payfrock, who is an activity coordinator at an assisted-living community in Minneapolis. "This was a way to leave them my thoughts, to give them a part of myself."

Payfrock didn't know it at the time, but she had written each of her children an *ethical will.* Whereas legal wills bequeath material wealth, ethical wills dispense emotional and spiritual wealth. "It's a way to pass on your values, share lessons learned, express love, and address any regrets," says Barry Baines, the medical director of a hospice in Minneapolis and author of *Ethical Will: Putting Your Values on Paper.* Preparing such a document is not easy, since it requires earnest self-examination. But writers and recipients of ethical wills say the result is an invaluable legacy.[1]

SOCIAL MEDIA WILL

Social media is part of daily life, so what happens to the online content that you created once you die? If you are active online, you should consider creating a statement of how you would like your online identity to be handled, like a social media will. You should appoint someone you trust as an online executor. This person will be responsible for the closure of your email addresses, social media profiles, and blogs after you die. Take these steps to help you write a social media will:

- Review the privacy policies and the terms and conditions of each website where you have a presence.
- State how you would like your profile to be handled. You may want to completely cancel your profile or keep it up for friends and family to visit. Some sites allow users to create a memorial profile where other users can still see your profile but can't post anything new.
- Give the social media executor a document that lists all the websites where you have a profile, along with your usernames and passwords.
- State in your will that the online executor should have a copy of your death certificate. The online executor may need this as proof in order for websites to take any actions on your behalf.

POWER OF ATTORNEY

durable power of attorney A legal document authorizing someone to act on one's behalf.

Related to the concept of a living will is a durable power of attorney also known as a health care proxy. A **durable power of attorney** is a legal document authorizing someone to act on your behalf. At some point in your life, you may become ill or incapacitated. You may then wish to have someone attend to your needs and your personal affairs. You can assign a durable power of attorney to anyone you choose.

The person you name can be given limited power or a great deal of power. The power given can be special—to carry out certain acts or transactions—or it can be general—to act completely for you. A conventional power of attorney is automatically revoked in a case of legal incapacity.

LETTER OF LAST INSTRUCTION

In addition to your will, you should prepare a *letter of last instruction.* This document, also known as after-death wishes, though not legally enforceable in some states, can provide your heirs with important information. It should contain the details of your funeral arrangements. It should also contain the names of the people who are to be notified of your death and the locations of your bank accounts, safe-deposit box, and other important items listed on page 663.

my life 3

In addition to a will, I should prepare a letter of last instruction.

Even though a letter of last instruction is not legally binding, it can provide heirs with important information. It should contain preferences for funeral arrangements as well as the names of the people who are to be informed of the death. For information on topics such as letters of last instruction, wills, trusts, living wills, and power of attorney, visit www.nolo.com/lawcenter/index.

Will planning sheet

1 Distinguish among the four types of wills.
2 What are the two formats of wills?
3 What are the steps in writing your will?
4 What is an ethical will?
5 What is a power of attorney?
6 What is a letter of last instruction?

Types of Trusts and Estates

LO19-4

Appraise various types of trusts and estates.

A trust is a property arrangement in which a trustee, such as a person or a bank trust department, holds title to, takes care of, and in most cases manages property for the benefit of someone else. The creator of the trust is called the **trustor** or *grantor.* A bank, as trustee, charges a modest fee for its services, generally based on the value of the trust assets. All trust assets added together are known as an *estate.*

It is a good idea to discuss with your attorney the possibility of establishing a trust as a means of managing your estate. Basically, a **trust** is a legal arrangement through which a trustee holds your assets for your benefit or that of your beneficiaries. Trusts are used for everything from protecting assets from creditors to managing property for young children, disabled elders, or even the family pets.

Trusts are either revocable or irrevocable. If you establish a **revocable trust,** you retain the right to end the trust or change its terms during your lifetime. Revocable trusts avoid the often lengthy probate process, but they do not provide shelter from federal or state estate taxes. You might choose a revocable trust if you think you may need its assets for your own use at a later time or if you want to monitor the performance of the trust and the trustee before the arrangement is made irrevocable by your death. If you establish an **irrevocable trust,** you cannot change its terms or end it. The trust becomes, for tax purposes, a separate entity, and the assets can't be removed, nor can changes be made by the grantor. Therefore, an irrevocable trust offers tax advantages not offered by a revocable trust. Irrevocable trusts often are used by individuals with large estates to reduce estate taxes and avoid probate.

trustor The creator of a trust; also called the *grantor.*

trust A legal arrangement through which one's assets are held by a trustee.

revocable trust A trust whose terms the trustor retains the rights to change.

irrevocable trust A trust that cannot be altered or ended by its creator.

my life 4

If I establish a trust, it will avoid probate and transfer my assets immediately to my beneficiaries.

Basically, a trust is a legal arrangement that helps manage the assets of your estate for your benefit or that of your beneficiaries. One of the benefits of establishing a trust is that it avoids probate and transfers your assets immediately to your beneficiaries.

BENEFITS OF ESTABLISHING TRUSTS

Your individual circumstances dictate whether it makes sense to establish a trust. Here are some common reasons for setting up a trust. You can use a trust to

- Reduce or otherwise provide for payment of estate taxes.
- Avoid probate and transfer your assets immediately to your beneficiaries.
- Free yourself from management of your assets while you receive a regular income from the trust.
- Provide income for a surviving spouse or other beneficiaries.
- Ensure that your property serves a desired purpose after your death.

Trustee services are commonly provided by banks and, in some instances, by life insurance companies. An estate attorney can advise you about the right type of trust for you.

TYPES OF TRUSTS

There are many types of trusts, some of which are described in detail below. Each of these types has particular advantages. Choose the type of trust that is most appropriate for your family situation.

credit-shelter trust A trust that allows married couples to leave everything to each other tax free.

CREDIT-SHELTER TRUST A **credit-shelter trust** was perhaps the most common estate planning trust. It is also known as a *bypass trust,* a *"residuary" trust,* an *A/B trust,* an *exemption equivalent trust,* or a *family trust.* It is designed to allow married couples, who can leave everything to each other tax free, to take full advantage of the exemption that allows $5.25 million (in 2013) in every estate to pass free of federal estate taxes.

The American Taxpayer Relief Act of 2012 (ATRA), enacted on January 2, 2013, provides a permanent $5.25 million gift and estate tax exemption (indexed for inflation) for individuals and $10.5 million for married couples. Therefore, a married couple will not pay any estate tax if their estate is less than $10.5 million. Estates above these amounts are taxed at 40 percent. However, the "permanent" $5.25 million may not be permanent.

disclaimer trust A trust designed for a couple who do not yet have enough assets to need a credit-shelter trust but may need one in the future.

DISCLAIMER TRUST A **disclaimer trust** is appropriate for a couple who do not yet have enough assets to need a credit-shelter trust but may need one in the future. For example, a newly practicing physician who will soon finish paying off college loans might want to take this approach. With a disclaimer trust, the surviving spouse is left everything but has the right to disclaim some portion of the estate. Anything disclaimed goes into a credit-shelter trust. This approach gives the surviving spouse the flexibility to shelter any wealth from estate taxes. However, if the estate fails to grow as expected, the survivor isn't locked into a trust structure.

living trust A trust that is created and provides benefits during the trustor's lifetime.

LIVING, OR INTER VIVOS, TRUST A **living trust,** or *inter vivos trust,* is a property management arrangement that you establish while you are alive. Well-structured estate plans often start with a living trust that becomes irrevocable at death, dividing itself into several other types of trusts, such as a credit-shelter trust. You simply transfer some property to a trustee, giving him or her instructions regarding its management and disposition while you are alive and after your death.

In the past several years, many people have opted for a living trust instead of a will, or in addition to one. But bare-bones living trusts, which start at $1,500, are overhyped and often misunderstood. (See How To . . . Feature: How to Make Sure a Living Trust Offer Is Trustworthy. They do not, for example, bypass estate taxes or protect you from

HOW TO...

Make Sure a Living Trust Offer Is Trustworthy

Misinformation and misunderstanding about estate taxes and the length or complexity of probate provide the perfect cover for scam artists who have created an industry out of older people's fears that their estates could be eaten up by costs or that the distribution of their assets could be delayed for years. Some unscrupulous businesses are advertising seminars on living trusts or sending postcards inviting consumers to call for in-home appointments to learn whether a living trust is right for them. In these cases, it's not uncommon for the salesperson to exaggerate the benefits or the appropriateness of the living trust and claim—falsely—that locally licensed lawyers will prepare the documents.

Other businesses are advertising living trust "kits": consumers send money for these do-it-yourself products but receive nothing in return. Still other businesses are using estate planning services to gain access to consumers' financial information and to sell them other financial products, such as insurance annuities.

What's a consumer to do? It's true that for some people, a living trust can be a useful and practical tool. But for others, it can be a waste of money and time. Because state laws and requirements vary, "cookie- cutter" approaches to estate planning aren't always the most efficient way to handle your affairs. Before you sign any papers to create a will, a living trust, or any other kind of trust:

- Explore all your options with an experienced and licensed estate planning attorney or financial adviser. Generally, state law requires that an attoney draft the trust.
- Avoid high-pressure sales tactics and high-speed sales pitches by anyone who is selling estate planning tools or arrangements.
- Avoid salespeople who give the impression that AARP is selling or endorsing their products. AARP does not endorse any living trust product.
- Do your homework. Get information about your local probate laws from the Clerk (or Registrar) of Wills.
- If you opt for a living trust, make sure it's properly funded—that is, that the property has been transferred from your name to the trust. If the transfers aren't done properly, the trust will be invalid and the state will determine who inherits your property and serves as guardian for your minor children.
- If someone tries to sell you a living trust, ask whether the seller is an attorney. Some states limit the sale of living trust services to attorneys.
- Remember the *Cooling Off Rule.* If you buy a living trust in your home or somewhere other than the seller's permanent place of business (say, at a hotel seminar), the seller must give you a written statement of your right to cancel the deal within three business days. The cooling off rule provides that during the sales transaction, the salesperson must give you two copies of a cancellation form (one for you to keep and one to return to the company) and a copy of your contract or receipt. The contract or receipt must be dated, show the name and address of the seller, and explain your right to cancel. You can write a letter and exercise your right to cancel within three days, even if you don't receive a cancellation form. You do not have to give a reason for canceling. Stopping payment on your check if you do cancel in these circumstances is a good idea. If you pay by credit card and the seller does not credit your account after you cancel, you can dispute the charge with the credit card issuer.
- Check out the organization with the Better Business Bureau in your state or the state where the organization is located before you send any money for any product or service. Although this is prudent, it is not foolproof: there may be no record of complaints if an organization is too new or has changed its name.

(*continued*)

HOW TO... Continued

FOR MORE INFORMATION

To learn more about estate planning strategies, talk with an experienced estate planning attorney or financial adviser and check out the following resources:

AARP: 1-800-424-3410; www.aarp.org. Ask for a copy of *Product Report: Wills & Living Trusts.* AARP does not sell or endorse living trust products.

American Bar Association, Service Center, 541 N. Fairbanks Ct., Chicago, IL 60611; 312-988-5522; www.abanet.org/publiced/publicpubs.html.

Council of Better Business Bureaus Inc., 4200 Wilson Blvd., Suite 800, Arlington, VA 22203-1838; 703-276-0100; www.bbb.org/.

National Academy of Elder Law Attorneys Inc., 1604 North Country Club Rd., Tucson, AZ 85716; 520-881-4005; www.naela.org/.

National Consumer Law Center Inc., 77 Summer Street, 10th Floor, Boston, MA, 02110-1006; 617-542-8010; www.consumerlaw.org/.

Source: www.ftc.gov/os/2000/07/livingtrusts/cams.htm, accessed May 9, 2013.

creditors. What they do is avoid probate—which, in states such as Florida and California, can drag on for a couple of years and eat up as much as 5 percent or 10 percent of the estate's assets in administrative fees. With a living trust, you can change the terms while you're living, and your successor trustee, usually a family member, distributes the property without court interference when you die.

Living trusts are a must if you own property in more than one state, since your heirs will not be subjected to multiple probate proceedings. Unlike wills, which become public as soon as they are filed with the probate court, living trusts are private documents. They can be handy for other situations as well, such as disinheriting estranged family members. The biggest mistake made in estate planning? You sign the documents setting up the trust but don't follow through with the tedious task of retitling all of your property, such as real estate, stocks and bonds, and bank accounts, in the specific name of the trust. A living trust has these advantages:

- It ensures privacy. A will is a public record; a trust is not.
- The property held in the trust avoids probate at your death. It eliminates probate costs and delays.
- It enables you to review your trustee's performance and make changes if necessary.
- It can remove management responsibilities from your shoulders.
- It is less subject to dispute by disappointed heirs than a will is.
- It can guide your family and doctors if you become terminally ill or incompetent.

However, a living trust can be complicated and involves higher costs than creating a will, and funding a trust can be time consuming.

testamentary trust
A trust established by the creator's will that becomes effective upon his or her death.

TESTAMENTARY TRUST A **testamentary trust** is established by your will and becomes effective upon your death. Such a trust can be valuable if your beneficiaries are inexperienced in financial matters or if the potential estate tax is substantial.

Like a living trust, a testamentary trust provides the benefits of asset management, financial bookkeeping, protection of the beneficiaries, and minimizing of estate taxes.

Newly acquired property can always be added to your trust. But what if you forget to change the title on some of your assets? A simple pourover will, written when the trust agreement is drafted, is the answer. A *pourover* will is a simple document stating that anything you may have neglected to place in your trust during your lifetime should be placed in it at your death. While assets passing under a pourover will are generally probated, a small amount may be excluded from a probate.

LIFE INSURANCE TRUST In many families, the proceeds of life insurance policies are the largest single asset of the estate. A **life insurance trust** is established while you are living. The trust receives your life insurance benefits upon your death and administers them in an agreed-on manner. Such a trust can be canceled if your family or financial circumstances change or if you wish to make new plans for the future.

life insurance trust A trust whose assets are derived at least in part from the proceeds of life insurance.

Although common estate planning tools, life insurance trusts "aren't for the faint of heart," says one tax attorney. They require careful monitoring so that they don't run afoul of gift tax rules.

As you can see, trusts are complicated; therefore, you should seek a competent estate attorney in preparing this legal document. The purpose of all types of trusts is to preserve your estate for your heirs. (Read the Financial Planning for Life's Situations: Other Types of Trusts feature).

ESTATES

As mentioned earlier, your estate is everything you own (see Exhibit 19-4). It includes all of your property—tangible and intangible, however acquired or owned, whether inside or outside the country. It may include jointly owned property, life insurance and employee benefits. Thus, an important step in estate planning is taking inventory of everything you own, such as

DID YOU KNOW?

In common-law states (most states), spouses are not considered co-owners of property unless it has been jointly titled. Surviving spouses are entitled to inherit a portion of the deceased spouse's property.

1. Cash, checking accounts, savings accounts, CDs, and money market funds.
2. Stocks, bonds (including municipals and U.S. savings bonds), mutual funds, commodity futures, and tax shelters.
3. Life insurance, employee benefits, and annuities.
4. Your home and any other real estate, land and buildings, furniture, and fixtures.

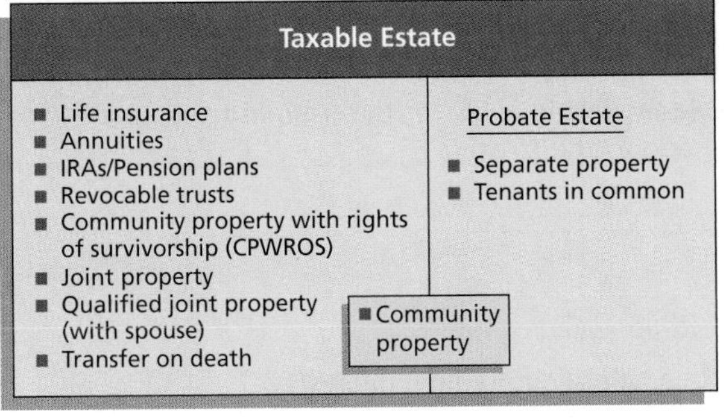

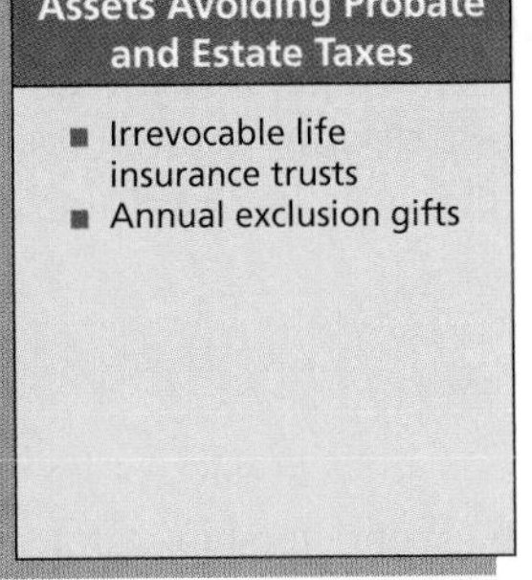

Exhibit 19-4

What is your estate?

Your estate consists of everything you own.

This exhibit shows which assets are included in your probate estate, the much larger number of assets included in your taxable estate, and the very few assets that can avoid both probate and estate taxes.

Source: *Planning Your Estate* (A. G. Edwards, 1996), p. 6.

OTHER TYPES OF TRUSTS

GRANTOR RETAINED ANNUITY TRUST (GRAT)

If you are worried about estate taxes, consider one of today's most popular alternatives. A grantor retained annuity trust (GRAT) not only shelters valuable assets that you can pass on to your heirs with minimal taxes but also lets you receive an annuity for as long as the trust lasts.

MARITAL-DEDUCTION TRUST

With a marital-deduction trust, you can leave to your spouse any money that doesn't go into a credit-shelter trust. Whatever the amount, it is free of estate tax when you die, since it qualifies for the marital deduction. Perhaps the most popular form of marital trust is the *qualified terminable interest property trust,* or *Q-TIP.* Here the surviving spouse gets all trust income, which must be distributed at least once a year, and sometimes receives access to the principal as well. When the spouse dies, the assets go to whomever you specified in the trust documents. The trust assets are then taxed as part of the surviving spouse's estate.

SELF-DECLARATION TRUST

A self-declaration trust is a variation of the living trust. Its unique feature is that the creator of the trust is also the trustee. The trust document usually includes a procedure for removing the creator of the trust as the trustee without going to court. Typically, one or more physicians or family members, or a combination of physicians and family members, have removal power. If the creator of the trust is removed, a named successor trustee takes over.

CHARITABLE REMAINDER TRUST

With a charitable remainder trust, you retain the right to the income but transfer that right to the charity upon death. If you have highly appreciated assets, it is a great way to improve your cash flow during your retirement and pursue a charitable interest at the same time. The biggest drawback is that you have to give away the asset irrevocably.

QUALIFIED PERSONAL RESIDENCE TRUST

A qualified personal residence trust (QPRT) lets you get your home or vacation home out of your estate. You give your home to a trust but live in it for a term of, say, 10 years. At the end of that time, the home belongs to the continuing trust or to the trust beneficiaries, depending on how the trust is written.

CHARITABLE LEAD TRUST

A charitable lead trust pays a specified charity income from a donated asset for a set number of years. When the term is up, the principal goes to the donor's beneficiaries with reduced estate or gift taxes. Such a trust has high setup and operating costs, however, which may make it impractical unless the assets involved are substantial. For this reason, it is a vehicle for very wealthy people, allowing them a way to keep an asset in the family but greatly reducing the cost of passing it on.

GENERATION-SKIPPING TRUST

A generation-skipping trust allows you to directly leave a substantial amount of money to your grandchildren or great-grandchildren. If you have a large estate, you should explore a generation-skipping (or dynasty) trust. Over time, it can save millions of dollars in taxes and can be used to help all of those family members who come after you.

SPENDTHRIFT TRUST

If your beneficiary is too young or unable to handle money wisely, consider a spendthrift trust. Here the beneficiary receives small amounts of money at specified intervals. It prevents the beneficiary from squandering money or losing it in a bad investment.

OTHER TYPES

There are still other types of specialized trusts. For example, a *pourover trust* is usually dormant during your lifetime, but can be activated if you become disabled. It can be used to manage your insurance, qualified pension or profit-sharing plan proceeds, and your probate estate. A *Q-DOT (qualified domestic trust)* is for spouses who are not U.S. citizens. It provides the same marital deduction benefit that is available to citizen spouses. A GRUT (grantor retained unitrust) and a *personal residence GRIT (grantor retained income trust)* permit grantors to use favorable rules for determining the amount of gift made to the trust.

5. Farms, grain, livestock, machinery, and equipment.
6. Proprietorship, partnership, and close corporation interests.
7. Notes, accounts, and claims receivable.
8. Interests in trusts and powers of appointment.
9. Antiques, works of art, collectibles, cars, boats, planes, personal effects, and everything else.

In the community-property states (Arizona, California, Idaho, Louisiana, Nevada, New Mexico, Texas, Wisconsin, and Washington), where each spouse owns 50 percent of the property, half of the community assets are included in each spouse's estate. **Community property** is "any property that has been acquired by either of the spouses during the marriage, but not by gift, devise, bequest or inheritance, or, often, by the income therefrom." In the other, non–community-property states, property is included in the estate of the spouse who owns it. The way you own property can make a tax difference.

community property Any property that has been acquired by either spouse during the marriage.

JOINT OWNERSHIP

Joint ownership of property between spouses is very common. Joint ownership may also exist between parents and children, other relatives, or any two or more persons. While joint ownership may avoid *probate* (official proof of a will), creditor attachment, and inheritance taxes in some states, it does not avoid federal estate taxes. In fact, it may increase them.

There are three types of joint ownership, and each has different tax and estate planning consequences. First, if you and your spouse own property as *joint tenants with the right of survivorship (JT/WROS),* the property is considered owned 50–50 for estate tax purposes and will automatically pass to your spouse at your death, and vice versa. No gift tax is paid on creating such ownership, nor, due to the unlimited marital deduction, is any estate tax paid at the first death. However, this type of joint ownership may result in more taxes overall at the surviving spouse's later death than would be the case with a traditional marital share will, discussed earlier.

DID YOU KNOW?

In community-property states, spouses are generally considered co-owners of any property acquired during marriage. These states include Arizona, California, Idaho, Louisiana, Nevada, New Mexico, Texas, Wisconsin, and Washington.

Second, if you and your spouse or anyone else own property as *tenants in common,* each individual is considered to own a proportionate share for tax purposes, and only your share is included in your estate. That share does not go to the other tenants in common at your death but is included in your probate estate and subject to your decision as to who gets it. While there are no gift or estate tax consequences between spouse joint owners, gifts of joint interests to children or others can create taxation.

Tenancy by the entirety, the third type of joint ownership, is limited to married couples. Under this type of joint ownership, both spouses own the property; when one spouse dies, the other gets it automatically. Neither spouse may sell the property without the consent of the other.

Joint ownership is a poor substitute for a will. It gives you less control over the disposition and taxation of your property. Your state laws govern the types and effects of joint ownership. Some states require that survivorship rights be spelled out in the deed, or at least abbreviated (for example, JT/WROS). Only your attorney can advise you on these matters.

LIFE INSURANCE AND EMPLOYEE BENEFITS

Life insurance proceeds are free of income tax, excluded from probate, and wholly or partially exempt from most state inheritance taxes. These proceeds are included in your estate for federal estate tax purposes if the policy contains any incidents of ownership such as the right to change beneficiaries, surrender the policy for cash, or make loans on the policy.

Assignment of ownership to your beneficiary or a trust can remove a life insurance policy from your estate. But if your spouse is the intended beneficiary, you do not need to assign ownership, since the proceeds will be free of estate tax due to the marital deduction.

Death benefits from qualified pension, profit-sharing, or Keogh plans are excluded from your estate unless they are payable to it or unless your beneficiary elects the special provision for averaging income tax in lump-sum distributions.

If there is "too much" money in your qualified retirement plan when you and your spouse die, your heirs could lose up to 80 percent in federal and state income taxes, estate tax, and the "excess accumulation" tax. Proper estate planning can minimize such confiscatory taxes.[2]

LIFETIME GIFTS AND TRUSTS Gifts or trusts with strings attached, such as retaining the income, use, or control of the property, are fully included in your estate at their date-of-death value, whether your rights are expressed or implied. For example, if you transfer title of your home to a child but continue to live in it, the home is taxed in your estate. Or if you put property in trust and retain a certain amount of control over the income or principal, the property is included in your estate even though you cannot obtain it yourself. Also, if you are the beneficiary of a trust established by someone else and you have general rights to the principal during life or the power to appoint it to anyone at death, that amount is included in your estate.

SETTLING YOUR ESTATE

If you have had a will drawn, you are *testate* in the eyes of the law, and an executor (named in your will) will carry out your wishes in due time. If you have not named an executor, the probate court (the court that supervises the distribution of estates) will appoint an administrator to carry out the instructions in your will.

If you don't have a will, you become *intestate* at your death. In that case, your estate is put under the control of a court-appointed administrator for distribution according to the laws of the state in which you reside.

Some assets pass outside of the will directly to your beneficiaries. These assets that avoid probate include proceeds from life insurance, annuities, investments in your Individual Retirement Accounts (IRA), qualified retirement plans such as 401 (k)s, 403 (b)s, SEPs, and trust property. Jointly owned property such as, home, cars, bank accounts, etc. automatically pass to the surviving co-owner without probate.

Trust comparison sheet

PRACTICE QUIZ 19-4

1 Differentiate among the various types of trusts.
2 What is included in an estate?
3 What are the three types of joint ownership?

Federal and State Estate Taxes

LO19-5

Evaluate the effects of federal and state taxes on estate planning.

The tax aspects of estate planning have changed considerably due to recent major changes in the federal tax structure. The maximum tax rate on estates and gifts, for example, is gradually declining. However, as Exhibit 19-5 shows, estate settlement costs can quickly deplete an estate.

You can reduce your taxable estate by giving away assets to anyone during your lifetime. (But don't give away assets just to reduce your estate tax liability if you may need those assets in your retirement.) No gift tax is due on gifts of up to $14,000 (in 2013) to any one person in any one year. (A married couple, acting together, may give up to $28,000 to one person in one year.)

Exhibit 19-5

The erosion of probate and estate taxes

	Gross Estate	Settlement Costs	Net Estate	Percent Shrinkage
Elvis Presley	$10,165,434	$ 7,374,635	$ 2,790,799	73%
John D. Rockefeller	26,905,182	17,124,988	9,780,194	64
Clark Gable	2,806,526	1,101,038	1,705,488	39
Walt Disney	23,004,851	6,811,943	16,192,908	30

Source: Public court records, state probate courts.

EXAMPLE: Reducing an Estate by Gifting

Suppose that on December 31, 2013, Michael gave $14,000 worth of shares of a stock mutual fund to his son. On January 2, 2016, these shares are worth $31,000. As a result of this gift in 2013, Michael has removed from his estate the $14,000 gift plus $17,000 of appreciation, for a total of $31,000. All of this has been accomplished at no gift tax cost.

TYPES OF TAXES

Federal and state governments levy various types of taxes that you must consider in planning your estate. The four major taxes of this kind are estate taxes, estate and trust income taxes, inheritance taxes, and gift taxes.

I can reduce my taxable estate by giving away assets to anyone during my lifetime.

Yes. You can reduce your taxable estate by giving away assets to anyone, but don't give away assets if you may need those assets during your retirement years.

ESTATE TAXES An **estate tax** is a federal tax levied on the right of a deceased person to transmit his or her property and life insurance at death. Estate taxes, levied since 1916, have undergone extensive revision since the mid-1970s. The Economic Recovery Tax Act of 1981 made important tax concessions, particularly the unlimited marital deduction and the increased exemption equivalent.

Then, the Economic Growth and Tax Relief Reconciliation Act of 2001 brought important changes to the federal estate, gift, and generation-skipping transfer (GST) taxes, including a potential one-year repeal of the estate and GST taxes after 2009.

estate tax A federal tax on the right of a deceased person to transfer property and life insurance at death.

Under the American Taxpayer Relief Act of 2012 (ATRA), with intelligent estate planning and properly drawn wills, you may leave all of your property to your surviving spouse free of federal estate taxes. The surviving spouse's estate in excess of $10.5 million (in 2013) faces estate tax of 40 percent.

All limits have been removed from transfers between spouses during their lifetimes as well as at death. Whatever you give your spouse is exempt from gift and estate taxes. Gift tax returns need not be filed for interspousal gifts. There is still the possibility, however, that such gifts will be included in your estate if they were given within three years of your death.

ESTATE AND TRUST FEDERAL INCOME TAXES In addition to the federal estate tax, estates and certain trusts must file federal income tax returns with the Internal Revenue Service. Generally, taxable income for estates and trusts is computed in much the same manner as taxable income for individuals. Under the Tax Reform Act

Form **706** (Rev. August 2012) Department of the Treasury Internal Revenue Service

United States Estate (and Generation-Skipping Transfer) Tax Return

▶ Estate of a citizen or resident of the United States (see instructions). To be filed for decedents dying after December 31, 2011, and before January 1, 2013.
▶ Information about Form 706 and its separate instructions is at *www.irs.gov/form706*.

OMB No. 1545-0015

Part 1—Decedent and Executor

1a Decedent's first name and middle initial (and maiden name, if any) | 1b Decedent's last name | 2 Decedent's social security no.
3a County, state, and ZIP or foreign country and postal code, of legal residence (domicile) at time of death | 3b Year domicile established | 4 Date of birth | 5 Date of death
6b Executor's address (number and street including apartment or suite no.; city, town, or post office; state; country; and ZIP or postal code) and phone no.
6a Name of executor (see instructions)
6c Executor's social security number (see instructions)
Phone no.
6d If there are multiple executors, check here ☐ and attach a list showing the names, addresses, telephone numbers, and SSNs of the additional executors.
7a Name and location of court where will was probated or estate administered | 7b Case number
8 If decedent died testate, check here ▶ ☐ and attach a certified copy of the will. | 9 If you extended the time to file this Form 706, check here ▶ ☐
10 If Schedule R-1 is attached, check here ▶ ☐ | 11 If you are estimating the value of assets included in the gross estate on line 1 pursuant to the special rule of Reg. section 20.2010-2T(a) (7)(ii), check here ▶ ☐

Part 2—Tax Computation

1	Total gross estate less exclusion (from Part 5—Recapitulation, item 13)		1
2	Tentative total allowable deductions (from Part 5—Recapitulation, item 24)		2
3a	Tentative taxable estate (subtract line 2 from line 1)		3a
b	State death tax deduction		3b
c	Taxable estate (subtract line 3b from line 3a)		3c
4	Adjusted taxable gifts (see instructions)		4
5	Add lines 3c and 4		5
6	Tentative tax on the amount on line 5 from Table A in the instructions		6
7	Total gift tax paid or payable (see instructions)		7
8	Gross estate tax (subtract line 7 from line 6)		8
9a	Basic exclusion amount	9a	
9b	Deceased spousal unused exclusion (DSUE) amount from predeceased spouse(s), if any (from Section D, Part 6—Portability of Deceased Spousal Unused Exclusion)	9b	
9c	Applicable exclusion amount (add lines 9a and 9b)	9c	
9d	Applicable credit amount (tentative tax on the amount in 9c from Table A in the instructions)	9d	
10	Adjustment to applicable credit amount (May not exceed $6,000. See instructions.)	10	
11	Allowable applicable credit amount (subtract line 10 from line 9d)		11
12	Subtract line 11 from line 8 (but do not enter less than zero)		12
13	Credit for foreign death taxes (from Schedule P). (Attach Form(s) 706-CE.)	13	
14	Credit for tax on prior transfers (from Schedule Q)	14	
15	Total credits (add lines 13 and 14)		15
16	Net estate tax (subtract line 15 from line 12)		16
17	Generation-skipping transfer (GST) taxes payable (from Schedule R, Part 2, line 10)		17
18	Total transfer taxes (add lines 16 and 17)		18
19	Prior payments (explain in an attached statement)		19
20	Balance due (or overpayment) (subtract line 19 from line 18)		20

Under penalties of perjury, I declare that I have examined this return, including accompanying schedules and statements, and to the best of my knowledge and belief, it is true, correct, and complete. Declaration of preparer other than the executor is based on all information of which preparer has any knowledge.

Sign Here ▶ Signature of executor ▶ Date
▶ Signature of executor ▶ Date

Paid Preparer Use Only Print/Type preparer's name | Preparer's signature | Date | Check ☐ if self-employed | PTIN
Firm's name ▶ | Firm's EIN ▶
Firm's address ▶ | Phone no.

For Privacy Act and Paperwork Reduction Act Notice, see instructions. Cat. No. 20548R Form **706** (Rev. 8-2012)

Dealing with the financial aspects of a person's death can be a difficult burden.

of 1986, trusts and estates must pay quarterly estimated taxes, and new trusts must use the calendar year as the tax year.

INHERITANCE TAXES An **inheritance tax** is levied on the right of an heir to receive all or part of the estate and life insurance proceeds of a deceased person. The tax payable depends on the net value of the property and insurance received. It also depends on the relationship of the heir to the deceased.

Inheritance taxes are imposed only by the state governments. Most states levy an inheritance tax, but the state laws differ widely as to exemptions, rates of taxation, and the treatment of property and life insurance. A reasonable average for state inheritance taxes would be 4 to 10 percent of your estate, with the higher percentages on larger amounts.

Over the past few years, many states have been phasing out their inheritance tax provisions, usually over a period of three or four years. This apparently reflects a desire to retain older and wealthy citizens as residents and to discourage them from leaving the states where they have lived most of their lives to seek tax havens in states such as Florida and Nevada. Increasingly, state legislatures have been questioning the equity of further taxes at death and are opting instead for sales and income taxes to provide state revenues. As of 2013, 30 states do not impose estate or inheritance tax

inheritance tax A tax levied on the right of an heir to receive an estate.

gift tax A federal and state tax on the privilege of making gifts to others.

GIFT TAXES The federal and state governments levy a **gift tax** on the privilege of making gifts to others. A property owner can avoid estate and inheritance taxes by giving property during his or her lifetime. For this reason, the federal tax laws provide for taxes on gifts of property. The tax rates on gifts used to be only 75 percent of the tax rates on estates, but since 1976 the gift tax rates have been the same as the estate tax rates. Indeed, the tax rates are now called *unified transfer tax rates.*

Many states have gift tax laws. The state gift tax laws are similar to the federal gift tax laws, but the exemptions and dates for filing returns vary widely among the states.

As discussed earlier, the federal gift tax law allows you to give up to $14,000 each year to any person without incurring gift tax liability or having to report the gift to the IRS. Note that the Taxpayer Relief Act of 1997 increased this amount in $1,000 increments, depending on rates of inflation in future years. Gifts from a husband or a wife to a third party are considered as having been made in equal amounts by each spouse. Consequently, a husband and wife may give as much as $28,000 per year to anyone without incurring tax liability.

Exhibit 19-6 summarizes the important provisions of the Economic Growth and Tax Relief Reconciliation Act of 2001 and the American Taxpayer Act of 2012 pertaining to estate planning.

TAX AVOIDANCE AND TAX EVASION

A poorly arranged estate may be subject to unduly large taxation. Therefore, you should study the tax laws and seek advice to avoid estate taxes larger than those the lawmakers intended you to pay. You should have a clear idea of the distinction between tax avoidance and tax evasion. *Tax avoidance* is the use of legal methods to reduce or escape taxes; *tax evasion* is the use of illegal methods to reduce or escape taxes.

CHARITABLE GIFTS AND BEQUESTS Gifts made to certain recognized charitable or educational organizations are exempt from gift, estate, and inheritance taxes. Accordingly, such gifts or bequests (gifts through a will) represent one method of reducing or avoiding estate and inheritance taxes.

Exhibit 19-6 Estate tax law changes

The Economic Growth and Tax Relief Reconciliation Act of 2001 brought important and significant changes to the federal estate, gift, and generation-skipping transfer (GST) taxes, including a potential one-year repeal of the estate and GST taxes after 2009.

Tax Year	Highest Estate Tax Rate (%)	Gift Exemption ($ million)	Estate Exemption Unified or Credit Amount ($ million)	GST Tax Exemption ($ million)	Notes
2001	55	0.675	0.675	0.675	
2002	50	1.00	1.00	1.00*	Estate tax exemption is raised to $1 million; top estate tax is cut to 50 percent.
2003	49	1.00	1.00	1.00*	Top estate tax is cut to 49 percent.
2004	48	1.00	1.50	1.50	Estate tax exemption rises to $1.5 million; top estate tax rate is cut to 48 percent.
2005	47	1.00	1.50	1.50	Top estate tax is cut to 47 percent.
2006	46	1.00	2.00	2.00	Exemption rises to $2 million; top rate declines to 46 percent.
2007	45	1.00	2.00	2.00	Top rate declines to 45 percent.
2008	45	1.00	2.00	2.00	No change.
2009	45	1.00	3.50	3.50	Exemption rises to $3.5 million.
2010	0	1.00	Repeal	Repeal	Estate tax is completely repealed.
2011	35	1.00	5.00	5.00	
2012	35	5.12	5.12	5.12	
2013	40	5.25	5.25	5.25	Exemption rises to $5.25 million. Top estate tax rises to 40 percent.

* Adjusted annually for inflation.
Source: www.irs.gov, accessed May 9, 2013.

CALCULATING THE TAX

The estate tax is applied not to your total gross estate but to your net taxable estate at death. *Net taxable estate* is your testamentary net worth after subtracting your debts, liabilities, probate costs, and administration costs. These items, all of which are taken off your estate before calculating your tax, are cash requirements to be paid by your estate.

DEBTS AND LIABILITIES In arriving at your taxable estate, the amount of your debts and other creditor obligations are subtracted. You are liable for the payment of these debts while living; your estate will be liable at your death. Your debts may include mortgages, collateralized loans, margin accounts, bank loans, notes payable, installment and charge accounts, and accrued income and property taxes. They may also include your last-illness and funeral expenses.

PROBATE AND ADMINISTRATION COSTS Your estate administration costs will include fees for attorneys, accountants, appraisers, executors or administrators and trustees, court costs, bonding and surety costs, and miscellaneous expenses.

These administration costs may run 5 to 8 percent of your estate, depending on its size and complexity. While the percentage usually decreases as the size of the estate increases, it may be increased by additional complicating factors, such as handling a business interest.

Next, deductions are made for bequests to qualified charities and for property passing to your spouse (the marital deduction). That leaves your net taxable estate, to which the rates shown in Exhibit 19-6 on page 683 are applied to determine your gross estate tax.

Inheritance and estate taxes in your own state are additional costs, and these costs are not deductible in arriving at your taxable estate. In fact, you may have to pay inheritance taxes in two or more states, depending on the location of your property.

PAYING THE TAX

If, after having used various estate tax reduction techniques, you must still pay an estate tax, you should consider the best way to pay it. The federal estate tax is due and payable in cash nine months after your death. State taxes, probate costs, debts, and expenses also usually fall due within that time. These often result in a real cash bind, because people rarely keep a lot of cash on hand. They derived their wealth from putting their money to work in businesses, real estate, or other investments. Estate liquidity— having enough cash to pay taxes and costs without selling assets or borrowing heavily—is often a problem.

One way to handle the estate tax is to set aside or accumulate enough cash to pay it when it falls due. However, you may die before you have accumulated enough cash, and the cash you accumulate may be subject to income tax during your lifetime and to estate tax at your death.

Another way to handle the estate tax is for your family to sell assets to pay taxes. The first assets to be sold might be stocks, bonds, gold or silver coins, and similar liquid assets. However, these assets may be the source of your family's income after your death, and the market for them may be down. Assets such as real estate may also be sold, but prices on forced sales are usually only a fraction of the fair value.

Your family could consider borrowing; however, it is unusual to find a commercial lender that will lend money to pay back-taxes. If you do find one, it may require personal liability. In any event, borrowing does not solve the problem; it only prolongs it, adding interest costs in the process.

Borrowing from the IRS itself in the form of deferred payments or installments may be possible for reasonable cause. Tax extension and installment payment provisions are helpful, but they still leave a tax debt to be paid by your heirs at your death. Paying that debt, even over an extended period of time, could be a real burden and severely restrict their income and flexibility.

Life insurance may be a reasonable, feasible, and economical means of paying your estate tax. Instead of forcing your family to pay off the estate tax and other debts and costs by borrowing or selling, you can, through insurance, provide your family with tax-free cash at a fraction of the cost of borrowing.

Estate tax projection and settlement costs

PRACTICE QUIZ 19-5

1 What are the four types of taxes to consider in planning your estate?
2 How is estate tax calculated?
3 What are the various ways to handle the payment of estate tax?

my life stages for estate planning . . .

YOUR PERSONAL FINANCE DASHBOARD

A personal finance dashboard with key performance indicators can help you monitor your financial situation and guide you toward financial independence.

Estate planning is essential not only to ensure that your assets are distributed in the way you choose, but also to make sure that your loved ones are not left with difficult or costly problems. Planning for your estate and taxes as well as writing a will are just a few of the steps you can take to have a secure financial future for yourself and your loved ones.

YOUR SITUATION: Have you prepared a valid will? Do you have several copies of the documents needed for processing insurance claims and settling your estate? Have you selected an executor who is willing to perform the tasks involved in carrying out a will? If you have children, have you selected a guardian to care of them in the event that you and your spouse die at the same time? Have you prepared a power of attorney and a letter of last instructions? Other personal financial planning actions you might consider during various stages of your life include:

. . . in college

- You may not be wealthy, but make a will
- Prepare a durable power of attorney and a living will
- Carry a card in your wallet that states you have advance directives

. . . in my 20s

- Make sure to prepare a will
- Give a copy of your advance directives to family members and/or friends

. . . in my 30s and 40s

- Decide who will take care of your children if you and your spouse die in an accident
- Review your power of attorney every few years
- Keep the original copies of your living will, durable power of attorney, and letter of last instructions where they are easily found
- Give your doctor a copy of your advance directives for your medical record

. . . in my 50s and beyond

- Review your estate plan. With a proper estate plan, you can avoid underfunded and backlogged courts
- Tell your children what you intend to leave for them in your will and why
- Make a list and share detailed financial information about your assets with your spouse
- Provide a copy of your advance directives to a hospital and/or your nursing home

(continued)

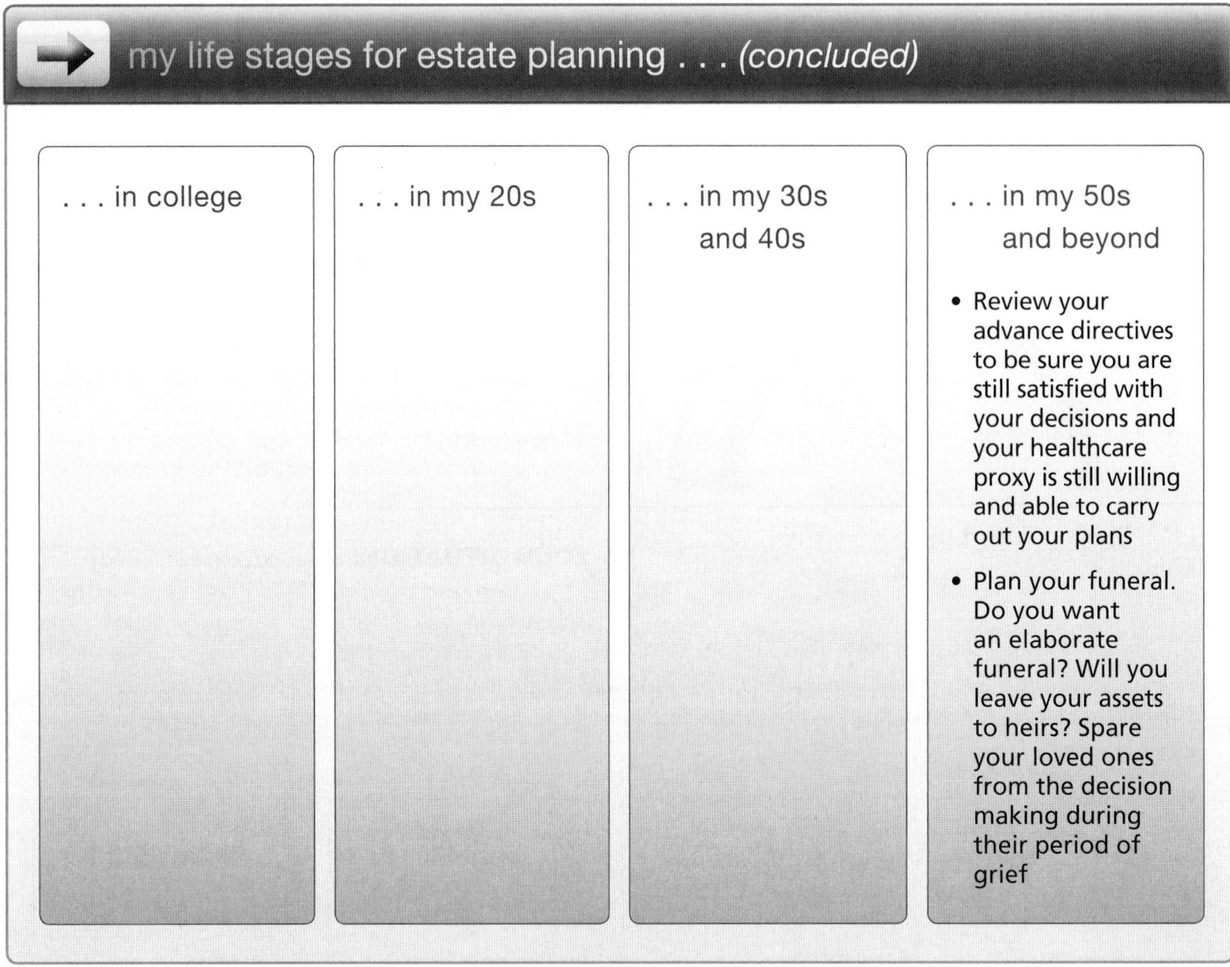

SUMMARY OF LEARNING OBJECTIVES

LO19-1

Analyze the personal aspects of estate planning.

Estate planning is an essential part of retirement planning and an integral part of financial planning. The first part of estate planning consists of building your estate; the second part consists of transferring your estate, at your death, in the manner you have specified. The personal aspects of estate planning depend on whether you are single or married. If you are married, your estate planning involves the interests of at least two people, and more if there are children. Never having been married does not eliminate the need to organize your financial affairs.

LO19-2

Assess the legal aspects of estate planning.

In the event of death, proof of claims must be produced or the claims will not be processed. Among the papers needed are birth certificates, marriage certificates, legal name changes, and military service records. Every adult should have a written will, which is the legal declaration of a person's mind as to the disposition of his or her property after death. Thus, a will is a way to transfer your property according to your wishes after you die.

LO19-3

Distinguish among various types and formats of wills.

The four types of wills are the simple will, the traditional marital share will, the exemption trust will, and the stated dollar amount will. A will can be simple or complex depending on your personal and financial circumstances.

A *simple will* leaves everything to the spouse. Such a will is sufficient for most smaller estates. However, if you have a large or complex estate, a simple will may not meet your objectives. It may also create higher overall taxation, because everything would be taxed in your spouse's subsequent estate.

LO19-4

Appraise various types of trusts and estates.

Establishing a trust can be an excellent way to manage your estate. Trusts are revocable or irrevocable. Popular forms of trusts include credit-shelter trusts, grantor retained annuity trusts, disclaimer trusts, marital-deduction trusts, living trusts, self-declaration trusts, testamentary trusts, life insurance trusts, charitable remainder trusts, qualified personal residence trusts, charitable lead trusts, generation-skipping trusts, and spendthrift trusts. An attorney's help is needed to establish a trust.

If you establish a *revocable trust,* you retain the right to end the trust or change its terms during your lifetime. If you establish an *irrevocable trust,* you cannot change its terms or end it. However, an irrevocable trust offers tax advantages not offered by a revocable trust.

LO19-5

Evaluate the effects of federal and state taxes on estate planning.

The tax aspects of estate planning have changed considerably due to recent major changes in the federal tax structure. The four major federal and state taxes you must consider in planning your estate are estate taxes, estate and trust income taxes, inheritance taxes, and gift taxes.

The federal estate tax is due and payable in cash nine months after your death. State taxes, probate costs, debts, and expenses also usually fall due within that time.

KEY TERMS

adjusted gross estate 666
beneficiary 667
codicil 670
community property 679
credit-shelter trust 674
disclaimer trust 674
durable power of attorney 672
estate 660
estate planning 660
estate tax 681
ethical will 672
exemption trust will 666
formal will 667
gift tax 682
guardian 669
holographic will 667
inheritance tax 682
intestate 664
irrevocable trust 673
life insurance trust 677
living trust 674
living will 670
prenuptial agreement 670
probate 666
revocable trust 673
simple will 666
stated dollar amount will 667
statutory will 667
testamentary trust 676
traditional marital share will 666
trust 673
trustee 669
trustor 673
will 664

SELF-TEST PROBLEMS

1. In 2013, you gave $14,000 worth of stock to your best friend. In 2016, the stock is valued at $25,000.

a. What was the gift tax in 2013?

b. What is the total amount removed from your estate in 2016?

c. What will be the gift tax in 2016?

2. On December 31, 2013, George gives $14,000 to his son and $14,000 to his son's wife. On January 1, 2014, George gives another $14,000 to his son and another $14,000 to his son's wife. George made no other gifts to his son and his son 's wife in 2013 and 2014. What is the gift tax?

Solutions

1. a. Since you can give up to $14,000 to anyone in 2013, there is no gift tax.

b. Total amount removed from your estate in 2016 is $14,000 + $11,000 = $25,000.

c. Gift tax will be zero in 2016.

2. There is no gift tax in 2013 or in 2014 since George gave $14,000 to his son and his son's wife in each of the two years.

FINANCIAL PLANNING PROBLEMS

Problems 1, 2, and 3 are based on the following scenario:

In 2013, Joshua gave $14,000 worth of XYZ stock to his son. In 2014, the XYZ shares are worth $25,000.

LO19-5 **1.** *Calculating the Gift Tax.* What was the gift tax in 2010?

LO19-5 **2.** *Calculating the Gift Tax.* What is the total amount removed from Joshua's estate in 2014?

LO19-5 **3.** *Calculating the Gift Tax.* What will be the gift tax in 2014?

LO19-5 **4.** *Calculating the Gift Tax.* In 2013, you gave a $14,000 cash gift to your best friend. What is the gift tax?

Problems 5, 6, and 7 are based on the following scenario:

Barry and his wife Mary have accumulated over $4 million during their 45 years of marriage. They have three children and five grandchildren.

LO19-5 **5.** *Calculating the Gift Tax.* How much money can Barry and Mary gift to their children in 2008 without any gift tax liability?

LO19-5 **6.** *Calculating the Gift Tax.* How much money can Barry and Mary gift to their grandchildren?

LO19-5 **7.** *Calculating the Gift Tax.* What is the total amount removed from Barry and Mary's estate?

LO19-5 **8.** *Calculating the Estate Tax.* The date of death for a widow was 2008. If the estate was valued at $2,129,000 and the estate was taxed at 45 percent, what was the heir's tax liability?

LO19-5 **9.** *Calculating the Estate Tax.* Joel and Rachel are both retired. Married for 50 years, they've amassed an estate worth $2.4 million. The couple has no trusts or other types of tax-sheltered assets. If Joel or Rachel dies in 2008, how much federal estate tax would the surviving spouse have to pay, assuming that the estate is taxed at the 45 percent rate?

FINANCIAL PLANNING ACTIVITIES

LO19-1 **1.** *Preparing a Written Record of Personal Information.* Prepare a written record of personal information that would be helpful to you and your heirs. Make sure to include the location of family records, your military service file, and other important papers; medical records; bank accounts; charge accounts; the location of your safe-deposit box; U.S. savings bonds; stocks, bonds, and other securities; property owned; life insurance; annuities; and Social Security information.

LO19-2 **2.** *Using the Internet to Obtain Information about Wills.* Visit Metropolitan Life Insurance Company's website at www.lifeadvice.com. Using this information, prepare a report on the following: (*a*) Who needs a will? (*b*) What are the elements of a will (naming a guardian, naming an executor, preparing a will, updating a will, estate taxes, where to keep your will, living will, etc.)? (*c*) How is this report helpful in preparing your own will?

LO19-3 **3.** *Preparing the Letter of Last Instructions.* Prepare your own letter of last instructions.

LO19-3 **4.** *Determining Criteria in Choosing a Guardian.* Make a list of the criteria you will use in deciding who will be the guardian of your minor children if you and your spouse die at the same time.

LO19-4 **5.** *Using the Internet to Obtain Information about Estate Planning.* Visit the Prudential Insurance Company of America website at prudential.com/estateplan. Gather information on various estate planning topics such as an estate planning worksheet; whether you need an estate plan; when to update your plan; estate taxes, wills, executors, trusts, etc. Then prepare a report to help you develop your estate plan.

FINANCIAL PLANNING CASE

Estate Planning

A married couple, Linda and Charles, have just learned about the death of their friend, Lloyd, and wondered whether Lloyd had provided for his family. Charles admits he doesn't even have a will. What would happen to their children if Charles died today?

Rick Fenelli, an estate planning attorney, explains that the first step in estate planning is to identify all of your assets. He reminds us that most people forget that life insurance proceeds are fully taxable by Uncle Sam.

Linda and Charles believe their net worth is not much, even though they own a home, a savings account, 401(k)s, and a few IRAs. Their attorney friend calculates that Linda and Charles have a net worth of about $1 million. The couple is startled. The attorney friend explains that they already have a will even though they never wrote one. The will is written by the state and it's called "probate." Dying without a will is called "dying intestate."

Questions

1. What triggered Charles and Linda to start thinking about planning their estate?
2. According to attorney Rick Fenelli, what is the first step in estate planning?
3. Who writes your will if you don't?

PERSONAL FINANCIAL PLANNER IN ACTION

Developing an Estate Plan

Most people do not think they have enough assets to do estate planning. However, the planned transfer of resources with the use of a will, trusts, and other legal vehicles is a necessary phase of your total financial plan.

Your Short-Term Financial Planning Activities	*Resources*
1. Investigate the cost of a will. Decide on the type of will and provisions appropriate for your life situation.	PFP Sheet 67 www.mtpalermo.com www.prudential.com www.nolo.com
2. Using the IRS and other websites, identify recent estate tax law changes that may affect your financial planning decisions.	www.irs.com www.banksite.com/calc/estate
3. Compare the benefits and costs of different trusts that might be appropriate for your life situation.	PFP Sheet 68 www.webtrust.com
Your Long-Term Financial Planning Activities	*Resources*
1. Develop a plan for actions to take related to estate planning.	PFP Sheet 66 www.naepc.org
2. Identify saving and investing decisions that would minimize future estate taxes.	PFP Sheet 69

CONTINUING CASE

Estate Planning

Life Situation	*Financial Data*	
Shelby, age 45	Monthly Gross Income	$8,000
Mark, age 46	Living Expenses	$6,500
Two children, ages 19 and 13	Assets	$230,000
	Liabilities	$85,000

Since Shelby and Mark Lawrence are less than 20 years away from retirement, they are also concerned with various estate planning actions. They have talked about a will and investigated the benefits of several types of trusts. However, they have not taken any specific actions.

Questions

1. What types of estate planning activities should the Lawrences consider at this time?
2. Explain how Shelby and Mark might use the Personal Financial Planner sheets on Estate Planning Activities and Will Planning.

DAILY SPENDING DIARY

"This current spending information allows me to better plan for the future needs of my family."

Directions

Your "Daily Spending Diary" can provide you with ongoing information that will help you manage your current finances while planning for future family needs.

Analysis Questions

1. What information from your spending patterns can help you plan for the long-term needs of you and family members?
2. What estate planning activities are you planning to take action on in the next few years?

The Daily Spending Diary sheets are located in Appendix D at the end of the book and on the student website at www.mhhe.com/kdh.

appendix A

Education Financing, Loans, and Scholarships

The desire to pursue higher education has grown steadily since the 1940s. According to the Census Bureau, in 1940 approximately 5 percent of the population held a bachelor's degree. Today, that percentage has grown to greater than 30 percent. The increase in demand for education has created an expansion in many areas, including the number of higher education schools, the development of different types of degree programs, and specialization in occupations, which has contributed to the overall higher cost of a college education.

Increasing Costs of Education

As college enrollments have swelled, increases in tuition, especially over the last decade, have been significant. Not only are there major increases in the number of traditional students coming straight from high school, but the number of those who are returning to school to "retool" and change careers has risen greatly as well. Some students are even staying in school to ride out an undesirable job market. A very common issue for many of these students is the need to find ways to pay for tuition, books, school fees, and living expenses while they pursue an education.

What is driving the increase in demand for education? Some of the main drivers appear to be higher projected salaries with additional education and reduced potential for unemployment. Numerous studies have shown a correlation between additional education and higher salaries. In addition, lower unemployment rates are correlated with higher education levels. (See Exhibit A-1). However, along with additional education comes the opportunity costs associated with it: lost wages while in school and tuition and living costs to attend school. Funding and repaying these educational pursuits is the primary focus of this appendix.

For some students, being accepted by their "dream college" can be a euphoric experience. The more earth-bound question is: How do you pay for the education? This question clearly should be asked before applying to schools, but school endowments and additional assistance provided frequently add to the challenge of determining the full costs until the college applications are accepted and the financial aid process begins.

The majority of students fund their education through a combination of loans, scholarships, grants, savings, and current earnings. Loans have specific repayment terms, but scholarships and grants do not need to be repaid and thus are sometimes referred to as *free money.* Yet nothing in life is free, as the saying goes, and although there are no repayment requirements, you will have to put in some time and effort to find these scholarships. Information and websites for scholarships will be provided later in this appendix.

DID YOU KNOW?

The average student loan balance in 2012 was $24,803, up from $15,000 in 2005.

Source: Federal Reserve Bank of New York, 2012 Q4, *Quarterly Report on Household Debt and Credit (accessed May 3, 2013).*

Exhibit **A-1**

Education, Unemployment & Wages

Education Pays...

Education Pays in higher earnings and lower unemployment rates

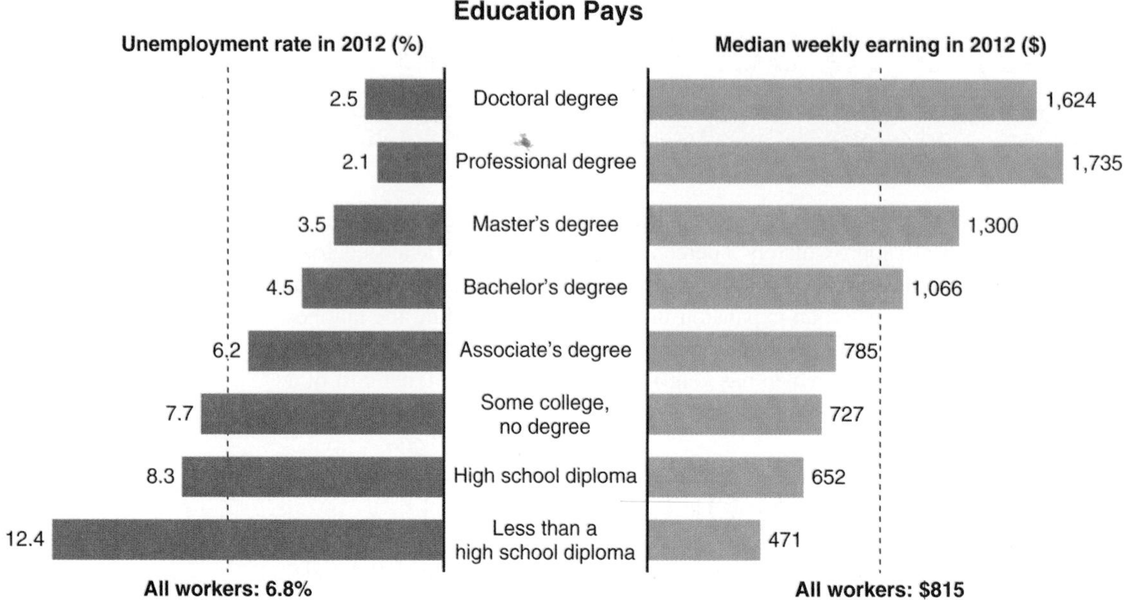

Note: Data are for persons age 25 and over. Earnings are for full-time wage and salary workers.
Source: Bureau of Labor Statistics. Date Accessed: May 5, 2013.

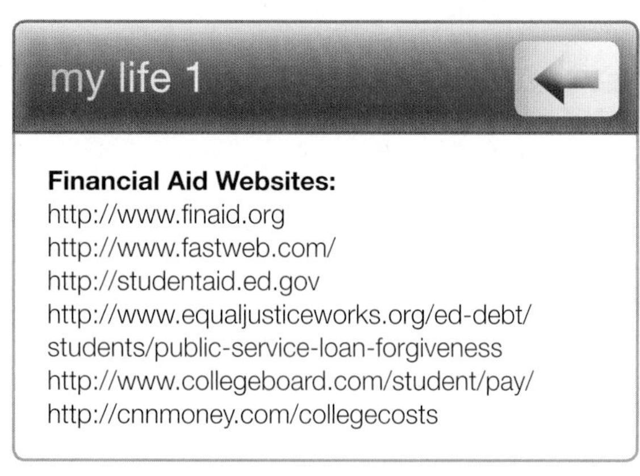

FAFSA (Free Application for Federal Student Aid)

The very first step in funding your education, whether with loans or certain grants, is completing and submitting the FAFSA (Free Application for Federal Student Aid) form. Many state and institutional aid programs also require that this form be remitted before they consider providing any type of funding. After the FAFSA has been processed, you will receive notification of your estimated family contribution (EFC). For dependent students being claimed on their parents' tax return; the amount of parental income, assets, and college savings accounts will be important factors in determining the amount of the EFC. For an independent student, individual assets will also be carefully considered in determining eligibility for aid.

The schools that the student designated on the FAFSA will receive notification that the FAFSA has been processed. Once the admission application is accepted, the schools will take the FAFSA information and prepare a financial aid package. The goal is to evaluate each student's situation and provide the best possible selection of aid. In many cases, the aid package will not be able to cover the full cost of attendance. In addition, the federal student aid may be reduced based upon other aid that has been awarded (scholarships, state aid, etc.).

The financial aid package received from the school will often include a combination of grants, loans, and work-study options. The student will be sent an award letter with each portion designated (see Exhibit A-2). Each of these aid types will now be reviewed with the goal of understanding which selection requires repayment and the terms of acceptance.

Exhibit A-2

Sample award package

Sample Financial Aid Award Package	
Total cost of attendance	$20,000
Expected family contribution (EFC)	$ 1,823
Outside scholarship	$ 1,000
Financial need	$17,177
Federal Pell Grant	$ 3,700
State scholarship grant	$ 1,500
Institutional grant	$ 7,500
Federal Perkins Loan	$ 1,000
Federal direct loan	$ 1,477
Federal work-study	$ 2,000
Total award	$17,177

GRANTS

A grant is money that is given and does not need to be repaid. It can be used to pay for education, training, books, tuition, or any school-related expenses. Students who have demonstrated financial need may receive grants. The most common type is the federal Pell Grant that offers a maximum of $5,645 for the 2013–14 academic year. This maximum amount can change each year and has increased significantly in the past few years. For the most up-to-date numbers, visit http://studentaid.ed.gov. The Pell Grant will only be disbursed for a maximum of 12 semesters. Another grant that is available is the Federal Supplemental Educational Opportunity Grants (FSEOG). It can be worth up to $4,000 annually. You must receive a Pell Grant to be eligible for the FSEOG grants. This grant is typically provided to those who have demonstrated exceptional financial need.

The Teacher Education Assistance for College and Higher Education (TEACH) grant may also be available depending on the types of courses and the student's future career. This grant provides up to $4,000 annually and requires a signed TEACH grant agreement that the student will fulfill their teaching requirement within eight years of graduation or leaving school.

Another relatively new grant is the Iraq and Afghanistan service grant. These are available to students whose parents have died as a result of military service in Iraq or Afghanistan after 9/11. The grant offers a maximum of $5,645 for the 2013–14 academic year.

In addition to the federal grants, many states offer grants that are distributed through the schools' financial aid office, called institutional grants. Certain colleges and schools also provide grants to women and minority groups and to students in certain degree programs to encourage enrollment.

LOANS

Education loans can be a significant part of the financial aid package. These types of loans have become a significant part of the outstanding consumer debt. It has been reported by the Federal Reserve Bank of New York and the U.S. Department of Education that the total amount of student loans distributed in recent years was $100 billion annually. Additionally, they have reported that the total loan balances outstanding are expected to grow to over $1 trillion, an amount greater than the total owed nationally on consumer credit cards.[1]

Federal education loans that are available today originate from the Direct Loan program. Each college's financial aid office disburses the funds provided by the U.S. Department of Education.

The interest rates and fees can change annually and are adjusted by the federal government. The current range for interest rates for federal loans is between 3.4% and 6.8%.[2] These rates are expected to rise in the future.

Education loans are typically divided into four main categories:

1. *Stafford Loans*
   a. Stafford Loans were initially called the Federal Guaranteed Student Loan Program. In 1988, the loans were renamed to honor U.S. Senator Robert Stafford, based on his work with higher education.
   b. The Stafford Loans are the most frequently disbursed loans. They are typically disbursed directly from the financial aid office directly to the student. (*Note:* The Stafford Loan can also be disbursed through a private lender, which will be discussed later).
   c. One key element to the Stafford Loan is how the interest accrues while the student is in school. In some cases of extreme need, the federal government will make the interest payments during the time that the student is in school and for certain grace periods. This type of loan is commonly referred to as a *subsidized loan.* Subsidized loans are no longer available for graduate or professional education programs.
   d. However, the more common scenario is that the interest is the responsibility of the borrower while in school and during the grace period. Two options exist for handling the interest: pay the interest while still enrolled in school or have the interest added to the balance of the loan. The borrower must carefully calculate the cost of allowing this interest to add on to the loan. This process is commonly called *negative amortization* and occurs when the amount of the loan exceeds the original amount borrowed. This not only adds to the amount of the loan but can extend the time for repayment. This type of loan is commonly referred to as an *unsubsidized loan.*
   e. The maximum amounts allowed for the Stafford Loans vary considerably based on many factors including: the student's current year in school, type of schooling, subsidized versus unsubsidized cumulative amounts, and dependency status. The federal website with the most up-to-date information is: http://studentaid.ed.gov.

2. *Perkins Loans*
   a. Perkins Loans are named after Carl D. Perkins, a former member of the U.S. House of Representatives from Kentucky. Mr. Perkins was an advocate for higher education, as well as a strong supporter of education for underprivileged students.
   b. The Perkins Loan is typically provided to students who have demonstrated exceptional financial need. This program is run by the individual schools, which serve as the lender, using money provided by the federal government. This type of loan is provided only in a subsidized form; it offers a very low interest rate, a long repayment schedule of 10 years, and a slightly longer grace period to begin repayment.

c. Although each school's financial aid office will determine the amount each student receives, there are still annual and cumulative limits for this loan. For the 2013–14 academic year, the maximum Perkins Loan allowed for undergraduate students is $5,500 with a cumulative maximum of $27,500. For graduate students, the annual maximum is $8,000 and a cumulative maximum of $60,000.

3. *Parent Loans (PLUS loans),* formerly known as the Parent Loan for Undergraduate Students, now referred to as the PLUS loan for parents or the Grad PLUS loan for Graduate Students.

   a. There are times when parents of dependent children want to contribute financially to help with educational expenses. If they do not currently have funds to contribute, they may apply for a loan. After July 1, 2010, all new PLUS loans are provided by the government and can only be obtained by contacting the financial aid office of the school, not a private lender. Currently, there is no maximum amount; however, the parent may only borrow amounts not covered by student's current financial aid package, up to the total cost of attending the school.
   b. For the PLUS loans, the parent is responsible for repaying the loan. The parent's creditworthiness is a factor in determining whether the loan will be granted. If the parent does not qualify, the student may have the option of taking out additional unsubsidized Stafford loans.
   c. One variant of the PLUS loan program is the Grad PLUS loan which allows graduate students to borrow for educational expenses.
   d. The PLUS loans and the Grad PLUS loans have higher interest rates than the Stafford and Perkins loans so, they should be considered very carefully.

4. *Private Student Loans (also called Alternative Student Loans).*

   a. Private student loans should also be considered very carefully. They tend to have higher interest rates than the government programs. In addition, the interest rates are commonly variable which can make the payments more challenging to manage.
   b. The three most common reasons that borrowers choose private student loans are:
      1. To fund additional education expenses above the limits that the other programs provide.
      2. There is no requirement for a FAFSA form to be completed. The loan is based upon the creditworthiness of the borrower.
      3. To provide additional flexibility over the government loans to the borrower in terms of repayment or deferral while the student is in school.

In addition to traditional student loans, a new form of nontraditional lending has also started to be used to fund education expenses. It is known as *social lending* or *peer-to-peer lending*. This newest form of student loan comes from the private sector. The basic premise is that borrowers can post relevant information and stories regarding why they need money, and prospective lenders or individuals can view the information and choose to fund these aspirations. A large majority of social lending has been in the form of short-term lending, six months to three years. Thus, student lending has been a little slower to catch on primarily due to the time frame for repayment. However, a few websites have started to offer longer repayment periods. Examples of social lending sites are: www.greennote.com, www.prosper.com, and www.lendingclub.com

REPAYING YOUR LOANS

Acquiring the funds to attend school is only the beginning of the financial aid process. The much more lengthy part of the process is the repayment. Many of the different types of loans have differing *grace periods* before the first payment is due:

- Stafford Loans require repayment to begin six months after the student no longer attends school or has dropped below half-time enrollment.
- Perkins Loans require repayment to begin nine months after the student no longer attends school or has dropped below half-time enrollment.

- Federal PLUS Loans, which are typically taken out by parents or graduate students, require repayment to begin 60 days after the loan is disbursed. The repayment can sometimes be deferred while the student is in school, but the interest will still accrue, much like an unsubsidized Stafford Loan.

Once repayment begins, federal loan borrowers have numerous options to consider regarding repaying the loan. The most common plans are:

1. *Standard Repayment.* This is one of the most common repayment plans. A fixed monthly amount is paid for a repayment term not to exceed 10 years.
2. *Extended Repayment.* This option lowers the monthly payment amounts. The length of the repayment term is up to 25 years. One point to consider is the increase in the amount of total interest that will be paid over this time period.
3. *Graduated Repayment.* This repayment plan allows borrowers to make lower payments as they start their careers and then slowly increase the amount of the monthly payment over the life of the loan.
4. *Income-Contingent Repayment.* This repayment plan is designed to provide the borrower with some leniency in terms of the amount to be repaid. The monthly payments are recalculated annually, based on the borrower's most recent reported income as well as total debt amount. The length of the repayment is up to 25 years. If the borrower follows through with the entire repayment plan, any remaining balance will be forgiven. One thing to keep in mind, the forgiven amount will be considered taxable income to the borrower.
5. *Income-Sensitive Repayment.* This repayment plan is similar to the income contingent repayment plan. The income-sensitive plan allows the borrower the option to set the monthly payment amount based upon a percentage of gross monthly income. The length of this repayment is limited to 10 years.
6. *Income-Based Repayment. (IBR)* This repayment plan is currently calculated as 15 percent of discretionary income. To calculate discretionary income: take your adjusted gross income (see Chapter 3) and subtract 150 percent of the poverty line for your state and family size. The plan provides a reduction to the previously discussed income contingent and Income-Sensitive Repayment Plans. This program provides forgiveness beyond a 25-year time period, if all prior payments were made timely. This newer repayment plan was included in the College Cost Reduction and Access Act of 2007.
7. *Pay as You Earn Repayment.* This is the newest repayment option that is available for direct loans disbursed after 10/1/11. The repayment amount is capped at 10 percent of discretionary income (See IBR plan above to calculate). This program provides forgiveness beyond a 20-year time period, if all prior payments were made timely. The plan does require proof of a partial financial hardship to qualify for the more favorable terms compared to the IBR plan.

All seven plans are available for student loans, but only the first three plans are available for PLUS loans to parents.

DID YOU KNOW?

Between 2007 and 2011, state and local funding to colleges and universities decreased by 18.4 percent for full-time undergraduate students.

Source: http://collegecost.ed.gov/statespending.aspx, (accessed May 7, 2013).

CONSOLIDATION LOAN

Another attractive repayment option for borrowers is the combination of all their student loans into one loan, and thus one convenient monthly payment. Just like the extended repayment plan, this method will lower the total monthly payment amount and increase the length of the loan up to 30 years. Remember to carefully consider the increase in the amount of total interest that will be paid over this time period. Unless you are struggling to make the individual loan payment amounts, typically there is no advantage to consolidating loans other than ease of administration (i.e., one payment).

Private loans may have the option of refinancing to obtain a lower interest rate based on an improved credit situation for the borrower. However, in most cases, a federal consolidated loan does not offer this option.

STUDENT LOAN DEFAULT STATISTICS

The ease of obtaining money and the ever-increasing student loan balances that new graduates must begin to repay have created many challenges. These issues combined with a significant number of graduates that are all vying for a smaller pool of available jobs has created some very unfortunate side effects relating to students' abilities to repay loans. The percentage of student loan borrowers that are more than 90 days late on their student loan payments has increased significantly since 2004 (see Exhibit A-3).

Default rates on student loans have increased dramatically for students that have attended all types of higher education institutions: public, private, and for-profit. Student loans will typically not be included in bankruptcy. There are no limitations on the number of years that the lender can seek repayment. For federal student loans, the government can garnish wages, take tax refunds, or take other federal benefits for which you might be eligible. Careful consideration should be given to the costs associated with repaying loans.

LOAN DEFERMENT

Loan deferments allow you to temporarily stop making payments on existing student loans. The most common reasons for the deferments are reenrollment in school, demonstrated financial hardship, unemployment, and military deployment.

LOAN FORGIVENESS

Loan forgiveness is the option to have all or a portion of your student loan forgiven (paid off on your behalf). The most common forgiveness options are for volunteer work or public or military service.

The Public Service Loan Forgiveness Program was established by the College Cost Reduction & Access Act of 2007. Under this program, full-time, qualifying public service employees that make 120 qualifying loan payments on eligible Federal Direct loans will have the balance of their Federal Direct Loans forgiven. Eligibility for the public service position includes working for the government or an organized nonprofit organization, service in the Peace Corps or AmeriCorps, or even working for a private organization that provides public service.

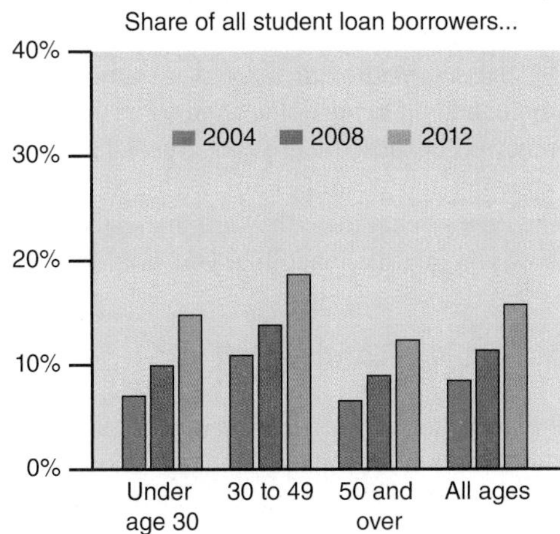

Federal Reserve Bank of New York Consumer Credit Panel/Equifax. Date Accessed: May 4, 2013.

Exhibit A-3

Proportion of student loan borrowers 90+ days delinquent

Many of the above mentioned organizations also have specific programs to allow a portion of the loan to be canceled even sooner. For example:

- The Peace Corps provides partial cancellation of Perkins Loans (15 percent for each year of service, up to 70 percent in total).
- AmeriCorps volunteers who serve for 12 months can receive $4,725 to be used towards cancellation of their loan.
- Military service also offers a cancellation program. Students who enlist in the Army National Guard may be eligible for up to $10,000 of cancellation of student loans.
- In addition, there are a variety of other programs for teachers who serve in low-income areas, work with students with disabilities, or work in high-need schools. Law students can also find loan forgiveness programs for serving with nonprofit or public interest organizations. Medical students may also be eligible for loan forgiveness for performing certain medical research or working in low-income or remote areas. It is strongly advised that you review each program's requirements for eligibility, conditions of employment, and repayment to ensure that you are a good candidate for the program.

LOAN CANCELLATION (DISCHARGE)

In very special circumstances, student loans may be permanently canceled. The most common situations include:

- Death.
- Total and permanent disability.
- Fraud by the school (e.g., in the event of forged promissory notes, the school owes the lender a refund).
- Bankruptcy (very rare because the bankruptcy court would need to establish that repayment would create a significant hardship).

SCHOLARSHIPS

Scholarships, just like grants, do not have to be repaid. Scholarships do have to be reported on the FAFSA or to the financial aid office, if awarded later. Big-name scholarships (e.g., Coca-Cola & Prudential) receive an extraordinary amount of applicants, but there are many other places to consider. Examples include: rotary clubs, churches, professional associations, and local or regional businesses. Although the reward amounts may be smaller, they might add up to big dollars and some may have the benefit of being renewed in subsequent years. Special attention should be spent on knowing the deadlines for each scholarship. Carefully research the type of candidate they are interested in helping and tailor your information to show how you qualify, much like you would do with a résumé.

WORK-STUDY PROGRAMS

Aside from loans, there are other ways to earn money to pay for educational expenses. The Federal Work-Study Program is available at many schools. It is commonly included as part of the financial aid package. Students who decline this option are expected to fund the amount from another source. Some students like the options that the program offers: they can work on campus without needing additional transportation, apply to a variety of positions that interest them, and get to know faculty and staff that they may want to work with on teaching or research assignments. Some students decline the option in favor of higher paying jobs off-campus. You should consider very carefully the opportunity costs with this decision: fuel costs, commuting time, wardrobe needs, and so on.

Decision Making for Financial Aid

Navigating the process of financing an education can be very daunting and time consuming, but the rewards are very high. Finding the money for school and repaying the loans in a manner that works best for your personal situation can lead to long-term success, improved credit scores, higher salaries, and a lower potential for future unemployment. One excellent source for choosing a school, and the financial aid package for your needs, is the College Affordability and Transparency Center (http://collegecost.ed.gov/). This is a one-stop website that you can use to evaluate a college based upon net price, average student debt, state funding, graduation rates, and much more. It is very important for your financial future that you find the most affordable education that fits your budget, future career, and your long-term financial goals.

appendix B

Financial Planners and Other Information Sources

"ATM fees rise."

"Global currency fluctuations may affect consumer prices."

"Mortgage interest rates remain constant."

These are just a few of the possible influences on personal financial decisions that occur each day. While this book offers the foundation for successful personal financial planning, changing social trends, economic conditions, and technology will influence your decision-making environment. An ability to continually update your knowledge is a skill that will serve you for a lifetime.

Various resources are available to assist you with personal financial decisions. These resources include printed materials, financial institutions, courses and seminars, software and apps, online sources, and financial planning specialists.

Current Periodicals

As Exhibit B-1 shows, a variety of personal finance publications are available to expand and update your knowledge. These periodicals, along with books on various personal finance topics, can be found in libraries and online.

Exhibit B-1

Personal financial planning publications

Personal finance is constantly changing. Keep up with new developments through the following publications:

Bloomberg Personal Finance	www.bloomberg.com
Businessweek	www.businessweek.com
Consumer Reports	www.consumerreports.org
Financial Times	www.ft.com
Forbes	www.forbes.com
Fortune	www.fortune.com
Kiplinger's Personal Finance	www.kiplinger.com
Money	www.money.com
U.S. News & World Report	money.usnews.com
The Wall Street Journal	www.wsj.com
Worth	www.worth.com

Financial Institutions

Some financial advisers, such as insurance agents and investment brokers, are affiliated with companies that sell financial services. Through national marketing efforts or local promotions, banks, credit unions, insurance companies, investment brokers, and real estate offices offer suggestions on budgeting, saving, investing, and other aspects of financial planning. These organizations frequently offer financial planning workshops, publications, and online information.

Courses and Seminars

Colleges and universities offer courses in investments, real estate, insurance, taxation, and estate planning to enhance your personal finance knowledge. The Cooperative Extension Service, funded through the U.S. Department of Agriculture, has offices located at universities in every state and in many counties. Programs of these offices include community seminars and continuing education courses in the areas of family financial management, housing, wise buying, health care, and food and nutrition. In addition, Cooperative Extension Service offices offer a variety of publications, videos, and software to assist consumers. Libraries and community organizations often schedule free or low-cost programs on career planning, small-business management, budgeting, life insurance, tax return preparation, and investments.

Personal Finance Software and Apps

Computer software and apps are available to help you with personal financial planning activities, from selecting a career to writing a will. These programs can analyze your current financial situation and project your future financial position. Specialized programs are also available for conducting investment analyses, preparing tax returns, and determining the costs of financing and owning a home. Remember, an app cannot change your saving, spending, and borrowing habits; only *you* can do that. However, your smartphone or tablet can provide fast and current analyses of your financial situation and progress.

A spreadsheet program, such as Excel, can assist with various financial planning tasks. Spreadsheet software can store, manipulate, create projections, and report data for activities such as

- Creating budget categories and recording spending patterns.
- Maintaining tax records for different types of expenses such as mileage, travel expenses, materials and supplies, and business-related costs.
- Calculating the growth potential of savings accounts and investments.
- Monitoring changes in the market value of investments.
- Keeping records of the value of items for a home inventory.
- Projecting needed amounts of life insurance and retirement income.

An online search for "personal finance spreadsheets" can help you locate various ready-to-use templates. In addition, Excel spreadsheet templates are available for each of the Personal Financial Planner sheets at www.mhhe.com/kdh.

Online Financial Planning Information

A wide range of online sources are available to assist you with various personal financial planning activities. Some of the most useful websites providing current information on various personal finance topics include:

- *Money* magazine at www.money.com
- *Kiplinger's Personal Finance* at www.kiplinger.com
- The Motley Fool at www.fool.com
- "About Financial Planning" at financialplan.about.com
- Bankrate at www.bankrate.com
- Money Central at www.moneycentral.msn.com
- The Federal Reserve System at www.federalreserve.gov

Additional websites are offered at the end of each chapter in the *Your Personal Financial Planner in Action* feature.

When conducting an online search, be precise with your descriptive words. For example, use "mortgage rates" instead of "interest rates" to obtain information on the cost of borrowing to buy a home. Use "résumés" instead of "career planning" for assistance on developing a personal data sheet.

Financial Planning Specialists

Various specialists provide specific financial assistance and advice:

- *Accountants* specialize in tax matters and financial documents.
- *Bankers* assist with financial services and trusts.
- *Certified financial planners* coordinate financial decisions into a single plan.
- *Credit counselors* suggest ways to reduce spending and eliminate credit problems.
- *Insurance agents* sell insurance coverage to protect your wealth and property.
- *Investment brokers* provide information and handle transactions for stocks, bonds, and other investments.
- *Lawyers* help in preparing wills, estate planning, tax problems, and other legal matters.
- *Real estate agents* assist with buying and selling a home or other real estate.
- *Tax preparers* specialize in completing income tax returns and in other tax matters.

Many of these specialists offer services that include various aspects of financial planning. A financial planner's background or the company he or she represents is a good gauge of the financial planner's principal area of expertise. An accountant is likely to be most knowledgeable about tax laws, while an insurance company representative will probably emphasize how to use insurance for achieving financial goals.

WHO ARE THE FINANCIAL PLANNERS?

Many financial planners represent major insurance companies or investment businesses. Financial planners may also be individuals whose primary profession is tax accounting, real estate, or law. Over 250,000 people call themselves financial planners. Financial planners are commonly categorized based on four methods of compensation:

1. **Fee-only planners** charge an hourly rate that may range from $75 to $200, or may charge a fixed fee of between less than $500 and several thousand dollars. Other fee-only planners may charge an annual fee ranging from .04 percent to 1 percent of the value of your assets.
2. **Fee-offset planners** start with an hourly fee or an annual fee. This charge is reduced by any commission earned from the sale of investments or insurance.
3. **Fee-and-commission planners** earn commissions from the investment and insurance products purchased and charge a fixed fee (ranging from $250 to $2,000) for a financial plan.
4. **Commission-only planners** receive their revenue from the commissions on sales of insurance, mutual funds, and other investments.

Consumers must be cautious about the fees charged and how these fees are communicated. Studies reveal that financial planners who say they offer "fee-only" services actually earned commissions or other financial rewards for implementing the recommendations made to their clients.

DO YOU NEED A FINANCIAL PLANNER?

The two main factors that determine whether you need financial planning assistance are (1) your income and (2) your willingness to make independent decisions. If you earn less than $50,000 a year, you probably do not need a financial planner. Income of less than this amount does not allow for many major financial decisions once you have allocated for the spending, savings, insurance, and tax elements of your personal financial planning.

Taking an active role in your financial affairs can reduce the need for a financial planner. Your willingness to keep up to date on developments related to investments, insurance, and taxes can reduce the amount you spend on financial advisers. This action will require an ongoing investment of time and effort; however, it will enable you to control your own financial direction.

When deciding whether to use a financial planner, also consider the services provided. First, the financial planner should assist you in assessing your current financial position with regard to spending, saving, insurance, taxes, and potential investments. Second, the financial planner should offer a clearly written plan with different courses of action. Third, the planner should take time to discuss the components of the plan and help you monitor your financial progress. Finally, the financial planner should guide you to other experts and sources of financial services as needed.

HOW SHOULD YOU SELECT A FINANCIAL PLANNER?

You can locate financial planners by using a telephone directory, contacting financial institutions, or obtaining references from friends, business associates, or professionals with whom you currently deal, such as insurance agents or real estate brokers.

When evaluating a financial planner, ask the following:

- Is financial planning your primary activity, or are other activities primary?
- Are you licensed as an investment broker or as a seller of life insurance?
- What is your educational background and formal training?
- What are your areas of expertise?
- Do you use experts in other areas, such as taxes, law, or insurance, to assist you with financial planning recommendations?
- What professional titles and certifications do you possess?

- Am I allowed a free initial consultation?
- How is the fee determined? (Is this an amount I can afford?)
- Do you have an independent practice, or are you affiliated with a major financial services company?
- What are sample insurance, tax, and investment recommendations you make for clients?
- My major concern is _____. What would you suggest?
- May I see a sample of a written financial plan?
- May I see the contract you use with clients?
- Who are some of your clients whom I might contact?

Also, make sure you are comfortable with the planner and that the planner can clearly communicate. This type of investigation takes time and effort; however, remember that you are considering placing your entire financial future in the hands of one person.

HOW ARE FINANCIAL PLANNERS CERTIFIED?

While state and federal regulation of financial planners exists, the requirements for becoming a financial planner vary from state to state. Some states license individual investment advisers; other states license firms but not individual advisers. A few states regulate neither individual advisers nor firms. Federal regulation requires that the Securities and Exchange Commission (SEC) monitor the largest financial advisers.

Many financial planners use abbreviations for the certifications they have earned. Some of these abbreviations are quite familiar, for example, CPA (certified public accountant), JD (doctor of law), and MBA (master of business administration); others include:

- CFP—Certified Financial Planners have expertise in insurance, investments, taxation, employee benefits, retirement and estate planning.
- ChFC—Chartered Financial Consultants are trained in the areas of finance, insurance, and investing.
- CFA—Chartered Financial Analysts have focused training in portfolio management and security analysis.
- RIA—Registered Investment Advisers provide investment advice and are registered with the SEC or a state securities agency.
- EA—Enrolled Agents are tax specialists certified by the Internal Revenue Service.
- RFC—Registered Financial Consultants have training in insurance, investments, taxes, and estate planning.
- AEP—Accredited Estate Planners emphasize wills, trusts, and estate taxes.
- CRP—Certified Retirement Planners address long-term financial planning activities.
- AICPA PFP—Personal Financial Planning Specialists are certified public accountants with additional financial planning training.
- AFC—Accredited Financial Counselors are certified by the Association for Financial Counseling and Planning Education.

Additional information on these and other financial planning designations is available at www.myfinancialadvice.com.

While these credentials provide some assurance of expertise, not all planners are licensed. The Federal Trade Commission estimates that fraudulent planners take consumers for tens of millions of dollars in bad investments and advice each year. Financial planning activities such as insurance and investment security sales are regulated. Be wary, and investigate any financial planning action you are considering.

You may contact the following organizations and agencies for further information about certification and regulation of financial planners:

- National Association of Personal Financial Advisors at 1-888-333-6659 (www.napfa.org).
- Certified Financial Planners Board of Standards at 1-800-487-1497 (www.cfp.net).
- Financial Planning Association at 1-800-945-4237 (www.fpanet.org).
- North American Securities Administrators Association at 1-202-737-0900 (www.nasaa.org).
- National Association of Insurance Commissioners at 816-842-3600 (www.naic.org).
- Securities and Exchange Commission at 1-800-732-0330 (www.sec.gov).
- American Institute of Certified Public Accountants at 1-800-862-4272 (www.aicpa.org).

appendix C

Consumer Agencies and Organizations

Various government agencies and private organizations offer information and assistance on financial planning and consumer purchasing topics. These groups can serve your needs when you want to:

- Research a financial or consumer topic area.
- Obtain information for planning a purchase decision.
- Seek assistance to resolve a consumer problem.

Section 1 provides an overview of federal, state, and local agencies and other organizations you may contact for information related to various financial planning and consumer topic areas. Section 2 covers state consumer protection offices that can assist you in local matters.

Section 1

Most federal agencies may be contacted through the Internet; several websites are noted. In addition, consumer information from several federal government agencies may be accessed at www.consumer.gov.

Information on additional government agencies and private organizations available to assist you may be obtained in the *Consumer Action Handbook,* available at no charge from the Consumer Information Center, Pueblo, CO 81009 or online at www.pueblo.gsa.gov.

Exhibit C-1

Federal, State, and Local Agencies and Other Organizations

Topic Area	Federal Agency	State, Local Agency; Other Organizations
Advertising False advertising Product labeling Deceptive sales practices Warranties	Federal Trade Commission 1-877-FTC-HELP (www.ftc.gov)	State Consumer Protection Office c/o State Attorney General or Governor's Office National Fraud Information Center (www.fraud.org)
Air Travel Air safety Airport regulation Airline route	Federal Aviation Administration 1-800-FAA-SURE (www.faa.gov)	International Airline Passengers Association 1-800-527-5888 (www.iapa.com)

Continued

Exhibit C-1 Continued

Topic Area	Federal Agency	State, Local Agency; Other Organizations
Appliances/Product Safety Potentially dangerous products Complaints against retailers, manufacturers	Consumer Product Safety Commission 1-800-638-CPSC (www.cpsc.gov)	Council of Better Business Bureaus 1-800-955-5100 (www.bbb.org)
Automobiles New cars Used cars Automobile repairs Auto safety	Federal Trade Commission (see above) National Highway Traffic Safety Administration 1-800-424-9393 (www.nhtsa.gov)	AUTOCAP/National Automobile Dealers Association 1-800-252-6232 (www.nada.org) Center for Auto Safety (202) 328-7700 (www.autosafety.org)
Banking and Financial Institutions Checking accounts Savings accounts Deposit insurance Financial services	Federal Deposit Insurance Corporation 1-877-275-3342 (www.fdic.gov) Comptroller of the Currency (202) 447-1600 (www.occ.treas.gov) Federal Reserve Board (202) 452-3693 (www.federalreserve.gov) National Credit Union Administration (703) 518-6300 (www.ncua.gov)	State Banking Authority Credit Union National Association (608) 232-8256 (www.cuna.org) American Bankers Association (202) 663-5000 (www.aba.com) U.S. savings bond rates 1-800-US-BONDS (www.savingsbonds.gov)
Career Planning Job training Employment information	Coordinator of Consumer Affairs Department of Labor (202) 219-6060 (www.dol.gov)	State Department of Labor or State Employment Service
Consumer Credit Credit cards Deceptive credit advertising Truth-in-Lending Act Credit rights of women, minorities	Consumer Financial Protection Bureau 1-855-411-2372 (www.consumerfinance.gov) Federal Trade Commission 1-877-FTC-HELP (www.ftc.gov)	CredAbility 1-800-251-2227 (www.cccsatl.org) National Foundation for Credit Counseling (301) 589-5600 (www.nfcc.org)
Environment Air, water pollution Toxic substances	Environmental Protection Agency 1-800-438-4318 (indoor air quality) 1-800-426-4791 (drinking water safety) (www.epa.gov)	Clean Water Action (202) 895-0420 (www.cleanwater.org)

Continued

Topic Area	Federal Agency	State, Local Agency; Other Organizations
Food		
Food grades Food additives Nutritional information	U.S. Department of Agriculture 1-800-424-9121 (www.usda.gov) Food and Drug Administration 1-888-463-6332 (www.fda.gov)	Center for Science in the Public Interest (202) 332-9110 (www.cspinet.org)
Funerals		
Cost disclosure Deceptive business practices	Federal Trade Commission 1-877-FTC-HELP (www.ftc.gov)	Funeral Service Help Line 1-800-228-6332 (www.nfda.org)
Housing and Real Estate		
Fair housing practices Mortgages Community development	Department of Housing and Urban Development 1-800-669-9777 (www.hud.gov)	National Association of Realtors (www.realtor.com) (www.move.com) National Association of Home Builders (www.nahb.com)
Insurance		
Policy conditions Premiums Types of coverage Consumer complaints	Federal Trade Commission (see above) National Flood Insurance Program 1-888-CALL-FLOOD	State Insurance Regulator American Council of Life Insurance (www.acli.com) Insurance Information Institute 1-800-331-9146 (www.iii.org)
Internet/Mail Order		
Damaged products Deceptive business practices Illegal use of U.S. mail	Internet Crime Complaint Center (www.ic3.gov) U.S. Postal Service 1-800-ASK-USPS (www.usps.gov)	Direct Marketing Association (212) 768-7277 (www.the-dma.org)
Investments		
Stocks, bonds Mutual funds Commodities Investment brokers	Securities and Exchange Commission (202) 551-6551 (www.sec.gov) Commodity Futures Trading Commission (202) 418-5000 (www.cftc.org)	Investment Company Institute (202) 293-7700 (www.ici.gov) National Association of Securities Dealers (202) 728-8000 (www.nasd.com) National Futures Association 1-800-621-3570 (www.nfa.futures.org) Securities Investor Protection Corp. (202) 371-8300 (www.sipc.org)

Continued

Exhibit C-1 Continued

Topic Area	Federal Agency	State, Local Agency; Other Organizations
Legal Matters Consumer complaints Arbitration	Department of Justice Office of Consumer Litigation (202) 514-2401	American Arbitration Association (212) 484-4000 (www.adr.org) American Bar Association 1-800-285-2221 (www.abanet.org)
Medical Concerns Prescription medications Over-the-counter medications Medical devices Health care	Food and Drug Administration (see above) Public Health Service 1-800-621-8335 (www.usphs.gov)	American Medical Association 1-800-336-4797 (www.ama-assn.org) Public Citizen Health Research Group (202) 588-1000 (www.citizen.org/hrg)
Retirement Old-age benefits Pension information Medicare	Social Security Administration 1-800-772-1213 (www.ssa.gov)	AARP (202) 434-2277 (www.aarp.org)
Taxes Tax information Audit procedures	Internal Revenue Service 1-800-829-1040 1-800-TAX-FORM (www.irs.gov)	Department of Revenue (in your state capital city) The Tax Foundation (202) 464-6200 (www.taxfoundation.org) National Association of Enrolled Agents 1-800-424-4339 (www.naea.org)
Telemarketing 900 numbers	Federal Communications Commission 1-888-225-5322 (www.fcc.gov)	National Consumers League (202) 835-3323 (www.nclnet.org)
Utilities Cable television Utility rates	Federal Communications Commission 1-988-225-5322 (www.fcc.gov)	State utility commission (in your state capital)

Section 2

State, county, and local consumer protection offices provide consumers with a variety of services, including publications and information before buying as well as handling complaints. This section provides contact information for state consumer protection agencies. In addition to the primary offices listed here, agencies regulating banking, insurance, securities, and utilities are available in each state. These may be located through an online search or by going to the *Consumer's Resource Handbook* at http://publications.usa.gov/USAPubs.php.

Many state consumer protection offices may be accessed through the website of the National Association of Attorneys General at www.naag.org or with an online search for your state consumer protection office using "(*state*) consumer protection agency."

To save time, call the office before sending in a written complaint. Ask if the office handles the type of complaint you have or if complaint forms are provided. Many offices distribute consumer materials specifically geared to state laws and local issues. Call to obtain available educational information on your problem.

State departments of insurance may be accessed online at www.naic.org/state_web_map.htm.

The websites of state tax departments are available at www.taxadmin.org/fta/link/default.php or www.aicpa.org/yellow/yptsgus.htm.

appendix D

Daily Spending Diary

Effective short-term money management and long-term financial security depend on spending less than you earn. The use of a Daily Spending Diary will provide information to better understand your spending patterns and to help you achieve desired financial goals.

The following sheets, which are also available at www.mhhe.com/kdh, can be used to record *every cent* of your spending each day in the categories provided. Or you can create your own format to monitor your spending. You can indicate the use of a credit card with (CR). This experience will help you better understand your spending habits and identify desired changes you might want to make in your spending activities. Your comments should reflect what you have learned about your spending and can assist with changes you might want to make. Ask yourself, "What spending amounts can I reduce or eliminate?"

Many people who take on this task find it difficult at first and may consider it a waste of time. However, nearly everyone who makes a serious effort to keep a Daily Spending Diary has found it beneficial. The process may seem tedious at first, but after a while recording this information becomes easier and faster. Most important, you will know where your money is going. Then you will be able to better decide if that is truly how you want to spend your available financial resources. A sincere effort with this activity will result in useful information for monitoring and controlling your spending.

Daily Spending Diary

Directions: Record *every cent* of your spending each day in the categories provided, or create your own format to monitor your spending. You can indicate the use of a credit card with (CR). Comments should reflect what you have learned about your spending patterns and desired changes you might want to make in your spending habits. (*Note:* As income is received, record in Date column.)

Month: _____ Amount available for spending: $ _____ Amount to be saved: $ _____

Date (Income)	Total Spending	Auto, Transportation	Housing, Utilities	Food (H) Home (A) Away	Health, Personal Care	Education	Recreation, Leisure	Donations, Gifts	Other (note item, amount)	Comments
Example	*$83*	*$20 (gas) (CR)*		*$47 (H)*		*$2 (pen)*	*$4 (DVD rental)*	*$10 (church)*		*This takes time but it helps me control my spending*
1										
2										
3										
4										
5										
6										
7										
8										
9										
10										
11										
12										
13										
14										
Subtotal										

Date (Income)	Total Spending	Auto, Transportation	Housing, Utilities	Food (H) Home (A) Away	Health, Personal Care	Education	Recreation, Leisure	Donations, Gifts	Other (note item, amount)	Comments
15										
16										
17										
18										
19										
20										
21										
22										
23										
24										
25										
26										
27										
28										
29										
30										
31										
Total										

Total Income	Total Spending	Difference (+/−)	*Possible Actions:* amount to savings; areas for reduced spending; other actions . . .
$ ______	$ ______	$ ______	

Daily Spending Diary

Directions: Record *every cent* of your spending each day in the categories provided, or create your own format to monitor your spending. You can indicate the use of a credit card with (CR). Comments should reflect what you have learned about your spending patterns and desired changes you might want to make in your spending habits. (*Note:* As income is received, record in Date column.)

Month: ______ **Amount available for spending: $** ______ **Amount to be saved: $** ______

Date (Income)	Total Spending	Auto, Transportation	Housing, Utilities	Food (H) Home (A) Away	Health, Personal Care	Education	Recreation, Leisure	Donations, Gifts	Other (note item, amount)	Comments
1										
2										
3										
4										
5										
6										
7										
8										
9										
10										
11										
12										
13										
14										
Subtotal										

Date (Income)	Total Spending	Auto, Transportation	Housing, Utilities	Food (H) Home (A) Away	Health, Personal Care	Education	Recreation, Leisure	Donations, Gifts	Other (note item, amount)	Comments
15										
16										
17										
18										
19										
20										
21										
22										
23										
24										
25										
26										
27										
28										
29										
30										
31										
Total										
Total Income **$ ________**		**Total Spending** **$ ________**		**Difference (+/−)** **$ ________**		***Possible Actions:*** **amount to savings; areas for reduced spending; other actions . . .**				

Daily Spending Diary

Directions: Record *every cent* of your spending each day in the categories provided, or create your own format to monitor your spending. You can indicate the use of a credit card with (CR). Comments should reflect what you have learned about your spending patterns and desired changes you might want to make in your spending habits. (*Note:* As income is received, record in Date column.)

Month: ______ **Amount available for spending: $** ______ **Amount to be saved: $** ______

Date (Income)	Total Spending	Auto, Transportation	Housing, Utilities	Food (H) Home (A) Away	Health, Personal Care	Education	Recreation, Leisure	Donations, Gifts	Other (note item, amount)	Comments
1										
2										
3										
4										
5										
6										
7										
8										
9										
10										
11										
12										
13										
14										
Subtotal										

Date (Income)	Total Spending	Auto, Transportation	Housing, Utilities	Food (H) Home (A) Away	Health, Personal Care	Education	Recreation, Leisure	Donations, Gifts	Other (note item, amount)	Comments
15										
16										
17										
18										
19										
20										
21										
22										
23										
24										
25										
26										
27										
28										
29										
30										
31										
Total										
Total Income **$ ______**		**Total Spending** **$ ______**		**Difference (+/−)** **$ ______**		***Possible Actions:*** **amount to savings; areas for reduced spending; other actions . . .**				

Daily Spending Diary

Directions: Record *every cent* of your spending each day in the categories provided, or create your own format to monitor your spending. You can indicate the use of a credit card with (CR). Comments should reflect what you have learned about your spending patterns and desired changes you might want to make in your spending habits. (*Note:* As income is received, record in Date column.)

Month: ______________ **Amount available for spending: $** ______________ **Amount to be saved: $** ______________

Date (Income)	Total Spending	Auto, Transportation	Housing, Utilities	Food (H) Home (A) Away	Health, Personal Care	Education	Recreation, Leisure	Donations, Gifts	Other (note item, amount)	Comments
1										
2										
3										
4										
5										
6										
7										
8										
9										
10										
11										
12										
13										
14										
Subtotal										

Date (Income)	Total Spending	Auto, Transportation	Housing, Utilities	Food (H) Home (A) Away	Health, Personal Care	Education	Recreation, Leisure	Donations, Gifts	Other (note item, amount)	Comments
15										
16										
17										
18										
19										
20										
21										
22										
23										
24										
25										
26										
27										
28										
29										
30										
31										
Total										

Total Income **$** ____________	**Total Spending** **$** ______________	**Difference (+/−)** **$** ______________	***Possible Actions:*** **amount to savings; areas for reduced spending; other actions . . .**

Endnotes

CHAPTER [6]

1. Peter Pae, "Credit Junkies," *The Wall Street Journal,* December 26, 1991, p. 1.
2. Statistical Abstract of the United States 2012, Table 1187, www.census.gov, accessed March 7, 2013.
3. Adapted from *Guide to Online Payments,* Federal Trade Commission, www.ftc.gov, accessed March 8, 2013.
4. Adapted from William M. Pride, Robert J. Hughes, and Jack R. Kapoor, *Business,* 12th ed. (Mason, OH: Cengage Learning, 2014), p. 541.

CHAPTER [7]

1. National Credit Union Administration, www.ncua.gov/news/pages/nw20130301CUEarnings.aspx, accessed March 15, 2013.
2. Wenli Li, "What Do We Know about Chapter 13 Personal Bankruptcy Filings?" *Business Review,* Federal Reserve Bank of Philadelphia, Fourth Quarter 2007, p. 25.

CHAPTER [11]

1. The Census Bureau website at www.census.gov, accessed March 18, 2013.
2. The government long term website at www.longtermcare.gov, accessed March 19, 2013.
3. Eve Tahmincioglu, "The Catch-22 of Long Term Care Insurance," *Kiplinger's Personal Finance,* May 1997, pp. 97–102.
4. HealthCare.gov website at http://www.healthcare.gov/, accessed March 20, 2013.
5. Kathleen Sebelius, "Affordable Care Act at 3: Looking Forward and Expanding Access," Health Care Blog, HealthCare.gov, accessed March 22, 2013.
6. Rob Engstrom, "Three Years Ago Today," U.S. Chamber of Commerce (Washington, DC), http://www.uschamber.com/healthcare, accessed March 23, 2013.

CHAPTER [12]

1. American Council of Life Insurers, *2012 Life Insurance Fact Book,* p. 66, www.acli.com, accessed March 16, 2013.
2. Ibid.
3. Ibid.
4. Ibid.

CHAPTER [13]

1. U.S. Bureau of the Census, *Statistical Abstract of the United States 2012* (Washington, DC: U.S. Government Printing Office), Table 1187 (www.census.gov).
2. Joseph McClain, "American Consumers Start 2013 with a Staggering Average Household Credit Card Debt of $15, 422," the Yahoo! News website at www.yahoo.com, accessed January 31, 2013.
3. Lucy Lazarony, "Credit Cards Teaching Students a Costly Lesson," the BankRate.com website, at www.bankrate.com, accessed February 1, 2013.
4. The BankRate.com website at www.bankrate.com, accessed February 2, 2013.
5. The Yahoo! Finance website at http://finance.yahoo.com, accessed February 3, 2013.
6. "Money 101 Lesson 4 'Investing Your Money Basics,'" the CNN/Money website at http://money.cnn.com/magazines/moneymag/money101/lesson4, accessed February 5, 2013.
7. Ibid.
8. "Vanguard Portfolio Allocation Models," the Vanguard website at www.vanguard.com, accessed February 5, 2013.
9. Ibid.
10. "Money 101 Lesson 4 'Investing Your Money Basics,'" the CNN/Money website at http://money.cnn.com/magazines/moneymag/money101/lesson4, accessed February 5, 2013.
11. William J. Bernstein, "The Online Asset Allocator," the Efficient Frontier website at www.efficientfrontier.com, accessed February 6, 2013.
12. "Money 101 Lesson 4 'Investing Your Money Basics,'" the CNN/Money website at http://money.cnn.com/magazines/moneymag/money101/lesson4, accessed February 5, 2013.
13. Suze Orman, *"The Road to Wealth,"* (New York: Riverbend Books, 2004), p. 371.
14. The Mutual Fund Education Alliance website at www.mfea.com, accessed February 6, 2013.

CHAPTER [14]

1. The McDonald's Corporation website at www.mcdonalds.com, accessed February 19, 2013.
2. "Money 101 Lesson 4, 'Investing Your Money Basics,'" the CNN/Money website at http://money.cnn.com/magazines/moneymag/money101/lesson 4, accessed February 5, 2013.
3. "Vanguard Portfolio Allocation Models," the Vanguard website at www.vanguard.com, accessed February 5, 2013.
4. Ibid.
5. "Money 101 Lesson 4, 'Investing Your Money Basics,'" the CNN/Money website at http://money.cnn.com/magazines/moneymag/money101/lesson 4, accessed February 5, 2013.
6. The Yahoo! Finance website at http://finance.yahoo.com, accessed February 19, 2013.
7. The MSN Money website at www.money.msn.com, accessed February 24, 2013.
8. The Investopedia.com website at www.investopedia.com, accessed February 26, 2013.
9. Chris Dieterich, "Xoom Soars in Trading Debut," *The Wall Street Journal* website, accessed February 15, 2013.
10. The NYSE Euronext website at www.nyse.com, accessed February 27, 2013.
11. The NASDAQ website at www.nasdaq.com, accessed February 27, 2013.

CHAPTER [15]

1. The Ford Motor Company website at http://corporate.ford.com, accessed March 14, 2013.

CHAPTER [16]

1. The Mutual Fund Education Alliance website at www.mfea.com, accessed March 25, 2013.
2. The Investment Company Institute website at www.ici.org, accessed March 26, 2013.
3. Ibid.
4. Ibid.
5. Ibid.
6. Bill Barker, "Loads," the Motley Fool website at www.fool.com, accessed March 26, 2013.
7. The Vanguard Group website at www.vanguard.com, accessed March 25, 2013.

8. "Index Investing: Index Funds," the Investopedia website at www.investopedia.com, accessed March 28, 2013.
9. "Index Funds vs. Actively Managed Funds," the Bankrate.com website at www.bankrate.com, accessed March 27, 2013.
10. John Bogle, "The First Index Mutual Fund: A History of Vanguard Index Trust and the Vanguard Index Strategy," the Vanguard Group website at www.vanguard.com, accessed March 25, 2013.
11. "Morningstar Mutual Fund Screener," the Morningstar website at www.morningstar.com., accessed March 29, 2013.
12. "Money 70: Best Mutual Funds and ETFs," *Money Magazine: Investor's Guide 2013,* the CNNMoney website at www.money.cnn.com, accessed March 29, 2013.

CHAPTER [17]

1. Alex Musatov and Danielle Di Martino Booth, "Foreclosures' Silver Lining: They Could Restrain Rent Inflation," *Economic Letter,* Federal Reserve Bank of Dallas, March 2013, p.1.
2. 2013 NAR Investment and Vacation Home Buyers Survey, www.realtor.org-releases/2013/04/2012-vacation-home-sales-up-investment, accessed April 23, 2013.
3. Ibid.
4. World Gold Council website, www.gold.org, accessed May 2, 2013.
5. *Bloomberg Businessweek*, "All the World's an Auction," February 7, 1999.

CHAPTER [18]

1. Eric Schine, "There's Never Any Reason for Us to Be Bored," *Bloomberg Businessweek,* July 21, 1997, pp. 70–76.
2. Social Security Administration website at www.ssa.gov/pressoffice/basicfact.htm, accessed May 3, 2013.
3. Carol Kleiman, "Firms Shifting Retirement Planning, Risk to Workers," *Chicago Tribune*, January 19, 1992.

CHAPTER [19]

1. Excerpted from Kate Murphy. "The Virtues and Values of an Ethical Will," *Bloomberg Businessweek,* April 7, 2002, p. 83.
2. American Society of CLU and ChFC. *Looking Beyond Your Current Estate Plan,* 1997.

APPENDIX [A]

1. www.newyorkfed.org/householdcredit/ (2012 Q4, *Quarterly Report on Household Debt and Credit),* accessed May 3, 2013.
2. http://studentaid.ed.gov/types/loans/interest-rates

Photo Credits

CHAPTER [1]

Page 2: © CNCCRAY/Alamy/RF.
Page 6: © Comstock Images/Getty Images.
Page 15: © Mark Scott/Photographer's Choice RF/Getty Images.
Page 25: © Press Association via AP Images.

CHAPTER [2]

Page 46: © Peter Dazeley/Getty Images.
Page 48: © BananaStock/PictureQuest.
Page 53: © Royalty-Free/Corbis.
Page 60: © Justin Sullivan/Getty Images.

CHAPTER [3]

Page 86: © Cultura/Seb Oliver/Getty Images.
Page 95: © Digital Vision Ltd./SuperStock.
Page 100: © Digital Vision/PunchStock.
Page 107: © Purestock/Getty Images.

CHAPTER [4]

Page 116: © Photodisc/Getty Images.
Page 119: © Johan Ronn/Getty Images.
Page 136: © AP Photo/Paul Sakuma.

CHAPTER [5]

Page 154: © William Andrew/Photographer's Choice/Getty Images.
Page 156: © Bonnie Kamin/PhotoEdit.
Page 172: Reproduction of image permitted under General Public License Agreement (GPL).
Page 174: © Tara Moore/Taxi/Getty Images.

CHAPTER [6]

Page 186: © Comstock Images/Punch Stock.
Page 198: © Rudi Von Briel/PhotoEdit.
Page 203: © 1996–2010 Mighty Net, Inc. All rights reserved. CreditReport.com is a trademark of Mighty Net, Inc.
Page 204: © Digital Vision/Getty Images.
Page 215: © PRNewsFoto/Newsweek.

CHAPTER [7]

Page 228: © Roberts Publishing Services. All rights reserved.
Page 230: © Tetra Images/Corbis/RF.
Page 248: © AP Photo/Kervork Djansezian.
Page 251: © Kayte M. Deioma/PhotoEdit.

CHAPTER [8]

Page 266: © AP Photo/Robert F. Bukaty.
Page 269: © Ken Welsh/Getty Images.
Page 274: © Ed Bock /Corbis.
Page 283: © Jupiterimages/Comstock Images/Getty Images.
Page 289: © Bob Daemmrich/PhotoEdit.

CHAPTER [9]

Page 298: © C. Borland/PhotoLink/Getty Images.
Page 303: Listing from craigslist. © 2013 craigslist, inc.
Page 309: © Ryan McVay/Getty Images.
Page 312: © Jupiterimages/Getty Images.
Page 321: © Digital Vision/Getty Images.

CHAPTER [10]

Page 334: © Comstock.
Page 337: © AP/Jupiterimages/RF.
Page 342: © Frederick McKinney/Getty Images.
Page 349: © Liz Roll/FEMA.
Page 354: © Keith Brofsky/Getty Images.

CHAPTER [11]

Page 366: © Realistic Reflections.
Page 378: © Rolf Bruderer/Blend Images.
Page 380: © Florian Franke/Purestock/SuperStock.
Page 386: © Brand X Pictures/PunchStock.
Page 394: Public domain image from the U.S. Department of Health & Human Services.

CHAPTER [12]

Page 406: © Stockbyte/PunchStock.
Page 409: © Image Source/PunchStock.

CHAPTER [13]

Page 442: © Adam Gault/Getty Images.

CHAPTER [14]

Page 480: © Comstock Images/Jupiter Images.

CHAPTER [15]

Page 520: © Paris Pierce/Alamy.

CHAPTER [16]

Page 554: © Adam Gault/OJO/Getty Images.
Page 557: © Brian Zak/Sipa Press via AP Images.

CHAPTER [17]

Page 590: © Mario Beauregard/Getty Images.
Page 596: © Bill Ross/Corbis.
Page 599: © Prawel Gaul/Getty Images.
Page 605: Photo displayed on touristlink.com. © TouristLink.com. All rights reserved.
Page 607: © Royalty-Free/Corbis.

CHAPTER [18]

Page 616: © Brand X Pictures.
Page 618: © Purestock/SuperStock.
Page 629: © Digital Vision/Getty Images.
Page 647: © Ariel Skelley/Getty Images/RF.

CHAPTER [19]

Page 658: © Jules Frazier/Getty Images.
Page 661: © Tetra Images/Getty Images/RF.
Page 664: © PaloAlto/PunchStock.
Page 668: © Image Source/PunchStock.
Page 682: Reproduction of form permitted under General Public License Agreement (GPL).

Index

[A]

[C]

[E]

[F]

[G]

[H]

[I]

[J]

[K]

[L]

[M]

[N]

[Q]

[R]

[S]

[T]

[U]

[V]

Preface

This Personal Financial Planner is designed to help you create and implement a personal financial plan.

Items to consider when using this Personal Financial Planner

1. Since these sheets are designed to adapt to every personal financial situation, some may be appropriate for you at this time while others will not be used until later in your life.
2. The sheets are referenced to specific pages in the textbook. To help you use these sheets with the appropriate text material, the following textbook icon (appearing as appropriate with the Practice Quizzes) will refer you to the appropriate sheet.

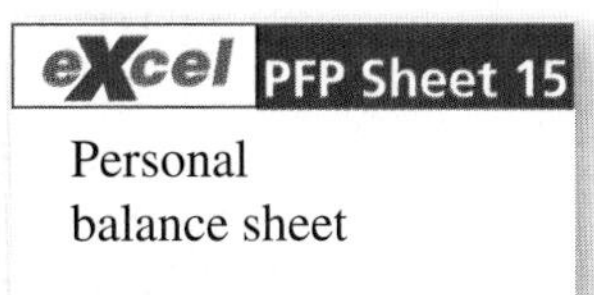

3. Some sheets will be used more than once (such as preparing a personal cash flow statement or a budget). You are encouraged to photocopy additional sheets as needed, or print additional copies from the Excel templates at www.mhhe.com/kdh.
4. To assist you with using online information sources for financial planning activities, suggested websites and apps are presented on the sheets.
5. Finally, remember personal financial planning is an ongoing activity. With the use of these sheets, textbook material, and your efforts, an organized and satisfying personal economic existence can be yours.

Personal Financial Planner

Table of Contents

Name: ____________________ Date: ____________________

Personal Data

Purpose: To provide quick reference for vital household data.

Instructions: Provide the personal and financial data requested below. This sheet is also available in an Excel spreadsheet format at www.mhhe.com/kdh.

Suggested websites: www.money.com www.kiplinger.com www.moneycafe.com

Name		
Birth date		
Marital status		
Address		
Phone		
E-mail		
Social Security no.		
Driver's license no.		
Place of employment		
Address		
Phone		
Position		
Length of service		
Checking acct. no.		
Financial institution		
Address		
Phone		

Dependent Data

Name	Birth date	Relationship	Social Security no.

What's Next for Your Personal Financial Plan?

- Identify financial planning experts (insurance agent, banker, investment adviser, tax preparer, others) you might contact for financial planning information or assistance.
- Discuss with other household members various financial planning priorities.

Name: ______________________ Date: ______________

Financial Institutions and Advisers

Purpose: To create a directory of personal financial institutions and financial planning professionals.

Instructions: Supply the information required in the spaces provided. This sheet is also available in an Excel spreadsheet format at www.mhhe.com/kdh.

Suggested websites: www.20somethingfinance.com www.bankrate.com

Attorney

Name ______
Address ______
______
Phone/Fax ______
Website ______
E-mail ______

Primary Financial Institution

Name ______
Address ______
______
Phone/Fax ______
Website ______
Checking acct. no. ______
Savings acct. no. ______
Loan no. ______

Insurance (Home/Auto)

Agent ______
Company ______
Address ______
______
Phone/Fax ______
Website ______
Policy no. ______
E-mail ______

Credit Card 1

Issuer ______
Address ______
______
Phone/Fax ______
Website ______
Acct. no. ______
Exp. date ______
Limit ______

Credit Card 2

Issuer ______
Address ______
______
Phone/Fax ______
Website ______
Acct. no. ______
Exp. date ______
Limit ______

Tax Preparer

Name ______
Firm ______
Address ______
______
Phone/Fax ______
Website ______
E-mail ______

Insurance (Life/Health)

Agent ______
Company ______
Address ______
______
Phone/Fax ______
Website ______
E-mail ______
Policy no. ______

Investment Broker

Name ______
Address ______
______
Phone/Fax ______
Website ______
E-mail ______
Acct. no. ______

Real Estate Agent

Name ______
Company ______
Address ______
______
Phone/Fax ______
Website ______
E-mail ______

Investment Company

Name ______
Address ______
______
Phone ______
Fax ______
Acct. no. ______
E-mail ______
Website ______

Suggested App:
- Ask Dave Ramsey

What's Next for Your Personal Financial Plan?

- Talk to various personal and professional contacts to determine factors to consider when selecting various financial planning advisers.
- Identify additional financial planning contacts that you might consider using in the future.

Name: ______________________ Date: ______________

Personal Financial Goals

Purose: To identify personal financial goals and create an action plan. (pp. 15–18)

Instructions: Based on personal and household needs and values, identify specific goals that require action. This sheet is also available in an Excel spreadsheet format at www.mhhe.com/kdh.

Suggested websites: www.financialplan.about.com www.planwise.com www.20somethingfinance.com

Short-Term Monetary Goals (less than one year)

Description	Amount needed	Months to achieve	Action to be taken	Priority
Example: pay off credit card debt	*$850*	*10*	*Use money from pay raise*	*High*

Intermediate and Long-Term Monetary Goals

Description	Amount needed	Months to achieve	Action to be taken	Priority

Nonmonetary Goals

Description	Time frame	Actions to be taken
Example: set up system for personal financial records and documents	*Next 2–3 months*	• *Locate personal and financial records and documents.* • *Set up spreadsheet for various spending, saving, borrowing categories.*

What's Next for Your Personal Financial Plan?

- Based on various financial goals, calculate the savings deposits necessary to achieve those goals.
- Analyze current economic trends that might influence various saving, spending, investing, and borrowing decisions.

3

Personal Financial Planner

Personal Financial Planner 4

Name: ______________________ Date: ______________________

Current Economic Conditions

Purpose: To monitor selected economic indicators that might influence your saving, investing, spending, and borrowing decisions. (pp. 11–15)

Instructions: Using *The Wall Street Journal,* an Internet search, or other sources of economic information, obtain current data for various economic factors. This sheet is also available in an Excel spreadsheet format at www.mhhe.com/kdh.

Suggested websites: www.bls.gov www.federalreserve.gov www.wsj.com www.ft.com

Economic Factor	Recent Trends	Possible Financial Planning Actions
Example: Mortgage rates	*Decline in mortgage rates*	• *Consider buying a home.* • *Consider refinancing an existing mortgage.*
Interest rates		
Consumer prices		
Other: __________		
Other: __________		
Other: __________		

Suggested App:
• The Wall Street Journal

What's Next for Your Personal Financial Plan?

- Determine the economic factors that could affect your personal financial decisions in the next few years.
- Identify actions to take as a result of various current economic trends.

Name: ______________________ Date: ______________

Time Value of Money

Purpose: To calculate future and present value amounts related to financial planning decisions. (pp. 19–23; 34–45)

Instructions: Use a calculator or future/present value tables to compute the time value of money. This sheet is also available in an Excel spreadsheet format at www.mhhe.com/kdh.

Suggested websites: www.dinkytown.net www.kiplinger.com/tools www.grunderware.com

Future Value of a Single Amount

(Use Exhibit 1–A in Chapter 1 Appendix)

- to determine future value of a single amount
- to determine interest lost when cash purchase is made

$$FV = PV\,(1+i)^n$$

current amount	times	future value factor	equals	future value amount
$ ______	×	$ ______	=	$ ______

Future Value of a Series of Deposits

(Use Exhibit 1–B in Chapter 1 Appendix)

- to determine future values of regular savings deposits
- to determine future value of regular retirement deposits

$$FV = \text{Annuity}\,\frac{(1+i)^n - 1}{i}$$

regular deposit amount	times	future value of annuity factor	equals	future value amount
$ ______	×	$ ______	=	$ ______

Present Value of a Single Amount

(Use Exhibit 1–C in Chapter 1 Appendix)

- to determine an amount to be deposited now that will grow to desired amount

$$PV = \frac{FV}{(1+i)^n}$$

future amount desired	times	present value factor	equals	present value amount
$ ______	×	$ ______	=	$ ______

Present Value of a Series of Deposits

(Use Exhibit 1–D in Chapter 1 Appendix)

- to determine an amount that can be withdrawn on a regular basis

$$PV = \text{Annuity}\,\frac{1-\frac{1}{(1+i)^n}}{i}$$

regular amount to be withdrawn	times	present value of annuity factor	equals	present value amount
$ ______	×	$ ______	×	$ ______

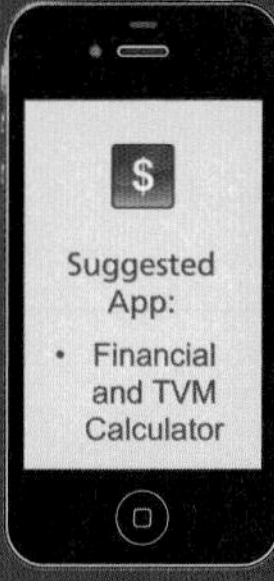

Note: A financial calculator or spreadsheet software may be used for future value and present value calculations.

What's Next for Your Personal Financial Plan?

- Identify various financial goals that require time value of money calculations.
- Research current interest rates to determine a rate that you might use when calculating time value of money for various personal financial goals.

Name: ______________________ Date: ______________

6

Personal Financial Planner

Career Research Sheet

Purpose: To become familiar with work activities and career requirements for a field of employment. (pp. 48–54)

Instructions: Using various information sources (library materials, interviews, websites), obtain information related to one or more career areas of interest to you. This sheet is also available in an Excel spreadsheet format at www.mhhe.com/kdh.

Suggested websites: www.mappingyourfuture.org www.ajb.dni.us

Career Area/Job Title		
Nature of the work General activities and duties		
Working conditions Physical surroundings, hours, mental and physical demands		
Training and other qualifications		
Job outlook Future prospect for employment in this field		
Earnings Starting and advanced		
Additional information		
Other questions that require further research		
Sources of additional information Publications, trade associations, professional organizations, government agencies, websites		

Suggested App:
- Job Search Organizer

What's Next for Your Personal Financial Plan?

- Identify various employment activities and industries of interest to you.
- Discuss existing and future career opportunities with various people.

Name: ______________________ Date: ______________

Career Contacts

Purpose: To create a guide of professional contacts. (pp. 56–59)

Instructions: Record the requested information for use in researching career areas and employment opportunities. This sheet is also available in an Excel spreadsheet format at www.mhhe.com/kdh.

Suggested websites: www.rileyguide.com www.careerjournal.com

Name ______________________

Organization ______________________

Address ______________________

____

Phone ____________ Fax ____________

Website ____________ E-mail ____________

Date of contact ______________________

Situation ______________________

Career situation of contact ______________________

Areas of specialization ______________________

Major accomplishments ______________________

Name ______________________

Organization ______________________

Address ______________________

____

Phone ____________ Fax ____________

Website ____________ E-mail ____________

Date of contact ______________________

Situation ______________________

Career situation of contact ______________________

Areas of specialization ______________________

Major accomplishments ______________________

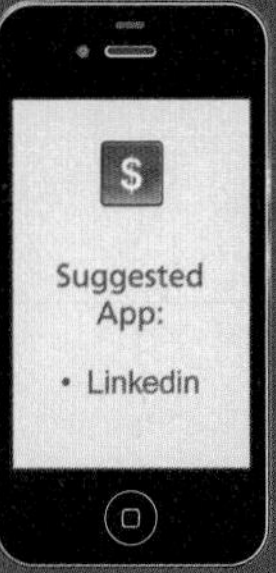

What's Next for Your Personal Financial Plan?

- Identify various people whom you might contact to obtain career information.
- Prepare specific questions to ask people about career fields and the application process.

Name: ______________________ Date: ______________

Résumé Planning

Purpose: To inventory your education, training, work background, and other experiences for use when preparing a résumé. (pp. 75–79)

Instructions: List dates, organizations, and other data for each of the categories given below. This sheet is also available in an Excel spreadsheet format at www.mhhe.com/kdh.

Suggested websites: www.monster.com www.rileyguide.com

Education

Degree/programs completed	School/location	Dates

Work Experience

Title	Organization	Dates	Responsibilities

Other Experience

Title	Organization	Dates	Responsibilities

Campus/Community Activities

Organization/location	Dates	Involvement

Honors/Awards

Title	Organization/location	Dates

References

Name	Title	Organization	Address	Phone

Note: See Exhibit 2-B, Page 77 for résumé format suggestions.

What's Next for Your Personal Financial Plan?

- Create a preliminary résumé and ask others for suggested improvements.
- Conduct research to obtain samples of effective résumé formats.

Suggested App:
- Pocket Résumé

Name: ______________________________ Date: ______________

Cover Letter Planning

Purpose: To outline an employment cover letter. (pp. 80–81)

Instructions: Prepare the preliminary draft of a cover letter for a specific employment position. This sheet is also available in an Excel spreadsheet format at www.mhhe.com/kdh.

Suggested websites: www.monster.com www.rileyguide.com

Name ______________________________

Title ______________________________

Organization ______________________________

Address ______________________________

Phone ______________________________

Fax ______________ E-mail ______________

Information about

Employment position available ______________________________

Organizational information ______________________________

Introduction: Get attention of reader with distinctive skills or experience; or make reference to a mutual contact.

Development: Emphasize how your experience, knowledge, and skills will benefit the needs of the organization in the future.

Conclusion: Request an interview; restate any distinctive qualities; tell how you may be contacted.

Note: See sample cover letter (Exhibit 2-C) on page 81.

What's Next for Your Personal Financial Plan?

- Research examples of effective cover letters.
- Prepare a preliminary cover letter and obtain comments for improvements from others.

Name: ______________________ Date: ______________

10

Prospective Employer Research

Purpose: To obtain information about an organization for which an employment position is available. (p. 81)

Instructions: Use research sources to obtain the information requested below. This sheet is also available in an Excel spreadsheet format at www.mhhe.com/kdh.

Suggested websites: www.careerbuilder.com www.hoovers.com www.annualreports.com

Organization ______________________

Address ______________________

____

Contact ______________________

Title ______________________

Phone ______________________

Fax ______________ E-mail ______________

Website ______________________

Title of position ______________________

Major products, services, and customers

Locations of main offices, factories, and other facilities

Major historical developments of the company

Recent company and industry developments

Required skills and experience

Major responsibilities and duties

Employee benefits

Other comments

Suggested App:
- Job Compass

What's Next for Your Personal Financial Plan?

- Prepare a list of organizations and information you might obtain when researching these companies.
- Conduct library and online research about specific organizations in which you are interested.

Name: ______________________ Date: ______________

Interview Preparation

Purpose: To organize information and ideas for a job interview. (pp. 81–85)

Instructions: Prepare information for the items listed. This sheet is also available in an Excel spreadsheet format at www.mhhe.com/kdh.

Suggested websites: www.rileyguide.com www.careerbuilder.com

Organization ______________________

Address ______________________

____

Contact ______________________

Title ______________________

Phone ______________________

Fax ______________ E-mail ______________

Website ______________________

Title of position ______________________

Date/time/location of interview ______________________

Required skills and experience

Major responsibilities and duties

Questions you expect to be asked

Major ideas you plan to emphasize

Questions you plan to ask

Other comments

What's Next for Your Personal Financial Plan?

- Prepare preliminary answers for potential interview questions. (see p. 82)
- Have others ask you questions in a practice interview setting.

12

Personal Financial Planner

Name: ______________________ Date: ______________________

Employee Benefits Comparison

Purpose: To assess the financial and personal value of employment benefits. (pp. 62–65)

Instructions: When comparing different employment situations or when selecting benefits, consider the factors listed below. This sheet is also available in an Excel spreadsheet format at www.mhhe.com/kdh.

Suggested websites: www.benefitnews.com www.dol.gov/ebsa

Organization		
Location		
Phone		
Contact/title		
Health insurance Company/coverage Cost to be paid by employee		
Disability income insurance Company/coverage Cost to be paid by employee		
Life insurance Company/coverage Cost to be paid by employee		
Pension/retirement Employer contributions Vesting period Tax benefits Employee contributions		
Other benefits/estimated market value • vacation time • tuition reimbursement • child/dependent care • other ______________		
Website to access benefit information		

Suggested App:
- 401(k)

What's Next for Your Personal Financial Plan?

- Talk to various people about their employee benefits.
- Conduct research to obtain information on various employee benefits required by law and those commonly provided in various industries.

Name: ______________________ Date: ______________

Career Development and Advancement

Purpose: To develop a plan for career advancement. (pp. 65–66)

Instructions: Prepare responses for the items listed. This sheet is also available in an Excel spreadsheet format at www.mhhe.com/kdh.

Suggested websites: www.careerjournal.com www.careerplanning.about.com

Current position ______________________

Address ______________________

____

Phone ______________________

Fax ______________ E-mail ______________

Website ______________________

Current responsibilities and duties

Accomplishments

Career goal within the next year

- Required skills and experience
- Plans to achieve that goal

Career goal within the next two years

- Required skills and experience
- Plans to achieve that goal

Career goal within the next five years

- Required skills and experience
- Plans to achieve that goal

What's Next for Your Personal Financial Plan?

- Talk with others about the career development activities in which they have participated.
- Prepare a list of formal and informal career development activities in which you might participate.

14

Personal Financial Planner

Name: ______________________ Date: ______________

Financial Documents and Records

Purpose: To develop a system for maintaining and storing personal financial documents and records. (pp. 89–91)

Instructions: Indicate the location of the following records, and create files for the eight major categories of financial documents. This sheet is also available in an Excel spreadsheet format at www.mhhe.com/kdh.

Suggested websites: www.bankrate.com www.kiplinger.com www.usa.gov

Item	Home File	Safe Deposit Box	Computer File, Online, Other (specify)
1. Money management records			
• budget, financial statements			
2. Personal/employment records			
• current résumé, Social Security card			
• educational transcripts			
• birth, marriage, divorce certificates			
• citizenship, military papers, passport			
• adoption, custody papers			
3. Tax records			
4. Financial services/Consumer credit records			
• unused, canceled checks			
• savings, passbook statements			
• savings certificates			
• credit card information, statements			
• credit contracts			
5. Consumer purchase, housing, and automobile records			
• warranties, receipts			
• owner's manuals			
• lease or mortgage papers, title deed, property tax info			
• automobile title			
• auto registration			
• auto service records			
6. Insurance records			
• insurance policies			
• home inventory			
• medical information (health history)			
7. Investment records			
• broker statements			
• dividend reports			
• stock/bond certificates			
• rare coins, stamps, and collectibles			
8. Estate planning and retirement			
• will			
• pension, Social Security info			

Suggested App:

• Manilla

What's Next for Your Personal Financial Plan?

- Select a location for storing your financial documents and records.
- Decide if various documents may no longer be needed.

Name: ______________________ Date: ______________

Personal Balance Sheet

Purpose: To determine your current financial position. (pp. 92–94)

Instructions: List the current values of the asset categories below; list the amounts owed for various liabilities; subtract total liabilities from total assets to determine net worth. This sheet is also available in an Excel spreadsheet format at www.mhhe.com/kdh.

Suggested websites: www.money.com www.lifeadvice.com

Balance Sheet as of ______________________

Assets

Liquid assets

Checking account balance ______

Savings/money market accounts, funds ______

Cash value of life insurance ______

Other ______ ______

Total liquid assets . . . . ______

Household assets & possessions

Current market value of home ______

Market value of automobiles ______

Furniture ______

Computer, electronics, camera ______

Jewelry ______

Other ______ ______

Other ______ ______

Total household assets . . . . ______

Investment assets

Savings certificates ______

Stocks and bonds ______

Retirement accounts ______

Mutual funds ______

Other ______ ______

Total investment assets . . . . ______

Total assets . . . . ______

Liabilities

Current liabilities

Charge account and credit card balances ______

Loan balances ______

Other ______ ______

Other ______ ______

Total current liabilities . . . .

Long-term liabilities

Mortgage ______

Other ______ ______

Total long-term liabilities . . . . ______

Total liabilities . . . . ______

Net Worth ______

(assets minus liabilities)

What's Next for Your Personal Financial Plan?

- Compare your net worth to previous balance sheets.
- Decide how often you will prepare a balance sheet.

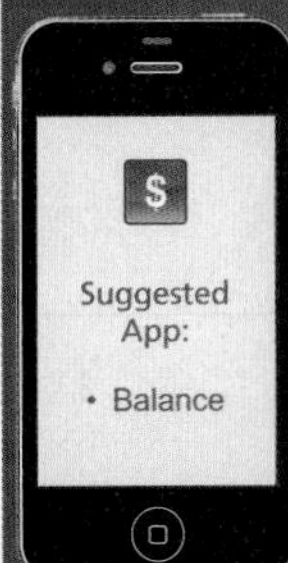

Name: ______________________ Date: ______________

16

Personal Financial Planner

Personal Cash Flow Statement

Purpose: To maintain a record of cash inflows and outflows for a month (or three months). (pp. 95–98)

Instructions: Record inflows and outflows of cash for a one- (or three-) month period. This sheet is also available in an Excel spreadsheet format at www.mhhe.com/kdh.

Suggested websites: www.asec.org www.clevelandsaves.org

For month ending ______________

Cash Inflows

Salary (take-home) ______________

Other income: ______________

Other income: ______________

Total Income . . . . [ ]

Cash Outflows

Fixed expenses

Mortgage or rent ______________

Loan payments ______________

Insurance ______________

Other ________ ______________

Other ________ ______________

Total fixed outflows . . . . ______________

Variable expenses

Food ______________

Clothing ______________

Electricity ______________

Telephone ______________

Water ______________

Transportation ______________

Personal care ______________

Medical expenses ______________

Recreation/entertainment ______________

Gifts ______________

Donations ______________

Other ________ ______________

Other ________ ______________

Total variable outflows . . . . ______________

Total outflows . . . . [ ]

Surplus/Deficit . . . . [ ]

Allocation of surplus

Emergency fund savings ______________

Financial goals savings ______________

Other savings ________ ______________

Suggested App:

• Expensify

What's Next for Your Personal Financial Plan?

- Decide which areas of spending need to be revised.
- Evaluate your spending patterns for preparing a budget.

Name: ______________________ Date: ______________________

Cash Budget

Purpose: To compare projected and actual spending for a one- (or three-) month period. (pp. 98–105)

Instructions: Estimate projected spending based on your cash flow statement, and maintain records for actual spending for these same budget categories. This sheet is also available in an Excel spreadsheet format at www.mhhe.com/kdh.

Suggested websites: www.betterbudgeting.com www.mymoney.gov www.thesimpledollar.com

	Budgeted Amounts			
Income	**Dollar**	**Percent**	**Actual Amounts**	**Variance**
Salary				
Other ______				
Total income		**100%**		
Expenses	<<<<<<<<<	<<<<<<<<<<<	<<<<<<<<<<<	<<<<<<<<<<
Fixed expenses	<<<<<<<<<	<<<<<<<<<<<	<<<<<<<<<<<	<<<<<<<<<<
Mortgage or rent				
Property taxes				
Loan payments				
Insurance				
Other ______				
Total fixed expenses				
Emergency fund/savings	<<<<<<<<<	<<<<<<<<<<<	<<<<<<<<<<	<<<<<<<<<<
Emergency fund				
Savings for ______				
Savings for ______				
Total savings				
Variable expenses	<<<<<<<<<	<<<<<<<<<<<	<<<<<<<<<<<	<<<<<<<<<<<
Food				
Utilities				
Clothing				
Transportation costs				
Personal care				
Medical and health care				
Entertainment				
Education				
Gifts/donations				
Miscellaneous				
Other ______				
Other ______				
Total variable expenses				
Total expenses		**100%**		

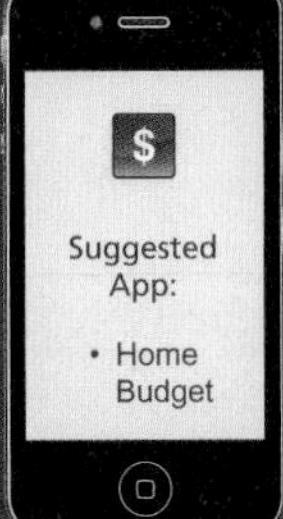

What's Next for Your Personal Financial Plan?

- Evaluate the appropriateness of your budget for your current situation.
- Assess whether your budgeting activities are helping you achieve your financial goals.

Name: ____________________ Date: ____________

Annual Budget Summary

Purpose: To see an overview of spending patterns for a year. (pp. 103–104)

Instructions: Record the monthly budget amount in the first column and actual monthly spending in the appropriate column. This sheet is also available in an Excel spreadsheet format at www.mhhe.com/kdh.

Suggested websites: www.mymoney.gov www.bls.gov/cex

Expense	Monthly Budget	Actual Spending					
		Jan	Feb	Mar	Apr	May	Jun
Savings							
Mortgage/rent							
Housing costs							
Telephone							
Food (at home)							
Food (away)							
Clothing							
Transportation							
Credit payments							
Insurance							
Health care							
Recreation							
Reading/education							
Gifts/donations							
Miscellaneous							
Other ______							
Other ______							
Total							

Expense	Actual Spending						Year Totals	
	Jul	Aug	Sep	Oct	Nov	Dec	Actual	Budget
Savings								
Mortgage/rent								
Housing costs								
Telephone								
Food (at home)								
Food (away)								
Clothing								
Transportation								
Credit payments								
Insurance								
Health care								
Recreation								
Reading/education								
Gifts/donations								
Miscellaneous								
Other ______								
Other ______								
Total								

What's Next for Your Personal Financial Plan?

- Decide which areas of spending need to be revised.
- Evaluate your spending patterns for preparing a budget.

Name: ______________________________ Date: ______________

College Education Savings Plan

Purpose: To estimate future costs of college and calculate needed savings. (pp. 107–108; Appendix A)

Instructions: Complete the information and calculations requested below. This sheet is also available in an Excel spreadsheet format at www.mhhe.com/kdh.

Suggested websites: www.statefarm.com/lifevents/lifevents.htm www.kiplinger.com

Estimated Cost of College Education

Current cost of college education $ ________

(including tuition, fees, room, board, books, travel, and other expenses)

Future value for ________ years until starting college at an expected annual inflation of ________ percent (use future value of $1, Exhibit 1-A in Chapter 1 Appendix or a financial calculator) × $ ________

Projected future cost of college adjusted for inflation . . . . = $ ________

Estimated Annual Savings Needed

Projected future cost of college adjusted for inflation . . . . **(A)** $ ________

Future value of a series of deposits for ________ years until starting college and expected annual rate of return on savings and investments of ________ percent (use Exhibit 1-B in Chapter 1 Appendix or a financial calculator) **(B)** $ ________

Estimated annual deposit to achieve needed education fund . . . . **A** divided by **B** $ ________

What's Next for Your Personal Financial Plan?

- Identify savings and investment plans that could be used to save for long-term goals.
- Ask others to suggest actions that might be taken to save for long-term goals.

19

Personal Financial Planner

20

Personal Financial Planner

Name: ______________________ Date: ______________________

Income Tax Estimate

Purpose: To estimate your current federal income tax liability. (pp. 120–127)

Instructions: Based on last year's tax return, estimates for the current year, and current tax regulations and rates, estimate your current tax liability. This sheet is also available in an Excel spreadsheet at www.mhhe.com/kdh.

Suggested websites: www.irs.gov https://turbotax.intuit.com/tax-tools/calculators/taxcaster/

Gross income (wages, salary, investment income, and other ordinary income)		$	
Less Adjustments to income (see current tax regulations)		− $	
Equals Adjusted gross income		= $	
Less Standard deduction **or**	Itemized deduction		
↓	medical expenses (exceeding 10% of AGI)		$
	state/local income & property taxes		$
	mortgage, home equity loan interest		$
	contributions		$
	casualty and theft losses		$
	moving expenses, job-related and miscellaneous expenses (exceeding 2% of AGI)		$
Amount − $	**Total**		− $
Less Personal exemptions		− $	
Equals Taxable income		= $	
Estimated tax (based on current tax tables or tax schedules)		$	
Less Tax credits		− $	
Plus Other taxes		+ $	
Equals Total tax liability		= $	
Less Estimated withholding and payments		− $	
Equals Tax due (or refund)		= $	

$

Suggested App:

- TaxCaster

What's Next for Your Personal Financial Plan?

- Develop a system for filing and storing various tax records related to income, deductible expenses, and current tax forms.
- Using www.irs.gov and other websites, identify recent changes in tax laws that may affect your financial planning decisions.

Name: ______________________________ Date: ______________

Tax Preparer Comparison

Purpose: To compare the services and costs of different income tax return preparation sources. (pp. 138–139)

Instructions: Using advertisements and information from tax preparation services, obtain information for the following. This sheet is also available in an Excel spreadsheet at www.mhhe.com/kdh.

Suggested websites: https://www.turbotax.intuit.com/tax-tools/ www.hrblock.com

	Local Tax Service	National Tax Service	Local Accountant
Company name			
Address			
Telephone			
E-mail			
Website			
Cost of preparing Form 1040EZ			
Cost of preparing Form 1040A			
Cost of preparing Form 1040 with Schedule A (itemized deductions)			
Cost of preparing state or local tax return			
Cost of electronic filing			
Assistance provided if IRS questions your return			
Other services provided			

What's Next for Your Personal Financial Plan?

- Talk with people about their experiences when using a tax preparation service.
- Compare the costs and benefits of using a tax preparation service with preparing your own taxes with tax software.

22

Personal Financial Planner

Name: ______________________________ Date: ______________________

Tax Planning Activities

Purpose: To consider actions that can prevent tax penalties and may result in tax savings. (pp. 142–147)

Instructions: Consider which of the following actions are appropriate to your tax situation. This sheet is also available in an Excel spreadsheet at www.mhhe.com/kdh.

Suggested websites: www.irs.gov https://www.turbotax.intuit.com/tax-tools/

	Action to be taken (if applicable)	Completed
Filing Status/Withholding		
• Change filing status or exemptions because of changes in life situation.		
• Change amount of withholding because of changes in tax situation.		
• Plan to make estimated tax payments (due the 15th of April, June, September, and January).		
Tax Records/Documents		
• Organize home files for ease of maintaining and retrieving data.		
• Send current mailing address and correct Social Security number to IRS, place of employment, and other sources of income.		
Annual Tax Activities		
• Be certain all needed data and current tax forms are available well before deadline.		
• Research tax code changes and uncertain tax areas.		
Tax Savings Actions		
• Consider tax-exempt and tax-deferred investments.		
• If you expect to have the same or lower tax rate next year, accelerate deductions into the current year.		
• If you expect to have the same or lower tax rate next year, delay the receipt of income until next year.		
• If you expect to have a higher tax rate next year, delay deductions because they will have a greater benefit.		
• If you expect to have a higher tax rate next year, accelerate the receipt of income to have it taxed at the current lower rate.		
• Start or increase use of tax-deferred retirement plans.		
• Other.		

Suggested Apps:
- IRS2go
- iDonatedit

What's Next for Your Personal Financial Plan?

- Identify saving and investing decisions that would minimize future income taxes.
- Develop a plan for actions to take related to your current and future tax situation.

Name: ______________________ Date: ______________

Financial Services Planning

Purpose: To indicate currently used financial services and to determine services that may be needed in the future. (pp. 156–165)

Instructions: List currently used services with financial institution information (name, address, phone, website) and services that are likely to be needed in the future. This sheet is also available in an Excel spreadsheet format at www.mhhe.com/kdh.

Suggested websites: www.bankrate.com www.creditunion.coop www.findabetterbank.com

Types of financial services	Current financial services used	Additional financial services needed
Payment services (checking, debit card, online payments, money orders)	Financial institution:	
	Address:	
	Phone:	
	Website:	
Savings plans (savings account, certificates of deposit, savings bonds)	Financial institution:	
	Address:	
	Phone:	
	Website:	
Credit accounts (credit cards, personal loans, mortgage)	Financial institution:	
	Address:	
	Phone:	
	Website:	
Other financial services (investments, trust account, tax planning)	Financial institution:	
	Address:	
	Phone:	
	Website:	

What's Next for Your Personal Financial Plan?

- Assess whether the current types of and sources of your financial services are appropriate.
- Determine additional financial services you may wish to make use of in the future.

Name: ______________________ Date: ______________

24

Saving to Achieve Financial Goals

Purpose: To monitor savings for use in reaching financial goals. (pp. 165–169)

Instructions: Record savings plan information along with the amount of your balance or income on a periodic basis. This sheet is also available in an Excel spreadsheet format at www.mhhe.com/kdh.

Suggested websites: www.fdic.gov www.savingsbonds.gov

Regular Savings Account

Acct. no. ______________

Financial institution ______________

Address ______________

____

Phone ______________

Website ______________

Savings goal/Amount needed/Date needed:

____

Initial deposit: Date ________ $________

Balance: Date ________ $________

Date ________ $________

Date ________ $________

Date ________ $________

Certificate of Deposit

Acct. no. ______________

Financial institution ______________

Address ______________

____

Phone ______________

Website ______________

Savings goal/Amount needed/Date needed:

____

Initial deposit: Date ________ $ ________

Balance: Date ________ $ ________

Date ________ $ ________

Date ________ $ ________

Date ________ $ ________

Money Market fund/account

Acct. no. ______________

Financial institution ______________

Address ______________

____

Phone ______________

Website ______________

Savings goal/Amount needed/Date needed:

____

Initial deposit: Date ________ $ ________

Balance: Date ________ $ ________

Date ________ $ ________

Date ________ $ ________

Date ________ $ ________

U.S. Savings Bonds

Purchase location ______________

____

Address ______________

____

Phone ______________

Website ______________

Savings goal/Amount needed/Date needed:

____

Purchase date: ________ Maturity date: ________

Amount: ________ Maturity date: ________

Purchase date: ________ Maturity date: ________

Amount: ________ Maturity date: ________

What's Next for Your Personal Financial Plan?

- Assess your current progress toward achieving various savings goals. Evaluate existing and new savings goals.
- Plan actions to expand the amount you are saving toward various savings goals.

Suggested App:

- SmartyPig

Name: ______________________ Date: ______________

Savings Plan Comparison

Purpose: To compare the benefits and costs associated with different savings plans. (pp. 165–173)

Instructions: Analyze advertisements and contact various financial institutions to obtain the information requested below. This sheet is also available in an Excel spreadsheet format at www.mhhe.com/kdh.

Suggested websites: www.bankrate.com www.fdic.gov

Type of savings plan: (regular savings account, certificate of deposit, money market account, other ________)			
Financial institution			
Address/Phone			
Website			
Annual interest rate			
Annual percentage yield (APY)			
Frequency of compounding			
Insured by FDIC, NCUA, other			
Maximum amount insured			
Minimum initial deposit			
Minimum time period savings must be on deposit			
Penalties for early withdrawal			
Service charges, transaction fees, other costs or fees			

What's Next for Your Personal Financial Plan?

- Based on this savings plan analysis, determine the best types for your current and future financial situation.
- When analyzing savings plans, what factors should you carefully investigate?

Name: ______________________ Date: ______________

26

Payment Account Comparison

Purpose: To compare the benefits and costs associated with different checking/payment accounts. (pp. 174–179)

Instructions: Analyze advertisements and contact various financial institutions (banks, savings and loan associations, or credit unions) to obtain the information requested below. This sheet is also available in an Excel spreadsheet format at www.mhhe.com/kdh.

Suggested websites: www.bankrate.com www.checkfree.com

Institution name			
Address			
Phone			
Website			
Type of account (regular checking, interest-earning account, or other ________)			
Minimum balance for "free" checking			
Monthly fee for going below minimum balance			
"Free" checking accounts for full-time students?			
Online banking services			
Other fees/costs			
• printing of checks			
• stop payment order			
• overdrawn account			
• certified check			
• ATM, other charges			
Banking hours			
Location of branch offices and ATM network			

Suggested App:
- Money Pass (ATM locator)

What's Next for Your Personal Financial Plan?

- Are your current payment activities best served by your current payment methods (checking account, cash card, online payments)?
- Talk with others about their online payment experiences.

Name: ______________________ Date: ______________________

Payment Account Cost Analysis

27

Personal Financial Planner

Purpose: To compare the inflows and outflows of a checking account. (pp. 174–179)

Instructions: Record the interest earned (inflows) and the costs and fees (outflows) as requested below. *Note: Not all items will apply to every checking account.* This sheet is also available in an Excel spreadsheet format at www.mhhe.com/kdh.

Suggested websites: www.bankrate.com www.checkfree.com

Inflows (earnings)

Step 1

Multiply average monthly balance $ ______ by average rate of return ______ % to determine annual earnings

Outflows (costs)

Step 2

Monthly service charge $ ______ × 12 = $ ______

Average number of checks written per month ______ × charge per check (if applicable) × 12 = $ ______

Average number of deposits per month ______ × charge per deposit (if applicable) × 12 = $ ______

Fee incurred when going below minimum balance ______ × times below minimum = $ ______

Lost interest: opportunity cost ______ % × required minimum balance $ ______ = $ ______

= [ ]

Total estimated inflow $ ______

Total estimated outflow $ ______

Estimated inflows less outflows =

Net earnings for account ______

− **Net cost for account** ______

+/−$ ______

Note: This calculation does not take into account charges and fees for such services as overdrafts, stop payments, ATM use, and check printing. Be sure to also consider those costs when selecting a checking account.

What's Next for Your Personal Financial Plan?

- What actions can you take to minimize checking/payment account costs?
- Talk to others about the actions they take to minimize checking account costs.

Name: ______________________ Date: ______________

Checking Account Reconciliation

Purpose: To determine the adjusted cash balance for your checking account. (pp. 179–180)

Instructions: Enter data from your bank statement and checkbook for the amounts requested. This sheet is also available in an Excel spreadsheet format at www.mhhe.com/kdh.

Suggested websites: www.bankrate.com www.checkfree.com

Date of bank statement ______________

Balance on bank statement $ ______

Step 1

Subtract total of outstanding checks (checks that you have written but have not yet cleared in the banking system)

Check No.	Amount	Check No.	Amount

– $ ______

Step 2

Add deposits in transit (deposits you have made but have not been reported on this statement)

Date	Amount	Date	Amount

+ $ ______

Adjusted cash balance . . . . $ ______

Current balance in your checkbook ______

Step 3

Subtract fees or other charges listed on your bank statement

Item	Amount	Item	Amount

– $ ______

Subtract ATM withdrawals, debit card payments, and other automatic payments. – $ ______

Step 4

Add interest earned + $ ______

Add direct deposits + $ ______

Adjusted cash balance . . . . $ ______

(The two adjusted balances should be the same; if not, carefully check your math and check to see that deposits and checks recorded in your checkbook and on your statement are for the correct amounts.)

What's Next for Your Personal Financial Plan?

- Develop a plan to monitor your payment records.
- Select actions to reduce banking service costs.

Name: ____________________ Date: ____________________

Consumer Credit Usage

Purpose: To create a record of current consumer debt balances. (pp. 200–205)

Instructions: Record account names, numbers, and payments for current consumer debts. This sheet is also available in an Excel spreadsheet format at www.mhhe.com/kdh.

Suggested websites: www.bankrate.com www.ftc.gov

Automobile, Education, Personal, and Installment Loans

Financial institution	Account number	Current balance	Monthly payment

Charge Accounts and Credit Cards

Other Loans (overdraft protection, home equity, life insurance loan)

	Totals		

$$\text{Debt payment-to-income ratio} = \frac{\text{Total monthly payments}}{\text{net (after-tax) income}}$$

What's Next for Your Personal Financial Plan?

- Survey three or four individuals to determine their uses of credit.
- Talk to several people to determine how they first established credit.

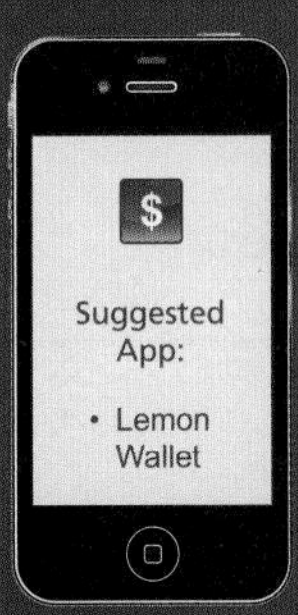

Name: ______________________ Date: ______________

30

Personal Financial Planner

Credit Card Comparison

Purpose: To compare the benefits and costs associated with different credit cards and charge accounts. (pp. 230–245)

Instructions: Analyze ads and credit applications and contact various financial institutions to obtain the information requested below. This sheet is also available in an Excel spreadsheet format at www.mhhe.com/kdh.

Suggested websites: www.bankrate.com www.banx.com

Type of credit/charge account			
Name of company/account			
Address/phone			
Website			
Type of purchases that can be made			
Annual fee (if any)			
Annual percentage rate (APR) (interest calculation information)			
Credit limit for new customers			
Minimum monthly payment			
Other costs: • credit report • late fee • other _________			
Restrictions (age, minimum annual income)			
Other information for consumers to consider			
Rewards program			

What's Next for Your Personal Financial Plan?

- Make a list of the pros and cons of using credit or debit cards.
- Contact a local credit bureau to obtain information on the services provided and the fees charged.

Name: ______________________ Date: ______________

Consumer Loan Comparison

Purpose: To compare the costs associated with different sources of loans. (pp. 230–245)

Instructions: Contact or visit a bank, credit union, and consumer finance company to obtain information on a loan for a specific purpose. This sheet is also available in an Excel spreadsheet format at www.mhhe.com/kdh.

Suggested websites: www.eloan.com www.bankrate.com

Amount of loan $ __________

Type of financial institution

Name			
Address			
Phone			
Website			
Amount of down payment			
Length of loan (months)			
What collateral is required?			
Amount of monthly payment			
Total amount to be repaid (monthly amount × number of months + down payment)			
Total finance charge/cost of credit			
Annual percentage rate (APR)			
Other costs • credit life insurance • credit report • other __________			
Is a cosigner required?			
Other information			

What's Next for Your Personal Financial Plan?

- Ask several individuals how they would compare loans at different financial institutions.
- Survey several friends and relatives to determine whether they ever cosigned a loan. If yes, what were the consequences of cosigning?

32

Name: ______________________ Date: ______________

Unit Pricing Worksheet

Purpose: To calculate the unit price for a consumer purchase. (p. 272)

Instructions: Use advertisements or information obtained during store visits to calculate and compare unit prices. This sheet is also available in an Excel spreadsheet format at www.mhhe.com/kdh.

Suggested websites: www.consumer.gov www.consumerworld.org

Item ______________________

Date	Store/Location	Brand	Total price	÷	Size	=	Unit Price	Unit of Measurement

Highest unit price

Store ______________________

Date ______________________

Lowest unit price

Store ______________________

Date ______________________

Difference: ______________

Wisest consumer buy/Best overall store

Reasons

Suggested App:

- Grocery Gadget

What's Next for Your Personal Financial Plan?

- Talk to others about actions they take to get the most for their money.
- Prepare a list of local and online shopping locations that provide the best value.

Name: ______________________ Date: ______________________

Consumer Purchase Comparison

Purpose: To research and evaluate brands and store services for purchase of a major consumer item. (pp. 268–284)

Instructions: When considering the purchase of a major consumer item, use ads, catalogs, an Internet search, store visits, and other sources to obtain the information below. This sheet is also available in an Excel spreadsheet format at www.mhhe.com/kdh.

Suggested websites: www.consumerreports.org www.mysimon.com

Product:

____

Exact description (size, model, features, etc.):

____

Research the item online and in consumer periodicals for information regarding your product

Source ______________________ Source ______________________

Date ______________________ Date ______________________

____

What buying suggestions are presented in these information sources?

____

Which brands are recommended in these information sources? Why?

____

Contact or visit two or three stores or online sources that sell the product to obtain the following information:

	Buying location	Buying location	Buying location
Company name			
Address			
Phone/website			
Brand name/cost			
Product difference from item above			
Guarantee/warranty offered (describe)			

Which brand and at which store would you buy this product? Why?

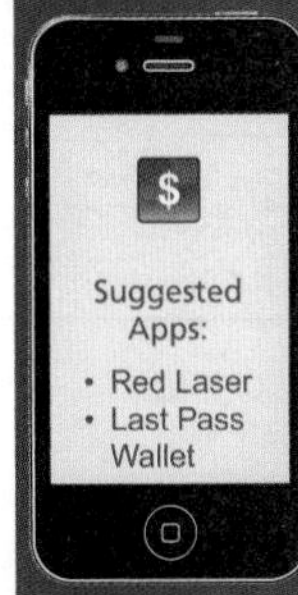

What's Next for Your Personal Financial Plan?

- Which consumer information sources are most valuable for your future buying decisions?
- List guidelines to use in the future when making major purchases.

Personal Financial Planner

34

Name: ______________________ Date: ______________________

Transportation Needs

Purpose: To assess current and future transportation needs. (pp. 275–280)

Instructions: Based on current needs and expected needs, complete the information requested below. This sheet is also available in an Excel spreadsheet format at www.mhhe.com/kdh.

Suggested websites: cars.about.com www.kbb.com

Current situation: Date ______________________

	Vehicle 1		Vehicle 2
Year/Model		Year/Model	
Mileage		Mileage	
Condition		Condition	
Needed repairs		Needed repairs	
Estimated annual costs		**Estimated annual costs**	
Gas, oil, repairs		Gas, oil, repairs	
Insurance		Insurance	
Loan balance		Loan balance	
Estimated market value		Estimated market value	

Expected and projected changes in transportation needs

Personal desires and concerns regarding current transportation

Analysis of Future Desired Transportation Situation

Description of new vehicle

Time when new vehicle is desired

Financing resources needed

Available and projected financial resources

Concerns that must be overcome

Realistic time when transportation choice may be achieved

Suggested App:
• KBB

What's Next for Your Personal Financial Plan?

- Talk to others about their experiences with public transportation.
- Identify financial and personal factors that affect your transportation spending decisions.

Name: ______________________ Date: ______________

Used-Car Comparison

35

Personal Financial Planner

Purpose: To research and evaluate different types and sources of used cars. (pp. 277–280)

Instructions: When considering a used-car purchase, use advertisements and visits to new and used car dealers to obtain the information below. This sheet is also available in an Excel spreadsheet format at www.mhhe.com/kdh.

Suggested websites: www.carbuyingtips.com www.kbb.com

Automobile (year, make, model)			
Dealer/Source name			
Address			
Phone			
Website			
Cost			
Mileage			
Condition of auto			
Condition of tires			
Radio			
Air conditioning			
Other options			
Warranty (if applicable)			
Items in need of repair			
Inspection items: • any rust, major dents?			
• oil or fluid leaks?			
• condition of brakes?			
• proper operation of heater, wipers, other accessories?			
Other information			

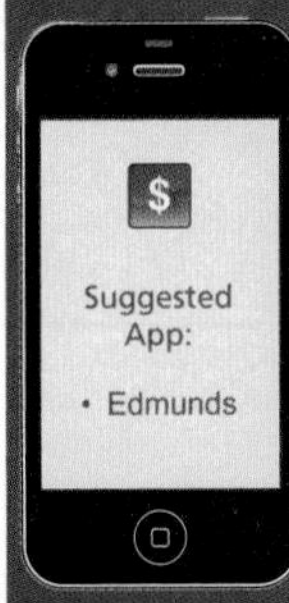

What's Next for Your Personal Financial Plan?

- Maintain a record of automobile operating costs.
- Prepare a plan for regular maintenance of your vehicle.

Name: ______________________________ Date: ______________

Buying or Leasing a Motor Vehicle

Purpose: To compare costs of buying and leasing an automobile or other vehicle. This analysis should compare two situations with comparable payment amounts, even though the length of the agreements may differ. (pp. 278–279)

Instructions: Obtain costs related to leasing and buying a vehicle. This sheet is also available in an Excel spreadsheet format at www.mhhe.com/kdh.

Suggested websites: cars.about.com www.leasesource.com

Purchase Costs

Total vehicle cost, including sales tax ($ _________)

Down payment (or full amount if paying cash) $ ____________

Monthly loan payment $ _________ times _________ months
(this item is zero if vehicle is not financed) $ ____________

Opportunity cost of down payment (or total cost of the vehicle if bought for cash)

$ _________ times number of years of financing/ownership times

_________ percent (interest rate which funds could earn) $ ____________

Less: estimated value of vehicle at end of loan term/ownership $ ____________

Total cost to buy .... $

Leasing Costs

Security deposit $ _________ $ ____________

Monthly lease payments $ _________ times _________ months $ ____________

Opportunity cost of security deposit:
$ _________ times _________ years times _________ percent $ ____________

End-of-lease charges (if applicable)* $ ____________

Total cost to lease .... $

*Such as charges for extra mileage.

What's Next for Your Personal Financial Plan?

- Prepare a list of future actions to use when buying, financing, and leasing a car.
- Maintain a record of operating costs and maintenance actions for your vehicle.

Name: ______________________ Date: ______________

Comparing Cash and Credit Purchases

37

Personal Financial Planner

Purpose: To compare the costs and benefits of cash and credit. (pp. 277–284)

Instructions: When considering a major consumer purchase, complete the information requested below. This sheet is also available in an Excel spreadsheet format at www.mhhe.com/kdh.

Suggested websites: www.consumerreports.org www.mysimon.com

Item/Description ______________________

Cash Price

Selling price	$ ______
Sales tax	$ ______
Additional charges (delivery, setup, service contract)	$ ______
Discounts (employee, senior citizen or student discounts, discounts for paying cash)	$ ______
Net cost of item times percent interest that could be earned times years of use to determine opportunity cost	$ ______
Total financial and economic cost when paying cash	$

Credit Price

Down payment	$ ______
Financing: monthly payment times months	$ ______
Additional financing charges (application fee, credit report, credit life insurance)	$ ______
Product-related charges (delivery, setup)	$ ______
Discounts that may apply	–$ ______
Total financial and economic cost when using credit	$

Other Considerations

Will cash used for the purchase be needed for other purposes?

Will this credit purchase result in financial difficulties?

Do alternatives exist for this purchasing and payment decision?

Note: Use Sheet 33 to compare brands, stores, features, and prices when making a major consumer purchase.

What's Next for Your Personal Financial Plan?

- Develop a plan to save for major purchases in the future.
- Create a list of personal factors to consider when comparing cash and credit purchases.

Name: ______________________ Date: ______________________

Auto Operation Costs

Purpose: To calculate or estimate the cost of owning and operating an automobile or other vehicle. (pp. 282–283)

Instructions: Maintain records related to the cost of categories listed below. This sheet is also available in an Excel spreadsheet format at www.mhhe.com/kdh.

Suggested websites: www.consumerreports.org www.autobytel.com

Model year ______________ **Make, size, model** ______________________

Fixed Ownership Costs

Depreciation*

Purchase price $ ________ divided by estimated life of ________ years $ ____________

Interest on auto loan

Annual cost of financing vehicle if buying on credit $ ____________

Insurance for the Vehicle

Annual cost of liability and property $ ____________

License, registration fee, and taxes $ ____________

Cost of registering vehicle for state and city license fees $ ____________

Total fixed costs (A) .... $ ____________

Variable Costs

Gasoline

________ estimated miles per year divided by ________ miles per gallon of ________ times the average price of $ ________ per gallon $ ____________

Oil changes

Cost of regular oil changes during the year $ ____________

Tires

Cost of tires purchased during the year $ ____________

Maintenance/repairs

Cost of planned or other unexpected maintenance $ ____________

Parking and tolls

Regular fees for parking and highway toll charges $ ____________

Total variable costs (B).. $ ____________

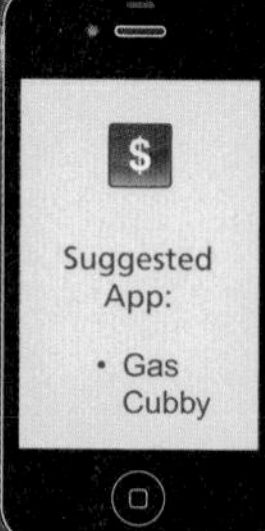

Total costs (A+B) $ ____________

Divided by miles per year ____________

Equals cost per mile $ ____________

*This estimate of vehicle depreciation is based on a straight-line approach—equal depreciation each year. A more realistic approach would be larger amounts in the early years of ownership, such as 25–30 percent in the first year, 30–35 percent in the second; most cars lose 90 percent of their value by the time they are seven years old.

What's Next for Your Personal Financial Plan?

- Talk to others to obtain suggestions for reducing auto operation costs.
- Prepare a list of local businesses that provide the best value for motor vehicle service.

Name: ____________________ Date: ____________________

Legal Services Comparison

Purpose: To compare costs of services from different sources of legal assistance. (pp. 289–290)

Instructions: Contact various sources of legal services (lawyer, prepaid legal service, legal aid society) to compare costs and available services. This sheet is also available in an Excel spreadsheet format at www.mhhe.com/kdh.

Suggested websites: www.ftc.gov www.fraud.org www.nolo.com

Type of legal service			
Organization name			
Address			
Phone			
Website			
Contact person			
Recommended by			
Areas of specialization			
Cost of initial consultation			
Cost of simple will			
Cost of real estate closing			
Cost method for other services—flat fee, hourly rate, or contingency basis			
Other information			

What's Next for Your Personal Financial Plan?

- Determine the best alternative for your future legal needs.
- Maintain a file of legal documents and other financial records.

Personal Financial Planner

40

Name: ______________________ Date: ______________

Housing Needs

Purpose: To assess current and future plans for housing. (pp. 300–303)

Instructions: Based on current and expected future needs, complete the information requested below. This sheet is also available in an Excel spreadsheet format at www.mhhe.com/kdh.

Suggested websites: homebuying.about.com realestate.msn.com

Current situation ______________ Date ______________

Renting		Buying	
Location		Location	
Description		Description	
Advantages		Advantages	
Disadvantages		Disadvantages	
Rent $		Mortgage payment $	
Lease expiration		Balance $	
		Current market value	

Expected and projected changes in housing needs

Personal desires and concerns regarding current housing situation

Analysis of Future Desired Housing Situation

Description of new housing situation	
Time when this situation is desired	
Financing resources needed/available	
Concerns that must be overcome	
Realistic time when housing of choice may be achieved	

Suggested App:
- Redfin

What's Next for Your Personal Financial Plan?

- List personal factors that would affect your decision to rent or buy.
- Talk with various people about factors that affect their housing decisions.

Name: ______________________ Date: ______________________

Renting or Buying Housing

Purpose: To compare cost of renting and buying your place of residence. (pp. 303–307)

Instructions: Obtain estimates for comparable housing units for the data requested below. This sheet is also available in an Excel spreadsheet format at www.mhhe.com/kdh.

Suggested websites: www.homefair.com www.newbuyer.com/homes

41

Personal Financial Planner

Rental Costs

Annual rent payments (monthly rent $ ______ × 12)	$ ______
Renter's insurance	$ ______
Interest lost on security deposit (deposit times after-tax savings account interest rate)	$ ______
Total annual cost of renting	$

Buying Costs

Annual mortgage payments	$ ______
Property taxes (annual costs)	$ ______
Homeowner's insurance (annual premium)	$ ______
Estimated maintenance and repairs	$ ______
After-tax interest lost because of down payment/closing costs	$ ______
Less: financial benefits of home ownership	
Growth in equity	$ – ______
Tax savings for mortgage interest (annual mortgage interest times tax rate)	$ – ______
Tax savings for property taxes (annual property taxes times tax rate)	$ – ______
Estimated annual depreciation	$ – ______
Total annual cost of buying	$

What's Next for Your Personal Financial Plan?

- Determine whether renting or buying is most appropriate for you at the current time.
- Prepare a list of circumstances or actions that might change your housing needs.

42

Personal Financial Planner

Name: ______________________ Date: ______________

Apartment Rental Comparison

Purpose: To evaluate and compare rental housing alternatives. (pp. 303–307)

Instructions: When in the market for an apartment, obtain information to compare costs and facilities of three apartments. This sheet is also available in an Excel spreadsheet format at www.mhhe.com/kdh.

Suggested websites: apartments.about.com www.taa.org

Name of renting person or apartment building			
Address			
Phone			
E-mail, website			
Monthly rent			
Amount of security deposit			
Length of lease			
Utilities included in rent			
Parking facilities			
Storage area in building			
Laundry facilities			
Distance to schools			
Distance to public transportation			
Distance to shopping			
Pool, recreation area, other facilities			
Estimated utility costs: • electric • telephone • gas • water			
Other costs			
Other information			

Suggested App:
• Pad Mapper

What's Next for Your Personal Financial Plan?

- Which of these rental units would best serve your current housing needs?
- What additional information should be considered when renting an apartment?

Name: ______________________________ Date: ______________

Housing Mortgage Affordability

43

Purpose: To estimate the amount of affordable mortgage payment, mortgage amount, and home purchase price. (pp. 316–317)

Instructions: Enter the amounts requested, and perform the required calculations. This sheet is also available in an Excel spreadsheet format at www.mhhe.com/kdh.

Suggested websites: www.kiplinger.com www.mortgagecalculator.org

Personal Financial Planner

Step 1

Determine your monthly gross income (annual income divided by 12). $ ______________

Step 2

With a down payment of at least 5 percent, lenders use 33 percent of monthly gross income as a guideline for PITI (principal, interest, taxes, and insurance), and 38 percent of monthly gross income as a guideline for PITI plus other debt payments (enter 0.33 or 0.38). × ______________

Step 3

Subtract other debt payments (such as payments on an auto loan), if applicable. − ______________

Subtract estimated monthly costs of property taxes and homeowners' insurance. − ______________

Affordable monthly mortgage payment .... $ ______________

Step 4

Divide this amount by the monthly mortgage payment per $1,000 based on current mortgage rates (see Exhibit 9–9, text p. 317). For example, for a 10 percent, 30-year loan, the number would be $8.78). ÷ ______________

Multiply by $1,000. × $1,000

Affordable mortgage amount .... $ ______________

Step 5

Divide your affordable mortgage amount by 1 minus the fractional portion of your down payment (for example, 0.9 for a 10 percent down payment). ÷ ______________

Affordable home purchase price .... $ ______________

Note: The two ratios used by lending institutions (Step 2) and other loan requirements are likely to vary based on a variety of factors, including the type of mortgage, the amount of the down payment, your income level, and current interest rates. For example, with a down payment of 10 percent or more and a credit score of at least 720, the ratios might increase to 40/45 or 45/50 percent in the above analysis.

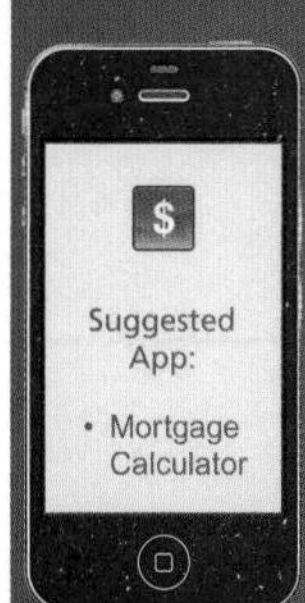

What's Next for Your Personal Financial Plan?

- Identify actions you might need to take to qualify for a mortgage.
- Discuss your mortgage qualifications with a mortgage broker or other lender.

Name: ______________________ Date: ______________

Mortgage Comparison

Purpose: To compare the services and costs for different home mortgage sources. (pp. 319–322)

Instructions: When obtaining a mortgage, obtain the information requested below from different mortgage companies. This sheet is also available in an Excel spreadsheet format at www.mhhe.com/kdh.

Suggested websites: www.bankrate.com   www.hsh.com

Amount of mortgage $ __________ Down payment $ __________ Years __________

Company		
Address		
Phone		
Website		
Contact person		
Application fee, credit report, property appraisal fees		
Loan origination fee		
Other fees, charges (commitment, title, tax transfer)		
Fixed rate mortgage		
Monthly payment		
Discount points		
Adjustable rate mortgage		
• time until first rate change • frequency of rate change		
Monthly payment		
Discount points		
Payment cap		
Interest rate cap		
Rate index used		
Commitment period		
Other information		

What's Next for Your Personal Financial Plan?

- What additional information should be considered when selecting a mortgage?
- Which of these mortgage companies would best serve your current and future needs?

Suggested App:
- Mortgage Rates

Name: ____________________ Date: ____________________

Mortgage Refinance Analysis

Purpose: To determine savings associated with refinancing a mortgage. (p. 322)

Instructions: Record financing costs and amount saved with new mortgage in the areas provided. This sheet is also available in an Excel spreadsheet format at www.mhhe.com/kdh.

Suggested websites: www.interest.com www.mortgage-net.com

Costs of refinancing:

Points $ ____________________

Application fee $ ____________________

Credit report $ ____________________

Attorney fees $ ____________________

Title search $ ____________________

Title insurance $ ____________________

Appraisal fee $ ____________________

Inspection fee $ ____________________

Other fees $ ____________________

Total refinancing costs .... **(A)** $ __________

Monthly savings:

Current monthly mortgage payment $ ____________________

Less:

New monthly payment $ ____________________

Monthly savings .... **(B)** $ __________

Number of months to cover finance costs

Refinance costs (A) divided by monthly savings (B)

(A) ________________ ÷ (B) ________________ = ________________ months

What's Next for Your Personal Financial Plan?

- Monitor changing mortgage rates to determine if any actions are necessary.
- Talk with a mortgage broker about expected trends in mortgage rates.

Name: ______________________ Date: ______________

46

Personal Financial Planner

Insurance Policies and Needs

Purpose: To establish a record of current and needed insurance coverage. (pp. 336–341)

Instructions: List current insurance policies and areas where new or additional coverage is needed. This sheet is also available in an Excel spreadsheet format at www.mhhe.com/kdh.

Suggested websites: www.personalinsure.about.com www.iii.org

Current Coverage		Needed Coverage
Property insurance		
Company	______	
Policy no.	______	
Coverage amounts	______	
Deductible	______	
Annual premium	______	
Agent	______	
Address	______	
Phone	______	
Website	______	
Automobile insurance		
Company	______	
Policy no.	______	
Coverage amounts	______	
Deductible	______	
Annual premium	______	
Agent	______	
Address	______	
Phone	______	
Website	______	
Disability income insurance		
Company	______	
Policy no.	______	
Coverage	______	
Contact	______	
Phone	______	
Website	______	
Health insurance		
Company	______	
Policy no.	______	
Policy provisions	______	
Contact	______	
Phone	______	
Website	______	
Life insurance		
Company	______	
Policy no.	______	
Type of policy	______	
Amount of coverage	______	
Cash value	______	
Agent	______	
Phone	______	
Website	______	

What's Next for Your Personal Financial Plan?

- Talk with others to determine the types of insurance they have.
- Conduct a Web search for various types of insurance on which you need additional information.

Name: ______________________ Date: ______________

Home Inventory

Purpose: To create a record of personal belongings for use when settling home insurance claims. (pp. 344–345)

Instructions: For areas of the home, list your possessions including a description (model, serial number), cost, and date of acquisition. Also consider photographs and videos of your possessions. This sheet is also available in an Excel spreadsheet format at www.mhhe.com/kdh.

Suggested websites: www.knowyourstuff.org www.statefarm.com/_pdf/home_inventory_checklist.pdf

Item, description	Cost	Date acquired
Attic		
Bathroom		
Bedrooms		
Family room		
Living room		
Hallways		
Kitchen		
Dining room		
Basement		
Garage		
Other items		

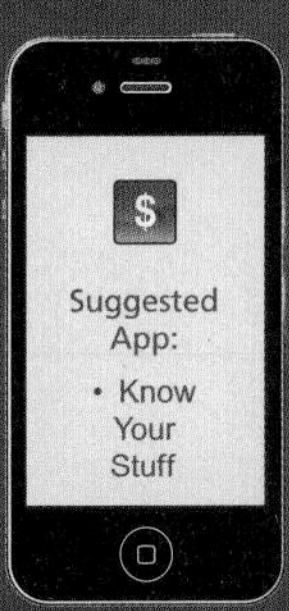

What's Next for Your Personal Financial Plan?

- Determine common items that may be overlooked when preparing a home inventory.
- Talk to an insurance agent to determine how best to document your property in the event of an insurance claim.

Name: ______________________ Date: ______________________

Property Insurance

Purpose: To determine property insurance needed for a home or apartment. (pp. 343–350)

Instructions: Estimate the value and your needs for the categories below. This sheet is also available in an Excel spreadsheet format at www.mhhe.com/kdh.

Suggested websites: www.personalinsure.about.com www.insure.com www.iii.org

Real Property

(this section not applicable to renters)

Current replacement value of home $ ______________

Personal Property

Estimated value of appliances, furniture, clothing, and other household items (conduct an inventory) $ ______________

Type of coverage for personal property

actual cash value ☐

replacement value ☐

Additional coverage for items with limits on standard personal property coverage such as jewelry, firearms, silverware, photographic, electronic and computer equipment

Item	Amount

Personal Liability

Amount of additional personal liability coverage desired for possible personal injury claims $ ______________

Specialized Coverages

If appropriate, investigate flood or earthquake coverage excluded from home insurance policies $ ______________

Note: Use Sheet 49 to compare companies, coverages, and costs for apartment or home insurance.

What's Next for Your Personal Financial Plan?

- Talk to others about the amount of coverage for their home and property.
- Research the main factors that affect home insurance costs in your region.

Name: ______________________________ Date: ______________________

Apartment/Home Insurance Comparison

Purpose: To research and compare companies, coverages, and costs for apartment or home insurance. (pp. 350–351)

Instructions: Contact three insurance agents to obtain the information requested below. This sheet is also available in an Excel spreadsheet format at www.mhhe.com/kdh.

Suggested websites: www.netquote.com www.iii.org www.insurancequotes.org/home-insurance/

Type of building: ☐ apartment ☐ house ☐ condominium

Location: ______________________________

Type of construction ______________________ Age of building ______________________

Company name			
Agent's name, address and phone			
E-mail, website			
Coverage: Dwelling $ Other structures $ (does not apply to apartment/condo coverage)	**Premium**	**Premium**	**Premium**
Personal property $			
Additional living expenses $			
Personal liability Bodily injury $ Property damage $			
Medical payments Per person $ Per accident $			
Deductible amount			
Other coverage $			
Service charges or fees			
Total Premium			

What's Next for Your Personal Financial Plan?

- Conduct a survey to determine common reasons that renters do not have renter's insurance.
- Determine cost differences for home insurance among various local agents and online companies.

Name: ______________________________ Date: ______________________________

Automobile Insurance Comparison

Purpose: To research and compare companies, coverages, and costs for auto insurance. (pp. 356–359)

Instructions: Contact three insurance agents to obtain the information requested below. This sheet is also available in an Excel spreadsheet format at www.mhhe.com/kdh.

Suggested websites: personalinsure.about.com www.insquote.com

Automobile (year, make, model, engine size) ______________________________

Driver's age __________ Sex __________ Total miles driven in a year __________

Full- or part-time drive? __________ Driver's education completed? __________

Accidents or traffic violations within the past three years? ______________________________

Company name			
Agent's name, address and phone			
E-mail, website			
Policy length (6 months, 1 year)			
Coverage: *Bodily injury liability* Per person $	**Premium**	**Premium**	**Premium**
Per accident $			
Property damage liability per accident $			
Collision deductible $			
Comprehensive deductible $			
Medical payments per person $			
Uninsured motorist Per person $			
Per accident $			
Other coverage			
Service charges			
Total Premium			

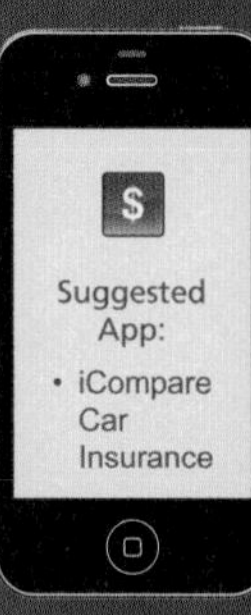

What's Next for Your Personal Financial Plan?

- Research actions that you might take to reduce automobile insurance costs.
- Determine cost differences for auto insurance among various local agents and online companies.

Name: ______________________________ Date: ______________________

Health Care Insurance

Purpose: To assess current and needed medical and health care insurance. (pp. 373–381)

Instructions: Assess current and needed medical and health care insurance. Investigate your existing medical and health insurance, and determine the need for additional coverages. This sheet is also available in an Excel spreadsheet format at www.mhhe.com/kdh.

Suggested websites: www.insure.com www.lifehappens.org www.ehealthinsurance.com

Insurance company	
Address	
Type of coverage	☐ individual health policy ☐ group health policy ☐ HMO ☐ PPO ☐ other ________
Premium amount (monthly/quarterly/semiannually/annually)	
Main coverages	
Amount of coverage for	
• Hospital costs	
• Surgery costs	
• Physician's fees	
• Lab tests	
• Outpatient expenses	
• Maternity	
• Major medical	
Other items covered/amounts	
Policy restrictions (deductible, coinsurance, maximum limits)	
Items not covered by this insurance	
Of items not covered, would supplemental coverage be appropriate for your personal situation?	
What actions related to your current (or proposed additional) coverage are necessary?	

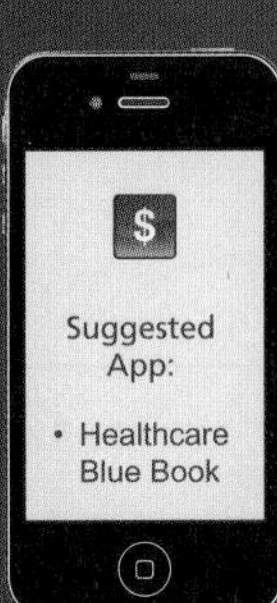

What's Next for Your Personal Financial Plan?

- Talk to others about the impact of their health insurance on other financial decisions.
- Contact an insurance agent to obtain cost information for an individual health insurance plan.

52

Personal Financial Planner

Name: ______________________ Date: ______________________

Disability Income Insurance

Purpose: To determine financial needs and insurance coverage related to employment disability situations. (pp. 396–399)

Instructions: Use the categories below to determine your potential income needs and disability insurance coverage. This sheet is also available in an Excel spreadsheet format at www.mhhe.com/kdh.

Suggested websites: www.ssa.gov www.clarkhoward.com/categories/insurance/disability-insurance/

Monthly Expenses

	Current	When Disabled
Mortgage (or rent)	$ ________	$ ________
Utilities	$ ________	$ ________
Food	$ ________	$ ________
Clothing	$ ________	$ ________
Insurance payments	$ ________	$ ________
Debt payments	$ ________	$ ________
Auto/transportation	$ ________	$ ________
Medical/dental care	$ ________	$ ________
Education	$ ________	$ ________
Personal allowances	$ ________	$ ________
Recreation/entertainment	$ ________	$ ________
Contributors, donations	$ ________	$ ________
Total monthly expenses when disabled		$ ________

Substitute Income	Monthly Benefit*
Group disability insurance	$ ________
Social Security	$ ________
State disability insurance	$ ________
Worker's compensation	$ ________
Credit disability insurance (in some auto loan or home mortgages)	$ ________
Other income (investments, etc.)	$ ________
Total projected income when disabled	$ ________

If projected income when disabled is less than expenses, additional disability income insurance should be considered.

*Most disability insurance programs have a waiting period before benefits start, and they may have a limit as to how long benefits are received.

What's Next for Your Personal Financial Plan?

- Survey several people to determine if they have disability insurance.
- Talk to an insurance agent to compare the costs of disability income insurance available from several insurance companies.

Name: ______________________________ Date: ______________________

Life Insurance

53

Purpose: To estimate life insurance coverage needed to cover expected expenses and future family living costs. (pp. 411–414)

Instructions: Estimate the amounts for the categories listed. This sheet is also available in an Excel spreadsheet format at www.mhhe.com/kdh.

Suggested websites: www.insure.com http://financialplan.about.com/cs/insuranc1/a/LifeInsurance.htm

Household expenses to be covered

Final expenses (funeral, estate taxes, etc.) (1) $ ____________

Payment of consumer debt amounts (2) $ ____________

Emergency fund (3) $ ____________

College fund (4) $ ____________

Expected living expenses:

Average living expense $ ____________

Spouse's income after taxes $ – ____________

Annual Social Security benefits $ – ____________

Net annual living expenses (a) $ ____________

Years until spouse is 90 ____________

Investment rate factor (see below) (b) ____________

Total living expenses (a × b) (5) $ ____________

Total monetary needs (1 + 2 + 3 + 4 + 5) $ ____________

Less: Total current investments $ – ____________

Life insurance needs $ ____________

Investment rate factors

Years until Spouse Is 90

	25	30	35	40	45	50	55	60
Conservative investment	20	22	25	27	30	31	33	35
Aggressive investment	16	17	19	20	21	21	22	23

Note: Use Sheet 54 to compare life insurance policies.

What's Next for Your Personal Financial Plan?

- Survey several people to determine their reasons for buying life insurance.
- Talk to an insurance agent to compare the rates charged by different companies and for different age categories.

Name: ______________________ Date: ______________

Life Insurance Comparison

Purpose: To research and compare companies, coverages, and costs for different insurance policies. (pp. 423–431)

Instructions: Analyze ads and contact life insurance agents to obtain the information requested below. This sheet is also available in an Excel spreadsheet format at www.mhhe.com/kdh.

Suggested websites: www.insure.com www.accuquote.com www.selectquote.com

Age			
Company			
Agent's name, address, and phone			
E-mail, website			
Type of insurance (term, straight/whole, limited payment, endowment, universal)			
Type of policy (individual, group)			
Amount of coverage			
Frequency of payment (monthly, quarterly, semiannually, annually)			
Premium amount			
Other costs: • Service charges • Physical exam			
Rate of return (annual percentage increase in cash value; not applicable for term policies)			
Benefits of insurance as stated in ad or by agent			
Potential problems or disadvantages of this coverage			

Suggested App:
• LIFE Foundation

What's Next for Your Personal Financial Plan?

- Talk to a life insurance agent to obtain information on the methods they suggest for determining the amount of life insurance a person should have.
- Research the differences in premium costs among various types of life insurance companies.

Name: ______________________ Date: ______________

Investment Objectives

Purpose: To determine specific goals for an investment program. (pp. 444–449)

Instructions: Based on short- and long-term objectives for your investment efforts, enter the items requested below. This sheet is also available in an Excel spreadsheet format at www.mhhe.com/kdh.

Suggested websites: www.fool.com www.betterinvesting.org

Description of goal	Amount	Date needed	Investment goal (safety, growth, income)	Level of risk (high, medium, low)	Possible investments to achieve this goal

What's Next for Your Personal Financial Plan?

- Use the suggestions listed in Chapter 13 to perform a financial checkup.
- Discuss the importance of investment goals and financial planning with other household members.

Name: ______________________ Date: ______________________

Investment Risk

Purpose: To assess the risk of various investments in relation to your personal risk tolerance and financial goals. (pp. 450–455)

Instructions: List various investments you are considering based on the type and level of risk associated with each. This sheet is also available in an Excel spreadsheet format at www.mhhe.com/kdh.

Suggested websites: www.marketwatch.com http://finance.yahoo.com

		Type of Risk		
Level of risk	Loss of market value (market risk)	Inflation risk	Interest rate risk	Liquidity risk
High risk				
Moderate risk				
Low risk				

Suggested App:

• The Motley Fool

What's Next for Your Personal Financial Plan?

- Identify current economic trends that might increase or decrease the risk associated with your choice of investments.
- Based on the risk associated with the investments you chose, which investment would you choose to obtain your investment goals.

Name: ______________________ Date: ______________________

Investment Information Sources

Purpose: To identify and assess the value of various investment information sources. (pp. 466–469)

Instructions: Obtain samples of investment information from at least three sources that you might consider to guide you in your investment decisions. This sheet is also available in an Excel spreadsheet format at www.mhhe.com/kdh.

Suggested websites: www.streetinsider.com http://finance.yahoo.com

	Item 1	Item 2	Item 3
Information source, organization			
Address			
Phone, e-mail			
Website			
Overview of information provided (main features)			
Cost			
Ease of access			
Evaluation: • reliability • clarity • value of information compared to cost			

What's Next for Your Personal Financial Plan?

- Based on the information that you provided on this form, choose one source that you believe is not only easy to use, but also provides quality information that would help you obtain your financial goals.
- Choose a specific investment and use the "best" information source that you identified above to conduct a more thorough evaluation of the chosen investment alternative.

Name: ______________________ Date: ______________

58 Corporate Stock Evaluation

Purpose: To identify a corporate stock that could help you obtain your investment goals. (pp. 489–501)

Instructions: Use Internet research or library materials to answer the questions on this personal financial planning sheet. This sheet is also available in an Excel spreadsheet format at www.mhhe.com/kdh.

Suggested websites: finance.yahoo.com www.marketwatch.com

Note: No checklist can serve as a foolproof guide for choosing a common or preferred stock. However, the following questions will help you evaluate a potential stock investment. Use stock websites on the Internet and/or use library materials to answer these questions about a corporate stock that you believe could help you obtain your investment goals.

Category 1: The Basics

1. What is the corporation's name? ______________________
2. What are the corporation's address and telephone number? ______________________
3. Have you requested the latest annual report and quarterly report? ☐ Yes ☐ No
4. What information about the corporation is available on the Internet? ______________________
5. Where is the stock traded? ______________________
6. What types of products or services does this firm provide? ______________________
7. Briefly describe the prospects for this company. (Include significant factors like product development, plans for expansion, plans for mergers, etc.) ______________________

Category 2: Dividend Income

8. Is the corporation currently paying dividends? If so, how much? ______________________
9. What is the current yield for this stock? ______________________
10. Has the dividend payout increased or decreased over the past five years? ______________________
11. How does the yield for this investment compare with those for other potential investments? ______________________

Category 3: Financial Performance

12. What are the firm's earnings per share for the last year? ______________________
13. Have the firm's earnings increased over the past five years? ______________________
14. What is the firm's current price-earnings ratio? ______________________
15. How does the firm's current price-earnings ratio compare with firms in the same industry? ______________________
16. Describe trends for the firm's price-earnings ratio over the past three years. Do these trends show improvement or decline in investment value? ______________________
17. What are the firm's projected earnings for the next year? ______________________
18. Have sales increased over the last five years? ______________________
19. What is the stock's current price? ______________________
20. What are the 52-week high and low prices for this stock? ______________________
21. Do the analysts that cover this stock indicate this is a good time to invest in this stock? ______________________
22. Briefly describe any other information that you obtained from Morningstar, Value Line, Standard & Poor's, or other sources of information. ______________________

A Word of Caution

When you use a checklist, there is always a danger of overlooking important relevant information. This checklist is not all-inclusive, but it does provide some questions that you should answer before making a decision to invest in stock. Quite simply, it is a place to start. If you need more information, *you* are responsible for obtaining it and for determining how it affects your potential investment.

What's Next for Your Personal Financial Plan?

- Identify additional factors that might affect your decision to invest in this corporation's stock.
- Develop a plan for monitoring an investment's value once a stock is purchased.

Name: ______________________ Date: ______________

Investment Broker Comparison

Purpose: To compare the benefits and costs of different investment brokers. (pp. 502–504)

Instructions: Compare the services of an investment broker based on the factors listed below. This sheet is also available in an Excel spreadsheet format at www.mhhe.com/kdh.

Suggested websites: www.fool.com   www.placetrade.com

Broker's name		
Organization		
Address		
Phone		
Website		
How much money is required to open an account		
What type of retirement accounts are offered?		
Can I talk with a real person when I need assistance?		
Online services offered		
Minimum commission charge		
Commission on 100 shares of stock at $50/share		
Fees for other investments: • corporate bonds • mutual funds • stock options		
Other fees: • annual account fee • inactivity fee • other		

What's Next for Your Personal Financial Plan?

- Using the information you obtained, choose a brokerage firm that you believe will help you obtain your investment goals.
- Access the website for the brokerage firm you have chosen and answer the questions on pages 502–503 in your text.

Name: ______________________ Date: ______________

60

Corporate Bond Evaluation

Purpose: To determine if a specific corporate bond could help you obtain your financial goals. (pp. 537–544)

Instructions: Use the Internet or library sources to answer the questions below. This sheet is also available in an Excel spreadsheet format at www.mhhe.com/kdh.

Suggested websites: finance.yahoo.com/bonds www.bondsonline.com

Category 1: Information about the Corporation

1. What is the corporation's name? ______________
2. What are the corporation's website address and telephone number? ______________
3. What type of products or services does this firm provide? ______________
4. Briefly describe the prospects for this company. (Include significant factors like product development, plans for expansion, plans for mergers, etc.) ______________

Category 2: Bond Basics

5. What type of bond is this? ______________
6. What is the face value for this bond? ______________
7. What is the interest rate for this bond? ______________
8. What is the dollar amount of annual interest for this bond? ______________
9. When are interest payments made to bondholders? ______________
10. Is the corporation currently paying interest as scheduled? ☐ Yes ☐ No
11. What is the maturity date for this bond? ______________
12. What is Moody's rating for this bond? ______________
13. What is Standard & Poor's rating for this bond? ______________
14. What do these ratings mean? ______________
15. What was the original issue date? ______________
16. Who is the trustee for this bond issue? ______________
17. Is the bond callable? If so, when? ______________
18. Is the bond secured with collateral? If so, what? ☐ Yes ☐ No ______________

Category 3: Financial Performance

19. What are the firm's earnings per share for the last year? ______________
20. Have the firm's earnings increased over the past five years? ______________
21. What are the firm's projected earnings for the next year? ______________
22. Have sales increased over the last five years? ______________
23. Do the analysts indicate that this is a good time to invest in this company? ______________
24. Briefly describe any other information that you obtained from Moody's, Standard & Poor's, or other sources of information. ______________

A Word of Caution

When you use a checklist, there is always a danger of overlooking important relevant information. The above checklist is not a cure-all, but it does provide some questions that you should answer before making a decision to invest in bonds. Quite simply, it is a place to start. If you need other information, *you* are responsible for obtaining it and for determining how it affects your potential investment.

What's Next for Your Personal Financial Plan?

- Talk with various people who have invested in government, municipal, or corporate bonds.
- Discuss with other household members why bonds might be a valid choice for your investment program.

Name: ______________________________ Date: ____________________

Mutual Fund Investment Information

Purpose: To identify and assess the value of various mutual fund investment information sources. (pp. 568–574)

Instructions: Obtain samples of several investment information sources that you might consider to guide you in your investment decisions. This sheet is also available in an Excel spreadsheet format at www.mhhe.com/kdh.

Suggested websites: www.morningstar.com www.mfea.com

	Item 1	Item 2	Item 3
Information source, organization			
Internet address or location where information can be found			
Overview of information provided (main features)			
Cost, if any			
Ease of access			
Evaluation • Reliability • Clarity • Value of information compared to cost			

What's Next for Your Personal Financial Plan?

- Talk with friends and relatives to determine what sources of information they use to evaluate mutual funds.
- Choose one source of information and describe how the information could help you obtain your investment goals.

Name: ______________________ Date: ______________

Mutual Fund Evaluation

Purpose: To determine whether a specific mutual fund could help you obtain your investment goals. (pp. 568–574)

Instructions: Use the Internet or library sources to answer the questions below. This sheet is also available in an Excel spreadsheet format at www.mhhe.com/kdh.

Suggested websites: www.morningstar.com finance.yahoo.com/funds/

Category 1: Fund Characteristics

1. What is the fund's name? what is the fund's ticker symbol?
____
2. What is this fund's Morningstar rating?
____
3. What is the minimum investment?
____
4. Does the fund allow telephone or Internet exchanges? ☐ Yes ☐ No
5. Is there a fee for exchanges? ☐ Yes ☐ No

Category 2: Costs

6. Is there a front-end load charge? If so, how much is it?
____
7. Is there a redemption fee? If so, how much is it?
____
8. How much is the annual management fee?
____
9. Is there a 12b-1 fee? If so, how much is it?
____
10. What is the fund's expense ratio?
____

Category 3: Diversification

11. What is the fund's objective?
____
12. What types of securities does the fund's portfolio include?
____
13. How many different securities does the fund's portfolio include?
____
14. How many types of industries does the fund's portfolio include?
____
15. What are the fund's five largest holdings?
____

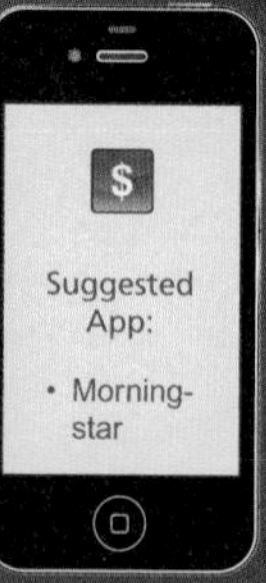

Category 4: Fund Performance

16. How long has the fund manager been with the fund?
____
17. How would you describe the fund's performance over the past 12 months?
____
18. How would you describe the fund's performance over the past five years?
____
19. How would you describe the fund's performance over the past 10 years?
____
20. What is the current net asset value for this fund?
____
21. What is the high net asset value for this fund over the last 12 months?
____
22. What is the low net asset value for this fund over the last 12 months?
____
23. What do the experts say about this fund?
____

Category 5: Conclusion

24. Based on the above information, do you think an investment in this fund will help you achieve your investment goals? ☐ Yes ☐ No
25. Explain your answer to question 24.
____

A Word of Caution

When you use a checklist, there is always a danger of overlooking important relevant information. This checklist is not a cure-all, but it does provide some questions that you should answer before making a mutual fund investment decision. Quite simply, it is a place to start. If you need other information, *you* are responsible for obtaining it and for determining how it affects your potential investment.

What's Next for Your Personal Financial Plan?

- Identify additional factors that may affect your decision to invest in this fund.
- Develop a plan for monitoring an investment's value once various mutual funds are purchased.

Name: ______________________________ Date: ______________________

Retirement Planning

Purpose: To consider housing alternatives for retirement living and to plan retirement activities. (pp. 622–630)

Instructions: Evaluate current and expected needs and interest based on the items below. This sheet is also available in an Excel spreadsheet format at www.mhhe.com/kdh.

Suggested websites: www.aarp.org retireplan.about.com

Retirement Housing Plans

Description of current housing situation (size, facilities, location)

Time until retirement __________ years

Description of retirement housing needs

Checklist of Retirement Housing Alternatives

__________ present home

__________ house sharing

__________ accessory apartment

__________ elder cottage housing

__________ rooming house

__________ single-room occupancy

__________ caretaker arrangement

__________ professional companionship arrangement

__________ commercial rental

__________ board and care home

__________ congregate housing

__________ continuing care retirement community

__________ assisted-living facility

__________ nursing home

Personal and financial factors that will influence the retirement housing decision

Financial planning actions to be taken related to retirement housing

Retirement Activities

What plans do you have to work part-time or do volunteer work?

What recreational activities do you plan to continue or start? (Location, training, equipment needs)

What plans do you have for travel or educational study?

What's Next for Your Personal Financial Plan?

- Survey local senior housing facilities to determine the types of services available to seniors.
- Make a list that suggests the best housing options for seniors.

Name: ______________________________ Date: ____________________

Retirement Plan Comparison

Purpose: To compare benefits and costs for different retirement plans (401K, IRA, Keogh, SEP). (pp. 630–646)

Instructions: Analyze advertisements and articles, and contact your employer and financial institutions to obtain the information below. This sheet is also available in an Excel spreadsheet format at www.mhhe.com/kdh.

Suggested websites: retireplan.about.com www.aarp.org

Type of plan			
Name of financial institution or employer			
Address			
Phone			
Website			
Type of investments			
Minimum initial deposit			
Minimum additional deposits			
Employer contributions			
Current rate of return			
Service charges/fees			
Safety insured? By whom?			
Amount			
Payroll deduction available			
Tax benefits			
Penalty for early withdrawal: • IRS penalty (10%) • Other penalties			
Other features or restrictions			

What's Next for Your Personal Financial Plan?

- Survey local businesses to determine the types of retirement plans available to employees.
- Talk to representatives of various financial institutions to obtain suggestions for retirement plan investments.

Name: ______________________________ Date: ______________________

Retirement Income Forecast

Purpose: To determine the amount needed to save each year to have the necessary funds to cover retirement living costs. (pp. 645–646)

Instructions: Estimate the information requested below. This sheet is also available in an Excel spreadsheet format at www.mhhe.com/kdh.

Suggested websites: www.ssa.gov www.pensionplanners.com

Estimated annual retirement living expenses

Estimated annual living expenses if you retired today $ ____________

Future value for ______ years until retirement at expected annual income of ______% (use future value of $1, Exhibit 1–A of the Chapter 1 Appendix) × ____________

Projected annual retirement living expenses adjusted for inflation . . . . (A) $ ____________

Estimated annual income at retirement

Social Security income $ ____________

Company pension, personal retirement account income $ ____________

Investment and other income $ ____________

Total retirement income . . . . (B) $ ____________

Additional retirement plan contributions (if B is less than A)

Annual shortfall of income after retirement (A − B) $ ____________

Expected annual rate of return on invested funds after retirement, percentage expressed as a decimal $ ____________

Needed investment fund after retirement A − B . . . . (C) $ ____________

Future value factor of a series of deposits for ______ years until retirement and an expected annual rate of return before retirement of ______ % (use Exhibit 1–B of the Chapter 1 Appendix) (D) $ ____________

Annual deposit to achieve needed investment fund (C divided by D) . . . . $ ____________

What's Next for Your Personal Financial Plan?

- Survey retired individuals or people close to retirement to obtain information on their main sources of retirement income.
- Evaluate various investment options for an individual retirement account.

Name: ______________________ Date: ______________

Estate Planning

Purpose: To develop a plan for estate planning and related financial activities. (pp. 660–663)

Instructions: Respond to the following questions as a basis for making and implementing an estate plan. This sheet is also available in an Excel spreadsheet format at www.mhhe.com/kdh.

Suggested websites: www.nolo.com www.estateplanning.com

Are your financial records, including recent tax forms, insurance policies, and investment and housing documents, organized and easily accessible?	
Do you have a safe-deposit box? Where is it located? Where is the key?	
Location of life insurance policies. Name and address of insurance company and agent.	
Is your will current? Location of copies of your will. Name and address of your lawyer.	
Name and address of your executor.	
Do you have a listing of the current value of assets owned and liabilities outstanding?	
Have any funeral and burial arrangements been made?	
Have you created any trusts? Name and location of financial institution.	
Do you have any current information on gift and estate taxes?	
Have you prepared a letter of last instruction? Where is it located?	

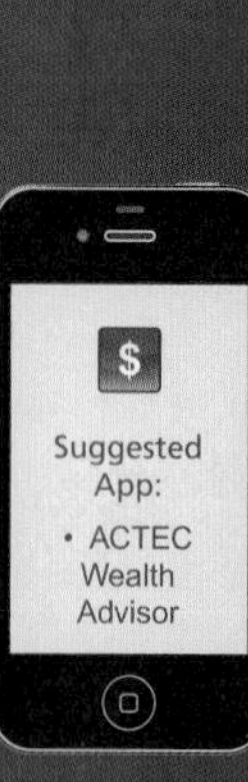

What's Next for Your Personal Financial Plan?

- Talk to several individuals about the actions they have taken related to estate planning.
- Create a list of situations in which a will would need to be revised.

Name: ______________________ Date: ______________

Will Planning

Purpose: To compare costs and features of various types of wills. (pp. 666–673)

Instructions: Obtain information for the various areas listed based on your current and future situation; contact attorneys regarding the cost of these wills. This sheet is also available in an Excel spreadsheet format at www.mhhe.com/kdh.

Suggested websites: www.netplanning.com www.estateplanninglinks.com http://wills.about.com/

Type of will	Features that would be appropriate for my current or future situation	Cost Attorney, Address, Phone

What's Next for Your Personal Financial Plan?

- Create a list of items that you believe would be desirable to include in a will.
- Obtain the cost of a will from a number of different lawyers.

Name: ______________________ Date: ______________

Trust Comparison

Purpose: To assess the features of different types of trusts. (pp. 673–680)

Instructions: Research features of various trusts to determine their value to your personal situation. This sheet is also available in an Excel spreadsheet format at www.mhhe.com/kdh.

Suggested websites: www.estateplanning.com/ www.savewealth.com

Type of trust	Benefits	Possible value for my situation

What's Next for Your Personal Financial Plan?

- Talk to legal and financial planning experts to contrast the cost and benefits of wills and trusts.
- Talk to one or more lawyers to obtain information about the type of trust recommended for your situation.

Suggested App:

- Trusts & Estates Plus

Name: ______________________ Date: ______________

Estate Tax Estimate

Purpose: To estimate the estate tax based on your financial situation. (pp. 680–684)

Instructions: Enter the data requested below to calculate the tax based on current tax rates. This sheet is also available in an Excel spreadsheet format at www.mhhe.com/kdh.

Suggested websites: www.irs.gov www.savewealth.com

Gross Estate Values

Personal property	$ ________	
Real estate	$ ________	
Joint ownership	$ ________	
Business interests	$ ________	
Life insurance	$ ________	
Employee benefits	$ ________	
Controlled gifts/trusts	$ ________	
Prior taxable gifts	$ ________	
Total estate values		$ ________

Deductible Debts, Costs, Expenses

Mortgages and secured loans	$ ________	
Unsecured notes and loans	$ ________	
Bills and accounts payable	$ ________	
Funeral and medical expenses	$ ________	
Probate administration costs	$ ________	
Total deductions		−$ ________
Marital deduction		−$ ________
Taxable estate		=$ ________
Gross estate tax*		$ ________

Allowable Credits

Unified credit	$ ________	
Gift tax credit	$ ________	
State tax credit	$ ________	
Foreign tax credit	$ ________	
Prior tax credit	$ ________	
Total tax credits		−$ ________
Net Estate Tax		$ ________

*Consult the Internal Revenue Service (www.irs.gov) for current rates and regulations related to estate taxes.

What's Next for Your Personal Financial Plan?

- Research the history of the estate tax law to find out when the law was first implemented and how it has changed over the years.
- Research the inheritance and gift tax laws in your state.

Name: ______________________ Date: ______________

Financial Data Summary

Date > > > > > > > > >					
Balance sheet summary					
Assets					
Liabilities					
Net worth					
Cash flow summary					
Inflows					
Outflows					
Surplus/deficit					
Budget summary					
Budget					
Actual					
Variance					

Date > > > > > > > > >					
Balance sheet summary					
Assets					
Liabilities					
Net worth					
Cash flow summary					
Inflows					
Outflows					
Surplus/deficit					
Budget summary					
Budget					
Actual					
Variance					

Name: ______________________ Date: ______________

Savings/Investment Portfolio Summary

Description	Organization contact/phone/ website	Purchase price/date	Value/ date	Value/ date	Value/ date	Value/ date

Name: ______________________ Date: ______________

Progress Check—Major Financial Goals and Activities

Some financial planning activities require short-term perspective. Other activities may require continued efforts over a long period of time, such as purchasing a vacation home. This sheet is designed to help you monitor these long-term, ongoing financial activities.

Major financial objective	Desired completion date	Initial actions and date	Progress checks (date, progress made, and other actions to be taken)

Name: ______________________ Date: ______________

Money Management, Budgeting, and Tax Planning—Summary

As you complete the various sheets in this *Personal Financial Planner,* transfer financial data, goals, and planned actions to the following summary sheet. For example:

Sheet	Actions to be taken	Planned completion date	Completed (√)
14 (Financial documents and records)	Locate and organize all personal financial documents	Within 2–3 months	
20 (Current income tax estimate)	Sort current tax data, compute estimate to determine tax amount	February 15	√

(Text Chapters 3–4; Sheets 1–22)

Sheet	Actions to be taken	Planned completion date	Completed (√)

Name: ______________________________ Date: ______________

74 Banking Services and Consumer Credit—Summary

(Text Chapters 5–7; Sheets 23–31)

Sheet	Actions to be taken	Planned completion date	Completed (√)

Name: ______________________ Date: ______________

Consumer Buying and Housing—Summary

(Text Chapters 8–9; Sheets 32–45)

Sheet	Actions to be taken	Planned completion date	Completed (√)

Name: ________________ Date: ________________

Insurance—Summary

(Text Chapters 10–12; Sheets 46–54)

Sheet	Actions to be taken	Planned completion date	Completed (√)

Name: ______________________ Date: ______________

Investments—Summary

(Text Chapters 13–17; Sheets 55–62)

Sheet	Actions to be taken	Planned completion date	Completed (√)

Name: ______________________ Date: ______________

Retirement and Estate Planning—Summary

(Text Chapters 18–19; Sheets 63–69)

Sheet	Actions to be taken	Planned completion date	Completed (√)

Is There A Better Time To Start Planning

Taking this course is the first step towards understanding personal finance. Take it to the next level by applying what you've learned in class to your own personal life and financial plan. Don't have a financial plan yet? Let's get started!

The **Personal Financial Planner Sheets** are located at the end of the text: fill them in and keep them with you for your own reference. The worksheets correlate with topics and financial situations in the book. They ask you to consider your own financial life and goals, and record your plan for each event.

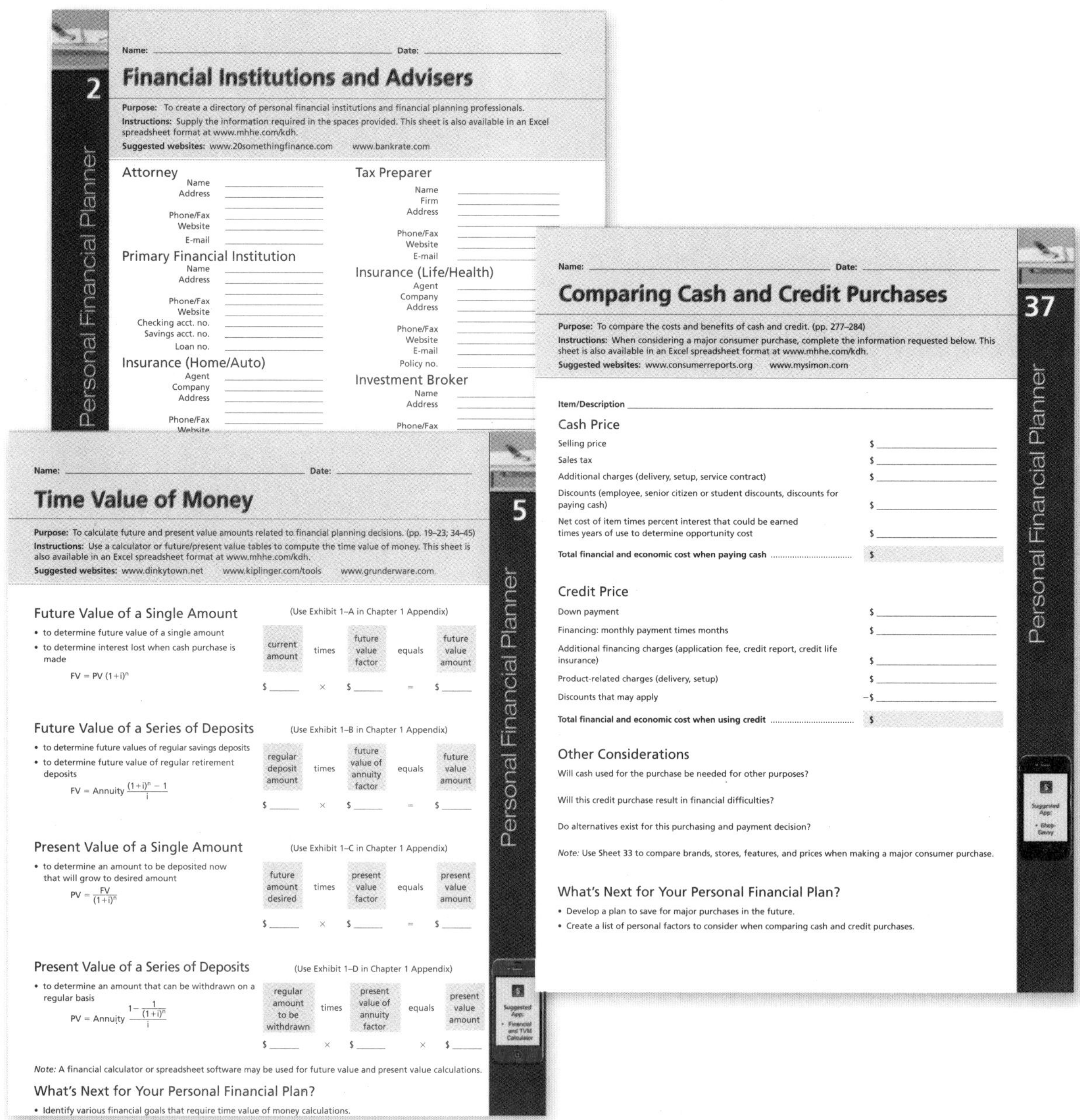

Personal Financial Planner

2

Name: Date:

Financial Institutions and Advisers

Purpose: To create a directory of personal financial institutions and financial planning professionals.
Instructions: Supply the information required in the spaces provided. This sheet is also available in an Excel spreadsheet format at www.mhhe.com/kdh.
Suggested websites: www.20somethingfinance.com www.bankrate.com

Attorney
Name
Address
Phone/Fax
Website
E-mail

Primary Financial Institution
Name
Address
Phone/Fax
Website
Checking acct. no.
Savings acct. no.
Loan no.

Insurance (Home/Auto)
Agent
Company
Address
Phone/Fax
Website

Tax Preparer
Name
Firm
Address
Phone/Fax
Website
E-mail

Insurance (Life/Health)
Agent
Company
Address
Phone/Fax
Website
E-mail
Policy no.

Investment Broker
Name
Address
Phone/Fax

Personal Financial Planner

5

Name: Date:

Time Value of Money

Purpose: To calculate future and present value amounts related to financial planning decisions. (pp. 19–23; 34–45)
Instructions: Use a calculator or future/present value tables to compute the time value of money. This sheet is also available in an Excel spreadsheet format at www.mhhe.com/kdh.
Suggested websites: www.dinkytown.net www.kiplinger.com/tools www.grunderware.com

Future Value of a Single Amount (Use Exhibit 1–A in Chapter 1 Appendix)
- to determine future value of a single amount
- to determine interest lost when cash purchase is made

$FV = PV(1+i)^n$

current amount times future value factor equals future value amount
$ ____ × $ ____ = $ ____

Future Value of a Series of Deposits (Use Exhibit 1–B in Chapter 1 Appendix)
- to determine future values of regular savings deposits
- to determine future value of regular retirement deposits

$FV = \text{Annuity}\,\frac{(1+i)^n - 1}{i}$

regular deposit amount times future value of annuity factor equals future value amount
$ ____ × $ ____ = $ ____

Present Value of a Single Amount (Use Exhibit 1–C in Chapter 1 Appendix)
- to determine an amount to be deposited now that will grow to desired amount

$PV = \frac{FV}{(1+i)^n}$

future amount desired times present value factor equals present value amount
$ ____ × $ ____ = $ ____

Present Value of a Series of Deposits (Use Exhibit 1–D in Chapter 1 Appendix)
- to determine an amount that can be withdrawn on a regular basis

$PV = \text{Annuity}\,\frac{1 - \frac{1}{(1+i)^n}}{i}$

regular amount to be withdrawn times present value of annuity factor equals present value amount
$ ____ × $ ____ × $ ____

Note: A financial calculator or spreadsheet software may be used for future value and present value calculations.

What's Next for Your Personal Financial Plan?
- Identify various financial goals that require time value of money calculations.

Suggested App:
- Financial and TVM Calculator

Personal Financial Planner

37

Name: Date:

Comparing Cash and Credit Purchases

Purpose: To compare the costs and benefits of cash and credit. (pp. 277–284)
Instructions: When considering a major consumer purchase, complete the information requested below. This sheet is also available in an Excel spreadsheet format at www.mhhe.com/kdh.
Suggested websites: www.consumerreports.org www.mysimon.com

Item/Description

Cash Price

Selling price	$
Sales tax	$
Additional charges (delivery, setup, service contract)	$
Discounts (employee, senior citizen or student discounts, discounts for paying cash)	$
Net cost of item times percent interest that could be earned times years of use to determine opportunity cost	$
Total financial and economic cost when paying cash	$

Credit Price

Down payment	$
Financing: monthly payment times months	$
Additional financing charges (application fee, credit report, credit life insurance)	$
Product-related charges (delivery, setup)	$
Discounts that may apply	–$
Total financial and economic cost when using credit	$

Other Considerations
Will cash used for the purchase be needed for other purposes?
Will this credit purchase result in financial difficulties?
Do alternatives exist for this purchasing and payment decision?

Note: Use Sheet 33 to compare brands, stores, features, and prices when making a major consumer purchase.

What's Next for Your Personal Financial Plan?
- Develop a plan to save for major purchases in the future.
- Create a list of personal factors to consider when comparing cash and credit purchases.

Suggested App:
- Shop-Savvy